440871

THE WILL OF ZEUS

STRINGFELLOW BARR

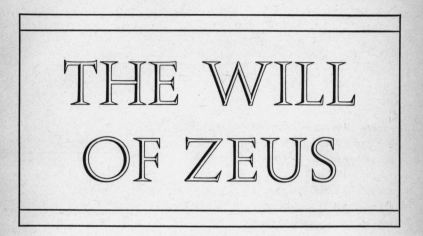

THE WILL
OF ZEUS

A HISTORY OF GREECE
FROM THE ORIGINS OF
HELLENIC CULTURE TO THE
DEATH OF ALEXANDER

A DELTA BOOK · 1965

A DELTA BOOK

PUBLISHED BY DELL PUBLISHING CO., INC.

750 THIRD AVENUE, NEW YORK, N.Y. 10017

COPYRIGHT © 1961 BY STRINGFELLOW BARR

DELTA® TM 755118, DELL PUBLISHING CO., INC.

ALL RIGHTS RESERVED

REPRINTED BY ARRANGEMENT WITH J.B. LIPPINCOTT COMPANY

PHILADELPHIA AND NEW YORK

LIBRARY OF CONGRESS CATALOG CARD NUMBER: 61-8681

COVER ILLUSTRATION BY CHARLES KATINAS

FIRST DELTA PRINTING—JANUARY, 1965

MANUFACTURED IN THE UNITED STATES OF AMERICA

For permission to quote from copyright material, thanks are due:

to the Harvard University Press for passages from the various Loeb Classical Library volumes listed on p. 455 and in the Notes, pp. 457-77; reprinted by permission of the publishers and The Loeb Classical Library.

to the University of Chicago Press for passages from *The Complete Greek Tragedies*, edited by David Grene and Richmond Lattimore, 4 vols. (Chicago, 1959), as follows: from vol. I, Aeschylus, *Oresteia, The Persians, Prometheus Bound*, © 1953, 1956, 1942, by The University of Chicago; from vol. III, Euripides, *The Trojan Women, Heracles*, © 1956 by The University of Chicago.

to the University of Michigan Press for passages from Xenophon's *Anabasis: The March Up Country*, translated by W. H. D. Rouse (Ann Arbor, Mich., 1958).

to Basil Blackwell, Publisher, for passages from Kathleen Freeman's *Ancilla to the Pre-Socratic Philosophers* (Oxford, 1948); reprinted by permission of Sir Basil Blackwell.

The chapter-page decorations are reproduced by courtesy of Ginn & Company, from drawings of Greek coins which appeared in A *History of Greece for Colleges and High Schools*, by Philip Van Ness Myers.

To Scott Buchanan
who led me to Hellas again

PREFACE

THIS book tries to tell what the ancient Greeks said and did and what seemed to them important. It was never this book's primary purpose to compile the known events of Hellenic history; I have therefore omitted much. I have tried, wherever possible, to let the Greeks tell the tale themselves, and I hope that my effort to let them speak will excuse the unusual length and frequency of my quotations. I have not justified my narrative by pointing out the contributions ancient Greece made to our civilization, because I judge Greek culture to have been so important in its own right as to need no such justification. On the other hand, neither I nor my readers can forget, when we encounter the Greeks, whatever insights we may have gained by living through the glories and miseries of the twentieth century, its destructive wars, its bloody revolutions. We cannot forget the hopes and fears these cataclysms have engendered in our hearts or the questions they have engendered in our minds. It was partly by the light of these questions that I have written this book. I have tried to avoid moralizing, opining, and assigning rewards and punishments. When it has seemed necessary to discuss controversial points, I have used notes in the back of the book for that purpose. The number affixed to each note occurs twice and only twice in this volume: once in the section devoted to notes, pages 457-77, and once in the text itself at the point to which the note applies.

The gap between history and legend, between the truth of courtroom testimony and the truth of a poem was smaller in ancient Greece, even for the better historians, than it is for professional historians today. This has led me to risk annoying the reader with phrases like "according to later tradition" whenever I have felt that the poetic truth of legend had begun to replace the truth of testimony.

I have risked another annoyance, the annoyance of recapitulation, either explicit or by allusion. I have assumed that a reader who may have forgotten his Greek history may not easily recall a character or event mentioned many pages earlier, especially if his reading of this book should have to be an interrupted reading. I hope the reader who does not need such reminders will forgive me.

Nobody to my knowledge has ever reduced to consistency the spelling of Greek names. The names Plato, Solon, and Meno all end in Greek with the same two letters. But in English we never say Platon, never say Solo, and we write Meno for the man in Plato's dialogue of that name and frequently write the same man's name as Menon in the *Anabasis* of Xenophon—not Xenopho! When Greek names ending in ōn were transliterated into Roman letters by authors who wrote in Latin, the last letter was dropped, at least in the nominative case, and the name passed into English in that form. Other such names bypassed Latin, or are now made to bypass it by authors who write in English, whereupon such familiar spellings as Alcibiades and Cyrus become Alkibiades and Kyros. But unless Sappho's Lesbos is to become Lesbus and holy Delos is to become Delus, why should Phoenician interests in Cyprus become Phoinikian interests in Kypros? In general, I have kept the Latin spellings where these were familiar in English and have transliterated other names straight from Greek. But I am under no illusion that I have solved a persistent problem.

Even common nouns can offer a problem. When we took over the word hybris from Greek, we followed the regular rules for transliteration from Greek letters to our own Roman letters, but now writers on Greek tragedy show signs of preferring to write hubris, presumably because, while the Greek letter upsilon could be transliterated into a Latin *y* without changing its sound, that sound changes abruptly when the *y* reaches English, and to this our modern writers object. I shall join them in writing the word as hubris on the day I can draw a chemical compound of hudrogen and oxugen from the hudrant. In the present volume, I have pedantically stuck to hybris.

In presenting quotations, I was confronted with the thorny problem of choosing a translation. Other things being equal, I have chosen the translations in the Loeb Classics, thereby furnishing the reader who wishes to check further with both a reputable Greek text and an English translation facing it in one readily available edition. At other times my strong preference for some other translation prevailed. And occasionally I have made my own translation, where the Greek yielded a meaning important for my story but not fully captured in the translations at hand.

Many of the events in Greek history, especially in the earlier period, cannot be dated precisely, and I have reluctantly fallen back on such phrases as "about 432," or "c. 432" in the Chronological Summary. Finally, since all the events in this volume occurred before the Christian era, there seemed no point in placing B.C. after any date.

The work on this book extended, with interruptions, over a period of twenty-six years, and was sustained by the generous help of many persons and several institutions. In 1935 a grant from the Institute for Research in the Social Sciences, in the University of Virginia, permitted me to start on a longer road than I then foresaw as necessary. In 1957 the Old Dominion Foundation made a grant to Rutgers University which provided me with a research associate for three years. In addition the Foundation and Rutgers jointly financed a year's leave of absence from teaching in order that I might the sooner finish my journey. During the past three years Dr. William Dix, Librarian of Firestone Library, Princeton University, and members of his staff hospitably supplied my research associate and me with facilities rarely duplicated in this country. In 1957 Professor R. P. Blackmur of Princeton University invited me to conduct a Christian Gauss Seminar on the problems I confronted, and I owe the members of that Seminar thanks for their friendly attacks and suggestions.

I am grateful for patient criticism from Baldwin Barr, Scott Buchanan, Francis Fergusson, R. W. B. Lewis, and Dennis O'Brien, and for assistance far beyond the call of duty from Stewart Richardson, my editor at Lippincott. None of them can be held responsible for my failures, since I did not always follow their advice. Finally, the assistance of Cary T. Peebles, my research associate, over the past three years has often amounted to collaboration, and without her advice, criticism, and unremitting labor this book would not exist. The other persons who helped me are too numerous to mention here, but I must speak of the many students I have taught since 1924 who looked at Hellenic history with fresh eyes and who raised good questions.

STRINGFELLOW BARR

January 20, 1961
Princeton, New Jersey

CONTENTS

Preface .... PAGE ix

Maps .... following PAGE xvi

1. THE WORLD OF ACHILLES AND ODYSSEUS 3

2. A RACE OF IRON 27

3. THE LAWGIVERS, LYCURGUS AND SOLON 48

4. FOR NONE SAVE ONLY ZEUS IS FREE 73

5. THE SCHOOL OF HELLAS 121

6. THE AGONY OF HELLAS 166

7. THE PHILOSOPHER KING 233

8. THE POLIS IN FLIGHT AND THE THIRTEENTH GOD ... 299

9. FROM THE VOYAGE OF PLATO TO THE EMPIRE OF
   ARISTOTLE 352

10. ALEXANDER'S WORLD POLIS 393

Chronological Summary 443

Bibliographical Note 453

Notes 457

Index.. 479

MAPS

Drawn by Guy Fleming

MAINLAND GREECE AND GREECE-IN-ASIA

WESTERN GREECE

THE MINOAN-MYCENAEAN WORLD

THE AGE OF GREEK COLONIZATION

EUROPEAN BATTLES OF THE PERSIAN WARS

THE LEAGUE OF DELOS AND THE SPARTAN ALLIANCE

THE ANABASIS OF XENOPHON

ALEXANDER'S EMPIRE

MAINLAND GREECE AND GREECE-IN-ASIA

SCALE OF MILES

0   40   80

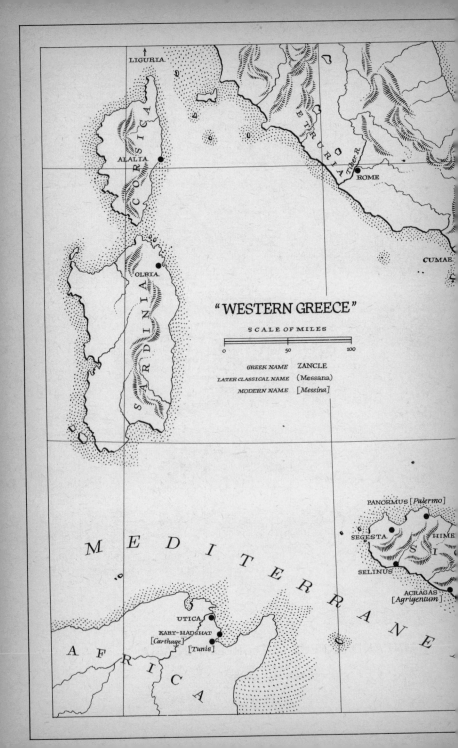

LIGURIA

CORSICA

ALALTA

ETRURIA

TIBER R.

ROME

SARDINIA

OLBIA

CUMAE

"WESTERN GREECE"

SCALE OF MILES

0   50   100

GREEK NAME	ZANCLE
LATER CLASSICAL NAME	(Messana)
MODERN NAME	[Messina]

MEDITERRANE

PANORMUS [Palermo]

SEGESTA

SI

HIME

SELINUS

ACRAGAS
[Agrigentum]

UTICA

KART-HADSHAT
[Carthage]

[Tunis]

AFRICA

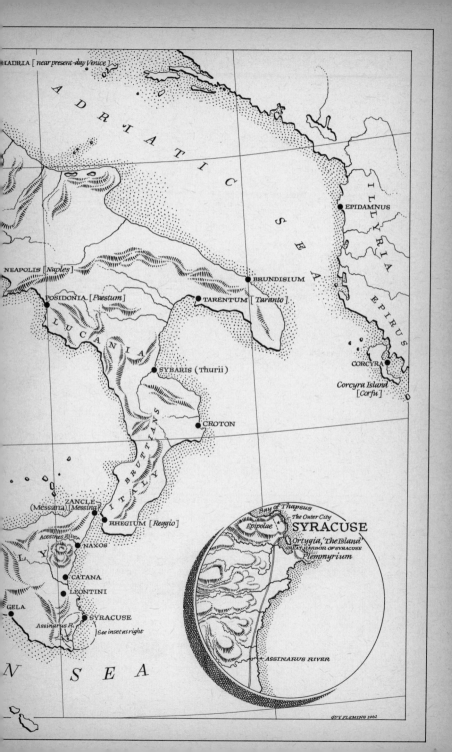

HADRIA [near present-day Venice]

ADRIATIC SEA

ILLYRIA

EPIDAMNUS

EPIRUS

NEAPOLIS [Naples]

BRUNDISIUM

POSIDONIA [Paestum]

TARENTUM [Taranto]

LUCANIA

CORCYRA

Corcyra Island [Corfu]

SYBARIS (Thurii)

CROTON

BRUTTIANS

ITALY

ZANCLE (Messana) [Messina]

RHEGIUM [Reggio]

Acesines River

NAXOS

LY

CATANA

LEONTINI

GELA

SYRACUSE

Assinarus R.

See inset at right

N SEA

Bay of Thapsus

The Outer City

Epipolae

SYRACUSE

Ortygia, The Island

GREAT HARBOR OF SYRACUSE

Plemmyrium

ASSINARUS RIVER

GUY FLEMING 1961

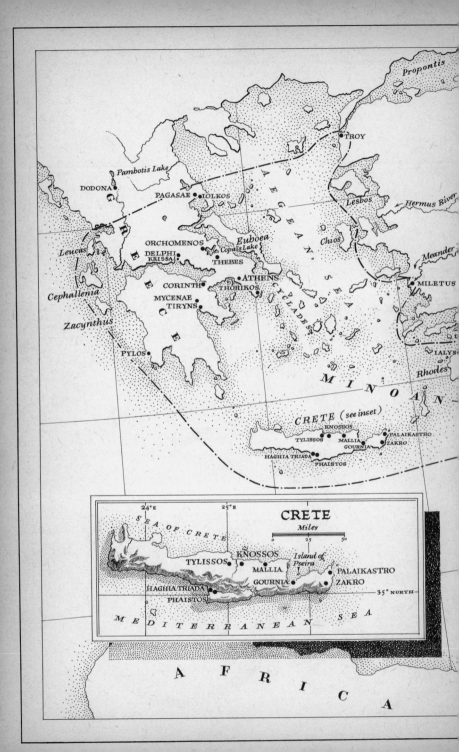

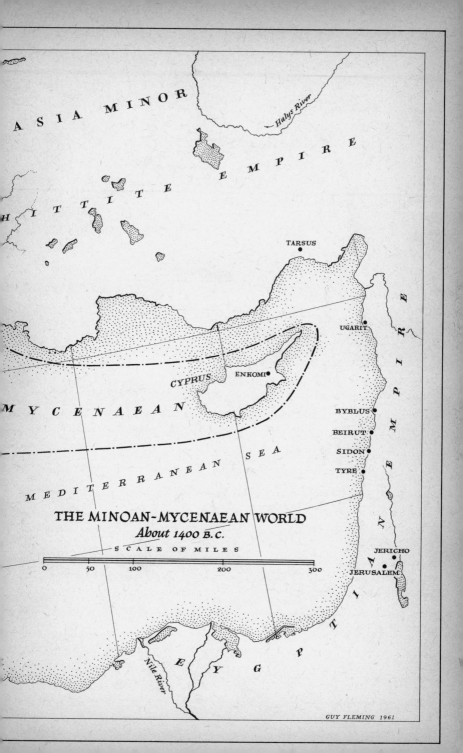

THE MINOAN-MYCENAEAN WORLD
About 1400 B.C.

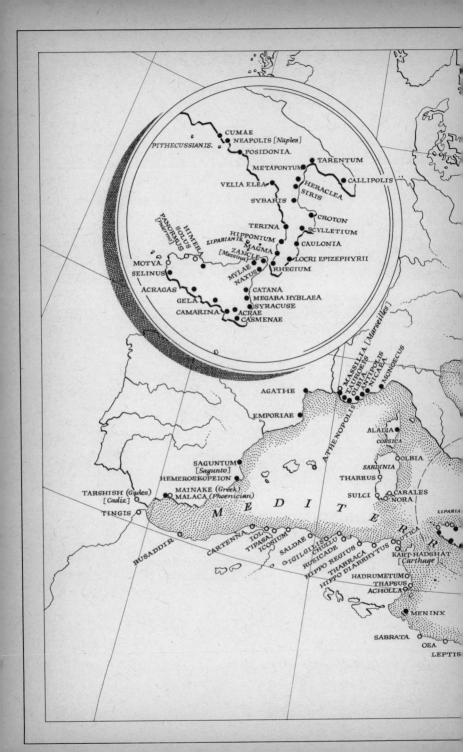

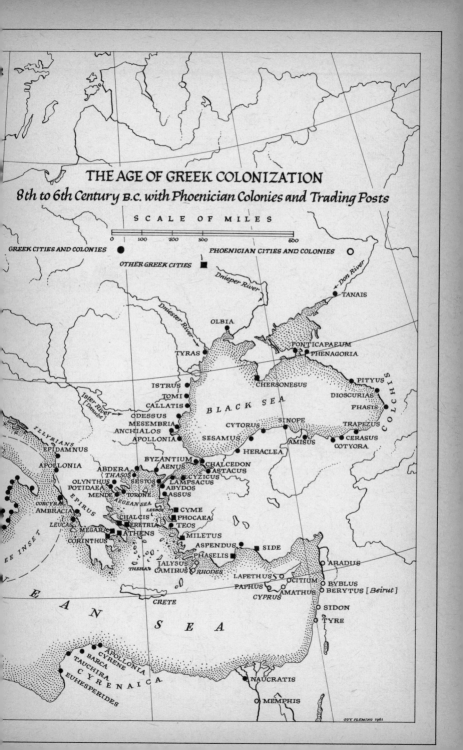

THE AGE OF GREEK COLONIZATION
8th to 6th Century B.C. with Phoenician Colonies and Trading Posts

SCALE OF MILES

0   100   200   300   600

GREEK CITIES AND COLONIES ●

OTHER GREEK CITIES ■

PHOENICIAN CITIES AND COLONIES ○

Dnieper River

Don River

TANAIS

Dniester River

OLBIA

PONTICAPAEUM
PHENAGORIA

TYRAS

Ister River
Danube

ISTRUS
TOMI
CALLATIS
ODESSUS
MESEMBRIA
ANCHIALOS
APOLLONIA

CHERSONESUS

PITYUS

DIOSCURIAS
PHASIS

COLCHIS

BLACK SEA

CYTORUS   SINOPE
SESAMUS
AMISUS
HERACLEA

TRAPEZUS
CERASUS
COTYORA

ILLYRIANS
EPIDAMNUS
APOLLONIA

BYZANTIUM
AENUS   CHALCEDON
ASTACUS
ABDERA
THASOS   CYZICUS
OLYNTHUS   SESTOS   LAMPSACUS
POTIDAEA   ABYDOS
MENDE   TORONE   ASSUS
CORCYRA
AMBRACIA   *LESBOS*   CYME
EPIRUS   *AEGEAN SEA*   PHOCAEA
LEUCAS   CHALCIS   TEOS
MEGARA   ERETRIA
CORINTHUS   ATHENS   MILETUS
ASPENDUS   SIDE
PHASELIS
THERA   IALYSUS
CAMIRUS   *RHODES*
LAPETHUS   OCITIUM   ARADUS
PAPHUS   BYBLUS
CYPRUS   AMATHUS   BERYTUS [*Beirut*]
CRETE   SIDON
TYRE

SEE INSET

EAN

SEA

APOLLONIA
CYRENE
BARCA
TAUCHIRA
CYRENAICA
EUHESPERIDES

NAUCRATIS

MEMPHIS

GUY FLEMING 1961

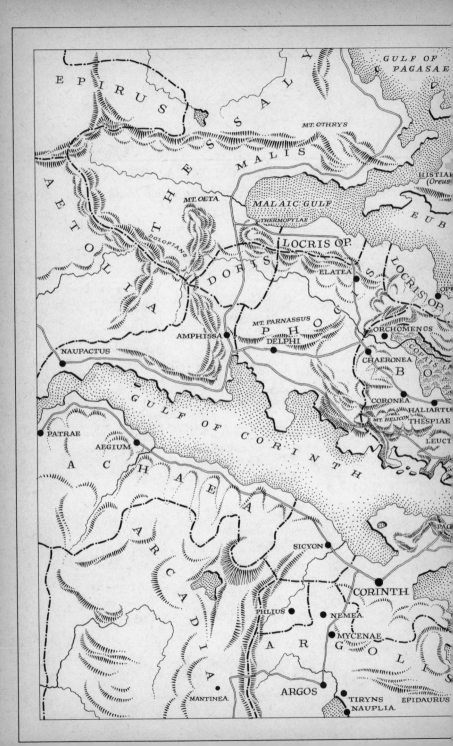

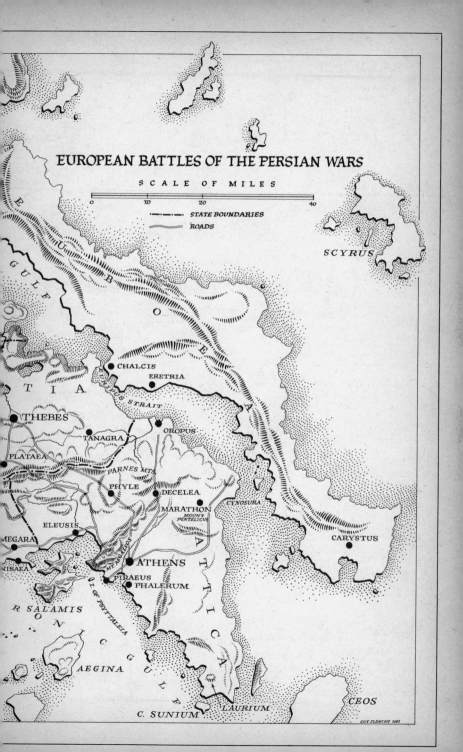

EUROPEAN BATTLES OF THE PERSIAN WARS

SCALE OF MILES

STATE BOUNDARIES
ROADS

SCYRUS

GULF

EUBOEA

TIA

CHALCIS

ERETRIA

THEBES

TANAGRA

OROPUS

PLATAEA

PARNES MTS.

PHYLE

DECELEA

MARATHON

MOUNT
PENTELICUS

CYNOSURA

ELEUSIS

MEGARA

CARYSTUS

NISAEA

MT AEGALUS

ATHENS

I. OF PSYTTALEIA

PIRAEUS

PHALERUM

R SALAMIS

ON

IC

GULF

AEGINA

ATTICA

C. SUNIUM

LAURIUM

CEOS

GUY FLEMING 1961

EPIDAMNUS

LYCHNITIS LAKE

APOLLONIA

Aous River

Apsus River

EPIRUS

CORCYRA

DODONA

THESPROTIA

LEUCAS

ACARNANIA

AMBRACIA

ARGOS

PAEONIANS

Axius River

LYNCESTIS

MACEDONIA

AEGAE

PELLA

THERMA

METHONE

PYDNA

PERRHAEBIA

LARISSA

CRANNON

THESSALY

PHERAE

PHARSALUS

HALUS

Haliacmon R.

MAGNESIA

Strymon River

Nestus River

CRENIDES

ABD

AMPHIPOLIS

EION   GALEPSUS

THASOS

CHALCIDICE

OLYNTHUS

POTIDAEA

MT. ATH

MENDE

SCIONE

AEGEA

SCIATHOS

ICOS

PEPARETHOS

POLYAEGOS

SCYROS

OREUS

Achelous River

Inachus R.

AETOLIA

LOCRIS

DELPHI

CALYDON

NAUPACTUS

LOCRIS OZOLIAN

PATRAE

GULF

AEGIUM

OF CORINTH

OPUS

CHAERONEA

CORONEA

BOEOTIA

OENOPHYTA

THEBES

LARYMNA

CHALCIS

ERETRIA

DELIUM

OROPUS

TANAGRA

DECELEA

CARYS

CEPHALLENIA   ITHACA

PALE

CRANI   SAME

PRONNI

ZACYNTHUS

CYLLENE

ELIS

OLYMPIA

Alpheus River

ACHAEA

ARCADIA

SICYON

CORINTH

PHLIUS

MANTINEA

ARGOS

ARGOLIS

MEGALOPOLIS

TEGEA

MESSENE

MESSENIA

PYLOS

SPHACTERIA

PAGAE

MEGARA

NISAEA

SALAMIS

ATHENS

PIRAEUS

ATTICA

AEGINA

EPIDAURUS

TROEZEN

HERMIONE

SPARTA

Eurotas River

LACONIA

MT. LAURIUM

CEOS

CYTHNOS

SERIPHOS

SIPHNOS

MELOS

ANI

CYTHERA

SICILY

<u>RHEGIUM</u>   *CITY ON SIDE OF ATHENS IN THE PELOPONNESIAN WAR.*

<u>HIMERA</u>   *CITY ON SIDE OF SPARTA IN THE PELOPONNESIAN WAR.*

LIPARA

PANORMUS

MESSINA

RHEGIUM

AEGATES ISLDS

SEGESTA

MT. AETNA

HIMERA

NAXOS

SELINUS

CATANA

ACRAGAS

LEONTINI

MEGARA HYBLAEA

SYRACUSE

GELA

CAMARINA

T H

THASOS

AEGEA

C

R

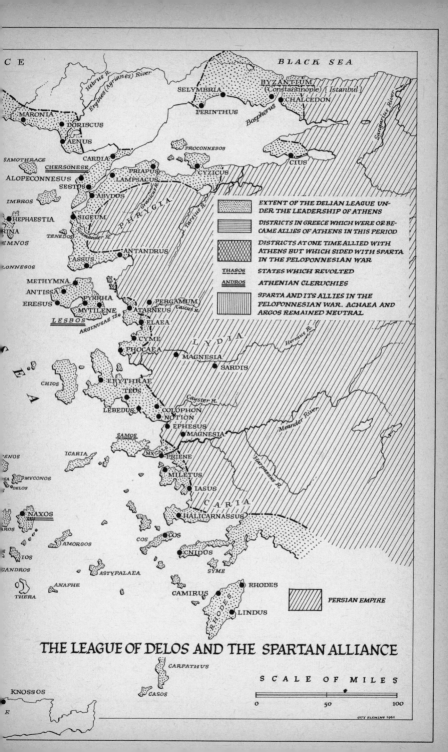

THE LEAGUE OF DELOS AND THE SPARTAN ALLIANCE

Map labels and legend:

BLACK SEA

C E

Hebrus R.
Ergines (Agrianes) River

MARONIA
DORISCUS
AENUS

SELYMBRIA
BYZANTIUM (Constantinople) Istanbul
CHALCEDON
PERINTHUS
Bosphorus
Sangarius River

SAMOTHRACE
CHERSONESE
ALOPECONNESUS
SESTOS
ABYDOS
CARDIA
PRIAPUS
LAMPSACUS
PROCONNESOS
CYZICUS
CIUS

IMBROS
HEPHAESTIA
SIGEUM
PHRYGIA
Granicus R.
Rhyndacus R.

RINA
EMNOS
TENEDOS
Scamander R.
ANTANDRUS
ASSUS
LONNESOS

METHYMNA
ANTISSA
ERESUS
PYRRHA
MYTILENE
ATARNEUS
PERGAMUM
Caicus R.
ELAEA
LESBOS
ARGINUSAE Is.
CYME
PHOCAEA
MAGNESIA
LYDIA
SARDIS
Hermus R.

CHIOS
ERYTHRAE
TEOS
LEBEDUS
COLOPHON
NOTION
EPHESUS
MAGNESIA
Cayster R.
Meander River

ENOS
ICARIA
MYCONOS
DELOS
SAMOS
MYCALE
PRIENE
MILETUS
IASUS
Harpassus R.
CARIA

NAXOS
ROS
AMORGOS
COS
COS
CNIDOS
HALICARNASSUS

IOS
GANDROS
ASTYPALAEA
SYME

ANAPHE
THERA
CAMIRUS
RHODES
RHODES
LINDUS

LEGEND

- EXTENT OF THE DELIAN LEAGUE UNDER THE LEADERSHIP OF ATHENS
- DISTRICTS IN GREECE WHICH WERE OR BECAME ALLIES OF ATHENS IN THIS PERIOD
- DISTRICTS AT ONE TIME ALLIED WITH ATHENS BUT WHICH SIDED WITH SPARTA IN THE PELOPONNESIAN WAR
- THASOS — STATES WHICH REVOLTED
- ANDROS — ATHENIAN CLERUCHIES
- SPARTA AND ITS ALLIES IN THE PELOPONNESIAN WAR. ACHAEA AND ARGOS REMAINED NEUTRAL
- PERSIAN EMPIRE

CARPATHUS
CASOS

KNOSSOS
E

SCALE OF MILES
0   50   100

GUY FLEMING 1961

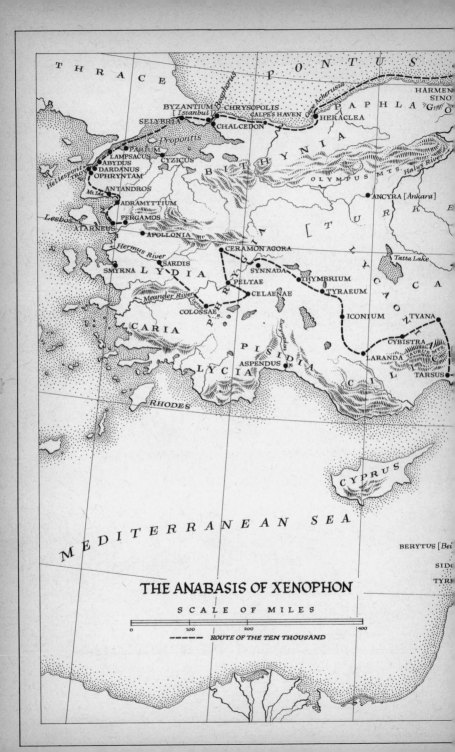

THE ANABASIS OF XENOPHON

SCALE OF MILES

0   100   200   400

- - - - - *ROUTE OF THE TEN THOUSAND*

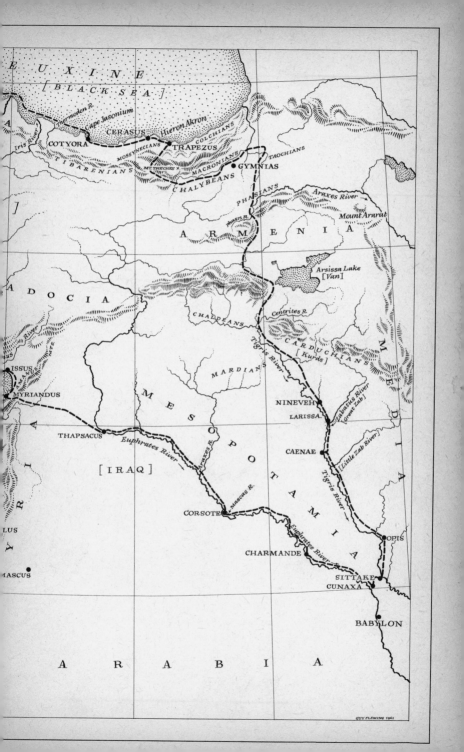

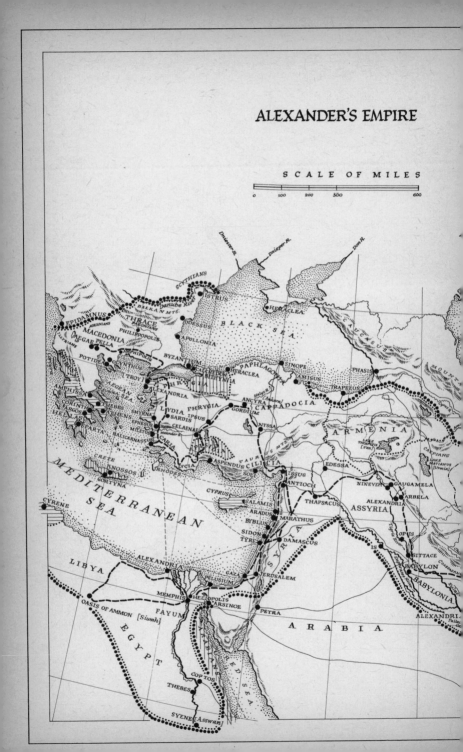

ALEXANDER'S EMPIRE

SCALE OF MILES

0   100   200   300   600

UNDER ALEXANDER, DIRECT RULE
ALLIED STATES
INDEPENDENT STATES
ALEXANDER'S ROUTE
ROUTES OF HIS GENERALS
LAND ROUTES
SEA ROUTES

And thus the will of Zeus was being brought to fulfilment.

—THE ILIAD, I, 5
Murray translation

The absence of romance in my history will, I fear, detract somewhat from its interest; but if it be judged useful by those inquirers who desire an exact knowledge of the past as an aid to the interpretation of the future, which in the course of human things must resemble if it does not reflect it, I shall be content.

—Thucydides, I, 22
Crawley translation

1

THE WORLD OF ACHILLES AND ODYSSEUS

SOME eight centuries before Christ a world was born, the Hellenic world. It emerges to view from the obscure shadows of a Dark Age. It learns to live in freedom under law; to imagine and create a magnificent art, a magnificent literature of tragedy, comedy, history, philosophy, mathematics, science. It tries to keep open the paths that lead from things to ideas and back again to things. It develops a wider commerce both in things and in ideas. It grows rich and waxes fat and imposes its will. It tries to base, on force, on military empire, and on domestic slavery, a wider freedom and a wider law. It fails, and itself passes under the yoke of a conqueror. It dares less, and asks less of life; it grows weary and skeptical; and at last it submits to the sword and governance of Rome. It becomes part of a Roman Empire that absorbs, dilutes, and extends Hellenic culture. Within its womb a new community is born, the Chris-

tian community. Its own gods die or withdraw from men. In the East
the shell of Empire protects a new, Byzantine culture; and in the West,
shell and all collapse, and civilization disintegrates into a new Dark Age.
This book will try to tell the story of the Hellenic world from its first
emergence to the death of Alexander the Great half a millennium later,
when the Hellenic world passes into its Hellenistic phase.

Hellenic culture was born not only out of the meager soil of Greece
and the island-studded Aegean Sea, but also out of myth—out of myths
that dealt with gods and men and with commerce between them, out of
myths put in the mouths of minstrels by a Muse, the goddess daughter of
Zeus, father of gods and men alike. And of all the myths that engendered
that culture out of soil and sea, two were by all odds the most powerful: the
myth of Achilles' wrath, which Homer sang in his epic poem, the *Iliad*,
and the myth of Odysseus' questing voyage, which the same poet[1] sang in
his epic, the *Odyssey*. Both myths were acts: they were verbs, not nouns or
adjectives. In the world of Achilles he and his fellow Achaeans acted in
battle, and their Trojan opponents acted also. Even the gods participated
in the confused struggle on the plains of Troy, some on one side, some on
the other: in this myth, the *Iliad*, even the gods acted. This thrust and
energy perhaps accounted for the fact that Hellenic culture, which did not
wholly create either *Iliad* or *Odyssey*, was nevertheless in large part created
by them. He who reads them today knows that Achilles has at last been
slain and that his soul has gone down to the House of Hades; he knows
that Odysseus has lost all his ships and all his comrades and has stooped
alone to kiss the soil of his native Ithaca. And yet the reader knows, too,
in a different way, that Achilles still fights beneath the walls of Troy and
that Odysseus' black ship, if not his fleet of ships, still skims the wine-dark
sea, seeking whatever Odysseus meant by Home. Are these two illusions,
or poetic insights, of the reader due to the same driving energy that the
Muse put in Homer and that Homer put in his two myths?

4

Neither of these epic myths is history; or they are history so transmuted into poetry that the historian has had to re-transmute them, so far as he could, before he could trust them. Some of the events they record did indeed happen, even in the historian's sense, in the early twelfth century. The Homer who composed the *Iliad* may have lived in the ninth century, and it can be argued that the Homer who composed the *Odyssey* probably lived in the eighth. Since both poems may well have contained minstrel lays composed long before that, the worlds they picture may really correspond in large part with what the historian means by reality. But which parts? From the historian's point of view, both epics contain contradictions and anachronisms. The historian Herodotus, in the early fifth century, and also Thucydides, in the late fifth, would have qualms about the historic value of the poetic legends. But the poets who were to write the great Attic tragedies—Aeschylus, Sophocles, Euripides—would turn to these legends and to others like them, confident that their audiences would recognize the doings of their ancestors. It was indeed through these legends that the fifth-century Greek could continue to belong both to his ancestors and to his gods. Peering back through the long childhood images of the eleventh, tenth, and ninth centuries, peering back through the murk of a Dark Age, these worlds of Achilles and Odysseus were the chief things he remembered. Moreover, modern archaeological research has confirmed a surprising proportion of these transmuted memories. The world of Achilles is therefore fully worth entering.

The immediate world of Achilles is the plain of Troy. It lies between that walled hill city and the mouth of the Hellespont, where the Achaean host have beached the swift, black ships that brought them from Greece and the Aegean Isles, and where they have built themselves huts behind a moat and palisade. They are commanded by Agamemnon, king of Mycenae; and their several contingents are commanded by lesser chieftain-kings. Their most celebrated fighter is Achilles, who has brought a force from a little kingdom in southern Thessaly. These Achaeans are ancestors of the Hellenes, the classical Greeks of history.

It is the tenth year of the siege of Troy. The Achaeans' attack was provoked by Alexander, or Paris, son of Priam, the aged king of Troy. Paris, while a guest of Agamemnon's brother Menelaus, chieftain-king of Sparta, abducted Menelaus' wife, the beautiful Helen. Agamemnon, most powerful of Achaean monarchs, therefore led his fellow kings in a kind of crusade

5

to rescue Helen, to avenge the dishonor Paris had done Menelaus, and to sack and despoil wealthy Troy. To avenge insult, to seize wealth, and to win glory and immortal fame among men, Achilles has spent these years on the plain of Troy, fighting the Trojans and their allies and pillaging the countryside for cattle and women.

Now in the tenth year of this crusade, the god Apollo has sent a pestilence to slaughter the Achaean besiegers. Apollo has acted because one of his priests has prayed him to do so; and his priest has prayed him because Agamemnon holds captive a daughter of the priest, has made her his concubine, and has refused a rich ransom for her.

With the Achaeans perishing from plague, Achilles calls a general assembly, which he has a right to do, and proposes to Agamemnon, general leader of the host, that they consult some soothsayer as to why Apollo, sender of plagues, is angry with the Achaeans. At once an Achaean soothsayer stands up and announces that he can answer that question if Achilles will swear to protect him against one whom all the Achaeans obey, which can only mean Agamemnon. Achilles immediately promises. Whereupon the soothsayer declares that Apollo will not cease to slay them until Agamemnon's concubine has been returned to her father and without ransom.

Agamemnon stands angrily, abuses the soothsayer, declares publicly that he loves this girl more than his wife and queen at home, yet that, rather than see the folk perish, he will return her. But she is his meed of honor, and he demands that she be replaced with some other prize. Instantly Achilles speaks and accuses Agamemnon of wanting more than his share of the booty. Agamemnon threatens to seize a meed of honor from some other king, maybe from Achilles himself, but orders his own concubine returned. The crusade that crossed the sea to right a wrong and avenge the theft of a woman is torn with strife on another point of honor and over another woman, Achilles' captive, Briseis of the fair cheeks. Agamemnon announces next that he will take Briseis, Achilles' meed of honor, so Achilles may know how far greater Agamemnon is than Achilles. Achilles draws his sword. But the goddess Athena comes, makes herself visible to Achilles alone, forbids him to slay Agamemnon, yet permits him to revile the leader. Achilles thereupon swears a mighty, public oath to withdraw his forces from the struggle to their ships until the war shall turn against them, until all the Achaeans shall long for his help, and until Agamemnon shall tear his heart within him for anger that he did in no wise honor the best of the Achaeans. But Achilles declines to defend Briseis by force. Agamemnon has her brought to his hut, and Achilles and his forces temporarily withdraw from the Trojan War.

If this clash had been a mere conflict between two petty clan chieftains about women they had seized for booty; if, indeed, a boastful barbarian pirate had actually sulked in his tent, deserted the ranks, and left his comrades to die, all because his vanity was wounded, one of the world's great poems could not have emerged from the quarrel and no amount of poetic language could have made it emerge. But in terms of Achilles' world, what is at stake is honor and the praise and prizes honor rightly demands if this world is to have meaning. Captive women can be enjoyed physically, but that is not the central point. The point is that meeds of honor for which heroes freely and gladly choose to risk their lives cannot be lightly yielded. They are the outward and visible signs of things that are neither outward nor visible, things that govern the actions of warriors like Achilles. None of his peers considers him a sulky boy or a vain braggart, nor does any of the gods who take sides in the war. Achilles, man of action, is not only quick to seize his sword; he is quick to state his case in the assembly, and he is quick to pray. He does, indeed, speak most often in contest, in order to persuade or threaten, in order to have his way, to work his will. He does, indeed, pray most often to persuade the gods to help him do what he has already decided to do. But he also obeys the gods, as he expects lesser men to obey him. The gods are more powerful than he is and therefore clearly merit his obedience.

In battle other warriors, friend and foe alike, find Achilles ferocious, like a beast of prey. But the epithet Homer frequently uses with his name, as with the names of many other warriors, is "godlike." He and the heroes around him are like gods and also like beasts. Physically, they are made in the image of the gods to whom they pray. It is true that the gods are taller, stronger, swifter, fairer, wiser, and happier. Their meed of honor is unquestionably greater than Achilles' meed or even Agamemnon's, precisely because their excellence is greater. In being jealous of his honor, Achilles is strongly confirming his right to the epithet, godlike. The gods are jealous of men who try to usurp their rights and functions. They are also jealous of each other in cases of overlapping jurisdiction and in cases that violate the hierarchical order on Mount Olympus.

The Homeric warrior-kings do not, when they feast, eat ambrosia. They slaughter the cattle they have seized, cut them up, put the pieces on spits, roast, and eat them; but they do not eat until they have burned the thigh-bones, wrapped in rich fat, in sacrifice to the gods. Unlike the gods, these warriors drink no nectar. They drink wine at their feasts, but only after they have poured a little on the ground in libation to the gods. In short they share their feasts with the gods, although these are only earthly feasts and never the nectar and ambrosia served on Olympus. A number of the gods take part in the Trojan War; they advise the combatants; they conceal or whisk away warriors who are in mortal danger; they even fight physically in the melee. More than that, they wound each other and are wounded by men. It is true that where the human warrior bleeds blood, the divine warrior bleeds a liquid called ichor. But, like men, the gods suffer pain and fear, hate and love and grief.

Like men, the gods marry. Like men, they commit adultery, especially Zeus, the father of gods and men. They marry and commit adultery with each other; they occasionally marry human beings; and they often commit adultery with human beings. Generally, it is a god who loves a woman; but sometimes, too, a goddess loves a man. The offspring is almost always human, practically never a god. Achilles himself is the son of a goddess, the sea nymph Thetis, and he is not the only warrior present who can boast of a divine parent. Nearly all of the Achaean heroes trace their ancestry to a god, often to Zeus himself.

It is in this context that Achilles withdraws to his hut and awaits the slaughter of his Achaean comrades to teach the leader of the host a proper respect for him. It is in the context of a war that rages in heaven as well as on earth, "and thus the will of Zeus was being brought to fulfilment."[2] The world in which Achilles moves is therefore penetrated and guided by another world, a divine world, and one which even the godlike Achilles cannot enter. There is a kind of community that includes all gods and all men; yet, between gods and men there is a great gulf fixed. Men are mortal, and the gods are not. In the world of Achilles perhaps the commonest designation of the gods is "the Immortals." Gods are not outside time: they have beginnings but no endings. Most of them were born of divine mothers, but they will never die. They do not even suffer grievous old age, as men must if they outlive youth and strength. Moreover, when Achilles' hour comes, not even his divine mother can gain him entrance into the heaven of Mount Olympus. His soul will descend, wraithlike, to the House of Hades, not, indeed, to torment, but to a kind of half-life devoid of all Achilles loves. Achilles must frequently risk his life in battle because that is the way his world is organized for godlike rulers of men; but he enters battle, knowing he stakes his all. His all, and yet not quite all: Achilles himself will be obliterated; but, until that moment, he may hope to act in such a way that he will leave immortal fame behind him, that men will make songs about him, and that the songs will not die. He himself must die, in youth and glory or in any case after grievous old age and perhaps with no glory; but, if he defends his honor manfully now, it is precisely his honor that will survive, that will be immortal like a god.

It is therefore the enduring thing about Achilles that has withdrawn him and his forces from the war and has made him nurse his wrath in his hut. That part of himself that cannot hope to endure—his youth and beauty and strength and the inestimable joy of living and acting on this earth— these he stands ready to stake again, instantly, once his honor is again free of the taint that Agamemnon has placed upon it.

The *Iliad* reports Achilles' action in and on his world. Almost at the beginning of the poem, he quarrels with Agamemnon and withdraws his forces from the war. The poem has almost sung itself out when he resumes his role in battle. Meanwhile, the fortunes of war swing uncertainly back and forth, and most of the poem narrates what other men than Achilles did on the plain beneath the walls of Troy. Where now is the man of action? Indeed, where now is the hero of the poem?

But Achilles is acting during these weary days as surely as Zeus, who, unlike a number of the Olympic gods, never fights in person on the plain. Achilles' will, like the will of Zeus, is being fulfilled. As Achilles predicted, the Achaeans are driven back to the wall they have built around their beached ships. Agamemnon swallows his pride, admits that he has played the fool, and sends friends of Achilles to his hut to offer apologies; to offer to return Achilles' meed of honor, the woman Achilles loves; and to offer gifts of reconciliation. Achilles is courteous to his friends but grimly declines Agamemnon's offers. Finally, the Trojans begin to fire the ships and thereby to cut the Achaeans off from escape.

Then Patroclus, Achilles' most loved friend and companion in arms, begs Achilles' armor from him that he may join his hard-pressed friends and terrify the Trojans. Achilles consents, and his beloved Patroclus is killed in battle by the Trojans' leading champion, Hector, who, like Paris, is a son of King Priam. Achilles' wild grief for the young Patroclus turns his wrath against Hector, reconciles his tense will with the will of his leader, Agamemnon, and leads him back into battle. Once more it is not only his honor that acts; it is his body, clothed in fresh armor fashioned by a god at the request of Achilles' goddess mother. He goes forth to battle again, knowing that he will shortly die—though his death does not occur in this particular poem. He slays Hector, drags his corpse behind his war chariot past the walls of the city to shame him even in death, and returns to his camp to bury Patroclus, his beloved.

This time Achilles' wrath is not merely redirected; it is purged by his overwhelming grief. And when the aged King Priam ventures secretly from Troy to ransom the torn body of his son—which the gods have miraculously healed after each desecration—Achilles joins his grief to Priam's and together they weep. The body is returned, and the poem ends with the funeral games in Troy, to speed the spirit of Hector to the House of Hades. The theme of the epic, announced in the initial invocation of the Muse, was the wrath of Achilles; and the wrath has worked itself out to the end, to grief and a kind of understanding, an understanding of his friend's death and of his own death to come. A war that has been fought by the will of Zeus between gods as well as between men is also about to work itself out, and its end reaffirms death, the end to which all men come, even godlike men who hold it less important to stay alive than to live their kind of life. What remains is a song about these men, a song that has not died as they had to die, and especially a song about Achilles.

Homer reports that the wall and trench with which the Achaean host had defended their beached ships remained intact so long as Hector lived and Achilles' wrath endured and Troy remained unsacked. But it had been built against the will of the gods. So, when all the bravest of the Trojans had died and the Achaeans had gone back in their ships to their dear native land, then Posidon, god of the sea, took counsel with Apollo and caused all the rivers that flowed down from Mount Ida to sweep against the wall for nine days. And Zeus rained continually. And Posidon's sea waves pounded, there by the river banks where "many shields of bull's-hide and many helms fell in the dust, and the race of men half-divine." Posidon swept away the foundations of beams and stones that the Achaeans had laid with toil, and made all smooth along the strong stream of the

Hellespont, and again covered the great beach with sand, when he had swept away the wall.[3]

So much else has been covered too by sand. Who were the Achaeans? Where did this semi-divine race come from? Our meager evidence, most of it based on archaeological diggings, will as yet yield no history of this folk which can command the agreement of modern scholars. Some two thousand years before Christ, war bands of Achaeans found their way into Greece, and such inroads continued for centuries. These Achaeans were a pastoral people who may have come from the shores of the Caspian or from the nearer Danube basin. They took over the Thessalian plains and, by 1700, they had seized the whole of Greece. They were a warrior class and a minority; and, although their conquered subjects, known as Pelasgians, accepted the language of the intruder, the conqueror in turn was partially assimilated to the local customs.

The land they had entered was a beautiful land but in some ways mysterious. Like the Balkan highlands they had just passed through, it was mountainous. Indeed, four-fifths of it was covered by mountains, which reached heights of only three to five thousand feet in the Attic peninsula but elsewhere included peaks like Parnassus, over eight thousand, and cloud-capped Olympus, nearly ten. Most of the valleys that contained good pasture or arable land were small. The higher mountains were forested with oak and maple, with yew and cypress, with silver fir, pine, and other conifers. Lower down, glades were numerous and shrubs like smilax and ivy flourished. In general, forests were less dense, less towering, less dark than some of those through which the invaders had passed in their long trek toward Greece. Hunting was good. There were the lion, leopard, lynx, panther, bear, wild boar, roe, together with small game like hare, partridge, thrush, quail, and lark.[4] The rare plains could support horse breeding, and even on the mountain slopes there was forage sufficient for cattle. The winters brought rain, but they were rendered mild by a thing the invaders were least familiar with, an omnipresent sea. No point in Greece was more than sixty miles from the Mediterranean, and most of the places in which the war bands settled were far nearer than that. They had left the large lakes behind them in their trek, and they had left the large rivers. Greek rivers were mostly too small to navigate, even if the invader had known how. They usually carried too much sediment to furnish good drinking water. Moreover, Greece was limestone country, full of subterranean cavities, and the rivers had a disconcerting way of disappearing underground. By the same token, it was a land of fresh and delicious springs. The summers were hot, in proportion as one went inland from the sea and its cooling breezes, and were so dry that the glorious profusion of spring flowers was succeeded by dust and dry earth. But it was an invigorating climate, even in summer: it would not enervate the Northern warriors.

The small valleys furnished agricultural oases where spelt and even wheat would grow, and the omnipresent sea offered other nutritious food that these landsmen and herdsmen had not learned to eat: sardines, anchovies, tunny, octopus, squid, oysters. The sea was strange and the Achaeans lacked even a name for it. They called it "the salty" or "the flat" or "the road,"[5] until they adopted from the natives the un-Achaean word, *thalassa*, which would become the regular Greek word for sea. Everywhere this sea and their newly conquered land interpenetrated. The drowned river valleys of a long-subsided coastline formed bays and gulfs and little sheltering harbors that the newcomers did not know how to use. The mountain chains ran out into the Aegean to form peninsulas, turned often into a last, sharp rock cliff, plunged beneath the mysterious sea, and then reared as occasional peaks in a long line of mountain-islands. Standing on such a final cliff, the invader warrior could look off to stepping stones that beckoned man eastward across the Aegean to the coast of Asia Minor. At no point in the Aegean could a sailor get more than forty miles from land, and this in a climate that was generally sunny and in an air that was generally crystal clear.

Having the means of producing bread and meat, the Achaean invader brought with him the sheep that produced his wool and the women's knowledge of spinning and weaving. So food and clothing were his. And for shelter he had good clay in the valleys from which to make sun-dried brick, and, in many places, excellent, soft, and easily worked stone for more pretentious dwellings or for temples. In short, he had found a fairly good home. With his bronze long-sword and his bull's-hide shield he could hope to hold it. There were numerous deposits of copper to make more swords, if he could but find the tin to turn his copper into bronze.

At about the time that the Achaeans entered Pelasgian Greece and carved out little kingdoms for themselves, an advanced civilization was already flourishing on the island of Crete to the southeast. Crete lay strategically between Egypt, the Cyclades, Mainland Greece, and Asia Minor, and during the third millennium B.C. she had become an important commercial center. Before the period 2000-1700, when the Achaeans were conquering Pelasgian Greece, Crete had gained naval control of the Aegean, built large palaces for her kings, developed a fine pottery for export, and a hieroglyphic writing in which to do business. Her goods now penetrated not only Egypt, which already possessed an ancient culture, but also Cyrenaica on the coast of present-day Libya, and Mainland Greece. In Greece, her wares reached as far as central Phocis, perhaps by way of Corinth, which had long traded with the Cyclades. Corinth, in turn, lay on one of the rare roads of Greece, a road that connected Cephissus in Attica with Tiryns in the Argolid, in the eastern Peloponnese. Tiryns, like Corinth, had long traded with the nearby islands of the Cyclades, and now dealt with Crete.

About 1700, when the Achaeans had completed their conquest of Greece, the great royal palaces in Crete, at Knossos, Mallia, and Tylissos, were all sacked[6] and burned, perhaps by rebellious Cretans, perhaps by the Achaeans of Greece. But a new dynasty built a palace at Phaestos and a splendid new one at Knossos, and Crete flourished again. In fact, the art forms she now created excelled her earlier work. She reduced her hieroglyphic writing to a more convenient linear script. Political power seems to have become centralized at Knossos, where the new palace covered some five acres and contained not merely a throne room and royal living quarters, but administrative offices with archives and inventories. Royal factories turned out exquisite pottery, sculpture, and marquetry. Delicate frescoes recorded a luxurious court life. The thalassocracy, or sea power, of this later Crete was fully restored in the Aegean, and Cretan colonies appeared in Miletus on the coast of Asia Minor and on the island of Rhodes. Probably, during the sixteenth and early fifteenth centuries, Crete was the middleman for commerce between wealthy Egypt and the whole Aegean area.

This was the great age of Minoan civilization, an elegant, gracious, and sophisticated culture that not only exchanged commodities with the Achaean Greeks but powerfully influenced their minds and their taste. The Argolid took over the cultivation of the vine and the olive, those crops that would centuries later make Greece's fortune. Palaces rose at Mycenae and Tiryns, in which Achaean ladies imitated the dress and ornaments of Crete. The interior walls of these palaces were covered with Cretan paintings, probably by painters imported from Crete. But there were important differences. The paintings and other locally produced art work compared unfavorably with the great works of Crete. The subjects the artist chose, or that were chosen for him by his half-civilized Achaean patrons, did not express the gay, lovely, tranquil, dancing Cretan world, but tended especially to war and the chase. For although this Argolid was now, if not a political colony of Crete, at least its cultural colony, yet it possessed limited powers of assimilating the elegance of metropolitan Crete.

A thousand years later, the Athenian historian Thucydides would assert that Minos, ruler of Crete, sent his sons as lieutenants, or vice-regents, to his foreign possessions. But the Greeks retained only faint memories of Minos and his empire. They told of a king and great lawgiver of Crete; of Theseus of Athens and the annual tribute ancient Athens had been compelled to send to Minos, a tribute of seven youths and seven maidens; of how Minos' daughter, the princess Ariadne, fell in love with Theseus and helped him slay the Minotaur, half man and half bull, in the tortuous labyrinth. The modern world has now excavated the vast and labyrinthine palace of Knossos and has uncovered the frescoes in which courtiers gaze down while athletes, both men and women, engage in graceful acrobatic feats on the backs of formidable bulls. But so far as history is concerned, the bull and Minos got somehow mixed up in the Achaean legends, as indeed they really are mixed in the name of the monster, Minotaur. Historians now suspect that for many years every king of Crete was a Minos, as every king of Egypt was a Pharaoh. So the historian calls this civilization, which created one of the great arts of all human history, Minoan; or, because of its sea power and its control of the Aegean, simply Aegean. If the present work of decoding its writing fares well, perhaps we shall some day know the secret history of a great civilization, a civilization which radiated art forms into Achaean Greece.

Meanwhile, we possess archaeological evidence that the Mycenaean culture which those radiations helped create existed in varying degrees not only at Mycenae and the nearby hill fortress of Tiryns but, between 1600 and 1400, at such places as Krissa, Delphi, Aegina, Chalcis in Euboea, Thebes, Orchomenos, Thorikos, Iolkos, Pagasae, Athens and the whole of

Attica and finally in distant Thessaly itself. In Boeotia attempts were made to drain Lake Copaïs. In the little Mycenaean kingdoms, the Achaean governing class was learning the art of seafaring, was trying its hand at piracy, and discovering the advantages of peaceful barter with the Cretans. Later, they may have outflanked the Cretans and traded directly with Egypt. About 1400, Knossos, Gournia, Pseira, Zakro, and Palaikastro in Crete met destruction, and Egyptian documents ceased to mention the Keftiu, the men of Crete. The Mycenaeans, with their mixed heritage of Achaean conqueror from the north, of Pelasgian vanquished in Greece, and of civilized Cretan overlord, seem to have conquered Crete itself. Minoan art declined, and what remained of Minoan culture was what her once subject peoples had been able to assimilate and adapt. The center of gravity of the Aegean world had apparently shifted to the Argolid, the land of Mycenae and Tiryns.

Perhaps for a modern, the essential symbol of the shift is the contrast between the spacious and luxurious palace at Knossos, where the queen, at least, possessed plumbing and even a water-closet, and the heavy hill-fortress palaces of Tiryns and Mycenae, where dwelt the Achaean warrior-kings. Where the palace at Knossos had enjoyed the flat roof of so much Mediterranean architecture, the palaces of these half-barbarian imitators of Knossos were crowned with the gabled roofs that recalled the snowy northlands from which the chieftain-kings' ancestors had come, on their long march into sunny southern Greece. And where braziers sufficed to heat the palace of Knossos, the fortress-palace of the Argolid was built around a Great Hall, in the center of which was a fireplace. Above it was a roofed-over aperture to allow the smoke to escape.

At both Tiryns and Mycenae immense new fortifications were built, for the age of a lawgiver, armed with decisive sea power, gave way now to an age of political decentralization. And yet it was also an age of expansion. The Achaeans took over Rhodes, and founded cities, and traded from there with mighty Egypt. They took over Cyprus, penetrated Asia Minor and Egypt itself. They went into Sicily. But they never built a centralized political empire. They seized widely separated sites and set up petty kingdoms. They carried on the arts they had learned from Minoan culture, but these arts declined. Art forms degenerated. As one would expect, techniques in weapon-making remained high. Except in Crete, writing practically disappeared.

It was marauding Achaeans like these who attacked Troy and built the wall and ditch that Posidon and Apollo would destroy. Only a few decades later other destruction came to Greece. Down through Epirus came men with iron weapons, the Dorians, and threw Achaean Greece into great confusion. Many of its inhabitants fled into Attica, whose meager soil could hardly attract the new and fierce invaders. From Attica refugees passed on across the islands of the Aegean to Asia Minor. The Dorians, like the Achaeans, spoke a Greek tongue. But where the Achaeans appropriated Pelasgian Greece, came to terms with it, and together with their subjects adopted a coarsened variant of Minoan culture, the Dorians proved more ruthless than the Achaeans and less assimilative. Their war bands seized parts of central Greece, most of the Peloponnese, and passed on to Melos, Rhodes, and, later, Doris, the southern portion of the Aegean coast of Asia Minor. Mycenaean culture could not recover from this onslaught, and Mainland Greece entered her Dark Age, an age of military and political confusion, of oral tradition in which the art of writing disappeared, of subsistence agriculture on the land, frequently carried on by serf labor, and of piracy rather than trade by sea.

Achilles' wrath against Agamemnon, his grief over the death of Patroclus, his slaying of Hector, the grief he shared with Priam, and the understanding born of grief all happened in the last year of the siege of Troy. When the minstrels sang the *Iliad*, the song made clear that Achilles would not survive the city's fall.

But Odysseus, the hero of the *Odyssey*, having survived the war, spent ten years in wandering about the Mediterranean in quest of his home. Both men acted. Both men were warrior-kings who fought at Troy. Both men sought immortal fame. Both men enlisted the aid of the immortal gods. But even in the *Iliad*, Odysseus is "wise Odysseus"; the epithet "wise" is never once affixed to Achilles' glorious name. He is godlike Achilles, but not godlike in wisdom. And though Achilles was forced by catastrophe to a kind of understanding at last, Odysseus from the start deliberately and continuously sought to understand. He sought to know. He longed to know the unfamiliar, mysterious, and terrible reaches of the cruel sea. He longed to see strange cities and converse with strange men. It is true he was trying to get home, that he was king of Ithaca and that therefore home was Ithaca; but his restless mind kept diverting him. He loved Ithaca, but he kept looking for a home which Ithaca could but reflect. He loved his queen, Penelope, yet he lay with a goddess, the nymph Calypso, who was even more beautiful, and immortal as well. Achilles' world was war, its glory and horror, the lust of battle, the pride of victory, the thrill of the nearness of death, the fear that unloosened the knees of men, and the song the minstrel would one day sing. Odysseus' world was the unknown sea, exploration, discovery, search, learning. The ordeals he underwent were the ordeals of a learner, and the goddess who guided his voyage was the goddess of wisdom, Athena.

Zeus once told Ares, god of war, to his face that he was the most hated of all the gods on Olympus. Yet Ares was an immortal god. The Achaean chieftain-kings who fought at Troy for ten long years often execrated war, as soldiers will, but war intoxicated them too. For another ten long years the sea waged unequal combat with Odysseus, who wanted to find his home; but Posidon, the god of the sea, was Zeus's own brother and almost the equal of Zeus in honor. And like countless other sailors Odysseus both hated the sea and loved it. The sea was salt and barren and unharvested —though the Greek would one day learn to harvest it—and Odysseus yearned to die, in his longing to see his native land or only to see the smoke that curled up from its dwellings.[7] There were times, as in his rescue from the sea on the shores of Phaeacia, when he could sink down in the reeds of a river to kiss the earth, the giver of grain.[8] And yet this barren sea that gave no grain beckoned him; bore him to strange places where he could learn the world beyond beloved Ithaca; in short, taught him. Taught him, and therefore changed him: when at last he reached the shores of Ithaca itself, he knew it not after his long absence, for about him the goddess of wisdom herself had shed a mist. Under her guidance Odysseus entered his kingdom. But he entered it disguised as a beggar, and therefore saw an Ithaca he had never before seen.

And because he came as a beggar, no man knew him. Only his hound, Argos, who lay neglected at his door, knew him. But Argos was old and, though he wagged his tail, he lacked the strength to rise and greet his master, and "the fate of black death seized him straightway when he had seen Odysseus in the twentieth year."[9] Even when his childhood nurse, Euryclea, had recognized him by a scar, his wife Penelope could not recognize him, either disguised as a beggar, or bathed and suitably dressed and transfigured by Athena. But since Penelope too knew guile, she put him to trial by leading him to suppose that the bridal bed he had long ago built for himself and her had been moved; and, speaking in anger, he showed that he knew the bed. Then her knees were loosened where she sat, and her heart melted, for she knew her husband. So was Odysseus recognized in three ways, by dog, by nurse, and by wife.

Though Odysseus returned to his kingdom as a beggar, he never ceased to be an Achaean warrior-chieftain, capable of indignant wrath. He was as ruthless as Achilles when the hour had come to slay the suitors in his own Great Hall and to punish their insolence. Had not his grandfather chosen a name for him, when he was but a baby, that suggested "Child of Wrath"[10]? But he knew the limitations of wrath, too; and Achilles could scarcely have said, as Odysseus did to his host, the king of Phaeacia, "for we are quick to anger, we tribes of men upon the earth."[11] It was Odysseus, too, when still disguised as a wandering beggar, who said to his queen, Penelope: "I am a man of many sorrows."[12]

He could experience wrath, and he also desired glory. When the Cyclops, Polyphemus, the one-eyed cannibal giant, had shut up in his cave both Odysseus and his comrades and had begun to devour those comrades, Odysseus by his own statement devised evil in the deep of his heart, "if in any way I might take vengeance on him, and Athene grant me glory."[13] When he had blinded the Cyclops and his ships were slipping silently out to sea from the shore where the blind giant raged, Odysseus endangered his own life and the lives of all his comrades by a triumphant boast worthy of Achilles himself. He called back to shore exultantly:

Cyclops, if any one of mortal men shall ask thee about the shameful blinding of thine eye, say that Odysseus, the sacker of cities, blinded it, even the son of Laertes, whose home is in Ithaca.[14]

It was then that the blinded Cyclops successfully prayed to his father, the sea god Posidon, to delay Odysseus' return to Ithaca.

But throughout most of his voyage Odysseus was busy less with either vengeance or glory than with solutions to hard and dangerous problems and with learning; and it was a Phaeacian challenger to athletic contests, not the Odysseus he challenged, who made the very Achaean assertion that "there is no greater glory for a man so long as he lives than that which he achieves by his own hands and his feet."[15] Odysseus' greatest glory was achieved by seeking and learning.

It was the ship and the oar that symbolized Odysseus, not the sword or the shield nor yet the bow that he nevertheless knew so well how to wield. It was the ship and the oar that brought the Achaeans to Troy to win glory with the sword; they would one day take them homeward; and they were the warriors' last resource if all should be lost and the host should be forced to escape destruction. But in the *Iliad* the ships were mostly beached. In the *Odyssey* it was a swift, black ship that took Odysseus through so many of his ordeals, and the even more marvelous ship of the Phaeacians that at last laid the sleeping Odysseus on the Ithacan shore. Achilles stayed at Troy; he slew Hector to avenge Patroclus and to be remembered as the fairest, bravest, and deadliest warrior of the host. Odysseus of many wiles dared sail and see, passed through many ordeals, and reached a home that was more than the Ithaca he had left twenty long years before.

His adventures took him even beneath the depths of the earth to the House of Hades, where he found the wraiths of Achaean warriors still discussing honor and glory and fame, while thronging about the wraith of Achilles. And Agamemnon's ghost spoke to the ghost of Achilles:

> Fortunate son of Peleus, godlike Achilles, that wast slain in the land of Troy far from Argos, and about thee others fell, the best of the sons of the Trojans and Achaeans, fighting for thy body; and thou in the whirl of dust didst lie mighty in thy mightiness, forgetful of thy horseman- ship. . . . Thus for seventeen days alike by night and day did we bewail thee, immortal gods and mortal men . . . Thus not even in death didst thou lose thy name, but ever shalt thou have fair renown among all men, Achilles[16]

—whereas Agamemnon had survived the war and had reached home, only to be murdered ingloriously by an adulterous wife and her paramour. His son Orestes had indeed avenged him; and Athena would urge the son of Odysseus to be valiant like Orestes "that many an one of men yet to be born may praise thee."[17] The spirit of Amphimedon sympathized with Agamemnon's feeling that he had lost his full glory by not falling when Achilles fell, and praised Odysseus' wife for knowing how to wait:

> therefore the fame of her virtue shall never perish, but the immortals shall make among men on earth a pleasant song in honor of constant Penelope.[18]

When Odysseus had reached home, had reconnoitered a difficult political situation, and had finally slain the suitors, the father of the first suitor whom Odysseus had slain urged vengeance in public assembly:

> For a shame is this even for men that are yet to be born to hear of, if we shall not take vengeance on the slayers of our sons and our brothers.[19]

Neither Odysseus nor the men and women of Odysseus' world were immune from this primal call to glory, a glory that would reach men yet to be born. And yet Odysseus in his hollow, black ship, sailing under the protection of the goddess of wisdom, faced his ordeals for another reason.

Though he valued the immortality of fame as Odysseus, sacker of cities, even the son of Laërtes, whose home was in Ithaca, he accepted grievous old age and even grievous death. According to a statement[20] of Athena to Odysseus' son, Telemachus, death is common to all, and the gods themselves could not ward it off from a man they loved when fate decreed his hour had come. Was that why Odysseus' paramour for seven years, the goddess Calypso, who held him on her wooded isle, could not persuade Odysseus to let her make him both immortal and ageless? Did he doubt her power to make him the gift of immortality and to spare him the trials that yet stood between himself and home? Or did he fear that immortality with Calypso would deprive him of the self-knowledge and self-fulfillment implicit in his search for his own proper home? He already knew that the hero, Heracles, took his joy in the feast among the immortal gods and dwelt on Mount Olympus as the son and son-in-law of Zeus himself. But he had also met the phantom of Heracles in the House of Hades. He had slept with Circe, whose magic wand turned men to swine, even though they retained the minds of men, and he had rescued his companions from that swinishness. But neither the immortality of the gods on the one hand nor the brutishness of animals on the other could ensnare him: he steered between them as surely as he steered between Scylla and Charybdis.

He remained, throughout, the wise Odysseus; Odysseus of many wiles; Odysseus, the wise and crafty-minded; Odysseus, the peer of the gods in counsel; neither immortal like the gods, nor yet sunk in animality; and the goddess who guided him homeward against the vengeance of the wrathful Posidon's treacherous sea was Athena, goddess of wisdom. It was this same Athena who assured his son that Odysseus "will contrive a way to return, for he is a man of many devices."[21] But she never ceased to supplement his unusual wisdom with her own divine wisdom. Part of his own wisdom, indeed, consisted in scrupulously following hers. His reward was to see many cities and to learn the minds of many men. As for the immortality of fame, there were more ways to win fame than by muscle and brawn and the long-sword of gleaming bronze and the willingness to die. Could a bronze sword, backed with muscle, outwit the treacherous sea? Human intelligence was better and more godlike than brute force. That was why Odysseus could boast to his gentle host, the king of the Phaeacians: "I am Odysseus, son of Laertes, who am known among men for all manner of wiles, and my fame reaches unto heaven."[22] Fame was a perquisite of wisdom, even among the immortal gods, perhaps especially among the immortal gods.

True, the wisdom Odysseus displayed was primarily a practical wisdom, a shrewdness, a cunning. But the gods favored that, too; or certainly some of them did. Old Autolycus, the maternal grandfather of Odysseus, who had chosen to name him Man of Wrath, had, according to Homer, "excelled all men in thievery,"[23] thanks to the god Hermes, who understood the art well. It was this shrewdness, this cunning, that enabled Odysseus to escape the countless dangers of a Mediterranean world filled with magic, like the wand and potions of Circe and like Hermes' herb to counteract those potions: "Moly, the gods call it."[24] It was the wisdom, too, of his wife, Penelope, and the wisdom of his son, Telemachus, guided by Athena, that laid the groundwork for Odysseus' return and triumph. Athena had endowed Penelope not only with that most valuable of women's skills in Homeric society, a knowledge of fair handiwork, but also "an understanding heart, and wiles."[25] She knew how to weave a web that would serve as shroud for Odysseus' aging father; but she also knew how to unravel it at night and delay its completion and therefore how to postpone her choice of suitors in case her true lord might yet return.

Although Odysseus left eleven of his twelve ships safely behind, he insisted on taking his own ship and its crew to the land of the Cyclopes. He wanted to learn who these Cyclopes were, whether they were cruel, and wild, and unjust, or whether they loved strangers and feared the gods in their thoughts.[26] And even after it became clear that he and his crew were in danger, even after his comrades had besought him to leave, he waited at Polyphemus' cave "to the end that I might see the man himself, and whether he would give me gifts of entertainment."[27] When he was forced to pass the man-devouring, sweetly singing Sirens, he took Circe's advice. He stopped the ears of his crew against that overpowering song, but he had them lash him to the mast with ears unstopped, that with delight he might listen to the voice of the two Sirens.[28] And he was richly rewarded, for the Sirens, according at least to their own boast, "know all things that come to pass upon the fruitful earth."[29] Odysseus wanted to know all too, not merely for immediate practical reasons, but because it is the nature of man to desire knowledge. His voyage had the practical aim of getting himself and his comrades back to the Ithaca they had left behind them twenty long years before. But Odysseus converted a return trip into an exploration; into a kind of education; into an intellectual, not a merely physical, adventure.

The cost of standing in battle, shield to shield, beside Achilles was high; but so was the cost of exploration in Odysseus' ship. There were those men whom the Cyclops had devoured in his blood-spattered cave. There were those others who had, at least temporarily, been turned by Circe into swine. There were the ghastly narrows between Scylla and Charybdis, and these must be followed through. Odysseus knew in advance that, rowed they never so swiftly, the six-headed monster Scylla would yet have time to seize six of his crew. Yet, if the men were warned of this, they might stop rowing at the crucial moment and huddle together in the hold, and then there would be more than six men lost. So he approached the strait, with that special kind of heavyheartedness that the leader is often forced to bear alone. When the monster struck, the six victims "cried aloud, calling upon me by name for that last time in anguish of heart."[30] While she devoured them, they stretched out their hands toward him in their awful death struggle, and, "Most piteous did mine eyes behold that thing of all that I bore while I explored the paths of the sea."[31] The passage between Scylla and Charybdis was, of course, inevitable; but the blood-smeared cave of the Cyclops was not. And when, later, one of Odysseus' followers called him "reckless Odysseus" and recalled that it was "through this man's folly"[32] that those men too had perished, Odysseus must have learned, or learned again, what the restless mind of the thinker could cost those he loved, and could cost the thinker, too.

Part of his wisdom lay in his love of law and justice, and part in his obedience to the gods. For he was a civilized man, and the cannibalism in Polyphemus' cave led him to a more general inference: that the Cyclopes were savages, an overweening and lawless folk, who did not even practice agriculture.

> Neither assemblies for counsel have they, nor appointed laws, but they dwell on the peaks of lofty mountains in hollow caves, and each one is lawgiver to his children and his wives, and they reck nothing of one another.[33]

Polyphemus, despite the fact that he was own son to Posidon, boasted frankly that they recked nothing of Zeus nor of the blessed gods, "since verily we are better far than they."[34] Whereas Zeus himself spoke to Athena of "godlike Odysseus, who is beyond all mortals in wisdom, and beyond all has paid sacrifice to the immortal gods."[35]

Alone at last, on a beach in his beloved Ithaca, yet not recognizing his country through the protective mist Athena had shed about him, he saw a young man approach who told him where he was. Crafty Odysseus began to pose as a newcomer from Crete and began to spin a yarn about how he had reached Ithaca. Athena—for the young man was indeed flashing-eyed Athena in disguise—was so delighted by the imaginative zest of his deception that she smiled and stroked Odysseus' cheek and told him who she was. She then touched him with a wand that transformed him into an aged beggar, ordered him to return to his home without telling anyone who he actually was, and took counsel with him how he might dispose of the importunate wooers who had now for three years lorded it in his halls. But his lies about Crete also led her to say: "Bold man, crafty in counsel, insatiate in deceit, not even in thine own land, it seems, wast thou to cease from guile and deceitful tales."[36] She found him also "soft of speech, keen of wit, and prudent."[37] She declared that he was best of all men in counsel and in speech and claimed that she herself among all the gods was "famed for wisdom and craft."[38] She gave him interesting instructions: he was to make trial of his wife and the others in his kingdom before disclosing his identity; and meanwhile, he was to "endure thy many griefs, and submit to the violence of men."[39] Was this, perhaps, the price that every man must pay who would know and understand, and not merely conquer with the sword? In any case, Athena's admonition led the returned king to take on himself the person of a helpless beggar and to gain for the first time in his life the knowledge of his kingdom that only a beggar could gain.

Achilles had frequently prayed, to get the gods to help him work his unexamined will. But Odysseus knew what Achilles did not: that, since the gods understood more than men, it was possible to get from them a more godlike kind of aid: they could help a man not only to slay his enemies; not only to outwit them; but to understand and to know. It was this that made his odyssey a wise man's pilgrimage and a learning of the human condition. Wisdom brought him a sense of proportion that Achilles lacked, and so this seaman's yarn was suffused with a humor which the *Iliad*, with all its power and majesty, conspicuously lacked.

In the world of Achilles human courage, even the lionlike courage of Achilles himself, was not adequate to the human problem. Something, wisdom could do: it was crafty Odysseus' ruse of the wooden horse, filled with Achaean warriors, that at last brought Troy low. But the sack of Troy brought to Odysseus himself a second ten years of trial and made him a man of many sorrows. For in his world human wisdom, even his many devices, were not adequate to the human predicament either. At Troy Odysseus shared the fame of wisdom with ancient Nestor, king of Pylos; and it was later, at Pylos, that Nestor's own son informed a visiting stranger that all men had need of the gods.[40] Ironically, it was to a goddess, Athena, disguised as the friend and guide of Odysseus' son, now come to Pylos to seek news of his still-missing hero-father, that the information was given. Ironically, that information was given at a sacrifice offered to Posidon, the sea god, who had just spent ten years delaying what Athena had labored to bring about, the return of Odysseus to Ithaca.

Nestor's son merely voiced what every wise man knew: that all men had need of the gods. But this still left difficulties. Beyond the hundred and one daily rituals that kept this terrible need fresh in men's minds, there still were difficulties, even for those wise enough, as Odysseus himself was clearly wise enough, to know that there were things they did not know. Not even the gods knew everything, or they could not have deceived each other. That they knew more than men and that they appeared to men and advised them, seemed certain. But it was troubling that, in those direct encounters of the divine and human, the god was almost always disguised, usually as some human friend of the human party to the encounter. At the conclusion of such an encounter, the god might turn into

24

a sea eagle or some other bird and fly off: Athena repeatedly withdrew in this fashion from the human world of Odysseus. Human witness was uncertain: Athena appeared to Odysseus in the hut of his swineherd, Eumaeus; but Telemachus was there and "did not see her before him, or notice her; for in no wise do the gods appear in manifest presence to all."[41] Yet Telemachus was not blind to gods, as witness the fact that a moment later, when Athena had beckoned Odysseus from the hut, had touched him with a golden wand, and had transfigured him, "his dear son marveled, and, seized with fear, turned his eyes aside, lest it should be a god."[42] And Odysseus reassured him:

> Be sure I am no god; why dost thou liken me to the immortals? Nay, I am thy father, for whose sake thou dost with groaning endure many griefs and submittest to the violence of men.[43]

But Telemachus, who had "not noticed" Athena, reasoned that only a god could transform himself from an aged beggar into this handsome, kingly man. This sort of transfiguration of man by god happened repeatedly, both in Odysseus' world and in that of Achilles.

A god could put courage in an Achilles or wisdom in an Odysseus. Did not Athena herself "put strength and courage"[44] in Telemachus's heart when he dreaded going among the unfriendly wooers of his mother, to the extent even of making him a "godlike man"[45]? But in urging the voyage to Pylos, she promised that she, or some god, would put wisdom in his mind. Telemachus shrank from encountering Nestor, renowned for his wise words, since he himself was "as yet all unversed in subtle speech."[46] Her answer told something of the relation of gods and men: "Telemachus, somewhat thou of thyself devise in thy breast, and somewhat heaven [daimōn] too will prompt thee."[47] If Telemachus sounded childishly timid, yet in his world men were keenly aware of the mysterious work of what Homer repeatedly called "wingèd words," those symbols that conveyed invisible thoughts from the mysterious recesses of one human mind to the mysterious recesses of another.

Often the gods communicated to men by dreams. But could a dream be trusted? Penelope told Odysseus, her still-disguised husband, that her absent lord had appeared to her in a dream and had foretold his return. But when Odysseus urged her to accept the dream as true, she replied sadly: "Stranger, dreams are baffling and unclear of meaning, and in no wise do they find fulfilment in all things for men."[48] Some dreams were true and some were false, and how could Penelope tell which class her dream belonged to? As a matter of fact, although Penelope presumably did not know it, Zeus had sent a dream to Agamemnon at Troy precisely in order to deceive him into fighting and losing.

Wingèd words, dreams, and gods disguised as men were heard or seen by some bystanders and not by others. Could the human mind be sure of any of them, in its doomed effort to understand its world? Yet some wingèd words seemed to fly straight, from mind to mind; Penelope herself admitted that some dreams came true; and some men had been certain they encountered a god. Should words, then, "remain unwingèd"[49]—that is, should men keep silence? And cease to search their dreams for meaning? And believe the god they were sure they saw was probably but a man? After all, Odysseus, who spoke wingèd words, and urged belief in a dream, and walked and talked with gods—even Odysseus admitted that "Nothing feebler does earth nurture than man, of all things that on earth are breathing and moving."[50] For just this reason he made use of prayer, of signs and tokens, and of words. After the events in the *Odyssey* had all occurred, and Odysseus had understood his kingdom in a new way, and his wife, and his son, did he obey the injunction Tiresias gave him beneath the earth in the House of Hades? Did he reaffirm his belief in the invisible world of the gods that penetrated his own? Did he reaffirm his faith in the power of things to serve as symbols, in the power of his world to have meaning, even to be transfigured?

Tiresias ordered him, when the suitors had been slain, to take a shapely oar and strike inland until he came to men who had never heard of the sea, or of ships, or of the oars that serve ships as wings. And this should be a sign to him: when a wayfarer should mistake the oar on Odysseus' shoulder for a fan with which to winnow grain, then Odysseus should erect the oar in the earth and sacrifice to the god of the sea, Posidon. Later, after a long and prosperous life, death would come to Odysseus—from the sea. Tiresias, of course, was a prophet, with more faith in symbols than most men dared to hold.

2

A RACE OF IRON

THE tales of Achilles' ruinous wrath and of Odysseus' restless quest were not only mighty poems for bards to sing at the feasts of
chieftain-kings and their nobles. They were the collected memories of a
people who had gone to earth beneath the onslaught of the Dorian tribes—
the Mycenaean people, who had achieved a coarsened version of the elegant
life of ancient Crete, of its Minoan sea power, its Minoan law and order.
The *Iliad* and the *Odyssey* and the lesser epics of the Homeric Cycle,
like the legends of Theseus, king of Athens; of Perseus, who reigned in
Tiryns, who slew the Gorgon Medusa, and who founded Mycenae itself;
of King Minos of Crete and his wife's monstrous son, the Minotaur, shut
up in the Labyrinth to feed on human victims; of Oedipus, prince of
Corinth, who in ignorance slew his father and married his mother and
ruled Thebes; of Jason and his Argonauts, who sailed to the Black Sea
in search of the Golden Fleece, and of Medea, the barbarian queen Jason
brought back from his voyage; all these oral legends served the early Greeks
as history. But it was a history that had been half forgotten and that had

been transmuted into poetry, so that the history of many centuries of
Minoan culture, of Mycenaean power, of Achaean and Dorian invaders
from the north, of the struggle between the invaders' Olympic gods and
the local gods of the settled population the invaders overran, of the great
Achaean crusade to Troy, and of the political disintegration and military
disorder that followed the coming of the Dorians—this history became
scrambled, jumbled, like the geological strata of the Grecian land itself,
folded by volcanic action, eroded by later rivers, partly drowned in the
sea, with only a peak emerging here and there as an island. Invader and
invaded had alike gone to earth, to seek their food from the meager soil
of Greece, in little isolated communities huddled for protection around
the hill fortress of some king. The knowledge of writing disappeared, and
where the past lived on, it had to live in song and the spoken word. Art
languished, and the scenes of war and the chase that graced the walls and
drinking cups of long-buried Mycenaean lords gave way now, in the tenth
century, to the primitive geometrical designs on pot and vase and amphora,
designs that were painted in some strongly local style, since a pot would
rarely sell now far from the home of the man who had made it and painted
it. In parts of Greece, clear into the seventh century, this geometric art
would endure.

Even the physical remains of Mycenaean palaces were no longer understood: the massive stone walls of the royal fortresses at Tiryns and Mycenae,
and the roads that led from those ruined fortresses northward to Corinth,
paved with stone and supplied with necessary bridges, now seemed beyond
the power of mortal men to build. They had been built, men thought,
by the Cyclopes.[51] Growing their own food, making their own clothing,
building their own houses, these huddled farmers understood little of
commerce, either between their own communities or with the outside
world.

But the outside world was beginning to seek them out. With the breakup
of Minoan power the ships of Phoenicia began to nose their way among
the islands of the Aegean and along the cliffs and into the innumerable
bays of Mainland Greece. The Phoenicians were a Semitic people with
a trading tradition. The Greeks called them *Phoinikes*, Red Men, perhaps
because their skins were swarthier than Greek skins, perhaps because one
of their most successful commodities was crimson-to-purple cloth, dyed
with the juice of the murex, a shellfish that flourished off the Phoenician

coast and that the Phoenician traders were now finding also among the islands of the Aegean. For a while the men of Sidon dominated this trade. By the twelfth century, Sidon's colony, Tyre, rivaled the mother city; and between the tenth and eighth centuries Tyre was the chief port of the entire Mediterranean and Tyrian purple became a commercial term. The Tyrians not only traded; they colonized. They founded Utica on the North African coast, and Palermo in Sicily. Besides Tyre and Sidon, Phoenician trading centers developed at Beirut; at nearby Byblus; and, in distant Spain, where the Phoenicians went in search of metals, they founded Tarshish on the Atlantic coast itself, at the site of modern Cadiz. Beyond such distant trading posts they went for tin, either to the Scilly Isles off Cornwall, or to northwest Spain. Precisely where the tin lay was a jealously guarded secret. For although iron was now gradually replacing bronze in the making of agricultural tools, the processes for hardening it were still poorly developed, and most weapons of war continued to be made of bronze.[52] Bronze could not be made without both copper and tin; and, whereas there were numerous deposits of copper in the eastern Mediterranean, tin was still scarce and highly valued.

The Phoenicians were not empire-builders; they were shrewd businessmen. Few of their trading posts, therefore, ever developed into powerful cities. The most brilliant exception was Kart-hadshat, or New City, which the Tyrians founded at least as early as the eighth century a few miles from the site of modern Tunis. Kart-hadshat, which others would some day call Carthage, possessed fine harborage at a point commanding the main sea passage that connected the eastern Mediterranean and the western. It proved a strategic strong point; and for food it could draw on plentiful and rich wheatlands.

But in general, Phoenicians clung to the coastlines and devoted themselves to trade, and their homeland could not ward off powerful military empires like the Assyrian or the Chaldean. Sennacherib of Assyria conquered Phoenicia in 701; and though it was freed from the Assyrian yoke by the fall of Nineveh in 612, it was gobbled up again, this time in 574 by the Chaldean emperor, Nebuchadnezzar. But even before Nineveh fell, the Red Men's dazzled customers in Greece had learned to rove the sea and were taking over the sea lanes. In the eighth century the Phoenicians still dominated the western Mediterranean; but by about 600 the Greeks of Phocaea in Ionia had founded or taken over Marseilles, which they called Massilia, and could tap the Rhone River route for both tin and amber.

In the early days of their trade with the Greeks, the Phoenicians must have thought of that trade as in large part trinkets for barbarians. For unlike the Greeks, or at least the Mainland Greeks, the Phoenicians were in touch with ancient, powerful, and luxurious civilizations. One of the few return cargoes they could make real profit from was the slaves they bought or kidnaped on their Aegean run. In return, the Greeks got more than trinkets. The tin and other products the Red Men brought had to come from somewhere, and eventually the Greeks took to the sea to find the source. Although the Phoenician art objects tended to be merely copies of the art of other peoples, the Phoenicians were middlemen for better things than they made, and the wares they brought led Greek potters from their primitive geometric ornamentation of pots to a style that more and more represented the objects the artist saw about him.[53] More important, perhaps, was another art the Greeks acquired from the Phoenicians, the art of writing. The Greeks took over the Phoenician alphabet and adapted it to the various dialects of their own tongue. Not even the now dimly remembered Minoans had possessed a true alphabet. Minoan writing had represented syllables, rather than simple sounds. The Greek alphabets had been constructed around the ninth century, in Ionia.[54] Perhaps Homer[55] wrote down the *Iliad* when he composed it, whether or not he wove into it lays that antedated writing. In any case, when the Ionians of Asia Minor and the peoples of Mainland Greece began to take over the Aegean from the Phoenician traders, their early ventures into trade were buttressed by the power to write.

The Aegean Sea furnished a unique school for mariners,[56] a school no other part of the Mediterranean was so well equipped to provide. True, in winter there could be terrible storms, but the Greek sailor did not commonly try to use the Aegean in winter. Even in summer the Aegean was subject to dangerous squalls; yet a ship could often avoid these if it kept close to land, and this the Greek sailor habitually did. Lacking a compass, he depended heavily on landmarks. He soon learned that the stars could guide him—but not on a cloudy night. He lacked the art of tacking against the wind, but his ship was small enough to row; and in a calm he could always fall back on oars. His ship was also too small for the storage of much food or for a convenient place to cook it: normally, therefore, he beached his ship by night and cooked his morning and evening meals ashore. Since for long he carried no anchor, his ideal port was a sheltered beach. Around the middle of the seventh century he developed a wooden anchor, weighted with a lump of metal or a stone; and in the early sixth century metal anchors came into use. With a good anchor, a ship could take refuge from foul weather in a deep-water harbor, even when the harbor lacked a beach.

By the seventh century, if a craft happened to be a warship, it would most likely be a penteconter, a fifty-oared ship with twenty-five men rowing on each side, with two sweeps in the rear to serve as rudders, and with a very small deck at each end. Or it might be a sort of longboat with a long deck and with two tiers of oars, a bireme. In either case, the basic source of a warship's power was human muscle: a warship must be able to count on its power even in a calm, and sails could be at best an auxiliary source, useful only when the wind was right. The penteconter was basically the same kind of swift, black ship that took Achilles to the land of Troy and that bore Odysseus home to Ithaca. The bireme was an improvement, because it packed more motive power into a given length. However, if a Greek sailed a merchantman, she would have been a roundish tub, whose shipwright had sacrificed speed to gain more space for cargo.

All in all, what with the storms and the pirates, life at sea was thoroughly dangerous. The Aegean was indeed a school; it was also a graveyard. But the profits of merchant adventurers in a Greece just learning to exchange commodities were very heavy. On all sides, the blue Aegean beckoned, to danger and to wealth.

Transportation by land could not compete with the sea lanes. Those roads which the one-eyed giants had built remained almost the only roads in Greece. The Greeks did eventually build several short paved roads, with artificially incised ruts for the cartwheels: such were the sacred roads that led from Athens to nearby Eleusis, from Sparta to Amyclae, from Elis to Olympia. But most roads in Greece were mere tracks for pedestrians or pack animals. Even had there been vehicular roads, the designers of harness had proven considerably less skillful than the designers of ships, with the curious result that draft animals could not compete with the oar. Oxen were too slow, so the Greek attempted to make ox harness serve for an ass or a mule. The attempt failed. A draft animal which should have pulled, had he been pulling with his shoulders instead of his throat, fifteen times the load a man could pull actually in this badly designed harness drew only some four times as much, and the mule could already carry that much as a pack animal. Finally the Greek never developed a good enough horseshoe to increase the animal's traction: the carter used removable horseshoes of metal, leather, or even straw. If the sea lanes had invited less urgently, would the Greek merchant have invented a better harness and a better shoe for his draft animals? Would he have built paved roads too, despite the mountainous terrain? Perhaps, but the sea invited him, and the Greek merchant followed where it led.

The Aegean Sea served as a school, not only to Mainland Greece, but to those Greeks, whether they spoke Aeolian Greek or even Ionian or Dorian, who had crossed that sea from the Greek peninsula and colonized the west coast of Asia Minor. In fact, by the close of the Greek Dark Ages, the Aegean Sea rather than European Greece was the geographical center of Hellas. Hellas was clustered around it rather than merely lying west of it.

Nobody knew exactly when the Ionian Greeks had settled in their home, but the pressure of the Dorian invasion had a good deal to do with their original crossing from Europe. The ancient Minoan Empire had never gained much foothold there, since the coast of Asia Minor was then dominated by the powerful kingdom of the Hittites in the mountainous hinterland. But, when pressure from Assyria weakened the Hittites' hold on their Aegean coastline, it was opened to settlement from Mainland Greece. There was no organized Greek invasion: the Greeks came in small parties and included men of Achaean stock as well as of pre-Achaean. In Ionia they found fertile bottom land to cultivate and neighbors able to transmit to them through trade the ideas and crafts developed by the great Near Eastern empires. Of all the Greeks in Asia, the Ionians especially took to the sea. And they early produced an impressive literature. According to later Greek tradition, Homer himself was an Ionian. Following the epics that were composed by him or ascribed to him, there was an outburst, in the eighth and seventh centuries, of lyric poetry that extended from the funeral dirge to martial or festive or patriotic themes.

It was in these two centuries, moreover, that the Greeks on both sides of the Aegean further developed their most characteristic political form, the small city-state, the *polis*. Originally, the polis was the hill fortress of the chieftain-king. Later the word included the cluster of houses that huddled at the foot of that hill, and the hill itself became the *acropolis* or "high city." Eventually the polis included acropolis, huddled houses, and in addition all the agricultural territory surrounding them. It was under the leadership of the chieftain-king that the settled war band formed this city-state, in which the king and his council of nobles ruled and announced their decisions to the assembly of all free males. The nobles, from being the roving warriors who followed the king in raids, tended to form a stable landed aristocracy, ready to defend their little polis, though ready also to make forays, to steal women and cattle. Or, in the good months of July and August, a noble might fit out a ship and turn pirate, or trader, or both.

Since the noble had seized the best land in the city-state, he alone was well enough off to wear proper bronze armor and, above all, to keep a horse. It was the Assyrians, not the Greeks, who had introduced cavalry in the ninth century, but by the eighth the Greek noble's proudest title was Horseman, or Knight. Actually, the Greek, like the Assyrian horseman, was not a true cavalryman: he used the horse, which he rode bareback,[57] to give him mobility between battles; he did not fight on horseback. These Knights, then, were actually mounted infantry. Yet their mounts did give them speed in pursuit. As for the war chariot the Achaeans had used at Troy, that had disappeared, even though the terms that described its two occupants, the fighter and the driver, long survived in an honorific sense, and even though the chariot was still used for an athletic event, the highly honored chariot race. Finally, except in a few localities like the plains of Thessaly, the roughness of Greek terrain severely limited the usefulness of cavalry in war.

The noble defended the polis with his life, and more and more he assumed the right to govern what he defended. During the eighth and seventh centuries, king after king lost all, or a portion, of his powers to his nobles. Monarchy gave way to the aristocratic republic in one polis after another, although kingship usually survived as an elective office, with very limited powers. Custom had always given the council the right to discuss and advise. Now this same council gained the right to vote and decide and, through officials of its own choice, to execute. Law was still unwritten, customary law, which the gods revealed; but they revealed it only to the noble, and only the noble could judge cases by the light of this revealed knowledge. The noble was one of the *Aristoi*—the Best People, who had inherited the right to rule from ancestors who were also the Best People and who, indeed, were occasionally immortal gods. But he must share the rule with other nobles and needed, therefore, not only to wield a sword in battle but to wield words in council.

As for the peasants, the noble despised them. Living in his town house in the polis, where he could keep an eye on politics, he watched the peasants plod in from the country, toil-stained, half-clad. In battle these same peasants formed an undisciplined rabble of under-armed, under-armored men. The noble called them Sheepskin-wearers or Club-bearers, as at Sicyon; or Dustyfeet, as at Epidaurus; or Half-clad, as at Argos; or merely the Poor, the *Penestai*, as in Thessaly, where they were actual serfs, bound to the soil. Just as the noble frequently believed that he himself, in descent at least, was partly a god, the Dustyfoot must have struck him as being partly a brute, certainly unfit to share in the mysterious art of statecraft and hardly fit to share in defending the state in battle.

But just as Achilles could stand up in the Achaean assembly before Troy, take the herald's wand that gave him the right to speak, and call Agamemnon, leader of the host, dog-faced,[58] so Thersites also, the Dustyfoot from the ranks, railed publicly at Agamemnon. True, Odysseus beat him for his impudence, but according to Odysseus it was not the first time Thersites had railed. Now, four centuries later, even the noble who chose to dwell in town, at least part of the year, away from his land can hardly have had the impersonal relationship to those who served him that money would some day bring to the rich. These early nobles were rooted in the soil, like the peasants who worked for them. They ate better food, wore better clothes, and lived in better houses than Dustyfoot; but by later standards, the material gap cannot have been great. It was the spiritual gap that counted.

The noble retained an image of himself that was like the image of Achilles in the poem the noble had heard sung when men feasted in the great hall. He imposed his will, like the powerful gods themselves. Early in the seventh century Archilochus of Paros would state the ideal in a poem:

> In the spear is my kneaded bread, in the spear my Ismarian wine,
> when I drink I recline on the spear.[59]

Even the most land-bound noble retained the conqueror's predatory pride and felt he had the right to seize what he desired.

He felt also a mystical interest in the blood tie. He was passionately bound to his kindred: to those who lived about him, to his ancestors who had already lived out their lives and perished, to his unborn descendants. In the early days of the Greek polis, family pride and family vendetta were towering obstacles to law and justice. There was wergild, or blood money, for murder done; compurgation, in which the relatives and friends of an accused man assembled and swore to his innocence; ordeal by fire; and, even in war, a kind of Truce of God[60] for religious festivals. The ghost of a murdered man drove his kinsmen to avenge his death, and later, to prosecute his murderer in court. The polis still left such prosecution to the slain man's natural defenders, those who shared his blood, some of which had been spilled. This blood tie was so strong that the descendants of a man who had committed an impious act could be polluted by that act. But when the propinquity of the polis had begun to tell—of this polis, this little island of growing order in a sea of disorder—then murder could pollute the entire community, and the polis would take steps to cleanse itself by punishing the offender.

Next to ruling and fighting, the noble loved athletic contests; poetry, especially the *Iliad* and the *Odyssey*; and music. Like Achilles, he sought imperishable honor. Perhaps the best material symbol of that immaterial prize was the materially worthless wreath of laurel that a man could win at Olympia. There the great festivals and competitions were held as early as 776, and by the sixth century the Olympics were drawing Greek competitors from all over the Mediterranean area to Olympia and competitions like the Olympics were taking place regularly at Delphi, at Isthmus, at Nemea. In those places, too, honor could be won by the Best People, people less anxious to live than to live well, people not afraid of death by battle but hopeful that men would make a song about them. At the Sacred Games they sought to excell and to have their excellence recognized.

But the nobles did more than convert monarchies into aristocratic republics, more than rule those republics and defend them with their blood. For it was during their rule that the republics of Mainland Greece and Asia Minor alike planted colonies, westward as far as Sagunto on the Mediterranean coast of Spain; eastward as far as Phasis on the eastern coast of the Black Sea; northward as far as Olbia, not far east of the modern city of Odessa; and southward as far as the coasts of modern Tunisia and Libya. Acting at home in the image of Achilles, the nobles led or sent forth explorers and colonists in the image of Odysseus, men who took to the sea to enrich themselves by trade, like the Phoenicians whom they supplanted in the Aegean, and, like them, to practice piracy. Like them, they bought or captured slaves. But, hunting for things to trade, they also found land to till.

Out to those lands, especially to the rich lands of southern Italy and of eastern Sicily while the Phoenicians held the western part of the island and kept the Strait of Gibraltar closed, streamed the Greek colonists. Most often, though not always, it was by fighting rather than by negotiation that they secured their new land; and when they had secured it, they promptly established an independent city-state, a polis, like the little city-states at home. As a rule they were not sent out by governments. The colonists went as groups of individuals, seeking their fortune where land was more plentiful than at home. But they went with the blessing of the aristocratic republic at home, and they carried their religious beliefs and customs with them. They even carried sacred fire from the altar of the mother-city, the *metro*-polis. Usually, their memories bound them to the polis from which they came. But sometimes more than one polis contributed colonists to a given venture.

Their newly founded cities served purposes which the colonists had not had in mind. They supplied markets for industries, notably pottery, at home. And the time came when they could send back badly needed wheat to feed their metropolis. By adding the rich wheatlands of southern Italy, Sicily, North Africa, and what are now southern Russia and the Turkish shores of the Sea of Marmora to the total means of production of the Greek peoples, the colonies permitted eventually a division of labor that was economically desirable. The home-country had never had enough wheatlands; or, at least, not under the land system that prevailed. The poor, the misfits, the restless, the ambitious, the merely adventurous now dreamed of new lands where they could carve out new lives for themselves. Their departure relieved the tension between rich and poor and the pressure for reform, and many a noble was glad to see the malcontents depart.

By an apparent paradox, when wheat and metals began to flow back from the colonies, the little city-states that colonists had gone out from grew more populous than before the emigration. They were supported by trade with the colonies, by manufactures for colonial markets, by a more specialized and more suitable agriculture at home, especially an agriculture that developed the vine and the olive on terraced slopes where neither wheat nor barley could ever have yielded profit. The bulk of the pottery that went out to the colonies consisted of huge amphorae that carried wine or olive oil. Wine was drunk everywhere in the Greek Mediterranean, although it was habitually mixed with water. To drink wine straight was to resemble the barbarian Thracians north of the Aegean. Olive oil found a multitude of uses. It took the place of the butter of Northern peoples: the Greeks flavored food with it, and cooked with it, too. It supplied the little clay lamps of Greece with illuminating oil. It was what the Greek athlete rubbed down with when he wished to cleanse his body. Or the unpressed fruit was eaten for food. In short, the olive was basic to Greek life; and it was a curious fact that when Greece sent out its colonists in all directions and to great distances, there were few Greek settlements where the olive could not be grown. Both the Mediterranean and the Black Sea tempered and softened the climate of the lands that bordered them: the sea protected the North African coast from the blast of summer heat that afflicted the hinterland, and it protected the Greek in southern Russia or on the French coast from the blast of winter cold that would kill an olive tree a few miles inland. The colonization of the eighth and seventh centuries merely won for the Greek farmer the natural limits of the arts he knew. Yet all the distant lands he settled in he organized politically in small, independent city-states; and everywhere these city-states wrangled and warred with each other, sometimes for the possession of land, the life-giver, but more and more for trade.

Despite these wars between the new colonies, the founding of new cities did much to create unity among Greeks everywhere. By their language, by their customs, by their gods, Hellenes everywhere found themselves set apart from the 'barbarians' and therefore more conscious of their own unity. The fact that many colonies had been founded by emigrants from more than one city-state in Mainland Greece and Greece-in-Asia tended toward the same sense of unity. Even in Mainland Greece, the aristocrats' sense of blood had always made for marriages between noble families in different city-states. Especially in Calabria, the toe of the Italian boot, which comprised the whole of what the Greek colonists termed "Italy," this common sense of being Hellenes developed strongly. And it was in southern Italy that the Greek colonies grew so numerous and so rich that the Hellenes would later call it Great Hellas.[61]

Where Greek colonists went to found some new polis, whether on the shores of the western Mediterranean or on those of the Black Sea, Minoan Crete and later the Mycenaean states had often got there first, centuries before. Whatever else the tale of Odysseus recorded, it also remembered sea routes that were later closed. For the Sicilian towns with which the Mycenaeans had traded had by the ninth century moved inland, to escape the piracy which was the sea's version of the Dark Ages. Essentially, then, the aristocratic republics of the ninth and eighth centuries were opening up a New World. In it they discovered fewer one-eyed giants, and six-headed monsters, and Sirens, and nymphs like Calypso, and magicians like Circe than the long-dead Odysseus had encountered, but they did discover Great Hellas, a land of broader fields and greater wealth. In a sense, like so many colonists, they discovered what Odysseus had restlessly sought: home. For they found at least the good earth often lying idle, land that would have already opened to another's plow in the city-states from which they had just sailed.

By the middle of the sixth century the Hellenes had founded their little city-states rather thickly on the shores of the Dardanelles, which they called the Hellespont. They had penetrated the Black Sea, which they called the Pontus, or open sea, or sometimes the Euxine, or Hospitable Sea—a title they may have given it to propitiate it, since they found rough sailing there. They scattered colonies on the western coast of the Black Sea, and a few on its other coasts. They had already settled the shores of the Propontis, which was the vestibule to the Pontus proper, the Black Sea. They had founded many colonies on the coasts of Sicily, except in the extreme west, and many in southern Italy, from Cumae, near the present site of Naples, to Tarentum, on the heel of the boot. They held both sides of the strategic strait between Italy and Sicily: Messina, which they called Messana, on one side; Reggio di Calabria, which they called Rhegium, on the other. Similarly, at the southern mouth of the Bosphorus, the Ox-ford, which connects the Black Sea with the Propontis, Chalcedon grew up on the eastern shore, and, on the western, the strategic city of Byzantium, which would not for many centuries be called Constantinople. A few colonies were planted on the coast of Epirus and even of Illyria, as far north as modern Albania. On the French coast of the Mediterranean six colonies sprang up, beginning at Marseilles, the Greek Massilia, and stretching westward. There were three on the northern part of Spain's east coast; three on the coast of what is now Libya; five on the south coast of Asia Minor and in Cyprus. There were even two 'treaty ports' in Egypt itself. In short, colonists created a string of Hellenic cities, whose citizens could be found scattered along the shores of the Mediterranean, and the Black Sea too, like frogs about a pond.[62]

Some of these new and distant Greek city-states remained relatively unimportant except for the grain or fish or timber or other things they could furnish in exchange for oil or wine or woolen cloth, but Western Greece evolved a characteristic colonial life of its own. That life was somehow larger and easier than in Mainland Greece, if only because there was more land. Where cities grew rich, as Sybaris did at a strategic spot on the westernmost shore of the present Gulf of Taranto, there developed a degree of luxury that made the Sybarite a byword in Mainland Greece. The Western Greeks loved athletic competition as much as their cousins in the old country, and regularly sent contestants to the Olympics and the other great religious games. They would never equal the final achievements of Mainland Greece in literature or philosophy or the plastic arts; and they would tend to import their art from home. But they would turn early toward medicine, engineering, and the practical art of rhetoric that fitted one for a political career. All that, however, would be in the future.

The geographical expansion of Mainland Greece and Greece-in-Asia involved three economic stages. In the first, merchant adventurers were scouting for metals and selling petty luxuries to the natives, the barbarians, in the fashion of the Phoenicians, whom they were crowding out of many markets. This was why, according to tradition, the first Greek colony on Italian soil was planted not on the nearest and richest Italian land but at Cumae, north of Naples, where there was trade in metals with the Etruscans farther north; and this was why Cumae remained the northernmost outpost of Hellas in Italy. Later, Neapolis, New City, now Naples, was founded farther south, as so many other cities were, farther southward still, and much nearer the mother-cities at home. For the merchant-adventurer stage of colonization was giving way to the stage of permanent settlements by land-hungry settlers, even where those settlers kept at least one eye on trade. It was only in a third stage that Mainland Greece and Greece-in-Asia effected a division of labor between themselves and the colonies they had sent out. Only then was there heavy commerce. The colonies which the Ionian city-state, Miletus, for example, had planted on the southeastern and northern shores of the Black Sea would greedily buy Milesian woolen fabrics in exchange for wheat, timber, metals, salted fish, and slaves.

In order for this cycle of metal-hunting and trinket trade, of land settlement, and of heavy commerce to complete itself, two very special devices were badly needed and happily found: the art of writing, which the Phoenicians helped the Greeks to invent, and the art of coining money.

From Asia, the Greeks got the practice of coining money. By the early seventh century the kingdom of Lydia, which lay just behind Ionia in the mountains of western Asia Minor, had developed coins out of an earlier exchange token. This token was the bean-shaped 'dump' of electrum, an alloy of gold and silver sometimes called white gold, which the Lydians found in river beds, already blended by nature. The great empires of Egypt, Babylonia, and Assyria had made the transition from cattle as a medium of exchange to metal bars or ingots. But these, though more convenient than cattle, had to be weighed and their purity assayed if they were to fulfill their function. This problem had been met by having the government weigh and assay, and then stamp the metal as a guarantee of its value. The Lydian 'dump' was stamped in this way. But the royal Lydian government improved this little bean-shaped nugget of electrum by flattening it to a disk, placing it on an anvil, and striking it with an intaglio die which impressed a bas-relief design. It was this practice that spread from Lydia, first to neighboring Ionian city-states like Miletus and Samos, but soon to Aegina, the cities of Euboea, and the cities of Mainland Greece.[63] Since gold was scarce in the Greek world, the cities of European Hellas struck their coins from silver. Normally they were imprinted with the symbol of some god.

The spoken, wingèd word had now found its equivalent symbol in the written word; and the bar of metal had found its own equivalent symbol in the coin. These two transformations liberated both word and coin from serious limitations of space. The word could now be heard across the Aegean, across the whole Mediterranean, and to the farthest shore of the Black Sea, wherever another person lived who could read Greek. The coin traveled with greater ease and speed than ever metal bars could. But both symbols, the word and the coin, introduced complicated problems. In theory both were merely means of exchange, in the one case for images and ideas, in the other case for material objects. Together they promoted and enlarged the commerce in ideas, and the commerce in commodities. They should, therefore, have promoted community. But words, whether uttered or written, could lie, as well as tell the truth. Money, at first merely the means that would help a man exchange goods with his neighbor, to the advantage of both, could be turned from a means into an end. The exchange of goods could be carried on for the purpose of making money.

In the Greek city-states, and especially in those with easy access to the sea, coinage wrought a revolution. Slowly men shifted further and further from raising and making the things they used, to making and raising things in order to get coin, since it appeared that coin was the one thing that could always command other men's labor or possessions, whether in Hellas or in foreign lands. This shift produced disastrous consequences for the poor. It was only the rich, which at first meant only the nobles, who had enough surplus goods to acquire a share of the new power that coined money gave. Coin was still scarce, which meant that the few who had got hold of it could demand very high interest from those who needed money. Money developed the division of labor and special skills. The man who had been able in the old days to supply all his own wants, barring acts of the gods which might bring famine or pestilence, now began to need money to buy services as well as goods. The old family system of land ownership gave way to private personal ownership. Farms that had once rented for a fixed share of the crop now rented for a fixed sum of money: if the crop failed, the tenant was lost. And he was literally lost, because his creditor might legally seize, not only his personal possessions, not only the tools with which he labored, but his very person itself. In short, his creditor might sell him as a thing into slavery. When some city-states shifted from grain-growing to vines and olives, and when grain began to be imported from better grain lands abroad, the farmer without capital could not participate in this new division of labor. It took some five years for an olive tree to bear and it took nearer fifteen to get full production. The man without capital could not wait that long for his returns. Finally, since the laws were administered only by the nobles, since they were not even written down and were known only to the nobles, and since the revolution that was ruining so many of the poor was increasing the wealth and power of the nobles, abuses were numerous and conditions were growing steadily more desperate.

The noble, who scorned the peasant because he could not find in him the virtues which he himself prized and was ready to die for, often felt the smoldering hate for the peasant that any normal man would tend to feel for the man he had wronged. In the early, vigorous days of the aristocracy, the noble discharged a genuine social function: the defense of the state and the administration of the state. His privileges were related to those functions and morally supported by them. But now something was happening that he could scarcely have foreseen, something that would rob him of his function and therefore something that would make his position and privileges seem unjust. Moreover, this happened just when the personal relationship that existed between noble and peasant in the old life together on the land was yielding place to the impersonal relationship, the cash nexus, of buyer and seller, of creditor and debtor. Yet it was just that personal relationship which must often have mitigated the inequalities of wealth. Now it was vanishing.

In the economic revolution through which Hellas passed not every man who prospered was a noble. Sometimes a Dustyfoot might through energy or shrewdness or sheer luck acquire some of the new power that movable wealth was introducing into a community where once power had come from land alone. Lacking the prestige of birth, of descent from the gods, of the right to rule the polis, such a merchant was nevertheless winning the prestige of wealth. At last this new power enabled him to play a new role on the field of battle. Around 700,[64] in the cities of Eretria and Chalcis, a new type of soldier appeared: the heavy-armed foot soldier, the hoplite. He fought, not as the half-armed, half-armored member of a rabble of peasants following the mounted nobles, but in a disciplined military formation known as the phalanx. He was able to find enough money to clothe himself in bronze armor, and he fought shield to shield with his hoplite comrades in a solid formation often eight lines deep. He learned to stand firm against pursuit by horsemen. He fought, not like Achilles for the glory of his lineage or himself, but to defend the polis where he lived and throve. It no longer took noble blood to defend that polis; and the hoplite inevitably came to wonder why it should take noble blood to rule it. The aristocratic republic, which in so many city-states had peacefully taken over or forcibly seized the duties and honors of the chieftain-king, now fought a rear-guard action against the new man whom trade had brought to birth, the well-to-do Dustyfoot who could defend his polis and longed to share in its rule to foster his own interests and to protect his way of earning his bread. The use of coin had increased the nobles' power to exploit their peasants' labor, and now it lost the nobles their exclusive power to rule the polis.

Here again, as in the case of so many similar revolutions in other civilizations, the new men lacked the confidence in themselves and in each other necessary to seize the government. But the discontent they generated, when added to the discontent of Dustyfeet less fortunate than themselves, was a standing invitation to some noble, more selfishly ambitious, or more clear-sighted, or merely more just, to lead a revolution. And thus arose the tyrant. In the beginning, it was the tyrant who led the peasant toward freedom.

When these revolutions first occurred, the term tyrant was not a term of abuse or opprobrium. It was morally neutral. The word itself came, as coins did, from the kingdom of Lydia, by way of Ionia.[65] It meant a person who had seized monarchical power by force. In the seventh century, in a number of Greek cities, tyrannies of this sort were established; and for obvious political reasons they favored the opponents of the nobles they had overthrown. They favored commerce and industry, and they might even see fit to lighten the lot of the peasants. Where the chieftain-king's power had rested on personal loyalty, religious sanction, and hallowed custom, the power of the new monarch, the tyrant, rested on popular hatred of the nobles and on money to pay the tyrant's personal bodyguard.

Despite all the Greeks who turned mariner, most Greeks still did what Greeks had done all through the Dark Ages and would keep on doing: they farmed. They found a poet who could speak for them as not even Homer had spoken, Hesiod. Later Greeks might think of him chiefly as the author[66] of the *Theogony*, in which he traced the lineage of the Olympic gods, and thereby expanded the divine lore which men had already learned from the *Iliad* and the *Odyssey*. But his greatest poem was a farmer's, not a warrior's, poem: *Works and Days*. It was written in the epic meter of the *Iliad*, and, although Homer's epics were greater than anything Hesiod ever wrote, *Works and Days* achieved a special greatness of its own.[67] Although the specific "works" described in *Works and Days*

43

are farm tasks, and the "days" discussed are largely those of good omen or bad omen for farm operations, what Hesiod was really writing about was justice, human and divine; and work, labor, the lot of man on earth. About justice and about work he wrote with true poetic passion. The glory and misery of war that Achilles knew did not directly interest him. Neither did the "unfruitful sea,"[68] the "grey, discomfortable sea,"[69] which he thoroughly disliked and feared, nor the restless drive of the explorer to know. What he knew was the bountiful earth, "the wide-bosomed Earth,"[70] from whom were descended both gods and men. What he knew, or thought he knew, was that although once men lived on earth "free from ills and hard toil,"[71] now they must work or perish. Was it some dim folk-memory of Minoan wealth and power that led him to sing how a golden race of men had once "lived like gods without sorrow of heart, remote and free from toil and grief"[72]? Then had come a silver race. Then a bronze race of men, who had strong, bronze armor, but no iron, and who were destroyed by their own hands.[73] Could this, too, be a folk-memory? A memory of the Mycenaeans, who weakened each other through incessant wars, who had finally fought at Troy, and who had been submerged and thrown into disorder by the Northern Dorians, a race that according to tradition had brought in iron? In any case, the bronze race was followed by a generation of "heroes," who also disappeared, but who now dwelt on the Isles of the Blessed on the shore of the Ocean. At last a generation of iron appeared, the men whom Hesiod saw about him; and he cried out:

> Thereafter, would that I were not among the men of the fifth generation, but either had died before or been born afterwards. For now truly is a race of iron, and men never rest from labor and sorrow by day, and from perishing by night.[74]

Centuries of turmoil had succeeded the fall of Mycenae and its world, centuries of labor and sorrow by day and perishing by night. Those centuries were ending now: many a chieftain-king had founded a settled polis, and the polis had become a republic, though an aristocratic republic in which few men ruled, and before long the colonists would go out, and human existence, at least for those at the top, would become less full of labor and sorrow. Even for some of the others, it would become in many ways more significant and more exciting to live. But Hesiod had no way of knowing all this. *Works and Days* was based on harsh personal experience, not on a colonial expansion that had not even begun. It was the experience of a smallholder, wringing a living from a farm at the foot of Mount Helicon, in southern Boeotia, in the eighth century.[75]

Hesiod's father had been a merchant sailor in the thriving port of Cyme on the coast of Asia Minor, and had failed in business. He salvaged enough to buy a farm, or clear one as a pioneer, here near the village of Ascra, and to leave it on his death to his two sons, Hesiod and Perses. *Works and Days* was addressed directly to Perses and sharply rebuked him for bribing the court of nobles which settled the inheritance. But the poem was also a hymn to Zeus, who ruled the invisible world of the gods as well as the hard world of those men who belonged to a race of iron; to Zeus who loved justice, and who in the long run would punish those who bought and sold crooked judgment. Hesiod was as indignant at being legally robbed of land that was rightfully his as Achilles was when his superior, Agamemnon, robbed him of his meed of honor, the woman Briseis. But he was sure that injustice would be punished. For the Fates

> pursue the transgressions of men and of gods; and these goddesses never cease from their dread anger until they punish the sinner with a sore penalty.[76]

Zeus had

> thrice ten thousand spirits, watchers of mortal men, and these keep watch on judgements and deeds of wrong as they roam, clothed in mist, all over the earth.[77]

Indeed, Justice herself, also

> wrapped in mist, follows to the city and haunts of people, weeping, and bringing mischief to men, even to such as have driven her forth in that they did not deal straitly with her.[78]

It was to right these injustices that Zeus "humbles the proud and raises the obscure."[79]

Hesiod rebuked the nobles for accepting bribes and seizing what was not their own and dealing out crooked justice. He made no explicit objections to government by the Best People. He was a moral reformer, but not a political one. More than either, he was a poet, heavyhearted at man's injustice to his fellow man, and at violence as a substitute for justice.

Heavyhearted, and indignant. On this earth, sang the farmer, man's destiny was to work, and then work. Neither begging nor robbing would substitute for *ergon*, work. This was why he explained to Perses, his brother, how the farmer's work was done and on which days it was likeliest to be best done. The warning of the thrice ten thousand spirits who kept watch on judgments was brusquely addressed to the nobles themselves.

Fighting would not help. Zeus

has ordained this law for men, that fishes and beasts and winged fowls should devour one another, for right is not in them; but to mankind he gave right which proves far the best.[80]

Evil action was easy and the road to it was smooth. "But between us and Goodness the gods have placed the sweat of our brows."[81] "Both gods and men are angry with a man who lives idle."[82] Wealth should not be seized: "god-given wealth is much better."[83] This was why he urged his rapacious brother to "work upon work,"[84] and to "work the work which the gods ordained for men."[85]

As for *Eris*, or Strife, she was not one goddess but two, a good Eris and a bad. The Eris who led neighbor to vie with neighbor in productive work was wholesome for men.[86] But Hesiod hated the Eris who fostered war, the Eris Achilles followed, as he hated the sea Odysseus followed. And in the *Theogony*, a poem in which, taught by the Muses whom he invoked, he told which god was descended from which, or married which, or gave birth to which, he told also where this second, evil Eris came from and what her evil progeny was. This second and "hard-hearted Strife"[87] was born of Night, who also bore Deceit and hateful Age.

But abhorred Strife bare painful Toil and Forgetfulness and Famine and tearful Sorrows, Fightings also, Battles, Murders, Manslaughters, Quarrels, Lying Words, Disputes, Lawlessness and Ruin, all of one nature . . .[88]

Despite the hardness, the toughness, and the peasant grumbling about the crops and the farmer's life, *Works and Days* could have been written only by a man who loved the earth, this earth that he was forced to till if he would eat. The country images of the weather, the hills, the birds, the flowers kept bursting through the dour descriptions of man's plight. In the *Theogony* Hesiod[89] said he saw a divine vision. The Muses, who danced on soft feet atop Mount Helicon about the altar of Zeus, were in the habit of going abroad by night, veiled in thick mist, to utter their song.

46

And one day they taught Hesiod glorious song while he was shepherding his lambs under holy Helicon, and this word first the goddesses said to me—the Muses of Olympus, daughters of Zeus who holds the aegis:

"Shepherds of the wilderness, wretched things of shame, mere bellies, we know how to speak many false things as though they were true; but we know, when we will, to utter true things."

So said the ready-voiced daughters of great Zeus, and they plucked and gave me a rod, a shoot of sturdy laurel, a marvelous thing, and breathed into me a divine voice to celebrate things that shall be and things that were aforetime; and they bade me sing of the race of the blessed gods that are eternally, but ever to sing of themselves both first and last.[90]

They were veiled, as the Homeric gods so often were, in thick mist; and none would expect a wretched thing of shame, a mere belly, to pierce through that mist with his eyes. But Hesiod did.[91] Nor would one expect the Muses to hand him the rod that would authorize him to speak, that would literally inspire him with a divine voice. But this the Muses did. And the divine voice celebrated things that would yet be and things that had already been.

This, of course, was Hesiod's interpretation of what happened to him that night at the foot of holy Helicon. But he himself stated that the goddesses were veiled in a thick mist. The later Greeks, whose memories were the *Iliad* and the *Odyssey*, firmly believed that, after Homer, the other great authority on the immortal gods was Hesiod. And the manner of life the small aristocratic republics fought to defend and carried in their hollow ships to the other small cities that they founded all over the Mediterranean world was a manner of life shown to them by the gods, largely through Homer and Hesiod. That manner of life would make the Greeks an inspired race and not mere bellies and wretched things of shame. And thanks in large measure to Hesiod, they would learn not only to die gloriously, not only to search ceaselessly for man's home, but to work the work which the gods ordained for men. Indeed, some of them would even learn, in the very midst of war and slavery and oppression, to accept the law that Zeus had ordained for men, that they differed from fishes and beasts and winged fowls, who devoured one another, for right was not in them; but to man he gave right, which proved far the best.

47

3

THE LAWGIVERS,
LYCURGUS AND SOLON

IT WAS on the Asian shore of the Aegean, not on the European, that the Hellenes first emerged from the Dark Age that followed the Dorian invasion. In Europe, where Minos the Cretan lawgiver had become a confused memory and where even Tiryns and Mycenae had turned into legend, men had re-entered the womb of their mother, the earth. And from that spacious womb a new agrarian, feudal society had been born, lived out its rough childhood, and was still uncouth when the cities of Asian Greece began to develop something that Minos himself would have recognized as a good life for men. The Dorian invasion that had thrown Mycenaean Greece into chaos had driven many of its victims to flee across the Aegean to the nearby coast of Asia Minor. Because of the many islands, the refugees at no time needed to lose sight of land. In Asia Minor they found a balmier climate than the one they had left, and a relatively wide and fertile littoral to settle. Some of the refugees were Achaeans, some were the Pelasgians whom the Achaeans had conquered. They may well have taken with them a larger share of Mycenaean ideas and skills than could survive in Mainland Greece. On the Asian shore they may well have found more of those ideas and skills. In the north, Aeolians settled the littoral of Phrygia and Mysia, and their settlements came to comprise Aeolis. In the center, Ionians who would claim to have sailed from Attica founded settlements that came to be called Ionia. But all of these refugees, and even a thrust of Dorians who followed the Cyclades islands to found Doris on the southernmost portion of this same inviting shore, were exposed to the fertilizing influences of the great and ancient civilizations of the Middle East, like Babylonia and Assyria. Their new home turned out, therefore, to be a hothouse in which their own skills, images, and ideas went through a rapid forcing stage. Ionia, especially, developed powerful and wealthy and luxurious cities when the city-states of Mainland Greece were by comparison small and rustic communities. In Europe, on the other hand, Greeks of the young cities for long came into contact only with their uncouth cousins to the north, such as the tribesmen of Macedonia or Epirus. Even in the western Mediterranean the Greek colonists met mostly with barbarous tribes and confronted few civilized foreigners except their trade competitors: seafaring men of Phoenicia, Carthaginians, Etruscans.

One of the Homeric Hymns, this one the Hymn to the Delian Apollo, described a religious festival of the Ionians in the Isle of Delos, the land the god loved best:

> for there the long robed Ionians gather in your honour with their children and shy wives: mindful, they delight you with boxing and dancing and song, so often as they hold their gathering. A man would say that they were deathless and unaging if he should then come upon the Ionians so met together. For he would see the graces of them all, and would be pleased in heart gazing at the men and well-girded women with their swift ships and great wealth.[92]

A goodly portion of this great wealth was concentrated in the Ionian city of Miletus. Strategically situated on a promontory, this city had four sheltered harbors and easy communications inland by the Meander River. There was flat, fertile land for wheat, flanked by hillside vineyards and orchards. On the plateau behind, there was ample pasturage for the sheep whose wool nourished the city's famous cloth manufacture. With a mixed but thoroughly Hellenized population, Miletus became by the sixth century the busiest and most populous of Greek cities anywhere. For two centuries Milesians had colonized the Black Sea. They had established a special trading post on the coast of Egypt. Everywhere they traded their famous goods for the food, the raw materials, and the slave labor they required. They processed the skins and precious metals of neighboring Lydia, the wool of Phrygia, the hemp of Colchis at the foot of the Caucasus, and iron from the Chalybes, a little south of Colchis. The Milesians turned out furniture, especially beds. Except in Mainland Greece, their customers not only wanted pottery; they wanted pots that were filled with oil or wine. Wealthy customers in Western Greece—especially southern Italy and Sicily—bid for Milesian rugs and the Milesians' magnificent purple cloth.

In the sixth century this great wealth of the long-robed Ionians came under the gentle protectorate of a partially Hellenized monarch, Croesus of Lydia. The Ionians had steadily refused to convert the Panionian League, a primarily religious association, into some sort of political and military unit capable of defending them. So, one by one, Croesus had conquered their cities. Lydian garrisons took over the Ionian cities, and those cities paid Croesus an annual tribute; otherwise, they governed themselves. Croesus enforced a peace between them, a peace which their mutual jealousy had hitherto prevented. Their rustic cousins across the Aegean might affect to despise them for surrendering their freedom; but they admired them, too, and envied them their wealth. The Ionians loved money and luxury and elegance. In their trailing robes, fastened with golden grasshopper pins, their arms loaded with finely wrought gold and jewels, the men promenaded along their cities' handsome avenues. Their wives, escorted by many slaves, displayed their elaborate costumes, their hair and their breasts perfumed. Pleasure had conquered them quite as much as Croesus had; but, while they feasted and sang, Croesus descried a mounting danger in the East.

However, Ionia was more than pleasure, and more than business. In the plastic arts, in architecture, in music, in poetry, in natural philosophy Ionians pioneered; and their dialogue in the arts and sciences penetrated Mainland Greece and involved the Western Greeks as well. Mainland Greece was still building Doric temples out of wood and brick long after

Ionia had learned to use marble. The Ionian sculptor likewise learned to use marble, and to cast hollow bronze statues too. The sculpture helped the architect develop the narrow, fluted marble column with the gracefully voluted Ionic capital. He invented the caryatid, or marble statue of a woman, placed to serve as a temple column; and, in order to portray the long-robed Ionians, he pioneered in the study of elaborate drapery. At its worst, his art struck the Mainlander as luxurious, fussy, prettified, effeminate; but at its best, the Mainlander found it gracious, smiling, delicate, and utterly charming. Throughout the sixth century, Mainland Greece went to school to Ionian sculptors and architects.

Greece-in-Asia, which had dreamed the first great poems, the epics of Homer, now originated another kind of poetry, a poetry of short songs sung to a lyre, or to a cithara, or to a flute. In the case of the choral lyric, both musical notes and dance steps went with the poem. The poet departed from the dactylic hexameter of Homer and Hesiod and invented various metrical forms. He no longer sang, one after another, tales about the great heroes of the past. Increasingly, the poet talked about himself, about the deeds he himself had done, the passions he himself had suffered.

This poetry could be savagely satirical and morally revolutionary. To a Greek, for example, to throw away one's shield in battle was the very hallmark of cowardice. Yet in the seventh century Archilochus of Paros could cry:

> The shield I left because I must, poor blameless armament! beside a bush, gives joy now to some Saian, but myself I have saved. What care I for that shield. It shall go with a curse. I'll get me another e'en as good.[93]

Or he could be tersely witty:

> The Fox knoweth many things, the Hedgehog one great thing.[94]

Later in the same seventh century, the Aeolian poet, Alcaeus of rich Lesbos, sang his aristocratic disdain of the new merchant class, in which "money maketh man,"[95] his aristocratic hatred of the tyrant Myrsilus, and his savage exultation at news of the tyrant's death:

> Now must a man get drunk and pledge with strength since Myrsilus is dead.[96]

The poems of Alcaeus called on his friends to drink sweet wine, to pile up the fire while a winter storm raged outside—or in summer to drink wine in the grateful shadow of some sheltering rock.

Early in the sixth century Ionia gave Hellas Anacreon of Teos, although a Persian invasion would eventually drive him to emigrate from Ionia to Thrace. A love affair with a Thracian girl led Anacreon to sing naughtily:

Pray, why do you look askance at me, my Thracian filly, and shun me so resolutely as though I knew nothing of my art? I would have you to know I could bridle you right well and take rein and ride you about the turning-post of the course. But instead you graze in the meadows and frisk and frolic to your heart's content; for you have not a clever breaker to ride you.[97]

Anacreon visited the court of Polycrates, the celebrated tyrant of Samos, who also played patron to a poet of southern Italy, Ibycus of Rhegium. When the Persians captured and crucified Polycrates, Anacreon went to the court of Hipparchus, tyrant of Athens, where he charmed men with his drinking songs and love lyrics. Like so many of the melodious, witty, sensual poems Ionian poets sang, Anacreon's poems were haunted by the remembrance of oncoming Death. But he lived to be eighty-five.

Neither Anacreon nor Alcaeus nor Archilochus, with all their wit, with all their beauty of image, could match the torrential force of an Aeolian poet, born like Alcaeus in lovely Lesbos. But this other Lesbian was a woman, Sappho, a friend of Alcaeus, an aristocrat like him. She was born about 612. In Lesbos she directed a sort of school, based on the cult of Aphrodite, in which girls were educated and prepared for marriage. Sappho's deep attachments to her young charges would survive only in slight fragments, but in fragments burning with passion. A Mainland Greek might find Lesbos sophisticated, worldly-wise, half-mocking, pleasure-loving; at best, gracious, smiling, melodious. But these few remaining words out of Lesbos, sung by one woman, would always live, searing and terrible words, words inspired by the great Goddess of Love, so that it was rightly that Alcaeus, and others too, called Sappho "holy." It was as if an Aeolian woman had suddenly reminded her hearers that Aphrodite was first worshiped in Eastern lands and that the soul of Asian Greece was most truly itself when it stood stricken, not indeed by the pleasant desire for wine, women, and song, but by all-destroying love. For Asia Minor knew, more clearly than Mainland Greece, the frightening power of this Great

Goddess, whether men called her Aphrodite, or Astarte, or Ishtar. It was this dread goddess that holy Sappho served. She wrote:

It is to be a God, methinks, to sit before you and listen close by to the sweet accents and winning laughter which have made the heart in my breast beat fast, I warrant you. When I look on you, Brocheo, my speech comes short or fails me quite, I am tongue-tied; in a moment a delicate fire has overrun my flesh, my eyes grow dim and my ears sing, the sweat runs down me and a trembling takes me altogether, till I am as green and pale as the grass, and death itself seems not very far away. . . .[98]

And again:

> The Moon is gone
> And the Pleiads set,
>   Midnight is nigh;
> Time passes on,
> And passes; yet
> Alone I lie.[99]

Ionia and Lesbos gave Greece these early poets, but Ionia gave her also her earliest philosophy. For most of her first philosophers either lived or wrote in Ionia; or left Ionia to teach in Mainland Greece or in the West; or came to Ionia from elsewhere. At Miletus, Thales, Anaximander, and Anaximenes devoted themselves to natural philosophy, to a search for a common material principle or base to which the varied and changing phenomenal world about them could be reduced. Pythagoras fled Polycrates' tyranny in Samos to teach in Croton, in southern Italy, and to found there a sort of ascetic order of both men and women. This Pythagorean order for a while governed Croton. Its master taught the necessity of purifying the soul, largely through intellectual discipline. He sought to explain the phenomenal world by applying mathematics to it. Also to Western Greece, to Elea, came Xenophanes from his native Colophon; he was another political refugee. Although Xenophanes admitted more than one god in his pantheon, he was certain that one of those gods was supreme over all others. He blamed Homer and Hesiod, who had "ascribed unto the Gods all that is reproach and blame in the world of men, stealing and adultery and deceit."[100] He declared that rainbows were not the goddess Iris but merely "a cloud, purple and red and yellow to view."[101]

And he scorned the Greeks' habit of making their gods in their own image:

> Now if horses or oxen or lions had hands or power to paint and make the works of art that men make, then would horses give their Gods horse-like forms in painting or sculpture, and oxen ox-like forms, even each after its own kind.[102]

And:

> The Aethiop saith that his Gods are snub-nosed and black, the Thracian that his have blue eyes and red hair . . .[103]

"There's one God," wrote Xenophanes again, "greatest among Gods and men, who is like to mortals neither in form nor mind."[104]

In Ephesus, Heraclitus speculated on the unity-in-change of the world about him. Some of these Ionian thinkers wrote in verse; but in the sixth century others became the earliest writers of Greek prose, a medium that was proving useful to another intellectual venture, the first writing of history.

All in all, Greece-in-Asia, and especially Ionia, had by the end of the sixth century played an extraordinary role in the history of Hellas. These Asian Greeks had moved from the simplicity of children to adult awareness, and sometimes even to middle-aged disillusionment, in three brief centuries. That they made that passage early was natural, given their contact with the old ways and thoughts and dreams of Asia, an Asia past her full bloom. Ionian artists, Ionian poets, Ionian musicians, Ionian philosophers would scatter westward through the Greek world and guide that tardier world's first steps toward more beautiful images, more expert crafts, profounder thoughts. If it was primarily in Ionia that the Hellenic world had encountered the immemorial ways of Asia, how would Asia affect the political life of Hellas? That question was answered, at least provisionally, when Croesus, the wealthy and half-Hellenized king of Lydia, made himself suzerain of the semi-autonomous city-states of Greece-in-Asia. Politically, it seemed, Asian Greeks were destined to be ruled by non-Hellenic Asians. Meanwhile, Mainland Greece had received the gift of Ionia's vision. And Mainland Greece was more sheltered than Ionia, from annexation by non-Hellenic military states, from the too swift absorption of non-Hellenic ideas, and from the confusion bred by wealth too speedily acquired.

By the sixth century no other city-state in Mainland Greece enjoyed such prestige as Lacedaemon, or Sparta. In the first place Sparta directly ruled a larger territory than even Athens, her nearest competitor. Hollow Lacedaemon, the land from which Helen of Troy had fled with Paris when she deserted her husband, King Menelaus, for that Trojan prince, lay in the southeast portion of the Peloponnese, between two mountain ranges. Geologically, Lacedaemon had been a lake bottom. When the Dorian invasion came, a band of Dorians seized this fertile valley and united four small villages into a polis, officially "the City of the Lacedaemonians," informally "Sparta." The entire territory which the Spartiates first governed was named Laconia. Two leading families shared the government: from early times Sparta had two kings, one from each of these two families.

As the number of Spartans increased and as land grew scarce, Sparta followed the usual pattern of the Greek polis: the nobility managed to monopolize most of the land. But Sparta did not attempt to solve her problem as did Corinth, another leading Dorian state, by repeatedly sending out colonies. Instead, toward the end of the eighth century, she attacked Messenia, across the mountains to her west, a populous state with even more fertile farm land than Laconia had. The First Messenian War took some twenty years of hard fighting. The dispossessed Messenians were subjected. As Sparta's fighting poet, the lame Tyrtaeus, would later put it, they were "galled with great burdens like asses, bringing to their lords under grievous necessity a half of all the fruit of the soil."[105] Each Spartiate family was assigned its portion of the land and its fruits in addition to what the family had been assigned at home in Laconia. But violence between conqueror and conquered broke out again: Messenia revolted about 640 and was with difficulty quelled in the Second Messenian War; and by the sixth century Sparta had been transformed into an aristocratic, conservative state unique in Greek history.

According to tradition this conservative state had been shaped by a great lawgiver named Lycurgus, who had lived long before, though tradition was uncertain as to just how long before. Lycurgus' father, one Eurypon, was one of the two kings of Sparta. In Sparta too, the usual tensions developed between the wealthy landowner and the poorer citizen; and Lycurgus' father was stabbed while trying to make peace during a riot. Lycurgus' elder brother, Polydectes, inherited his family's crown; but Polydectes himself died shortly afterwards without issue, and the crown passed to Lycurgus. Then Lycurgus discovered that his brother's widow was with child and he insisted that, if this posthumous child of the late king should be a boy, this boy must reign; he himself would step aside and would act as regent to his nephew-king. The child did turn out to be a boy, and Lycurgus did step aside and was greatly admired for acting on his just decision.

But there were also Spartans who accused him of secretly aiming to recover royal power. To avoid suspicion, Lycurgus determined to travel abroad until his nephew should come of age, marry, and beget a son to succeed him. He traveled in Crete, the storied land of Minos, the law-giver.[106] From Crete, with its excellent laws, he voyaged to luxurious Ionia, in order to understand what happened when the laws of a polis did not impose a simple and severe regime on its citizens. There he discovered the poems of Homer, which he copied to take home with him to Sparta. Some historians claimed that he visited Egypt, too, and one even insisted that he had gone as far as India and talked with the gymnosophists, or naked philosophers, there. Meanwhile, this inquiring traveler, this ex-regent of Sparta who could have remained king had he been a little less scrupulous, was longed for in his own polis. The people considered their present kings undistinguished and lacking in leadership and wanted Lycurgus back. Even the kings wished for his return, on the chance that he could control their subjects' insolence. From Egypt or from India or from elsewhere Lycurgus returned. Judging that Spartan society was sick and that only the most drastic reforms would save the polis, he went to Delphi and consulted Apollo. The priestess gave him an oracle:

Dear to Zeus thou hast come to my well-stored temple, Lycurgus,
Dear to Zeus and to all who dwell in the courts of Olympus.
Art thou a man or a god? 'Tis a god I deem thee, Lycurgus.[107]

According to one tradition, Apollo then gave him a constitution for Sparta. He returned to Sparta, put down the unruly populace, strengthened the aristocracy, and established his new order. He retained Sparta's two kings, who continued to perform the offices of high priest and, at least to some extent, those of supreme judge, and who commanded Sparta's army in the field. But he set up also, by a *rhetra*, or compact, especially obtained from Delphi, a Council of Elders, or Senate, the *Gerousia*. This Senate contained the two kings and twenty-eight other members at least sixty years old, elected for life. The Senate wielded enormous powers, especially in foreign affairs. It was the Spartan version of the aristocratic council which replaced kingship in most Hellenic states. As for the restive populace, those men over thirty formed the *Apella*, or Assembly. They could initiate no laws. They cast no ballots. They did not deliberate. They merely acclaimed by shouts those measures of the Senate that they approved. Indeed, at some period later than Lycurgus' day, two kings of Sparta were said to have changed the famous compact so that, if the popular Assembly tried to amend the laws submitted to it, the Senate could dismiss the Assembly. Apollo, the Spartans claimed, sanctioned this change too. But now the Senate grew tyrannical and, more than a century after Lycurgus, the kings managed to establish a board of five Ephors, or Overseers, to check the insolence of the Senate and to defend the rights of all Spartans. The Overseers were elected by the people, from the people, for a term of one year.

Lycurgus also judged that one of the principal causes of the disorder Sparta had suffered from was the fact that land was concentrating in the hands of the rich. His remedy was heroic: he would do away with the bad eris, or strife, of competitive money-making, of greed, and luxury, and recover the good eris, the competition for honor. He persuaded his fellow citizens to turn over all land to the polis. Then he assigned equal lots of land to all Spartiates and equal lots of other land in Laconia to the *Perioeci*, or Dwellers-round-about. The subject population, what survived of the pre-Dorian stock,[108] became state serfs called Helots. These Helots were assigned to the lots of the Spartiates and were compelled to produce a modest, fixed amount of food for their masters. All beyond their masters' rations they might keep for themselves.

But Lycurgus knew that money was the great cause of the tensions between rich and poor that had threatened to destroy the polis, and here too his remedy was heroic. He caused all gold and silver coin to be withdrawn and he issued in its place a clumsy iron money, too heavy and of too little value to invite hoarding or other misuse. The new currency had the further advantage of isolating Sparta from the merchants of luxuries, the teachers of rhetoric, the wandering soothsayers, the pimps, the goldsmiths, the silversmiths, in short from all those who had swarmed in from abroad when there had been real money, current throughout Greece, to be made there. As for craftsmen, Lycurgus turned their attention to the few useful articles like chairs, tables, and beds that his new-style Spartan would still need: let them make these few things beautiful and not waste their time on baubles.

Tradition recounted that the rich were outraged by losing the luxuries which gold and silver had once bought for them; that they stoned Lycurgus from the market place, and that he fled to a temple. Before he reached sanctuary, a youth named Alcander smote him with his staff and blinded one eye. When the Spartans saw him bloody and half-blinded, they repented, and delivered Alcander to him to punish. Lycurgus commended them, led Alcander home, dismissed his servants, and bade Alcander tend his needs. In doing so, Alcander discovered that Lycurgus was neither rough nor self-willed, but gentle, calm, self-disciplined, and diligent. He became Lycurgus' devoted disciple. Moreover, the contrite Spartans ceased henceforth from carrying staves into their Assembly.

Lycurgus counted on training and ingrained habits, rather than legal statutes, to maintain his and Apollo's polis. One of his Delphic compacts even forbade written laws, when once his basic rhetras had established *eunomia*, the state of being well-lawed. Another rhetra, rather than forbidding luxurious dwellings, forbade the citizen to build his house with any tools but the ax and the saw. With no fine house to furnish, who would want silver-footed couches, purple coverlets, or gold drinking cups? Another compact forbade frequent expeditions against the same foe; why school that foe to fight better next time? Tradition would ascribe all these compacts to Delphi and to Apollo, who knew the will of his father, Zeus. They were *themis*, the will of the gods, made *diké*, or human justice, by the mediating wisdom of Lycurgus the lawgiver.

When his polis had been reconstituted and was healthily functioning, Lycurgus announced to his fellow Spartans that one great matter remained, and on this matter he must go to Delphi again. Then he made them swear an oath to keep his laws until his return, and set out for Delphi. There he sacrificed to Apollo and asked if his laws were good. Apollo answered that they were, and that the city would continue to be held in highest honor so long as it remained faithful to the laws of Lycurgus. Lycurgus wrote down this oracle and sent it back to Sparta. He had performed man's highest function: by translating *themis* into *diké*, divine law into human law, for the common good of his fellow men, he had in some sense joined earth to heaven. His one remaining problem was to hold his fellow men to his divinely dictated compacts; and, since they had sworn not to subvert his laws until he returned to Sparta, he could bind his countrymen for all time only by ending his life. He therefore abstained from food until he died of starvation. His body was brought home to his polis and buried. According to tradition, a bolt of that lightning which only Zeus could wield struck his tomb. The Spartans built a temple to him and worshiped him as a god.

This, men said, was how Sparta had won her eunomia, her state of being well-lawed. It was true that on many points traditions conflicted; but at least as myth they were true: they contained the high poetic truth that Homer's tale of Achilles contained. In part, at least, they were supported by historical fact, as Homer's Achilles was.

Sparta had never turned to the sea, as Corinth had done. Corinth, like Sparta, was a Dorian state; but Corinth straddled an isthmus. And her famous *diolkos*, a track with rollers for moving ships across the high ground between, connected two seas that beckoned forth to trade. One sea led to the Aegean islands, the Greek coast of Asia Minor, the Black Sea, Syria, Palestine, and Egypt; the other sea, to northwestern Greece, Italy, and Sicily. No wonder Corinth became for a time the leading center of trade in Mainland Greece. No wonder she sent out colonies that grew to be important cities and even to be rivals of their mother-city. But Sparta's coast was bare of good harbors, and much of it lay between two capes, Malea and Taenarum, which all Greek sailors dreaded. Indeed, Cape Taenarum was one of the entrances to Hades.[109]

Nevertheless, in the seventh century Sparta was open to ideas and skills from many lands. She welcomed foreigners. She had relations with Rhodes, Cyprus, Cyrene. Samos aided Sparta in her second struggle with Messenia. The powerful kingdom of Lydia sought her friendship. Sparta practiced the arts of peace too: she had her own architects, her celebrated potters, her weavers, her leather-workers, her metal-workers, her sculptors in wood, although many of these artists were indeed foreign-born. Like rich Miletus, she dyed purple cloth. She had her famous temples, like the Brazen House of Athana—as the Spartan called Athena in his broad Dorian Greek. Sparta's dancers, her singers, her musicians were renowned. Indeed, the choral lyric flourished at Sparta as nowhere else. It was, for example, for Spartan maidens that Alcman, although he came from Sardis in Lydia, wrote his famous choral lyrics. Spartans won numerous victories at the various panhellenic games. At the Olympics between 720 and 576, out of eighty-one athletes who won the victor's laurel crown, forty-six were reported to be sons of Sparta.

That was in the eighth and seventh centuries, long after the period to which tradition assigned Lycurgus. Yet by the sixth century, the arts seemed to disappear and the laws of Lycurgus were firmly entrenched. By then the City of the Lacedaemonians contained three classes of men. First came the Spartiates, who ruled and fought but never labored. Next came the Dwellers-round-about, who governed their own cities, but were forced to pay tribute to Sparta, to farm the royal domains and temple domains, and to serve in the Spartiates' army in the lower ranks. These Dwellers-round-about were forbidden to intermarry with their Spartiate masters. They earned their living by farming, raising stock, fishing, mining; by producing woolen cloth, lumber, and pottery; and above all by supplying the army. They held a monopoly of all the business life of the state, such as still existed; and some of them acquired wealth. Lastly came the Helots, or serfs, owned by the polis and each assigned to a Spartiate to farm the piece of land allotted for his support. The Helot's master could neither sell him nor free him, since he belonged to the state. He was forced to deliver to his master annually an amount of barley, of fruit, of olive oil, and of wine sufficient to free his master of all economic functions. But since his master was required to live simply, this placed no heavy burden on the Helot. The rest of what he produced he kept, and some Helots were quite well off. The Helot might be compelled to follow his Spartiate master to war, as a servant or even as a light-armed infantryman; but if he was, he was allowed to pillage freely.

To each his function. Whether or not the relations of these three classes reflected in part the original Dorian conquest, those relations were by the sixth century essentially relations of force with a minimum of consent. It is true that, at least in theory, all classes served the state. It is true that the dominant class received for its service honor, danger, no private property, harsh discipline, a daily and arduous military training, and stark subsistence. But the Dwellers-round-about were at their mercy and were looked down upon; the Helots were held under by a reign of terror. The Helots might, indeed, eat better food than their Spartiate masters, but they had no rights at law whatever. They were forbidden to carry arms except on campaign. They were forbidden to assemble after nightfall.

Once a year the five Overseers proclaimed a state of siege under which any Spartiate was permitted to murder a Helot with impunity.[110] Young Spartiates hunted down Helots at night as part of their military training. A secret police, known as the *Krypteia*, watched the Helots constantly for signs of revolt and quietly murdered any serf who seemed likely to start trouble.

Sixth-century Hellas was still a basically aristocratic society, and the Greek aristocrats' forebears, whether Achaean or Dorian, had been hardy Northern barbarians, who had fought their way into Mycenaean Greece and had ultimately wrecked a civilization. In the Dark Age that followed they had become landed nobles, fighting, ruling, and living on the labor of those whose lives they had spared. Their image was Achilles, the descendant of Zeus, who chose a brief life and the immortality of fame over a long life of ease—Achilles, who chose, not to live long, but to live well, and to obey his father's command "to be ever the best and to excel all other men."[111] But the sea, trade, and money had softened these nobles and, in many cities, even robbed them of the right to rule. Here, now, was Sparta, which had restored Achillean glory to the polis, and had created a school of virtue—of aristocratic virtue. She had placed courage in battle first. But she had also banned intemperance, the love of pleasure that had so largely transformed the warrior class elsewhere. She had forbidden gold and silver and had continued the use of her ancient iron money. The gay Ionian poets and musicians were gone from Sparta, and poetry had been put to its proper use: the inculcation of the aristocratic virtues. Her lame poet-general, Tyrtaeus, had sung:

> For 'tis a fair thing for a good man to fall and die fighting in the van for his native land . . . to a young man all is seemly enough, so long as he have the noble bloom of lovely youth, aye a marvel he for men to behold, and desirable unto women, so long as ever he be alive, and fair in like manner when he be fallen in the vanguard. So let each man bite his lip with his teeth and abide firm-set astride upon the ground.[112]

Let Dwellers-round-about and Helots fear pain and follow pleasure! Shorn of private property and taught to obey the law at all costs, was the Spartiate not the just man? Practical, shrewd, and even cunning, could he not fairly be considered wise?

Was not Hellas right to admire a kind of man who was fair in his dealings with his fellow citizens, self-controlled, brave unto death, pious? And this in a world so full of men who were unfair, greedy, cowardly, and foolish? If Lycurgus' laws were not the best in Hellas, why could no other army in the Hellenic world stand up to the Spartans in battle? To do so would be to count on green troops against a seasoned and expert regular army, the only regular army of any size in the Greek world. In other Hellenic states it was not only the aristocrats who looked on the City of the Lacedaemonians as the school of Hellas, even though it was a school that most men would have lacked the courage to attend.

Hellas could admire Sparta all the more because, around 550, under the guidance of one of her famous Overseers, Chilon, she ceased her aggressive expansion and intervened in other Hellenic states only to help put down tyrants and restore freedom—the traditional freedom of the nobles, who were normally pro-Spartan. Her policy, domestic and foreign, became a stubborn rear-guard action against change. Old ways were best. A nation of soldiers, she avoided wars wherever she could with honor. Could any war be fought without leaving an enemy at her back—her sullen Helots? And in that sea of Helots, there in hollow Lacedaemon, watchful Sparta lay, proud that she was unwalled. Or rather, proud that her only wall consisted of the tough, willing bodies of her ceaselessly drilled citizens, bodies trained to obey by a city that claimed to be a school of moral virtue.

The man who was born into that school passed through many ordeals. When he was born, he was presented not only to his father—as were Greek babies elsewhere—to decide whether he was to live or die; here, the elders of his father's tribe had to decide also. Would he make a strong man? Would his father's allotment and its fixed yield suffice to support this newcomer? If he was spared, he was turned over to his mother until he was seven—for his father lived, not at home, but among his fellow soldiers. At seven he was placed, along with other little boys, in the hands of a young man to train. There followed a rigorous instruction and test after test. If successful, at the age of twenty he too was placed in charge of a group of boys to train. He taught them to bear pain, to speak only when spoken to, and then only to the point, to respect their elders, to obey absolutely, to harden their bodies, to eat sparingly, to forage by night for any additional food they might need, and to suffer flogging if caught— not because they had stolen but because they had clumsily allowed themselves to be detected. Lycurgus, noting that it was rivalry which produced good athletes at the games and good choruses, had determined to match the young men of Sparta "in an eris of valor,"[113] in that kind of eris that was dearest to the gods, and in the highest sense political—the eris that would set the standard of a brave man's conduct, and in which each party would exert itself to the end that it might never fall below its best, and that, when the time came, every member of it might support the Polis with all his might.

When a young man became a trainer of boys, he applied for admission to an eating club, for Lycurgus had decreed that all Spartan citizens should mess together daily, on the simplest of food, and in groups or clubs of about fifteen members. A young trainer could gain admission to a club only by the consent of all its members, but once admitted he would belong to his club for forty years, if he lived that long, unless degraded for cowardice or inability to keep up his subscription. At mess, the trainer had the right to eat Lycurgus' black broth, which was said to be palatable only to those who had first plunged into the cold waters of the River Eurotas.

To the club mess-tables the boys in training were brought as part of their education. There they heard the conversation of men who lived hard lives and were proud of it, who knew how to die but not how to surrender. Laconians prided themselves on speaking laconically, and they treasured and quoted terse, pithy, acid repartee, and the rough, soldierly jest that a soldier should know how to take. If war came, the members of each club would march off together to the sound of the flute, wearing heavy bronze armor, a crimson[114] tunic, and a plumed helmet, their hair long in the old way, and on their lips perhaps one of Tyrtaeus' marching songs.

Now a full-fledged member of the army, a young man could hope to earn promotion by serving with distinction. If his performance was brilliant, he might even gain membership in the special royal guard, the Three Hundred. If he married, the State would make sure that he married a strong and healthy woman, able to bear future soldiers, nor could he quit his barracks to sleep at home until he was thirty. If he failed to beget children, he might invite a companion to sire children for him. His wife, who had herself received strenuous athletic training in order to fit her to mother strong future soldiers, would be expected to consent to be loaned out in this fashion. If the men went off to war, their wives assumed considerable political responsibilities in their absence. At sixty, the Spartiate would be released at last from his military service, would live at home, and would be eligible for that highest elective honor, membership in the Senate.

There was room in this somewhat hierarchical society for a perverse brutality, but could not its admirers claim that brutality existed everywhere? There was also room for the kind of immortality Achilles sought and perhaps for a better kind than he sought. For besides the individual immortality of deathless fame for heroism in battle, there was a subtler ideal of immortality: one might die oneself, but that would not so much matter if one's own death served the continuing life of Sparta, the City of the Lacedaemonians. To that second aim all had been sacrificed: pleasure, even bare comfort, gaiety, gentleness, most of the beauty of the arts, much of the free motion of the human mind. But, in return, the Spartiate achieved the heroic life of danger, the taut will, the sense of triumph that drove the daring horseman to choose the dangerous horse. The horse that Sparta was riding was each Spartan's own subordinates; was Sparta's restless allies; was jealous, neighboring Argos, with memories of her mighty, Mycenaean past; was the rebellious Helots, sullenly dreaming of freedom or rising in desperate revolt; was each man's own fears, each man's own appetites, conquered at last or at least cowering in silence. Living under this tension, a man gained the respectful companionship of brave and expert warriors. A man gained Sparta, a city like no other.

In the seventh century the aristocratic republic of Athens governed more territory than any other state in Hellas except Sparta. But, whereas the Dorians who settled Sparta had subjected by military conquest first Laconia and then neighboring Messenia, Athens had long ago persuaded the rulers of the various small communities throughout Attica to merge their governments with that of Athens.[115] The citizens of those communities received full rights as citizens of Athens. The Athenian government now controlled some thousand square miles, although about two-fifths of it was mountainous[116] and therefore yielded little but timber, charcoal for fuel, and some pasturage. This decision of Attica to unite may have been partly responsible for the Athenian legend that the people of Attica had always lived there. Partly responsible, too, was the fact that the destructive Dorian conquest, which had created Sparta, had bypassed Attica—perhaps because the Attic land was conspicuously poorer than some of the areas the Dorians seized, such as Laconia and the even richer Messenia.

Although less rich in good land than hollow Lacedaemon, Attica possessed what Laconia signally lacked—a number of excellent harbors. Moreover, it was a peninsula thrust into the Aegean and therefore thrust toward Asia Minor and rich Ionia. Attic traditions agreed with Ionian that it was from Attica that the Ionians had emigrated to Asia Minor. Athens had sent out no colonies in the eighth or seventh century. When the sea did at last call her to trade, Miletus in Ionia and her own near neighbors, Corinth, Chalcis, and Aegina, were already trading far and wide.

As with all the more advanced Hellenic cities, Athens had moved early from a monarchy, in which a normally hereditary king governed with the advice of a council of nobles, to an aristocratic republic in which the king lost all but his priestly functions. In the seventh century the nobility not only deliberated but decided. By 686 three archons, or rulers, each elected for one year, and themselves nobles, formed the executive. One of them, the king-archon, had taken over the monarch's last remaining duties, which were chiefly religious. Another, the *polemarch*, or leader in battle, directed the armed forces. The third archon was civil head of the state. But it was the nobles who controlled the Athenian republic. Were they not the Eupatrids, the "Well-fathered"? They alone owned war horses. They alone enjoyed the right of "iron-bearing"—the right to bear arms in life, and later in their tombs. They alone could do justice because they alone knew *themis*, they alone *diké*. Of written law there was none. The popular Assembly, which in Athens was called the Ecclesia, exercised little power.

In Attica as in many other city-states, the shift from growing food to eat to growing crops for money, from barley and wheat to exportable wine and olive oil, brought greater wealth to the wealthier nobles and increased misery for the bulk of the peasants. At some time in the seventh century, blue blood made a partial concession to silver money. Political rights began now to reflect wealth—but only wealth in land. The nobility remained dominant. But since family ownership and inalienability of land were giving way, since more and more land could be individually owned and could be bought and sold, those who made money in commerce could secure greater rights by buying land. The nobles began marrying non-noble heiresses. Social barriers were crumbling. More merchant ships, and even warships, were built, and those who rowed these ships were most certainly not nobles. The effect was like the effect of the shift all over Greece from cavalry to heavy-armed infantry. Those who defended the commonwealth with their bodies would more and more demand the right to help govern it with their minds. It appeared less and less likely that the noble, by mystic right of blood, was alone able to read the will of the gods, alone able to apply that will by interpreting unwritten customary law which he alone knew, alone able to deliberate on essential measures for the good of the whole polis. The Greek colonists who had gone out to Italy and Sicily had broken with so many customs; had indeed often included in their number men from so many different states with so many differing customs, and so many poor men who sought not only land but an escape from the scorn and oppression of the Best People; had, finally, met so many new conditions to which the good old ways were irrelevant, that they were compelled to contrive constitutions and laws in writing for all to read. The experience of these Western colonists shook in turn even the stay-at-homes in the mother-cities of Mainland Greece.

As the Athenian nobles turned more and more into merchants, their ancient privileges seemed less and less to operate in the common interest; their monopoly of law and justice seemed correspondingly less justified, their decisions less and less to be trusted. Under pressure, the nobles made a concession: they placed the surveillance of the legal system in the hands of a special commission. But social discontent continued. A young noble named Cylon, son-in-law of Theagenes, the tyrant-ruler of neighboring Megara, tried with Theagenes' help to seize the Acropolis and restore by force the disappearing privileges and prestige of the Athenian nobility. Cylon's attempt to seize power was put down by a popular insurrection, led by a nobleman of the pro-reform family of Alcmeonid. Nevertheless, enough disorder followed, and enough private vendettas, to force action. The archon Dracon was furnished in 621 with extraordinary powers to reform criminal justice.

Dracon's principal achievement was to substitute public trial and punishment for family vendetta and private vengeance. To ensure that necessary shift he made public punishment so severe that later generations, not faced by his problems, would declare that Dracon's laws were written, not in ink, but in blood. But, thanks to Dracon, the force of the whole Athenian community was placed behind law. Legal evidence and reasoned argument replaced endless and unreasoning vendetta; law was no longer the monopoly of the Well-fathered but of the polis; and, to that end, it was written law.

Despite this triumph of human reason, the land of Attica continued steadily to fall into fewer and fewer hands. The peasant fell further into debt. Sometimes he sold his land, paid his debt, and went into exile. Sometimes he could not meet his debt, and under traditional law his creditor had legal power to seize him, his wife, and his children, and sell them all as slaves. Finally, the peasant might sometimes yield up his land, remain as tenant, and accept the status of serf, required to turn over to his lord five-sixths[117] of his harvest; the sixth share, he retained, and he was therefore called a *hectemor*, or sixth-sharer.

Throughout Attica discontent ripened toward rebellion. The peasants demanded that the lands of the nobles be confiscated, as had happened in certain other city-states, and redistributed among those who tilled it. The rich, whether noble or non-noble, wanted to develop further their monopoly of the land. Athens, "the oldest land of Ionia," was "being slain."[118] Only eunomia,[119] the state of being well-lawed, could save her from falling into that wrong kind of strife, of physical violence, of eris, that Hesiod had so much dreaded for man.

Lycurgus had tried to find eunomia for Sparta. He had shut Sparta off from the ideas that were current in Greece, from the silver and gold coins that were current, and had shut her in with her iron money and her iron thoughts and, above all, with her iron will. He had turned her citizens into a professional standing army imposing its will on Dwellers-round-about and Helots alike. He had tried to abolish all inequality of wealth for his citizen-soldiers by reducing all to a subsistence wage, supplied in kind by state serfs. What was left of industry and commerce he delegated to the Dwellers-round-about. He gave the gods their due, the kings their due, and his warriors theirs.

Other cities, commercial ones like Athens' neighbors, Megara and Corinth, had turned to tyranny to guide the state from rule by landed nobles to rule by trade and money, to economic development, to the arts of Ionia on which Sparta had turned her back, to the future, not the past.

Between the Scylla of Spartan renunciation and the Charybdis of popular dictatorship the Athenians tried to steer their political course into the unknown future. They sought Hesiod's other kind of eris, when neighbor vied with neighbor in productive work, the eris that is wholesome for men. To reach their goal they freely elected, about 594, a leader to show the way. His name was Solon. They made him archon and they gave him extraordinary powers to find eunomia for Athens.

Solon was a noble, whose family had been wealthy landowners; but he was no rustic conservative. His father had been openhanded toward others and had impaired the family fortune: Solon's response was not to join those of his fellow nobles who wanted to squeeze Dustyfoot harder, but to take to commerce and the sea and repair his inheritance by his own work. He became a successful merchant, who understood the economic problems Athens now faced. He was also a poet, whose poems were political pamphlets, written in the elegiac[120] couplets which Ionia had invented. He was an undoctrinaire reformer, who sought political equilibrium for a polis that was reeling from dissension between large landowner and peasant. Naturally, many of his fellow landowners hoped he would put down popular discontent with a firm and ruthless hand. Naturally, many of the peasants hoped he would redistribute the land. He neither repressed the poor nor confiscated the lands of the rich. What he did do was to abolish the peasants' debts, to forbid enslavement for debt, to limit the size of landed estates, to bring back those whom debt had driven into exile and those who had been carried there as slaves—"men," he wrote in one of his pamphleteering poems, "that no longer spake the Attic speech because they had wandered so far and wide."[121] "By fitting close together right and might"[122] he did these things—that is, he made force the servant of justice and of law.

The Athenian census already distinguished between the *hippeis*, or cavalrymen, men rich enough to report for military service mounted on their own horses, and the *zeugitai*, men rich enough to keep a yoke of oxen and to serve as heavy-armed infantry. To these two classes, Solon added two more, the Five-hundred-Bushelers, whose title reflected their annual income, and the *thetes*, or Wage-earners. Eligibility for office was no longer based on birth and wealth, but on wealth alone, though in general the wealthy were still the Well-fathered. Which offices a man was eligible for depended on which of the three top classes he belonged to. The fourth class, the Wage-earners, could not hold office. Alongside the aristocratic Senate, or Council of the Areopagus, Solon established a Council of Four Hundred to prepare the agenda for the popular Assembly, in which even the Wage-earner sat, could join in debate, and could vote. Finally, Solon established courts, whose membership was selected by lot from the popular Assembly.

Solon clearly did not judge the Wage-earners ready for equal political rights, but his new constitution permitted every citizen to take some part in the political process of self-government, and it rendered inevitable a growth in that participation. By imposing severe penalties for idleness, he reflected Hesiod's respect for ergon, for work, and he encouraged Hesiod's good kind of eris. He encouraged the same good strife by reforming the currency and by reforming weights and measures. In his new constitution, he also invited all Athenians to a higher form of this good strife, the eris of making law and of judging cases under the law the citizen helped make. Athens would inevitably move nearer to a community of free men, able by fitting close together right and might to seek justice together in an open society. For such a society, however dimly Solon may have descried it in the future, he laid the strong foundations; and, although he was a widely traveled man, he could have found no model for such a society in any land he had come to. In his own Odyssean imagination and intellect he had found the route to a kind of home for free beings. On this home, precisely because it was free, some of the divine light of another home was shed—the home of the gods, Olympus.

He could appeal in his poems to Zeus, who punished human violence, and to the other Olympians whom the Achaean and Dorian invaders had discovered and worshiped before they ever entered Greece. But in the poem in which he claimed to have fitted close together right and might, he spoke of quite another god, or rather goddess. She was that goddess whom the Pelasgians of the great days of Crete and Mycenae had worshiped for centuries, before the Achaean and Dorian war bands had swarmed in from the North. She was the Great Mother, the Earth. Solon had removed the boundary stones on which farm mortgages were recorded and had loosened the strangle hold of the rich upon the life-giving land. And "Right good witness shall I have in the court of Time," he wrote,

> to wit the Great Mother of the Olympian Gods, dark Earth, whose so many fixed landmarks I once removed, and have made her free that was once a slave.[123]

He had freed the energies of the earth as he had freed the energies of his fellow Athenians—their political energies, their commercial energies, their industrial energies. He offered no vast blueprint of some future human equality. From time to time, he even made an aristocrat's hard judgment on the folly and envy of the classes beneath his own. But he did know how to detect energy, divine or human, actual or potential.

Lycurgus the Lawgiver had taken the stubborn stance of godlike Achilles, who could pray and fight and love and hate, but who lacked wily Odysseus' will to think and skill to think. As for the work that Hesiod glorified, and that Odysseus had also will and skill to do, Lycurgus left that to ungodlike underlings, whose task it was to live unhonored lives. Meanwhile the Polis would be the armed and disciplined Spartiates, each of whom knew how to "bite his lip with his teeth and abide firm-set astride upon the ground." It was the ideal of an aristocrat, and of an aristocrat hard pressed by the changes coming over Hellas.

Although in the seventh century Sparta was open to the arts of other lands, in the sixth she turned in on herself, broke off almost all friendly contact with other Greek cities, and became a garrison state, fearful of foreign attack, and, if anything, yet more fearful of rebellion by those whom the Spartiates had brutally subjected. Paradoxically, the society she then proceeded to construct, a society men ascribed to Lycurgus the Lawgiver—Did he indeed live? If he did, when? Was he god or man?—became the admiration of Hellas, and not merely of the rich or the Well-fathered. The Greek mind was fascinated by Lycurgus' eunomia; by a certain symmetry in the Lycurgan constitution; by the laconic repartee of these Laconians—a repartee full of suppressed violence; by their single-minded courage on behalf of their polis; by their readiness to die in the grand manner of Achilles; by their self-control in the face of corrupting pleasures, their freely chosen life of hardship, their swift obedience to lawful authority; and by their whole air of time-honored virtue such as men had displayed in the good old days.

Solon of Athens, though himself an aristocrat, was a poet, a man of imagination and intellect, a man whom later generations would place among the Seven Sages of Greece. He followed, not Achilles, but wise Odysseus. He discovered and invented. The Spartans whom Lycurgus had molded by his stern discipline said that Homer was a poet for warriors, Hesiod for serfs.[124] But Solon the Lawgiver by a gentler discipline molded his Athenians toward both the justice and the work that had inspired Hesiod to sing.

As one of the Seven Sages, he commonly got credit for two epigrams as famous as any that Greece had yet produced: "Know thyself" and "Do nothing too much"[125]—that is, moderation in all things. He had sought to apply this second formula to Athens' most basic problem: how to change peacefully from a polis in which men husbanded the feminine earth, plowed her yielding body, sowed seed in her womb, and from her womb received the things their own bodies required—from a polis in which noble blood and ancient custom and family ties ruled, to a new polis that men could scarcely yet comprehend. In this new polis men produced olive oil and wine to sell for money and to ship to distant lands. The oil and wine were shipped in exquisitely painted pots of Attic clay. The money from their sale abroad bought grain to make bread with or dried fish or leather hides from grazing countries or better timber for ships than one could any longer hope to find on the cut-over mountainsides of Attica. Somehow, in this change from growing things for use to growing things to sell, the rich seemed to get richer and the poor to get poorer. In other Greek cities some man, usually a noble, had used force to make himself tyrant, and in the name of justice for the poor had destroyed freedom. Solon strove hard to protect the poor against the greed of the rich and the rich against the envy of the poor without resort to the usual Greek device: tyranny, a dictatorship, violence instead of reason. Before he laid down his powers, he made all citizens swear an oath to support the new constitution which had disappointed so many. Further to forestall violence, he ingeniously required that if violence did break out every citizen must openly take sides: he feared the withdrawal of moderates when and if the hotheads acted. Then he deliberately withdrew from Athens and voyaged to Egypt and Cyprus.

In the short run, Solon failed. Violence between rich and poor quickly broke out. Parties formed: the People of the Plain, composed of nobles and successful peasants, who wanted to abolish Solon's reforms; the People of the Coast, composed of men who lived by commerce, shipping, and fisheries, of craftsmen, and of poor but free peasants; and the Mountaineers, composed of the goatherds in the mountains of Attica but also of the poorest men everywhere, who were still determined to confiscate and redistribute the land. An ambitious noble, Pisistratus, seized the leadership of the Mountaineers. Solon, who had returned to his disordered polis and was watching the shrewd moves of Pisistratus, launched more of his pamphlet-poems to warn Athens that Pisistratus wanted to be tyrant; but he warned to no avail. At the opportune moment Pisistratus used the true and tried device: he rushed into the Agora, covered with blood and crying out that his political opponents had sought to assassinate him. A confederate promptly proposed that he be given a guard of fifty men armed with clubs. Once he secured his personal guard, he of course seized the Acropolis, and Athens had her tyrant at last.

That was in 561, thirty-three years after Solon had first assumed power—constitutionally. Now he had to watch this comedy played to its expected, bitter end. The aged statesman hung up his shield and spear before the door of his house, as a symbol that other men, perhaps younger men, must take over the defense of freedom. But Solon knew how much easier it was to permit a tyrant to seize power than to get rid, not only of a tyrant, but of the political habits tyranny might breed. Was his dream of a free society, of citizens seeking justice together through common deliberation, a dream beyond the power of men to realize? Would Pisistratus rule the men of Athens as animals are ruled, and then Pisistratus's sons, and his sons' sons?

Meanwhile, Pisistratus showed him great deference. A year or two after freedom fell, Solon died.

4

FOR NONE
SAVE ONLY ZEUS
IS FREE

SOLON had been no mean poet, but he may not have completely read his own symbolic act when he hung up his arms before the door of his dwelling. For it was basically by bringing arms to Solon's peaceful revolution that Pisistratus, tyrant of Athens, defended the gains of that revolution. He, too, fitted close together right and might, as Solon had done; but he increased the proportion of might in Solon's formula. Even then, during the thirty-three years between his seizure of power in 561 and his death in 528 or 527, his political opponents succeeded in exiling him twice, for a total of fourteen years. The first time he was exiled, his property was confiscated and sold; but he maneuvered his way back to power by marrying the daughter of his political opponent, Megacles. Exiled a second time, he later landed on the coast of Attica at the head of an army of mercenaries, occupied Marathon, reconquered his country, and ruled it.

The sequence of events had been instructive. The Athenian aristocracy had tried, and failed, to govern Athens under Dracon's written laws. As violence mounted, the aristocrats had agreed with their opponents to elect Solon as dictator[126] with extraordinary powers to arbitrate differences. Although extraordinary, these powers had been strictly constitutional. Despite the oath which all citizens had sworn to obey Solon's new laws, tensions between rich and poor had again produced anarchy. Thereupon Pisistratus had secured his bodyguard of men with clubs, by deception but without openly violating the constitution; then he had ignored the constitution and had seized the citadel on the Acropolis. Driven from Athens twice, he had hired mercenary troops and conquered power by force of arms.

The fact remained that he used that power to protect and develop Solon's reforms. In effect, he forced the rich and Well-fathered of Athens to keep the oath that Solon had exacted of all citizens before he deliberately went on his travels. It was as if the doctor had failed through the obstinacy of the patient and a ruthless surgeon had taken over. Pisistratus gained the reputation of a wise and moderate ruler, a reputation not many Greek tyrants had gained. He kept the forms of Solon's constitution, merely seeing to it that only his supporters held office. He guarded the interests of the peasant, redistributed the lands of exiled nobles, built an aqueduct and undertook other public works that employed the poor in the city of Athens. Since Athens could now count on grain from her Black Sea trade, he encouraged the farmer to produce wine as well as olive oil for export.

Moreover, Pisistratus and the two sons who succeeded him built temples and altars to the gods, especially a new temple to Athens' divine patroness, Athena, goddess of wisdom; and began a great Doric temple to Olympian Zeus. To decorate these temples and altars, they brought over famous sculptors from Ionia and from the Aegean Isles; and painters decorated the walls of these buildings with frescoes. The Ionian sculptors, and the Athenian sculptors who learned their art from them, turned from brilliantly painted statues of limestone to statues carved from marble. Both statues and temples, first of wood and then of limestone, had invited paint, if only to hide the irregularities of the material. But when the Ionians taught the Athenians to carve their statues and build their temples out of marble, the painters less and less often covered them with their brilliant and varied colors. The sculptor noted that the more regular surface did not need color; besides, the better Greek marbles were simply too beautiful to spoil by concealing their translucent radiance. Instead, he tinted the statue, enough to give a flush to the portions that represented human skin, and colored perhaps the hair and eyes and lips. Or he contented himself with the waxing process called *ganosis*, to bring out the mellow tone. The statues in low relief or high relief that decorated the pediments of temples and the friezes along their sides were no longer brightly colored against a plain background. At about the time that potters changed from black figures on red ground to red figures on black, the artists who created the statues on pediment or frieze left their white marble statues uncolored against a solidly painted ground.

But what most distinguished the statues of this period was not a matter of technique, not a matter of gay color, or of ganosis, or of their stiff, formal, almost Egyptian style. It was their aristocratic bearing, shown alike in god and godlike youth, in goddess and in girl. It was the fact that the sculptor ignored the transient, the particular; what he sought was the universal and eternal. He saw, for example, in a child, not the large head and half-formed features of childhood but only another case of man, and he carved the boy merely as a small man. And for the fleeting emotion on the human face, he substituted the mysterious, discreet smile,[127] the smile a god might wear, or even a godlike youth, even a godlike youth who was wounded, who was dying. These marble gods and youths were not concerned with the obvious but with what was, for most men, hidden. And yet, alongside this aristocratic and reticent and radiant sculpture, artists were painting delicately shaped pots and jars and amphorae and lamps, some indeed displaying the heroic but many of them covered with the scenes of everyday Hellenic life, with its work, its play, its pleasure and vices, its comedy, and its laughter.

To Athens came the artists; to Athens came the poets. From the nearby Aegean island of Ceos came the lyric poet Simonides to the court of the tyrant sons of Pisistratus. When the gay poet, Anacreon, came, Athens even sent a trireme to conduct him from Samos. Not content with making more impressive the Great Panathenaic festivals, in which athletes from all over Greece competed, chariots raced, rhapsodes recited Homer, and musicians sang or played, Pisistratus also founded the Great Dionysiac festivals to appeal to the people—for Dionysus was a favorite god of Dusty-foot.

A central feature of the Great Dionysiac was a chorus of singers, disguised as followers of Dionysus and chanting tales of his adventures. Then it became a custom to have the leader step forward and sing responses to the dithyrambic verses of the rest of the chorus. Later, from being merely the leader of a chorus, he took to impersonating a god—and a kind of dramatic dialogue was born, a dialogue in words and in dance, a dialogue between god and man. Pisistratus organized these performances and established prizes for which their authors might compete in yet another eris.

Pisistratus and his two sons were not the only tyrants who favored those gods and heroes whom the populace most loved. Periander of Corinth and Clisthenes of Sicyon went further: they frowned on the ancient religious family rites of the nobles. In favoring Dionysus, the god of the grape, of wine, of the union of man with god, of death and resurrection, in favoring Demeter, who made the peasants' crops grow, Pisistratus was drawing on the deepest beliefs of the poor, on ancient religious hopes and fears that the nobles, with their Olympic deities, in general did not share. The Eleusinian mysteries were celebrated each spring at Eleusis, a town near Athens that dated back to ancient Minoan days; and the secret rites to Demeter promised eternal life to all initiates, even slaves.

In their foreign policy the Pisistratids gained a firm grip on the Helles-pont to secure Athens' access to Black Sea grain, and they also staked out claims in Thrace where precious metals and timber were to be had. Athens began to crowd out Corinth as the leading commercial city of Greece. Her wine, her olive oil, and her pottery were now shipped out to every part of the Mediterranean.

Pisistratus was succeeded in 527 by his eldest son, Hippias, who was assisted by his brother, Hipparchus. Fourteen years after the father's death an attempt was made to assassinate both brothers, and the younger one was indeed killed. Four years later still, Hippias was driven out of Athens by a Spartan army, co-operating with exiled Athenian nobles. The long tyranny had ended, partly because of certain setbacks in foreign policy, but partly because tyranny had largely lost its function by doing its work too well. It had lasted, with interruptions, from 561 to 510—over half a century. It had fostered, against the landlords, a commercial and industrial society, a society self-confident and ready to govern itself in freedom.

Backed by Spartan military intervention, the nobles now tried to abolish Solon's reforms, which Pisistratus and his sons had retained, and to re-establish the aristocratic republic. But Solon's reforms and Pisistratus's administration had created a new Athenian republic and one whose problems the landed noble was ill equipped to solve. The new society soon found a leader—Clisthenes, member of the aristocratic family of Alcmeonid, a family which, like Solon's, had long looked to the future, toward the sea and adventure; not back toward the land or custom or the past. The nobles found means of banishing Clisthenes, but this counter-revolution of the old nobility was stopped in its tracks by a popular rising. The Spartan garrison and the intransigent nobles were forced to quit Athens. Clisthenes then returned to Athens and completed the revolution in which Dracon, Solon, and Pisistratus, whose work had covered more than a century, had each played a vital role. In a few months he had reorganized the constitution of Athens. In particular, he effected three major reforms.

The first of these reforms was to divide Attica into one hundred districts known as demes. Citizenship in the deme, not membership in one of the four Ionic tribes, now gave citizenship in the polis. This freed the polis and its common good from the bad eris between ancient tribes and families. With their powerful religious traditions and passionate loyalties, these groups had kept Athena's Polis the contested prize of great families.

Clisthenes' second reform was to admit to citizenship many of the metics, foreigners whom the laws protected but who could not help make law, and he admitted many former slaves as well. He provided that henceforth the son of a citizen should inherit citizenship regardless of his mother's status. He then divided his hundred demes into ten new 'tribes' of ten demes each; but he saw to it that each tribe should contain nearly the same number of demes from each of the characteristic regions of Attica, regions that had already produced three opposing factions: the Mountain, the Plain, and the Coast. The effect of forming his new, artificial tribes out of scattered demes was to prevent any one tribe from representing in concentrated form a single, basic economic interest. To the rich he left their family rites and even the ancient rites of the four Ionic tribes that he had just superseded politically. But by composing his new tribes of widely scattered demes and by enrolling many metics and freedmen as citizens he fatally weakened the power of the great landed families, with their local retainers and clients.

Clisthenes' third reform was to introduce the legal device of ostracism. Once a year the popular Assembly deliberated on whether any citizen should be required to go into exile for ten years on the grounds that his presence in Athens was a threat to the constitution. If the Assembly voted to hold an ostracism, a second vote was taken. Then, if six thousand citizens[128] wrote the same name on an *ostrakon*, or potsherd, the man named must leave Athens for ten years. But he did not lose his citizenship, his goods were not confiscated, he did not even suffer disgrace. In fact, it was only the man of great ability who was likely to be ostracized, yet the possibility of ostracism was a constant deterrent to overweening political ambition.

The reforms of Clisthenes completed Solon's work for him, and their success proved that Solon's failure had been more apparent than real. The result was a kind of eunomia that no Greek ever heard of as existing outside Hellas. In Athena's Polis women, children, slaves, foreign residents, and some of the sons of non-citizens were still excluded from a share of making law, of administering it, and of judging those accused of infringing it. Yet Athens came nearer to being a self-governing community than anything man had dreamed of in the Mediterranean world. Every citizen lived in freedom under law, and this law was the fruit of debate, of argument, of reason, of Hesiod's good kind of eris in action. The rivalry of Athenian potters and other craftsmen had already produced a standard of workmanship famous throughout the Mediterranean. But now the clash of political argument was leading Athenians of every class to a constant, responsible consideration of the common good. The good potter sought beauty in his work. In the Assembly the same potter could seek the good by taking part in the city's search for good law. But that kind of search involved an intellectual discipline that encouraged men to search together by eris for what was true, regardless of whether this truth appeared immediately applicable to the making of a beautiful, useful pot or even to the making of a good and useful law.

By fitting close together right and might, Athens was learning to seek and to understand, to make and to demonstrate. But during the same

many Greeks wanted
Apollo himself at Delphi.
ted on a tripod, she went into
ent words. A prophet stood by, who
verse. All over the Hellenic world men quoted
these verses.

Sometimes the oracles thus issued were fairly specific. More often, their language was dark, ambiguous, ironic—in short, oracular. The truth they purported to convey was poetic truth and required interpretation. It came to men disguised, as Athena so often came to Odysseus. Specific questions were likely to elicit general answers or answers which, like so many other poems, wore an air of being specific yet irrelevant.

Faced with the question of whether to attack Cyrus the Persian and try to restore his brother-in-law to the Median throne, Croesus sent rich gifts of gold and silver to the god Apollo at Delphi together with this message: "Shall Croesus send an army against the Persians . . . ?" The Delphic oracle's reply was characteristic: "that if he should send an army against the Persians he would destroy a great empire."[129] Croesus was delighted. Like many other men who consulted the Delphic oracle, he was eager that Apollo should advise him to do what he, Croesus, had already made up his mind to do. He attacked Cyrus, and by doing so he promptly destroyed a great empire—his own. After his defeat, he sent another delegation to Delphi. Its members were instructed to ask Apollo "if he were not ashamed that he had persuaded Croesus to attack the Persians, telling him that he would destroy Cyrus' power . . ."[130] Apollo retorted that he had but prophesied that

if he should lead an army against the Persians he would destroy a great empire. Therefore it behoved him, if he would take right counsel, to send and ask whether the god spoke of Croesus' or of Cyrus' empire. But he understood not that which was spoken, nor made further inquiry: wherefore now let him blame himself.[131]

Should he not have made further inquiry? At a minimum, Apollo had challenged him to recognize that it was easier to start a war than to predict its outcome. A god could scarcely have given more important advice, and the advice was more important, because more general, than the answer Croesus imagined he heard. His willfulness not only cost him an empire: it cost the Greek states in Asia their easy Lydian yoke and left them to face the rapi

Faced with the threat o
sent embassies to Sparta, renow
to get help, but none came. The city o
tant and dangerous expeditions. Thales of Miletus, the p
posed that the Ionian city-states form one large state, as the various tiny
states of Attica had done centuries before; that the religious alliance
known as the Panionian League convert itself into a government capable
of the common defense. Bias of Priene, a statesman accounted one of the
Seven Sages, advised that all the Ionians quit Asia, sail west to the great
island of Sardinia, and there set up a common polis. And in fact most of
the citizens of Phocaea did emigrate to Alalia, a colony which they had
already founded in Corsica, while the citizens of Teos sailed to the coast of
Thrace and founded Abdera.

But Thales' advice was ignored; no common defense was achieved; and,
one by one, Cyrus picked off the Greek cities of Asia, along with those
on the Hellespont. Then Cyrus turned eastward and conquered various
peoples clear to the Jaxartes River. By 538 he had turned back and had
taken Babylon. Persia was preparing to conquer Egypt when Cyrus died.
His son and successor, Cambyses, conquered Egypt and annexed it. From
the Hellespont to the Pamir Mountains, northeast of modern Afghanistan,
from the Nile to the Caucasus and to the Jaxartes River beyond Samarkand, a single mighty empire stood. The lands that several empires had
once governed—the Egyptian, the Babylonian, the Assyrian, the Hittite—
were all governed now by the King of Kings. The whole Fertile Crescent
was his, and the Arabian tribes of the desert were his allies. Nothing like
this political colossus had ever been known to the Greeks.

The Persian Empire, though it could brutally repress rebels and could
transplant whole populations if need be, gave on the whole just government. Above all, the laws of the Medes and Persians brought a kind of
universal peace to the Middle East. The Empire also improved agriculture, irrigated dry lands, built needed roads. It respected local religions
and local customs. But, to the Ionian cities, it was a sorry substitute for
Croesus of Lydia. Croesus had been halfway adopted into the Hellenic
family and so had many of his Lydian subjects. The Ionians were now a
tiny fringe of a vast empire, ruled from remote Susa by a Great King, an
empire with no leanings toward Greek gods or Greek ways. Worse still,

the Great King had seized control of the grain route from the Black Sea and had opened it to Ionia's ancient Phoenician rivals, Tyre and Sidon. The Phoenicians were also subjects of the Great King and now after all these decades they were again competing in the commerce of the Aegean itself.

Cyrus the Great had built most of this empire, except for Egypt, which his son Cambyses had added. When Cambyses died, his conquering army was still in Egypt. A Persian noble, Darius, led that army home. Three years later Darius was King of Kings. Less than a decade later he turned to his northern and western frontiers. He crossed the Bosphorus on a pontoon bridge built by an Ionian engineer of Samos, and conquered the tribes of eastern Thrace. In 512 he reached the Danube River. An Ionian fleet serving the Great King sailed through the Black Sea and up the Danube to join Darius' army. There the fleet formed another pontoon bridge. While the Ionians held the bridge, Darius warred against the nomadic Scythians on the steppes.[132] But the Scythian horsemen were too much for him: the quick attacks of the Scythians and their instant disappearances into vast and empty steppes left the Persian army in sore straits, and Darius at last retreated to the pontoon bridge across the Danube. Even so, after he returned to Asia, his empire still extended to the Danube. News of his disasters on the steppes caused Byzantium and several neighboring Greek city-states to revolt; but a Persian army shortly reconquered them, and the Greek cities of Asia saw their vital grain route from the Black Sea again under the control of Persia, again open to their competitors, the merchants of Phoenicia.[133]

In 499 the cities of Ionia rose against Darius' world empire. The revolt was not well organized or even well planned. It was occasioned in large part by the political intrigues of Aristagoras, tyrant of Miletus. Once it had broken out, Aristagoras surrendered his tyranny and voyaged to Greece to secure the aid of the two leading states there, Sparta and Athens. The Spartan kings refused to move: their state was interested in retaining its hegemony over Mainland Greece; it was neither a colonizing nor a trading state; one of its kings, Cleomenes, was at odds with the other king, Demaratus; Aristagoras admitted that Persia was so vast that it took three months to march from the sea to the Great King's capital at Susa; and finally, Cleomenes correctly judged that the Ionian Revolt was militarily doomed.

Though Sparta refused to budge, the democratic Assembly of Athens saw the matter differently. According to tradition the Ionian cities had been founded hundreds of years before by colonists from Attica. Darius, who had ruled the Ionian cities through local tyrants, now harbored the last of the tyrants at Athens, the hated Hippias, son of Pisistratus; and Hippias was busily if vainly trying to persuade the King of Kings to restore him by force as tyrant of Athens. Moreover, by closing off the Black Sea, Darius had endangered not only Ionia's trade but the trade of Athens. In that region Athens sold her olive oil, her wine, her now famous pottery, and the other works of industrious Athenian minds and hands. And Athens bought timber, fish, and grain from the Black Sea states. For Athens, as for Ionia, the Black Sea was a larder. So the Assembly voted to send twenty triremes. To these twenty, Eretria in Euboea added five: Miletus had once aided Eretria in a war against Chalcis. Between them, Athens and Eretria brought the Ionian rebels some 2,000 fighting men.

In the spring of 498 the expedition reached Ionia, where the Persians were getting ready to besiege Miletus. Thereupon the Ionians, with their Athenian and Eretrian allies, marched on the provincial capital of Sardis and took it. During the sack of Sardis, fire broke out and largely destroyed the city, including the temple of Cybele, the Earth Mother. But the Greek army was decisively beaten that summer; the Spartan judgment on the revolt appeared to be confirmed; and the Athenian force sailed home. Cyprus now joined the Ionian Revolt. So did the Greek cities of the Hellespont and the Propontis, clear up to Byzantium. So did Caria. But in the summer of 494 an Imperial Persian fleet composed of Phoenicians, Egyptians, Cilicians, and loyal Cypriots decisively defeated a smaller Ionian fleet off the island of Lade. The King's forces assaulted Miletus, ringleader of the rebellion, captured it, and razed it. They slaughtered or deported most of its male citizens; they enslaved its women and children and resettled them at the mouth of the Tigris River, where it emptied into the distant Persian Gulf. By the following summer the rebellion had been everywhere put down.

"Lord, remember the Athenians!" This admonition, according to reports, a slave of Darius' had been ordered to pronounce three times whenever the Great King dined. Certainly, there seemed little to prevent Darius from launching a punitive expedition against Athens and Eretria for aiding their Ionian cousins to rebel against the King of Kings. Sparta's two kings, Cleomenes and Demaratus, quarreled on. Athens was torn by faction: when the democratic, commercial, and naval interests had insisted on sending help to Miletus, the oligarchs tended to view the expedition as provocative meddling in Persian domestic affairs. The Athenian democracy was badly shaken by the news of the destruction of Miletus; and when the Athenian dramatist Phrynichus represented the fall of Miletus in a tragedy, the audience wept. The government thereupon fined Phrynichus and forbade the tragedy to be played. Meanwhile, Corinth was having trouble with her colonies. Aegina was brooding over her defeat in a war with Athens; Argos, over a recent defeat by Sparta. The northern city-states were clearly leaning toward Persia. Thessaly and Phocis were distrustful of each other. Greek colonies on the shores of the Black Sea, of the Propontis, of the Hellespont, and of Thrace had fallen to the Great King. The various city-states, intent on their wars with each other, from time to time appealed for Persian support against their neighbors. Clisthenes himself, when Athens' neighbors had attacked her in 506 and enemy forces had started to close in upon her, had sent an embassy to solicit Persian aid. These ambassadors even consented to offer the traditional earth and water to the Great King, but on their return to Athens they were disavowed. The Athenians therefore got no Persian aid against their Greek neighbors. When Hippias was expelled from Athens and sought Persian help to re-establish his tyranny, he was only one of a succession of Greeks who had gone up to Sardis to persuade the Persian governor there to intervene, either to help their polis against other Greek states or to help their faction against another faction in their own polis.

In Western Greece, the Hellenic city-states, weakened by wars with one another and by civil wars inside many states, were threatened by the Etruscans, the Italiots, and above all by the mighty Phoenician city on the African coast, Carthage. The Western Greeks were now being pushed back by Carthage in Corsica, in Sardinia, in Gaul, in southern Spain; and even in Sicily the Greeks were in danger. If Darius should indeed "remember the Athenians" and strike—at them, at Eretria too, or perhaps at all of Mainland Greece—the home countries could hardly expect their colonists in the western Mediterranean to come to their rescue. Whether Darius negotiated with Carthage or not, events would negotiate for him. A Graeco-Persian war would furnish Carthage her best chance of sweeping

Greek merchants from the western seas at a moment when no restless Athens or Eretria could bother about Sicily.

Greece-in-Asia had been reconquered and swallowed up in the maw of the mighty Persian Empire. And Mainland Greece might well have seemed to Darius a cauldron of anarchy. It was a cauldron that had boiled over once already to Persia's hurt, when Athens and Eretria had insolently aided the Great King's Greek subjects in Ionia to rebel against the laws of the Medes and Persians. It might boil over again. Mainland Greece was a serious frontier problem for a world empire. Yet the anarchy it presented might be expected to simplify the problems of a punitive expedition.

In 492 Darius struck. His young son-in-law, Mardonius, led a large army and fleet through Ionia to the Hellespont. In view of the fact that the tyrants who governed the Ionian cities had fomented the recent Ionian Revolt against the Persian Empire, Mardonius had deposed most of them and had established democratic governments in their place. After all, Persia's interest in Ionia was not in the forms of local government: Persia merely wanted tributary governments on whose loyalty she could depend. Arrived at the Hellespont, Mardonius first used his navy to ferry his army across to the European shore, and then to reduce the nearby island of Thasos, while his army conquered much of Macedonia and annexed it to the Empire. Next, the fleet coasted down to Acanthus, on the north shore of the first of the three peninsulas which Chalcidice thrust southeastward into the Aegean Sea. This first finger, called Acte, began with an isthmus about a mile and a quarter wide and fairly level. Then a spine of hills started down it and turned into a range of mountains. As the Persian ships moved down the coast, the mountains on their right grew higher until there loomed up at the tip of Acte a huge shape, like a vast pyramid. It was Mount Athos, towering over 6,000 feet out of the sea. Among the Greek sailors who plied the route to the Black Sea, Mount Athos was greatly feared.

On a momentous day Darius' navy started to round this cape to punish Athens and Eretria for aiding his rebellious Ionians, and perhaps to subject other Greek states as well. Immediately, a violent north wind sprang up and shattered his fleet against Athos. It was later reported[134] that almost 300 vessels were destroyed and nearly 20,000 men. Some of the men were dashed against the rocks; some died of exposure; many of them did not know how to swim and were drowned; the survivors gazed on the

Aegean Sea blossoming with dead men.[135] Boreas, the god of the north wind, had saved Hellas from the Persian fleet. But it was Thracian tribesmen who meanwhile attacked and defeated the army. Even Mardonius, its commander, was wounded. Mardonius fought the Thracians again, conquered them, and made them subject to Persia. But, with his fleet shattered, he postponed the punishment of Athens and retreated to Asia.

Darius did not forget the Athenians: he merely made more careful preparations. He now sent out heralds to various states in Mainland Greece and in the Aegean Isles to demand earth and water, the symbols of obedience. At the same time he ordered his seaport towns, including those in Ionia, to provide warships and horse transports. Many of the Greek states sent earth and water, despairing of defense against the Eastern colossus. Then, in the spring of 490, two years after Mardonius had lost his ships off Athos, Darius launched a second punitive expedition against those two meddling cities, Athens and Eretria. With the expedition went Hippias, the deposed tyrant of Athens, ready to serve as the Great King's local governor. This time there would be no Athos: this second army, cavalry and all, would proceed straight across the Aegean by way of the islands, conquering them as it went. The expedition included some 50,000 men.[136] The island of Naxos was taken by surprise. Those inhabitants who did not flee to the mountains were captured and sold as slaves; their houses and temples were burned. Apollo's holy island of Delos was, indeed, spared; but other islands were subdued. At last the conquerors reached the southern tip of Euboea, a few miles from Athens, and ravaged Carystus. Sailing northward up the strait, they assaulted Eretria.

Athens had intended, if Eretria were attacked first, to dispatch to her aid 4,000 Athenians whom she had sent as outsettlers[137] to nearby Chalcis on the Euboean coast. But there was clearly a group of pro-Persians in Eretria who favored surrender; other Eretrians had fled to the mountains of Euboea; and Athens ordered her colonists back across the strait to help defend Attica, whose turn to receive the blow was evidently next. After six days of fighting, Eretria was betrayed by two of her citizens, and fell. The temples were burned in revenge for those that had been burned at Sardis when Ionia revolted. The people were taken captive and eventually resettled near Susa, the capital of the Great King. The island of Euboea, just off the coast of Attica, now became the advanced base of Persia's expeditionary force. From Euboea Hippias guided the conquerors to the nearby Attic shore where a plain would give scope to the Persian cavalry. Half a century before, Hippias had landed here with his father, Pisistratus, who was then returning from his second exile. Now that he was an old man, he was about to win his throne again.

Some twenty miles away, news reached the Athenian generals that the Persians had beached their ships on the shore below Marathon and had pitched camp. Should the Athenians attack them there or await their onslaught? On September 3, 490, the generals dispatched a professional runner to Sparta, some 140 miles away over rough country. His name was Phidippides. He finished his Marathon race in two[138] days; and even so he had time left for a conversation with the god Pan, whom he met en route—or so he reported when he returned to Athens. Pan had asked the runner why the Athenians neglected him; he had often helped them, and would do so again. Phidippides also reported that, for reasons connected with a religious festival, the Spartans could not march to battle before the next full moon. Luckily, Plataea, a small Boeotian town just across the frontier, which had sought alliance with Athens as a protection against Thebes and her Boeotian confederacy, promised to send prompt help.

Ten thousand heavy infantry marched from Athens to the high ground northwest of the Plain of Marathon. One thousand Plataeans joined them there. They camped in the holy grounds of a temple built to Heracles, high up a rocky valley, where they could readily guard the two roads that led to Athens. Below lay the Plain of Marathon between the small but rugged mountains and the Bay. The plain was over four miles long, but marshes occupied each end. The Persians had chosen—or Hippias had chosen for them—a camping spot next to the northeastern marsh. The distance from the mountains to the shore varied from one and a half to two miles, which gave the Persian cavalry room for maneuver against an army without cavalry. The Imperial fleet was anchored along the northeast end of the crescent-shaped shore, snugly protected by the hilly promontory of Cynosura.

Neither side was in a hurry to fight. The best strategy for the Persians was to watch for a signal, flashed by a shield in the sunlight to tell them treason had done its work in Athens and that their sympathizers were ready to help them take the city, preferably while the Athenian army was still absent. So they waited. The obvious strategy for the Athenians and their Plataean allies was to wait until the Spartans could join them. So they, too, were willing to wait. But, even so, the Athenians were the better placed. If the Persians chose to attack them, they would have to come up a narrow valley where numbers would not count and where cavalry could not do its proper work. If they started for Athens, they would expose their right flank to sudden assault from high ground. If they re-embarked, they would be, for a brief time at least, highly vulnerable. For about a week the Athenian army waited, and both sides watched.

The Athenian polemarch, or battle chief, had called a council of war with his ten generals, one from each Clisthenic tribe. Some of them argued that the Greeks were heavily outnumbered. Given the delay at Sparta, they ought to return to Athens, some twenty-four miles away, and protect the city. But one of them, Miltiades, argued for fighting it out on the Plain of Marathon. Miltiades had come recently from the Thracian Chersonese, where he had inherited a frontier kingdom from his uncle of the same name and had also ruled as tyrant over colonists from Athens. He knew the Persians well. Pisistratus had at one time banished his father. The sons of Pisistratus had hired assassins to kill his uncle. Now Hippias, one of Pisistratus's sons, had guided a Persian fleet to the shore a few miles down the valley where Miltiades argued for attack.

Miltiades persuaded some of his fellow generals and he persuaded Callimachus, the battle chief, who presided over the military council. He won his argument. In accordance with Athenian law the ten generals took turns, each for one day, as field commander. Those who had voted with Miltiades yielded their days to him. Even so, perhaps because he knew that his tyranny in the Chersonese rendered him suspect at Athens, he waited for his legal day. Or perhaps he chose that day because it was then that the Persians chose to move, both by land and sea. Persian forces started southward down the shore of the Bay of Marathon, and other Imperial forces started re-embarking to take the ninety-mile sea route around Cape Sunium to Athens. When part of the latter forces and all of the cavalry mounts had re-embarked, Miltiades' army started down the valley.

Within a mile of the Persian forces they formed for battle. Callimachus commanded the right wing. The Plataeans took the left. To cover the longer Persian formation, and perhaps also because he had ideas of his own, Miltiades made his two wings heavy and stretched his line between them perilously thin. The Imperial command had placed its picked troops,

Persians and Sacans, opposite that weak center. Miltiades' chief danger was not enemy cavalry—they were now safely in the ships. His chief danger was from the Persian arrows until his heavy infantry could close hand-to-hand and make its superior weapons and superior armor felt. So he ordered his line forward at a run[139] for this last mile. The Persian forces, seeing this smaller army[140] attack them at a run, thought the Greeks must have lost their senses. The elite Persian center fought steadily, broke Miltiades' weak center, and started to chase the Athenians back toward the hills. For a long time the two armies fought. Then Miltiades closed the pincers upon the victorious Persian center.

At this point the god Pan put into the hearts of the Persians one of those sudden, irrational, Panic fears, which taught Hellenic armies to pray to him. There was wild disorder, and the Imperials fled toward those ships that were still beached or were anchored in shallow water. The Athenian soldiers were calling for fire in order to destroy the enemy ships, now ready to carry the foe against their sacred polis. The ships tried to shove off. In the melee on the beach, Callimachus the battle chief performed doughty deeds, then gave his life for his polis. Cynegirus, brother of the tragedian, Aeschylus, seized the stern of an escaping ship; an enemy ax chopped off his hand; and he died on the beach. But seven ships were captured. The rest of the fleet escaped; a distant shield flashed in the sunlight and gave the sign of treason; and the Great King's fleet started for Phalerum, the port and arsenal of Athens. On the blood-stained beach they had left behind them were 6,400 dead. The Athenians lost only 192, for the battle had ended in Panic slaughter.

But Athens was still in danger: the Persian fleet could still sail around Cape Sunium at the tip of Attica and hope to reach Athens in nine or ten hours. Despite their long battle, the little Athenian army made a forced march back to their threatened polis. Who had flashed the bronze shield from the summit of Mount Pentelicus? What friend of Hippias or what aristocratic opponent of the new democracy at Athens? Nobody ever found out. When the Persian fleet reached Athens, the very Athenian army that had just that day destroyed an army of the Great King at Marathon, grimly awaited a second round. The Persian fleet sailed back to Asia.

A second time, the mighty Persian Empire had failed to conquer Greece. Two years before it had been Boreas, the north wind, or perhaps

Posidon, great god of the sea, who had destroyed the fleet of the Great King off Mount Athos. Now it was Athens, unaided by the leading military state in Greece, Sparta. When 2,000 Spartans did reach Attica after a forced march of three days, the mighty invaders had already sailed away, defeated; and the Spartans marched to Marathon, not to risk their lives but to view the dead warriors from Asia. Athens had indeed been supported on the day of Marathon by 1,000 Plataeans. But, according to the reports of her army, the gods had fought on her side too, as some of the gods had once fought for the Achaeans from Greece on that other plain centuries ago beneath the walls of Troy. The god Pan had kept his promise to the runner, Phidippides, that he would help Athens, and the Athenians showed their gratitude by setting up a shrine to Pan in a cave on the slope of the Acropolis. The hero, Theseus, who as king of Athens long ago had, according to tradition, peacefully united all Attica, had been seen fighting in the Athenian ranks at Marathon. An unknown warrior, dressed like a countryman and armed only with a ploughshare, fought there too. Later, when he could not be found, the Athenians sent to Delphi to ask Apollo's oracle who this could have been. Apollo replied that they should worship the hero Echetlus, him of the Ploughtail.[141]

Darius, King of Kings, was angered by the defeat of his army on the plain below Marathon and by his second failure in two years to subdue Mainland Greece. This second failure was bound to make for restlessness in Thrace and Macedonia, so recently brought under Persian law, and even in recently reconquered Ionia. But Egypt was first to revolt. Darius thereupon set about mustering enormous forces, sufficient to reconquer Egypt and to avenge Marathon too by annexing Greece. This time, he proposed to command his forces himself. Then, suddenly, after a reign of thirty-six years, he died. Although he had conquered less territory for the Persian Empire than Cyrus the Great, its founder, yet Darius the Great had done much to reorganize its administration; and he had ruled his empire well. At his death he had already designated which of his sons should rule: Xerxes now mounted the throne. Along with that throne he inherited the Empire's Greek problem and its Egyptian problem.

Egypt he reconquered. The Greek problem was more complex, if only because, unlike Egypt, Greece was not itself an empire but a collection of small states torn by wars among themselves, by the bad eris between rich and poor inside many of the individual states, and by intervention in each other's internal strife. On all three counts Xerxes could have truthfully declared that Mainland Greece did not know how to govern itself, and that in addition the intervention by Athens and Eretria in Ionia had proven that Mainland Greece was determined to prevent the Persian Empire from governing Greece-in-Asia. Meanwhile, he was being urged to settle this Greek problem once and for all by the powerful family of the Aleuadae, who ruled Larissa in Thessaly and longed to rule more; by Demaratus, the Spartan king, who had finally been deposed, had fled to the court of Darius, and now wanted Darius' son Xerxes to restore him to power; by another deposed king, Scythas of Zancle in Sicily; by the descendants of Pisistratus, who longed to be restored as the reigning dynasty of Athens; and by these Pisistratids' oraclemonger, Onomacritus, who kept finding—or forging—oracles which promised Greece to Persia.

Xerxes now spent three years in the most thorough preparations for massive war that the Mediterranean and Middle Eastern world had ever witnessed. He made an alliance[142] with Carthage that was calculated to keep the Greeks of the western Mediterranean too busy defending their own states to answer any calls for help that might come from Mainland Greece. He sent his ambassadors throughout Mainland Greece, demanding earth and water. Most of the states in northern Greece, uncertain that Athens could, or that Sparta would, defend them, promptly medized— that is, submitted to a Persian Empire which the Greeks had traditionally called Median. But, even in central Greece, the oligarchic rulers of many cities in Boeotia medized too. And in more distant Peloponnesus, Argos, always against the Spartans, who had robbed her[143] of her Homeric hegemony, made a secret treaty with Xerxes. To Athens and Sparta Xerxes sent no ambassadors. Both cities had once killed heralds whom his father had sent.

The army and navy which Xerxes proposed to hurl at Greece would be far too large to transport straight across the Aegean, on the pattern of 490 and Marathon. Neither would Xerxes risk rounding dangerous Mount Athos, where his father, Darius, had already lost a fleet in 492. He would not even try to ferry his army across the Hellespont as Darius had done in that same catastrophic first attempt on Greece. Instead he set Phoenician and Egyptian engineers to work to construct a double pontoon bridge across the Hellespont at Abydos, a matter of less than two miles. Persian engineers bridged the Strymon River in Macedonia. To avoid Athos, the same Persian engineers cut a canal across the isthmus of the peninsula of Acte which wholly bypassed Athos and was wide enough to allow two triremes to pass through abreast. Moles at each end extended into the sea to keep the two mouths of the canal from silting up.

The Greeks were puzzled that Xerxes should dig this canal, since their own ships crossed the Isthmus of Corinth on a wooden track with rollers, Corinth's famous *diolkos*. They suspected ostentatious pride. But they overlooked two facts. First, a canal at Corinth would have needed to be perhaps three times as long as the one that Xerxes dug across Acte and would have had to run through higher ground at that. Second, Xerxes had ampler labor power at his disposal than anything the Greeks could command. In addition to his canal and his bridges, Xerxes also established huge depots of supplies in a line that extended clear to the mouth of the Axios River in Macedonia.

Nevertheless Xerxes' problem of moving several hundred thousand men from all over his vast empire on foot, on horse, on camel, and of keeping them supplied with food and water, was formidable. Besides, the divine powers which had destroyed his father's fleet twelve years ago struck, too, at him. A tempest smashed the two parallel pontoon bridges that were to bring his monstrous herd of men across the Hellespont from Asia into Europe. The huge cables, cables of flax made by the Phoenicians, cables of papyrus made by the Egyptians, that bound the anchored ships together in lines for nearly two miles, had snapped.

Xerxes ordered the Hellespont scourged with three hundred lashes and addressed defiant words to it; he commanded that a pair of fetters be thrown into it to bind it to his will; he sent it word that it was but just that no man offer it sacrifice, since it was a turbid and briny river. For the briny water flowed from the Black Sea; that sea was constantly increased by great rivers like the Danube, the Dniester, the Dnieper, and the Don; and the scourged and fettered waters ran down to the Mediterranean at some seven knots. The Greeks, when they heard that Xerxes had scourged the Hellespont, were horrified by his hybris, by this insolence in the face of divine powers. As this huge army, this human war-tempest, moved under arms toward their lovely land, were they heartened by the fact that its leader was defying not only Athens, not only Greece, but the gods that watched over both and that would surely punish pride and blasphemy?

The pontoon bridge was rebuilt, and it was a Greek engineer who rebuilt it, an Ionian of Samos named Harpalus. Three hundred sixty ships, anchored side by side, composed the floating base of one bridge; three hundred fourteen, the other. Again they were bound together with cables. On these cables plank was laid, and over the plank, first brush, then earth. Fences were built on both sides of each bridge so that the animals would not be frightened of the briny, rebellious river that flowed beneath. Xerxes had yoked the neck of the sea.[144]

The day fixed for beginning the crossing arrived. At dawn Xerxes himself poured a libation from a golden phial into the sea he had earlier scourged and fettered. He then prayed to the Sun for the success of his expedition into Europe. Now he cast the golden phial into the waters of the Hellespont, and with it a golden bowl and a Persian sword. Then Xerxes and his Persian warriors crossed; and of these the 10,000 picked troops known as the Immortals wore garlands on their heads. Finally, the contingents of his subject provinces started crossing under the lash, and later tradition would recount that it took this polyglot army seven days and seven nights to complete its crossing.

At Doriscus Xerxes ordered his army and navy renumbered. The army may have contained some 360,000 combatants. A confused throng of servants, concubines, and supply men followed it. And the navy that supported it contained 1,207 triremes, mostly from Egypt, Phoenicia, or Ionia, although perhaps only 700 or 800 were fighting ships, as distinguished from supply ships and transports. It was a formidable force.[145] It is true that the higher naval officers were Persians with no naval tradition; that the loyalty of the recently rebellious Ionians might depend only on fear for their families, in Asia, and therefore at the mercy of the Great King; that, with the exception of the Persians, few of the soldiers or sailors of Xerxes showed enthusiasm for the war. They had come against Europe because they had to come. Finally, even if the gods should not grow jealous of this one man's godlike power, there were two great enemies to be dreaded, the land and the sea: the largely unknown land ahead might lead these vast forces to famine, and the uncertain sea might strike this fleet off a coast with too few harbors to shield it from storms. Such was the warning of the Great King's uncle, Artabanus. In any case, the invasion army embodied might rather than right, brute force rather than an appeal to justice, blind will rather than questing intellect, and its strategy tended toward the hammer blow rather than the planned maneuver or the skillful thrust. How can man will the waves of the sea to calm? How can he make food spring from a strange and mountainous and none too fertile land? They were entering a hard land, a treacherous sea, to fight hard men who were preparing to defend their hearths. In their favor, they had overwhelming numbers, though marching under the lash and preparing to fight under the lash. This multitude was supported or hindered by cooking women, concubines, and eunuchs. Persian hybris and confidence in force, wealth, and luxury—on a scale never dreamed of by Cyrus, founder of this empire —were preparing to drive a mammoth army of conquered subjects from many lands against desperate courage and the ingenuity that necessity might mother.

On the beach near Doriscus, Xerxes, riding in a chariot, reviewed his vast army. He rode past his Persians with their coats of mail and their breeches, their wicker bucklers and their quivers, their short spears, long bows, and reed arrows, and their daggers hanging from their girdles. The Medes were equipped in the same way and so were the Cissians, and the Hyrcanians who came from the southeastern shore of the Caspian Sea. The Assyrians wore bronze helmets, with Egyptian-style shields and spears and daggers. They carried wooden clubs studded with iron, and wore linen breastplates. Xerxes' chariot passed the Bactrians, carrying bows made of reeds and short spears; and the Sacans, a Scythian folk, with tall, stiff-pointed caps on their heads and breeches on their legs, and carrying their native bows, daggers, and axes. He drove past troops from India, wearing garments of 'tree-wool,' or cotton, and armed with reed bows and iron-tipped arrows; past Areians, Parthians, Caspians, Pactyes, and past Sarangas with knee-high boots. His Arabian contingent carried bows which, when unstrung, curved backward. His Ethiopians wore leopard skins and lion skins; their long-bows were made of strips of palm wood, and their short arrows were tipped with sharpened stone; the Ethiopians carried also spears tipped with the horn of the gazelle, and their clubs were studded. Half of each Ethiopian's body was painted white with gypsum and half was red with vermilion. The eastern Ethiopian soldiers each wore the skin of a horse's head on his, with the mane for his crest, and the horse's ears erect; his shield was made from the skin of a crane. The Libyans wore leather clothing and charred their wooden javelins. The Lydians were equipped more or less in the Greek style. The Thracians wore fox-skin caps, many-colored mantles, fawn-skin boots on their feet and legs. They were armed with javelins, daggers, and shields. Of all these peoples, the Persians were the most richly adorned. They brought with them an abundance of gold. Carriages bore their concubines and servants. Camels and other pack animals bore their food.

Of the various national contingents many, but not all, included cavalry. The Sagartian cavalry used lassoes. The cavalry of India rode swift horses; they also used chariots drawn by horses and wild asses. The Arabians were mounted on camels, and rode in the rear so that their animals would not panic the horses.

When Xerxes had reviewed his army, he reviewed the linen-winged warships of his Imperial navy. The ships were drawn down the beach, launched, and anchored in a line. Xerxes alighted from his chariot, boarded a Sidonian vessel, and sat under a golden canopy while he was carried past the prows of the ships and while on each trireme his marines stood to arms.

The Imperial navy's 1,207 triremes came from Phoenicia, Egypt, Cyprus, Cilicia, Pamphylia, Lycia, Caria, Doris, Ionia, and the Aegean Islands. The best ships were brought by the Phoenicians, and the best of the Phoenician ships had sailed out of Sidon. Besides the 1,207 triremes, there were ships of thirty oars and of fifty oars, light galleys, and huge transports for horses. On all the triremes there were fighting marines: Persians, Medes, and Sacans.

Xerxes was well satisfied. He summoned Demaratus, the deposed Spartan king.

"You are a Greek, . . ." said Xerxes. "Now therefore tell me this: will the Greeks offer me battle and abide my coming? . . ."[146]

"O King," answered Demaratus, the Spartan,

seeing that you bid me by all means speak the whole truth, and say that which you shall not afterwards prove to be false,—in Hellas poverty is ever native to the soil, but courage comes of their own seeking, the fruit of wisdom and strong law; by use of courage Hellas defends herself from poverty and tyranny. Now I say nought but good of all Greeks that dwell in those Dorian lands; yet it is not of all that I would now speak, but only of the Lacedaemonians; and this I say of them; firstly, that they will never accept conditions from you that import the enslaving of Hellas; and secondly, that they will meet you in battle, yea, even though all the rest of the Greeks be on your side. But, for the number of them, ask me not how many these men are, who are like to do as I say; be it of a thousand men, or of more or of fewer than that, their army will fight with you.[147]

Xerxes was smiling but incredulous. Demaratus reminded him that Sparta had made him, Demaratus, an exile without a polis, while Xerxes' father, Darius, had received, protected, and supported him. As to the Spartans:

> fighting singly they are as brave as any man living, and together they are the best warriors on earth. Free they are, yet not wholly free; for law is their master, whom they fear much more than your men fear you. This is my proof—what their law bids them, that they do; and its bidding is ever the same, that they must never flee from the battle before whatsoever odds, but abide at their post and there conquer or die. If this that I say seems to you but foolishness, then let me hereafter hold my peace; it is under constraint that I have now spoken. But may your wish, O king! be fulfilled.[148]

Xerxes made a jest of Demaratus' answer, but treated the Spartan kindly. Under the presidency of Sparta, thirty-one of the warring states of Greece had met at the Isthmus of Corinth to concert a common defense in the autumn of 481, before Xerxes' monstrous herd of men had even crossed the Hellespont. Those northern states which were most exposed, like the states in Thessaly, were cautious about promising to fight until they could judge whether the states of central and southern Greece were prepared to help defend them. A defensive alliance, the Panhellenic League, was formed. Feuds between states were hastily patched up. Athens and her neighbor, Aegina, were persuaded to end their war. It was inevitably agreed that Sparta would lead the army. But who would lead the navy? Sparta had the strongest army in Greece; however, under the guidance of a statesman of genius, Themistocles, a man of relatively obscure origins but with an imagination and wiliness worthy of Odysseus, Athens had just built the strongest navy. The urgent necessity of her war with Aegina had happily coincided with a chance strike at her state-owned silver mines at Laurium. By this year of invasion Athens had built, with her new funds, 147 ships[149] ready for action and was holding 53 more in reserve. If Sparta had the right to command the Allied armies, Athens had the same right to command the Allied navies. But the rapid rise of Athenian power had aroused so much jealousy and fear that the congress at the Isthmus demanded that Sparta should command the Allied navies too, even though Sparta was no sea power. The congress was able to muster some 35,000 heavy infantry and some 40,000 light-armed followers.[150]

If only the Thessalians would join, the Allies could send cavalry too, against the formidable cavalry of the invader. Out of all the states of Mainland Greece, only Thessaly, and to a far lesser extent Boeotia, bred horses extensively and maintained a real cavalry. And most of the Boeotian cities had already followed Thebes's example and medized. As Xerxes approached the Hellespont, those Thessalians who opposed the medizing Aleuadae of Larissa announced that they would join the Greek alliance provided the Allies would fight on their northern border. The Allies therefore sent 10,000 heavy infantry to hold the narrow Pass of Tempe. The Vale of Tempe led for nearly five narrow miles from Macedonia, between Mount Olympus, home of the Twelve Great Gods, and the less imposing Ossa, into Thessaly. Here in the Vale of Tempe, the Allies were joined by Thessalian horse. But learning there were alternate routes from Macedonia into Thessaly, the Allies withdrew at just about the time that Xerxes' army marched triumphantly across that briny river, the Hellespont. Thessaly now medized and added her cavalry to the monster army that was headed south for Athens.

One of the most alarming aspects of the coming storm was the attitude of the gods. Not only was a man of godlike power[151] now marching against Athens, but the Delphic oracle was apparently advising the embassies of various Greek states that their governments should medize. When an Athenian embassy sought Apollo's counsel, he replied through the mouth of the Pythoness:

> Wretches, why tarry ye thus? Nay, flee from your houses and city,
> Flee to the ends of the earth from the circle embattled of Athens! . . .[152]

and Apollo went on to predict that fortresses and temples would alike be burned. The two Athenian envoys were dismayed. But where Croesus of Lydia understood not that which was spoken, nor made further inquiry, the envoys from Athens took suppliant boughs in their hands and made further inquiry, praying aloud to Apollo:

98

> Lord, regard in thy mercy these suppliant boughs which we bring to thee,
> and give us some better answer concerning our country; else we will not
> depart out of thy temple, but abide here till we die.[153]

Confronted by this obstinate and urgent faith, Apollo spoke a second
oracle. His language was full of the poetic ambiguity and obscurity that
clothed so many of his famous oracles; but he seemed to be saying that
Athena, divine protectress of Athens, was trying in vain to secure the help
of Zeus for her city; that all Attica would be lost to Xerxes, but that Zeus
would permit a wood-built wall to protect the Athenians; that they should
withdraw from Athens rather than await there the armies of Xerxes; that,
even then, they would meet him in battle; and, finally, that "Salamis, isle
divine" would "destroy children of women."

This second oracle sounded at least more merciful than the first, so
the envoys wrote it down and took it back to Athens. Then, when they
read it before the Athenian Assembly, the argument began. Some of the
older citizens, who had lived on, and loved, the Attic soil before the
younger citizens of Athens had turned to the sea, to ships, and to commerce, thought that the wood-built walls were the thorn hedge that had
once upon a time fenced in the Acropolis. They should therefore retire
to the Acropolis and defend that. But others insisted that the wood-built
walls were the walls of their ships. They should flee all of Attica and take
to the sea. Then they should fight Xerxes' fleet near Salamis, isle divine,
which lay a quarter of a mile off the Attic coast a short distance above the
Piraeus and indeed near to Athens itself. The professional interpreters of
oracles pointed out that Salamis would destroy them. No, said the wily
Themistocles, who had caused Athens to build her present excellent fleet
and who had moved her naval base from exposed Phalerum to the now partially fortified and nearer harbor at Piraeus, if the children of women whom
Salamis would destroy were Athenians, Apollo would not have called that
island "divine" but would have called it by some word like "cruel." Apollo,
he declared, meant that Salamis would destroy the Persian fleet, if the
Athenians would but quit Attica, Acropolis and all, and take to their ships.
Themistocles won the debate.

But the Greek states were troubled not only by those other oracles of
Apollo that seemed to urge submission. They were also troubled because
in most states the aristocrats, who were fighting a losing battle against
rising democracies, were defecting to Persia. The Best People were un-

moved by the heroic opposition of the Athenian democrats. If the people who were not Best, instead of turning sailor or shipbuilder, merchant or politician, had stayed on the land and tilled the farms of the landowning nobles; if they had left law to the nobles, who knew from of old how to translate divine law into civil law and how to govern the polis; then there might well have been no Athenian or Eretrian intervention in aid of the Greek King's rebellious Ionian subjects and no invasion of Greece.

Among the aristocrats who remained unmoved by the efforts to rally Hellas against the invading Xerxes was the famous Theban poet, Pindar. Pindar wrote victory odes for nobles and even tyrants, for men descended from gods, men who strove in the ancient, traditional, athletic contests like the Olympic Games; who won crowns of laurel for their skill and endurance; and whose excellence in sport reminded Pindar of the excellence their ancestors had shown in war. But it was excellence for the sake of excellence, not for the sake of grain routes to the Black Sea or of timber from Thrace. It was an excellence that strove, not for progress, but for perfection. Even the aristocrat, the descendant of a god, could not excel but by the grace of the Olympian.

> Creatures of a day, what is anyone? What is he not? Man is but a dream of a shadow; but when the Zeus-given gleam of sunlight comes, a radiance rests on men, and a gentle life.[154]

Pindar looked, for significance, not outward beyond the sea, but upward, toward the gods; not toward a prosperous future but toward the permanent and immortal, contained and reflected in the present, heroic, striving moment. The god-descended noble, the god-descended runner or chariot-driver at the Olympic Games, or at the Pythian, the Nemean, or the Isthmian, could fulfill himself and make his life a sign of eternity only because he lived the present moment to the full, and because a radiance rested on him. That Pindar might remain neither the dream of a shadow nor the creature of a day, but endure, that those victorious athletes for whom he wrote his odes might also endure, he looked to the gleam of Zeus-given light that had brought courage to Achilles, that he also might endure, and he did not look to the restless cunning of Odysseus.

As to Apollo, who spoke the will of Zeus through his oracles at Delphi, was it so sure that, as many charged, his priests were corrupted into medizing? The Athenian envoys who would not take no for answer had inquired further, and Apollo had told them that Zeus would permit a wood-built wall to protect the Athenians. There all inquiry ceased, and whether they or their sons or their sons' sons would prove but creatures of a day and what would ultimately befall their Polis if they fought, and which children of men Salamis, isle divine, would ultimately destroy, was never disclosed to them, if only because they did not ask.

Despite the hope in Apollo's second oracle, given when the envoys of Athens had insisted on making further inquiry—assuming Themistocles had read the oracle rightly—the men of Athens could hope for little either from the gods or from the gods' descendants, the nobles, in most of the cities of Greece. When the Allies fell back from the narrow Pass of Tempe and abandoned Thessaly, the next obvious place to defend eastern Greece south of the Malaic Gulf was a narrow pass between sheer mountains and the sea, connecting Malis and Locris. The pass ran from east to west for about a mile along the south shore of the Malaic Gulf, near the western cape of the long island of Euboea. At each end of the mile, the pass became so narrow as to suggest two gates. In fact, the gates were scarcely wider than a cart road. The area between them widened somewhat, but the flow from a number of hot mineral springs created a morass. Many years before, the Phocians had deliberately guided the hot, sulphurous water into the pass so as to keep the pass from being used by Thessalian raiders who might come against them. For the same reason, they had built a wall, which was now in ruins, across the path near the western gate. Because of the hot springs and the two narrow gates, the whole pass was called Thermopylae, or the Hot Gates. At Thermopylae a huge army would enjoy little advantage over a small force of men who knew how to die. It is true that a circuitous, little-known path over the mountain that flanked the pass could furnish a detour, but this mountain trail could also be guarded.

The Allies, in congress at the Isthmus, decided to guard the Pass of Thermopylae and at least to delay the enemy there. They also decided to send the Allied fleet to Artemisium, on the northernmost coast of Euboea. There it could guard the entrance to the strait that separated that island from the mainland. In case of necessity, it could fight the Great King's fleet inside the strait, where the narrow waters would serve as a naval Thermopylae for a small but determined force. And it could keep an eye on the coast to the rear of the men who must hold Thermopylae.

In the summer of 480 Leonidas, one of the two kings of Sparta, marched a force of 300 chosen Spartans from the Isthmus to Thermopylae. All his men were mature citizens who had already fathered sons to defend Sparta in future years. With them marched upwards of 4,900 men from other Greek cities, even including 400 Thebans, unsympathetic with the medizing policy of the oligarchs who governed Thebes, and perhaps some Helots from Lacedaemonia and other light troops. The Allied command claimed that this was only an advance guard. Sparta delayed sending more men for the moment, because a religious festival detained them at home. Unkind critics would later declare that, since she really wanted to hold the line, not in central Greece, but at the Isthmus of Corinth, she had sent only a token force to the coming battle at the Hot Gates. But Sparta was not alone in delaying. Other states delayed on the grounds of another religious festival, the Olympic Games. In any case, given the size of Xerxes' army and given the remarkable strategic value of Thermopylae, Leonidas commanded only token forces.

Meanwhile, the Allied fleet was posted off Artemisium, but when some of their scouting vessels reported that the much larger Persian fleet was following down the east coast of the peninsula of Magnesia, the Allies somewhat fearfully withdrew down the strait between Euboea and the mainland. Then, according to later report, Posidon, the sea god, and Boreas, the north wind, suddenly raised a fearful storm off Magnesia, where most of the enemy fleet were anchored, and for three days the sea rose in waves of death, as it had risen against the Achaean conquerors, homeward bound from fallen Troy.[155] Four hundred warships were destroyed, together with unnumbered supply ships and transports. The gods had struck an even deadlier blow at the navy of Xerxes than the blow they had struck twelve years earlier at his father's navy off Mount Athos. After the storm, the still formidable Persian fleet withdrew for a few days to the Gulf of Pagasae.

The huge Persian land forces now arrived outside the Hot Gates and encamped. At sight of this overwhelming host, this "mighty flood of men,"[156] many of Leonidas's army lost heart. Most of the Peloponnesian contingents wanted to fall back to the Isthmus of Corinth where with reinforcements they might at least save the Peloponnese. This proposal naturally angered the contingents of Phocians and Locrians, whose little countries would instantly fall to the Persian host. Leonidas decided to stay, and sent messengers to the Allied cities to demand reinforcements, since he and his forces were too few to stand against Xerxes' huge army, even in the narrow pass between the Hot Gates.

Xerxes sent a mounted scout to spy out the Greek position. Most of the Greeks were hidden behind the ancient wall which the Phocians had built and which Leonidas's men had now repaired; but the Lacedaemonians were posted outside the wall. Here, on this mid-August day, between the mountain's rock cliffs and the sea, some of them were practicing gymnastic exercises. Others were busy combing their hair, which they wore long, as did all Spartans, in the fashion of their forefathers. When the scene was reported to the Great King, he found it so laughable that he summoned the deposed Lacedaemonian king, Demaratus, whom he had brought with him to Greece, and demanded an explanation. Now it was Demaratus' fellow king Cleomenes who had brought about his deposition. Cleomenes was now dead, and a few miles away his son-in-law Leonidas held the narrow pass. To the Great King's questions about his amusing handful of opponents, combing their hair and ignoring certain doom, Demaratus answered, with due deference but with Spartan stubbornness, that "these men are come to fight with us for the passage, and for that they are preparing"[157]; the Lacedaemonians, he added, always adorned their hair before risking their lives.

But Xerxes would not believe him. Four days he waited for the Greeks to withdraw and save themselves—as indeed most of the contingents under Leonidas wished to do. Then he grew angry. He ordered his Median and Cissian troops to attack, capture the Greeks, and bring them alive into his presence. For a whole day the Medes and Cissians fought the Greeks and lost many men, but to no avail. The second day, Xerxes ordered out the Immortals. But the Lacedaemonians, favored by the narrowness of the pass, by greater length of spear, and by cleverer tactics, slew many of the Immortals, lost relatively few men themselves—and held the pass. The third day Xerxes hoped to find the Greeks exhausted; but the contingents of the various cities took turns fighting. And they held the pass.

Meanwhile, a Greek from Malis, a state abutting Thessaly which had medized when the Allies abandoned Tempe and left the northern states to their fate—this Greek, whose name was Epialtes, informed Xerxes of the mountain trail that detoured the Hot Gates. The Phocian contingent had been ordered by Leonidas to hold this trail. Xerxes thereupon sent his Immortals by night and by this trail across the mountain that flanked Thermopylae. They were guided by Epialtes.[158] On this still August night, the Phocians' first warning that Persians were at hand was the noise of dried oak leaves beneath Persian feet. Under a rain of arrows and convinced that the Persians had come especially to attack them, they fled to the top of the mountain and prepared to die. The Immortals let them flee and hurried on to trap Leonidas from the rear.

Leonidas was warned by his seer, Megistias, that he and his little band were to die next morning. Then deserters brought them word that they were outflanked. When day dawned, their own sentries rushed down from the heights to tell them that they would soon be bottled up in the pass.

Following their custom, the Greek forces held a council, and many advised retreat. Leonidas thereupon sent back those who were eager to return to their respective cities. Leonidas and his Spartans remained at the post to which they had been ordered. The Thespian contingent chose to remain at their side. The Thebans, his most dubiously loyal contingent, Leonidas detained against their will. Did he have hopes of reinforcements? Or was he merely determined to obey when someone had blundered? Or did he recall an oracle which the Spartans had received from Delphi at the beginning of the war? Apollo had told them that Xerxes, mighty as Zeus, would either lay waste Sparta or else kill one of their kings. Perhaps Leonidas thought his death at Thermopylae would save his polis. Finally, Leonidas may have sent back the other contingents, not to their cities, but to attack the Persian Immortals and to protect the contingents that still held the pass.

Xerxes rose when the sun rose, and offered libations, but he delayed the assault until later in the forenoon to give his Immortals time to make their detour and to strike simultaneously with his own forces at the eastern gate from the rear of Leonidas. Having chosen to die, Leonidas and his little band shifted tactics. On the three previous days they had fought from behind the Phocian wall. Now they went beyond it; and, while the Persian officers scourged their men to advance, the Greeks mowed them down. Most of the Greeks had by now broken their heavy spears and were working with swords. In that work Leonidas fell, and over his body the Greeks fought, as the heroes in Homer had fought to retrieve the body of Patroclus. Just then word came that the Persian Immortals were approaching from the rear. The Greeks promptly withdrew behind the Phocian wall and took position on a hillock near the eastern gate. During the withdrawal, the Thebans suddenly threw down their arms and surrendered. Of those on the hillock, the men who still had swords worked with them; the others worked with their fists and their teeth. But Persian arrows rained down; to the west the Phocian wall was breached; the hillock was now ringed round; and, to a man, the Greeks fell. After the war, the Amphictyonic League would erect pillars where they fell, one to all the Peloponnesians who died at Thermopylae and one to the Spartans alone. Each pillar would bear an inscription, a laconic inscription, composed by the poet Simonides. For all those who fell, Simonides would write:

> Here four thousand of the Peloponnese once fought with three thousand thousand.[159]

And for the Spartans alone:

> Stranger, go tell the Lacedaemonians that we lie here obedient to their word.[160]

When Xerxes examined the bodies of the fallen Greeks, the body of Leonidas was identified. Xerxes ordered the head struck off and the body crucified. Twenty thousand men of Xerxes' army had been slain.

While Leonidas fought at the Hot Gates, things were happening at sea too. For a while Xerxes' battered navy licked its wounds in the Gulf of Pagasae, but it was still large enough to strike dread in the Allied fleet off Artemisium. Several of the Greek contingents wanted to draw back, and the people in the island of Euboea were begging for time to evacuate their children and slaves before Euboea was abandoned. Luckily, the Euboeans hit on the plan of giving Themistocles, who commanded the Athenian contingent, a handsome bribe of thirty talents. Themistocles promptly distributed modest fractions of this sum to the recalcitrant Allied commanders. The fleet stayed.

The Persians now decided that, before attacking the Allied fleet, they should close the southern end of the Euripus, the strait that lay between Euboea and the mainland, in case the Allies should attempt to use it as an escape corridor. So they detached 200 ships and sent them around

Euboea. Then the main Persian fleet sighted the Greek ships approaching from Artemisium. There was a battle, and by superior tactics the Greeks captured thirty ships from the Persians. Night put an end to the fighting, and the Allies returned to Artemisium.

But with night the sea once more rose in waves of death, and in this new storm it was the 200 Persian ships on their voyage around Euboea that were entirely lost. Cheered by news of this event and by the timely arrival of 53 additional ships from Attica, the Allies struck again, this time at some Cilician ships from the Persian navy, and destroyed them. At the end of this second day, they withdrew again to Artemisium.

On the third day the two main fleets fought a pitched battle and both were badly mauled, with no clear victory for either side.

Shortly thereafter, an Athenian ship that had waited offshore near Thermopylae to obtain news of the outcome reported back that the pass was lost. Central Greece now lay open to the Great King's land forces and the Allied fleet hurriedly withdrew to that divine isle, Salamis, to cover the evacuation of Attica. But the wily Themistocles found time as his Athenian contingent sailed round Attica to cut inscriptions on the rock cliffs wherever the Persian fleet was likely to stop for fresh water. The inscriptions read:

> Men of Ionia, you do wrongly to fight against the land of your fathers and bring slavery upon Hellas. It were best of all that you should join yourselves to us; but if that be impossible for you, then do you even now withdraw yourselves from the war, and entreat the Carians to do the same as you. If neither of these things may be, and you are fast bound by such constraint that you cannot rebel, yet we pray you not to use your full strength in the day of battle; be mindful that you are our sons and that our quarrel with the foreigner was of your making in the beginning.[161]

Whether or not Xerxes believed that the Ionians would change sides, he would be likely to distrust them, perhaps to the point of not sending them into battle.

Meanwhile, the huge Persian army was moving south toward Athens. But part of it made a detour to seize the rich votive offerings of Apollo's temple at Delphi. The Delphians asked the god whether they should bury his treasures, but he replied through his priestess that it was unnecessary: he was able to protect his own. The Delphians ferried their women and children across the Gulf of Corinth to Achaea, while most of the men sought refuge on the heights of Mount Parnassus. On came the Persians. A frightful storm burst. Two crags split off from Mount Parnassus, and rolled down on the Persian forces, killing a large number.[162] The Persian forces fled; the Delphians dashed from their hiding places and slaughtered many of the Great King's men; and it was later reported that two armed warriors, of more than human stature, joined in the chase and in the slaughter.

The Peloponnesian land forces, under the command of the dead Leonidas's brother, were now busily building a wall across the Isthmus of Corinth. They were determined not to defend anything north of that point. The Persians therefore occupied Boeotia, collected fresh cavalry there, and reached the frontier of Attica with so many Greek reinforcements as to be stronger than before Thermopylae.

The ships of Athens now proceeded to remove the inhabitants of Attica —some to Salamis, some to Troezen in the Argolid, and some to the land of their recently reconciled enemy, the Aeginetans. From various parts of the Greek peninsula and from some of the islands, more ships hurried in. There was even one ship from southern Italy, from the Greek city of Croton. At the Allied base at Salamis there were now 378 triremes, not counting a number of the old-fashioned penteconters.

A council of war was held, and most of the commanders of contingents urged moving the Allied fleet to the Isthmus, since Attica was lost. Indeed, word came that the Persians had marched through Boeotia, where they had burned Plataea—whose men alone had fought beside the men of Athens ten years before at Marathon. The Persians had also burned Thespiae, whose men had stood by Leonidas and fallen with him at Thermopylae. They were now ravaging Attica and burning everything. At Athens they found a deserted city: the polis, the human community, had quit this sacred ground on Apollo's advice. A few citizens had disobeyed the proclamation to quit Attica and had taken refuge in the Acropolis, which they had boarded up with wooden plank, apparently wagering their lives that they had read the oracle's phrase better than Themistocles and that a wood-built wall would protect them. The Persians came; despite a long and heroic resistance the wager was lost; the Persians slew every Athenian; and they burned Athena's temple in vengeance for those temples of Sardis in Lydia that had been burned when Athenians and Eretrians had aided the Ionian rebels against the King. Marathon, too, was avenged: Lord, remember the Athenians. Many captains of Greek naval contingents, when they heard the fate of Athens, quit the council, went on board their ships, and made ready to fall back to the Isthmus.

But they reckoned without the cunning of Themistocles. First he persuaded the Spartan admiral to call them again into council, and Themistocles argued. To no avail. The commander of the Corinthian fleet pointed out bitterly that a man with no polis should have no vote. Themistocles declared that he had a polis greater than Corinth so long as Athens had 200 fully manned ships, for no other polis in Greece could beat them off. Then he played his trump card: the Athenians would collect their households, voyage to Siris in Italy, and settle there, leaving the rest of them to face the Persians alone. At that, the Spartan admiral came about.

Themistocles and the captains of the contingents from Megara and Aegina, city-states which, like Athens, were faced with desertion by the Peloponnesians, seemed to have won the argument. But the Peloponnesians managed to call another council of war and threatened to outvote them. Thereupon, Themistocles slipped quietly out of the meeting and sent a messenger to the Persians, declaring himself a secret friend of the Great King and urging Xerxes to attack quickly and bottle up the Allied fleet in the narrow straits between Salamis and the mainland. During the night, the Persians took his advice.

But now, while the Allied captains still argued, Themistocles was called out of the meeting by the Athenian, Aristides. Aristides had been a political opponent of his, had been ostracized by the democratic Assembly, and had gone into exile. He came now from Aegina to inform Themistocles that the Allied fleet was encircled. Themistocles told him of his ruse and pointed out that if he, Themistocles, conveyed Aristides' message to the wrangling captains, they would not believe him: Aristides himself should tell them. Even then, most of the wranglers were incredulous, until a deserter from the Persian fleet confirmed the news. It was dawn now. There was nothing left but to fight.

A recent earthquake, a deep bellowing thunder beneath the earth,[163] had caused the Allied Greek captains to offer prayers to the gods; to beg help of those two brother heroes, Ajax and Teucer, who had sailed from Salamis to fight at Troy; and to send a trireme to Aegina to fetch statues of other members of their family. At sunrise of the morning after Xerxes

sealed the strait, the Greeks manned their ships, and at that moment
the trireme returned from Aegina with the sacred images. The Allied fleet
had scarcely put out when the Great King's navy attacked. Most of the
Greek triremes began to back water; but one charged an enemy ship. It
was later reported, too, that the vision of a woman appeared and demanded of the Greeks, "Sirs, what madness is this? how long will you
still be backing water?"[164] Then the vision issued commands in a voice
loud enough for the whole Greek fleet to hear. A Greek trumpet sounded.
The Greek paean rose and echoed against the hills of Salamis. A Greek
voice cried out:

> O Greek sons, advance! Free your fathers' land, free your sons, your
> wives, the temples of your fathers' gods, the tombs of your forefathers.
> Now you fight for all you love.[165]

The Greeks, especially the men of Aegina and of Athens, now found
the rhythm of their oars and drove the bronze beaks of their triremes
against the sides of the enemy ships or sheared off their oars. Between the
craggy Isle of Salamis and the nearby Attic shore, they did their skillful
work. The Aeginetans faced mainly the Great King's Ionian ships; and,
despite the message of Themistocles inscribed on the sea cliffs and urging
them to change sides or at least fight halfheartedly, most of the Ionian
ships fought well, far better than at Artemisium a few weeks before. The
Athenians faced Xerxes' best contingent, the Phoenicians. Back of the
Phoenicians, high on the shore of Attica, with Mount Aegaleos towering
behind, the Great King himself sat on a white marble throne with silver
feet, to watch the Greeks' defeat, while his scribes stood at his side to write
down the names of whichever of his captains should distinguish themselves most. Farther to the right rose the Acropolis of the city they had
left; and from the Acropolis looked down upon their ships the half-burned
temples of their gods. The massive Imperial navy, crowded into narrow
waters, fell into disorder and the Great King's ships through mischance
rammed and smashed each other. His ships capsized and showed their
bellies. Their bronze jaws gaped. The narrows became a bloody mass of
wreckage. Corpses

> glutted beaches and the rocks.
> Every warship urged its own anarchic
> Rout; and all who survived that expedition,

Like mackerel or some catch of fish,
Were stunned and slaughtered, boned with broken oars
And splintered wrecks: lamentations, cries
Possessed the open sea, until the black
Eye of evening, closing, hushed them . . .[166]

The Athenian squadron under Themistocles drove many of the Phoenician warships against the tiny, rocky island of Psyttaleia, that lay between Salamis and Athens' port city, the Piraeus. From dawn to twilight the battle had raged. It was on tiny Psyttaleia that Xerxes had posted some picked fighters with orders to rescue any men they could who might survive a wrecked Imperial ship and to kill any Greek sailors or infantry who might survive a wreck of their own. When the Imperial fleet fled in disorder, Aristides ferried Athenian infantry to Psyttaleia and slaughtered the Imperials to the last man. The victorious Allies towed to Salamis all the wrecks they could find. Although the beaten Imperial fleet had withdrawn to Phalerum, the Allies assumed that they would have to fight again. Night fell, while "the sea-dyed corpses" still whirled "vagrant on cragged shores."[167]

The battle of Salamis was fought on September 29[168] in the year 480. It lasted all day, and it went as Themistocles expected it to go. It was he who had created the Athenian navy. The "fountain of silver"[169] at Laurium had nourished it. Long and hard practice had taught it skill and a kind of discipline at which the dogged Spartan army could barely guess. Athenian ingenuity and flexibility made it a terrible instrument. The war with Aegina had tempered it, and it was not by chance that the navies of Aegina and Athens distinguished themselves at Salamis above all others. Though the ships were manned by oarsmen who were not descended from the gods, yet they looked on themselves as free-born sons of Athens, governing themselves by reason and law, no victims of oligarchic or tyrannical force. They and their scattered, exiled families were part of a polis torn loose from its native soil, but with the image of lovely Attica in their hearts and the promise of Apollo to protect them.

The Persian fleet was defeated, demoralized, and disaffected. During the battle, some of the Phoenicians who escaped from the melee in the narrow straits accused the Ionians of treason and of destroying Phoenician vessels. Xerxes, watching the defeat from his marble throne near the Attic shore, just then happened to witness the heroic behavior of an Ionian ship. Turning on these Phoenician informers in one of his sudden rages, he ordered their heads cut off, that cowards like themselves should no longer be able to accuse better men. By the time the battle was lost, it was doubtful whether either of the main elements in his navy, the Phoenician or the Ionian, could be fully counted on.

Would Thrace and Macedonia rebel? If so, would they break the bridge at the Hellespont? And what of Ionia? The warships of the Great King fled toward the Hellespont. Unsupported by a fleet, the army withdrew northward. A message had already gone to Susa that Athens had been burned. By a stretch of the royal imagination, the destruction of Athens could be pictured, along with the sack of Eretria and the submission of many Greek states, as the real point of the whole horrible enterprise. Now another message went to inform Susa of the catastrophe at Salamis. Mardonius, brother-in-law of Xerxes, persuaded the King to give him a force[170] of picked men and to return to Asia with the rest. Mardonius chose the Persian Immortals and other Persian troops, including the Great King's personal guard of a thousand horse; the contingents of Medes, of Sacans, and of Bactrians from northwest Afghanistan, and Indians from the Punjab; and certain distinguished fighters from other provinces of the empire. Then he and his army wintered in Thessaly. The bridge over the Hellespont had been destroyed by another storm, but the fleet ferried the Great King and his army back to Asia. Mardonius planned the campaign of 479.

The Greeks divided the booty, built temples to the gods who had saved them, set up captured Phoenician ships as trophies of their great victory, and of their booty sent the first fruits to Apollo at Delphi. As to the prize of valor for the captain who had most distinguished himself, the wrangling captains again could not agree; but all of them voted the second prize to Themistocles.

The Great King's fleet was ordered to Samos to watch restless Ionia. The Athenians returned to their empty city and countryside and began reconstruction. The Allied fleet withdrew to Aegina. The Ionians sent envoys to Sparta and begged the Spartans to lead the Allies to Asia and liberate Ionia. Cautious Sparta did not budge. So the Ionians went to Aegina. They succeeded in getting the Allied fleet to move as far eastward as the island of Delos.

Sparta, at the command of a Delphic oracle, sent heralds after Xerxes. They were given an audience and solemnly announced: "The Lacedaemonians . . . demand of you, King of the Medes! that you pay the penalty for the death of their king, whom you slew while he defended Hellas."[171] The King of Kings never had been able to understand the Greeks. Now he laughed. Pointing to Mardonius, he said, "Then here is Mardonius, who shall pay . . . such penalty as befits them."[172] The irony was worthy of a Delphic oracle; but might this irony raise questions for Xerxes as well as for the Spartans?

From Athens the wily Themistocles sent a secret message to Xerxes that, as a service to the Great King, he had persuaded the Allies not to pursue his navy northward nor to break down the bridges at the Hellespont. The message was untrue of course, but who could tell whether Xerxes might not be useful some day to Themistocles? Then Themistocles, who seemed to possess an equal talent for giving and accepting bribes, secretly blackmailed some of the island states in the Aegean that had medized by threatening them with punishment for their treason to Greece.

Mardonius was convinced that his picked force, now wintering in Thessaly, could reduce Greece if only he could detach the Athenians and thereby break the sea power of the Greeks. He therefore sent Alexander,[173] king of the Macedonians, to propose an alliance between Athens and the Persian Empire. When news of this proposal reached Sparta, the Lacedaemonians were thoroughly alarmed and rushed envoys to Athens. They pointed out to the Athenians that Athens had really started the war by aiding the Ionian revolt a dozen years earlier, and had done it without consulting Sparta. How could Athens, which loved freedom, now help the Persians reduce all other Greeks to slavery? The Spartans promised to see that the Allies should bear the expense, for the duration of the war, of supporting Athens' civilian population, since Athens had lost two years' harvest at Persian hands.

To Alexander the Athenians replied:

> So long as the sun keeps its course, we will never join alliance with Xerxes. Nay, we shall oppose him unceasingly, trusting in the aid of those gods and heroes whom he has lightly esteemed, whose houses and whose images he has burnt with fire.[174]

They then rebuked the Spartan envoys for suspecting that the Persians could bribe them. Because the Persians had destroyed their temples and their images of the gods, because of their common brotherhood with other Greeks, their common language, their common altars, and their common way of life, it would ill become Athenians to be false. They thanked the Spartans for offering to help them, but declined to be a burden to the Allies. But they pointed out that by rebuffing Mardonius's offer, they invited a second invasion. They therefore begged Sparta to hurry and join them in occupying Boeotia.

The Athenians were right in their fear of a second invasion. When Mardonius received their refusal of his offer, he quickly occupied Boeotia himself. The Lacedaemonians, relieved of their alarm, were busily celebrating another religious festival. More important, they were now completing the wall across the Isthmus, which was to shelter the Peloponnesians from invasions such as Athens had to endure. Athens, Megara, and Plataea, all of them situated beyond the protecting wall, sent envoys to Sparta to reproach her and beg help, but the Spartans played for time.

The Thebans urged Mardonius to stay in Boeotia and to break up the Greek alliance by a judicious distribution of bribes to the Allied states. But with Sparta and her Peloponnesian allies delaying, Mardonius chose to move into exposed Attica and, for the second time in ten months, the Persians seized Athens. For the second time they captured an empty city: the Athenians had taken to their ships again and had placed their families on Salamis. Again the Athenians pleaded with Sparta to help them fight the Persian army, this time in Attica. At last Sparta, reflecting however tardily that if Athens really should in despair switch her sea power to the side of Persia, the wall Sparta had built at the Isthmus would do her little good, sent her army to the Isthmus. Medizing Argos promptly warned Mardonius that a Peloponnesian army which the Argives were too weak to attack was on its way. In June, 479, Mardonius leveled partially rebuilt Athens, wasted the countryside, and withdrew to Boeotia: Attica, with its mountainous frontiers, could have proved a trap for his army; and besides, Attica offered his powerful cavalry no advantage comparable with the plains of Boeotia.

In August of 479 the two armies converged near Plataea. Mardonius commanded an army of some 125,000 men, including 24,000 Greek heavy infantry and 1,000 Greek cavalry. Pausanias, the Spartan regent, commanded around 40,000 Greek heavy infantry, including contingents he had picked up from Megara, Athens, and Plataea.[175] But Pausanias was without cavalry, and Herodotus reported[176] that the Persian and Theban cavalry, especially the mounted archers, sorely harassed the Allied forces. From Lacedaemon Pausanias had brought 5,000 heavy-armed Spartan infantry, with 35,000 light-armed Helots to attend them and 5,000 Dwellers-round-about, who formed his right wing. The left wing was held by 8,000 heavy-armed Athenians, under the command of Aristides. Spartan and Athenian were preparing now to fight shoulder to shoulder at Plataea because they needed each other. The Allied army that faced Mardonius included contingents—some of them very small—from Lacedaemonia, Athens, Tegea, Corinth, Potidaea, Orchomenos, Sicyon, Troezen, Lepreum, Mycenae, Tiryns, Phlius, Hermione, Eretria, Styreia, Chalcidice, Ambracia, Leucas, Anactorium, Pale, Aegina, Megara, and Plataea.

Mardonius's cavalry continually harassed the Allied army and even succeeded in badly disorganizing its lines of supply. But for days there was no general pitched battle, while prophets on both sides consulted the auspices. Cut off from water, Pausanias was forced to withdraw by night more than a mile farther westward. But he handled his withdrawal badly. The Megarians, Phliasians, and Corinthians fell back on Plataea. The Athenians failed to effect complete junction. One of the Spartan battalion commanders decided it was dishonorable to withdraw, as Pausanias had ordered, and the other leaders lost hours trying to persuade him. Indeed, when dawn broke, Persian scouts found only his battalion still near the original line.

On August 27, 479, Mardonius attacked. His picked Persian troops closed with the Lacedaemonians and Tegeans; the Athenians were not even in sight. The Boeotians and the other medizing Greeks in his army followed but in some disorder. Pausanias, when the Persian cavalry attacked him, sent word to the Athenians, beseeching their prompt aid. But the Athenians by this time were fighting off Mardonius's Greek allies and could send no help. Pausanias prepared therefore to defend himself with only some 50,000 Lacedaemonians and 3,000 Tegeans, but few of these were heavy infantry, and most of them were light-armed Helots. The Spartans were sacrificing to the gods but could not get favorable auspices. The Persians set up their shields for a fence and rained arrows on Pausanias's men.

Pausanias lifted his eyes to the temple of Hera in nearby Plataea and prayed to her for help. The men of Tegea did not wait for him to finish: they charged the Persians. Just then the Spartans' sacrifices started showing favorable omens, and they too charged the Persians. The Persians threw away their bows and fought now at the line formed by their fence of shields. When the fence was overthrown, they seized the Spartans' spears and broke them off: they fought bravely, but were less well armed than the Spartans and less skilled at close combat. As at Marathon ten years earlier, they were more dangerous when shooting arrows from a distance than they were when fighting hand to hand. Where Mardonius, riding a white charger, fought, surrounded by a thousand especially chosen Persians, the Lacedaemonians bought their ground dear.

Then Mardonius was slain, along with his picked troops, and Spartan heavy armor and Spartan skill in close combat and Spartan discipline began to tell. The Imperial army fled and took refuge in its fortified camp outside Thebes, a camp surrounded by a wooden stockade with towers. The Theban cavalry covered the Persian retreat; and, indeed, of all the Greeks who had medized and who had served in Mardonius's army, the Thebans alone fought hard, bravely, and skillfully. Meanwhile one of the Great King's favorite generals, Artabazus, who had disapproved when Xerxes granted Mardonius his army and had again disapproved when Mardonius insisted on a pitched battle instead of holding Thebes and counting on bribery to dissolve the Greek Alliance—Artabazus now, when he approached the battleground and found Mardonius's men already in flight, turned the 40,000 men in his corps toward the Hellespont and home, leaving the remains of Mardonius's forces to their fate in the wooden fortress outside Thebes.

Pausanias and his Lacedaemonians assaulted the fortress, but made little headway, for the Spartans lacked skill in assaulting walls. Then the Athenians, who possessed that skill, arrived. After several days, they scaled the wall and breached it too, and the Greek Allies poured in. The rest was massacre—a

> sacrificial cake of clotted gore
> Made at Plataea by Dorian spear.
> And corpses piled up like sand . . .[177]

Mainland Greece was free at last.

The Allies buried their relatively few dead. Of the heavy infantry who fought, 91 Spartans lost their lives, 52 Athenians, and 16 Tegeans. The Mantineans arrived too late for the battle. They begged Pausanias to let them pursue Artabazus and his 40,000 men, now fleeing toward the Hellespont, but the Lacedaemonians refused to allow them to pursue fleeing men.

In fulfillment of the oracle, Mardonius had paid with his life for the death of Leonidas. The men of Xerxes' ruined army were either dead or enslaved or streaming toward the Hellespont and Asia, leaving an immense and rich spoil, of which the Greeks awarded a tithe to Apollo's temple at Delphi. Thebes was forced to surrender its pro-Persian oligarchs, whom Pausanias took to Corinth and put to death without trial. Plataea, on whose soil the victory had been won, was voted heavy compensation. She, on her part, undertook to render religious honors yearly at the tombs of the Greeks who had fallen and to hold every fifth year athletic contests like the Olympic Games, to be known as the festival of Eleutheria—that is, of Freedom. The Allies exchanged oaths to protect the sovereignty of Plataea against the Thebans' constant efforts to rule her. And they dissolved the Boeotian federation. The Allies then solemnly swore to maintain the Panhellenic League against Persia and to meet annually at Plataea.

Five centuries later the Eleutheria would still be held. At break of day a trumpeter would sound the signal for battle and then lead the procession. Behind him would come the wagons loaded with myrtle wreaths, then the black bull, then the freeborn youths bearing the jars of wine and milk for the libations and the pitchers of oil and myrrh. No slave would be allowed to help, for the men whom this procession would honor died for freedom. Then would come the chief magistrate of Plataea, robed in purple, carrying on high a water jar from the city's archive chamber, and in his other hand a sword. Arrived at the graves of those who died for freedom, he would take water from the sacred spring and wash their gravestones with his own hands and anoint them with myrrh. Then he would slaughter the black bull at the funeral pyre; pray to Zeus the Liberator, and to Hermes as guide of the dead;[178] and summon the brave men who died for Hellas to come to the banquet and drink its copious draughts of blood. Finally, he would himself drink wine and would pour a libation saying: "I drink to the men who died for the freedom of the Hellenes."[179]

After Salamis, word had come that Greeks in Sicily had won another victory for Hellas. It was even reported that they had done it on the very day that the Greek Allies had battered Xerxes' fleet at Salamis. For, presumably in concert with Xerxes, Carthage had struck at Sicily. Like Persia, Carthage was constantly being invited by Hellenic cities to aid them in their ferocious quarrels with each other. Like Persia's Phoenician subjects of Tyre and Sidon, Phoenician Carthage keenly felt the competition of Greek merchants. In 480 a Greek tyrant, whom the city of Himera on the northern coast of Sicily had recently expelled, appealed to Carthage to help him regain his lost throne—as Hippias, son of Pisistratus, had got Persian help in order to win back the tyranny of Athens. Carthage exploited the occasion. One of the two magistrates who headed the oligarchic republic of Carthage was the general-in-chief, Hamilcar, son of a Carthaginian father and a Syracusan mother. He now convoyed a large army[180] of mercenaries, recruited from Carthage, Libya, Spain, Sardinia, Corsica, and from Liguria, south of the Alps, to Panormus, a Greek city on the future site of Palermo. He then marched on nearby Himera and laid siege to the city. Himera appealed to Gelo, tyrant of Syracuse, for help. At this time Syracuse was, along with Athens and Sparta, one of the three great cities of Hellas; and Athens and Sparta had vainly solicited Gelo's aid when Xerxes was preparing to strike. Gelo marched against Hamilcar's mercenaries, destroyed his army, enslaved thousands of prisoners, and captured immense booty.

When the Allied fleet had moved from Aegina to the island of Delos, envoys from Ionia promptly followed it there and again begged its Spartan admiral to liberate Ionia. The Persian fleet was still based on the island of Samos, where it was keeping an eye on Greece-in-Asia. When the Ionian fleet went to Samos to defeat it, the Persian fleet dismissed the disaffected Phoenicians and cautiously withdrew to the mainland promontory of Mycale. There a Persian army of 60,000 men was stationed to forestall a second Ionian revolt, like the revolt that had precipitated the three attempts to conquer Mainland Greece. Under protection of these forces, the sailors of the Persian navy beached their ships and threw up a rampart of stones and tree trunks to protect both the ships and themselves. There the Allied fleet found them. The Spartan commander immediately repeated the stratagem of Themistocles on the sea journey from Artemisium around Attica to Salamis; but he did it by a herald's voice rather than by inscriptions.

Men of Ionia, you that hear us, take heed of what I say! for in no
case will the Persians understand aught of my charge to you: when we
join battle, let a man remember first his freedom, and next the watchword "Hebe": and let him that hears me not, be told of this by him
that hears.[181]

This stratagem the Persians met by disarming the Samians, whom they
rightly suspected of conspiring with the Allies. Since they suspected the
Milesians also, they sent them up into the heights of Mycale, allegedly
to guard the approaches to the Persian camp.

Just as the Greek Allies prepared to attack, a *phēmē*, or voice from
heaven,[182] sped through all the army, and a herald's wand was observed
lying on the shore where the waters of the sea began, as if it had floated
over with news from Greece. According to the phēmē, the Allies had
defeated the Persians in Boeotia. The Allies at Mycale had been de-
pressed by the knowledge that even now Mardonius might be overwhelming their comrades at home. They were aware that if their comrades had
won at home and if Mycale should prove a victory too, then the Aegean
Isles would be liberated and the Hellespont could be shortly cleared.
Heartened by the phēmē and by the herald's wand, the Greeks grew eager
for battle. Their line was so established that the Athenians had either
beach or other level ground before them, but the Lacedaemonians had
to advance through a ravine and among hills. The Persians prepared to
fight outside their stockade; and, just as at Plataea, they stood their shields
upright in a line to form a barrier. The Athenians, and the contingents that
flanked them—the men of Corinth, of Sicyon, and of Troezen—saw a
chance to break through the Persian shields before the Lacedaemonians
could make contact with the enemy, and they went to work in earnest.

The Persians fought hard behind their barrier of shields. Even after the
barrier was broken down, they stood their ground for a long time. But
they finally retreated inside the palisade where the ships lay beached.
However, the Athenians and Corinthians and Sicyonians and Troezenians
managed to crowd in after them and, unlike the stockade outside Thebes
that furnished temporary refuge for the Great King's men after the battle of
Plataea, this wall at Mycale never demanded Athenian skill at breaching.
When the Allies had once rushed inside the fortified area, all the Imperial
troops surrendered except the native Persians. The Persians fought on.
But then the Lacedaemonians arrived; the Samians turned on the Persians

with whatever weapons they could seize; and, finally, the other Ionians turned on them too. Some of the Persians managed to escape from this slaughterhouse of men and to flee to the hills where they had posted the Milesians, who knew the country, to act as guides in case of disaster. But the Milesian guides deliberately led the Persians into ambushes and in the end joined the Allies in slaughtering the refugees. Some managed to escape. The Greek losses were not light, but the Persian losses were frightful.

Ionia was once more free. And according to later tradition,[183] the Allies had won the battle of Plataea in the morning, and their comrades in Asia had won the battle of Mycale toward evening, of that same day, August 27, 479.

It was now some twenty years since Athens and Eretria had intervened in the Ionian Revolt and had thereby drawn down Darius' wrath on Mainland Greece. Shipwrecked at Athos, beaten at Marathon, halted at Thermopylae, badly defeated at Salamis by Greek triremes, routed at Plataea by Greek infantry, the Persians had failed even in Asia, and the second Ionian revolt was on.

But what was to prevent the mighty Persian Empire from quelling the second revolt, as she had quelled the first, once the Mainland Greeks had sailed home? The Peloponnesians answered this problem in their traditional way. They urged that all Greeks should be removed from this lovely, luxurious, but perilous coast. How could the Mainland Greeks, even after Salamis, even after Plataea, even after Mycale, hope to protect Greeks in Asia against the vengeance of the King of Kings? Why should the Greeks not content themselves with holding the sea, the islands, and the Hellespont? But where could the Greeks of the Asian coast be resettled? The Peloponnesians suggested seizing for their use the seaport towns of those Mainland Greeks who had medized in the hour of Greece's awful peril. But the Athenians objected that Ionia had been settled by men from Attica centuries ago and that Ionia must be defended. It was not only sympathy and Ionian pride that led Athens to refuse to evacuate Ionia. It was to the Ionians' and to her mutual advantage that the Persian Empire be shut off from the Aegean Sea as well as from the Hellespont and the Black Sea beyond it. The Ionians, like the Athenians, and quite unlike most Peloponnesians, were seafarers, sea fighters, and merchants; and Athens had the word of Apollo himself that in the hour of gravest danger her polis must be based on ships. The Peloponnesians yielded.

The first task was to break down the bridges at the Hellespont. The Allies thought these were still standing and were still inviting Asians to invade Europe, but when they reached Abydos on the Hellespont, they found the gods had done their work for them some ten months before.

The Spartan commander and the Peloponnesians under him now considered the war closed. But not the Athenians. Athens had long possessed important interests in the Chersonese, the peninsula that formed the western shore of the strategic Hellespont. It was from this Chersonese that Miltiades, later the hero of Marathon, had fled the Persians a year before their first invasion. The Chersonese was still held by a Persian governor; and its strongest fortress was Sestos. So while the Peloponnesians sailed away to their homes in triumph, the Athenians toiled through the autumn of 479, laying siege to Sestos. When the city had been reduced to stark famine, the Persian garrison managed to escape and their victims inside joyfully opened the gates of the city wall. The Athenians seized the treasures of the Persian governor, including the massive cables of hemp and the cables of papyrus that had borne the Great King's yoke of continents.[184] These they took home as trophies to dedicate in their temples to those gods who had so often saved the freedom of Hellas.

THE SCHOOL OF HELLAS

IN 489, when Miltiades, hero of Marathon, had suffered fiasco in his attack on Paros, it was Xanthippus who prosecuted him for deceiving the Athenian people. Xanthippus was a noble. He had married Agariste, niece of the great constitutional reformer, Clisthenes. Like him, Xanthippus opposed the return either of oligarchy or of tyranny. In 485 Athens ostracized Xanthippus, as she exiled Aristides two or three years later. Like him, Xanthippus was recalled under the general amnesty of 480, when Thermopylae had fallen and when the Athenians had left their city silent and deserted and had set forth for Salamis, for heroism, and for triumph.

About 490, the year of victory at Marathon, a son was born to Xanthippus and was named Pericles. He was about five when his father went into exile. The boy's uncle, Megacles, had been ostracized two years earlier. Pericles was ten when the women and children were hurried from Athens, some to the divine isle of Salamis, some to Aegina, some to Troezen. The young Pericles was taken to Salamis, that island so near Athens, which, ninety years before under the urging of Solon, Athens had seized, colonized, and made part of Athena's Polis. According to later tradition,[185] beside the trireme that bore Pericles swam his dog, refusing to be left behind. He made the island and then, exhausted, fell dead. In Salamis Pericles must have witnessed, as Xerxes did, the fleet of Xerxes and the fleet of the Greek Allies confront each other at dawn in the narrow waters. He must have heard the paean rise from the Allied fleet; have heard the trumpets' blast; have seen the even stroke of foaming oars. He may even have caught the Greek words ringing across the sounding straits and calling on the sons of Greece to free their fathers' tombs.

The next year, 479, Xanthippus was elected archon; then *strategos*, or commander. He commanded the Athenian contingent at the battle of Mycale, which freed the Ionians from Persian rule. It was Xanthippus and his Athenian troops who opposed the Spartans' plan of evacuating the Ionians to Greece. In the spring of 478, it was Xanthippus who besieged Sestos on the Hellespont, when the Peloponnesians had returned to Greece. The Persian garrison fled, Sestos surrendered, Xanthippus pursued the Persians, massacred many of them at Aegospotami and crucified their leader for his many cruelties while governor. It was Xanthippus who brought back to Athena's temple those two eloquent trophies—the cable of hemp and the cable of papyrus, which had supported Xerxes' impious bridge from Asia into Europe.

An Athenian boy of Pericles' clan would spend his first seven years in the women's quarters with his mother. He was then schooled by men. First he learned to read and write and reckon, on his little wooden tablet covered with soft wax to take the stylus' mark. Then he studied music, which included not only melody, not only the flute, the lyre, singing, and the dance, but the epic poets, Homer and Hesiod, and lyric poets like Solon, Mimnermus, Theognis. Music and poetry were expected to form his soul, to gentle and to civilize him. Was not music the lore of the Muses of Olympus, daughters of Zeus, who danced on soft feet about his altar on holy Helicon where Hesiod shepherded his lambs? Hesiod heard them sing and learned from them. But most men clearly did not. Hesiod saw them; but they often went abroad, clothed in thick mist, through which most men could not see. The poems and melodies they could teach to men must open the heart of the young Athenian to things mere reasoning could not fathom; must bring his heart into harmony with wiser minds and deeper knowledge than any race of iron could hope to find without the Muses' aid.

The boy Pericles was also taken to an outdoor gymnasium, the *palaestra*, where he learned to run, to leap, to wrestle, to throw the discus and the javelin, his body stripped beneath the Attic sun. In such fashion he would be hardened; he would learn courage and endurance. A young noble like Pericles, who could expect some day to serve in the cavalry, would in addition learn to ride and handle horses. From eighteen to twenty, he did his military service—a year of active duty, followed by a year of garrison duty. Then he was a full-fledged citizen with all the rights of a free man, member of a free polis.

In Pericles' boyhood the barbarians had come, bent on destroying freedom, on restoring a tyrant to Athens, on reducing Athens to the status of a subject city. The Athenians had closed ranks. The polis had twice uprooted itself and taken to the fleet and to Salamis. Twice its members had swarmed home to the smoking ruins of their temples and their homes. Tensions there still were, between rich, landowning nobles harking back nostalgically to their lost feudal power, and the new, raw democracy, bred by commerce and the sea, disciplined by the potter's wheel, the flaming forge, the shipyard, and the grueling work on the rowing pads of the swift, bronze-beaked triremes. But shared disaster, shared hardship, and shared ultimate triumph over tyranny and barbarism alike had redefined for all Athenians the very words tyrant and barbarian. Tyrant no longer meant merely a man who had seized power to rule in the interest of merchant and wage-earner against a decadent and rapacious nobility: tyrant meant the foe of freedom. Rich and poor alike had gazed in admiration at the bronze group of the two tyrannicides who had assassinated Pisistratus's younger son and had planned to assassinate Hippias too— gazed in admiration, that is, until this famous bronze had been stolen from the polis by Xerxes and taken to Susa, capital of the barbarians. As for this other word, barbarian, it no longer meant merely non-Hellene;[186] it was beginning to mean a man incapable of establishing a free polis or even of knowing what polis meant.

The schoolboy Pericles had watched free men, rich and poor alike, defeat overwhelming numbers of barbarians, mere slaves of one master, of him they called the King of Kings. Athenians, too, had a master, the Law.

But they demanded *isonomia*, equality before the law. And they demanded *isegoria*, equality in discussion, the free competition of ideas in the agora, the market place, before a rule was voted into law. In short, they governed themselves, and that was a new and exhilarating thing to do. They were learning to substitute reason for force, right for might. Or, more accurately, they were determined that the might of Athena's Polis should clearly serve the right, and that what was right should be determined by reason and free debate. They were determined to achieve, not only freedom, but law and justice.

In this democratic dream, men's minds and bodies were alike provided for. Through the medium of money they freely exchanged the material objects their bodies might require. Through the medium of words they freely exchanged the ideas their minds required. Yet not all the might of the polis had been tamed and made to serve right. Some money was used to oppress those who had none; some words were used to deceive the ignorant. And there were many persons in the polis still who did not share isegoria or help to make the laws they were nevertheless forced to obey. Athenian boys like the young Pericles were carefully taught to speak wingèd words. But their sisters were not. Athenian women were taught the domestic arts and could expect neither to hold office, nor to vote, nor even to participate in public discussion. Nor could the metic, or foreign resident, do any of these things, no matter what wealth he might amass in the business life of the Piraeus. Nor could the slaves; and, as the wealth of Athens grew, slaves became more and more numerous. Finally, although the common hardships of all Athenians, twice driven to abandon Attica, had created politically a kind of sacred union of democrats and aristocrats, yet nobles with permanent democratic leanings, nobles such as Pericles' father, Xanthippus, were rare. The Areopagus, that most conservative body in the machinery of government, in which only ex-archons could sit but where these had seats for life, regained some of its ancient rights to supervise the entire operation of government. In the Persian crisis, the Areopagus had behaved well. When that crisis was over, would the nobles not use it again to thwart the progress of equality? Would the nobles not feel in their bones, as they had always felt—these descendants of Achaean invaders who had bought Hellas with their blood and who commonly claimed descent from the very gods they had taught the conquered to worship—would these nobles not feel that they could make juster laws than ignorant and ignoble peasants and craftsmen? Might they not again feel justified in using might to assert their right, the right of the Best to rule? Inside the Polis of Athena, then, the dream of equal freedom under law was far from realized: the poor man, the man who was not Well-fathered, the slave, the woman, the metic were all in varying degrees shut out.

But what of the relations between the free men of Athens and the citizens of some other Hellenic polis, who spoke approximately the same tongue, who worshiped the same gods, not to mention the outer world of non-Hellenes, of barbarians? The other Hellenes lived under other laws, perhaps under laws like those of Sparta, perhaps, in backward northwestern Greece, under a form of monarchy or a later form of landed aristocracy. If the men of Athens and the men of Sparta disagreed on right, to what court could they turn? Both cities were sovereign states, obeying no human law but their own. Would disputes between those cities have to be settled by force and fraud? In default of a court, administering equal law, made by citizens in equal and free debate, must Athenians and Spartans turn to diplomatic deception and, at the last, to war? To Ares, whom Homer's Zeus clearly declared the most hated of all the gods on high Olympus? To Ares, who is "just and slays him who slays"[187]? If so, what of the fact that the nobles of Athens, or most of them, were frankly pro-Spartan and even imitated the Spartans' dress and manner? Neither the simmering hatred between rich and poor nor the constant threat of foreign war with some neighboring sovereign Greek state promised well for Solon's dream of fitting right with might. A new Hellenic community was emerging, knit together by growing commerce and relatively speedy transportation. Although individual city-states had achieved law internally, Hellas had not yet achieved law.

After the second occupation of Athens had ended and after what was left of the Persian army had fled northward from destruction at Plataea, the Athenians returned a second time to find their houses, except for those which Persian leaders had lately occupied, largely destroyed, Xanthippus' house among them. Xanthippus himself was still besieging Sestos on the Hellespont, when Pericles was taken home from Salamis to the city.

Themistocles now enjoyed, as a result of the victory off Salamis in 480, something of the prestige which had come to Miltiades after the battle of Marathon ten years before. It is true that men distrusted his cleverness, his wiliness; but his lively imagination and his ingenuity in practical affairs compelled them to follow him. In any case, they did trust Aristides, and Aristides was working with him to restore their common polis. On the eve of Salamis, in Themistocles' darkest hour, when the squadrons of the Peloponnesians seemed bent on deserting the Athenian fleet, it was Aristides, the recalled political exile, who had brought his political enemy the glad tidings that the Persians had bottled up the Greeks in the very spot where Themistocles wanted them. Because the Allies distrusted the man of many wiles, he had persuaded Aristides to convince them they must seek decision off Salamis. It had taken little persuasion. With or without Hesiod's help, Aristides could distinguish between the two strifes: the blind strife between two lusts for power and the good strife of common rivalry for the common good, the rivalry in excellence that stirred the aristocratic poet Pindar, the rivalry not for private gain but for the materially worthless laurel wreath the Olympic victor won. And therefore Aristides had said, "Let the rivalry between us be now as it has been before, to see which of us two shall do his country more good."[188] The Greek word he used for "rivalry" was the same word Hesiod had used when he spoke of the good kind of strife: *eris*. Now with both Themistocles and Aristides back in their ruined common city, Aristides stood by the good strife.

Themistocles imagined the Athenian polis as an island, a peninsula no more—an island defended by the wooden walls of her swift, beaked ships. He "wished to attach the whole city to the sea,"[189] where its new strength lay, by building a new wall for Athens, as he had fifteen years before built a wall for her new port at the Piraeus. The first task was not to rebuild private homes, but to make the polis an island. So all set to work— old men, women, and children, every able-bodied person not with the fleet. They traced a wall some five and a half miles long around their polis, to enclose a bigger space than the old wall had. Along that line, they dug a ditch some five feet deep and seven or eight feet wide. They filled it with heavy stones, some of them stones from their ruined homes, some from the city's public buildings, even some columns from grave monuments; and they cemented these stones together. Then they continued the wall upward with unfired brick—for the present to a height of ten or eleven feet. The width varied from seven or eight feet to fifteen. In nine days, the foundations were done. In a month their city was stoutly walled against further attack.

When Athens' new wall began to rise, other states grew alarmed and persuaded Sparta to protest. Spartan envoys urged the Athenians not to wall their city, but on the contrary to help her raze the walls of all cities that stood north of the Isthmus. Then, if the barbarians should come again, they could not shelter their forces behind city walls as they had done at Thebes before the battle of Plataea. It was the old Spartan policy of abandoning everything beyond the Isthmus if and when danger should strike Hellas. But the Spartans reckoned without Themistocles. He persuaded the Athenians to send him to Sparta to negotiate, and meanwhile to delay sending Aristides and a third ambassador. By one ruse after another he stalled for time, while the old men, the women, and the children of Athens feverishly walled their polis in. At last, he was able to face the Lacedaemonians and tell them frankly that Athens was already walled and quite able to look out for her own interests. He reminded them that Athens had shown better judgment than the Spartans had in the night before Salamis. Either all the cities in the Panhellenic League, which had been formed to fight Xerxes, would dismantle their fortifications—which unwalled Sparta knew, alas, they would not do—or Athens would keep hers too. He insisted that a walled Athens was an advantage to all Hellas. The Spartans, outwitted as usual, swallowed their resentment.

Then Themistocles turned to his true love, the Piraeus, with its three superb ports less than five miles from Athens. He had begun a wall around the Piraeus some years before, when he was archon. Now he finished it. He also enlarged the town of Piraeus in modern style. Athens, like other cities, had emerged from the Dark Ages of Greece with little, crooked, unplanned streets. Now Hippodamos of Miletus laid out a new Piraeus with three straight, parallel avenues, intersected at right angles by a fourth. Also he furnished the new port town with a spacious agora, or market place, in the Ionian manner. Did Themistocles secretly wish the Athenians would move their capital to up-to-date Piraeus? Whether he did or not, religious piety as well as simple sentiment would have blocked any such proposal. So Themistocles, always with his inward eye fixed on that image of an island, "fastened the city to the Piraeus, and the land to the sea."[190] The city's patron-goddess, Athena Polias, now stood armed to defend her people. The walls of Athens and Piraeus were her shield; the Athenian fleet was her spear.

In the summer of 478, when Xanthippus, father of Pericles, had taken Sestos, the Spartans in their turn again took up the sword. An Allied army left for Thessaly under the command of Leutychides, one of Sparta's two kings and commander of the Allied forces at Mycale when Xanthippus commanded the Athenian contingent there. But, whereas Xanthippus succeeded at Sestos, the Spartan king's expedition against the Persians failed. Sparta then sent out a small naval force under Pausanias, who had commanded the Greek Allies at Plataea and who was regent for the young son of Leonidas, the hero of Thermopylae. Pausanias subjected part of the island of Cyprus; then headed north and took Byzantium. But success promptly went to Pausanias's head. At the temple of Posidon on the Black Sea, he dedicated a bronze crater describing himself as "Pausanias, ruler of vast Hellas."[191] Then men remembered that when the Panhellenic League had set up a gold tripod at Delphi as a trophy and votive offering for the victory at Plataea, Pausanias on his own authority had inscribed it,

> When as captain of the Hellenes he had destroyed the Persian host, Pausanias dedicated this memorial to Phoebus [Apollo].[192]

The Lacedaemonians had promptly chiseled off his inscription and replaced it with the names of all the cities whose men had fought at Plataea. Now, on the Hellespontine shore, he was making himself generally hated by the Allies. They found him overbearing, as the Spartans often seemed, with that discourtesy which the Spartans often paraded as masculine candor and soldierly brevity. He was accused of conspiring with the King of Kings in order that he might be ruler of all Greece. He dressed in the Persian manner and maintained a bodyguard of Medes and Egyptians. He scandalized his carefully frugal subjects at home by having his table served in the Persian style. It was rumored that he was intriguing with the Helots and fomenting a rebellion. Sparta ordered him home. There he was caught corresponding with Persia; he took sanctuary in the Spartan temple to 'Athana' called the Brazen House; he was starved into weakness; he was dragged out lest his death defile Athena's holy ground; and he died.

Pausanias's command of the expeditionary forces was turned over to an obscure Spartan, a ship's captain; but the Allies had had enough and rejected Sparta's traditional claim to hegemony. The islanders of Samos, Chios, and Lesbos demanded that Athens lead them. More specifically, they demanded that the trustworthy Athenian, Aristides, organize the common Hellenic defense. For Pausanias's absurd and treasonable behavior had merely dramatized Sparta's unfitness to lead in a war whose purposes she could not share and perhaps did not wholly grasp: the common defense, not merely of the Peloponnese, but of the whole Aegean community.

In the spring of 476, when Pericles was fourteen, delegates from Ionia and the Isles began arriving in Athens to establish formally what the Allies had agreed on for the defense of Hellas and freedom: the League of Delos. It was not a government, not even a federal one. Its member states remained sovereign; and in its deliberative assembly each state, no matter how small or weak, was to have one vote. The common assembly would sit once a year on the Isle of Delos, birthplace of Apollo, where for centuries the long-robed Ionians with their swift ships had gathered for their religious festivals, for boxing and dancing and song. There, too, the League would establish a common treasury, a thing never done by Sparta's Peloponnesian Alliance nor even by the Panhellenic League formed to fight off Xerxes.

The program of the League of Delos was to free those Hellenic cities which the King of Kings still held and, meanwhile, to pillage his empire. The means to carry it out included a joint army and, above all, a joint navy. Ships cost money, and the League Assembly had to decide the painful question of naval quotas. Since everybody trusted Aristides, the delegates turned over to him the allocation of quotas. The important islands of Samos, Chios, Lesbos, and Naxos contributed ships. But most of the new League's member states possessed only obsolete war vessels; most of them lacked timber with which to build new ones; some of the smaller states would have had to combine resources to furnish even one modern trireme; and most states preferred to make a fixed money contribution. Aristides calculated their joint contribution at 460 talents a year. This *phoros*, or tribute, they would pay to the League's Treasury at Delos. Then he assessed each member state's contribution according to its capacity to pay. The Treasury would turn over all these funds to Athens, with her shipyards, her imported timber, and her skilled shipwrights; and Athens would recruit the ships' crews from her own population and from the other cities of the League. Everybody was well satisfied with Aristides' handling of an unpopular task.

The decision to commute the tribute from ships to money perhaps implied more than the delegates at Athens guessed; as, indeed, the shift long before from subsistence agriculture to a money economy had implied more for Athens than Athens herself had guessed. Money had turned out to possess an unexpected tendency to concentrate economic and even political power. It was now agreed that Athens would in effect serve as the executive branch of this new shadow government of Aegean Hellas. It was true that the power of the purse would be in the hands of something that resembled a legislative branch, the League Assembly at Delos. The tribute would indeed flow to Delos, but no Samian or Chian or Lesbian or Naxian ship would report to Delos for active duty. Instead, they would report to Themistocles' new port town of Piraeus with its three harbors. If Solon's element of right in politics remained at holy Delos, the money tribute of most League members placed Solon's element of might in Athens' hands. Finally, the delegates who established this lopsided League with Athens made no provision for secession from it. The urgent fact was still Persia, and no member state could be spared from the war of liberation born at Marathon and Salamis. Hellas was riding a wild beast.

Meanwhile, Themistocles faced a new political rival, young but able. His name was Cimon. He was the son of Miltiades, hero of Marathon, by a Thracian princess whom Miltiades had married when he was tyrant of the Chersonese. Cimon was around twenty when his father died in prison, to which the Athenians had sent him after the fiasco of his expedition against the island of Paros. The son was tall, handsome, curly-haired, with a soldierly eloquence of the sort practiced by the Spartans and by those Athenian aristocrats who wistfully imitated them. He loved to drink, to sing, to make love. The ruin of his father's fortunes left him poor. But he married off his sister to a mineowner named Callias, perhaps the richest man in Athens at the time, and Callias paid the heavy fine Miltiades had bequeathed to his son. Cimon then married a wealthy heiress. A second wife was a granddaughter of Megacles, who, like Clisthenes and Pericles' mother, was a member of the Alcmeonid family. Cimon had fought brilliantly at Salamis, had been elected general about a year later, had showed himself a born military leader like his father and an ingenious ship's architect besides. Like other noblemen, he had served in the cavalry; but when Themistocles was persuading the Athenians to take to their ships, and when the land-loving nobles had hesitated, Cimon had gaily led a procession of them up to the Acropolis, carrying in his hands his horse's bridle. This he dedicated to Athena; he took down a shield which hung on the wall, made a prayer to the goddess, and led his noble fellow horsemen down to the sea.

When this half-Thracian, aristocratic, picturesque kinsman by marriage of the young Pericles entered active politics at Athens, there was little danger that he would collide with Aristides, who was engrossed with the League of Delos and its difficult new problems. But he could hardly hope to co-operate with the social newcomer, Themistocles, devious, slippery with money, distrusted, brilliant, overbearing, sarcastic, a hater of Cimon's beloved Sparta. Themistocles, too, had a foreign mother, some even said a Thracian; but she was no princess. His father was indeed an Athenian, but he was not among the Well-fathered.

Cimon's rise was swift. When he was elected general, the Spartan regent, Pausanias, had not yet been ordered home; he had taken possession of Sestos, the town which Xanthippus' Athenians had finally reduced, and had seized Byzantium. Cimon managed to force him out of both, and in 475 drove the Persians out of nearby Eion. Then he planted a colony of Athenian cleruchs, or citizen outsettlers, to hold it; but the colony was massacred by Thracians a few years later.

Cimon tried in vain to clear the Persians from Doriscus. Then he turned to the island of Scyros, where a nest of pirates had been preying on Aegean shipping. Inevitably one of the tasks of Athens, as head of the League of Delos, would for some years remain that of making the Aegean safe for Hellenic commerce. Scyros, once cleared of pirates, could also complete a chain of ports from Attica to Euboea to Scyros to the Hellespont. The island was conquered, the pirates were sold as slaves, and another cleruchy, this one successful, was established. Then Cimon somehow found on the island, or claimed to find, the bones of Athens' early king, Theseus; for Theseus, men said, had died four centuries before in Scyros and had been buried there. Cimon took the hallowed bones of the hero in his own trireme and bore them triumphantly to Athens. It was the military and political career of Cimon which unfolded itself before the eyes of a kinsman by marriage, a youth still under twenty, Pericles, son of Xanthippus.

Cimon's clash with Themistocles was not long in coming. For Cimon, Athens' policy was clear: to finish defeating Persia, and, through the League of Delos, to control the Aegean, leaving Sparta predominant on land in

Mainland Greece. But Themistocles wanted to use Athens' new power to confound her only Hellenic rival, Sparta. The clash ended in a vote of ostracism, in 472, and it was Themistocles who was forced into exile. He went to Argos, that city of ancient jealousy toward Sparta, and proceeded to carry on a one-man diplomatic duel with Lacedaemon.

Themistocles in his duel with Sparta and with oligarchy seemed to be winning. Argos underwent a democratic revolution. The oligarchs were driven out of Elis, which proceeded to adopt a democratic constitution modeled on that of Athens. The imitation went further than popular government even: Elis achieved a synoecism, as Athens had done centuries before, and made Elis the polis of many neighboring towns which had previously been sovereign. In Arcadia, the city of Mantinea did the same thing: she organized democratic government and collected the citizens of five little cities into one polis. In 473-472, Tegea, in Arcadia, declared war on domineering Sparta, but met defeat. Most of the small cities of Arcadia adopted a common coinage and defied Sparta. But aid from Argos failed to arrive, and this coalition, too, was suppressed by Sparta. Sparta now reorganized her reluctant allies and placed their military contingents under Spartan officers. What role did the exiled Themistocles play in these rebellions against Lacedaemon? In any case, he conspired with Pausanias, before the regent's death on holy ground beside Athana's Brazen House in Sparta. When the Spartans uncovered their conspiracy, they demanded that Athens punish the ostracized Themistocles with death, and Themistocles was summoned back to Athens. He promptly fled to Corcyra; was refused refuge there; went to the king of the Molossians, a half-civilized Hellenic folk in the western part of Mainland Greece; with the king's aid reached Pydna, a Macedonian port; and then shipped to Ephesus in Ionia. Athens sentenced the refugee to death. When Xerxes died in 464 and Artaxerxes succeeded him as King of Kings, Themistocles went to the Great King's court. There he reminded Artaxerxes that he had warned his father that the Greek Allies would destroy his Hellespontine bridge and cut off his escape; and Artaxerxes greatly honored him as the King's friend. He was even assigned, as a gift, the revenues of three Ionian cities. His long and arduous odyssey ended at Magnesia near the Meander River in Asia Minor, where he lived until his death.

For Themistocles was indeed an Odysseus. True, he was no king as Odysseus was: he was even considered baseborn. But he possessed the wily

Odysseus' quick mind, his capacity for ruse, his audacity, and an almost animal cunning against his antagonists. He would have gladly risked the boasts Odysseus made as the Ithacans' ship bore him to sea and Cyclops raged. Had Themistocles not annoyed Athens by his arrogance in the days before ostracism drove him forth? For example, he had built a temple near his dwelling, dedicated to Artemis, Best Counselor, to remind the Athenians that it was his advice in the days of Salamis that had saved their skins.

Themistocles' exile, followed in a few years by Aristides' death, left Cimon pre-eminent in Athens. He continued his task of destroying the pirates that infested the Aegean Sea. He forced the city of Carystus, in southern Euboea, to join the Delian League. Naxos tried to secede from the League, and Cimon conquered her and reduced her, not to her old status of member, but to the new status of subject city. Naxos was the first member of the League to lose its formal sovereignty. At the head of 200 warships, Cimon liberated the coasts of Caria and Lycia from Persian control. About 468 he destroyed a fleet of the Great King's ships at the mouth of the Eurymedon on the southern coast of Asia Minor; disembarked and defeated a land army; re-embarked and captured a Phoenician fleet that was coming to the rescue of the Great King's now destroyed naval force. He returned to Athens in triumph. After the battle of the Eurymedon, the Delian League controlled most of the Greek cities from Euboea to the Bosphorus, from Pamphylia to the Black Sea, some 200 cities in all. Athens meanwhile had become the commercial metropolis of the eastern Mediterranean. Cimon and his moderate conservatives now seemed beyond political attack, and the rehabilitated Council of the Areopagus, that constitutional bastion of the Best People, bore daily witness to the forces back of Cimon.

Those were the political facts that confronted Pericles, now nearing thirty. But he discerned also a less well-recognized fact. The Athenian workingmen, who belonged to the fourth category of citizens in Solon's constitution and were still excluded from high offices, were growing restless. It is true that, since Solon's categories had long been calculated in money and since the value of money had steadily declined, more and more voters had graduated to a higher category. But there were still many in the lowest grade who had manned the oars at Salamis and yet remained at a political disadvantage in the polis they had risked their lives to save. These men were rallying to the standard of Ephialtes, a political leader of good family but democratic beliefs, who was now ranged against the powerful Cimon and his conservative aristocrats. Pericles, though rich, belonged both by preference and family tradition to the minority of nobles in favor of the emergent democracy. He was slow to enter the fray: he belonged to a suspect social class and both his father, Xanthippus, and his uncle, Megacles, had suffered the ostracism that brilliant leaders so often incurred.

In the spring of 472, Pericles had gained some public fame as choregus of a successful tragedy—the *Persians* of Aeschylus, which dramatized the insolence of Xerxes and his catastrophe at Salamis. As choregus, Pericles had assumed the duty of providing and training the chorus. But eight years later, he took the real plunge into public life. Cimon, triumphant at the Eurymedon, had undertaken to clear out the few remaining Persian garrisons in Thrace. In the process he collided with one of Athens' most powerful allies, Thasos, a city which had commercial and mining interests in Thrace. Thasos thereupon seceded from the League of Delos. The League Council declared her in rebellion; and Cimon, after an arduous siege of two years, forced Thasos to surrender, seized her fleet, and levied a heavy cash indemnity. However, despite this triumph, Ephialtes and the democrats charged him with coddling Alexander, the king of Macedonia, and with dragging out the siege of Thasos to please his beloved Sparta. But it was Pericles who formally called him to account on a charge of accepting bribes from Alexander. And, although Cimon won acquittal and with it the first round of a struggle with the democrats, the fight continued.

In the summer of 464 a frightful earthquake destroyed Sparta. Thereupon, the Helots rose in rebellion; two cities of the Dwellers-round-about revolted; Messenia rose. After a long, hard fight the Spartans drove their rebellious subjects back to the stronghold of Mount Ithome. Here some of the ancestors of the rebels had made their last desperate stand over two centuries before, when Sparta had first conquered Messenia. Now in the fifth century, a Spartan army again laid siege to the natural fortress of Ithome. But the Spartans were notoriously inept at sieges, where the Athenians were clever, and perhaps men once more remembered that it was wily Odysseus, not staunch Achilles, who ended the ten long years of siege when Troy fell. The Spartans appealed to Athens for aid, not against Persians, not on the sea, but on the land, Sparta's own element, and against Sparta's own rebellious subjects.

In the Athenian Assembly, Ephialtes argued that Sparta should be left to her fate. But Cimon argued for sending aid. The moderate aristocrats whom Cimon led had accepted the sea, and commerce, and war with the Persians, and even a League of Delos that excluded the ancient military city they admired and often imitated. But they were unwilling to accept the democratic view of men like Ephialtes and Pericles that now, when Persia had been pushed back, Sparta was the rival to be feared and watched. The alliance of Athens with Sparta had for long been an uneasy one, held together by the common fear of the Persian invasion. Even so, they had in fact fought shoulder to shoulder against the polyglot army of Asia at Plataea; and under the common mound at Thermopylae the men of Sparta lay, obedient to her commands. When Cimon exhorted the Athenians "not to suffer Hellas to be crippled, nor their city to be robbed of its yoke-fellow,"[193] he won his debate and led an army of 4,000 heavy infantry, including the Best People, to Ithome. This middle-aged, conservative, landowning noble had won, even with the use of a farmer's metaphor, not a seaman's. Yet, only the earthquake and the Helot revolt had prevented Athens' yoke-fellow from fulfilling her secret promise to aid Thasos in its revolt against Athens by invading Attica. Sparta's secret promise[194] to Thasos remained an unread footnote to the thesis of Ephialtes and of his political lieutenant, Pericles, that the true enemy of Athenian sea power was Sparta and that with a trireme no ox could be yoked.

At Ithome the Spartans grew suspicious: might not these revolutionary Athenians, even Athenian aristocrats, change sides and aid the rebels? The Spartans requested them, and them alone among all the allies who had come to Sparta's rescue, to go home. The Assembly at Athens was furious. While the more aristocratic Athenians were serving at Ithome, Ephialtes took advantage of their absence to push through the Assembly laws removing from the Areopagus its recently recovered powers to supervise the operation of the state, to punish officials, and to inquire into the private lives of citizens. It retained only certain religious functions, including the right to judge those accused of polluting their polis with premeditated murder. Cimon led back his humiliated forces from Ithome and promptly made an ill-timed effort to restore to the Areopagus the powers the democrats had just removed. In 461, a few months after his humiliation at Ithome, Cimon was charged with being a friend of the Lacedaemonians and an enemy of the people[195] and was ostracized. Athens then prepared to ally herself with Thessaly and Argos. The Panhellenic League, which had won the great battles of Salamis, of Plataea, and of Mycale, was finished. Shortly after the ostracism of Cimon, his chief political opponent, Ephialtes, was assassinated.

The aristocratic party lay in ruins. Many members of that party had lost their lives in battle. Sparta's insult at Ithome had destroyed the party's prestige. Cimon was in exile, and there was no leader capable of replacing him. On the democratic side, Themistocles, ostracized too, had died in exile a year before Cimon's ostracism. Now Ephialtes was gone, and his leadership had been inherited by Pericles, who had helped him curtail the powers of the Areopagus and to place the state in the hands of the whole body of citizens. Now, at last, the whole Assembly made the laws; the Council of Five Hundred executed them; the popular courts judged those who broke them. The Confederacy of Delos, headed by the people of Athens, controlled and policed Aegean Hellas; Persia had been pushed back; the uneasy alliance with Sparta was broken; and, by land, the people of Athens leaned on two new allies: Thessaly in the north with her formidable cavalry; Argos in Peloponnese, the traditional enemy of neighboring Lacedaemon.

The new Hellas coming to birth inside the old was conceived by fear of Persian might. It loved justice; and its enthusiastic choice of Aristides the Just to apportion the contributions of its sovereign members expressed its Solonian determination to bind right to might. But, alas, the necessities of war gave might a persistent advantage. The Council of the League did indeed meet, not at Athens, but in holy Delos; and the Treasury of the League was kept in Delos too. But Athens controlled the League's navy. When, about 469, Naxos tried to secede, Cimon had not only crushed her, but degraded her from ally to subject city. In 454 the Treasury of the League was transferred to Athens. True, it was transferred by consent and not by force. It was Samos, not Athens, which moved that it be transferred on the grounds that it would be safer there. For Athens controlled the League's ships and the League's money: in short, Athens controlled the might, as her own aristocracy had controlled the might in Athens before Solon joined it to the people's right. What Athens was tempted to do, and did, was to place both ships and money at the disposal of the Athenian Assembly: the Council of the League ceased to meet and its functions were taken over by that Assembly. Athens joined the League's might to the Athenian democracy's right. The inevitable result was a growing resentment among her Allies.

The truth is that democratic Athens, victorious over Persia and in control of the new League of Delos, displayed that same exultant pride and overweening ambition that had led the Odyssean Themistocles to ostracism from Athens and that had also led Pausanias to death at Athana's Brazen House in his native Sparta. Solon's commands, "Know thyself" and "Nothing too much," were forgotten, as limitless prospects of glory and profit opened up. For sixteen years the Athenian democracy tried its hand at military conquest.

Athens seized Naupactus from the Ozolian Locrians, which gave her considerable control over the westbound traffic of her commercial rival, Corinth. Megara quarreled with Corinth about their common frontier and made alliance with Athens. Athens promptly built a double line of walls from the citadel of Megara to its southern port, Nisaea, and garrisoned Megara. Athens thereby blocked the east road from Sparta into central Greece. She besieged her other chief commercial rival, Aegina; captured that city; and forced Aegina to join her League of Delos, to surrender her fleet, and to pay tribute. While doing all these things, Athens audaciously launched a large expedition to aid a revolt against Persia which had broken out in the Egyptian delta, a rich granary for an Athens always interested in grain. But, in 457, Sparta forced the cities of Boeotia back into a league under Theban domination, to serve as a counterpoise to the growing power of neighboring Athens. A Spartan army in Boeotia was stirring up trouble for Athens, whose citizens were now busy connecting Athens with the Piraeus by a double line of walls like those they had built between Megara and her port, Nisaea. The ostracized Cimon came to the Athenian army, which was encamped on Boeotian soil, and begged to fight again for Athens. But the democrats refused his plea. A battle followed at Tanagra; Athens' Thessalian cavalry deserted, and the Athenians lost. On a motion of Pericles, the Athenian Assembly recalled Cimon from some four years of ostracism.

Some two months after Tanagra Athens had won all Boeotia but Thebes; the vanquished cities were required to furnish contingents to her armies. She also subjected Phocis and Opuntian Locris. Now, in addition to her maritime empire, which had evolved out of a voluntary league of sovereign states, she controlled most of her near neighbors and had protected her land frontiers, so often crossed in the past by hostile armies. She dominated the eastern, civilized portion of central Greece from Thessaly to the borders of Corinth. She had not only gained a new protection for the frontiers of Attica; she had won a Mainland empire which Themistocles could scarcely have approved. Nevertheless, she prudently completed the Long Walls. One wall connected Athens to her port, Piraeus, some four miles away. A second wall ran from Athens to Phalerum, the ancient harbor to the east of triple-harbored Piraeus. The triangle Athens-Piraeus-Phalerum was now a single island of the sort Themistocles had always longed for.

But in 454 a Persian army attacked and defeated the force which Athens had sent to Egypt to aid rebellion there. The Athenian army was then surrounded, and burned its ships to keep them out of Persian hands. At last the Athenians capitulated on condition that they should be allowed to withdraw in peace from Egypt. They started by foot across the Libyan desert, but only a handful reached the Greek city of Cyrene on the Libyan coast. Meanwhile, a fleet of fifty triremes, sent to Egypt as reinforcements, was almost completely destroyed by the Persians. According to later tradition, the Egyptian expedition cost Athens some 35,000 men, of whom 6,000 were Athenian citizens. No Greek army had ever suffered so catastrophic a defeat. It was precisely this catastrophe and the fear that a Persian fleet would once more appear in the Aegean that had prompted Samos to propose moving the Treasury of the League of Delos from Apollo's exposed island to the temple of Athena in Athens.

Another, and a subtler change, was coming over the League of Delos. Athens' policy toward her allies had been relatively free of political doctrine. When, in 457, she had liberated the Boeotian cities from Thebes, she recalled their exiles, oligarchs included. She was not fighting to spread democracy but to build a continental empire north of the Isthmus. In the years that followed, however, and in many of her subject cities, pro-Spartan oligarchs led rebellions against Athenian imperial control, and democratic Athens found herself aiding the local democratic opponents of these oligarchs. If, therefore, she robbed other cities of their sovereignty, she at least found herself liberating democrats in them from the oligarchs who oppressed them.

The Egyptian disaster and the restlessness in Athens' new empire led Pericles to set Cimon the task of negotiating another peace with Sparta; and, in the spring of 450, Cimon effected his five-year truce. Then Pericles turned to Persia again: Artaxerxes' Phoenician fleet, which had put down the rebellion in Egypt, was under orders to restore the Great King's authority in Cyprus. Athens sent Cimon to the rescue with 200 ships. But Cimon, already ill, died during the campaign of 450-449; and, although his forces gained a face-saving victory at Salamis in Cyprus, a costly campaign netted Athens nothing more substantial than a chance to negotiate with Persia. Cimon's rich brother-in-law, Callias, was sent to Susa. Whether a formal treaty was in fact drawn up or not, in 449-448 began the Peace of Callias, characterized by the following abstentions. Persia would send no Black Sea warship of hers west of the Bosphorus. She would send no Mediterranean warship of hers nearer the Aegean than Phaselis on the southern coast of Asia Minor. Athens, on her side, would attack no territory of the King of Kings. Athens' lonely battle for freedom had begun four decades before on the shore of Marathon, and tradition would recount that Callias had taken part in the battle. The new Athenian Empire and the Persian Empire had now, by long trial of strength and great military disasters on both sides, found their common frontier. Pericles and the Athenian democrats were left free to deal with the city which the late Cimon had called Athens' yoke-fellow, Sparta.

But Themistocles' urge toward the sea and away from the land seemed justified: Athens' Mainland empire, so recently won, began to dissolve. Anti-Athenian oligarchs seized control of some of the cities of Boeotia, and Athens intervened. In the summer of 447, a small army of volunteers—which Pericles deemed quite inadequate—marched into Boeotia: near the town of Coronea, it suffered complete disaster. Boeotia was lost; and with Boeotia gone, it became strategically impossible to hold either Phocis or Opuntian Locris. By the end of 447, all central Greece was lost. The next summer most of the cities in the neighboring island of Euboea rose, and Pericles himself led an army to Euboea to restore Athenian control. They had hardly disembarked when news came that Megara, on Attica's western flank, had massacred its Athenian garrison and allied itself with Corinth. The Isthmus was open again to Sparta and her Peloponnesian allies; the five-year truce with Sparta, negotiated by Cimon, expired; and Sparta promptly led her Peloponnesian allies into Attica. Then, somewhat mysteriously, they withdrew. Pericles returned to Euboea; subjected it, confiscated the lands of the anti-Athenian oligarchs, planted colonies of Athenian cleruchs, and tightened Athenian control of Euboea's city-states. Meanwhile, those who had led the Peloponnesians against Athens were charged on their return with having accepted bribes to withdraw. They fled Sparta and were condemned to death in contumacy.

Both yoke-fellows were now exhausted. Late in 446, Callias once more went on embassy, this time with nine other envoys, this time to Sparta. A Thirty Years' Peace was negotiated. Athens gave up all claim to her continental empire, except for Naupactus, that strategic station at the mouth of the Gulf of Corinth. Aegina would stay in the League of Delos, but as a sovereign, not a subject, state. Athens agreed not to receive any dissatisfied allies of Sparta into her League of Delos, and Sparta agreed not to receive into her Peloponnesian League any state that seceded from the League of Delos. Any neutral state might join either league it wished to join. Argos, which had recently broken with Athens and made her peace with Sparta, had nevertheless not formally joined the Peloponnesian League, and Athens was left free to treat with her.

But, with Megara gone, and the eastern coast road to Attica once more open, Athens would be exposed to Spartan attack if the Thirty Years' Peace should collapse. Her country population might, of course, take refuge in the Themistoclean island formed by Athens, Piraeus, and the Long Walls. But though the North Wall ran to Piraeus and the South Wall met the sea at Phalerum, yet the marshy shore of the bay that lay between was inconveniently long to defend against attack by sea. Pericles thereupon replaced the South Wall with a middle wall, paralleling the North Wall and leaving a corridor between them some 200 yards wide, like the bar of a dumbbell, connecting ancient Athens with her triple-harbored port of Piraeus. The man-made island became safer than ever, and it still ruled an Aegean empire largely composed of islands made by nature. For the first time since 480, for the first time since Thermopylae, Artemisium, Salamis, and Plataea, there was peace in Greece.

Athens' meteoric career of conquest and violence had lasted fourteen years and had ended in defeat on the Mainland and catastrophe in Egypt. If this catastrophe did not bring recognition and understanding to all her citizens, yet her chief citizen, Pericles, had learned. He himself had led some of his city's recent campaigns, and not without success. But he now left to others the dream of assaulting Egypt again, or of attacking grain-rich Sicily or even Carthage or Etruria in central Italy. His own plan was to consolidate Athens' grip on the basically maritime League of Delos; and to enlarge it by persuasion, not by force. He often held Athens' highest office: from 443 to his death, he was elected general every year, and several times before that. Since 461, when Cimon, leader of the aristocrats, had been ostracized and Ephialtes, leader of the democrats, had been assassinated, Pericles had led the Athenian democracy. When Cimon died in 450-449, a relation of his by marriage, Thucydides—not the historian of that name—took over the leadership of the rich and Well-fathered; but in 443 or 442 Thucydides was ostracized. The democracy then governed Athens without serious challenge. Athens in turn virtually governed the League of Delos. Culturally, though not politically, she even governed Hellas. She had achieved peace with Persia and at least a truce with the state that Pericles most distrusted—Sparta, with her Peloponnesian League, with her fear and hatred of Athenian democracy, of Athenian wealth, of Athenian prestige, above all, of Athenian expansion.

To preserve this new Athenian Hellas, Pericles increased the navy of the League of Delos and kept one squadron always on maneuver for eight months of the year. He developed grappling irons to aid in boarding enemy ships. The booty his father's army had taken at Sestos on the Hellespont after the final liberation of Ionia had been used in part to convert Athens' so-called cavalry from a contingent of mounted infantry with very limited functions to a genuine cavalry, trained to fight on horseback. Pericles therefore developed horse transports. The oarsmen who manned his navy were now paid three obols a day, in addition to their cash allowance for food. They were recruited from the thetes, the fourth and lowest class of citizens, the Wage-earners; but they were recruited also from the poorer class in the cities of Athens' allies, a class that was usually pro-Athenian. From the thetes also he recruited an enlarged force of light infantry, and the number of archers was increased from the 700 who fought in the Persian War to 1,600, plus 200 horse-archers. Even the heavy infantry came to be paid; and the state provided an allowance for feeding the cavalryman's mount.

As usual, the poor man who was invited to risk his life for the state demanded a greater share in governing it. That had happened in the old days in the aristocratic republics of Greece, when heavy infantry started usurping the role of the nobles who went to war on horseback. Now in the middle of the fifth century the highest office, the archonship, was opened to the third class of citizens, the zeugitai, and in practice to the fourth, the thetes. But if all classes were to participate in government, the juryman must be compensated in part for the workday lost. The aristocrats, with their tradition of free service to the state, objected to the large courts of paid jurymen, whom the nobles regarded as too lazy to work and as drunk with self-importance. But the large juries had at least the great virtue of being too numerous to bribe in a society where bribery was a serious problem. In general, Athens' cash economy and her economic inequality made payment for both civil duties and military duties inevitable, if freedom was indeed to mean that a man must obey only those laws which he had first had a chance to vote on, after free debate, open to all. Finally, the prestige and superior education of aristocrats like Pericles gave them still a near-monopoly of high office provided they showed themselves loyal to the ideas of equality of debate and equality before the law.

This dream of a free society guided a polis of perhaps 410,000-420,000,[196] of whom a good half lived in the city of Athens and its port, the Piraeus. Of this total, there may have been around 208,000 slaves and 70,000 metics, or foreign residents. There may have been some 138,000 free Athenians. But of these only the adult males voted and were eligible for office: there may have been some 41,700 of them. Few as these full citizens were, in 451 on the motion of Pericles they reversed the slow expansion of freedom that Dracon, Solon, and Clisthenes had striven for, that had inspired Athens' heroic courage under the onslaughts of a vast, despotic Persian Empire, that men had died for at Marathon and at Salamis, that had rallied Ionia and the Isles to Athenian leadership, that attracted to Athens the admiration and even the emulation of most of Hellas. In 451 wealth, comfort, and enjoyment were increasing; the number of metics and slaves was increasing; the control of her allies by Athens was increasing. It is true that some metics were gaining citizenship, though not always by honest methods. And the son of an Athenian citizen had always been a citizen, even though his mother might be a foreigner. In 451 a law proposed by Pericles provided that no man should be a citizen of Athens unless both parents had been citizens—though the mother, of course, would in any case neither have voted nor held office.

This closure of naturalization was highly symbolic. The new law would have denied citizenship to Clisthenes, to Miltiades, to Themistocles, to Cimon, to the great historian, Thucydides. All of them had had foreign mothers. Indeed, Athenian aristocrats had always been quick to marry the daughters of other aristocrats—or, anyhow, of rich men—whether native or foreign: high birth transcended frontiers. Against the privilege of birth or wealth the Athenian democracy had waged political war; today the Athenian citizen, rich or poor, enjoyed legal equality and freedom. But under Pericles' new law the political and economic benefits of freedom would be reserved to those who had inherited freedom, as a new privilege, a kind of property. It would be reserved by force: by the enforced law of the polis against metic and slave, by the enforced will of Athens against ally and commercial rival and military rival alike. Athens, which had so long explored with Odysseus, would now dig in her heels with Achilles—so far, at least, as her political life was concerned.

Her closed citizenry would not only determine to have and to hold Athens against all newcomers. By the system of cleruchies, so detested by the Allies, this closed citizenry would establish colonies recruited from its own ranks, colonies in the Thracian Chersonese, in Lemnos, in Imbros, in Andros, in Naxos, in Eretria, in Thracian Brea, in Oreus, in Amisus and Astacus on the Black Sea, in Aegina. The land for Athenian settlers was at first paid for by a reduction in tribute, but later Athens merely seized it. It is true that the land she seized was often confiscated from anti-Athenian oligarchs. But it was seized; and often the new Athenian landlords allowed the former owners to work the land for the landlords' benefit. Surely these cleruchies must have reminded at least a few Athenians of the Messenians the Spartans had reduced to helotry when they had conquered Messenia centuries ago. By the will of Athens, some 10,000 Athenians in all were settled as cleruchs, to help find livelihood for the poor of Athens, to solve Athens' population problem, to keep an eye on restless allies and to guard trade routes.

However, under the guidance of Pericles, the yoke of Athens was not a crushing one. Her government brought a considerable measure of economic unity to the new Aegean Hellas, encouraged the exchange of commodities and hence the wiser use of local resources, and enriched her own unenfranchised metics. Athens became the undisputed emporium of Aegean Hellas; and her oil and wine and pottery were going even to Western Greece, even to distant Etruria. Her ships policed the seas that had once been preyed upon by pirates.

She brought also a kind of intellectual unity, and she was the center of the literary and artistic life of the Hellenes. Her rich Attic dialect was beginning to serve as the common tongue of Hellas, the medium for the exchange of ideas. Her coin, bearing the famous image of Athena's sacred owl, was beginning to serve as the common coin of the Aegean, the medium for the exchange of Greek commodities. Her imposing system of law was being widely copied by her Allies. That system spread in part because she took over a portion of the judicial function of the governments of her Allies. Athenian courts came to handle acts against the League and to hear appeals against sentences of death, of exile, of confiscation of goods—if only to protect her supporters in Allied lands from discontented oligarchs. Still, her Hellenic subjects were not free in Athens' own sense of freedom.

Was it Pericles' sense of how far Athens was substituting might for right that led him in 448 to call a Panhellenic Congress at Athens? Or, since he had every reason to expect that jealous Sparta would refuse, was it mere diplomatic maneuver, an effort to convey to Hellas that Athens sought consensus and not a Spartan blind obedience? In any case, he proposed that all Hellenes take common counsel on a plan to rebuild the temples the Persian barbarian had destroyed and to police the seas that connected their city-states together. Sparta refused, and nothing came of Pericles' plan for a Panhellenic Congress. Hellas remained dangerously cleft in three parts: Athens' League of Delos, Sparta's Peloponnesian League, and a neutral and hesitant and divided world of shifting petty alliances.

Five years later, in 443, Pericles launched another common effort, of a kind that had a long and familiar tradition, though for a new purpose. He founded Thurii, near the ancient site of Sybaris in southern Italy. He invited Hellenes, not only from Athens, but from all Greece to join in the settlement. The new city of Thurii was laid out by that same Hippodamos of Miletus who had laid out the geometrical avenues of Piraeus. It grew rich. Its citizens included famous men: Herodotus, the historian; Protagoras, the sophist, who became its official lawgiver; Empedocles, the natural philosopher; and others. But within a decade Thurii was drifting away from Athenian political influence.

Late in 441, Athens' most powerful ally, Samos, quarreled with one of Athens' subject cities, Miletus, and defeated her in battle. Miletus appealed to Athens for help, and Athens demanded that Samos submit her quarrel to Athenian arbitration. Samos refused. Thereupon Pericles sailed for Samos at the head of forty vessels, and the oligarchs who had governed

Samos withdrew to the mainland to seek Persian aid against Athens—against Athens, which had taken the leadership only a few short decades before in rescuing Samos and the other Ionian states from their Persian rulers. In 441 Pericles placed a democratic government in power and withdrew. But the oligarchs, with their Persian mercenaries, returned to Samos and declared the independence of Samos. Pericles had already written off Athens' briefly held land empire in order to control more securely the League of Delos. When Byzantium followed Samos and revolted, he struck hard. But it was not until the spring of 439, after a most costly war, that Pericles and his fleets forced Samos to capitulate. She was forced to surrender her fleet, raze her fortifications, pay a heavy indemnity, accept a democratic government, and become a subject city. Pericles returned to Athens in triumph. Byzantium, and some of her restless neighbors, were promptly subdued; but during the war some of the Carian allies had ceased to pay tribute. Rather than risk a clash with Persia, Pericles avoided an immediate further suppression.

The Samian revolt was instructive. It was obvious that the voluntary League of Delos had turned into an Athenian Empire, in which Athens controlled the joint navy and the joint finances. In 434 she would even forbid her Allies to coin money, although the right of coinage was one of the Greek city-states' proudest sovereign prerogatives. On the other hand, Samos was not the only Allied city in which it was chiefly the wealthy class that hated Athenian control and in which the lower class tended to look on the imperial city as protector. Moreover, aside from championing the democrats and aside from policing the seas for the benefit of merchants everywhere, Athens held another and important advantage in her battle for Hellenic unity under her own hegemony. She had become the dazzling and exciting center of the cultural life, not only of her new empire, but of all Hellas. She represented a concentration such as no Hellene had known in any country anywhere, of architecture, sculpture, painting, music, philosophic inquiry, and especially of drama. If she had failed to expand the constitution of Clisthenes into some sort of true political union of city-states, if she had failed to develop the Council of the League from a diplomatic assembly of sovereign states to a common government of elected representatives, nevertheless she herself did represent every Hellene everywhere who wanted to enter the great conversation which Hellas was becoming. Even her fleet of fighting triremes looked, in the light of this achievement, less like naked force and tyranny, more like the might that must be joined to right if law and justice were ever to operate in fact. And although only the hated Athenian cleruchs could, by going to Athens, lawfully claim a seat in her Assembly, where free men governed themselves, yet plenty of other Hellenes could, and did, go to Athens to help build the temples and paint the pictures and carve or mold the statues that made human existence come alive, that made the earth a more luminous dwelling place for man; or to argue about those intangible but powerful things the Athenian called ideas, things that only the mind's eye could see. It is true that neither these Hellenic visitors, or immigrants, nor—since the Periclean law of 451—their sons nor their sons' sons could ever help make law at Athens. Yet they could be sure of a welcome to all who cared about what was good or what was true or what was beautiful. They could be sure of a certain civilized gentleness, a certain courtesy in human intercourse, that marked off Athens from Sparta.

It was thus that Polygnotus, the painter, could come from Thasos to work beside Phidias, the native Athenian sculptor, and watch him plan with Pericles a temple to Athena. And what other temple in Hellas made so noble a home for a god as the Parthenon? Ictinus would help design it; Callicrates would carry out his plans. Mnesicles would design the magnificent approach to it—the Propylaea. Phidias, already famous for the colossal statue of Zeus at Olympia, would create inside the Parthenon the colossal statue of Athena, her flesh formed of ivory, her vesture of pure gold. Around the outside walls not only would the sculptor carve in marble bas-relief the figures of gods and men but the painter would decorate the background in brilliant red and blue. And painters like Polygnotus and Micon would paint life-size frescoes on the walls of the Painted Portico in the market place and on temple walls too, in the city that lay below Athena's hill. When the fleets returned to Athens from their sweeping cruises through the Aegean or the Black Sea, and long before they sighted the Acropolis, they would see on the high cliffs at the southern tip of Attica the tall marble columns of a temple to Posidon. And as they approached Athens on a sunny day they would behold high on the Acropolis the spear point and plume of an heroic statue of Athena, Athena of Battles, standing jealous guard over the land she most loved.

The statues that Greek sculptors carved in marble, in the years when Pericles was leader of Athens and her Aegean empire, differed profoundly from those the tyrant Pisistratus had beheld. The stiffly formal figures with their long robes hanging in vertical lines; the masculine heads with their almost Assyrian ringlets; the mysterious, secret smile; even the brilliantly painted limestone from which these gods and goddesses, these godlike youths and maidens, had been formed—all these things gave way now before a different sort of god, a different sort of youth or maid. The sculptor evoked them from exquisite marble, often the marble of Paros, from which sunlight did not glance away but into whose translucent outer edges sunlight caressingly melted. This marble was painted little or not at all. But what stirred the wonder of the beholder was not the superior matter in which the sculptor found his image or the exquisite skill with which he could now guide his questing chisel. It was rather the image he discovered, the incredibly graceful naked youth in all his muscled strength and sudden glory; the gently curved body of goddess or woman, draped in garments that fell in curved folds of exquisite harmony. It was the grave, serene face, so often lightly tinged with melancholy. Perhaps there was something that soared invisibly upward from those older and ruder statues of the sixth century, as if it would quit an imperfect world for a world where all would be perfection, and perhaps this something was missing from the technically perfect statues of Periclean Athens. But at least that other perfection, that no man's naked eye would ever see, had somehow, if incompletely, come down from where the gods dwelt, as radiant light comes down, and had clothed itself in marble and in bronze. If these later statues hinted less at beauty eternal, they now embodied more, here and now in Athens and in the other cities of Hellas. What spring had promised, summer had almost fulfilled. And if summer in turn appeared to promise autumn, summer was still a gift whose beauty could come but from the gods themselves.

But it was not only her temples and her statues and her paintings that gave meaning to life at Athens. It was also her music, her dancing, her literature. Pericles reorganized the Great Panathenaic Festival, which rejoiced Athena and her people for ten days of every fourth year. In Festival time a great procession of the people followed the maidens who bore the yellow wool garment they had woven for the goddess. They climbed the high Acropolis to the old temple which Athena shared with Erechtheus, whom she herself had reared—him, the son of Earth herself, who had ruled Athens as king in her half-remembered past. Animal sacrifices were held and the people ate meat with their goddess; then they clothed her in her newly made robe. There were competitions by those who recited, by those who played musical instruments and sang. The young men ran and leapt and wrestled; threw the discus and the javelin; engaged in the Pyrrhic dance of armed warriors to win the prize of an ox; raced on horseback; ran in the torch race, holding a flaming torch while protecting its flame with a shield.

Around 446, a Greek world traveler from Asia Minor read aloud to the Athenians something new in their experience and gained a prize of two talents. This composition, like a famous tragedy of Aeschylus, dealt with Xerxes' pride and punishment and with the leading role of Athens in the Hellenic fight for political freedom. But it was not poetry. It was not even written in meter but in prose. It began:

> What Herodotus the Halicarnassian has learnt by inquiry is here set forth: in order that so the memory of the past may not be blotted out from among men by time, and that great and marvelous deeds done by Greeks and foreigners and especially the reason why they warred against each other may not lack renown.[197]

Herodotus's word for inquiry was the Greek word *historia,* and without any adequate precedent he had just invented history—more specifically a history of the recent Persian War. Like Homer, he wrote about a war, and like Homer he wanted men to remember. As in Homer's *Iliad,* so in Herodotus's history the deathless gods sometimes appeared and aided the men who faced death, and who faced even the forgetfulness of later generations. It is true that Herodotus reported the divine interventions without always believing they occurred. Moreover the basic purpose had shifted from the purpose of Homer. Witnesses were called up and the causes of events were argued about. And the search for causes drove Herodotus back in time to Cyrus the Great and the rise of the Persian Empire; back, even, to Croesus of Lydia, who should have made further inquiry of Apollo before attacking Cyrus; back, even, to Homer's Trojan War. The search for causes drove him outward in space. He traveled to Egypt, to Libya, to Syria, perhaps to Mesopotamia, to the northern coast of the Black Sea. Throughout much of his work he was more the geographer and anthropologist than the historian. The strange customs he saw or heard of, the strange anecdotes he collected—these he repeated with contagious relish. He was often misinformed by those he questioned, but he clearly made enormous effort to learn what really did take place. His history became the first great prose work of Hellenic literature.

At the foot of the Acropolis stood the temple to Dionysus, the popular god of wine and ecstacy, who possessed his frenzied followers and who had died and been reborn to save them from their sins. Here, during religious festivals ever since the days of Pisistratus, a new kind of competition had been held, a competition by those who wrote tragedies. Here, in 472, the poet Aeschylus had presented his tragedy of the *Persians*, less than a decade after Xerxes had watched from his silver-footed throne while his fleet was destroyed in the narrow waters off the Isle of Salamis. This was the tragedy for which Pericles had served as choregus. Did Aeschylus make Salamis his scene of action or the Greek triumph his subject? On the contrary, he made the palace of Xerxes in Susa his scene, and he made his subject the insolent pride of Xerxes, his pride and its punishment by the gods, acting through the Greeks at Salamis. But Pericles was a young noble when he helped produce the *Persians*, and politically unknown; even Aeschylus was still in his fifties. Aeschylus continued to pour out tragedies: he may have written as many as ninety[198] dramas. During the early years of his career he, like other tragedians who competed before the temple of Dionysus, had to offer three tragedies, followed by a satyr play, a sort of grotesque farce. Each tragedy was complete in itself; but in Aeschylus's case the trilogy of tragedies often displayed an intelligible structure of its own. He first competed in 499, when he was twenty-six. In 484, four years before Salamis, he won his first victory. He may himself have fought at Salamis; he had certainly fought at Marathon. He remained the leading tragedian of Hellas until his death in Sicily in 455.

After Pericles came to power, Aeschylus's only performance at Athens was the trilogy known as the *Oresteia*, followed by a satyr play called the *Proteus*. The trilogy included the *Agamemnon*, the *Libation-Bearers*, and the *Eumenides*. The *Oresteia*[199] of Aeschylus exemplified the extraordinary role of tragic drama in Athenian and Hellenic life. Its performance was an act of religious devotion. It was presented to a god who was beloved by the common people and whose worship involved man's deepest and least understood longings more completely perhaps than did the worship of any other god on Olympus. It was presented to a god, son of Zeus, born of a mortal woman. In it, the arts of the poet, the musician, the choreographer were harmoniously combined. This half-opera had to be played in the open air to an audience seated on wooden benches against the southern slope of the Acropolis, with an all-male cast of masked actors to whom special high shoes gave majestic stature. The drama had to come to life with only the simplest of stage settings. The *Oresteia* was a feast of awareness, in which citizens of every level of intelligence, of every political conviction, of every economic class, joined with their god.

The plot of the *Oresteia* was not something Aeschylus had contrived in order to astonish a gaping crowd. On the contrary, he merely retold one of the best-known tales from the Homeric Cycle, from the corpus of epic poems that had nurtured Hellas for hundreds of years. It was a tale of those dimly remembered Mycenaean days before the eruption of the Dorians into Greece more than half a millennium ago. It was a tale of dynastic families, of bloody violence, of vengeance blindly trying to serve the function of public law; a tale of greatness brought low; and, above all, a tale of the suffering through which a man might win understanding and release. The plot did indeed come from Homer's world, and Aeschylus himself, according to later tradition, remarked modestly that his tragedies were but slices of meat from Homer's mighty dinners.[200] But where the *Iliad* merely told, through the mouth of the rhapsode who sang or declaimed it, what the men of old had done and said and suffered, the *Oresteia* made them do and say and suffer these things before the spectator's very eyes, while their cadenced, magic words rang out against the steep slope of the holy Acropolis itself. The *Oresteia* carried the spectators back through the centuries to the day when Agamemnon, having sacked Troy, returned in triumph to his palace so few miles south of where the spectators sat, only to be done to death by his queen, Clytemnestra. But, if it carried the spectators back in time to the return of the conquerors from Troy, it carried Mycenae forward too. Agamemnon's palace at Mycenae was magically transported to neighboring Argos, which has just made common cause with Athens to hold the Spartans in check.

The bloody vendetta of which Clytemnestra's murderous act was but a part would proliferate hopelessly until her son Orestes would kill her; until the tormented matricide, pursued by the frightful Furies of the nether world, would seek Apollo's advice at Delphi; until Apollo would escort Orestes to Athens, home of law and justice; until Athena herself would

preside over a formal court, whose judges would be members of the Areopagus—of that Areopagus whose traditional power to judge blood-guilt not
even Ephialtes or Pericles had torn from it; and until this court, presided
over by Divine Wisdom herself, would acquit the matricide, Orestes. Nor
could the tragic cycle end until Athena had assigned the avenging Furies,
now robbed of their prey, to sanctuary in a cave, a cave in the side of the
very hill on which the Areopagus still heard such cases when the *Oresteia*
was played. The Furies were given a new name, the Gracious Goddesses,[201]
and undertook to bless the city of Athens. Ancient vengeance for the blood
that had been spilt, especially kinsman's blood, had been reconciled with
wisdom and reason and law. Man as moral agent had through great suffering been purified; and through the direct intervention of the gods the Polis,
the human community, had been saved from anarchy.

This was the trilogy, the tragedy-in-three-tragedies, that Athena's Polis
was allowed to live in, to pass through, to understand, to remember. And
it was this new art form, tragedy, fashioned and perfected in Athens out
of ancient elements collected hither and yon, that conquered the Hellenic
spirit. As for the *Oresteia* itself, it was the work of an aristocrat, born in
the holy town of Eleusis, goal of pilgrims, of those who, burdened with
sin, longed for a life beyond death. It was the work of an aristocrat who
had fought at Marathon for a city already turning toward democratic rule,
toward equality before Law, toward the right of every citizen to speak in
the Assembly as an equal of all his fellows. Here in the Theater of Dionysus
every citizen could see man face to face with his gods, face to face with his
neighbor, speaking wingèd words, listening, thinking, acting. He could see
man acting; he could see an actor acting. The actor in the play was a
reflection of another man who acted, yet not in a theater. And by an effort
of imagination, he could see the historical Agamemnon act, all unconscious
that real acts in history might at some later day appear to men like mere
reflections of the actions in a tragedy. This was an experience calculated
to help the Athenian look at his own acts, to be aware of them, to live,
not the life of the somnambulist, but the life of a man who was fully alive,
alive to himself and to the persons about him. It was an experience calculated to give him not a childish optimism, not a foolish sentimentality,
but the tragic sense of life that it was not a child's lot to possess.

Work of the caliber of Aeschylus's tragedies was well-nigh bound to
provoke challenge; and it was chiefly Sophocles who responded. He was

born in Colonus, a little town a little north of Athens, in 495, five years
before Aeschylus fought at Marathon. When the Persian fleet met catastrophe in the narrow, crowded waters off Salamis, Sophocles was a lad of
fifteen; and, when a trophy was dedicated after the battle, it was Sophocles
who led the chorus that danced and sang around the trophy. Sixteen years
after Aeschylus's first triumph in tragedy and only ten years before the
Oresteia, Sophocles won first prize.[202] He was only twenty-seven, and his
defeated opponent was Aeschylus. Sophocles lived about ninety years, and,
according to later tradition, he wrote around 125 dramas,[203] of which
some 24 won first prize. Like Aeschylus, he was an aristocrat and a soldier
as well as a tragic poet. He held several public offices. When Pericles sailed
in 440 to quell the revolt of Samos, one of his generals was Sophocles.

In Sophocles' hands, the structure of tragedy, with its high conventions,
changed. The trilogy, or tragedy-in-three-tragedies, he attempted only once.
Although gods and heroes might appear, the source of dramatic human
action had somehow shifted from gods to men. But the men were likely to
be the legendary kings and heroes of Hellas, who represented in their
single persons the whole human community. This symbolizing of a community by a person enabled Sophocles, like Aeschylus, to deal with that
community, with the political problems of war and peace, of tyranny and
freedom under law, with law made by gods as against law made by men
alone; and yet to deal at the same time with persons, not with faceless
crowds. These were persons who loved, hated, thought, deliberated, made
choices, acted, and suffered. As in the tragedies of Aeschylus, they were
men who wielded power, who grew proud and misused power, who therefore grew blind and deaf, who listened less well, and who suffered the
catastrophe that could bring understanding.

Technically, Sophocles increased the chances for listening and hence
the opportunities for turning the deaf ear. He increased the chances for
true communion with god and communion with other men. For where
dialogue in Aeschylus might involve two characters at any given moment,
besides the chorus, in Sophocles the dialogue might involve three. The
point of interest correspondingly shifted still further from the chorus, which
took less and less part in the action, but rather observed and commented.
Although there were now more characters ready to speak, they seemed
readier to speak with each other than with the gods. In place of the tremendous religious tension that led the spectator of Aeschylean drama up

from human action to the action of the gods, the tension in Sophoclean drama often led the spectator more from one man's act and purpose to the clashing purpose and counter-act of other men.

The tragedy that won Sophocles his most enduring fame was *Oedipus the King*. Like Croesus, king of Lydia, Oedipus consulted the oracle at Delphi. Like Croesus, he consulted him inadequately. For Oedipus wanted to keep buried memories hidden. He had been brought up to consider himself the legitimate son of the king and queen of Corinth. A fellow reveler at a banquet cast doubt on his parentage. When he consulted the oracle, he was told only that he would slay his own father and wed his own mother. He jumped to the conclusion that the oracle alluded to the king and queen of Corinth—although whether he was indeed their son was precisely the problem that had taken him to Delphi in the first place. He determined to avoid Corinth; he rushed blindly off toward Thebes. On the road he met an old man and his servants; he quarreled over the right of way; he slew the old man. He arrived at plague-ridden Thebes; freed it from plague by reading the riddle of the sphinx; gained, by way of reward, the hand of its middle-aged, recently widowed queen, Jocasta, and became king of Thebes. All this happened before the action of Sophocles' tragedy began: Oedipus's precipitate misreading of the oracle; his failure to make further inquiry; the slaying where three roads met of a man old enough to be his father; his triumphant reading of the riddle; his consequent marriage with the widowed queen; the coming of a new plague to Thebes. Then the action of the drama itself began.

The blind prophet Tiresias announced that the plague was a moral pollution: Jocasta's first husband, the late king, had been murdered. The murderer must be identified and banished if the Polis was to be cleansed and the plague driven out. Oedipus, with enormous pride in his power to read dark words, with enormous recurrent suspicion that his kingly authority was being threatened by treason, and with a proud determination to find the murderer, to do justice, and to save his people for a second time, embarked on his quest to find—himself. But such was his overweening pride that, though the dialogue of the drama offered him many opportunities to learn the hideous truth and to know himself, to know who he was, he could not listen, he could not understand, but threatened those who, wittingly or unwittingly, provided the clues he needed.

In the end he found the murderer—and himself, but not before his mother, wife, and queen had discovered who she and he both were and had taken her own life. He found himself murderer of his own father, husband of his own mother, half-brother of his own sons, father of his two half-sisters, nephew of his brother-in-law, Creon, who now became his king and not his subject: he found himself a man with eyes who could not see. Thereupon he tore out his offending eyeballs and went into banishment.

Among many others things, the *Oedipus* recalled Solon's commandment, "Know thyself." It suggested strongly that this commandment was hardest to obey for those who wielded power, since power tended to blind. In recalling this commandment of Solon's, it pictured these blinding effects of power just as Athens was becoming the most powerful state in Greece, an imperial city quick to scotch rebellion, the wealthy market place of the eastern Mediterranean. To her were crowding the artistic talents of Hellas; to her were crowding the masters of Hellenic literature. And to her crowded the sophists, lecturers and publicists who taught what was known or believed about the world the Greek inhabited and, above all, the art of rhetoric, that would enable their pupils to face political debate or judicial prosecution alike and win the war of words. Some pupils adopted from the sophists who taught them the convenient conviction that knowledge was but opinion, that everything was relative, that morals were but mores, that law was a convenient human convention, that the ancient myths about the gods were old wives' tales, and that might made right.

It was in the context of Aeschylus's tragic vision of the will of Zeus and the will of other gods fulfilling itself through the free choices of men; and it was even more in the succeeding tragic vision of Sophocles, of men who have seized the initiative but must still consult the will of Zeus, as transmitted by Apollo and his oracle at holy Delphi;—it was by this prismatic light that Pericles ruled democratic Athens, but by persuasion, not by force. From Damon he had learned music and the curious personal harmony, serenity, gentleness, and courtesy that contrasted so strongly with the bluff, hearty manner of his fellow aristocrat, Cimon, that cavalryman turned successful admiral. A statesman, a soldier, and an admiral himself, Pericles yet appeared strangely withdrawn and aloof, so that his political enemies derisively called him Olympian Zeus; but he was so cogent in debate, in a polis more and more attentive to the appeal to reason and to the charm of skillful speech, that his gentle mastery of that polis could not be overthrown. Like Solon, he was a man of both thought and action, and this at a moment in Athenian history when war and violence more and more threatened the marriage of thought and action. As to his gentleness, a tale was told that when a scurrilous and uncouth citizen followed him all day long, heaping insults upon him, he made no reply; and, when this stream of abuse followed him clear to his own doorway that evening, he still made no comment, except to order his servant, now darkness had fallen, to light a torch and escort his assailant safely home.

From Zeno the Eleatic, Pericles learned the power of close argument. Indeed, Zeno was sometimes called its inventor. But Zeno also sought the One, to which the many shifting phenomena of an ever-changing world might be reduced. So did, according to some, the founder of the Eleatic school in southern Italy, Xenophanes of Colophon, that enlightened Ionian poet, philosopher, and theologian who made such sport of Hellenic polytheism. Besides Damon's music and Zeno's brilliant dialectic, Pericles received for years the constant gift of Anaxagoras's thought. Anaxagoras had come from Clazomene in Ionia in 456 and was Pericles' intimate companion. He was learned in mathematics and medicine; he speculated in natural philosophy; and he taught the doctrine that neither air, nor fire, nor earth, nor water had originated our universe but that this universe had been made out of such elements by *Nous*—that is, by mind, intellect. Certainly it was to intellect that Pericles turned as to a court of last resort.

And yet, despite this Ionian tendency to trace all things to one primal cause, despite this Odyssean tendency toward intellectual light, toward quiet reflection, the question, and attentiveness, it was Pericles who sponsored the exhilarating program of housing the traditional, numerous gods of Athens in magnificent new temples. It was Pericles who worked intimately with Phidias to crown the Acropolis and Athens and Hellas with marble that could speak, with columns that would soar, with bas-relief that would remember the community of gods and men, that would glorify and validate a polis as something other than a herd of clever animals; that would certify it as other for all men at all hours of the day wherever the eye glanced and regardless of their varying intellectual powers; that would give work to the unemployed and would thereby consecrate Athens' surplus labor to an expression of adoration for the gods, of adoration from all the men of all the cities of her new empire, of adoration from all Hellenes ready to adore.

The tongues of many lands were now spoken on the busy docks of the Piraeus. The compelling might of the Athenian fleets patrolled the Aegean and kept the allied and subject cities obedient to the Athenian people. The delicate foods and delectable luxuries that flowed in on Athens tempted at least her richer citizens with a new vision that might blur the tragic sense or the rule of intellect, a vision of comfort and pleasure and a high standard of living, far from the stark simplicities of food and clothing and shelter amidst which she had fought for human freedom. Nevertheless, life in Pericles' Athens possessed an extraordinary luminous significance. There was plenty to worry about; most men were still poor; many had lost through slavery their full rights as men; yet human existence in Athens was at least phosphorescent with meaning, as it was in the great tragedies of Aeschylus and Sophocles.

Even the men of birth and money were partially won over by Pericles, by his moderation, by his prudence, by his obvious loftiness of spirit. Their aristocratic claim that quality be recognized, Pericles so clearly met; but they still regretted the breach with aristocratic, conservative Sparta and its rigorous, simple life. They challenged their own city's right to use the tribute of other League members, not for defense but to deck out Athens in baubles like some harlot. They were rendered uneasy by the Periclean democracy's growing tendency to overthrow their fellow nobles and fellow rich in Allied cities, to confiscate their lands, and to settle Attic rustics and craftsmen as cleruchs on those lands.

To the charge that Athens had no right to use the tribute of the League members, levied for the common defense, in order to beautify the capital city of a single member, Pericles replied that the Allies had no right to object so long as Athens protected them from Persia. They now contributed only money and they received protection. Besides, the construction program brought employment to the needy. Had Aristides,[204] who first divided the burden of the common defense, been alive now, would he have accepted the first of these arguments? But the Allies were in no condition any longer to object, and the work went on.

In 453, when he was nearing forty, Pericles married. Two sons were born of this marriage; but the parents separated by mutual consent when the boys were still small, and the mother remarried. Pericles did not remarry. He took into his home Aspasia, an extraordinary, highly cultivated woman from Miletus, who presided for years over a salon for the writers and artists and thinkers and statesmen of Athens, at a time when Athenian women, even of high family, were given little formal education and could provide little intellectual companionship for men like Pericles. He kept his two sons with him, and ultimately had a son by Aspasia. By virtue of Pericles' own law of 451, since Aspasia was not an Athenian, her son could not look forward to citizenship in his native polis. In addition to these three boys, Pericles took into his own home as wards two other boys, whose father, Clinias, a kinsman of Pericles, had fallen in the battle of Coronea in 447, the battle in which Athens lost control of Boeotia. These two wards were named Alcibiades and Clinias. Of these two, Alcibiades early showed brilliance of mind, a headstrong will, and a soaring ambition.

In 443, the aristocratic opponents of Pericles formed a coalition with the more radical democrats. This coalition dared not attack Pericles personally: his superior abilities were too obvious. He was a less great soldier than Cimon had been; he lacked the infallible animal cunning of a Themistocles and Themistocles' marvelous talent for improvised solutions. But he was as incorruptible as Aristides the Just; he was a prudent commander in the field; and, once he and Athens had surrendered their territorial ambitions to landward, both his foreign and domestic policies were essentially those of Themistocles. Above all, his intellectual attainments were conspicuously higher than those of either Cimon or Aristides or Themistocles, at a time when Athenian hegemony in Hellas was as much intellectual as military. He was the great persuader in a polis more sensitive to argument and persuasion than perhaps any other in Hellas.

Invulnerable in himself, he was forced to watch his opponents attack him in the persons of his intimates. His teacher of music, Damon, had already been ostracized around 444. In 432 Anaxagoras, who had taught him that Intellect ordered the universe and who had kept Pericles' own intellect active and inquiring in areas closed to his opponents, was prosecuted for atheism toward the many gods of Hellas and for pro-Persian sympathies. Pericles helped him escape from Athens to Lampsacus on the Hellespont, where he founded a school. When Pericles' mistress, Aspasia, was prosecuted on the same two counts, Pericles managed to get her acquitted. Phidias, his great collaborator on the Parthenon and other temples, was accused of misappropriating some of the gold destined for his colossal gold and ivory statue of Athena, in the inner sanctum of the Parthenon. But the gold had been applied in thin, removable plates. When removed and weighed, it was not found wanting. The political opposition thereupon prosecuted Phidias for impiety. When he had designed a frieze on a wall of the Parthenon, showing the Battle of the Amazons, could not he and Pericles too be discovered in the design that decorated Athena's shield? Still in prison and under trial, the greatest of Athens' sculptors died—and the scandalmongers whispered that Pericles had poisoned him to forestall incriminating testimony.[205]

Meanwhile the comic poets like Cratinus were deriding Pericles, his policies, his mistress, his friends. He was the Olympian, withdrawn, arrogant. He was Squill-head, Onion-head; for despite the grave beauty of his features, his head was unduly elongated, and this defect caused sculptors to portray him with his helmet unvisored but in place.

While his opponents crowded in upon him, like hounds around a stag, war came nearer. The growing power of Athens caused a growing fear in Sparta. It caused even more fear in Athens' commercial rival, Corinth. Even among Hellenic states outside both power blocs, the sense of impending collision was driving the weak to take sides. The brutal fact was that the Hellenic community, united by common gods, by common religious shrines, by a common literature and common plastic arts, by a growing philosophic tradition and a growing commerce in material goods, had as yet found no way to establish a common government. Hellas lived in that deceptive and dangerous anarchy in which the community was ungoverned but in which its parts—in the case of Hellas, each city-state, each polis—had made the difficult transition from private vendetta to public law, based on court evidence, on general published rule, and on judicial application of that rule by reasoned argument. This was the transition that the *Oresteia* of Aeschylus recorded, in all its agony and in all its final triumph. This was the law of which the exiled Spartan king, Demaratus, spoke, on that Samothracian beach, to Xerxes, when the Great King had passed in review his vast, polyglot army and his magnificent navy: "What their law bids them, that they do."[206]

But Simonides' terse epitaph on the Three Hundred who fell at Thermopylae referred the reader not to Hellas but to the Spartans: "Obedient to their word we lie." One could not lie down in death, obedient to the word of Hellas, because Hellas possessed no government to make laws. Hellas was armed against herself: private vendetta between city-states still gave Hellas rule by violence—the violence of one polis against another.

The nearest thing to Hellenic law that had been devised was the law of Athens. It was imposed on the city-states that now formed her empire. It was imposed partly by the Hellenic community's desperate need of a common government, partly by the high reputation of Athenian courts, and in the last analysis by force of arms, as witness the end of the Samian revolt. But those who made that law were citizens neither of Samos nor of any other ally; they were citizens of Athens. And the essential point of the freedom for which men had died at Marathon, at Thermopylae, at Salamis, at Plataea, at Mycale, the essential point of the recent war that had freed the Boeotians and other Hellenes from Athenian domination was that a man should help make the laws he lived under if he were to be truly free. Only then could law rightly be his master.

Athens stood for the unity of Hellas under law, and, if necessary, under imposed law. Sparta stood for the independence of every polis against a law imposed by force from outside its community of citizens. The clash between them drew ominously nearer. It was predictable that the necessary military incidents would not be lacking. One of them happened in 433 at Corcyra, an island state off the west coast of Greece, on the grain route from Sicily. A second occurred in the same year at Potidaea, a tributary city of Athens in the Chalcidic peninsula, not many miles from the canal that Xerxes had dug to avoid the dangerous cape at Mount Athos. Both Corcyra and Potidaea were originally colonies of Athens' enemy, Corinth. A third incident occurred when Megara, so recently part of Athens' Mainland empire, allied herself with Corinth, and when, as a counter-measure, Athens closed the markets of her whole empire to Megara's goods in the spring of 432. That autumn Sparta's allies persuaded her to demand that Athens make concessions to Corinth and Megara or fight. Pericles, convinced that war with Sparta was inevitable, persuaded Athens to reject this ultimatum and to offer to submit to arbitration by a third party, as provided for in the Thirty Years' Peace. The Athenian offer to arbitrate was not accepted.

In 431 an army of Spartans, other Peloponnesians, and Boeotians occupied Acharnae, the most populous Attic deme outside of Athens. Some six miles away in Athens many Athenians wanted to attack, but Pericles had determined to follow where the wily Themistocles had led. He abandoned the Attic countryside and packed the country population inside the walled island that comprised Athens, its triple port of Piraeus, and the corridor that connected them. Their cattle and sheep and goats were sent across the strait to Euboea and to other islands. Athens still controlled the sea. She could live on imported foodstuffs. Meanwhile, she would harry the coasts of the Peloponnese until Sparta and her Peloponnesian League should tire of the war and should sue for peace.

Inside the walls the country people crowded wretchedly, in this city whose clever folk they so much distrusted. They slept in temples, in the towers on the city wall, in Piraeus, in the long walled corridor that connected Athens with her port. They huddled sorrowfully among the household furnishings they had salvaged and watched with horror from the walls while the enemy ravaged their orchards and vineyards and grain fields, so toilsomely husbanded over the decades. They outnumbered the city-dwellers. The polis that Pericles ruled, that the sea and the distant lands obeyed, with its foreign slaves and busy docks, its luxury and its power, its idle and garrulous and litigious citizens—this polis was still, if one merely counted heads, mainly a rural polis, a polis of ploughing and reaping, of herding, of pruning the vine, of beekeeping, and of the relentless work of the sort that Hesiod had prescribed in song. Conservative, pious, fond of their ancient traditions, slow-moving and slow-speaking, what could the men who carried on this work know of the clever, greedy, lazy, restless, skeptical city and its ways? Only the old could remember how, nearly fifty years before, with the vast armies of the Great King approaching, they had abandoned their fruitful countryside, had abandoned even Athens itself, to take to the ships and die for the right of the survivors to come home. Now, crowded in their unsanitary quarters, uprooted and homesick, they grumbled and lamented. Pericles tried to conciliate them by sending out raiding parties of cavalry to protect the fields nearest Athens. But he declined to convoke the Assembly for fear the hotheads would force a military blunder. Then, when the long summer campaign was over, he followed Athenian custom and held a state funeral for those who had fallen for Athens in the first year of the Peloponnesian War.

It was he who had pronounced, nine years before, a funeral oration over the bones of those who had fallen in the Samian revolt, and men still repeated his phrases. One could not see these fallen heroes now, he had then declared; neither could one see the gods, "but from the honors which they receive, and the blessings which they bestow, we conclude that they are immortal."[207] And so it was with the heroes who died suppressing the rebels at Samos. And in that same oration, he had cried that the Polis had lost its youth and the year had lost its spring. Now it fell to his lot to pronounce another oration, this one over the bones of those who had fallen in the first year's fighting of another, more ominous war.

Like a victory ode of Pindar that leaped upward from victory in the games to the victor's god-descended ancestors who also won victories and won them on storied battlefields, the funeral oration of Pericles leaped from the present occasion and the newly fallen heroes to their heroic ancestors who had kept Athens free, to their fathers who had won for her an empire, and to the battles which those present had fought to extend that empire. But, he asked, under what kind of government and out of what sort of habits and customs had such greatness grown? "It is true," he answered,

> that our government is called a democracy, because its administration is in the hands, not of the few, but of the many; yet while as regards the law all men are on an equality for the settlement of their private disputes, as regards the value set on them it is as each man is in any way distinguished that he is preferred to public honours, not because he belongs to a particular class, but because of personal merits; nor, again, on the ground of poverty is a man barred from a public career by obscurity of rank if he but has it in him to do the state a service. And not only in our public life are we liberal, but also as regards our freedom from suspicion of one another in the pursuits of every-day life; for we do not feel resentment at our neighbour if he does as he likes, nor yet do we put on sour looks which, though harmless, are painful to behold. But while we thus avoid giving offense in our private intercourse, in our public life we are restrained from lawlessness chiefly through reverent fear, for we render obedience to those in authority and to the laws, and especially to those laws which are ordained for the succour of the oppressed and those which, though unwritten, bring upon the transgressor a disgrace which all men recognize.[208]

> And our city is so great that all the products of all the earth flow in upon us, and ours is the happy lot to gather in the good fruits of our own soil with no more home-felt security of enjoyment than we do those of other lands.[209]

> We are also superior to our opponents in our system of training for warfare. . . . In the first place we throw our city open to all the world and

we never by exclusion acts debar any one from learning or seeing anything which an enemy might profit by observing . . . for we place our dependence, not so much upon prearranged devices to deceive, as upon the courage which springs from our own souls when we are called to action.[210]

For we are lovers of beauty yet with no extravagance and lovers of wisdom yet without weakness. Wealth we employ rather as an opportunity for action than as a subject for boasting; and with us it is not a shame for a man to acknowledge poverty, but the greater shame is for him not to do his best to avoid it. . . . We alone regard the man who takes no part in public affairs, not as one who minds his own business, but as good for nothing; and we Athenians decide public questions for ourselves or at least endeavour to arrive at a sound understanding of them, in the belief that it is not debate that is a hindrance to action, but rather not to be instructed by debate before the time comes for action. For in truth we have this point also of superiority over other men, to be most daring in action and yet at the same time most given to reflection upon the ventures we mean to undertake . . .[211]

Then came an extraordinary statement. Pericles was, after all, making a patriotic oration. It was scarcely surprising that the Athens he described did not exist concretely, either in the now abandoned Attic countryside or behind the walls of the man-made island Themistocles had imagined, or even in the wooden walls of Athens' watchful fleets. It existed only as an ideal, yet an ideal toward which Athens had steadily been tending. Even if his oration were construed as an effort to console by flattery, it was extraordinary by what high and central point in his discourse he chose to flatter—he who knew his audience so well, knew what they wanted to be or even to seem to be.

In a word, then, I say that our city as a whole is the school of Hellas . . .[212]

He said more: he spoke of those things that such an oration had to speak of before he dismissed his fellow citizens:

grief, I know, is felt, not for the want of the good things which a man has never known, but for what is taken away from him after he has once become accustomed to it.[213]

162

But he had already summed up in a sentence his hopes for his city, in a universe ruled by Nous, by Intellect.

When the winter of 431-430 closed, the Spartans and their allies again invaded Attica and ravaged it; but a worse enemy than Sparta struck an even harder blow at the school of Hellas: a frightful plague broke out in the crowded city, and, during the hot and stifling summer that followed, turned Athens into a city of horrors. Men believed the epidemic had started on the upper Nile; that it had swept Egypt and Libya and most of the Great King's empire. Then it broke out in the Piraeus, for it came from the sea that Hesiod so much dreaded, from the sea whence so many modern ills had come. Thucydides, who contracted the disease himself but recovered, carefully set down its symptoms, its fearful crisis, and the ghastly death that frequently followed. With it came a frightening demoralization that loosened the bonds that held the polis together. Crowded in their stifling, improvised cabins, idle, disconsolate, the refugees from the Attic countryside died like flies. Faced with probable death, and hence with a probable escape from retribution, at least in this life, many Athenians did things they had always feared to do or had always been ashamed to do.

Meanwhile Athens struggled on with the war. She sent a fleet to ravage the coast of Peloponnese, but the plague attacked the fleet. She sent an army to conquer rebel Potidaea, but the plague attacked the army. Pericles himself lost his two legitimate sons. He lost his sister. He lost most of his friends. His eldest son had, in any case, quarreled with him over money matters and was publicly slandering him. But when the younger son died too and the moment came for Pericles to lay a wreath upon the dead, he did what he had never yet done in public: he wept.

Nevertheless the Olympian kept his courage. The Athenians, watching their city fill with corpses and their countryside with enemy troops, murmured against his leadership. At last, in despair, they insisted on suing for peace, but failed to secure it. Then they turned on Pericles. He called an assembly. He rebuked them for breaking under their private misfortunes and reminded them that

> even though a man flourishes in his own private affairs, yet if his country goes to ruin he perishes with her all the same. . . . Since, then, the state may bear the misfortunes of her private citizens but the individual cannot bear hers, surely all men ought to defend her.[214]

"Nor must you think," he warned,

> that you are fighting for the simple issue of slavery or freedom; on the
> contrary, loss of empire is also involved and danger from the hatred in-
> curred in your sway ... for by this time the empire you hold is a tyranny,
> which it may seem wrong to have assumed, but which certainly it is
> dangerous to let go.[215]

This very point the Corinthians had made on the eve of the war when they
were urging hesitant Sparta and her other allies to combine against imperial Athens. The Peloponnesians, they had cried, ought not to prove

> degenerate sons of our fathers, who liberated Hellas, whereas we, so far
> from making this liberty secure, should be allowing a city to be established
> as a tyrant in our midst, though we claim the reputation of deposing the
> monarchs in single states.[216]

Pericles won the debate on policy, but resentment against him for
Athens' disasters was so high that he was prosecuted for embezzlement.
His accounts were examined for a period of fifteen years. There was one
sum of some ten or twenty talents that he could not account for and that
he had probably used to bribe an invading Spartan king in 446. He was
fined some fifty talents and lost his civic rights. But his integrity was perfectly well known; his wisdom was desperately needed; and he was shortly
restored to power. Indeed, a few months later, the Assembly at his request
granted rights of citizenship to the son whom Aspasia, his Milesian mistress, had given him, a son now some sixteen years old. He, too, was named
Pericles.

In the autumn of the following year, 429, the Olympian fell ill. According to later tradition, it was the plague; and though it was but a light
attack, it slowly used him up. According also to tradition, when a friend
visited him, Pericles ruefully showed him an amulet the women of his
household had hung around his neck. Pericles had so hated superstition and
had always so serenely followed reason. As he lay dying, he might well
reflect that he had not even wholly completed the group of buildings that
crowned the Acropolis—for example the new temple known as the Erechtheum, and even certain details of the queenly Parthenon itself. The
Hephaesteum, erected to the glory of Hephaestus, blacksmith son of mighty
Zeus, and to Athena Hephaestia, patron god and patron goddess of the
busy artisans of Athens, especially of her blacksmiths and her potters—

even the Hephaesteum had not yet been formally dedicated. Pericles had learned by grim experience to expect that, once he was gone, the Athenian democracy would most likely lose its head, would perhaps commit some fatal folly in the war that now raged into its third year. He left no political heir capable of guiding and restraining the Assembly.

While he lived, Athens was the school of Hellas in a double sense. She incited other Hellenic states by her contagious example to achieve democratic freedom, a freedom in which law was the conclusion of debate, of deliberation on the common good by all citizens, regardless of birth or wealth. But she was a school also for her own Athenian citizens, a learning polis, where men learned to make useful and beautiful objects and to defend the polis with their swords, their oars, and their lives; where men could listen to great music in the Odeum that Pericles had built near the Acropolis, partly from the masts and spars of captured Persian ships; could listen to rhapsodes recite Homer and to Herodotus the Halicarnassian read his history of the Persian Wars; could sit in the open-air theater of the god Dionysus and watch the heroes of Aeschylean tragedy act, suffer, and learn; could look up to the Acropolis and gaze on as lovely temples as man had ever built; could wrestle naked in the Attic sunlight in the palaestra and make their bodies strong and swift and skillful and beautiful, like the bodies of the gods themselves; could make law in the Assembly and render judgment under law in the courts; could stroll in the Agora and argue about the nature of man and his destiny, or listen to lectures by sophists, or simply talk with the merchants and sailors from strange and distant lands who crowded the water front of Piraeus. And yet, the citizens of Athens had clearly not developed the wisdom to govern their polis without unusual leadership. When Pericles had died, who would be competent to lead? Above all, when he died, he would bequeath this lovely city, this school of Hellas, but, alas, this tyrant-city too, a most deadly war. That war now threatened to bring Athens at last to her knees and to destroy once and for all the semblance of Hellenic unity which she had built out of her blood, out of her toil, out of her overweening pride.

In the autumn of 429 Pericles died.

6

THE AGONY OF HELLAS

THE WAR the dying Pericles bequeathed to his successors was a war in which both sides fought for Hellenic freedom. Half a century earlier both sides had fought, shoulder to shoulder, for the right of Hellenes to make the laws which they themselves obeyed and not to obey those of the Great King. On the beach at Marathon, in the bloody Pass of Thermopylae, between the rock cliffs and the sea, in the waters north of Artemisium, and in the narrow straits of divine Salamis, men had died for that freedom. And, when the Asian army of Mardonius had broken at Plataea, it was to Zeus Eleutherius, Zeus the Liberator, that the Hellenes dedicated annual sacrifices; for Mainland Greece was free. Then Athens willingly, and Sparta with hesitation, had freed Greece-in-Asia, on another beach, at Mycale. The two leading cities of Mainland Greece now diverged. For Sparta, freedom had been saved; but Athens and the Asian Greeks first fought to open the Hellespont and then formed the League of Delos to protect Aegean Hellas and the sea lanes that made Aegean Hellas possible. From a league to defend Hellenic freedom Aegean Hellas evolved into an Athenian Empire. The thrust of that empire was toward trade, money, sea power, and government by the people, the Demos—that is, toward democracy. More and more, whatever support Athens found for her rule she found among the populace in each of the cities she governed. More and more, the Well-fathered and the wealthy in each subject city, sure of their right to rule their own polis, conspired against the imperial capital of this new Hellenic empire.

Aegean Hellas flourished. Its political unity brought, within its jurisdiction, something approaching peace. Freed by Athenian naval power from the piracy that had cursed the Aegean, freed from the competition of the Great King's Phoenician merchants, Hellenic trade expanded. The standard of living in Athens' empire rose. If an ordinary citizen in one of the subject cities could not always find work and bread in trade or industry, he might hope to find a bench and a seaman's wage in one of the imperial triremes that Athens built with the tribute from his own, or another, city. As for the intellectual, the artist, the philosopher, he would find a gracious welcome at Athens, the undisputed capital of thinking, feeling Hellas. Even the enterprising merchant might move his business there. Though he could no longer hope, except by a special grant from the Assembly, to become a citizen, he might certainly hope to grow rich and to enjoy life in the loveliest and liveliest city in all Hellas. The statues and temples, the mural paintings, the music, the soaring tragedies and ribald comedies, the exciting conversation, and the civilized, courteous daily life of Athens were his.

The price of this new order was the loss of sovereignty, though not the loss of local self-government. For the ordinary citizen of a polis in Aegean Hellas, the part he played in governing his city might actually be increased. The noble, and the rich merchant too, who wanted to make the laws this humbler citizen must obey, threatened his freedom far more than Athens seemed to do. Even his polis, if it happened to be a small one, was protected by Athens against its more powerful neighbors, as the merchant and dock-worker of Athens had once been protected by the tyrant Pisistratus against the rapacious Athenian noble. The brutal fact remained that this small polis, if it should decide to secede from the League of Delos, now become an empire, must reckon with the might of Athens. Indeed, this polis was at the mercy of the triremes and infantry of Athens precisely as every single Athenian had once been at the mercy of the tyrant Pisistratus's bodyguard. If a subject polis claimed it suffered from injustice, such as Athens' doubling the tribute in 425, the only court it could carry its grievance to would be a court in Athens. Was this freedom?

Opposed to Athens and her Aegean empire stood Sparta and her Peloponnesian League. Sparta fought, at least in theory, for the sovereignty of each polis. But she maintained her leadership by supporting the Well-fathered and the well-to-do against the mob in each polis with which she was allied. Although some of her allies, such as Corinth and Megara, lived by trade rather than by the plough, Sparta herself did not. She still put her faith in the eunomia of Lycurgus, in tradition, in the shield and spear of the heavy infantry, in the courage and iron discipline of that infantry, in the virtues of the aristocrat. She still counted on the terror her army inspired both at home and abroad. In short, Sparta stood guard over an older Hellas, a Hellas that was dying, but a Hellas that was still a glorious and moving tradition. For the new problems of adventurous, enterprising, commercial Aegean Hellas she offered no solutions; she promised only freedom from Athens.

Both Spartan and Athenian, then, loved freedom under law. If ever in Hellenic history there had been need of a good strife, a good eris, a fruitful dialogue, it had been during the last years of peace as the hundreds of Greek city-states watched and as war, the evil eris, approached. If Pericles could have assembled his Panhellenic Congress, could its delegates have explored freedom by means of the good eris? Could they have devised a Solonian joining of right with might throughout the new Aegean Hellas?[217]

A new, emerging Hellenic community, with not only a common tongue, common gods, and common customs, but with an economy that was more and more common too, remained a collection of small city-states, each one a sovereign polis. The polis remained the largest area of man-made law. Of necessity, the polis, when it differed with a neighbor, took law into its own hands and fought for what it believed was justice, was freedom under law. At best, both sides sometimes submitted their disputes to arbitration. In short, they behaved toward each other as noble families had done before the polis had replaced vendetta with a court of law. It was as if that important step, which Aeschylus, in the Oresteia, had shown men taking under the guidance of Athena, goddess of wisdom, required more imagination, perhaps more mutual confidence, more spiritual energy, than Greeks could any longer muster. It was as if they had, with the help of the gods, expanded their comprehension of the human community from family to polis, but could not win through to a vision of a still wider human community, of free men living by reason and not violence. What blinded them? Was it the residual violence, the bad eris, between rich and poor that still smoldered beneath the surface of community life, or wildly erupted and threatened to destroy life, liberty, property, and polis? Or was it the other way around? Did the eris between Demos, the People, on the one hand, and on the other the Oligoi, the few—that is, the Best People and especially the rich people—did this evil eris of democratic revolution and oligarchic counter-revolution spring from the artificial assumption that, though man clearly needed law, yet one's own small polis was somehow the whole of mankind?

By the autumn of 429, when Pericles lay dying, War was taking over from Law, "but war, which robs men of the easy supply of their daily wants, is a rough schoolmaster and creates in most people a temper that matches their condition."[218] From the beginning of the war, whomever the Lacedaemonians caught in ships off the coast of Peloponnese, whether soldier, sailor, or civilian, whether Athenian or neutral, they put to death. In reprisal, in 430, when Athenians in Thrace captured envoys from Sparta and her allies, bound for the Great King's court to beg for money and other help against Athens, they killed them without trial. When the Athenians besieged and blockaded Potidaea, hunger within that city led to cannibalism. When Potidaea surrendered, the entire population was driven into exile. The plague in crowded, besieged Athens brought not only a loss of some one-third of her population, including 4,400 hoplites and 300 cavalry, but a terrifying demoralization of those who remained. Plataea, for nearly a century the ally of Athens, and sole sharer of Athens' glory at Marathon, was betrayed by her own oligarchs to Thebes. But she held out for four years. When Athens failed to send the aid she had promised, the Plataeans surrendered to a Lacedaemonian army on condition they would be tried. Five Lacedaemonian judges, determined to please their Theban allies, asked the Plataeans one by one, only one question: whether they had done the Lacedaemonians and Lacedaemon's allies any service in the war. The Plataeans could only answer no, and they were led out singly and slain to a man.

War was indeed taking over, and even the original policy for the war itself, laid down by Pericles, grew blurred, as violence led to violence. Pericles had wanted to collect the people of Attica into the man-made island of Athens and Piraeus, to allow the Peloponnesians to ravage the countryside, and never risk battle against Sparta's vastly superior land forces; meanwhile to keep firm control of the sea, and to make sudden and damaging raids on the coasts of Laconia and the Peloponnese. He wanted Athens to hold tight her subject allies and above all not to attempt fresh conquests. Sparta would soon grow sick of a futile war, which she had not the money to prolong, and would make peace. The war would have demonstrated that Sparta's professionalized citizen-army was indeed supreme on land but that Athens' imperial navy was equally superior at sea.

What that navy could do, the Athenian admiral Phormio had shown in the last months of Pericles' life. Other Greek navies were still using the trireme in the way that Athenian cavalry had until recently used the horse: to transport infantry. Arrived at the battlefield, this mounted infantry had dismounted and had fought it out, as other men fought it out. But Greek triremes too, once they had come to battle, used grappling irons on the enemy triremes while the marines they carried fought it out. Later, Greek cavalry had learned to fight from horseback and had learned to turn its horses into combat weapons. And Phormio's triremes had turned into weapons, too. Pericles' training routine that kept 60 battle craft constantly at sea during the best eight months of the year had created crews with such consummate skill that Phormio, with 20 ships, could outmaneuver 47 Peloponnesian ships, later increased to 77, in the Gulf of Corinth, could row rapidly around them in a steadily constricting circle, then wheel and ram their wooden flanks with the bronze beaks of his vessels or shear off their oars, or merely crowd them into colliding fatally with each other. Or, with one daring, wheeling ship, he could throw them into utter confusion. His crews went at their hard, skillful work in silence, that they might hear their officers' commands. Their officers learned to exploit the familiar behavior of wind and current, to co-ordinate their own work with the work of the sea, and so to destroy their enemies. Those officers knew their work and watched for the propitious day just as surely as had Hesiod, who knew the land but feared the sea. The ships of Athens inspired in men the same awe and admiration as the heavy infantry of Sparta. Sparta's naval disasters nonplused her, and she suspected misconduct and cowardice. But Phormio knew that Spartan courage was based on hard-won knowledge, knowledge of the spear and sword. The knowledge the Spartan lacked was a knowledge equally hard to win, knowledge of what the sea was and of what a ship could do about it. As the arts of peace declined, the arts of war developed. War, that rough schoolmaster, taught men not only how to die like heroes, but how to kill other men efficiently.

In the year after Pericles' death, Mitylene, a city on the coast of Lesbos facing the Asian mainland, revolted against Athens and appealed to Sparta and Boeotia for aid. The other towns of Lesbos, with the single exception of Methymna, joined in the revolt, and indeed set up a common polis with Mitylene. Mitylenian envoys attended the Olympic Games of 428, stood in the temple of Zeus, and put their case. So Sparta sent a fleet; and simultaneously she ravaged Attica more thoroughly than before to distract Athens from her problem in Lesbos. But the Spartan fleet loitered; provisions failed at Mitylene; and Salaethus, whom Sparta had sent ahead of the fleet to take charge of the city's defense, now decided to provide even the democrats with heavy arms and armor in order to fight his way out of the beleaguered city. Once armed, the democrats promptly mutinied against their oligarchic government, demanded that the oligarchs distribute the provisions they were hiding, and threatened that otherwise they would surrender the city to the Athenians. Fearful that the democrats would turn them over to a besieging Athenian army for instigating rebellion, the oligarchs themselves surrendered the city, on condition that they be allowed to send an embassy to Athens before anyone should be punished. The Athenian general, Paches, agreed. Along with the envoys, he sent to Athens the Spartan Salaethus and the oligarchs who had instigated the revolt.

The democratic party which still governed Athens was no longer led by Periclean appeals to reason. The war had brought to the top the rope merchant, Eucrates; Lysicles, a sheep dealer; Hyperbolus, a lamp manufacturer; and above all, a rich tanner named Cleon. Cleon was widely denounced by his opponents as a harsh and violent demagogue, ill-born, vulgar, domineering, cynical, venal, a master of invective. But he was a militant leader of Demos against a conservative party that did not relish the war. He was a militant imperialist, because imperial expansion brought economic benefits to Demos.

Cleon saw the Mitylenian revolt in black and white. In addition to the execution of Salaethus, the Spartan, he demanded of the Assembly that they decree the death of the oligarchic Mitylenians now imprisoned in

Athens, the death of every adult male in Mitylene, and slavery for the women and children. Diodotus, a moderate, opposed his motion. The prospect that rebellion might spread throughout their empire and leave them at the mercy of Sparta frightened the Athenians. Mitylene had revolted even though Chios and Lesbos were the only parts of the Athenian Empire still allowed to supply a quota of ships as against money tribute. This fact angered the Athenians, and they carried Cleon's motion. Orders were sent to Paches at Mitylene to execute the murderous decree.

But the Athenians shortly repented of their cruelty, another meeting of the Assembly was called, and a hot debate ensued. Then Cleon spoke again. He declared that Athens was a tyrant-city, obeyed by her allies out of fear, not love. The term tyrant, of course, had been applied by the Olympian himself to his beloved School of Hellas. But Pericles would not have agreed with Cleon's next point: that Athens ruled by force alone and that her allies obeyed her not out of loyalty but out of fear. Cleon's point was that the Athenian Empire was governed by might, a might that need not be joined with right. He rebuked his fellow citizens for not holding more firmly to their decisions and declared he had often observed that a democracy was incompetent to govern others; that "simpler people for the most part make better citizens than the more shrewd."[219] He attacked those who wanted to review the decree against Mitylene. These orators, he declared, were acting for gain. Or, at best, they were taking advantage of the Assembly's great weakness: to vote for the more eloquent, not the more cogent speaker. The members of the Assembly were prone to confuse legislative deliberation with contests for orators, to be "spectators of words and hearers of deeds."[220] There was no reason to punish only the aristocrats at Mitylene; the democrats had participated in the rebellion. Cleon warned the Athenians against pity, delight in eloquence, and clemency: they were the chief threats to an imperial state.

> I can sum up what I have to say in a word. If you take my advice, you will do not only what is just to the Mytilenaeans but also at the same time what is expedient for us; but if you decide otherwise, you will not win their gratitude but will rather bring a just condemnation upon yourselves; for if these people had a right to secede, it would follow that you are wrong in exercising dominion. But if, right or wrong, you are still resolved to maintain it, then you must punish these people in defiance of

equity as your interests require; or else you must give up your empire and in discreet safety practise the fine virtues you preach.[221]

Next Diodotus, the man who had spoken against Cleon's brutal motion, spoke again. He first parried Cleon's attack on that glory of Athens, free speech. He insisted that wise action must be based on deliberation; haste made for folly. If frank advice was to be met with the charge of bribery, then orators would have to resort to deceit to win the Assembly to even the wisest proposal: even "the man whose proposals are good must lie in order to be believed."[222]

Then the man whose proposals were good perhaps lied in order to be believed. Instead of appealing to the compassion which he might have assumed in many members of his audience and then showing how that compassion was a reflection of wisdom and for that reason practical, Diodotus bowed to the lesson which war had taught the Athenians: to be realistic, without compassion; to serve only their immediate interests; to sit in Athens and mete out cold-blooded massacre; to treat other men not as opponents in a dialogue, not even in the dialogue of battle and death, but as objects; not as ends, like themselves, but as means. After all, that was what these freedom-loving democrats considered their own slaves, at least in law. They were means to the good life of their free masters. Either Diodotus was now himself holding this view of such things as force and freedom, right and might; or he was afraid to risk statesmanship against a cynical politician. The issue, he declared, was not what wrong Mitylene had done but what was the wise course for Athens. Mitylene and Athens were not involved in a lawsuit: the problem was how best to make Mitylene useful to Athens again. Diodotus denied that the mass death sentence would deter other allies from rebellion: the death sentence had never yet deterred men from crime. If rebellion was to spell death, other rebels in the future would merely be more desperate fighters.

And do you consider, too, how great a mistake you would make in another point also by following Cleon's advice. At the present time the populace of all the cities is well disposed to you, and either does not join with the aristocrats in revolting, or, if forced to do so, is hostile from the beginning to those who stirred up the revolt; and so, when you go to war, you have the populace of the rebellious city as your allies. If, however, you destroy the populace in Mitylene, which took no part in the revolt, and which voluntarily put the city into your hands as soon as it got hold of arms, in the first place you will be guilty of killing your benefactors, and, in the second place, you will bring about what the influential men most wish: the next time they instigate a revolt among our allies they will at once have published it abroad that the same punishment is ordained for the innocent and for the guilty. Why, even if they were guilty, you should pretend not to know it, to the end that the only class that is still friendly to us may not become hostile.[223]

Then Diodotus again denied appealing to either pity or clemency; urged passing sentence on those rebels who had been brought to Athens for punishment, advised letting the others alone; and sat down. The debate went on. But, in the end, Diodotus's plea for the higher realism, combined perhaps with a compassion which neither he nor any other man dared to show, won by a bare majority. Cleon's decree for massacre was repealed. By this time the trireme they had sent to Mitylene, bearing death and slavery in its hold, had gained a start of about twenty-four hours, but it was bent on so horrible a mission that its crew had rowed halfheartedly. A second trireme was sent after it, bearing life and mercy. The Mitylenian envoys had provided wine and barley for the crew and had promised a large reward if they should reach Mitylene in time. So the oarsmen, as they rowed, ate their barley cakes, kneaded with wine and oil, and they took turns sleeping and rowing. When they arrived, Paches had received the decree of death and was about to start the butchery. The butchery never took place.

The Athenians did not impose tribute on Lesbos. Instead, they confiscated all the land of the island, except that held by loyal Methymna, and divided it into 3,000 allotments. A tenth of these they turned over to the gods. The rest were assigned to Athenian outsettlers, chosen by lot; and the outsettlers rented them to their former owners to work. Athens demolished the walls of Mitylene and seized her navy.

The revolt of Mitylene was suppressed in 427, in the fifth year of the war, but not before Plataea, faithful ally of Athens in Boeotia, had fallen that same summer and had been razed to the ground by the Peloponnesians. In this same year, the plague broke out a second time in Athens, although this time it lasted not two years, but one. Attica was invaded again. Yet, when Leontini, a city in Sicily, sent Gorgias, the famous rhetorician, to beg for Athenian help against Syracuse, Athens sent twenty triremes. In 433, two years before war with Sparta began, she had renewed her treaties with Leontini and Rhegium, a city just across the strait from Messina; and before the war began she was already active in the waters off the west coast of Mainland Greece, where the route to Sicily lay. Now that war had come, Sicily and southern Italy were more interesting than ever to Athens, since some of the Peloponnesian cities depended on grain from those areas. But in this same eventful year, 427, something else happened off the west coast of Mainland Greece that shed a lurid light on one aspect of the war, an aspect that was steadily growing in importance. Civil war broke out in Corcyra.

Corcyra, on the island now called Corfu, had been founded, or taken over from Eretrians, about 625, by colonists from Corinth. With the help of Corinth, Corcyra had founded a colony called Epidamnus, at the site of modern Durazzo, on the coast of Illyria. By 435 the democrats of Epidamnus had expelled the oligarchs, and the oligarchs joined the barbarous Illyrian tribesmen of the mainland to harass the democrats. The democrats appealed for help to their mother-city, Corcyra. When aid was refused, they asked Apollo at Delphi whether they should appeal to Corcyra's mother-city, Corinth, and Apollo advised them to do so. Corinth helped Epidamnus; and Corcyra, annoyed by Corinthian meddling, defeated a Corinthian fleet at sea. Corcyra then proposed a defensive alliance with Athens. Since Athens did not want the second naval power of Hellas aligned against her, she agreed. When Corinth attacked Corcyra's fleet, Athens helped her ally. This collision in 433 between Athens and Corinth led to the revolt of Potidaea in Chalcidice, a city which paid tribute to Athens but was closely bound to its mother-city, Corinth. The affair of Epidamnus and the affair of Potidaea had done much to precipitate the war between Athens and the Peloponnesians. For it was chiefly Corinth that had persuaded Sparta to issue her ultimatum to Athens.

In 427, a group of Corcyrean oligarchs whom Corinth had taken prisoner in a naval battle were released on condition that they should detach Corcyra from her alliance with Athens. These oligarchs entered the Senate-house of Corcyra, attacked the leaders of the popular party and slew them. Then a street battle between oligarchs and democrats broke out, and both sides sent into the countryside and offered freedom to any slaves who would join them. Most of the slaves joined the democrats; whereupon the oligarchs hired 800 mercenaries from the mainland. Another street battle broke out: the democrats fell on the oligarchs, while from the tops of houses women pelted the oligarchs with tiles.

Next day an Athenian general, Nicostratus, arrived with 12 ships and with 500 heavy infantry from Messene. Nicostratus tried to make peace and bring the ringleaders of these riots to trial. But violence again broke out. The pro-Athenian democrats began killing the pro-Spartan oligarchs. Next, they

> went into the temple of Hera, persuaded about fifty of the suppliants there to submit to trial, and condemned them all to death. But most of the suppliants, not having consented to be tried, when they saw what was happening set about destroying one another in the sacred precinct itself, while a few hanged themselves on trees, and still others made away with themselves as best they could. And during the seven days that Eurymedon [an Athenian admiral sent to reinforce Nicostratus], after his arrival, stayed there with his sixty ships, the Corcyraeans continued slaughtering such of their fellow-citizens as they considered to be their personal enemies. The charge they brought was of conspiring to overthrow the democracy, but some were in fact put to death merely to satisfy private enmity, and others, because money was owing to them, were slain by those who had borrowed it. Death in every form ensued, and whatever horrors are wont to be perpetrated at such times all happened then— aye, and even worse. For father slew son, men were dragged from the temples and slain near them, and some were even walled up in the temple of Dionysus and perished there.[224]

Thucydides at this point noted that the war propagated revolution:

> for afterwards practically the whole Hellenic world was convulsed, since in each state the leaders of the democratic factions were at variance with the oligarchs, the former seeking to bring in the Athenians, the latter the Lacedaemonians. And while in time of peace they would have had no pretext for asking their intervention, nor any inclination to do so, yet now that these two states were at war, either faction in the various cities, if it desired a revolution, found it easy to bring in allies also, for the discomfiture at one stroke of its opponents and the strengthening of its own cause. And so there fell upon the cities on account of revolutions many grievous calamities, such as happen and always will happen while human nature is the same, but which are severer or milder, and different in their manifestations, according as the variations in circumstances present themselves in each case. For in peace and prosperity both states and individuals

have gentler feelings, because men are not then forced to face conditions of dire necessity; but war, which robs men of the easy supply of their daily wants, is a rough schoolmaster and creates in most people a temper that matches their condition.[225]

War not only made men's deeds brutal; it twisted men's words:

The ordinary acceptation of words in their relation to things was changed as men thought fit. Reckless audacity came to be regarded as courageous loyalty to party, prudent hesitation as specious cowardice, moderation as a cloak for unmanly weakness, and to be clever in everything was to do naught in anything.[226]

The cause of all these evils was the desire to rule which greed and ambition inspire, and also, springing from them, that ardour which belongs to men who once have become engaged in factious rivalry. For those who emerged as party leaders in the several cities, by assuming on either side a fair-sounding name, the one using as its catch-word "political equality for the masses under the law," the other "temperate aristocracy," while they pretended to be devoted to the common weal, in reality made it their prize; striving in every way to get the better of each other they dared the most awful deeds, and sought revenges still more awful. . . . The result was that though neither had any regard for true piety, yet those who could carry through an odious deed under the cloak of a specious phrase received the higher praise. And citizens who belonged to neither party were continually destroyed by both, either because they would not make common cause with them, or through mere jealousy that they should survive.[227]

So it was that every form of depravity showed itself in Hellas in consequence of its revolutions, and that simplicity, which is the chief element of a noble nature, was laughed to scorn and disappeared, while mutual antagonism of feeling, combined with mistrust, prevailed far and wide. . . . And it was generally those of meaner intellect who won the day; for being afraid of their own defects and of their opponents' sagacity, in order that they might not be worsted in words . . . they boldly resorted to deeds. Their opponents, on the other hand, contemptuously assuming that . . . there was no need to secure by deeds what they might have by wit, were taken off their guard and perished in greater numbers.[228]

. . . At this crisis, when the life of the city had been thrown into utter confusion, human nature, now triumphant over the laws, and accustomed even in spite of the laws to do wrong, took delight in showing that its passions were ungovernable, that it was stronger than justice and an enemy to all superiority. . . . Indeed, men do not hesitate, when they seek to avenge themselves upon others, to abrogate in advance the common principles observed in such cases—those principles upon which depends every man's own hope of salvation should he himself be overtaken by misfortune.[229]

In 426, the year after Mitylene fell and the Peloponnesians razed Plataea and civil war broke out in Corcyra, Athens sent a general named Demosthenes around the Peloponnese to ravage the western coast and outlying islands of Mainland Greece. There Demosthenes was persuaded by the Messenians to attack neutral Aetolia and eventually to pass eastward through Phocis and attack Boeotia from the rear. Meanwhile Nicias and an Athenian army were attacking Boeotia from the east. Aetolian tribesmen were, indeed, numerous and warlike; but they used only light armor and lived in unwalled villages scattered far apart. Almost untouched by the commerce in goods and ideas that had civilized the cities on the Aegean coast of Mainland Greece, they still lived the sort of life all Greeks had once lived. Some of them spoke a Greek which the Athenians could barely understand. Some of them ate their meat raw. Even civilians carried arms. This plan of Demosthenes to conquer central Greece was a reversion to the land imperialism that had followed Cimon's ostracism, that had dazzled Pericles in his younger days of power, that had ended in instructive disaster, and that violated the formula of Themistocles, which Pericles had fervently adopted: Athens was an artificial island whose destiny lay on the sea. The lesson was now learned all over again, and it was written in blood. Among the wooded mountains of Aetolia, tribesmen armed with bow and arrow and familiar with the terrain fell on the heavy infantry of Athens as they wandered in pathless gullies. At last Demosthenes' men lost their way in a forest and the wild tribesmen set the forest afire. The survivors escaped to the sea and took ship back to Athens. Demosthenes, afraid of punishment in Athens, stayed behind. Luckily, a little later, at the head of a force of Acarnanians, he retrieved his military reputation, first by saving the city of Naupactus from an army of Peloponnesians and Aetolians, and then by defeating an army of the Peloponnesians and Aetolians at Olpae on the Ambracian Gulf.

In this sixth year of the war, numerous earthquakes occurred, some of which caused destructive tidal waves on the coasts. In consequence an army of Peloponnesians which was preparing to invade and ravage Attica as usual, when it had reached the Isthmus, turned back, and Attica was spared. Three years earlier, the plague at Athens had apparently shortened a similar invasion. These invasions, which happened in five of the first ten summers of the war, had failed to provoke Athens to the land battle Sparta desired. Nor could the Peloponnesians face a decisive battle with Athens by sea. But the confused struggle in many theaters of war was teaching Athens more than improved naval tactics. Demosthenes, at least, was learning about forests, forest fires, and what light infantry could do with the somewhat despised bow against the traditional heavy infantry of Greece. On their side, Spartans were acquiring some knowledge of the sea and of the skills that sea power could teach. If they were learning their new art more slowly than Athens was learning hers, that was because Athenian infantry could drill not only on islands but on any other land Athenian triremes could defend, while Sparta's raw navy was largely barred by Athens from the drill ground it needed—the sea.

In general, however, the war was destructive, demoralizing, and indecisive. Sparta's traditional caution and conservatism lost her many valuable opportunities, such as the chance to liberate Mitylene. Her bad political judgment in foreign affairs often cost her the support of potential allies. But the Athenian democrats were capable of the same bad judgment, as Diodotus pointed out in his debate with Cleon. And Athens' chief mistake was worse: after the death of Pericles, her cleverness, her quick-wittedness, her inventiveness, her Themistoclean talent for brilliant improvisation repeatedly led her to gallop in all directions, as it were; to fail to concentrate on her main objective, victory through attrition. Pericles had wanted only to convince Sparta that Athens' empire could not be taken from her. The constant use of force was dulling the intelligence of both sides and reducing statesmanship to cunning tactics, far too short-ranged to achieve a solution of the problems common to all Hellas. And it was in Hellas, after all, that both Athens and Sparta were privileged, or condemned, to live.

It was not until 425, the seventh year of the war, that Athens unexpectedly won a serious advantage over Sparta. In the previous year, Athens' allies in Sicily requested help against the growing power of Syracuse and in 425 Athens sent out forty ships, with orders to stop off at Corcyra on their way. For Corcyra, now under democratic government, was suffering from raids by some 500 of her exiled oligarchs who had stationed themselves on a nearby mountain and were receiving help from the Peloponnesians. The Athenians also allowed Demosthenes, the hero of tribal warfare in Acarnania, to go with the Athenian squadron and use it on the Peloponnesian coast if opportunity beckoned. The fleet was forced by a squall to take shelter behind the small peninsula of Pylos, which lay off the western coast of Messenia in southwest Peloponnese. It had been Demosthenes' plan to fortify the hill at the tip of this peninsula. Pylos lay some forty-five miles from Sparta. There was abundant stone and timber with which to wall it off. Moreover, this was the ancient country of Demosthenes' friends, the Messenians, whose ancestors Sparta had "galled with great burdens like asses"230 nearly a century earlier. Only three decades before, the Athenians had rescued some Messenian exiles and had settled them at Naupactus to guard the narrowest part of the Corinthian Gulf. They were now Athens' most loyal allies in the west country. Only the year before they had shared Demosthenes' disaster among the wild Aetolian tribesmen. Only the year before they had taken the chief honors when he defeated the Peloponnesians and their Ambraciot allies at Olpae. He now believed that, with their help, he could raise a Messenian rebellion against the hated Spartan overlords, provided he could make a fortified Pylos, with its ample harborage, a safe base for insurrection.

The commanders of the fleet failed to share his vision. They wanted to hurry on to Corcyra and then to Sicily. But the storm raged on, and partly from boredom the Athenian soldiers suddenly set to work and in six days built the fort Demosthenes longed to see in being. Sparta, though nearby, lay quiet. Her army was, as so often at this season, invading Attica. A religious festival was in progress, as religious festivals so frequently were. Anyhow, the Spartans were confident they could drive off the Athenians whenever they chose to do so. The Athenian commanders now left Demosthenes five of their ships, to which were added two Messenian privateers, and a garrison for his new fort. Then they hurried toward Corcyra. South of his little fortified hill on Pylos lay an island, Sphacteria, nearly three miles long, about half a mile wide, hilly and wooded like Pylos. The Spartans came. They occupied Sphacteria with 420 heavy infantry and their attendant Helots. Though Demosthenes had sent after the Athenian fleet for help, a Peloponnesian fleet from Corcyra got there first and blocked the narrow[231] inlets to the harbor behind Pylos and Sphacteria. The outer shore of Pylos offered no harborage and the Athenians could not hope to base a fleet on it. The Lacedaemonians then prepared to attack Pylos both by land and sea, and Demosthenes manned his land fortifications and the rocky outer shore of Pylos. Ship after ship tried to force a landing, even at the cost of wrecking itself on the rocks. The Spartan who most distinguished himself was a ship's captain named Brasidas, who was severely wounded trying to force his way ashore. All one day and most of the next a spectacle continued that amazed contemporaries: an Athenian army was fighting from the land, where usually Sparta's power was overwhelming—and was defending land that was part of Sparta's own domain at that—against Spartans coming from the sea, where normally the fleets of Athens were supreme. The Spartans failed to force a landing. Then the Athenian fleet returned from Corcyra.

The Peloponnesian fleet would not come out to meet it. But next day, for some reason, the Spartans neglected to close the inlet. The Athenian fleet sailed in, badly battered the Peloponnesians, and proceeded to blockade the Spartan forces on Sphacteria. Sparta was thoroughly alarmed. She requested an armistice to permit her to send envoys to Athens. Meanwhile, Sparta undertook to turn over to the Athenians what was left of her fleet at Pylos, together with all warships then in Laconia. Sparta agreed to make no attack on Demosthenes' fort, and Athens, no attack on the Spartan forces blockaded on Sphacteria. Sparta should be allowed to ship in provisions to Sphacteria. An Athenian ship should carry the Spartan envoys to Athens, and on the envoys' return, Athens would give back to Sparta all the ships now turned over to her. The armistice was accepted.

Arrived at Athens, the Spartan envoys addressed the Assembly with dignity and moderation. They proposed that Athens and Sparta make peace and insist that their allies respect the agreement. They even proposed an alliance between Sparta and Athens. Cleon, the leader of the democratic war party in Athens, persuaded the Assembly, which had recently longed for release from a war that stretched endlessly ahead, to take advantage of Sparta's predicament at Sphacteria and to demand back cities Athens had surrendered two decades ago in order to obtain the so-called Thirty Years' Peace. Since two of these cities were in Megara and none of them belonged to Sparta, the Spartan envoys were scarcely in a position to agree. What they proposed was that the Assembly appoint commissioners with whom they might try to negotiate mutually acceptable terms. Immediately, Cleon assailed them violently for wanting to go behind the backs of the Athenian people. Rather than lose credit with Sparta's allies by trying to negotiate in public with a popular assembly and convinced that the Athenians would agree to no acceptable terms anyhow, the envoys returned to Pylos and Cleon had his war.

When the Spartans now demanded their ships back, the Athenians refused to return them on the grounds that the Spartans had already broken the armistice by attacking Demosthenes' fort. This charge the Spartans denied, and hostilities were resumed. Many Helots won freedom by managing to carry provisions by night to the seaward shore of Sphacteria in small boats. Winter was coming on, and Athens began to worry. It would be difficult to convoy provisions in winter seas to her besieged garrison on Pylos and to the Athenian ships patrolling the inner shore of Sphacteria. The Assembly thoroughly regretted taking Cleon's advice. At this juncture Cleon rose to defend his policy. He pointed at Nicias, one of the ten elected generals of Athens and the leader of the conservatives in Athens ever since the death of Pericles. If, said Cleon tauntingly, the Assembly had men for generals, they could take Sphacteria and capture the Spartans now on it. If he, Cleon, were general, he could do it himself within twenty days. Nicias promptly rose and resigned his office in favor of Cleon. Cleon showed reluctance, but the Assembly clamored that he should go. Cornered, he went. Lacking military knowledge himself, he chose Demosthenes, who was still at Pylos, as his colleague. The conservatives were delighted: either the expedition would succeed and Athens would capture the Spartans, or, better still, it would fail, and Athens would get rid of their opponent, Cleon.

Demosthenes had not dared attack Sphacteria hitherto because the Spartans had the protection of a wood, and Demosthenes had learned the year before in Aetolia what that could mean. But, meanwhile, through an accident, the bulk of the forest on Sphacteria had burned and the danger of ambush was gone. Then Cleon arrived with reinforcements. In addition to his heavy infantry, Demosthenes threw into Sphacteria men from his ships' crews and—something which, again, Aetolia had taught him to value—archers, who would attack the flanks and rear of the Spartans. These light troops landed with sinking hearts at the thought of attacking the famous heavy infantry of Sparta, but they soon learned that they could succeed. The Spartans were not trained to cope with these nimble bowmen. Dust and ashes rose from the newly burned wood and blinded the Spartan infantry. They were exhausted from lack of adequate food. They were finally caught between a cross fire of arrows and began retreating. Cleon and Demosthenes, anxious to capture them alive and take them back to Athens, called on them to lay down their arms. A truce was arranged, and the Spartans sent to the Lacedaemonians on the mainland to ask for instructions. The reply came back: "The Lacedaemonians bid you decide your case for yourselves, but do nothing dishonorable."[232] The Spartans on Sphacteria surrendered. Of the 420 heavy infantry, 292 Lacedaemonians remained alive, of whom some 120 were Spartans.

Hellas was thunderstruck. A Spartan force had surrendered rather than die. What was it Demaratus had said to Xerxes on the beach near Doriscus? The Spartans "must never flee from the battle before whatsoever odds, but abide at their post and there conquer or die."[233] Those words were signed at Thermopylae. But now, when someone tauntingly asked of one of the Spartans who had surrendered on Sphacteria whether his slain comrades were brave men, the Spartan answered that any arrow which could distinguish a brave man from a coward would be a very valuable weapon.[234] Some of the exiled Messenians in Demosthenes' army were making incursions on the mainland of their ancient country. Helots were deserting from the Spartan army. Again Spartan envoys went to Athens, but Athens was in no mood to negotiate. Cleon had made good his boast that he himself could capture Sphacteria and bring its defenders alive to Athens within twenty days; he had done so; and the democratic war-party was drunk with victory.

In the same year, 425, the Athenian fleet continued to Corcyra and helped the democrats force the surrender of the Corcyrean oligarchs on the mountain nearby. Formally, they surrendered to Athens, but the democrats tricked them into breaking an agreement they had made with the Athenians and the oligarchs were given up to their opponents, who

shut them up in a large building; afterwards they led them out in groups of twenty and marched them down between two lines of hoplites stationed on either side, the prisoners being bound to one another and receiving blows and stabs from the men who stood in the lines, if any of these perchance saw among them a personal enemy; and men with scourges walked by their sides to quicken the steps of such as proceeded too slowly on the way.

In this manner about sixty men were led out and killed without the knowledge of the men who remained in the house, who supposed that their companions were being led out in order to be transferred to some other place. But when they perceived what was going on, or were told by somebody, they appealed to the Athenians and urged them, if they wished to kill them, to do so with their own hands; and they refused thenceforth to leave the house, and declared that they would not allow anyone to enter if they could prevent it. Nor had the Corcyraeans themselves any intention of trying to force their way in by the doors, but climbing on to the top of the building and breaking through the roof they hurled tiles and shot arrows upon them from above. The men inside tried to defend themselves as best they could, and at the same time most of them set to work to destroy themselves by thrusting into their throats the arrows which the enemy had shot or by strangling themselves with the cords from some beds that happened to be in the place or with strips made from their own garments. Thus for the greater part of the night—for night fell upon their misery—dispatching themselves in every fashion and struck by the missiles of the men on the roof, they perished. When day came the Corcyraeans loaded the bodies on wagons, laying them lengthwise and crosswise, and hauled them out of the city; but the women who had been captured in the fort were sold into captivity. In such fashion the Corcyraeans from the mountain were destroyed by the popular party, and the revolution, which had lasted long, ended thus, so far at least as this war was concerned; for there were no longer enough of the oligarchs left to be of any account. But the Athenians sailed for Sicily, whither they had set out in the first place, and proceeded to carry on the war in conjunction with their allies in the island.[235]

The next year the Athenians, who still held their base at Pylos, managed, with Nicias as general, to seize the island of Cythera, about six miles south of Laconia, and from the island made repeated and unexpected raids on the coast of Laconia itself. Morale at Sparta sank. A famous rhetra of Lycurgus was being justified: they had fought Athens long enough for Athens to learn how to ravage more thoroughly at least the coasts of their own Laconia. The Spartans were alarmed by the possibility of a Helot revolt. They sent repeated embassies to Athens in a vain effort to negotiate peace. They had lost confidence in their own strategy. In desperation they organized a force of cavalry and even of archers—

they, citizens of an unwalled polis, who had from time out of memory counted on heavy infantry and despised light-armed bowmen. They were not even able to save their Aeginetan allies, whom they had settled in Thyrea on their Argolid frontier in the first year of the war, when the Athenians had driven them out of Aegina and converted that island into a colony of Athenian outsettlers. The Athenians raided Thyrea, killed many of the colonists from Aegina, captured the rest, and took them to Athens. There, out of their ancient hatred for Aegina, they slew without mercy all the Aeginetan prisoners. The same year, under the leadership of Hermocrates of Syracuse, the Sicilians assembled at Gela and put an end to the war in which Athens had for years taken part. The Athenian fleet sailed home to Athens; but there the Assembly banished two commanders and fined a third, Eurymedon, for having quit Sicily. By now the Athenian war party had reached that point of optimism where a setback could be ascribed only to treachery or cowardice.

Before the year 424 closed, the Athenians captured Nisaea, the port of Megara facing Salamis, with the help of a democratic faction in Nisaea. But they failed to win Megara itself, since just then a Peloponnesian force moved up, led by that Spartan who had most distinguished himself in the attack on Demosthenes at Pylos, Brasidas. But the success at Nisaea set the Athenians dreaming again of the land empire they had once won and lost when Pericles was young. Supported by democrats in Boeotia, they launched a three-pronged attack on that country. At Delium they suffered overwhelming defeat. Meanwhile, Brasidas had managed to march northward through Thessaly with 1,700 infantry. The people of Thessaly were pro-Athenian, but the country was governed by pro-Spartan oligarchs. Even so, Brasidas needed tact and speed if Sparta were to reach Perdiccas, a Macedonian king, and Athens' subject cities in Chalcidice. Both Perdiccas and these cities were soliciting Sparta's aid. Perdiccas wanted help against a neighboring Macedonian king, and the subject cities were eager to revolt.

The Spartans had sent Brasidas north for several reasons. They hoped to divert Athens from her raids on their coasts. They saw a chance to send 700 of their Helots out of the country, armed as heavy infantry. So frightened were they of a Helot insurrection that they even called on all Helots who claimed to have distinguished themselves against the enemy to come forward and receive their liberty. Some 2,000 did. Free at last, they crowned themselves and visited the temples. All of them disappeared, and no one seemed to know how. The Spartans had calculated that their ruse would deliver into their hands the most spirited and hence the most dangerous of their restless state serfs.

Brasidas was not only a brave fighter and a skillful strategist, who moved rapidly and decisively. He had the ability as a speaker as well as the tact that most Spartans notoriously lacked. But, above all, he had a policy, something beyond merely injuring the enemy. He promised in the name of Sparta that she would not interfere with the political constitution of any city she might help to free itself from Athenian domination. But, as Brasidas said at Acanthus,

> if you meet these offers of mine with the plea that you cannot join us, but, because you are well-disposed to us, claim that you should not suffer by your refusal, and maintain that the liberty I offer seems to you to be not without its dangers, and that it is right to offer it to those who can receive it but not to force it on anyone against his will, I shall make the gods and heroes of your country my witnesses that, though I come for your good, I cannot persuade you, and I shall try, by ravaging your territory, to compel you; and in that case I shall not consider that I am doing wrong, but that I have some justification, for two compelling reasons: first, in the interest of the Lacedaemonians, that with all your professed good-will toward them they may not, in case you shall not be brought over, be injured by the money you pay as tribute to the Athenians; secondly, that the Hellenes may not be prevented by you from escaping bondage. For otherwise we should not be justified in acting thus, nor are we Lacedaemonians bound, except on the plea of some common good, to confer liberty on those who do not wish it. Nor, again, are we seeking after empire, but rather we are eager to stop others from acquiring it; and we should do wrong to the majority, if, when we are bringing independence to all, we permitted you to stand in the way. In view of these things, deliberate wisely, and strive to be the first to inaugurate freedom for the Hellenes and to lay up for yourselves undying fame; thus you will save your own property from injury and confer upon your whole state the fairest name.[236]

On into the cold Macedonian winter he fought. He liberated Acanthus and a number of Athens' other subject cities. At last he reached Athens' most valuable possession on the northern coast of the Aegean, the city of Amphipolis, on the Thracian bank of the river Strymon. Amphipolis commanded the resources of nearby Mount Pangaeus. Three miles downstream, at the mouth of the Strymon, lay the port of Eion. Across the river from Amphipolis lay the smaller city of Argilus. Argilus admitted Brasidas, and Spartan sympathizers in Argilus were in secret correspondence with fellow conspirators inside Amphipolis. There were two Athenian commanders charged with protecting the area. One of them, Eucles, was inside beleaguered Amphipolis. The other, Thucydides, the historian, was at the Isle of Thasos, half a day's sail away. Eucles got word to Thucydides to come quickly and help defend Amphipolis, and Thucydides with seven ships sailed promptly to Eion. But by that time, Brasidas had persuaded Amphipolis to admit him. He failed to dislodge Thucydides from Eion.

Athens was thoroughly alarmed. The navy counted heavily on Amphipolis for the timber it constantly needed, and the gold and silver mines Amphipolis also commanded had helped finance the war. The bridge at Amphipolis now gave Peloponnesians access to the Thracian coast and perhaps to the Hellespont itself, Athens' life line to Black Sea grain. Brasidas, by proclaiming the liberation of Hellas and by acting with model clemency, was encouraging Athens' Mainland possessions to revolt, where Spartan tactlessness and brutality during the revolt of Mitylene had produced the opposite effect. Torone fell. Lecythus fell. By the spring of 423, the Athenians were ready to sign a one-year armistice with Sparta. This would give them a chance to plan defenses against Brasidas. The Spartans hoped to convert the armistice into a peace and thereby get back the Spartan prisoners whom Cleon and Demosthenes had triumphantly brought home from the island of Sphacteria.

The one-year armistice was concluded, but Brasidas's political warfare had now so shaken Athenian rule in Chalcidice that city after city came over to him. When the armistice terms officially reached Chalcidice, Brasidas objected that one of the cities he had acquired, Scione, had revolted two days before the date on which the armistice had been signed; he accordingly refused to give Scione back. This point of Brasidas's Athens denied, and Cleon got a decree from the Assembly that Scione should be reduced and all its citizens put to death. Brasidas had now become entangled in the politics of his ally, Perdiccas the Macedonian. Athens sent Nicias and another commander to Chalcidice with 50 ships and over 1,700 troops. Perdiccas suddenly changed sides, allied himself with Athens, and persuaded the Thessalians not to allow Peloponnesian reinforcements for Brasidas to pass through. For Sparta to reinforce him by sea was, of course, impossible: as usual, the sea belonged to Athens' navy. Straight through the one-year truce the struggle in Thrace continued. Elsewhere, the armistice proved effective.

The next year, 422, when the armistice had ended, Cleon persuaded the Athenian Assembly to let him go to Thrace. He took 1,200 heavy infantry, 300 horse, and 30 ships from Athens, and a larger land force of allies. His brilliant success at Pylos, when his political opponent, Nicias, had resigned as general, made him confident he could drive out Brasidas, who had first won fame at Pylos too, and that he could regain Athens' jewel, Amphipolis. Outside of the walls of Amphipolis, he awaited reinforcements of troops from Perdiccas of Macedonia as well as a contingent of Thracian mercenaries. The impatience of his troops to attack induced him to lead them near the city walls. Brasidas made a sudden sally; Cleon's troops panicked; he himself fled and was killed. But Brasidas, too, was wounded. He was carried back into the city and lived long enough to learn that once more he was victorious. He had been the most intelligent, and therefore the most dangerous, opponent the ten years of warfare had brought against Athens. He had won his first fame in the Spartan assault from the sea on Pylos and died three short years later at Amphipolis in Thrace. Sparta had never given him adequate support, partly because Athens held the sea and because sending reinforcements to Brasidas by land was not always possible, given Thessaly's dubious and fluctuating attitude; but partly also because he was envied by other Spartans at home. He had been skillful, tactful, gentle, modest, honest, and loyal to Sparta. But he had also been those things in Thrace; and two generations before, Pausanias, another Spartan general, had taught Sparta caution in exporting generals there. Pausanias had been arrogant, harsh, foolish, and treasonous. Now Brasidas was dead and, with Sparta's allies standing to arms, he was buried at public expense in the market place of Amphipolis. The citizens of this polis that he had liberated ceased to pay public honors to their Athenian founder and decreed those honors now to the Spartan hero, Brasidas, with annual games and offerings.

With Cleon and Brasidas dead, Athens and Sparta negotiated a peace, to be binding for fifty years. The treaty was largely the work of Nicias, the Athenian general, and Pausanias's son, Plistoanax, the restored king of the Lacedaemonians. The conservative Nicias was now the most influential leader in Athens. He had, for years, even when Cleon defeated him in matters of policy, been more respected than Cleon, largely because he was above bribery, whereas few Athenian politicians were. He was Well-fathered, he was rich, he was no oligarchic schemer against democracy, he had won an excellent record as a general, and he discharged his political and religious duties to the polis with zeal and generosity. It is true that his religion seemed to incline him to superstition and to an inordinate interest in auguries and prophecies, that he was timid when faced with demagogues like Cleon, and that he was quick to buy off informers and blackmailers. Much of his income he derived from the state silver mines at Laurium, which he leased and worked with a large number of slaves at a handsome profit. The peace he negotiated with Sparta brought him immense popularity in war-weary Athens and was commonly called the Peace of Nicias.[237]

Just before the Thirty Years' Peace a quarter of a century earlier, Plistoanax had been deposed as one of Sparta's kings. With the recently built land empire of Athens crumbling, and Plistoanax about to invade Attica, the king had unaccountably led his army home again. He had therefore been charged with accepting a bribe from Pericles. He had fled to western Arcadia and had built a house for himself, half of which lay conveniently within the sanctuary of a temple to Zeus. But, whenever the Lacedaemonians sent envoys to Delphi to consult Apollo they were told by the god to bring home the seed of the demigod son of Zeus—Plistoanax, the Heraclid, the descendant of Zeus's hero son, Heracles. The Spartans had finally brought him back. His enemies were now murmuring that he had bribed the prophetess at Delphi and that his unjust restoration was the cause of their many disasters in the present war with Athens. Plistoanax could hope to end the accusation by ending the disasters, and the best way to end the disasters was to negotiate a peace with Athens. He and Nicias made peace.

The Peace of Nicias provided that Amphipolis would be given back to Athens. Certain other cities were to be restored. Any citizens of these places who did not wish to remain under Athenian leadership would be permitted to emigrate, taking their property with them. The cities were to be self-governing, provided they paid their contributions to Athens as originally assessed by Aristides. Athens was to free certain other cities, though she retained her strong point at Pylos. All prisoners on both sides were to be released, including of course the Spartans captured at Sphacteria. It was Sparta's determination to recover these last that had made her return Amphipolis. The ten-year butchery seemed to be over at last, but it was a bad sign that when Sparta and her allies voted to accept the treaty, Boeotia, Corinth, Elis, and Megara voted nay.

Hellas lay exhausted and demoralized; but meanwhile, three famous Athenians had been commenting on the war. When the Peloponnesian War began, Thucydides judged it would be the greatest war Hellenic man had yet known, and he had begun to chronicle its events. He displayed in his history neither the buoyant confidence nor the charming, childlike curiosity nor the zest for anecdote of Herodotus, who had so recently won his prize from the Athenians for his history of Persia's invasion of Hellas. "The absence of romance in my history," wrote Thucydides,

> will, I fear, detract somewhat from its interest; but if it be judged useful by those inquirers who desire an exact knowledge of the past as an aid to the interpretation of the future, which in the course of human things must resemble if it does not reflect it, I shall be content. In fine, I have written my work, not as an essay which is to win the applause of the moment, but as a possession for all time.[238]

Thucydides served in the war he wrote about. An aristocrat, like Pericles, he rallied early to Pericles' leadership and democratic program. When he was around the age of thirty, Pericles died, and Thucydides watched with disgust the self-interest and fumbling of the Olympian's successors. When Amphipolis fell, Thucydides and his fellow commander in Thrace, Eucles, were banished for their failure to save the city from the Spartan, Brasidas. In exile, Thucydides had a chance to watch the progress of the war from the new vantage point of neutral and even enemy lands. Had the drama of Aeschylus and Sophocles taught him the tragic sense of life that matured to intellectual adulthood so many citizens of Athens? Had Aeschylus and Sophocles taught him to discern in the hurrying events of the Peloponnesian War the pattern of a vast tragedy of which Athens was the hero? As a polis suddenly risen to power and pride, Athens developed the blindness of power, the faith in violence, the necessity to give hostages to fortune, the hybris of Agamemnon on his return from Troy and of Oedipus at Thebes. The attempt of Athens to solve one problem led to the creation of other problems. She grew confused, lost her purpose, redoubled her efforts, and arrived at the Peace of Nicias, a peace that promised more violence to come. There would be suffering that would inspire in Thucydides and his readers both pity and terror, and perhaps bring in the end frightful and chastening catastrophe and, through suffering, a kind of knowledge. Just such knowledge had come also, if not always to the tragic heroes of Aeschylus and Sophocles, then at least to some of those who watched their tragedies before the temple of the god Dionysus.

Herodotus, too, had found in a chain of historic events the same tragic pattern. Herodotus's hero had been Xerxes, or Xerxes and his powerful empire. Xerxes had hurled the strength of that empire at the little city-states of Greece, had exulted in his pride, his hybris, had affronted the gods themselves, and had suffered great catastrophe. But there was an exuberant faith in human existence in Herodotus, a gaiety and serenity reminiscent of the mysterious smile on the faces of those painted limestone statues which Ionia and Athens had created in the sixth century. And his confident faith in the power and justice of Zeus recalled somehow the robust and soaring faith of Aeschylus in the midst of the horror and disaster he projected in his plays.

Thucydides, on the other hand, with heavy heart was watching his beloved Athens pick up the power and cares and cruelties of empire. He was watching freedom turn to license and folly. He was watching Hellas tear itself to pieces, as it polarized into pro-Athenian demos and pro-Spartan oligarchy, and as polis after polis was torn apart and plunged into civil strife. His history exhibited therefore some of the gravity as well as some of the elaborate skill that his readers could see in some marble statue of the days of Pericles, with its still serene but slightly melancholy face. His careful account of events displayed the intricate plot and the skillful, sophisticated study of human motive and human conflict that Sophocles had exhibited more than Aeschylus; and, just as in many of Sophocles' tragedies, so in this history by Thucydides, the gods were somehow in the background and even there did not transcend their reported interventions. In Thucydides' sober report, oracles certainly affected decisions of state. Professional diviners certainly influenced men like the rich and pious Nicias. Oaths were often kept because men believed the gods existed, or might exist. But the necessities of man's own existence, his urgent and clamorous physical existence, reduced the gods to stage properties more than they did in Herodotus's history of an earlier war. Herodotus's tragedy of Xerxes, unlike Thucydides' tragedy of the School of Hellas, was rendered luminous by the triumph of human freedom, which Zeus the Liberator granted as boon to those who stood ready to die for freedom's sake.

Thucydides' tragic sense of life did not lead him away from concern for historical fact, but it did supply him with a sure and severe sense of relevance: he knew which of his many facts held permanent significance for his own and for future generations.[239] It led him also to use a kind of dramatic dialogue, in the shape of formal speeches, that gave a due content of thought and purpose to both sides in the bloody conflict and kept that conflict from sinking to the level of mere animal violence. He warned his readers in advance that he could not vouch for the strict accuracy of the speeches, even when he had heard them personally; but he adhered "as closely as possible to the general sense of what was actually said."[240]

Another Athenian who found himself living through this war did not try to write its history, for he was born a poet. Euripides started life around 485, a year before Aeschylus won his first prize for tragedy, and Euripides was already around thirty when Aeschylus, now in his last years, departed for Sicily. That had left Sophocles unrivaled in tragic poetry at Athens. Euripides presented his own first tragedy in 455, the year Aeschylus died. Out of some ninety plays[241] he wrote, only four won him victory. In his latter years he lived in Thessaly and at the court of King Archelaus in Macedonia, where he died about 406. Sophocles, though a decade older, outlived him a year. Tragedy did not normally treat of contemporary themes, except by implication; and Euripides therefore commented on these war-torn years only in a very special sense. But, compared with the slightly older Sophocles, who after all lived through the same horrors, his tragedies reflected in curious ways the disintegration of Hellas. The very plots of his plays faltered when compared with those of Aeschylus and Sophocles, as if life were becoming less intelligible, less whole. Euripides excelled less in plot than in character; and, even here, where his two elder fellow poets showed the heart of man by what man did and thought as well as felt, Euripides psychologized and analyzed. He was often less interested in those who performed great actions than in those who suffered great passions. He was especially interested in the weak and oppressed—in women, in children, in slaves. It was not the heroic, masculine, ruthless courage of Achilles that shone from a tragedy like the

Trojan Women, but the agony and grief of the victims, such as the dead
Hector's mother, Hecuba, who lived through the deliberate murder of
Hector's tiny son, hurled from the walls of Troy when Troy was sacked
and burned. In the *Trojan Women* the old queen held the tiny corpse
of her grandson in her arms and cried:

Lay down the circled shield of Hector on the ground:
a hateful thing to look at; it means no love to me.
Achaeans! All your strength is in your spears, not in
the mind. What were you afraid of, that it made you kill
this child so savagely? That Troy, which fell, might be
raised from the ground once more? Your strength meant nothing, then.
When Hector's spear was fortunate, and numberless
strong hands were there to help him, we were still destroyed.
Now when the city is fallen and the Phrygians slain,
this baby terrified you? I despise the fear
which is pure terror in a mind unreasoning.

O darling child, how wretched was this death. You might
have fallen fighting for your city, grown to man's
age, and married, and with the king's power like a god's,
and died happy, if there is any happiness here.
But no. You grew to where you could see and learn, my child,
yet your mind was not old enough to win advantage
of fortune. How wickedly, poor boy, your fathers' walls,
Apollo's handiwork, have crushed your pitiful head
tended and trimmed to ringlets by your mother's hand,
and the face she kissed once, where the brightness now is blood
shining through the torn bones—too horrible to say more.
O little hands, sweet likeness of Hector's once,
now you lie broken at the wrists before my feet;
and mouth beloved whose words were once so confident,
you are dead; and all was false, when you would lean across
my bed, and say: "Mother, when you die I will cut
my long hair in your memory, and at your grave
bring companies of boys my age, to sing farewell."
It did not happen; now I, a homeless, childless, old
woman must bury your poor corpse, which is so young.
Alas for all the tendernesses, my nursing care,
and all your slumbers gone. What shall the poet say,

what words will he inscribe upon your monument?
Here lies a little child the Argives killed, because
they were afraid of him. That? The epitaph of Greek shame.
You will not win your father's heritage, except
for this, which is your coffin now: the brazen shield.

O shield, who guarded the strong shape of Hector's arm:
the bravest man of all, who wore you once, is dead.
How sweet the impression of his body on your sling,
and at the true circle of your rim the stain of sweat
where in the grind of his many combats Hector leaned
his chin against you, and the drops fell from his brow!

Take up your work now; bring from what is left some robes
to wrap the tragic dead. The gods will not allow us
to do it right. But let him have what we can give.

That mortal is a fool who, prospering, thinks his life
has any strong foundation; since our fortune's course
of action is the reeling way a madman takes,
and no one person is ever happy all the time.[242]

This was Euripides' comment on war's glory. It was as if the Peloponnesian War had broken him, had broken his dramatic plots, had left
his sweetly lyrical choruses without dramatic function, had left his most
typical tragedies filled with pathos whenever they did not border perilously
on melodrama. It was as if the gods—or Aeschylus's gods, anyhow—had
withdrawn for all time to Olympus, and could be introduced on the stage
now only by a derrick[243] which let them down from above. It was as if even
then the gods could not convince all of the spectators, could not, perhaps,
convince Euripides himself. Did he not make Heracles, own hero son of
Zeus, speak with blasphemous melancholy to Theseus?

Then Zeus—whoever Zeus may be—begot me
for Hera's hatred. Take no offense, old man,
for I count you my father now, not Zeus.[244]

Further on in the same tragedy, Heracles made another Euripidean statement to Theseus. And if all agreed that Heracles was the son of Zeus, many
believed that Theseus was the son of Posidon, Zeus's own brother. Faced
with the gods of Homer and Hesiod, faced with the gods of his con-

temporaries, Aeschylus and Sophocles, this time Euripides made Heracles
say:

> but I do not believe the gods commit
> adultery, or bind each other in chains.
> I never did believe it; I never shall;
> nor that one god is tyrant of the rest.
> If god is truly god, he is perfect,
> lacking nothing. These are poets' wretched lies.[245]

Whether it was his religious skepticism or the weakened structure of
his dramatic plots, his four victories in the contests for tragedies were
disappointingly few. But may not his deepest frustration have derived from
the fact that, as Hellas moved into what looked like a death agony of
vengeance and violence and as fear and hate and even bloodshed tore
the Polis itself apart, the audience for real tragedy began to disintegrate?
That audience had formed, in the great days of Aeschylus, a Polis in the
ancient sense, a community of gods and men engaged in a dialogue
of words and deeds, in full personal encounter: persons all, divine and
human, never mere things. There had indeed been nameless crime, searing
remorse, but also redemption from pollution, for god, for man, and for
the Polis too. But there had always remained community, whether in hus-
banding the meager, crowded land, or in seeking a like home far beyond the
sea, or in fighting Asians at day's end on some bitter battlefield, or in
the rhythm of the oars as the triremes charged, or in the great religious processions when men broke bread with their gods, or here in the Theater
of Dionysus where, with high and ancient ritual, with painted scenery,
with dance and song, men who had acted in all these dramas of their
common life watched others act out before them in formal mask and
costume the actions that made men what men were, a community of
feeling, thinking, speaking persons, and not a lonely herd of dumb beasts.

The decade of blood that bought the fragile Peace of Nicias provoked
a comment also from a third Athenian, this time neither an historian nor
a tragedian but the comedian, Aristophanes. He brought out his first
comedy[246] in 427, the year in which Cleon argued for mass murder in
Mitylene, in which Plataea fell, and in which civil war broke out in Corcyra.
His comedy won first prize and by the time the Peace of Nicias came,
six years later, he had already surpassed in fame older and more famous
rivals such as Eupolis and Cratinus.[247] While Attic tragedy portrayed the

noble and the great and the godlike, Attic comedy portrayed the ignoble, the low, the coward afraid of his own shadow, the glutton and the woman-izer, the absurdly impractical man, the inveterate cheat. It showed these petty people and their acts and laughed at them hilariously and infec-tiously. Precisely because men had the power to learn how to be brave, to exercise self-control, to make wise practical decisions, to treat their fellow men justly—in short, precisely because a man could learn to let his mind and will guide his bodily appetites—the all too familiar sight of the man whose bodily appetites guided his mind and will into petty catastrophe awoke ridicule and restored sanity.

Comedy had sprung from the ancient village comus, or revel, in which buffoons fought, in which actors hurled ribald insults at each other or at members of the audience, in which the chorus sang and danced, often with obscene gestures, and in which the action was likely to end with the comic hero being borne off in hilarious triumph to the bed of his new bride. In Athens, comedy had inherited or developed as many conventions as tragedy: the comic mask, the grotesque costume, the painted scenery, the song of the chorus, gloriously bawdy, or sometimes a movingly beautiful lyric that pictured the Attic countryside, the unrestrained dance, and the frequent gibes at contemporary events, at the very important people who gave themselves airs, even at persons in the audience. The obscenity that abounded in most comedies was not something slipped in to spice dull lines, it was integral to the play. That any animal as godlike as man should remain so much an animal as to be constantly fornicating, urinating, and defecating—especially if he defecated from terror—struck Athens as enormously funny.[248]

To achieve his Olympic laughter, Aristophanes had to submit to the strenuous discipline of Thalia, the comic muse.[249] For example, when the *Acharnians* showed a private citizen of Athens, weary of the war, now in its seventh year, making a private peace with Sparta, Aristophanes got good comedy. The year that Nicias was negotiating his peace with Sparta, Aristophanes' laughter came loud and clear. He presented the *Peace* at the Great Dionysia, and on the day after that festival Athens and Sparta agreed on the terms of peace. In the *Peace* a low character named Trygaeus, despairing of ever seeing the long war end, had determined to climb to heaven and try to get Zeus himself to stop the war. But Trygaeus' ladder had broken, so now he tried riding to heaven on a huge dung beetle.

At this point the stage derrick Euripides so often used to lower a god to earth was employed to help the dung beetle, with Trygaeus astride him, to soar above the theater and to reach Zeus in heaven. Yet, on his precarious voyage, Trygaeus had time to cry out:

> Ah! machinist, take great care of me. There is already a wind whirling round my navel; take great care or, from sheer fright, I shall form food for my beetle.[250]

To portray the cowardice of a comic hero by making him fear that he would defecate was a typical Aristophanic device. And the freedom for an actor to address the audience or a stagehand without fear of destroying the dramatic illusion was also Aristophanic. For in a sense there was no illusion to destroy. The spectators lost themselves in tragedy, lived it with the persons represented before them, and could not safely be reminded that they were only at the theater. But a comedy could remind them. They were not expected to identify themselves too profoundly with the characters represented: these characters were obviously too contemptible, too ridiculous, for real sympathy. Comedy mocked the great men who controlled war and peace. It mocked the spectators who let them do it. It mocked itself. It even mocked the gods.

Trygaeus reached Zeus's palace in heaven only to learn from Hermes that Zeus and the other gods had become so annoyed with the follies of the Greeks that they had retired to the farthest end of the dome of heaven and had placed Polemos, or War, in their own dwelling with full power to do as he pleased with the Greeks. But why? asked Trygaeus. "Because," answered Hermes,

> they have afforded you an opportunity for peace more than once, but you have always preferred war. If the Laconians got the very slightest advantage, they would exclaim, "By the Twin Brethren! the Athenians shall smart for this." If, on the contrary, the latter triumphed and the Laconians came with peace proposals, you would say, "By Demeter, they want to deceive us. No, by Zeus, we will not hear a word; they will always be coming as long as we hold Pylos."[251]

Moreover, War had cast Peace into a pit and had now brought a huge mortar in which to pound up all the cities of Greece. But War needed a pestle. He sent his slave, Tumult, to Athens to fetch one, but Athens' pestle, "the tanner who ground Greece to powder,"[252] was lost, for

Cleon had fallen at Amphipolis. Tumult was then sent to Sparta, but Sparta had lent her pestle to the Thracians, who had lost it; for Brasidas, the spectators in the theater knew, had died at Amphipolis too.

Then the Chorus, composed of laborers and farmers from various Greek states, helped Trygaeus hoist Peace out of the pit where War had thrown her. At last she emerged; and with her, Opora, goddess of Fruitfulness, and Theoria, goddess of Spectacle. But Peace was angry. After the battle of Pylos, she complained, she had offered Athens a truce three times, only to have the Assembly vote each offer down. Trygaeus finally persuaded Peace that Athens was really done with war. Then he returned to Athens and to the spectators of the play, accompanied by the two lovely companions of Peace: Fruitfulness and Spectacle. And Trygaeus remarked,

> Ah! it's a rough job getting to the gods! my legs are as good as broken through it.

Then, turning to the spectators,

> How small you were, to be sure, when seen from heaven! you had all the appearance too of being great rascals; but seen close, you look even worse.[253]

A delegation of armorers arrived, terrified by the prospect of losing their swollen war profits, but Trygaeus scorned them. He offered to buy a couple of helmet crests to use for dusting the table and to buy a breastplate to use as a thunder-mug. Then the beautiful Fruitfulness, whom Hermes had given Trygaeus to wed, appeared onstage. The bridegroom was borne triumphantly off, to the traditional bridal cry, "Oh! Hymen! oh! Hymenaeus!"

In some ways, the commentary of Aristophanes the comic poet on the ten terrible years of massacre, vengeance, betrayal, and brutalization was more pregnant than either the somber account of Thucydides the historian or the tragic pathos of Euripides, as first Hellas and then the Polis itself began to disintegrate. For through sane laughter Aristophanes achieved a godlike view of the war. His comic hero had ridden on a dung beetle to the palace of Zeus himself and had seen men as the gods could always see them, and "How small you were, to be sure, when seen from heaven!" It was a rough job getting to the gods. Possibly Aeschylus himself could no longer have done it; for the audience, the Polis, had too far lost the tragic sense of life. In a measure, Euripides did it, but his tragic world lacked the wholeness of the tragic deed, and, anyhow, did the gods exist? Thucydides got nearer, if not to the gods, then at least to ideas, to intelligibility, by writing, not tragedy, but history. But, when the Polis had slipped; when, seen from heaven, it looked smaller and smaller; when, seen close, it looked worse; then, perhaps, only a dung beetle could take one to the gods for help. Not to see the face of Zeus, who had withdrawn from men in disgust, but at least to talk with the caretaker of his palace, Hermes. And Hermes could give crucial information on how to find Peace.

Since the Peace of Nicias was never signed by Sparta's chief allies, Athens agreed to an alliance with Sparta for fifty years, under which Athens gave back the prisoners from Sphacteria. This was Nicias' idea, and by it Athens lost her chief means of exerting pressure on Sparta to fulfill Sparta's part of the bargain. Foremost of those at Athens who wished to cancel the new treaty with Sparta was Alcibiades, the former ward of Pericles and now a political rival of Nicias.

Alcibiades was still in his early thirties. He came of illustrious lineage, and although the people of Athens insisted on political democracy, a famous family name was still a help to a young man ambitious to lead. Alcibiades' father, Clinias, had fallen at Coronea in 447, the battle Pericles would have chosen not to fight, the battle that symbolized the end of his early dream of expansion on the mainland. This Clinias was not only a eupatrid, one of the well-fathered; he belonged to a clan whose actual name was Eupatrid. His wife was an Alcmeonid, as was the mother of Pericles, and as Clisthenes had been.

The home in which Alcibiades grew up was not only the political center of Athens: it was also a center of philosophy and of art and of letters. Moreover, his brilliant, restless mind led him to join the young men who gathered around the philosopher Socrates. Socrates recognized his brilliance; fell under the spell of his personal beauty and the enormous personal charm for which the young man was famous throughout Athens; tried to strengthen him in his search for wisdom; and recognized his dangerous love for applause. This exuberant, dazzling, handsome youth, by turns ingratiating and imperious, drunken reveler and victorious athlete, adored by women, imitated—even to a slight speech defect—by other young dandies about town, attracted older men to the romantic homosexual relation which Hellenic custom allowed, but did not attract Socrates.

Socrates wanted, not the young man's body, but his mind. He wanted to provoke that mind to do its proper work. In the summer of 432 both of them left with the heavy infantry for Potidaea, which was rebelling against Athens. There, muffled miserably against the cold of a northern winter, its soldiers' feet wrapped in fleeces, the army conducted its siege; there Socrates and Alcibiades were messmates. Socrates saved Alcibiades' life in battle; and, when the generals wished later to award the prize of valor to the famous young blood, Alcibiades insisted in vain that it should go to Socrates. Eight years later they met on another battlefield, when the Boeotians defeated the Athenians at Delium. The heavy infantry was in rout. This time Alcibiades was serving in the cavalry and was able to protect Socrates on the retreat.

That same year, 424, Alcibiades, still under thirty, tried his hand at private diplomacy. Trading on the fact that his father's father, also named Alcibiades, had served as proxenus, or honorary consul, for Sparta, the youthful politician tried to negotiate a peace that would include a return of the prisoners from Sphacteria. Sparta preferred to deal with his political opponent, Nicias. When the Peace of Nicias was signed and the alliance with Sparta had been concluded, and when Sparta had proven unable or unwilling to persuade her allies to carry out her side of the agreement, Alcibiades vigorously attacked Nicias for having given back the prisoners, and entered into private negotiations with Argos to stir her up against Sparta. Argos had stayed out of the ten-year war, had thereby grown prosperous, was in the hands of her democratic party, and was interested. Alcibiades now urged Argos that she, Mantinea, and Elis ally themselves with Athens as protection against Sparta's domination of the Peloponnese.

Sparta became alarmed and sent envoys to Athens with full power to negotiate with the Council there. Alcibiades, to save his Argive alliance, thereupon promised the Spartan envoys that if, when they should appear before the popular Assembly, they would state that they lacked full powers, he would undertake to secure the withdrawal of the Athenian garrison from Pylos. This time, his private diplomacy succeeded. When asked in the Assembly if they had full powers, the envoys denied that they had them. Alcibiades thundered out a denunciation of them. In the end, Alcibiades got his anti-Spartan alliance. Shortly thereafter he was elected one of the generals of Athens.

During the next year Alcibiades led 1,000 heavy infantry to the Peloponnese to defend Argos, but his plans foundered on the complexities of Peloponnesian politics and nothing decisive came of them. In fact, in 418, when Nicias was elected a general again, Alcibiades failed to win a third annual term. Also, his Peloponnesian Alliance was decisively defeated by Sparta at Mantinea in August of 418, and Argos made a treaty with the Spartans. Athens was once more learning that she had no future as a land power in Mainland Greece. Sparta's prestige, shattered by the surrender of her heavy infantry on the island of Sphacteria, was restored throughout Hellas. Tension between Nicias and Alcibiades grew, and for the first time in 26 years an ostracism was held. When the voting was over, it was the popular leader, Hyperbolus the lamp manufacturer, who was ostracized. But Hyperbolus seemed to the Athenians so unworthy of the penalty inflicted on some of their greatest, and hence potentially dangerous, leaders that the device lost its function. In 417-416 Alcibiades was again elected a general.

Since the war had broken out in 431, the Dorian islands of Thera and Cythera had both been annexed by Athens. Even the island of Melos, colonized by Laconians long ago, had been pillaged by Nicias in 426, but the city of Melos had held out. In 416 an Athenian fleet of thirty-eight ships sailed to the island with 3,420 troops and tried to negotiate admission to the city of Melos. Thucydides, whom Athens had eight years before banished for arriving too late from Thasos to save Amphipolis from Brasidas, recorded the negotiations of the Athenian commanders for a peaceful surrender of the city. The Melian oligarchy would not allow the Athenians to address their popular assembly, perhaps because in most islands the populace was pro-Athenian. So the Athenian envoys presented their case to the magistrates:

> Well, then, we on our part will make use of no fair phrases, saying either that we hold sway justly because we overthrew the Persians, or that we now come against you because we are injured, offering in a lengthy speech arguments that would not be believed; nor, on the other hand, do we presume that you will assert, either that the reason why you did not join us in the war was because you were colonists of the Lacedaemonians, or that you have done us no wrong. Rather we presume that you aim at accomplishing what is possible in accordance with the real thoughts of both of us, since you know as well as we know that what is just is arrived at in human arguments only when the necessity on both sides is equal,

and that the powerful exact what they can, while the weak yield what they must.[254]

Melians: As we think, at any rate, it is expedient (for we are constrained to speak of expediency, since you have in this fashion, ignoring the principle of justice, suggested that we speak of what is advantageous) that you should not rule out the principle of the common good, but that for him who is at the time in peril what is equitable should also be just. . . . And this is not less for your interest than for our own, inasmuch as you, if you shall ever meet with a reverse, would not only incur the greatest punishment, but would also become a warning example to others.

Athenians: But we on our part, so far as our empire is concerned, even if it should cease to be, do not look forward to the end with dismay. For it is not those who rule over others, as the Lacedaemonians also do—though our quarrel is not now with the Lacedaemonians—that are a terror to the vanquished, but subject peoples who may perchance themselves attack and get the better of their rulers. . . . what we desire is to have dominion over you without trouble to ourselves, and that you should be saved to the advantage of both.

Melians: And how could it prove as advantageous for us to become slaves, as it is for you to have dominion?

Athenians: Because it would be to your advantage to submit before suffering the most horrible fate, and we should gain by not destroying you.

Melians: And so, you mean, you would not consent to our remaining at peace and being friends instead of enemies, but allies of neither combatant?

Athenians: No; for your hostility does not injure us so much as your friendship; for in the eyes of our subjects that would be a proof of our weakness, whereas your hatred is a proof of our power.

Melians: Do your subjects regard equity in such a way as to put in the same category those that do not belong to you at all and those—your own colonists in most cases and in others revolted subjects—who have been subdued by you?

Athenians: As to pleas of justice, they think that neither the one nor the other lacks them, but that those who preserve their freedom owe it to their power, and that we do not attack them because we are afraid. . . .

Melians: . . . And in this what else are you doing but strengthening the enemies you already have, and bringing upon you, against their inclination, others who would never have thought of becoming your enemies?

Athenians: Not so, for we do not reckon those as the more dangerous to us who, dwelling somewhere on the mainland and being free men, will defer for a long time taking any precautions against us, but rather those who dwell in some of the islands, both those who, like you, are subject to no control, and those who are already exasperated by the necessity of submission to our rule. . . .

Melians: Surely, then, if you and your subjects brave so great a risk, you in order that you may not lose your empire, and they, who are already your slaves, in order that they may be rid of it, for us surely who still have our freedom it would be the height of baseness and cowardice not to resort to every expedient before submitting to servitude.

Athenians: No, not if you take a sensible view of the matter . . . rather the question before you is one of self-preservation—to avoid offering resistance to those who are far stronger than you.

Melians: But we know that the fortune of war is sometimes impartial and not in accord with the difference in numbers. And for us, to yield is at once to give up hope; but if we make an effort, there is still hope that we may stand erect.

Athenians: Hope is indeed a solace in danger, and for those who have other resources in abundance, though she may injure, she does not ruin them; but for those who stake their all on a single throw—hope being by nature prodigal—it is only when disaster has befallen that her true nature is recognized, and when at last she is known, she leaves the victim no resource wherewith to take precautions against her in future. This fate, we beg of you, weak as you are and dependent on a single turn of the scale, do not willingly incur; nor make yourselves like the common crowd who, when it is possible still to be saved by human means, as soon as distress comes and all visible grounds of hope fail them, betake them- selves to those that are invisible—to divination, oracles, and the like, which, with the hopes they inspire, bring men to ruin.

Melians: We, too, be well assured, think it difficult to contend both against your power and against fortune, unless she shall be impartial; but nevertheless we trust that, in point of fortune, we shall through the divine favour be at no disadvantage because we are god-fearing men stand- ing our ground against men who are unjust; and as to the matter of power, that the alliance of the Lacedaemonians will supply what we lack, since that alliance must aid us, if for no other reason, because of our kinship with them and for very shame. . . .

Athenians: Well, as to the kindness of the divine favour, neither do we expect to fall short of you therein. For in no respect are we departing from men's observances regarding that which pertains to the divine or from their desires regarding that which pertains to themselves, in aught that we demand or do. For of the gods we hold the belief, and of men we know, that by a necessity of their nature wherever they have power they always rule. . . . But as to your expectation regarding the Lacedaemonians, your confident trust that out of shame forsooth they will aid you—while we admire your simplicity, we do not envy you your folly. We must indeed acknowledge that with respect to themselves and the institutions of their own country, the Lacedaemonians practise virtue in a very high degree; but with respect to their conduct towards the rest of mankind . . . one may declare that of all men with whom we are acquainted they, most conspicuously, consider what is agreeable to be honourable and what is expedient just. . . .[255]

The argument continued. Then the Athenians urged the Melians to think it over, and withdrew. The Melians decided not to yield and to hope for help from Sparta and the gods. The siege began. Twice the Melians made fairly successful sorties. But, after some months, the city was betrayed from within, and the authorities surrendered unconditionally. All the grown men were put to death. The women and children were sold into slavery. Athens resettled the island with 500 outsettlers. The strong had done what they could, and the weak had done what they were forced to do. Prophecies and oracles seemed what the envoys of Athens had claimed they were, inventions that delude. Whether the gods the envoys professed did, as they claimed, rule wherever they could, whether, indeed, all men did it, at least, in this case, the Athenians did. By their own professed theology, their deed was godlike.

Hesiod, who hated the wrong kind of eris, the eris of violence and war, had declared that Zeus "has ordained this law for men, that fishes and beasts and wingèd fowls should devour one another, for right is not in them, but to mankind he gave right which proves far the best."[256] But Melos was devoured. In 427 Mitylene had barely escaped the same fate. Mitylene was indeed in theory a free city, supplying ships, not tribute, and she had turned against her own ally. In 421 Scione had defected and had received the punishment of Melos. But Melos was a neutral, and the negotiations at Melos which Thucydides reported went further than to countenance massacre: they enunciated doctrine, about men, about the gods, including Zeus whose daughter was Justice.

The punishment of Melos was voted on the motion of Alcibiades. At Athens, Alcibiades had attained new heights of popularity. He won office, he won prizes for choruses, he entered seven four-horse chariots in the races at the Olympic Games. Euripides, who could write so movingly of the vanquished, could write of victors too. Pindar's great odes had celebrated the athletic victories of those whose ancestors had won great victories on the field of battle. Euripides sang of Alcibiades:

> But I will sing thy praises, son of Cleinias. A noble thing is victory, noblest of the noble to do what no Greek had ever done, be first and second and third in the chariot-race, and go unwearied yet, wreathed in the olive of Zeus, to make the herald cry you.[257]

No man in Athens was more gossiped about. His luxurious manner of life, his drunken revels, his courtesans, his highhandedness and studied insults, the Ionian effeminacy of his dress, his trailing purple robes, his golden shield shocked and angered his conservative elders. If the young blades followed and imitated him, what of Athens as a whole? The god Dionysus would answer that question in Aristophanes' comedy, the *Frogs*: "She loves and hates, and longs still to possess."[258] And, when the poet Aeschylus appeared in the same comedy, he advised Athens how to treat her hero:

> No lion's whelp within thy precincts raise;
> But, if it *be* there, bend thee to its ways![259]

The very year of the massacre of Melos, Alcibiades saw opportunity for greatness open: Segesta, Athens' Sicilian ally, was calling for help against its neighbor Selinus, and Selinus was backed by Syracuse, which had recently swallowed up Leontini. Athens had been allied with Segesta for 38 years and with Leontini for 17. Only 11 years earlier, the year Athens crushed the Mitylenian revolt, she had sent 20 ships to help Leontini against Syracuse, but Syracuse had persuaded her neighbors, including Athens' allies, to make peace. Now Segesta was pointing out that powerful, Dorian Syracuse, daughter of Athens' enemy, Corinth, was likely some day to unite all Sicily and come to the aid of the Dorians of Peloponnese against Athens. Less hypothetical than that aid was the fact that the Peloponnese counted on grain from Sicily as Athens counted on grain from the Hellespont and beyond.

The Athenian Assembly voted an expedition of 60 triremes to go to

Sicily. They appointed Nicias, Alcibiades, and Lamachus to command, and granted them full powers. Their instructions were to help Segesta against her neighbor Selinus; to restore Leontini, which Syracuse had depopulated; and "to settle all other matters in Sicily as they might deem best for the Athenians."[260] Nicias argued against the expedition. He pointed out that the peace which bore his name was ignored by some of Sparta's allies; that Athens' tributary allies in Chalcidice were still in rebellion; while Sicily, even if conquered, would be difficult to hold and govern. "And," added Nicias,

> if there be anyone here who, elated at being chosen to command, exhorts you to sail, considering—especially as he is too young to command—only his own interest, how he may get admiration for his raising of fine horses, and then, because that is very expensive, how he may also get some profit from his command, do not afford this man, at the cost of the state, opportunity to make a personal display, but rather consider that such men damage the public interest while they waste their own property, and that the matter is one of great seriousness, and not such as a youth may decide and rashly take in hand.
>
> It is of such youths, when I see them sitting here in answer to the appeal of this same man, that I am afraid; and I make a counter-appeal to the older men, if any of you sit by one of these, not to be shamed into fear lest he may seem to be a coward if he do not vote for war, and not, though that may be *their* feeling, to have a morbid craving for what is out of reach, knowing that few successes are won by greed, but very many by foresight; on the contrary, on behalf of our country, which is now running the greatest risk it has ever run, hold up your hands in opposition . . . and let us not make allies, as we are wont to do, whom we must assist when they fare ill, but from whom we shall get no help when we are ourselves in need.[261]

Clearly, Alcibiades, the warmest advocate in the Assembly for the Sicilian expedition, had to reply:

> It belongs to me more than to others, Athenians, to have command—for I must needs begin with this, since Nicias has attacked me—and I think, too, that I am worthy to command. For those things for which I am railed at bring glory to my ancestors and myself, as well as advantage to my country. For the Hellenes, who had previously hoped that our state had been exhausted by the war, conceived an idea of its greatness that even transcended its actual power by reason of the magnificence of my

display as sacred deputy at Olympia, because I entered seven chariots, a number that no private citizen had ever entered before, and won the first prize and the second and the fourth, and provided everything else in a style worthy of my victory. For by general custom such things do indeed mean honour, and from what is done men also infer power. And again, although whatever display I made in the city, by providing choruses or in any other way, naturally causes jealousy among my townsmen, yet in the eyes of strangers this too gives an impression of strength.[262]

Moreover, he continued,

look at my public acts and see whether I execute them worse than an-other. I brought together the greatest powers of the Peloponnesus without great danger to you or expense and forced the Lacedaemonians to stake all upon a single day at Mantinea; and in consequence of this, though vic-torious in the field, even yet they have not firm confidence.

Thus did my youthfulness and my seemingly abnormal folly cope with the power of the Peloponnesians in fitting words and with a spirit that inspired faith win assent. And now be not afraid of it, but while I am still in the flower of youth, and Nicias has the reputation of good luck, make the most of the services of us both.[263]

Far from not helping Athens, Alcibiades insisted the Segestaeans did help by keeping Syracuse too preoccupied in Sicily to aid her Dorian cousins in the Peloponnese against Athens.

And it is not possible for us to exercise a careful stewardship of the limits we would set to our empire; but, since we are placed in this position, it is necessary to plot against some and not let go our hold upon others, be-cause there is a danger of coming ourselves under the empire of others, should we not ourselves hold empire over other peoples. And you cannot regard a pacific policy in the same light as other states might, unless you will change your practices also to correspond with theirs.

Calculating, then, that we shall rather strengthen our power here if we go over there, let us make the voyage, that we may lay low the haughty spirit of the Peloponnesians, as we shall if we let men see that in con-tempt of our present peaceful condition we even sail against Sicily; and that we may, at the same time, either acquire empire over all Hellas, as in all probability we shall, when the Hellenes there have been added to us, or may at least cripple the Syracusans, whereby both ourselves and our allies will be benefited. . . . In short, I declare that a state which is ac-customed to activity would very quickly be ruined by a change to inactivity; and that those men live most securely whose political action is least at variance with existing habits and institutions, even when these are not the best.[264]

To discourage the Assembly, Nicias shifted tactics and demanded more ships and men than had been proposed. To his dismay, the Assembly promptly and enthusiastically voted them. The Athenians, their decision now made, longed to see their great armada sail. The city, so recently impoverished by the plague, was rich again and ready to invest its wealth in war. The older citizens believed so great a force would either win or at least escape disaster. A new generation had grown up that had seen little or no battle, and the young men were excited by the prospect of distant adventure. With so many Athenians eager for the attack on Sicily, the few who feared disaster feared also to appear disloyal if they voiced their doubts.

The poorer citizens, who did not live on mining concessions like the wealthy Nicias, had learned from Cleon and from experience the economic benefits of empire; it meant employment, as soldier, as sailor, as shipbuilder, or as paid juror in the courts. They knew that these wages were paid out of tribute received from Athens' subject cities and that more subject cities meant more tribute. In the old days many of them lived on the land. Since then they had been forced into the city by Spartan invasions or drawn there by the prospect of wages in a thriving city. They were now uprooted, urbanized, and anxious to share in the luxuries they saw about them. Many of them lived by their wits in a society that was teaching them daily how easy and pleasant it was for the strong to exploit the weak. Conquests in this distant island in the west meant relief from want and maybe, even, a chance for wealth and ease.

While the polis prepared its grand armada, it was suddenly thrown into hysterical panic by a mysterious event. In a single night, around June 7 of 415, most of the traditional Herms, the blocks of stone carved at the top into a bust of the god Hermes and left uncarved in the lower portion, which commonly stood in the doorways of both temples and private dwellings, were badly mutilated. This sacrilege was taken as an evil omen for the great expedition. Rewards were offered for the desecrators. Informers were busy. Just then some resident aliens and slaves testified that other sacrileges had occurred. Other images had been mutilated by young men in a drunken frolic, and mock celebrations of the Eleusinian mysteries had been held in private houses. The enemies of Alcibiades promptly tried to incriminate him: it was all a scheme of this insolent and notorious flouter of ancient convention to overthrow the Athenian democracy.

Alcibiades denied the charges and demanded trial. But his opponents were afraid the army would support him. The Argives and Mantineans who had joined in the expedition had done so out of confidence in his leadership. The expedition was now nearly ready to sail. So his opponents insisted on deferring the trial until after the campaign. It was about midsummer. Most of the allies and the supply ships had been ordered to muster at Corcyra, on the route to Sicily.

But the Athenians themselves and the allies that were present went down to the Peiraeus at dawn on a day appointed and proceeded to man the ships for the purpose of putting to sea. And with them went down also all the general throng, everyone, we may almost say, that was in the city, both citizens and strangers, the natives to send off each their own, whether friends or kinsmen or sons, going at once in hope and with lamentations —hope that they would make conquests in Sicily, lamentations that they might never see their friends again, considering how long was the voyage from their own land on which they were being sent. And at this crisis, when under impending dangers they were now about to take leave of one another, the risks came home to them more than when they were voting for the expedition; but still their courage revived at the sight of their present strength because of the abundance of everything they saw before their eyes. The strangers on the other hand and the rest of the multitude had come for a spectacle, in the feeling that the enterprise was noteworthy and surpassing belief.

For this first armament that sailed for Sicily was the costliest and most splendid, belonging to a single city and with a purely Hellenic force, that had ever up to that time set sail. . . . And the fame of the armament was noised abroad, not less because of amazement at its boldness and the splendour of the spectacle than on account of its overwhelming force as compared with those whom they were going against; and also because it was the longest voyage from home as yet attempted and undertaken with the highest hopes for the future as compared with their present resources.

When the ships had been manned and everything had at last been put aboard which they were to take with them on the voyage, the trumpeter proclaimed silence, and they offered the prayers that were customary before putting out to sea, not ship by ship but all together, led by a herald, the mariners as well as the officers throughout the whole army making libations with golden and silver cups from wine they had mixed. And the rest of the throng of people on the shore, both the citizens and all others present who wished the Athenians well, also joined in the prayers. And when they had sung the paean and had finished the libations, they put off, and sailing out at first in single column they then raced as far as Aegina. The Athenian fleet, then, was pressing on to reach Corcyra, where the rest of the armament of the allies was assembling.[265]

In Syracuse opinion was divided on whether to attack the Athenian fleet before it could cross the Ionian Sea to Italy, to call on Carthage to help defend Sicily, to call on Sparta to invade Attica again, or whether to await the armada's coming and then defend Syracuse. Meanwhile, the armada met with a chilly reception from the Greek cities on the coast of Italy; in Sicily Segesta turned out to be quite unable to supply the funds she had promised: Alcibiades, Nicias, and Lamachus held a council of war. Nicias urged that they try to settle Segesta's dispute with Selinus, coast past the port cities of Sicily to display their power, and go home. Alcibiades wanted to negotiate for allies before striking Syracuse. Lamachus, who was a more experienced soldier than either of his colleagues, correctly guessed that Syracuse had not completed her preparations for defense, and was for striking now. The three men compromised on the plan of Alcibiades. But the cities of Sicily were distrustful of the Athenian armada and almost all of them refused to co-operate. The armada was ominously big. Its purpose was ill-defined, even in the minds of the Athenians at home. Its purpose was divided in the minds of those who led it. It necessarily wore an air of blind force and one could not argue with blind force. Where one could not argue, what was there to negotiate?

At Athens, the hysteria over the mutilated Herms and the parody of the holy mysteries had continued; rumor flew that oligarchic subversives planned a tyranny. About a hundred suspects were rounded up, some were executed, and others escaped abroad with a price on their heads. The tyrant-state which had so often imposed its will by force on other states and which had declared through the mouths of its generals at Melos that, in the eyes of gods and men, might made right, now wondered if it was itself destined for the fate of Corcyra: civil war. There appeared to be men inside the polis who were prepared to apply the Melian formula at home, godless men who would enthrone might over right in the School of Hellas itself. But where were they? The enemies of Alcibiades made it clear that in all likelihood he was one of them. They persuaded the Assembly to summon him home for trial. The official city trireme, the Salaminia, was ordered to Sicily to escort Alcibiades' trireme back to Athens, bearing Alcibiades himself and some others who were accused. At Thurii, in Italy, the group of suspects jumped ship and disappeared. Alcibiades, now an outlaw, crossed in a trading vessel to Cyllene, a port in Peloponnese; the Salaminia returned to Athens; and the Assembly passed sentence of death on all the refugees from justice.

The armada was now in the hands of Nicias, who had never at any point approved of the expedition; and of Lamachus, a good soldier but without prestige in the army. The general who really believed in the expedition was in exile with a price on his head. The advice Aristophanes had put in the dead Aeschylus's mouth concerning Alcibiades had been ignored: Athens, having reared a lion in the state, had failed to humor him. The rest of the summer was frittered away by Nicias and his remaining colleague. The Syracusans recovered from their earlier alarm. Winter came. Nicias and Lamachus by a stratagem lured the Syracusan army to nearby Catana to attack them there. Then they swiftly embarked with their whole army by night; landed on the coast north of Syracuse; and seized Epipolae, or Overtown, a long hill overlooking Syracuse and its Great Harbor. Epipolae was now fortified; and when the Syracusans returned from their wild goose chase to Catana, Nicias defeated them. But Nicias despaired of taking Syracuse without more cavalry, without more money, and without the Sicilian allies he hoped his recent victory would now bring him, and he therefore led his army back to Sicilian Naxos and Catana for the winter. Under the leadership of Hermocrates, Syracuse began to rebuild her armed forces and to urge Corinth and Sparta to send help. Corinth agreed to help, and sent envoys along with the Syracusan envoys to Sparta. Arrived there, they found unexpected support—from Alcibiades, who had audaciously taken refuge in the city he had so much harmed.

The Spartans agreed to help; but, as usual, they delayed. Whereupon Alcibiades addressed them. He defended himself for stirring up Sparta's allies against her five years before: had Sparta not snubbed him when he tried to help her get back the prisoners from Sphacteria? He defended himself for co-operating with the Athenian democracy: he gladly admitted that democracy was absurd, as witness what the extreme democrats had just done to him; but he had had to adjust to the facts of political life. Then he came to the business at hand:

We sailed to Sicily, first, to subdue the Siceliots, if we could, and after them the Italiots also; and then to make an attempt upon the empire of the Carthaginians and upon the city itself. If these things, either all, or at least the greater part of them, succeeded, then we intended to attack the Peloponnesus, bringing here the whole Hellenic force that had joined us there, hiring besides many barbarians, both Iberians and others of the peoples there that are admittedly the most warlike of the barbarians at the present day, and building many triremes in addition to our own, as Italy has timber in abundance. Laying a blockade with these triremes round the Peloponnesus, and at the same time attacking it with our infantry by land, having thus taken some of its cities by assault and walled in others, we expected easily to reduce it, and after that to have sway over the whole Hellenic race. As to money and food, for making any of these projects more feasible, the additional territory acquired in Sicily would of itself furnish these in sufficient quantity, independently of our home revenues.[266]

But now, he continued, unless Sparta acted quickly, Sicily would fall to Athens and the Peloponnese would be in grave danger. Sparta should send heavy infantry to help Syracuse. Even more important, she should send a Spartan to organize the resistance. Then they must occupy Decelea in Attica, the move Athens had always feared most. It would cut off Athens from her silver mines at Laurium and encourage her subject allies to neglect paying their tribute.

The accomplishment of any of these projects promptly and more zealously depends, men of Lacedaemon, upon you. . . . And I claim that no one of you shall think more harshly of me because I, who once seemed to be a lover of my city, now make assault with all my might upon her, in concert with her bitterest enemies; nor do I think that my word should be suspected on the score of the outcast's zeal. . . . the worse enemies are not those who, like you, have merely hurt their enemies, but those who have forced their friends to become foes. And as to love of country—I have it not when I am wronged, but had it when I possessed my civil rights in security. . . . And the true patriot is not the man who, having unjustly lost his fatherland, refrains from attacking it, but he who in his yearning for it tries in every way to get it back. So I urge you, Lacedaemonians, to use me without misgiving for any danger and for any hardships, recognising that, according to the saying which is on everybody's lips, if as an enemy I did you exceeding injury, I might also be of some sufficient service to you as a friend, in so far as I know the affairs of the Athenians, while I could only conjecture yours. And I urge, too, that you yourselves now, convinced that you are deliberating about interests that are of the greatest importance, shrink not from sending an expedition into Sicily, and also into Attica, in order that, by keeping a small detachment on the island, you may preserve the large interests you have over there and may overthrow the power of the Athenians both present and prospective, and after that may yourselves live in security and be accepted by all the Hellenes of their free will, not by force but through affection, as their leaders.[267]

The Spartans took Alcibiades' advice. Although they did not immediately fortify Decelea in Attica, they did send a Spartan general, Gylippus, to command the Syracusans and to find out in Syracuse what other help must be sent. Nicias, meanwhile, received money and cavalrymen from Athens, with instructions to find their mounts in Sicily. He had had almost no luck in rallying the civilized coast cities to his banner, but he did get men and even some money from the interior. He now began, in the summer of 414, to run a wall from the Bay of Thapsus, north of Syracuse, where his own fleet was stationed, to the Great Harbor of Syracuse, south of the city. He built a circular fort and from that point started one wall north toward the bay and another south toward the harbor. Cut off from help by land, Syracuse could then be cut off by his fleet from help by sea and must be forced to surrender. The Syracusans started building a counter-wall to prevent Nicias' south wall from reaching the Great Harbor. This counter-wall the Athenians succeeded in destroying. The Syracusans then attempted a palisaded trench to prevent Nicias' wall from reaching the Great Harbor. This, too, the Athenians attacked and destroyed. But they paid a price: Lamachus was killed in action. Of the three commanders under whom the grand armada had sailed, one was in Sparta, a second was dead, and the only one left had disapproved of the expedition. But provisions and even some allies were coming in, and victory seemed to beckon. Morale inside Syracuse was sinking. Where was the help from Sparta? The Syracusans started proposing terms to Nicias. They began to accuse each other of treachery. They appointed new commanders.

Word reached Nicias that Gylippus, the Spartan commander, had touched Tarentum in Italy. But Gylippus apparently had so few ships that Nicias concluded he must be bent only on piracy. Gylippus therefore sailed unhindered to Himera on the north coast of Sicily, collected some troops, and marched on Syracuse. After losing one battle and winning another, he managed to build another counter-wall that effectually destroyed Nicias' last hope of leading his own wall, which had now reached the Great Harbor in the south, all the way to the Bay of Thapsus in the north.

Nicias appealed to Athens. From being the besieger, he was now the besieged. He was cut off by Gylippus from obtaining supplies by land, and even supply by sea was becoming precarious. Slaves were deserting from the Athenian fleet. So were other sailors who had signed on merely for high pay and in the hope of booty. Some of the latter had bribed their captains to accept Sicilian slaves in their places and were themselves scattering to engage in trade. Nicias appealed for another fleet and another army as large as those he had led to Sicily; for more money; and for a general to replace him, since he was suffering from a serious disease of the kidneys.

The Athenian Assembly voted another army and navy, money, and two new generals, but they refused to accept Nicias' resignation. His two new colleagues were to be Demosthenes, who had fought in Aetolia and shared with Cleon the glory of capturing the Spartans on Sphacteria, and Eurymedon, who had co-operated with the democrats in the revolution at Corcyra and who had later been involved in Athens' unsuccessful efforts in Sicily.

Gylippus, the Spartan, was showing some of the prompt strategy and deft diplomacy that no Spartan had shown abroad since the death of Brasidas; but Gylippus was not Nicias' only enemy. At Sparta, Alcibiades was tirelessly inciting action. It was largely due to Alcibiades that Gylippus had gone to Sicily. Now, in the winter of 414-413, he was still urging the Spartans to invade Attica, in order to discourage Athens from sparing too much help for Nicias, and to seize and fortify Decelea as a permanent base from which to ravage Attica more systematically. In the spring, Agis, one of Lacedaemon's two kings, wasted Attica and fortified Decelea. The new fort was no more than fourteen miles from Athens and about the same distance from the frontier of Athens' bitter enemy, Boeotia. It blocked off a supply route from Euboea, Athens' nearest breadbasket, through the port of Oropus. It blocked communications with Laurium, where Nicias' mining interests lay, and where a fountain of silver had nourished Athens' war against the Peloponnesians, as it had once nourished her war against Xerxes. More than 20,000 slaves, including many artisans, escaped from the Athenians to the Spartans.

Sparta also sent 1,600 heavy infantry to Gylippus in Sicily: men from Boeotia, Corinth, Sicyon, together with Helots and emancipated Helots from Lacedaemonia. Meanwhile, Demosthenes left Athens for Syracuse with 65 ships, 1,200 Athenian heavy infantry, and as many islanders as Athens could muster.

The Great Harbor was some three miles across from north to south, with a mouth about a mile wide. North of the mouth lay 'the Island,' the oldest part of Syracuse. South of it, the land extended to a point called Plemmyrium. Here Nicias had built three forts where he could base his ships. Gylippus, backed by Hermocrates, the Syracusan commander, persuaded the Syracusans to attack the dread Athenian fleet; and though the Athenians won, a simultaneous land assault by Gylippus captured Plemmyrium and the supplies stored there. The Athenian fleet fell back on the northern shore of the harbor, near where their north-south wall reached the water's edge. Syracusan vessels could not guard both sides of the harbor mouth, and any ships that brought in supplies for Nicias were subject to attack.

Meanwhile, Demosthenes and his reinforcements had joined forces with an Athenian fleet of thirty ships, had picked up some heavy infantry from Argos, troops from the western coast of Mainland Greece, and from Thurii in southern Italy, and were said to be approaching Syracuse. The 1,300 Thracian archers he had hoped to include in his forces had reached Athens too late to join the expedition, so the Athenians sent them home by ship with orders to do what harm they could to the enemy. Landing on the northern coast of Boeotia, they attacked a small town called Mycalessus and butchered all the men, women, children, and even animals that they could find. In particular, they attacked a boys' school and massacred all the students. In the eyes of Hellas the massacre brought no glory to the School of Hellas. The massacre sprang from orders to wild tribesmen to do the enemy all the harm they could, and those orders caricatured the original orders to the three commanders of the Sicilian armada to settle all other matters in Sicily as they might deem best for the Athenians. It caricatured even the massacre of Melos: why spare the women and children and animals? Athenian purpose was less and less defined and could command less and less respect in Hellas. War as skillful surgery had turned into war as butchery and buccaneering. Small wonder that Sicily began to rally to Gylippus against what felt more and more like an explosion of arrogant and mindless violence from Athens.

The Syracusans had finally dared to meet an Athenian fleet and, though they had suffered defeat, it was a defeat that fell far short of catastrophe. Heartened, they now prepared to attack again by sea and land. Besides, a Corinthian squadron had recently fought an Athenian squadron in the Corinthian gulf, where the latter had been stationed to guard the supply line from Athens to Sicily. Although here again the results slightly favored the Athenians, a new naval device of the Corinthians had proven itself brilliantly. The device consisted of strengthening the prow and cheeks of the Corinthian triremes so that they could be used with devastating effect in prow-to-prow collisions. The prows of seven Athenian triremes were thus staved in. The Syracusans now copied this device. The skillful Athenian crews, already rendered less skillful by desertions, lacked space for their customary maneuvers, which generally ended with ramming the sides of the enemy ships. The Syracusan triremes simply charged head-on, and their newly enforced bronze beaks staved in the weaker bronze beaks of the Athenian vessels. The darters on the decks of the Syracusan triremes did their work well. And, worst of all, darters in small boats dashed in close to the Athenian ships and attacked their sailors. The Syracusans won a decisive victory and drove the Athenians back to their improvised base.

Then, to the dismay of Syracuse, Demosthenes and Eurymedon arrived from Athens with a new fleet of over 70 triremes, with nearly 5,000 heavy infantry, with Hellenic and barbarian darters, and with slingers and archers as well. Demosthenes did not propose to imitate Nicias, who had wasted a whole winter while Syracuse grew strong. He urged that the army immediately attack Gylippus' counter-wall, take it, and complete Nicias' wall from the Great Harbor clear to the Bay of Thapsus. If this effort succeeded, it ought to be possible to starve out Syracuse. If it failed, they should return to Athens instantly and not risk losing both army and fleet. In short, for Nicias' paralysis, he wanted to substitute decisive action.

The Athenian army attacked the counter-wall by night. A confused struggle ensued; for a while the Athenians were gaining; but in the end they met severe defeat. Demosthenes now voted to quit Sicily and fight in Mainland Greece, where Sparta's occupation of Decelea was pressing hard on Athens. But Nicias, though he had not approved of the war in the first place and had frittered away the period during which Syracuse might have been taken, insisted on staying. He did not want to face the Athenian Assembly and the usual accusations of bribery and malfeasance. The pro-Athenian party in Syracuse was secretly encouraging him to believe that Syracuse was in an even worse plight than its besiegers. The besiegers stayed.

Then Gylippus returned from recruiting a fresh army among the Sicilian cities, and fresh infantry also reached him from the Peloponnese. The Athenian army, encamped on marshy ground beside the Great Harbor, was ravaged by sickness and thoroughly discouraged. At last even Nicias agreed to withdraw from Sicily. At that moment an eclipse of the moon occurred, which was taken as a bad omen. The army wanted to delay. Nicias' soothsayer declared they should wait "thrice nine days" before departing, and Nicias had never in his career failed to exhibit the most pious respect for divination. The besiegers stayed.

The Syracusans got wind that the Athenian armada planned to quit the siege of Syracuse, but they did not propose to let the Athenians retreat to some other point on the island only to make trouble later. They launched another sea and land attack on the besiegers. The land attack by Gylippus was indecisive, but the Athenian fleet was again defeated and its ships driven ashore. During the battle Eurymedon, whom Athens had sent out with Demosthenes to help Nicias, was slain. Athens, confronted with cities in Sicily which were already ruled by democrats, had been unable to seduce them by offering to free them from oppressive oligarchs. She had been unable to crush them by force. Not only her land forces but also her fleet had been decisively defeated. The failure of the expedition was clear for all to see. What was left of it would, when the omens permitted, go home. But the Syracusans, who had only recently despaired of saving their city, no longer wanted to drive the armada off: they wanted to destroy it. Now would come the kill; now would come the freeing of Hellas from the tyrant-state, Athens. The Syracusans began to block up the Great Harbor by mooring vessels across its mouth.

The Athenians fortified their little base on the harbor shore and staked their fleet on a final naval battle. They planned, if they lost, to burn their ships and fight their way by land to the nearest friendly place they could reach. They succeeded in manning some 110 ships for the final struggle. To protect their ships against the strong-beaked Syracusan triremes, they prepared grappling irons. They would close quickly and fight, in the antiquated style, a land battle on the decks of ships. Nicias made a last appeal to his Athenians and to their allies, then ranged his land forces along the shore at his base, while Demosthenes led his fleet toward the blocked mouth of the harbor. The Syracusans stretched hides over the prows and gunwales of their ships so that the grappling irons of the Athenians would slip harmlessly off and leave them free to ram Athenian prows, back water, and ram again. The Syracusans, with around ninety ships, deployed their fleet at various points around the Great Harbor and posted their land forces around the shore. In this vast arena, with the two armies looking on, the two fleets fought long and hard. The Athenian soldiers watched from the shore in an agony of fear and hope, their bodies swaying with the fortunes of their comrades, who were victorious at one point in the melee of ships, overwhelmed at another. Some Athenian spectators were overjoyed that they might once more behold Athens and at the same moment other spectators wailed aloud their grief and despair. Then, at last, the Athenian fleet broke, and its triremes fled for shore. There was complete panic.

Demosthenes convinced Nicias that they should try again next morning to force their way through the blockade at the mouth of the Great Harbor. They still had about sixty ships left to the enemy's less than fifty. But the men were now wholly demoralized and refused to go on board. The fleet was lost. The Athenians burned the few triremes that the enemy, after the Athenians panicked, had not seized and towed away. There remained the problem of getting as many men as possible, both from the army and the navy, out of the area before Gylippus should block the roads. The Syracusan Hermocrates sent men who would pose as pro-Athenian to warn Nicias against a night march on the grounds that the roads were already blocked. So the besieged besiegers stayed on.

After this, when it seemed to Nicias and Demosthenes that adequate preparations had been made, the departure of the army at last took place —on the third day following the sea-fight. And it was terrible, not in one aspect only of their fortunes, in that they were going away after losing all their ships, and, in place of high hopes, with danger threatening both themselves and their State, but also in that, on the abandonment of their camp, it fell to the lot of each man to see things that were painful both to sight and mind. The corpses were still unburied, and whenever a man saw one of his own friends lying dead, he was plunged into grief commingled with fear; and the living who were being left behind, wounded or sick, far more than the dead seemed piteous to the living, and were more wretched than those that had perished. For turning to entreaty and lamentation, they drove the men to distraction; begging to be taken along and calling aloud upon each one if they saw anywhere a comrade or a kinsman, clinging to their tent-mates now going away and following after them as long as they were able, and then, when the bodily strength of one or another failed, falling behind, though not without faint appeals to the gods and lamentations; so that the whole army, being filled with grief and in such perplexity, found it hard to depart, even out of a country that was hostile, and though they had endured already sufferings too great for tears and feared for the future what they might still have to suffer. There was also a general feeling of dejection and much self-condemnation. For indeed they looked like nothing else than a city in secret flight after a siege, and that no small city; for in the entire throng no fewer than four myriads were on the march together. And of these, the rest all bore whatever each could that was useful, while the hoplites and the horsemen, contrary to their wont, carried their own food, some for want of attendants, others through distrust of them; for there had been desertions all along and in greatest numbers immediately on their defeat. But even so they did not carry enough, for there was no longer food in the camp. Furthermore, the rest of their misery and the equal sharing of their ills—although there was in this very sharing with many some alleviation—did not even so seem easy at the moment, especially when one considered from what splendour and boastfulness at first to what humiliating end they had now come. For this was indeed the very greatest reversal that had ever happened to an Hellenic armament; for it so fell out that in place of having come to enslave others, they were now going away in fear lest they might rather themselves suffer this, and instead of prayers and paeans, with which they had sailed forth, were now departing for home with imprecations quite the reverse of these; going too as foot-soldiers instead of seamen, and relying upon hoplites rather than a fleet. And yet, by reason of the magnitude of the danger still impending, all these things seemed to them tolerable.[268]

But the roads and fords were now blocked. Cavalry and archers harassed the retreating Athenians. Food and water were scarce. So they abandoned their westerly route into the interior of Sicily. Then they tried by a night march to throw Gylippus off the scent, and struck for the coast and Catana. They reached the sea, but again they found the Syracusans blocking the ford of a river they must cross. Demosthenes' rear guard had meanwhile during the night march lost contact with the forces under Nicias, was ambushed in a walled olive orchard, and was showered with murderous arrows. At last Demosthenes surrendered, on condition that the lives of his men would be spared. Some 6,000 men laid down their arms.

Then the forces of Nicias, exhausted and suffering from thirst, pushed on toward the Assinarus River.

And when they reached it, they rushed in, no longer preserving order, but everyone eager to be himself the first to cross; and at the same time the pressure of the enemy now made the crossing difficult. For since they were obliged to move in a dense mass, they fell upon and trod one another down, and some perished at once, run through by their own spears, while others became entangled in their trappings and were carried away by the current. The Syracusans stood along the other bank of the river, which was steep, and hurled missiles down upon the Athenians, most of whom were drinking greedily and were all huddled in confusion in the hollow bed of the river. Moreover, the Peloponnesians went down to the water's edge and butchered them, especially those in the river. The water at once became foul, but was drunk all the same, although muddy and dyed with blood, and indeed was fought for by most of them.[269]

Nicias finally surrendered and begged Gylippus to stop the butchery. The official prisoner list was not long. Many prisoners had been hidden by their captors to be sold as slaves. Of these, some escaped later to friendly Catana. The slaughter had been the worst of the war. Nicias and Demosthenes, against the will of Gylippus, were executed by Syracuse and her allies. And despite Nicias' fatal blunders at Syracuse, Thucydides judged him "a man who, of all the Hellenes of my time, least deserved to meet with such a calamity, because of his course of life that had been wholly regulated in accordance with virtue."[270] The remaining official prisoners were deposited in some stone quarries. There, exposed to broiling sun by day and autumnal chill by night, to the cries of their wounded and dying, and to the stench of their dead, they were allowed a daily ration of one pint of water and one pint of grain. After seventy days some of the survivors were sold, but the Athenians and those from Sicily or Italy who had been guilty of joining the Athenians remained in the stinking quarries a total of eight months.

The great expedition was over. As at Melos, Athens had appealed to the principle that the strong do what they can and the weak suffer what they must, to the law of the pack, not of the polis. At Melos they had declared, in defiance of Zeus, who had reputedly taught men justice: "of the gods we hold the belief, and of men we know, that by a necessity of their nature wherever they have power they always rule."[271] It took Thucydides only a few lines to weigh the fruits of their policy:

> This event proved to be the greatest of all that had happened in the course of this war, and, as it seems to me, of all Hellenic events of which we have record—for the victors most splendid, for the vanquished most disastrous. For the vanquished, beaten utterly at every point and having suffered no slight ill in any respect—having met, as the saying goes, with utter destruction—land-force and fleet and everything perished, and few out of many came back home.[272]

When news of this vast catastrophe reached Athens, of this greatest event of all that had happened in the course of the war, her citizens at first declined to believe it. But when they became convinced, they passed, through rage at those who had persuaded them to send their armada to Sicily, to unprecedented panic. They had lost not only an experienced army; they were almost without ships or money to build ships, and almost without crews to man them if built. Would the Syracusan fleet now close in on Athens?

The subject cities of Athens dreamed of freedom from the tyrant city at last. Some of them sent envoys to seek aid of Agis, the Spartan king who held Decelea in Attica; others sent to Sparta itself. The neutrals in the war reflected that it would have been their turn next had Syracuse fallen and began to consider joining in the crusade against the oppressor before it was too late to share in the coming victory. Sparta levied contributions of ships from among her allies. The Persian governor Tissaphernes was promising Sparta to subsidize an army if she would send one to liberate the Ionian subject cities of Athens. The Persian governor Pharnabazus was bidding against him, to get Sparta to liberate Athens' subject cities on the Hellespont instead. The oligarchs of Chios, who wanted help, seconded Tissaphernes. So did Alcibiades. The Spartans sent seven ships to Chios and Alcibiades went with them.

He had stayed in Sparta some two years. As usual, he had ingratiated himself with many persons. He who had trailed a purple robe at Athens left his hair untrimmed in Spartan style, took cold baths, ate coarse bread and Sparta's famous black broth. But with King Agis away and occupying Decelea, Alcibiades seduced his wife, Queen Timaia, and she bore him a son. Spartan custom had always condoned the loan of a wife to a friend as the means of obtaining an especially fine son, and Alcibiades now mockingly declared that he had neither been misled by passion nor by a desire to insult the king but by the wish that descendants of his might be kings of the Lacedaemonians. He went unpunished, but the Spartan authorities may well have been glad to see the end of him. Since the queen had not been loaned by her husband but requisitioned like that other queen of Sparta, Helen of Troy, King Agis, on campaign in Attica, was furious.

Ionia turned out to be a paradise for a man with Alcibiades' gift for intrigue. Tissaphernes wanted to use the Spartans and their allies as mercenaries to recover from Athens Ionian cities whose tribute would then go to him. Sparta wanted to use Tissaphernes as paymaster for her navy in order to deprive Athens of her Aegean empire, since tribute from that empire was Athens' only means of tyrannizing over Mainland Greece and even threatening Sparta's hegemony in the Peloponnese. Pharnabazus hoped to wean the Spartan fleet away from Tissaphernes so that it might enable him to replace Athens in the region of the Hellespont. Out of this complex of cross purposes, Alcibiades was determined to find leverage that would force Athens to recall him in triumph to the city he loved and wanted to possess. The method he chose was to convince the Athenians that he enjoyed Tissaphernes' complete confidence and that, if they wanted to defeat Sparta and save their empire, they must make him, their condemned exile, their agent. His method of retaining the confidence of Tissaphernes was to urge him privately to subsidize the Spartan fleet enough to keep it fighting the Athenians but not enough to let it win. When both sides were exhausted, Tissaphernes could, unmolested, gather up the stakes. Alcibiades would still have to face the problem of deceiving the Spartans, but a few months after he reached Ionia the Spartan government grew weary of his schemes and his effrontery and sent orders to its commanders to kill him. Alcibiades got wind of the orders and instantly fled to Tissaphernes.

Meanwhile, a democratic revolution occurred at Samos; and Athens, confident the new democratic regime would yield her fidelity and aid, decreed that Samos should be independent. Alcibiades then entered into secret negotiations with the officers of an Athenian force stationed at Samos and persuaded them with ease that if only Athens would get rid of "the villainous mob-rule that had banished him"[273] he would return to Athens and make Tissaphernes help her against Sparta. With some difficulty, these officers persuaded their soldiers and sailors that Athens should modify her constitution. The men grumbled, but the prospect of good pay from a Persian subsidy was tempting and they made no trouble. The officers then sent envoys to Athens; and these addressed the Assembly. The vision of a Persian subsidy persuaded the Assembly to adjust their constitution at least until peace could be won. Alcibiades' officer friends returned to Samos, put it back into the hands of its oligarchy, ignored Alcibiades, and started again for Athens, restoring oligarchies in a number of the subject states as they went. At Athens political murders had begun, and the officers called an Assembly at Colonus, just outside Athens, and persuaded it to set up a Council of Four Hundred, who would rule in the emergency and would eventually call into being a citizenship of Five Thousand, all of whom must be able to serve their country without pay. The Four Hundred disposed of troublemakers by execution, prison, or exile, and opened negotiations for peace with Sparta.

Meanwhile, at Samos, the democrats seized power again, with the help of soldiers and sailors from the Athenian camp. Then news came of the oligarchic seizure of power in Athens by the Four Hundred. The soldiers and sailors held an Assembly, deposed their oligarchic officers, and elected officers they felt they could trust. In effect they declared that they, encamped in Samos, were the Polis, and not the Four Hundred who now oppressed Athens. It was they who owned a fleet, not the Four Hundred. It was therefore they and not these oligarchic tyrants in Athens who could collect the tribute from the islands. As for the war with Sparta, the base for that was in any case not Athens but Samos. If the oligarchs at home did not restore the democratic constitution, the camp at Samos would exclude Athens from the sea. If the camp brought Alcibiades back from exile, he would in return bring it alliance with the Great King. And if all else failed, the camp possessed a fleet strong enough to win its members new lands to settle.

Once, long before, as Xerxes marched southward, the whole Polis, noble and democrat, rich and poor, man, woman, and child, had left Athens and gone to divine Salamis. Now, a democratic army and navy had appropriated the Polis and located it on another and more distant island, Samos. Themistocles at Salamis, within sight of silent, deserted Athens and reproached by an Allied captain that he could no longer speak for a city, had also seen that so long as Athens had her fleet her citizens could settle where they pleased.

The leaders of this new, democratic Polis-in-exile then, in effect, invited that general-in-exile, Alcibiades, to the camp at Samos. Alcibiades continued his bluff of many months and reported that Tissaphernes had solemnly promised him to subsidize the Athenian forces "if he could but trust the Athenians'" and that "he could place confidence in the Athenians only on condition that he, Alcibiades, should be restored in safety and become surety to him."[274] The army believed him and promptly elected him a general; and in effect he took charge of the Polis-in-exile. Its Assembly now clamored to go to Athens and put down the oligarchs. But Alcibiades refused: he must immediately see Tissaphernes and concert strategy. He was determined to show his new constituents in the Athenian camp that he enjoyed the Persian governor's confidence. He was also determined to show the Persian that he could now speak from military strength. He was no longer a lonely exile. He was head of an army and a fleet. To get those things, he had had to lie, to betray, and above all to bluff.

On his return to Samos envoys from the Four Hundred arrived and tried to conciliate the Athenian forces. They failed, and there were cries from the audience to kill the envoys and sail against the Four Hundred in Athens. It was Alcibiades who dissuaded them and pointed out that, while they were sailing against Athens, the enemy would certainly seize their empire in Ionia and around the Hellespont. When the envoys returned to Athens, the Four Hundred made a desperate attempt to obtain peace from Sparta on almost any terms. But, in the autumn of 411, Euboea revolted, all of the island except Oreus was lost, and a fleet of 36 triremes which the oligarchs had sent to defend Euboea was overwhelmed by 42 Peloponnesian ships and suffered the loss of 22 vessels. The fall of Euboea struck home as not even the great catastrophe at Syracuse had done: with Attica in the hands of King Agis at Decelea, food from Euboea was more desperately needed than ever. The camp at Samos was in full revolt. Athens had too few ships to defend Piraeus against the attack they felt sure was imminent. An Assembly was called. The Four Hundred were deposed. All who could afford a suit of armor were to belong to 'the Five Thousand,' a body the

Four Hundred had always talked about but had never actually created. Nobody should receive pay for public office. And the Assembly voted to recall Alcibiades and other exiles. A message was sent him, beseeching him and the camp at Samos to keep pressing the enemy. Most of the hated Athenian oligarchs fled to Decelea and the Spartan king. The Peloponnesian fleet, sick of hearing Tissaphernes' promises of a Phoenician fleet, which never came and which quite possibly was never available to him, deserted its paymaster for Pharnabazus, whose province included the Hellespont.

The naval campaign now shifted to the Hellespont. But Tissaphernes went there too; Alcibiades visited him—and was arrested and sent to Sardis. He escaped. In the spring of 410 a Peloponnesian fleet, now under the command of Mindarus, was badly defeated by the Athenians, off Cyzicus on the Propontis. Alcibiades, Theramenes, and Thrasybulus slipped a fleet of 86 ships through the Hellespont, unseen, and surprised Mindarus. They sank or captured about 60 triremes, and Mindarus was killed. The Athenians intercepted a laconic message to Sparta from Mindarus' successor: "The ships are gone. Mindarus is dead. The men are starving. We know not what to do."[275] When news of the victory at Cyzicus was received, the old democratic constitution was restored. Under Alcibiades' leadership, the Athenian forces won back complete control of the grain route, including the Bosphorus. But while Alcibiades won glory in the north, affairs nearer home presented a sharp contrast. King Agis still held Decelea and therefore Attica. Euboea was gone. Megara had won back her eastern port, Nisaea. Chios was lost again. Corcyra threatened to become neutral. And, after all these years, Sparta had at last regained Pylos. In the spring of 407 Alcibiades learned that the Athenian Assembly had once more elected him a general.

Now he chose to come home, not because he had been grudgingly recalled in 411 when the Four Hundred fell, but because he was a conquering hero who had again secured his city's life line to the grain supply of the Black Sea. Or did Athens look on him as a hero? As a matter of fact, opinion was still divided. He collected troops at Samos and twenty ships. He sailed to the Ceramic Gulf in southwest Asia Minor and collected a hundred talents. Then he cautiously sailed near Athens to learn for himself how he would be received. When his ship reached Piraeus, after his exile of eight years, a crowd awaited him. On seeing a group of his relatives and

personal friends, he was reassured, and went up to Athens, with his friends
protectively surrounding him, and addressed the Council and Assembly.
He denied the old charge of sacrilege and claimed he had been unjustly
treated. No one spoke in opposition: by now the Assembly would not have
tolerated it. He was voted extraordinary powers[276] to save his polis. His
first act was to conduct in person the procession of the Eleusinian mysteries.

There was no question either of the death sentence or of the curse placed
upon him for sacrilege, when toward the end of October, 407, he sailed
with a fleet of a hundred triremes. Eight years before, he had sailed out of
Athens with 134 ships, bound for Sicily and conquest, but he had been
only one of three commanders of that doomed expedition and he had
sailed under a cloud, accused of desecrating the holy mysteries of Eleusis.
This time, before he sailed, he had organized and led the first annual pilgrimage that Athenians had made in years, by land along the Sacred Way
to Eleusis, his troops guarding the holy procession. He had made it under
the nose of the Spartan King Agis at Decelea—of Agis, whose queen he,
Alcibiades, had seduced, while conspiring in Sparta against Athens, to bring
Athens to her senses again. There were indeed dissenting voices, but, as he
sailed from Piraeus with his hundred ships, he was the hero of his polis.
He had already opened the Hellespont; now he must reconquer those of
the Ionian cities still in a state of revolt. On the way, he attacked Andros,
but failed to take the city, and returned to Athens' main base at Samos.

But fate had pitted against him two new and formidable antagonists.
One was Lysander, whom Sparta had sent out to command her forces, perhaps the ablest man she had sent out since Brasidas. The other was the
Persian prince, Cyrus, to whom the Great King had turned over most of
Tissaphernes' province and a mandate to finish the war with Athens. Cyrus
was much struck with Lysander's ability and honesty and raised the wage
of the seamen in Lysander's fleet, settled arrears of pay, and gave the
seamen a month's pay in advance. In 407, Alcibiades, finding it necessary to
be away from his fleet, committed it to the care of a favorite of his, Antiochus, captain of Alcibiades' own ship. He also ordered him not to attack
Lysander's fleet, now lying at Ephesus. During his absence, Antiochus disobeyed, allowed Lysander to trap him into a battle, and lost. Opinion in
Athens turned against Alcibiades, the Assembly replaced him, and Alcibiades fled to one of his private castles on the Hellespont, built on his
last campaign in those regions.

Meanwhile, things were going badly for Athens too. With the backing of Cyrus, the Peloponnesians built their fleet up to 140 ships. The Athenian commander, Conon, with only 70 vessels, was attacked outside Mitylene and lost 30 precious triremes, and the rest of his fleet was blockaded in the harbor. Athens was now desperate. She borrowed the gold and silver dedications from the temples on the Acropolis, melted them down, built a new fleet of 150 triremes, and sent it to relieve Mitylene. The Peloponnesians met the new Athenian fleet near the Arginusae, a cluster of tiny islands between Lesbos and the mainland. Lysander's term of office had expired and now, in 406, his successor Callicratidas commanded the Peloponnesians. He was overwhelmed; 70 of his ships were sunk or captured, and he himself was killed. But the eight Athenian commanders in charge were accused at Athens of criminal negligence: they had delayed rescuing the crews of 25 triremes that had been wrecked in battle, until a rising storm had rendered rescue impracticable. Two commanders had since fled. The other six were illegally tried in a group, before the Assembly itself and not in court. Although Alcibiades' friend, Socrates, who happened to be presiding that day, refused to put the illegal motion to the vote, a vote was nevertheless taken, and all six of the commanders were executed. One of them was Pericles, son of Aspasia and the great Pericles.

The battle of Arginusae had given the eastern Aegean back to Athenian sea power, so Sparta sued for peace. Athens, elated by her newly re-won power, rejected Sparta's proposals. Again Sparta turned to Lysander. Under Spartan law he could not officially serve as admiral a second time, but he was sent as secretary to his successor in office with real power to direct operations. Toward the end of summer, 405, Lysander sailed to the Hellespont and captured Lampsacus. An Athenian fleet which followed him beached across the Hellespont from Lampsacus at Aegospotami, or Goat's River. From his neighboring castle Alcibiades noted the Athenian camp and rode over to urge the commanders in charge to fall back on Sestos, about two miles downshore, so that the crews could secure provisions without leaving their fleet. The commanders paid no heed and ordered him off: it was they who were in charge, not Alcibiades. Soon thereafter his fears were realized. Lysander, with some 200 vessels, fell on the Athenian fleet when it was unprepared: only nine ships escaped. Most of the men were captured. Lysander then called together his allies and invited proposals on what was to be done with the Athenian prisoners. The allies charged the Athenian Assembly with having declared that, if their fleet won, their commanders would cut off the right hand of every man they might capture. One Athenian commander, Philocles, who had captured two ships, was accused of having thrown every man on them overboard. It was decided to execute every prisoner who was an Athenian, except one man who had opposed the motion made in the Assembly. As to Philocles, Lysander ordered his throat cut.

The man-made island, Athens-Piraeus, would now learn the price islands had to pay when they lost the sea. But news of her final defeat did not immediately reach Athens.

> It was at night that the Paralus [an official State trireme] arrived at Athens with tidings of the disaster, and a sound of wailing ran from Piraeus through the long walls to the city, one man passing on the news to another; and during that night no one slept, all mourning, not for the lost alone, but far more for their own selves, thinking that they would suffer such treatment as they had visited upon the Melians, colonists of the Lacedaemonians, after reducing them by siege, and upon the Histiaeans and Scionaeans and Toronaeans and Aeginetans and many other Greek peoples. On the following day they convened an Assembly, at which it was resolved to block up all the harbours except one, to repair the walls, to station guards, and in all other respects to get the city ready for a siege. They busied themselves, accordingly, with these matters.[277]

Lysander of Sparta now held the sea, and Lysander was made of iron. Unlike some other commanders Sparta had sent out, he scorned personal gain, avoided luxury, and wore his hair long. Incorruptible himself, he freely corrupted others. He lied, he bribed, he was notorious for his cruelty. He conquered city after city, abolished democratic government everywhere, and installed oligarchies backed by Spartan garrisons. He methodically rounded up every Athenian he could find and offered him safe-conduct to Athens or the risk of death if caught elsewhere. He had determined to blockade Athens by sea, while King Agis held it blockaded by land, until famine should open it; hence, the more people it had to feed the better.

King Pausanias marched an army up from Sparta to join King Agis, and Lysander closed his sea blockade of Piraeus with 150 ships. With no fleet, no allies, and little food, Athens closed ranks and restored political rights to those she had disfranchised. People had begun to starve, but for a while she made no effort to negotiate. Then, when all her supplies of food were exhausted, she sent ambassadors to Agis. She offered to become the ally of Sparta, if only she might keep Piraeus and her walls.

Sparta insisted the Athenians must tear down a portion of the Long Walls for about a mile and a quarter—enough, in short, to convert the man-made island into a peninsula, accessible to control by Spartan land forces for the first time in over half a century. The negotiations dragged on, while famine gripped Athens harder. Then the Athenians grew more amenable and gave their ambassadors full powers to go to Sparta and negotiate with the Lacedaemonians and their allies. Thebes, Corinth, and many other allies opposed a treaty: they favored destroying Athens. But the Spartans retorted that they would not enslave a Greek city which had done so much for Greece. Had not Athens first defeated the Persian invaders at Marathon? And fought at Sparta's side at Salamis, at Plataea, at Mycale? Athens could now have peace if she would destroy the Long Walls and the walls of Piraeus, surrender all but twelve of her ships, allow her exiled oligarchs to come home, and subordinate her foreign policy to Sparta's.

> So Theramenes and his fellow-ambassadors brought back this word to Athens. And as they were entering the city, a great crowd gathered around them, fearful that they had returned unsuccessful; for it was no longer possible to delay, on account of the number who were dying of the famine. On the next day the ambassadors reported to the Assembly the terms on which the Lacedaemonians offered to make peace; Theramenes acted as spokesman for the embassy, and urged that it was best to obey the Lacedaemonians and tear down the walls. And while some spoke in opposition to him, a far greater number supported him, and it was voted to accept the peace. After this Lysander sailed into Piraeus, the exiles returned, and the Peloponnesians with great enthusiasm began to tear down the walls to the music of flute-girls, thinking that that day was the beginning of freedom for Greece.[278]

It was April of the year 404, twenty-seven years after Sparta had invaded Attica and thereby precipitated the Peloponnesian War.

And Alcibiades? The thirty oligarchs who ruled Athens after her fall from power were nominally charged by the Assembly, acting under pressure from their conqueror, Lysander, with drawing up a new constitution. But first the thirty inaugurated a reign of terror. Now that Sparta, which had condemned Alcibiades to death, was taking over the Hellespont, he fled to the Persian governor, Pharnabazus. So the 'Thirty Tyrants' officially banished him. Then one of them, Critias, persuaded Sparta that the democrats in Athens would never willingly submit to government by their betters so long as they could hope that some day Alcibiades might come home. Once more Sparta sent orders, this time to Lysander, to see that Alcibiades was killed. Lysander persuaded Alcibiades' Persian host to have him slain. The men sent to kill him found him in a village in Phrygia, where he was living with a courtesan. They went at night to his house and, not daring to enter it, they set it afire. Alcibiades dashed out and scattered them with his sword, but they slew him with javelins and arrows. His mistress wrapped his body in her own garments and gave him the most brilliant funeral she could provide. But this whole story of his death survived as only a dubious legend. Some men said that it was neither Lysander nor the Spartans nor the Persian, Pharnabazus, who took his life. These men claimed it was not a courtesan with whom he was living but the daughter of a well-known family; that Alcibiades had seduced her; and that it was her brothers who fired the house and killed him. Others claimed that he went to Pharnabazus with the project of imitating that earlier famous exile from Athens, Themistocles; and that he also, Alcibiades, planned to go up to Susa to the palace of the Great King. There he would offer to help the King put down his new rival for power in the Aegean, Lacedaemon. In any case,[279] Alcibiades died when he was about forty-six years old, in the year 404, the same year the Athenian Empire died.

Indeed, he and the Athenian democracy mirrored each other. He was beautiful, and so was Athens; he loved beauty, and so did she; he had taste, and so had his city. He displayed a captivating charm at a time when the charm of Athens captivated all Hellas. He had the quick adaptability of Odysseus, and Athens had it too. He was courageous, and often rash. Was not Athens both? Like his city, he struck hard at his enemies. He displayed an insolence, a hybris, such as the gods hated, and so did his polis. And like her, he was dramatic, both in word and deed. He had an imagination that led him to dream of conquering Italy and Carthage when Amphipolis still defied her metropolis, and tradition would record that in those same months, before their splendid armada sailed off for Sicily, the people of Athens also dreamed dreams of unlimited glory. For both Alcibiades and Athens desperately wanted fame and always wanted money. In the west, could they not find both? Both he and she were quickly diverted if opportunity suddenly beckoned. They were changeable in fortunate times, obstinate and persevering when the times seemed hopeless.

When dark days came, they both refused to give up. After complete catastrophe in Sicily, to the amazement of all Hellas Athens won a naval victory at Cynossema in 411 and an overwhelming victory off Cyzicus in 410. After her defeats in 407 at Notion and off Mitylene, she melted down the gold and silver ornaments in her temples, built a new fleet, and overwhelmed her foes again at Arginusae in 406. But in that terrible summer of 405 and in the hungry winter that followed, she came at last to know that the sword and the oar had failed her. And in April, 404, her Long Walls came down. For his part Alcibiades had repeatedly risen from disaster. After his city had placed a price on his head, he taught Sparta to humble her. After he had left Sparta for Ionia and had got news that Sparta, too, had condemned him to death, he went alone to Tissaphernes, the Persian governor; he bluffed the Athenian forces at Samos into believing that he could bring Athens the subsidies Persia now gave Sparta, if only Athens would get rid of the extreme democracy that had banished and condemned him; was elected a general; led the reconquest of the route to the Black Sea and Athens' daily bread; returned in triumph to Athens; lost Athens' confidence and was replaced; retreated to his Hellespontine castle; tried to rescue an Athenian fleet from its folly and bad strategy; saw that fleet's ruin; and then—according to at least one of the traditions that grew up about him—planned to find new leverage as an advisor to the Great King himself. Where the city had been surrendered and forced out of its sheltering walls by famine, Alcibiades had been surrounded and forced out of his house by fire—if another of the legends of Alcibiades was correct. And he was forced out to die, sword in hand, under a hail of arrows.

Athens was his mistress, not his wife, and he loved her with possessive passion. She would be his, or nobody's. They were capable of doing each other great injury, but they longed with passion for each other. And, indeed, where else but Athens could he hope to be happy? Where else but in this witty polis would he find the conversation that could feed his mind? Where else the beauty that shone down from the Acropolis? Where else so sophisticated a community of men, "feeding on the most illustrious wisdom," as Euripides wrote, "and walking delicately in the most radiant air"[280]? In short, what other place than Athens was truly civilized? What could one do in the long months at Sparta, except perhaps eat black broth, take cold baths, and seduce a Spartan queen? Then, at least, Sparta would have a half-Athenian king to reign over her dour, laconic, cautious army of drill sergeants. In Athens, in the Agora, there was something no Spartan would ever grasp, something he would scorn as idle chatter: there was good talk, a communion of men's minds, a duel of wits, and if Socrates happened to be present, a joint search into the invisible realm of ideas, vaster and more mysterious than Sicily itself.

7

THE PHILOSOPHER KING

IN APRIL, 404, when the twenty-seven years of butchery and devastation, of hatred and deception, of suspicion and betrayal, of heroic sacrifice and black grief had ended, when to the sound of flutes the Long Walls came down that Hellas might be free, and when empire was gone, Socrates of Athens was sixty-six years old. He had been a boy of about ten when Pericles and democracy came to power in Athens. He had been a young man of twenty-four when Pericles abandoned the idea of empire in Mainland Greece and focused on sea power, islands, and distant coasts. He was thirty-one when the revolt of Samos was quelled; and at thirty-seven he served in the heavy infantry at the siege of rebel Potidaea. He was thirty-nine when Sparta and her allies invaded Attica, and the Great War, the long agony of Hellas, began. Then came Pericles' famous funeral oration, in which he declared that this polis of Socrates was the School of Hellas; then the frightful plague; the drop in Athenian morale; and another great speech from Pericles, in which he warned the Athenians that their polis was a tyrant-city, ruling her allies by force, and that it was too late to turn back from the path of empire. Now, a quarter of a century later, when Socrates was an old man, the Long Walls came down. In a sense, he too had followed the path of empire. It had led him not only to Potidaea, but also to take part in the Athenian rout at Delium in 424. In 422 it led him to fight in the battle of Amphipolis, in which fell both Cleon of Athens and Brasidas of Sparta, those two 'pestles' who had ground up the cities of Hellas in the mortar of war.

But Socrates' understanding had already been formed in pre-war Periclean Athens, in the polis which created the Parthenon to crown its holy Acropolis; which created the music one heard in the Odeon at the foot of that same Acropolis; which created in the nearby theater of the god Dionysus the majestic religious tragedies of Aeschylus and the more complex tragedies of Sophocles; and which created the mural paintings in the arcaded Agora. It was the polis in which Herodotus read aloud his history of the defense of Hellenic freedom against the vast imperial forces of Xerxes; the polis which gathered up the philosophers from all over Hellas, with their speculations on the nature of matter and the universe; the great sophists, ready to lecture, for a fee, on rhetoric and on many other subjects, the great artists—and the great merchants. For Athens' port, the Piraeus, joined to her by the impregnable Long Walls in a man-made island ruling natural islands, was now the main emporium of the Mediterranean world, an emporium where money was no longer a mere medium for the exchange of commodities but was often an end in itself, an emporium where strange tongues could be heard and strange costumes seen. Athens was also the headquarters of a powerful fleet of swift triremes, ready to police the trade routes against pirates, ready to collect the tribute imposed on her subject cities, ready to guarantee the grain route from the Black Sea that a polis which Attic farms could no longer feed might continue nevertheless to eat. She was the most populous polis in Hellas: counting her slaves and her metics, she contained perhaps over 400,000 souls. She was the richest city in Hellas, richer even than her jealous commercial rival, Corinth. To impose her will, she had easily the most powerful navy, much stronger than that of her nearest competitor, Corcyra.

If the Piraeus was the Mediterranean's leading center for the exchange of commodities, Athens was its leading center for the exchange of words. For, among other things, this polis was an unending conversation. At its best, it was a noble conversation, the noblest that Hellas had achieved.

It was a communion of men's minds that sought communion with the gods themselves, a conversation through which a community of men learned together. When Simonides had written that "Polis teaches man,"[281] might he not have had in mind that the true polis was in essence a conversation, a conversation about important matters? Perhaps he even knew that conversations were conducted not merely in speculative words that jointly sought a truth common to all men in the polis, nor in deliberative words that sought their common good in council, assembly, or court of justice. Perhaps he knew a conversation could also occur between architects, not in words but in temples, between sculptors who carved or modeled statues, between painters who spoke on walls or only on vases and kitchen pots, between all artists and their other fellow citizens; and that it raised questions and essayed answers in a common search for beauty.

Yet, either because the docks and warehouses and shops of the Piraeus were too close, or because the physical appetites of philosopher, statesman, or artist were too clamorous, the citizens of Athena's Polis bought and sold, not only oil and wine and pots and woolen cloth, but words and statues too. The sophist might turn word merchant to teach men the false argument that deceived, that bore false witness in assembly or court, the poet might write what was neither true nor beautiful but what would gain a prize, the artist might consciously or unconsciously build or carve or paint the meretricious.

These were some of the problems that faced the polis into which, in 470, Socrates had been born. His father was a sculptor in stone and a friend of Lysimachus, son of Aristides the Just. The mother of Socrates, Phaenarete, was in her later years an expert midwife. When Socrates was young, he studied, as other Athenian boys did, music and gymnastic. Music meant Homer and other poetry as well as music in the usual sense; gymnastic trained one in grace of movement as well as in strength and endurance. Socrates also acquired some knowledge of geometry and astronomy. He started out in his father's occupation, sculpture or stonecutting. But he became enamored of the speculations of the Ionians on the nature of matter, and together with a friend named Chaerephon and other young men tried to acquire the natural science of his day.

However, his interest slowly shifted to the intellectual and moral nature of man, to man's place in his polis, to what made the polis itself good or evil. Finally, he combined a deep interest in religion with a ceaselessly questing mind. Did his interest in religion spring, at least in part, from a direct and powerful intuitive experience he had known intermittently since childhood? This intuition took the form of a kind of voice, a divine spirit that dwelt within him, a sign, that often warned him not to do something he was about to do, but never gave positive advice.

During the period of his friendship with Socrates, Chaerephon was so impressed with his friend's intellectual powers that he journeyed to Delphi and boldly asked Apollo to tell him whether anyone was wiser than Socrates. The oracle replied that there was no man wiser. When this reply was reported to Socrates, he was troubled:[282] he did not believe he was wise at all, but neither did he believe that the god would lie. That Apollo should appear to speak in a riddle was of course no cause for astonishment: everybody knew that oracles were often ironical. Cassandra, the Trojan prophetess in Aeschylus's *Oresteia* spoke in that style; so did the prophet Tiresias in Sophocles' *Oedipus the King*. The problem was to keep the conversation going, to assume the oracle made sense, to assume therefore that one must discover in what sense the words were delivered. When Croesus, king of Lydia, had lost an empire to Cyrus of Persia and had then sent envoys to rebuke Apollo for deceiving him with the promise that, should he attack Cyrus, a great empire would fall, had not Apollo calmly pointed out to the Lydian envoys that Croesus should have inquired further? That was precisely what Socrates now proposed to do. He would try to find another man who was clearly wiser than himself and then go to Delphi and confront Apollo with his discovery. He would say to the god, "Here is a man who is wiser than I am, but you said that I was the wisest."[283]

Socrates picked out a leading Athenian politician and questioned him narrowly. But though the politician he had picked out "was thought wise by many, and still wiser by himself,"[284] his confused and conflicting answers to Socrates' questions made it clear that he was anything but wise. Also he apparently realized he had made a fool of himself, for he was angry. So Socrates left him, saying to himself as he went away:

Well, although I do not suppose that either of us knows anything really beautiful and good, I am better off than he is,—for he knows nothing and thinks that he knows; I neither know nor think that I know. In this latter particular, then, I seem to have slightly the advantage of him.[285]

He went to others, with the same result. They always started the conversation sure of their wisdom. Then they became confused and contradicted themselves. Then they felt shown up and became angry. Socrates concluded from a series of such examinations "that the men most in repute were all but the most foolish; and that others less esteemed were really wiser and better."[286] After the politicians, he tried poets, whom he questioned about "some of the most elaborate passages in their own writings,"[287] only to discover that poets apparently wrote out of inspiration, not out of their own wisdom. Yet, because they really had written good poetry, they imagined they were the wisest of men in other matters also. He tried artisans, with the same results.

The method of close, logical questioning that Socrates used normally led the answerer to self-contradiction. Socrates did not denounce the answerer's opinions. He merely elicited from him, step by logical step, opinions which conflicted so glaringly that the answerer grew furious. Yet Socrates was faultlessly courteous. He treated the firmly announced opinions of other men as he had treated the oracle of Apollo: their answers often appeared to him false, but he assumed, for the purposes of the discussion, that the fault lay in him, not in them. He continued, patiently and apologetically, until they fell into pitfalls that not even their pride of authorship could protect them from seeing. They thereupon guessed that Socrates had all along seen these pitfalls coming; yet it was not Socrates, but their own words that landed them in a refutation. The Greek word for refutation, *elenchos*,[288] had an older and primary meaning: disgrace, dishonor. When their own words refuted them, they felt disgraced and dishonored, and by Socrates, or at least in front of Socrates. It was with Socrates that they remained angry.

And Socrates? He concluded that the riddling words of the oracle which had been given to his friend, Chaerephon, really meant that no man was truly wise, that only God was wise, and that the only human wisdom that Socrates or any other man could possess was to know that his own wisdom meant nothing. In that case, what could a mere man do? He could inquire further. This was what Socrates invariably and persistently did and it was his unique characteristic. Indeed, he construed the oracle given to Chaerephon as a mission given to him, Socrates, to keep inquiring further. "Obedient to the god,"[289] he kept inquiring. To do so, he accepted the poverty that Pericles, in his great funeral oration, had declared was no disgrace in Athens. To continue to inquire, he joyfully embraced poverty, which Pericles had declared it was disgraceful not to do something about. Pericles was of course talking about material possessions, those that satisfy the body's wants. But Socrates, by focusing on possessions that satisfied the mind's wants, in effect restated the Periclean formula: ignorance was no disgrace; the only disgrace was not doing anything about ignorance. Socrates had not always been poor: as late as 431, when he fought at Potidaea, he had fought in the heavy infantry, which the very poor could not enter because of the cost of equipment. But, at least in the later years of his mission, he wandered about Athens in a single garment, in all weather, and without sandals. The diet of Athenians, excepting some of the rich, was a matter of bread, mixed wine and water, olives, vegetables, salads, dried fish, and all of them scantly rationed with perhaps a piece of meat on the days of public sacrifice. Yet even in Athens Socrates' diet was conspicuously scant and simple. Antiphon, the sophist, once remarked to him:

> you are living a life that would drive even a slave to desert his master. Your meat and drink are of the poorest: the cloak you wear is not only a poor thing, but is never changed summer or winter; and you never wear shoes or tunic.[290]

"But," objected Socrates, "my belief is that to have no wants is divine; to have as few as possible comes next to the divine."[291]

He embraced poverty, partly to gain freedom from the preoccupations that a higher standard of living would have brought him, partly to gain the leisure for a kind of inquiry that was clearly a full-time job, partly because he found it brought him a sort of health which physical pleasures would have quickly stolen away. He had observed that doctors were busy chiefly with treating the effects of overindulgence. Most Athenians would inevitably regard Socrates as a barefoot, garrulous eccentric but essentially one of the sophists or teachers of wisdom. But the other sophists tended to lecture and to teach others to make speeches too: Socrates disliked speech-making and monologuing and preferred a very special form of conversation, dialectic, in which one person—either person of the two who consented to play the game of dialectic—questioned the other. In this game, skillful play normally started with a request for a definition, a request meant to invite a brief answer. Then the questioner asked a second brief question and got a second brief reply. By brief question alternating with brief reply, the game went on. The skillful questioner would try to make his question elicit the implications of the first reply—of the first, tentative definition, the first hypothesis, as it were—until, short logical step by short logical step, the answerer reached a conclusion so palpably absurd that he himself either rejected it or else refined his first hypothesis and tried again to survive in this trial by ordeal.

This game of dialectic was none other than old Hesiod's good eris, that good strife, or free competition, that set potter against potter and minstrel against minstrel. But in dialectic it was clear ideas that must be shaped, not pots, argument that must vie with argument, not song that must outdo song.

Alongside of this good eris, again as in Hesiod, stood an evil eris that superficially resembled it. Indeed, eristic was its common name. Both were contests. But in true dialectic, questioner and answerer alike came out victorious. Both of them at the end were likely to discover that the original definition or opinion with which the cross-examination had started was false. If they were concerned with truth, they were glad to be rid of a false opinion. Socrates learned early that the ignorant man abounded in unexamined opinions: the ignorant man was the opinionated man. If the falseness of one of his opinions neared the surface of his mind, he fell into a psychic panic, as the hero of Sophocles' *Oedipus the King* did whenever his search for the man who had murdered the former king confronted him with troubling words that might have meant not only that it was he who had murdered, but that the victim was his own father, and his wife, Queen Jocasta, his own mother. At the end of a dialectical process, Socrates' opponent in the good eris all too often assumed that the *elenchos* which meant refutation was really the *elenchos* that meant dishonor and disgrace. Since the habits of Socrates' opponent had usually been the habits of eristic dispute, not of a common dialectical search, the opponent often valued his opinions not because they were demonstrably true but because they were his own. It was therefore a point of honor or prestige to get them agreed to, true or false though they might be. When the intellectual wrestling match ended in the opponent's logical fall, the opponent was concerned with his single defeat, Socrates with their joint victory. The examined opinion had for Socrates passed through an ordeal of its own, like the ordeal of a tragic hero in one of the plays of Aeschylus or of Sophocles. It had met catastrophe, and out of catastrophe might come understanding; out of hybris and defeat, a kind of victory.

By such encounters Socrates made many bitter enemies, especially among the very important people in his polis. The more important they were, the more face they had to lose. And they often lost it in front of others. As the questions and answers continued and his victims felt the jaws of logic closing on them, they somehow mistook the grip of logic for the grip of Socrates. Was their increasing discomfiture precisely the disgrace and dishonor which they, with their eristic habits, had hoped to inflict on Socrates? That Socrates was unusually courteous, even in a polis renowned for courtesy, mysteriously added insult to injury—or smugness to injury. That he was gay and humorous, with the gaiety and humor that sprang from freedom, freedom from wealth and the hostages given to wealth, made him still more insufferable, like an executioner who put men to the rack while jesting about no laughing matter. Those whom he questioned accused him of knowing in advance the correct answers to his questions. For example, in 404, when Sparta installed an oligarchical government in defeated Athens, a member of this government, Charicles, ordered Socrates to stop asking questions of young men.

"Suppose," asked Socrates gently, "I want to buy something, am I not even then to ask the price if the seller is under thirty?"

"Oh, yes," answered Charicles, "you may in such cases. But the fact is, Socrates, you are in the habit of asking questions to which you know the answer: so that is what you are not to do."[292]

But Charicles, too, was judging Socratic dialectic by eristic: he was judging argument as a means to discover the truth or falsity of an opinion by argument for the sake of apparent victory regardless of the truth. The same basic misunderstanding made men doubt the kind of statement Socrates once made to his friend, Charmides:

> And at this moment I pursue the argument chiefly for my own sake, and perhaps in some degree also for the sake of my other friends. For is not the discovery of things as they truly are, a good common to all mankind?[293]

The same misunderstanding made men doubt even the kind of statement Socrates once made to Callicles:

These truths . . . would seem now to have been fixed and riveted by us, if I may use an expression which is certainly bold, in words which are like bonds of iron and adamant; and unless you or some other still more enterprising hero shall break them, there is no possibility of denying what I say. For my position has always been, that I myself am ignorant how these things are, but that I have never met any one who could say otherwise, any more than you can, and not appear ridiculous.[294]

Socrates clearly stood ready to re-examine the issues.

The intellectual good manners of Socrates, the courtesy and even the deference he showed to all comers, were the courtesy and deference he owed formally to a fellow inquirer. This formal courtesy sprang from his deference to truth. He never offered deference to birth or fame or wealth, except with a kind of gentle irony, which the eristic debater, if he detected it, would be likely to interpret as sarcasm. But it was irony, and Socrates loved and used irony because it raised a question, as Apollo's irony in his first answer to Croesus had raised a question, and because, as in a good oracle, irony therefore invited thought. Irony to a wealthy and important Athenian would at least raise the question of whether either the wealth or the importance of a man need have any relevance either to the correctness of his opinions or to his desire to learn; of whether, indeed, a man's worldly status need bear at all on his ordeal by question.

In a polis where famous sophists taught for high fees, Socrates steadfastly refused to accept money for his teaching. How could he, since he did not teach?[295] And how could he teach, since he claimed no knowledge? He was merely trying to learn and maybe to help others to learn, though he sometimes admitted he did know one or two things: for example, that one must try to know. He remarked once to his friend Meno,

> Some things I have said of which I am not altogether confident. But that we shall be better and braver and less helpless if we think that we ought to enquire, than we should have been if we indulged in the idle fancy that there was no knowing and no use in seeking to know what we do not know;—that is a theme upon which I am ready to fight, in word and deed, to the utmost of my power.[296]

He knew too, or firmly believed he knew, what he meant by the word knowledge. Speaking to Meno on the same occasion, he said:

> I too speak rather in ignorance; I only conjecture. And yet that knowledge differs from true opinion is no matter of conjecture with me. There

are not many things which I profess to know, but this is most certainly one of them.[297]

The level of Socrates' irony was general and universal, a level of the permanent and timeless. There was no climbing to that level by syllogisms, since syllogisms could lead only downward from the general to the special, from the universal to the particular. To help his companions up, he cast down rope ladders of analogy, of metaphor; he played the poet; he jested; he teased when they tired and he caressed them with his words when they struggled to climb up; he punctured their vanity when they were complacent. He wanted them to think, as he wanted himself to think. When Theaetetus struggled vainly to answer a difficult question the argument had posed, Socrates comforted him:

These are the pangs of labour, my dear Theaetetus; you have something within you which you are bringing to the birth.

Theaet. I do not know, Socrates; I only say what I feel.

Soc. And have you never heard, simpleton, that I am the son of a midwife, brave and burly, whose name was Phaenarete?

Theaet. Yes, I have.

Soc. And that I myself practise midwifery?

Theaet. No, never.

Soc. Let me tell you that I do though, my friend: but you must not reveal the secret, as the world in general have not found me out; and therefore they only say of me, that I am the strangest of mortals and drive men to their wits' end. Did you ever hear that too?

Theaet. Yes.

Soc. Shall I tell you the reason?

Theaet. By all means.

Soc. Bear in mind the whole business of the midwives, and then you will see my meaning better:—No woman, as you are probably aware, who is still able to conceive and bear, attends other women, but only those who are past bearing.

Theaet. Yes, I know.

Soc. The reason of this is said to be that Artemis—the goddess of childbirth—is not a mother, and she honours those who are like herself; but she could not allow the barren to be midwives, because human nature cannot know the mystery of an art without experience; and therefore she assigned this office to those who are too old to bear.

Theaet. I dare say.

Soc. And I dare say too, or rather I am absolutely certain, that the midwives know better than others who is pregnant and who is not?

Theaet. Very true.

Soc. And by the use of potions and incantations they are able to arouse the pangs and to soothe them at will; they can make those bear who have a difficulty in bearing, and if they think fit they can smother the embryo in the womb.

Theaet. They can.

Soc. Did you ever remark that they are also most cunning matchmakers, and have a thorough knowledge of what unions are likely to produce a brave brood?

Theaet. No, never.

Soc. Then let me tell you that this is their greatest pride, more than cutting the umbilical cord. And if you reflect, you will see that the same art which cultivates and gathers in the fruits of the earth, will be most likely to know in what soils the several plants or seeds should be deposited.

Theaet. Yes, the same art.

Soc. And do you suppose that with women the case is otherwise?

Theaet. I should think not.

Soc. Certainly not; but midwives are respectable women who have a character to lose, and they avoid this department of their profession, because they are afraid of being called procuresses, which is a name given to those who join together man and woman in an unlawful and unscientific way; and yet the true midwife is also the true and only matchmaker.

Theaet. Clearly.

Soc. Such are the midwives, whose task is a very important one, but not so important as mine; for women do not bring into the world at one time real children, and at another time counterfeits which are with difficulty distinguished from them; if they did, then the discernment of the true and false birth would be the crowning achievement of the art of midwifery—you would think so?

Theaet. Indeed I should.

Soc. Well, my art of midwifery is in most respects like theirs; but differs, in that I attend men and not women, and I look after their souls when they are in labour, and not after their bodies: and the triumph of my art is in thoroughly examining whether the thought which the mind of the young man brings forth is a false idol or a noble and true birth. And like midwives, I am barren, and the reproach which is often made against me, that I ask questions of others and have not the wit to answer them myself is very just—the reason is, that the god compels me to be a midwife, but does not allow me to bring forth. And therefore I am not myself at all wise, nor have I anything to show which is the invention or birth of my own soul, but those who converse with me profit. Some of them appear dull enough at first, but afterwards, as our acquaintance ripens, if the god is gracious to them, they all make astonishing progress; and this in the opinion of others as well as in their own. It is quite clear that they never learned anything from me; the many fine discoveries to which they cling are of their own making. But to me and the god they owe their delivery. And the proof of my words is, that many of them in their ignorance, either in their self-conceit despising me, or falling under the influence of others, have gone away too soon; and have not only lost the children of whom I had previously delivered them by an ill bringing up, but have stifled whatever else they had in them by evil communications, being fonder of lies and shams than of the truth; and they have at last ended by seeing themselves, as others see them, to be great fools. Aristeides, the son of Lysimachus, is one of them, and there are many others. The truants often return to me, and beg that I would consort with them again—they are ready to go to me on their knees—and then, if my familiar [*daimōn*] allows, which is not always the case, I receive them, and they begin to grow again. Dire are the pangs which my art is able to arouse and to allay in those who consort with me, just like the pangs of women in childbirth; night and day they are full of perplexity and travail which is even worse than that of the women. So much for them. And there are others, Theaetetus, who come to me apparently having nothing in them; and as I know that they have no need of my art, I coax them into marrying some one, and by the grace of God I can generally tell who is likely to do them good. Many of them I have given away to Prodicus, and many to other inspired sages. I tell you this long story, friend Theaetetus, because I suspect, as indeed you seem to think yourself, that you are in labour—great with some conception. Come then to me, who am a midwife's son and myself a midwife, and do your best to answer the questions which I will ask you. And if I abstract and expose your firstborn, because I discover upon inspection that the conception which you have formed is a vain shadow, do not quarrel with me on that account, as the manner of women is when their first children are taken from them. For I have actually known some who were ready to bite me when I deprived them of a darling folly; they did not perceive that I acted from good will, not knowing that no god is the enemy of man—that was not within the range of their ideas; neither am I their enemy in all this, but it would be wrong for me to admit falsehood, or to stifle the truth. Once more, then, Theaetetus, I repeat my old question, 'What is knowledge?' —and do not say that you cannot tell; but quit yourself like a man, and by the help of God you will be able to tell.

Theaet. At any rate, Socrates, after such an exhortation I should be ashamed of not trying to do my best. Now he who knows perceives what he knows, and, as far as I can see at present, knowledge is perception.

Soc. Bravely said, boy; that is the way in which you should express your opinion. And now, let us examine together this conception of yours, and see whether it is a true birth or a mere wind-egg:—You say that knowledge is perception?[298]

When the famous sophist, Protagoras of Abdera, visited Athens shortly before the Great War began, one of Socrates' young friends awoke him at dawn. Protagoras had gone to the home of the wealthy Callias; so had Hippias of Elis, Prodicus of Ceos, and several other wise men. Hippocrates persuaded Socrates to take him to Callias' home and present him to the great sophist. Arrived at the vestibule of Callias' house, Socrates and Hippocrates fell into philosophic argument and argued long before knocking. The porter had already had enough of sophists: when they knocked, he grumbled that Callias was not at home and slammed the door in their faces. But they finally got in. Socrates later described what they saw:

When we entered, we found Protagoras taking a walk in the cloister; and next to him, on one side, were walking Callias, the son of Hipponicus, and Paralus, the son of Pericles, who, by the mother's side, is his half-brother, and Charmides, the son of Glaucon. On the other side of him were Xanthippus, the other son of Pericles, Philippides, the son of Philomelus; also Antimoerus of Mende, who of all the disciples of Protagoras is the most famous, and intends to make sophistry his profession. A train of listeners followed him; the greater part of them appeared to be foreigners, whom Protagoras had brought with him out of the various cities visited by him in his journeys, he, like Orpheus, attracting them by his voice, and they following. I should mention also that there were some Athenians in the company. Nothing delighted me more than the precision of their movements: they never got into his way at all; but when he and those who were with him turned back, then the band of listeners parted regularly on either side; he was always in front, and they wheeled round and took their places behind him in perfect order.[299]

The irony Socrates put into describing Protagoras and his adoring disciples invited his companion to gauge the distance between the peripatetic lecture and the healthily rough give-and-take of dialectic. Physically as well as intellectually, the great Protagoras was followed. Physically and intellectually, those who followed him got out of his way when he and his thought turned. And once more, "in perfect order," they followed.[300]

Then, casually, the famous, elderly Protagoras and the then young Socrates engaged. But Protagoras quickly threw aside the brief give-and-take of dialectic and soared into a long and rhetorically skillful oration. At last it ended, and Socrates remarked that many orators, including Pericles, could pronounce a fine discourse,

> but then when one has a question to ask of any of them, like books, they can neither answer nor ask; and if any one challenges the least particular of their speech, they go ringing on in a long harangue, like brazen pots, which when they are struck continue to sound unless some one puts his hand upon them; whereas our friend Protagoras can not only make a good speech, as he has already shown, but when he is asked a question he can answer briefly; and when he asks he will wait and hear the answer; and this is a very rare gift. Now I, Protagoras, want to ask of you a little question, which if you will only answer, I shall be quite satisfied.[301]

Now, at least for a short while, Socrates held the great man to the brief answer. But as the going began to get rough for a man with great face to lose, and fees, too, Protagoras grew hesitant, evasive, then ruffled and excited—and made a longer speech, so eloquent that his adoring followers broke into a cheer. Then Socrates:

> Protagoras, I have a wretched memory, and when any one makes a long speech to me I never remember what he is talking about. As then, if I had been deaf, and you were going to converse with me, you would have had to raise your voice; so now, having such a bad memory, I will ask you to cut your answers shorter, if you would take me with you.
> What do you mean? he said: how am I to shorten my answers? shall I make them too short?
> Certainly not, I said.

But short enough?

Yes, I said.

Shall I answer what appears to me to be short enough, or what appears to you to be short enough?

I have heard, I said, that you can speak and teach others to speak about the same things at such length that words never seemed to fail, or with such brevity that no one could use fewer of them. Please therefore, if you talk with me, to adopt the latter or more compendious method.

Socrates, he replied, many a battle of words have I fought, and if I had followed the method of disputation which my adversaries desired, as you want me to do, I should have been no better than another, and the name of Protagoras would have been nowhere.

I saw that he was not satisfied with his previous answers, and that he would not play the part of answerer any more if he could help; and I considered that there was no call upon me to continue the conversation; so I said: Protagoras, I do not wish to force the conversation upon you if you had rather not, but when you are willing to argue with me in such a way that I can follow you, then I will argue with you. Now you, as is said of you by others and as you say of yourself, are able to have discussions in shorter forms of speech as well as in longer, for you are a master of wisdom; but I cannot manage these long speeches: I only wish that I could. You, on the other hand, who are capable of either, ought to speak shorter as I beg you, and then we might converse. But I see that you are disinclined, and as I have an engagement which will prevent my staying to hear you at greater length (for I have to be in another place), I will depart; although I should have liked to have heard you.[302]

Socrates had early in life displayed a memory for complicated conversation that was extraordinary, yet his plea of a bad memory contained an element of truth: he found it hard to remember the unrelated items in a rhetorical explosion set off for purposes of display; and he could not imagine how a series of such explosions could advance the dialectical search he had drawn Protagoras into. But his wealthy host, Callias, begged him to stay. At last Socrates said:

Let me tell you then what I will do in order that the conversation and discussion may go on as you desire. If Protagoras is not disposed to answer, let him ask and I will answer; and I will endeavour to show at the same time how, as I maintain, he ought to answer: and when I have answered as many questions as he likes to ask, let him in like manner answer me;

and if he seems to be not very ready at answering the precise question asked of him, you and I will unite in entreating him, as you entreated me, not to spoil the discussion. And this will require no special arbiter—all of you shall be arbiters.

This was generally approved, and Protagoras, though very much against his will, was obliged to agree that he would ask questions; and when he had put a sufficient number of them, that he would answer in his turn those which he was asked in short replies.[303]

Protagoras promptly shifted the theme of their argument to a doubtfully relevant passage of the poet Simonides; tried to trip Socrates up in argument; and again elicited cheers from his followers. Thereupon Socrates made a very long speech, delicately parodying the intricate literary criticism which sophists like Protagoras loved. Indeed, Hippias quite missed his irony and was so inspired that he asked permission to propound his own interpretation of the passage in Simonides. "Nay, Hippias," said Alcibiades; "not now, but at some other time." Then Socrates said:

I wish Protagoras either to ask or answer as he is inclined; but I would rather have done with poems and odes, if he does not object, and come back to the question about which I was asking you at first, Protagoras, and by your help make an end of that. The talk about poets seems to me like a commonplace entertainment to which a vulgar company have recourse; who, because they are not able to converse or amuse one another, while they are drinking, with the sound of their own voices and conversation, by reason of their stupidity, raise the price of flute-girls in the market, hiring for a great sum the voice of a flute instead of their own breath, to be the medium of intercourse among them: but where the company are real gentlemen and men of education, you will see no flute-girls, nor dancing-girls, nor harp-girls; and they have no nonsense or games, but are contented with one another's conversation, of which their own voices are the medium, and which they carry on by turns and in an orderly manner, even though they are very liberal in their potations. And a company like this of ours, and men such as we profess to be, do not require the help of another's voice, or of the poets whom you cannot interrogate about the meaning of what they are saying; people who cite them declaring, some that the poet has one meaning, and others that he has another, and the point which is in dispute can never be decided. This sort of entertainment they decline, and prefer to talk with one another, and put one another to the proof in conversation. And these are the models which I desire that you and I should imitate. Leaving the poets, and keeping to ourselves, let us try the mettle of one another and make proof of the truth in conversation. If you have a mind to ask, I am ready to answer; or if you would rather, do you answer, and give me the opportunity of resuming and completing our unfinished argument.

I made these and some similar observations; but Protagoras would not distinctly say which he would do. Thereupon Alcibiades turned to Callias, and said:—Do you think, Callias, that Protagoras is fair in refusing to say whether he will or will not answer? for I certainly think that he is unfair; he ought either to proceed with the argument, or distinctly to refuse to proceed, that we may know his intention; and then Socrates will be able to discourse with some one else, and the rest of the company will be free to talk with one another.

I think that Protagoras was really made ashamed by these words of Alcibiades, and when the prayers of Callias and the company were super-added, he was at last induced to argue, and said that I might ask and he would answer.

So I said: Do not imagine, Protagoras, that I have any other interest in asking questions of you but that of clearing up my own difficulties. For I think that Homer was very right in saying that

'When two go together, one sees before the other,'

for all men who have a companion are readier in deed, word, or thought; but if a man

'Sees a thing when he is alone,'

he goes about straightway seeking until he finds some one to whom he may show his discoveries, and who may confirm him in them. And I would rather hold discourse with you than with any one, because I think that no man has a better understanding of most things which a good man may be expected to understand, and in particular of virtue. For who is there, but you?—who not only claim to be a good man and a gentleman, for many are this, and yet have not the power of making others good—whereas you are not only good yourself, but also the cause of goodness in others. Moreover such confidence have you in yourself, that although other Sophists conceal their profession, you proclaim in the face of Hellas that you are a Sophist or teacher of virtue and education, and are the first who demanded pay in return. How then can I do otherwise than invite you to the examination of these subjects, and ask questions and consult with you?[804]

So again they tried, Socrates asking, Protagoras answering. But Socrates led the argument to a certain stage and then pointed out to Protagoras that somehow they had shifted sides and must start again. "And," he added, "if you have no objection, as I said at first, I should like to have your help in the inquiry."

But Protagoras had throughout the long discussion aimed at another goal than Socrates. Socrates contested with Protagoras as a means to their jointly discovering the truth. Had Protagoras accepted his invitation to a joint search because the search was a contest he had hoped to win? And because the contest was held before an audience of fellow sophists and prospective pupils? He had been, after all, as Socrates had pointed out, the first sophist to "proclaim in the face of Hellas" that he was a sophist, that he taught virtue, and demanded pay for his teaching. This particular contest, or exhibition of his skill, had not proven wholly satisfactory. So he excused himself:

> Socrates, I am not of a base nature, and I am the last man in the world to be envious. I cannot but applaud your energy and your conduct of an argument. As I have often said, I admire you above all men whom I know, and far above all men of your age; and I believe that you will become very eminent in philosophy. Let us come back to the subject at some future time; at present we had better turn to something else.[305]

Had the compliment to Socrates been not ironical, as had been those of Socrates to him, but conciliatory? If it was a shade patronizing—well, was not Protagoras the older man and a great deal the more famous? If Socrates' courtesy to him had been wholly ironical, it nevertheless showed him deference because Protagoras was a human being and he might therefore at any moment rise from eristic to dialectic, from the bad eris to the good.[306] Perhaps Protagoras's courtesy to Socrates was a generous invitation to share personal glory and professional prestige, the polite offer of one professional intellectual to conspire with another. Perhaps it suggested an offer to split with a famous colleague the limited fund of respect and money which a lay public was prepared to afford to intellectuals as a group.

This conspiracy of the intellectuals did not escape the sharp eyes of Aristophanes. At the Great Dionysia of 423 he presented the *Clouds*. It won only third prize. In the *Clouds* Aristophanes pilloried the sophists, those wise men who taught for pay and who especially taught men to argue successfully, whether they wished to debate in the Assembly or the Council on public measures or whether they wished to prosecute others or defend themselves in the courts. In the *Clouds*, a rustic from the Attic countryside named Strepsiades, who had married above himself socially and now lived in Athens, was struggling with the unpaid bills of his spendthrift son Phidippides. Phidippides was mad about horses and loved the expensive, aristocratic sport of chariot-racing, the sport at which the great Alcibiades excelled. Next door to Strepsiades' home the spectators beheld a house full of learned sophists who studied under the direction of Socrates. They studied natural philosophy, astronomy, geography, geometry, and especially the air: had not Anaximenes, the Ionian, and his followers found in air, not only the basic substance of the material universe, but the source of mind itself? Here now was Socrates, suspended in a basket from the derrick that enabled the gods in Euripides' tragedies still to appear to men. Here was Socrates observing loftily:

> I have to suspend my brain and mingle the subtle essence of my mind with this air, which is of the like nature, in order clearly to penetrate the things of heaven. I should have discovered nothing, had I remained on the ground to consider from below the things that are above; for the earth by its force attracts the sap of the mind to itself. It's just the same with the water-cress.[307]

This house of Socrates and his studious companions was "the Thoughtery of wise souls."[308] And they not only studied nature; like other sophists they could teach one how to present a bad policy in the Assembly and make it sound like a good one, to go to court with guilty hands and yet persuade the judges to acquittal. So Strepsiades wished to enroll and to learn the skill that could defraud his creditors. In the Thoughtery Socrates presented him to the Clouds, or to the chorus dressed as clouds, as "the only goddesses; all the rest are pure myth."[309] But what of Zeus? Does he not make it rain? Not at all: the Clouds do, by bumping against each other. But doesn't Zeus cause them to bump? Not at all: the aerial Whirlwind does that.

But Strepsiades turned out too stupid to learn the esoteric knowledge of the Thoughtery. The chorus of Clouds advised him to send his son instead. Strepsiades went home, informed his son that Whirlwind had driven out Zeus and was now King, and persuaded him to study at the

Thoughtery; meanwhile he himself staved off his creditors with his newly acquired sophistry and with threats of force. Phidippides returned home fully corrupted by the Thoughtery, gave his father a sound thrashing, and calmly defended his action with elaborate sophistry. This was too much for the old man. "Oh!" he cried, "what madness! I had lost my reason when I threw over the gods through Socrates's seductive phrases."[310] He called his servants and burned the Thoughtery over the heads of these evil men, crying:

> Ah! you insulted the gods! You studied the face of the moon! Chase them, strike and beat them down! Forward! they have richly deserved their fate—above all, by reason of their blasphemies.[311]

The real Socrates, of course, was conspicuous for declining pay; he did not scoff at the gods of his polis, although he did reject, as degrading, myths about them which he thought unworthy of the godhead; he was punctilious in prayer and sacrifice; he early turned from Ionian speculations on the nature of matter; he turned instead to the mission Apollo had placed on him to ask questions and to seek the good life for man and the good life of the polis. Yet any ordinary spectator who witnessed the *Clouds* was most likely accustomed to think of Socrates as a sophist—a word which was originally as free of obloquy as the word tyrant had once been. If asked to name a sophist, such a spectator would have been likely to name Socrates—that ubiquitous, eccentric, talkative fellow, with his bare feet, his single garment, his snub nose, flanging nostrils, thick lips, and bulging eyes. True, the other sophists did not wander the streets exchanging ideas with all comers. On the contrary, they lectured in private to young men who could afford to pay well for instruction. It was also true that this well-known eccentric did not conduct a school. But in the years when Chaerephon's admiration for Socrates' intellectual abilities had driven him to Delphi to consult Apollo about him, he and Chaerephon and other young men really had studied natural philosophy together.[312] So the eccentric Socrates came to personify in the *Clouds* those sophists who marketed ideas as commodities, those who taught men to use words not as the medium of exchange for the ideas that might lead to a common truth but as weapons in the war of words, weapons fitted to deceive, to confuse, to injure. The Athens of Aristophanes, now in the ninth year of a demoralizing war, was more and more inclined to use words in just that way. Did not the great Thucydides, speaking of the bloody revolution at Corcyra and of those which followed elsewhere, note one of the effects of substituting violence for reason: that ordinary words lost their traditional meanings and took on new and more cynical meanings?

If Aristophanes' caricature was somewhat irresponsible in those dangerous years, it did not reflect a lack of friendship for Socrates. Indeed, when Socrates' friend Agathon gave a banquet[313] to celebrate his having won first prize for his first tragedy, both Socrates and Aristophanes were among his guests. The banquet was held a few months before the great armada was to sail against Syracuse. Alcibiades, who came late to the party, had already been named one of the three generals to command the expedition which he, more than any other man, was responsible for launching. Socrates even wore sandals to celebrate the occasion, finery, as he explained, because Agathon was such a fine man. After dinner, when the drinking began, the usual flute girl appeared, but was told to leave: they wanted to talk. They had met for a banquet, and their Greek word for banquet was symposium, a drinking together. But, being Athenians, they wanted to think together too—or, at a minimum, to talk together. They decided to take turns at making an extemporaneous eulogy of the great and glorious god, Love, or Eros. Phaedrus delivered a highly rhetorical speech in praise of the homosexual love which Dorian states like Sparta encouraged in their armies as an incitement to valor and which the laconizing aristocrats of Athens tended to cultivate. Pausanias's speech demanded that love be more than merely sensual. The turn of the comic poet Aristophanes came next, but he had developed hiccoughs; so Eryximachus, who was a doctor, exchanged turns with him, meanwhile ordering him to hold his breath. The doctor then gave an ingenious and playfully pedantic speech likening love between persons to other forms of attraction in matter, animate and inanimate. Then Aristophanes, his hiccoughs now cured, delivered a thoroughly Aristophanic discourse, picturing the sexual union of man and woman as a reunion of the two halves of a previously round animal with two faces, four arms, and four legs. Zeus, it appeared, had sliced these monsters in two, and sexual desire was their longing for the wholeness of which Zeus had deprived them. Then the host, Agathon, the tragic poet, gave a wordy speech in purple prose, a dithyrambic glorification of Eros, god of love. And Socrates' turn came.

Socrates began with a few simple questions to Agathon, and the dialectic disclosed that erotic love was a desire, a want, a need, a lack. Before Socrates was through, he had pictured Love as the longing of the soul for the eternal and the divine. Love was not himself beautiful, but longed for the beautiful, a *daimōn*, "the mediator who spans the chasm"[314] between man and God—or so Socrates claimed to have learned from a wise woman, Diotima of Mantinea, who came once to Athens to purify the polis and thereby delayed the coming of the great plague for ten years. Nor was Love wise: he was a lover of wisdom, a philosopher. The soul's longing that men called Love could lead a man to the fair woman who might bring him a sort of immortality through posterity, or even to the vision which led Homer to father a great poem and Lycurgus and Solon to father wise laws. Love could lead a man up a kind of ladder from perceiving and loving a beautiful form to loving all beautiful forms, to the beauty of institutions and laws, to the beauty of the various sciences, to a science of beauty everywhere, until at last such a man could behold pure beauty itself, beauty bare, unspecified, simple, everlasting. This, too, was only what the wise Diotima had told him, but Socrates claimed to believe her. Just as he finished delivering his encomium, they heard a great knocking at the door and the notes of a flute girl.

"A little while afterwards," according to Plato's later report,

> they heard the voice of Alcibiades resounding in the court; he was in a great state of intoxication, and kept roaring and shouting "Where is Agathon? Lead me to Agathon," and at length, supported by the flute-girl and some of his attendants, he found his way to them. "Hail, friends," he said, appearing at the door crowned with a massive garland of ivy and violets, his head flowing with ribands. "Will you have a very drunken man as a companion of your revels? Or shall I crown Agathon, which was my intention in coming, and go away? For I was unable to come yesterday, and therefore I am here to-day, carrying on my head these ribands, that taking them from my own head, I may crown the head of this fairest and wisest of men, as I may be allowed to call him. Will you laugh at me because I am drunk? Yet I know very well that I am speaking the truth, although you may laugh. But first tell me; if I come in shall we have the understanding of which I spoke? Will you drink with me or not?"[315]

They begged him to stay. Alcibiades drank deep and bade Socrates drink the same quantity.

"Observe, my friends," he said, "that this ingenious trick of mine will have no effect on Socrates, for he can drink any quantity of wine and not be at all nearer being drunk."[316]

Then the drunken general-elect of the coming expedition to Syracuse threatened an encomium of his own, and what he proposed to praise was Socrates.

What are you about? said Socrates; are you going to raise a laugh at my expense? Is that the meaning of your praise?

I am going to speak the truth, if you will permit me.

I not only permit, but exhort you to speak the truth.

Then I will begin at once, said Alcibiades, and if I say anything which is not true, you may interrupt me if you will, and say 'that is a lie,' though my intention is to speak the truth. But you must not wonder if I speak any how as things come into my mind; for the fluent and orderly enumeration of all your singularities is not a task which is easy to a man in my condition.

And now, my boys, I shall praise Socrates in a figure which will appear to him to be a caricature, and yet I speak, not to make fun of him, but only for the truth's sake. I say, that he is exactly like the busts of Silenus, which are set up in the statuaries' shops, holding pipes and flutes in their mouths; and they are made to open in the middle, and have images of gods inside them. I say also that he is like Marsyas the satyr. You yourself will not deny, Socrates, that your face is like that of a satyr. Aye, and there is a resemblance in other points too. For example, you are a bully, as I can prove by witnesses, if you will not confess. And are you not a flute-player? That you are, and a performer far more wonderful than Marsyas. He indeed with instruments used to charm the souls of men by the powers of his breath, and the players of his music do so still: for the melodies of Olympus are derived from Marsyas who taught them, and these, whether they are played by a great master or by a miserable flute-girl, have a power which no others have; they alone possess the soul and reveal the wants of those who have need of gods and mysteries, because they are divine. But you produce the same effect with your words only, and do not require the flute; that is the difference between you and him. When we hear any other speaker, even a very good one, he produces absolutely no effect upon us, or not much, whereas the mere fragments of you and your words, even at second-hand, and however imperfectly repeated, amaze and possess the souls of every man, woman, and child who comes within hearing of them. And if I were not afraid that you would think me hopelessly drunk, I would have sworn as well as spoken to the influence which they have always had and still have over me. For my heart leaps within me more than that of any Corybantian reveller, and my eyes rain tears when I hear them. And I observe that many others are affected in the same manner. I have heard Pericles and other great orators, and I thought that they spoke well, but I never had any similar feeling; my soul was not stirred by them, nor was I angry at the thought of my own slavish state. But this Marsyas has often brought me to such a pass, that I have felt as if I could hardly endure the life which I am leading (this, Socrates, you will admit); and I am conscious that if I did not shut my ears against him, and fly as from the voice of the siren, my fate would be like that of others,—he would transfix me, and I should grow old sitting at his feet. For he makes me confess that I ought not to live as I do, neglecting the wants of my own soul, and busying myself with the concerns of the Athenians; therefore I hold my ears and tear myself away from him. And he is the only person who ever made me ashamed, which you might think not to be in my nature, and there is no one else who does the same. For I know that I cannot answer him or say that I ought not to do as he bids, but when I leave his presence the love of popularity gets the better of me. And therefore I run away and fly from him, and when I see him I am ashamed of what I have confessed to him. Many a time have I wished that he were dead, and yet I know that I should be much more sorry than glad, if he were to die: so that I am at my wit's end.

And this is what I and many others have suffered from the flute-playing of this satyr. Yet hear me once more while I show you how exact the image is, and how marvellous his power. For let me tell you; none of you know him; but I will reveal him to you; having begun, I must go on. See you how fond he is of the fair? He is always with them and is always being smitten by them, and then again he knows nothing and is ignorant of all things—such is the appearance which he puts on. Is he not like a Silenus in this? To be sure he is: his outer mask is the carved head of the Silenus; but, O my companions in drink, when he is opened, what temperance there is residing within! Know you that beauty and wealth and honour, at which the many wonder, are of no account with him, and are utterly despised by him: he regards not at all the persons who are gifted with them; mankind are nothing to him; all his life is spent in mocking and flouting at them. But when I opened him, and looked within at his serious purpose, I saw in him divine and golden images of such fascinating beauty that I was ready to do in a moment whatever Socrates commanded: they may have escaped the observation of others, but I saw them. . . .[317]

Then Alcibiades remembered their days at the siege of Potidaea:

there we messed together, and I had the opportunity of observing his extraordinary power of sustaining fatigue. His endurance was simply marvellous when, being cut off from our supplies, we were compelled to go without food—on such occasions, which often happen in time of war, he was superior not only to me but to everybody; there was no one to be compared to him. Yet at a festival he was the only person who had any real powers of enjoyment; though not willing to drink, he could if compelled beat us all at that,—wonderful to relate! no human being had ever seen Socrates drunk; and his powers, if I am not mistaken, will be tested before long. His fortitude in enduring cold was also surprising. There was a severe frost, for the winter in that region is really tremendous, and everybody else either remained indoors, or if they went out had on an amazing quantity of clothes, and were well shod, and had their feet swathed in felt and fleeces: in the midst of this, Socrates with his bare feet on the ice and in his ordinary dress marched better than the other soldiers who had shoes, and they looked daggers at him because he seemed to despise them.

I have told you one tale, and now I must tell you another, which is worth hearing,

'Of the doings and sufferings of the enduring man'

while he was on the expedition. One morning he was thinking about something which he could not resolve; he would not give it up, but continued thinking from early dawn until noon—there he stood fixed in thought; and at noon attention was drawn to him, and the rumour ran through the wondering crowd that Socrates had been standing and thinking about something ever since the break of day. At last, in the evening after supper, some Ionians out of curiosity (I should explain that this was not in winter but in summer), brought out their mats and slept in the open air that they might watch him and see whether he would stand all night. There he stood until the following morning; and with the return of light he offered up a prayer to the sun, and went his way. I will also tell, if you please—and indeed I am bound to tell—of his courage in battle; for who but he saved my life? Now this was the engagement in which I received the prize of valour: for I was wounded and he would not leave me, but he rescued me and my arms; and he ought to have received the prize of valour which the generals wanted to confer on me partly on account of my rank, and I told them so (this, again, Socrates will not impeach or deny), but he was more eager than the generals that I and not he should have the prize. There was another occasion on which his behaviour was very remarkable—in the flight of the army after the battle of Delium, where he served among the heavy-armed,—I had a better opportunity of seeing him than at Potidaea, for I was myself on horseback, and therefore comparatively out of danger. He and Laches were retreating, for the troops were in flight, and I met them and told them not to be discouraged, and promised to remain with them; and there you might see him, Aristophanes, as you describe, just as he is in the streets of Athens, stalking like a pelican, and rolling his eyes, calmly contemplating enemies as well as friends, and making very intelligible to anybody, even from a distance, that whoever attacked him would be likely to meet with a stout resistance; and in this way he and his companion escaped—for this is the sort of man who is never touched in war; those only are pursued who are running away headlong. I particularly observed how superior he was to Laches in presence of mind. Many are the marvels which I might narrate in praise of Socrates; most of his ways might perhaps be paralleled in another man, but his absolute unlikeness to any human being that is or ever has been is perfectly astonishing. You may imagine Brasidas and others to have been like Achilles; or you may imagine Nestor and Antenor to have been like Pericles; and the same may be said of other famous men, but of this strange being you will never be able to find any likeness, however remote, either among men who now are or who ever have been—other than that which I have already suggested of Silenus and the satyrs; and they represent in a figure not only himself, but his words. For, although I forgot to mention this to you before, his words are like the images of Silenus which open; they are ridiculous when you first hear them; he clothes himself in language that is like the skin of the wanton satyr—for his talk is of pack-asses and smiths and cobblers and curriers, and he is always repeating the same things in the same words, so that any ignorant or inexperienced person might feel disposed to laugh at him; but he who opens the bust and sees what is within will find that they are the only words which have a meaning in them, and also the most divine, abounding in fair images of virtue, and of the widest comprehension, or rather extending to the whole duty of a good and honourable man.

This, friends, is my praise of Socrates.[318]

There was laughter. They jested a little. Then a stray band of revelers entered and great confusion ensued. Aristodemus, who had come with Socrates to the banquet, fell asleep:

he was awakened towards daybreak by a crowing of cocks, and when he awoke, the others were either asleep, or had gone away; there remained only Socrates, Aristophanes, and Agathon, who were drinking out of a large goblet which they passed around, and Socrates was discoursing to them. Aristodemus was only half awake, and he did not hear the beginning of the discourse; the chief thing which he remembered was Socrates compelling the other two to acknowledge that the genius of comedy was the same with that of tragedy, and that the true artist in tragedy was an artist in comedy also. To this they were constrained to assent, being drowsy, and not quite following the argument. And first of all Aristophanes dropped off, then, when the day was already dawning, Agathon. Socrates, having laid them to sleep, rose to depart; Aristodemus, as his manner was, following him. At the Lyceum he took a bath, and passed the day as usual. In the evening he retired to rest at his own home.[819]

Perhaps the truth which Alcibiades spoke in his cups, that Socrates' words cast an enchantment on him; that his dialectic reduced him to shame; that he had often wished Socrates were dead; but that, though he often fled, he was inexorably drawn back—perhaps this experience was based chiefly on the fact that, when he talked with Socrates, he found another human mind fully meeting his own mind to a degree he never experienced in conversation with any other man. Perhaps, also, this exhilarating sense of communing with another was based on one thing more than on any other: Socrates listened. He listened to Apollo's oracles; he listened to the opinions of other men; he listened as the poets and artists of Athens must have listened to the Muse, in quietude of spirit. He listened to—or gazed inward at—ideas, standing at Potidaea for twenty-four hours, lost in thought, while the light-hearted, pleasure-loving Ionians in the besiegers' camp gazed at him curiously. This boon companion at banquets, this rigorous master of deductive argument, had somewhere learned the even rarer art of contemplation, perhaps from listening to the voice of his own *daimōn*, a voice that had spoken to him intermittently since childhood. His listening was not of the sort that flattered the vanity of the chatterer. On the contrary, he was renowned for deflating vanity.

But, for the young men who came to him, his attentiveness gave a dimension to human intercourse that brought them alive. His awareness awakened those who were intellectual sleepwalkers. Had not Heraclitus once written that the world was one and common to those who were awake?[320] The conversations these young men had taken part in over the years so often had been blind collisions. Now there was no collision, but engagement. This man listened. In a city more given to listening than most, he out-listened all competitors: the result was a kind of communion that gave back to the polis some of the ancient excitement Simonides had expressed, when he had written, "Polis teaches man."[321]

Indeed, in the most famous of all his conversations, Socrates imagined and he caused his companions to help him imagine, what a truly listening polis would be like, and hence what a truly human community would be like, a community seeing by intellectual light. At some time around 421[322] he and Glaucon, the elder brother of Plato, went down to Piraeus to attend the festival of Bendis, a Thracian goddess corresponding to the Hellenes' Artemis. Polemarchus, son of a wealthy metic named Cephalus, persuaded them to stay for the evening and for good talk. Included among the guests was a famous sophist from Chalcedon, Thrasymachus. The company fell to talking about justice, about what a just man was. Various definitions ran the dialectical gauntlet: that the just man was one who spoke the truth and paid his debts; that he was one who did good to his friends and evil to his enemies; or perhaps one who did good to his friends only when his friends were good, and evil to his enemies only when his enemies were evil. None of the definitions survived the short questions which Socrates so gently and persistently put.

But the famous sophist of Chalcedon was growing restless. As Socrates reported next day, in recounting the conversation to a friend,

> Several times in the course of the discussion Thrasymachus had made an attempt to get the argument into his own hands, and had been put down by the rest of the company, who wanted to hear the end. But when Polemarchus and I had done speaking and there was a pause, he could no longer hold his peace; and, gathering himself up, he came at us like a wild beast, seeking to devour us. We were quite panic-stricken at the sight of him.
>
> He roared out to the whole company: What folly, Socrates, has taken possession of you all? And why, sillybillies, do you knock under to one

another? I say that if you want really to know what justice is, you should not only ask but answer, and you should not seek honour to yourself from the refutation of an opponent, but have your own answer; for there is many a one who can ask and cannot answer. And now I will not have you say that justice is duty or advantage or profit or gain or interest, for this sort of nonsense will not do for me; I must have clearness and accuracy.

I was panic-stricken at his words, and could not look at him without trembling. Indeed I believe that if I had not fixed my eye upon him, I should have been struck dumb: but when I saw his fury rising, I looked at him first, and was therefore able to reply to him.

Thrasymachus, I said, with a quiver, don't be hard upon us. Polemarchus and I may have been guilty of a little mistake in the argument, but I can assure you that the error was not intentional. If we were seeking for a piece of gold, you would not imagine that we were 'knocking under to one another,' and so losing our chance of finding it. And why, when we are seeking for justice, a thing more precious than many pieces of gold, do you say that we are weakly yielding to one another and not doing our utmost to get at the truth? Nay, my good friend, we are most willing and anxious to do so, but the fact is that we cannot. And if so, you people who know all things should pity us and not be angry with us.

How characteristic of Socrates! he replied, with a bitter laugh;—that's your ironical style! Did I not foresee—have I not already told you, that whatever he was asked he would refuse to answer, and try irony or any other shuffle, in order that he might avoid answering?

You are a philosopher, Thrasymachus, I replied, and well know that if you ask a person what numbers make up twelve, taking care to prohibit him whom you ask from answering twice six, or three times four, or six times two, or four times three, 'for this sort of nonsense will not do for me,'—then obviously, if that is your way of putting the question, no one can answer you. But suppose that he were to retort, 'Thrasymachus, what do you mean? If one of these numbers which you interdict be the true answer to the question, am I falsely to say some other number which is not the right one?—is that your meaning?'—How would you answer him?

Just as if the two cases were at all alike! he said.

Why should they not be? I replied; and even if they are not, but only appear to be so to the person who is asked, ought he not to say what he thinks, whether you and I forbid him or not?

I presume then that you are going to make one of the interdicted answers?

I dare say that I may, notwithstanding the danger, if upon reflection I approve of any of them.

But what if I give you an answer about justice other and better, he said, than any of these? What do you deserve to have done to you?

Done to me!—as becomes the ignorant, I must learn from the wise—that is what I deserve to have done to me.

What, and no payment! a pleasant notion!

I will pay when I have the money, I replied.

But you have, Socrates, said Glaucon: and you, Thrasymachus, need be under no anxiety about money, for we will all make a contribution for Socrates.

Yes, he replied, and then Socrates will do as he always does—refuse to answer himself, but take and pull to pieces the answer of some one else.

Why, my good friend, I said, how can any one answer who knows, and says that he knows, just nothing; and who, even if he has some faint notions of his own, is told by a man of authority not to utter them? The natural thing is, that the speaker should be some one like yourself who professes to know and can tell what he knows. Will you then kindly answer, for the edification of the company and of myself?

Glaucon and the rest of the company joined in my request and Thrasymachus, as any one might see, was in reality eager to speak; for he thought that he had an excellent answer, and would distinguish himself. But at first he affected to insist on my answering; at length he consented to begin. Behold, he said, the wisdom of Socrates; he refuses to teach himself, and goes about learning of others, to whom he never even says Thank you.

That I learn of others, I replied, is quite true; but that I am ungrateful I wholly deny. Money I have none, and therefore I pay in praise, which is all I have; and how ready I am to praise any one who appears to me to speak well you will very soon find out when you answer; for I expect that you will answer well.

Listen, then, he said; I proclaim that justice is nothing else than the interest of the stronger. And now why do you not praise me? But of course you won't.

Let me first understand you, I replied. Justice, as you say, is the interest of the stronger. What, Thrasymachus, is the meaning of this? You cannot mean to say that because Polydamas, the pancratiast, is stronger than we are, and finds the eating of beef conducive to his bodily strength, that to eat beef is therefore equally for our good who are weaker than he is, and right and just for us?

That's abominable of you, Socrates; you take the words in the sense which is most damaging to the argument.

Not at all, my good sir, I said; I am trying to understand them; and I wish that you would be a little clearer.[323]

The year of 421, when these men talked together about justice, was the year of the Peace of Nicias. Six years before, the Assembly had debated on whether to massacre all the adult males of reconquered Mitylene. In another five years Athens really would massacre the conquered Melians after warning them of what the sophist Thrasymachus was already shouting at Socrates: that might made right. But Socrates remained unconvinced, not because he was unable to face the harsh realities of his brutalized world but because he rejected the childish notion that brute force could successfully parade as logical proof. He therefore quietly continued to question Thrasymachus, who now cried out that Socrates argued like an informer.

Indeed, Thrasymachus, and do I really appear to you to argue like an informer?

Certainly, he replied.

And do you suppose that I ask these questions with any design of injuring you in the argument?

Nay, he replied, 'suppose' is not the word—I know it; but you will be found out, and by sheer force of argument you will never prevail.

I shall not make the attempt, my dear man; but to avoid any misunderstanding occurring between us in future, let me ask, in what sense do you speak of a ruler or stronger whose interest, as you were saying, he being the superior, it is just that the inferior should execute—is he a ruler in the popular or in the strict sense of the term?

In the strictest of all senses, he said. And now cheat and play the informer if you can; I ask no quarter at your hands. But you never will be able, never.

And do you imagine, I said, that I am such a madman as to try and cheat Thrasymachus? I might as well shave a lion.

Why, he said, you made the attempt a minute ago, and you failed.

Enough, I said, of these civilities. It will be better that I should ask you a question: Is the physician, taken in that strict sense of which you are speaking, a healer of the sick or a maker of money? And remember that I am now speaking of the true physician.[324]

And so it went: brief, probing question followed brief, probing question; with Thrasymachus entangled in his own contradictions, yet sure of his practical experience of a wicked world; with Socrates gently coaxing him on, throwing down his ladder of analogies from everyday life, trying to help him climb to a clear idea, to some recognizable principle:

And the pilot likewise, in the strict sense of the term, is a ruler of sailors and not a mere sailor?

That has been admitted.

And such a pilot and ruler will provide and prescribe for the interest of the sailor who is under him, and not for his own or the ruler's interest?

He gave a reluctant 'Yes.'

Then, I said, Thrasymachus, there is no one in any rule who, in so far as he is a ruler, considers or enjoins what is for his own interest, but always what is for the interest of his subject or suitable to his art; to that he looks, and that alone he considers in everything which he says and does.

When we had got to this point in the argument, and every one saw that the definition of justice had been completely upset, Thrasymachus, instead of replying to me, said: Tell me, Socrates, have you got a nurse?

Why do you ask such a question, I said, when you ought rather to be answering?

Because she leaves you to snivel, and never wipes your nose: she has not even taught you to know the shepherd from the sheep.

What makes you say that? I replied.

Because you fancy that the shepherd or neatherd fattens or tends the sheep or oxen with a view to their own good and not to the good of himself or his master; and you further imagine that the rulers of states, if they are true rulers, never think of their subjects as sheep, and that they are not studying their own advantage day and night. . . .[325]

Then Thrasymachus, conscious that his argument was breaking down, hurried into one of those long and complicated tirades, such as Protagoras, too, had launched, and concluded emphatically:

And thus, as I have shown, Socrates, injustice, when on a sufficient scale, has more strength and freedom and mastery than justice; and, as I said at first, justice is the interest of the stronger, whereas injustice is a man's own profit and interest.

Thrasymachus, when he had thus spoken, having, like a bathman, deluged our ears with his words, had a mind to go away. But the company would not let him; they insisted that he should remain and defend his position; and I myself added my own humble request that he would not leave us. Thrasymachus, I said to him, excellent man, how suggestive are your remarks! And are you going to run away before you have fairly taught or learned whether they are true or not? Is the attempt to determine the way of a man's life so small a matter in your eyes—to determine how life may be passed by each one of us to the greatest advantage?

And do I differ from you, he said, as to the importance of the enquiry?

You appear rather, I replied, to have no care or thought about us, Thrasymachus—whether we live better or worse from not knowing what you say you know, is to you a matter of indifference. Prithee, friend, do not keep your knowledge to yourself; we are a large party; and any benefit which you confer upon us will be amply rewarded. For my own part I openly declare that I am not convinced, and that I do not believe injustice to be more gainful than justice, even if uncontrolled and allowed to have free play. For, granting that there may be an unjust man who is able to commit injustice either by fraud or force, still this does not convince me of the superior advantage of injustice, and there may be others who are in the same predicament with myself. Perhaps we may be wrong; if so, you in your wisdom should convince us that we are mistaken in preferring justice to injustice.

And how am I to convince you, he said, if you are not already convinced by what I have just said; what more can I do for you? Would you have me put the proof bodily into your souls?

Heaven forbid! I said; I would only ask you to be consistent; or, if you change, change openly and let there be no deception. . . .[326]

Again, the gentle, gentle, relentless questions, the faultless memory for the thread of argument, the attentive ear that heard the word, but also the mind's eye that saw the idea, half-clothed in mist, behind the word, until the crucial admission was made, and Socrates could say,

Then the just has turned out to be wise and good and the unjust evil and ignorant.

Thrasymachus made all these admissions, not fluently, as I repeat them, but with extreme reluctance; it was a hot summer's day, and the perspiration poured from him in torrents; and then I saw what I had never seen before, Thrasymachus blushing. As we were now agreed that justice was virtue and wisdom, and injustice vice and ignorance, I proceeded to another point:

Well, I said, Thrasymachus, that matter is now settled; but were we not also saying that injustice had strength; do you remember?

Yes, I remember, he said, but do not suppose that I approve of what you are saying or have no answer; if however I were to answer, you would be quite certain to accuse me of haranguing; therefore either permit me to have my say out, or if you would rather ask, do so, and I will answer 'Very good,' as they say to story-telling old women, and will nod 'Yes' and 'No.'

Certainly not, I said, if contrary to your real opinion.[327]

More questions. An admission. And Socrates:

Then the just is happy, and the unjust miserable?
So be it.
But happiness and not misery is profitable.
Of course.
Then, my blessed Thrasymachus, injustice can never be more profitable than justice.
Let this, Socrates, he said, be your entertainment at the Bendidea.
For which I am indebted to you, I said, now that you have grown gentle towards me and have left off scolding. Nevertheless, I have not been well entertained; but that was my own fault and not yours. As an epicure snatches a taste of every dish which is successively brought to table, he not having allowed himself time to enjoy the one before, so have I gone from one subject to another without having discovered what I sought at first, the nature of justice. I left that enquiry and turned away to consider whether justice is virtue and wisdom or evil and folly; and when there arose a further question about the comparative advantages of justice and injustice, I could not refrain from passing on to that. And the result of the whole discussion has been that I know nothing at all. For I know not what justice is, and therefore I am not likely to know whether it is or is not a virtue, nor can I say whether the just man is happy or unhappy.[328]

As so often before, he had not found what he was looking for—in this case, the true nature of justice. The whole of Hellas was being torn to pieces by men who charged each other with injustice: had the charge no meaning? True, those who conversed that summer night had found some of the things justice was not, things men had mistaken for justice itself, and there was some negative gain in that. The argument had once more done for Socrates what his *daimōn* had often done for him: it had vetoed, but it had not yielded the secret of what he ought to do, what he ought to believe. Except that, by implication, it told him to inquire further. And that is precisely what one of his young companions, Glaucon, begged him to do. So at it they went again, while the long night wore on—at this game of dialectic. Wild Thracian to the north, laconic Spartan to the south, would have looked on this game with an equal disdain. But this was Athens.

Socrates then somewhat playfully proposed that since men spoke not only of a just man but of a just polis, and since a polis was bigger than a man, maybe they could first locate justice in a polis and then the more readily locate it in the individual man. And so it came about that for most of the night Socrates, with what help he could conscript, imagined an ideal polis, a polis that was just because its citizens were just and that was in turn capable of educating citizens to be just. Polis teaches man.

First, thought Socrates, a polis was brought into being because men needed each other's skills and because a division of labor between them and an exchange of their products made human life better. The farmer could produce food; the builder, houses; the weaver, clothing; and, asked the barefoot Socrates, "shall we add to them a shoemaker, or perhaps some other purveyor to our bodily wants?"[329]

Slowly the list of craftsmen grew: carpenters, smiths, toolmakers, herdsmen, wage-laborers, even merchants and sailors. For this simple polis would want to exchange products with other communities. For exchange there would need to be money. Playfully, Socrates embarked on a lyrical description of a happy polis with a primitive economy. But Glaucon cut in:

> Yes, Socrates, he said, and if you were providing for a city of pigs, how else would you feed the beasts?
>
> But what would you have, Glaucon? I replied.
>
> Why he said, you should give them the ordinary conveniences of life. People who are to be comfortable are accustomed to lie on sofas, and dine off tables, and they should have sauces and sweets in the modern style.
>
> Yes, I said, now I understand: the question which you would have me consider is, not only how a State, but how a luxurious State is created; and possibly there is no harm in this, for in such a State we shall be more likely to see how justice and injustice originate. In my opinion the true and healthy constitution of the State is the one which I have described. But if you wish also to see a State at fever-heat, I have no objection. For I suspect that many will not be satisfied with the simpler way of life. They will be for adding sofas, and tables, and other furniture; also dainties, and perfumes, and incense, and courtesans, and cakes, all these

not of one sort only, but in every variety; we must go beyond the neces-
saries of which I was at first speaking, such as houses, and clothes, and
shoes: the arts of the painter and the embroiderer will have to be set in
motion, and gold and ivory and all sorts of materials must be procured.

True, he said.

Then we must enlarge our borders; for the original healthy State is no
longer sufficient. Now will the city have to fill and swell with a multitude
of callings which are not required by any natural want; such as the whole
tribe of hunters and actors, of whom one large class have to do with
forms and colours; another will be the votaries of music—poets and
their attendant train of rhapsodists, players, dancers, contractors; also
makers of divers kinds of articles, including women's dresses. And we
shall want more servants. Will not tutors be also in request, and nurses
wet and dry, tirewomen and barbers, as well as confectioners and cooks;
and swineherds, too, who were not needed and therefore had no place in
the former edition of our State, but are needed now? They must not be
forgotten: and there will be animals of many other kinds, if people eat
them.

Certainly.

And living in this way we shall have much greater need of physicians
than before?

Much greater.

And the country which was enough to support the original inhabitants
will be too small now, and not enough?

Quite true.

Then a slice of our neighbours' land will be wanted by us for pasture
and tillage, and they will want a slice of ours, if, like ourselves, they ex-
ceed the limit of necessity, and give themselves up to the unlimited
accumulation of wealth?

That, Socrates, will be inevitable.

And so we shall go to war, Glaucon. Shall we not?

Most certainly, he replied.

Then, without determining as yet whether war does good or harm, thus
much we may affirm, that now we have discovered war to be derived from
causes which are also the causes of almost all the evils in States, private
as well as public.[330]

Was Socrates' picture of a primitive polis designed merely to tease his
listeners into demanding a more Periclean polis, a high human culture?
Certainly what Glaucon called a city of pigs would have furnished Socrates

himself with all the material goods he needed or desired, plus the finery of a pair of sandals. But he assented gaily enough to expand his city of pigs into a luxurious city, with an army ready to make war. Indeed, as he ironically observed, it might be easier in a luxurious city to see how justice and injustice originated. In passing, one could note one consequence of "the unlimited accumulation of wealth": "And so we shall go to war, Glaucon. Shall we not?"[331] In any case this conversation contained not only taut logical necessities but humor and satire and repartee. In the hands of this sculptor and son of a sculptor, or in his words and the words of his companions, the image of a polis slowly took shape, a polis in which the boys who would one day have to defend it would study music and poetry, as the present company had done themselves, to make their souls gentle and receptive; to teach them, in fact, to listen. But the music and the poetry would have to be of the right kind. Not even Homer, whom Socrates revered and appeared to know by heart, would be allowed to tell to the young base stories about the gods and heroes, nor would there be the Lydian music that relaxed and over-softened. There would be stirring Dorian music. Then, of course, there must be gymnastic, to discipline and free the body's strength and grace, to school the youth in courage and endurance.

From among these Guardians of the Polis, the ablest would be picked out and trained in wisdom that they might know how to rule. Those who remained merely soldiers, Socrates speculated, might better be renamed Auxiliaries. The bulk of the population, requiring neither the wisdom to rule nor the courage and endurance to fight, would produce and exchange the material goods the polis would need. Their special virtue should be temperance or self-control. The polis Socrates had now imagined was an aristocracy, a government by the Aristoi, the Best People. But they were best, not because of the military virtues of the ancient, feudal aristocracies of Hellas; they were best because they had been tested and found wisest. The ancient aristocracies had forfeited their right to rule, partly by their avarice, which had led them to monopolize the wealth of the polis, partly by family vendettas that had bred faction and split the polis. Socrates forbade his Guardians to own private property, as Lycurgus had forbidden his Spartiates. But where Lycurgus merely put severe limits on marital life, Socrates—laughing at the audacity of his prescription—forbade marriage, in order to prevent his rulers from substituting the private good of the family for the common good of the polis. These Guardians whom he had called into being would be assigned by their magistrates temporary mates from among women as rigorously educated as themselves, in order to procreate their class. Except for this eugenic breeding, male and female Guardians alike would remain chaste. Neither artisan nor laborer nor businessman could participate in governing the polis, although they alone could hold private property. Only the wise must govern.

But there were things not even the wise knew, such as the services and rites and sacrifices due to the gods. For this last kind of knowledge, suggested Socrates, we must turn to the oracle of Apollo. Was not Apollo "the spokesman of his father, Zeus"[332]?

Even if the wise ought in fact to govern, how find the wise? And how secure the consent of the less wise to be governed by the wise? To the second question Socrates in effect imagined a myth worthy of Hesiod. His future citizens would be isolated in childhood and would be taught that the Earth was the common mother of them all; that they were therefore all brothers; but that some of them were golden and destined to rule, some were silver and destined for the army, and some were of iron or bronze and would neither rule nor fight. As to the first problem, the problem of finding the wise, that would have to be done through the most strenuous education.

They had built their imaginary state. It was ruled by the wise, defended by the brave, obeyed by those concerned with its material needs. These three functions were performed by specialized classes: golden Guardians, silver Auxiliaries, and the men made of baser metals. When each of the three classes performed well the function for which it was responsible, then, they decided, there was a just polis.

Turning from the polis to the single human being, Socrates and his colleagues in political sculpture saw the human intellect as corresponding to the ruling Guardians, with wisdom as its specific virtue; saw spirit, or drive, as corresponding to the Auxiliaries, with courage as its virtue; and saw the physical appetites as corresponding to the producing, exchanging, money-making class, with self-control as the specific virtue of the appetites. The man whose intellect governed his spirit or drive, as well as his physical appetites—the man, otherwise stated, who was wise and courageous and self-controlled—would be a just man who would choose to act justly, regardless of rewards and punishments, either in this life or another.

But how should these wise Guardians be educated? Most of this long night's conversation had been lighthearted, humorous, fanciful, free of literal-mindedness, part debate and part story-telling, emphatically not constitution-making of a schematic sort. But on the point of education for wisdom, Socrates grew earnest. He reminded his companions that they lived in two interpenetrating worlds, the world of things the physical eye could see by the light of the sun and the world of ideas which only the mind's eye could see—and then only by virtue of an intellectual light, shed by something he preferred to call the Idea of the Good. To educate Guardians wise enough to govern a polis was to help them to move freely between this visible world and that intelligible world—and thereby to find intelligibility in the concrete world they must deal with. An unprincipled man could not govern wisely; no man could deal with cases without knowing what they were cases of. Socrates now suggested, as so often, an analogy that might help his companions to intuit—in fact, an analogy that fruitfully burst forth into a cluster of analogies and proportions.

Imagine a line, he suggested, and divide it unequally, so that AB is to BC as AD is to DB and as BE is to EC. Let BC represent things the body's eye can see and let AB represent the things which only the mind's eye can see—the intelligibles. Imagine EC to represent only images and reflections, like the reflections in water and in mirrors. The objects they reflect, he suggested, the objects his companions called real, could be represented by BE. Now Socrates invited them to enter AB, the world of the intelligibles, the world of understanding—the world, he might have added, in which Oedipus saw more clearly once he had destroyed his physical eyesight. But that world, too, had a higher and a lower division. In DB there dwelt abstract ideas like triangle and circle— perfect triangularity and perfect circularity—which the intellect of the geometer had seized, or abstracted, from the imperfect triangles and circles the physical eye had seen in BE. The triangles in BE, however, were merely approximate and never permanent, because they were made out of changing matter. Those in DB were immaterial, eternal, perfect, unchanging. Such was the world of every mathematician. But the sciences which dealt with the eternal objects of DB all depended, as geometry did, on certain basic assumptions, certain axioms, which everybody took for granted.

Now he invited his audience to ascend to the last subdivision of the line

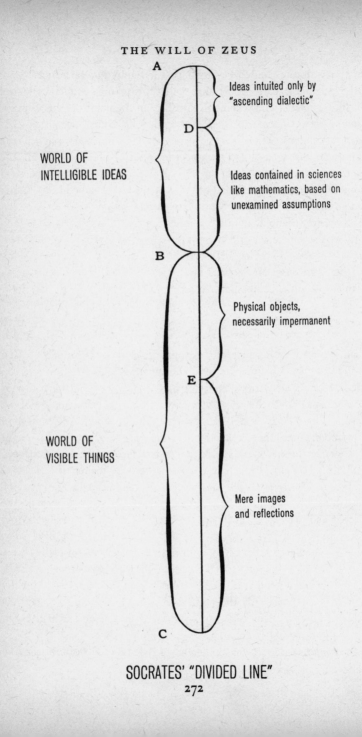

A

Ideas intuited only by
"ascending dialectic"

D

WORLD OF
INTELLIGIBLE IDEAS

Ideas contained in sciences
like mathematics, based on
unexamined assumptions

B

Physical objects,
necessarily impermanent

E

WORLD OF
VISIBLE THINGS

Mere images
and reflections

C

SOCRATES' "DIVIDED LINE"

he had imagined, a subdivision where the deductive logic of DB could not suffice, and where only dialectic could guide:

> And when I speak of the other division of the intelligible, you will understand me to speak of that other sort of knowledge which reason herself attains by the power of dialectic, using the hypotheses not as first principles, but only as hypotheses—that is to say, as steps and points of departure into a world which is above hypotheses, in order that she may soar beyond them to the first principle of the whole; and clinging to this and then to that which depends on this, by successive steps she descends again without the aid of any sensible object, from ideas, through ideas, and in ideas she ends.[333]

Socrates' ladder that led from the world of sensory perception and unexamined opinion to the world of clear ideas and knowledge led toward truth itself, as another ladder he had described to the drunken Alcibiades and his fellow revelers led toward beauty itself. Glaucon thought he understood, though by no means perfectly. Glaucon, though he came of an aristocratic family, was a child of Periclean democracy, a society whose love of free speech and equality before the law was not unconnected with Socrates' willingness to talk with anybody who was willing to search, but a society which inevitably misled the ignorant into supposing that what they could not understand was not understandable. Had Glaucon, then, contracted from his master some of the art of listening that made it possible to learn, some of the intellectual courtesy that made Socrates formally assume that, when another man seemed to be talking nonsense, it was his, Socrates', fault that communication failed? And that the cure for such failure, whether one conversed with an apparent dolt or with Apollo himself, was to inquire further and find out if what seemed to have no sense could be important truth if only the riddling word, the dark saying, were understood in another sense? In any case, Glaucon continued now to listen. And, as if to rescue him from groping, Socrates shifted his figure of speech and cast down another ladder:

> And now, I said, let me show in a figure how far our nature is enlightened or unenlightened:—Behold! human beings living in an underground den, which has a mouth open towards the light and reaching all along the den; here they have been from their childhood, and have their legs and necks chained so that they cannot move, and can only see before them, being prevented by the chains from turning round their

heads. Above and behind them a fire is blazing at a distance, and between the fire and the prisoners there is a raised way; and you will see, if you look, a low wall built along the way, like the screen which marionette players have in front of them, over which they show the puppets.

I see.

And do you see, I said, men passing along the wall carrying all sorts of vessels, and statues and figures of animals made of wood and stone and various materials, which appear over the wall? Some of them are talking, others silent.

You have shown me a strange image, and they are strange prisoners.

Like ourselves, I replied; and they see only their own shadows, or the shadows of one another, which the fire throws on the opposite wall of the cave?

True, he said; how could they see anything but the shadows if they were never allowed to move their heads?

And of the objects which are being carried in like manner they would only see the shadows?

Yes, he said.

And if they were able to converse with one another, would they not suppose that they were naming what was actually before them?

Very true.

And suppose further that the prison had an echo which came from the other side, would they not be sure to fancy when one of the passers-by spoke that the voice which they heard came from the passing shadow?

No question, he replied.

To them, I said, the truth would be literally nothing but the shadows of the images.

That is certain.

And now look again, and see what will naturally follow if the prisoners are released and disabused of their error. At first, when any of them is liberated and compelled suddenly to stand up and turn his neck round and walk and look towards the light, he will suffer sharp pains; the glare will distress him, and he will be unable to see the realities of which in his former state he had seen the shadows; and then conceive some one saying to him, that what he saw before was an illusion, but that now, when he is approaching nearer to being and his eye is turned towards more real existence, he has a clearer vision,—what will be his reply? And you may further imagine that his instructor is pointing to the objects as they pass and requiring him to name them,—will he not be perplexed? Will he not fancy that the shadows which he formerly saw are truer than the objects which are now shown to him?

Far truer.

And if he is compelled to look straight at the light, will he not have a pain in his eyes which will make him turn away to take refuge in the objects of vision which he can see, and which he will conceive to be in reality clearer than the things which are now being shown to him?

True, he said.

And suppose once more, that he is reluctantly dragged up a steep and rugged ascent, and held fast until he is forced into the presence of the sun himself, is he not likely to be pained and irritated? When he approaches the light his eyes will be dazzled, and he will not be able to see anything at all of what are now called realities.

Not all in a moment, he said.

He will require to grow accustomed to the sight of the upper world. And first he will see the shadows best, next the reflections of men and other objects in the water, and then the objects themselves; then he will gaze upon the light of the moon and the stars and the spangled heaven; and he will see the sky and the stars by night better than the sun or the light of the sun by day?

Certainly.

Last of all he will be able to see the sun, and not mere reflections of him in the water, but he will see him in his own proper place, and not in another; and he will contemplate him as he is.

Certainly.

He will then proceed to argue that this is he who gives the season and the years, and is the guardian of all that is in the visible world, and in a certain way the cause of all things which he and his fellows have been accustomed to behold?

Clearly, he said, he would first see the sun and then reason about him.

And when he remembered his old habitation, and the wisdom of the den and his fellow-prisoners, do you not suppose that he would felicitate himself on the change, and pity them?

Certainly, he would.

And if they were in the habit of conferring honours among themselves on those who were quickest to observe the passing shadows and to remark which of them went before, and which followed after, and which were together; and who were therefore best able to draw conclusions as to the future, do you think that he would care for such honours and glories, or envy the possessors of them? Would he not say with Homer,

'Better to be the poor servant of a poor master,'

and to endure anything, rather than think as they do and live after their manner?

Yes, he said, I think that he would rather suffer anything than entertain these false notions and live in this miserable manner.

Imagine once more, I said, such an one coming suddenly out of the sun to be replaced in his old situation; would he not be certain to have his eyes full of darkness?

To be sure, he said.

And if there were a contest, and he had to compete in measuring the shadows with the prisoners who had never moved out of the den, while his sight was still weak, and before his eyes had become steady (and the time which would be needed to acquire this new habit of sight might be very considerable), would he not be ridiculous? Men would say of him that up he went and down he came without his eyes; and that it was better not even to think of ascending; and if any one tried to loose another and lead him up to the light, let them only catch the offender, and they would put him to death.

No question, he said.

This entire allegory, I said, you may now append, dear Glaucon, to the previous argument; the prison-house is the world of sight, the light of the fire is the sun, and you will not misapprehend me if you interpret the journey upwards to be the ascent of the soul into the intellectual world according to my poor belief, which, at your desire, I have expressed—whether rightly or wrongly God knows. But, whether true or false, my opinion is that in the world of knowledge the idea of good appears last of all, and is seen only with an effort; and, when seen, is also inferred to be the universal author of all things beautiful and right, parent of light and of the lord of light in this visible world, and the immediate source of reason and truth in the intellectual; and that this is the power upon which he who would act rationally either in public or private life must have his eye fixed.

I agree, he said, as far as I am able to understand you.

Moreover, I said, you must not wonder that those who attain to this beatific vision are unwilling to descend to human affairs; for their souls are ever hastening into the upper world where they desire to dwell; which desire of theirs is very natural, if our allegory may be trusted.

Yes, very natural.

And is there anything surprising in one who passes from divine contemplations to the evil state of man, misbehaving himself in a ridiculous manner; if, while his eyes are blinking and before he has become accustomed to the surrounding darkness, he is compelled to fight in courts of law, or in other places, about the images or the shadows of images of justice, and is endeavouring to meet the conceptions of those who have never yet seen absolute justice?

Anything but surprising, he replied.

Any one who has common sense will remember that the bewilderment of the eyes are of two kinds, and arise from two causes, either from coming out of the light or from going into the light, which is true of the mind's eye, quite as much as of the bodily eye; and he who remembers this when he sees any one whose vision is perplexed and weak, will not be too ready to laugh; he will first ask whether that soul of man has come out of the brighter life, and is unable to see because unaccustomed to the dark, or having turned from darkness to the day is dazzled by excess of light. And he will count the one happy in his condition and state of being, and he will pity the other; or, if he have a mind to laugh at the soul which comes from below into the light, there will be more reason in this than in the laugh which greets him who returns from above out of the light into the den.

That, he said, is a very just distinction.

But then, if I am right, certain professors of education must be wrong when they say that they can put a knowledge into the soul which was not there before, like sight into blind eyes.

They undoubtedly say this, he replied.

Whereas, our argument shows that the power and capacity of learning exists in the soul already; and that just as the eye was unable to turn from darkness to light without the whole body, so too the instrument of knowledge can only by the movement of the whole soul be turned from the world of becoming into that of being, and learn by degrees to endure the sight of being, and of the brightest and best of being, or in other words, of the good.

Very true.

And must there not be some art which will effect conversion in the easiest and quickest manner; not implanting the faculty of sight, for that exists already, but has been turned in the wrong direction, and is looking away from the truth?

Yes, he said, such an art may be presumed.

And whereas the other so-called virtues of the soul seem to be akin to bodily qualities, for even when they are not originally innate they can be implanted later by habit and exercise, the virtue of wisdom more than anything else contains a divine element which always remains, and by this conversion is rendered useful and profitable; or, on the other hand, hurtful and useless. Did you never observe the narrow intelligence flashing from the keen eye of a clever rogue—how eager he is, how clearly his paltry soul sees the way to his end; he is the reverse of blind, but his keen eye-sight is forced into the service of evil, and he is mischievous in proportion to his cleverness.

Very true, he said.

But what if there had been a circumcision of such natures in the days of their youth; and they had been severed from those sensual pleasures, such as eating and drinking, which, like leaden weights, were attached to them at their birth, and which drag them down and turn the vision of their souls upon the things that are below—if, I say, they had been released from these impediments and turned in the opposite direction, the very same faculty in them would have seen the truth as keenly as they see what their eyes are turned to now.

Very likely.

Yes, I said; and there is another thing which is likely, or rather a necessary inference from what has preceded, that neither the uneducated and uninformed of the truth, nor yet those who never make an end of their education, will be able ministers of State; not the former, because they have no single aim of duty which is the rule of all their actions, private as well as public; nor the latter, because they will not act at all except upon compulsion, fancying that they are already dwelling apart in the islands of the blest.

Very true, he replied.

Then, I said, the business of us who are the founders of the State will be to compel the best minds to attain that knowledge which we have already shown to be the greatest of all—they must continue to ascend until they arrive at the good; but when they have ascended and seen enough we must not allow them to do as they do now.

What do you mean?

I mean that they remain in the upper world: but this must not be allowed; they must be made to descend again among the prisoners in the den, and partake of their labours and honours, whether they are worth having or not.[334]

Each of the Guardians of the Republic, each of the future rulers of the polis they were imagining, must somehow in his education be "liberated and compelled suddenly to stand up and turn his neck round and walk and look towards the light." This turning round, this conversion, was the essence of liberal education. Compared with the practical instruction the famous sophists were offering to would-be politicians and exhibitionistic young gentlemen, Socrates' words were the words of a mystic. What was this invisible world? Was it there that he went during those fits of abstraction like the one at Potidaea? Was he really lost in thought? Or merely trying not to be lost in feckless action, merely trying to find himself—or, in the words inscribed at Delphi, to know himself? If the Guardians would also know themselves, they must come out of the underground den and begin to see things in their true light. Already taught to listen by music and poetry, already toughened by strenuous gymnastic, they must now enter the difficult world of the intelligibles—not yet its subdivision where dialectic would be learned but that less arduous area, the mathematical sciences. When they had learned there to deal skillfully with such easily abstracted ideas as triangle and circle, there would be time—say, when they were thirty—to pass upward to the much more difficult abstractions, like man, or polis, or justice.

But even when men who had undergone long training in both mind and body should have been magically placed in power in this polis Socrates had imagined, the ideal polis could not hope to endure. The aristocracy of the wise and brave would degenerate into a timocracy; the lover of wisdom would yield place to the lover of *time*, honor. In effect, the gold men would yield authority to the silver, the philosophers to the soldiers. And these silver men, lacking wisdom, would slowly discover the delights of private property, of money, of faction—as indeed the timocrats of seventh-century Hellas, who of course called themselves aristocrats, had turned to money; then timocracy would yield to oligarchy, or rule by the Oligoi, the few—which in practice would mean the rich. Socrates had that very evening pointed out[335] that not a single Greek polis of his day was actually one polis. It was two: the polis of the rich and the polis of the poor. The oligarchy, with or without civil war or foreign intervention, would in the end give way to democracy. And, where the principles of oligarchy were thrift and avarice, the principles of democracy were liberty and pleasure. Democracy hated discipline and authority. Socrates remarked:

By degrees the anarchy finds a way into private houses, and ends by getting among the animals and infecting them.

How do you mean?

I mean that the father grows accustomed to descend to the level of his sons and to fear them, and the son is on a level with his father, he having no respect or reverence for either of his parents; and this is his freedom, and the metic is equal with the citizen and the citizen with the metic, and the stranger is quite as good as either.

Yes, he said, that is the way.

And these are not the only evils, I said—there are several lesser ones: In such a state of society the master fears and flatters his scholars, and the scholars despise their masters and tutors; young and old are all alike; and the young man is on a level with the old, and is ready to compete with him in word or deed; and old men condescend to the young and are full of pleasantry and gaiety; they are loth to be thought morose and authoritative, and therefore they adopt the manners of the young.

Quite true, he said.

The last extreme of popular liberty is when the slave bought with money, whether male or female, is just as free as his or her purchaser; nor must I forget to tell of the liberty and equality of the two sexes in relation to each other.

Why not, as Aeschylus says, utter the word which rises to our lips?

That is what I am doing, I replied; and I must add that no one who does not know would believe, how much greater is the liberty which the animals who are under the dominion of man have in a democracy than in any other State: for truly, the she-dogs, as the proverb says, are as good as their she-mistresses, and the horses and asses have a way of marching along with all the rights and dignities of freemen; and they will run at any body who comes in their way if he does not leave the road clear for them: and all things are just ready to burst with liberty.

When I take a country walk, he said, I often experience what you describe. You and I have dreamed the same thing.

And above all, I said, and as the result of all, see how sensitive the citizens become; they chafe impatiently at the least touch of authority and at length, as you know, they cease to care even for the laws, written or unwritten; they will have no one over them.

Yes, he said, I know it too well.

Such, my friend, I said, is the fair and glorious beginning out of which springs tyranny.[336]

Socrates now proceeded to give a hideously accurate picture of the cruelty and violence that tyranny did often bring. The tyrant was a man who made the interest of the stronger serve for justice, and he was wretched. So were his enslaved fellow citizens. No, the happy polis was the just polis; and the happy man, the just man. Of this wise man he spoke:

> He will look at the city which is within him, and take heed that no disorder occur in it, such as might arise either from superfluity or from want; and upon this principle he will regulate his property and gain or spend according to his means.
> Very true.
> And, for the same reason, he will gladly accept and enjoy such honours as he deems likely to make him a better man; but those, whether private or public, which are likely to disorder his life, he will avoid?
> Then, if that is his motive, he will not be a statesman.
> By the dog of Egypt, he will! in the city which is his own he certainly will, though in the land of his birth perhaps not, unless he have a divine call.
> I understand; you mean that he will be a ruler in the city of which we are the founders, and which exists in idea only; for I do not believe that there is such an one anywhere on earth?
> In heaven, I replied, there is laid up a pattern of it, methinks, which he who desires may behold, and beholding, may set his own house in order. But whether such an one exists, or ever will exist in fact, is no matter; for he will live after the manner of that city, having nothing to do with any other.
> I think so, he said.[337]

The long discussion was ending. Socrates had convinced his hearers that treating others unjustly made one even unhappier than being treated unjustly by them; that, whether or not there was an after-life with rewards and punishments, the just life was the happier life here and now. But having convinced them, he chose to assume that the soul of man was indeed immortal. He did not try to prove it: on more than one occasion he made it clear that he knew no proof, but only signs and evidence. So now, instead of presenting an argument, he told a tale, to finish off the evening. A man named Er, a Pamphylian, had been slain in battle, but his body did not decay, and ten days after he died he returned to life and told his friends what he had seen in that other world. A kind of purgatory he had seen; he had seen the mouth of a kind of hell; from other souls he had heard news of a kind of heaven, where there were visions of inconceivable beauty.

The evening at the Piraeus ended. Socrates had imagined a kind of polis, a kind of human community, that he had never seen except with the mind's eye. Would it ever exist? One had no proof that it was impossible.[338] But neither was it likely. Meanwhile, as he observed to Glaucon, there was one thing a man could do, even in a most imperfect polis. He could order that city within him, his own soul, after the pattern laid up in heaven of the polis they had just imagined.

During these same years, Socrates' friend, Aristophanes, was having his say, too, on man and his polis. The very year after he and Socrates banqueted at Agathon's and heard the drunken Alcibiades declare his subjection to Socrates, the comic poet presented the *Birds*. With Nicias besieging Syracuse and with Athens dreaming of conquests that would cut off Sicilian and Italian grain from her enemies in Peloponnese, Aristophanes imagined two Athenian rogues founding Cloudcuckooland in the sky, a city of birds, a pattern laid up in heaven by two ridiculous, cowardly clowns, where the animal appetites could rule supreme, unhampered by reason and wisdom. This delightful polis intercepted the smoke that rose from men's sacrifices to satisfy the gods. So the gods were quickly reduced by famine and one of the Athenian rogues received as his bride a beautiful young woman, Basileia, or Sovereignty, who made Zeus's lightning bolts for him. Their marriage would place him on the throne of Zeus.

So much for a heavenly city far from the wise and virtuous community Socrates would imagine for Glaucon and his other friends. But by the time Socrates and Glaucon had imagined their just polis, Aristophanes presented another utopia, this time his own Athens, but an Athens in which a woman named Lysistrata had persuaded the women of Hellas to stop sleeping with their husbands until their husbands should put an end to the Great War. And in 392, when Socrates was dead, Aristophanes built still another imaginary polis, the *Ecclesiazusae*, in which women ruled instead of men and property was held in common.

By then, Euripides, whom Aristophanes and the other comic poets mocked so often for his newfangled tragedies, had withdrawn from Athens, which never till after his death was generous with prizes for his drama. About four years before the fall of Athens, Euripides left for Magnesia in Thessaly and then for the court of King Archelaus in Macedonia, where he wrote his *Bacchae*. There he shortly died, some two years before Lysander laid the Long Walls of Athens low and made the School of Hellas subject to Sparta.

Democracy had fallen. The exiled or refugee oligarchs swarmed joyfully home. Theramenes, the moderate, who had established in 411 a moderate constitution only to see an Athenian victory the next year at Cyzicus restore the old democratic constitution, now tried again. His party combined with the extreme oligarchs who had returned from exile. Their leader Critias had been one of Socrates' companions, a disciple of the Sicilian sophist Gorgias, an orator and poet. Cowed by their brutal conqueror, Lysander, the Athenian Assembly voted to establish a provisional government of thirty men, charged with establishing a constitution and meanwhile governing Athens. Each of Athens' ten tribes would supply three men, one chosen by Critias, one chosen by Theramenes, and one by the Assembly. In the summer or fall of 404, the Thirty were chosen. Technically, Athens was again a sovereign state, while the cities subject to her, despite Brasidas' promises of liberation and autonomy, were now governed by small groups of vengeful oligarchs, generally committees of ten called decarchies, chosen by Lysander. But when Lysander had seen the Thirty safely installed and the rest of the Long Walls and the walls around Athens and Piraeus pulled down, and when he had set forth with his fleet for a triumphant return to Sparta, he took all but twelve of Athens' warships with him. Then the Thirty, to make sure of their rule, managed to secure a Spartan garrison, which they undertook to maintain until, as they said, "they could put the 'scoundrels' out of the way and establish their government."[339]

Critias and his extremists promptly turned the Thirty into an engine of terror. At first they arrested and executed the political informers under the previous democracy and other men hateful even to the democrats. Then they began killing men for no reason other than their support of the democracy which had exiled Critias. His moderate colleague, Theramenes, demurred. When the extremists began to kill from personal enmity or merely to confiscate property, the strain between Critias and Theramenes increased. The extremists even made up a list of metics, or resident aliens, to kill and despoil, among them one Leon of Salamis. To implicate as many citizens as possible in their crimes and thereby give their terrified subjects a motive for supporting them, they ordered groups of citizens to arrest these innocent metics. Socrates was one of five citizens ordered to produce Leon. Socrates refused. And Critias did not punish him. In a few months, according to later reports, 1,500 victims met their death; 5,000 others were banished.

Of the moderates among the Thirty, Theramenes alone dared protest publicly against Critias and his terror. He counted on persuading the newly created Council to back him up in his demand that the Thirty produce their constitution and end their interim government. In October, 404, by a show of force, Critias frightened the Council into striking Theramenes' name from the list of citizens. Then the Thirty condemned him to death. The executioner handed him the cup of poison. He threw out the last drops, exclaiming: "Here's to the health of the noble Critias!"[340] One of the young Athenians who backed the provisional government until its violence and injustice alienated them later reported the death of Theramenes and added: "I deem it admirable in the man that when death was close at hand, neither self-possession nor the spirit of playfulness departed from his soul."[341] In that same autumn, the exiled Alcibiades was hunted down in Asia Minor and slain.

Meanwhile, a group of exiled Athenian democrats were gathering in Thebes, under the leadership of Thrasybulus, one of the heroes of the Athenian naval victory of Cynossema seven years earlier. Other refugees from the terror in Athens were in Corinth and Megara. All these cities had fought alongside Sparta against democratic, imperialist Athens. But Sparta's high-handed refusal to share the spoils of their joint victory, combined perhaps with the tales of horror coming out of prostrate Athens, predisposed them to shelter the intended victims of the Thirty. In December, 404, Thrasybulus set out from Thebes with a little band of seventy intrepid exiles and seized a mountain fortress on the Athenian frontier. The Thirty tried to reduce it, but a violent snowstorm caused them to withdraw to Athens. From all sides volunteers now poured in to Thrasybulus. The Thirty sent against them the Spartan garrison and two squadrons of cavalry, only to have these forces ambushed by night. Thrasybulus killed 120 of them and, best of all, seized provisions and the arms of the fallen. The Thirty next sent an offer to Thrasybulus to join their government. He refused. With opinion at Athens rising against them, the Thirty seized Eleusis and Salamis as refuges in case they were driven from Athens. Meanwhile they evacuated from Athens to Piraeus some 5,000 men not of their party. Thrasybulus and his force promptly joined the 5,000 there and took possession of the heights of Munychia.

Every city in Hellas, Socrates had once said on an evening in the Piraeus, near where Thrasybulus' army of exiled democrats stood, was not one city, but two: a city of the rich and a city of the poor. That had become cruelly apparent at Corcyra, at the beginning of the long war which had ended a year ago. During that war city after city had split into two cities, the poor turning to Athens for help, the rich, to Sparta. In Athens, Pericles had held the two cities together. Even after his death, when Nicias timidly led one city and Cleon the other, the struggle between them had remained a battle of words, often eristic and violent words, in the Assembly, not of weapons in the Agora. After the frightful disaster at Syracuse, when the subject cities of the Athenian Empire revolted, the strain in Athens increased. In 411, the democratic Assembly had been persuaded, at least for the duration of the war, to establish an oligarchic government. The extremists in that government appealed to Sparta for help. There was disorder; there was even political murder. But the oligarchic government lost Euboea; a moderate democracy took its place; and the extreme oligarchs fled to Decelea, the Attic fortress the Spartans then held. Thrasybulus' naval victory at Cynossema and the overwhelming victory which he and Theramenes and Alcibiades won the next year off Cyzicus enabled the democrats to upset Theramenes' moderate government and restore full democracy. The extreme oligarchs had now executed Theramenes at Athens, had perhaps caused the murder of Alcibiades in Asia Minor, and watched from Athens, the city of the rich, while Thrasybulus and his city of the poor held that hill in Piraeus.

Critias led his city of the rich against Munychia, and stormed up the hill. But his forces were badly defeated and he himself was slain. When a truce was declared so that the two armies might gather up their dead, some men from both sides fraternized. Then, reported Xenophon, one of Thrasybulus' men cried out to those from Athens:

> Fellow Citizens, why do you drive us out of the city? why do you wish to kill us? For we never did you any harm, but we have shared with you in the most solemn rites and sacrifices and the most splendid festivals, we have been companions in the dance and schoolmates and comrades in arms, and we have braved many dangers with you both by land and by sea in defence of the common safety and freedom of us both. In

the name of the gods of our fathers and mothers, in the name of our ties of kinship and marriage and comradeship,—for all these many of us share with one another,—cease, out of shame before gods and men, to sin against your fatherland, and do not obey those most accursed Thirty, who for the sake of their private gain have killed in eight months more Athenians, almost, than all the Peloponnesians in ten years of war. And when we might live in peace as fellow citizens, these men bring upon us war with one another, a war most utterly shameful and intolerable, utterly unholy and hated by both gods and men. Yet for all that, be well assured that for some of those now slain by our hands not only you, but we also, have wept bitterly.[342]

Those who listened, over the bodies of their common dead, were hastily marshaled back to Athens by their oligarchic officers, but it was too late. Opinion in Athens now sharply divided those who were afraid of punishment for their crimes if the Thirty were deposed from those who were sick of the Thirty and of their unbridled, cynical violence. The Thirty were voted out. Their worst violence had lasted eight months. Some of the extremists who had followed Critias then withdrew to Eleusis. There they composed an epitaph for Critias and the other oligarchs who had fallen at Munychia: "In memory of the brave men who once lanced the swollen pride of the damned democrats at Athens."[343]

The civil war between oligarchic Athens and democratic Piraeus continued, with metics, other foreigners, and even slaves joining Thrasybulus' democratic army, and with Athens' communications increasingly difficult. In despair, Athens and extremist Eleusis sent an appeal to Lysander. But the Ephors of Sparta declined to rescue those who had perpetrated the notorious terror at Athens. They sent one of their two kings, who bore the famous name Pausanias, and Pausanias set to work to reconcile the moderates in the Athenian Assembly with the motley army of democrats under Thrasybulus at Piraeus. By August, 403, he had succeeded. A general amnesty was declared. It excluded only the Thirty and a few others. Then Pausanias discreetly withdrew from Athens. On September 2, 403, the men from Piraeus returned to Athens, went up to the Acropolis, and offered sacrifice to Athena. When a united Assembly had been convoked, Thrasybulus read the terms of agreement and they were unanimously sworn to. Then he offered some advice, both to his late enemies, the city of the rich, and to his own city of the poor, now reunited with their goddess and their common polis:

> "I advise you," he said, "men of the city, to 'know yourselves.' And you would best learn to know yourselves were you to consider what grounds you have for arrogance, that you should undertake to rule over us. Are you more just? But the commons, though poorer than you, never did you any wrong for the sake of money; while you, though richer than any of them, have done many disgraceful things for the sake of gain. But since you can lay no claim to justice, consider then whether it is courage that you have a right to pride yourselves upon. And what better test could there be of this than the way we made war upon one another? Well then, would you say that you are superior in intelligence, you who having a wall, arms, money, and the Peloponnesians as allies, have been worsted by men who had none of these? Is it the Lacedaemonians, then, think you, that you may pride yourselves upon? How so? Why, they have delivered you up to this outraged populace, just as men fasten a clog upon the necks of snapping dogs and deliver them up to keepers, and now have gone away and left you. Nevertheless, my comrades, I am not the man to ask you to violate any one of the pledges to which you have sworn, but I ask you rather to show this virtue also, in addition to your other virtues,—that you are true to your oaths and are god-fearing men. . . ."[344]

The reconciliation proved extraordinary. Athens' love of free speech, her long tradition of equality before the law, her civilized manners, her skill and wise political compromise, her gift for commerce and industry magically revived. It was as if the vast tragedy which Thucydides described had brought her the Aeschylean wisdom that only suffering could bring. The tyrant-state that Pericles' clear eyes had seen in his beloved polis had been deposed: Sparta was tyrant now, a far harsher and more irresponsible tyrant than Athens had ever been, except at rare moments and in a few places. What remained was Pericles' other image, the School of Hellas, that and a conscious effort to get back to the laws of Solon, which sought to build a just polis, a common home for all free men, for rich and poor alike.

It was in this restored and chastened democracy, in this reconciled polis, that a charge was preferred against Socrates by a rich tanner named Anytus. He was a partisan of the moderate oligarch, Theramenes, whom the brutal

Critias had liquidated, and had played a leading role in the great reconciliation. He was deeply convinced that back of Athens' military catastrophe, back of her recent political disintegration, lay a religious and
moral decline. He was convinced that for that decline the atheistic natural
philosophers and morally skeptical sophists were largely responsible. Here
was Socrates, whom all the comic poets, not just Aristophanes, had
lampooned as an eccentric sophist. Socrates had once advised this tanner
not to confine his son's education to hides.[345] What was wrong, Anytus
had wanted to know, with this boy's taking over a business his father's
father had run before him? But Socrates' young men were always criticizing their elders. And who had his disciples been? A Critias, of all the
Thirty the greediest and most violent. An Alcibiades, licentious, insolent,
sacrilegious, traitor to his country. A Charmides, who had aided Critias
and had fallen when Critias fell in the unsuccessful attempt to storm the
hill that Thrasybulus held at the Piraeus.

Anytus left the formal prosecution to Meletus, an unsuccessful tragic
poet,[346] who had been angered[347] by Socrates' comments on poets and poetry. The indictment read to this effect: "Socrates is guilty of rejecting the
gods acknowledged by the state and of bringing in strange deities: he is
also guilty of corrupting the youth."[348] The penalty proposed was death.
It soon became apparent that the object of the indictment was not to
take Socrates' life; it was to frighten him into withdrawing from Athens
and accepting exile. The trial took place in February, 399, before a tribunal
of 501 citizen judges. Among those present were a number of Socrates'
most devoted disciples, and among these disciples was a young aristocrat
named Plato, still under thirty, who would later report his master's speech
in his own defense.

The great ironist had rarely faced a more deeply ironical situation. His
judges assumed that they were judging him, and Socrates was completely
aware that the case was judging them. His judges were trying to determine his relation to the gods of their polis: Socrates was well known for
his piety, yet he constantly raised questions which his judges might well
deem impious. Under cross-examination, of the usual Socratic variety, he
easily led Meletus on the one hand to accuse him of being a complete
atheist and on the other of believing in new gods—but gods just the same.
So he brushed the accusation aside. He had always insisted that he did
not teach, since he laid no claim to knowledge. If lectures by sophists were

teaching, he of course spoke the truth; but his midwifery of ideas was a far more powerful form of teaching, and he knew it. Indeed, at one point in his speech, he dropped that particular irony and stated calmly that he would always practice and teach philosophy, a word which in the Greek he spoke meant, at least etymologically, not the wisdom, or *sophia*, that so many sophists professed to teach, but the love of wisdom.

Then this indicted atheist announced:

> For I do nothing but go about persuading you all, old and young alike, not to take thought for your persons or your properties, but first and chiefly to care about the greatest improvement of the soul. I tell you that virtue is not given by money, but that from virtue comes money and every other good of man, public as well as private. This is my teaching, and if this is the doctrine which corrupts the youth, I am a mischievous person. But if any one says that this is not my teaching, he is speaking an untruth. Wherefore, O men of Athens, I say to you, do as Anytus bids or not as Anytus bids, and either acquit me or not; but whichever you do, understand that I shall never alter my ways, not even if I have to die many times.[349]

That statement caused such a stir that he had to request his judges not to interrupt him. He continued:

> And now, Athenians, I am not going to argue for my own sake, as you may think, but for yours, that you may not sin against the God by condemning me, who am his gift to you. For if you kill me you will not easily find a successor to me, who, if I may use such a ludicrous figure of speech, am a sort of gadfly, given to the state by God; and the state is a great and noble steed who is tardy in his motions owing to his very size, and requires to be stirred into life. I am that gadfly which God has attached to the state, and all day long and in all places am always fastening upon you, arousing and persuading and reproaching you. You will not easily find another like me, and therefore I would advise you to spare me.[350]

He spoke of his military service to the state, only to make the point that he ought not here in court any more than in battle to fear death. He reminded his judges that, after the battle off Arginusae seven years before, in the days of the democracy, when they wanted to try the generals in a batch and therefore illegally, he alone had refused to vote to submit their cases to the Assembly in that form. He reminded them that, in the later days of the oligarchy, when the Thirty had ordered him and four others to arrest Leon of Salamis, he alone had risked his life by refusing.

Then he switched back to a meaning of the word teach that he was fond of and, in a context that made his meaning clear, stated that he never taught or professed to teach anybody: he conversed with people, with anybody who wanted to converse with him. He identified companions of his in the court and challenged his accusers to produce a witness who could testify to his having morally damaged some youth.

He reminded his judges that sometimes the accused produced his children or relations in court to weep and thereby move the judges. He had a wife, too, and three sons, one almost a man and two small ones, but he felt that leading them in now would be "discreditable to myself, and to you, and to the whole state."[351] It was not his function as the accused to ask a favor of the judges; it was his function to inform and convince them. It was their function "not to make a present of justice, but to give judgment."[352] They had sworn to the gods to do justice; and if— the old irony returning like bubbling waters from some inexhaustible spring—

> if, O men of Athens, by force of persuasion and entreaty I could over-power your oaths, then I should be teaching you to believe that there are no gods, and in defending should simply convict myself of the charge, of not believing in them. But that is not so—far otherwise. For I do believe that there are gods, and in a sense higher than that in which any of my accusers believe in them. And to you and to God I commit my cause, to be determined by you as is best for you and me.[353]

The judges prepared to vote. Were his friends in the court moved by his running so true to form? He had been calm, humorous, gentle in his personal behavior, but his line of argument had been as rigorous, as inexorable, as disquieting as always. His accusers had hoped he would flee Athens before his trial came up. He had not only stayed. He had forced his judges to face up to the issue. He had forced them to make a genuine choice. For it was his accusers, not he, who wanted to evade the issue, who wanted not to choose, who merely wanted the gadfly to go away and stop stinging. He had encountered them physically in court and he had done his best to encounter their minds there as well. He showed no signs of wanting to die, although the young Xenophon, who loved and admired him but who was absent in Asia Minor, would later guess in his own, secondhand account of the trial, that, being now around seventy, Socrates dreaded grievous old age and wanted to die. If his judges should now vote him innocent, he would know that the trial had taught them something, about law, about a polis, about membership in a polis. That would be a triumph, not because he feared to cease living physically, but because learning and thinking were always a triumph for man.

The judges voted by 281 to 220 that he was guilty. Under Athenian law he was now required to propose a penalty alternative to the one Meletus had proposed. Legally, the judges must choose one of the two penalties proposed. If he proposed one that showed a little contrition, 31 votes might shift in his direction and he would escape death. This would be his last chance. But the irony of the trial continued: on his own premises, it was his judges who should be given one last chance—to see the point, and so in effect to reverse an unjust decision.

Socrates gave them that last chance:

> Reflecting that I was really too honest a man to be a politician and live, I did not go where I could do no good to you or to myself; but where I could do the greatest good privately to every one of you, thither I went, and sought to persuade every man among you that he must look to himself, and seek virtue and wisdom before he looks to his private interests, and look to the state before he looks to the interests of the state; and that this should be the order which he observes in all his actions. What shall be done to such an one? Doubtless some good thing, O men of Athens, if he has his reward; and the good should be of a kind suitable to him. What would be a reward suitable to a poor man who is your benefactor, and who desires leisure that he may instruct you?[354]

The answer: free meals at the expense of the polis—a reward sometimes given to citizens who had deserved well of their country. Nor, he hastened to add, was he trying to be impudent, any more than when he refused to bring his family to court to weep and beg for mercy. He was merely trying to state truthfully what he, Socrates, considered a just penalty, or rather a just return for what he had actually done. He was, he went on, not afraid of death, since he did not have knowledge of what followed this present life. Would the just penalty be imprisonment? But why? A fine? He had no money. Exile? If Athens could not tolerate him, what other polis would? Unless, of course, he stopped examining himself and others:

but precisely this sort of inquiry was the greatest good of man and, besides, "the unexamined life is not worth living."[355] Then he said:

> Well, perhaps I could afford a mina, and therefore I propose that penalty: Plato, Crito, Critobulus, and Apollodorus, my friends here, bid me say thirty minae, and they will be the sureties. Let thirty minae be the penalty; for which sum they will be ample security to you.[356]

It was as if he had relented and had offered to join a game that children were playing, rather than appear to them incomprehensibly obstinate.

The judges again sustained his accuser, this time by a larger vote: 360 to 141. His companions, who had tried to purchase his life, recognized this sort of outcome from long experience: his persistent return to what he regarded as the true issue had once more aroused anger.

A third time he spoke. He prophesied to those who had voted his death that they would get the polis an evil name by killing him. And he informed them that by pleading his case in the manner they would have approved he could have escaped death.

> The difficulty, my friends, is not to avoid death, but to avoid unrighteousness; for that runs faster than death. I am old and move slowly, and the slower runner has overtaken me, and my accusers are keen and quick, and the faster runner, who is unrighteousness, has overtaken them. And now I depart hence condemned by you to suffer the penalty of death,— they too go their ways condemned by the truth to suffer the penalty of villainy and wrong; and I must abide by my award—let them abide by theirs. I suppose that these things may be regarded as fated,—and I think that they are well.[357]

To those who voted for his acquittal he wanted to show "the meaning of this event"[358]—he who had always sought for meaning. He told them that the divine sign within him, which had so often checked him from some word or deed, had today not checked him once. And as to death, if it was not merely an eternal sleep, it might lead him to another place where he could converse with Orpheus, Hesiod, Homer, Ajax, Agamemnon, and Odysseus.

> What infinite delight would there be in conversing with them and asking them questions! In another world they do not put a man to death for asking questions: assuredly not. . . . I am not angry with my condemners, or with my accusers; they have done me no harm, although they did

not mean to do me any good; and for this I may gently blame them. . . .

The hour of departure has arrived, and we go our ways—I to die, and you to live. Which is better God only knows.[859]

But he could not legally be executed until a sacred ship which had been sent to Apollo's Isle of Delos should return. In his prison cell, his devoted friend Crito tried to persuade Socrates to let him bribe his jailers and spirit him away to friends of Crito's in Thessaly. Desperately Crito advanced every conceivable argument, and Socrates—questioned him, of course. The arguments would not stand up. Granted that the judges who voted him guilty had done evil, he himself could not escape now without breaking the laws of his polis. Should he, too, do evil? The distraught Crito yielded.

On his last day a group of devoted companions visited his cell and they argued the day away on the subject of immortality. Once more, according to Phaedo's eye-witness account to Echecrates, he let down his ladder of analogies, not to prove anything but to provoke insights. Once more he charmed them with poetic myth. It was clear that he had faith in the immortality of the soul. It was equally clear that he knew of no way to construct a logical proof of immortality:

A man of sense ought not to say, nor will I be very confident, that the description which I have given of the soul and her mansions is exactly true. But I do say that, inasmuch as the soul is shown to be immortal, he may venture to think, not improperly or unworthily, that something of the kind is true. The venture is a glorious one, and he ought to comfort himself with words like these, which is the reason why I lengthen out the tale. Wherefore, I say, let a man be of good cheer about his soul, who having cast away the pleasures and ornaments of the body as alien to him and working harm rather than good, has sought after the pleasures of knowledge; and has arrayed the soul, not in some foreign attire, but in her own proper jewels, temperance, and justice, and courage, and nobility, and truth—in these adorned she is ready to go on her journey to the world below, when her hour comes. You, Simmias and Cebes, and all other men, will depart at some time or other. Me already, as a tragic poet would say, the voice of fate calls. Soon I must drink the poison; and I think that I had better repair to the bath first, in order that the women may not have the trouble of washing my body after I am dead.

When he had done speaking, Crito said: And have you any commands for us, Socrates—anything to say about your children, or any other matter in which we can serve you?

Nothing particular, Crito, he replied: only, as I have always told you, take care of yourselves; that is a service which you may be ever rendering to me and mine and to all of us, whether you promise to do so or not. But if you have no thought for yourselves, and care not to walk according to the rule which I have prescribed for you, not now for the first time, however much you may profess or promise at the moment, it will be of no avail.

We will do our best, said Crito: And in what way shall we bury you?

In any way that you like; but you must get hold of me, and take care that I do not run away from you. Then he turned to us, and added with a smile:—I cannot make Crito believe that I am the same Socrates who have been talking and conducting the argument; he fancies that I am the other Socrates whom he will soon see, a dead body—and he asks, How shall he bury me? And though I have spoken many words in the endeavour to show that when I have drunk the poison I shall leave you and go to the joys of the blessed,—these words of mine, with which I was comforting you and myself, have had, as I perceive, no effect upon Crito. And therefore I want you to be surety for me to him now, as at the trial he was surety to the judges for me: but let the promise be of another sort; for he was surety for me to the judges that I would remain, and you must be my surety to him that I shall not remain, but go away and depart; and then he will suffer less at my death, and not be grieved when he sees my body being burned or buried. I would not have him sorrow at my hard lot, or say at the burial, Thus we lay out Socrates, or, Thus we follow him to the grave or bury him; for false words are not only evil in themselves, but they infect the soul with evil. Be of good cheer then, my dear Crito, and say that you are burying my body only, and do with that whatever is usual, and what you think best.

When he had spoken these words, he arose and went into a chamber to bathe; Crito followed him and told us to wait. So we remained behind, talking and thinking of the subject of discourse, and also of the greatness of our sorrow; he was like a father of whom we were being bereaved, and we were about to pass the rest of our lives as orphans. When he had taken the bath his children were brought to him—(he had two young sons and an elder one); and the women of his family also came, and he talked to them and gave them a few directions in the presence of Crito; then he dismissed them and returned to us.

Now the hour of sunset was near, for a good deal of time had passed while he was within. When he came out, he sat down with us again after his bath, but not much was said. Soon the jailer, who was the servant of the Eleven, entered and stood by him, saying:—To you, Socrates, whom I know to be the noblest and gentlest and best of all who ever came to this place, I will not impute the angry feelings of other men, who rage and swear at me, when, in obedience to the authorities, I bid them drink the poison—indeed, I am sure that you will not be angry with me; for others, as you are aware, and not I, are to blame. And so fare you well, and try to bear lightly what must needs be— you know my errand. Then bursting into tears he turned away and went out.

Socrates looked at him and said: I return your good wishes, and will do as you bid. Then turning to us, he said, How charming the man is: since I have been in prison he has always been coming to see me, and at times he would talk to me, and was as good to me as could be, and now see how generously he sorrows on my account. We must do as he says, Crito; and therefore let the cup be brought, if the poison is prepared: if not, let the attendant prepare some.

Yet, said Crito, the sun is still upon the hill-tops, and I know that many a one has taken the draught late, and after the announcement has been made to him, he has eaten and drunk, and enjoyed the society of his beloved; do not hurry—there is time enough.

Socrates said: Yes, Crito, and they of whom you speak are right in so acting, for they think that they will be the gainers by the delay; but I am right in not following their example, for I do not think that I should gain anything by drinking the poison a little later; I should only be ridiculous in my own eyes for sparing and saving a life which is already forfeit. Please then to do as I say, and not to refuse me.

Crito made a sign to the servant, who was standing by; and he went out, and having been absent for some time, returned with the jailer carrying the cup of poison. Socrates said: You, my good friend, who are experienced in these matters, shall give me directions how I am to proceed. The man answered: You have only to walk about until your legs are heavy, and then to lie down, and the poison will act. At the same time he handed the cup to Socrates, who in the easiest and gentlest manner, without the least fear or change of colour or feature, looking at the man with all his eyes, Echecrates, as his manner was, took the cup and said: What do you say about making a libation out of this cup to any god? May I, or not? The man answered: We only prepare, Socrates, just so much as we deem enough. I understand, he said: but I may and must ask the gods to prosper my journey from this to the other world—even so—and so be it according to my prayer. Then raising the cup to his lips, quite readily and cheerfully he drank off the poison. And hitherto most of us had been able to control our sorrow; but now when we saw him drinking, and saw too that he had finished the draught, we could no longer forbear, and in spite of myself my own tears were flowing fast; so that I covered my face and wept, not for him, but at the thought of my own calamity in having to part from such a friend. Nor was I the first; for Crito, when he found himself unable to restrain his tears, had got up, and I followed; and at that moment, Apollodorus, who had been weeping all the time, broke out in a loud and passionate cry which made cowards of us all. Socrates alone retained his calmness: What is this strange outcry? he said. I sent away the women mainly in order that they might not misbehave in this way, for I have been told that a man should die in peace. Be quiet then, and have patience. When we heard his words we were ashamed, and refrained our tears; and he walked about until, as he said, his legs began to fail, and then he lay on his back, according to the directions, and the man who gave him the poison now and then looked at his feet and legs; and after a while he pressed his foot hard, and asked him if he could feel; and he said, No; and then his leg, and so upwards and upwards, and showed us that he was cold and stiff. And he felt them himself, and said: When the poison reaches the heart, that will be the end. He was beginning to grow cold about the groin, when he uncovered his face, for he had covered himself up, and said—they were his last words—he said: Crito, I owe a cock to Asclepius; will you remember to pay the debt? The debt shall be paid, said Crito; is there anything else? There was no answer to this question; but in a minute or two a movement was heard, and the attendants uncovered him; his eyes were set, and Crito closed his eyes and mouth.

Such was the end, Echecrates, of our friend; concerning whom I may truly say, that of all the men of his time whom I have known, he was the wisest and justest and best.[360]

Crito had decently closed the eyes of a man who had spent his life learning to see things no physical eye could see. That man had clearly believed that, after death, he would see those things more clearly, as Oedipus saw them more clearly once he had blinded himself, and as Tiresias, the blind seer, could so perfectly see. Crito also closed the dead man's mouth, the lips that Athens had been so determined to seal. But those questioning lips had already done their work. The questions they framed had thrown a new light on the whole history of Hellas from the Dark Ages to the tranquil death in the prison cell, on Hellenic man's effort to achieve a polis that participated in two worlds. It must be a community of both gods and men. It must express the will of eternal gods, who only half revealed themselves to men; of invisible ideas that could, though only with humility and travail, be embodied in concrete things; of universal freedom and justice applied to practical politics and the unruly passions of men; of the kind of intellect for which every answer posed the next question. It must be an anagogical polis, in which all things led the understanding upward, in which the thing was read as sign, in which symbol soared, and in which to live, though often painful, must never be meaningless. It must be a polis in which not only the mind's eye should see but the heart could feel, and in which carved temple, statue of cast bronze, mural panel, or note of flute or lyre, should open the heart of man, guide his foot in delicate dance and his voice in exultant song. It must be a polis in which person intimately confronted person, a polis whose citizens were not things.

All those longings of Hellas had been brought to focus in the Athens that gave Socrates birth, in the polis that Pericles proudly called the School of Hellas. And though she was also a tyrant-state, which compelled physical submission, yet her intellectual and aesthetic vocation compelled the minds and souls of Hellenes from Spain to Cyprus, from Libya to the Russian steppes. For Athens represented Hellas; she was the mouthpiece of Hellas, even when Hellas fought against her. And the mouthpiece of Athens was Socrates, even when Athens slew him. If the whole history of Hellas, all the way up to 399, was a kind of Aeschylean tragedy, in which understanding must be won through suffering, then of that tragedy Socrates was the hero.

Other characters represented more perfectly than he specific aspirations and achievements of the Hellenic spirit. Though he started life as a sculptor, he was no Phidias. Though he sometimes wrote poetry, as when alone in his prison cell he turned Aesop's *Fables* into verse, he was no Aeschylus. He loved jest, but he was no Aristophanes. He understood what law was, but it was Solon and Clisthenes, not he, who in some sense legislated Athens into existence. He imagined a polis, and Pericles ruled one. He was a good soldier, but no Themistocles. He was as just as Aristides the

Just, but he held no high office. Yet essentially, Hellas was quest. Hellas sought to know and to understand. And in tireless quest Socrates stood supreme, the key actor in the great drama called Hellas.

At the Piraeus with Glaucon and the others, when they had imagined a more perfect polis, he had not greatly cared whether final decision rested with one philosopher king or a number. In a very real sense he himself was the uncrowned philosopher king of Athens. There was an ancient myth in Hellas, though not only in Hellas, that the king must die. Now he had died. In his court defense he had not sought death, whether, as Xenophon later guessed, in order to avoid the ills of grievous old age, or to call attention to his ideas on man and the polis. The philosopher king died because he refused to quit his quest. Did not his death perfect his reign and extend it to men of all times and in all places? Did not his wingèd words before an Athenian court reach even to Achilles, who had willed, not to live long, but to live well? Did they not reach beyond Athens to Hellene and barbarian alike? For they had put the enduring and ironical question, to man, in polis: Who am I?

8

THE POLIS IN FLIGHT
AND
THE THIRTEENTH GOD

IN THE SPRING of 401, some two years before his death,
Socrates was asked for advice by one of his young friends, Xenophon.
Xenophon had received a letter from an old family friend, a Theban named
Proxenus. Cyrus, younger brother of Artaxerxes II, new King of Kings, had
induced Proxenus "to get as many men as he could and join him, since he
was about to attack the Pisidians, who were making themselves a nuisance
to his country."[361] So Proxenus had raised a force of mercenaries and had
gone to Cyrus. If Xenophon would join him there, he promised

to introduce him to Cyros, who was, he said, more than home and country to himself. Xenophon read his letter, and consulted Socrates the
philosopher about this trip. Socrates had a suspicion that there might be

some state objection to his being friendly with Cyros, because Cyros had favoured the Lacedaimonians in their war against Athens; so he advised Xenophon to go to Delphi and inquire of the oracle about this journey. Accordingly Xenophon went and asked Apollo what god he should sacrifice and pray to, that he might best accomplish the journey he had in mind, and come back safe and successful. Apollo named the gods to whom he must sacrifice.

When he came back he told the oracle to Socrates. But Socrates blamed him because he had not asked first whether it was better for him to go or to stay, but just decided to go, and then asked how he could best do it. "But," said he, "since you did ask that, you must do what the god bids."[362]

So Xenophon sacrificed to the gods whom Apollo's oracle had named and joined Proxenus and Cyrus of Persia in Sardis.

The decision was a fateful one. It was the subsidies of Cyrus that had enabled the Spartans to destroy the Athenian Empire, to starve Athens herself to her knees, to place a Spartan garrison on the holy Acropolis, and to back up the bloody Critias in his anti-democratic terror. Xenophon, then in his early twenties, son of a landowner from an estate some nine miles northeast of Athens, member of the class of knights, politically conservative and glad to have Athens again allied to her yoke-fellow Sparta, had served in the cavalry under the Thirty. Now the democracy was back in power. Now he was joining his Theban friend, to whom Cyrus the Persian was "more than home and country." And, from Socrates' point of view, Xenophon had consulted the oracle, as Croesus and so many others had done, the wrong way. He had not asked what he should do but which gods he should conscript to help him do what he had already made up his mind to do.

The Greek mercenary force he joined at Sardis contained some 12,900 infantry, of whom 10,600 were heavy-armed. On March 6, 401, Cyrus led them eastward out of Sardis. Not even Proxenus knew that it was not the hill tribes of Pisidia whom Cyrus was leading them against but the King of Kings himself. Of the Greeks, only the Spartan Clearchus, their commander, knew.

However, when they got as far as Cilicia, it seemed to be clear to all that they were marching against the king. Most of them followed for shame of one another and Cyros, although they feared the journey and went against their will; and one of these was Xenophon.[363]

At Tarsus the Greeks balked, and some of the mercenaries even stoned Clearchus. But Clearchus cleverly succeeded in convincing them it was unsafe to turn back, and Cyrus lied about his reasons for wanting to reach the Euphrates River. Although the Greeks were still suspicious, a 50-per-cent increase in pay decided them to follow on. At Thapsacus on the Euphrates, Cyrus told the higher Greek officers the truth: they were marching against the King and against Babylon. This time it took a bonus to get the Greeks in motion again, but they crossed the river and followed Cyrus down the left bank toward the famous city, marching through the Syrian desert with its sweet-smelling plants, hunting the wild asses, whose meat tasted like venison but was tenderer, hunting the ostrich, the bustard, the gazelle. When they neared the King's army, Cyrus made fresh promises in case of victory and then reviewed his forces. Cyrus had his Greek mercenaries, a much larger number of Asian troops, a few scythe-bearing chariots. His brother, King Artaxerxes, had a much larger force than his, more scythed chariots, but no Greek mercenary force.[364] On a September morning at the village of Cunaxa, a few miles from the site of modern Baghdad, the Great King struck. The Greek mercenaries of Cyrus raised the paean, charged at the double, and completely scattered the forces opposite them. But Cyrus himself was less lucky. He managed to attack the King his brother personally, and even to wound him, but he himself was killed. Instead of attacking the Greeks, Artaxerxes then withdrew: anyhow the death of Cyrus had brought the Greek expedition to ruin. When the Greeks returned to their camp for breakfast, there was nothing to eat: the camp had been pillaged.

When the Great King sent word that they were to lay down their arms, they refused. They wanted to get home to Greece, but how? They had marched nearly 1,500 miles from Sardis. They could not possibly go back the way they had come: they lacked the necessary provisions to cross the desert. Tissaphernes, the royal governor whom Cyrus had replaced at Sardis, offered to guide them northward toward the Black Sea. And so, with Tissaphernes' army leading, the Greeks started up the left bank of the Tigris toward the great eastern mountains of modern Turkey. They reached the Great Zab, which flowed into the Tigris.

But there was distrust between the two armies. Where, wondered the

Greeks, was Tissaphernes guiding them? Would they be ambushed? On the Persian side, there was fear of this desperate army of Greek mercenaries, which, like some hostile polis, moved through the heart of the Persian Empire. How get rid of them? At last Clearchus, the Spartan commander, decided to seek a conference with Tissaphernes and to try for some sort of firmer understanding. Tissaphernes invited the Greek leaders to his quarters; there he seized Clearchus, Proxenus, Menon, and two other Greek leaders and sent them to the Great King; the remainder of the delegation were massacred. Then he sent fresh demands to the Greek army to lay down their arms.

In Xenophon's judgment, Clearchus the Spartan, principal commander of the Greeks, had been a harsh, cruel, but efficient leader. After refusing to return to Sparta with an expedition he was leading to the Hellespont, he had been sentenced to death for disobedience, and had turned soldier of fortune. War was his passion. He was about fifty when the Great King beheaded him. Xenophon's friend Proxenus was likewise beheaded; he was only about thirty. Xenophon mourned Proxenus as a man too gentle and too honorable to command his mercenary force. Of Menon, the Thessalian general, Xenophon had a low opinion, and he heard without sorrow that he had not merely lost his life like the other generals but had met slow death by torture. When Xenophon came later to write the history of their Anabasis, their March Up Country, he pictured the army, now largely bereft of leadership:

> They could not sleep for sorrow, longing for home and parents, for wives and children, which they never expected to see again. In this state they all tried to rest.[365]

> There was a man in the army named Xenophon, an Athenian, who was neither general nor captain nor private . . .[346]

> And now in their desperate plight, he was unhappy like the rest and could not sleep; but he did snatch a nap, and then he saw a dream. He thought there was lightning and a thunderbolt fell on his father's house, and all was in a blaze. He woke at once in terror; the dream he judged to be good in one way, because amid troubles and dangers he seemed to see a great light from Zeus, but in another way he feared, because he considered the dream to come from Zeus the king and the blaze of fire seemed to be all round, so he feared difficulties would fence him in all round, and he might not be able to get out of the country of the king.[367]

Xenophon called together the officers who had served under his friend Proxenus, pointed out that the Persians had broken their oaths and thereby aligned the gods on the side of the Greeks, and said:

> They are men easier to wound and to kill than we are if the gods give us victory as before.
>
> Perhaps others are now thinking the same, but in heaven's name don't let us wait for someone else to come and pat us on the back and say, Go it. Here's a grand enterprise! Let us take the lead and show the others how to be brave! Show yourselves the best of officers, and as worthy to be captains as the captains themselves! Count on me, if you are willing to make the start; I will follow you, or if you order me to lead, I will not make my youth an excuse, but I think I am old enough to keep danger from myself![368]

With one dissenting vote, the subordinates of Proxenus chose this young Athenian to lead their contingent. Then they collected officers from the other contingents and by midnight about a hundred officers were in council. Xenophon was called on to speak. He urged them instantly to appoint new officers to replace those the army had now lost. This was done, and then they convened a general assembly of the whole army, just as the Council at Athens might have convened the Assembly of all citizens. A Lacedaemonian officer addressed them, then the newly appointed general of the Arcadian contingent spoke.

> Then Xenophon rose; he was arrayed for war in his finest dress. "If the gods grant victory," he thought, "the finest adornments are most proper for such a victory; if I must die, after grand ambitions I would meet my end in grandeur."[369]

He insisted that with God's help there were many good hopes of safety. Someone in the audience sneezed. This was a good omen; the soldiers recognized it as such by kissing their hands to heaven; and Xenophon instantly cried:

> While we were speaking of safety came an omen of Zeus the Saviour! Then I think we should vow to this god a thanksgiving for salvation as soon as we reach the first friendly country, and vow a sacrifice to the other gods according to our ability. Whoever agrees with this, let him hold up his hand.[370]

All held up their hands. Then they made their vow and chanted the paean. Xenophon now spoke at length. He reminded them that the Persians had come long ago to punish Athens. At Marathon the Athenians had beaten them. Then Xerxes had come by land and sea with an innumerable host. The ancestors of this audience he was addressing had beaten them. The Greeks would beat them again. No cavalry? They would need none. No provisions? They would seize provisions. Rivers impassable? All rivers could be passed if you went far enough toward the source. Even if the army could not escape, it was strong enough to settle down and defy the King, as some of the hill tribes had in fact done.

> But I am afraid that if we once learn to live idle in luxury, and to dally with the fine big women and girls of the Medes and Persians, we may be like the lotus-eaters and forget the way home!
>
> I think, then, that we must first try to reach Hellas and our own people, and show the Hellenes that they are poor only because they want to be, when they could bring their paupers over here and see them rich. But don't forget, men, that all these good things belong to the conquerors; and now it is necessary to say how we can travel most safely and fight most successfully.[371]

Next he proposed that they burn their baggage train. All hands would be needed to fight. But the chief thing was complete obedience to discipline. The Persians had treacherously killed the Greek leaders: the Persians must find that the Greeks could obey new leaders. He called for a vote approving his plans.

> Or if anyone has anything better, let him speak up boldly and say so, even if he is a private soldier, for our common safety is our common need.[372]

The Greek army started north toward the high mountains, a Greek polis on the march, a panhellenic polis like the one Pericles dreamed that Thurii might be, a footloose polis like Athens herself, but one prepared to move much further than Salamis, into the towering, unknown mountains. Nearly a century and a half before, when Cyrus had conquered Lydia, had not the Phocaeans deserted their hearths and planned their city elsewhere, on some islands off Chios? Had they not then sworn a solemn oath to move to Corsica? For their common safety had been their common need. Only a few weeks before Cyrus had known that if he could but slay his brother, the Great King, the leaderless Imperial host would rally to himself. When Cyrus was slain, the Persians assumed that his Greek followers could only lay down their arms. But Clearchus and the other Greek generals had taken charge. Surely, if these too could be got rid of, their army would be forced to surrender. Not at all: the army turned polis and struck out for the mysterious highlands. Their common safety was their common need; their habits of self-government bound them together, their sneezes were omens, and their trust was in Zeus the Savior.

The long ordeal began. The Persian archers could outrange the Cretan archers who served in the retreating polis. And Xenophon had been wrong about not needing cavalry. Persian cavalry constantly harassed the rear guard, which Xenophon and Clearchus' successor, the young Timasion, commanded. Xenophon concluded that slingers and horsemen must be found. Some 200 men of Rhodes were collected who understood slings and whose leaden bullets had twice the range of the stones, as big as a human fist, which the Persian slingers hurled. Horses hitherto used as pack animals were examined and some fifty were found fit for cavalry. By the time the retreating army reached the ruins of Nineveh, the Rhodian slingers and the newly formed cavalry were holding Tissaphernes at bay. The Cretans were collecting and using the spent arrows of the Persians. Moreover, in some of the villages they found lead to make bullets for the slings and plenty of gut to use in the slings themselves. The moving polis was in some sense importing the goods it required, but importing them by moving to where they were. Sometimes it found a well-provisioned village and spent a few days there, partly to let its surgeons tend the wounded, partly to eat the good wheat meal stored there and drink the wine and let their horses feed on the stored-up barley.

It took them seven days of constant fighting to pass through the mountainous country of the wild Kurds, at whose hands they suffered more losses than all those Tissaphernes had been able to inflict. Then they started across Armenia, shadowed by Tiribazus, the King's local governor, who kept an eye on them but did not attack. It was now late autumn and the heavy snowfalls began. Once they marched through snow six feet deep. The army lost animals, slaves, soldiers.

Men also were left behind who had been blinded by the snow or lost their toes by frostbite. It did some good to the eyes if the men marched holding something black before their eyes; for the feet, to keep them moving without rest all the time and to take off the shoes at night. But if any slept with shoes on, the straps worked into the feet and the shoes froze; for the old shoes were gone, and they had to make them of raw leather from untanned hides newly flayed.[373]

They came to underground houses, filled with people and animals. There they got provisions, including an unfamiliar drink, beer:

barley-wine in tubs; there were barley-grains floating on the wine at the rim, and straws lay there, large and small, without knots. If you were thirsty, you picked up one of these and sucked through it. It was very strong wine if drunk neat, and the taste was delicious when you were used to it.[374]

A village headman proved hospitable. And he also taught Xenophon how to wrap bags round the hooves of his horses so they would not sink to their bellies in the snow. In some villages the people feasted them:

everywhere on the same table were piles of lamb, kid, pork, veal, fowl, with all sorts of cakes, both wheaten and barley. When one would show goodwill by drinking your health, he dragged you to the bowl, and you must duck your head and gulp it up like a bullock.[375]

Through the countries of the Taochians and the Chalybeans they stumbled on until they reached a sizable city called Gymnias. Thence they marched five days to Mount Theches.

When the first men reached the summit and caught sight of the sea there was loud shouting. Xenophon and the rearguard, hearing this, thought that more enemies were attacking in front; for some were following behind them from the burning countryside, and their own rearguards had killed a few men and captured others, and taken wicker shields, covered with raw hairy oxhides, about twenty. But when the shouts grew louder and nearer, as each group came up it went pelting along to the shouting men in front, and the shouting was louder and louder as the crowds increased. Xenophon thought it must be something very important; he mounted his horse, and took Lycios with his horsemen, and galloped to bring help. Soon they heard the soldiers shouting "Sea! sea!" and passing the word along.

Then the rearguard also broke into a run, and the horses and baggage animals galloped too. When they all reached the summit then they embraced each other, captains and officers and all, with tears running down their cheeks. And suddenly—whoever sent the word round—the soldiers brought stones and made a huge pile. Upon it they threw heaps of raw hides and sticks and the captured shields . . .[376]

And so they sacrificed to their gods. They still had to get through the country of the Macronians, but luckily a man in the Greek army, who had been a slave in Athens, recognized these highlands as his native land and was able to negotiate safe passage. They now reached the Colchians, those distant barbarians Jason had reached when his Argonauts had sought the Golden Fleece, barbarians whose passionate princess, Medea, Euripides had immortalized. The Colchians massed their forces in order to hold a mountain pass. Xenophon formed the Greek army in company columns and prepared them to fight their way through. Then he addressed the soldiers:

"Men, these whom you see alone are left in the way, to keep us from reaching at once the place we have been seeking so long. These men, if we can, we must devour raw!"[377]

Then the word went round to offer their prayers; they prayed aloud, and chanted the battle-hymn, and advanced.[378]

The enemy fell into panic. In two more days the Greeks were in Trapezus, on the shore of the Black Sea, that vast water the Greeks had always called the Euxine, the Hospitable[379] Sea.

They had left Sardis, so near the Aegean, in spring. They had fought the fateful battle of Cunaxa, outside the mighty walls of Babylon, in September. They had crossed the highlands of eastern Turkey in the dead of winter. Now it was February, and they had gained the sea, and to a Greek the sea was the road home. Meanwhile, the citizens of Greek Trapezus provided them with a market, and made them gifts; and, with the encouragement of their hosts, the wandering army spent about thirty days despoiling the nearby Colchian tribes.

After this they prepared the sacrifice which they had vowed; they had cattle enough to sacrifice fully to Zeus Saviour and Heracles and the other gods, all they had vowed.

They held also a contest of games and sports on the hill where they were encamped. To find a racecourse and superintend the games they chose one Dracontios, a Spartan noble who had been banished as a boy for striking a boy with his knife and killing him by accident.

After the sacrifice they gave over the hides to Dracontios, and told him to take them to his ground. He pointed to the hill where they stood, and says he, "This hill is the best possible place to race wherever you like." "Oh," said they, "and how can they wrestle on this hard bushy ground?" He said, "So much the worse for the man who gets a fall." There was the two hundred yards for boys, mostly captives; in the long race the Cretans ran, more than sixty of them; others did wrestling and boxing and both combined, and it was a fine sight; there were plenty of entries, and plenty of rivalry with all their comrades looking on. There was horse-racing too; they had to ride down the precipice into the sea, and back again to the altar. On the way down most of them rolled along; on the way up the horses could hardly walk up that sheer steep. What shouts, what roars of laughter, what cheers![380]

After the sacrifices and games, the moving, pillaging panhellenic polis met and deliberated on the best way to get home.

First Leon, a Thurian, rose, and spoke as follows:

"To speak for myself, sirs, I'm tired out by this time, with packing up and marching and doubling and carrying arms and falling in and keeping guard and fighting. I want a little rest now from these hardships. We have the sea, then let's go by sea the rest of the way, lying flat like Odysseus, till we get to Hellas."

There was great cheering at this, "Good! Good!" and someone else said the same, and so said all of them. Then Cheirisophos rose, and said:

"I have a friend, sirs, Anaxibios, who is now Lord High Admiral at home, as it happens. If you will send me there, I think I shall bring you back ships of war and transports to carry you. If you want to go by sea, wait until I return; I won't be long."

On hearing this, the men were delighted and voted that he should sail, the sooner the better.[381]

But suppose Chirisophus should fail to secure sufficient sea transport? Xenophon persuaded the army to borrow warships from Trapezus and seize merchant vessels. They would pay and maintain the crews. He also tried to organize the pillage on which the army counted for food. He persuaded the coast cities to repair the roads, so they could march to the Hellespont if they had to; and the cities acceded, because they were all fearful of this mercenary force and eager to be rid of them. When Chirisophus did not return and when they themselves failed to capture enough transports and when provisions grew scarce, they put on board the ships they had those who were sick, those over forty, the boys and women they had seized during the long march, and most of the baggage, and sent them westward to Cerasus, another colony of Sinope. The rest of the army made the journey on foot in three days. At Cerasus the generals reviewed and numbered their troops. There were 8,600 men left, about two-thirds of those who had fought at Cunaxa. The rest had been killed in action, or lost in the mountains, or had perished in the snow, or had been captured, or had died of disease. They now divided the booty. They reserved a tithe for Apollo and Artemis, and entrusted shares of it to their generals, including Xenophon.

The army started westward again. Then men marched through strange lands, among people who used dolphin blubber in place of olive oil.

When they were among friends on this march the people held shows for them of rich men's children, fatted children fed on boiled chestnuts, tender and very white, and almost as broad as they were long, with backs and breasts variegated and tattooed all over in flower patterns. They ran after the women in the camp and wanted to lie with them in broad daylight, which was their own custom. All the men and women were fair-skinned. The army said that these were the most savage of all they had seen in their travels, and the farthest away from Hellenic customs. They would do in public what other human beings would do in private, and when they were alone they did what people do in company, talk to themselves and laugh at themselves, stop and dance anywhere as if they were showing off.[382]

They tried to get more ships from the city of Sinope to come and fetch them.

Meanwhile, Xenophon looked upon all these men-at-arms, and all those targeteers, and the bowmen and slingers and horsemen, too, and all fit from long practice—he saw all these on the Euxine, where so great a force could never have been collected without vast expense, and he thought it would be fine to found a city there, and to add territory and power to Hellas.[383]

The army heard of his desire and murmured. They wanted to go home. But, now that their common danger had decreased, discipline was declining fast. The Greek cities of the coast were increasingly alarmed, as Sicily had once been alarmed by Athens' grand armada, with its concentration of force and its ill-defined purpose. This same combination now gave Xeno-phon's army of mercenaries the appearance of a very large animal with a very small brain. Repeatedly, during the summer of 400, as the army slowly made its way toward the Bosphorus, Xenophon toyed with the idea of colonizing, especially at Calpe's Haven, which lay on the Black Sea coast only a score of miles east of Byzantium, only half a day's journey by oar. He would give this brainless, thrashing animal a purpose. Xenophon later wrote:

Calpe's Haven lies halfway on the voyage between Heracleia and Byzan-tion. It is a promontory jutting out into the sea; the part by the sea being a sheer cliff, height where it is least no less than twenty fathoms, and facing the land a neck about four hundred feet wide. The space inside the neck is enough for ten thousand inhabitants. The harbour under the cliff has a beach towards the west. There is a spring of plentiful sweet water close beside the sea commanded by the promontory. There is abundance of all sorts of wood, and particularly a great deal of fine wood for shipbuilding close to the sea. The highland stretches into the country some two or three miles, good soil without stones; and the part along the seashore is longer still, set thick with much timber of all sorts. The rest of the country for a long way round is good, and has many villages full of people; the land bears barley and wheat and pulse of all sorts, millet and sesame, figs enough, plenty of grapes, good wine-grapes too, and everything else except olives. So much for the country.

They encamped on the beach beside the sea. They would not camp on a place which might be turned into a city, and they thought indeed that they had really been brought there by some scheme of persons who wanted to found a city. For most of the soldiers had not been driven by poverty to this expedition; but it was the fame of Cyros which had brought them, some had followers with them, some had spent money themselves, and a few others had run away from home—they had left father and mother, or even children too, hoping to return with wealth for them, since they had heard how others had made their fortunes with Cyros. Men such as these wished to return safe to Hellas.[884]

When at last they reached Byzantium and the Spartan admiral Anaxibius closed the city's gates against them, they forced their way in. Xenophon had to remind them that the Lacedaemonians now controlled Hellas. If the Lacedaemonians had but recently brought his own city, imperial Athens, to her knees, they could certainly reduce Byzantium and they could punish any mercenary army that had seized it. To everybody's relief, at that moment

a certain Coiratadas arrived; he was a Theban on his travels, not a banished man but one with a fever for generaleering, ready with his services if army, city, or nation wanted a good commander. He came and said he was ready to lead them to what is called the Delta of Thrace, where they could get all sorts of good things; until they got there, he would find plenty of food and drink. While he was speaking, the answer came from Anaxibios: that if they were obedient they should never be sorry for it; he would report it to the authorities at home, and he would himself do all he could for them. Accordingly, the soldiers accepted Coiratadas for their general, and went outside the walls. Coiratadas arranged to be there the next day with victims for sacrifice, and a seer, and food and drink for the army. When they were outside, Anaxibios closed the gates and proclaimed that any soldier caught inside would be sold as a slave.[385]

A new Spartan governor arrived and found 400 sick men from Xenophon's army whom his predecessor had quartered in Byzantium. The new governor promptly sold them as slaves. The Theban buccaneer, Coiratadas, who had hired the army, sacrificed repeatedly in a vain effort to get favorable auspices; then he disappeared. The generals could not agree where to lead their rootless, hungry polis next. An exiled Thracian prince named Seuthes hired the army in hopes of winning back his father's kingdom. All through the harsh Thracian winter they served him, but the pay was irregular; and so, hearing that Sparta had decided on war with their old enemy Tissaphernes and would willingly pay them well, some 6,000 followed Xenophon across the Hellespont back into Asia Minor. They passed near Troy and then marched to Pergamos. There in March, 399, Xenophon turned over his 6,000 men to the Spartan commander, Thibron. Scarce fifty miles to the southeast lay Sardis, whence Cyrus had led them bravely forth two long years before. It was an expedition that had taken them some 4,000 miles.

Meanwhile, several things had happened to Xenophon. A month before his old master, Socrates, had been condemned to death in Athens. A month later the city that condemned Socrates would condemn Xenophon himself, in his absence, to exile:[386] had he not served under Cyrus, whose pay had enabled Sparta to destroy the Athenian Empire? According to Xenophon's own later account of the great expedition, he reached Pergamos with scarcely more worldly goods than Socrates, and had to sell his horse in order to pay his passage home. But luckily the wife of a Greek exile at Pergamos told him of a wealthy Persian who lived in a nearby castle. Xenophon led his followers against this fat prey, bagged the Persian, his wife and children, many other captives, horses, and cattle. Of this rich plunder Xenophon was voted the lion's share. But there was more booty in the Persian provinces yet to be won, and fame too: he stayed on in Persia's Aegean provinces to serve in the Spartan army.

During the first four decades of the fourth century the disintegration of the Hellenic state system that had produced the Peloponnesian War continued unabated. Athens had failed to give her lost empire a workable constitution. Sparta and her Peloponnesian allies had fought the long war to liberate Athens' subject allies. Sparta promptly garrisoned those she liberated and collected for herself the tribute they had before paid Athens. She restored oligarchies in them. She dominated and bullied her allies in Mainland Greece. She lacked any real interest in the new economic problems of the Aegean and Asian Greeks. Sparta still vaunted the laws of Lycurgus, but Lysander's conquests had flooded her with the gold and silver which Lycurgus the Lawgiver had strictly forbidden. Inequalities of wealth bred discontent and Sparta was even forced to nip an incipient revolution within the ranks of the Spartiates themselves, while always the Dwellers-round-about and the Helots sullenly nursed their grievances. Her principal allies in the Peloponnesian War, states like Thebes and Corinth, had been ruthlessly shouldered aside when Sparta appropriated the empire of fallen Athens.

In less than a decade from the fall of Athens, Sparta's allies in Greece were ready to rise against her. A Spartan army was plundering Phrygia, nominally to complete the liberation of Greece-in-Asia. It was Persian money that had enabled Sparta to destroy Athens; now, with a Spartan army ravaging her western provinces, Persia used her money again, but this time to subsidize Sparta's discontented allies in Mainland Greece. Thebes, Athens, Corinth, and Argos thereupon headed an insurgent alliance. Within three years Sparta was so hard pressed that she solicited Persia to impose peace on the warring Greeks. She failed; but there was still hope, for the Great King was bound to be alarmed by signs of Athenian recovery in the Aegean.

In the fourth century the problem of every state that aspired to power was money. In one of the last comedies Aristophanes wrote, a querulous old man declared to Wealth:

> See here, everything that's done is done through you. You and you alone are the cause of everything. Why, even in war, it's the side you're on that wins.[387]

Even under Pericles it had been money that had built and manned the fleet. During the Peloponnesian War both sides more and more often hired mercenaries, either Greek or barbarian. When the long war ended in 404, all Hellas was flooded with men who had never mastered any trade but war. A whole generation had grown up amidst violence, violence between polis and polis, between rich and poor inside the polis. Returning from war to a ravaged homeland, to its disrupted commerce, and to unemployment, the former soldier looked, as Xenophon had looked, to foreign service: under a Persian prince eager to seize his brother's crown, or under a Thracian princeling like Seuthes, or even under an unknown Theban buccaneer with a fever for generaleering, full of promises of good pillage in the Thracian countryside. Hundreds of years ago, Hellas had been founded by marauding bands. The new marauders of the fourth century, unlike their remote Achaean or Dorian ancestors, fought for money. They plundered village storehouses and made off with cattle and kidnaped natives, but only in part to enjoy food or women. Much of what they seized, they sold for cash. Unlike their heroic ancestors they were the children of a cash economy, which even Sparta had now entered.

By the 380's, an Athenian captain of mercenaries named Iphicrates, who was born the son of a leather-worker, a little north of Marathon, had begun to revolutionize Greek warfare. Against this ingenious professional, the locked shields of the stubborn citizen soldiers of Sparta's heavy infantry proved an inadequate defense. For centuries Spartans had fought in ranks for a sacred polis, a little in the spirit of Homeric single combat. As early as 425, on the island of Sphacteria, Spartan heavy infantry had learned that this obstinate courage could not ward off arrows from lightly armed and swiftly moving troops under Demosthenes and Cleon. In the decades that followed, men like Xenophon were learning, often from

Persian opponents, the true uses of archers and slingers and cavalry. This Athenian professional, Iphicrates, now developed systematically both light infantry and cavalry. To his infantry he assigned the javelin, the bow, a lengthened lance, a lengthened sword, together with a light wicker shield covered with hide. Iphicrates' light-armed troops were trained to move fast, to surprise the enemy, to harass him, to maneuver rapidly. To his light cavalry he assigned the lance. Already on a winter's day in 390, near Corinth's port, Lechaeum, he had fallen on King Agesilaus' heavy infantry and taught all Greece what his own kind of light troops could do. Of the Spartan hero's heavy infantry 250 out of some 600 had been killed.

The new mercenary and the new warfare that money had created were subject to one important weakness. In Pericles' time, when a citizen Assembly voted for a campaign, a citizen general was likely to get the funds he required to win it, if only because the men who voted, or their relatives, or their immediate friends, would have to fight it. But a fourth-century Assembly might vote the campaign and then vote quite inadequate sums to some professional like Iphicrates. The professional had then to hire an army of mercenaries and embark on the campaign, only to find later that he must resort to brutal requisitions abroad or even encourage pillaging an ally to keep his professionals from quitting.

Faced with the Aristophanic fact that in war the side the money was on would win, and knowing from experience that Persia was where the big sums of money were, by 386 Sparta became in a sense herself a mercenary. For she induced the Great King to put Persia's money on Sparta once again, or in any case to publish the fact that she would do so if the Greek states did not make peace. No confederation or alliance except Sparta's Peloponnesian League would be permitted. To obtain those terms, Sparta abandoned the Asian Greeks. In effect she sold Greece-in-Asia to the Great King in return for the right to dominate Mainland Greece. The many little leagues that were springing up had to be dissolved. The anti-Spartan coalition knew it could not confront Sparta's Peloponnesian League backed by Persian gold. To make war, they would have required mercenaries, and only money could buy them. The meeting of interests between Sparta and Persia took the form, not of a treaty, but of a terse announcement made in 386 by the King of Kings:

> King Artaxerxes thinks it just that the cities in Asia should belong to him, as well as Clazomenae and Cyprus among the islands, and that the

other Greek cities, both small and great, should be left independent, except Lemnos, Imbros, and Scyros; and these should belong, as of old, to the Athenians. But whichever of the two parties does not accept this peace, upon them I will make war, in company with those who desire this arrangement, both by land and by sea, with ships and with money.[388]

The Great King's announcement ended with the right words: *kai chremasin*, and with money. Persian money had started the war. The power of Persian money now stopped it. Was it the memory of Leonidas standing firm at Thermopylae while Thebes and many other Greek states medized and either helped Xerxes assault Greece or did not hinder him, that caused a bystander to cry out to Xenophon's Spartan hero, King Agesilaus: "Alas for Greece, now that the Spartans are medizing." "Are not," replied the king, "the Medes the rather spartanizing?"[389] Agesilaus' reply was in the great Spartan tradition of the pithy, laconic epigram. But it concealed a brutal fact: that the monetizing of war had just led to the sale of Greece. Scarcely ninety years before, Persian gold had failed to prevent the catastrophe of Xerxes at Salamis, at Plataea, at Mycale, or even his loss of Greece-in-Asia.

Persia had often subsidized Greek against Greek to keep them from meddling in Persian affairs. But, more than once in the fourth century, the Great King needed Greek soldiers in order to put down rebellion, in Egypt or in some other province. Peace among the Greeks was then needed. With the rise of the mercenaries, one of diplomacy's functions was to regulate the market in mercenaries. War was an industry that consumed mercenaries, and therefore money; it produced captives, therefore slaves, therefore money from the sale of slaves. War also produced booty, which again produced money when mercenaries sold it. Slaves made life comfortable for free citizens, which made free citizens less willing to face war, which created a market for mercenaries. Free citizens were often unwilling to tax themselves sufficiently to provide adequate pay for the armies they hired, and so their armies plundered. These sudden shifts in military campaigns prolonged old wars and started new ones. To keep all these processes going, one prime mover was required: money.

After the King's declaration of 386, the Spartans grew more highhanded than ever, and it was their hybris, their insolence, that undid them. Theban oligarchs betrayed Thebes to a Spartan army; a resurgent, democratic Thebes, led by Pelopidas, ejected its Spartan garrison. Within a decade,

ม military genius, Epaminondas, had reorganized the Theban army. The new Theban phalanx, fifty shields deep, met the famous Spartan line, which was only twelve shields deep, at Leuctra in July, 371, and by its weight the phalanx broke the line. Then Epaminondas began periodic invasions of Laconia. Indeed, having just missed capturing Sparta, he laid waste southern Laconia itself, stirred up a serf rebellion in Messenia, and refounded the city of Messene on the slopes of famous Mount Ithome. Persia, having subsidized Sparta, then Athens, then Sparta again, chose now to place her money on Thebes. The year after Sparta's defeat at Leuctra, the tyrant Jason of Pherae, Epaminondas' ally, who had united all Thessaly and might have disputed the hegemony that Epaminondas was wresting from Sparta, was assassinated, and his death cut short the further growth of Thessalian power. In 362, Epaminondas fought a great battle at Mantinea. Although he once more beat a Spartan army, he lost his own life, and the pre-eminence of Thebes did not long survive him. Athens, too, had made another bid for hegemony. She had constructed a confederacy for the second time. She had tried to avoid features like the tribute and the cleruchies, which had aroused revolt against her former confederacy once it had turned empire. But she failed a second time to devise political institutions through which her new union might govern itself in freedom. She was constantly weakened by the revolts of her allies.

Throughout the confused events that marked successive bids for power by Sparta, by Thessaly, by Thebes, by Athens again, one fact was clear. Greek city-states could be briefly brought into alliance, and sometimes on a small scale into political union, only by a common fear of conquest or else by a common hatred of arbitrary force and a common rebellion against it. The kaleidoscopic shifts in alliances that went on during these four decades were basically scrambles for security in a constantly shifting balance of power. The shifts continued not only between alliance and alliance but also inside most states between oligarchy and democracy.

Xenophon, the Athenian exile, tried to give in his *Hellenica* an account of Greek history from 411, the point at which Thucydides broke off, to 362, when Epaminondas the Theban defeated Sparta at Mantinea and fell in action. Xenophon had served under King Agesilaus in Asia in 396-394. When Sparta's allies rose against her and the Ephors swiftly recalled Agesilaus and his army to save Sparta, Xenophon, still an exile from Athens, followed him to Greece. When Agesilaus won an empty victory over the Thebans and Athenians at Coronea, in Boeotia, Xenophon fought under him and then retreated with him to Peloponnese. The Spartans gave the exile an estate near Olympia. There, with a wife and two small sons, he lived the life of a retired army officer and country noble and there he wrote a book on the *Republic of the Lacedaemonians*, praising the laws of the wise Lycurgus, at least a portion of his *Memorabilia*, recounting the actions and sayings of Socrates, and began a treatise on estate management, and another on horsemanship.[390]

Plato had written his *Apology*, a report of Socrates' defense in court. So Xenophon also wrote an *Apology*, his own defense of their common master. His writings about Socrates showed a less luminous person than the person revealed in the *Dialogues* of Plato. But there was no essential contradiction between them. Like Plato he saw in Socrates great goodness. Unlike Plato, he moralized about that goodness. He assumed that Socrates chose death, not—as Plato's Socrates himself declared—because he had no other right choice open, but because he feared the evils of old age. His portrait of Socrates was the picture of a philosopher painted by a gallant soldier, a wily strategist, a practical man of action, a country gentleman, conventional, unspeculative, ambitious, uncritical of his own motives, a man who was not greedy or covetous but who valued money and position, though he valued fame and honor even more. In place of the dialectical view of virtue that interested the Socrates whom Plato presented, Xenophon displayed a sort of basic decency, supported by a naïve casuistry. He possessed an enormous zest for life and a great capacity for friendship and loyalty. He looked outward, not inward. All these traits were reflected in his easy, simple, sometimes rather circumstantial style.

His knack for straightforward narrative and his eye for vivid detail made his *Anabasis* a delight to read. But his more ambitious effort to relate the political and military history of Greece for the half-century following the period which Thucydides covered lapsed for the most part into something more like chronicle than history. The *Hellenica* did indeed contain brief passages that were memorable; but the important questions were often not only unanswered, they even went unasked. For this, Xenophon was only in part responsible. Even Thucydides had flagged in the latter portion of his own history. After the great catastrophe at Syracuse, the Peloponnesian War increasingly lost its inner meaning. The confrontation of ideas that kept its early stages dialectical and tragic and therefore human and intelligible, more and more gave way to mere violence and counter-violence, to the conflict of passions rather than of ideas. Was it death that made Thucydides break off his writings seven years before the flutes had played and the walls of Athens had come down? Or had the later years of the war so lost meaning that his subject began to bore and depress him? The vast tragedy he had mounted for the readers of all time had stupidly refused to end. It was at that perilous moment in the plot that Xenophon tried to take up the history of Greece. In theory he could have traced Sparta's seizure of Athens' empire, the hybris Sparta showed as oppressor of Mainland and Aegean Greece, her cynical recourse to the Great King to guarantee her supremacy, and finally the loss of her hegemony; but Sparta's statesmen worked by the light of too few ideas for even a Thucydides to have cast their polis as tragic hero. The rise and fall of Spartan hegemony furnished a pattern that Xenophon could have used to greater advantage in the *Hellenica* than he did, but even if he had so used it, he could not have achieved the universal human significance of Thucydides.

With the weakening of Sparta's power after the battle of Leuctra in 371, Sparta relinquished to Elis the district near Olympia where the pleasant estate of Xenophon lay. He accordingly moved to Corinth. Two years later Athens, alarmed by the rise of Theban power, allied herself with Sparta; and two years after that, Athens revoked the decree which had exiled Xenophon. A year or two later he returned to Athens, after an absence of nearly forty years. Then, at the battle of Mantinea in 362, the point at which he left off his history of Greece, one of his sons was killed in action while serving in the Athenian cavalry, fighting for the two cities his father loved best, Athens and Sparta, for the moment yoke-fellows once more, as Cimon had long ago prescribed.

Two years after his son's death at Mantinea, Xenophon's old commander, King Agesilaus of Sparta, died. Xenophon wrote a laudatory biography of the man under whom he had fought in Asia and at Coronea. He continued and completed an historical romance about another king, another leader of men: the *Education of Cyrus*. The hero of this tale was not the Cyrus whom Xenophon had followed to the waters of Babylon but Cyrus the Great, who founded the Persian Empire. Even before King Agesilaus died, Xenophon had written of that other master of his, that very different hero, Socrates. Did he wish to emulate Plato's picture of Socrates in the *Symposium*, in which Socrates and others had praised love and the riotous Alcibiades praised Socrates? In any case, Xenophon wrote his own *Symposium*, in which the conversation was more boisterous, often trivial, sometimes flat. Shortly after Agesilaus died, he wrote, not too skillfully, a dialogue dealing with the life of the typical tyrant. He finished his essay on horsemanship and wrote another on the cavalry commander. He finished his history of Greece, the *Hellenica*, down to that battle at Mantinea, in which one of his own sons had fallen; and he finished his *Memorabilia* of Socrates. Around 354 Xenophon died.

Xenophon was a child of the Peloponnesian War. He had seen imperial Athens humbled. He had seen Sparta, Thebes, and Athens fail successively to unite Mainland Greece. It had been Athens' second failure to find a common purpose and common political institutions for herself and for her allies that had lost her much of the power which she had in part recaptured. But it had been also a desperate lack of money. And so the last work Xenophon composed was his *Ways and Means*, apparently addressed to his city's Council of Five Hundred. In it he urged an income tax; hotels, erected by the state for foreign merchants and visitors; a fleet of state-owned merchant vessels; and better exploitation of the state silver mines at Laurium. Also he prescribed peace. He was a cavalryman and he had loved adventure, but he had always prided himself on being practical and useful to others. He admired Socrates because he was so practical, so useful.

The Hellenic world in which Xenophon died was a far different world from the one that had formed his mind and character. Protagoras the sophist had scandalized Hellas in the fifth century by announcing that man was the measure of all things; but by the fourth, a man's money seemed to be a simpler, more concrete measure. The old landed nobility that had created the polis as an aristocratic republic ruled by the Best People had now been partly killed off in the perpetual wars between polis and polis. Its specific virtue had been courage; its aim, honor in this life and fame after death. But, as Socrates implied, it lacked the wisdom that transcended even honor; and when the sea opened and trade grew and money multiplied, it came to love money. It retained some traditional prejudices against trade; its members would still have preferred to seize rather than to haggle and save and scheme like a merchant. But as generation followed generation, blue blood and silver coin mixed; an aristocracy that had really been a timocracy was transformed into an oligarchy; the Best People became merely the richest, the few, *hoi Oligoi*. Beneath them were the many, *hoi Polloi*, the poor.

The blooded aristocrat like Cimon, or Pericles, or even, potentially, Alcibiades, had attracted the many, the poor, by a certain nobility of soul. These aristocrats had displayed a grandness of manner, some mysterious power to represent the aspirations even of the lowly. Their wealth was their perquisite, not their essence. Their scorn of vulgarity and pettiness and servility struck some resonance even in the vulgar, the petty, and the servile. But the man who was merely rich, especially if he happened to be clearly vulgar too, was distinguished not by what he was but by what he had. What he had, any other man could have who was strong enough or sly enough to get it away from this rich man or to get wealth like it elsewhere. By the time Xenophon died, then, class cleavage in Hellas existed more explicitly between rich and poor than it had ever done before. In some oligarchies the oligarchs actually took an oath: "And I will be hostile to the people and will plan whatever evil I can against them."[391] The aristocrat had excited admiration; the oligarch ruled by economic force. If the oligarch thought of himself as an aristocrat, few of those who hated or feared or used him shared his opinion. Few were taken in by his romantic love of Sparta: he would have loathed its black broth and grueling physical drill. The oligarch was no Spartan ascetic. On the contrary, the oligarch was learning the uses of physical luxury; and ever since Lysander had flooded Sparta with booty and money the oligarch had been learning luxury even in Sparta.

The fourth century was marked by a sharp drop in population. In 431 Athens had scarcely more than 40,000 voters. By 390 she had only 30,000; by 310 she would have 20,000. Constant wars, the famines and plagues caused by wars, the destruction of productive capital such as olive trees and vines and farm houses and draft animals, took their toll. Thousands of Greek captives were sold into slavery, often abroad, although by way of compensation thousands of foreign slaves were imported. Exposure of unwanted children had always been acceptable practice and had always been legal.[392] In most states the father decided; in Sparta, the state. In Sparta, in 480, the Spartiates furnished over 8,000 heavy infantry; on the eve of the terrible defeat at Leuctra in 371, there were less than 2,000; less than half a century later Aristotle[393] would put them at 1,000.

Not only was the population diminishing; what was left of it was migrating from the countryside to the city. The farmers whom Pericles had summoned into his walled, artificial island when Sparta invaded Attica had been homesick and unhappy in the city. But, as the long war had gone on and as the ravages of Attica had increased, many of them had learned to be city folk in Athens, or port folk or sailors in Piraeus. At Athens, also, thousands of outsettlers who had farmed in the islands had been driven back to hungry, besieged Athens to give her more mouths to feed. In Attica they had found no land to take up and became city men. Finally, the smallholder, whose ancestors had lived a hard life and sold only the small surplus of food they and their household did not need for themselves, could not compete in cash farming with the men of means who were buying up small plots here and there or seizing them for debt; who could carry these plots in years of lean crops; and who could squeeze profit out of them with slave labor or cheap labor and by improved methods and equipment. For methods did improve: rotation of crops, a metal point for the ancient wooden plow, legumes in place of fallow, better irrigation, better manuring, seed selection, better choice of crop according to soil. But all these improvements called for money. A technical literature on agriculture sprang into being, but for capitalist investors in land, not for smallholders.

In the city, industry and commerce were growing also. In industry cloth production, flour production, and bread baking were partly shifting now from home to shop, and shops were likely to be manned by slaves. The father of the orator Demosthenes, for example, operated a sword factory manned by some thirty-two slaves and a couch factory manned by twenty slaves.[394] In commerce navigation was improving, especially whenever Athenian sea power was in a position to police the seas for pirates. Commercial companies were forming. Banking facilities were increasing. Attic pottery was sold from one end of the Mediterranean to another. Not only Athens, but Ephesus in Asian Greece, Cyzicus on the Propontis, Byzantium at the southern entrance of the Bosphorus, Olbia on the Scythian coast of the Black Sea, Cyrene on the coast of Libya, Massilia on the present site of Marseilles, and scores of other ports prospered. Above all, strategically placed as a port of call, Syracuse became the most populous city in Hellas.

In this new, money-loving Hellas, the upper class had lost much of its social function. Its members no longer looked on military service as a duty or even, what it had originally been, the prerogative of a fighting aristocracy. The status of mercenary had caused a shift in army nomenclature.[395] In the fifth century a mercenary was an *epikouros*, or helper, a skilled professional assisting amateur citizen-soldiers. The term signified nothing about the money the helper earned. In the first half of the fourth century he was less reticently called a wage-earning peltast, or light infantryman. By the close of the fourth century he was merely a *stratiōtes*, a member of an army, a soldier. Being hired was no longer a distinguishing characteristic. It was natural that, with the professionalizing of warfare, athletics tended to turn professional too. The hard, sunburnt body of the free Athenian often turned white and soft, like the body of an upper-class Asian. One took one's ease.

Political leadership, like military leadership, was no longer a function of noble blood. Like generalship, it tended to fall into the hands of the professional, as the operations, especially the fiscal operations, of the polis grew more complex. As to the statesman's problem of public persuasion, that task went more and more to the professional persuader, the phrasemaker, the paid speech-writer, the orator. In 354, about the year Xenophon died, a thirty-year-old orator named Demosthenes made his first speech in a court trial and his first oration before the Athenian Assembly. The speeches of the new orators were not delivered on the Olympian level of the speeches the great Pericles had made. They reminded one more of the violent style and personal invective which, according to Thucydides, the tanner Cleon first introduced into the Assembly. These orators spoke before an audience of connoisseurs, who were too often guilty of the civic crime Cleon had charged the Assembly with in his day: they voted not for what they deemed wisest for the polis but for the speaker they most enjoyed hearing. Indeed, the speeches which men like Demosthenes wrote, learned by heart, delivered before the Assembly, and then published became perhaps the most characteristic form of literature in the fourth century.

Both literature and art ceased to be the confident enterprise of a close-knit polis and began to express a population of lonelier individuals than before, of less intuitive individuals, more analytical, harder to lead to the heights, more eager for pleasure and for the one thing that seemed to buy pleasure with the least effort. Money could propitiate the gods, pay the speech-writer, bribe the statesman, buy the use of beautiful women, buy

the richest food, the best wine, the most skillful cook, and even pay the
doctor who repaired the harm these pleasures might do the body. Money
could buy the soldier's courage, or anyhow the mercenary's skill, and within
the polis mercenaries might win their paymaster a tyrant's throne. Even
for the least ambitious and the least daring, money could purchase ease
and comfort and pleasure, and even friends, or at least parasites, to share
one's pleasures.

As the invisible world of revealed gods and intuited ideas receded from
most men's experience, and as the attention of most men focused with
a feverish new interest on the world the senses knew, literature and art
faithfully recorded the shift. Great tragedies were no longer being written.
The theater sometimes revived Euripides, whose plays were more admired
now than when he was still alive. There were even revivals of Sophocles.
But to the fourth century Aeschylus appealed less than either. The things
Aeschylus was most concerned with, the gods, the justice the gods taught
men, the polis that bound men together, the truly heroic man or woman,
seemed more and more remote. Aeschylus was too deeply religious, too
deeply aristocratic, too bound by—or freed by?—conventions no longer
comprehended. He was too intellectually strenuous.

Comedy had had to change too. Aristophanes had laughed uproariously,
but at things he considered central and important: at man's failure to find
his true relation to the gods, at man's failure to achieve polis, community
—in short, his failure to find a genuinely human existence, a life worthy
of being lived. And since Aristophanes believed such a life could be lived
only in a polis that intimately associated man both with his gods and with
his fellow citizens, some of his finest comedies were profoundly political.
But now, in the fourth century, the polis, and the sense of polis, were in
decline. Both the relation between god and man and the relation between
man and his political community interested audiences less. The successors
of Aristophanes wrote less of the citizen and more of the individual and
his private affairs. These later writers were less joyous, less confident, less
boisterous, less bawdy. For the infinitely playful, they substituted the
cleverly contrived, the technically expert. For high-spirited obscenity they
substituted wittily suggestive innuendo. They parodied the myths about
the gods, myths that had lost much of their power to move and could be
handled now as amusing scandal. The literary conventions of comedy,
which had sprung out of forgotten religious rites, in part distintegrated,

and comedy was left free to be merely amusing. It could help the relieved spectator to descend comfortably from the sublime to the foolish, from wisdom to knowledgeability, from a troubling, striving faith to amused and self-flattering incredulity. It diverted. It relaxed.

The architect and the sculptor followed the same descent. Now that both tragedy and comedy carried a lighter load of significance, now that both had lost some of their ancient ritual power to unite and lift, the architect compensated in part for that loss by building magnificent marble tiers to replace the rude wooden seating of the outdoor theater and by designing more elaborate staging. Athens might have no great tragedians left, but those she still had could be heard in more elegant surroundings. In these splendid surroundings an Athenian could hear his favorite actor, regardless of the play. It had once been unimportant what actor spoke from behind his conventional mask, and an Aeschylus might himself write the play and also act in it. But now the professional actor flourished and found his enthusiastic followers able to applaud his virtuosity even in a second-rate tragedy or comedy.

The architect still built temples as dwellings for the gods, but his vision of beauty had somewhat changed. One of the marvels of the fifth-century Parthenon was its perfect marriage of Dorian masculinity with the feminine grace of Ionia. In the fourth century, it was as if the softer, more delicate spirit of Ionia had finally won out. And why not? Athenian life now resembled the life of sixth-century Ionia far more than Periclean Athens had resembled it. The aesthetic solutions of Ionia found a resonance in the new Athens. Softness, delicacy, daintiness, ornateness, and even prettiness were the marks of that resonance. Even by 407, alongside the Parthenon with its strong Doric columns, Athens had completed another temple, the Erechtheum, a temple with tall, slender Ionic columns. The roof of one of its porches rested on the heads of a row of young maidens in marble: caryatids, priestesses of Artemis, and caryatids too were first carved in Ionia. The solution was devised with technical brilliance; but compared with the grave and masculine Dorian columns of the nearby Parthenon, it remained a bit contrived, a bit forced, its emphasis more on means than on ends. The Erechtheum lacked the wholeness of the Parthenon. Its sculptured details exhibited skill, delicacy, and sensuous grace rather than the majesty one saw in the friezes of Athena's stately dwelling. The shift exemplified in the Parthenon and the Erechtheum continued in the fourth century.

But the architects did not stop at making the new dwellings for their gods more human, more delightful. They were also building costlier, handsomer homes for men, or rather for rich men. The fifth-century aristocrats of Athens had kept their homes in the country and had maintained only humble dwellings in town for their occasional use. The soaring temples of Athens' gods had once stood in marked contrast with the simple dwellings of the men, whether rich or poor, who worshiped those gods. But in the fourth century the rich lived more continuously in the city, even if they owned farmland outside, and they now employed architects to build them more elaborate dwellings. Moreover, when the architect or sculptor or painter went to other lands, it was less now to build other temples to the same great gods of Hellas than to build a palace or a splendid tomb for the truly rich man, the monarch or tyrant. In general, the artist was treating men as if they were gods.

Sculptors, too, turned from the gods to men. They did indeed continue to model or carve statues of Apollo and Aphrodite and the other gods, but their gods were more and more like men: the Apollo of sculptors like Praxiteles was likely now to display a beauty that was merely human and a grace that was even slightly effeminate; and their Aphrodite was less a superhuman being than a voluptuous, desirable, and even coy woman. On the other hand, portrait statues and busts of the rich or famous multiplied and were made more specifically true to life. In earlier days, gods were shown as larger then men; small boys looked like diminutive men. But now the sculptor carefully distinguished between the fully developed features of a man and the more blurred features of a child.[396] Also, he took pains to note that the child's head was larger in proportion to his body than a man's would be. The earlier sculptors had thought of the boy as a man, imperfectly developed but essentially a man. Their successors saw in a boy something different from a man, and something different from other boys of the same age. It was the same story with the transient emotion reflected on a human face. Instead of the masklike smile of the sixth century and the serenity of the fifth, sculptors like Scopas now portrayed not only transient emotions but even violent emotions. Finally, just as the fourth-century actor emerged, metaphorically, from behind his mask and became no longer anonymous but a personal favorite of his public, so the architect and sculptor strove to be original: a so-called school or style might be associated less with a polis than with a famous and admired virtuoso in his art.

In art, as in literature, the individual had been freed from his polis. Otherwise stated, he had lost his community and stood alone. Was it this aloneness that made him look for a man, some man who could save Hellas, some man of the very type that would have provoked a legal ostracism from an earlier polis? As life grew more urban, more complex, more impersonal, the yearning for a person grew concurrently. Was this yearning connected with Xenophon's hero-worship of King Agesilaus? Was it connected with Xenophon's constant obsession with the charismatic qualities of the true military leader? With the ability of Epaminondas and Pelopidas to lead Thebes and Boeotia in a few years to the brief hegemony of Mainland Greece? With Xenophon's historical romance about Cyrus the Great? With the fascination exerted at Athens and elsewhere by the orator, who knew how to exalt his audience to a sense of at least emotional community? More importantly, did this search for a person in part account for the mingled dread and hope with which Mainland Greece watched the sudden rise of a new king of barbarous Macedonia to the north, a king whose name was just becoming famous at Athens during the last few years of Xenophon's life?

That king was Philip II. The Macedonia into which he was born was mountainous, like Greece. But the lowlands around the Thermaic Gulf north of Thessaly and a number of plains on the plateaus upcountry supplied plentiful grain for bread and ample pasturage for farm stock and specifically for horses. Like Thessaly and Boeotia, Macedonia had never been forced by hunger to turn to the sea. Besides, Greek maritime states like Chalcis and Corinth had early planted colonies on its coasts, especially on the trident-shaped peninsula which had come to be called Chalcidice. It was they, and not the Macedonians, who exploited and exported the country's timber and metals to Greece. Later it was imperial Athens. Macedonia remained, therefore, like the western portion of Mainland Greece, archaic, tribal, monarchical, and largely feudal, a country of horses rather than of ships, a country more like the past self of Greece than Greece was.

The Greeks looked down on Macedonians as backward, as lacking true arts or letters or politics, as not being Greek, although Herodotus reminded the Greeks that Alexander I of Macedonia had claimed to be Greek, had demanded and obtained the right therefore to compete in the Olympic Games; and although Thucydides reported that Alexander's family, the Temenid dynasty, came from Argos. The kings of Macedon not only claimed to be of Greek stock. In the true style of the Greek king or noble, they claimed descent from the same savior hero as the Spartan kings: Heracles, son, by a human mother, of Zeus himself. The king's subjects could manage to talk with Greeks without an interpreter, whereas a Thracian could not. The Macedonian dialect indeed contained Illyrian words, words like *sarissa*, the name for a very long pike used by Macedonian soldiers; but these same soldiers could not understand the language of the dangerous neighbors from whom they had borrowed such words. Some of their place names, like the names of their months, bore witness to the fact that, like the more civilized Greeks to the south, they were the racial product of the Achaean and Dorian invaders and of a population these conquerors had subdued. Alexander I not only competed at Olympia: he cultivated the great Theban poet Pindar, who knew how to write victory odes worthy of royal competitors, and he received the historian Herodotus at his court.

Alexander's son Perdiccas reigned during the Peloponnesian War and had his hands full maintaining his kingdom's independence while Brasidas was on campaign. Perdiccas' successor, Archelaus, built roads and fortresses, moved his capital from Aegae to Pella, reorganized his army. Like his father, Archelaus tried to bring Greek civilization to Pella. He commissioned the famous painter Zeuxis to decorate his palace with murals; brought in Timotheus of Miletus, famous for his reforms in music; attracted from Samos the epic poet Choerilus and from Athens the young friend of Socrates, the tragic poet Agathon. Certainly Zeuxis was no Polygnotus; his painting sometimes strove for a realism and a pathos that Polygnotus would not have sought. But Zeuxis was praised for his improved techniques; and, in any case, Polygnotus was not available: his painting days belonged a generation before, and the hellenizing Archelaus took what the Hellas of his own day could still offer. Agathon, too, was a far cry from Aeschylus or Sophocles; but, a few years before Athens finally surrendered to Lysander in 404, Euripides had moved to Thessaly, and Archelaus brought him to his court. There Euripides composed his last tragedies, including the *Bacchae* and *Archelaus*, and there he died.

It was Archelaus' grandfather who had won for his family the right to participate in the panhellenic games at Olympia. The grandson set up new games in Macedonia at Dion, where men would compete in racing, in music, and in drama. Appropriately, Dion lay in Pieria, traditionally considered a favorite abode of the Muses, those daughters of Zeus whom Hesiod had heard singing on holy Helicon. Just south of Dion towered Mount Olympus, where Zeus himself dwelt, on the frontier between Macedonia and Hellas. About 399, the year in which Athens executed Socrates, Archelaus was assassinated, and for seven years coronations and assassinations alternated rapidly. Then Amyntas III came to the throne. By 370, when he died, Amyntas had managed to rescue his kingdom from pressure by the wild Illyrians, had skillfully maneuvered his way through the tangled antagonisms of Greek politics, and had reduced his feudal princes in the highlands to obedience.

Amyntas' eldest son, Alexander I, reigned two years; then his mother arranged his assassination so that she and Ptolemy, her son-in-law and lover, might rule. But the Chalcidian League was backing another candidate for the throne. The murderous queen called in Athens' brilliant professional general of mercenaries, Iphicrates, as support against the League. Her husband had adopted Iphicrates as his son, to please a Thracian king whose daughter the Athenian general had married. Aside from this somewhat personal tangle, Athens was opposed to the Chalcidian League, which was supporting Amphipolis against reconquest by Athens. But then friends of the Macedonian queen's dead husband called on Pelopidas of Thebes to lead an army of mercenaries against the queen and her lover Ptolemy. Ptolemy bribed the mercenaries and agreed to serve only as regent and as guardian of the queen's two remaining sons, Perdiccas and Philip. He also turned over to Thebes fifty hostages, including Philip. Philip was about fifteen when he went to Thebes, and he stayed there for some three years. In 365, Perdiccas came of age and demanded the crown. Ptolemy refused; Perdiccas contrived his assassination and his mother, the queen, having caused the murder of her eldest son in order that she and her lover might reign, consoled her widowhood by learning to read.

Her second son, Perdiccas III, carried on the hellenizing tradition of his court at Pella, interested himself in philosophy and geometry and received at his court a pupil of Plato's. He was an able administrator; and with the aid of an Athenian exile, he reorganized his kingdom's finances. The Illyrians again started trouble in the northwest. In 359 he led an army against them, but he was overwhelmingly defeated. Some 4,000 Macedonians fell in battle; among them was the king. His infant son succeeded him, with Philip as regent. The Paeonians were attacking from the north; the Thracians were attacking from the east and backing a claimant to the throne; and Athens was backing another claimant with her fleet.

Philip was only twenty-three when he became regent of Macedonia. He had been born the year the Spartans seized by treachery the citadel of Thebes. He was eleven when news came that Epaminondas, the Theban general, had decisively defeated a Spartan army at Leuctra. Epaminondas had smashed through the famous Spartan line, twelve shields deep, with his newly developed phalanx or wedge of heavy infantry, fifty shields deep. At the front of the phalanx he had placed the Sacred Band, led by his friend Pelopidas. Four years after Leuctra, Philip, as one of the hostages to Thebes, came to know both Epaminondas and Pelopidas, and there he was lodged in the home of another great Theban general, Pammenes. By then Epaminondas had three times invaded the Peloponnese, had broken all precedent by ravaging the heart of Laconia itself, and had barely missed taking Sparta. Pelopidas had twice invaded Thessaly. Although Athens still headed her second maritime league, it was Thebes that dominated Mainland Greece. She dominated largely through the military genius of Epaminondas and his ingenuity in developing new tactics.

Although Thebes, too, sometimes used mercenaries, her victories were won primarily by citizen-soldiers fighting as heavy infantry or as cavalry, citizen-soldiers who had spent their lives largely as the Macedonians had done, in farming, hunting, and fighting, citizen-soldiers who were neither merchants nor seamen. Boeotia, unlike Macedonia, had produced a Hesiod and even a Pindar; the men of Attica nevertheless looked down on Boeotians as not living what Pericles had described as the good life. Despite her two coasts, Boeotia kept her hand from the ship's tiller, kept her hand on the plow. By turning her back on the sea, she partially turned her back both on commerce in goods and on commerce in ideas. Her name itself suggested cow country, and precisely so Athenians viewed her. While Philip was living in Thebes, Epaminondas did make a precipitate effort to match Athens at sea, but Thebes's naval career, though not inglorious, was brief. Given the Boeotian economy, a navy was essentially artificial; and money soon failed.

A young, hellenized Macedonian prince could learn lessons here in Thebes. He could admire Athens at a distance as a city of ideas, as a city of ships, a city turned toward the sea. He could admire the aristocratic, military tradition of Sparta and her extraordinary hold on the imagination of aristocrat and oligarch throughout Greece. But he would remember that Thebes had humbled Sparta, and that it was in Thebes that men were really thinking about the occupation of princes, war. For Thebes was effecting her own revolution in warfare and it was a different revolution from that of Iphicrates. Were Macedonia to acquire this new Theban knowledge, could she not put it to even more effective use than Thebes?

In 359, Philip became regent, then king, of Macedonia. He bought off, or fought off, the various foes that threatened her. Between his return from Thebes and his assuming the post of regent, he had been assigned a semi-independent principality. There he had trained in the latest Theban fashion 10,000 infantry and 600 cavalry. They had crushingly defeated the Illyrian clans. But he had learned in Thebes that the new warfare, even with his citizen-soldiers, would require a standing army, professionally trained, able to keep the field the year round, and that this took money. His brother, Perdiccas, had deserted an alliance with Athens and had, to the fury of Athens, defended against Athenian troops Amphipolis, guardian of the gold mines of Mount Pangaeus and guardian too of the ship's timber that could be floated down the Strymon River. To pacify Athens, Philip declared Amphipolis an independent polis. He also returned without ransom the Athenians he had captured in a battle with Athens' claimant to his throne and even made a secret treaty with Athens. Under that treaty Philip himself was to conquer Amphipolis and then turn her over to Athens, while Athens was to turn over her ally, Pydna, a free Greek city on the Macedonian coast, to Philip. In 357 he marched to Amphipolis and demanded that it surrender. The Amphipolitans begged for Athenian help. But Athens, neutralized by her secret treaty with Philip, delayed. Philip brought up his rams, breached the walls of Amphipolis, and the city fell. He then declined to keep his promise in the secret treaty to yield his prey to Athens.

Athens, faced with a revolt among her allies, did nothing to recover

Amphipolis. Since she was either morally or physically unable to deliver Pydna to Philip, a few months later he marched on Pydna, secured help from traitors inside, and seized the city. Philip now converted the nearby mining town of Crenides, on Mount Pangaeus, into the city of Philippi, and began to exploit the gold. Before long, he was receiving the immense revenue of a thousand talents a year. No other state that he would have to deal with, except Persia, enjoyed a revenue anywhere near that figure. By 348-347 Philip was striking a new gold coin, the *philippeion*. Had he learned in his Greek exile why the right of coinage, the right to emit the medium which made possible the commerce in things, was prized almost as much by the polis as was the word, the medium which made possible the commerce in ideas? Or that it took coins as well as words to support a commercial community?

Whether or not he reflected on such things, Philip now held the means to do what neither Pericles of Athens nor Lysander and Agesilaus of Sparta nor Epaminondas and Pelopidas of Thebes could possibly have done. No one of these three sovereign city-states, even considered along with its subject states, could properly be called a nation. No one of them ever devised institutions capable of making Hellas a nation in the political sense. But Philip now led a kind of nation, and that nation held nearly twice the territory of its Greek neighbor Thessaly, and, on the rare occasions when Thessaly was united, it was the most extensive single political unit in Mainland Greece. Once Philip had finally integrated his wild highlanders of the western hinterland into his kingdom, Macedonia was not only extensive but populous, and Philip could muster 80,000 fighting men able to equip themselves at their own expense. In terms of Greek warfare, this was an immense force. Nor were they the subject slaves of a King of Kings, fighting unwillingly under the lash. They loved fighting. They were a nation of fighting nobles and peasants, owing allegiance to a king who, given Macedonia's troubled history, was primarily commander-in-chief. It was a nation that had passed through none of the frustrations and disillusionments, none of the intellectual skepticism and debilitating ease, of most of the Greek city-states to the south. Its new monarch knew Greek life at first hand, admired the Athens Pericles had called the School of Hellas, had every reason to be wary of the imperializing city which Pericles had called a tyrant state. Philip knew the Greeks' increasing love of money; he knew their increased respect for force and fraud; he knew both the skill and the fickleness of the Greek mercenary. His money brought to his court the Greek knowledge and Greek administrative skill he wanted, and Greek administrators and civil servants were spreading in Macedonia the Attic dialect in which Xenophon wrote, the dialect that had now become the common tongue of educated Hellenes everywhere.

Not only was Philip's army large. It combined the patriotic loyalty of Epaminondas' Thebans, the constant drill that had once made Spartan infantry supreme over her neighbors' citizen levies, the innovating tactics of the new mercenaries of Athens. But where the Athenian general of mercenaries, Iphicrates, had already lengthened the pike of the light infantryman, Philip lengthened the traditional Macedonian lance, the sarissa, to over twenty feet for the men in the rear rank. And since the length of the sarissa varied with the rank its user marched in, a formidable porcupine of spear points held off Philip's enemies while his other infantry and his cavalry deployed and maneuvered for attack. The flood of golden philips from the mines of Mount Pangaeus kept Philip's armies in the field the year round, sure of the regular wage on which Athens' expert mercenaries could never depend. Thus Philip's army was a knife that never turned and cut his hand, as Athens' mercenary armies turned and cut hers when, lacking pay, they pillaged their city's own allies.

Philip never used force unless amicable negotiation, fraud, and bribery had all failed. In diplomacy he lied as fast as the Greeks did, if not even faster; but he lied with much more method and in terms of the long view. In his handling of his army he was a ruthless disciplinarian, a generous rewarder of merit, and expert in choosing the right man for the right task. Above all, he had clear-cut policies, and his opponents had not. He had single-minded purpose, and his purpose dictated means and ends. His most persistent opponent, Athens, followed conflicting purposes, and the conflict kept her means and ends confused. Philip's purpose was to unite under his leadership Hellas and Macedonia. He would thereby bring political order to the Greeks and Hellenic culture to his half-barbarous Macedonians. His golden philips bore on one side a head of Apollo, who interpreted to men the will of his father Zeus, and on the other a two-horse chariot with its ambiguous Pindaric overtones of Achilles' eris against the Trojans and the eris of the holy races held at the Olympic Games.

By the summer of 356 Philip had taken Potidaea and had eliminated the Athenians from the Chalcidic peninsula, he had put an end to the inroads of the Illyrians and Paeonians, and he had pushed his eastern, Thracian frontier from the Strymon River to the Nestus River, to the far side of gold-laden Mount Pangaeus. In that same single summer[397] he received news that Parmenion, one of his generals, had won a final victory over the Illyrians; that his horses had won the chariot race at the Olympic Games; that his wild Epirote wife, Olympias, had borne him a son and heir, whose name would be Alexander.

Except for the city of Methone on the Thermaic Gulf, Philip had cleared his coast of colonial control by Athens and he had done it without open war. He did not want war with Athens. Athena's polis remained the symbol of Hellenic culture, and his overriding aim was to merge that culture with the semi-barbaric vitality, the military power, and the economic resources of Macedonia. In his own phrase Athens was the Theater of Glory.[398] However, he wanted Methone, and in 353 he laid siege to it. Athens, as usual, delayed too long, and Methone fell. In the battle Philip lost one eye; he also lost his troubled peace with Athens.

Philip was now ready for intervention in Greece. Happily, an ideal opportunity arose. In 356 Thebes had become involved in the affairs of Phocis and persuaded the Amphictyonic League, an organization of neighboring states formed to protect Delphi and its oracle, to fine certain rich Phocians on a charge of sacrilege. When the fines were not paid on time the Amphictyons assigned the lands of the accused to the temple of Apollo. The victims determined to resist, appointed one Philomelus general, and hired mercenaries. Philomelus then seized Delphi and used the treasures of the temple, treasures he insisted he was merely borrowing from Apollo, to raise mercenaries and defend Phocis. He insisted also that the little town of Delphi belonged to Phocis and was not a sovereign holy enclave, and he got promises of help from Athens, from Sparta, and from some other Greek states. But one forced loan from Apollo led to another, as more and more mercenaries were hired. The war, being a holy war, was fought with extraordinary ferocity. At last, in 354, whether or not because the god objected to forced loans, Philomelus was disastrously defeated and committed suicide.

His lieutenant Onomarchus took over. Onomarchus not only continued to borrow from the god in order to raise mercenaries. A dream convinced him that the gods were on his side.[399] He melted down the gifts of bronze and iron accumulated by Apollo and made armor of them. He melted down the gold and silver gifts Apollo had received since the time of Croesus of Lydia, and minted them; and some 10,000 talents sufficed to bring him the mercenaries he needed and to corrupt the leaders in other states. The sacred war to protect Apollo had brought an unexpected result: Apollo was being turned into money.

It was the culmination of a long process. The Hellenes had more than once become confused over the relation of Apollo and money. Whether or not Apollo correctly informed men of the will of Zeus, the information had to pass through several corruptible human agents. There was, first, the Pythia, the priestess, who sat on her tripod, went into a trance, and murmured or mumbled the god's message or cried it out in words that often sounded quite unintelligible. Secondly, there were the priests, who commonly put the message into hexameter verse, the ancient meter of Homer and Hesiod. More than once in Greek history the priests had been charged with accepting bribes. But even if the priests were faithful translators, their messages had a way of sounding like riddles, cynically calculated to cover all contingencies. Wooden walls might conveniently have meant either ships or the stockade around the Acropolis. A Croesus eager to attack Cyrus, or a Xenophon eager to serve another Cyrus, might jump to conclusions instead of really listening, really questioning. Obviously, if bribes could deflect the oracle, whether Apollo's part in it, or the Pythia's, or the part the priests played, there was room for cynicism. If the final oracle was ambiguous, was its ambiguity merely a cloak for ignorance, an effort to cover all contingencies? Ever since those terrible days nearly a century and a half before when Xerxes and his monstrous herd drew nearer and nearer and when Apollo had issued more than one warning not to oppose the invader, Apollo—or his temple servants—had been accused of medizing in Hellas' greatest hour of peril; and Delphi had lost face correspondingly.

In any case the gods themselves had in some sense withdrawn from among men. Xenophon, who must have remembered how they helped the heroes fight at Troy and who may have read in Herodotus of how they still appeared to men when Xerxes struck, could have found no such theophanies in Thucydides' history, the very history he himself completed; he was able to find only the religious hysteria over the mutilated Herms at Athens, the costly pride of piety that Nicias displayed before Syracuse, and the auspices and omens that the least pious general always had to respect. Xenophon himself wrote:

> If anyone is surprised at my frequent repetition of the exhortation to work with God, I can assure him that his surprise will diminish, if he is often in peril, and if he considers that in time of war foemen plot and counterplot, but seldom know what will come of their plots. Therefore there is none other that can give counsel in such a case but the gods.[400]

And he had, of course, earned the rebuke of Socrates by conscripting Apollo at Delphi when he was bent on serving Cyrus in Asia. But if it was not to learn the will of Zeus that one now went to Delphi, if one no longer listened in quietude of spirit, if Delphi was something to be used, along with the god who dwelt there, a case could be made for melting down the god and minting him into coin, the medium through which all things could be obtained, including victory in war.

The relation of Phocis to the panhellenic shrine within her territory was also a debatable point; and if the Phocians were now correct in asserting that Delphi, with its profitable pilgrim trade, had always belonged to them, was Onomarchus in principle doing more than the Athenians had done during the Peloponnesian War when they borrowed the holy statues and other gifts from the Parthenon to save Athena's city? The Phocians had firmly declared they would return the equivalent of Apollo's treasures as soon as they had fought off the invasion of the busybody Amphictyonic League. Still, the ransacking of Delphi had reached the proportions of an orgy of plunder. A god was indeed being melted down and minted, a god not merely of the Phocians but of Hellenes everywhere.

Philip saw his chance. When the Thessalian League joined the Boeotians against the sacrilegious Phocians, Onomarchus allied himself with the rulers of Pherae in Thessaly, enemies of the League, and the League appealed to Philip. Philip marched south into Thessaly. But Onomarchus, on whom Apollo's gold had temporarily conferred the military supremacy of central Greece, marched into Thessaly too and defeated Philip twice, so severely that Philip withdrew into Macedonia. The following year Philip returned and, in a battle fought near the Thessalian port of Pagasae, he killed or captured a third of the Phocian army. Among the slain lay Onomarchus, who had minted a god. Onomarchus had been a formidable soldier and a skillful statesman. But Philip was now busy defending Apollo against sacrilege: he ordered his prisoners thrown into the sea and he crucified the corpse of Onomarchus. That was in 352. Then he organized the quarreling cities of Thessaly in a league under his own control and thereby imposed a peace which Thessaly had badly needed for half a century. Her cities would govern themselves, on condition that their armies would stand ready to serve Philip. He especially needed Thessalian cavalry, which had always been the best in Greece.

Strengthened by his new resources, Philip dedicated a statue to Apollo, collected the combined forces of Macedonia and Thessaly, and started for the Pass of Thermopylae to continue the war on Phocis. But the allies of Phocis got to the famous Hot Gates first. Even Athens acted promptly this time; she sent a fleet, 5,000 heavy infantry, and 400 horse. Sparta sent 1,000 men; Achaea, 2,000. The Thessalians of Pherae, whom Philip had defeated, also arrived with 2,000 mercenaries. Even assuming that Philip had found the means of outflanking Thermopylae and attacking its defenders from both ends, as Xerxes had, it would have been a politically stupid move. The image which Philip was busily and carefully presenting to Greece was that of the ruler of the largest state in Greece leading a panhellenic holy war against the violators of Greece's holiest shrine. The image he was determined not to present was that of a barbarian king leading, like Xerxes, an assault on Hellas. Philip did not want to conquer Greece, least of all Athens. He wanted to rally Greece to his leadership. If he marched on Phocis, he must somehow march in Greece's name. His path could lead through Thermopylae; or, if need be, through bloodshed; but not through both at once.

Meanwhile, the sacrilegious but determined Phocians fought on against the Thebans, under a brother of Onomarchus, until that brother fell ill and died, then under their crucified leader's son. Even when Thebes secured a subsidy from Persia in return for a promise of mercenaries, the minted god kept Phocian mercenary guerillas in the field. At last, in 347-346, the temple treasure was exhausted, the mercenaries were grumbling, and the war petered out. Meanwhile Philip had defeated Cersobleptes, king of Thrace, and forced him into an alliance. The Athenian Assembly hurriedly voted an armament to prevent Philip from cutting off her grain route from the Black Sea. But then word came that Philip was dead, and Athens postponed her expedition.

Though Philip was not dead, he was at least temporarily ill. He was now violently attacked in an oration delivered before the Assembly of a Greek polis. Worse still, the polis was Athens. The orator's name was Demosthenes. He was young: he was the same age as Philip. His father had been a well-to-do Athenian businessman, who produced among other things swords for the army. But the father died when Demosthenes was but seven, and the boy's guardians betrayed their trust. Demosthenes determined to sue his guardians in court when he came of age and he prepared himself by studying under the orator Isaeus. He was too delicate to follow the usual course of gymnastics. He haunted the courts and the Assembly and practiced rewriting the speeches he heard there. He studied Thucydides' history and relived the glories of his polis in the great days of Pericles. When he came to speak publicly, he noticed his defects. So he practiced declaiming with pebbles in his mouth, and he practiced gesticulation before a mirror. He pleaded his case against his guardians and won back at least a part of his inheritance. He became a professional speech-writer and made considerable money at the profession. He served repeatedly as trierarch, or officer charged with fitting out a trireme for the state; and, armed with his gift for speaking, he entered politics.

Most men of Demosthenes' economic class followed the conservative statesman Eubulus, who stood for sound fiscal policy and peace at almost any price. Mercenary warfare fell heavily on the rich. It even threatened the pleasures of the poor, for it soon became evident that the polis could not continue its custom of free tickets to the great religious dramatic festivals if its resources must go to war. Demosthenes set himself against this peace policy on the grounds that Philip clearly proposed to conquer Greece. His oratory won him enormous acclaim but not the prompt action he pleaded for. By 351 he was excoriating the Assembly for its apathy, in his first great philippic:

> Or tell me, are you content to run round and ask one another, "Is there any news today?" Could there be any news more startling than that a Macedonian is triumphing over Athenians and settling the destiny of Hellas? "Is Philip dead?" you ask. "No, indeed; but he is ill." And what is that to you? Even if something happens to him, you will soon raise up a second Philip, if that is the way you attend to your affairs; for even this Philip has not grown great through his own unaided strength so much as through our carelessness.[401]

337

Demosthenes' forensic war on Philip continued tirelessly. His orations were enormously admired. But, even when he could arouse the Athenians to action, the action was usually too little and too late to stop Philip. Undoubtedly, Demosthenes fought under a great handicap. As he himself later complained to the Athenian Assembly, Philip's advantages were many:

> In the first place, he was the despotic commander of his adherents: and in war that is the most important of all advantages. Secondly, they had their weapons constantly in their hands. Then he was well provided with money: he did whatever he chose, without giving notice by publishing decrees, or deliberating in public, without fear of prosecution by informers or indictment for illegal measures. He was responsible to nobody: he was the absolute autocrat, commander, and master of everybody and everything. And I, his chosen adversary—it is a fair inquiry—of what was I master? Of nothing at all! Public speaking was my only privilege: and that you permitted to Philip's hired servants on the same terms as to me. Whenever they had the advantage of me—and for one reason or another that often happened—you laid your plans for the enemy's benefit, and went your ways.[402]

Philip did indeed have more money, an army he could keep in the field the year round, the secrecy of dictatorship, and a dictator's power to command. And Demosthenes was justified, when he cried to the Athenian Assembly in his first philippic:

> in your present condition you would be unable, even if the opportunity offered, to take over Amphipolis, having neither a force nor a policy ready to hand.[403]

But, while Demosthenes himself gave good advice about mobilizing the force, his own policy was to stop Philip, as Athenians of another generation had stopped Xerxes at Marathon, at Salamis, at Plataea, at Mycale. Those other Athenians, however, had been poorer, tougher men than these; they had been full of boundless hope and spiritual vigor. They had not known the glories and miseries of imperial power, nor the treasons and brutalities of the Peloponnesian War, nor the disillusionments of an empire's collapse. They had not seen the rise of their own polis to power, nor its corruption by that power, nor its failure to bring peace and justice to a Hellas still dispersed in its many small, sovereign city-states. The Athenians who had stopped Xerxes had not seen Sparta take her turn and fail, or Thebes take hers. They had not witnessed Athens' effort to reconstitute her old Aegean empire, nor the second disintegration of that empire. Granted that the Athenians of Philip's time no longer wanted to serve in battle, their unwillingness was not all cowardice: war had become professionalized and Greece was awash with expert fighters looking for employment. Granted they loved the pleasant life of Athens and its civilized ease; that they liked listening to the brilliant rhetorical fireworks of Demosthenes and the other professional orators better than the hard work of real political life. To do that hard work intelligently, they needed a cogent purpose; yet they, like Demosthenes, lacked a real policy. Was not the problem that called aloud for a policy the political organization of Greece? Yet Demosthenes never dealt with that problem.[404]

Demosthenes' orations, therefore, though they exhibited great skill and intricate workmanship, fell short of their target. Moreover, in their personal vituperation of Philip and of those Athenian orators who opposed Demosthenes, they often sank to the level of bitter impotence. On his own assumptions, indeed, Demosthenes proved a better prophet than his opponents did: when Philip deceived them as to his determination to gain control of Mainland Greece, he did not deceive Demosthenes. Demosthenes therefore tasted some of the agony that Cassandra tasted in Aeschylus's *Agamemnon*: it was Apollo's cruel gift to her that she should see future events but should always fail to persuade others that she saw them. Demosthenes had something of the same cruel gift, which lent him at least the appearance of lonely grandeur. But was not the future he saw partly the product of his own incapacity to find a solution to the real problem?

Lacking the procreative idea, Demosthenes redoubled his rhetorical flourishes; and thereby managed unwittingly to justify the cutting remarks on rhetoric which Socrates had once made[405] to the famous sophist, Gorgias. Rhetoric inflated Demosthenes, as it had the sophist Protagoras, whom Socrates was dragged at dawn to admire. How much inflated it left Demosthenes, he himself discovered afresh whenever Phocion, the statesman and general, the pupil of Socrates' disciple Plato, would rise and make one of his simple, laconic statements. Then it was as if Lycurgan Sparta herself were rebuking the garrulity, the flattery, the florid excitement of this Athenian, with his carefully elaborated, studiedly emotional, thoroughly memorized calls to greatness, each gesture in its proper place. Demosthenes dreaded Phocion. According to later tradition, when Phocion would approach the rostrum, the great orator would remark to his friends: "Here comes the pruning-knife of my speeches."[406]

It was Isocrates of Athens who nearly saw the problem. He was eighty-five years old when Demosthenes delivered his first philippic before the Athenian Assembly. He was born in the great age of Pericles in 436, five years before the long Peloponnesian War broke out. He was the son of a prosperous manufacturer of flutes. He knew Gorgias the sophist, and Socrates too. But where Plato was attracted by Socrates' questioning mind, Isocrates saw chiefly the side of him that Xenophon saw, the moral side. Like Demosthenes, Isocrates was drawn toward oratory and the political life. But a weak voice and a certain lack of assurance diverted his ambition, and he therefore wrote speeches for others. More importantly, he started a school, which became the only institutional rival of the Academy set up a few years later by Plato. There he taught the art of discourse. He conceived of this art as not merely the composition of speeches, but the liberal education that alone enabled the orator, not merely to say things well, but to know what should be said. Indeed, he thought of himself as a philosopher. Although Socrates had prophesied, when Isocrates was young, that he would go beyond all other speech-writers because he already showed some impulse toward philosophy, yet Isocrates had turned from the intellectual rigors of philosophic thought to the realm of the practical. His school attracted students from all over Hellas, from the Black Sea to Sicily. He was a true Athenian in his love of the word. Writing autobiographically when he was an old man of eighty-two, he praised the art of discourse:

> We ought, therefore, to think of the art of discourse just as we think of the other arts, and not to form opposite judgements about similar things, nor show ourselves intolerant toward that power which, of all the faculties which belong to the nature of man, is the source of most of our blessings. For in the other powers which we possess, as I have already said on a former occasion, we are in no respect superior to other living creatures; nay, we are inferior to many in swiftness and in strength and in other resources; but, because there has been implanted in us the power to persuade each other and to make clear to each other whatever

we desire, not only have we escaped the life of wild beasts, but we have come together and founded cities and made laws and invented arts; and, generally speaking, there is no institution devised by man which the power of speech has not helped us to establish. For this it is which has laid down laws concerning things just and unjust, and things honourable and base; and if it were not for these ordinances we should not be able to live with one another. It is by this also that we confute the bad and extol the good. Through this we educate the ignorant and appraise the wise; for the power to speak well is taken as the surest index of a sound understanding, and discourse which is true and lawful and just is the outward image of a good and faithful soul. With this faculty we both contend against others on matters which are open to dispute and seek light for ourselves on things which are unknown; for the same arguments which we use in persuading others when we speak in public, we employ also when we deliberate in our own thoughts; and, while we call eloquent those who are able to speak before a crowd, we regard as sage those who most skilfully debate their problems in their own minds. And, if there is need to speak in brief summary of this power, we shall find that none of the things which are done with intelligence take place without the help of speech, but that in all our actions as well as in all our thoughts speech is our guide, and is most employed by those who have the most wisdom.[407]

The theory that speech was most employed by those who had the most wisdom would have seemed unlikely to Phocion, the laconic meat-cleaver of Demosthenes' forensic displays. Indeed, it would have seemed unlikely to Socrates.

Although Isocrates deserted early in life his profession of paid speech-writer, he became Athens' leading publicist, her leading commentator on political affairs. Even so, his writings were almost invariably cast in the form of speeches. Somewhat as Thucydides, writing in the great age of Greek tragedy, cast his history in the form of tragedy, so Isocrates, writing at a time when the oration was the leading literary form of Greece, cast his own comments in the form of speeches, although these speeches were never delivered from a platform. He believed that Athens had many rivals in contests of the body but that "in the training of the mind everyone would concede that we stand first."[408] He urged that Athenians "get our youth to look down upon a life of ease and be willing to give their minds to their own improvement and to philosophy."[409]

Miltiades won at Marathon, he reminded his readers, Themistocles led Athens to power, Pericles made both the Acropolis and the homes of Athenian citizens overflow with wealth, not only because they were well-born and well spoken of, but because they knew how "to think and speak."[410] Isocrates devoted his life to Greek culture, the kind of culture befitting a gentleman; to a broad, general education. But the role of philosophy in this training would be not architectonic, as in the life of Socrates, but in a sense ornamental, an amenity rather than a stern guide. Isocrates was no barefoot inquirer; he was a successful, well-to-do, somewhat vain, and kindly man. Like Xenophon, he wanted to be useful.

Like Xenophon, also, he wrote in the Attic dialect and helped make that dialect familiar in all corners of the Hellenic world as the Greek spoken by educated men. Where the Attic of Xenophon's *Anabasis* was used in simple, soldierly sentences to convey vividly events a soldierly man had witnessed, Isocrates elaborated a complex periodic sentence, full of subtle and graceful rhythms, and consciously aimed at giving to the ear some of the pleasure that poetry had once given. Attic shared the strength, without the harshness, of Doric; it shared the grace, without the softness, of Ionic. In the matter of coin, Macedonian philips might be competing hard with Athenian owls as the medium men now used to exchange commodities, or the medium they now misused in order to accumulate power without limit or to satisfy appetites that never ceased growing. But even Macedonians were learning the Attic words that men used when they exchanged ideas, as, alone among animals, men could do; or that men misused in order to substitute for common deliberation the virtuoso performance of the spellbinder. And now that poetry had yielded first place to prose, prose came to the rescue and served to stir emotions. Orators like Demosthenes and Isocrates became the literary models of Hellas.

In addition to presiding over his school, in which men could be taught to think and speak without the Socratic rigors of Plato's Academy, Isocrates for decades preached Hellenic unity through a joint attack on Persia. In 380, seven years before Athens had formed her second confederacy, shortly after the Great King's announcement of 386 in effect forbade the Greek states to unite, and in the very years when a Spartan garrison was occupying Thebes, Isocrates wrote a *Panegyric* to Athens:

And so far has our city distanced the rest of mankind in thought and in speech that her pupils have become the teachers of the rest of the world; and she has brought it about that the name "Hellenes" suggests no longer a race but an intelligence, and that the title "Hellenes" is applied rather to those who share our culture than to those who share a common blood.[411]

Isocrates urged Athens, guardian and transmitter of this culture, to lead Hellas on a sacred mission, the conquest of Persia. In 368 he urged Dionysius I, tyrant of Syracuse, to do it; in 356, he urged it on Archidamus, son of Xenophon's leader, King Agesilaus. Agesilaus had in some sense done it. In 342, he wrote a letter urging it on Philip. But four years before the letter to Philip, when Isocrates was ninety, he had written a much longer *Address to Philip*. For a third of a century he had been looking for a lever to raise Hellas from the anarchy and misery and bloodshed in which it had floundered. The aged Athenian publicist, who had based a long and famous career on his faith in words and their power to persuade, pointed out to the still young king that beyond any of the Hellenes he, the king, was

possessed of both wealth and power, which are the only things in the world that are adapted at once to persuade and to compel; and these aids, I think, even the cause which I shall propose to you will need to have on its side. For I am going to advise you to champion the cause of concord among the Hellenes and of a campaign against the barbarian; and as persuasion will be helpful in dealing with the Hellenes, so compulsion will be useful in dealing with the barbarians. This, then, is the general scope of my discourse.[412]

Isocrates insisted that the mutual hatreds that separated so many Greek cities were counterbalanced by their willingness to ally themselves with former enemies in the name of expediency and by their common need of protection against one another. He retraced the confused, discouraging course of recent Hellenic history. He showed what certain leaders had accomplished against worse odds than would face Philip if, first, he composed the quarrels of the Greek cities, and, second, led them all against Persia. Look at what Xenophon and his fellow mercenaries had done against the Great King when they fought him at Cunaxa under Cyrus. There was now rebellion in the Persian Empire. Philip should emulate his ancestor, Heracles, who helped the Hellenes. What fame would be Philip's if he conquered the Persian Empire or, at any rate, its western provinces and undertook

> to establish cities in this region, and to settle in permanent abodes those who now, for lack of the daily necessities of life, are wandering from place to place and committing outrages upon whomsoever they encounter?[413]

If Philip would plant such military colonies on the eastern frontier of the Hellenic world in Asia, he would give an economic function to the mercenaries, the refugees, the uprooted, and he would at the same time restore order in Hellas. At a minimum he could free Greece-in-Asia from Persian control. There were other descendants of Heracles, but each clung to his own polis, while Philip was above cities and could, like Heracles, consider all Hellas his fatherland. And then the old man summarized his thesis, prompted by "the divine will"[414]:

> I assert that it is incumbent upon you to work for the good of the Hellenes, to reign as king over the Macedonians, and to extend your power over the greatest possible number of the barbarians. For if you do these things, all men will be grateful to you: the Hellenes for your kindness to them; the Macedonians if you reign over them, not like a tyrant, but like a king; and the rest of the nations, if by your hands they are delivered from barbaric despotism and are brought under the protection of Hellas.[415]

At his most thoughtful, Isocrates was urging that Philip restore order in Hellas and then maintain it by an economic and colonial expansion at Persia's expense. At his worst, was he trying to drain off the violence which now led Greek to murder Greek and to let it vent itself in the murder of the Great King's non-Hellenic subjects? Aeschylus had suggested in his *Oresteia* that, once violence was let loose, it required more than the counter-violence to purge it out of the human community. It required law. But Isocrates did not prescribe law. Unlike Demosthenes, he knew that the problem was not to stop Philip and restore the greatness of Athens under Pericles. He knew that the problem was anarchy in Hellas as a whole, the violence of polis against polis. Not having found a solution to the problem of violence, he ceaselessly advocated exporting it. But he was also exploiting a deep urge in Hellas.

The urge to emigrate, to colonize, sometimes man by man, more often in bands, not only caused the citizens of Phocaea to swear a mighty oath to move their polis to Corsica, but permitted the men of the Athenian navy at Samos to fancy that they, and not the oligarchs at home, were the real polis. It was the same urge that had prompted Xenophon to gaze hungrily at Calpe's Haven on the Black Sea; that had led Aristophanes to imagine Cloudcuckooland, a comic paradise, a polis founded in between the world of the gods and the world of men. Even Socrates had imagined a heavenly polis in the clear world of ideas that every earthly polis could at best but imitate. Practically, poetically, philosophically, Hellas showed signs of flight from the polis which men had known to a polis poignantly sensed if dimly seen, a home that might be Ithaca or might be another shore Odysseus had not yet beheld.

While Demosthenes thundered out his denunciations of the barbarian, Philip, who was determined to put an end to Hellenic freedom, or more accurately to end the right of Greek cities to make war on each other and to subject each other—Philip continued methodically with his own plan to wed Macedonian strength and discipline to what was left of the Hellenic culture Isocrates admired and taught. He used and misused words quite as skillfully as Demosthenes. For Demosthenes' carefully written, brilliantly delivered orations, he substituted his diplomatic fencing, his personal charm, his golden philips. He played on the fears and hates that set Greek polis against Greek polis. He allowed his opponents to intercept messages which he had planted for the purpose. He spread rumors. He treated Athens as he might have treated one of his numerous mistresses: he courted her, he made her gifts, he slapped her when he felt he had to, he admired her and was fascinated by her. And Athens? Through Demosthenes' bitter, eloquent mouth she denounced and insulted him, she sent envoys and made up with him, she stirred up his neighbors against him. She still commanded the Aegean Sea and made what trouble she could for him with her fleet. But when by 348 Philip had reduced the Greek cities of Chalcidice, he controlled the coast from the border of Thessaly to the Chersonese.

In July, 346, Philip appeared again with an army at the Pass of Thermopylae. Opposing him was Phalaecus, son of Onomarchus, the Onomarchus who had minted the god Apollo to defend his country, Phocis. But internal squabbles in Phocis had driven out Phalaecus, and he and his mercenaries now held Thermopylae. Philip tried negotiation. Phalaecus asked for time, and sent to Athens for help. His mercenaries' pay was in arrears and they were growing restive. The Athenian Assembly was passing resolutions against Philip but would clearly not send adequate support. Thereupon Phalaecus sold the Pass to Philip. Philip marched south to help Thebes destroy the sacrilegious Phocians and to avenge Apollo. Phocis was devastated and the Delphians they had driven out ten years before were restored to their polis and its sacred temple. Through his oracle, Apollo thanked Philip, and the Amphictyons elected him to replace Phocis on their Council. By autumn he sat in the president's chair at the Pythian games.

Within four years, the cities of Thessaly had elected Philip archon of their League for life. He improved his navy and negotiated alliances in the Peloponnese with Messenia, Megalopolis, Elis, Argos. The polis he wanted most to conciliate was Athens, but at Athens Demosthenes was loudly charging that Philip was planning to destroy the city. Both Demosthenes and the orator Aeschines, bitter forensic foes, had served on Athenian embassies that had recently made peace with Philip, and both now engaged in mutual recriminations concerning the roles they had played while on mission. Demosthenes traveled through the Peloponnese trying to inflame people there against Philip. Meanwhile Philip marched into Epirus, where his Epirote wife's royal father had died, and secured the succession for his wife's brother. Then he conquered Thrace; dethroned Cersobleptes; made his kingdom a province of Macedonia; landed troops on the Chersonese; and attacked Byzantium. Athens' grain route was thereby endangered, and she sent a naval force that was able to save Byzantium. Demosthenes had by now so aroused Athenian fears that he was able to secure a law distributing more equitably the burden of fitting out triremes, and another law that diverted to military purposes the money previously reserved to buy admission for the poor to the great religious festivals. Having failed at Byzantium to secure the grain route and, with it, control of the food supply of Athens and other Greek cities, Philip struck northward and shattered an army of Scythians. But on the way home, he was attacked by wild tribesmen and was himself wounded in the thigh. The wound threatened to gangrene. He returned to his capital at Pella for the winter of 339-338.

In March a message arrived from the Amphictyonic League. Another political scuffle, involving the charge of another act of sacrilege, had broken out. The Amphictyons were in vain appealing to Athens and Thebes to punish the Locrian city of Amphissa. Now they appealed to Philip. Once more the defender of Apollo marched south to do his religious duty toward all Hellas. He went as far as Elatea in Phocis and then proposed to Thebes that she join him in pillaging Attica, or failing that, give him free passage through Boeotia. Athens sent envoys, including Demosthenes, who persuaded Thebes to desert her alliance with Philip and combine with Athens against him. Philip marched into Boeotia.

Near Chaeronea, around August of 338, he faced his Greek opponents: Thebans, with their Sacred Band in front, Athenians, mercenaries from Corinth, Achaeans, and contingents from a group of small cities. Philip himself faced the Athenians. His son, Alexander, now eighteen, faced the Thebans. The opposing armies were about equal in number: some 30,000 infantry and about 2,000 horse.[416] But Philip's troops were better trained, better armed, and much better commanded. Demosthenes finally had his hour: a Greek army was defending Greece against northern barbarians not many miles from Plataea, where a Greek army had defeated the Persian barbarians, and he, Demosthenes, stood in the ranks of the Athenians. On the Greek left the Athenians fought well, even though Philip badly outgeneraled them. But the Greek center gave way and suffered heavy losses. For a moment the right wing of the Athenians appeared to be gaining, and one of their generals, Stratocles, started yelling that they would push on to Macedonia. But the Athenian advance opened a gap in the Greek line. Into it Alexander and his cavalry promptly charged. Macedonian infantry followed the cavalry. And while the infantry by a flank attack rolled up the Greek line, Alexander's cavalry encircled the Thebans' Sacred Band. Philip threw the Athenians into a rout; some 1,000 were killed, some 2,000 were captured. The rest fled, Demosthenes among them. The Sacred Band, which had made the army of Thebes so formidable in the days of Epaminondas and Pelopidas, kept their tradition, to conquer or to die. They died to a man.

Chaeronea gave Greece to Philip, and he knew it. According to later tradition, he invited his officers to a feast, the sort his Macedonians loved, with plenty of women, plenty of music, plenty of wine. The usual heralds who came to seek permission to collect the Greek dead for burial were kept waiting. Athens had offered an alliance to Thebes on a motion by Demosthenes, and when the Macedonians had feasted,

> Philip waxed insolent for joy, and going forth in revel rout to see the bodies of the slain, and being in his cups, recited the beginning of the decree introduced by Demosthenes, dividing it into feet and marking off the time:—
>
> "Demosthenes, son of Demosthenes, of Paeania, thus moves."[417]

Among the Athenian prisoners stood Demades, an orator famed for his incisive speech. Now he spoke to Philip: "King, when Fate has cast thee for Agamemnon, art not ashamed to play Thersites?" The allusion to Homer, fount of the Hellenic culture which Philip had set out to win for his half-barbarian Macedonians, brought him to his senses. He tore the festive garlands from him; the wine cups and flutes were flung down and trodden underfoot; he ordered Demades to be set free, and went away ashamed.

The victor treated Thebes harshly. He garrisoned her citadel, the Cadmea, with Macedonian troops, and turned Thebes over to the tender mercies of some 300 men she had exiled for supporting Philip. It was from Thebes that, as a boy, he had learned the art of war. Now he repaid her in the coin war commonly used. For Philip had learned Homer, too: "Ares is just and slays him who slays."[418] But Athens must be an exception. He was determined not to appear her victor any more than she had forced him to play that role already. He gave back her prisoners; and, unlike Thebes, the city he still courted was not asked for ransom. Athens had strengthened her walls with tree trunks and even with gravestones, but her conqueror led no soldier across her frontier. When she sent envoys, he gave them an offer of alliance to take home, and sent Demades, his rebuker, with them. He also sent his regent, Antipater, and his son, Alexander, whose troops had broken the Thebans at Chaeronea. Even Demosthenes refrained from urging a last, desperate stand behind the walls: there were no besiegers to fight with. Freedom was lost, but at least he was chosen to pronounce an oration over those who fell at Chaeronea. As for Isocrates, he was now ninety-eight; and he wrote one last letter to Philip, in which he pointed out that

> on account of the battle which has taken place, all are compelled to be prudent and to desire that which they surmise you wish to do and to

say, namely, that they must desist from the madness and the spirit of aggrandizement, which they were wont to display in their relations with each other, and must carry the war into Asia. . . . No achievement could be more glorious, more useful to the Greeks, or more timely than this will be.[419]

Of the city-states of Mainland Greece, Sparta alone refused to submit. Philip ravaged Laconia, but the unwalled polis still would not recognize him as leader of the Greeks. He demanded the honor of Laconian citizenship for himself, and Sparta replied in her old grand manner, as Achilles might have done, that at least Philip could not prevent the Spartans from dying for their country. At last he diminished her territory and left her to sulk: to overwhelm her militarily would have blurred the image he wanted to present to Hellas.

Before the year of Chaeronea was spent, Philip convoked a congress of the Greek states to meet at Corinth. Early in 337, the delegates assembled. They represented all of Mainland Greece except Sparta, and even some of the islands and some of the Greek states in Thrace. Philip submitted a plan for a general peace between all the Greek states represented. They were to form a panhellenic league, and the league was to sign an offensive and defensive alliance with Macedon. All existing frontiers were confirmed. The league was charged with arbitrating all future disputes between member states. No member state could change its constitution by force, and no state was to permit the banished citizens of another state to organize on its soil a military expedition against their home government. In theory, therefore, both war and revolution, those twin evils of Hellas, each a contributing cause of the other, were quite simply abolished. Every state was to enjoy full local autonomy and full freedom of the seas. No city need accept a foreign garrison, except those cities already garrisoned by Macedonians to insure the common defense: Thebes, Chalcis, Corinth, and Ambracia. No city would be required to contribute money to the league, but all would be required to contribute military or naval contingents when needed. The king of Macedonia was to be ex officio Hegemon, or leader, of the Hellenes, and in theory would exercise the executive functions of the panhellenic league. In addition to its leader, the league would possess a council, called the Synhedrion of the Hellenes. This league council would be composed of delegates plenipotentiary, and each member state would be allowed delegates in proportion to its military contributions. If any member state should break the peace, the league was to call on the executive—the king of Macedon—to mobilize the military contingents of the remaining members and to discipline the recalcitrant.

If the cities which established this council could have viewed it as the common representative assembly of all the citizens of all the member cities; if all the citizens of each state had elected their delegates to this panhellenic congress; and if the congress' new League of Corinth had been empowered to impose taxes; then might not a common government have made a genuine step toward freedom under law? In such a case, the idea of polis, which had already been twice extended, might have been extended once more, and a genuine, free, federal government might have emerged. But the weakness of the League of Corinth, together with its tight alliance with the king of Macedon, placed all real power in his hands. The dialectic between the freedom of Periclean democracy and the Spartan championship of sovereign independence for every polis had first been transformed into the eristic of the Peloponnesian War and of the increasingly senseless wars that followed, and the eristic had now ended in a peace imposed by a veiled despotism.

At Corinth Philip also announced his intention of invading the Persian Empire; and the member states of the new League of Corinth promised contingents for a crusade in which the Greeks no longer felt any real desire to take part. Their participation was clearly intended only as a token, but Philip still might hope that the joint enterprise would serve to weld together the force of Macedonia and the renowned culture of the Greeks. By the spring of 336 he had sent a fraction of his army to hold the Hellespont, in order that he might cross it into Asia, as Xerxes had crossed it a century and a half before, coming from that same Asia into Europe against the little city-states of Hellas. Philip of course consulted the Delphic oracle, not on whether to attack Persia, but on whether he would be victorious when he attacked. And Apollo answered: "The bull is crowned; the consummation is at hand; the sacrificer is ready."[420] Philip construed this oracle to mean that the crowned King of Kings was the bull and he, Philip, the man who would sacrifice him, the way one would sacrifice a real bull garlanded for slaughter at the altar.

He delayed leading the main force across to Asia. He had repudiated his Epirote wife Olympias, the mother of Alexander, on the charge of adultery. He himself, since their marriage, had acquired a number of wives, often for dynastic reasons. He now married Cleopatra, daughter of one of his generals, Attalus. He faced a long absence from his kingdom. Olympias had left in rage for the court of her brother, Alexander, king of Epirus. Would she stir up this brother against Philip while Philip was absent in Asia? To neutralize Olympias, Philip offered her brother the hand of his own and Olympias's daughter, who bore the same name as her new stepmother, Cleopatra. The offer was accepted. Olympias and Alexander returned to Macedonia for the wedding.

With the Delphic Apollo safely conscripted to his banner, Philip offered costly and magnificent sacrifices and solemnized the marriage of his daughter at Aegae, the capital of Macedonia before Archelaus had moved his court to Pella, and still the religious center of the royal family. Guests were invited from all over Greece. Many Greek cities sent golden crowns; and one crown came from Athens. She was grateful, or desired to appear grateful, for Philip's treatment of her in defeat and helplessness. Philip did his best to make the occasion one of reconciliation between Hellene and half-Hellene, between Greek and Macedonian. Neoptolemus, a famous tragedian, wrote verses on the coming expedition into Asia and gave a command recitation. There were music, dancing, feasting, athletic games, dramatic performances. Then, at a ceremony in the public theater, packed with guests, a pompous procession entered. Its members filed in, bearing twelve images of the Twelve Great Gods of Hellas, and "the image of Philip, clothed like the gods in every respect, made the thirteenth, hereby arrogating to himself a place, as if he would be enthroned among the gods."[421] Philip and his friends arrived. Philip commanded his friends to go before him into the theater and his guards to stand back. Then he prepared to enter alone, clothed in white, the admired conqueror, ruler of Macedonia and Hellas, the self-appointed sacrificer of the Bull of Persia. At that moment a youth, a favorite of Philip's, leapt forward, drew a dagger from beneath his cloak, and plunged it into the king's side. The Bull of Macedonia fell dead at his slaughterer's feet, and Apollo's oracle was fulfilled.

FROM THE VOYAGE OF
PLATO TO THE EMPIRE
OF ARISTOTLE

WHEN SOCRATES, in his prison cell, drank the cup of hemlock which his polis offered him, his followers were alarmed. It was the restored democracy of Thrasybulus that had condemned him and it was easy to picture him as anti-democratic. He had declared he could not teach because he had no knowledge; but he remained for many the Socrates of his friend Aristophanes' comedy, the *Clouds*, corrupting the young Phidippides for profit, a typical sophist among his disciples, aloft in his basket above his Thoughtery. And who were his disciples? The handsome, brilliant, insolent young aristocrat, Alcibiades, who had profaned the holy mysteries and defaced the Herms. Had not Socrates gone to his death on a charge of not believing in the gods of his own polis, he who in the *Clouds* had declared that Zeus was no longer king, but Whirlwind was king? Then his disciple Alcibiades, summoned home from Sicily, had fled to Sparta, that mainstay of oligarchs throughout all Hellas. Had this barefoot sophist not taught Critias too? Critias had been the bloodiest of the thirty tyrants who, with a Spartan garrison back of them, had established the oligarchic terror at Athens after her empire was lost and hunger brought her to her knees. Among Socrates' disciples also had been the young Charmides, Critias's nephew, who had fallen with his uncle in the battle of Munychia. It was over their dead bodies that the democrats who held the Piraeus had won the right to re-enter Athens and re-establish law, freedom, and democracy.

So it was that when Socrates died his friends were in fear, and a small group of them withdrew to neighboring Megara. There they were protected by Euclides, who had been with Socrates when he drained his last cup. Among those whom Euclides sheltered was Socrates' young friend Plato.

Plato was about thirty when he went to Megara. He had been born in 428-427, a year or so after Pericles died. His father, Ariston, was an Athenian noble whose family claimed descent from the ancient kings of Athens, and through them from Posidon, god of the sea and brother of Zeus himself. Plato's mother, Perictione, was a sister of Charmides, niece of Critias, and a collateral descendant of Solon, who gave law to Athens.

When the long Peloponnesian War finally ended, and when the Thirty, under Critias, seized power, they invited Plato to join them. He was twenty-three. He had been reared in a home where public service was taken for granted. He was a member of the Athenian landed aristocracy which now proposed to take back some of the power the rising commercial democracy had steadily acquired. Plato's stepfather, indeed, had been an active follower of Pericles. But after Pericles' death the democracy had gone from folly to folly and had led Athens to exhaustion and ruinous defeat. The young Plato enthusiastically backed the reforming oligarchs. But when he witnessed the executions and confiscations and when he saw the Thirty trying to force his "aged friend Socrates"[422] to share their guilt by fetching the innocent Leon of Salamis to his death, Plato was indignant and withdrew. When the Thirty fell, he once more wanted to enter public life. He was impressed by the moderation of the restored democracy; but when that democracy sentenced Socrates to death, he despaired of both political parties. He was convinced that the written laws as well as the customs of his own polis had become profoundly corrupted. There was nothing reassuring about the oligarchies which victorious Sparta had installed in the subject cities she seized from Athens; nor indeed about the Spartiates themselves, since Lysander's booty had vindicated the Delphic oracle that "love of money and nothing else will ruin Sparta."[423] Everywhere still, polis struggled against polis; within each polis the city of the rich and the city of the poor fought for the upper hand; and the struggle between classes stimulated and complicated the struggle between sovereign city-states. Plato was not the only Hellene to be horrified by the political chaos of Hellas or by the moral and intellectual chaos it reflected. Was the chaos curable? Plato concluded that there would be

> no cessation from evils until either the class of those who are right and true philosophers attains political supremacy, or else the class of those who hold power in the States becomes, by some dispensation of Heaven, really philosophic.[424]

The witnesses to the moral and intellectual chaos which Plato discerned behind the incessant wars and revolutions of the fourth century were numerous: skeptics, relativists, materialists, distrusters of civilization, romantics who sought in nature escape from what was artificial and conventional. The atomist, Democritus of Abdera, had written, "We know nothing in reality; for truth lies in an abyss."[425] As to the polis, that small, intense communion of gods and men, "to a wise man, the whole earth is open; for the native land of a good soul is the whole earth."[426] As for justice, Thrasymachus of Chalcedon, the famous sophist who argued so angrily with Socrates that evening at the Piraeus, was not the first to insist that justice was the interest of the stronger, that might made right. "Rule," said Democritus, "belongs by nature to the stronger."[427] To Protagoras's insistence that man was the measure of all things, Metrodorus of Chios added, "Everything exists which anyone perceives."[428] As for Socrates' brave faith that knowledge differed from mere opinion, this same Metrodorus held that "None of us knows anything, not even whether we know or do not know, nor do we know whether not knowing and knowing exist, nor in general whether there is anything or not."[429] As to the gods, Critias, the bloody leader of the Thirty and uncle of Plato's own mother, wrote a satirical play, a play in which one of the characters disposed of the gods as speedily as he himself disposed of his political opponents:

> Then, when the laws forbade them to commit open crimes of violence, and they began to do them in secret, a wise and clever man invented fear of the gods for mortals, that there might be some means of frightening the wicked, even if they do anything or say or think it in secret. Hence he introduced the Divine, saying that there is a God flourishing with immortal life, hearing and seeing with his mind, and thinking of everything and caring about these things. . . . Thus, I think, for the first time did someone persuade mortals to believe in a race of deities.[430]

Socrates' old opponent, the sophist Antiphon, handled justice with sophistication:

> Justice, then, is not to transgress that which is the law of the city in which one is a citizen. A man therefore can best conduct himself in harmony with justice, if when in the company of witnesses he upholds the laws and when alone without witnesses he upholds the edicts of nature. For the edicts of the laws are imposed artificially, but those of nature are compulsory. And the edicts of the laws are arrived at by consent, not by natural growth, whereas those of nature are not a matter of consent.
>
> So if the man who transgresses the legal code evades those who have agreed to these edicts, he avoids both disgrace and penalty; otherwise not. But if a man violates against possibility any of the laws which are implanted in nature, even if he evades all men's detection, the ill is no less, and even if all see, it is no greater. For he is not hurt on account of an opinion, but because of truth. The examination of these things is in general for this reason, that the majority of just acts according to law are prescribed contrary to nature. . . .
>
> We revere and honor those born of noble fathers but those who are not born of noble houses we neither revere nor honour. In this we are, in our relations with one another, like barbarians, since we are all by nature born the same in every way, both barbarians and Hellenes. And it is open to all men to observe the laws of nature, which are compulsory. Similarly all of these things can be acquired by all, and in none of these things is any of us distinguished as barbarian or Hellene. We all breathe into the air through mouth and nostrils, and we all eat with hands.[431]

When Plato turned in revulsion from the violence between polis and polis and the violence between rich and poor, he looked for causes, as

Socrates before him had looked. And what he saw in the thinking of men like Democritus, Thrasymachus, Protagoras, Critias, and Antiphon was that Hellas was sick. Wars and revolutions, demoralizing as they had been, were only symptoms. The real disorder was an intellectual and moral confusion which precluded both the search for truth and the making of good law. The real disorder lay deeper. Zeus was no longer king, but Whirlwind was king.

When Plato was about forty, he visited several Hellenic cities in southern Italy and Sicily. At Tarentum, according to later tradition, he observed the school which the Pythagoreans were setting up under Archytas. The Socrates of the Platonic dialogues had consistently shared the Pythagorean interest in mathematics as the door to philosophy. At Syracuse the tyrant, Dionysius I, had recently fought two successful wars against Carthage, had driven the Carthaginians out of all Sicily except its western corner and had gained control of every Hellenic polis in the island. He had recently crossed the Strait of Messina and subjected a group of cities in the toe of the Italian peninsula. He was the most powerful despot in Hellas when Plato visited Syracuse. There Plato met the tyrant's son-in-law, Dion, then about twenty years old. Plato was repelled by the high living and low thinking that cursed the wealthy cities of Italy and Sicily even more, in his judgment, than they cursed Mainland Greece. He was not surprised that a population of men who lived to satisfy their physical appetites should live also in a continual state of revolution, oscillating between tyranny, oligarchy, and a disordered democracy. But in the young Dion he found a lively intellect and a responsive one. Dion underwent something like a Socratic conversion, withdrew from the dissipated life of the tyrant's court, and started cultivating his mind. His decision naturally made him many enemies.

Meanwhile, Dionysius I extended the power of Syracuse up both coasts of Italy. The Celts had come down from the north and had invaded both Etruria and Latium. Dionysius also pillaged in Etruria and then garrisoned Corsica. In 387 the Celts seized Rome, a small republican city-state of Italic farmers, and sent an embassy to Dionysius, who now recruited Celtic mercenaries. Dionysius was working up the west coast of the Adriatic, founding Ancona, founding Hadria at one of the mouths of the Po, where the amber of northern Europe reached the Mediterranean. His power was felt even on the far shore of the Adriatic, among the Illyrians.

When, in 387, at Sparta's instigation, the Persian King of Kings laid claim to Greece-in-Asia and backed Sparta's hegemony over Mainland Greece, Dionysius I of Syracuse effectually controlled Western Greece. This man who had been born the son of a donkey-driver had risen fast. No wonder Isocrates of Athens saw in him, before he thought he saw in Philip II of Macedon, the savior who would bring peace and order to all Hellas.

But, like the Macedonian dynasts, this self-made Sicilian was not content with his military and economic power. Like them, he craved the culture, the artistic and intellectual aura, that only Mainland Greece could confer. This ruthless pillager of temples wanted to win personal fame at the holy games of Olympia, wanted to win first prize at Athens for a tragedy from his own pen. To import thinkers and writers and artists for Syracuse, as Hiero had done, would not satisfy him. The men he wanted at Syracuse were the engineers who built him powerful catapults for his armies and who understood the new science of ballistics. But Dionysius wanted to be his own poet. When the Olympics of 388 were held, he sent not only a magnificently equipped delegation and his best race horses; he also sent the best rhapsodes money could hire to recite the poems he himself had written. But the Athenian orator Lysias excited the throng at Olympia against this sacrilegious tyrant who subjected Hellenic cities with his barbarian mercenaries. The Syracusan delegation was not allowed to perform the sacrifices. Their splendid pavilion was attacked. Dionysius' horses failed to win prizes. When his poems were read, people refused to listen. It was a bitter cup, but the temple robber obstinately continued making gifts to the holy places of Mainland Greece.

After Thebes had defeated Sparta at Leuctra, and Athens shifted to the side of Sparta, both of these allies tried to get mercenaries from Dionysius to check the rising power of Thebes under Epaminondas. In 368 Dionysius sent Sparta a band of Celts, but Athens got no help until she fulfilled one of his highest ambitions. In no Hellenic competition had he ever won more than second or third prize with a tragedy until in February of 367 his *Ransom of Hector* was presented at Athens and won first prize. He celebrated his great victory with a drinking bout, took to his bed, and died.

The son of Dionysius succeeded him. Dionysius II was still a young man. He had been reared, not as a donkey-driver's son, but as son and heir of the most powerful Hellenic ruler of his day. Understandably, he lacked his father's drive; understandably, he shared his love of high living. But his brother-in-law, Dion, whom Plato had infected with such a love of justice and of reason, had successfully interested a few of his companions in mathematics and philosophy, and Dion hoped that the young monarch might vindicate Socrates' wistful statement, reported or imputed in Plato's dialogue, the *Republic*, that until philosophers became kings and rulers, "or until kings, or if not kings, the sons of kings or princes, are divinely inspired with a true love of true philosophy,"[432] then the miseries of the cities of Hellas must continue. Here was the son of a prince, who had inherited absolute power; his brother-in-law, Dion, believed he could be educated. Dion sent an urgent plea to Plato, in Athens, to come to Syracuse.

A score of years earlier Plato had visited Syracuse for a few months. If, as later tradition claimed, he met Dionysius I, he could hardly have seen in him a possible philosopher king. On the contrary, Dionysius displayed, despite his great abilities, most of the traits that the *Republic* ascribed to the typical tyrant. With no hope of converting this ruler into a philosopher, Plato on his return to Athens had followed the other route. He had bought a piece of property just outside the city walls in a grove sacred to the hero Academus. There he established a school, which from its location came to be known as the Academy. If he could not make an existing ruler philosophic, he could at least train philosophers capable of ruling, or of advising those who already ruled and who might seek advice. Isocrates' school had already been founded, and was also aimed at a more systematic preparation for public life than the lectures of itinerant sophists could furnish. But the Academy undertook to provide an intellectual discipline far more drastic than anything Isocrates wanted to give, or could have given. In fact, the Academy undertook a kind of study that Plato in the *Republic* had prescribed for the Guardians: mathematics and metaphysics. Isocrates could not see why a statesman should sweat over geometry or mathematical astronomy or engage in the, to him, insubstantial argument which some of Plato's later dialogues exemplified.

It was in this Academy that Plato's pupils learned to ascend the divided line from the world of visible things to the world of invisible ideas; from changing, physical objects, through the unchanging, abstract ideas of mathematics, to the investigation of the assumptions on which mathematics rested, to ideas that could only be intuited by dialectic, and at last to the Idea of Good itself. It was here in the Academy that men learned to turn around, or turn their minds around, away from the shadowland in which Demosthenes, and even Isocrates in large part, operated—from the world of practical men, of the struggle for political power, of aims that had not passed through the Socratic ordeal by dialectic. And having turned around, they left the semi-darkness of popular opinion and climbed out of the cave into daylight, and might even strengthen the mind's eye until it could gaze upon the sun itself, the Idea of the Good. By that sun's clear light they analyzed the principles of jurisprudence. And by that same light they recognized their duty to descend into the cave again when needed; so that more than one Hellenic polis turned to Plato's Academy for expert advice on constitutional reform. And more than one of Plato's pupils went forth from the Academy to study the practical problems which such cities faced; to fit principle to case and the idea of justice to concrete situation; and to make law.

It was from this Academy, too, that Dion now urged its founder to come forth, into the Sicilian and Italian world of power and insolence and self-will, the world which the donkey-driver's son had built out of the luxury-loving, money-getting cities of Western Greece. Dion insisted that he was not alone in desiring true law for this empire and that his brother-in-law, the new ruler, Dionysius II, was eager to educate himself to rule well under law. Dionysius himself seconded the plan, and Dion wrote that "now, if ever . . . all our hopes will be fulfilled of seeing the same persons at once philosophers and rulers of mighty States."[433]

Plato was wary. He still had great confidence in Dion, but it was not Dion who ruled at Syracuse. Years later he wrote:

> Holding this view and in this spirit of adventure it was that I set out from home,—not in the spirit which some have supposed, but dreading self-reproach most of all, lest haply I should seem to myself to be utterly and absolutely nothing more than a mere voice and never to undertake willingly any action . . .[434]

Besides, Dion, who was his friend, was asking his help. By going, Plato said,

> I freed myself from guilt in the eyes of Zeus Xenios and cleared myself from reproach on the part of Philosophy, seeing that she would have

been calumniated if I, through poorness of spirit and timidity, had incurred the shame of cowardice.[435]

At Syracuse those of Dionysius's friends who dreaded reform convinced Dionysius that Dion was plotting against him, and Dion was exiled. Plato thought Dionysius's suspicions were the fruit of monstrous slanders, but Dionysius's throne was a dangerous seat. It was at this court in his father's day that the sword of Damocles became legend. Could Dionysius help feeling that in an important sense, though not in a literal sense, Dion and even Plato wanted to use him? And was not the plan to use the sovereign, for no matter what high purpose, a form of usurpation? Somewhere in their hearts, perhaps unknown to themselves, might not disloyalty lurk? As it had lurked in the heart of Marsyas, whom Dionysius had advanced to positions of high command? Marsyas had dreamed that he had killed Dionysius, and Dionysius reasoned that the dream reflected a purpose and executed Marsyas.[436]

But Dionysius did not relish the reputation of having driven Plato from his court, and he begged Plato to stay. Indeed, he made it impossible for him to leave: he housed him in the citadel, from which no ship's captain would have dared accept Plato as passenger to Athens. He wanted Plato to praise him, Dionysius, rather than Dion; but his fear of the anti-reform element at his court made him chary of any serious study with Plato. At last the captive philosopher received permission to go home to Athens and his Academy. Naturally there were plenty of people to ridicule his adventure and to ascribe it to personal ambition, to vanity, to credulity, to the intellectual's naïveté when faced with the cruel realities of practical power politics. A tyrant had indeed turned to a philosopher, not to get his help in radically re-examining the function of ruler, but to get his advice on how to achieve his already chosen goals. In short, Dionysius had turned to Plato in the same way as the youthful Xenophon had turned to Apollo.

Dionysius's treatment of Dion went from bad to worse. He confiscated Dion's property. He gave Dion's wife to another man. In 361 Plato made his third voyage to Syracuse, in a special trireme sent by Dionysius to fetch him, and tried in vain to conciliate the two brothers-in-law, ruler and exile. At Syracuse, Plato worked on the draft of a common constitution for the Hellenic states of Dionysius's empire. But nothing came of it, and with difficulty he again got leave to return to Athens.

In 357 Dion landed with a small force in southwestern Sicily and won his way to the control of Syracuse. He had wanted to bring Syracuse a free constitution, but the political cross-currents were too much for him: he became himself tyrant. Then Callippus, one of Plato's pupils at the Academy, who had come with Dion to Sicily to liberate Syracuse, arranged for his murder and became tyrant. And so it went until the Syracusans begged Corinth, the mother-city of Syracuse, to rescue them. Corinth sent Timoleon, who restored order and even defeated an army Carthage sent into Sicily. Then he quietly laid down his powers and retired to a country estate, which the grateful Syracusans had given him.

Socrates had been executed in 399, and about 387 Plato had founded the Academy. During the dozen years that intervened Plato had written a group of dialogues[437] in which Socrates played the leading role. From the time Plato was forty to the time he entered his sixties, he wrote little or nothing and labored at his teaching and research in the Academy. Then he wrote more dialogues, but in a different tone. They were less dramatic, less poetic, more analytical; in some, Socrates played only a minor role; in some he did not even appear.

These later dialogues, like the earlier, simpler, more dramatic ones, were written for the general public. Plato's most serious teaching took place in the Academy, and he held to the Socratic reservations about written philosophy. Like Socrates, he was not interested in creating a philosophic system. Like Socrates, and despite his publication of the *Dialogues*, he was convinced that men could best seek truth together in the dialectical give-and-take of the spoken word, where the inadequacy of all words can most quickly be corrected, and where the powers of intuition are heightened. Perhaps he remembered Pindar's cry to men:

Creatures of a day, what is anyone? What is he not? Man is but a dream of a shadow; but when the Zeus-given gleam of sunlight comes, a radiance rests on man, and a gentle life.[438]

In any case he was sure that, in the higher reaches of Socrates' divided line, no written treatise could help. Contemplation and communion with ideas prepared the way for that gleam of sunlight Zeus could send to illuminate the shadow, man, and to shed the radiance of grace on his heart and mind. Knowledge of the ideas "is brought to birth in the soul on a sudden,"

Plato himself wrote, "as light that is kindled by a leaping spark, and thereafter it nourishes itself."[439]

Of the later dialogues, written in Plato's late sixties and seventies, the *Timaeus* was unique, because it dealt mainly with subjects Socrates had turned away from in his youth, cosmology, physics, physiology, and because no other Platonic dialogue did. Socrates appeared in it as a listener, while Timaeus speculated on the creation of the universe. Timaeus came from Locri, in southern Italy, and his speculation drew on the mathematical tradition of the Pythagoreans and the atomist tradition of Empedocles. Plato himself never appeared as a speaker in any of his dialogues. But this speculation on the origin of the material universe was not placed in Socrates' mouth either. Timaeus undertook to imagine or intuit the world in which any polis must operate, including the one Socrates had the day before imagined in the *Republic*.

God, as Timaeus imagined, created the cosmos; and this visible, tangible world he created according to an eternal and unchanging pattern; and being perfectly good himself, he desired that it should resemble him in goodness. He endowed the cosmos with soul and mind, so that it was a vast and living animal. He made it out of the four elements the Ionians had written of: earth, air, fire, and water. He made it spherical and rotating. It was impossible to make a material universe eternal and at rest, like the divine idea it copied. So he made a moving image of eternity, which men called time, and gave us past, present, and future, whereas God himself eternally is. He made the stars and planets, which were themselves gods and alive.

As for gods like Zeus and Hera, cosmogonies like that of Hesiod must be accepted. The men of old claimed to be descendants of the gods, and presumably these men knew their own family history. But these gods were not the Creator, the Demiurge, the Artisan, who created them and men and all. When these gods had been created, the God who created them commanded them to create other living creatures, men and animals; but the Creator reserved to himself the work of creating souls for men, since these souls, he told the gods, were

> the part of them worthy of the name immortal, which is called divine and is the guiding principle of those who are willing to follow justice and you . . .[440]

Then the subordinate gods furnished men with mortal bodies and gave them food and made them grow and received them again in death.

Because man was given this double nature of soul and body, his youth was turbulent; later he became less subject to his appetites and if given proper education

> he attains the fulness and health of the perfect man, and escapes the worst disease of all; but if he neglects education he walks lame to the end of his life . . .[441]

The four traditional elements—earth, air, fire, and water—out of which men's bodies and all other matter were composed, were made of atoms that were regular geometrical solids, and the solids could all be reduced to triangles. And the triangles? The triangles, which were forms and hence knowable by the mind, were imposed on space. And space, having in itself no form, was not knowable. One could say only that it was the receptacle of all forms, the mother of all material things.

In this mathematical but live[442] universe, man moved and had his being—his double being. Because he had a mortal body, his mouth was designed to receive food; and because he had an immortal soul, it was designed to emit "the river of speech, which flows out of a man and ministers to the intelligence" and "is the fairest and noblest of all streams."[443] And "every man ought always to begin his speaking and his thinking with the gods,"[444] as if all true speech were a prayer and a communion. Because he had a mortal body, he was given eyes to guide him to what his body needed; and because he had an immortal soul his eyes could perceive the ordered movement of the stars in time—time, the moving image of eternity; his mind's eye could detect their mathematical harmony; and he could even order his own soul. And Timaeus concluded:

> We may now say that our discourse about the nature of the universe has an end. The world has received animals, mortal and immortal, and is fulfilled with them, and has become a visible animal containing the visible—the sensible God who is the image of the intellectual, the greatest, best, fairest, most perfect—the one only-begotten heaven.[445]

This tentative, humble, reverent, soaring account of the universe around Plato came from the ivory tower of the Academy, in which both the orator Demosthenes, crying defiance against Philip, and the publicist Isocrates, inviting Philip to lead Hellas, would alike have scorned to dwell.

But the *Timaeus* marked the Academy as not merely a withdrawal from the madness of Hellas' social disintegration but also as the expansion of mind from polis to universe, of mind probing the nature of man, the nature of matter, the most distant stars, the cunningly devised body of man, the ecology of the living earth. In time as well as in space the probing mind went, clear back to the Creation, to the dawn of time itself, to all that man remembered or half remembered. Had not the poet Alcman written long ago that Memory was "she that looks with the mind"[446]? Necessarily back to creation and necessarily forward to the future, since this living animal, the universe, bore everywhere the signature of purpose. And because all things were infused with purpose, all things were turned toward God and served his will. Man, having intellect, was created "the most religious of animals,"[447] but all animals were religious in the sense that their existence fulfilled the will of God. Necessarily backward to creation went Timaeus, necessarily forward; although it was not Timaeus but another and earlier Pythagorean who wrote that men perish because they cannot join the beginning to the end.[448] It was not Plato in the Academy but Demosthenes in the Assembly and Isocrates the political pamphleteer who sought neither the beginning nor the end. Demosthenes and Isocrates were both great talkers, either from a real platform or from an imaginary platform. They loved words and practical action. "The Athenian citizen," wrote Plato, "is reputed among all the Hellenes to be a great talker."[449] But they had never ascended from the cave to the light. It was one of the tasks of the Academy to induce this ascent.

The last dialogue the aged Plato wrote was the *Laws*. It was decades since he had written his *Republic*, in which Socrates imagined a polis on earth with some of the goodness that rendered luminous the heavenly pattern by which every polis must be judged. Now, in his old age, with a lifetime of reflection behind him and with the plight of Hellas far more parlous than in the days of Socrates, Plato set himself the task of sketching another, a more immediately realizable constitution for a new polis, for a colony. The *Laws* was technically a dialogue, in which a Cretan, a Lacedaemonian, and an Athenian Stranger discussed law, as they walked from Knossos, where Minos the lawgiver had ruled, to the grotto and temple of Zeus on Mount Ida. But there was little of the old sparkle that graced the dramatic dialogue in the *Republic*. Was the

Athenian Stranger the aged Plato himself? All three characters in the dialogue were elderly men. Crete and Lacedaemon were famous for their laws. It was Zeus himself who had given law to Crete; and if Lycurgus had received his rhetras from Apollo at Delphi, at least Apollo was reputed to interpret the will of Zeus. And so the three old men conversed; but the conversation threatened constantly to become a lecture delivered by the Athenian Stranger.

Law, the Stranger held, came from God, for not man, as Protagoras the sophist had proclaimed, but "God ought to be to us the measure of all things."[450] Man might well be a puppet of the gods, pulled by many cords this way and that. Some cords were of hard iron, but one cord alone was the golden cord of reason, soft because made of gold, beautiful and gentle, not violent. It was to this cord that a man must hold fast. For law was the expression of reason in the polis, "the distribution of mind"[451] in polis. And where mind was properly distributed, where law represented persuasion by reason and not mere brute force, men could develop not only the human goods of health, beauty, strength, and the proper amount of wealth, but the divine goods of wisdom, self-control in the face of pleasure, courage in the face of pain, and justice—the four kinds of virtue Socrates had talked of in the *Republic*. Long ago, Cronus, father of Zeus, had placed animals under the rule of divine spirits. Today, men ought to place themselves, through law, under reason, the golden cord which connected men with the gods.

In short, the Athenian Stranger, or Plato in his old age, had turned the talk from the *Timaeus* back to the double theme of the *Republic*: how to live a good, just, and happy life individually; and, since man could be wholly man only in the human community, only in polis, how to frame such laws for a polis as to make it a good, just, and happy human community. The Plato of the *Laws* was once more, like Socrates, overwhelmingly interested in finding answers to those two problems.

And yet so long as Hellas, or even Mainland Greece, could devise no law common to all the persons in it and able to put an end to the vendetta between polis and polis, there was little chance that any polis, no matter how good its laws, would escape being pulled apart by forces from beyond its own frontiers. But nowhere in his dialogues did Plato face that problem, not even in the *Laws*. His small city-state remained the only source of enforceable law, a polis armed against its neighbor, unable to protect its citizens except by a force in being that could not but cause a neighboring polis fear, could not but incite it to arm, could not but create, therefore, a peril to itself.

Socrates had sought the answers to the question of a good life for the polis and a good life for the citizen by starting conversations. And each conversation momentarily created, whether in the gymnasium, in the Agora, or even outside the city walls, a miniature, intense, and fleeting polis that seemed to some to threaten the tyrant-city, Athens. Plato had institutionalized that kind of conversation by creating the Academy, by providing something like the continuous, arduous education that Socrates himself had said the rulers of a just polis would need to have. And where Socrates had left in part to chance the persons he argued with, Plato had followed the path, in some ways harder, of trying to educate an actual ruler. When it came to setting up his ideal Republic, Socrates had playfully resorted to his old Phoenician tale of citizens born of a common mother the earth, some of whom were made of gold and hence were wise enough to rule. Plato, in the *Laws*, was prepared to launch his state if only an educable tyrant could be found.

If a truly wise legislator wanted to reform an existing society, Plato's Athenian Stranger thought the legislator's best chance was such a tyrant. A constitutional monarch would lack the necessary power. A democracy would be harder to persuade than either. Hardest of all to persuade would be an oligarchy, for here each member of the ruling group considered himself a potentate. Was Plato willing to compromise much further than Socrates in order to meet the more desperate moral and political chaos he now faced? He had hoped against hope that a tyrant like Dionysius, so like the evil portrait of a tyrant which Socrates had sketched in Plato's *Republic*, could become a philosopher king. But how free had Dionysius been to fulfill Plato's hope, to convert the corrupt power he held into the kind of power good law required? Was his distrustful treatment of Plato a confession, which perhaps a Socrates would have grasped, that he, Dionysius, was the chief slave of the system he had inherited? Socrates had never turned to the mighty for the redemption of polis. He and Plato both knew, what Solon had known before them, that the just polis required both right and might, that law had to be both just and enforceable. Either a philosopher must secure the might of a king; or else a king who already wielded might must be educated until he could discern justice and follow it. But Socrates went to no Syracuse. Plato did, though he went neither happily nor hopefully. In the *Laws* he was willing to forgo placing all authority in the hands of an aristocracy of wisdom and to seek a stable blend of monarchy and democracy, provided only the government was essentially a government of laws and not of men. There must be a consent of the governed. The laws should persuade even more by reason than by force: that is why the Athenian Stranger insisted that all laws should have preambles that would explain their legitimate purpose.

To the principle that men needed a government of laws, not merely of men, the slave was an exception. The laws did of course protect both master and slave, although the *Laws* proposed some very severe ordinances for slaves. But, within a legally defined area, the slave was governed, not by law at all, but by his master. Antiphon might insist that all men, barbarian and Hellene alike, were subject to the laws of nature; that they all breathed the air through mouth and nostrils and ate with their hands. And in the *Laws* the Athenian Stranger might hold that the sacred and golden cord of reason connected all men to gods; that law was to be obeyed because it expressed this reason; and that reason was beautiful and gentle, not violent. But did the golden cord reach the slave? Was his relation to the master who had bought him, who now owned him, and who might yet sell him, a relation of reason or of violence? The Athenian Stranger thought that the master should be even more scrupulously just to a slave than to his own equals; but he also knew that good, if firm, treatment helped to prevent revolt. It was better too not to have all slaves come from the same foreign country, speaking the same language. At most, the *Laws* urged softening what was in essence a relation of force. But the Athenian Stranger never asked what effect this relation of force— or, for that matter, the relation of force between sovereign polis and sovereign polis—was likely to have on the sacred and golden cord of reason.

The Athenian Stranger's laws sanctioned not only the use of force called war and the use of force called slavery but also the use of force called censorship. Like Socrates in the *Republic*, he censored poets. Indeed, unlike Socrates, he regulated beliefs about the gods. Those who denied that the gods existed, or that they took care of men, or that their actions were always just were to be prosecuted for impiety. Impiety would bring an imprisonment of at least five years; and a second offense would bring death, and death without burial at that. Would Plato have urged an attempt to control religion if in his last years he had not felt a desperate need to shore up the society he saw crumbling about him, a need which perhaps some of the judges who had voted for Socrates' death also had felt when they meted out death to Socrates, on a charge that included impiety? Certainly, the *Laws* tried to come to terms with an increasingly brutalized society, as the *Republic* had not. The freedom of speech, of which Pericles had boasted, assumed that men were adult. But could physically grown-up children, armed, greedy, and violent, be told things about the gods that sanctioned their own lawlessness?

As to the Athenian Stranger's censorship of the poets, Plato's fear of what poetry could do to the soul was based on direct experience. Many of the dialogues, notably the *Republic* and the *Symposium*, could have been written only by a man who was both a philosopher and a poet. Even in his last dialogue, the *Laws*, with its sometimes tedious lists of proposed statutes, his poetic gifts often broke through. Moreover, although neither he nor other writers of his generation any longer wrote their philosophic discourses in verse, as the early Ionians had often done, Plato himself wrote poems:

> Leaving behind the sounding surge of the Aegean we lie on the midmost of the plains of Ecbatana. Farewell, Eretria, once our glorious country; farewell, Athens, the neighbor of Euboea; farewell, dear Sea.[452]

Among other poems he wrote were:

> I am the tomb of a shipwrecked man, and that opposite is the tomb of a husbandman. So death lies in wait for us alike on sea and land.[453]

> I throw the apple at thee, and thou, if thou lovest me from thy heart, take it and give me of thy maidenhead; but if thy thoughts be what I pray they are not, take it still and reflect how short-lived is beauty.[454]

> Thou lookest on the stars, my Star. Would I were heaven, to look on thee with many eyes.[455]

> Some say the Muses are nine, but how carelessly! Look at the tenth, Sappho from Lesbos.[456]

He knew the magic power of poetry over those whose souls were open to poetry, and he knew that the fictions of poetry could both tell the truth and tell lies. It was as if he, not Hesiod, had met the Muses, the ready-voiced daughters of great Zeus, while he, not Hesiod, was shepherding his lambs under holy Helicon. And it was as if the Muses had sung to him, Plato: "we know how to speak many false things as though they were true."[457]

He bore the great epics of Hellas, sung or recited over the centuries, in his heart and memory. He bore there also, like an atavistic memory of the landed aristocracy from which he had sprung, the instinct to colonize, as the nobles of the eighth and seventh centuries had done. Western Greece, that land of opportunity for Mainland Greeks, where Plato went three times, had furnished the word Sybarite, the proverbial term for a man that lived in luxury. The cities of Western Greece had never become holy ground like Athens or Sparta or Argos or Delphi or Olympia. Most of them remained primarily centers of economic expansion. Intellectually, Syracuse excelled more in mechanics than in literature. Although great temples were built, as at Posidonia, the West tended to import its poets and philosophers and artists. Characteristically, the art in which the Sicilian cities most excelled was the designing of coins, and the education for which the West was most famous was training in rhetoric. It was somehow right that the coin and the word should be cultivated there. Both were means: means by which the men of a polis could exchange commodities and exchange ideas. But both could become means to power and almost ends in themselves. Even more than in Mainland Greece, the man of means had come into his own. Nevertheless, despite his revulsion from the Italians and Syracusans who spent their existence "in gorging food twice a day and never sleeping alone at night, and all the practices which accompany this mode of living,"[458] Plato went three times to Syracuse. And, had he achieved the success he never expected to achieve, he might himself have colonized in the somewhat raw but less tradition-bound world of Western Greece. He might have founded the polis, or at least have made Syracuse and its dependent cities into communities that would reflect the pattern Socrates saw laid up in heaven.

Plato never forgot poetry. He never forgot the need to colonize. Nor did he ever forget law. He admired the laws of Lycurgus, although he recognized that they made Sparta what Socrates in the *Republic* called a timocracy, whose goal was honor and whose special virtue was courage, and not what Socrates called an aristocracy, whose goal was justice and whose special virtue was wisdom. Sparta was governed by men trained as warriors rather than by men trained as statesmen, by Socratic auxiliaries rather than by Socratic guardians. Lacking wisdom, its timocracy had largely turned into oligarchy. Plato knew, as Solon had known, that the highest gift the gods could give to a polis was a just law. When Athens, "the oldest land in Ionia," was "being slain"[459] by class hatred, Solon had stood off envious pauper and grasping landowner alike, and had tried to bring his polis justice. Where Solon had hung up his armor at the door of his house when Pisistratus seized power, Plato, despite his scorching description of tyranny in the *Republic*, journeyed to Syracuse in the forlorn hope of educating a tyrant. Such a tyrant might add reason and law to naked force, might make laws that would bring reason and order to the life of his subjects, and

> these things, I say, the laws, as we proceed with them, will accomplish, partly persuading, and partly when natures do not yield to the persuasion of custom, chastising them by might and right, and will thus render our state, if the Gods co-operate with us, prosperous and happy.[460]

For Plato was certain that no polis could be free that did not hold fast to reason, the golden cord that joined the minds of men to the will of God. The forlorn hope perished, and he returned to Athens.

No polis could be free that would not use might to defend its freedom against outsiders who would subject it. In Plato's dialogue, the *Critias*, Critias—not to be confused[461] with the Critias who imposed a bloody terror on Athens in 405—recounted to Socrates and Hermocrates and Timaeus, who had finished describing the creation of the universe and its material structure, an ancient tale that Solon himself had brought back from Egypt. According to this tale, Athens had once, nine thousand years before, led the defense of the Mediterranean world against the wealthy and powerful peoples who dwelt in the vast island of Atlantis beyond the Pillars of Heracles, in the western ocean, an island later sunk by an earthquake. The tale brought memories of the gallant fighters at Marathon.

What disturbed Plato was not the heroic defense of Mainland Greece against Xerxes, but the Greeks' later betrayal of the freedom they had saved. Men exercised freedom not merely by rejecting the arbitrary will of invading despot or of domestic tyrant but by reverence for law, the polis' equivalent of self-control and justice in the soul of the individual citizen. No army, not even one of heroic Marathon fighters, could guarantee that internal freedom. For many years Sparta's freedom had survived precisely because, thanks to Lycurgus' reforms, "Law became with them supreme king over man instead of men being despots over the laws."[462] Aeschylus's statement, "For none save only Zeus is free,"[463] was echoed by Plato when he freely accepted one form of slavery for man:

> For as regards both slavery and freedom, when either is in excess it is wholly evil, but when in moderation wholly good; and moderate slavery consists in being the slave of God, immoderate, in being the slave of men; and men of sound sense have Law for their God, but men without sense Pleasure.[464]

Law "for their God" precisely because real law expressed reason, and reason was of God.

Plato could have drunk with a clear conscience the toast drunk annually at the graves of those who had fallen at Plataea, "I drink to the men who died for the freedom of the Hellenes."[465] But because of what Hellas had done with the freedom men died for at Plataea, Plato could have drunk another toast that would have stirred him even more deeply. In the cell in which Socrates had drunk of a cup not filled with wine, had Plato then been present with those other friends of Socrates, he could have drunk to the man who died for the freedom of the Hellenes, the man who loved freedom under law and bore witness to the end that the citizen who would be truly loyal would strive at the cost of life itself to use the reason God had given him. For Socrates had known what Plato declared in the *Laws* concerning the Hellenes who had freely died for freedom: "Education certainly gives victory, although victory sometimes produces forgetfulness of education."[466]

When the School of Hellas had passed through Melos, through Syracuse, to great catastrophe, to famine and surrender, and her conquerors had thought that tearing down her walls would prove to be "the beginning of freedom for Greece,"[467] it was not walls that kept freedom out of Greece. The bloody oligarchy that sought to silence the questioning Socrates and the restored democracy that silenced him forever taught Plato once and for all that the evil was radical and lay in the minds of those who governed, whether as democracy or oligarchy. Other Hellenic cities were busy documenting the same point. If freedom and justice were to be found, somebody's mind had to be changed—either the mind of a Dionysius or the minds of men who might advise the rulers of any given polis. The true nature of law had to be rediscovered, or the intolerable anarchy of Hellas would continue. The problem was not one of rhetoric or of orators; it was a problem of ethics and jurisprudence. It was one which only disciplined minds could solve. So Plato founded the Academy.

The Academy, which lacked the power of a government, was nevertheless the School of Athens, which was the School of Hellas. It dared turn toward high theory at a moment when the practical men of Hellas were diligently, if quite unintentionally, destroying Hellas. The Academy could hope to house a saving remnant and to become a miniature polis, a community of men sufficiently awakened intellectually to achieve communication. Could it save Hellas? The more relevant question was whether Hellas or any other community could find salvation by any other route. It was a miniature polis because, as Simonides had written, Polis teaches man.[468] Granted that it was another polis in flight, yet it had withdrawn in order to think. To leave the shadows in the cave for the clear sunlight outside was, as Socrates knew, a withdrawal that angered those whose necks remained chained, those who had never turned around, had never been converted to the question, the search, to faith in mind and in ideas.

Plato was no Pericles: he did not rule a state, much less an empire, while arguing with philosophers and planning with architects and sculptors. To unite thought and action in that pre-eminent degree was perhaps no longer possible in Hellas. But Plato also bore two worlds within him, the world of poetic insight and the world of close, cool-headed analysis. He was spiritual kith and kin to Homer and the great tragedians; he also wrote the most powerful philosophic discourses Hellas had known. In him were harmoniously blended rigorous thought and a lofty imagination; and his was at least the courage, if not often the chance, to enter the political arena.

The polis of Pericles had witnessed most of the great tragedies of the Athenian theater and the beginnings of its great comedies. According to later tradition Plato in his early youth wrote tragedies himself.[469] In the *Laws* he admitted into the polis both comedy and tragedy, though under careful censorship. Comedy he thought necessary, because "serious things cannot be understood without laughable things"[470]—a principle of which he himself had always made generous use in presenting his philosophic speculations, so often phrased with a deft sense of comedy. But comedy presented and laughed at vice; and he wanted no free citizen to act in comedies. To impersonate those who were cowardly or greedy or foolish or unfair was corrupting. To laugh at their weakness was to reject such weakness. As to tragedies, Plato's legislators should say to the poets who wrote them,

> we also according to our ability are tragic poets, and our tragedy is the best and noblest; for our whole state is an imitation of the best and noblest life, which we affirm to be indeed the very truth of tragedy. You are poets and we are poets . . .[471]

The well-ordered polis, in which and in which alone a man could live the noblest life, taught noble living even more adequately than tragedies enacted in some theater could do. But did he mean to imply also what he had reported or imputed in the *Republic*, that given the limitations of the human condition, even the most wisely governed polis must in the end, like a tragic hero, fail? In any case, the *Dialogues* were philosophy cast in dramatic form, comic or tragic or both by turns, as Thucydides' history had been cast in dramatic form. Plato could see human life as tragedy, but he could also see it through the laughing eyes of Aristophanes. And, although Aristophanes' caricature of Socrates, whom Plato loved, perhaps helped bring the cup of hemlock, Plato could nevertheless write a couplet:

> The Graces, seeking for themselves a shrine that would not fall, found the soul of Aristophanes.[472]

Finally, Plato loved not only drama but music and the plastic arts. Whether the tradition[473] that he painted was true or not, his writings were filled with brilliant and sensitive images, painted or sculptured in sensitive, musical prose.

But above all he was the child of war and revolution. The Peloponnesian War was only in its fourth year when Plato was born, and it was not until he was twenty-four that his famished polis surrendered, and the oligarchic terror began. He had been a mere baby when civil war had turned Corcyra into a cage of snarling animals. For the rest of his long life he watched the disintegration of Hellas by revolution and by war, a war in which he himself had fought with distinction, as Socrates had done.[474] He was still alive when Demosthenes stirred Athens with his *First Philippic*, but Plato felt a profound distrust for oratory. Like Xenophon and Isocrates, Plato dreamed of a ruler: of a king, or a malleable young prince, or even a tyrant. But in any case a man, a person, a mind. As for Demosthenes' eloquent pleas to Hellas to unite against Philip, Plato might have quoted to him that line from the *Agamemnon* of Aeschylus: "Great your design, your speech is a clamor of pride."[475] Better to lead a minute polis in flight from the Agora to the grove of the hero Academus, to remember, to reflect, to study, to understand, than to rally the planless power of Hellas against the planned power of Philip.

Plato died at the age of eighty, in 348-347. And centuries later it would be written:

> Plato, however, when he was now at the point of death, lauded his guardian genius [*daimōn*] and Fortune because, to begin with, he had been born a man and not an irrational animal; again, because he was a Greek and not a Barbarian; and still again, because his birth had fallen in the time of Socrates.[476]

Like Socrates, Plato had borne witness, although in a different fashion, to his love of the truth and to his vision of the Good. With the memory of that vision Socrates had descended into the cave most men inhabit, had seen their necks chained, had released them that they might climb with him out of the cave where the sun illuminated reality; and at the cost of his life had served notice on his judges that he would remove those chains again. But Plato, too, left the luminous upward search of the Academy and entered the shadowland of Sicilian politics in the barest hope of freeing other men. His descent into darkness was no less a witness to his faith in light than that of Socrates had been. His life was in danger at Syracuse. He courted ridicule in Athens as the impractical intellectual eager to play the statesman, as the professed lover of wisdom who was in fact the sycophant of power. Was the cup of failure which Plato drained at Syracuse less bitter than the hemlock in the cup of Socrates?

When the eighteen-year-old Aristotle entered the Academy around 366, he came as a foreign student. He entered the School of Hellas which Plato had founded inside Athens a score of years after it had first opened. In choosing Plato's Academy and not the celebrated school which Isocrates directed, Aristotle had chosen hard intellectual discipline and inquiry as against a course of studies designed to provide a general, if superficial, culture, and a preparation, especially in public speaking, for practical life. Though not an Athenian, Aristotle was a Hellene both by race and culture. He had been born in 384 in Stagira, a few miles up the eastern coast of the Chalcidic peninsula from the point where long ago Xerxes had dug his canal and a few miles from Amphipolis, which Thucydides, the admiral and historian, had reached too late. Stagira was originally a colony of Chalcis and Andros, and Aristotle's mother came from Chalcis itself. His father was a member of the medical guild, or clan, of Asclepius, and served at Pella as court physician to Amyntas III, father of Philip of Macedon. Both of Aristotle's parents died when the boy was young. Whether or not Aristotle spent any part of his boyhood at Pella, the growing power of Macedon was one of the facts of his youth. Whether or not his father's medical practice influenced him directly, his family background was neither aristocratic, like Plato's, nor socially humble: it was professional and scientific.

For twenty years, until Plato died, in 348-347, Aristotle studied and pursued his research at the Academy. At Plato's death, his nephew, Speusippus, succeeded him as head of the Academy. Was it because Speusippus tended from Aristotle's point of view to turn philosophy into mathematics that Aristotle, now about thirty-six, left the Academy? In any case, he and another member of the Academy, Xenocrates, joined a third Academic, Hermeias, on the Asian mainland near the island of Lesbos. Hermeias, once a slave, later a student at the Academy, had risen to be tyrant of Atarneus. Aristotle married the adoptive daughter, or perhaps the niece, of Hermeias and for three years lived at nearby Assus, where Hermeias had established a sort of philosophic institute and where Aristotle continued his studies in biology. Then, perhaps because Hermeias was betrayed, was sent to Susa, and was there executed by the Great King, Aristotle moved to nearby Mitylene on the coast of Lesbos. In 343-342, when Aristotle was around forty-one, Philip of Macedon offered him a post as tutor to his thirteen-year-old son Alexander. The post promised not merely honor and profit: the education of princes was one of the cardinal aims of the Academics. Had not Plato himself felt bound to go to Syracuse for the same purpose? Aristotle stayed at the Macedonian court until after the death of Philip. During his tutorship, he wrote at least two treatises for the young prince, one on monarchy and one on colonies.

Soon after Philip's death, in 336, Aristotle returned to Athens, but he did not rejoin the Academy, even though Xenocrates, his friend who had gone to Asia with him a dozen years earlier, had succeeded Speusippus as head. Instead, he started a school of his own. Outside Athens stood a grove sacred to Apollo Lyceius, or Apollo the Wolf God, and hence known as the Lyceum, a grove that Socrates had loved. In the Lyceum stood several buildings, and a covered colonnade. Not being an Athenian citizen, Aristotle could not purchase land. But he rented this property and started his school, and the Lyceum soon became famous. Like most schools it contained a *peripatos*, or walk, where the members of the Lyceum could stroll while conversing, and at the Lyceum they strolled enough to earn for themselves the title Peripatetics. When the Lyceum was founded, Isocrates had been dead for three years; the Lyceum succeeded his school as the chief rival of the Academy. The Lyceum was equipped with a considerable library, the largest yet formed in Hellas. It possessed maps and a museum of specimens for scientific study. Its members partook of common meals, and once a month held a symposium. Aristotle walked and discussed problems with his disciples, but above all he lectured. Although he had written dialogues, some of them bearing the same names as certain dialogues by Plato, the give-and-take of dialogue never played the role in his life which it played in the lives of Socrates and Plato. Those of Aristotle's works that would survive were essentially lectures or notes for lectures, and although these works commonly started off with a survey of the opinions of other thinkers on the subject and even of what the common man in the Agora opined, it was Aristotle himself who quickly took the floor, to rectify, to clarify, to render explicit.

Aristotle was indeed the intellectual son of Plato, as Plato in a somewhat different sense was the son of Socrates. But Aristotle's descent from Socrates was descent in a double sense. Socrates did of course insist on both the ascending and descending dialectic: on the motion of the mind from the thing to idea, from the visible to the invisible, from concrete to abstract, from the abstract idea itself to the more general idea implicit in it, and also on the motion by deduction from these high ideas back to things. He had reticently tried to describe this ascent and descent of the mind when he used the metaphor of the divided line. Socrates had tried to awaken reason in others, to play midwife to them when they conceived —when they conceived ideas, grasped concepts. But unlike the famous sophists he encountered, he denied that he had knowledge he could transfer to others; denied that he was a teacher; took no pupils; accepted fees from no man. He inquired further, until his inquiries angered and alarmed the Athenians and they silenced him with death. He left no written philosophy behind him.

Plato institutionalized the dialectical search, accepted pupils, wrote and published. True, the writings he published were dialogues, though the later ones somewhat resembled lectures. Nevertheless, he remained Socratic in his dislike of the dogmatic, in his reverence for the truth still sought and not yet found, in his poetic insight, his humor, his commitment to his polis.

Aristotle, compared with either Socrates or Plato, was a professional intellectual, an alien resident at Athens, a distinguished professor. He neither practiced Socratic irony nor shrank, like Socrates, from publishing the written word. He eschewed the oracular, avoided the purposeful ambiguity of the poet. Though he wrote at least some verse, he was not a poet. His wit was sharp, but the sheet lightning of humor was missing. His genius was a superb common sense, a powerful and active mind, which observed tirelessly, described accurately, analyzed completely. For Aristotle, to know was to classify and systematize. Neither Socrates nor Plato built a philosophical system. Aristotle did. Socrates declared in his trial that he knew he knew nothing; Aristotle knew that he knew. What he knew, he was prepared to transmit. What he knew turned out to be a vast summary, an inventory, of Hellenic knowledge, corrected, ordered, made explicit.[477]

That knowledge he divided into three branches: the theoretical, the practical, the productive. To deal properly with any of them, a man must think logically, and in the *Organon*, or Instrument, Aristotle attempted to furnish the thinker with rules of thought that would enable him to think accurately and well. If a man thought theoretically, he would be seeking knowledge merely for its own sake, and because, as Aristotle himself stated in one of the most gallant Greek sentences yet written, "All men desire by nature to know."[478] But theoretical knowledge could itself be usefully divided. There was theology, the science of God, which he also called "first philosophy," since all other knowledge depended on it. His treatise on this first philosophy, later known as the *Metaphysics*,[479] dealt not with any class of material things such as men or animals or plants, which lived and moved and had their being on earth, but with abstract being as such.

A second theoretical science, or group of sciences, dealt with the objects of nature. A third dealt with mathematics: numbers and magnitudes. All these theoretical sciences were studied by man, not to learn what to do or how to make something, but merely to understand them.

Aristotle's theoretical sciences covered roughly what Plato's *Timaeus* had covered. But though it was not easy to find anything in Aristotle's treatises in theoretical science that had not been implied or suggested by the *Timaeus*, between them, nevertheless, a gulf yawned. For one thing, what the *Timaeus* stated poetically and provocatively, Aristotle stated at length, in detail, explicitly. Again, while the *Timaeus* portrayed God as the Creator, direct or indirect, of man and the world he dwelt in, Aristotle's God, the Unmoved Mover, had not created matter, which was co-eternal with God; and while the *Timaeus* imagined or intuited a God that found the world good, Aristotle's God neither intervened in nor gave a thought to the world. He contemplated the only thing worthy of his contemplation, himself. His only intervention in man's world was to exert an influence like the influence a loved person exerts on those who love him. As in the *Timaeus*, the whole earth and everything in it yearned toward him, and this fact gave to Aristotle's physics as well as his biology a strongly teleological cast. Finally, Aristotle's distrust of the Academy's tendency to mathematicize nature turned his physics and his astronomy away from number and quantity toward quality; and his distrust of the eternal forms of Socrates and Plato led him to insist that the form or essence of a class of things could exist only in concrete individuals, only in the matter they formed. For despite his metaphysical speculations, it was the downward dialectic of deductive science, not the upward dialectic of metaphysics, that occupied him most. He abstracted, he deduced, he applied, he observed, he classified.

His practical sciences dealt with *praxis*, with human action, with conduct. And since man was a "political animal,"[480] a polis animal, who could not achieve a good life alone, all ethical problems, all problems of how a man should act, were closely connected with the nature of the state and the science of politics. In the *Nicomachean Ethics* and the *Politics* Aristotle therefore studied the problems of man-in-polis, problems that Socrates had discussed in Plato's *Republic* and that the Athenian Stranger had expounded in Plato's *Laws*. It had been characteristic of Plato that in each of those two dialogues he had fused ethics and politics, and it was characteristic of Aristotle that, while insisting his two treatises made one whole, he nevertheless dealt with that whole in two treatises.

In the *Physics*, Aristotle created a network of terms with which the human intellect might grasp and hold the ceaselessly changing world of matter about him. There was Plato's "form," of course: the idea that made men call all things of a certain kind by the same name, like man, or animal, or plant. There was the matter in which this form was embodied. And there was the resulting substance. All the matter men had ever perceived was formed matter or substance, was in short matter of some kind: matter itself was therefore a mere abstraction like form. Nobody had ever seen or touched pure matter. But he declined to reduce this unsensed matter to mathematics, as Timaeus had invited Socrates to do.

These substances, these things, among which man lived, were in ceaseless motion: motion from place to place, or motion from small to large as in growth, the motion of being born and coming into being, of dying and passing out of being, of changing color or temperature or some other quality. It was this changing world of formed and reformed matter which the physicist, or philosopher of nature, studied.

These substances had powers, or potentialities. A learner had the power to learn, and this power was actualized, developed, realized, when he had used it and had learned. An unhealthy man had the power to be healed, and it was the doctor's function to actualize this power. Seeds had power to become plants, bronze to become a statue, bricks to become a house; and even a stone lying on the ground had the power to be moved. To understand learners and unhealthy men and raw bronze and stones, one needed to understand their powers and what causes could actualize those powers. There were, Aristotle held, always four causes in the material universe: the material, the efficient, the formal, and the final. In the case of a marble statue, the material cause was the block of marble from which a statue could be hewn. That marble had the power to become a statue only if other causes operated; nevertheless, without it, no marble statue could be caused. Unlike some of the early Ionian philosophers of nature, Aristotle declined to believe that matter could be the ultimate, sole cause of the universe. There had to be a sculptor, wielding a chisel: there had to be what Aristotle called the efficient cause. Even then, putting a man and a chisel and a block of marble together need not cause a statue. The man must have an idea, a Platonic form, of what he wanted to make: this was the formal cause of a statue's coming into being. But such a man could conceive such an idea or imagine such a statue, and still nothing would happen unless he had also the will and purpose to impress this form on the substance, marble, a substance which was itself a case of formed matter. His will and purpose were the end, the *telos*, which the sculptor had in view, and hence Aristotle could not envisage a physical universe that was purely mechanical and without purpose. This purposed end was the final cause. When the seed became a plant, nature, which Aristotle occasionally called God and nature, merged the formal cause and final cause, and out of a seed purposely formed a plant.

The skein of such terms as form, matter, power, actualization, and the four causes, which did such yeoman service in the *Physics*, Aristotle used also in the *Nicomachean Ethics* and the *Politics*. He concluded in the *Ethics* that the object of all men was happiness, though they differed as to the appropriate means to reach this end: some thought money would get them there, some thought honor would, some chose other means as their immediate, intermediary ends. Aristotle undertook in the *Ethics* to demonstrate that virtue, or, more precisely, a group of virtues, were the principal means. He undertook to name these virtues, to define them and classify them. The virtues, he argued, were essentially habits of making right choices, and their corresponding vices were habits of choosing wrongly. He assailed the view of Socrates and Plato, which appeared to him to reduce all virtue to knowledge, to trace all vice to ignorance. He insisted that a man sometimes knows what is right but does its opposite. In the sphere of practical action a man must actualize his power to act courageously by performing a courageous act. If he does this often enough he acquires the habit, or virtue, which men call courage, and he himself then and only then becomes a courageous man. It was the same with the other principal moral virtues: temperance, or self-control; prudence, or practical wisdom; and justice, or fair dealing. A man who lacked these four virtues would be cowardly, greedy, foolish, and crooked.

But, since the completely actualized man is one who can think well in the field of theory as well as act properly in practical life, a man should also actualize into habits his latent power to do certain things intellectually. Aristotle believed he could identify five ways in which the human intellect acted. It could make; and the habit of making skillfully, whether a man painted a picture or built a bridge, Aristotle identified as art, which he called one of the intellectual virtues. The intellect could also demonstrate, follow an argument, construct an ordered science like geometry; and the habit of doing these things well he called the intellectual virtue, science. The intellect could choose, in practical affairs, between things that were good and things that were bad for human beings; and prudence therefore had to be placed in this list of intellectual virtues, even though it had already been presented from another point of view as a moral virtue. The intellect had the power to intuit, and this power, when actualized by use into a habit, was the virtue of intuition. The intellect could, by subtly combining acts of intuition with acts of demonstration, or science, act wisely in the area of speculation and pure theory: such acts produced the virtue of *sophia*, speculative wisdom, as distinguished from practical wisdom, or prudence. The five intellectual virtues, then, were art, science, prudence, intuition, and speculative wisdom; and the last-named was man's highest and most godlike virtue. The virtuous man was the only man who could achieve happiness, because happiness was full activity, full operation, complete functioning; and only the virtuous man possessed the full use of the powers proper to man; the only man in full working order was the virtuous man.

Aristotle's conviction that the power to contemplate was the highest of human powers led him to another gallant statement. The great poets of the Hellenic past had warned man against the willful arrogance, the hybris, of imagining, in the intoxication of good fortune and success, that any man could wield the power the gods wielded. "Strive not," wrote Pindar, "to be a Zeus . . . Mortal aims befit mortal men."[481] And again, when Chiron the centaur restored a dead man to life, Zeus slew both of them, which led Pindar to cry: "Seek not, my soul, the immortal life."[482] But Pindar was talking about self-will, based on the lack of self-knowledge. Aristotle would have agreed, though in different terms perhaps, that a man ought not to set his will against the will of Zeus. But he knew of one act of God that, without hybris, man might and ought to imitate:

If then the intellect is something divine in comparison with man, so is the life of the intellect divine in comparison with human life. Nor ought we to obey those who enjoin that a man should have man's thoughts and a mortal the thoughts of mortality, but we ought so far as possible to achieve immortality, and do all that man may to live in ac-

cordance with the highest thing in him; for though this be small in
bulk, in power and value it far surpasses all the rest.[483]

And yet, if no peril of hybris lurked in contemplation, did the peril not
confront the intellect the moment it re-entered the world of things?
Aristotle himself had undertaken not merely to wonder at this intricate
cosmos of concentric celestial spheres, of the earth, its plants and animals,
its men, and the polis, that "partnership of free men"[484]; he had also undertaken to bring it to order, at least in his own mind, and to that extent to
rule it. Plato's mind, too, had roved upward in space to the shining stars,
moving on their appointed rounds, and backward in time to the lost con-
tinent of Atlantis, described to Solon by the priests of Egypt. But he had
imagined and conceived undogmatically. He had seized no distant terrain
as his own, as his colony, his empire of the intellect. Aristotle classified and
defined and intellectually appropriated the marvels of this vast cosmos,
this cosmos that yearned toward God. He divided and subdivided, often
illuminatingly, sometimes a little obsessively and pedantically. If he warned
Philip against imperialist adventures in Asia, was he not himself in some
sense seizing the philosophic hegemony of Hellas? This sometimes gave
his argument the eristic tone that Socrates always considered such a poor
substitute for the dialectical.[485] But the note of professional rivalry in
Aristotle's works suggested Philip's imperialism less than a related trait
in his writings: his determination to achieve a certain neatness in his
map of the cosmos, to make it conform to a system, and often to ignore the
questions raised by his own answers to previous questions. By and large, his
statements were those neither of a midwife nor a gadfly, but those of a
judge rendering a verdict. By and large, they did not invite further dialogue
from his reader. They invited him to fill in the detail of a world that
Aristotle had made Aristotle's world. The conquest of that world wore the
air of triumph, and what remained for the conqueror's successors was the
work of mopping up, the work of pacification.

None the less, it was a brilliant conquest. Perhaps it was a necessary
conquest, in the same sense that Philip's conquest of Mainland Greece was
a necessary one. The dialectic of freedom had broken down in Hellenic
politics, and Isocrates was not the only Hellene prepared to welcome
Philip, to have him end the interminable eristic of war and revolution in
Hellas. But back of that political breakdown was another crisis. The gods

had largely withdrawn from Hellas, at least from its educated class. The relation of man to man was increasingly impersonal. Faith in ideas was yielding to skepticism, and free moral choices seemed to be narrowing toward animal survival. Hellenic man was lonely and frightened and he looked for shelter. Aristotle's system offered shelter. It was a better shelter than any other thinker offered, as Philip's empire was a better empire. If each in his way was an empire-builder, at least each responded to a genuine need.

To his *Politics* Aristotle brought the same diligent observation he had brought to his biological research. And though he, like his teacher and his teacher's teacher, was concerned to discover the ideal polis, the polis in which men could most fully develop both their moral virtues and their intellectual virtues, he wrote mostly in the vein of the *Laws*, not of the *Republic*. He wanted to apply sound political principle to the actual condition of Hellas. Like Socrates and Plato he discarded the notion that law was merely the rule of the stronger, that might made right, that laws were purely conventional and were not the embodiments of reason in the polis. The polis, he was convinced, was as essential to man's nature as the family. To function properly, the polis had to have a proper size. A polis of ten citizens could not be self-sufficient, but a polis of 100,000 would be absurd and no polis at all. Barbarians, ruled by despots, could live in huge cities; but no huge city could be a partnership of free men. Such partnerships permitted free men to govern themselves responsibly through reason and law and thereby provided the necessary conditions for the exercise of both the moral and intellectual virtues. Indeed, such freedom actualized man, made him most completely man, where the relationship of force or might did not. For that reason Aristotle looked on tyranny as a degradation of monarchy, on oligarchy as a degradation of aristocracy, on a democracy led by demagogues as a degradation of the sort of moderate, constitutional democracy Theramenes had briefly achieved in Athens in 411. He knew that revolution introduced force and tended to destroy the rule of reason even when its aim was to increase it.

A good polis, like a good man, needed good habits and a certain stability, and Aristotle's anxiety to restore such stability to the cities of Hellas, rent asunder by the ceaseless struggle of rich and poor, led him to prescribe a large middle class as the best device for steadying the state. He knew that the moral virtue of a good man is guided by intellect, that the moral act is voluntary and deliberate, not a mere reflex produced by animal training. But what he most emphasized in his *Ethics* was training and habit, and the fact that in practice courage, for example, was a mean between two extremes, rashness and cowardice; and he urged his reader to aim at the mean. Where Socrates sought the formal cause of virtue, knowledge, Aristotle tended to focus on its efficient cause. It was as if, in a world that threatened to brutalize its inhabitants and then collapse into final anarchy, he wanted not only to steady the polis with a middle class but also to steady the citizen by helping him acquire good civic habits, as a parent might help a child or a general might help raw recruits. Plato's talk about the moral virtues had reflected the aristocrat's insight into the heroic; Aristotle's, the middle-class professional man's insight into the advantages of moderate behavior. Where Plato's Socrates defined courage as knowing what is to be feared and not to be feared, Aristotle set for man the more modest, less inspiring goal of acquiring good moral habits with or without insight, by repetition and by the prudent rule of thumb: aim at the mean, or a little to whichever side of it would best compensate for one's recognizable failings.

But the kindred evils of war, slavery, and the money that came from booty and was invested in mercenaries remained in the *Politics* essentially unprescribed for. Had Aristotle's method been less that of the lecturer who already knew and more that of the questioner jointly exploring a problem with others, he might indeed have followed through on some of his own ideas, which, given his method, went unexplored. In explaining, for example, that a good polis needed citizens who were full of spirit like the barbarian peoples of Europe but who were also intelligent and skillful like the subjected peoples of Asia, he observed with satisfaction:

> But the Greek race participates in both characters, just as it occupies the middle position geographically, for it is both spirited and intelligent; hence it continues to be free and to have very good political institutions, and to be capable of ruling all mankind if it attains constitutional unity.[486]

But he was too full of his mean between two extremes to follow the insight contained in those last words, "if it attains constitutional unity," or to consider how Hellas might devise common political institutions. Or, if Macedonian hegemony had now rendered that question academic, to consider how such a political union might conceivably include Macedonia. And it was perhaps characteristic of a fourth-century Hellene, whether he were Aristotle or Isocrates, that when he thought of political union, capable of substituting law and reason for the interstate anarchy of Hellas, he should think of union not as a device for replacing force with reason so much as a device for joining forces and imposing the Hellenes' will upon their neighbors.

Again, if his readers sought his advice on that other glaring case where might made right in Hellas, on slavery, so largely itself a product of war and an incitement to make war, here too he lacked Socrates' capacity for detecting in an apparent irrelevancy an unexpected trail that might lead toward truth. Some thinkers, Aristotle observed,

> maintain that for one man to be another's master is contrary to nature, because it is only convention that makes the one a slave and the other a freeman and there is no difference between them by nature, and that therefore it is unjust, for it is based on force.[487]

But

> the manager of a household must have his tools, and of tools some are lifeless and others living (for example, for a helmsman the rudder is a lifeless tool and the lookout man a live tool—for an assistant in the arts belongs to the class of tools), so also an article of property is a tool for the purpose of life, and property generally is a collection of tools, and a slave is a live article of property. And every assistant is as it were a tool that serves for several tools; for if every tool could perform its own work when ordered, or by seeing what to do in advance . . . if thus shuttles wove and quills played harps of themselves, master-craftsmen would have no need of assistants and masters no need of slaves.[488]

It was clear that Aristotle was talking, not about the relatively few slaves employed in producing articles for sale, but about the large number the Hellenes used for domestic servants. But when he admitted that there would be no need of slaves if quills automatically played harps and if other less musical domestic services could be performed by automatic devices—an alternative he clearly considered absurd—did he not lay a poor groundwork for the rest of his argument?

> These considerations therefore make clear the nature of the slave and his essential quality: one who is a human being belonging by nature

not to himself but to another is by nature a slave, and a person is a human being belonging to another if being a man he is an article of property, and an article of property is an instrument for action separable from its owner. But we must next consider whether or not anyone exists who is by nature of this character, and whether it is advantageous and just for anyone to be a slave, or whether on the contrary all slavery is against nature. And it is not difficult either to discern the answer by theory or to learn it empirically. Authority and subordination are conditions not only inevitable but also expedient; in some cases things are marked out from the moment of birth to rule or to be ruled.[489]

Just as the soul ought to rule the body, and the king ought to rule his subjects; just as man ought to rule other animals, and it is an advantage to domestic animals to be ruled by their masters, "since this gives them security"[490]; just as, "between the sexes, the male is by nature superior and the female inferior, the male ruler and female subject"[491]; so

all men that differ as widely as the soul does from the body and the human being from the lower animal (and this is the condition of those whose function is the use of the body and from whom this is the best that is forthcoming)—these are by nature slaves, for whom to be governed by this kind of authority is advantageous, inasmuch as it is advantageous to the subject things already mentioned. For he is by nature a slave who is capable of belonging to another (and that is why he does so belong), and who participates in reason so far as to apprehend it but not to possess it; for the animals other than man are subservient not to reason, by apprehending it, but to feelings. And also the usefulness of slaves diverges little from that of animals; bodily service for the necessities of life is forthcoming from both, from slaves and from domestic animals alike. The intention of nature therefore is to make the bodies also of freemen and of slaves different—the latter strong for necessary service, the former erect and unserviceable for such occupations, but serviceable for a life of citizenship (and that again divides into the employments of war and those of peace); but as a matter of fact often the very opposite comes about—some persons have the bodies of free men and others the souls; since this is certainly clear, that if persons were born as distinguished only in body as are the statues of the gods, everyone would say that those who were inferior deserved to be these men's slaves. And if this is true in the case of the body, there is far juster reason for this rule being laid down in the case of the soul; but beauty of soul is not so easy to see as beauty of body. It is manifest therefore that there are

386

cases of people of whom some are freemen and the others slaves by nature, and for these slavery is an institution both expedient and just.[492]

Aristotle did not defend the subjection, as tools or mere means to another's will, of those who were slaves by law but not by nature. Only those who were slaves by nature, because they participated in reason so far as to apprehend it but not to possess it, were better off for being slaves. But why the hurried observation that, if only domestic tasks could be done by automatic tools, their services would not be needed? Was this relevant to the argument? Could not the fact that this observation was made, no matter how hurriedly, have suggested to a Socrates the question whether Aristotle's real reason for endorsing slavery as natural was that he felt a natural desire to enjoy the service of slaves, since that service freed his time and gave him leisure to think and teach and write?

Might not Aristotle's own conclusion, that man could secure the full use of his latent powers only by actualizing those powers into their appropriate moral and intellectual virtues, have suggested to him that what he called a natural slave was merely an unactualized man—that is, an uneducated one? That he did not take this step was all the more remarkable in that no Hellene, not even Plato, ever insisted more strenuously on the duty of the polis to educate its citizens if it was to govern by reason and consent and not by mere force.

When somebody asked him how the educated differed from the uneducated, Aristotle answered, "As much as the living from the dead."[493] The polis he wanted was a polis of living men. Had not Heraclitus written: "To those who are awake, there is one ordered universe common to all, whereas in sleep each man turns away from this world to one of his own"[494]? Because education actualized men's powers, it converted men from sleepwalkers into citizens. For only those who possessed the habits of acting justly, courageously, temperately, and prudently, and of using their intellects to purpose could hope to govern their own polis well, whether such persons were monarchs, or oligarchs, or democrats. Nor could any others use wisely those two extraordinary means to true community, those two powerful and easily misused media, those two sets of symbols: words and coins.

As to words, Aristotle's *Organon*, or treatise on logic, had gone far in examining words as well as ideas. And, in his grand encyclopedic arrangement of human knowledge into the speculative sciences, the practical sciences, and the productive sciences, he inserted among the productive sciences a treatise on *Rhetoric*, along with a treatise on *Poetics*. The *Rhetoric* was a handbook on how to make persuasive speeches, which the citizens of a free polis must know how to make if common deliberation was to proceed. The *Poetics* told how to make poems, in a society that lived in part by the epics men recited and the dramas, whether tragic or comic, that men needed if they were to be alive and awake.

On money, his thought followed the Platonic tradition: money was good when it served as a convenient medium for the exchange of material goods. But the use of money to make more money was an evil. Since the temptation to convert the means, money, into an end was an all too frequent phenomenon, Aristotle quoted Solon's warning: "But of riches no bound has been fixed or revealed to men."[495] Aristotle held that "a man cannot expect to make money out of the community and to receive honor as well."[496] Since of those who sought the good life many thought to find it in physical pleasure, and since physical pleasure could be bought with money, the many aimed in practice at piling up money. The aim of the military art was victory, but the mercenary often made that aim money. The aim of the medical art was to cause health in the patient, but the doctor could pervert its aim into the making of money. The management of money for the purpose of providing the necessities of life was the perfectly legitimate *oikonomikē*, or household art of economics, and Aristotle never attempted a treatise on political economy, the 'household art' of a whole polis. He noted that this household art was esteemed, but that trade for the purpose of making money was

> justly discredited (for it is not in accordance with nature, but involves men's taking things from one another). As this is so, usury is most reasonably hated, because its gain comes from money itself and not from that for the sake of which money was invented. For money was brought into existence for the purpose of exchange, but interest increases the amount of the money itself (and this is the actual origin of the Greek word: offspring resembles parent, and interest is money born of money); consequently this form of the business of getting wealth is of all forms the most contrary to nature.[497]

He then proceeded to discuss commercial practices, including monopoly, "a universal principle of business"[498]; and told a tale about Thales of

Miletus, who had founded the early Ionian philosophy and was commonly considered, like Solon, one of the Seven Sages.

> Thales, so the story goes, because of his poverty was taunted with the uselessness of philosophy; but from his knowledge of astronomy he had observed while it was still winter that there was going to be a large crop of olives, so he raised a small sum of money and paid round deposits for the whole of the olive-presses in Miletus and Chios, which he hired at a low rent as nobody was running him up; and when the season arrived, there was a sudden demand for a number of presses at the same time, and by letting them out on what terms he liked he realized a large sum of money, so proving that it is easy for philosophers to be rich if they choose, but this is not what they care about. Thales then is reported to have thus displayed his wisdom, but as a matter of fact this device of taking an opportunity to secure a monopoly is a universal principle of business . . .[499]

He had managed to come to terms with war and slavery, but not with the commercial and banking operations of Athens, operations which had done so much to create his Hellenic community. That community was still without common government, was a community of city-states, most of them split internally by democrat and oligarch, and divided externally from each other by a long history of battle and bloodshed. Aristotle in his detailed analysis of the varieties of government sometimes skirted the problem: the Greek race would be "capable of ruling all mankind if it attains constitutional unity."[500] But he did not follow that train of thought, since it did not fit into his arrangement of his material. He was discussing something else, as he was busy doing when his active mind opened that other trail, the relative uselessness of natural slaves if their work could be done by machinery.

He stuck to the polis; yet even Demosthenes the orator could have told him that Aristotle's former patron, Philip II of Macedonia, had already put an end to the polis by effectually robbing it of its sovereignty. Aristotle had performed a magnificent service in historical research by collecting his 158 city-state constitutions. But he did not think of political science as merely historical or descriptive or theoretical; he classified it as a practical science, to be studied as a guide to political action. It would have been fair to ask him, since the polis was in decline, how should men act politically once more?

When he passed from the practical sciences to the productive and faced the problem of analyzing drama, he was again in a sense too late. He wrote as if he admired Sophocles' *Oedipus the King* more than any other tragedy, but the days of Aeschylus and Sophocles and even Euripides were now long past. Their tragedies were presented in the Theater of Dionysus at Athens as revivals for a polis which could no longer write tragedies of that stature. Through the mind of this alien resident from the north, Athens was reflecting on a political organization that was no longer adequate to her problems and on dramas she could no longer conceive. The fact remained that the polis was one embodiment of that human community in which apparently all men must learn to dwell: in that sense polis could never die. And because man's destiny was tragic, Oedipus could not die, any more than Homer's Achilles could die. Aristotle undertook neither to write an epic nor a tragedy nor any other long poem; he undertook to analyze them as literary forms. How much analysis he could pack into few words he showed when he came to the problem of defining tragedy:

> Tragedy is, then, a representation of an action that is heroic and complete and of a certain magnitude—by means of language enriched with all kinds of ornament, each used separately in the different parts of the play: it represents men in action and does not use narrative, and through pity and fear it effects relief to these and similar emotions.[501]

Then, having offered his definition, he proceeded to expand and explain it. But the idea in his definition that perhaps shone most brilliantly came from the medical tradition, the tradition of his father's family. The relief which men got from their emotions when they witnessed tragedy Aristotle expressed by the Greek word *katharsis*, the regular medical term for a purge. The Athenian polis assembled twice a year under religious auspices, and tragedies were played, tragedies that stirred up the spectators' emotions and then by dramatic resolution drained them safely off. This was an insight Plato never had, or at least never put in his dialogues. And yet, Socrates in the *Republic* had used the medical metaphor in speaking even of a polis which neither he nor those who talked with him were ever likely to see on earth. For, once Glaucon had scorned Socrates' bucolic "city of pigs,"[502] Socrates had proceeded to imagine a fevered[503] state. Well, the fever men called civilization needed purging; tragedy was perhaps one of the cures.

If applying the medical notion of catharsis to his study of tragedy reflected Aristotle's most brilliant insight in his *Poetics*, then one of his most Platonic insights into narrative poetry in general was that "poetry is something more scientific and serious than history, because poetry tends to give general truths while history gives particular truths."[504] And finally, his most Hellenic insight was that what tragedy, and indeed all drama, essentially imitated or represented was not character or elevated diction, though these were needed. The essence of drama was action, human action. The very word drama, Aristotle asserted, came from the Dorians, who claimed to have invented both tragedy and comedy. The very word came from the Dorian word *dran*, to act, to do. It was what the characters did and not primarily what they were that made a tragedy dramatic. It was not characterization but plot. The point was profoundly Hellenic, as was for that matter Attic tragedy itself. For the Hellene loved action, including the action of the imagination and the reason. Achilles acted. It was through acts, Aristotle had insisted in the *Ethics*, that man acquired the moral virtues; it was through acts of choice. It was even by acts that he acquired the intellectual virtues. And it was precisely because it was an action of the intellect, moreover an action freed from the passions, relatively free from being acted upon through the body, that contemplation could be viewed by Aristotle as man's highest act. After all, the God he wrote about in his *Metaphysics*, a God completely immaterial, the Unmoved Mover of the whole cosmos, was pure Act.

For a dozen years Aristotle taught at his Lyceum and classified his universe. His wife died, leaving him a daughter. He remarried, and his second wife gave him a son, named Nicomachus for Aristotle's father, the royal physician to Amyntas III. Then, like Socrates, he was charged with impiety. Was his real crime his relations with his old pupil, King Alexander of Macedon, and with Alexander's regent for Hellas, Antipater? There was a wave of anti-Macedonian sentiment in Athens at the time. In any case, the evidence adduced against him was that he had written a hymn, a poem that could be properly addressed only to a god, and had indited it to Hermeias, the Academic, tyrant of Atarneus and Assus; and that he had also written an epitaph for a statue of Hermeias at Delphi. In 323, the year Alexander died, Aristotle left Athens for Chalcis in Euboea, his mother's native city, now under Macedonian control, observing that he would not permit the polis which killed Socrates to sin twice against philosophy.[505]

He left his old companion, Theophrastus, the botanist, in charge of the Lyceum. Aristotle's problem was different from that of Socrates. Socrates was an Athenian citizen and did not feel free to flout the laws of his own polis. Besides, Socrates, though he did not claim to know that man was immortal, expressed a lively faith that man was. Aristotle's writings were ambiguous on this point, but leaned away from personal immortality.

In 322 when he was sixty-two, and a year after he fled Athens, Aristotle died; and the tradition that grew out of his life would picture him as a bald man with thin legs, small eyes, and a lisp, a well-dressed man not given to ascetic living, a man with a mocking wit.

10

ALEXANDER'S
WORLD POLIS

WHEN Philip of Macedon, the Thirteenth God, was
murdered and his son Alexander mounted his throne, the young king was
twenty. He inherited more than a throne. Through his father he was
descended from Achilles; from the Argive hero, Perseus; and from Heracles,
the hero born of a human mother and of Zeus himself, a hero who by
arduous labors benefited the Hellenes and who by the will of Zeus was
raised to the rank of god. Philip bequeathed Alexander courage in battle,
the lessons in strategy and tactics learned in Thebes during the great days
of Epaminondas and the phalanx, and a magnificently trained, expertly
officered army.

From his mother Olympias, the rejected Epirote princess, Alexander
inherited a passionate and mystical nature. And though each of his
parents came from a dynasty which claimed to be Greek, Philip's own
mother had come from wild Illyria. Although Philip had made a number

of political marriages, he had married Olympias for love. He had met her on the Isle of Samothrace, during her initiation into a mystery cult, when he was twenty-seven and she was twenty. Tradition would report that, as an unusually zealous and inspired Bacchante, or woman worshiper of the wine god Dionysus, she used to distribute to her fellow revelers tame serpents, which coiled about the women's wands as they danced wildly, and that this spectacle terrified the men.

Through his tutor Aristotle, Alexander became heir to Greek poetry and to Greek political and ethical thought. He loved Aristotle, he used to say, more than he did his father Philip; for while Philip had given him life, Aristotle had taught him how to live a noble life.[506] He read Homer, loved Achilles, and learned sections of the *Iliad* by heart. He read Greek tragedy, especially Euripides, who had written his last plays at the Macedonian court. He read the great lyric poets. In a period when Greek thinkers were desperately turning toward monarchy and colonization, Alexander learned from Aristotle the problems which both ideas involved. After three years with Aristotle, at the age of sixteen he had served as regent in Philip's absence on campaign; had led an army himself against a Thracian tribe; and had founded a military colony, which he named Alexandropolis—the polis of Alexander. He had been eighteen when Philip and he had won control of Mainland Greece at Chaeronea, and it had been Alexander's cavalry charge that broke the Sacred Band of Thebes. After that battle, he had done what Philip had never done: he had entered holy Athens itself, the symbol of all poetry and philosophy, the unchallenged School of Hellas.

But if he inherited from Philip a greatly expanded kingdom and the hegemony of Mainland Greece, the inheritance had to be claimed in the Macedonian manner. Philip's death was the signal for some of the feudal lords of Macedon to rise and to conspire in favor of Alexander's infant half-brother, Philip's son by Cleopatra, the rejected Olympias's successor. There were, as usual, murders and executions before the throne could be guaranteed. Olympias herself saw to it that the infant claimant was murdered in Cleopatra's lap and that Cleopatra was forced to hang herself. Alexander of Macedon and Darius III of Persia ascended their thrones in the same year, 336. Both had waded through blood to be king.

In Athens, Demosthenes had received a secret message that his archfoe, the barbarian Philip, was dead. Demosthenes was at the time in mourning for his daughter, but on hearing the news he changed to his best clothes, placed a garland on his head, and offered a public sacrifice of thanksgiving. He spoke disparagingly of Alexander as a child and a silly madman.[507] Athens ordered a sacrifice of thanks to the gods and passed a decree in honor of Philip's murderer. The other Greek states prepared to defend themselves against Macedonia. With the promptness of a Philip, Alexander led his Macedonians southward; the Greek cities helplessly submitted. Alexander took no reprisals; the League of Corinth elected Alexander Hegemon in Philip's place; and the Greeks again agreed to support the crusade that Philip had planned to lead against the King of Kings, Darius III.

In 335, Alexander subdued the Triballians and the Getae in the northeast in a campaign that took him beyond the Danube; and subjected, with frightful slaughter, the Illyrians to his northwest. He was still in Illyria when news came that the Greek cities were in rebellion. Exiled democrats had seized Thebes, which Athens was promising once more to defend. Alexander led an army southward in fourteen days, collected contingents from Phocis and Boeotia, and laid siege to Thebes. In a single day's assault, Thebes fell. The League of Corinth conveniently voted for the city's destruction. Alexander razed it to the ground: except for the citadel, now garrisoned again with Macedonians, only the temples of Thebes were spared, her temples and the house of Pindar the poet. Some 6,000 Thebans were said to have been slain; some 8,000 men, women, and children were sold into slavery. The incipient Greek revolt ended in October, 335, and Athens sent Alexander congratulations. He replied by demanding the surrender of five anti-Macedonian politicians, including Demosthenes. But in the end, when Athens had agreed to prosecute them herself, Alexander relented. Like Philip, he was always gentle with Athens.

In the following spring he crossed the Hellespont into Asia, at the head of some 40,000 men, of which over 5,000 were cavalry. The great panhellenic crusade that Isocrates had longed for had begun at last. In the expeditionary force were 12,000 Macedonians; 12,000 Greeks, including Allied contingents and mercenaries, a mixed group of Thracians, Paeonians, Agrianians, Triballians, Odrysians, and Illyrians from beyond Macedonia's northern frontiers; and a contingent of archers from Crete. The panhellenic crusade was therefore about two-fifths Hellenic in race. Moreover, of that two-fifths many went, as Xenophon and his polis in flight had gone before them, for pay and pillage and adventure. The rest reflected no enthusiasm on the part of Greek states for war with Persia.

Although Alexander had inherited from Philip a consolidated Macedon, a superb army, and the well-publicized project of a panhellenic crusade, he inherited neither an adequate navy nor an adequate war chest. Philip's navy was too weak to open and keep open communications by sea. Alexander's Greek allies had navies, but those allies were halfhearted and he chose not to exact naval contingents from them. Athens, for example, with a navy of 400 triremes, supplied him with only a token force of 20 ships. As to his finances, his long-term natural resources, notably his gold mines on Mount Pangaeus, were abundant; but when Philip died, the royal treasury was deeply in debt, and the booty Alexander's northern campaigns had brought in had only in part liquidated that debt.

In addition to his infantry and his cavalry, Alexander's army was supported by an artillery that included siege towers on wheels, rams for breaching walls, light catapults for hurling javelins, heavy catapults for launching huge stones. There were trained sappers and pontoon builders, architects, surveyors, geographers, botanists, and even historians. There was an excellent baggage train and commissariat. Aristotle, who had now returned to Athens to found his Lyceum, sent with Alexander his nephew, Callisthenes of Olynthus, philosopher and historian; and Alexander planned to send back to Aristotle scientific specimens and data. The empire Alexander proposed to win was not unrelated to the empire of the mind which Aristotle would win, and would win moreover with Alexander's financial support. Both master and pupil desired by nature to know,[508] and then to organize.

When Alexander crossed the Hellespont, he entered the vastest empire known to the Hellenic mind, an empire which had absorbed the earlier empires of Babylonia, Assyria, and Egypt, as well as Greece-in-Asia. Its wealth was a subject of fable. Although it had failed in the days of Xerxes to conquer Mainland Greece by force, it had in recent decades largely controlled Greece by judicious subsidy and bribe, and bribes and subsidies were still being offered to stir up the Greeks against Macedonia. But it was an empire which had grown fat with success; its provincial governors frequently revolted; and its most dependable soldiers were the mercenaries its gold drew from Mainland Greece. At the moment, it was defended by a huge polyglot army, containing hard fighters from the Persian and Afghan highlands and Greek mercenaries, but an army poorly organized, poorly disciplined, and poorly commanded. The Persian Empire was likewise defended by a navy of some 400 ships, drawn as usual from Phoenicia and Ionia, and commanded by an able Greek, Memnon of Rhodes. But Memnon's navy was never fully manned. The Empire, like its king, Darius III, was middle-aged, slow, hesitant, and purposeless.

Alexander had indeed inherited the project of a panhellenic war of revenge, but there were stronger practical reasons for attacking the Persian Empire than revenge for Xerxes' invasion. The Greek mercenaries under Darius III, the Persian gold that continued to buy friends in Greece, the Ionian ships in Memnon's navy, and Memnon's sea power in the Aegean were all symptoms of the fact that money had inextricably commingled Persian and Greek affairs. Those affairs needed ordering, and Alexander proposed to order them.

Arrived in Asia unopposed, he went to Troy, now only a village, and entered the temple of Athena, where he dedicated his own arms and took in their place armor and weapons which the Achaeans had dedicated when the then great city of Priam had fallen eight long centuries before. Then he offered sacrifice and held games on the plain where Achilles had slain Hector. Alexander laid a wreath on Achilles' tomb, and his dearest friend Hephestion laid one on the tomb of Patroclus, beloved companion of Achilles. Then he declared Troy free, restored its democracy, and abolished the tribute exacted by Persia.

At the small Granicus River Alexander met a Persian army, including cavalry and several thousand Greek mercenaries. His second in command, Parmenion, a veteran general of Philip's army, urged him to wait till morning to attack, but Alexander judged otherwise. He fought his way across the Granicus, while the Persian leaders concentrated their tactics on killing Alexander. And, indeed, at one point Spithridates, governor of Lydia, nearly cut him down, but Clitus the Black, who commanded Alexander's cavalry guard, saved him. The Persians broke; but Alexander made little effort to pursue them. He was too busy massacring the Greek mercenaries in the Persian forces. Of those left alive, he captured some 2,000, and sent them in chains to Macedonia to forced labor "because they had violated Greek public opinion by fighting with Orientals against Greeks."[509] He then sent 300 captured suits of armor to Athens as an offering to Athena, whose temple Xerxes had once burned, and inscribed them:

"Alexander, son of Philip and the Greeks, save Lacedaemonians, these spoils from the Persians in Asia."[510]

He announced that he had come to free the Greek cities, both from the tribute levied by Persia and from the oligarchies through which Persia controlled Greek cities. A wave of democratic revolutions swept Greece-in-Asia. Memnon, who still held the Aegean for Persia, would have liked to reply in kind and to raise a democratic revolution in Mainland Greece, where Alexander's regent also governed through oligarchies. But the League of Corinth dared not move. Alexander held too many hostages: Allied army contingents, individual mercenaries, the 2,000 Greek prisoners he had captured on the Granicus. Meanwhile Memnon's Ionian crews were deserting with their ships: the oarsmen came from the poorer families; now they went home to join other democrats in their liberated cities. So democratic freedom spread. At Ephesus Alexander had to protect the oligarchs for fear of an indiscriminate slaughter.

At Miletus, a Persian garrison backed by a Persian fleet threatened to block Alexander's southward march. Parmenion urged him to order his own small fleet into action, since the Persian fleet which opposed him was even smaller. Alexander refused: he would conquer the Persian fleet on land. Miletus fell; and, when 300 mercenaries escaped to an island ready for a last-ditch stand, he bought their services for his own army. Then, short of funds for his fleet, he dismissed all his ships except the twenty that Athens had furnished. He besieged and took Halicarnassus, restored Ada, the deposed queen of Caria, allowed her to adopt him as her son, and left an army of 3,200 mercenaries to finish reducing her enemies. He himself spent the winter of 334-333 quelling the hill tribes of Lycia and Pisidia. He also conquered Pamphylia.

In the spring he went to Gordium. There in the acropolis stood a chariot, set up long ago by King Midas of Phrygia as a thank-offering to Zeus. The yoke of this chariot was fastened to the tongue by a rope made of bark from the cornel tree. The two ends of the rope were concealed in the knot and there was a local tradition that whoever could untie that knot would become lord of Asia. Aristobulus, one of Alexander's Greek technicians, reported later that Alexander merely drew out a wooden pin driven through the tongue of the chariot and the knot then fell apart, but a legend would grow that he tried and failed to untie the knot and that he thereupon drew his sword, cut through the knot, and exclaimed: "I have loosed it";

also that thunder and lightning that night seemed to certify that the prophecy had been fulfilled and that Alexander would indeed rule Asia. The cutting of the Gordian knot would become a symbol, along with Alexander's reported effort to consult the Delphic oracle before he ever came to Asia. At Delphi he had wanted to know, like Xenophon before him, whether his mission in Asia would prove successful. But the priestess would not enter the temple; he had reached Delphi on one of the inauspicious days. Then, according to the tale, Alexander tried to drag her into the temple; whereupon the priestess cried out, "Thou art invincible, my son!" Alexander took the complaint for a prophecy, decided he had had his oracle, and departed. But at least up to his visit to Gordium he had untied more political knots in Asia than he had cut with the sword. He had subverted Persian power and its subservient tyrants and oligarchies with his declaration that he was liberating Greece-in-Asia. Up to his visit to Gordium, the impatience the Delphi story imputed to him had not been one of his vices, although Parmenion, the general he had inherited from Philip, might think it was.

From Gordium Alexander marched east to Ancyra and then south to the mountain pass known as the Cilician Gates. By reaching the pass before he was expected by the enemy, he got through without the loss of a man. He entered Tarsus, which the Persians had just evacuated. There he fell ill of a fever. His Greek friend and physician, Philip, prescribed a purge. While Philip was preparing the draught, a note arrived from Parmenion. Alexander read it, took the cup from Philip, handed him the note, and while Alexander drank the prescribed draught, Philip read, "Beware Philip! I learn that Dareius has bribed him to murder you."[511]

At the mystery celebrations in Eleusis, there were things recited, things shown, things done. All three kinds of things were counted on to convey truth. The scene with the Greek doctor took its place alongside the arms Alexander had dedicated at Troy, the Greeks he had sent in chains to Macedonia for helping Persians against Greece, the Persian panoplies sent to Athens, the cutting of the Gordian knot, as things done, things done to convey meaning, symbolic actions that spoke louder than words, especially to soldiers and to masses of frightened civilians.

From Tarsus, after his recovery, Alexander moved southeastward down the Syrian coast. Then he learned that Darius was in his rear with an army. He addressed his officers. These were not provincial governors, he said, that they would now fight, but the Great King himself. This would be the decisive battle. He addressed individual officers by name and recalled individual deeds of heroism they had already performed. He spoke of Xenophon and his famous march through the mountains to the Black Sea. The officers cheered. After a night's sleep, they moved toward Darius. In the afternoon, on a November day of 333, near Issus, the two armies clashed. Despite the vast military potential of his empire, Darius at Issus commanded about the same number[512] of troops as Alexander, mostly Persian cavalry and a heavy infantry of Greek mercenaries. Alexander fought on his own right wing where he had massed his cavalry, and it was a cavalry charge that crumpled the Persian lines. Darius fled; but his Greek mercenaries gave the Macedonians a rough fight, and when the battle was lost they managed to retire in good order to Tripolis, where they took ship for service in Egypt.

The battle of Issus brought Alexander both triumph and challenge. In theory, he could have pacified the mountainous interior of Asia Minor and have striven for the frontier which Isocrates of Athens had urged on Philip: a line from Cilicia, where Alexander now was, north to the Greek city of Sinope on the Black Sea. But such a frontier would have meant little from a military point of view. Darius had indeed been badly beaten. He had lost prestige; he had lost a valuable contingent of Greek mercenaries; he had even lost his mother, wife, and two daughters, who were captured when he had fled. He had also lost a considerable treasure, stored as war chest at Damascus. This, Parmenion and his Thessalian cavalry had promptly seized; and by now Alexander badly needed it. But Darius had not lost his predominance at sea, and Alexander therefore stuck to his plan of conquering the Great King's remaining Mediterranean seacoast. He would thereby leave the enemy's fleet without bases, and he would cut off Persian subsidies to Sparta and other troublemakers in Greece. He knew that Phoenicia and Egypt were already restless. Darius would doubtless raise a fresh army: he would have to be dealt with later.

Alexander headed south toward Phoenicia. Marathus opened its gates, and at Marathus a letter arrived from Darius. It gently took exception to the aggressions of Philip and Alexander and justified the writer's own acts. The battle of Issus "had gone as some god had willed it."[513] As king to king, he begged Alexander to restore his mother, wife, and two daughters; and on his side he offered friendship and alliance. Alexander answered:

Your ancestors invaded Macedonia and the rest of Greece and did us much harm, though we had done none to them; I have been duly appointed Commander-in-Chief of the Greeks, and invaded Asia desiring to take vengeance on Persia; but it was you who began the mischief. You assisted Perinthus, which wronged my father; and Ochus sent a force into Thrace, which is under our sovereignty. My father was murdered by conspirators, whom you instructed, as you yourselves boasted in your letters, before all the world; you assassinated Arses with the help of Bagoas, and seized the throne unjustly and, according to Persian law, illegally, doing grievous wrong to Persians; you sent improper letters to the Greeks about me, urging them to declare war upon me. You despatched sums of money to the Lacedaemonians and certain other Greeks, and when no other city received these, save only the Lacedaemonians, and when your envoys corrupted my friends and sought to destroy the peace I had made in Greece, I took up arms against you; but it was you who started the quarrel. And whereas I conquered in battle first your generals and satraps, and now yourself and your own force, and hold the country—by the gift of heaven—I hold myself responsible for all of your troops who did not die in the field but took refuge with me; indeed they are with me of their own free will and of their will serve in my army. Regard me then as Lord of all Asia and come to me. If you fear lest by coming you may receive some ungracious treatment at my hands, send some of your friends to receive proper pledges. When you come to me, request and receive your mother, wife, and children, and what you will. You shall have whatsoever you persuade me to give. And in future when you send, send to me as Supreme Lord of Asia, and do not direct what you require as on equal terms, but tell me, as lord of all your possessions, if you have need of aught; otherwise I shall take steps concerning you as a misdemeanant. If you claim your kingdom, stand your ground and fight for it and flee not, since I will pursue you whithersoever you go.[514]

When did he decide that he was Supreme Lord of Asia? And how far did his Asia extend? Events had decided the first question, events and peoples and terrain. The second question no man could yet decide. But the letter was based on a role that Alexander had accepted: he was functioning in Asia as its sovereign, and more completely than Darius ever had done. He was not merely marauding. He was cutting as few Gordian knots as possible. He was organizing and administering. He was liberating Ionian cities from tribute, although he was also accepting contributions, officially voluntary, from those cities to help him complete his task. He was trying to do justice and protect law. He was treating Darius' captured family with an honor worthy of the family of a deposed king. That is, he was respecting the crown, but treating Darius himself as his own subject. On the day after the battle of Issus, according to one tradition,[515] he and Hephestion went alone to Darius' pavilion to show deference to the captive queen mother. They went dressed and armed alike, and the queen mother prostrated herself before Hephestion, since he appeared the taller. When she learned her mistake, she was confused, but Alexander denied that she was mistaken, on the grounds that Hephestion also was an Alexander. The remark was not merely a graceful way of reassuring an anxious captive; it was the illuminating pun of a man who was feeling for his role in history, almost feeling for his identity. Both he and Hephestion were Alexanders; the name meant a defender of men. Both he and Hephestion wanted to defend men; that was why they were fighting in Asia; that was why Alexander must be Lord of Asia.

Where Persia's provincial governors exercised the right of coinage, Alexander usually reserved that right to himself. There would be a common coinage, even though the Greek cities were allowed to coin too. He had won control of scarcely half of Asia Minor, but what he held was the valuable half, especially the Mediterranean coast and the great highways. Of the other half, much had never been governed by Persia either.

The Phoenician ports of Byblus and Sidon surrendered without fighting. Tyre, feeling secure on its rock island a half mile off the coast, played for time. Alexander asked leave to enter the city and sacrifice to the god Melkart, whom he identified with his ancestor, Heracles. Alexander assembled his officers and spoke:

My friends and allies, so long as Persia is supreme at sea I cannot see how we can march in safety to Egypt. Nor, again, is it safe to pursue Dareius, leaving in our rear the city of Tyre, of doubtful allegiance, and Egypt and Cyprus still in Persia's hands, especially in view of the state of Greek affairs. There is a fear lest the Persians, again seizing the coast places, when we have gone in full force toward Babylon and Dareius, should with a larger army transfer the war into Greece, where the Lacedaemonians are at the moment fighting us; and Athens is kept in its place for the present by fear rather than goodwill towards us. But with Tyre once destroyed, Phoenicia could all be held, and the best and strongest part of the Persian navy, the Phoenician element, would most probably come over to us. For neither the rowers nor the marines of Phoenicia will have the courage, if their cities are in our hands, to sail the sea and run its dangers for the sake of others. After this Cyprus, moreover, will either come readily to our side or be captured easily by a naval raid. Then if we hold the sea with our Macedonian ships, and the Phoenician navy too, and with Cyprus ours, we should firmly hold the sea-power, and in virtue thereof our expedition to Egypt would be easy. Then, when we have possession of Egypt, we shall have no cause for uneasiness for Greece and our own home, and we shall make the expedition to Babylon, with security at home, and with our enhanced prestige, with the whole sea cut off from Persia and all the country this side of Euphrates.[516]

The siege of Tyre began. Alexander built a causeway from the mainland to the island, and his engineers rolled out wooden siege towers to attack the massive city walls. The Tyrians ran a fireship against the causeway, and managed to burn Alexander's siege towers. Then Alexander succeeded in getting ships from Sidon; for, hearing the news of his successes in Phoenicia, the Persian fleet was disintegrating. In all he collected 220 ships and seized control of the sea around Tyre. A combined sea and land assault breached the great walls. In July, 332, after holding out for seven months, Tyre fell. During the siege, the Tyrians had captured men from one of Alexander's ships and had murdered them high on their wall in the sight of all: the victorious Macedonians now took vengeance. Some 8,000 Tyrians were slaughtered. Thousands of others were sold into slavery. And Alexander sacrificed to Melkart-Heracles and dedicated in his temple the siege engine that had finally breached the wall.

Meanwhile, he had received a second message from Darius. This time Darius offered 10,000 talents for his mother, wife, and two daughters. He offered to cede to Alexander all his provinces between the Euphrates and the sea. He offered a daughter in marriage, royal friendship, and alliance. These terms Alexander read to his staff. "If I were Alexander," said Parmenion, "I would accept these terms." "And so indeed would I," replied the young king, "were I Parmenion."[517] Being Alexander, he wrote Darius that he needed no money from Darius, nor to receive a part of his empire in place of the whole, since both the king's treasures and the king's country were already his. If he chose to marry a daughter of Darius, he would marry her with or without permission. If Darius wanted friendship, he must come to Alexander to ask it. Darius prepared to fight again.

From Tyre Alexander moved through Palestine toward Egypt. Palestine submitted, except for the strongly fortified city of Gaza, the last city before he would reach the desert that separated him from Egypt. Gaza was held by the eunuch Batis, with a strong force of Arab mercenaries. The besieged city fought hard, and Alexander himself was wounded in the shoulder by a catapult. But the siege engines that took Tyre now arrived. The walls of Gaza were battered above ground and sapped below ground, and on the fourth assault the Macedonians poured in. The Arabs fought on desperately till all were killed; the women and children were sold into slavery; and Gaza was repopulated with local tribesmen and refortified.

In late November, 332, Alexander crossed the desert in seven days to the Delta city of Pelusium, and there he found his fleet awaiting him. The Persian provincial governor of Egypt, Mazaces, had no military force capable of saving Egypt and so he surrendered the country to him. Alexander sent his fleet upriver to Memphis while he and his army followed the right bank up to Heliopolis. There he crossed over to Memphis and sacrificed to Apis the bull god and to the other gods of Egypt. It was the slaying of the sacred Apis by the half-mad Cambyses that had ushered in Persia's conquest and subjection of Egypt. Alexander's sacrifice to Apis ushered it out. He was now the new Pharaoh of Egypt.

Alexander next visited the northwestern corner of the Delta and founded there a city to serve as a strategic center of shipping and commerce, and he called his new city Alexandria. Then, taking a small force, he followed the coast of Libya westward till he was north of the Oasis of Ammon; for, as Pharaoh, he was officially the son of this Egyptian god. At the oasis was an oracle, which ranked in the Greek world with the oracle of Delphi and with the ancient oracle of Dodona in Olympias's native Epirus. For the Greeks identified Ammon with Zeus himself, who spoke to men at Dodona in the rustling of the leaves of oak trees and whose son Apollo spoke for him at Delphi. Pindar had sung of Libya's cities "fostered of men near the foundations of Zeus Ammon."[518] Herodotus had written that "Amun is the Egyptian name for Zeus,"[519] and had spoken of "the Ammonians, who follow the worship of the Zeus of Thebes."[520]

Through a sandy, waterless waste Alexander and his force marched southward; and, when an unexpected rain fell, they could only guess it was some god who saved them. Among the drifting dunes the guides lost their way, and again they were saved, as if by gods. Ptolemy, a general, later reported that two serpents led them, even talking serpents; but Aristobulus, the technician, said it was two crows who guided them to the divine oasis. Here they found olives and palms and garden trees, nourished by heavy dew. The priest greeted Alexander, some said, as son of Ammon, which Alexander had to be, since only Ammon's son could be Pharaoh. Others claimed the priest called him explicitly son of Zeus.[521] Still others insisted the priest had tried to address him in Greek, had mispronounced the word for son, and had merely seemed to say, O son of Zeus.[522]

In any case, Alexander spoke alone with the oracle and reported after his consultation that he had received the answer his soul required, a report that settled nothing. Did the priest tell him he was the son both of Zeus Ammon and of Philip the Thirteenth God? That would have been good Egyptian theology but might seem too ingenious to the Greek world, a world accustomed to gods who lay, or were said by the ancient poets to lie, with mortal women. The men of Tyre might not boggle at Egyptian theology, and Alexander in a letter to the Tyrians called himself "son of Ammon, child of King Philip."[523] To his mother he wrote that he "received certain secret responses, which he would tell to her, and to her alone, on his return."[524] A philosopher in Egypt named Psammon told him that "all mankind are under the kingship of God, since in every case that which gets the mastery and rules is divine."[525] But this could have been mere flattery to an absolute monarch. Alexander himself put it differently when he said that "although God was indeed a common father of all mankind, still, He made peculiarly His own the noblest and best of them."[526] Was he, then, son of Ammon, or of Zeus, only in the sense that all men were his sons, even though he, Alexander, resembled Zeus more than the others because, like Zeus, and by his permission, he ruled? At Ephesus the famous Greek painter, Apelles, had done his portrait and had shown him as wielder of the thunderbolt. Like his divine father? As he pondered certain secret responses, Ephesus was scarce two years behind him. Since then, he had hung up his arms at Troy and had honored with sacrifices and games his ancestor, Achilles, grandson of Zeus. He had broken the army of the King of Kings at Issus and had himself been crowned Pharaoh of Egypt, son of Ammon.

Alexander had a disciplined mind, a mind that analyzed military and political problems and directed him in his choice of means. But he had none of the Athenians' sophisticated skepticism. He was a Macedonian, with the ardor of an earlier generation of Athenians; son of a wild and passionate queen who was addicted to mystery religions. He understood that man's nature itself was a mystery and that there were some things man could communicate only by things recited, things shown, things done. A man did deeds in battle himself that made other men do deeds. He cut knots. A man sacrificed to Melkart of Tyre, who was really his ancestor Heracles, benefactor of the Hellenes, son of Zeus by a mortal mother, himself raised to godhead after death by Zeus, who ruled all. A man must know which verse from Homer or Euripides to recite, in order to illuminate the minds of men as no amount of oratory could.

In some later traditions, Alexander knew he was son of Zeus; in others he was less sure. On her marriage night, had not a thunderbolt struck the womb of Olympias? Philip had found his wife in her bed, a serpent lying beside her: had Zeus, who had come disguised to other mortal women as a bull or as a swan, now taken a serpent's form? At the marriage feast when Philip wedded Cleopatra, Attalus, Philip's general and the bride's uncle, had called drunkenly on the guests to pray the gods for a legitimate heir to the kingdom. Alexander had hurled a cup at Attalus and cried: "But what of me, base wretch? Dost thou take me for a bastard?"[527] Then Philip, in a drunken rage, had drawn his sword against his son, had tripped and fallen. And Alexander had mocked, "Look now, men! here is one who was preparing to cross from Europe into Asia; and he is upset in trying to cross from couch to couch."[528]

That was at a banquet, and at Macedonian banquets wine flowed fast. But it was also at a banquet that the young Oedipus was told he was not the son of the king and queen of Corinth. And in Sophocles' play Oedipus had agonized, in his fashion, over the ancient and very Socratic question, "Who am I?" Perhaps, Oedipus suggested at one point in the play, he was the son of Mount Cithaeron. Alexander's relations with Philip had been often strained, and Philip had repudiated Alexander's mother. No more than any other man did Alexander know who his father was, and the drunken Attalus's insult could be true. Again in a later tradition,[529] when Alexander asked the high priest of Ammon whether any of his father's murderers had escaped him, the priest bade him be guarded in his speech, since his was not a mortal father. But even if that tale was historically true, the priest might merely have been saying in a forceful way that in the eyes of Ammon, Ammon himself was the young Pharaoh's father. And, whatever the mystery of man's nature, whatever the difference between fact and metaphor, there was every political reason for accepting and exploiting the Egyptian solution: that he was the son of Ammon. As for his Greek and Macedonian friends, he could afford ironic banter. Wounded, he could fall back on Homer and remark, "This, my friends, that flows here, is blood, and not 'Ichor, such as flows from the veins of the blessed gods.' "[530] Or, again, he could regret wistfully a mortality he was ready to admit and remark "that sleep and sexual intercourse, more than anything else, made him conscious that he was mortal."[531]

Alexander returned to Memphis; and the south wind left him unscathed although, according to Herodotus, it was this same south wind that had buried Cambyses' army of 50,000 in sand nearly two centuries before. He reorganized the government of Egypt, received envoys from various states, sent Parmenion back to Asia with orders to bridge the Euphrates, and in July, 331, he and his army crossed the Euphrates at Thapsacus, and then crossed the Tigris. Darius, meanwhile, had mustered another army, which included 40,000 cavalry and some 16,000 heavy infantry. He could no longer recruit Greek mercenaries, and he had only 2,000 left.[532] His archers had already proven they could not cope with Macedonian cavalry. His generals had therefore collected cavalry contingents from all parts of his shrinking empire and had revived the use of the scythed chariots that Xenophon's men had faced when Cyrus the Younger fell. Besides 200 scythed chariots, he had 15 elephants.

On September 30, 331, Alexander's army of 40,000 foot and 7,000 horse confronted the larger army of Darius near the village of Gaugamela, not far from the ruins of Nineveh and only thirty-five miles from the town of Arbela. Should he engage immediately? Most of his officers said yes, but Parmenion wanted to wait and to reconnoiter first. This time Alexander agreed with Parmenion; he reconnoitered. Then he reassembled his officers and spoke to them briefly. This battle, he declared, would be neither for Lowland Syria nor for Egypt but for the sovereignty of all Asia. Both for them and for him all Asia meant the Persian Empire, including its conquests in the Punjab, the Land of the Five Rivers, of which four were tributaries of the fifth, the Indus. Then he ordered them to mess where the army now stood and to get some rest.

That night Parmenion came to his commander's tent and urged him to attack the enemy by night and to hope for panic in the Persian ranks. Alexander replied that he would not steal a victory. His decision did more than impress his followers with his confidence. It guaranteed his own troops against the panic that fighting in darkness might easily cause on either side. But, in any case, his problem was not the purely military one of defeating Darius a third time. It was the political problem of convincing the subjects of Darius that a third defeat at Alexander's hands was no accident but accurately reflected Alexander's invincibility.

Next day the two armies maneuvered for position and Darius' Sacan contingent of 1,000 cavalry, sheathed in chain mail, struck. The fighting was hard. But the scythed chariots were successfully evaded and finally their drivers and horses were cut down. In the end a cavalry charge by Alexander and his picked corps of young Macedonian noblemen known as the Companions broke the Persian line. As at Issus, Darius fled, this time toward Media, while his mercenary Greeks managed to delay pursuit. On the left, Parmenion had been outgeneraled, and Parthian and Indian horse had split the Macedonian phalanx in two. But Parmenion recovered; news of Darius' flight demoralized the Persian army; and it too fled. Alexander pursued it till dark, cutting it to pieces. Then he and his men rested till midnight, when they chased it again as far as Arbela. Afterward, when his army was well rested, he marched against Babylon.

The Persian governor of Babylonia, Mazaeus, opened the bronze gates of Babylon and received him with honor. Thereupon, Alexander confirmed Mazaeus as governor of Babylonia, although he placed the military power of the province in the hands of a Macedonian general. This was the first time he had left a Persian governor in charge even of civil affairs. He sent one of his officers to Phoenicia to hold his sea communications open with Europe and, if necessary, to help Antipater, his regent in Europe, against Sparta. For King Agis of Sparta had finally declared open war on Macedonia. Sparta had never joined the League of Corinth, which Philip had founded and which Alexander now officially headed. Sparta had not helped Athens and Thebes when Philip and Alexander crushed them at Chaeronea. Now, too late, she attacked. Near Megalopolis Antipater's Macedonians and his Greek Allies defeated King Agis. Agis was killed in battle, and Sparta was forced to join the League of Corinth.

Alexander stayed for more than a month in Babylon. In Egypt he had exploited the blasphemous behavior of its Persian conqueror, Cambyses;

now in Babylon he exploited the blasphemies of Xerxes, who had destroyed many of Babylon's temples, including the temple of its greatest god, Marduk. Alexander ordered all the temples rebuilt and, by sacrificing to Marduk, made himself Marduk's vicar, the rightful ruler of Babylonia. He now held approximately the territory which Cyrus the Great and his son Cambyses had conquered, either in the west or in the south. He controlled Greece-in-Asia, the whole Fertile Crescent from the Persian Gulf to Palestine, as well as the rich kingdom of Egypt. But, as he worked that month in Babylon, the whole Iranian plateau, the whole of modern Iran and Afghanistan, was nominally in the hands of Darius. Somewhere in those towering mountains was Darius himself. There, too, and relatively near, was Susa, the capital of the Persian Empire and Babylon's only rival as leading city. For many decades Greek envoys and Greek captives had 'gone up' to Susa, following the royal road from Sardis near the Aegean. Also, not far beyond Susa in the home province of the Persian dynasty, stood Parsa and Pasargadae. It was from these mountain fastnesses that decade after decade had poured forth the archers and horsemen who seized the Fertile Crescent, who conquered Egypt, and assaulted Mainland Greece.

In a twenty-day march, Alexander reached Susa. In its treasury were 50,000 talents, which he seized. Reinforcements reached him from Macedonia, and he sent his regent, Antipater, 3,000 talents. At Susa he found also the bronze group of Harmodius and Aristogiton, the Athenian tyrannicides who slew Hipparchus, son of Pisistratus. Xerxes had seized these bronzes when he occupied Athens, and now Alexander returned them to Athens. Alexander took over the royal military academy which trained the sons of Persian nobles to lead the Great King's armies. These young nobles thereby became his hostages for the behavior of their fathers, and at the same time Darius' chief source of future officers was cut off.

Then Alexander struck at Parsa, which the Greeks renamed Persepolis, so swiftly that its garrison had no time to remove its royal treasure of 120,000 talents. And at nearby Pasargadae, where Cyrus the Great lay buried, he seized 6,000 more. Persepolis stood on a high plain, and there on artificial terraces at the foot of a mountain was ranged a group of palaces. These were reached by a stairway, wide enough for ten horsemen to ride up it abreast. Darius I, whose fleet had been lost at Mount Athos, had leveled these rock terraces and had constructed a palace and an audience hall whose roof was supported by a hundred columns. Xerxes had completed the group, and here the Macedonians gazed at his lofty colonnaded porch, guarded by colossal winged bulls of the sort a simpler generation of Persians had first seen in Assyria. The capitals of his columns were carved in the shape of crouching bulls. These magnificent palaces, symbols of Persian pride and oppression, Alexander decided to burn. In vain Parmenion argued that this property was now Alexander's and that burning the royal palaces would convince Asians that he had come to pass through in triumph, not to rule. Alexander was determined to take vengeance for the wrongs the dynasty had done Greece, wrecking Athens, burning temples. And he had every reason to believe that his act of vandalism would impress Babylon, whose great temple, E-sagila, Xerxes had burned, and the Egyptians, whose religious beliefs Cambyses had flouted. Later, of course, the Greeks would tell how Thaïs, an Athenian mistress of one of his generals, Ptolemy, had incited Alexander at a drunken orgy to set the torch to the Great King's splendor. In any case, for days the Macedonian army pillaged the town below the palace. Persepolis was laid low, and it was here at Persepolis that Alexander first got word that Antipater had defeated Sparta.

In the summer of 330 he marched to Ecbatana, in Media. Ecbatana was the summer capital of the kings of Persia, and Herodotus had written[533] of the Median king's stronghold, crowning a hill, coated with silver and gold. In this citadel Alexander stored the gold and silver ingots from the various treasuries of Darius, and ordered Harpalus, his imperial treasurer, to mint them into money for his empire. He left Parmenion to protect his treasury at Ecbatana and to take charge of communications with the imperial army. The terrible vengeance Alexander had taken on Persepolis symbolized the end of the panhellenic crusade against Persia. Antipater had Mainland Greece under control, and Alexander's Greek soldiers were therefore no longer needed as hostages for the good behavior of the states they had come from. So he paid off all his Greeks, including the Thessalians, gave them a handsome bonus, and sent them home, except for those soldiers who might prefer to engage individually as mercenaries.

Alexander's role and function now shifted, as the inexorable result of his own victories. His hero, Achilles, had gone to Asia to avenge at Troy the theft of an Argive queen. Alexander had led his Greeks and Macedonians to Asia, ostensibly to avenge Persia's attacks on Mainland Greece. But if his panhellenic war of vengeance had now ended, it had ended not without irony. At Salamis and at Plataea, the Hellenes had fought in order that their small, free city-states should not be ruled by the Great King; and now the Great King ruled them, though he had been born in Macedonia, not in Susa or Persepolis. His garrisons occupied Greece; and though formally Athens and Sparta and the other states of Greece were his allies and though they paid no tribute, no intelligent Greek could doubt who controlled Mainland Greece.

But Alexander's own fate did not lack irony either. He had come to conquer Asia, and now he was enmeshed in the affairs of a disintegrating empire. He was learning the full force of Aristotle's teaching[534] that the purpose of war is peace, as the purpose of business is leisure, and as the training of the body is for the sake of the soul. What would be the conditions of a just and durable peace? When Darius, after his defeat near Issus, had tried to negotiate, Alexander had demanded that Darius recognize him as Lord of Asia, and he had held to that position at Tyre. Since that time, he had annexed everything of consequence that Darius ruled, up to the Iranian plateau, and had even occupied the provinces of Persis and Media. But Darius was somewhere to the northwest, still alive, still undeposed. Peace could not be organized under two warring heads. The victories Alexander had won had left many problems unsolved. The sword could not solve them: it could only decide who was responsible for solving them. One of these problems, even under a King of Kings, was the consent of the governed, if the empire was ever to be more than occupied territory. When Alexander confirmed the Persian Mazaeus in his governorship of Babylonia, he was already involved in the problem of consent.

Aristotle envisaged three types of just war. Men might justly prepare for war, not to

> enslave those who do not deserve slavery, but in order that first they may themselves avoid becoming enslaved to others; then so that they may seek suzerainty for the benefit of the subject people, but not for the sake of world-wide despotism; and thirdly to hold despotic power over those who deserve to be slaves.[535]

Assuming Alexander agreed with this view, he could justify his war. First, he was attempting to end Persia's secular efforts to enslave Hellas. Secondly, he might hope to benefit the subject peoples who were being badly ruled by a decadent and exploitative Perisan dynasty. Thirdly, he might subject to his will, as one would subject animals, the hill tribes, who were both barbarous and dangerous. But problems could still remain. Both Aristotle and Plato thought that the ideal polis should be small, but no Greek polis yet, not Athens, not Sparta, not Thebes, had devised a constitution for a new human community that had slowly been emerging and that no city-state could contain. The small polis of the philosophers' dreams seemed doomed by history to collide fatally with its neighbor or to be pulled apart by revolution. The affairs of Hellas, of Macedonia, and of Persia were hopelessly entangled. If polis meant a human community of gods and men, then commerce and money and ideas had created a kind of polis out of the whole known civilized world, a polis out of the cosmos, a cosmopolis. Not even Philip's dream was large enough, his polis composed of Macedonia and Hellas, in which Macedonia would contribute a ruler, a disciplined army, money, adequate land, and peace within this new, enlarged polis, while Hellas, and especially Athens, would contribute the ideas, the civilization.

No, Philip's dream was too small. It was clear that the new cosmopolis included not only Greece-in-Asia but Egypt, with a far older culture than that of Hellas, and ancient Babylonia, and Persians like Mazaeus whom Alexander was learning to respect. The real problem was to find the frontiers of cosmopolis. They must be militarily defensible. So far as possible, they must include all civilized peoples, and perhaps some that were just now becoming civilized. They must exclude, so far as possible, all those barbarians who in Aristotle's words deserved to be slaves. It was this political problem that Alexander faced, high on the plateau of Media, among strange peoples, who wore strange costumes and spoke strange tongues. Even had he wanted to rule all these peoples despotically, by terror, he could not hope to do it. He had used force to secure their momentary obedience; to make that obedience permanent, he must give law, he must guarantee justice, he must arouse loyalty. To do these things, he must first destroy Darius; Darius must be viewed as a pretender to the throne he had forfeited. And Alexander must shift his own role, at least in Asia, from European conqueror to Asian King of Kings. He appointed Persian governors for Media and for Media Paraetacene and prepared to track down Darius.

In midsummer of 330 he heard that Darius was collecting reinforcements and withdrawing toward Bactria, a province in the northeastern portion of what is now Afghanistan. Alexander moved by forced marches eastward, with the desert of Parthia on his right and the lofty Elburz Range on his left. Word came that two of Darius' provincial governors had deposed him. The next news stated that one of the governors, Bessus of Bactria, had been acclaimed king by his Bactrians and by most of the followers of Darius. Would the eastern provinces, provinces noted for their tough fighters, now rise against Alexander? With a detachment of horse Alexander speeded his pursuit. At last, near the site of modern Shahrud, they came on Darius. One of his provincial governors and the commander of the cavalry with Darius had wounded him and had fled. Before Alexander rode up, Darius had died. Alexander covered the dead king's body with a purple cloak and sent it to Persepolis to the royal tomb.

Darius had occupied, if only briefly and by dubious means, Alexander's own imperial throne, and royalty was to be respected. The enemy was not the corpse of Darius, whom Alexander had overthrown in battle, but Bessus, governor of Bactria, who had helped betray his king and who now sought to seize the crown. Those Persian nobles who had remained loyal to Darius, Alexander now honored. When the Greek mercenaries of Darius surrendered, he released all those who were in Persian service before the conclusion of the alliance between Macedonia and the League of Corinth. The others he ordered to join his own forces at the same rate of pay.

Word came that Bessus was wearing the royal tiara, had collected an army of Bactrians and of Persians who had fled to Bactria, and was trying to raise the Scythians. The province of Areia was up, and the Areians were marching to the support of Bessus. Alexander quelled Areia and founded another Alexandria on the site of modern Herat. This was a land of fortresses and villages and he wanted cities. He appointed a Persian to govern Areia. Then he headed south to the royal residence of Phrada, not far short of the Helmund River.

Here in the east, while Bessus mustered an army against him, conspiracy flared within his own general staff. He learned that Philotas, the one remaining son of Parmenion and commander of the Companions, had conspired against him. Once before, in Egypt, Philotas had been accused of conspiracy, but Alexander had refused to believe him disloyal. Philotas was now tried by court-martial, was judged guilty, and was shot down by javelins, along with several fellow conspirators. The traitor's father, Parmenion, remained a problem. Had he shared in his son's conspiracy? Whether he had or not, would he seek revenge? Parmenion had been Philip's right-hand man; Alexander had inherited him along with Philip's army. Alexander had rarely followed Parmenion's advice, and Alexander had consistently been proven right. Parmenion had all but failed him at Gaugamela, the final, crucial battle with Darius. Parmenion's enemies were suggesting that he had not wanted Alexander to win, and Alexander had left him at Ecbatana, far to the rear, in charge of communications. But Parmenion was popular both with the Macedonian soldiers and the Greek mercenaries of Alexander. Parmenion symbolized Macedonian military conquest as distinguished from the political problems of pacifying Asia which now confronted a King of Kings.

Alexander's title to the Persian throne was clouded by the claim of Bessus. Bessus was of the blood royal, was in the field with an army, and held the wild northeast provinces. In short, although Alexander had now overrun most of the Empire, the succession was still in doubt. The Macedonian way and the Persian way of handling this problem had been illustrated when Alexander and Darius mounted their thrones in 336. The two ways were identical and traditional: the way was murder, murder of claimants, of conspirators, and of the kinsmen of claimants and conspirators. Alexander simultaneously faced a powerful claimant to his Persian throne and a popular father of a conspirator. Therefore he sent word to three of his generals in Media to put Parmenion to death. The power Philotas had held as commander of the Companions' cavalry Alexander now decided to entrust to no man. He divided the cavalry in two sections and put one section in the hands of Hephestion, the friend he loved most, and one in the hands of Clitus the Black, the boyhood friend who had saved his life at the battle of the Granicus. Clitus' command included the royal horse-guard.

At Phrada, Alexander founded yet another Alexandria. He marched south to the Helmund River through the country of the Ariaspian tribesmen, who were also called the Benefactors, because about two centuries earlier they had helped Cyrus in his campaign against the Scythians. Alexander, who now held Cyrus' throne, did not subjugate the Benefactors, both because of their services to the crown and because of "his own observation that they were not governed like the other tribesmen of these parts, but also claimed to practise justice, like the best of the Greeks."[536] He reduced the southeastern provinces of the Persian Empire, Drangiana, Gedrosia, and Arachosia, fighting in mountain snows on short provisions. But now Areia, with the help of troops sent by Bessus, blazed into revolt; Alexander sent back forces, which suppressed this rebellion, while he himself marched up the valley of the Helmund into Bactria, founding another Alexandria on the way.

Then, in the spring of 329, Alexander crossed the snow-covered Hindu Kush, which his army called Mount Caucasus and which really was part of the vast broken range that swept from the Caucasus Mountains to the Himalayas. Like Xenophon's men in other Asian mountains less far from home, they suffered from cold and snow blindness. On the far side of the mountains in Bactria, they found that Bessus had ravaged the country to impede their march; Bessus and his army then crossed the Oxus River into the province of Sogdiana and burned their boats behind them. Alexander's men also crossed the Oxus, lying flat on skins stuffed with rushes.

When two Sogdian nobles revolted from Bessus and notified Alexander that they had arrested Bessus and were ready to give him up, Alexander sent a detachment under Ptolemy to fetch the pretender to the throne. Bessus was brought to Alexander naked, bound, wearing a wooden collar, and was stationed by the roadside while the army of Alexander marched past. When Alexander himself reached Bessus, he "asked him why he had first seized Dareius, who had been his king, his relative, and his benefactor, then led him about in chains, and then murdered him."[537] Bessus pleaded that he was only one of many who had done these things. Alexander ordered him scourged; during the scourging the herald was to proclaim the crimes Alexander had just reproached Bessus with. Then Bessus was sent to Bactra to await final judgment. Alexander, King of Kings, had done provisional justice to a rebel against Darius, King of Kings, now honorably interred among his royal predecessors.

Alexander next took possession of the royal summer palace at Maracanda, modern Samarkand, and reached the Jaxartes River, the northeastern frontier of Darius' empire. There he summoned the great nobles of Sogdiana to meet with him. Instead, the Sogdians rose in revolt and massacred five garrisons he had left behind him. In the space of two days Alexander and his army put down the Sogdians with hideous slaughter. Then he marched against Cyropolis, the City of Cyrus, razed it, and built his own frontier fortress on the south bank of the Jaxartes River, to protect Cosmopolis from the wild Scythians on the other side. This new city he called Alexandria the Farthest, and he peopled it with tough veterans, both Greek mercenaries and Macedonians. Now his soldiers prepared to cross the river on stuffed hides, as they had earlier crossed the Oxus. He frightened the Scythians who patrolled the farther bank with an attack by catapults, moved his men across the river, outgeneraled the enemy, but was unable to pursue them far. He had come down with dysentery and was carried back into camp. The pursuit had taken place in great heat, the army had suffered from thirst, and he himself had drunk foul water. The pursuit had carried him north almost as far as the site of modern Tashkent.

News came that Spitamenes, one of the two nobles who had surrendered Bessus to Alexander and one of the great nobles of Sogdiana who had revolted and had besieged Maracanda, had ambushed some of Alexander's forces and all but annihilated them. By forced marches Alexander reached Maracanda in four days, but Spitamenes had heard he was on the way and had fled.

The army had gone through two years of savage fighting; Alexander therefore led it back to winter quarters at Bactra, even though Spitamenes was safe at Bokhara, unpunished for his recent ambush of Alexander's men. During that winter of 329-328 at Bactra, Alexander was busy receiving reinforcements from Europe and mercenaries from Greece-in-Asia, treating with his neighbors beyond his new northern frontier, planning the reduction of Sogdiana. Bessus was tried for treason and condemned. His punishment was again Persian: his ears and nose were cut off and he was sent back to Ecbatana to be executed. An ally from south of the Aral Sea offered to show Alexander a northern route to the Black Sea, but Alexander was determined, as soon as Spitamenes had been put down and Sogdiana pacified, to move into India. For in India the Persians had once held, and later lost, a province.

In the spring of 328, Alexander moved across the Oxus again, conquered Spitamenes in a hard summer campaign, and tied down the province of Sogdiana with a network of fortified posts.

That same summer at Maracanda both hybris and catastrophe entered Alexander's life. Unlike his father Philip, he was not inordinately given either to women or to wine. During six years of campaigning in Asia, when he could have possessed any woman he saw, including the daughters of Darius, during six years at the head of an army in which the Macedonians at least could generally be counted on to drink hard and in which thousands of soldiers were followed by their concubines, his own evident continence astonished those who knew him, and his habit of lingering long over his wine rather than getting drunk was a matter of common gossip. But the strain of those six years was taking its toll, even in a man still under twenty-eight. Macedonian and Greek warfare alike demanded that he plan his battles, infuse his men with courage by speech, and fight with the best of them when they closed with the enemy. He knew fatigue and thirst, and if his men both feared and adored him, if he exerted on them that indefinable magnetic charm Xenophon noted in the great military leader, it was partly because he so clearly asked more of himself than of others. During those six years he had known illness and he had known wounds. He had even known the deepest wounds of all, betrayal by those he trusted.

But in addition to mapping his strategy and fighting in the melee of battle as his ancestor Achilles had fought, he was conducting political warfare, receiving embassies, planning cities with his architects, cities that would create civilizing commerce, cities that would serve as forts to protect Cosmopolis. Worse still, he was struggling with his most difficult problem of all: Who am I? Son of Philip, son of Ammon, or son of both, however that might be? He was certainly king of Macedonia, king in an almost Homeric sense, among fighting nobles who demanded that respect be mutual. He was simultaneously Pharaoh of Egypt, and his Egyptian coins showed a Heracles with the features of his divine descendant, Alexander. Coins later pictured Alexander with the ram's horns of Ammon showing through his locks of hair. His mint at Babylon commonly issued coins which bore the initial M for Metropolis: was not Babylon the mother-city, in size, in economic power, and in strategic location for commerce, of his entire Cosmopolis? But about 324 an issue from the Babylonian mint would sum up his political problem. It would show him as a god, wearing a Greek breastplate and sword, a Macedonian cloak, a half-Greek and half-Persian helmet, and carrying in his right hand the thunderbolt of his father, Zeus. He was king of ancient Babylonia and the chief servant of Baal-Marduk; here now in distant Bactra he wore the tiara of the Great King, a Great King who controlled Hellas because he had launched a war of vengeance against an empire, now his own, which had in turn once dared threaten the freedom of Hellas; a Great King who had decided somewhere along his route to be Lord of Asia, meaning the Asia which Darius had tried to rule. And now he, Asia's conqueror, was trapped by Asia. To prevent his conquest from fading out of memory as a raid by marauding Macedonians, he had found himself discharging the function of Great King, doing the *ergon*, the work, of Asia's king, appointing Persians to rule provinces, absorbing Persian forces into his Macedonian army. He unquestionably wanted as a fighting man the glory, the earned fame for excellence, for which Achilles strove on the Trojan plain, the earned fame hymned in Pindar's odes. But he was a statesman, too. He knew that in many real senses Hellas and Macedonia and Egypt and Babylonia and the peoples of the Iranian plateau were a community; but his Macedonians did not know it and they had begun to sense that the young king they had followed through so many hardships was somehow eluding them. They began to feel they had been merely used by Alexander.

And then, one night in Maracanda, Alexander and his friends drank in the true Macedonian fashion. They had many things to forget, the massacres of natives, the things men had always done in war. Alexander and many others present were clearly drunk. The talk turned to the Homeric heroes, Castor and Pollux, brothers of Helen of Troy, and it turned also to the question of whether the brothers were indeed sons of Tyndareus or sons of Zeus himself, as Heracles was. There were flatterers present who urged that the deeds of Alexander were greater even than those of Heracles. Then Clitus the Black, who was in his cups, and who had for long disliked Alexander's apparent transformation from Macedonian soldier-king to Asian despot, grew angry that the deeds of the heroes of old, now divine beings, should be belittled. It was not Alexander alone, he cried, who had done these things, but the Macedonians. Alexander turned to two of his Greek guests: "Do not the Greeks appear to you to walk about among Macedonians like demi-gods among wild beasts?"[538] When someone present spoke slightingly of Macedonian Philip, Clitus praised Philip's achievements in comparison with those of Alexander. He reminded Alexander of the day, six strenuous years before, when they had fought their first Asian battle beside the Granicus, and when he, Clitus, had saved the king's life. He raised his right hand proudly: "This very hand, Alexander, saved you then!"[539] But Alexander happened to share more with Achilles than courage and the love of fame: he shared his kindling wrath, a wrath he had learned generally to control. Tonight wine had stolen his self-control; like Philip at another banquet, he leapt up to strike Clitus. His friends restrained him, and he called for his bodyguard. But the bodyguard discreetly refrained from intervening in the brawl. And so, he shouted, he had come to the same pass as Darius, when Bessus had held him prisoner: he was king in name only. He snatched a spear from a guard. Ptolemy managed to get the drunken Clitus out of the banquet hall. But Clitus broke loose; and when he heard Alexander calling out "Clitus!" he entered by another door, crying: "Behold, here is Clitus, Alexander!"[540] and Alexander launched the spear into his body.

The murder sobered Alexander. Some reports asserted that he immediately tried to kill himself. In any event, he took to his bed and lay for three days without food, crying out the names of Clitus and of Clitus' sister, Lanice, who had nursed Alexander as a baby, and calling himself the slayer of his friends. It was later said that Anaxarchus the Sophist, when he found Alexander moaning in grief, laughed at him and insisted that, just as whatever Zeus did was just, so whatever a great king did should be held just, both by himself and by others. It was also reported that Alexander was somewhat consoled by this argument.

But neither the wine that caused the brawl, nor the murder, nor the repentance, nor the consolation was the basic problem. The basic problem remained: Who was Alexander; where was Cosmopolis; and what was Alexander's relation to Cosmopolis? Aristotle's nephew Callisthenes, the court historian, had sent back to Greece his account of the conquest of Asia, so far as it had gone, and Callisthenes' history made it clear who Alexander was: he was the son of Zeus; Apollo's oracle at Didyma, near Miletus, had said so; the priest of Ammon in the oasis in the Libyan desert had said so. These stories fitted in neatly with the gossip that Philip had doubted whether Alexander was his own son; they fitted also with Olympias's claims[541] that she had borne a son to a god. Everybody knew that the Macedonian dynasty descended from Heracles, and Heracles was certainly a son of Zeus. If Zeus had fathered Heracles, he could certainly have fathered Alexander. But the problem was more complicated even than his unknown paternity. Heracles had later been raised by Zeus to godhood. So had Castor and Pollux. Did Zeus intend to do the same thing for Alexander?

Some of the Greek sophists, like Anaxarchus, who were present at Alexander's court when he was at Bactra, and some of the Persians and Medes at court, agreed with Alexander that the question of his possible divinity should be raised over the wine at a coming banquet. There Anaxarchus opened the discussion. He argued that clearly Alexander would be honored as a god after his death. Why not now? And Macedonians ought to prefer him as a god to Heracles, who was but an Argive, or to Dionysus, who was but a Theban. Others agreed and urged that those present prostrate themselves here and now before Alexander. Actually, the subjects of the King of Kings had always prostrated themselves before their monarch, without thereby implying that he was divine. But Macedonians had no such ceremonial, and the proposal of prostration this evening left those Macedonians who were present glumly silent. It was not they but Callisthenes who spoke. He argued that only gods should be accorded the honor of prostration. Then, surprisingly, in view of what he had written in his history, he pointed out that he was advising, not

some Cambyses or Xerxes, but a son of Philip, by race a descendant of Heracles and of Aeacus, whose forefathers came from Argos to Macedonia, and long held sway there, not as tyrants but as constitutional monarchs of Macedonia. But not even to Heracles himself were divine honours paid by the Greeks while he yet lived; nay, even after his death they were not paid before an oracle was given by the god of Delphi that Heracles was to be honoured as a god. If, however, we must think in foreign fashion, since our discussion takes place in a foreign country, yet even so I beg you, Alexander, to remember Greece, for whose sake all your expedition took place, to add Asia to Greece. Moreover, consider this also, on your return to Greece will it be Greeks, the most free of all mankind, whom you will compel to bow down before you, or will you perhaps exempt the Greeks, and shackle the Macedonians with this shame? or will you draw a line thus in the matter of honours for all the world, that by Greeks and Macedonians you shall be honoured as a man, but by foreigners only in this foreign fashion? But if it is said of Cyrus son of Cambyses that Cyrus was the first of men to receive this homage of bowing to the ground, and that therefore this humiliation became traditional with Persians and Medes, yet you must remember that this very Cyrus was brought to a better mind by Scythians, a poor but free people;

Dareius too by other Scythians, Xerxes by Athenians and Lacedaemonians, and Artaxerxes by Clearchus and Xenophon and their Ten
Thousand, and Dareius now by Alexander, as yet unworshipped by pros-
trations.[542]

Alexander was angered, but the Macedonians were clearly pleased.
Alexander curtly ordered them not to adopt the custom of prostration.
There was silence. But, then, led by their eldest, the Persians rose one by
one and prostrated themselves before their king. Even Hephestion, Alexander's dearest friend, and one or two other Macedonians joined in. But
Callisthenes had touched a nerve: Who lived in Cosmopolis, and what
was their relation to Alexander to be? To the Macedonians Cosmopolis did
not exist; only Macedonia existed, and the foreign provinces which the
Macedonians had conquered with the sword under the able leadership of
Philip's son, whom they dearly loved. To the Persians Cosmopolis offered
something like equality with their conquerors, something like law and
justice under their traditional monarchy, in which the reigning monarch
was indeed a European but a European who had increasingly accepted the
costume and the customs of Persia.

Not long after the murder of Clitus, another conspiracy was discovered,
this time of the Royal Pages, young Macedonian nobles who attended the
king. One of them, Hermolaus, offended Alexander while hunting, and
Alexander's very Macedonian punishment was to have Hermolaus whipped
and his horse taken from him. Hermolaus was furious, and persuaded
other pages who were friends of his to conspire with him to assassinate
Alexander. When the conspiracy was discovered, the conspirators were
executed. But Hermolaus, the ringleader, happened to be a pupil of
Callisthenes, who had dared instruct the king on the difference between
gods and men. The pages claimed that they had been urged on by Callisthenes. Callisthenes was therefore accused and convicted, although later
accounts differed as to whether he died of illness while a prisoner or
whether he was first tortured and then hanged. Some men claimed that
Hermolaus at his trial declared that no freeborn man could endure the
arrogance, the hybris, of Alexander; that Philotas had been unjustly put
to death; and that Parmenion's execution was even more unlawful. They
said Hermolaus spoke too of the murder of Clitus, of Alexander's adoption
of the Persian costume, of his heavy drinking, of his continued preference
for prostration. The plot of the Royal Pages increased the strain between

Alexander and his Macedonians, between the expanded polis that Philip had bequeathed his son, if indeed he was his son, and the vaster Cosmopolis that Alexander was determined to construct and rule.

In the same year as the Pages' conspiracy, 327, Alexander besieged the Sogdian Rock, a high hill with sheer cliffs, which was considered impregnable. A number of Sogdians had taken refuge on the Rock, and Oxyartes, one of the Sogdian feudatories who had revolted from Alexander, had secretly sent his wife and daughters there. Alexander offered large money prizes to those who would scale the sheerest cliff, so sheer it had been left wholly unguarded. Some 300 tried it, with iron pegs and flaxen ropes; some 30 of those fell to their death and the bodies were forever lost in the snow; the rest seized the summit of the crag and signaled their arrival. The Sogdians panicked and surrendered. Among the captives was Oxyartes' daughter, Roxana. It was later reported that it was because Alexander fell in love with her that he married her. Whether that report was true or false, the marriage had important political implications for the ferocious war in Sogdiana and Alexander's ability at last to end it.

After this, he reorganized his army and prepared to march down the narrow valley of the Cophen River, the modern Kabul, to the Khyber Pass and into 'India.' That meant the Punjab province in modern Pakistan and whatever else the kings of Persia had once held. Alexander had left most of his mercenaries in the various cities he had founded. But Antipater, having defeated Sparta, was now able to send him some seasoned troops under the command of Clitus the White. The sons of a few great Persian nobles were included in the Royal Squadron once commanded by Clitus the Black, which Alexander himself had, since the murder of Clitus, commanded. He sent home much of his European cavalry and recruited some of the excellent cavalry he had just defeated in the eastern provinces. He entered India with a smaller army than the one he had brought across the Hellespont seven years earlier; not more than 30,000 at most. But there trailed behind his fighting force a moving polis of concubines, children, technicians, writers, traders, and auxiliary services.

Alexander believed that India was a peninsula jutting eastward from the Iranian Plateau and that beyond it flowed the Ocean Stream. He did not know whether the Indus was the upper Nile or whether it flowed into Ocean and never came near Egypt. To help him explore, he had brought out from Egypt and Phoenicia both shipwrights and sailors. For he was interested not only in completing the conquest of anything that had belonged to Persia; he wanted also to find the defensible frontiers of Cosmopolis, frontiers which might prove in the east to be Ocean. He did not know how far the steppes extended in the north; he himself had been turned back by sickness when he was still short of the area of modern Tashkent. But a case could be made anyhow for the Jaxartes as his northern frontier and for the exclusion of the Scythian nomads from Cosmopolis. Buddha had lived and died, but Alexander knew nothing of Buddha's India; Confucius had lived and died, but Alexander knew nothing of China.[543] His Cosmos, his world, could not include them. He was not even familiar with Herodotus' claim that Darius I had sent ships under a Greek named Scylax down the Indus and around Arabia to the Red Sea.[544]

Alexander sent Hephestion and Perdiccas with the baggage and part of the army down the Kabul River. With them went an Indian ally, Taxiles, who had come to seek Alexander's aid against his aggressive Indian neighbor Porus. Alexander bore northward of the Kabul valley to protect Hephestion and Perdiccas from attack by tribesmen on the left flank. This supporting movement led to very hard fighting, in strange and wild country. He spared a town named Nysa, because its chief magistrate convinced him that, when the god Dionysus had conquered the Indians and was returning toward the Greek Sea, with his discharged soldiers following him as Bacchic revelers, he had founded Nysa; and the magistrate showed the Macedonians the god's beloved ivy growing and assured Alexander it grew nowhere else in India. Alexander hoped this information would fill his soldiers with longing to follow him beyond the limits of Dionysus's conquest. His homesick soldiers crowned themselves with the ivy and sang hymns to the god, and Alexander himself sacrificed to Dionysus. Later, the tale was also told that they found a cave in which, undoubtedly, Prometheus had been chained when the eagle of Zeus fed daily on his liver, till Heracles delivered him. Moreover, the army saw cattle branded with the image of a club, additional evidence that Heracles, who always bore a club, had reached India before them. In any case, some of the cattle they made off with were so handsome that Alexander sent breeding stock back to Macedonia. They also assaulted the impregnable rock they called Aornus, which Heracles, or some Indian god they identified with Heracles, had failed to capture. The descendant of Heracles took the rock.

Alexander joined up with Hephestion and Perdiccas at the Indus, which Hephestion had bridged; and marched to Taxila, the city of their ally. Here for the first time they saw a great Indian city, famous alike for its commerce and its learning. Here the Brahmans, who had long ago come out of the northwest mountains like the later Persians and now the Macedonians, taught their doctrines. Alexander's men held athletic contests and cavalry games. His ally Taxiles furnished him 700 horse, and they all set out for the next river, the boundary of Porus' kingdom. This river was the Jhelum, known to them as the Hydaspes. There they found Porus on the farther bank awaiting them, with his cavalry and his 200 war elephants. After a desperate battle, Alexander finally broke his opponent's army, and Porus surrendered. When Alexander asked Porus how he wished to be treated, he answered, "Treat me, Alexander, like a king."[545] Alexander made him his ally and treated him with the same grave courtesy he had shown the royal family of Persia.

Where Alexander's camp had stood, near the battlefield, he founded a city, Alexandria Nicaea, or Alexandria Victorious. The horse which Philip had given him when a boy because he alone had had the combined courage and intelligence to break him in, the horse he had used throughout his conquest of the Persian Empire, died on the battlefield itself, not of any wound but of old age and exhaustion. His name was Bucephalus, so there Alexander founded Alexandria Bucephala. For Porus' benefit he subdued some nearby tribes. Then, in early July, 326, though the monsoon rains were on and the Chenab in flood, he crossed that river and the Ravi too, and after desperate fighting, stormed and took Sangala. Next, he continued southwest to the Beas, the last of the Five Rivers which were tributary to the lower Indus.

But here at the Beas the army began to grumble. The monsoon rains and humid heat of July had taken their toll. Alexander had already marched some 11,185 miles since leaving Amphipolis. The fighting at Sangala had been costly, and rumor had it that across the river dwelt people kin to the fighters the army had just been up against, and that these people had more and better war elephants. But it was more than that. Alexander summoned his chief officers and addressed them:

> I observe that you, Macedonians and allied forces, are not following me into dangers any longer with your old spirit. I have summoned you

together, either to persuade you and go forward, or to be persuaded by you and turn back.[546]

Had they not, he asked, won rich reward for their labors to date? He named off the provinces of the vast empire they had conquered. Were they afraid of the tribesmen of India? He described the weakness of these tribesmen, not too accurately. Did his officers want to know how much farther they must go? He insisted they had almost reached the Ganges River and the eastern sea already. This sea connected with the Caspian and with the Indian Gulf, which in turn connected with the Persian Gulf. From there the fleet could sail round to Libya, clear to the Pillars of Heracles, and the Mediterranean coast from Egypt to the Pillars could be theirs, as well as the whole of Asia, boundaries God himself had set for the whole earth. However, if the natives beyond this Beas River were left unsubdued, most likely their new and unconsolidated empire would collapse and all their labor to date would then be wasted. "But," he continued,

> do you abide constant, Macedonians and allies. It is those who endure toil and who dare dangers that achieve glorious deeds; and it is a lovely thing to live with courage, and to die, leaving behind an everlasting renown.[547]

Did they not know that "our forefather," meaning his ancestor Heracles, would never have won fame by staying at home in Tiryns or Argos, nor even have been made a god? Dionysus, too, faced dangers. The Macedonians had now won the rock of Aornus, which Heracles had tried in vain to win, and passed beyond Dionysus' city of Nysa.

> If then while you were bearing labours and bearing dangers I had led you, myself, your leader, without labours and without dangers, you would not unnaturally have become weary in your hearts; when you alone had all the labours, and were procuring the prizes thereof for others; but it is not so; our labours are shared in common; we bear an equal part in dangers; the prizes are open to all. For the land is yours; it is you who are its viceroys; the greater part of the treasure comes to you, and when we master all Asia, then—by Heaven!—I will not merely satisfy you, but will surpass the utmost hope of good things for each of you, I will send home all who desire to go home or will myself lead them back; those who stay, I shall make to be envied by those who go back.[548]

He had finished. For a long time, his officers were silent. He invited them, if they disagreed, to say so. But the silence continued. Then Coenus, son-in-law of Parmenion, spoke:

> Seeing that you, sir, do not yourself desire to command the Macedonians tyrannically, but expressly state that you will lead them on only by gaining their approval, and failing this you will not compel them, I shall not speak these words on behalf of us here present, who, being held in honour beyond the rest, have, most of us, already received the prizes of our labours, and in virtue of our authority, because we have power, are in all things heartily ready beyond others to forward your interests; rather I shall speak for most of the army.[549]

Carefully, respectfully, he pointed out how few of the original army were left; how some had been settled in the newly founded cities, many of them unwillingly; how some had been left behind, wounded; how of all Alexander's original host, only a small fraction remained, and these weakened in body and weary of spirit. "But do not be a leader of unwilling troops."[550] Coenus urged Alexander to postpone his Indian campaign eastward until another time, with another army. And he urged on his king the self-restraint that warded off hybris and catastrophe.

Some of the bystanders applauded, some wept; but Alexander was angry. He dismissed them. Next day he called them in again. He would, he announced, compel no Macedonian to go with him against his will. He had other subjects who would follow him. The Macedonians could go home and could tell their friends they had left their king to face his foes without them. Then, like another Achilles, he withdrew to his tent and waited for them to change their minds. He waited for three days, seeing no one. Outside, there was sullen, obstinate silence. Then he prepared to go without them, and sacrificed before crossing the Beas; but at the sacrifices the auspices proved unfavorable. He conferred with his intimates. Then he publicly proclaimed that he was turning back.

The army shouted for joy; many soldiers wept. They crowded to the royal tent and invoked blessings on their king. He set up twelve huge altars to the twelve great gods of Olympus, sacrificed upon them, and held athletic contests and cavalry exercises. Everything east of the Jhelum he formally assigned to his former enemy, Porus, to rule. He would never find his eastern frontier, nor a coast of Ocean for his Greeks to colonize.

But the army had only partly won the contest of wills, for he was determined not to go back the way he had come: he would explore the Jhelum downstream. He completed the building of his fleet, a fleet of between 800 and 1,000 ships. Nearchus the Cretan would command it. Alexander had seen crocodiles in the Indus and nowhere else except in the Nile; what looked like Egyptian beans grew near the Indus. He wrote his mother he thought he had discovered the sources of the Nile, but the Indians insisted the Indus flowed through two mouths into the Great Sea, so he corrected his letter to Olympias.

At dawn of a November day in 326 he embarked; he poured a libation into the Jhelum and libations to his ancestor Heracles and other gods; the bugle sounded, and the ships started in order downstream, with the boatswains calling the stroke to their crews, and with the chanteys the crews sang reverberating from the high banks. The natives, astonished by their first view of horse transports, came running to the banks and followed along, singing their wild, strange songs. Most of his army followed along the two banks too, infantry, cavalry, and some 200 elephants which he had acquired. On the way down he stopped to conquer the Mallians, who were reportedly preparing to resist him. Crossing a desert to a walled city of theirs, he surprised many of them unarmed outside the walls: he killed thousands of them.

Some of the Mallians had taken refuge in a city of the Brahmans: the city was taken and some 5,000 Indians were slaughtered. The remaining Mallians made their last stand in another of their walled cities, their greatest. Convinced that some of his own men were hanging back from scaling the walls, Alexander seized a ladder and climbed the wall himself. Peucestas, the royal shield-bearer, followed, carrying the sacred shield of Athena which Alexander had brought from Troy and which always protected the king in battle. Others tried to follow, but the ladder broke. Alexander was now a target for arrows. He leapt down inside the city, while Peucestas and two others followed. There they fought alone; one was killed, and Alexander was wounded almost mortally by an arrow. Just then the Macedonians broke in. Some of them carried off the king, on his shield. The others slaughtered the Mallians inside, man, woman, and child.

The Mallian campaign was one of the most savage Alexander had ever fought, whether because many of the Mallians preferred death to surrender, or because Alexander's men were frightened by signs of a general uprising, or because they were eager to get home and therefore quick to punish brutally the least resistance. When news spread that Alexander had fallen, his army feared they would be trapped amidst these uncharted rivers, swamps, and deserts, and be wiped out. The men suspected that those Indian peoples who had not yet attacked were held in check only by their fear of Alexander. To reassure the army, the wounded king was brought past them in his boat. The awning was removed. He raised an arm, and the army shouted, and some of his men wept for joy. The ship stopped and a litter was brought. But he demanded a horse; the men clapped wildly and the banks echoed the sound. He rode nearly to his tent, dismounted, and walked. Then the army went wild with relief and joy.

Alexander continued his southward march, subduing tribesmen, executing Brahmans who had incited revolts, receiving embassies, founding cities. When he reached Pattala, where the Indus divided, he began to build a great harbor with docks and then explored the western outlet to the sea. There his navy, unaccustomed to tides, was alarmed by a sudden tidal bore that rushed upstream and even destroyed some of the ships. At last, in July, 325, he sailed out into the Indian Ocean, where he sacrificed bulls to Posidon, god of the sea. He explored the eastern outlet and built another harbor and dockyards. Then he prepared to dispatch Nearchus and his fleet westward along the coast toward Mesopotamia while he himself led his army along beside it to dig wells and establish depots of food for the navy. When the southwest monsoons should stop blowing in October, Nearchus would start. But local tribesmen were threatening, and Nearchus started in September.

The land march through the Gedrosian desert proved deadly, with attacks by tribesmen, with provisions running short, with his guides losing their way. So great was the heat that the men could march only at night. They were reduced to eating their baggage animals and to burning their carts for firewood. The sick and the exhausted followed the army as long as they could, then sank into the sand like men who drowned at sea. The stragglers died. The horses and mules sank into the sand dunes, stumbled, and fell. Sometimes in the desert there were myrrh trees, and the Phoenician traders with the army collected the valuable gum and loaded it onto their mules. Sometimes the spikenard grew so plentifully that, when the marching army trod it underfoot, the perfume filled the desert air. What looked like giant thistles grew on stalks so high and so strong that the spikes dragged horsemen from their horses, and the stalks yielded juice that tasted sharper than the juice of figs in spring at home. When they finally found provisions, Alexander tried to send some to the desert coast for the navy; but the men charged with carrying them, in their hunger pillaged them. The wadis, or arroyos, either lacked water altogether or fresheted in the night from sudden rains upcountry and swept away animals and tents and even weapons. Water was often so scarce that once when some was found it barely filled a helmet; it was offered to Alexander. He thanked those who brought it but, unwilling to drink while his men thirsted, he poured it out into the sand. And the gesture heartened his suffering men. At last, after more than sixty days, they reached the Anamis River, where Craterus joined them after a more northerly march through the Mulla Pass, bringing the bulk of the baggage, the siege train, the sick and wounded, the elephants, and an army escort. Here at the river Alexander founded another Alexandria, and his army rested while he anxiously awaited news of the fleet.

The fleet had its own hardships. They carried provisions for ten days and water for five. Sometimes the barren coast yielded fish, which the natives dried and ground into meal, sometimes it yielded wild dates, sometimes nothing. The fleet had its own adventures too. They discovered the island of a mermaid, who changed sailors into fish. They met a number of whales, which spouted water into the air, and the sailors were so startled that they dropped their oars. Nearchus encouraged his men and ordered them to turn their ships' prows toward the monsters, then raise their battle cry and charge them. The bugles blared, the men shouted and splashed their oars, and at the last, dangerous moment the whales dived. They discovered stone-age tribes with wooden spears who lived on raw fish, on flocks of sheep which had only fish to eat, and on bread made from fish meal. After a grueling voyage of eighty days they reached the Anamis River, ragged, shaggy-haired, and weak, but with the loss of only four ships; and there they made contact with Alexander and the army. Army and navy feasted and held athletic contests. From India to the Arabian Gulf the coast of Asia had been methodically explored.

Alexander returned to the province of Persia and found his empire in considerable disorder. Some of the provincial governors had enrolled mercenaries and had become in effect rulers of sovereign states. Some were guilty of extortion and other oppression. In Media and Carmania pretenders to Alexander's throne had appeared. As symbol of the disintegration of empire, the tomb of Cyrus the Great had been broken open and robbed. The inscription over the door still cried out, "Mortal! I am Cyrus, son of Cambyses, who founded the Persian empire, and was Lord of Asia. Grudge me not, then, my monument."[551] Alexander repaired the tomb and tried to repair the empire.

But there were other omens of the mortality of men and of empires. In India he had come on a group of Indian wise men standing in a meadow, where they were accustomed to hold their disputations. When they saw Alexander and his army, they said nothing but stamped the ground with their feet. When Alexander's interpreter asked what this action meant, they replied,

> O King Alexander, each man possesses just so much of the earth as this on which we stand; and you being a man like other men, save that you are full of activity and relentless, are roaming over all this earth far from your home, troubled yourself, and troubling others. But not so long hence you will die, and will possess just so much of the earth as suffices for your burial.[552]

At Taxila, in India, he saw wise men who went naked; he admired their endurance and wanted to persuade one of them to join him. In a later tradition, their leader rejected the proposal: he himself, the Indian declared, was just as much the son of Zeus as Alexander was. He needed nothing from Alexander, since he was already content with what he had. He noted that those who were wandering over land and sea were no better off for it all, and were still doomed to wander. But one of their number did agree to go, covered with the reproaches of his fellow philosophers for serving some other master than God. The renegade was called Calanus.

In the province of Persia, Calanus fell ill for the first time in his life. But he declined medical care, decided he was ready to die, and requested that a pyre be built. In vain Alexander argued with him. So a military procession marched to the pyre, with Calanus borne on a litter. He was crowned with garlands in the Indian fashion and was singing Indian hymns to the gods of India. He mounted the pyre and distributed to his friends the precious gifts that had been placed on it. He said farewell to

Alexander's generals; but to Alexander he said merely that he would see him again at Babylon. The pyre was lighted; Calanus never flinched; and while the trumpets sounded and the army raised the battle cry and the elephants trumpeted, Alexander watched in sorrow as Calanus died.

But he himself was still alive, and the responsibilities he bore were heavier than those of any other man in his Cosmopolis. He was only thirty-two. But he was exhausted. He had been on campaign in Asia for ten hard years. He had suffered illness at Tarsus; had been wounded at Issus; had been wounded severely at the siege of Gaza. He had lost part of his tibia, fighting the Scythians near the Jaxartes; had been struck in the neck by a stone at Cyropolis; had suffered a debilitating attack of dysentery north of the Jaxartes, again fighting the Scythians. He had been wounded fighting the Aspasians in India, and the arrow planted in his breast when he stormed the city of the Brahmans had nearly proved fatal. He had driven himself mercilessly in the mountain snows of the Hindu Kush and again in the terrible march through the burning desert sands of Gedrosia. But above all, like Odysseus, he was a man of many sorrows and he was still looking for his Ithaca: some way to persuade his generation to cease their petty strife and enter his Cosmopolis.

So now at Susa, with his faithless provincial governors executed and replaced, with the desecrated tomb of his empire's founder repaired or under repair, he tried to weld the disparate elements of that empire. He persuaded eighty of his officers to marry girls of the native aristocracy. He himself, though he never accepted the idea of a king's harem, did take a second wife, one of Darius' two daughters, Barsine,[553] and Hephestion, now the second man of the empire, married the other. But the mass wedding went further: some 10,000 soldiers married their native concubines, to all of whom the king gave dowries. He then undertook to pay the debts of all his men.

In addition to his attempt to fuse the cultures of Cosmopolis by mass marriage, he enlisted in his army 30,000 native youths who had been given Macedonian military training and now wore Macedonian dress. He himself wore Persian dress. So did Peucestas, who had also learned to speak Persian and governed the province of Persia. But if Alexander sought to make his Cosmopolis something which Persians as well as Macedonians could feel loyal toward, yet it was the Athens of Aristotle and the Lyceum, of the Parthenon he had seen and the tragedies of Euripides he had read, and no polis in Asia, not even mighty Babylon, that represented in his mind civilization. Athens, for him, was the kind of society in which all of man's powers, moral, intellectual, and physical, could be most nearly actualized. In Aristotle's terms, it was a polis in which men could acquire the moral and intellectual virtues and thereby happiness, and in which some men through contemplation might briefly achieve a happiness that God knows eternally. Yet, try as Alexander might, Greece remained sullen. He had felt it necessary to destroy Thebes and to defeat Sparta, but he had wistfully cherished Athens; and, in form at least, though only in form, he was the Hegemon, the freely chosen leader, of the Hellenes of Mainland Greece.

The Mainland Greeks resented the peace between their cities which Alexander's deputy, Antipater, imposed. The oligarchies he supported had exiled thousands of democrats now adrift in Greece, some of them ready to serve anybody in need of mercenaries. But Greece could no longer endanger his rear while his hands were tied in Asia. He wanted to reconcile the Hellenes, polis with polis, oligarch with democrat. If he broke his sworn covenant with the League of Corinth, if in effect he annexed Greece instead of preserving appearances, he could order the cities to amnesty their exiled democrats. Instead he chose a more complicated method, a proclamation at the Olympic Games of 324: to restore all exiles and have someone propose his own deification. Obeying a god would not, formally at least, be the same thing as bowing to Macedonian power.

Thousands of hopeful exiles crowded Olympia and awaited the word of Alexander in Asia. All the cities sent envoys, and Athens sent Demosthenes. Nicanor, son-in-law of Aristotle, served as Alexander's messenger, and the royal message in effect ordered the cities to recall their political refugees. Nicanor also suggested that the cities accord divine honors to Alexander. There was grumbling, but educated Greeks no longer felt as strongly about the Olympic deities as Callisthenes had implied when he rejected the ceremony of prostration before the King. According to later tradition Sparta's decree on the subject preserved her reputation for laconism: "Since Alexander wants to be god, let him be god."[554] The Athenian orator, Demades, who had always served Macedon, was fined for proposing that Athens also accept Nicanor's suggestion. As for Macedon's bitter enemy, Demosthenes, he "conceded in the Assembly that

Alexander might be the son of Zeus and Poseidon too, if he wished."[555] Most cities sent envoys to Babylon, with instructions to treat Alexander as a god but to try to evade the order to recall the exiles.

Soon afterwards, Alexander joined his fleet on the Eulaeus River, sailed down to the Persian Gulf, and up the Tigris, clearing it of the weirs which the Persians had installed to block enemy ships. At Opis on the Tigris he summoned his Macedonian forces, told them he was sending home to Macedonia those whom age or service wounds had weakened, and promised them a generous bonus. Instead of being pleased, the whole army read his decision in the context of his new Persian soldiers, of his introduction of foreign cavalry into the ranks of the proud Companions, and of his own frequent use of Persian dress. They again concluded that they had been used and were now being discarded. They demanded that all of them, and not merely the incapacitated, be sent home and that Alexander carry on the war himself with the help of his father.

Alexander's old Achillean wrath flamed. It might well have flamed even if the unspeakable horrors of the Indian campaign and the misconduct of his provincial governors and the burden of administration had not made him more irritable. But, in addition, there was the gnawing problem of Cosmopolis, of the strain between conquerors and conquered, of his own tangled relationship with many peoples of many and varied customs, and even of the unresolved question, Who am I? The phrase "with the help of his father" was too obvious an allusion to miss, and too obvious to forgive for a king grown accustomed to the sort of respect his Asian and Egyptian subjects must perforce yield, even had there been no theological doubts in his own mind, even if the whole matter of divinity had been merely a coldly calculated political hoax.

In any case, he leapt from the platform from which he had been speaking, pointed out thirteen ringleaders to his officers, and ordered them executed. A dead silence followed. Then he remounted the platform and spoke:[556]

I now propose to speak, Macedonians, not with a view to checking your homeward impulse; so far as I am concerned, you may go where you will; but that you may know, if you do so go away, how you have behaved to us, and how we have behaved to you. First then I shall begin my speech with my father Philip, as is right and proper. For Philip found you vagabonds and helpless, most of you clothed with sheepskins, pasturing a few sheep on the mountain sides, and fighting for these, with ill success, against Illyrians and Triballians, and the Thracians on your borders; Philip gave you cloaks to wear, in place of sheepskins, brought you down from the hills to the plains, made you doughty opponents of your neighbouring enemies, so that you trusted now not so much to the natural strength of your villages as to your own courage. Nay, he made you dwellers of cities, and civilized you with good laws and customs. Then of those very tribes to whom you submitted, and by whom you and your goods were harried, he made you masters, no longer slaves and subjects; and he added most of Thrace to Macedonia, and seizing the most convenient coast towns, opened up commerce to your country, and enabled you to work your mines in peace. Then he made you overlords of the Thessalians, before whom you had long died of terror, and humbling the Phocians, made the highroad into Greece broad and easy for you, whereas it had been narrow and difficult. Athens and Thebes, always watching their chance to destroy Macedon, he so completely humbled—ourselves by this time sharing these his labours—that instead of our paying tribute to Athens and obeying Thebes, they had to win from us in turn their right to exist. Then he passed into the Peloponnese, and put all in due order there; and now being declared overlord of all the rest of Greece for the expedition against Persia, he won this new prestige not so much for himself as for all the Macedonian people.

All these noble deeds of my father towards you are great indeed, if looked at by themselves, and yet small, if compared with ours. I inherited from my father a few gold and silver cups, and not so much as sixty talents in his treasure; and of debts owed by Philip as much as five hundred talents, and yet having myself borrowed over and above these another eight hundred, I set forth from that country which hardly maintained you in comfort and at once opened to you the strait of the Hellespont, though the Persians were then masters of the sea; then, crushing with my cavalry Dareius' satraps, I added to your empire all Ionia, all Aeolia, Upper and Lower Phrygia, and Lydia; Miletus I took by seige; all else I took by surrender and gave to you to reap the fruits thereof. All good things from Egypt and Cyrene, which I took without striking a blow, come to you; Coele-Syria, and Palestine and Mesopotamia are your own possessions; Babylon is yours, Bactria, and Susa; the wealth of Lydia, the treasures of Persia, the good things of India, the outer ocean, all are yours; you are satraps, you guards, you captains. So what is left for myself from all these toils save the purple and this diadem? I have taken nothing to myself, nor can anyone show treasures of mine, save these possessions of yours, or what is being safeguarded for you. For there is nothing as concerns myself for which I should reserve them, since I eat the same food that you eat, and have such sleep as you have—and yet I hardly think that I do eat the same food as some of you, who live delicately; I know, moreover, that I wake before you, that you may sleep quietly in your beds.

Yet you may feel that while you were enduring the toils and distresses, I have acquired all this without toil and without distress. But who of you is conscious of having endured more toil for me than I for him? Or see here, let any who carries wounds strip himself and show them; I too will show mine. For I have no part of my body, in front at least, that is left without scars; there is no weapon, used at close quarters, or hurled from afar, of which I do not carry the mark. Nay, I have been wounded by the sword, hand to hand; I have been shot with arrows, I have been struck from a catapult, smitten many a time with stones and clubs, for you, for your glory, for your wealth; I lead you conquerors through every land, every sea, every river, mountain, plain. I married as you married; the children of many of you will be blood-relations of my children. Moreover, if any had debts, I, being no busybody to enquire how they were made, when you were winning so much pay, and acquiring so much plunder, whenever there was plunder after a siege—I have cancelled them all. And further, golden coronals are reminders to the most part of you, both of your bravery and of my high regard—reminders that will never perish. Whosoever has died, his death has been glorious; and splendid has been his burial. To most of them there stand at home brazen statues; their parents are held in esteem, and have been freed from all services and taxes. For while I have led you, not one of you has fallen in flight.

And now I had in mind to send away those of you who are no longer equal to campaigning, to be the envy of all at home; but since you all wish to go home, depart, all of you; and when you reach home, tell them there that this your King, Alexander, victor over Persians, Medes, Bactrians, Sacaeans, conquerer of Uxians, Arachotians, Drangae, master of Parthyaea, Chorasmia, Hyrcania to the Caspian Sea; who crossed the Caucasus beyond the Caspian gates, who crossed the rivers Oxus and Tanais, yes, and the Indus too, that none but Dionysus had crossed, the Hydaspes, Acesines, Hydraotes; and who would further have crossed the Hyphasis, had not you shrunk back; who broke into the Indian Ocean by both mouths of the Indus; who traversed the Gadrosian desert—where none other had passed with an armed force; who in the line of march captured Carmania and the country of the Oreitans; whom, when his fleet had sailed from India to the Persian Sea, you led back again to Susa—tell them, I say, that you deserted him, that you took yourselves off, leaving him to the care of the wild tribes you had conquered. This, when you declare it, will be, no doubt, glorious among men, and pious in the sight of heaven. Begone![557]

He leapt from the platform again and passed swiftly into the royal headquarters. The Macedonians, who had been deeply moved by his speech, simply stood there silent, without purpose, like bereaved children. Neither that day nor the next was he seen. On the third day he summoned picked men among the Persians and began commissioning them. As news that one famous unit after another was passing into Persian hands, the Macedonians broke down. They ran to his quarters, threw their arms in submission before his door, and begged to be let into the presence of the man they had followed through such untold horrors, the man whose incredible triumphs they had also shared, the man they had come so deeply to adore. They wept. Alexander came out. When he saw them humble and loving, he melted; he, too, shed tears. Callines, a famous officer in the superb Companions' cavalry, said:

> This, O King, is what grieves the Macedonians, that you have made Persians your kinsmen and Persians are called 'Alexander's kinsmen,' and they are permitted to kiss you; but no Macedonian has tasted this privilege.[558]

And the King said quickly,

> But all of you I regard as my kinsmen, and so from henceforth I call you.[559]

All who desired to were allowed to kiss him. And they marched off to their camp, singing the victory paean.

The reconciliation that caused that paean of victory grew, at least in symbol, into a wider reconciliation and another song of victory over conflict. For Alexander gave a feast, to which he invited not only his Macedonians but the Persians and men from many other nations of those he now ruled. Some 9,000 guests sat at Alexander's cosmopolitan feast and prepared to break bread together. Greek seers and Persian magi alike officiated. When the hour for wine came, Alexander and those at his table poured the same libations to the gods with wine from the same great bowl; and the whole throng joined them, each group making libation with wine from its own bowl. And they all drank, all in each group from its own common bowl; and they all sang together one paean. Three centuries afterwards it would be related in Greece that Alexander "believed that he came as a heaven-sent governor to all, and as a mediator for the whole world"[560]; that

> those whom he could not persuade to unite with him, he conquered by force of arms, and he brought together into one body all men everywhere, uniting and mixing in one great loving-cup, as it were, men's lives, their characters, their marriages, their very habits of life. He bade them all consider as their fatherland the whole inhabited earth, as their stronghold and protection his camp, as akin to them all good men, and as foreigners only the wicked; they should not distinguish between Grecian and foreigner by Grecian cloak and targe, or scimitar and jacket; but the distinguishing mark of the Grecian should be seen in virtue, and that of the foreigner in iniquity; clothing and food, marriage and manner of life they should regard as common to all, being blended into one by ties of blood and children.[561]

How close to that later report did his words really come? At least he prayed for all sorts of blessings, including *Homonoia* and *Koinonia*, Harmony and Fellowship, in the empire, between Macedonian and Persian. In Alexander's own mind, what did Opis mean? A sacramental initiation into the Cosmopolis he had brought to birth? A quick, shrewd effort to convert his personal reconciliation with the Macedonians into one that would include the Persians and permit one ruler to rule two such different races?

But what, in Homer's mind, had the *Iliad* meant? That the war in which the warrior Achilles found release, work to do, a chance to excell, and fame, was desirable? Or that Ares, god of war, was justly the most hated god on Olympus? Alexander kept the *Iliad* under his pillow while on campaign; and if Homer had not taught him the complexity of that question, he could have learned it from the glories and miseries of his own war, from the field where Achilles had fought to the blood which his men, and he himself, had mixed with the monsoon rains of India. Now he wanted peace, the consent of the governed, and the friendship between the governed which Aristotle knew every polis must have and which Alexander as statesman knew Cosmopolis must therefore have. But Alexander had always shown the ability to use the symbol: whatever he said at Opis, it was not a lecture on political philosophy. It was things recited, things shown, things done.

Meanwhile, he needed the wisdom of Solon and of Lycurgus, too, if he was to bring the genuine peace his victories in war had made him responsible for. A mammoth task of organization faced him. Olympias plagued him with letters, complaining that his regent in Europe, Antipater, was arrogant; and Antipater's constant cry was that the queen mother was high-tempered and interfering. Alexander remarked that Antipater could never understand that one tear of Olympias would outweigh all Antipater's dispatches; and on another occasion, that his mother was exacting a heavy price from him for her nine months' housing of him. He ordered Antipater to join him in Asia with fresh Macedonian troops and sent back the invalided Craterus to take his place. Craterus conducted with him some 10,000 Macedonian veterans, now reconciled with their king and more than willing to go home.

And then, in the autumn of 324, Hephestion, who had been to Alexander what Patroclus had been to Achilles, fell ill at Ecbatana and in seven days was dead. Alexander was wild with grief. For three days he tasted no morsel of food. He would have agreed with Pericles that heroes have the whole earth for their tomb;[562] nevertheless, the body of Hephestion was burned on an immense pyre at Babylon, and 3,000 contestants took part in the funeral games. Alexander assuaged his grief by a winter campaign against the Cossaeans, a hill tribe between Ecbatana and Babylon who lived on brigandage and whom the Persians had failed to bring to heel. The Cossaeans were destroyed.

In the spring Alexander returned to Babylon, where he received envoys from the Libyans; and from Italy, Bruttian, Lucanian, and Etruscan envoys. He ordered an expedition to explore the Caspian Sea. To encourage commerce, he founded another Alexandria at the mouth of the Tigris. He laid plans to plant a colony of Phoenician seafarers on the east coast of the Persian Gulf and began at Babylon a harbor and dockyards for merchantmen: he wanted commerce with India. He planned to lead a joint military and naval expedition to find a route around Arabia to Egypt: he wanted a commercial sea route between Babylon and Egypt. While the fleet was being prepared, he improved the irrigation system of Mesopotamia.

Alexander was still not quite thirty-three. He still radiated the youth, strength, health, and beauty of person that made him seem to those around him so much more alive, more awake, than other men. He would have agreed with Heraclitus that all those who are awake have one ordered universe common to all, whereas in sleep each man turns away from that common world to a private world of his own.[563] Was not Alexander, being among those few who were awake, trying in agony to point out to those who slept, the common universe, the Cosmopolis that was adumbrated around them? Much of his courtesy, his politeness, to others was the politeness of the *polites*, the citizen, of that new and opening world. Aristotle, who saw the difference between the educated man and the uneducated man as the difference between the man awake and the man asleep, could have asked with justifiable pride why on earth his famous pupil should not be wide awake. But it was the pupil, and not the master, who was dealing with the opposite of the *polites*, or citizen; and in Greek that opposite was called *idiotes*. In the context of emergent Cosmopolis, Demosthenes' patriotic tirades were more idiotic than polite. For city-state patriotism had become the private world of idiocy.

Alexander had already proven himself a consummate general, and part of that proof lay not only in what he did with an army to win victory but in what he did as a statesman after victory with those who had submitted. He thought of himself as a Hellene, creating a Hellenized new world, but to many Athenians besides Demosthenes he was an outsider. It would have been hard for any cultivated Athenian in the disillusioned, commercialized Athens of the late fourth century to see himself as Achilles and to feel Achilles acting in himself. Perhaps it would have been hard for him to feel the kind of wonder Odysseus felt when faced with a strange sea and a half-descried coast. Or to feel the urgency of a Solon longing to bring law in place of violence. Alexander did not feel himself a member of Hesiod's race of iron but of an earlier race of heroes. The Mainland Greeks could call him tyrant as they liked: he had at least freed Greece-in-Asia from its Persian master. And no disciple of Aristotle was likely to desire human freedom in the sentimental terms of a Demosthenes. He showed the awareness of Aeschylus, and of Aristotle, that only Zeus was free and that in the last analysis man won freedom only by imitating

439

God, or at least God's act of understanding. He wanted all that polis meant to Pericles, but he knew it could no longer be found in a city-state: he wanted the polis to be a school that civilized and ennobled its members. He was a questioner, like Socrates, but as a king, he was doomed to employ not only wisdom, but force. He hated the obstinate, blind, bestial strife which destroyed polis, the kind of strife that the Peloponnesian War became, that the revolution in Corcyra became, with results fatal for Hellas. He was punctilious in his observances of Greek official religion, as Xenophon had known that warfare made men be; but he knew of religious problems which Xenophon never dreamt of. He could be as cunning, as harsh, as politic as Philip; but one of his many other fathers, Aristotle, had inspired him with a moral nobility, a capacity for disinterested inquiry, and a kind of grace of spirit that Philip did not exhibit.

Above all, Alexander's sureness in performing the symbolic act had turned him into myth long before that hot June in Babylon when he planned to explore, perhaps to annex, the coasts of fabled Arabia. His acts generated meanings, meanings capable of breeding further meanings; and he supplemented his acts, as Odysseus had supplemented his, with dreams, signs, tokens, wingèd words, and prayers, to conquer and grasp and comprehend a world which the sword alone could never wholly conquer, nor the most royal scepter hold. His acts generated meanings as surely as did the acts of any hero in Greek tragedy, whether Orestes or Oedipus, until it became hard to disentangle the historic truth about him from the truth Aristotle had considered more philosophic than history: poetic truth.

Nevertheless, he had thus far failed to weld his empire into one. Labor as he might to pacify, to reconcile, to mediate between men, Cosmopolis throbbed with repressed violence. If he dreamed of all men as brothers under their common father Zeus, with himself as son of Zeus in some special sense, charged to make the will of Zeus the will also of men, yet he was a savior with a sword, and, at least in the myth his actions had created, the knot at Gordium had been cut, not untied. True, he had become Lord of Asia; but in what sense Lord? A Lord who brought what appeared, indeed, when the libations were being poured at Opis, like Harmony and Fellowship throughout Cosmopolis. But a Lord who, battle by battle, found himself not only breaking judiciously Darius' resistance at Issus but murdering Black Clitus in drunken rage, murdering

Parmenion with the swords of others, massacring natives in his northeast provinces, and massacring even more savagely in India, so that part of the myth he had already created before this year of 323 was that of blood and agonizing death, of depopulation, of drunken orgy and barbarous vandalism, of an insane striving for world conquest, and above all of the paranoiac, sacrilegious hybris of a man determined to be God. Did part of the tenseness, the irritability, which he had given vent to in these later years, come from the horrified discovery that, though he had indeed forced open Asia's door to the more rapid expansion of Greek commerce in commodities and ideas, yet his dream of a Cosmopolis worthy to be the polis of Zeus was an empty dream? That his attack on Persia had not even exorcised the violence that had so degraded Hellas, as Isocrates had perhaps hoped his father Philip might have exorcised it? That to reconcile men would require something other than a sword or even something opposite to it? And that now all one could do was shed more blood, this time in Arabia?

Around the beginning of June, Alexander and his friends sacrificed, partly in thanksgiving for many blessings already received and partly because his seers were troubled by curious omens of misfortune. Then they feasted and drank late into the night. He started to retire but a trusted Companion named Medius persuaded him to come with him for a smaller, final party. The royal diaries reported that he drank merrily with Medius, bathed and slept, dined with him and again drank late, then again bathed. Then he slept where he was because he felt unwell. He was running a fever. But he continued to confer with his officers about the Arabian expedition, which was due to leave in four days' time. It was hot. They took him across the wide Euphrates in a boat to a garden, and there he bathed and again rested. Next day he lay in his room, talking to Medius, and planned to meet his officers the following morning. Though he ran a high fever the whole night, he nevertheless kept his morning appointment with his admiral, Nearchus, and the others and gave directions for the great expedition. The fever continued, but next day the conferring continued too. By night he was very ill; yet on the day after that he was still planning with his officers. But the following day, he ordered his officers to wait in the court. He was brought back across the river to the palace. When the officers followed and were ushered in, he knew them but he could no longer speak.

For two nights and two days more the fever raged. The royal diaries reported that his soldiers begged to be admitted to see him. They filed past. He could not speak, but his eyes showed he knew them. In the temple of Sarapis, an Egyptian god who often gave medical advice, some of the king's friends kept vigil. They asked the god whether the king should be brought to the temple too, for prayer and healing. The oracle replied that it would be better for Alexander if he remained where he was. Meanwhile, neither in his recent conferences nor earlier had he dealt with the problem of succession in case of his death. Roxana was now with child. Was he counting on a son? On his own health, which always after illness had returned? On his own extraordinary good fortune in battle, that could be counted on in Arabia as elsewhere? According to some reports his Companions, before the fever had stolen his power of speech, asked him to whom he left his empire, and he replied, "to the strongest."[564] Others said that he, who had so lately ordered the magnificent athletic contests at the funeral of Hephestion, added that he foresaw a great funeral contest on his own death. Did he speak in despair? In weariness? In grim irony?

CHRONOLOGICAL SUMMARY

Circa 2000-1700	Achaean invasion of Mainland Greece.
c. 1700	Destruction of Minoan palaces at Crete.
c. 1600-1500	Crete the entrepôt for Egypt and the Aegean.
c. 1600-1100	Mycenaean Age in Mainland Greece.
c. 1400	Collapse of Minoan power.
c. 1200-1180	Trojan War.
c. 1150	Dorian invasion; coming of iron; beginning of Dark Age; development of Phoenician trade; migrations from Mainland Greece to Asia Minor.
c. 900-800(?)	Construction of Greek alphabet in Ionia. Composition of the *Iliad*. Introduction of cavalry to Greece.
c. 800-700(?)	Hesiod. Composition of the *Odyssey*.
c. 800-600	Growth of city-state. Development from monarchy to aristocracy to, sometimes, tyranny. Greek colonization.
c. 800-500	Ionian school of lyric poetry.
776	First Olympic Festival.
c. 740-720	Spartan conquest of Messenia.
701	Phoenicia conquered by Assyria.
c. 700-600	Development of coinage. Tyrtaeus.
c. 700-500	Ionian school of philosophy.

c. 700	First hoplites.
c. 640	Second Messenian War.
c. 632	Cylon tries to seize Acropolis.
621	Dracon's legal reforms at Athens.
c. 600	Phocaeans found or take over Marseilles; tap Rhone River route to northern Europe.
c. 594	Solon archon of Athens.
c. 585-546	Thales *floruit.*
574	Phoenicia taken over by Chaldea.
c. 570	Athenian conquest of Salamis.
c. 561	Pisistratus becomes tyrant of Athens.
c. 560-546	Ionia a protectorate of Croesus of Lydia.
c. 555-552(?)	First exile of Pisistratus.
c. 552	Pisistratus's restoration and second exile. Cyrus the Great of Persia conquers Medes.
546	Cyrus conquers Lydia.
c. 539	Cyrus takes Babylon.
529	Death of Cyrus.
c. 527	Death of Pisistratus. Hippias and Hipparchus succeed him at Athens.
525	Cambyses of Persia annexes Egypt.
514	Hipparchus assassinated.
512	Darius of Persia conquers Thrace to Danube.
510	Spartan army liberates Athens from Hippias.
508-507	Sparta fails to restore aristocracy at Athens. Clisthenes destroys political power of tribes.
506	Attica repels attack by Peloponnesians, Boeotians, and Chalcidians. Plants outsettlers.
c. 505-366	Peloponnesian League.
499	Ionia revolts from Persian Empire.
498-438	Pindar *floruit.*

c. 498	Athens at war with Aegina. Ionians, Athenians, Eretrians take Sardis and are then defeated.
494, SUMMER	Persia's fleet defeats Ionia's at Lade. Miletus razed.
493, SUMMER	Collapse of Ionian Revolt.
492	Darius leads first Persian expedition against Mainland Greece.
490, SPRING	Darius leads second Persian expedition against Mainland Greece.
490, SEPTEMBER(?)	Battle of Marathon.
489	Miltiades defeated at Paros. Prosecuted at Athens.
485	Athens ostracizes Xanthippus.
484	Aeschylus's first victory in dramatic competition.
483-482	Athens ostracizes Aristides. Themistocles turns Athens to the sea.
481-461	Panhellenic league against Persia.
480	Xerxes leads third Persian expedition against Mainland Greece. Athens recalls Xanthippus and Aristides under general amnesty. Sicilians defeat Carthaginians at Himera.
480, AUGUST(?)	Battles of Thermopylae and Artemisium.
480, SEPTEMBER(?)	Battle of Salamis.
479, JUNE	Mardonius invades Attica.
479, AUGUST 27(?)	Battles of Plataea and Mycale.
c. 479-478	Xanthippus besieges Sestos.
478-476	Rebuilding of walls of Athens.
476	Foundation of League of Delos.
475	Cimon takes Eion, near Amphipolis.
473-472	Democratic revolts in Peloponnese.
472	Production of Aeschylus's *Persians*, with Pericles as choregus.

472	Themistocles ostracized in clash with Cimon.
470-469	Naxos revolts from League of Delos; is reduced by Athens.
468	Aeschylus defeated by Sophocles in dramatic competition.
c. 468	Cimon destroys Persia's fleet at Eurymedon.
464	Death of Xerxes. Accession of Artaxerxes. Themistocles at Persian court.
464, SUMMER	Spartan earthquake. Helot rebellion.
c. 462	Themistocles dies in exile.
462-461	Laws passed depriving Areopagus of power to oversee Athenian constitution.
c. 461-456	Construction of Long Walls from Athens to Piraeus.
461	Cimon ostracized. Ephialtes assassinated. Pericles heads democratic party at Athens.
459	Athens aids Egypt's revolt against Persia.
458	Production of Aeschylus's *Oresteia*.
457	Spartan alliance defeats Athenians at Tanagra. Athens gains control of Boeotia and Phocis at Oenophyta. Cimon recalled from exile.
455	Production of Euripides' first tragedy.
454	Failure of Athens' expedition to Egypt. Treasury of League of Delos moved to Athens.
451-446	Five-year truce between Athens and Sparta.
450-449	Death of Cimon on campaign.
449-448	Peace of Callias between Athens and Persia begins.
c. 448	Pericles tries to convene Panhellenic Congress.
447	Athens loses Boeotia at Coronea, and finally control of central Greece.
447-432	Building of Parthenon.
446-445	Thirty Years' Peace between Athens and Sparta begins.

446	Athens subjects Euboea. Megara revolts.
c. 446	Herodotus reads his *History* at Athens.
c. 444	Athens ostracizes Damon, Pericles' friend.
443	Pericles founds Thurii.
440-439	Revolt and reduction of Samos and Byzantium. Pericles' first funeral oration.
438	Phidias's statue of Athena set up in Parthenon.
435	Sea fight between Corinth and Corcyra over Epidamnus.
434	Athens forbids Allies to coin money.
433	Athens renews treaties with Leontini and Rhegium. Alliance between Megara and Corinth. Athenians assist Corcyra against Corinth. Revolt of Potidaea from League of Delos.
432	Prosecution at Athens of Anaxagoras, Pericles' friend. Athens closes markets to Megara.
431-421	Peloponnesian War.
431	Athens expels Aeginetans and resettles island.
c. 431	Athens exiles Phidias.
430	Phormio fights Peloponnesians in Gulf of Corinth. Pericles' second funeral oration (March).
c. 429-422	Cleon foremost political leader at Athens.
429, AUTUMN	Death of Pericles.
428-427	Revolt of Mitylene.
427-425	Corcyrean revolution.
427	Surrender of Plataea. Production of Aristophanes' first comedy, the *Banqueters*.
426	Demosthenes invades Aetolia.
425	Athenians capture Pylos.
424	Athenians capture Cythera and Nisaea. Defeated at Delium. Brasidas leads Spartan expedition to Thrace; takes Amphipolis.

447

	Congress of Gela, in Sicily. Thucydides, the historian, exiled by Athens.
c. 424	2,000 freed Helots disappear in Sparta.
423	Athens makes one-year truce with Sparta. Production of Aristophanes' *Clouds*.
422	Cleon and Brasidas killed at Amphipolis.
421	Peace of Nicias between Athens and Peloponnese. Production of Aristophanes' *Peace*. Athens quells revolt of Scione in Chalcidice.
421-420	Defensive alliance between Athens and Sparta.
420	Alcibiades effects anti-Spartan alliance in Peloponnese.
418, AUGUST	Anti-Spartan alliance defeated at Mantinea. Argos makes treaty with Sparta.
416	Athenians massacre Melians.
415, C. JUNE 7	Desecration of Herms at Athens.
415, C. MIDSUMMER	Athens launches expedition to Sicily.
415, C. AUTUMN	Alcibiades ordered home for trial; escapes to Sparta; sentenced to death at Athens, *in absentia*.
414	Sparta intervenes in Sicily. Production of Aristophanes' *Birds*.
413	Sparta takes Decelea. Second Athenian expedition to Sicily. Massacre at Mycalessus by Thracian mercenaries. Athenian disaster in Sicily. Execution of Nicias and Demosthenes.
412	Athenian allies revolt.
411, JANUARY-FEBRUARY	Production of Aristophanes' *Lysistrata*.
411, JUNE	Council of 400 at Athens. 'Polis' at Samos elects Alcibiades general.
411, SEPTEMBER	Revolt of Euboea. Fall of Council of 400.
411, AUTUMN	Moderate constitution set up at Athens.

410	Athenians defeat Peloponnesian fleet at Cyzicus. Restoration of democracy at Athens.
409	Athenians lose Pylos and Nisaea.
407, SUMMER	Alcibiades, elected general by Athenian Assembly, returns to Athens.
407	Alcibiades' fleet trapped at Notion. Alcibiades flees to Hellespont. Conon trapped at Mitylene. Erectheum completed.
c. 406-367	Dionysius I tyrant at Syracuse.
406	Defeat of Peloponnesians at Arginusae. Trial of Athenian generals.
c. 406	Death of Euripides at Macedonian court.
405	Athenian disaster at Aegospotami. Production of Aristophanes' Frogs.
404	Fall of Athens' Long Walls. Thirty Tyrants installed at Athens. Death of Alcibiades and Theramenes.
403	Fall of Thirty Tyrants. General amnesty at Athens.
401, MARCH 6	Xenophon and the Ten Thousand begin their March Up Country.
401, SEPTEMBER	Cyrus slain at Cunaxa.
399, FEBRUARY	Trial of Socrates.
399, MARCH	End of Anabasis. Xenophon exiled by Athens.
394	Xenophon fights under Agesilaus against Athens at battle of Coronea.
c. 392	Isocrates founds school at Athens.
387	Celts seize Rome. Plato's first visit to Syracuse.
c. 387	Plato founds Academy at Athens.
386	Peace of Antalcidas, or King's Peace. Thessaly united under Jason of Pherae.
378-377	Second Athenian Confederacy.
371, JULY	Epaminondas defeats Spartans at Leuctra.

449

370-369	First and second Boeotian invasions of Peloponnese.
369-368	Pelopidas of Thebes invades Thessaly.
367	Dionysius I wins first dramatic prize at Athens. Dies. Succeeded by Dionysius II. Plato's second visit to Sicily.
c. 367	Philip of Macedonia taken to Thebes as hostage. Athens terminates Xenophon's exile.
c. 366	Third Boeotian expedition to Peloponnese. Aristotle enters Plato's Academy.
365-359	Perdiccas III active in Macedonia.
365	Xenophon returns to Athens.
362	Epaminondas defeats Sparta at Mantinea and dies in battle.
361	Plato's third visit to Syracuse.
359	Philip becomes regent, then king, of Macedonia.
357	Philip tricks Athens at Amphipolis. Dion takes over Syracuse.
356-346	The Sacred War.
356	Athenians driven from Chalcidice. Philip conquers Potidaea, Pydna, and defeats Illyrians.
354	Philomelus of Phocis commits suicide; Onomarchus takes over. Murder of Dion of Syracuse. Demosthenes' first oration in Athenian Assembly.
c. 354	Death of Xenophon.
353	Philip takes Methone.
352	Philip puts Thessaly in order. Marches to Thermopylae.
351	Demosthenes' *First Philippic*.
348-347	Philip takes Olynthus. Coins golden philips. Death of Plato.
c. 347	Aristotle leaves Plato's Academy for Assus.

346	Philip elected president of Amphictyony after ending Sacred War. Isocrates' *Address to Philip*.
343-342	Aristotle goes to Macedonian court as tutor to Philip's son, Alexander.
341	Philip dethrones Cersobleptes of Thrace, invades Chersonese, attacks Byzantium.
338, AUGUST(?)	Philip wins control of Greece at Chaeronea.
337	Philip establishes League of Corinth.
336	Philip assassinated at Aegae. Succeeded by Alexander. Accession of Darius III to Persian throne.
335	Alexander razes Thebes.
c. 335	Aristotle founds Lyceum at Athens.
334, SPRING	Alexander opens campaign in Asia. Battle of the Granicus.
333	Alexander at Gordium.
333, NOVEMBER	Battle of Issus.
332, JANUARY-JULY	Siege of Tyre.
332, WINTER	Alexander becomes Pharaoh of Egypt.
331, WINTER	Alexander founds Alexandria in Egypt and visits Ammon.
331, AUTUMN	Battle of Gaugamela (October 1). Babylon surrenders to Alexander. Sparta defeated at Megalopolis.
330	Alexander takes Persepolis. Death of Darius III Philotas and Parmenion executed.
329	Bessus of Bactria betrayed to Alexander.
328, SUMMER	Alexander murders Clitus.
327	Pages' conspiracy. Alexander marries Roxana. Start of Indian expedition (summer).
326	Alexander crosses the Indus. Battle of the Hydaspes, or Jhelum, River. Army balks at Beas River (July). Sails down Jhelum (November).

325, JULY   Alexander enters Indian Ocean.

324   Restoration of Greek exiles proclaimed (July-
                              August). Alexander marries Darius' daugh-
                              ter, Barsine. Alexander at Opis. Death of
                              Hephestion (autumn).

323   Alexander dies at Babylon. Aristotle charged
                              with impiety; flees to Euboea.

322   Death of Aristotle.

BIBLIOGRAPHICAL NOTE

THE READER of the foregoing pages may wish to know more about the events of Greek history than this book has told him. He may therefore wish me to supply him with some sort of reading list. Of the hundreds of books by modern scholars which I read in preparation for writing this history, and of the hundreds of others I had to consult, there are indeed some that I am tempted to urge on anybody who has been my traveling companion thus far. But which books I would recommend to any given reader would depend on the special interests this history might have awakened in him.

If the many omissions in my narrative leave the reader hungry for more historical detail, I would recommend that he try one of four general histories of Greece written by modern historians. Perhaps the best known in this country is J. B. Bury: *A History of Greece* (2d ed., London, 1913). But in several ways this work has been recently superseded by N. G. L. Hammond: *A History of Greece* (Oxford, 1959). Hammond's text is enlivened and illuminated by a happy use of quotation.

Those who read French will find a more readable account than either in Gustave Glotz: *Histoire Grecque* (with the collaboration of Robert Cohen; 4 vols., Paris, 1925-38). Glotz exhibits the capacity for synthesis so frequently found in French historians. But if the reader chooses Glotz, he will confront several difficulties. First, volumes III and IV are out of print and exceedingly difficult to find. Secondly, although, unlike Bury and Hammond, Glotz gives an extensive bibliography for each chapter, the titles in these bibliographies are listed with comments addressed rather to the scholar than to the general reader. Thirdly, although Glotz is equipped with that indispensable tool, historical imagination, his inferences seem to me sometimes bolder than the evidence he cites can justify. Despite this word of caution I heartily recommend Glotz's history for a general view of the subject.

Above all three of these works, in terms of total intellectual achievement, I would rate George Grote's A *History of Greece* (12 vols., London, 1846-56). It was written before a century of historical and archaeological labor had further clarified many problems. It was written before Schliemann had unearthed Troy and Mycenae, before Evans had uncovered Knossos. It was written by an English Radical, whose view of the world now seems fatally limited, and this limitation becomes especially apparent in his treatment, for example, of Demosthenes and Philip. But his history has greatness, and it is an intellectual scandal that it should now be out of print. Fortunately, many good public libraries still possess Grote's work.

These general histories are the only works by moderns that I shall list here. What I really recommend to my reader is to read or re-read the Greeks themselves, and this for two reasons. First, nobody today could construct a history of Hellenic culture without the aid of the thousands of scholars, whether in ancient Alexandria or in our own modern world, who have labored with the pen and with the spade to render the documents available and ready for use. But too often we know what the Greeks said chiefly by knowing what our modern scholars say they said. Only a first-hand knowledge of the text brings the commentary into perspective. Secondly, it is not possible to narrate or even understand the history of a culture without immersion in that culture. The precise date of a battle cannot matter much if we have no insight into what led men to fight it.

I was not led to write *The Will of Zeus* by what modern historians have written, much as I owe to them, but by a direct and sometimes shattering encounter with the Greeks themselves. And even then I would not have written but for the hope that I could help bring about direct encounter or re-encounter between the Greeks and my reader, an encounter that would necessarily differ in many ways from my own.

I therefore urge the reader of this Bibliographical Note to turn next to the Greeks themselves. If he has already read them, he will already know they bear many readings. I make bold to urge that he read them as Socrates consulted the god at Delphi and not as Xenophon consulted him—that is, that he listen and reflect rather than try to discover the answers to specific questions he has already formulated, on the assumption that we moderns already know all the good questions. Ideally, of course, he should read them in the original Greek. However, the past few decades have fortunately witnessed the translation of many Greek works, and in many of these translations the intellectual light shines through with unmistakable brilliance. No snobbish talk about originals versus translations should deter the modern reader who cannot read Greek. If he wants still richer rewards, he can reflect that many men, from the Romans to ourselves, have learned Greek, even late in life.

The Greek authors listed below appear in the Loeb Classical Library, now published in this country by the Harvard University Press. It is their works on which I have drawn most heavily for this history. For the reader who knows even a little Greek, or will take the time to learn a little, the Loeb Classics offer the advantage of a double text: Greek on the left-hand page and an English translation on the right. The Loeb translations were made by many scholars and, as one might expect, are in varying degree successful. All or most of the extant works of the following authors are available in Loeb:

Aeschylus	Homer
Aristophanes	Isocrates
Aristotle	Pindar
Arrian	Plato
Demosthenes	Plutarch
Euripides	Sophocles
Herodotus	Thucydides
Hesiod	Xenophon

I have also drawn on the following collections of poems in Loeb:

> *The Greek Anthology*
> *Greek Elegy and Iambus*
> *Lyra Graeca*

A convenient collection of the fragments which survive from the writings of the pre-Socratic philosophers can be found in Kathleen Freeman's *Ancilla to the Pre-Socratic Philosophers* (Oxford, 1948). These fragments appear in English, keyed in with the Greek texts published in *Die Fragmente der Vorsokratiker*, edited by Hermann Diels (3 vols., Berlin, 1951-52).

Finally, I should like to call attention to certain other translations, some of them old favorites, some of them quoted in this history, some of them available also in paperback editions. Each of these translations has in some way or ways achieved great success in a difficult art:

Of Aeschylus, Euripides, and Sophocles—
> *The Complete Greek Tragedies*, edited by David Grene and Richmond Lattimore, 4 vols., Chicago, 1959.

Of Aristophanes—
> *The Complete Greek Drama*, edited by Whitney J. Oates and Eugene O'Neill, Jr., New York, 1938. Vol. II.

Herodotus: *The Persian Wars*, translated by George Rawlinson, New York (Modern Library), 1942.

Hesiod: *Works and Days, Theogony, The Shield of Herakles*, translated by Richmond Lattimore, Ann Arbor, Mich., 1959.

Homer: *The Iliad*, translated by Richmond Lattimore, Chicago, 1951.

Homer: *The Odyssey*, translated by T. E. Shaw, *i.e.*, T. E. Lawrence, New York, 1932.

Pindar: *Pythian Odes*, translated by H. T. Wade-Gery and C. M. Bowra, London, 1928.

Plato: *The Dialogues of Plato*, translated by Benjamin Jowett, 2 vols., New York, 1937.

Thucydides: *The Peloponnesian War*, translated by Thomas Hobbes, edited by David Grene, 2 vols., Ann Arbor, Mich., 1959.

Xenophon: *Anabasis: The March Up Country*, translated by W. H. D. Rouse, Ann Arbor, Mich., 1958.

And now, if you, my reader, choose to embark, or re-embark, on these Greek seas, may you, like Odysseus, see the cities and learn the minds of many men before you find home.

S. B.

NOTES

Books not fully identified in the Notes will be found so identified in the Bibliographical Note, p. 453.

CHAPTER ONE

1. If indeed the same poet wrote both poems. But was either the *Iliad* or the *Odyssey* the work of one man? The Homeric question is still a matter of vigorous debate.
2. Homer: *Iliad* I, 5. Loeb.
3. Ibid., XII, 5 ff.
4. A. Jardé in *The Formation of the Greek People*, New York, 1926, p. 28, gives this list, except for the lynx and the roe; but he implies that the lion, leopard, and panther were not found south of Macedonia in classical times. Yet see Herodotus VII, 125-26, on the lion. And all three species may well have ranged in Greece in 2000 B.C., when the Achaeans were probably arriving there. The δορκάς, or roe, was hunted in the Peloponnese in the fourth century, according to Xenophon: *Anabasis* V, iii, 10 (translated in Loeb as gazelle, but as roe in Liddell and Scott: *Greek-English Dictionary*, 8th ed.). Xenophon (*Scripta Minora*, On Hunting XI, 1, Loeb) claims that "lions, leopards, lynxes, panthers, and bears" were found in his day, not only in Thrace and in Asia Minor, but on Mount Pindus, the mountain range separating Thessaly from Epirus.
5. A. Jardé: *The Formation of the Greek People*, New York, 1926, p. 48.
6. Or destroyed by earthquake. This is a moot point among modern historians of Minoan civilization.
7. Homer: *Odyssey* I, 57-59. Loeb.
8. Ibid., V, 462-63.
9. Ibid., XVII, 326-27.
10. Ibid., XIX, 409.
11. Ibid., VII, 307.
12. Ibid., XIX, 118.
13. Ibid., IX, 316-17.

14. Ibid., IX, 502-5.
15. Ibid., VIII, 147-48.
16. Ibid., XXIV, 36-94.
17. Ibid., I, 302.
18. Ibid., XXIV, 196-98.
19. Ibid., XXIV, 433-35.
20. Ibid., III, 236-38.
21. Ibid., I, 205.
22. Ibid., IX, 19-20.
23. Ibid., XIX, 395-96.
24. Ibid., X, 305.
25. Ibid., II, 117-18.
26. Ibid., IX, 174-76.
27. Ibid., IX, 229.
28. Ibid., XII, 49-52.
29. Ibid., XII, 191.
30. Ibid., XII, 249-50.
31. Ibid., XII, 258-59.
32. Ibid., X, 436-37.
33. Ibid., IX, 112-15.
34. Ibid., IX, 276.
35. Ibid., I, 65-7.
36. Ibid., XIII, 293-95.
37. Ibid., XIII, 332.
38. Ibid., XIII, 299.
39. Ibid., XIII, 310.
40. Ibid., III, 48.
41. Ibid., XVI, 160-61.
42. Ibid., XVI, 178-79.
43. Ibid., XVI, 187-89.
44. Ibid., I, 320-21.
45. Ibid., I, 324.
46. Ibid., III, 23.
47. Ibid., III, 26-7.
48. Ibid., XIX, 560-61.
49. Ibid., XIX, 29; XVII, 57.
50. Ibid., XVIII, 130-31.

CHAPTER TWO

51. The Greeks of the Dark Ages, roughly the eleventh, tenth, and ninth centuries before Christ, had less historical understanding of what Minoan Crete had been, of what Mycenae had signified, than contemporary archaeologists have now acquired by 'digs' and by toilsome study of the forgotten writing of Minos' commercial empire. And the Greeks of Thucydides' day knew little more of Minoan Crete and Mycenae than their ancestors of the Dark Ages had known.

52. Margaret Wason: *Class Struggles in Ancient Greece*, London, 1947, pp. 19-31. Even if Wason underestimates the military importance of iron,

there is still a chance that it was not iron weapons but iron fighting men that the Achaean-Pelasgian society could not beat back.

53. That is, to the style which modern archaeologists call "Orientalizing."

54. The origins of the earlier Greek alphabets are matters of dispute.

55. On the moot question as to how Homer's *Iliad* and *Odyssey* were transmitted to modern times, see Cedric Whitman's discussion in *Homer and the Heroic Tradition*, Cambridge, Mass., 1957, particularly chap. 4.

56. A glance at a map of the Mediterranean will suffice to confirm this judgment.

57. The saddle would not be used for several centuries yet, although in the fourth century Xenophon would report the use of a pad.

58. Homer: *Iliad* I, 159. Loeb.

59. *Greek Elegy and Iambus* II, p. 99, Archilochus 2. Loeb.

60. Ἐκεχειρία. Glotz: *Histoire Grecque*, vol. I, p. 515. Justice often expressed itself in legal forms that we today associate with those other Middle Ages, our own, in Western Europe, centuries after the Greek polis had flourished and had perished.

61. The Romans would translate this phrase into Magna Graecia.

62. The simile is Plato's. *Phaedo*, 109B. Loeb.

63. The chronology of early coining by city-states is a vexed question. See Charles Seltman: *Greek Coins*, 2d ed., London, 1955, pp. 13-44.

64. I use here the date given by H. L. Lorimer in *Homer and the Monuments*, London, 1950. See chap. 5.

65. Probably, but not certainly. We first encounter the term in Archilochus of Paros, who applies it to the Lydian king, Gyges, a usurper.

66. Some modern scholars have doubted whether the *Theogony* was the work of Hesiod.

67. Poets presumably have as much right to tell their readers how to farm as scientists have. Naturally they sing when they do it.

68. Hesiod: *Theogony*, 737. Loeb.

69. Ibid., 440.

70. Ibid., 117.

71. Hesiod: *Works and Days*, 91. Loeb.

72. Ibid., 112-13.

73. Ibid., 152.

74. Ibid., 174-78. If the modern reader is tempted to reply that every generation believes that things are going to ruin, he might perhaps remember that sometimes it is true. The Minoan culture really had gone to ruin; and its Mainland derivative, the Mycenaean culture, had later gone there too.

75. In the fifth century the historian Herodotus guessed (Herodotus II, 53) that Homer and Hesiod lived not earlier than the ninth century. Modern historians cannot agree on the dates for either Homer or Hesiod. See, for example, Richmond Lattimore, pp. 12-13 of the Introduction to his translation of Hesiod, as against H. G. Evelyn-White in the Introduction to his translation of Hesiod in the Loeb edition.

76. Hesiod: *Theogony*, 220-22. Loeb.

77. Hesiod: *Works and Days*, 252-55. Loeb.

78. Ibid., 222-24.

79. Ibid., 6.
80. Ibid., 276-80.
81. Ibid., 289-90.
82. Ibid., 303-4.
83. Ibid., 320.
84. Ibid., 382.
85. Ibid., 397-98.
86. Ibid., 11-26.
87. Hesiod: *Theogony*, 224-25. Loeb.
88. Ibid., 226-30.
89. Or some disciple who put the words of the poem in Hesiod's mouth.
90. Hesiod: *Theogony*, 22-34. Loeb.
91. The reader will note that I have nowhere explained or assumed that the Greek gods were figments of the Greek imagination. I have refrained from doing so, partly because so many modern historians have done it at length, and partly because none of them has offered evidence that the gods did not exist. We cannot here fall back on the statistical method, since we do not know whether the Greeks who reported seeing a god have been as yet outnumbered by moderns who have asserted there were no gods to see. In any case the gods were often clothed in mist. I have decided to report in this volume what the Greeks reported, and I still seek evidence that they lied or were mistaken.

CHAPTER THREE

92. *Homeric Hymns* III, To Delian Apollo, 147-55. Loeb. The hymn to the Delian Apollo was probably sung as early as the eighth century.
93. *Greek Elegy and Iambus* II, p. 101, Archilochus 6. Loeb. The Saians were a people of Thrace.
94. Ibid., II, p. 175, Archilochus 118. F. L. Lucas, in *Greek Poetry for Everyman*, Boston, 1956, p. 234, translates this epigram: "Many a trick the wise fox knows;/ But the hedgehog has *one*, worth a lot of those."
95. Alcaeus, Fragment 12, in C. M. Bowra: *Greek Lyric Poetry*, Oxford, 1936, p. 161.
96. Ibid., Alcaeus, Fragment 93, p. 151.
97. *Lyra Graeca* II, p. 181, Anacreon 84. Loeb.
98. Ibid., I, p. 187, Sappho 2.
99. Ibid., I, p. 263, Sappho 111.
100. *Greek Elegy and Iambus* I, p. 201, Xenophanes 11. Loeb.
101. Ibid., I, p. 211, Xenophanes 32.
102. Ibid., I, p. 201, Xenophanes 15.
103. Ibid., I, p. 203, Xenophanes 16.
104. Ibid., I, p. 207, Xenophanes 23.
105. Ibid., I, p. 67, Tyrtaeus 6.
106. Tradition could later point to similarities between the Cretan and Spartan constitutions as evidence that Lycurgus did go to Crete. See K. M. T. Chrimes: *Ancient Sparta*, Manchester, 1949.
107. Herodotus I, 65. Loeb.
108. Presumably. But modern historians know little of the Dorian invasion.
109. Otto Kern, ed.: *Orphicorum Fragmenta*, Berlin, 1922, p. 65.

110. This custom of Sparta's often stirs the incredulity of modern historians. Yet it is perfectly consonant with other Spartan customs that modern historians cheerfully accept.

111. Homer: *Iliad* VI, 208. Lang, Leaf, and Myers translation, New York (Modern Library), 1935.

112. *Greek Elegy and Iambus*, I, pp. 69, 71, Tyrtaeus 10, lines 1-2, 27-32. Loeb.

113. Xenophon: *Scripta Minora*, Constitution of the Lacedaemonians IV, 2. Loeb.

114. Xenophon: *Scripta Minora*, Constitution of the Lacedaemonians XI, 3, states that the color made the tunic bear "least resemblance to women's clothing." But Plutarch in his *Moralia* III, Ancient Customs of the Spartans, 238F, says it was the color that least showed blood.

115. This synoecism was traditionally ascribed to Theseus.

116. The areas are from A. Jardé: *The Formation of the Greek People*, New York, 1926, p. 145.

117. It has sometimes been suggested that it must have been the landlord, not the tenant, who received one-sixth, since no peasant could have lived on so small a portion of his crop. But would a landlord, in a country where arable land was as scarce as it was in Greece, give up five-sixths of a crop for the factor of labor alone? In Iran today a tenant may receive anywhere from one-tenth to nine-tenths, but this depends on the province the land is in, and even more on who provides the seed, the draft animals, the tools, the manure, the irrigation water; on how much labor the particular crop requires; and finally on how scarce farm labor is. See Ann K. S. Lambton: *Landlord and Peasant in Persia*, London, 1953.

118. *Greek Elegy and Iambus* I, p. 143, Solon 28a. Loeb.

119. Ibid., I, p. 121, Solon 4, line 33.

120. The term elegy was a purely metrical term.

121. *Greek Elegy and Iambus* I, p. 151, Solon 36, lines 10-12. Loeb.

122. Ibid., I, p. 151, Solon 36, line 16.

123. Ibid., I, pp. 149, 151, Solon 36, lines 3-7.

124. H. T. Wade-Gery: *Essays in Greek History*, Oxford, 1958, p. 13.

125. *Greek Elegy and Iambus* I, p. 105, quoting from Suidas' Lexicon, on Solon. Loeb. Author's translation of μηδὲν ἄγαν.

CHAPTER FOUR

126. Αἰσυμνήτης, judge, umpire—a not uncommon Greek device.

127. Known in modern histories of Greek art as the archaic smile.

128. The 6,000 may have represented the necessary quorum out of which a majority sufficed to ostracize. On this point authorities differ.

129. Herodotus I, 53. Loeb.

130. Ibid., I, 90.

131. Ibid., I, 91.

132. Glotz, in his *Histoire Grecque*, vol. II, p. 18, believes he got as far as the Volga.

133. Ibid., vol. II, pp. 19-20. But Hammond (A *History of Greece*, p. 178) thinks Ionia's grievances were less economic than political.

134. Herodotus VI, 44. Loeb.

135. Aeschylus: *Agamemnon*, 659-60. Grene-Lattimore. Of the Achaeans, wrecked when returning from triumph over Troy.

136. Glotz's estimate. *Histoire Grecque*, vol. II, p. 33.

137. Herodotus VI, 100. Loeb. Glotz (*Histoire Grecque*, vol. II, p. 34) says 2,000, but does not defend his correction of Herodotus.

138. Herodotus (VI, 106, Loeb) says "the day after he left Athens."

139. Herodotus (VI, 112, Loeb) says they "charged at a run [δρόμῳ ἵεντο]." Some modern historians object that the Greeks could not run a mile with weapons and armor weighing around sixty pounds and still have strength for a hand-to-hand combat. Also that the long run would disorder their line, a line they traditionally counted on presenting unbroken, shield to shield.

But the Greek line might have been even further disordered if it had advanced at a walk under a shower of Persian arrows, when the Greeks themselves were without archers. The Greek strategy was to close quickly with the Persians. As to the objection that they would arrive too exhausted for hand-to-hand combat, the assertion is risky in view of the hard exercise and frugal fare to which the Greeks were accustomed from childhood upward. But actually δρόμῳ is often translated from Greek military histories as "at the double," or at a dogtrot.

It has been objected that the range of Persian bowshot was far under a mile and that there was hence no point in running until the Greeks came within range. But there is strong reason to suppose that the Greeks had other motives for a quick advance than to diminish the period of time during which Persian weapons could kill Greeks but Greek weapons could not kill Persians. It was to the advantage of the Greeks to catch the Persians at the vulnerable moment of embarkation and to catch those who expected to march south by land when these were ready to march but had not had time to get clear. Once the Greeks were detected advancing, it was to their advantage on both these scores to strike quickly.

140. Later Greek historians differ widely on the number in the Persian camp. Glotz (*Histoire Grecque*, vol. II, pp. 37-8) holds that, fearing reinforcements from Sparta, the Persians had begun re-embarking in order to sail around Sunium and attack the city of Athens. He suggests that the Persian army which fought the Greeks outnumbered the Greeks by "at least two to one."

141. Pausanias: *Description of Greece* I, xxxii, 5. Loeb.

142. Glotz reasonably follows Diodorus Siculus on the question of an alliance (*Histoire Grecque*, vol. II, p. 45, note 13).

143. Or, more precisely, nearby Mycenae.

144. The metaphor is that of Aeschylus in the *Persians*, line 72. Grene-Lattimore.

145. Glotz's estimates (*Histoire Grecque*, vol. II, pp. 49-50). Hammond (*A History of Greece*, p. 228) estimates the number "in the region of 500,000." A few decades after the invasion, Herodotus believed that the combined land and sea forces of Xerxes, including the recruits he picked up in Europe, ran to 2,641,610. He guessed that this fighting force was supported by an equal number of service troops and he therefore brought the grand total by the date of Thermopylae to 5,283,220. To this grand total he added uncounted "cook-

ing women, and concubines, and eunuchs" (Herodotus VII, 185-87, Loeb). Modern historians disagree widely on the size of Xerxes' forces. It is hard to imagine supplying such forces as Herodotus calculates, given the means of transport then available. For this and other reasons, recent historians at least agree that he grossly exaggerated the size of the invading forces.

146. Herodotus VII, 101. Loeb.

147. Ibid., VII, 102.

148. Ibid., VII, 104.

149. Glotz: *Histoire Grecque*, vol. II, p. 57.

150. Glotz's estimate. Ibid., vol. II, p. 60.

151. Herodotus VII, 56, 203. Loeb.

152. Ibid., VII, 140.

153. Ibid., VII, 141.

154. Pindar: *Pythian Odes* VIII, 95-7. Loeb. Author's translation.

155. Aeschylus: *Agamemnon*, 653. Grene-Lattimore.

156. Aeschylus: *Persians*, 88. Grene-Lattimore.

157. Herodotus VII, 209. Loeb.

158. Epialtes. I have followed the spelling in both Greek text and English translation of the Loeb Classics: Herodotus VII, 213, 214, 215, 218. Both Hammond (A *History of Greece*) and Glotz (*Histoire Grecque*) spell the name as Ephialtes.

159. *Lyra Graeca* II, p. 353, Simonides 118. Loeb.

160. Ibid., II, p. 353, Simonides 119, with author's substitution of "obedient" for "in obedience."

161. Herodotus VIII, 22. Loeb.

162. Herodotus (VIII, 37, 39, Loeb) reports that the rocks could still be seen in his day. Ingenious moderns have avoided the miraculous by pointing out that after the war, when the Delphic oracle was under criticism for medizing and serving Xerxes' cause, the Delphians were anxious to prove that they had not been spared by Xerxes but saved by a god and that they invented the story of the rocks. But the modern reader can accept the rocks without the embarrassment of accepting divine intervention. The rocks could have fallen, as countless similar rocks have fallen. Herodotus reports what witnesses inferred was divine intervention. Hammond (A *History of Greece*, p. 237) guesses that the Persian army had orders to spare the temple; reports that the rocks fell; and implies that both the Greeks and Persians believed the gods had intervened.

163. Aeschylus: *Prometheus Bound*, 993-94. Grene-Lattimore.

164. Herodotus VIII, 84. Loeb.

165. Aeschylus: *Persians*, 402-5. Loeb. Author's translation.

166. Ibid., 421-28. Grene-Lattimore.

167. Aeschylus: *Persians*, 275-77. Grene-Lattimore.

168. Glotz: *Histoire Grecque*, vol. II, p. 77. But J. A. R. Munro, in the *Cambridge Ancient History*, vol. IV, p. 313, gives September 23.

169. Aeschylus: *Persians*, 238. Loeb.

170. Herodotus (VIII, 113, Loeb) says Mardonius got 300,000 men, a figure scarcely acceptable if we take the estimate for the total army given by either Glotz or Hammond. See note 145.

171. Herodotus VIII, 114. Loeb.

172. Ibid.

173. Known to modern historians as Alexander I. Alexander the Great (356-323) is known as Alexander III.

174. Herodotus VIII, 143. Modern Library, 1942.

175. Herodotus (IX, 32, Loeb) guesses that, in addition to his 300,000 picked Asian troops, including cavalry, Mardonius commanded around 50,000 Greek infantry, not to mention Greek cavalry. He estimates (IX, 28-30) that Pausanias commanded 110,000 infantry, of whom only 28,000 were heavy-armed, but his calculations present difficulties. In any case historians consider his estimates for both Mardonius's army and that of Pausanias far too high. I have followed for both armies the estimates of Glotz: *Histoire Grecque*, vol. II, p. 86.

176. Herodotus IX, 39, 49. Loeb.

177. Aeschylus: *Persians*, 816-18. Grene-Lattimore.

178. Ἑρμηχθονίῳ.

179. Plutarch: *Lives* II, Aristides xxi, 5. Loeb.

180. Luigi Pareti, in his *Studi Siciliani ed Italioti*, Florence, 1914, pp. 141, 161, estimates Hamilcar's forces at 35,000-40,000 infantry.

181. Herodotus IX, 98. Loeb. But I have followed George Rawlinson's (Modern Library, 1942) translation of σύνθημα as "watchword," and I have inserted a comma after "him that hears me not" to clarify the sentence.

182. Herodotus (IX, 100, Loeb) would seem to have used *phēmē* in its original and primary sense. His translators tend to prefer its secondary sense of a mere rumor, the kind all armies abound in, and the kind some commanders purposely start.

183. See Herodotus IX, 101. Loeb.

184. Aeschylus: *Persians*, 736. Grene-Lattimore.

CHAPTER FIVE

185. Plutarch: *Lives* II, Themistocles x, 6. Loeb.

186. Scholars have guessed that *barbaros* was an onomatopoetic word intended to describe a man who could not speak Greek and could only cry *bar-bar* and utter other unintelligible sounds.

187. Homer: *Iliad* XVIII, 309. Loeb. I have followed the rendering given in Simone Weil's article, "The Iliad, or the Poem of Force," *Politics*, November, 1945.

188. Herodotus VIII, 79. Loeb.

189. Plutarch: *Lives* II, Themistocles xix, 2. Loeb.

190. Ibid., Themistocles xix, 3-4.

191. Karl Müller, ed.: *Fragmenta Historicorum Graecorum*, Paris, 1848-74, vol. III, p. 15: Nymphidis Heracleotae.

192. Thucydides I, cxxxii, 2. Loeb.

193. Plutarch: *Lives* II, Cimon xvi, 8. Loeb.

194. Thucydides I, ci, 2. Loeb.

195. Plutarch: *Lives* III, Pericles ix, 4. Loeb.

196. Glotz: *Histoire Grecque*, vol. II, pp. 224-28. These figures are for 431 and are all highly conjectural. No really dependable figures are available.

197. Herodotus, I, 1. Loeb.
198. Of these only seven tragedies survive in more than fragmentary form.
199. It is the only complete trilogy that has been transmitted to modern times. The *Proteus* has not survived.
200. Athenaeus: *Deipnosophists* VIII, 347e. Loeb.
201. In Greek the Furies are *Erinyes* and the Gracious Goddesses are *Eumenides*.
202. See Roy C. Flickinger: *The Greek Theater and Its Drama*, Chicago, 1922, p. 272, for the somewhat conjectural details on how the judges for dramatic contests were elected.
203. Only seven of his tragedies and one satyr play are still extant.
204. Aristotle (*Athenian Constitution* XXIII, 4 – XXIV, 2, Loeb) cannot be adduced to prove that Aristides planned the Athenian Empire and would have agreed with Pericles.
205. Plutarch: *Lives* III, Pericles xxxi, 5. Loeb. Like Léon Homo (*Périclès*, Paris, 1954, p. 281), I have followed Plutarch. Some authorities claim Phidias was exiled.
206. Herodotus VII, 104. Loeb.
207. Plutarch: *Lives* III, Pericles, viii, 6. Loeb.
208. Thucydides II, xxxvii, 1-3. Loeb. Luckily, his words were recorded, conceivably verbatim, by an Athenian of genius, Thucydides—not that other Thucydides, Cimon's son-in-law, who had tried to carry on the conservative opposition to Pericles and who had been ostracized for his pains.
209. Ibid., II, xxxviii, 2.
210. Ibid., II, xxxix, 1.
211. Ibid., II, xl, 1-3.
212. Ibid., II, xli, 1.
213. Ibid., II, xliv, 2.
214. Ibid., II, lx, 3-4.
215. Ibid., II, lxiii, 1-3.
216. Ibid., I, cxxii, 3.

CHAPTER SIX

217. The obvious solution, in the view of many modern historians, would have been some sort of common government, operated by elected representatives of all Hellas. Or, since this appeared impossible, the Athenian Empire could have been reorganized, the subjects of Athens could have been given the same rights as Athenians, and the Empire could have refrained from conquest and hoped that Hellenic states outside its borders would voluntarily choose to join it. Clisthenes, who restored and reformed the constitution of Solon, after the overthrow of the Pisistratid tyranny, had provided for a council whose members were elected by his new, artificial tribes. The Boeotian Confederacy, established in 447, was a federation of city-states with a kind of representative government. It was ruled by a common council if not by the Boeotarchs they chose. There were signs of federation in Thessaly. But, in general, these efforts toward federal union were made by oligarchs. The democrats showed a marked distrust for them and preferred primary assemblies, attended, at least in theory, by every free, adult, male citizen, regardless of

birth or wealth. See J. A. O. Larsen: *Representative Government in Greek and Roman History*, Berkeley, 1955.

218. Thucydides III, lxxxii, 2. Loeb.

219. Ibid., III, xxxvii, 3.

220. Ibid., III, xxxviii, 4.

221. Ibid., III, xl, 4.

222. Ibid., III, xliii, 3.

223. Ibid., III, xlvii, 1-4.

224. Ibid., III, lxxxi, 2-5.

225. Ibid., III, lxxxii, 1-2.

226. Ibid., III, lxxxii, 4.

227. Ibid., III, lxxxii, 8.

228. Ibid., III, lxxxiii, 1-4.

229. Ibid., III, lxxxiv, 2-3.

230. *Greek Elegy and Iambus* I, p. 67, Tyrtaeus 6. Loeb.

231. There are difficulties in Thucydides' assumption that both entrances were narrow. See George B. Grundy: "Investigation of the Topography of the Region of Sphacteria and Pylos," *Journal of Hellenic Studies*, vol. XVI, pp. 1-54.

232. Thucydides IV, xxxviii, 3. Loeb.

233. Herodotus VII, 104. Loeb.

234. Thucydides IV, xl, 2. Loeb.

235. Ibid., IV, xlvii, 3 – xlviii, 6.

236. Ibid., IV, lxxxvii, 2-6.

237. Plutarch: *Lives* III, Nicias ix, 7. Loeb.

238. Thucydides I, xxii, 4. Translated by Richard Crawley, Everyman's Library, 1910.

239. Cornford (F. M. Cornford: *Thucydides Mythistoricus*, London, 1907) suggests that Thucydides intended merely to report what was actually done and said, that he was unconsciously drawn into the pattern of Aeschylean tragedy, and that hence he was led to seek cause in personal motive rather than in economic conditions, for example. But though Cornford's study of Thucydides is most illuminating, I dissent from his analysis on two counts. First, I see no evidence for the statement that Thucydides' acceptance of the tragic pattern was unconscious. The author of a Greek tragedy was imitating life—not just any human life, it is true, but the life of a certain kind of person. Thucydides could have readily guessed, when the war began, that Athens was about to achieve tragedy and that for this reason coming events would be significant, hence worth recounting. Secondly, although the myth of economic determinism was not the myth he used, he was acutely aware of material causes. I invite the reader to read Thucydides with pencil in hand and to mark every passage with economic implications: if he does, he will badly deface his text. But where we moderns often make economic and sociological abstractions the only real agents in history, Thucydides focused mainly on human agents. See Cornford, especially chaps. 5 and 8.

240. Thucydides I, xxii, 1. Loeb.

241. Only eighteen of his tragedies and one satyr play survive.

242. Euripides: *Trojan Women*, 1156-1206. Grene-Lattimore.

243. The famous device of the *deus ex machina*, which some critics accused Euripides of overworking, as his only remaining means of saving himself from a poor plot.

244. Euripides: *Heracles*, 1263-65. Grene-Lattimore.

245. Ibid., 1341-46.

246. *The Banqueters*. Not extant. Aristophanes composed some forty comedies, of which eleven have survived.

247. No play by Eupolis or Cratinus is extant.

248. Unfortunately, most translators have not dared to translate Aristophanes without shamefully whitewashing the text. An honorable exception may be found in *The Complete Greek Drama*, two volumes edited by Whitney J. Oates and Eugene O'Neill, Jr. It is interesting that in this edition, except for the *Frogs*, an almost decorous play translated by Gilbert Murray, the extant comedies of Aristophanes have been most joyously rendered, and signed—"Translator Anonymous."

249. Aristophanes presumably knew about Thalia, since presumably he knew his Hesiod. But it was not until late Roman times, nearly a millennium after Aristophanes' death, that men discovered which Muse inspired comedy.

250. Aristophanes: *Peace*, 174-76. Oates-O'Neill.

251. Ibid., 211-19.

252. Ibid., 270.

253. Ibid., 819-23.

254. Thucydides V, lxxxix. Loeb.

255. Ibid., V, xc-cv, 3.

256. Hesiod: *Works and Days*, 276-80. Loeb.

257. *Lyra Graeca* III, p. 241, Euripides 1. Loeb. Fourth in the chariot race, not third, according to Alcibiades himself in Thucydides VI, xvi, 2. Loeb.

258. Aristophanes: *Frogs*, 1425. Oates-O'Neill.

259. Ibid., 1431-32.

260. Thucydides VI, viii, 2. Loeb.

261. Ibid., VI, xii, 2 – xiii.

262. Ibid., VI, xvi, 1-3.

263. Ibid., VI, xvi, 6 – xvii, 1.

264. Ibid., VI, xviii, 3, 4, 7.

265. Ibid., VI, xxx, 1 – xxxii, 2.

266. Ibid., VI, xc, 2-4.

267. Ibid., VI, xcii, 1-5.

268. Ibid., VII, lxxv, 1-7.

269. Ibid., VII, lxxxiv, 3-5.

270. Ibid., VII, lxxxvi, 5.

271. Ibid., V, cv, 2.

272. Ibid., VII, lxxxvii, 5-6.

273. Ibid., VIII, xlvii, 2.

274. Ibid., VIII, lxxxi, 3.

275. Xenophon: *Hellenica* I, i, 23-4. Loeb.

276. Ibid., I, iv, 20. As *hegemon autokrator*.

277. Ibid., II, ii, 3-4.

278. Ibid., II, ii, 21-3.

279. The various stories here given are all to be found in Plutarch: *Lives* IV, Alcibiades xxxvii, 4, xxxviii, and xxxix. Loeb.

280. Euripides: *Medea*, 828-30. Author's translation.

CHAPTER SEVEN

281. *Lyra Graeca* II, p. 336, Simonides 95. Loeb. Author's translation.

282. Plato: *Apology*, 21B. Jowett.

283. Ibid., 21C.

284. Ibid.

285. Ibid., 21D.

286. Ibid., 22A.

287. Ibid., 22B.

288. When the definite article preceding *elenchos* is neuter, the word means disgrace; when the article is masculine, the word means refutation.

289. Plato: *Apology*, 23B. Jowett.

290. Xenophon: *Memorabilia* I, vi, 2. Loeb.

291. Ibid., I, vi, 10.

292. Ibid., I, ii, 36.

293. Plato: *Charmides*, 166D. Jowett.

294. Plato: *Gorgias*, 509A. Jowett.

295. This was the reason Socrates himself gave. But there is irony in his word teach. In Socrates' view, dialectic was a far more powerful device for teaching than any lecture could be, provided that teach meant to help another human mind awaken, move, and work, and did not mean merely to transmit information or unproven opinion. But Socrates may also have feared that taking fees would corrupt the teaching function by substituting profit for truth as the teacher's goal.

The great British historian, George Grote (*History of Greece*, vol. VIII, p. 491), defends the sophists against the imputations in Plato's dialogues that they were intellectually corrupt. Grote discards the word sophist because of its invidious post-Platonic meanings and suggests that they be called "Professors or Public Teachers." Whether likening them to professors would clear sophists of intellectual corruption in Socrates' eyes would be a question worth exploring.

296. Plato: *Meno*, 86B-C. Jowett.

297. Ibid., 98B.

298. Plato: *Theaetetus*, 148-151E. Jowett. Although this conversation occurs in one of Plato's later dialogues, which are assumed to reflect his own thought far more than the thought of Socrates, it is thoroughly in character. Socrates' view of himself as an intellectual midwife was common knowledge.

299. Plato: *Protagoras*, 314E-315B. Jowett.

300. The scene gives a richer meaning to the phrase many teachers use: "Do you follow me?" Perhaps Socrates has such peripatetic questions in mind when, in Plato's *Cratylus*, he teases Cratylus and Hermogenes with his rapid-fire parody of the etymologists' speculations: "Pray observe how I gallop when I get on smooth ground." And "if I am not careful, before tomorrow's dawn I shall be wiser than I ought to be." (414B, 399A, Jowett.)

301. Plato: *Protagoras*, 329A-B. Jowett.

302. Ibid., 334C-335C.

303. Ibid., 338C-E.

304. Ibid., 347B-349A.

305. Ibid., 361D-362A.

306. Since Socrates' goal was the direct encounter of two minds, amicably wrestling together to find more truth, courtesy was the most probable means within his power of helping his opponent shift from the blindness and willfulness of self-interested eristic to the possible insights of disinterested dialectic. Socratic courtesy reminds one of Jesus of Nazareth's admonition that, when one man strikes another, the victim should offer him the other cheek to strike, thereby supplying the necessary condition for a direct encounter of two souls in mutual love, where striking back would supply the condition for the collison of two bodies in mutual hate. Mohandas K. Gandhi understood the admonition of Jesus, an admonition extremely unpopular in Western Christendom. Gandhi therefore advised that, in facing an opponent, one should always ascribe to him the highest motives capable of explaining his actions. He perhaps noted the tendency of Christians, with the aid of not too profound Marxians and Freudians, always to ascribe the lowest motives capable of explaining the actions of one's opponent. Obviously this formula offers great advantages to the self-righteous and saves energy. Similarly, it takes less energy in an argument to denounce an opponent for talking nonsense than to assume that what he says is true and to get his further help in understanding it. But the more courteous, and unusual, procedure at least permits the direct encounter of minds. Unfortunately, this sort of intellectual courtesy requires close listening. This requirement Socrates had learned to meet.

307. Aristophanes: *Clouds*, 228-34. Oates-O'Neill.

308. Ibid., 94.

309. Ibid., 365.

310. Ibid., 1476-77.

311. Ibid., 1506-9.

312. See A. E. Taylor: *Socrates*, London, 1953, pp. 55-93, for this deduction. When I first read this book, I rejected Taylor's inference, much as I had always admired his scholarship. On longer reflection, I was driven to accept his reconstruction of the events of Socrates' youth as highly probable.

313. A party portrayed in Plato's *Symposium*. Plato himself was not present. In that year, 415, he was only twelve or thirteen. Plato has Apollodorus recount to a companion the events and especially the conversation that occurred at the banquet. He in turn got the story from Aristodemus, and years later he got confirmation of some parts of it from Socrates himself. The speeches in the *Symposium* are therefore as unauthentic as some of those in Thucydides and should not be used as courtroom transcripts. Whether they represent essentially what was said poses a subtler problem.

314. Plato: *Symposium*, 202E. Jowett.

315. Ibid., 212D-213A.

316. Ibid., 214A.

317. Ibid., 214E-217A.

318. Ibid., 219E-222A.

319. Ibid., 223C-D.

320. Freeman: *Ancilla to the Pre-Socratic Philosophers*, Heracleitus 89.

321. *Lyra Graeca* II, p. 336, Simonides 95. Loeb. Author's translation.

322. A. E. Taylor, in his *Plato: The Man and His Work*, New York, 1936, pp. 263-64, guesses that the conversation Plato imagined as the *Republic* should be placed about 421. Paul Shorey, in the Introduction to his translation of the *Republic* in the Loeb edition, estimates that Plato wrote it between 380 and 370. Plato does not claim that he himself was present at the conversation the *Republic* purportedly records. The *Republic* comes no closer to history, therefore, than the *Symposium*, Plato's version of Socrates' account, rendered several decades earlier, of a long and intricate discussion that had occurred the night before. The *Apology*, on the other hand, purports to give Socrates' personal defense in a court of law, a defense which he and hundreds of persons, many of whom would still be alive when Plato wrote, had personally heard Socrates deliver. Thucydides, the historian, did indeed report both those speeches which he had heard and other speeches admittedly composed to fit a given occasion. But in the case of either category, Thucydides' basic purpose was the historian's purpose of recording as accurately as he could what some speaker had actually said. The basic purpose of Plato's dialogues, on the other hand, was to present philosophic dialectic of the sort his beloved Socrates engaged in. Viewed as historical document, the conversation presented in the *Republic* is therefore more like one of Sophocles' tragedies or Aristophanes' comedies than like any speech quoted by Thucydides, since at any given moment a speech in the dialogues may have even more bearing on Plato's thinking in the fourth century than on Socrates' thinking in the fifth. If a tape-recorder could have been used in Cephalus's home in Piraeus to record the conversation that took place there, the result would have been more factual, as we say nowadays, than Plato's recreation of such a conversation in his book the *Republic*. Whether it would have been a more truthful account would depend on the use to which a given historian put it. For the purposes of the present volume, it is perhaps no loss if Plato's mind is allowed to participate in the dialectic. 'The Platonic Socrates,' especially of the earlier dialogues, may be the most real, the most historical Socrates. We know Socrates by what his mind provoked Plato to write, not by what his voice might have caused a tape-recorder to record, if Hellas had produced tape-recorders instead of producing Plato.

323. Plato: *Republic* I, 336B-338D. Jowett.

324. Ibid., I, 341A-C.

325. Ibid., I, 342D-343C.

326. Ibid., I, 344C-345C.

327. Ibid., I, 350C-E.

328. Ibid., I, 354A-C.

329. Ibid., II, 369D.

330. Ibid., II, 372D-373E.

331. Does the "unlimited accumulation of wealth" fairly translate the contemporary American's 'ever rising standard of living'? Or does the American phrase intend that only the standard of the needy shall rise?

332. Aeschylus: *Eumenides*, 19. Grene-Lattimore.

333. Plato: *Republic* VI, 511B-C. Jowett.

334. Ibid., VII, 514A-519D.

335. Ibid., IV, 422E-423A.
336. Ibid., VIII, 562E-563E. Socrates was not concerned to offer a cyclic theory of history according to which every society followed the evolution: aristocracy to oligarchy to democracy to tyranny; or, otherwise stated, rule by the wise to rule by the brave to rule by the rich to rule by those who prize liberty and pleasure to rule by a tyrant. He and Glaucon both must have known that in historical fact the usual function of the Hellenic tyrant, whether Pisistratus of Athens or another, was to effect by force the transition from a timocracy of nobles turning into an oligarchy of the rich to an oligarchy tempered with democracy.
337. Ibid., IX, 591E-592B.
338. Ibid., VI, 499D, 502C.
339. Xenophon: *Hellenica* II, iii, 13. Loeb.
340. Ibid., II, iii, 56. Author's translation of τῷ καλῷ.
341. Ibid.
342. Ibid., II, iv, 20-22.
343. Scholiast Aeschines I, 39, 5. Edited by Wilhelm Dindorf, Oxon., 1852. μνῆμα τόδ' ἐστ' ἀνδρῶν ἀγαθῶν, οἳ κατάρατον δῆμον' Ἀθηναιών ὀλίγον χρόνον ὕβριος ἔσχον. Author's translation.
344. Xenophon: *Hellenica* II, iv, 40-2. Loeb.
345. Xenophon: *Apology*, 29. Loeb.
346. Or the poet's son. There is some doubt as to which.
347. Plato: *Apology*, 23E. Jowett.
348. Xenophon: *Memorabilia* I, i, 1. Loeb.
349. Plato: *Apology* 30A-C. Jowett.
350. Ibid., 30D-31A.
351. Ibid., 34E.
352. Ibid., 35C.
353. Ibid., 35D.
354. Ibid., 36B-D.
355. Ibid., 38A.
356. Ibid., 38B-C.
357. Ibid., 39A-B.
358. Ibid., 40A.
359. Ibid., 41C-42.
360. Plato: *Phaedo*, 114D-118. Jowett.

CHAPTER EIGHT

361. Xenophon: *Anabasis* I, i, 11. Rouse.
362. Ibid., III, i, 4-7.
363. Ibid., III, i, 10.
364. Modern historians commonly reject Xenophon's figures in *Anabasis* I, vii, 10-11. We have no other, more trustworthy source. See Glotz: *Histoire Grecque*, vol. III, pp. 37-9.
365. Xenophon: *Anabasis* III, i, 3. Rouse.
366. Ibid., III, i, 4. Loeb.
367. Ibid., III, i, 11-13. Rouse.
368. Ibid., III, i, 23-5.

369. Ibid., III, ii, 7.
370. Ibid., III, ii, 9.
371. Ibid., III, ii, 25-7.
372. Ibid., III, ii, 32.
373. Ibid., IV, v, 12-14.
374. Ibid., IV, v, 26-7.
375. Ibid., IV, v, 31-2.
376. Ibid., IV, vii, 21-6.
377. Ibid., IV, viii, 14.
378. Ibid., IV, viii, 16.
379. Translation disputed.
380. Xenophon: *Anabasis* IV, viii, 25-8. Rouse.
381. Ibid., V, i, 2-4.
382. Ibid., V, iv, 32-4.
383. Ibid., V, vi, 15-6.
384. Ibid., VI, iv, 3-8.
385. Ibid., VII, i, 33-7.
386. The exile is certain. The date is not. Neither is the charge. I have followed Edouard Delebecque: *Essai sur la vie de Xénophon*, Paris, 1957, on both points, and on much else. Many of the dates of Xenophon's life and some of the events as well are only informed guesses.
387. Aristophanes: *Plutus*, 181-85. Loeb. Author's translation.
388. Xenophon: *Hellenica* V, i, 31. Loeb. The King's announcement is called by modern historians either The King's Peace or the Peace of Antalcidas, Antalcidas being the Spartan general who negotiated the settlement.
389. Plutarch: *Lives* VII, Artaxerxes xxii, 2. Loeb.
390. Edouard Delebecque, in his *Essai sur la vie de Xénophon*, Paris, 1957, pp. 507-9, has made informed guesses at the dates of Xenophon's works. Though not citing those precise dates, I have followed his sequence.
391. Aristotle: *Politics* V, vii, 19. Loeb.
392. See Pierre Lavedan: *Dictionnaire illustré de la mythologie et des antiquités Grecques et Romaines*, 3d ed., Paris, 1954, article on "Exposition des enfants," p. 411.
393. Aristotle: *Politics* II, vi, 11. Loeb.
394. Demosthenes: *Private Orations*, Against Aphobus I, 9. Loeb.
395. H. W. Parke: *Greek Mercenary Soldiers*, Oxford, 1933, pp. 20-1.
396. Historians of art have sometimes written as if the earlier sculptors lacked the eye to see these differences or perhaps the skill to render them. Does it require more credulity to believe that the differences simply did not interest them?
397. In July, 356, according to Glotz: *Histoire Grecque*, vol. III, pp. 232-33. D. G. Hogarth, in *Philip and Alexander of Macedon*, New York, 1897, places the birth of Alexander in October.
398. Plutarch: Apothegms . . . of Kings and Great Commanders, Philip. In *Plutarch's Complete Works*, Thomas Crowell & Co., New York, 1909, vol. I, p. 26.
399. Diodorus Siculus XVI, 35, 1. Loeb.
400. Xenophon: *Scripta Minora*, The Cavalry Commander IX, 8-9. Loeb.

401. Demosthenes: *Philippics* I, 10-12. Loeb.

402. Demosthenes: *De Corona*, 235-37. Loeb.

403. Demosthenes: *Philippics* I, 12. Loeb.

404. Not, at least, in any of his surviving orations. This evidence is admittedly negative.

405. See Plato: *Gorgias*, especially line 465.

406. Plutarch: *Lives* VIII, Phocion v, 4. Loeb.

407. Isocrates: *Antidosis*, 253-57. Loeb.

408. Ibid., 302.

409. Ibid., 305.

410. Ibid., 308. Author's translation.

411. Isocrates: *Panegyricus*, 50. Loeb.

412. Isocrates: *Address to Philip*, 15-6. Loeb.

413. Ibid., 120-21.

414. Ibid., 149.

415. Ibid., 154.

416. The numbers are uncertain. I have followed Glotz: *Histoire Grecque*, vol. III, p. 359.

417. Plutarch: *Lives* VII, Demosthenes xx, 3. Loeb. Transliterated from the Greek: "*Dēmosthénēs/ Dēmosthénous/ Paianieùs/ tád' eîpen.*"

418. Homer: *Iliad* XVIII, 309. Loeb. I have followed the rendering given in Simone Weil's article, "The Iliad, or the Poem of Force," *Politics*, November, 1945.

419. Isocrates: *Letter to Philip* II, 2-3. Loeb.

420. Pausanias: *Description of Greece* VIII, vii, 6. Loeb.

421. Diodorus Siculus XVI, 92. Translated by G. Booth, London, 1814.

CHAPTER NINE

422. Plato: *Epistle* VII, 324E. Loeb.

423. Diodorus Siculus, Fragment 222, in H. W. Parke: *The Delphic Oracle*, 2 vols., Oxford, 1956, vol. II.

424. Plato: *Epistle* VII, 326A-B. Loeb.

425. Freeman: *Ancilla to the Pre-Socratic Philosophers*, Democritus 117.

426. Ibid., Democritus 247.

427. Ibid., Democritus 267.

428. Ibid., Metrodorus 2.

429. Ibid., Metrodorus 1.

430. Ibid., Critias 25.

431. Ibid., Antiphon 44.

432. Plato: *Republic* VI, 499B-C. Jowett.

433. Plato: *Epistle* VII, 328A. Loeb.

434. Ibid., 328C.

435. Ibid., 329B. Zeus Xenios was Zeus considered as the god of hospitality, who would govern Plato's relations with Dion and other hosts of his at Syracuse.

436. Plutarch: *Lives* VI, Dion ix, 5. Loeb.

437. I have followed A. E. Taylor's conjectural dating of the various

dialogues. See his *Plato: The Man and His Work*, New York, 1936, especially p. 21.

438. Pindar: *Pythian Odes* VIII, 94-8. Loeb. Author's translation.

439. Plato: *Epistle* VII, 341C-D. Loeb.

440. Plato: *Timaeus*, 41C. Jowett.

441. Ibid., 44C.

442. Those readers who are disturbed by Plato's image of the universe as "a living creature truly endowed with soul and intelligence" might be interested by a hauntingly similar account by a distinguished twentieth-century scientist, Pierre Teilhard de Chardin: *The Phenomenon of Man*, Introduction by Sir Julian Huxley, New York, 1960. The Platonic creation myth in the *Timaeus* should be much more intelligible to a modern scientist than to scientists of a century ago.

443. Plato: *Timaeus*, 75E. Jowett.

444. Plato: *Epistle* VIII, 352E-353A. Loeb.

445. Plato: *Timaeus*, 92C. Jowett.

446. *Lyra Graeca* I, p. 115, Alcman 124. Loeb.

447. Plato: *Timaeus*, 41E-42A. Jowett.

448. Freeman: *Ancilla to the Pre-Socratic Philosophers*, Alcmaeon of Crotona 2.

449. Plato: *Laws* I, 641E. Jowett.

450. Ibid., IV, 716C.

451. Ibid., IV, 714A.

452. *Greek Anthology* II, Bk. VII, 256. Loeb. Of the people of Eretria, whom Darius I had deported to the high plateau of Media, beyond even the furthest eastward march of Xenophon and his retreating polis of Greek mercenaries.

453. Ibid., II, Bk. VII, 265.

454. Ibid., I, Bk. V, 79.

455. Ibid., II, Bk. VII, 669.

456. Ibid., III, Bk. IX, 506.

457. Hesiod: *Theogony*, 27. Loeb.

458. Plato: *Epistle* VII, 326B-C. Loeb.

459. *Greek Elegy and Iambus* I, p. 143, Solon 28a. Loeb.

460. Plato: *Laws* IV, 718B. Jowett.

461. A. E. Taylor: *Plato: The Man and His Work*, New York, 1936, p. 437.

462. Plato: *Epistle* VIII, 354C. Loeb.

463. Aeschylus: *Prometheus Bound*, 50. Loeb. Author's translation.

464. Plato: *Epistle* VIII, 354E-355A. Loeb.

465. Plutarch: *Lives* II, Aristides xxi, 5. Loeb.

466. Plato: *Laws* I, 641C. Jowett.

467. Xenophon: *Hellenica* II, ii, 23. Loeb.

468. *Lyra Graeca* II, p. 336, Simonides 95. Loeb.

469. Diogenes Laertius: *Lives* III, Plato, 5-6. Loeb.

470. Plato: *Laws* VII, 816D-E. Jowett.

471. Ibid., VII, 817B.

472. *Greek Elegy and Iambus* II, p. 11, Plato 18. Loeb.

473. Diogenes Laertius: *Lives* III, Plato, 5. Loeb.

474. Ibid., Plato, 8.

475. Aeschylus: *Agamemnon*, 1426. Grene-Lattimore.

476. Plutarch: *Lives* IX, Caius Marius xlvi, 1-2. Loeb.

477. The discussion of Aristotle's works which follows is necessarily based on what survives. But what survives appears to be sometimes lectures strung together by later editors and sometimes not much more than notes for the lecturer—though hardly, as some have asserted, merely notes by pupils who had heard lectures. Aristotle was said to have published some finished literary productions, but these are not extant. His case is precisely the opposite of Plato's. In Plato's case the lecture notes, if he spoke from notes, perished; and the finished literary productions, the Dialogues, survived.

478. Aristotle: *Metaphysics* I, i, 1. Loeb. Author's translation.

479. Aristotle's *First Philosophy* acquired the name of the *Metaphysics* through an editorial accident. Some three centuries after his death, a scholar who listed his numerous works placed his *First Philosophy* after (*meta*) his *Physics*.

480. Aristotle: *Politics* I, i, 9. Loeb.

481. Pindar: *Isthmian Odes* V, 14-20. Loeb.

482. Pindar: *Pythian Odes* III, 109-10. Loeb. Author's translation. The Greek word is *athanaton*—immortal life.

483. Aristotle: *Nicomachaean Ethics* X, vii, 8. Loeb.

484. Aristotle: *Politics* III, iv, 7. Loeb.

485. Compare for example his grave refutation, in *Politics* II, i-ii, of Socrates' gay and witty assaults on private property (Plato: *Republic* V).

486. Aristotle: *Politics* VII, vi, 1. Loeb.

487. Ibid., I, ii, 3.

488. Ibid., I, ii, 4-5.

489. Ibid., I, ii, 7-8.

490. Ibid., I, ii, 12.

491. Ibid.

492. Ibid., I, ii, 13-15.

493. Diogenes Laertius: *Lives* V, Aristotle, 19. Loeb.

494. Freeman: *Ancilla to the Pre-Socratic Philosophers*, Heracleitus 89.

495. Aristotle: *Politics* I, iii, 9. Loeb.

496. Aristotle: *Nicomachaean Ethics* VIII, xiv, 3. Loeb.

497. Aristotle: *Politics* I, iii, 23. Loeb. The Greek word for offspring, interest, is *tokos*.

498. Ibid., I, iv, 6.

499. Ibid., I, iv, 5-6.

500. Ibid., VII, vi, 1.

501. Aristotle: *Poetics* VI, 2-3. Loeb.

502. Plato: *Republic* II, 372D. Jowett.

503. Plato: *Republic* II, 372E. Loeb: *phlegmainousan*.

504. Aristotle: *Poetics* IX, 3. Loeb.

505. Ammonius Hermeiou: *Vita Aristoteles*, Leiden, 1621, 68: Literally, "*Non concedam Atheniensibus bis peccare in Philosophiam.*"

CHAPTER TEN

506. Plutarch: *Lives* VII, Alexander viii, 3. Loeb.
507. Demosthenes' actual words (Plutarch: *Lives* VII, Demosthenes xxiii, 2, Loeb) are *pais* and *Margites*.
508. Aristotle: *Metaphysics* I, i, 1. Loeb.
509. Arrian I, 16, 6. Loeb.
510. Ibid., I, 16, 7.
511. Ibid., II, 4, 9.
512. W. W. Tarn (*Alexander the Great*, 2 vols., Cambridge, 1948, vol. I, p. 26) estimates Alexander's army at 25,000-29,000, but modern estimates of both armies differ widely.
513. Arrian II, 14, 3. Loeb.
514. Ibid., II, 14, 4-9.
515. Ibid., II, 12, 6-7.
516. Ibid., II, 17.
517. Plutarch: *Lives* VII, Alexander xxix, 4. Loeb.
518. Pindar: *Pythian Odes* IV, 15. Loeb.
519. Herodotus II, 42. Loeb.
520. Ibid., IV, 181. Amon-Re, great god of Thebes in Egypt, was called Ammon at his desert shrine.
521. Thus Callisthenes, Aristotle's nephew and the official historian of Alexander's expeditionary force. Callisthenes may have been present when the priest of Ammon greeted Alexander. In any case he later wrote that the priest called Alexander son of Zeus. On this whole matter, see W. W. Tarn: *Alexander the Great*, 2 vols., Cambridge, 1948, vol. II, Appendix 22.
522. Plutarch: *Lives* VII, Alexander xxvii, 5. Loeb.
523. Pseudo-Callisthenes: *The Life of Alexander of Macedon*. Translated and edited by E. H. Haight, New York, 1955, I, 35, 5.
524. Plutarch: *Lives* VII, Alexander xxvii, 5. Loeb.
525. Ibid., Alexander xxvii, 6.
526. Ibid.
527. Ibid., Alexander ix, 4.
528. Ibid., Alexander ix, 5.
529. Ibid., Alexander xxvii, 3-4.
530. Ibid., Alexander xxviii, 2. Also Homer: *Iliad* V, 340. Loeb.
531. Plutarch: *Lives* VII, Alexander xxii, 3. Loeb.
532. Hammond (*A History of Greece*, p. 615) says "perhaps 6,000."
533. Herodotus I, 98. Loeb.
534. Aristotle: *Politics* VII, xiii, 8. Loeb.
535. Ibid., VII, xiii, 14.
536. Arrian III, 27, 5. Loeb.
537. Ibid., III, 30, 4.
538. Plutarch: *Lives* VII, Alexander li, 2. Loeb.
539. Arrian IV, 8, 7. Loeb.
540. Ibid., IV, 8, 9.
541. Ibid., IV, 10, 2.
542. Ibid., IV, 11, 6-9.
543. These statements are based on purely negative evidence.

544. Herodotus IV, 44. Loeb.
545. Arrian V, 19, 2. Loeb.
546. Ibid., V, 25, 3.
547. Ibid., V, 26, 4.
548. Ibid., V, 26, 7-8.
549. Ibid., V, 27, 2.
550. Ibid., V, 27, 7.
551. Ibid., VI, 29, 8.
552. Ibid., VII, 1, 6.

553. Arrian gives her name as Barsine. Other historians called her Stateira and claimed that a Barsine had been Alexander's mistress since early in his Asian campaign.

554. C. Aelianus: *Varia Historia*, Leipzig, 1780, II, 19.

555. *Minor Attic Orators* II, Hyperides: Against Demosthenes, Fragment vii, col. 31. Loeb.

556. Flavius Arrianus, who quotes this speech, wrote his account of Alexander's conquests some five centuries after they occurred. His chief sources were Ptolemy, one of Alexander's generals, and Aristobulus, a Greek technician, both of whom served in Alexander's army and both of whom left histories of the campaign. Arrian does not specify his source for this speech and we have no guarantee that his version is verbatim. Neither are we in a position to impugn Arrian's version.

557. Arrian VII, 9-10. Loeb.
558. Ibid., VII, 11, 6.
559. Ibid., VII, 11, 7.
560. Plutarch: *Moralia* IV, On the Fortune of Alexander, 329C. Loeb.
561. Ibid., On the Fortune of Alexander, 329C-D.
562. Thucydides II, xliii, 3. Translated by Richard Crawley, Everyman's Library, 1910.

563. The Heraclitus fragment (89) follows: ὁ Ἡ. φησί τοῖς ἐγρηγορόσιν ἕνα καὶ κοινὸν κόσμον εἶναι, τῶν δὲ κοιμωμένων ἕκαστον εἰς ἴδιον ἀποστρέφεσθαι. Diels: *Die Fragmente der Vorsokratiker*. Translated in Freeman: *Ancilla to the Pre-Socratic Philosophers*.

564. Arrian VII, 26, 3. Loeb. Author's translation.

INDEX

Abdera, 82
Abydos, 92, 120
Academy, Plato's, 340, 342, 358-64, 366,
    372, 374-76, 378
Acanthus, 86, 186
Acarnanians, 178
Achaea, 107
Achaeans, 4-19, 32-34, 49, 61, 124, 327,
    347, 397
Acharnae, 159
Achilles, 4-10, 16-19, 22, 24-25, 34, 44,
    59, 61, 64, 70, 100, 134, 143, 192,
    332, 390, 393, 397, 405, 410,
    417-19, 426, 437-39
Acropolis, 33, 66, 72, 74, 91, 99, 107,
    109, 131, 146-47, 149-50, 155, 164-
    65, 227
Acte, 86, 93
Ada, 398
Aegae, 327, 351
Aegaleos, 109
Aegean Islands, 87, 96, 118
Aegean Sea, 5, 12, 30-32, 131, 133
Aegina, 14, 65, 79, 97-98, 107-9, 111,
    114, 117, 121, 137, 140, 143
Aeginetans, 107-9, 185
Aegospotami, 122
    battle of, 227-28
Aeolians, 49, 51-52, 82
Aeolis, 49
Aeschines, 346
Aeschylus, 5, 90, 190-92, 194-95, 323-24,
    439
    Agamemnon, 149-50, 339, 374
    Eumenides, 149-51
    Libation Bearers, 149-50
    Oresteia, 149-52, 158, 168, 236, 344

Aeschylus (continued)
    Persians, 109-10, 115, 134, 149
    Prometheus Bound, 371
    Proteus, 149
    translations, 455
Aetolians, 178, 180, 182
Afghanistan, 82, 409, 413
Africa, North, 36, 37
Agamemnon, 5-7, 9-10, 16, 19, 26, 34,
    149, 151, 190, 348
Agariste, 121
Agathon, 253-54, 259, 327
Agesilaus, 314-16, 318-19, 326
Agis, 214, 221-22, 224-25, 226, 228-29,
    408
Agrianians, 395
Ajax and Teucer, 108
Alalia, 82
Albania, 38
Alcaeus, poet, 51-52
    quoted, 51
Alcander, 58
Alcibiades, 157, 199-201, 205-14, 221-32,
    248-49, 251, 253-59, 273, 284-85,
    288, 320, 352-53
    on Socrates, 255-58
    speech on Sicilian expedition, 206-8
    speech to Spartans, 212-13
Alcmaeon of Crotona, quoted, 364
Alcman, poet, 59
    quoted, 364
Alcmeonids, 66, 77, 130, 199
Aleuadae, 92, 98
Alexander (Paris), 5-6, 55
Alexander I, 112, 134, 327-28
Alexander III, the Great, 333, 347-48,
    351, 375, 393-442, 464

Alexander III, the Great (*continued*)
  deification of, 351, 405-7, 418-20, 432-33
  empire, 409
  speech at the Beas, 424-25
  speech at Opis, 433-36
Alexandria (Anamis), 429
Alexandria (Bactria), 415
Alexandria (Egypt), 404
Alexandria (Farthest), 416
Alexandria (Herat), 413
Alexandria (Phrada), 414
Alexandria (Tigris), 438
Alexandria Bucephala, 424
Alexandria Nicaea, 424
Alexandropolis, 394
Alphabet, 30
Amazons, battle of, 158
Amber, 30, 356
Ambracia, 114, 349
Ambraciots, 180
Amisus, 143
Ammon, 404-7, 417, 419, 476
Amon-Re, 476
Amphictyonic League, 105, 333, 335, 346-47
Amphictyonic War, 333-36
Amphimedon, 19
Amphipolis, 186-90, 198, 328, 330-31, 375, 424
  battle of, 234
Amphissa, 347
Amyclae, 31
Amyntas III, 328, 375
Anabasis, Xenophon's, 299-312, 317
Anacreon, poet, 52, 75
Anactorium, 114
Anamis River, 429
Anaxagoras, 155, 157
Anaxarchus, 419-20
Anaxibius, 308, 310-11
Anaximander, 53
Anaximenes, 53, 251
Anchor, 31
Ancona, 356
Ancyra, 399
Andros, 143, 226, 375
Antalcidas, Peace of, 472
Antimoerus, 245
Antiochus, captain, 226
Antipater, 348, 391, 408-10, 422, 432, 438
Antiphon, sophist, 356, 367
  quoted, 355

Anytus, 287-89
Aornus, 423, 425
Apelles, painter, 405
Aphrodite, 52-53, 325
Apis, 404
Apollo, 16, 56-57, 80-81, 87, 91, 98-99, 100-101, 104, 106-7, 110-11, 116, 119, 129, 150, 154, 175, 236, 241, 259, 270, 300, 309, 331, 333-36, 339, 346-47, 365
Apollo Lyceius, 376
Apollodorus, 292, 296
Arabia, 438, 440-41
Arabians, 82, 95-96, 404
Arachosia, 415
Aral Sea, 416
Arbela, battle of, 407-8
Arcadia, 132, 189
Arcadians, 303
Archelaus, 192, 282, 327-28
Archidamus, 343
Archilochus, poet, 51
  quoted, 34, 51, 460
Archons, 65, 122, 124, 141-42
Archytas, 356
Areia, 413
Areians, 95
Areopagus, 68, 124, 133, 135-36, 151
Ares, 17, 125, 437
Argilus, 187
Arginusae, battle of, 227, 231, 289
Argonauts, 27, 307
Argolid, 13-15
Argos, 34, 64, 85, 92, 113, 132, 136, 140, 150, 200-1, 209, 215, 312, 327, 346
Argos (hound), 17
Ariadne, 14
Ariaspians, 414
Aristagoras, 83
Aristides, 108-10, 114, 121, 126-29, 131, 133, 137, 156-57, 189, 235, 244, 465
Aristobulus, 398, 405
Aristocracy, 33-35, 41-42, 45-46, 70, 74, 77, 99-100, 123-25, 130, 134-36, 142-43, 319-21, 353-54, 383
  in Athens, 65-66, 79
  in Sparta, 55-58, 61-62
  Socratic, 269, 279, 369-70
Aristodemus, 259
Ariston, 353
Aristophanes, 195-99, 250-53, 259, 323, 373

Aristophanes (*continued*)
  on Alcibiades, 205, 211
  Acharnians, 196-98
  Banqueters, 467
  Birds, 282, 345
  Clouds, 250-53, 352-53
  Ecclesiazusae, 282
  Frogs, 205, 467
  Lysistrata, 282
  Peace, 196-98
  Wealth, 313
Aristotle, 374-92, 394, 396, 432, 437,
  439-40, 475
  four causes, 379-80
  Metaphysics, 375, 377-78, 391, 475
  Nicomachean Ethics, 378-80, 382-88
  Organon, 377, 387-88
  Physics, 379-80
  Poetics, 388, 390-91
  Politics, 320, 378-80, 382-88, 411
  Rhetoric, 388
Armenia, 305
Arms and armaments, *see* Warfare
Arrian, as a historian, 477
  quoted, 401-3, 420-21, 424-26, 430,
  433-36
Arses, 401
Artabanus, 94
Artabazus, 115-16
Artaxerxes I, 132, 139
Artaxerxes II, 299, 301, 314-15
Artemis, 133, 309
Artemisium, 101-2, 105-6, 109
  battle of, 106
Asclepius, 296, 375
Ascra, 45
Asia Minor, 12, 13, 15, 16, 32, 39, 48-
  54, 81-84, 86
Aspasia, 156-57, 164
Assembly, in Athens, 65, 68-69, 78
  in Sparta, 57-58
Assinarus River, 220
Assus, 375
Assyrians, 29, 33, 49, 80, 95, 410
Astacus, 143
Astyages, 80
Atarneus, 375
Athena, 17, 19-21, 23-25, 59, 74, 99,
  107, 128, 131-32, 141, 146-47, 150-
  51, 157, 164, 168, 286, 397, 427
  Polias, 127
Athenaeus, quoted, 150
Athenian Empire, 139, 145, 166-67, 172-
  73, 222, 230, 285, 316, 339, 465-66

Athos, Mount, 86-87, 91-93, 102, 119,
  159
Atlantic, 29
Atlantis, 370, 382
Attalus, 351, 406
Attica, 11, 13, 15-16, 49, 64-65, 67, 77,
  79, 82, 87-88, 99, 106-7, 109-10, 113,
  139-40, 163, 174, 179-80, 214, 225
Autolycus, 21
Axios River, 93

Baal-Marduk, 417
Babylon, 82, 408-10, 431, 433, 438, 440
Babylonia, 49, 80-82, 411-12
Bactra, 416-17, 420
Bactria, 413, 415
Bactrians, 95, 111
Baghdad, 301
Bagoas, 401
Balkans, 11
Barbarians, 37, 123, 125, 343-45, 355,
  384, 464
Barsine, 431, 477
Basileia, 282
Batis, 404
Beas River, 424-25
Beer, 306
Beirut, 29
Bendis, 260, 266
Benefactors (tribe), 414-15
Bessus, 413-16
Bias of Priene, 82
Bireme, 31
Black Sea, 27, 35, 38, 40, 50, 74, 76,
  83-86, 93, 100, 119, 128, 133, 139,
  187, 225, 307, 309-10, 336
Boeotia, 15, 45, 92, 98, 107, 113, 118,
  137-39, 178, 190, 214-15, 329-30,
  347, 395
Boeotians, 159, 185
Boeotian League, 79, 88, 116, 465-66
Bokhara, 416
Boreas, 87, 90, 102
Bosphorus, 38, 83, 133, 139, 225, 310
Brahmans, 424, 427-28
Brasidas, 181, 185-88, 190, 198, 283
  speech at Acanthus, 186
Brea, Thrace, 143
Briseis, 6-7
Bronze, 12, 29, 33
Bruttians, 438
Bucephalus, 424
Buddha, 423
Bury, J. B., historian, 453

Byblus, 29, 402
Byzantium, 38, 83-84, 128, 131, 145, 310-11, 321, 346

Cadiz, 29
Calabria, 37
Calanus, 430-31
Callias, 130, 139-40, 245, 247, 249
    Peace of, 139
Callicles, 240-41
Callicrates, 146
Callicratidas, 227
Callimachus, 89, 90
Callines, 436
Callipus, 361
Callisthenes of Olynthus, 396, 419-21, 432
Calpe's Haven, 310, 345
Calypso, 17, 20, 38
Cambyses, 82-83, 404, 407-10
Caria, 84, 133, 398
Carians, 96, 106, 145
Carmania, 430
Carthage, 29, 85, 117, 140, 210, 356, 361
Carthaginians, 49
Caryatids, 51, 324
Carystus, 87, 133
Caspian Sea, 11, 438
Caspians, 95
Cassandra, 236, 339
Castor and Pollux, 418, 420
Catana, 211, 219-20
Caucasus, 50, 82, 416
Celts, 356-57
Ceos, 75
Cephalus, 260
Cephissus, 13
Ceramic Gulf, 225
Cerasus, 309
Cersobleptes, 336, 346
Chaerephon, 235-37, 252
Chaeronea, battle of, 346-48, 394
Chalcedon, 38
Chalcidian League, 328
Chalcidice, 86, 114, 159, 185, 187, 206, 326, 332, 345
Chalcis (Euboea), 14, 42, 65, 79, 84, 87, 326, 349, 375
Chalybeans, 306
Chalybes, 50
Charicles, 240
Charmides, 240, 245, 288, 353
Chenab River, 424

Chersonese, Thracian, 89, 120, 143, 345
Chilon, 62
Chios, 129, 172, 221, 225
Chirisophus, 308
Chiron, 381
Choerilus, poet, 327
Cilicia, 300, 400
Cilician Gates, 399
Cilicians, 84, 96, 106
Cimon, 130-31, 133-39, 141-42, 154, 157, 318, 320
Circe, 20-22, 38
Cissians, 95, 103
Cithaeron, Mount, 406
Citizenship (Athens), 77-79, 142-43, 146, 157, 167
City-state, see Polis
Clazomenae, 155, 314
Clearchus, 300-302, 305
Cleomenes, 83-84, 103
Cleon, 171-74, 179, 181-83, 187-89, 198, 208, 285, 322
    speech on Mytilene, 172-73
Cleopatra, daughter of Philip, 351
Cleopatra, wife of Philip, 351, 394, 406
Cleruchs, 79-80, 131, 139, 143, 146, 156, 174, 204, 316
Clinias, 157, 199
Clisthenes (Athens), 77-78, 121, 130, 142, 199, 465
    constitution of, 77-78, 85, 145
Clisthenes (Sicyon), 76
Clitus the Black, 397, 414, 418-19, 422
Clitus the White, 422
Clytemnestra, 150
Coenus, 426
Coinage, 40-41, 144-45, 331-32, 335, 369, 384, 402, 417, 459
Coiratadas, 311
Colchians, 307
Colchis, 50
Colonization, 32, 35-40, 50, 66, 79, 81
Colonus, 152, 223
Colophon, 53
Comedy, 195-98, 323-24, 372-73
Companions, Macedonian, 408, 413-14, 433, 436, 441-42
Confucius, 423
Conon, 227
Constantinople, 38
Copaïs, Lake, 15
Cophen River, 422
Copper, 29

Corcyra, 132, 159, 209, 225, 285, 373
  revolution at, 175-80, 183-84
Corfu, 175
Corinth, 13, 27-28, 53, 55, 59, 65, 67,
  76, 85, 108, 114, 116, 118, 137-39,
  158-59, 168, 175, 190, 205, 211,
  215-16, 229, 284, 312, 318, 326,
  347, 361
  Gulf of, 107
  Isthmus of, 59, 93, 97-98, 101-2, 107-
  8, 113, 127, 139, 179
  League of, 349-50, 395, 398, 408, 413,
  432
  speech of Corinthians, 164
Cornford, F. M., on Thucydides, 466
Cornwall, 29
Coronea, battle of, 99, 139, 157, 317-18
Corsica, 82, 85, 117, 304, 345
Cosmopolis (Alexander), 412, 416-17,
  419, 421-23, 431, 433, 437, 439-41
Cossaeans, 438
Cotton, 95
Council, 33
  in Athens, 45
  in Sparta, 56-57
Council of Four Hundred, 68, 223-25
Courts, at Athens, 69, 142, 144, 159,
  165, 288
Craterus, 429, 438
Cratinus, 158, 195
Crenides, 331
Creon, 154
Cretans, 308, 395
Crete, 12-15, 360, 364-65, 460
Critias, 230, 283-86, 288, 352-56
Crito, 292-96
Critobulus, 292
Crocodiles, 427
Croesus, 50, 54, 80-82, 98, 148, 153,
  236, 241, 300, 334
Cronus, 365
Croton, 107
Cumae, 38-39
Cunaxa, battle of, 301, 307, 309, 343
Cybele, 69, 84, 147
Cyclades, 13
Cyclopes, 18, 21-23, 28, 133
Cyllene, 211
Cylon, 66
Cyme, 45
Cynegirus, 90
Cynossema, battle of, 231, 284-85
Cynosura, 88

Cyprus, 15, 39, 59, 71, 84, 96, 128, 139,
  314, 402-3
Cyrenaica, 13
Cyrene, 59, 138, 321
Cyropolis, 415-16
Cyrus the Great, 80-83, 91, 95, 148, 236,
  409, 414, 420
  tomb of, 430
Cyrus, the younger, 226-27, 299-301, 304,
  310-11
Cythera, 184, 201
Cyzicus, 321
  battle of, 225, 231, 283

Daimōn, 25, 236, 259, 266, 374
Damascus, 400
Damocles, sword of, 360
Damon, 154-55, 157
Danube River, 11, 83, 93, 395
Dardanelles, 38
Darius I, 82-87, 91-92, 97, 119, 409-10,
  412-13
Darius III, 394-95, 397, 399-403, 407-15
Dark Age of Greece, 3, 5, 16, 32, 38, 48,
  127, 458
Decarchies, 283
Decelea, 212-16, 221-22, 224-25, 285
Delium, battle of, 185, 200, 234, 258
Delos, 87, 111, 117, 129-30, 136, 138,
  293
  League of, 129-31, 133-38, 140-41,
  144-45, 156
Delphi, 14, 80, 116, 128, 150, 333,
  335, 463
  games at, 35
Delphians, 106-7
Delphic Oracle, 56, 58, 80-81, 98-101,
  104, 112, 153-54, 175, 180-81, 189,
  236, 252, 270, 300, 333-35, 350-51,
  353-54, 399, 404, 420, 463
  quoted, 56, 81, 91, 98-99
Demades, 348, 432
Demaratus, 83-84, 92, 96-97, 103, 158,
  183
Demes, in Athens, 77-78
Demeter, 76; see Earth goddess
Demiurge, 362
Democracy, 85, 86, 161, 167, 383, 471
  at Athens, 77-79, 230-32
  Alcibiades on, 211-12
  Socrates on, 279-80
Democrats, 100, 123-24, 132, 134-35,
  138, 141, 145, 169, 171-72, 175-78,

183-84, 191, 208, 223-24, 228, 398, 432, 465
Democritus of Abdera, 354, 356
Demosthenes, general, 178-83, 187, 214-20
Demosthenes, orator, 321-22, 337-42, 345-48, 364, 373-74, 389, 394-96, 432-33, 439
  De Corona, 338
  Philippics, 337-38
Deus ex machina, 194, 467
Dialectic, Socratic, 237-44, 246-50, 259-60, 267, 359, 376-77, 468-69
Didyma, oracle at, 419
Diké, 58, 65; *see also* Justice
Diodotus, 173-74, 179
Diolkos, 59, 93
Dion, games at, 328
Dion, of Syracuse, 356, 358-61
Dionysiac festivals, 75-76, 196
Dionysius I, 343, 356-58
Dionysius II, 357-60, 366
Dionysus, 76, 149-50, 191, 205, 420, 423, 425
  Theater of, 151, 165, 195
Diotima, 254
Dnieper River, 93
Dniester River, 93
Dodona, oracle at, 80, 404
Don River, 93
Dorians, 16, 27, 32, 44, 48-49, 55, 61, 64-65, 96, 205, 207, 253, 327, 391
Doris, 16, 49
Doriscus, 94-95, 131, 183
Dracon, 66-67, 74
Dracontios, 307-8
Draft animals, 31-32
  harness, 31-32
  horseshoes, 32
Drama, 76, 145, 149-50, 465; *see also* Comedy *and* Tragedy
  Aristotle on, 390-91
Drangiana, 415
Durazzo, 175
Dustyfoot, 34, 42-43, 68, 76, 79; *see also* Thetes
Dwellers-round-about, 57, 60-61, 67, 134, 312

Earth goddess, 69, 84, 147; *see also* Demeter
Ecbatana, 368, 410, 414, 416, 438
Echecrates, 293, 296

Echetlus, 91
Education, Aristotle on, 387
  in Athens, 122-23, 161-62
  Isocratean, 340-42
  Platonic, 269-71, 277-78, 358-59, 371
  Spartan, 62-63
Egypt, 13, 15, 39, 50, 56, 71, 82-83, 91, 148, 400-407, 412, 422-23, 438
  Athens in, 137-38, 140
Egyptians, 84, 92-96, 128, 409-10
Eion, 131, 187
Elatea, 347
Elburz Mountains, 413
Elea, 53
Eleatic school, 155
Electrum, 40
Elenchos, 237-39, 468
Eleusis, 31, 76, 151, 284, 399
  mysteries, 208, 210, 226, 399
Eleutheria, festival of, 116
Elis, 31, 132, 190, 200, 318, 346
Empedocles, 144, 362
Epaminondas, 316, 326, 329-30, 357
Ephesus, 54, 132, 226, 321, 405
Ephialtes, 134-36, 141, 151
Ephors, 57, 61, 62
Epialtes, 103-4, 463
Epidamnus, 175
Epidaurus, 34
Epipolae, 211
Epirus, 16, 38, 49, 346
Er, myth of, 281-82
Erechtheum, 164, 324
Erechtheus, 147
Eretria, 42, 84-87, 92, 111, 114, 119, 143
Eretrians, 175, 368, 474
Ergon, 46, 418
Erinyes, 465; *see also* Eumenides
Eris, 46, 57, 63, 67-69, 77-78, 91, 126, 168-69, 239-40, 250, 332
Eristic, 239-40, 250, 350, 382, 469
Eros, 253-54
Eryximachus, 253
E-sagila, 410
Ethiopians, 95
Etruria, 140, 143, 356
Etruscans, 39, 49, 85, 438
Euboea, 40, 79, 84, 87, 101-2, 105-6, 131, 133, 139, 160, 214, 224-25, 285
Eubulus, 337
Eucles, 187, 190
Euclides, 353

Eucrates, 171
Eulaeus River, 433
Eumaeus, 25
Eumenides, 151, 465; see also Erinyes
Eunomia, 58-59, 67-68, 70, 78, 168
Eupatrids, 65, 68, 199; see also Aristocracy
Euphrates River, 403, 407, 441
Eupolis, 195
Euripides, 5, 192-99, 282-83, 323, 327-28, 394
  on Alcibiades, 205
  Archelaus, 328
  on Athens, 231
  Bacchae, 282, 328
  Heracles, 194-95
  Medea, 307
  translations, 455
  Trojan Women, 193-94
Euripus, 105
Euryclea, 17
Eurymedon, admiral, 176, 185, 214, 216-17
Eurymedon, battle of, 133
Eurypon, 55
Euxine, see Black Sea

Fertile Crescent, 82
Five-hundred-Bushelers, 68
Five Thousand, the, at Athens, 223-25
Four Hundred, the, at Athens, 223-25
France, colonies in, 37-39
Furies, 150-51; see also Erinyes

Gandhi, 469
Ganges River, 425
Gaugamela, battle of, 407-8, 414
Gaul, 85
Gaza, 404
Gedrosia, 415
Gedrosian desert, 428-29
Gela, 185
Gelo, 117
Gerousia, 56-57
Getae, 395
Gibraltar, Strait of, 36
Glaucon, 260, 262, 267-69, 273-82, 298, 390
Glotz, Gustave, historian, 453
Gods, 7-8, 17, 24-25, 47, 53-54, 69, 75-76, 98, 191, 194-95, 203-4, 303, 334-35, 364-65, 382-83, 405-6, 439-41, 460

Gods (continued)
  Aristotle on, 378, 380-81, 391
  in Herodotus, 148
  Olympic, 28, 47
  Plato on, 362-63, 371
  and the polis, 297
  Xenophanes on, 53-54
Golden Fleece, 27
Gordian Knot, 398-99, 440
Gorgias, 174, 283, 339-40
Gournia, 15
Granicus, battle of, 397-98, 414, 418
Great Hellas, 38; see also Western Greece
Great Mother, 69
Greece, fauna, 11, 457
  flora, 11
  geography, 11-12, 28
  roads, 31
Greeks, Aristotle on, 384, 389; see also Hellenes
Grote, George, historian, 454
  on sophists, 468
Gylippus, 213-20
Gymnias, 306
Gymnosophists, 56, 430

Hades, House of, 4, 9, 10, 19-20, 26, 59, 292
Hadria, 356
Halicarnassus, 398
Hamilcar, 117, 464
Hammond, N. G. L., historian, 453
Harmodius and Aristogeiton, 123, 409
Harpalus, 94, 410
Hectemor, 67
Hector, 10, 16, 193, 397
Hecuba, 193
Helen of Troy, 5, 6, 55, 222, 418
Helicon, Mount, 45-47, 122, 369
Heliopolis, 404
Hellenes, 5, 15, 39; see also Greeks
Hellespont, 5, 11, 38, 76, 82, 84-86, 92-94, 98, 111-12, 115-20, 128, 187, 221-22, 225-27, 230, 311, 350, 395-96
  bridges at, 92-94, 111, 120, 122, 132
Helmund River, 414-15
Helots, 57, 60-62, 64, 102, 114, 128, 134-35, 143, 180, 182-86, 215, 312
Hephaesteum, 164-65
Hephaestus, 164
Hephestion, 397, 402, 414, 421, 423-24, 431, 438, 442

Hera, 115, 176, 362
Heracles, 20, 88, 189, 307, 327, 344, 393, 402-3, 406, 417-20, 423, 425, 427
Heraclitus, 54, 477
  quoted, 439
Hermeias, 375, 391
Hermes, 21, 116, 197-99
Hermione, 114
Hermocrates, 185, 211, 215, 218, 370, 421
Hermolaus, 421-22
Herms, mutilation of, 208-210, 334, 352
Herodotus, 5, 96-97, 114, 144, 148-49, 165, 190-92, 327, 404, 407, 410, 423
  quoted, 96-99, 112, 118, 148, 158, 183
  translations, 455
Heroes, 7-9, 16-17, 19, 21-22, 24, 44
Hesiod, 43-47, 53, 68-71, 122, 126, 160, 170, 204, 239, 362
  date, 459
  quoted, 44-47, 368-69
  Theogony, 43, 46, 459
  translations, 455
  Works and Days, 43-47
Hiero, 357
Himera, 117, 214
Hindu Kush, 415
Hipparchus, 52, 76; see also Pisistratids
Hippeis, 68; see also Knights
Hippias, sophist, 245, 248
Hippias (tyrant), 76-77, 79, 84-85, 87-88, 90, 123; see also Pisistratids
Hippocrates, son of Apollodorus, 245
Hippodamus, 127, 144
Historia, 148
History, Aristotle on, 391
  cyclic theory, 471
  and legends, 27-28
  myths as, 4-5
  Thucydides on, 190
Hittites, 32
Homer, 4, 5, 30, 32, 47, 56, 70, 122, 148, 150, 254, 348, 394, 437, 458-59
  date, 459
  Iliad, 2, 5-10, 16, 18, 24, 27, 30, 35, 43, 148, 150, 437, 456
  Odyssey, 4, 5, 16-27, 35, 456
  quoted, 2, 4, 5, 8, 18, 19-26, 30, 32, 47, 125, 249, 348, 407
  translations, 456

Homeric Cycle, 27, 150
Homeric Hymn to Apollo, 49, 460
Hoplite, 42; see also Warfare
Hot Gates, see Thermopylae
Hybris, 93-95, 190, 230, 240, 315, 318, 381-82, 416-19, 421, 441
Hydaspes River, 424
Hyperbolus, 171, 201
Hyrcanians, 95

Ibycus, poet, 52
Ichor, 8, 407
Ictinus, 146
Ida, Mount, 364
Illyria, 38, 175
Illyrians, 327-30, 333, 356, 395
Imbros, 143, 315
Immortals (Persians), 94, 103-5, 111
India, 56, 416, 422-23, 427-28, 430
Indian Ocean, 428
Indians, 95-96, 111, 408
Indus River, 407, 422-24, 427-28
Infanticide, 320
Iolkos, 14
Ionia, 30, 32, 49, 56, 91, 129, 221-22, 226, 401
Ionian Revolt, 83-84, 86, 107-8, 112, 117, 119
Ionians, 30, 32, 49-52, 82-84, 94, 96, 106, 109-11, 119, 122
  philosophers, 53-54
  poets, 51-53
Iphicrates, 313-14, 328, 330, 332
Iran, 409
Irony, Socratic, 241-42, 246, 248, 250, 288-90
Isaeus, 337
Isegoria, 124
Isocrates, 340-45, 348-49, 357-58, 364, 382, 385, 395, 400, 441
  Address to Philip, 343-44
  Antidosis, 340-42
  Letter to Philip, 348-49
  Panegyric, 342-44
  on rhetoric, 340-41
Isonomia, 124
Issus, battle of, 400, 402
Isthmian Games, 35, 100
Italiots, 85
Italy, 36-38, 53, 175, 212
Ithaca, 4, 16-20, 22-24
Ithome, Mount, 134-36, 316

Jason, 27, 317

Jason of Pherae, 316
Jaxartes River, 82, 415-16, 423
Jhelum River, 424, 426-27
Jocasta, 153, 239
Justice, 42, 45, 46, 459; see also Diké
   Aristotle on, 380
   Socrates on, 262-67, 269, 281

Kabul River, 422-23
Keftiu, 15
Khyber Pass, 422
Kings, 33
   in Athens, 65
   in Homer, 8, 18
   in the polis, 43
   in Sparta, 55-57
Knights, 33; see also Hippeis
Knossos, 13-15, 364, 457
Krissa, 14
Krypteia, 61
Kurds, 305

Lacedaemon, see Sparta, Spartans
Laconia, 55, 65, 170, 184, 316, 329,
   349; see also Sparta
Laconisms, 63, 70, 105, 349
Lade, battle of, 84
Laertes, 21
Lamachus, 206, 211, 213
Lampsacus, 157, 227
Lanice, 419
Larissa, 92, 98
Latium, 356
Laurium, 97, 110, 189, 212, 214, 319
Law, 27, 33-34, 41-42, 46-47, 66-67, 69,
   74, 82, 123-25, 142, 151-52, 158-59,
   161-62, 165-68, 365, 367, 370-72
   aristocrats and, 100
   Aristotle on, 383
   of Athens, 78, 144
   of Crete, 56
   Dracon's, 66-67, 74
   Plato on, 369-72
   Spartan, 58-59, 62, 97
Lechaeum, 314
Lecythus, 187
Lemnos, 80, 143, 315
Leon of Salamis, 283-84, 290, 353
Leon of Thurii, 308
Leonidas, 102-5, 116, 128, 315
Leontini, 174-75, 205-6
Lepreum, 114
Lesbos, 51-53, 129, 171-74
Leucas, 114

Leuctra, battle of, 316, 318, 320, 329,
   357
Leutychides, 128
Libya, 36, 39, 117, 148
Libyans, 95, 438
Liguria, 117
Locri, 362
Locrians, 103, 137
Locris, 101
   Opuntian, 137, 139
   Ozolian, 137
Lucanians, 438
Lyceum, 259, 376
Lycia, 398
Lycians, 96, 133
Lycios, 306
Lycurgus, 55-64, 67, 70, 80, 254, 269,
   312, 365, 369, 371, 460
Lydia, 40, 43, 50-54, 59, 80, 82, 96
Lysander, 226-230, 283, 286, 312, 320
Lysias, 357
Lysicles, 171
Lysimachus, 235

Macedonia, 49, 86, 93, 98, 111, 185,
   192, 326-27, 331-32, 349-50, 385,
   408
   population of, 331
Macedonians, 347-48, 418, 420-22, 425-
   26, 436-37
Macronians, 307
Magnesia (Thessaly), 102, 282
Magnesia (on Meander River), 132
Malaic Gulf, 101
Malea, Cape, 59
Malis, 101, 103
Mallia, 13
Mallians, 427-28
Mantinea, 117, 132, 200-201, 207, 209
   battle of, 316, 318
Maracanda, 415-16, 418
Marathon, 74, 88-91, 108, 119, 121,
   149, 304, 370
Marathus, 400
Mardonius, 85-87, 111-19
Marduk, 409
Marmora, Sea of, 36; see also Propontis
Marseilles, 29-30, 39, 321
Marsyas, 255-56
Marsvas, Sicilian, 360
Massilia, 29-30, 39, 321
Mazaces, 404
Mazaeus, 408, 411-12
Meander River, 49, 132

Medea, 27, 307
Medes, 95-96, 103, 111, 128
Media, 80-81, 92, 408, 410-12, 430
  Paraetacene, 412
Medius, 441
Medusa, 27
Megacles, 73, 121, 130, 134
Megalopolis, 346, 408
Megara, 66-67, 79, 108, 113-14, 137,
  139-40, 159, 168, 181, 185, 190,
  225, 284, 353
Megistias, 104
Meletus, 288, 291
Melians, 263, 371; see also Melos
Melkart, 402-3, 406
Melos, 16, 201, 204-5, 210, 215, 221,
  228
  dialogue of, 201-4
Memnon, 397-98
Memphis, 404, 407
Menelaus, 5, 55
Meno, 241-42; see also Menon
Menon, 301; see also Meno
Mercenaries, 313-15, 322-23, 328, 332-
  33, 337, 346, 357
Mesopotamia, 148
Messene, 176, 316
Messenia, 55, 64-65, 134, 143, 178-80,
  183, 316, 346
  revolt of, 134-35
Messenian Wars, 55, 59
Messina, 38, 175, 356
Methone, 333
Methymna, 171, 174
Metics, at Athens, 77-78, 125, 142-43,
  280, 284, 286
Metrodorus of Chios, 354
Micon, 146
Midas, 398
Milesians, 118-19
Miletus, 5, 13, 40, 49-50, 53, 59, 65,
  82-85, 144-45, 398
Military, see Warfare
Miltiades, 89-90, 120-21, 125, 130, 142
Mimnermus, 122
Mindarus, 225
Minoan culture, 13-14, 16, 27, 30, 38,
  44
Minoan Empire, 32
Minos, 14, 27, 48, 56, 364
Minotaur, 14, 27
Mitylene, see Mytilene
Mnesicles, 146
Molossians, 132

Moly, 21
Money, Aristotle on, 388-89
  in Athens, 67
  effect on the polis, 40-42, 57-58, 124,
    130, 133, 142, 312-15, 319-20, 322-
    23
  effect on warfare, 313-15
  Persian use of, 397, 401
  Philip and, 331-32
  in Sparta, 57
Money economy and agriculture, 41, 321
Monopoly, Aristotle on, 388-89
Mulla Pass, 429
Munychia, battle of, 285-86, 353
Murex dye, 28-29
Muses, 4, 46-47, 122-23, 328, 368-69,
  467
Mycale, battle of, 117-19, 122, 128
Mycalessus, massacre at, 215
Mycenae, 13-15, 27-28, 114, 150
Mycenaean culture, 14, 16, 38, 44, 49
Myrsilus, 51
Myths, as history, 4-5, 59
  Platonic, 270, 281, 366, 370
Mytilene, 171-74, 179, 204-5, 227, 231,
  263, 275
  battle of, 231
  revolt of, 172-74

Naples, 38-39
Naupactus, 137, 140, 178, 180
Navigation, 30-31
Naxos, Island of, 87, 129, 133, 136, 143
Naxos (Sicily), 211
Neapolis, 39; see also Naples
Nearchus, 427-29, 441
Nebuchadnezzar, 29
Nemea, games at, 35, 100
Neoptolemus, 351
Nestor, 24-25
Nestus River, 333
Nicanor, 432
Nicias, 178, 182, 184, 187-89, 196, 199-
  201, 205-8, 211, 213-18, 220, 285,
  334-35
  Peace of, 188-91, 195, 199-200, 263
  speech of, 206
Nicostratus, 176
Nile, 82, 422, 427
Nineveh, 29, 305, 407
Nisaea, 59, 137, 185, 225
Notion, battle of, 231
Nysa, 423, 425

Ochus, 401
Odeon, 234
Odessa, 36
Odeum, 165
Odrysians, 395
Odysseus, 4, 5, 16-26, 34, 38, 70-71, 97, 132, 143, 439-40, 456
Oedipus, 27, 190, 406
Olbia, 35, 321
Oligarchs, 80, 85, 92, 116, 132, 138-39, 144-45, 169, 171, 175-78, 180, 183-84, 191, 201, 210, 223-24, 228, 283, 285, 287, 312, 315, 320, 366, 371, 398, 432, 465
Oligarchy, 279, 370, 383
Olive, 13, 37, 41
Olpae, 178, 180
Olympia, 31, 35, 146, 317-18
Olympias, 333, 346, 350-51, 393-94, 406, 419, 427, 438
Olympic Games, 35, 39, 59-60, 100, 102, 116, 126, 171, 205-7, 327-28, 332-33, 357, 432
Olympus, Mount, 7-9, 20, 69, 98, 122, 328
Omens, 217, 302, 305
Onomacritus, 92
Onomarchus, 333, 335-36, 345
Opis, 437-38, 440
Opora, 198
Oracles, 80-82, 92, 204, 259, 334-35, 403-4, 419, 422; see also Delphic Oracle
    in Thucydides, 191
Orchomenos, 14, 114
Orestes, 19, 150-51
Oreus, 143, 224
Oropus, 214
Ossa, Mount, 98
Ostracism, 78, 108, 121, 132-34, 136-37, 141, 201, 326, 461
Overseers, 57, 61, 62
Oxus River, 415-16
Oxyartes, 422

Paches, 171, 172, 174
Pactyes, 95
Paeonians, 329, 333, 395
Pagae, 59
Pagasae, Gulf of, 14, 102, 105, 335
Pages' conspiracy, 421-22
Pakistan, 422
Palaikastro, 15
Pale, 114

Palermo, 29, 117
Palestine, 404
Pamir Mountains, 82
Pammenes, 329
Pamphylia, 133, 398
Pamphylians, 96
Pan, at Marathon, 88, 90-91
Panathenaic Festivals, 75, 147-48
Pangaeus, Mount, 187, 330-33, 396
Panhellenic Congress, 144
Panhellenic League, 97, 116, 128-29, 136
Panionian League, 5, 50, 82
Panormus, 29, 117
Paralus, 228, 245
Paris, see Alexander (Paris)
Parmenion, 333, 397-400, 403, 407-8, 410, 413-14
Parnassus, Mount, 107
Paros, 121, 130
Parsa, 409
Parthenon, 146, 157-58, 164, 324, 335
Parthia, 413
Parthians, 95, 408
Pasargadae, 409
Patroclus, 9-10, 16, 105, 397, 428
Pausanias (in Plato's Symposium), 253
Pausanias, Spartan king, 114-16, 128-29, 131-32, 188
Pausanias, the younger, 228, 286
Pelasgians, 11-12, 15-16, 49
Pella, 327-28, 346, 351, 375
Pelopidas, 315, 326, 328-29
Peloponnese, 16, 163, 170, 178-80, 205, 207
Peloponnesian Alliance, 129, 201
Peloponnesian League, 140-41, 144, 160, 168
Peloponnesian War, 159-65, 168-89, 193, 195, 199-232, 313
Peloponnesians, 105, 108, 119-20, 126, 164
Pelusium, 404
Penelope, 17-19, 21, 25-26
Penteconter, 31
Pentelicus, Mount, 90
Perdiccas II, 185, 187-88, 327
Perdiccas III, 327-30
Perdiccas, Macedonian officer, 423-24
Pergamos, 311-12
Periander, 76
Pericles, 121-25, 127, 129, 130-38, 142-46, 149, 151-70, 172, 178-79, 185, 189-91, 199, 237-38, 246, 285, 313, 320, 353, 438

Pericles (*continued*)
  funeral oration, 160-63
  speech in 429 B.C., 163-64
Pericles, son of Pericles, 227
Peictione, 353
Perinthus, 401
Perioeci, *see* Dwellers-round-about
Peripatetics, 376
Persepolis, 409-10, 413
Perses, 45-46
Perseus, 27, 393
Persia, 80, 429
Persian Empire, 82-87, 91, 94-96, 112, 115, 139, 343-44, 396-99, 407, 409-11
Persian Wars, 80-120, 146
Persians, 88-90, 94-96, 115-20, 122, 125-26, 131-33, 137-39, 145, 148, 221-25, 300-305, 311-16, 331, 342, 350, 357, 411, 436-37
Persis, 411
Peucestas, 427, 431
Phaeacians, 17-19, 21
Phaedo, 293
Phaedrus, 253
Phaenarete, 235, 242
Phaestos, 13
Phalaecus, 345-46
Phalanx, 42, 316, 329, 408
Phalerum, 90, 99, 110, 138, 140
Pharnabazus, 221-22, 225, 230
Phaselis, 139
Phasis, 35
Phēmē, 118, 464
Pherae, 335-36
Phidias, 146, 155, 157-58, 465
Phidippides, 88, 91
Phidippides (*Clouds*), 251-52, 352
Philip II of Macedon, 326, 328-33, 335-38, 343-51, 357, 375, 382-83, 389, 393-95, 406, 414, 417-19
  and the polis, 412
Philip (physician), 399
Philippi, 331
Philippides, 245
Philips, golden, 331-32
Philocles, 227-28
Philomelus, 333
Philotas, 413-14, 421
Phliasians, 114
Phlius, 114
Phocaeans, 29-30, 82, 304, 345
Phocians, 101, 103-5, 345
Phocion, 339-41

Phocis, 13, 85, 137, 139, 178, 333, 335-36, 346-47, 395
Phoenicia, 400, 402, 408, 423
Phoenicians, 28-30, 49, 83-84, 92-94, 96, 109-11, 117, 133, 139, 167, 428, 438
Phormio, 170-71
Phrada, 413, 414
Phrygia, 49-50, 230, 312
Phrynichus, 85
Pieria, 328
Pindar, 100, 126, 161, 327, 395, 404, 418
  quoted, 100, 361, 381
  translation, 456
Piracy, 15, 16, 31, 33, 36, 38, 131, 133, 321
Piraeus, 70, 99, 124, 126-28, 130, 137-38, 140, 156, 159-60, 163, 165, 224-25, 228, 234, 284-86
Pisidia, 299-300, 398
Pisistratids, 76, 88, 91, 92; *see also* Hippias *and* Hipparchus
Pisistratus, 71-77, 88-89, 123, 147, 149, 167, 370, 409
Plague, 163-64, 169, 174, 179, 208
Plataea, 79, 107, 115, 118-19, 128, 135, 347, 371
  battle of, 113-16, 125
Plataeans, 88-91, 169, 174
Plato, 288, 292, 329, 353-56, 358-78
  Apology, 235-38, 288-93, 317, 470
  Censorship, 367-68
  Charmides, 240
  Cratylus, 468
  Critias, 370
  Crito, 293
  dialogues, 361-62, 376
  Epistles, 354, 359-62, 369-70
  Gorgias, 240-41
  Laws, 364-72, 378-79, 383
  Meno, 241-42
  Phaedo, 293-96
  poems, 368
  Protagoras, 245-50
  Republic, 260-82, 354, 358, 361-62, 364-69, 378-79, 390, 470
  Symposium, 253-59, 318-19, 368, 469
  Theaetetus, 242-45
  Timaeus, 362-63, 365, 378, 474
  translations, 456
Plemmyrium, 215
Plistoanax, 188-89

Plutarch, quoted, 126, 135, 160, 315, 333, 348, 371, 374, 406-7, 437
Polemarch, 65, 89
Polemarchus, 260
Polis, 32-37, 42, 124-26, 142-43, 153, 155, 158-60, 165, 167-69, 191, 195, 199, 224-26, 260, 297, 372; see also Cosmopolis
  Alexander and, 412, 439-40
  Aristotle and, 382-84, 387, 389-90
  army as, 303-5, 308
  Clisthenes and, 77-79
  Democritus on, 354
  early Athenian, 64-68
  and education, 373, 387
  extension of, 350
  fourth-century, 319-23
  ideal, search for, 345
  kinship in, 35
  money economy and, see under Money
  Plato on, 364-66
  Socrates and, 235-36, 267-70, 278-83, 291
  Solon and, 68-71
  Spartan, 55-57, 61, 63
  Thucydides on, 175-78
Polycrates of Samos, 52-53
Polydamas, 262
Polydectes, 55
Polygnotus, 146, 327
Polyphemus, 18, 21-23
Pontus, see Black Sea
Porus, 423-24, 426
Posidon, 10-11, 16-18, 20, 23, 26, 91, 102, 128, 146, 194, 353, 428, 433
Posidonia, 369
Potidaea, 114, 159, 163, 169, 200, 233-34
  revolt of, 175
  Socrates at, 257-59
Pottery, 28, 30, 37, 75, 78, 321
Praxiteles, 325-26
Pre-Socratics, 455
Priam, 5, 10, 16
Priene, 82
Prodicus, 244, 245
Prometheus, 423
Propontis, 38, 84-88; see also Marmora, Sea of
Propylaea, 146
Protagoras, 144, 245-50, 319, 339, 354, 356, 365
Proxenus, 200, 299-300, 302-3
Psammon, 405

Pseira, 15
Psyttaleia, 110
Ptolemy, general, 410, 415, 419
Ptolemy, Macedonian usurper, 328
Punjab, 407, 422
Pydna, 132, 330-31
Pylos, 24-25, 180-82, 184-89, 197-98, 225
Pythagoras, 53
Pythagoreans, 53, 356, 362, 364
Pythia, priestess, 81, 334, 399
Pythian Games, 100

Ravi River, 424
Red Sea, 423
Reggio di Calabria, 38
Rhegium, 38, 52, 175
Rhetras, 56, 58, 184
Rhodes, 13, 15, 16, 59
Rhodians, 305
Rhone River, 30
Rome, 356
Roxana, 422, 442
Russia, 36-37

Sacans, 90, 95-96, 111, 408
Sacred Band, Theban, 329, 347, 394
Sagartians, 96
Sagunto, 35
Salaethus, 171
Salaminia, 211
Salamis, 79, 99, 101, 106-11, 113, 117, 119, 121-27, 130, 133-34, 149, 152, 223-24, 284
  battle of, 109-111
Salamis (Cyprus), 139
Samarkand, 82, 415
Samos, 40, 52-53, 59, 111, 117-18, 121-22, 129, 136, 138, 144-45, 222-26, 348
  revolt of, 144-45, 152, 159-61
  revolution in, 222-23
Samothrace, 394
Sangala, 424
Sappho, 52-53
  quoted, 53
Sarangas, 95
Sarapis, oracle of, 442
Sardinia, 82, 85, 117
Sardis, 59, 107, 225, 300-301, 311, 409
  sack of, 84, 86-87
Scilly Isles, 29
Scione, 187, 204
Scopas, 325-26

Sculpture, 50-51, 74-75, 146-47, 325-26
Scylax, 423
Scylla and Charybdis, 20, 22
Scyros, 131, 315
Scythas, 92
Scythians, 83, 95, 346, 413-14, 416, 420-
    21, 423
Segesta, 205-7, 210
Selinus, 205-6, 210
Senate, in Sparta, 56-57
Sennacherib, 29
Serfs, 16, 67; see also Helots
Sestos, 120, 122, 125, 128, 141, 227
Seuthes, 311, 313
Seven Sages, 70-71, 82, 389
Shahrud, 413
Ships, 19, 31, 216; see also under Warfare,
    armaments, tactics
Sicilian expedition, 208-21
Sicilians, 356-59
Sicily, 15, 29, 36, 38, 85-86, 117, 140,
    175, 179, 185, 205-7, 211-21, 226
Sicyon, 34, 76, 114, 118, 215
Sidon, 29, 83, 96, 117, 402-3
Silenus, 255-56
Simmias, 293
Simonides, 75, 158, 248
    quoted, 105, 158, 235, 260, 372
Sinope, 309, 400
Sirens, 22, 38
Siris, 108
Slavery, Aristotle on, 385-87, 411
    for debt, 41, 67-68
    Socrates on, 280
Slaves, 116, 124-25, 142-43, 175, 215,
    286, 315, 320, 367
    in trade, 30, 36
Socrates, 199-200, 227, 233-85, 287-
    300, 317-19, 335, 338, 340-42,
    352-56, 364-72, 374, 380, 390, 440,
    469-71
    Alcibiades on, 255-58
    death of, 294-97
    on the polis, 345
    on rhetoric, 339
    trial of, 287-93
    Xenophon on, 317, 319
Sogdian Rock, 422
Sogdians, 415-16
Solon, 68-74, 77-78, 80, 122, 125, 130,
    136, 154-55, 254, 287, 353, 439
    constitution of, 68-69, 71, 74
    quoted, 69, 71, 137, 370, 388

Sophists, 154, 165, 234-35, 239, 241,
    244-45, 249-52, 288-89, 352-53, 468
Sophocles, 5, 151-54, 190-92, 195, 323
    Oedipus the King, 153-54, 236, 239,
        390, 406
    translations, 455
Spain, 35, 85, 117
Sparta and Spartans, 5, 31, 55-57, 64, 67,
    70, 79, 82-85, 88, 91-92, 97-98,
    102-5, 111-18, 125, 127-44, 156,
    158-60, 163-65, 168, 170-71, 175-
    76, 179-89, 199-201, 211-13, 216,
    221-25, 283-87, 300, 310-20, 329-
    30, 333, 336, 342, 349, 356-57, 370,
    400, 408, 410, 422, 432
    character of, 96-97
    population, 320
Spartiates, 57, 60-61, 64, 70
Speusippus, 375-76
Sphacteria, 180-83, 187, 190, 199-201,
    211, 313
Spitamenes, 416
Spithridates, 397
Stagira, 375
Stateira, 477
Stratocles, 347
Strepsiades, 251-52
Strymon River, 93, 186-87, 330, 333
Styreia, 114
Sunium, Cape, 89, 90
Susa, 82-83, 87, 111, 123, 139, 149, 230,
    409, 431
Sybaris, 39, 144
Sybarite, 39, 369
Syracuse, 114-16, 174, 179, 185, 205-7,
    210-13, 220-21, 321, 356-58, 360-
    61, 367, 369
Syria, 148, 301

Taenarum, Cape, 59
Tanagra, battle of, 137
Taochians, 306
Taranto, Gulf of, 39
Tarentum, 38, 214, 356
Tarshish, 29
Tarsus, 301, 399
Tashkent, 416, 423
Taxila, 424, 430
Taxiles, 423-24
Tegea, 114-16, 132
Teilhard de Chardin, Pierre, on living
    universe, 474
Telemachus, 20-21, 24-25
Temenids, 327

Tempe, Vale of, 98, 101
Teos, 52, 82
Thaïs, 410
Thales, 53, 82, 388-89
Thalia, 196, 467
Thapsacus, 301, 407
 Bay of, 213-16
Thasos, 86, 146
 revolt of, 134-35
Theaetetus, 242-45
Theagenes, 66
Thebes, 14, 27, 79, 88, 98, 102, 105, 113, 115-16, 118, 127, 137-38, 153, 169, 229, 284, 312, 315-19, 328-30, 333, 336, 342, 346-49, 357, 408
 destruction of, 395
Theches, Mount, 306
Themis, 58, 65
Themistocles, 97, 99, 101, 105-12, 117, 125-27, 130-33, 136-39, 142, 157, 159, 162, 178, 224, 230
Theognis, 122
Theophrastus, 392
Theoria, 198
Thera, 201
Theramenes, 225, 229, 283-85, 287, 383
Thermaic Gulf, 326, 333
Thermopylae, 101-3, 106, 119, 121, 135, 183, 336, 345-46
Thersites, 34, 348
Theseus, 14, 27, 91, 131, 195, 461
Thespiae, 107
Thespians, 104
Thesprotia, 80
Thessalian League, 335-36, 346, 465
Thessaly and Thessalians, 5, 11, 14-15, 33-34, 85, 92, 97-98, 101, 111, 128, 136, 138, 185, 188, 192, 316, 329, 331, 335-36, 410
Thetes, 68-69, 133, 141-42; *see also* Dustyfoot
Thetis, 8
Thibron, 311
Thirty Tyrants, the, 229-30, 283-84, 286, 288, 290, 353-54
Thirty Years' Peace, 140-41, 159, 181, 189
Thorikos, 14
Thrace and Thracians, 37, 52, 76, 82-83, 85, 87, 96, 100, 111, 130-31, 134, 169, 187-88, 190, 311, 327, 329, 333, 336, 346, 394-95
Thrasybulus, 225, 284-88, 352
Thrasymachus, 260-66, 354, 356

Three Hundred, the, at Thermopylae, 63, 101-3, 158
Thucydides, historian, 5, 14, 142, 163, 187, 198-99, 316-18, 341, 373, 466
 on civil war, 176-78
 economic interpretation, 466
 on history, 190
 on revolution, 183-84
 on Sicilian expedition, 209-10, 218-19, 220-21
 and tragedy, 191-92
 translations, 456
 quoted, 2, 128, 163-64, 172-74, 183-84
Thucydides, statesman, 141
Thurii, 144, 211, 215, 304
Thyrea, 185
Tigris River, 84, 301, 407, 433
Timaeus, 362-64, 370
Timaia, Queen, 222
Timocracy, 279, 320, 369-70
Timoleon, 361
Timotheus, 327
Tin, 12, 29, 30
Tiresias, 26, 153
Tiribazus, 305
Tiryns, 13-15, 27-28, 114
Tissaphernes, 221-26, 231, 301-2, 305, 311
Torone, 187
Tragedy, 5, 149-54, 190-99, 297, 323, 390-91, 440
 Aristotle on, 390-91
 and dialectic, 239-40
 Plato and, 372-73
 Thucydides and, 466
Trapezus, 307-8
Triballians, 395
Tripolis, 400
Troezen, 107, 114, 118, 121
Trojan War, 5-11
Troy, 4-10, 16, 24, 134, 193, 311, 397
Trygaeus, 196-98
Tunis, 29, 36
Tylissos, 13
Tyndareus, 418
Tyrants, 43, 67, 71-72, 74, 76, 79-80, 123, 172, 252, 319, 323, 358-60, 370, 383, 459, 471
 Socrates on, 280
Tyre, 29, 83, 117, 402-5, 411
Tyrian purple, 28-29
Tyrtaeus, 63
 quoted, 55, 61, 180

Utica, 29

Vine, 13, 37

Wage-earners, see Thetes
War, 169, 171, 215-16
    Aristotle on, 411
    Euripides on, 192-94
    of factions, 176-78
    mercenary, 313-15
    Socrates on, 268-69
Warfare, armaments, tactics, 179, 313-
        14, 316, 322, 330, 336; see also
        Mercenaries
    of Alexander, 396, 476
    archery, 182-84, 305
    Athenian, 141, 170
    bronze weapons, 12, 16
    cavalry, 33, 304-5
    chariots, 33, 407-8
    Corinthian naval armaments, 216
    Iphicratean, 313-14
    iron weapons, 16, 458-59
    Macedonian, 329, 332
    of Mardonius, 463-64
    money and, 313-15
    naval, 217-18
    sarissa, 327, 332
    of Xerxes, 94-6, 462-63
Wason, M., on weapons, 458-59
Weapons, see Warfare
Well-fathered, see Aristocrats
Western Greece, 39, 85-86
Women, Aristotle on, 386
    in Athens, 77-78, 124-25, 157
    in democracy, 280
    in Plato's polis, 270
    in Sparta, 63
Words and coins, 40, 144, 154, 177,
        331-32, 335, 369, 388, 402, 417
Writing, 14-16, 28, 30, 40, 66, 67

Xanthippus, father of Pericles, 121-22,
    124-25, 128, 131, 134

Xanthippus, son of Pericles, 245
Xenocrates, 375-76
Xenophanes, 155
    quoted, 53-54
Xenophon, 290, 301-13, 316-20, 332,
        340, 342-45, 400, 417, 440
    on Aegospotami, 228
    Anabasis, 299-312, 317, 342, 456
    Apology, 317
    Cavalry Commander, 319, 335
    Cyropaedia, 318, 326
    dates of works, 472
    Hellenica, 284-87, 316-18, 319, 371
    Memorabilia, 238, 240, 298, 317, 319
    On Horsemanship, 317, 319
    Republic of the Lacedaemonians, 317
    Symposium, 318-19
    Ways and Means, 319
Xerxes, 91-112, 115-17, 122-23, 127, 129,
        132, 134, 148-49, 158-59, 183, 191-
        92, 223, 304, 409-10
    army of, 94-96, 462-63
    navy of, 96-97
    and oracles, 334

Zab River, 301
Zakro, 15
Zancle, 92
Zeno, Eleatic, 155
Zeugitai, 68, 142
Zeus, 4, 8-10, 17, 20, 23, 26, 45-47, 59,
        69, 80, 99-101, 122, 125, 146, 189,
        191, 194, 196-97, 199, 204, 221,
        251, 253, 328, 352, 356, 362, 364-
        65, 371, 381, 393, 404-6, 417-19,
        430, 433, 439-41
    and justice, 45-46
    Liberator, 116, 166, 192
    Olympian, 74
    Savior, 303, 305, 307
    of Thebes, 404
    in tragedy, 154
    Xenios, 359, 473
Zeuxis, 327

THE ROMAN WORLD

Edited by **Sir John Boardman**, Professor Emeritus of Classical Archaeology and Art, Lincoln College, Oxford; **Dr Oswyn Murray**, Fellow and Tutor in Ancient History at Balliol College, Oxford; and **Jasper Griffin**, Professor of Classical Literature and a Fellow of Balliol College, Oxford.

THE seventeen contributors to *The Oxford History of the Roman World* are all distinguished authorities in their field. They are:

MICHAEL CRAWFORD, University College, London, *Early Rome and Italy*

†ELIZABETH RAWSON, Corpus Christi College, Oxford, *The Expansion of Rome*

P. G. M^cC. BROWN, Trinity College, Oxford, *The First Roman Literature*

MIRIAM GRIFFIN, Somerville College, Oxford, *Cicero and Rome*

ROBIN NISBET, Corpus Christi College, Oxford, *The Poets of the Late Republic*

DAVID STOCKTON, Brasenose College, Oxford, *The Founding of the Empire*

NICHOLAS PURCELL, St John's College, Oxford, *The Arts of Government*

R. O. A. M. LYNE, Balliol College, Oxford, *Augustan Poetry and Society*

JASPER GRIFFIN, Balliol College, Oxford, *Virgil*

ANDREW LINTOTT, Worcester College, Oxford, *Roman Historians*

DONALD RUSSELL, St John's College, Oxford, *The Arts of Prose: The Early Empire*

RICHARD JENKYNS, Lady Margaret Hall, Oxford, *Silver Latin Poetry and the Latin Novel*

ANTHONY MEREDITH, Campion Hall, Oxford, *Later Philosophy*

ROGER LING, University of Manchester, *The Arts of Living*

JOHN MATTHEWS, Queen's College, Oxford, *Roman Life and Society*

R. J. A. WILSON, Trinity College, Dublin, *Roman Art and Architecture*

HENRY CHADWICK, Peterhouse, Cambridge, *Envoi: On Taking Leave of Antiquity*

THE OXFORD
HISTORY OF
THE ROMAN
WORLD

EDITED BY

JOHN BOARDMAN
JASPER GRIFFIN
OSWYN MURRAY

OXFORD
UNIVERSITY PRESS

OXFORD

UNIVERSITY PRESS

Great Clarendon Street, Oxford OX2 6DP

Oxford University Press is a department of the University of Oxford.
It furthers the University's objective of excellence in research, scholarship,
and education by publishing worldwide in

Oxford New York

Athens Auckland Bangkok Bogotá Buenos Aires Cape Town
Chennai Dar es Salaam Delhi Florence Hong Kong Istanbul Karachi
Kolkata Kuala Lumpur Madrid Melbourne Mexico City Mumbai Nairobi
Paris São Paulo Shanghai Singapore Taipei Tokyo Toronto Warsaw

with associated companies in Berlin Ibadan

Oxford is a registered trade mark of Oxford University Press
in the UK and in certain other countries

British Library Cataloguing in Publication Data

Data available

Library of Congress Cataloging in Publication Data

The Oxford history of the Roman world/edited by John Boardman,
Jasper Griffin, Oswyn Murray.
p. cm.
Includes bibliographical references and index.
1. Rome—History—To 510 B.C. 2. Rome—History—Republic, 510–30
B.C. 3. Rome—History—Empire, 30 B.C.–284 A.D. I. Boardman,
John, 1927- . II. Griffin, Jasper. III. Murray, Oswyn.
937—dc20 DG231.094 1991 91–11763

ISBN-13: 978-0-19-280203-3

8

Printed in Great Britain by
Clays Ltd, St Ives plc

CONTENTS

List of Illustrations   vii

List of Maps   viii

INTRODUCTION   1
Jasper Griffin

1. EARLY ROME AND ITALY   13
Michael Crawford

2. THE EXPANSION OF ROME   50
Elizabeth Rawson

3. THE FIRST ROMAN LITERATURE   74
P. G. M^cC. Brown

4. CICERO AND ROME   90
Miriam Griffin

5. THE POETS OF THE LATE REPUBLIC   121
Robin Nisbet

6. THE FOUNDING OF THE EMPIRE   146
David Stockton

7. THE ARTS OF GOVERNMENT   180
Nicholas Purcell

8. AUGUSTAN POETRY AND SOCIETY   215
R. O. A. M. Lyne

9. VIRGIL   245
Jasper Griffin

10. ROMAN HISTORIANS   268
Andrew Lintott

11. THE ARTS OF PROSE: THE EARLY
    EMPIRE   288
Donald Russell

12. SILVER LATIN POETRY AND THE
    LATIN NOVEL   317
    Richard Jenkyns

13. LATER PHILOSOPHY   340
    Anthony Meredith

14. THE ARTS OF LIVING   362
    Roger Ling

15. ROMAN LIFE AND SOCIETY   388
    John Matthews

16. ROMAN ART AND ARCHITECTURE   413
    R. J. A. Wilson

17. ENVOI: ON TAKING LEAVE OF
    ANTIQUITY   449
    Henry Chadwick

Tables of Events   479
Index   507

LIST OF ILLUSTRATIONS

1. Interior of the Pantheon (c.AD 118–28). Painting by G. P. Pannini (before 1747). Washington, National Gallery of Art, Samuel H. Kress Collection, 1939. (Photo Museum).

2. Round Temple by the Tiber, Rome (end of 2nd century BC). Diam. approx. 17 m. (Fototeca Unione).

3. Pont du Gard, near Nîmes (late 1st century BC). Ht. 49 m. (Photo Michael Holford).

4. Reconstruction drawing of interior of House of Pansa at Pompeii. (British Library).

5. Painted wall-decoration from Boscotrecase (c.10 BC). Ht. 3.31 m. (including socle); length 3.27 m. Naples, Museo Nazionale 147501. (Photo Leonard von Matt).

6. Embossed silver wine-cup (1st century AD). Ht. 12.5 cm.; diam. 14.4 cm. Hildesheim, Römer-Pelizaeus Museum 3779.14. (Photo Staatliche Museen, Berlin).

7. Gemma Augustea: sardonyx cameo (between AD 14 and 37). Ht. 19 cm: width 23 cm. Vienna, Kunsthistorisches Museum. (Photo Arts Council of Great Britain).

8. Roman with the busts of his ancestors (late 1st century BC). Marble. Ht. 1.65 m. Rome, Palazzo Barberini 2392. (Photo Alinari).

9. Head of Pompey (106–48 BC). Marble (copy from original of 1st century BC). Ht. 26 cm. Copenhagen, Ny Carlsberg Glyptothek 733. (Photo Museum).

10. Head of Julius Caesar (100–44 BC) from Tusculum. Marble. Ht. 33 cm. (head 21 cm.). Turin, Museum of Antiquities. (Photo German Archaeological Institute, Rome).

11. Mother Earth relief, Ara Pacis, Rome (13–9 BC). Luna Marble. Ht. 1.57 m. (Photo Alinari).

12. Spoils from Jerusalem, Arch of Titus, Rome (soon after AD 81). Marble. Ht. 2.04 m.; length 3.80 m. (Photo Alinari).

13. Danube bridge: Trajan's column, Rome (AD 113). Cast. Ht of frieze
    approx 1.25 m. (Photo German Archaeological Institute, Rome).

14. Bronze statue of M. Aurelius (AD 166–80). Ht. 4.24 m. Rome,
    Piazza Campidoglio. (Photo Alinari).

15. Detail of the Canopus: Hadrian's Villa at Tivoli (between AD 124
    and 133). Length of crocodile (cast) 1.66 m. (Photo R. A. Ling).

16. Nile boat trip: mosaic from Tivoli (2nd century AD). Ht. 66.5 cm;
    width 67 cm. Cardiff, National Museum of Wales 32.93. (Photo
    Museum).

LIST OF MAPS

1. Italy   12
2. The Growth of Rome in Italy   14
3. The Roman Empire   143
4. The Growth of Roman Rule   152

NOTE

Cross-references to the companion volume to this book, *The Oxford
History of Greece and the Hellenistic World*, are given as (for example):
Vol. 1, p. 100.

Introduction

JASPER GRIFFIN

THIS book tells the story of the rise of Rome from its origins as a cluster of villages on the hills round the Forum to the possession of an empire which unified the Mediterranean world and a great deal besides. At its height the Roman Empire stretched from Northumberland to Algeria, from Portugal to Syria, from the Rhine to the Nile: it comprised the whole or part of the territory of what are now thirty sovereign states, and it was not until 1870 that Italy, for instance, achieved again the unity which Rome had imposed before the birth of Christ. The memory of that lost unity has haunted the mind of Europe.

The idea of Rome has given to the West several distinct myths, each full of resonance. There is the image of the stern and upright generals and consuls of the Republican period, great conquerors devoted to the service of their country. These were men like Cato, who after governing a province in Spain sold his horse so that the state should not have to bear the cost of transporting it back to Italy, and like Cincinnatus, who when the Senate summoned him to serve again as supreme commander was found hard at work ploughing his fields. Such a man deserved to have a great American city named after him. Their wives were women like Cornelia, mother of the Gracchi, who when a visitor displayed her jewellery called in her sons and said 'These are my jewels', and, later, Arria Paeta, who when the Emperor ordered her husband to commit suicide showed the way by stabbing herself with the words 'Look, it doesn't hurt'.

In later literature we find such figures in the tragedies of Corneille, and in Shakespeare's Brutus. Swift, in the third part of *Gulliver's Travels*, sends his hero to an island of necromancers, who at his desire call up the mighty dead. Gulliver tells us: 'I was struck with a profound veneration at the Sight of *Brutus*; and could easily discover the most consummate Virtue, the greatest intrepidity and Firmness of Mind, the truest Love of his Country, and general Benevolence for Mankind in every Lineament of his Countenance'. He goes on to say, 'I desired that the Senate of *Rome* might appear before me in one large Chamber, and a modern Representative, in Counterview, in another. The first seemed to be an Assembly of Heroes and Demy-Gods; the other a knot of Pedlars, Pick-pockets, Highwaymen and Bullies ...' In art we see such grand Romans depicted in the paintings of David: such subjects as Lucius Brutus condemning his own sons to death for treason to the Republic, and Horatius killing his country's enemy, although he is betrothed to his own sister.

In time the Republic gave place to an Empire. On the one hand the flamboyant personalities of the early Emperors, and the opulence of Imperial Rome, have created an ineffaceable picture of luxury and cruelty, which found expression in Flaubert, Gautier, and Victor Hugo, in *The Last Days of Pompeii*, and in Hollywood spectaculars from *Spartacus* to *Ben Hur*. But there also was the contrasting image: the straight and endless Roman roads which dominated the face of Europe, the matchless efficiency of the legions, and an Empire which brought peace for generations to a world where such a thing has at all times been far rarer than gold. Poems and stories of Kipling give that idea powerful expression: a self-denying and loyal military and administrative machine, protecting civilization from the barbarians across the frontier.

There have, of course, been other great civilizations in the history of the world. Ancient China, for instance, was an empire which lasted longer than Rome, and which produced great art and literature. But ancient Rome, with ancient Greece, has a special claim on the West, because our own culture has grown directly out of it. The remembrance was never lost that European society was the successor to an impressive earlier culture, even when, as we see from works like the medieval *Gesta Romanorum* (old stories collected and given Christian morals, often strikingly inappropriate) all sense of realistic history might be so completely vanished that in one story we find the Emperor Claudius marrying his daughter to the philosopher Socrates, who one day in the forest meets King Alexander. Rome was always a model for imitation and emulation, and thus two ideas were inbuilt: first, that one's own society was not the first in history; and second, that high civilization, once achieved, could be lost.

The Latin language, like Greek, belongs to the great Indo-European family which spread, in the course of many centuries, from an original centre somewhere south of the Caucasus into India, Iran, and Europe. The ancestors of the Romans must include many people who entered Italy from the north, probably not in one single group, reaching the site of Rome by about 1000 BC. There they mingled with other peoples: we can dimly discern different words and even different burial customs of elements later called 'Latin' and 'Sabine'. Until about 600 BC we find separate settlements on the Roman hills, that on the Palatine being traditionally the oldest. In the course of the sixth century the settlements amalgamated into one, and from then on Rome may be said to exist. Its traditional foundation date, 21 April 753 BC, with most of what we are told by later antiquity about Rome's early period, is essentially myth rather than history; but the tradition that Romulus, the founder, established a 'refuge' (*asylum*) to welcome refugees and outcasts to his new city may reflect a truth about the miscellaneous population of early Rome.

The city was much influenced by the Etruscans, a mysterious people then at their zenith in central Italy. They modified the

Indo-European inheritance considerably. It was their influence, for instance, that explains the triad of deities worshipped on the Capitol: Jupiter, Juno, and Minerva. That makes sense only in Etruscan terms. From Etruria also came the elaborate systems for discovering the divine purposes by means of omens, which were officially practised by Roman magistrates. Even their own names came to follow an alien pattern, the Indo-European single name (Menelaus, Siegfried), giving place to a complex style (Marcus Tullius Cicero). Etruria also transmitted the influence of Greece, especially in the visual arts.

Rome proved exceptional in aggressiveness and aptitude for war. Long years of campaigning reduced all of peninsular Italy to Roman domination by the early third century BC. The conquering city adopted many Greek refinements: her early coinage, for instance, is purely Greek in appearance. It was also hospitable to immigrants from other Italian communities, and generous in bestowing citizenship (but without the vote) on whole areas of Italy. Rome exacted tribute from subject Italian peoples in the form of soldiers; at the end of their military service they were settled in 'colonies', new towns which retained something of a military character, and which were intended to hold down and guarantee the security of conquered territories. The whole process made for a uniquely efficient machine for conquest.

Early Rome was characterized by a powerful public opinion, a strong public spirit, and a marked distaste for eccentricity and individualism. Despite the cultural influence of Greece, there was a powerful current of suspicion and dislike of highbrow foreign ways. A man should not lose touch with the soil, and the country was a morally better place than the town. The 'way of the ancestors' (*mos maiorum*) possessed a great moral force, and within the family, at least in the upper class, the father enjoyed a degree of power over his sons, even when they were grown men, which astonished the Greeks, and which is reflected in many stories of fathers who put their own sons to death and were admired for doing so. It is not difficult to imagine the stress produced in Romans by such pressures, and it is tempting to connect it with the double Roman obsession, on the one hand with parricide, and on the other with *pietas*, dutiful behaviour to parents, the archetype of which was the figure of Aeneas, founder of Rome, carrying his old father on his shoulders out of burning Troy. The anxiety engendered by such conflicts within the psyche, issuing in restless energy, might be part of the explanation for that astonishing fact, which seemed to the Romans themselves to be explicable only by constant divine favour: that this city, not particularly well sited or obviously well endowed, conquered the world.

Roman art and literature alike present the men of the Republic as tight-lipped, tight-fisted, and resolute. Such qualities as *parsimonia, severitas, frugalitas, simplicitas,* constantly praised, tell their own story; as does the moral ascendancy of a man like Cato, the quintessential peasant farmer magnified into a senator and consul. The names of many Roman grandees poignantly reveal their peasant origin. Cincinnatus and Calvus ('Curly' and 'Baldy'), Capito and Naso ('Big-head' and 'Nosey'), Crassus and Macer ('Fatty' and 'Skinny'), Flaccus and Bibulus ('Floppy' and 'The Drinker'), are the names of Roman consuls and poets, the inheritors of Etruscan kingly regalia and Greek aesthetic refinement.

Our richest and clearest evidence is for the late Republic, when the system was visibly breaking down, and when the old safeguards could no longer restrain the magnates from looting the provinces and even marching with armies on Rome in pursuit of their own aggrandizement. It is tempting to suppose that the reality had always been as venal and as ruthless. Yet it is clear that there had really been a change. When for fourteen years Hannibal led an invincible army about Italy urging Rome's Italian allies to revolt, the great majority of them stood firm; not much more than a hundred years later their grievances drove them to make war on Rome themselves. Roman justice and self-restraint, the public spirit which impressed Greeks when they met it in the second century BC, were not a myth.

The conquests of Alexander spread the language, architecture, and art of Greece as far to the East as India; the rise of Rome led eventually to the whole Mediterranean world and its 'fringe', as far as Britain, Romania, and Iraq, sharing in one recognizable culture with two great languages, Greek and Latin. Anything like modern nationalism was strikingly ineffective, and the Empire was not held down by force: for most of the first century AD, for instance, there was only one legion stationed in North Africa, and none at all in Spain. The Imperial administration insisted on two things: taxes must be paid, and law and order must be maintained. In most other respects the running of life was left to the cities, that is to say to the upper class who by their rank and wealth reckoned to run the cities. Culture was urban, literate, and remarkably uniform. The same books were studied by schoolboys all over this huge world, and whether in Provence, Turkey, or North Africa, cities arose whose layout and temples and public buildings shared the same repertory of forms and decorations. The silver on the table, the mosaics on the floor, the underfloor heating: a uniformity of style existed which is only now returning to our world.

That style was not, of course, all-inclusive. It was the creation of a leisured class, and Berber tribesmen or Illyrian goatherds doubtless felt little sympathy with it. The Empire must have depended on unfree labour to a much greater extent than Greece; and the slums of Rome show that many of the free urban poor lived lives of great poverty. Yet Rome was extraordinary among slave-owning societies in that slaves were constantly freed in great numbers, and the moment they were freed they became citizens. More than half of the thousands of epitaphs extant from imperial Rome are of freedmen and feedwomen. The poor citizen had the great public baths, public squares, parks, and forums, in which he reckoned to spend far more time out of his house than is normal in the colder and damper north.

Still darker aspects are not to be glossed over: the slave trade, infanticide, the gladiatorial shows, absolute power which could be in the hands of irresponsible or unbalanced men. Caligula and Nero, the spectacle of bloodshed and the sinister opulence of the orgy, have haunted the imagination of Europe. One of the ways in which the Roman Empire is interesting is that it shows certain sides of human nature developed to their fullest extent: 'Remember', Caligula used to say to people, 'that I can do anything to anybody.' The past is the laboratory in which human nature can be studied with security, perhaps the only way it can really be studied at all.

The ancients believed in the power and significance of great individuals. The daemonic Alcibiades, the imperturbable and ironic Socrates, the vehement Alexander: these stand beside such Romans as the all-conquering Caesar, the gallant but profligate Mark Antony, the demented aesthete Nero. The will to power incarnated in great individuals, the qualities of resolution, magnanimity, and pride: the ancients saw events very much in such terms. Such qualities as pride and magnanimity are essentially un-Christian. In the Middle Ages, and still more in the Renaissance, such pagan virtues, which Christian Europe had in reality by no means renounced, could be glorified in the persons and stories of the ancient world. Important human qualities which Christianity seemed to leave out, or which it rejected, could be depicted with sympathy in Achilles or Caesar, Helen or Cleopatra; in the rational suicide of Seneca or the passionate suicide of Dido.

The incompatibility of some pagan virtues with Christianity draws attention to an important aspect of the scope of this book. Jews and Christians are in principle not included—the *Envoi* looks forward to Christian Europe. Judaism and Christianity do not belong in a history of the classical world because they were too separate, too unclassical. The presuppositions of Jewish literature were essentially different from those of Greece and Rome, and so were its characteristic forms. Rome could come to terms with Judaism, which was at least an ancestral cult, if a bizarre one, more easily than with Christianity, which was not even respectably ancient, and which in vital respects contradicted the fundamental nature of the pagan state. Otherworldliness, celibacy, refusal to take an oath or offer the regular sacrifices—all this was more than official Rome could stomach, while the uncouth literary form of Christian writings, and their outlandish message, repelled the educated class: to the Greeks it seemed foolishness, St Paul admits of the Gospel. Yet there was a perspective in which, at least later, the classical world could be seen as necessary for the universal acceptance of the Christian revelation. The glorification of Socrates' condemnation and death as being a martyrdom, a triumph, which was proclaimed with all the literary genius of Plato, and accepted by the educated of Greece and Rome alike, prepared the way for the understanding of the Passion of Christ. The Roman Empire had pacified and united the world in time for the Gospel to be proclaimed everywhere. Rome the Imperial City became Rome the Holy City, and her bishops took the old Roman title of Supreme Pontiff. The universal claims of Rome assumed a sacerdotal form, but the continuity is obvious.

The classical tradition, a large fraction of the history of the West, is too vast a theme to be more than glanced at here. Greece and Rome provided the languages of the Western and Eastern Churches, when the unity imposed on the Mediterranean world finally broke in half with Rome's fall, and they continued to be the vehicle of intellectual communication for many centuries. The eastern Empire continued to call itself 'Roman' to its end, in 1453, but it did so in Greek. Some of ancient literature survived, including many masterpieces, although much more was lost. After great struggles and doubts on the part of Fathers of the Church it was widely, though never universally, accepted that the pagan classics could be read and taught by Christians. Virgil and Terence continued for a thousand years to be fundamental texts at schools in the West.

The idea of Rome never lost its fascination. Charlemagne went to the inconvenient Italian city to be crowned Emperor, and the struggle for and against a Roman Empire with universal claims dominated the history of Italy and Germany for hundreds of years. Napoleon revived it again, and Mussolini claimed to have 'restored the fasces' (whence 'fascists') and reconstituted an Empire for Rome. Shakespeare explored the dilemmas of power more deeply in his Roman tragedies than in his English history plays; Kipling, in some of his best poems and stories, took the Roman Empire as a paradigm of the British Raj. In the sphere of political reality the same idea can be seen. The trial of Warren Hastings for oppression and extortion in India was felt by all the participants to be an echo of the celebrated trials of Roman governors like Verres, denounced by Cicero. The word 'proconsul' was unselfconsciously applied to British colonial administrators.

The founders of new constitutions often took Roman models: thus there are Senates in France, Ireland, Italy, and the United States. The radical political wing could also find Roman models. French Revolutionaries took names like Gracchus, and claimed the inheritance of the tyrannicide Brutus and the Roman Republic. A German revolutionary movement named itself after the rebellious slave Spartacus; a left-wing magazine in Britain is still called *Tribune*. The Roman Church, of course, re-enacted the claims of the Empire on a different plane.

For the arts the influence of antiquity had three aspects: subject matter, form, and spirit. The myths of Greece were the other great subject of Renaissance art, along with Christian themes; the myths of Ovid were painted by Titian and Correggio, Rubens and Poussin; Mantegna, Piranesi, and David created visual images of Rome. Michelangelo began his career as a sculptor by creating works so closely modelled on ancient models that they passed as genuine antiques. The genres of ancient literature, too, lived on. Pastorals and epics, elegies and satires sprang up in every European language; the Italian musicians and patrons who created the first operas were trying to reconstruct the musical drama of antiquity; before Greek tragedy was understood, the rhetorical melodramas of Seneca were a formative influence on the tragedy which blossomed with Marlowe and Shakespeare. In another art the triumphal arch, the Doric, Ionic, and Corinthian capitals, the fountains with marble nymphs and river gods, the ornamental urns, all proliferated through the cities. The spirit is even more pervasive. David's Marat stabbed in his bath recalls the philosophical suicides of Rome; the grand manner of Raphael and Milton is inseparable from their classical studies; Dante claimed Virgil as his master, and for all the enormous difference of their styles the claim clearly expresses an important truth.

The English language itself is distinguished from its cousins in the Germanic branch of the Indo-European family by the very large number of words which have come into it from Latin and, to a lesser extent, from Greek; some directly, others through French or Italian. People sometimes talk as if such words were always massive and abstruse, like 'psychiatry' or 'prelapsarian', and indeed the vocabulary of abstract thought, of science and culture, is especially full of them. But the following sample of twenty-five may remind the reader that many short and basic words have the same source: act, art, beauty, colour, crime, fact, fate, fork, hour, human, idea, justice, language, law, matter, music, nature, number, place, reason, school, sense, sex, space, time.

Every generation approaches classical antiquity in a different way, draws different lessons from it, finds different things about it interesting. It is hoped that this book will help contemporary readers to understand something of its continuing significance and fascination.

MAP 1. ITALY

1

Early Rome and Italy

MICHAEL CRAWFORD

The central theme of this chapter is the Italian element in Roman history. Already under her early kings, before 509 BC, Rome was beginning to expand at the expense of her immediate neighbours. This process continued under the Republic, so that by the early third century Rome had no serious rivals south of the Po valley, where the Gauls remained an active threat. But Rome had not simply conquered Italy, she had also forced its different peoples to fight for her when required. The military manpower thus acquired was used first to defeat an invader from the east, then to win two wars against Carthage, then to conquer the whole of the Mediterranean basin.

The great wars of conquest after 200 BC form one of the themes of Chapter 2. But the relationship of Rome with Italy remained till the age of Augustus one of the determining factors in her history. The conquest of the Mediterranean basin led to changes in the economy of Italy, which from the end of the second century onwards generated a series of political crises, some of which form the theme of Chapter 4, but some of which are considered here, since they concern the relationship between Rome and Italy. At one level, these crises were resolved by the emergence of Augustus as Emperor; at another level, their resolution involved the final stages of the Romanization of Italy and the Italianization of Rome.

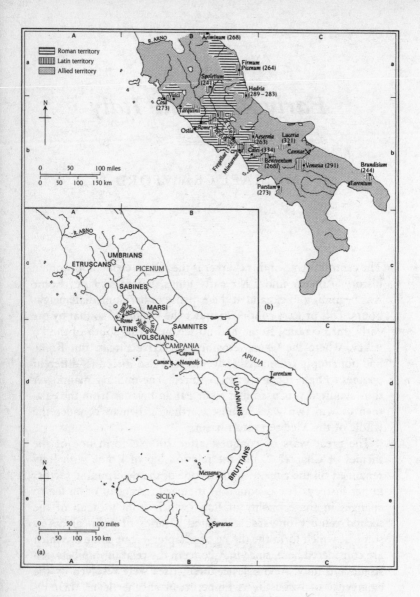

R. ARNO

Ariminum (268)

Firmum
Picenum (264)

Spoletium
(241)

Hadria
(289–283)

Vulci
Cosa
(273)

Tarquinii

Ostia

Rome

Aesernia
(263)

Luceria
(321)

Cannae

Cales (334)

Fregellae

Minturnae

Beneventum
(268)

Venusia (291)

Brundisium
(244)

Tarentum

Paestum
(273)

N

0   50   100 miles

0   50   100   150 km

(b)

R. ARNO

UMBRIANS

ETRUSCANS

PICENUM

SABINES

R. TIBER

R. ANIO

MARSI

Rome

R. LIRIS

R. TREBIA

SAMNITES

LATINS

VOLSCIANS

CAMPANIA

Capua

APULIA

Cumae

Neapolis

Tarentum

LUCANIANS

Messana

BRUTTIANS

SICILY

Syracuse

N

0   50   100 miles

0   50   100   150 km

(a)

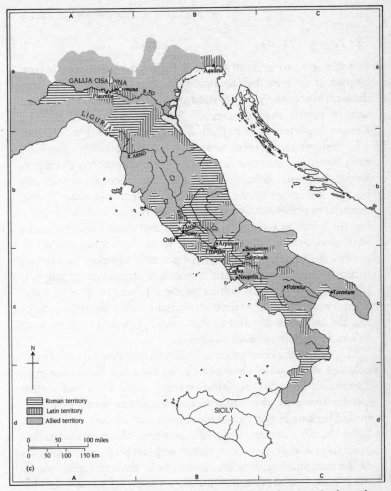

MAP 2. THE GROWTH OF ROME IN ITALY (*Facing bottom*): In the early period of her history, Rome was no more than one city among many in Italy, her territory restricted to the area immediately outside her wall, the Latins one tribe among others competing for mastery. (*Facing top*): By 241 BC not only did Roman territory spread south into Campania and south-east to the Adriatic, but a far-flung network of Latin colonies controlled much of the rest of Italy. (*Above*) By the time of the outbreak of the Social War, Roman and Latin territory had penetrated and isolated allied territory throughout Italy; the rebels of 91 were essentially the inhabitants of the last great block of allied territory in the central and southern Apennines.

The Peoples of Italy

In attempting to write of the early history of Rome, one is confronted at once by the fact that no account written earlier than
the late third century ever existed and that no continuous account
written earlier than the age of Augustus now survives. (The
Roman tradition of historical writing is discussed in Chapter
10.) Perhaps the gravest weakness in the literary tradition on
early Rome, however, is its ruthlessly Romanocentric character.
Before Polybius, Greek writers such as Aristotle occasionally
became conscious of the existence of Rome, and some of this
material is preserved, either directly or as used by later writers.
But the histories written by Etruscans and other local traditions
have disappeared almost without trace. It is thus extraordinarily hard to grasp the enormous diversity in ethnic formation,
social and economic structure, political organization, religion,
language, and material culture of the different peoples of Italy.
Rome succeeded in conquering and assimilating not only peoples
like the neighbouring and related Latins, but peoples who were
as like to herself as chalk to cheese.

The most distinctive group within Italy is formed by the Greek
colonies of the south, strung out along the coast from Cumae to
Tarentum. Founded as self-contained cities from the eighth
century onwards, they ensured that territories which they controlled became in every essential respect part of the Greek world.
From the fifth century onwards, however, these territories became increasingly subject to attack and conquest by the peoples
of the mountainous interior. Bruttians in the toe, Lucanians in
the instep, Samnites further north, a variety of small tribes including the Marsi to the east of Rome, were all anxious to control the fertile lands and established wealth of the coast. The
consequence, however, was sometimes very far from being a
process of take-over and barbarization.

These peoples of the mountainous interior spoke similar
languages (labelled as 'Italic' by scholars) and certainly in
historical times regarded themselves as related to each other.
Further north, the Latins on the coast and the Sabines and

Umbrians in the interior spoke languages belonging to the same 'Italic' group, but had a rather different history from the peoples further south. Legend regarded both Sabines and Latins as playing a part in the formation of the Roman state, and the history of the two peoples was always very closely intertwined. But the crucial influence both on Rome and on Umbria was Etruria. Here, from the eighth century onwards, there developed by a combination of internal evolution and outside, largely Greek, influence (the Etruscan language is neither Greek nor Italic) an advanced urban civilization; this civilization was essentially homogeneous, although the different Etruscan cities remained separate political entities.

Umbrian civilization in the early period was on the whole a pale imitation of Etruscan, and the Etruscan script was used to write the Umbrian language; but at Rome something rather different happened. The villages on the hills around what became the Forum linked up into a single city in the course of the sixth century; a similar process probably occurred at about the same time in the case of other Latin communities, such as Gabii or Praeneste. The material culture of archaic Latium has much in common with Etruscan; but Rome never became either culturally or politically a mere Etruscan dependency.

The story of Campania is even more complex. Here the Greek cities of the coast, principally Cumae and Neapolis, coexisted in the late archaic and classical period with an Etruscan principality based at Capua. The arrival of the Samnites in the fifth century did not lead to the destruction of the civilization which had emerged in Campania, although no Etruscan city survived as such and only Neapolis survived as a Greek city. Rather the Samnites became the new ruling class. The incorporation of this area by Rome in the fourth century was probably the most important formative experience in the history of the republic.

The contrast between Latium and Campania on the one hand and Picenum and Apulia on the other hand is instructive. In both areas a population which seems to have had little in common with the group of peoples extending from the Umbrians to the Bruttians underwent a certain development as a result of contact with the Greek world, in the case of Picenum passing Greek traders, in the case of Apulia the Greek city of Tarentum. But Picenum remained materially backward, barely literate, and hardly urbanized; and although Apulia came to possess a number of cities of native origin, the area seems to have run out of steam, culturally and politically, at the same time as did the Greek cities of the south, between the fourth and the third centuries.

Cutting across the ethnic differences there were important differences in economic and social structures. The Greek colonies were of course fully fledged *poleis*, and it is clear that places such as Etruscan Veii or Capua, Latin Rome or Praeneste, were in many respects similar. But much of central Italy remained without cities down to the age of Cicero. Here the pattern was of scattered villages and farmsteads, often within reach of a fortified hill-top, where it was possible to take refuge in time of war, but which was never built up or lived in, indeed which did not even fulfil the political or religious functions of a city. A clear example of this pattern of settlement is provided by Pietrabbondante, where the greatest of the Samnite sanctuaries, which served also as a meeting place, lay on the open hillside below a hill-top fort, both sanctuary and fort being completely detached from any trace of settlement.

One should not suppose, however, that the absence of cities meant the absence of settled agriculture. Naturally, the Greek *poleis* recruited their armies from the free peasant element of their populations, and the same was true of Rome. It must have been true also of the other communities of early Italy. For the Roman conquest of Italy involved a sequence of battles between the Roman heavy-armed infantry and that of their enemies; and the existence of heavy-armed infantry implies the existence of free peasants. This must be true for Etruria, although what our sources talk about is the serf element of the population (one thinks of Sparta where the helots supported a hoplite, not an aristocratic society); it must be true of Samnium, although our

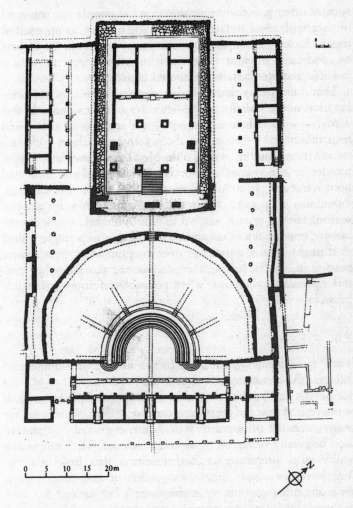

PLAN OF THE SANCTUARY AT PIETRABBONDANTE (*c.*100–91 BC). The grandest of the Samnite religious centres of the Republican period testifies to the wealth achieved by Italian merchants and bankers shortly before the Social War. The arrangement of a temple axially placed behind and overlooking a theatre is typical of central-Italian sanctuaries at this time.

sources often give the impression that the population consisted of shepherds. And in fact, if one travels in Italy, as opposed to merely looking at a map, one comes time and again on pockets of good land, often at a great height, where arable farming is possible and was certainly practised in antiquity.

That is not to say that there were no shepherds. And the combination of the Italian climate—hot dry summers and cold wet winters—with Italian geography—river and coastal plains and high mountains—meant that sheep farming took on a characteristic form found elsewhere in the Mediterranean. This involved pasture in the lowlands, often on farmland where grain had been harvested, from late summer till spring, and in the high mountains on grassland watered by melting snow for the hot season. Such a system, known as transhumance, might simply involve moving flocks up and down the side of a single valley; or it might involve movement over long distances, from winter pasture in Apulia, for instance, to summer pasture in the central Apennine mountains, when political conditions made this possible.

Early Rome

The city of Rome was formed by the linking of a number of villages; the consequence was that the Forum ceased to be used for burials and became the public open space of the new city. It is interesting that the great Etruscan city of Veii, which was for many years the principal rival of Rome, consisted of a plateau also originally occupied by separate villages. The comparison with Veii is interesting in another respect also; for Rome and Veii were not simply bigger, but orders of magnitude bigger, than any other community in the lower Tiber valley.

Certainly, Rome was a prize worth having, and Roman tradition was unanimous in holding that Rome was originally ruled by kings, and that two of the last three successors of Romulus, eponymous founder of the city and first king, were Etruscan adventurers, Tarquinius Priscus and Tarquinius Superbus. Their arrival in and seizure of power at Rome illustrates an important aspect of archaic society in central Italy as a whole, namely its openness to horizontal penetration. Just as in archaic Greece, tyrants and aristocrats of one *polis* intermarried with those of another, so in archaic Italy there was no rigid conception of citizenship to tie a man to the community of his birth. What is more, openness to horizontal penetration seems to have been true of all social levels; for in the years immediately after the fall of the monarchy at Rome, the Sabine aristocrat Appius Claudius and his retainers were admitted to membership of the community, he at the social level appropriate to his existing standing, they at the level appropriate to theirs. And when from the fourth century we can make reliable inferences about the nature of the relationship between Rome and other Latin communities, we can observe that an essential element of the relationship is freedom of movement between one community and another. It does not much matter whether this element of the relationship is a survival of a period when the Latins were a tribal community or whether it is the product of the diplomatic history of the sixth and fifth centuries. What matters is that it seemed acceptable in the context of archaic central Italian society.

In talking of the social level appropriate to the retainers of Appius Claudius, I have so far left on one side one of the crucial problems of early Roman history. Roman tradition is unanimous in holding that there existed already under the monarchy a group of families known as patricians which succeeded in the early years of the Republic in acquiring both a monopoly of secular and sacred office and almost complete control of the economic resources of the community. Those who were not patricians are presented by our sources as plebeians; this is the system they knew in their own day, but it is likely that the early community of the Romans included social groups which were neither patrician nor plebeian. What is clear is that there emerged with great rapidity a plebeian movement, which created an organization parallel to, and alternative to, that of the patrician state, in the course of what is known to scholars as the struggle of the orders. The plebeian organization set out to break the patrician monopoly of secular and sacred office in the Roman state and to reduce the extent of economic exploitation of the poor by the rich. In the pursuit of its first objective, the plebeian movement was wholly successful; and in the second century Cato could assume that there were no *formal* barriers in the way of any Roman citizen achieving the highest office of the state. We shall see shortly how plebeian economic aspirations were fulfilled.

I have used the term 'Roman citizen'; and the unitary concept of Roman citizenship is the result of the process I have been describing, at the end of which, if one was domiciled at Rome, one was either free and a Roman citizen or a slave. It cannot be too strongly emphasized that the openness of Roman society to plebeian mobility which is the corollary of this fact is *as far as we know* a feature unique to Rome; though it may have applied to other Latin communities, it probably did not apply to Etruscan communities, which continued to display, like some Greek communities, a range of statuses between slave and free.

But there is more. To the astonishment of Greek observers, a slave freed by a Roman citizen became a Roman citizen. And, as we shall see, Roman citizenship came to be available in due course not simply to members of Latin communities, but also to entire Italian peoples. Given the fact that by the time this occurred Rome was the dominant power in central Italy, this too is to be seen as involving the openness of Roman society to penetration from below.

I have talked in general terms of secular and sacred office in early Rome and of the creation of a plebeian organization parallel to that of the Roman state. Under the monarchy, presumably, the kings were in the habit of consulting a body of advisers, the institution which became in due course the Senate of the Republic. At the end of the sixth century the king holding office for life was replaced by two consuls holding office for one year at a time. There appear in addition in our sources for the early years of the Republic specialist financial officials (quaestors) and a variety of military offices. Probably the sources had no accurate information; but the supposition that there existed already under the monarchy a differentiated administrative structure is entirely reasonable; the method of appointment presumably changed from nomination to election with the arrival of the Republic. There also existed already under the monarchy two different ways in which the Roman people was organized as an assembly, the Comitia Curiata, the people organized in kin groups, and the Comitia Centuriata, the people organized in army units. The growth of the plebeian organization involved the creation of plebeian officials, of whom the most important were the tribunes of the plebs, and of another assembly, the Concilium Plebis or Comitia Tributa, the people organized by *tribus*, areas of domicile.

As the plebs achieved its aim of equality of political and religious rights with the patricians its organization was simply grafted on to that of the Roman state. The tribunes became for all practical purposes officials of the Roman state, the Concilium Plebis became with the name Comitia Tributa one of its assemblies. The plebeian organization, in creating its assembly, also preserved one of the most curious features of existing Roman assemblies, namely voting by groups. No Roman assembly ever reached a decision by a simple majority of those present and voting; each group, however defined, reached a decision in this way and the decision of the assembly was the decision of a majority of the groups.

In the case of the Comitia Centuriata, whose functions included the election of the consuls, the groups were organized in such a way as to facilitate the dominance of the rich. For, at any rate in its developed form in the middle Republic (the fourth and third centuries BC), the Comitia Centuriata contained a number of groups of men who were wealthy enough to serve as cavalrymen, a number of groups with a slightly lower property qualification, and so on. The richer the group, broadly speaking, the fewer men it contained; as a result their influence in the assembly was disproportionately large. Under the monarchy and in the early Republic the system was certainly less complicated, but the underlying principle is likely to have been the same. Of course this principle was not consciously formulated until much later, but its effect was that the wealthy, who paid more in taxes and on whom a greater burden fell in the defence of the community, had a greater say in the making of policy. It must be said, however, that the rich determined the outcome of a vote only if they were united—probably a rare occurrence. Obviously the nature and aims of the plebeian assembly were reflected in the fact that in it no advantage was conferred on the rich in the way in which the groups were formed.

Rome under the monarchy had a relatively differentiated administrative structure, and here too there is continuity of development from the earliest times onwards, as there was in the evolution of the different Roman assemblies. Throughout their history the Romans showed remarkable willingness to create new offices to take over specific functions from the consuls; thus the praetors came in due course to take over the specialized function of the administration of justice, the censors that of listing roughly every five years the members of the citizen body and the amount of their property liable to taxation, and of renewing the prayers of the Roman people for the favour of the gods. Throughout the Republic, indeed, until the anarchy of its last years, the census was the process whereby men were assigned their place in the community, as soldiers, taxpayers, and voters.

The Roman community did not consist simply of the citizens who belonged to it, together with their female, young, and slave dependants. It also included the gods, and Roman religious structures and history form in a number of very striking ways the mirror image of secular structures and developments.

In the first place, the relative complexity of the administrative structures of the early Republic is paralleled by the diversity of its priesthoods. There were from the start two major colleges, the *pontifices*, with the *pontifex maximus* at their head (and the

Vestal Virgins under his general control), and the *augures*; the former were concerned in general terms with sacrifices to the gods (the Vestal Virgins with the sacred hearth of the community), the latter with ascertaining the will of the gods, for instance by observing the flight of birds. And just as the state created new secular offices to meet new needs, so too in the field of religion new priesthoods were created from time to time. Moreover the priesthoods of the Republic were often held by men who also held secular office, with the difference that a priesthood was for life, a consulship for a year at a time. For at Rome religion and politics were not two worlds, but inseparable parts of the same world. One must not suppose that there was something 'wrong' with Roman religion because the world of the gods was involved in the world of political dispute.

Second, the plebeian organization, which developed in parallel to that of the Roman state, created also its own apparatus of cult, centring on the Aventine hill, outside the original boundary of the city of Rome, and involving the cult of Ceres, Liber, and Libera.

Finally, the readiness to innovate in the sphere of religion, which we have observed in the creation of new priesthoods and of a plebeian religious structure, operated also in a much wider context. Perhaps the most conspicuous feature of the religious history of the Republic is the steady importation of new deities, from Etruria, from elsewhere in Italy, or from overseas. The practice is not an indication of dissatisfaction with existing gods, but rather the reverse. Just as her citizens gave Rome her military strength, and Rome sought for most of her history constantly to increase their number, so also, as the gods helped Rome to win battles, the more gods one worshipped the better.

Apart from the creation of the militarily successful patrician–plebeian state, one other consequence of the struggle of the orders requires mention. Among the demands of the lower orders was the demand that the provisions of the Roman civil law be codified and recorded, in order that their interpretation should not be at the fancy of patrician office-holders. The result was the so-called Twelve Tables (traditionally *c.*450 BC), whose provisions still formed the basis of the Roman civil law in the age of Cicero. As a result of citations by writers of this and later periods, we have a fair idea of the original contents of the Twelve Tables; they reveal a society which is still that of a small agricultural community, but one in which the importance of the kin-group is already diminishing and in which there are already substantial numbers of slaves.

The Early Republic

The early years of the Republic were marked by an attempt on the part of the patrician families to achieve a monopoly of secular and sacred office. The fall of the monarchy also meant the partial loss of the superiority which Rome had achieved *vis-à-vis* her immediate neighbours. Furthermore, in the fifth century the Volscians emerged from the upper Liris valley and conquered most of the Trera valley and the coastal plain south of Rome. The first century and a half of the Republic saw first the reassertion of Roman leadership of the other Latin communities and then a long sequence of wars against the southern Etruscan cities, principally Veii (captured and destroyed in 396), and against the Volscians to the south. In the latter struggles Rome and the Latins could usually rely on the Hernicans, who had also suffered from Volscian expansion.

It was undoubtedly a period of economic difficulties which weighed heavily on the lower orders and exacerbated their resentment at patrician exclusiveness. At the same time the fact that some of the lower orders (not the very poor) contributed the manpower on which Roman military success depended conferred bargaining power which they were not slow to use. The erosion of patrician privileges went hand in hand with the steady acquisition of land by conquest, which was used to satisfy the economic aspirations of the lower orders. Such land either formed the territory of a new community, or *colonia*, possessing local self-government, or provided isolated plots of land for settlers not organized as a group. The Gallic sack of Rome in 390, traumatic though it must have been at the time, had little effect either on internal developments at Rome or on the process of conquest. The land acquired as a result of the capture of Veii was distributed to the poor at Rome, resulting in the creation of an enormous new reserve of peasant soldiers. By the middle of the fourth century Rome dominated south Etruria, no longer had anything to fear from incursions by tribes in the upper Anio valley, and was poised on the northern edge of Campania.

The crucial moment in the history of the Roman conquest of Italy came in 338. Most of the Latin communities around Rome, viewing her growing preponderance with alarm, attempted to reassert their independence. They were rapidly defeated and all, except the largest and most distant, incorporated in the Roman citizen body. From this time on, the original cities of Latium and the *coloniae* founded by them in association with Rome ceased individually or as a group to have any destiny separate from that of Rome. But Rome made the momentous decision to continue to found new communities with the status of Latin cities. Certainly later, and probably by now, Latin status *vis-à-vis* Rome and other Latin communities was defined essentially as involving rights of intermarriage, the enforceability of contractual obligations, and the right to change domicile, with the acquisition of the citizenship appropriate to the new domicile. The first of the Latin *coloniae* founded after 338 was Cales in northern Campania, founded in 334. The primary function of this and later *coloniae* was defensive, to hold down conquered territory or guard Roman territory against invasion. The foundation of a *colonia* was one way in which land acquired by conquest was used to relieve the poverty of the lower orders in Roman (and Latin) society; but *coloniae* of Latin status were also powerful factors making for the Romanization of Italy. They possessed from the outset constitutions modelled on that of Rome, and by their mere presence in an area previously without significant contact with Rome served to spread the Roman model of government. Recent archaeological evidence from Cosa (founded 273) suggests very strongly that Rome exported to the Latin *coloniae* her peculiar practice of voting in groups. But there is an even more important side to the foundation of Latin *coloniae*; it seems that membership was not limited to those who were already citizens of Rome or a Latin cummunity, but that any Italian ally was eligible. The Latin *coloniae* thus served to elevate large numbers of Italians to a status close to that of Roman citizenship. Neither this fact, however, nor the fact that Latin *coloniae* provided a context in which land was assigned to the poor meant that the *coloniae* were egalitarian or democratic foundations. A significant part of the population of Latin *coloniae* was more richly endowed with land than the rest, to provide a social élite and a governing class.

Both before and after 338 Rome also founded a number of *coloniae*, the members of which possessed Roman citizenship. These *coloniae* tended when founded to be smaller than *coloniae* of Latin status and to have guard duties of a very limited and precise nature, for instance at Ostia at the mouth of the Tiber or at Minturnae at the mouth of the Liris. But those possessed of Roman or Latin citizenship were eligible to take part in the settlements and Roman *coloniae* provided an avenue, even if not a very important one, whereby men whose families were of Italian origin could achieve Roman citizenship without moving to Rome.

Far more important as a means of creating new Roman citizens was the incorporation of entire Italian communities as citizens without the vote. Such communities possessed all the other rights of Roman citizens, primarily legal and social, and were also bound to perform all the duties of citizens, to pay taxes, and to fight. We do not know whether the act of conferring citizenship without the vote (perhaps sometimes withheld for reasons of distance or linguistic incompatibility) was intended as a reward or as a means of subjection, and perhaps it does not much matter. Large parts of Italy *became* Roman in this way, however, conspicuously the great Graeco—Etruscan—

Samnite city of Capua, and also Arpinum, later the birthplace of C. Marius and of Cicero. The details of the process whereby Capua and indeed much of Campania were in the middle of the fourth century incorporated in the Roman state are obscure and controversial. What matters is that what was by then the richest and most developed area of Italy entered the Roman sphere (below, pp. 32 f.).

The Unification of Italy

We have seen that there were a number of ways in which men belonging to different Italian communities, whether conquered or not, might come to acquire Roman citizenship or Latin status. But there are other aspects of the process whereby Rome succeeded not simply in conquering Italy, but also in moulding it into a single world. In the foundation of Latin *coloniae* Rome exported her own hierarchical pattern for the organization of society. The same general approach was extended to her dealings with the Italian allies. Systematically Rome sought out and privileged their upper classes; she supported them in a crisis, if they were faced with catastrophe from without or revolution from within; in normal times relations between Rome and any Italian community were conducted by means of the personal links between the upper orders of the two cities, based on a close community of interest and involving frequent contact, including intermarriage.

Given this network of personal relationships, it is not surprising that Rome found little difficulty in seeing that the principal demand she made on the communities of Italy was fulfilled. The demand was for troops, a fact which sets Rome apart from most other ancient empires and helps to explain the nature of Roman imperialism.

Most ancient empires demanded tribute from their subjects; superiority was symbolized by the demand, and its fulfilment provided tangible material rewards for having achieved rule

over others. Rome, clearly at a very early stage, simply extended
to other Italian peoples the demand for manpower which she
made on her own citizen body. The result was that the only
way in which she could symbolize the power she had over the
Volscians or the Etruscans was by demanding troops and the
only way in which she could derive any benefit was by using
the troops to acquire booty, land, and yet more power. It should
not be supposed, however, that the demand for troops necessarily fell on unwilling ears. For although Rome was less generous in distributing booty or land to her allies than she was
to her own citizens, she did share some of the ever-increasing
rewards of victory with them.

The Roman conquest of Italy was also accompanied by a
striking physical expression of the fact of a Roman presence.
Prior to its distribution, whether as isolated lots or in the territory of a *colonia*, conquered land was at any rate from the
late fourth century onwards measured and marked out by an
elaborate process eventually known as *centuriatio*. Initially,
perhaps from 334 onwards, land was divided into strips 10
actus wide (1 actus = *c*.35.5 m.); the lines of division were
known as *decumani*. In due course a full rectangular grid was
marked out; the transverse lines of division were known as
kardines. Just as in the simpler system the *decumani* were sometimes more or less than 10 *actus* apart, so in the developed system a grid of 20 × 20 *actus* was the norm, but not universal.
When such a grid was used, the result was 200 *jugera*, or a
centuria, within each square.

But this elaborate process was not used merely for measuring
the land; the lines of the grid were marked out by roads and
ditches which left an indelible mark on the countryside; they
patterned and structured its use for centuries, if not millennia,
and survive in many areas to this day, despite industrial development and mechanized farming.

On one hand, then, there was an almost violent expression of
Roman control of the land; but on the other hand, the pattern
of Roman-organized colonization in Italy facilitated the

acquisition of Latin, or eventually Roman, citizenship by Italians; it also permitted the presence and assimilation of existing ethnic elements. Thus the foundation of the Latin colony of Ariminum (in 268) in what had been Umbrian territory did not have an adverse effect on the major pre-Roman sanctuary of the area, outside the walls of the *colonia*; rather, as the offerings show, the sanctuary continued to be central to the life of the *colonia*, as it had been to that of the area before its foundation. At the other end of Italy, early inscriptions of the colony of Luceria (founded 314), on the borders of Samnite, Lucanian, and Apulian territory, show a mixed Latin-based dialect, which presupposes a mixed population.

A second-century inscription from Aesernia in Samnium (founded 263) shows a group of 'Samnites incolae', resident Samnites, clearly not citizens, but harmoniously established, going about their business and with their own form of corporate organization. And we know from literary sources that a large number of Samnites and Paelignians migrated to Fregellae in the early second century; we have no idea whether they became citizens, but their presence was clearly acceptable.

These examples of coexistence and assimilation come from those parts of Italy where the population may be defined as Italic, in general terms ethnically and linguistically close to the Latins. There were two areas of Italy where the story was rather different, Etruria and Gallia Cisalpina. In each case, a distinctive and remarkable culture was eventually submerged without trace, though for rather different reasons. In the case of Gallia Cisalpina, memories of the Gallic sack of Rome in 390 and the role played by his Gallic allies in Hannibal's invasion of Italy largely explain the brutality of the Roman conquest of the area. The first steps were taken already in the third century with the virtual destruction of the Senones, and the policy continued in the second century (below, pp. 38 f.). In Etruria the effect of the early wars in the fifth and fourth centuries had been to create a solid swathe of Roman or Latin territory in the south, leaving a few barely viable Etruscan enclaves, such as Tarquinii or Vulci.

In the north, Etruscan territory and culture remained intact, but in an increasingly isolated backwater.

Rome and the Greek Cities

In the sixth century, Greek culture had been mediated to Rome by Etruria. In the fourth century, with the absorption of Campania, Rome entered into close and direct contact with the Greek world, contact that was to increase in intensity and significance over the next three centuries. The Roman link with Campania was both symbolized and strengthened by the building of the Via Appia from Rome to Capua in 312, by Ap. Claudius Caecus as censor. It is likely that it was in this context that the first Roman silver coinage was produced, on the Greek model. The late fourth and early third centuries, indeed, saw the beginning of the rapid Hellenization of Rome. It was in this period that Rome absorbed from the Greek world an interest in the expression of the ideology of victory, a phenomenon which was not the least of the legacies of Alexander the Great. The consequence at Rome was the introduction of new cults of gods of war, gods of victory, Victory herself. It was in this period also that the cult of Hercules, heavily dependent on Greek models, became widespread in the Roman world, evidenced both by the institution by the state of new cults and by the upsurge in humble offerings to the new hero. At the same time a Greek influence on the material culture of the republic became even more apparent. At one level there is the sarcophagus of L. Cornelius Scipio Barbatus, found in the tomb of the Scipios on the Via Appia, which used Greek architectural motifs in its decoration. At another level, Rome began to produce around 330 her own local pottery, imitated from South-Italian or Etruscan red-figure pottery, known as Genucilia ware, and then in the early third century a fine black-slip pottery, imitative of Greek metal ware.

The late fourth century saw also the development by Rome of increasingly complex administrative structures, going beyond the simple adoption of coinage on the Greek model. It was certainly in this period that there evolved the developed structure of five census classes, each with different fiscal and military responsibilities.

The Defence of Italy and the First War against Carthage

The last serious wars fought by Rome against an Italian people were the wars against the Samnites. These were effectively over by 295, when the Samnites were defeated at Sentinum in northern Italy, along with Umbrian, Etruscan, and Gallic allies; for the Umbrian and Etruscan cities which remained independent had decided to make one last attempt to assert their freedom, while some of the Gallic tribes of the Po valley had decided to attempt to repeat the success of 390.

Fifteen years later the Romans met their first invasion from overseas. We have already seen that the Greek cities of the south were faced from the fifth century onwards by the territorial and political ambitions of their 'barbaric' neighbours (above, pp. 16 f.). Tarentum declined to compromise, as did Cumae or Posidonia, which had accepted the presence of a partially Samnite or Lucanian élite. Instead, she called to her aid a succession of Greek mercenary commanders. The last of these was Pyrrhus, king of Epirus, who was summoned in 280 to deal not with Tarentum's Lucanian neighbours, but with the Romans, who were now the principal threat to the independence of Tarentum.

It should be remarked that Tarentine opposition to Rome was by no means typical of the reaction of the Greek *poleis* of the south. Many welcomed the protection and alliance of Rome, both now and later. The obverse type of the issue of silver coins which Rome struck during the war against Pyrrhus should be seen as quite deliberately placing Rome on the side of civilization in the fight against barbarism. The type in question is a head of Apollo, the god who had become in 279 the symbol throughout the Greek world of the victory of the civilized over the barbarous, by reason of his defence of Delphi against a band of marauding Gauls. Rome too, as we have seen, had defeated a similar band, in 295, along with her other enemies.

Pyrrhus succeeded initially in winning a number of costly victories over the armies of Rome (hence the phrase 'Pyrrhic victory'). But he was in due course defeated at Beneventum and returned across the Adriatic. It was undoubtedly his defeat at the hands of Rome that caused the Greek historian, Timaeus of Tauromenium, writing in exile at Athens, to take notice of the new power in the West.

Shortly afterwards, this new power found itself at war with the other power in the West, Carthage, longer established as such and much better known in the Greek world as a result of the long series of bloody wars which she had fought with the Greeks in Sicily.

The earlier relations of Carthage with Rome had been pacific, and the two states had indeed made three treaties with each other, agreeing not to interfere in their respective spheres of interest. The treaties are preserved by Polybius. The earliest, belonging to the first year of the Republic, is the earliest Roman document known in something like its entirety.

In addition to the factors making for Roman expansion which we have already considered, others are evidenced by the outbreak of the First Punic War. Polybius reports that the Senate did not vote for action, but that the assembly did, and there is no doubt that sheer greed played a large part in swaying opinion. The action that led to war was to send an army to protect Messana, in the hands of a band of Italian mercenaries, against Hiero of Syracuse, despite the fact that the protection of Carthage had already been invoked. The action was in character; neither the Roman aristocracy nor the Roman state as a whole could ever resist the temptation to intervene when the chance arose.

The war lasted from 264 to 241 and was in effect a war for the control of Sicily, since Hiero of Syracuse decided at an early stage in the proceedings to throw in his lot with the Romans. Roman persistence won through, and Roman chicanery added Sardinia to the prize. Much is obscure about the way in which

Rome set about organizing her new acquisitions, but two points are worth making. In the first place, it is clear that the Italian model of a treaty which imposed on the defeated community the obligation to provide manpower at the behest of Rome was not applied; both Sicily and Sardinia were regarded as territories to be ruled and taxed. In the second place, a group of recently discovered inscriptions from Entella in western Sicily reveal at least one Italian in a semi-official position of influence under Roman auspices during the First Punic War, and probably profiting from the position.

Politics in the Middle Republic

Leadership in the wars that Rome fought in the fourth and third centuries was provided by the mixed patrician–plebeian nobility which had emerged as a result of the resolution of the struggle of the orders. Holders of the consulship or other high office and their descendants came to be regarded as forming the nobility under the new dispensation. It was this group that constituted the Senate in the traditional age of senatorial domination.

It must be said that our ignorance of how politics worked in this society is almost total. The problem arises at at least two levels, within the senatorial élite and between the élite and the population as a whole. Although what our sources tell us about this period, the period of the middle Republic, is no doubt heavily tinged with romanticism, it seems reasonable to suppose that both the élite and society as a whole were united to an extent that was clearly not true in the age of Cicero.

Obviously there was competition within the élite for office, power, and influence. We possess from the third century one early grave monument, that of L. Cornelius Scipio Barbatus (the inscription is later than the sarcophagus) and part of the *elogium* pronounced at the death of L. Caecilius Metellus, consul in 251. Neither the inscription of Barbatus nor the *elogium* on Metellus makes sense except in the context of a competitive aristocracy. Clearly there were moments of tension, as when an ancestor of Sulla (below, pp. 45, 97 ff.)

was expelled from the Senate for excessive display of wealth. But it is wildly unlikely that the fourth and third centuries were characterized by the bitterness and the unscrupulousness which marked political conflict in the age of Cicero. The consul of 251 was described as possessing great wealth, honourably acquired. Only the first part of this description could have been applied to Caesar.

When there was disagreement within the élite over policy, we simply do not know how it was resolved. It is, however, worth remarking that one modern theory, according to which entire *gentes* such as the Cornelii or the Caecilii operated as single entities, building stable alliances with other *gentes*, is almost certainly fantasy. The theory does not work for any period where we have first-hand evidence, and it is paradoxical to apply it when there is no such evidence; and men such as Barbatus and Metellus emerge as larger-than-life *individuals*, whose ambitions sometimes actually played a part in pushing Rome into war.

We are even more in the dark when it comes to understanding the nature of the relationship between the élite and the population as a whole. Again, of course, there was controversy, over matters which were to be characteristic causes of controversy in the second and first centuries; thus there was argument in 290 over the relative balance to be achieved in the use of conquered land in Sabinum between its distribution to the poor and its sale to the rich; and Polybius records a controversy aroused in 232 by the proposal to distribute land in Picenum and the south-east of the Po Valley. But Roman history in the fourth and third centuries is incomprehensible except on the assumption that the lower orders were largely satisfied with the leadership of the nobility and with the rewards to be won under their command.

Conventionally *clientela*, a traditional, often inherited relationship of dependence of one man on another, is regarded as the principal integrating factor in Roman society of the middle Republic. But other factors were surely at work. Although Rome, as we shall see in a moment, was already in the third century large in comparison with most ancient states, it was probably still a society where contact between different social levels was relatively easy; the number of enterprises, such as war and colonization, in which élite and people shared, ensured that the two remained relatively closely integrated. And now, as later, the élite could and did justify its actions to the population as a whole in terms of shared values; these values involved, among other things, the belief that the approval of the gods was necessary and that with it Rome could not fail.

The third century was not only, as Polybius observed, the high point in the development of the Roman body politic; it also marked the acme of the system of Italian alliances which Rome had built up, before the strains began to show. The last great Gallic invasion which Italy had to face was that of 225, and it is in the context of the preparations against it that Polybius describes the manpower resources available to Rome. To do so he drew on the account given by the first Roman historian, Q. Fabius Pictor, himself a witness of the events of 225. Although the list in Polybius contains some obscurities in detail, it fits with what else is known of Roman citizen numbers in this period and suggests that the Roman and Italian pool of men on which Rome could draw was of the order of 1–2 million.

Hannibal's Invasion: The Second Punic War

The existence of such a reserve enabled Rome to withstand the shock of Hannibal's invasion of Italy in 218. This invasion, the resources for which were provided by the Carthaginian acquisition of an empire in Spain, was a deliberate attempt to reverse the verdict of the First Punic War. Between 218 and 216, Hannibal, a brilliant general, was able to inflict a series of crushing and bloody defeats on the Roman armies sent to face him, culminating in the battle of Cannae in 216, and was able to detach a number of Rome's allies, notably Capua; at the same time, Carthage attempted to recover Sicily and in due course brought Syracuse over to her side.

But Rome was always able to field new armies to replace those which were lost, and most of her Italian allies never regarded Italy without Rome or Italy under Carthage as serious alternatives to the system with which they had become familiar. Rome first succeeded in confining Hannibal to Bruttium, while simultaneously recovering Sicily, seizing Spain, and fighting against Macedonia, which had allied with Carthage in 215 after the battle of Cannae, In due course the war was carried over to Africa; Hannibal was recalled from Italy in 203, to be defeated at the battle of Zama in 202; Carthage sued for peace and the attempt to dispute Roman hegemony in the western Mediterranean was over.

Hannibal's Legacy

What were the effects on Italy of fifteen years of warfare on Italian soil? It has been argued that the devastation of much of Italy by Hannibal led to the deracination of many Roman and Italian peasant soldiers and a shift to large farming enterprises owned by the élite and run by slave labour; whence the problems which Ti. Gracchus set out to resolve two generations later (below, pp. 41 f.). The argument is hard to maintain. Rome not only continued to field large armies of peasant soldiers throughout the Second Punic War, but undertook after it was over both the final conquest of the Po valley and a series of wars overseas (below, Ch. 2).

For those Italian communities that had allied with Hannibal, however, the consequences of his defeat were grave. The Bruttii were deprived of any form of communal institutions and were not even allowed a role in the armies levied by Rome, except as servants. They and many other communities lost land, a fact which lies behind some of the economic developments of the second century. Those communities which continued to provide troops for Rome were forced to provide disproportionately large contingents. In effect, if not in theory, second-century Italy was a single state ruled by Rome, with local government in the hands of its scattered communities, not a mosaic of independent states bound together by a network of alliances.

The principal Roman military effort in Italy after 201 was directed to the definitive conquest of the Po valley. The process had begun after the defeat of the Gallic invasion of Italy in 225, with the foundation in 218 of the *coloniae* of Cremona and Placentia. Rome picked up after the Second Punic War where she had left off, and the next generation saw both the military subjugation of the area and the settlement, either in *coloniae* or in scattered plots, of tens of thousands of Romans and Italians, from Placentia in the west to Aquileia in the east. Of the different Gallic peoples, the Boii simply ceased to exist, as had the Senones earlier. The Cenomani and Insubres survived, albeit with their freedom gone.

Both the nature of the landscape and the unfolding of the Roman conquest help to explain why Gallia Cisalpina is the area characterized more than any other by Roman centuriation (above, p. 30). As they moved across the largest plain in Italy, the Romans felt themselves bound by no existing political, social, economic, or even geographical pattern. A *tabula rasa*, the Po valley was imprinted for ever with the marks of the Roman presence, and absorbed over a whole generation much of the military and colonizing energy of the Roman people, energy which appears undiminished by the experience of the Second Punic War.

Meanwhile, however, the overseas wars which followed the Second Punic War were transforming the social and economic fabric of Italy. These wars had two consequences which concern us here. They led on the one hand to a steady professionalization of the Roman and Italian soldier. Strictly speaking, it is inappropriate to talk of such a thing as the Roman army at this date, quite apart from the fact that an army levied to fight for Rome consisted of a large number of notionally independent contingents. But whereas down to 201 it had been normal for a man to fight in the spare time left over from farming, it became increasingly common after 200 for men to serve abroad for years on end.

At the same time, the wealth of the Mediterranean was pouring into Italy, partly in the form of booty, partly in the form of payments exacted from defeated enemies. Some of this wealth was distributed to the lower orders on the occasion of the triumph celebrated at the conclusion of a successful campaign, but much ended up in the hands of the élite. Further wealth was acquired in the course of the administration of overseas territories or by lending money at exorbitant rates of interest to foreign communities.

What happened to all this money? Some of it, both that which remained under the control of the community and that which had passed into private hands, was expended on the erection of public, as well as private, buildings in Rome and Italy: Rome showed the way, with projects such as the linking of the temples (still visible) in the Largo Argentina into a single monumental complex. Similar projects, on a scale hitherto undreamt of, were carried out elsewhere in Italy. Thus the Latin *colonia* of Fregellae possessed before its revolt and destruction in 125–124 a gigantic sanctuary of Aesculapius—temple, portico on three sides, stone treasure chest, altar, water-supply, monumental access ramp.

Obviously, in so far as free labour was used in the execution of such projects, the lower orders benefited economically. And indeed the emergence of urban markets with considerable spending power is a necessary hypothesis to explain another important second-century development. For it seems clear that much of the new wealth of the Roman and Italian élite was invested in land, in large farming enterprises run by slave labour. These were essentially of two types, market gardens, olive groves, or vineyards on the one hand, transhumant sheep farming on the other. Both types of enterprise created a demand for land in central Italy, to the detriment of the peasant farmer, whose plot might be requested in purchase or sometimes even seized and whose access to common land on which he depended might be rendered more difficult. In concentrating central-Italian land in its hands, the Roman and Italian élite was to a certain extent acting against its own interests, since it needed to ensure a steady supply of men for the legions in order to organize its wars of conquest overseas. But men do not always act wholly rationally.

The Age of the Gracchi

A pattern seems to have emerged in the second century whereby peasant soldiers in central Italy surrendered their land and their rights to common land, from which they had in any case become detached in the course of long service overseas, and went to settle in the Po valley; their sons provided the next generation of soldiers. But with the pacification of that area, the great days of colonization came to an end, and there seems to have followed in the generation before 133 a steady build up of men without land of their own and without hope of land to go to. What Ti. Gracchus attempted to do was to reverse the trend in central Italy and increase the number of peasants at the expense of large-scale farming enterprises.

Elected tribune for 133 BC, he introduced a land bill limiting the size of holdings of public land, and redistributing the surplus to the people. The Senate retaliated by putting up another tribune, M. Octavius, to veto the proposal, and Tiberius was finally forced to procure his fellow tribune's deposition from the people. He further antagonized the Senate by seeking to interfere in the arrangements for the kingdom of Pergamum, left by will to the Roman people: the administration of foreign affairs was traditionally a prerogative of the Senate. Finally, in the disturbances caused by his attempt to secure re-election to the tribunate for a second term, he was murdered together with 300 of his supporters.

Perhaps the principal consequence of the attempts at reform in this period was the inextricable entangling of Italian with Roman politics. But there is a further process which must be considered before we can turn to this particular problem, the progressive Romanization of Italy. The golden age of Roman road-building is the generation or so before Ti. Gracchus; as a result the whole of Italy became linked together, both actually and symbolically, to a far greater extent than ever before.

Italy also became in the years after the Second Punic War a monetary and economic unity. Down to the end of that war there circulated in the different areas large numbers of coins produced by Italian communities other than Rome; after the end of the war few communities felt themselves sufficiently independent of Rome to produce coinage for themselves, and earlier issues rapidly disappeared from circulation. It was soldiers returning from service with the armies of Rome who carried Roman coinage into the remote backwaters of the Apennines. And it was the developing market economy of Italy in response to the wealth flowing in from the East that took the monetary and economic unity of Italy a stage further. Down to the middle of the second century there were some inequalities in the pattern of circulation of Roman coins in Italy, both in terms of types and in terms of quantity. These inequalities then disappeared, clearly a sign of the developing process of exchange of money for goods.

The armies of Rome were important in another respect also, as a powerful factor for linguistic unity. During and after the Second Punic War men were away from home for much longer than before, in an essentially Latin-speaking environment. Etruscan survived, as did the languages of Samnium and Lucania, but the rest were in the process of disappearing in the period before Ti. Gracchus.

The principal problem to be faced in dealing with Gracchus' legislation is that we simply do not know whether, let alone to what extent, it was intended to revive peasant farming, not only in Roman, but also in Italian communities in central Italy, although it must be the case that these were suffering from the same developments.

What is clear, however, is that Ti. Gracchus' attempt to resume public land in the hands of the rich in order to distribute it to the poor adversely affected the interests of Italian élites as well as those of the Roman élite. It was not long before the idea was floated of giving Roman citizenship to some or all Italians, partly to compensate them for reduced access to Roman public land, partly to give them a say in the making of policy in this sphere. Once floated, the idea would not go away, though it was not till 91 that the Italian demand for Roman citizenship exploded into war.

Meanwhile politics at Rome between 133 and 91 were marked by a series of attempts, analogous to that of Ti. Gracchus, to win for the Roman poor a larger share in the rewards of the Empire which as soldiers they had helped to win, whether those rewards were in the form of land or subsidized corn. The attempts often ended, as had that of Ti. Gracchus, in the violent death of their authors. Two must be mentioned specifically, the programme devised by Tiberius' brother C. Gracchus, in 123–122, which aimed not simply to improve the material lot of the poor, but also to shift the balance of power within the Roman state; and the career of L. Appuleius Saturninus, who in 103 and 100 set out, in alliance with the conqueror of Jugurtha of Numidia and of the Cimbri and the Teutones, C. Marius, to provide for the need of his veterans for land. The alliance between tribune of the plebs and general was one fraught with danger for the future.

The Division of the Spoils

One reason why the political argument at Rome over the division of the spoils of empire became so bitter in the last generation of the second century was precisely because these were becoming ever richer. In 133 the last king of Pergamum had actually left his kingdom to the Romans; the Roman acquisition of what became the province of Asia falls in the middle of the second great period of Roman acquisition of territory (not to be confused with acquisition of power), between Africa and Achaea in 146 and Provence in 121. The result was a rapid rise in the numbers of Romans and Italians living overseas, as tax-collectors, money-lenders, and slave-traders. Their activities happen to be principally documented in the East, and the greatest wealth was no doubt to be acquired there; but the process clearly went on in the West as well. What is important in this context is that Italians abroad were treated as equals with Romans by the people with whom they dealt; the lack of Roman citizenship was no doubt felt ever more acutely.

Other factors deserve a mention. There certainly took place in this period some genuine urbanization, as opposed to the embellishment of existing centres. For instance, at Bovianum and Saepinum, in central Samnium, where previously there had been scattered villages or farms and hill-forts as places of refuge, urban growth began on the plains below the hill-forts. At Monte Vairano, the hill-fort itself began to be permanently occupied. The Roman urban model of society was spreading. All these developments certainly made Italian communities feel even more acutely their formal inferiority and their lack of control over Roman policy. Romans sometimes behaved high-handedly to members of local élites. And the career of C. Marius—six times consul between 107 and 100, victor over Jugurtha, saviour of Rome from the Cimbri and Teutones—showed what could be achieved by an aristocrat from an Italian community which had been enfranchised.

At the same time, it is certain that the actual grievances of the allies were increasing, as Rome sought to avoid the consequences of her own lack of peasant soldiers by shifting ever more of the military burden on to her Italian allies. It is remarkable in these years how difficult Rome found it to defeat the relatively minor figure of Jugurtha of Numidia and how vulnerable she was to the Cimbri and Teutones. It was luck that brought them no nearer Rome than the Po valley. And one may wonder whether either Jugurtha or they would have been defeated without the skill of C. Marius.

Citizenship for Italy

By 91, it was no longer possible to evade the issue of granting Roman citizenship to the Italians, and when M. Livius Drusus' proposal to do so failed, half of Italy rose in revolt (the so-called Social War). Rome disarmed the revolt by agreeing to grant what she had at first refused and was able with the help of those who remained loyal to subdue the rebels who held out (for what, it is not clear).

The result was that the whole of peninsular Italy together with existing *coloniae* in the Po valley was organized into communities of Roman citizens. We are ignorant of the details of the process, but it was largely complete by 83. For it was in that year that L. Cornelius Sulla, who had in 88 fought a brief civil war in order to secure the command of the Roman armies in the East, returned to Italy. He was ruthless with particular communities or peoples which opposed him, but made no attempt to undo the enfranchisement or organization of Italy as a whole. In 89 the Po valley had been placed on the road to assimilation with peninsular Italy; Cn. Pompeius Strabo, the father of Magnus, gave the status of a Latin *colonia* to those communities in the Po valley and Liguria which were not already either Roman or Latin. Full Roman citizenship was delayed for more than a generation, but was granted by Caesar.

I have already drawn attention to the spread of the urban model in Italy. But what happened after the enfranchisement of Italy was of a rather different kind. Amidst all our ignorance, it is clear that new Roman communities were equipped with relatively homogeneous constitutions, appropriate to urban societies. Rome in fact found it difficult to think other than in terms of urban centres when dealing with other communities. The enfranchisement of Italy thus provided, with the creation of new Roman communities, a powerful spur to the development of urban centres. This in itself is likely to have been in turn a factor making for the Romanization of Italy.

There are at least two levels at which the phenomenon of Romanization needs to be considered. It is probably easiest to begin with the level of the élite. The Roman system had always been characterized by a relatively high degree of élite mobility. It was naturally rare for a man, none of whose family had ever held office, to reach the consulship, as did C. Marius and Cicero. But the ascent of a family to the consulship over several generations was a common enough phenomenon; and a man who ennobled himself and his descendants by being the first of his family to achieve the consulship or other high office was known as a *novus homo*, new man. Families from newly enfranchised communities, throughout the history of the republic, waited perhaps for a generation and could then begin their ascent to high office. The story was no different with the mass enfranchisement of Italy after 91–89; by the time of Augustus, the Roman Senate was full of members of the élites of recently enfranchised communities, many of whose descendants went on to hold the consulship. The avenues of advancement were those which had always applied, friendship with those already in positions of power, wealth, oratorical skill, military expertise (see Ch. 5 for Italian authors of the late Republic).

Much more difficult to assess is the Romanization of the population of Italy as a whole; we must admit that we can know nothing of the culture of an illiterate farm labourer, too poor even to be drafted into the armies of Rome. All our knowledge relates, if not to the élite, at least to those close to it. Given this limitation, there are four indicators worth considering of the survival or submergence of distinctive local cultures in Italy: language, religious practices, family structures, and funeral rites. The last, if valid, is particularly useful, since there is substantial archaeological evidence.

The evidence of language is striking. Northern Etruria remained substantially untouched by Roman influence down to 91. It is also an area where inscriptions in Latin down to the same date are conspicuous by their absence. In the generation after Sulla, however, bilingual inscriptions make their appearance, and within the lifetime of Cicero Etruscan had virtually disappeared. The case of Samnium is harder to assess, since the destruction wrought by Sulla in 82–81 means that there was little in the way of urban life till Caesar. Inscriptions in the local language, one of the varieties of what is known to modern scholars as Oscan, certainly disappear; but the argument from silence is dangerous. Further south in Lucania, however, the same pattern occurs, without any reason to suppose that Sulla was responsible; and indeed inscriptions in Oscan are here replaced by inscriptions in Latin. It is worth citing the evidence provided by the recent excavations at Rossano di Vaglio; here a rural Lucanian sanctuary was absorbed after Sulla into the administrative structures of the near-by city of Potentia.

The evidence for religious practices and family structures is exiguous; what there is suggests that during the lifetime of Cicero traces of religious diversity, such as different local calendars, disappeared and rules governing marriage and inheritance became steadily more uniform. The evidence relating to funerary practices is substantial, and is spread throughout Italy; it consistently portrays the replacement of distinctive local practices, often of great antiquity, by a relatively uniform set of customs. There remained, of course, enormous variety according to the wealth of the deceased, but that is another matter.

If it is true that the period between Sulla and Augustus saw an enormous advance in the level of Romanization achieved, it remains to ask why. The principal reason is to be sought in the process of veteran settlement between 59 and the early 20s BC. Beginning in 59 with the veterans from the eastern wars of Cn. Pompeius Magnus, enormous numbers of men, uprooted from their homes, serving together for long periods, were settled in groups far from their place of birth. The consequence for the next generation was the shattering of the existing social fabric both in the places of origin and in the communities where these men were settled. The Italian society of the early Empire which resulted was perhaps the most important and the most lasting consequence of the Roman revolution.

Further Reading

M. Beard and M. H. Crawford, *Rome in the Late Republic* (London, 1984), as well as providing a critical account of the main problems, contains a full account of the available translations of the ancient sources for Republican history as a whole and a full bibliography for the end of the Republic.

T. Cornell and J. Matthews, *Atlas of the Roman World* (Oxford, 1982) contains a good general account of Roman history and an excellent selection of maps and pictures.

Among histories of Rome, note R. M. Ogilvie, *Early Rome and the Etruscans* (London, 1976) and M. H. Crawford, *The Roman Republic* (London, 1978); H. H. Scullard, *History of the Roman World 753–146 BC*, 4th edn. (London, 1981), and *From the Gracchi to Nero*, 4th edn. (London, 1976); P. A. Brunt, *Social Conflicts in the Roman Republic* (London, 1971).

T. R. S. Broughton, *Magistrates of the Roman Republic* (New York, I–II, 1960 III, 1987), provides a year by year list of magistrates, with references to the sources and modern discussions.

For an analysis of recent work in the area, see M. H. Crawford, 'Rome and Italy', in *Journal of Roman Studies* 71 (1981), 153–60. Important books are E. T. Salmon, *Roman Colonisation* (London, 1969); *The Making of Roman Italy* (London, 1983), despite its narrowly political focus; A. N. Sherwin-White, *The Roman Citizenship*, 2nd. edn. (Oxford, 1973); E. Badian, *Foreign Clientelae* (Oxford, 1958); P. A. Brunt, *Italian Manpower* (Oxford, 1971); E. Gabba, *Republican Rome, the Army and the Allies* (Oxford, 1976); T. P. Wiseman, *New Men in the Roman Senate* (Oxford, 1971); E. T. Salmon, *Samnium and the Samnites* (Cambridge, 1967).

For the Roman political system, see H. F. Jolowicz and B. Nicholas, *Historical Introduction to Roman Law* (Cambridge, 1972); E. S. Staveley, *Greek and Roman Voting and Elections* (London, 1972).

For Roman religion, see the seminal article by J. A. North, 'Conservatism and change in Roman religion', in *Papers of the British School at Rome* 44 (1976), 1–12; also J. H. W. G. Liebeschuetz, *Continuity and Change in Roman Religion* (Oxford, 1979).

On the working of Roman politics, see M. Gelzer, *The Roman Nobility* (Oxford, 1969); P. A. Brunt, '*Nobilitas* and *Novitas*', in *Journal of Roman Studies* 72 (1982), 1–17; K. Hopkins, *Death and Renewal* (Cambridge, 1983), ch. 2.

On Rome and the outside world, see K. Hopkins, *Conquerors and Slaves* (Cambridge, 1978), ch. 1; W. V. Harris, *War and Imperialism in Republican*

Rome, 327–70 B.C. (Oxford, 1979); J. A. North, 'The Development of Roman Imperialism', in *Journal of Roman Studies* 71 (1981), 1–9; A. D. Momigliano, *Alien Wisdom* (London, 1975); W. V. Harris (ed.), *The Imperialism of the Roman Republic* (Rome, 1984).

For the transformation of Italy in the age of revolution, see L. Keppie, *Colonisation and Veteran Settlement in Italy 47–14 B.C.* (London, 1983).

2

The Expansion of Rome

ELIZABETH RAWSON

The Conquests of Rome

POLYBIUS thought that no one could be so worthless or indolent as not to wish to know how, and under what sort of government, the Romans had succeeded in less than fifty-three years in subjecting almost the whole inhabited world to their rule (below, pp. 271 ff.). We are now to consider Rome's expansion abroad from the beginning of the Punic Wars: but we will carry on the story after Polybius' death to the end of the Republic.

In 264 BC Rome controlled the whole of the Italian peninsula, except the Po valley ('Cisalpine Gaul'), and her defeat of Pyrrhus (above, p. 34) had attracted Greek interest. In that year a Roman army crossed to Sicily, partly to prevent the Carthaginians taking Messana and dominating the straits, and after twenty years' fighting, during which Rome turned herself into a naval power, she expelled the Carthaginians from the island. Part of it was left to friendly Syracuse and other Greek cities; for part Rome seems to have taken responsibility. In 237 she seized (on a poor excuse, but the islands were strategically vital now that Rome and Carthage were foes) Sardinia and Corsica, previously controlled by Carthage. In 227 two new magistrates were elected, for the 'jobs', *prouinciae*, of Sicily and Sardinia. Rome had also just intervened against the newly expansive and piratical Illyrians across the Adriatic, where a protectorate, including some Greek states, was established along the coast. When another and desperate clash with Carthage occurred (the Second Punic War) and Hannibal invaded Italy in 218, Roman forces were sent against his base in Spain, which they were not to leave again, though the peninsula was not wholly pacified till Augustus' day. Finally Hannibal was penned into the toe of Italy, and Scipio, who had fought with success in Spain and won over many tribes, moved the war to Africa itself, to which Hannibal was recalled only to be defeated at Zama in 202. Carthage lost territory to Roman allies in Africa and became another client state. On the other hand, the whole of Sicily became a province, for Syracuse had proved disloyal.

Hannibal's alliance with Philip V of Macedon had also led to Roman troops being deployed across the Adriatic, and finally to the Second Macedonian War, in which the King was defeated by T. Flamininus, though the kingdom was allowed to survive, and Greece proper was declared 'free' in 196; Roman influence in the whole area was, however, now paramount. Thus integrated into the world of the great Hellenistic powers, Rome involved herself in a victorious struggle, led by Scipio and his brother, against Antiochus III of Syria; again, though Rome annexed no territory, she cut down the power of Syria and arranged the affairs of the eastern Mediterranean as she pleased, to the advantage of her friends, the kingdom of Pergamum and the island republic of Rhodes.

The Romans after a time accused King Perseus, Philip's son, of disloyalty; he was crushed in 167 by Aemilius Paullus at the battle of Pydna, and Macedon was split into four tributary republics ('First', 'Second', and so on). There was no war with Egypt, the third of the great kingdoms that had emerged after Alexander's death, but she too almost became a protectorate, as was dramatically shown when a Roman envoy drew a circle with his staff around the person of the invading Antiochus IV and told him to order retreat before he stepped out of it. It is up to this point, from 220 BC, that Polybius' fifty-three years run. The fact that Rome had annexed little territory did not make

52 ·   *The Expansion of Rome*

him doubt that she had an Empire; the Greeks were used to seeing these based on alliances or leagues.

Polybius lived on to recount the anti-Roman movements in Macedon and Greece in 148, which were brutally put down, the city of Corinth being utterly destroyed. Macedon became a province and its governor was made responsible for Greece. Almost simultaneously Carthage, harassed by Rome's ally the King of Numidia, revolted, and was wiped from the face of the earth by the younger Scipio; her territory became the province of Africa. In 133 the last king of Pergamum died without a legitimate heir, leaving his kingdom to Rome (his motives are to some extent disputed), and part of it became the province of Asia. The need to safeguard the route to Spain, and obligations to Rome's old ally Massilia, led to fighting in Transalpine Gaul, and finally the establishment of a province in the area still called Provence.

However, towards the end of the second century Rome met with a number of defeats at the hands of barbarian enemies, notably Jugurtha in Africa and the northern Cimbri and Teutones who had invaded Italy (both wars were in the end successfully concluded by C. Marius). She was also preoccupied by internal problems brought to a head by the brothers Gracchi (above, pp. 41 f.), and from 91 with the 'Social' War against the Italian allies (above, pp. 45 f.). Upon this followed the first real civil war, leading to Sulla's brief dictatorship and his restoration of senatorial government. Understandably only small gains were made abroad in this period. Neglect of the East, which had allowed the rise of Mithridates of Pontus, who seized all Asia Minor, exploiting anti-Roman sentiment, and whose forces even invaded Greece, was ultimately remedied. The Roman general Pompey (below, pp. 101 ff.) decided that more direct rule was needed. He set up provinces in Syria (where the Seleucid kingdom had been in decline since its original defeat by Rome, with resulting disorder) and in Bithynia-Pontus in northern Asia Minor; he enlarged the 'province' of Cilicia, where Rome had for some time been trying to deal with pirates based on the wild coast. The rest of the East was put under selected kings and dynasts, at least some of whom paid tribute to Rome. The Empire had now reached the Euphrates, and Rome was in direct touch with Armenia and Parthia beyond it, kingdoms where the Greek cultural influence predominant in most of the Near East began to wear very thin.

Only a few years later, in 58 BC, C. Julius Caesar (below, pp. 107 ff.) became governor of southern Gaul and embarked on a war of conquest in the centre and north which even took him across the Rhine and the English Channel. He failed to make Britain tributary, but Gaul was organized as a province. This was the first of Rome's conquests remote from the Mediterranean or its extension the Black Sea, and led on to the successful Alpine and Balkan, and unsuccessful German, campaigns of Augustus. However the attempt by M. Crassus, the third member of the so-called First Triumvirate (below, pp. 109 ff.), to invade Parthia was a disaster, and the next major annexation completed the circuit of the Mediterranean: Cleopatra was encouraged by her Roman lover, Antony, to rebuild Egypt's power in the eastern Mediterranean, but they were defeated by Antony's rival for supremacy at Rome, the future Emperor Augustus.

The Evidence

No one disputes that the consequences for Rome of these conquests were vast, economically, socially, culturally, and politically. But to particularize raises hotly debated issues. The difficulties are due partly to the shortcomings of our sources. Polybius wrote a full and pretty reliable account of most of Rome's wars from 264 to 146, but his later books survive only in fragments and for the earlier ones he depended on previous writers whom he knew to be biased. Some of the missing parts of Polybius can be reconstructed from Livy, who sensibly used him for Rome's relations with the East; but Livy, who is again incompletely preserved (only in epitomes and derivatives after 167) also used the so-called annalistic tradition of his Latin-writing predecessors. Its reliability, and the extent to which it draws on documentary evidence, is disputed, but it certainly often distorts events for patriotic or dramatic ends (the desire of most historians to provide moral *exempla*, and their training in rhetoric, must be borne in mind). Of authors later than the Augustan Livy, the Greek historian Appian, who recounts many of Rome's wars, is notable, as is Plutarch, though the main interest of his *Lives* is in individual character. For Caesar's campaigns we have his own *Commentaries*, often disingenuous; and Cicero's speeches and letters throw much light on his own period, and incidentally on earlier ones. (A fuller account of the Roman historians is given in Ch. 10 below.)

To some extent the literary sources can be supplemented, especially in the Greek world, where there was a tradition of recording documents on stone (in the West bronze was often used for the less common inscriptions, and might be melted down for re-use). In all areas what survives does so by chance, often in fragments; but recent discoveries have changed our ideas in many respects. Archaeology proper shows us how in some parts of Italy in the second century subsistence agriculture gave way to larger slave-run estates producing for a market, and documents the growth of overseas trade with these more developed areas. But not all Italy has been, or can be, surveyed; and outside it most of the work has been concentrated in, this time, the western Mediterranean. And much trade leaves no trace; pottery and marble may survive, but what of slaves, corn, dried fish, spices? Still, we know that black-glazed table ware was exported from the western coast of central Italy to Gaul and Spain from the earlier second century, with an increasing number of the amphoras or wine-jars, of which it has been estimated that perhaps 40,000,000 were imported into Gaul between 150 BC and the end of the Republic. Wrecks of ships on their way to Rome from the East have also been found; works of art old and new (statues, that is; paintings would perish) have been recovered, with in one case such curiosities as old Greek inscriptions and a complex astronomical device. Finally numismatics, as coin hoards and other discoveries gradually fix the date of Greek and Roman issues, can tell us something of economic changes. But controversy still rages, for example about why, on several crucial occasions, Rome went to war.

Roman Imperialism

The central debate turns on the question: in what sense was Rome imperialist? It was once thought that Rome was not an aggressive power; that she had few contacts with the Greek world in the third century, apart from the old alliance with isolated Massilia, and was uninterested in the East: during the Hannibalic War her treaty with the Aetolians in northern Greece claimed only the movable booty from joint operations, the real estate being left to the Aetolians, and she campaigned without energy, making few, if any, other formal alliances. She was slow to annex, for example setting up in 167 four artificial 'independent' republics in Macedon. She sometimes refused lands bequeathed by will—notably Egypt in the early first century BC—while it took her twenty years to get round to organizing Cyrenaica, left to her in 96. It was further argued that the historians always showed Rome to have declared war for defensive reasons, or to assist allies to whom she had obligations and a reputation for *fides* (good faith) to keep up. For the idea of the *bellum iustum*, 'just war', undertaken in self-defence or to aid allies, obsessed her. Rome perhaps sometimes believed wrongly that she was under threat; there has been argument over whether there was, or Rome thought there was, a secret pact between Philip and Antiochus III in 200, and whether Perseus was really preparing war in the 170s. But if Rome's fears were mistaken, this showed her ignorance of the outside world. Polybius' belief that Rome aimed at world dominion was dismissed as the opinion of a Greek theorist, influenced by Thucydides on Athenian imperialism or by the career of Alexander; his own narrative refuted his general interpretation.

It was also argued that Rome rarely acted from economic

motives. Policy was made by senators, and they were forbidden by the Lex Claudia of 218 to own ships over a certain size, and barred from the lucrative public contracts which included supplying the armies and in time collecting provincial taxes. (Anyway such activities were thought low.) There soon came to be tension between the Senate and the contractors, *publicani*, who were mostly of the wealthy class later known as *equites* or knights, whose interests the Senate would oppose; some of the mines of Macedon were shut after 167 to prevent exploitation by the *publicani*. In addition, many of the *negotiatores* ('men of affairs'), engaged in money-lending, banking, trade, and even agriculture, whom we know from literary and epigraphic sources to have settled all over the Mediterranean world in the second century, were mostly, so it was held, until the Social War not citizens, but Italian allies, for whom Rome felt little responsibility. The names indeed of many are not Latin, and point to Oscan-speaking southern Italy, especially Campania (for instance, Stlaccius, found on the island mart of Delos). It has even been argued that most of what trade there was (it is still often minimized) was designed to supply Roman armies and Roman settlers, not to make a profit from the natives, though it had to be admitted that in the first century generals and *publicani* influenced policy, and Roman rule was detested for its greed.

This picture will not altogether do. Rome was in touch with the Greek world from an early date. And Roman society was militaristic. Polybius paints the Romans as above all soldiers of great discipline and ferocity: sacking a city, they even kill the animals. The Senate liked to keep the army in training. Young aristocrats were expected in Polybius' time to serve ten campaigns before standing for office; the top offices were basically military ones. Military prowess was valued above all things—*uirtus* meant primarily valour. The highest ambition was for a triumph, the pompous celebration of a major victory by a grand procession exhibiting the spoils of war, in which the victor was for a day almost equated with a god. (Triumphs proliferated in the second century and had to be regulated.) Only less regarded was the thanksgiving to the gods decreed by the Senate in the name of a victorious commander. Campaigns provoked by generals to earn a triumph undoubtedly occurred, even before the first century when the Senate lost control. A correspondent wished the unwarlike Cicero, then governor of Cilicia, 'enough fighting for a triumph', and he was himself shamefacedly eager for one. Admittedly, generals were often also anxious to end a war and take the troops home to grace the event.

If enough members of the oligarchy were to have a chance of distinction—and there was great pressure on the sons of aristocrats to emulate their ancestors—wars had to be almost continuous. There was resentment against men who, like Scipio, hogged big commands for years, and there was jockeying for appointment if a good war was in prospect. There might be disagreement about where to fight, but not about fighting somewhere. Roman aristocratic tradition was reinforced by Greek influence. Scipio already perhaps modelled himself on Alexander; Pompey notoriously did, adopting his hair-style and letting panegyrists exaggerate his youth at the time of his eastern conquests; Caesar is said to have wept in youth at the thought of the Macedonian, who had conquered the world at an age when he himself had done nothing. But there is public as well as personal glory; first-century Romans were intensely proud of their world Empire and set the globe on their coins.

The Economic Motive

All booty was legally at the general's disposal, though he was expected to give some to the Treasury and use some himself on public works, notably temples vowed in battle. Such buildings, apart from providing employment (to men who would support their employer at elections) kept a man's name, often emblazoned on the façade, before the public. And, as the standard of luxury—and later of electoral bribery—rose, spoil provided the quickest way to the wealth needed by the competitive upper class.

It was also the quickest way to wealth for the troops, to whom the general distributed part of the official booty—there was doubtless unofficial booty too, in spite of the rules. Although the really poor were not eligible for the army till the late second century, the (probably increasingly small) small-holders serving were often in debt to richer neighbours, and doubtless anyway eager to make their fortunes. Later, in a letter of 43 BC, D. Brutus tells Cicero that he has led his men against some Alpine tribes to meet their wishes. During the Italian wars victory had often led to conquered land being parcelled out among poor citizens. This happened much less after wars overseas, though the state acquired some land to rent out, to foreigners or citizens; but a few veterans were placed in the second century in Spain and the Balearics, and there was much settlement in Cisalpine Gaul. Gaius Gracchus, however, who, like his brother Tiberius, had a new vision of how the Empire could be used to support the poor of Rome, proposed colonies abroad; Saturninus, another demagogic tribune at the end of the second century, had a broad plan of transmarine settlement for both veterans, now including many landless, and the urban *plebs*. But in practice Caesar was the first to plant both classes abroad on any large scale.

It has also been suggested that, till the Social War, Rome's only way to profit from her alliances in Italy, since the allies paid no taxes, was to call them out to fight. Most Italian peoples had their own military tradition, and if at times they found Rome's demands oppressive, they took pride in their share in her victories, which many came to feel earned them a right to political equality and Roman citizenship. They did not always get an equal share of booty, but the grand buildings set up at some Italian shrines shortly before the Social War may show its deployment by local magnates; equally, the *negotiatores* hailing from Campania and elsewhere may have sometimes begun operations abroad by investing the profits of war. Pompeii documents the prosperity of Campania, partly the result of such *negotia*.

Booty included slaves—either those already such, or prisoners of war (the Romans perhaps rarely allowed ransom). Marxists, exaggerating the admittedly great importance of slavery in ancient society, have supposed that Roman conquests were fuelled by the need for slaves. No ancient source hints at this, but the sources are coy about the slave trade. Masses of slaves did result from Rome's wars; Aemilius Paullus, the victor of Pydna, is said to have sold 150,000 inhabitants of Epirus in northern Greece, on the Senate's order to deal harshly with the area; it became a virtual desert. Slaves were also acquired by trade; we are told that some Gallic chiefs were so fond of Italian wine they would give a slave for a single jar, and there is literary evidence for Gallic slaves in Italy. The geographer Strabo says that at the height of its prosperity about 100 BC Delos could handle 10,000 slaves a day (some originally kidnapped by pirates or slave-dealers, some foundlings or enslaved for debt, many bought from barbarian tribes in Thrace and elsewhere). It is not strange that servile revolts broke out in Italy and Sicily in the late second and early first centuries. Though the great expansion in the use of slaves in Italy on the land and on a smaller scale for skilled jobs, including teaching (these were mostly easterners) seems a result, rather than a cause, of the first transmarine conquests, it is likely that later the makers of Roman policy gave some thought to the supply; landowners needed slaves more than anyone, though they were used in every type of enterprise and small men too would profit from low prices.

The growing evidence for commerce after the Hannibalic War also makes it unlikely that senators were totally uninterested in trade. Italian exports were largely in agricultural produce, wine, and to some extent oil; great landowners may have traded in the name of freedmen, who could legally own big ships and were still bound to assist their masters, or sold their produce, sometimes still on the tree, to a merchant, as the elder Cato's agricultural treatise indicates. A gentlemanly distance was thus combined with profit. Even before Sulla enlarged the Senate (below, pp. 100 f.) there was intermarriage with rich non-senatorial families; and it has been shown that many of the far-flung *negotiatores* did come from parts of Italy given Roman citizenship well before the Social War. Certainly after Sulla many new senators had close relatives involved in business matters, while some probably refused to drop their own old interests; Cicero tells us in 70 that the Lex Claudia and similar measures were disobeyed, though Caesar may have reasserted them in 59. The rich also depended on luxuries from the East to sustain an increasingly sumptuous way of life; works of fine and applied art, rare foods and wines, skilled slaves, spices transmitted from distant climes.

Senators might lend money at interest; Cato, in the mid second century, did so through a freedman to finance trading voyages, and later senators made a corner in lending to ambassadors at Rome. It seems also that in the first century they could or did take shares in the great companies of *publicani* now farming some provincial taxes. Finally, in spite of friction between the classes, the system of patronage will always have meant that many business men could put pressure on individual senators to support their interests. It is thus hard to maintain that the Senate almost never had an eye to commercial interest, let alone other types of economic advantage.

Cicero indeed claims that Rome often went to war for her merchants. This is partly true, for example, of the First Illyrian War, though at that time and place they will in truth have been mostly Italians (trade in this region is not yet well documented archaeologically); but there was also mistreatment of envoys to avenge and perhaps appeals to answer. In 187 Rome laid down that Romans and Latins (and possibly Italians) should be exempt from harbour dues at Ambracia, and this may not have been the isolated action our sources suggest. The making of Delos a free port in 167 weakened Rhodes and benefited Roman and Italian traders. And Cicero indicates that some time before 129 Rome forbade Transalpine peoples (in southern Gaul; attempts to explain the notice away are perverse) to plant vines and olives, perhaps to protect her own trade in wine and oil. Admittedly this seems a unique measure; and Rome did not, for example, impose a common coinage over her sphere of influence, unlike Athens.

The one form of trade in which the state took a direct interest was that in corn. The urban *plebs* must not starve, the armies must be provisioned. With the increase in population at Rome corn (mainly wheat) from abroad had to be provided regularly, not just in crises (the rest of Italy still fed itself or even sent grain to Rome). Sicily annually gave up a tithe of its harvest as tax (and had from 73 to sell another to Rome at a fixed price if needed). After 146 the corn of Africa became vital. We now know that on one occasion in the second century a Roman magistrate got the Thessalians, in northern Greece, to bring corn to Rome; however, till the city became dependent on Egypt in the imperial age, the East was not often drawn on. Private merchants were responsible for the transfer of corn to Rome, but the Senate must have kept an eye on the situation. Most other basic raw materials, such as wood, were available in Italy, though the mines of Spain were important, and those of Macedon were soon reopened.

The Treasury became increasingly dependent on foreign revenues. At first Rome did not, it seems, always impose taxes, but just demanded reparations, or large sums for which no special justification was claimed; Antiochus III was mulcted of 1,500 talents. In civilized Sicily Rome took over the tax system existing under Syracuse, but it was perhaps gradually that proper taxes were imposed in Spain and the mines let. Contractors' fees, 'indemnities', taxes, and booty became so valuable that direct tax on citizens was abolished after Pydna, even though the armies, now serving all year round, were increasingly expensive to maintain. Taxes were sometimes lowered when an area was reorganized, but new customs dues, for example, were also imposed. Later, particularly after the Social War and Sulla's dictatorship, the state, with heavy wars on hand, faced severe financial problems; it now had to pay for the large part of the army previously financed by the Italian allies, and soon C. Gracchus' corn subsidies in Rome, abolished by Sulla, were reintroduced.

Cicero claimed in 66 that the only province to provide a surplus after defence and administration was Asia. But Plutarch says the tax income was doubled by Pompey's new arrangements. Gaul was also to contribute, and Egypt even more.

Finally, many senators made private fortunes from the Empire. Polybius believed that until his time Roman magistrates were remarkable for probity. Cato certainly reiterated that he had not made a sesterce from his service abroad. But Cicero's speeches illustrate the behaviour too common in his day, though we need not think that every governor was a Verres, emulated in rapacity by all his staff. Cicero himself was honest enough, and says in a letter from Cilicia that the other governors then in the East were all decent (though his own predecessor, Ap. Pulcher, was 'not a man, but some sort of wild beast'). The *Verrine Orations* detail every possible abuse, from conniving with pirates to stealing statues on such a scale that the Sicilian tourist trade was ruined. From the second century governors could be prosecuted for extortion, but it was hard for provincials to organize a trial at Rome, or to secure conviction, even at periods when it was the *equites*, not the senators, who formed, or formed a majority on, the jury.

The Reluctance to Annex

If senators and *equites*, private soldiers and the public Treasury, even the urban *plebs*, all profited from Rome's expansion, why was she so slow to annex territories that fell into her lap? Occasionally moral reluctance might be mooted: Flamininus refused to abolish the kingdom of Macedon at the Aetolians' demand, saying that it was unRoman to annihilate an enemy. There was hesitation about the final razing of Carthage, which was felt hard to justify to public, especially Greek, opinion; and the idea that states need an external threat to prevent corruption and decline was perhaps put forward. Not that the Romans doubted the morality of ruling an Empire as such; when the provocative Greek philosopher Carneades, in a lecture at Rome in 155, suggested that justice would demand that they should give up their conquests and return to shepherds' huts, there was outrage. At most, individual wars might be attacked as inspired by one's opponents' greed: thus Cato opposed a project of war with Rhodes in 167, and many objected to Crassus' Parthian campaign.

But it is significant that many people did just as well where annexation had not taken place. 'Kings, nations, and cities', even if technically 'free', were an integral part of the Empire. Some kings already claimed in the second century to be mere agents of Rome. Free states could be expected, or bound by treaty, to send aid in war; an increasing proportion of Rome's forces, especially in ships and cavalry, were 'auxiliary'. Where individuals are concerned, Verres carried off treasures from 'free' as well as from 'stipendiary' cities. Great Romans were patrons of dynasts and communities outside, as well as inside, the provinces, thus gaining power, prestige, and even profit— the line between gift and bribe was fine, as the friends of King Jugurtha of Numidia found. We can see how the Claudii, over two and a half centuries, extended their *clientela* in Greek-speaking lands, or how the Domitii Ahenobarbi, with an ancestor who had fought in southern Gaul and estates on the west coast of Italy, built up influence in the western Mediterranean. (A patron might be able to protect his clients from mistreatment; if he mistreated them himself it was hard for others to intervene.)

Trade and money-lending could be carried on almost better where there was no Roman governor for oppressed natives to appeal to, and where any action against *negotiatores* could be represented as anti-Roman. The wine trade stretched up into central Gaul well before Caesar's time, and when Cicero was in the East the unfortunate young King Ariobarzanes of Cappadocia ('Pious' and 'Pro-Roman' by style) was deep in debt to Roman moneylenders, including M. Brutus, that 'honourable man', and Pompey, a flock of whose agents were dunning him for interest. There is no sign that *negotiatores* wanted annexation;

Marius, a friend of the *equites*, did not extend the province of Africa. But Rome's power was there to protect or at least avenge them; Jugurtha's massacre of the hated *Italici* had been one of the causes of the war, and it is significant that if they called themselves *Italici*, the Greeks called them all *Rhōmaioi*, Romans.

Roman conservatism is also relevant. Rome had stretched the idea of the city-state to its limit, but not abandoned it; citizens had to vote in person, and not too many of the upper class at least should be on business abroad. The Senate, until Sulla, consisted of about 300 men, in practice all ex-magistrates; more provinces meant more offices. And the oligarchy, though continually replenished from wealthy outsiders—Marius was one—would not wish the process to be too rapid. It also feared individuals acquiring *regnum*, quasi-monarchic power, for which prolonged absence in a distant province could provide the base—though so might a war not ending in annexation. Sulla attempted to control ambitious governors by a law (flouted by Caesar in Gaul) forbidding among other things leaving one's province with an army without senatorial permission. The Senate set its face against annexing Egypt in the earlier first century partly because the untrustworthy and greedy Crassus wanted to be involved in it.

Furthermore, in the third and second centuries the army was not a standing one, but in theory raised annually, chiefly from the peasantry. Long and hard campaigns were unpopular with the troops, especially in Spain, not an area as rich in booty as the East. Cato said in 167 that Macedonia could not be annexed, because it could not be defended (in part from barbarians on its frontiers). The Romans indeed became anxious at this time about a decline in military quality, partly due to the decline, in some areas, of the peasant class; this was followed by a period, already mentioned, of military disasters, and that, as also noted, by one of financial stringency. No wonder many places were left to defend and police themselves.

Some peoples, too, were attached to their native rulers and

better left to them. And where the Greek cities were concerned, Rome discovered that 'liberation' was the best policy—perhaps already in Sicily and on the Adriatic coast, certainly when Flamininus, after defeating Philip of Macedon, declared Greece free at the Isthmian Games of 196, to frantic enthusiasm, and evacuated it completely. Some Greek cities had treaties with Rome (how many is disputed), which left them internal autonomy but bound them to give help in war (only treaties not described as equal bound them to respect the *maiestas* of the Roman People in all ways). Others were simply declared free unilaterally by Rome, a status which, it was in time discovered, she was ready unilaterally to revoke. The desire of Rhodes for a formal alliance in 167 shows this was felt to be some kind of safeguard; but in the end Rome refused to be shackled even by her treaties.

The policy of freedom for Greeks was not inspired by sentimental philhellenism, though Rome had more respect for Greek public opinion than she did for barbarian tribes, against whom her record was undoubtedly worse; rather its purpose was to reduce the power of Macedon and Syria. Rome did not apply it when it did not suit her: for example, she handed over various cities to her friends Pergamum and Rhodes. Under the Roman moral system, by which every *beneficium* had to be repaid by *officium* (act or sense of duty), the 'free' states were expected to conform to Rome's wishes. They did not always grasp this, a fact which contributed to the souring of Rome's relations with the various squabbling Greek states in the first half of the second century, until some of her generals began to behave to the Greeks, shortly before the war with Perseus, with brutality and contempt; this *noua sapientia*, as Livy called it, or new wisdom, was disapproved of by some prominent Romans, in vain.

The Protection of the Propertied Classes

In fact, even where the 'stipendiary' or tribute-paying inhabitants of a province were concerned, much responsibility was left to local communities, especially Greek cities. The Roman governor's duties were chiefly defence (hence the first of the great Roman roads outside Italy) and the administration of justice to Roman citizens; he could take cases between natives, but clearly not all of these, and Cicero says his (not unique) proclamation that he would take none was popular. The Romans made no attempt to impose uniformity; in some provinces a magistrate, the quaestor, was responsible for the collection of direct taxes, but probably only by overseeing local officials. In others both direct and indirect taxes were collected by tax-farmers, sometimes not even Roman, and these might have large staffs; even so, in some cases the cities did the basic work. These cities carried on their political life largely unhampered; when Pompey wanted to annex part of Pontus, he felt it best to found a group of Greek-style cities, if with larger territories than usual. As a result of this system the Romans, in spite of severe friction at times, developed a partnership with the upper classes who did much of the administration for them, and whom they defended against the cry of the poor for the division of land and abolition of debts that was sometimes heard.

Flamininus had left the cities of Greece in the hands of the well-off. Perseus appealed to the poor, though not only to them, for support; and anti-Roman feeling was often based on hostility to the rich—though it would be voiced by well-off leaders, jealous of whatever pro-Roman clique was in power, or genuinely idealistic or nationalistic. It is uncertain how far Rome intervened to make constitutions more oligarchic, as they tended to become; but we have on stone a letter from a governor of Macedon to a Peloponnesian city, of the late second century, which reveals that he has taken steps to crush social unrest there. Polybius, who came of a distinguished political family, thought a newly slavish adherence to Rome deplorable, but realized that dignified independence was only possible within narrow limits. He believed, however, that in spite of recent abuses and the new harshness Rome had given the Greek cities great benefits, and that the revolts of 148 were insane folly (these were again partly inspired by the poor, who would be less aware than the upper classes that Rome was too strong to resist).

Certainly Greek communities, from whatever motives, paid Rome every sort of honour. In early years her *fides*, the good faith to which communities were to entrust themselves, was much celebrated. From the early second century cults were founded to the goddess Roma (*Rhōmē* in Greek significantly means power); the poetess Melinno's hymn to Rome perhaps dates from this period. Cults were also set up to individuals, starting with Flamininus; Plutarch describes the ceremonies in his name still carried out in Euboea in his own day. The honour was gradually devalued: even Cicero was voted temples, which he refused in an attempt to keep the cities' expenditure within bounds. No wonder Roman statesmen began to feel themselves the equals of Hellenistic kings. Lesser honours—titles, statues—abounded, even for prominent *negotiatores*, such as the Cloatii who lent to and protected—or ran—the little town of Gytheum near Sparta in the early first century.

Even in the dark days of the Mithridatic War, when many places slaughtered the blood-sucking *negotiatores*, a few cities of Greece and Asia stayed loyal, if sometimes from traditional enmity to rebellious neighbours. Thus the Assembly at Aphrodisias in Asia Minor, where Rome honoured the shrine of Aphrodite, voted to go with every available man to help a Roman general, for 'without the protection of the Romans we do not even wish to live'. But the first century was a terrible time for many Greek cities. They suffered in the fighting against Mithridates, and Sulla exacted large sums to punish disloyalty and finance civil war. Piracy got out of hand, till Pompey suppressed it; so it seems did the *publicani*, till Caesar restricted their powers in Asia at least. Communities, like individuals, fell hopelessly in debt to Roman money-lenders. Cicero says in a speech of 66 (of course with an ulterior motive) 'it is hard to express, citizens, how loathed we are by foreign nations.' It was greed he blamed. The poverty of many cities is visible archaeologically; there was little new building. The East had not fully recovered when renewed civil wars broke out. Pompey and Caesar, Brutus and Cassius, Antony and Octavian, all financed their campaigns from Rome's subjects. When Judaea could not pay what Cassius demanded, he sold four towns and many officials into slavery; as Antony observed, this was unauthorized by the laws of war. Cassius also besieged the free city of Rhodes, so long a friend of Rome, and carried off all its wealth except the chariot of its patron god the Sun. An even older friend of Rome's, Massilia, had been taken by Caesar, for supporting Pompey.

And yet, through it all, many members of the upper class saw private and public advantage in—or no alternative to—supporting Rome. They cultivated ties with important Romans, whether in Rome themselves as ambassadors (a second-century inscription thanks a group of these for going round to the morning receptions of great nobles) or when putting up Roman governors on their way to, or on circuit in, the provinces. By the end of the Republic foreign *amici* had even begun to wield power in Rome as advisers to the great dynasts; Theophanes of Mytilene was an intimate of Pompey's, and L. Cornelius Balbus of Gades was Caesar's trusted agent. Though it had for long occasionally been granted as a reward for service in war, citizenship was first given on a larger scale by Caesar, in whose time the rule that Roman citizenship could not be combined with that of another state seems to have lapsed. The way was open for the gradual extension of privilege, ultimately even of senatorial rank, which was to hold the Empire together in succeeding centuries.

Hellenism at Rome

Co-operation between the Greek and Roman élites was possible because the Roman upper class, though loyal to much of its own tradition, became very Hellenized. Indeed, there were attempts to prove that the Romans *were* Greeks, descended not only from Trojan Aeneas, but from Evander the Arcadian (familiar from the *Aeneid*), or from Hercules, and their followers.

Some scholars held that Latin was a dialect of Greek. The attitude of many Romans to Greeks and Greek culture was, it is true, ambiguous; they believed in their own superiority in war and statecraft (and Cicero said other systems of civil law were puerile). Many people suspected customs that seemed softening or apt to distract from serious matters. Close and often unhappy experience of second-century Greeks led to these being characterized as effeminate, time-serving, politically inept (a useful justification of Empire), loquacious, and prone to abstract argument at the wrong time. Perhaps they had degenerated; there *are* some men worthy of ancient Greece, concedes Cicero (more philhellene than most), warning his brother to be wary of intimacies in his province. And the inhabitants of the now Greek-speaking cities of the East might be thought inferior to 'real Greeks'. But in Athens itself, which, like Delphi, Rome had treated with respect, Cicero expressed dismay at the arrogant treatment of the locals by his (strictly upright) suite.

Few well-off Romans, however, could resist the attractions of civilized Greek life, and some realized that it was only from the Greeks that they could learn much that the rulers of the world needed to know. Rome had perhaps never been wholly out of touch with the Greek world. Many of her gods had been identified with Greek ones, her art derived from Greek art; some Romans must always have known some Greek, and even perhaps read some Greek books. But a new epoch dawned in the mid third century, with the first plays on the Greek model in Latin (below, pp. 74 ff.), and (it seems) more formal schooling, in both tongues. In the Hannibalic War new Greek cults (and even the Great Mother from Asia) were introduced, to protect the city. The sack of Syracuse in 212 marked for Polybius the start of a taste for Greek art (a pity, he thought; states should stick to their own traditions); certainly innumerable statues and paintings were to be carried off to Rome in the next centuries. The physical face of the city was transformed as it became a great capital, though Polybius shows that its rustic air was mocked by cosmopolitan visitors in his day, and a truly Greek architectural style came a little later; marble was not much used for building purposes till later still.

But the upper classes' way of life was soon transformed. Historians tended to see Roman history in terms of moral decline, especially into avarice and luxury, and liked to mark its stages; some thought the booty brought back from Asia in 190, including handsome furniture, initiated the process. Polybius stressed the defeat of Macedon at Pydna and the wealth it brought: the young went mad for the worst aspects of Greek manners, pederasty, banquets to the sound of music, and so on. Cato had tried to outlaw, and then to tax prohibitively, various forms of luxury, and continued to inveigh against spending on handsome slaves or imported food, and adorning one's house with statues of the gods 'as though they were furniture'. But even Cato, as his buildings while censor and his own writings show, could not turn the clock back.

The crux of the matter was education, for to the Greeks their *paideia* was their culture. By tradition the upper-class Roman boy absorbed political and legal experience from his father's friends, and spent the campaigning season, from the age of seventeen, with the army. But the Greeks had developed a pattern of formal study, first of literature (primarily Homer), and then rhetoric and, for some, philosophy. Aemilius Paullus provided his sons with a bevy of Greek masters, even in music and hunting, and a philosopher doubling as drawing master. He also brought the royal library of Macedon to Rome, the first great Greek library to reach it. Polybius attests that there were now many Greek teachers there. Distinguished savants began to arrive, at first as envoys; the serious study of *grammatikē* was dated to the embassy of Crates of Pergamum, who broke his leg in an open sewer and lectured while immobilized. And in 155 Athens sent the heads of three philosophical schools, whose lectures caused a sudden rage for philosophy—though Cato, who thought philosophy 'mere gibberish', pressed the Senate to conclude their business quickly so that the young could return to learning from 'the laws and the magistrates'.

One must not exaggerate the depth of Greek influence at this period. There is evidence that Greek medicine was regarded with suspicion still, and in general the Romans were intellectually, as also artistically, clumsy and immature. Poetry was more developed than prose, though even poetry was crude, as Horace complained. Cicero thought that it was only towards the end of the century that orators really profited from the study of rhetoric, which taught one how to organize and argue, as well as ornament, a speech. What we know of prose literature suggests that the Romans, like many primitive peoples, found generalization and abstraction hard. It was only from about 100 BC, too, that they began to use traditional Greek logical structure in treatises, with explicit definitions of the subject and all key concepts, and careful division of the material into parts or aspects, instead of piling up information hugger-mugger like Cato in his agricultural treatise. And it was in the first century that Latin was refined into the splendid vehicle it was to be for prose as well as poetry, and that Latin authors colonized many new prose genres, including the philosophic treatise.

It was only now too that it became common for young gentlemen to study rhetoric or philosophy at Athens or Rhodes (more independent Alexandria seems to have been out of bounds), though sons of *negotiatores* were often educated in the East, and might go through a city's *ephēbeia*, a state-run training course now more cultural than military. The Mithridatic wars swept Greek refugees and captives to Rome, both classes including learned men; also great libraries. And they detained many Romans long years in the East. (The historian Sallust dated Rome's collapse into luxury from Sulla's campaigns in Asia.) Afterwards, Rome was equal to Alexandria as a magnet for Greek artists and intellectuals; there was patronage to be found almost nowhere else. And the Romans felt that they were, in one field after another, catching up with the Greeks. Cicero and his friend Atticus, admittedly exceptional men, must have met their Greek *amici* on fully equal terms.

In the West Rome felt she had little to learn, though an

isolated work on agriculture was translated by official order from
Punic. But the very fact that Romans rarely bothered to learn
western languages helped to prepare for an extension of privilege here too; for the native élites gradually took on the colours
of what seemed a superior, if at first often a hated, civilization.
Trade and the influx of settlers helped to Romanize. Rome rarely
consciously forwarded the process, though there was some encouragement in Spain of agriculture and urban settlement in
the valleys, to replace less controllable pastoral communities.
Though there was cultural prejudice against barbarians, there
was little racial prejudice. If barbarians gave up their ways
(beastly, like the habit of some Spanish tribes of washing their
teeth in urine, or less so, like those of the Gauls, whom Caesar
found intelligent and courageous, if unsteady), they could rise
above the status of barbarians; the geographer Strabo's description of southern Spain in the time of Augustus is illuminating
here. In fact, Balbus and his nephew from Gades (admittedly an
ancient and civilized Punic city) entered the Senate—though the
very idea shocked Cicero—before the son of Pompey's friend
Theophanes of Mytilene did so; and the Balbi were soon followed by a few Gallic nobles who, or whose fathers, owed the
citizenship to Caesar or Augustus. The lineaments of the Roman
Empire in its maturity were taking shape.

Further Reading

A translation of Polybius is most easily available in the Loeb edition; there is a
Penguin volume of selections, and F. W. Walbank's *Polybius* (California, 1972)
provides a good discussion of his work. Books of Livy are also available in the
Penguin Classics, and there are Loebs of his entire work and those of the other
authors mentioned. For Cicero see pp. 118 f.

The *Cambridge Ancient History* vol. viii (cf. also ix) gives a classic account, in
the chapters by M. Holleaux, of the older view of Roman expansion; it is soon
to be replaced by a new edition. For a more modern approach, see W. V. Harris,
War and Imperialism in Republican Rome 372–70 B.C. (Oxford, 1979), with
P. A. Brunt's chapter in *Imperialism in the Ancient World*, ed. P. D. A. Garnsey
and C. R. Whittaker, (Cambridge, 1978) and J. A. North, 'The Development
of Roman Imperialism' in *Journal of Roman Studies*, 1981. There is a good

general account in C. Nicolet, *Rome et la conquête du monde méditerranéen*, ii: *Genèse d'un empire* (Paris, 1978); cf. also R. M. Errington, *The Dawn of Empire: Rome's Rise to World Power* (Ithaca, NY, 1972).

E. Badian has followed up his important *Foreign Clientelae* (Oxford, 1958), with *Roman Imperialism` in the Late Republic* (Oxford, 1968) and *Publicans and Sinners* (Oxford, 1972). The first two sections of K. Hopkins, *Conquerors and Slaves* (Cambridge, 1978) deal with the transformation of Italian agriculture and economic life as a result of expansion; for *negotiatores* abroad, see A. J. N. Wilson, *Emigration from Italy in the Republican Age of Rome* (Manchester, 1966), less readable than J. Hatzfeld, *Les Trafiquants italiens dans l'orient hellénique* (Paris, 1919). See also J. H. D'Arms, *Commerce and Social Standino in Ancient Rome* (Cambridge, Mass. 1981); and M. H. Crawford, 'Rome and the Greek World: Economic Relations', *Econ. Hist. Review*, 1977; for the trade in corn, the first two chapters of G. Rickman, *The Corn Supply of Ancient Rome* (Oxford, 1980).

For study of individual figures, see F. W. Walbank, *Philip V of Macedon* (1940, repr. Hamden, Conn., 1967); R. M. Errington, *Philopoemen* (Oxford, 1969—Philopoemen was a leading figure in the Achaean League, admired by Polybius for his attitude to Rome); A. E. Astin, *Scipio Aemilianus* (Oxford, 1967) and *Cato the Censor* (Oxford, 1978).

For the East, see A. H. M. Jones, *The Greek City from Alexander to Justinian* (Oxford, 1966) and D. Magie's massive *Roman Rule in Asia Minor* (Princeton, 1950), also D. C. Braund, *Rome and the Friendly King* (London, 1984) and R. Mellor, *Thea Rhômé: The Worship of the Goddess Roma in the Greek World* (1975), also, now, A. N. Sherwin-White, *Roman Foreign Policy in the Greek East* (London, 1984) and E. S. Gruen, *The Hellenistic World and the Coming of Rome* (California, 1984), neither available when this chapter was written.

For Roman attitudes to foreigners, J. P. V. D. Balsdon's *Romans and Aliens* (London, 1979).

3

The First Roman Literature

P. G. M^cC. BROWN

Plautus

LATIN literature begins with a bang, with a dazzling display of virtuoso verbal fireworks in twenty comedies written by Plautus between about 205 and 184 BC. The start of Latin literature is conventionally dated to the performance of a play by Livius Andronicus at Rome in 240 BC, but these comedies by Plautus are the earliest works to have survived complete. They are modelled on Greek comedies, nearly all of them 'New Comedies' written by Menander and his contemporaries about 100 years before Plautus. Like the Greek comedies, they are written in verse. Greek comedies were written for performance in a permanent theatre at Athens, as central elements in a religious festival. Roman comedies were also performed at religious festivals, but they were one source of entertainment among many, and they were performed on a temporary stage erected for the occasion. Romans of all classes came to watch. We cannot tell to what extent Plautus adapted his style to the taste of his audience and to what extent he helped to form that taste; but he has imported into his plays a boisterousness and a broadness of comic effect which remind us more of Aristophanes (though there is much less obscenity) than of Menander.

The Greek originals of Plautus' plays have not survived, though a tattered papyrus published in 1968 contains the lines on which *Bacchides* ('The Bacchis Sisters') 494–561 are based and enables us to study Plautus' techniques of adaptation at first hand for this stretch of the play. Plautus has preserved the basic plot and sequence of scenes, but he has cut two scenes altogether, and at one point he reverses the order of entry of two characters so as to eliminate a pause in the action where there was an act-break in the original (Roman comedy was usually written for continuous performance, and the act- and scene-divisions found in modern editions do not go back to the authors). The tormented monologue of a young man in love has had some jokes added to it. Passages which would have been spoken without musical accompaniment in the original Greek are turned into passages in longer lines to be accompanied on a reed-pipe. Plautus' play is still set in Athens, and his characters have Greek-sounding names; but he has changed most of them from the original, most significantly that of the scheming slave who dominates the action: Plautus calls him Chrysalus (Goldfinger) and adds some colour to his part by punning on this name (240 'Goldfinger's got to get his fingers on some gold', 361–2 'He'll change my name from Goldfinger to Gallowsbird', etc.). The papyrus shows that this character in the original had the less striking name of Syrus (The Syrian), which adds spice to Chrysalus' boast at 649 that he is superior to run-of-the-mill slaves with names like Parmeno and Syrus—though the joke would doubtless have been lost on most of Plautus' audience.

The plots of the plays show considerable variety. In *Amphitruo*, Jupiter descends to earth disguised as Amphitruo in order to seduce the latter's wife Alcumena; when Amphitruo himself arrives home from a military expedition the next day, he is dismayed to discover from his wife's reception of him that she believes him to have spent the previous night with her. *Mercator* ('The Businessman') shows father and son in love with the same girl, as does *Casina* (named after the girl) in which one of the tricks used to thwart the father is the impersonation of Casina in the bedroom by a male slave. *Rudens* ('The Rope') is set on the coast of north Africa near Cyrene: a slave-dealer is shipwrecked there in a storm, and one of the girls in his possession turns out to be the long-lost daughter of a man living there in exile from Athens. But beneath the surface variety of the plays the basic structure of the plot (preserved from the Greek original) nearly always concerns the removal or overcoming of some apparent obstacle to the course of true love.

But Plautus' main interest was not so much in reproducing dramatic structures as in using them as an opportunity for virtuoso display. We have seen from *Bacchides* that he wrote a creative adaptation rather than a slavish translation of Menander's text. In many respects he can be said to have changed radically the type of comedy which the plays contain. Consistency of characterization and plot development are cheerfully sacrificed for the sake of an immediate effect. The humour resides less in the irony of the situation than in the cracking of jokes and the perpetration of puns. Instead of characters in a dramatic context we sometimes see comedians going through a routine. Three things in particular stand out: the glorification of the scheming slave, the musical element, and the creation of an imaginary world which is set in Greece but includes many Italian features.

Plautus did not invent the scheming slave: the Greek original of *Bacchides* was called *The Double Deceiver*, and the part played in it by Syrus must have been similar at least in outline to the part played by Chrysalus in Plautus' play. But Chrysalus dominates *Bacchides* not simply by his scheming (which is not particularly ingenious) but by his boasting. His plan to trick his master out of money is seen as a military campaign, and his description of it is embroidered at some points with triumph imagery which is peculiarly Roman. Chrysalus has an extended monologue in which he compares his campaign with that of the Greeks in the Trojan War (925 ff.):

They say the two brothers, the sons of Atreus, did a great deed when with their weapons and their horses, with their army and outstanding warriors, and with their thousand ships they overcame after ten years Priam's town of Troy, its fortifications built by the hands of gods. But that was less than a blister on the foot in comparison with the way I'm going to conquer my master without fleet, without army, without that great number of troops

—and so on for fifty lines, with a succession of fantastic and mutually contradictory parallels between the plot of the play and the events of the Trojan War. When he has completed his deception he boasts (1068 ff.):

That's the way to carry out your projects properly. Now I can triumph in style, laden with booty. Safe and sound, the city captured by a trick, I now lead my whole army home intact. But, spectators, don't be surprised that I'm not actually celebrating a triumph: everyone does that, I can't be bothered with it. All the same, my troops will be treated to a tipple. Now I shall take all this booty straight to the quaestor.

The effect of such passages is to focus our attention on Chrysalus' trickery as an achievement on its own account rather than as a necessary device to secure a sum of money to help a young man in love. The Plautine slave enjoys scheming for the sake of scheming and scarcely requires any further motivation for his actions.

Chrysalus' monologue on the Trojan War was written to be accompanied on a pipe, and we saw earlier that Plautus had increased the musical element in the passage of *Bacchides* which we can compare with its Greek original. In fact substantial portions of his plays would have been accompanied, a considerably larger part of them than of their originals. The effect of the music is entirely lost to us. But we can see that Plautus' language often becomes more colourful for these accompanied passages, and the music perhaps did no more than reinforce the effect of the words. Most striking are the so-called *cantica*, operatic arias and duets written in a variety of metres and displaying many features of high-flown style. They normally do little or nothing to further the action, and we know of nothing like them in Greek New Comedy. Chrysalus' 50-line monologue (his 'Troy-*canticum*') may have been expanded from a far briefer monologue in the original or it may have been spun altogether out of Plautus' head. A favourite type of *canticum*

comes in the mouth of a slave who rushes on to the stage in great
excitement to deliver an important piece of news. He is in a
hurry but takes time to utter a lengthy monologue on entry.
Thus the slave Acanthio at *Mercator* 111 ff.:

Strive with all your strength, struggle with might and main, to save
your young master by your efforts. Come on, Acanthio, drive away
your tiredness, don't indulge in idleness. I'm plagued by panting, I die
for want of wind. What's more, the pavements are packed with people
in my way: drive them off, knock them over, push them into the road!
What dreadful manners people have here! When a man's in a tearing
hurry, not one of them sees fit to make way for him. So you have three
things to do at once, when you've begun to do one: dash, bash and
brawl in the street!

Plautus is prodigal of his stylistic resources in the *cantica*, and it
is presumably no accident that a *canticum* often comes near the
beginning of a play where it is important to catch the audience's
attention.

We saw that Chrysalus' boasts at *Bacchides* 1068 ff. contained references to the Roman institution of the triumph and
to the quaestor, who was a Roman official. There is also a contemporary Roman reference in his remark about the frequency
of triumphs (whether this is taken as referring to the celebration
of triumphs by generals in real life or by slaves on the stage).
There is no attempt to sustain the illusion that we are watching
Greek characters in a Greek setting; and the dramatic illusion is
further broken by Chrysalus' explicit address of the audience.
This is altogether typical of Plautus. Sometimes he goes out of
his way to reminded the audience that his play is set in Greece, as
at *Stichus* 446–8 (where once again the audience is addressed):
'Don't be surprised that mere slaves can drink, make love and
accept invitations to dinner: we're allowed to do these things at
Athens.' But when his characters talk of a dissolute life-style
they speak of 'going Greek' (*pergraecari* or *congraecari*)—a
Roman and not a Greek way of putting it. There are many allusions to Roman practices and Roman officials; and when
the pimp Ballio addresses the members of his establishment

at *Pseudolus* 143 and 172 he speaks as a Roman magistrate issuing an official edict. In the *canticum* at *Menaechmi* 571 ff. Menaechmus of Epidamnus complains that he has wasted his day acting as *patronus* (protector) on behalf of a *cliens* (dependant) in a lawsuit. He begins with a general complaint:

What a completely crazy custom this is of ours, a terribly troublesome one! It's above all the top people who have this habit: everyone wants to have lots of clients; they don't ask whether they're good or bad. They ask more about the reputation of their clients' wealth than of their honesty. If a man's poor and not bad, he's regarded as worthless; if he's rich and bad, he's thought to be a worthy client.

As he proceeds to describe the duties of a patron, he mentions a number of Roman legal technicalities. The entire passage has to do with social practices at Rome in Plautus' day. In effect, the play is set simultaneously in Epidamnus and in Rome.

The element of social comment in this last passage is not typical. Plautus was above all an entertainer and a poet. He uses colloquial speech, but Romans presumably did not often speak in the alliterative style with which this passage opens: 'Ut hoc utimur maxime more moro molestoque multum!' He abounds in wordplay and puns (at *Rudens* 102 a roof whose tiles have been blown off in a storm lets the daylight through 'quam cribrum crebrius': it is 'more perforated than a percolator'), in startling personifications (*Rudens* 626 'twist the neck of wrongdoing'), and in riddling expressions (*Mercator* 361 'My father's a fly: you can't keep anything secret from him, he's always buzzing around'). It is the sheer enjoyment in playing with words that is the hallmark of Plautus' genius.

Terence

The next Latin works to have survived are six comedies written by Terence in the 160s BC. These too are based on Greek New Comedies and written in verse. But there is a world of difference between Terence and Plautus. We do not have any substantial portions of the Greek originals of Terence's plays; but (although we know him to have changed some things) he seems to have preserved far more carefully than Plautus the ethos and general construction of the Greek plays. Roman technical language is occasionally used, but not as obtrusively as by Plautus. There is a considerable musical element, but hardly anything as extensive or as exotic metrically as a Plautine *canticum*. Above all, the comedy remains essentially situation comedy, in which consistency of characterization and clarity of plot construction are of vital importance.

The plots are once again concerned with love affairs and with the misunderstandings which arise from ignorance. In *Andria* ('The Woman from Andros') Simo wants his son Pamphilus to marry the daughter of Chremes, a respectable Athenian citizen; but Pamphilus is in love with a girl from Andros (Glycerium) who appears to be far less respectable. Intrigues and counter-intrigues lead to a number of emotional complications, which are resolved by the discovery that Glycerium is herself a daughter of Chremes. In *Hecyra* ('The Mother-in-Law') a young man (another Pamphilus) has married a woman already pregnant (though he does not know this) as the result of being raped. When she gives birth to a child of which there is every reason to suppose that he is not the father, their marriage appears to be at an end. In the course of the play his wife's attempt to conceal her condition gives rise to various misunderstandings: in particular, we see her mother-in-law being blamed by her father-in-law for the breakdown of the marriage. But all ends happily when it is discovered that it was Pamphilus himself who had raped her one night when drunk in the street. (It seems that the Greek society portrayed in these plays was prepared to take a tolerant attitude to rape, as being a natural result of youthful drunkenness or high spirits. The girls in question led secluded lives, and young men had few opportunities to strike up acquaintance with them in a more leisurely way. Also, a citizen girl who had succumbed before marriage to a sustained campaign of seduction would have made a less sympathetic heroine than one who had been overcome by force. But the playwrights are not insensitive to the predicament of the victims of rape.) In *Eunuchus* ('The Eunuch') young Chaerea disguises himself as a eunuch in order to gain access to the bedroom of the girl with whom he is infatuated and there rapes her. The girl turns out to be the daughter of respectable Athenian parents, and Chaerea's father agrees to his marrying her. At the centre of the action is the prostitute Thais, who has taken the girl under her wing and is determined to help her find her parents. The picture of Thais is thrown into sharper relief by the fact that other characters in the play entertain quite unjustified suspicions of her behaviour.

These plots are less varied than those of Plautus, but their basic structure is not very different. The main difference between the two playwrights lies in the use which they make of their plots. Terence does not treat them as a springboard for extraneous jokes but preserves from the Greek originals the more elusive and ironic humour which arises out of a carefully constructed dramatic situation. We are told that Greek influence at Rome had increased considerably in the 160s, and Terence's plays have been taken as evidence that Greek refinement was now more widely appreciated than it had been by Plautus' less cultured audience. But there is a danger of exaggerating this difference. Some of the changes which Terence made to his Greek originals suggest that he was still aiming to appeal to a fairly unsophisticated kind of Roman. In adapting Menander's *Eunuchus* Terence has added from another play by Menander the characters of the boastful soldier and his fawning parasite, who bring with them some broad comic effects; and to Menander's *Adelphoe* ('The Brothers') he has added from a play by a different Greek author a scene of movement and violence in which a slave-dealer fails to prevent a young man from abducting one of the prostitutes he owns. Terence tells us of these additions in the prologues which he wrote to be delivered before the start of the plays themselves; and one of his prologues tells us something of the conditions in which his plays were performed. This is the prologue he wrote for the third performance

of *Hecyra*, describing how two previous attempts to stage it had
been failures:

The first time I began to perform this play, there was talk of a boxing
match, and there were also rumours that a tight-rope walker was going
to perform. Slaves were arriving, there was a din, women were shouting; and the result was that I had to give up before the end . . . . I put it
on again: the first act went down well, but then word got around that a
gladiatorial show was going to be given. People flew together, there was
an uproar, they were shouting and fighting for somewhere to sit. It was
impossible for me to hold my own against that.

Hecyra is the only play of Terence which we know to have had
difficulties with the public. His more boisterous *Eunuchus* was
an unprecedented success.

Terence's prologues are quite unlike anything we know of in
New Comedy or in Plautus. He uses them to conduct feuds with
his literary rivals and defend himself against criticisms which
they have made of him. They give us an exceptional glimpse of
the literary world in which he worked, though they do only give
his side of the arguments. If we can trust them, he was criticized
(among other things) for feebleness of style, for plagiarism, and
for combining more than one Greek original to construct a single
Latin play ('contamination', as his critics called it). Although
more faithful than Plautus to his originals, he seems not to have
been faithful enough for some of his contemporaries. We learn
of other innovations made by Terence from a commentary on
his plays written in the fourth century AD by the famous grammarian Donatus. We can deduce, for instance, from what Donatus tells us, that Terence has spun the first twenty lines of his
first play, *Andria*, entirely out of his own head. And one major
change which he has made to the openings of his plays is that
his prologues do not give the background to the plot (as those
of Menander and Plautus do). Perhaps he regarded that as an
artificial device, preferring to convey what information he could
more naturalistically in the mouths of his characters in the course
of the play. The result is that some opportunities for irony are

missed, since the audience do not always learn all that there is to learn until a late stage of the play.

Terence is thus a more enigmatic figure than Plautus. He chose to adapt Greek plays whose appreciation often demands some moral and emotional involvement, and he was faithful most of the time in reproducing their essential qualities; but he did not do so slavishly, and he added some scenes with a cruder comic effect. It was no doubt the liveliness of his *Eunuchus* that ensured its success in his lifetime; but it is the quieter elements in Terence's plays that have most impressed his readers in subsequent generations: his sympathetic portrayal of the problems and predicaments of individuals, and his concern for the serious issues underlying the comedy of his plays. These elements ensure that his plays repay thoughtful study more than those of Plautus can ever do. But they are probably reproduced from the original Greek plays; and there is room to doubt whether Terence himself always cared about the refinements he has reproduced, as we shall see in the case of *Adelphoe*.

One thing which was undoubtedly Terence's own achievement was the creation of a Latin literary style quite unlike that of Plautus or of any other previous writer. Although criticized for its feebleness in Terence's own life, it has since then been more generally admired for its elegance and clarity. Terence was the first Latin writer to reproduce the elliptical style of natural conversation. It is not a low colloquial style, but its clipped constructions have a realistic ring which is generally absent from Plautus.

Within a century of his death, Terence's plays had become school texts; and they have continued to be so for as long as we know Latin to have been studied in Europe, holding a central place in the school curriculum until the nineteenth century. He has been admired for his style and for his moral sentiments, which can be made to sound more uplifting than Terence intended by being quoted out of context: the most famous of all, 'Homo sum: humani nil a me alienum puto' ('I am a man: I regard all that concerns men as concerning me') comes in the mouth of a tedious old busybody who has been asked why he is poking his nose into his neighbour's affairs. Its effect in context is to make him look pompous and ridiculous. But Terence has not been much praised for his humour, partly no doubt because it depends for its effect on the context created by the plot of the play. In the following passage from *Adelphoe* (413 ff.) the old man Demea boasts to the slave Syrus (who has just returned from buying fish in the market) about the method he has used in bringing up his son to be well behaved. Demea believes his method to have been effective, whereas Syrus and the audience know that the son (now an adolescent) is living a much wilder life than Demea imagines. It is clear that Syrus is mocking Demea in the second half of the passage, but the absurdity of Demea's boasting is much more comic if we bear in mind how wrong he is about the effectiveness of his method of upbringing:

D. I take a lot of trouble over it; I don't let anything slip; I train him. In fact I tell him to look into the lives of others, as into a mirror, and to learn from their example. 'Do this', I say.
S. Quite right!
D. 'Don't do that.'
S. Clever!
D. 'This is praiseworthy.'
S. Just the thing!
D. 'This is blameworthy.'
S. Excellent!
D. Furthermore—
S. Well, look, I really haven't got time to listen now. I've got the fish I wanted; I must make sure nothing goes wrong with them . . . . To the best of my ability I give instructions to my fellow slaves just like the instructions you give: 'This is over-salted; this is burnt; this one hasn't been properly washed. That one's right: remember to do it like that next time.' I take a lot of trouble to teach them as well as my wits allow. In fact I tell them to look into the dishes, Demea, as if into a mirror, and I tell them what needs to be done.

Adelphoe is Terence's masterpiece. It was his last play and is the one that provokes most thought about a subject of perennial

importance. But there is reason to think that he has distorted
the balance of the play by striving for comic effect in its closing
scenes. The thought-provoking theme is the question of what
the relationship should be between a father and his adolescent
son. We have just seen Demea being mocked for his misplaced
confidence in a strict, didactic method of upbringing. His views
are contrasted with those of his brother Micio, who believes
that adolescent sons should be handled with openness and tolerance. Micio's method seems to be presented for most of the play
as the more humane and sympathetic one, and also the more
successful. Demea's blind confidence makes him an appropriate
comic butt, and Micio seems much more in control of events.
But towards the end of the play there is a startling reversal:
Demea starts to dominate at the expense of Micio, forcing him
to agree to a number of unwelcome proposals (not least that
he should marry a 'decrepit old woman'); and it looks as if the
final judgement of the play is that Micio's approach was over-
indulgent and excessively easy-going. This is very hard to reconcile with the rest of the play. Demea turns the tables on Micio
and makes us laugh; but we are left uncertain where our sympathies should lie. Many scholars feel that Menander would not
have written an ending so much at odds with the bulk of the play
and that it is Terence who has sacrificed consistency to a desire
to entertain or satisfy his Roman audience. But *Adelphoe* is not
only about tolerance and strictness; it is also concerned with
love between father and son and with lack of self-knowledge. Its
handing of these themes combines comedy with telling characterization. It is precisely because the play is otherwise so successful that the ending has been found a puzzle; and the merits of
the ending have long been hotly debated and will long continue
to be so.

Plautus and Terence have survived; and they have influenced
the European dramatic tradition. *Ralph Roister Doister* makes
use of Plautus' *Miles Gloriosus* and Terence's *Eunuchus*; *The
Comedy of Errors* is based on Plautus' *Menaechmi* and *Amphitruo*. Molière is one of many playwrights to have adapted the

latter play, and he also followed Plautus' *Aulularia* (in *L'Avare*) and Terence's *Adelphoe* (in *L'École des maris*) and *Phormio* (in *Les Fourberies de Scapin*). Boastful soldiers, rediscovered foundlings, and scheming servants have long been standard ingredients of comic writing, not only for the stage: although P. G. Wodehouse told me (when I wrote to ask him) that he had not read Plautus or Terence, his Jeeves is clearly heir to the tradition of the scheming servant.

Ennius

One author who has not survived except in fragments must be mentioned because of his importance in the development of Latin literature. This is Ennius (239–169 BC). We have more certain information about his life than about those of Plautus and Terence: born in Calabria, he was brought to Rome in 204 or 203 by M. Porcius Cato and gave lectures on poetry. He accompanied M. Fulvius Nobilior on his Aetolian campaign in 189 and wrote in praise of his patron's achievements. His name is also linked with those of other prominent Romans. One benefit which he derived from such patronage was the Roman citizenship, conferred on him in 184 (by Nobilior's son, according to the traditional but unreliable account).

Ennius was a more versatile writer than Plautus or Terence, composing tragedies, comedies, satires, and a number of minor works in addition to his epic *Annals*; but it was this last work that represented his greatest contribution to Latin literature. Covering in eighteen books the history of Rome from Aeneas' flight from Troy down to Ennius' own day, it was written during the last fifteen years or so of his life. We now have about 600 lines, many of them single lines and not all of them complete, from a work which may originally have had 20,000 or more. The lines which have survived have done so because they were quoted by later authors, often to illustrate a linguistic point or an Ennian reminiscence in Virgil. We do not always know their context, and it is often only in the barest outline that we can hope to reconstruct the sequence of events in a book of the *Annals*. But enough survives to make us regret keenly the loss of the rest. Ennius set the tone for Latin hexameter writing in the high style for the next century and a half. Lucretius and Virgil were considerably influenced by him, and if we had more of his work we should understand more of theirs.

Ennius' most important contribution was perhaps the hexameter itself, the traditional metre of Greek epic. He was not the first to write an epic in Latin: Livius Andronicus had written a translation of the *Odyssey*, and Naevius had written an epic about the First Punic War towards the end of the third century. But these authors both wrote in the jerky Saturnian metre. Ennius introduced the more smoothly flowing hexameter into Latin epic, and to go with the new metre he moulded a poetic diction which served as the basis for the style of his successors.

At the beginning of the *Annals* Ennius claimed to be a reincarnation of Homer: the ghost of Homer had revealed this to him in a dream. Many features of his epic were Homeric: a Council of the Gods, battle descriptions, and similes. But there is much which strikes a different note, not least the discussion of his own poetic activity at the beginning of the work. Another autobiographical passage opened Book vii, where Ennius contrasted his own craftsmanship with the crude composition of his predecessors. His self-conscious proclamation of his stylistic skill reminds us more of Callimachus than of Homer. His own style came to seem crude by later canons of taste; but it is clear that he devoted some care to it in full awareness of his role as a pioneer. There is also a moralizing streak which must have helped in the establishment of Ennius as a central author in the school curriculum until the time of Virgil. Over half the work was devoted to events of Ennius' lifetime, the Second Punic War and the subsequent remarkable expansion of Roman power. Ennius glorifies the military achievements of the Roman nobility and supports traditional Roman morality. Individual virtue is praised, as in the famous lines about Q. Fabius Maximus Cunctator:

> One man by his delays restored our nation.
> Our weal he put before his reputation.
> Thus now his glory shines more brightly yet
> In later years . . .

('Unus homo nobis cunctando restituit rem . . .'). Such glorification of an individual was perhaps not in the best Roman traditions; but the heroes of the *Annals* displayed virtues which were very much admired by Romans. And other passages combined profound reflection with stylistic vigour in a memorable way, for instance the following on the disruptive effects of war:

> Wisdom is driven out: violence holds sway.
> Sound speakers scorned, rough soldiers have their day.
> No longer with abuse or skilful speech
> Do men express their hatred, each to each.
> But now with weapons, not with writs, they fight;
> They strive to rule, press on with massive might.

Further Reading

There is an excellent survey of Early Latin Literature by A. S. Gratwick in *The Cambridge History of Classical Literature*, II, *Latin Literature* (1982), 60–171 (this survey forms the bulk of the first volume of the paperback edition of the Cambridge History, 'Part I: The Early Republic').

The Loeb Classical Library includes complete texts with translations of Plautus (in five volumes) and Terence (in two volumes); the fragments of Ennius are included in the volume *Remains of Old Latin*, I. In the Penguin Classics series nine plays of Plautus have been translated by E. F. Watling and all the plays of Terence by Betty Radice. There are also lively translations of selected plays of Plautus by Erich Segal (*Miles Gloriosus, Menaechmi, Mostellaria*: London, 1969), Christopher Stace (*Rudens, Curculio, Casina*: Cambridge, 1981), and James Tatum (*Bacchides, Casina, Truculentus*: Baltimore, 1983). John Barsby's edition of *Bacchides* (Warminster, 1986) includes a very successful verse translation and a full commmentary based on it; and Frances Muecke has produced a companion to the Penguin translation of *Menaechmi* (Bristol, 1987). The plays of Terence have been translated by Frank O. Copley, The Library of Liberal Arts (Indianapolis, 1967) and by P. Bovie and others (New Brunswick, NJ, 1974).

For Roman Comedy, the best general introduction in English is R. L. Hunter, *The New Comedy of Greece and Rome* (Cambridge, 1985). George E. Duckworth, *The Nature of Roman Comedy* (Princeton, 1952) provides a fuller account, though much of what he says about Greek New Comedy has been rendered obsolete by the discovery of substantial portions of plays by Menander since 1958. Both books are available in paperback.

The most important book on Plautus this century has been the book in German by Eduard Fraenkel, *Plautinisches im Plautus* (Berlin, 1922), which was reissued in an Italian translation with additional notes as *Elementi Plautini in Plauto* (Florence, 1960). Fraenkel was concerned to identify and evaluate the original features in Plautus' adaptations of Greek comedies. Erich Segal's book *Roman Laughter: The Comedy of Plautus* (Harvard, 1968; paperback edn., Oxford, 1987) is an entertaining and enthusiastic account of the 'festival' elements in Plautus' plays, the ways in which they invert everyday Roman values and behaviour.

Gilbert Norwood, *The Art of Terence* (Oxford, 1923; repr. New York, 1965), though outdated in some important respects, provides a very sympathetic appreciation of Terence and is the best book on him in English.

The fragments of Ennius' *Annals* have been edited by O. Skutsch, *The Annals of Q. Ennius* (Oxford, 1985).

4

Cicero and Rome

MIRIAM GRIFFIN

THIS chapter is devoted to the period which opens with the dictatorship of Sulla in 82 BC and closes with that of Caesar in 44 BC. It is concerned with the political life and death of the later Roman Republic.

Cicero

If we know more about these years than about any other period of Roman history, it is due principally to one man, Marcus Tullius Cicero. We have an abundance of speeches and letters written when he was deeply involved in day-to-day politics, either holding the highest offices of state or in contact with the men who were settling the future of the Mediterranean world. But it is not only political history that his works illuminate so brilliantly. When not at the centre of the stage, Cicero turned to literature of a more reflective sort and composed a corpus of theoretical works on philosophy and rhetoric richly adorned with contemporary examples and redolent of contemporary attitudes. Precisely because he was not an original thinker, Cicero helps us to recapture the intellectual habits of his generation.

The voluminous correspondence which Cicero maintained throughout all the vicissitudes of his adult life remains, however, his most valuable legacy to the historian. Some letters were private and not intended for publication; others were clearly written with a wider circulation in mind. Over 900 in number, they concern personal and cultural matters, as well as providing official and unofficial, public and private, views of the most important political events of the day. Of Cicero's most candid letters, those to his intimate friend Atticus, a younger contemporary was to write: 'Whoever reads the eleven books of the correspondence hardly feels the need of an organized history of the time.'

There is a dark side, however, to this picture. Cicero was an intelligent observer, but he was not detached; he was perceptive, but mercurial in mood and outlook; he was interested in other people, but, above all, obsessed with his own reputation. Moreover, his contemporaries have left little to serve as a corrective to his version of things. Their speeches, their works on philosophy and rhetoric have not survived intact, and much of what we know of them comes from Cicero. Over seventy letters from friends and acquaintances are preserved with Cicero's, but as they are mostly letters to him, they throw little light on matters outside his concerns. If it were not for Caesar's account of the Gallic and Civil Wars, Varro's antiquarian and agricultural writings, and some Roman legal documents preserved on stone or bronze, we might almost believe that the life of late-republican Rome, as we conceive it, was a creation of Cicero's fertile imagination.

We need, therefore, to ascertain how great is the distortion which the inevitable prominence of Cicero lends to our conception of the last and greatest phase of the Roman Republic. As regards Latin prose, we can rest easy. However regrettable the loss of works by other authors, either for their intrinsic merits or their value as evidence, Cicero rightly dominates the scene. There is copious testimony to the fact that the survival of so many of his works corresponds to their superiority in the eyes of the Romans themselves. After Cicero, no one could compose a speech in Latin, or a letter of any literary pretensions, or a work on philosophy or rhetoric, without author and audience being acutely conscious of the great exemplar. His works survived as textbooks in the grammar schools and models in the rhetorical schools. He was savagely criticized and passionately defended. Only his poetry was consistently and, as the remains show, justly ignored.

For the critic Quintilian (below, p. 293), Cicero was 'the name, not of a man, but of eloquence itself'. In what did the literary significance of Cicero consist? In oratory first of all, the indispensable accomplishment of an ancient politician. Cicero excelled in all three branches, deliberative, epideictic (display speeches), and forensic. His speeches before the Senate and people show us how he could present issues differently to different audiences, almost always with success. As consul he could turn the Roman populace against measures of debt relief and land distribution, though there were genuine shortages of currency and corn. At the end of his life he was able to persuade the Senate to vote official powers to Octavian, a revolutionary with a private army, in the name of the Republic. Epideictic oratory was less important as a genre at Rome, but it contributed vital ingredients, invective and eulogy, to different kinds of speech: if Cicero's praise of Pompey's achievements and Caesar's conquests moves us less than it did his contemporaries, we still find his absurd portrait of the ex-consul Piso in the speech *In Pisonem*, with his tame Epicurean philosopher and his mobile eyebrows, or his caricatures of the stern Stoic Cato and the pedantic jurist Sulpicius Rufus in the *Pro Murena*, hard to resist.

The most taxing and the most esteemed type of oratory at Rome was forensic. For at least twenty years, until his death in 43 BC, Cicero dominated the Roman courts, where arguments derived from law and fact counted for less than appeals to passion and prejudice. Though he boasted of being able to 'throw dust in the eyes of the jury', alleging in one case that there had been bribery in a *cause célèbre* and denying it in another four years later (and winning both cases), he was particularly famed for his ability to arouse and calm the emotions of jurors and spectators. He was for that reason regularly asked to give the concluding speech in defence.

The periodic style that Cicero developed, with its elaborately balanced clauses and careful rhythmic cadences, was less florid than that of Hortensius, the great rival of his youth, but by the end of his career it was becoming too ornate for the taste of the younger generation. Hence there is an apologetic element in his major works on rhetoric, which draw on Greek theory and on his own experience in order to present a picture of the perfect orator. In the *Brutus*, a history of Roman oratory written in 46 BC and ostensibly inspired by the death of Hortensius four years earlier, Cicero's own achievement is coyly represented as the climax of Roman eloquence. Here, as in the earlier *De Oratore* and the later *Orator*, Cicero lays great stress on the proper training for an orator, which he believed should not be just a matter of mastering techniques but of acquiring a broad education based on Greek culture. Cicero's hero, L. Licinius Crassus, to whom he had attached himself as an 'apprentice', had, as censor in 92, opposed the opening of schools to give rhetorical instruction in Latin alone: Greek was a richer language with an established tradition of great oratory that had to be mastered.

Though he regarded history and law as essential parts of the orator's education, it is Greek philosophy that Cicero recommends most strongly in these works: first because it imparts wisdom which the statesman needs to combine with eloquence, but also because it offers training in argument. These motives for interest in philosophy help to explain Cicero's choice of philosophical sect. Though he exposed himself to all the major schools, Epicureanism, which preached abstention from public life and had little interest in fine words, he gladly left to his friend Atticus. A Stoic philosopher named Diodotus lived in his house while he was still a boy and eventually died there: with him Cicero studied dialectic. His preference went to the teachers of the New Academy, the name given to a sceptical phase in the history of Plato's school, who taught that certain knowledge was not to be had, but that probability was an intellectually respectable basis for practical life. They were naturally committed to the Academic tradition of arguing both sides of a question, which gave excellent practice in speaking. Their beliefs also gave Cicero the freedom to choose what philosophical view he found most convincing on particular issues. For example, he was able without inconsistency to favour Stoic views on divine providence and on fundamental morality, while rejecting their view that oratory should be unemotional.

Though Cicero always maintained that public service should take precedence over study and writing, philosophy remained his favourite leisure activity. But it really came into its own when the political scene ceased to be hospitable to his talents. Given his priorities, it is not surprising that the first theoretical works he produced were the treatises on rhetoric we have mentioned and two works of political philosophy, *De Re Publica* and *De Legibus* ('On the State' and 'On the Laws'). But already in 46, two minor works gave the sign of things to come. *The Paradoxes of the Stoics* is a rhetorical *tour de force* in which Cicero defends these extreme formulations of Stoic doctrine, for instance, that virtue is the only good, and that all bad deeds are equally wicked. The work is dedicated to Cato's nephew Brutus and opens with praise of Cato for his ability to make his philosophy acceptable to the general public. Cato was then leading the Republican forces in Africa, which no doubt explains why Cicero wished to make amends for the ridicule he had heaped on his Stoicism some seventeen years earlier. Later in the year, after Cato's suicide, Cicero was to produce a moving eulogy of him.

By the next year he had embarked on a grand plan 'to provide for my fellow citizens a path through the noblest form of learning'. In the next two years he produced a dozen works, mostly in the dialogue form that Plato and Aristotle had invented, covering the three branches of ancient philosophy. The series began with the *Hortensius*, an exhortation to the study of philosophy now lost but whose impact can be judged from the words of St Augustine: 'That book changed my character and directed my prayers to you, Lord.' To the logical branch of philosophy, he devoted only one work, the *Academica*, which presented the sceptical standpoint of the New Academy. In the other two branches, he started with an 'academic' exposition of the views of the different schools on the most basic and general philosophical questions and then proceeded to defend his preferred doctrine on the more specific and practical questions. Thus in natural philosophy, the dialogue *On the Nature of the Gods* was followed by works *On Divination* and *On Fate*, and in moral philosophy the dialogue *On Ends*, discussing the goal of life as advocated by the different dogmatic schools, was followed by the *Tusculan Disputations* and *On Moral Obligations*, which defend the Stoic view of happiness and of duty.

Yet Cicero's purpose was not to preach particular philosophical doctrines. Indeed, even in his more dogmatic works, he asserts that there is no certain truth and defends his right to find different views more convincing according to the argumentation used on each occasion. His desire was to do the state some service and, in the process, to earn glory for himself when other avenues were closed. He made no claim to original philosophical ideas. What he had to contribute was his ability to reproduce Greek philosophy in eloquent Latin, to create a philosophical literature for Rome that could rival that of Greece, as Roman oratory already did. The eloquent orator would repay his debt to his education. Serious philosophical discourse had up to now been written in Greek: even Lucretius seems to have been regarded as a poet rather than as a philosopher. Cicero did not altogether reverse the pattern; but he had a firm follower in Seneca (below, pp. 300 ff.), and his ultimate heirs were the Latin Church Fathers. 'Latin philosophy, which before him was rough and ready, he polished by his eloquence', wrote a contemporary. He himself, in explaining how he could write so many books so quickly, says to Atticus: 'They are only copies and involve little effort; only the words are mine, of which I have a copious store.' There were Epicureans and Stoics who wrote in Latin before him, but they themselves, he says, made no pretension to stylistic elegance or even definition and arrangement. Though Cicero here exaggerates his role as a mere translator, which he elsewhere denies, there is no doubt that most of the evidence for his taking pains concerns not the meaning of the Greek doctrines but the choice of interlocutors and the problems of vocabulary. It was Cicero who fixed the correlation between Greek technical terms and the Latin word or words used to render them, because he was more interested in instructing all educated readers than in preaching to the converted. Not only does he often give the Greek original: he often discusses alternative translations and changes his mind in later works.

Before and after Cicero, it was common to complain of the deficiencies of Latin as a philosophical language. Cicero protested, with some justice, that new subjects in any language require the creation of new words, and that Greek philosophers too had resorted to neologisms. He himself introduced, for example, *qualitas, moralis*, and *beatitudo*, for 'quality', 'moral', and 'happiness' (it is suggestive that Rome, left to herself, needed no word for happiness). But though he patriotically maintained that Latin was potentially richer than Greek, it had certain fundamental limitations that were particularly serious for philosophical exposition: Latin was inhospitable to compound words, and it lacked the definite article. As Seneca was to complain, ' "Quod est" is a feeble substitute for Plato's *to on*,' ('that which exists'). Cicero often resorted to periphrasis, especially as he was aiming for eloquence, which meant respecting the genius of the language. 'We do not need to translate word for word, as unstylish translators do', he writes. The same consideration lead to the more irritating habit of translating Greek technical terms differently in different places, or by pairs of words, in accordance with his normal style. None the less, his achievement was immense. His greatest pagan successor, Seneca, though he added many new terms of his own to the Latin philosophical vocabulary, almost never rejected one of Cicero's translations: they permanently enlarged the resources of Latin.

That such a self-conscious stylist should also leave behind the most spontaneous personal letters may at first seem paradoxical. But it was part of Cicero's consummate talent for finding the right style for each occasion. The letters include official dispatches to the Senate on military affairs in his province which are quite different, in their formal simplicity, from the witty and entertaining picture of his duties that he gives his young friend Caelius, or the irritable coldness with which he addresses his inconsiderate predecessor Appius Claudius, or the bitter and anxious confidences he makes to his friend Atticus. The letters not only show us Cicero's literary versatility and the intricacies of Roman politics: they give us a glimpse of cultivated and sophisticated society—marriages and dowries, divorce and bereavement, property and investment, patronage and promotion, declamation and dinner parties. Above all, they furnish us with a more candid and intimate picture of an individual than we shall meet again until Marcus Aurelius and St Augustine.

Cicero's place in the political, military, and social history of Rome is not as secure as his place in cultural history. It is true that he held the major magistracies, that he suppressed a serious social revolt in his consulship, and that he governed a distant province for a year and might even have attained a triumph for his military achievements in the Taurus mountains, had the civil war not intervened. On the other hand, he can claim no part in the constitutional reforms or extensive conquests of his generation.

Sulla and his Legacy

The closest approximation to a historical account of Cicero's time written by a contemporary was eventually provided by Sallust (below, pp. 276 ff.). His monograph on the conspiracy of Catiline, the chief episode of Cicero's consulship, demonstrates to the full how difficult it was even for a contemporary witness of events to escape from Cicero's interpretation of them. Yet at the same time, the work exposes the misleading character of Cicero's version. For Sallust affords glimpses of the economic and social problems that afflicted the Italian peninsula and led to the unrest represented by Cicero as the work of a few aristocratic reprobates.

Sallust is valuable in another respect: he furnishes us with a starting-point for the period of the late Republic, namely, the dictatorship of L. Cornelius Sulla. He singled out the return of Sulla's booty-laden legions from the East, their seizure of the city by force, and the vindictiveness of Sulla's victory as the final turning-point in Roman conduct. Decline, he held, had set in when the destruction of Rome's mighty enemy Carthage left her without an incentive to self-discipline. Now personal greed and ambition came to dominate Roman political life. The historical perspective of Sallust, if not his diagnosis of the Republic's demise, can stand: it is not difficult to show that the age of Cicero was, in many respects, the legacy of Sulla.

Not only Catiline, whom Sallust specifically described as the product of the corrupt Sullan era, not only Crassus and Pompey, who were active partisans of Sulla, but Cicero, born in 106, Caesar, born in 100, and the younger Cato, born in 94, could remember the first armed conquest of Rome by a Roman, the proscriptions in which men all over Italy lost their property and their lives, and finally the astonishing abdication in 80 BC.

Though related by marriage to Sulla's enemy Marius, Cicero and his family, like many others, kept a low profile during the fighting and stayed in Rome when Sulla was away fighting Mithridates. Until 84, when Sulla's return was imminent, things were peaceful under the regime of Cinna and Marius; but the state was, as Cicero later described it, 'without law, without any semblance of authority'. As a result of the 'total dearth of orators', the young Hortensius Hortalus, only eight years older than Cicero, gained the limelight, and it was he whom Cicero opposed when he pleaded his first case after Sulla's return to Rome. Cicero's next two cases brought him face to face with the hardship inflicted on Italy by Sulla. The speech in defence of Roscius of Ameria in Umbria, delivered in 80, revealed the corrupt way in which Sulla's minions exploited the proscriptions and local feuds in the Italian towns for their own profit. In the second, delivered after Sulla had retired into private life, Cicero defended the rights of a woman of Arretium, one of the towns in Etruria from which Sulla had attempted to remove the rights of citizenship.

Cicero's attitude was not out of tune with the times. Many of Sulla's own allies had soon realized that the ruthlessness with which he destroyed his enemies and rewarded his friends could, in the long run, jeopardize his constitutional arrangements. To deflect the antagonism generated by his methods from the nobility that Sulla had left in charge, stories were circulated to the effect that this or that prominent supporter had queried the extent of the proscriptions, asking 'With whom shall we conquer?' The Metelli, the family of Sulla's wife, turned out in force to demonstrate sympathy with Roscius. Pompey, always adept at seeing how the wind was blowing, made a marriage alliance with them and successfully supported for the consulship of 78 a man no longer favoured by Sulla. This was Marcus Aemilius Lepidus, who was eventually to side with the dispossessed of Etruria when they attacked the Sullan colonists planted like garrisons on their land.

If Sulla had hoped that his confiscations would make his veterans prosperous and Italy secure, he was mistaken. The land allotted was often not of the best, while the forces that had been driving the small farmer off the land for a century—extended military service and capitalist farming by the rich—continued to operate. Some of the confiscated land had not actually been allocated and was held either by the original Marian partisans or by Sullan squatters. Threatened by every agrarian proposal, these men remained insecure in their tenure and hence ripe for revolution for the duration of the Republic.

Sulla's methods also left moral scars. The richest prizes had been used to keep and buy the loyalty of the upper orders. Leading men of the late Republic were known to be enjoying ill-gotten gains, and few consciences were absolutely clear. It is not surprising that in the seventies and sixties there were repeated attempts to revoke Sulla's exemptions and reclaim for the state treasury the price of proscribed property and the rewards given to agents of the proscriptions. One of Caesar's early claims to political notoriety was his willingness, as president of the murder court in 64, to accept charges against those who had killed for Sulla. Cicero was only too willing to exploit in his campaign for the consulship that year the threat this posed to his competitor L. Sergius Catilina whom men could still remember carrying the head of one of Marius' kinsmen through the streets of Rome to present it, still 'full of life and breath', to the dictator himself. Once elected, however, Cicero opposed a move to restore political rights to the sons of the proscribed, for, he argued, 'nothing could be crueller than to exclude men of such excellent families from political life, but the cohesion of the state is so dependent on Sulla's laws that it cannot survive their dissolution'.

Public Life at Rome

Most of Sulla's constitutional and legal arrangements survived to determine the character of political life throughout the late Republic. The dictator had laid down rules for the senatorial career, the *cursus honorum*, which were designed to ensure that men who finally found themselves, after holding the top magistracies, in command of armies and provinces would already have sat in the Senate for twenty years, absorbing its traditions and learning to set a high value on oligarchic cohesiveness. Holders of the quaestorship, the lowest office to carry senatorial rank, were now to number twenty a year, instead of eight, in order to maintain a Senate of 600. For the old council of 300 was inadequate to provide juries for all of Sulla's reorganized statutory courts where senators, as before C. Gracchus, were to be tried for public crimes by their peers. The number of officials required to administer Rome and its ten provinces was ensured, without damage to the prestige of the highest offices, by retaining two as the number of annual consuls and increasing the number of praetors from six to eight. Savage competition was built into the system, for every year saw twenty men spurred by initial success to hope for high office, fewer than half of whom would ever be elected praetor. It is therefore not surprising to find an increased emphasis on legislation against electoral corruption in the late Republic. Sulla's *lex de ambitu* carried the penalty of ten years' disqualification from public office; Cicero's *lex Tullia*, passed in his consulship, imposed ten years of exile.

Cicero's speeches give a vivid picture of a highly organized system for distributing largesse to the voters in various forms, from free seats at the games to outright bribes. In his indictment of C. Verres, who was on trial in 70 for extortionate practices as governor of Sicily, Cicero recounts how Verres tried to use his illicit gains to prevent Cicero's election to the aedileship in that year. One effect of the increased competition resulting from Sulla's measures was to make it even more difficult than before for a man of non-senatorial background to reach the higher offices, and Cicero wanted the aedileship, an optional office between quaestorship and praetorship, because it offered an opportunity to give games and win popularity. Despite Verres he was successful, but in that very year the electoral situation was made still more complex by the activity of the censors.

The year 70 was altogether momentous. For it was then, in the consulship of Cn. Pompeius Magnus and M. Licinius Crassus, outstanding partisans of Sulla, that the dictator's restrictions on the legislative and judicial powers of the tribunes of the *plebs* were removed, after nearly a decade of popular agitation. After his election, Pompey had made a speech combining this promise with an attack on the corruption of provincial governors and the senatorial juries who failed to punish them. A decade of expensive and prolonged war with accompanying food shortages had made the senatorial government vulnerable to criticism. Scandals involving marked ballots and lavish bribery had rendered the senatorial courts, despite the conviction of Verres, indefensible. If Sulla's senators were, as he probably hoped, less liable than their predecessors to acquit

their peers, since most of them would never enjoy the same opportunities, they were more vulnerable to bribes, since the new
men among them found maintaining a senatorial lifestyle a strain
and could not borrow easily in the expectation of later provincial profits. Though Pompey does not seem to have specified
how the judiciary was to be straightened out, he did not oppose
the passage of the *lex Aurelia* which gave the *equites* two-thirds
of the seats on the juries.

The censors of the year, friends of Pompey, ejected from the
Senate sixty-four members, mostly men who had proved themselves corrupt in the provinces or the courts. Their struggles to
recover senatorial rank by being elected to office again compounded electoral competition in the sixties, while other action
by the censors introduced a further element of uncertainty into
the electoral game. The Italians, who had gained the franchise at
the end of the Social War (above, pp. 45 f.) were at last enrolled
in the thirty-five Roman tribes. Henceforth candidates for office
had to consider a wider electorate, of whom at least the more
prosperous members might actually find it worth while to come
to Rome and vote. Thus when Cicero was planning his consular
campaign, he included in his schedule a visit to the governor of
Cisalpine Gaul (the Po valley) for 'the district is likely to count
heavily in the voting'.

Optimates and Populares

Sulla's legislation and the struggles that led to its modification
also had a profound effect on terminology and habits of thought.

It was in this period that the ideology or, on a cynical view,
the propaganda familiar to us from the works of Cicero and
Caesar became defined. The habit of mapping out the political
scene in terms of a Right and a Left by the words 'Optimates'
and 'Populares' could in fact be older than the days of Sulla, for
the programmes and methods of the Gracchi gave shape to such
a division. But it was Sulla's legislation that made explicit the
dominance of the Senate that had developed in the third and
second centuries BC and started to be seriously challenged in

the middle of the second. It was, in essence, Sulla's view of the proper balance of the constitution that became the bulwark of the Optimates. And it was the struggle over the modification of his laws, principally in 70, that gave definition to the *popularis ratio*.

In speaking of Optimates and Populares we are speaking of ideological labels, not of organized political parties. Indeed 'popularis', as applied to people, normally refers to leading politicians with a certain political style, not to leaders and followers, and usually to a succession of such leaders, not a group working together. A *popularis* was a politician who used and defended the powers of the popular assemblies and the popular office of tribune as a counterweight to senatorial authority and/ or championed such economic measures as land distribution, debt cancellation, and subsidized corn.

In the years immediately following the resurrection of the tribunate some ambitious men held the office and sponsored legislation that the establishment regarded as a threat. Gabinius even threatened to re-enact the most notorious act of Tiberius Gracchus (above, pp. 41 ff.) and depose his colleague from office rather than accept his veto. The kind of left-wing image affected by the tribune Rullus in 63 who, according to Cicero, grew his hair long and took to wearing dirty old clothes and a farouche expression; the self-advertisement of his colleague Labienus who put a statue of his uncle, the martyred tribune Saturninus, on the rostra—these were only to be expected of young men on the make; they might yet end as stalwart supporters of the Senate. For there is no warrant to assume sincerity, or even consistency, in the conduct of Roman politicians. Indeed the prime example of ambiguity and opportunism was the restorer of the tribunate himself.

Pompey

Though he had inherited from his father some connection with Marius' ally Cinna, Pompey raised an army of his father's clients in Picenum and joined Sulla on his return from the East. For his ruthlessness in destroying Sulla's enemies in Sicily and Africa he acquired the nickname 'teenage butcher'; for his selfish ambition he earned the distrust of his own side. From the dictator, who had treated him as an exception to his own rules and allowed him to command legions when he had not held public office, Pompey extorted a triumph. After being cut out of Sulla's will for supporting Lepidus, he then suppressed Lepidus' rebellion and used his troops to extort the Spanish command from the Senate. In Spain he managed to steal the limelight from Metellus Pius, who was already making headway against the rebel general Sertorius, and then returned to Italy to do the same to Crassus. After dealing with some fugitives from the rising led by the gladiator Spartacus, Pompey wrote to the Senate that Crassus had conquered the slaves, but that he himself had extirpated the war.

Pompey had nothing to lose by a shake-up of the Sullan system. He had made too many enemies to fit comfortably into Optimate politics: only the presence of his army in Italy had secured him senatorial dispensation to stand for the consulship without having held the lower offices. Now, after the popular measures of his consulship, enthusiastic tribunes secured for him from the people first, in 67, sweeping powers to clear the Mediterranean of pirates and then, in the next year, the command of the war against Mithridates, in which, true to form, he replaced Sulla's trusty officer L. Licinius Lucullus, who had been appointed some years ago by the Senate.

In Pompey's absence, Rome speculated on the manner of his return. Would the great man come home in a conservative or a radical mood? In the end he tried to manoeuvre a return in the company of his troops as in the past, but a move to recall him to suppress Catiline's forces was thwarted by the consul's decisiveness and the Optimates' determination. Eventually, towards the close of 62, Pompey dismissed his army at Brundisium and returned to confront the Senate of Sulla making its last stand.

Cicero, Pompey's exact contemporary, presents a similarly

complex, if less sinister, political image. By conviction he was a conservative, by temperament a moderate, while his municipal equestrian background gave him a certain perspective on the Roman scene. To enhance the favour his forensic work could bring him, Cicero identified himself with the rising star, prosecuting in 70 the man who had mistreated Pompey's Sicilian clients and going on to support the proposal to give Pompey the Mithridatic command. In the first he castigated the corruption of senatorial juries; in the second he lamented the sufferings of the Asian *publicani*. These were themes to attract the *equites*, but in 65 he defended Pompey's ex-quaestor Cornelius and the radical activities of his tribunate, with moving appeals to the ancient struggles of the *plebs*. His famous doctrine of the *concordia ordinum* (harmony of the orders) was more in line with Sulla, who had himself broadened the composition of the Senate: the upper orders, senators and *equites*, were to fulfil their different public obligations and co-operate against revolutionary movements. But when Cicero opposed a whole series of tribunician proposals which appealed to the rural and urban poor, he said, and no doubt partly believed, that he was a *popularis consul* safeguarding the true interests of the people.

Cicero believed that in 63 he had actually achieved the *concordia ordinum* and indeed a wider 'consensus of right-thinking men' against the subversive movement of Catiline. The Senate, too, was in elated mood and, led by a young man who succeeded by force of personality in persuading his peers that he embodied old republican morality, faced the demands of the triumphant Pompey in an uncompromising spirit. Pompey wanted a marriage alliance with Cato, but, to the disappointment of the women of his family, Cato said 'No'. Pompey wanted the Senate to ratify his eastern arrangements, which reversed many decisions of Lucullus, immediately and *en bloc*; Cato, a relative of Lucullus, and others said 'No'. Pompey wanted to distribute to his veterans and needy citizens Italian land, including the *ager Campanus* which even the Gracchi had spared; here even Cicero said 'No', for the rents from the Campanian land provided the closest, and hence the most reliable, source of public revenue.

Cato had the bit between his teeth. One of the effects of the civil wars of Sulla and Marius had been to deprive Rome of the men who should have been her senior statesmen. Those that were left were often too inclined, Cicero thought, to withdraw to their luxurious villas and fishponds and lead a life of cultured ease. Hence there was room for a strong character such as M. Porcius Cato to become a leader of the Senate before he had held the praetorship. Pompey was not his only target. Cato offended the *equites* by threatening the long-standing immunity from prosecution for bribery that equestrian jurors enjoyed. In addition he opposed making any concession to the *publicani* who had overbid for the tax-contract in Asia in the expectation that the province would quickly return to normal after the Mithridatic War. Here Cicero parted company with him. Cato was destroying the *concordia ordinum*: he behaved 'as if he were living in Plato's Republic and not in the cesspool of Romulus'.

Crassus

In the course of his crusade, Cato alienated not only Pompey but Crassus who had urged the tax-farmers to ask for a remission of their contract. The importance of Marcus Crassus is easier to demonstrate than to explain. He was a decent orator, but easily surpassed by Cicero; he was a talented general, but outclassed by Pompey and Caesar; he was rich, but hardly more so than Pompey when he returned home with his eastern booty. Like Pompey, Crassus had raised an army and joined Sulla on his return to Italy; unlike Pompey, he was a notorious profiteer in the proscriptions. What ancient writers liked to emphasize was his avarice and the political ambition he made it serve. He was said to have augmented his property by taking advantage of the frequent fires in Rome and the lack of a regular fire brigade: owners of burning buildings would sell them for a song, and Crassus, with his team of trained slaves, would repair and rebuild them for profit. A much quoted remark of his was, 'No man is rich who cannot support an army': the fact that Crassus could may help to explain how he obtained the command against Spartacus at a time of financial stress.

Less dramatic uses of his wealth included lending money to political associates free of interest, and providing lavish hospitality. The result, we are told, is that Crassus had considerable influence with the Senate. It is likely that he was one of the first to take the measure of the changed political conditions brought about by Sulla's doubling of the Senate's membership. The new men often needed money to maintain their new station, and they would relish invitations to dine with a noble of ancient family. But Crassus was not content to be a conservative politician. Shady and unorthodox himself, he liked to support black sheep and sponsor radical causes. Though resentful of Pompey's successes, he joined him as consul in 70 in restoring the rights of tribunes, and in successive years he supported several tribunes on trial. He also lent money to young aristocrats such as Caesar, or funded their electoral campaigns, as in the case of Catiline. Some of his more daring political initiatives were often unsuccessful: both of his projects as censor, to enfranchise the communities of Cisalpine Gaul and to exploit the will of the Egyptian king who left his country to Rome, were baulked by his colleague.

Caesar

While Cato preached and Pompey and Crassus fumed, an abler politician than any of them was planning how to exploit the situation. 'Caesar, from the outset and as it were by hereditary right the head of the popular party, had for thirty years borne aloft its banner without ever changing or even so much as concealing its colours.' So Mommsen wrote of the murdered dictator, 'the sole creative genius ever produced by Rome'. C. Iulius Caesar has been appreciably cut down to size in the past century, but it remains hard to deny that he was the most consistent politician of the late Republic.

Related by marriage to Marius and Cinna, he had escaped the proscriptions because of family connections on the other side. But tradition credited Sulla with the prediction that he would eventually destroy the Optimates for 'he harbours in him many a Marius'. In 70 he supported the restoration of the tribunes' powers and the amnesty granted to the followers of Lepidus, one of whom was his wife's brother. In youth Caesar had refused Sulla's request to divorce Cornelia, who was Cinna's daughter; when she died in 67 he delivered a public eulogy of her. In the same year, at the funeral of his aunt Julia, he displayed the images of her husband Marius, not seen since the days of Sulla. Then, as aedile in 65, Caesar restored to public view the trophies that Marius had brought back from his victories, and in 64 he countenanced the prosecution of Sulla's agents.

To the development of his *popularis* image Caesar brought all his considerable talent for publicity. In 63 he prosecuted Rabirius, first by an obsolete procedure dating from the time of the kings, then by trial before the popular assembly. Through this attempted vindication of the murdered tribune Saturninus, Caesar demonstrated not only his belief in the Gracchan principle that no citizen could be put to death without a trial authorized by the people, but also his grasp of ancient tradition and religious lore. For Caesar was aiming to be elected *pontifex maximus*, the head of the state religion. A similar combination of political principle and personal ambition had led him to support the bills granting Pompey his great commands. Then, in the last phase of the Catilinarian affair, he nearly succeeded in swaying senatorial opinion against the execution of the captured conspirators without trial, and he made clear his support for the recall of Pompey to deal with the rebel forces.

Caesar had become a much hated man in some quarters. When he returned from governing Spain early in 60, Cato led the Senate in blocking his request to be allowed to stand for the consulship in absence. Caesar wished to remain outside the sacred boundary of the city which he would then cross as part of his triumph, a privilege which the Senate had already granted him. The Senate further showed its reluctance to have him as consul by allocating as the consular provinces for that year the task of clearing out the woods and cattle-runs of Italy: there lurked the remnants of the bands of Spartacus and Catiline, the later, as some alleged, Caesar's own supporters.

The 'First Triumvirate'

Caesar gave up his triumph and retaliated by soliciting the support of those other victims of Cato's righteousness, Pompey and Crassus. Once elected consul for 59 BC, he reconciled the two rivals and set out to fulfil the promises he had made to them. Cato was therefore largely responsible for the formation of the so-called 'first triumvirate', and that moment, he later said, was the real beginning of the end for the Republic.

It is tempting to conjecture what might have happened had Caesar not been denied his triumph and the expectation of an important province after his consulship. Caesar was no radical fanatic: he had performed the requisite military service under two Sullan generals and not felt tempted to join the Marians under Lepidus and Sertorius. He was ultimately to say that his honour had always come before anything else; he held it dearer than his life. If he had not felt humiliated by the Senate, might he have proved a decorous consul, a rebel who had 'come round', as Cicero always hoped he would? Perhaps the answer does not matter so very much. Perhaps the same can be said even of that more obvious, but related, question: might civil war have been averted in 49? The interesting question for the historian is not whether any particular event is inevitable, but whether it is explicable. Why the fall of the Republic occurred exactly when and how it did is, after all, secondary to the main question: why did leading members of the Roman governing class, who themselves had most to gain from the existence of the Republic, destroy it, thereby committing political suicide?

The Romans, as we have said, thought of the issue in terms of moral degeneration. They believed that, whereas their ancestors had aspired to glory through service to the state, their contemporaries had come to put their own ambitions above the public welfare. The catalyst in the decline of traditional morality they felt to be the increase in Rome's power and wealth. The enormous opportunities for ruthless self-aggrandizement by individuals threatened the state in two directions. If her subjects were exploited, Rome might lose her Empire, for she had not the men or money to control such a vast area by brute force: an element of consensus in her rule was essential. Again, if some members of the governing class became a great deal more powerful than others, the essentially oligarchic system of the Republic would be replaced by one less beneficial to the governing class as a whole. Roman thinking ran on patriotic self-control where we might stress the need for institutional checks on the power of individuals. In fact some of the legislation they traditionally saw as encouraging the first can be interpreted as steps towards the second: sumptuary laws to limit conspicuous consumption and largesse, extortion laws to check greed and related abuses by Roman officials, canvassing laws to prevent men from buying their way into office on the profits of Empire. But certain changes, such as making generals strictly accountable for their booty, or taxing citizens enough so that the state could itself provide for discharged veterans, or creating a police force that could control political violence, were not in keeping with the closely guarded tradition of aristocratic independence. It was easier for the Senate to forgo a rich and strategic province such as Egypt, which might give excessive scope to one of its members, than to make the great generals, who behaved like kings abroad, toe the line when they returned home.

The standards of success were rising as the Empire grew. After the military triumphs of Marius in the West and Sulla in the East, Pompey would not have been satisfied with the normal one-year governorship after his consulship. Caesar, too, would be thinking of prolonged and extraordinary commands. Eventually Pompey could not bear an equal nor Caesar a superior. But the Republic was incompatible with the ascendancy of one

or two. It was also incompatible with the notion that great deeds
exempt one from the legal restraints placed on one's peers, an
idea Caesar is said to have voiced as he surveyed the enemy dead
after Pompey's defeat: 'They would have it so. Even I, Gaius
Caesar, *after my great achievements*, would have been convicted
in the courts, had I not sought help from my army.' Socrates
knew that the laws must be obeyed even when they led to an
unjust decision. By the start of the Civil War in 49 the laws of
Rome had been bent and ignored by powerful individuals too
often to seem worthy of obedience.

The expediency of conciliating Rome's subjects, however, had
been grasped by intelligent men of differing political complexion,
such as the Gracchi, Sulla, Pompey, Cicero, and Cato. Even
Caesar, who was to treat the conquered Gauls with great brutality, tightened up the extortion law. A more difficult issue was
how far to share the profits of empire with the whole citizen
body, for there was no conception of an impersonal 'government'
that bestowed specific benefits. The established tradition of
aristocratic largesse made it easy for men who legislated for the
distribution of land or money to gain the same credit and popularity as those whose generosity came from their own pockets.
Thus *popularis* moves to increase the welfare or power of the
equites or the *plebs* looked like threatening bids for individual
power. It was bad enough when a tribune of the *plebs* made
himself a nuisance in this way; still worse when the tribune was
in league with a senior magistrate. The year 59 presented the
spectacle of a consul who himself behaved like a tribune and had
the support, not only of a tribune, but of a general whose
veterans were on the scene. It is not surprising that on the brink
of civil war there were Optimates who feared nothing so much
as the thought of Caesar holding that office again.

Caesar's First Consulship

Caesar began, however, by attempting to secure a smooth passage for his legislation through tact and diplomacy. The settlement of Pompey's veterans had top priority, and in December

of 60 Caesar solicited the support, or at least the silence, of
the best orator in Rome, who had already sabotaged two previous attempts. Cicero was flattered, but decided to remain independent: he valued the opinion of Cato and others who had
called him 'Father of his Country' after his consulship. In March
Cicero confirmed Caesar's worst fears by indulging in critical
remarks about the state of public affairs. Caesar, with the co-
operation of Pompey (both in their priestly capacities), retaliated by carrying out a highly questionable adoption of Cicero's
personal enemy, Clodius, into a plebeian family so that he could
be elected tribune that summer. They no doubt hoped to lure
Cicero, this time by fear, into collaboration, but, if that failed,
Clodius would remove the nuisance. Cicero refused invitations
from Caesar to serve on his agrarian commission or accompany
him to his province (where he would have provided excellent
company in the long evenings). Cicero paid for his refusal by
being sent into exile in 58 for his execution of the conspirators
five years earlier. When he was recalled through Pompey's good
offices over a year later, he was easy to divert from further moves
towards independence.

It is important to realize that our best informant was not only
hostile to the coalition, but did not enjoy the confidence of its
members. Though Caesar's invitations amply demonstrate that
Cicero's political importance was not a figment of his own
vanity, he can offer us only his own intelligent speculations
on the motives and plans of those who came to control the
destiny of Rome.

Caesar's other attempt to employ diplomatic methods was
also unsuccessful. He carefully omitted from the agrarian proposal itself all the most controversial features of the earlier bills,
excluding the Campanian land from distribution, using only
Pompey's new revenues for purchase of land, and relying on
voluntary sale. He brought the proposal to the Senate and put it
to the Assembly, without senatorial sanction, only after meeting
with total and unreasoned opposition. Caesar's colleague in
office was Cato's son-in-law, M. Calpurnius Bibulus, whose

obstruction Caesar no doubt hoped to avert by impressing the body of the Senate with his sweet reasonableness. From now on, however, he showed how little he could be deflected from his course by shame or the pressure of public opinion. He affixed to the bill a clause, associated with Saturninus, that required the senators to swear individually to uphold it. Pompey and Crassus were induced to speak openly in its support and to promise to meet force with force. Against Optimate tribunes and his consular colleague, Caesar invoked the violence of the mob and Pompey's veterans. After the bill was passed, Caesar took all of his subsequent proposals directly to the people. His other bills ratifying Pompey's eastern settlement, granting a concession to the tax-farmers, recognizing the Egyptian king (who paid handsomely for the privilege), were passed without regard to opposition. Bibulus had resort to religious obstruction of an unorthodox kind and on an unprecedented scale: from his house he observed bad omens every day.

The intense opposition Caesar faced in passing measures that were addressed to real problems arose from fear of the political power he would thereby acquire with the *plebs*, with the veterans, with the *equites*, and with foreign potentates. Worse was still to come. The tribune Vatinius secured for him from the people a five-year command in Cisalpine Gaul and Illyricum: the first would enable him to keep a threatening eye on Rome when not on campaign, while the second offered him the opportunity for glory in forging the land route through the Balkans that Pompey's expansion of the eastern Empire now made imperative. In the end, politics interfered with the rational expansion of Rome, and Caesar extended the Empire north to the Channel and beyond. For his legislation, including the *lex Vatinia*, was vulnerable to subsequent attack because of the way it had been passed, and Caesar was therefore eager to gain the additional province of Gaul from the Senate. This he achieved through Pompey, whose continued loyalty he had secured through a marriage alliance.

Caesar was well aware, however, that Pompey was an

unreliable ally. Dependence on a junior, though it had achieved
its end, seemed to Pompey a humiliating position, which the
scurrilous edicts of Bibulus and the growing unpopularity of the
three only aggravated. As time rendered less vulnerable what
he had gained from Caesar, his hankering for respectability,
already demonstrated in 62, would reassert itself. But for a
while the malice of his enemies made him cling to the alliance
which was, in fact, renewed in 56, just as Cato's brother-in-law
was about to stand for the consulship. The presence of Caesar's
troops on leave in Rome ensured the election of Pompey and
Crassus instead, and they promptly renewed Caesar's command
in both Gauls and secured for themselves the control of Spain
and Syria for five years.

Crassus left for Syria and was killed a year later fighting the
Parthians. Caesar was tied up in Gaul and unable to cross the
Alps until the winter of 53/2. But Pompey, who chose to govern
Spain through legates and remain in the vicinity of Rome, was
in a position to exploit political developments. Electoral chaos
and gang violence eventually played into his hands since, as proconsul with the power to command and levy troops, he was the
obvious person to restore order. When Clodius was murdered at
the start of 52, the Senate had him elected sole consul. The death
of Caesar's daughter Julia in 54 had already ended Caesar's
family connection with him, and Pompey now seemed within
reach of recognition as leader of the traditional government.
But, to keep his options open, he supported a tribunician bill
which granted Caesar the right to stand for a second consulship in absence: he would be eligible for election in 49 after the
requisite ten-year interval had elapsed.

Civil War

Meanwhile a change in the method of appointing provincial
governors not only resulted in the dispatch of the reluctant
Cicero to govern Cilicia, but introduced complications into
Caesar's length of tenure in Gaul. Behind the legal question,

however, lay constitutional questions, and behind them lay a struggle for power more complex than the rivalry of Pompey and Caesar.

Cato's antagonism had removed any temptation Caesar may have felt to sacrifice his *popularis* image to his ambition. Instead, he remained true to the first as long as there was any risk to the second. Caesar now took his stand on the fact that the people had granted his command and the right to stand for the consulship in absence, which, he claimed, implied that he would still be in his province in the summer of 49. The Optimates had always disapproved of provincial commands granted by the people: they believed that the Senate should retain over foreign affairs the control it had acquired *de facto* as the only organ of government with a continuous existence and membership. Though sovereignty lay with the people, they did not agree with those Populares who held that the people could properly legislate on any matter, even without senatorial guidance. Had not the Republic long been thought of as 'the Senate and People of Rome'?

Marcus Marcellus, the consul of 51, tried to force the issue and recall Caesar a year early. Pompey tried to arrange a compromise, while nevertheless agreeing that the Senate ought to be obeyed. In 50 and early 49 Caesar had recourse to conciliatory offers, reinforced by the vetoes of friendly tribunes: when the diehards ignored them, he crossed the Rubicon, the river that marked the boundary of his province, in defence of their sacred rights—and of his honour.

Pompey went east to gather his forces, saying 'Sulla did it: why not I?' But the only resemblance lay in his threat of reprisals against his enemies. Speed and organization belonged to Caesar, and his policy of clemency captured public opinion.

Cicero, an honourable man trying to choose the side of the Republic, lamented that neither Pompey nor Caesar had any aim but *dominatio*. He could not do other than attribute blame to the protagonists, including the enemies of peace in the Senate, because he believed that the political system itself was blameless.

If Cato spoke as if living in Plato's Republic, Cicero had written that the Roman Republic surpassed even that utopia. In the late fifties, when chaos and violence had become the order of the day, he was moved to write two works of political philosophy based, in title and in content, on Plato's *Republic* and *Laws*. In the first he explained that Roman tradition had evolved a mixed constitution, which was the most balanced and stable kind. The laws he presented in the second work were designed for a future citizen body trained to virtue and resembled closely existing law and practice. What innovations there are in the part of the treatise that survives are designed to increase the power and authority of the Senate and senior magistrates.

Both *De Re Publica* and the roughly contemporary *De oratore* are set in the past when public affairs were in the hands of Scipio and Laelius or Lucius Crassus and Marcus Antonius. Cicero's answer to the problems of the Republic was the existence of statesmen or a statesman of their calibre who could serve as a model of conduct to others. He had never entertained such hopes of Pompey and Caesar, though he had once offered to play Laelius to Pompey's Scipio and was to offer advice to Caesar as dictator.

The Dictatorship

Caesar's victory destroyed the system within which he had wanted primacy. There is little sign that he enjoyed the task of reconstruction. Perhaps the only thing that rings true in Cicero's fawning speech *Pro Marcello*, delivered in 46, is his picture of the arbiter of men's destinies as weary of life. Until the spring of 45 Caesar could turn his attention to Rome's problems only in the intervals of fighting the civil war all over the Mediterranean. By March of 44, when he was killed, he was planning to leave Rome to fight the Parthians. Cicero was baffled. What of the programme he had outlined for him: the reorganization of the courts, the restoration of financial credit, the passing of moral legislation, the reform of political life? Caesar had in fact taken steps to ease the burden of debt. He had legislated against luxury and in favour of increasing the birth-rate. But Cicero could not grasp the difficulty of reforming Roman politics any more than he could appreciate Caesar's concern for Italy and the provinces.

In the short time he had, Caesar achieved enough to show how widely his mind ranged. The settlement of his veterans was to contribute to the restoration of Italian agriculture and man-power, for they were to be scattered up and down the peninsula, not planted like garrisons in the Sullan mode. Some of the administrative anomalies neglected since Italian towns became Roman *municipia* after the Social War were sorted out. The number of magistrates was increased to allow for the expanding number of provinces, and the unsatisfactory system of tax-collection by *publicani* based in Rome was discontinued, at least in Asia. Most important of all was the enfranchisement of Cis-alpine Gaul and the settlement of veterans and poor citizens in colonies abroad. The immediate effect of the colonies would be to cut down the urban population and, with it, public disorder and the cost of the corn dole. But in the long run the colonial policy, combined with Caesar's generosity in granting citizen-ship to individuals and communities, was to rejuvenate both the Roman legions and the Roman governing class. Caesar, who included some provincial aristocrats in his enlarged Senate, was perfectly aware of what he was doing.

The reform of Roman government was a different story. It was hard for a man of fifty to think afresh about the system that had so far determined his life: Caesar applied some traditional rem-edies, such as the abolition of certain urban clubs, the revision of criminal statutes, the restriction of the tenure of provincial commands. Accustomed to working at top speed in Gaul—he dictated letters to two secretaries while on horseback—Caesar had lost patience with the niceties of political life: Cicero com-plained that his own name was attached to senatorial decrees passed in his absence. Worse still, Caesar was about to leave for an indefinite period, having been made *dictator perpetuus* ('dictator without term'): perhaps he wanted to preclude any wrangles this time over his tenure of command, but it looked as if he had lost the will to restore the Republic. As dictator, he had shown no sign of relinquishing his stranglehold on the political machinery, designating governors, appointing many of the magistrates, and exercising personal jurisdiction. Hence the Ides of March.

After Caesar's death one of his intimates, Gaius Matius, was to lament: 'If he, for all his genius, could not find a way out, who is going to find one now?' Caesar knew that his peers disliked being kept waiting in his antechamber while he monopolized affairs. Yet what solution would they accept to the political chaos and armed conflicts he had brought to an end? Augustus was to avoid many of Caesar's mistakes, including the celebrated clemency which left his most determined opponents alive. Yet Augustus' solution was not so different, though he was more creative in adapting traditional language to describe his paralysis of the constitution. The greatest difference lay in the attitude of others. Another round of civil war had by then made peace in any form seem acceptable to those who survived. Augustus was young and had time to evolve a solution. The Catos and the Ciceros were gone. Who was there left who had seen the Republic?

Further Reading

PRINCIPAL ANCIENT SOURCES

The works of Cicero are readily available in translation. The Loeb Classical Library offers the complete works translated by different hands with facing Latin text. The Penguin Classical Series includes volumes of selected speeches in translation and, particularly worthy of note, a rendering of the letters by D. R. Shackleton-Bailey. This is a byproduct of his great edition and commentary, published by the Cambridge University Press, of which only the volumes of the *Letters to Atticus* contain a translation.

Other ancient works which contribute to our knowledge of the period can also be consulted in English. Sallust's monograph on the Conspiracy of Catiline appears in the Loeb and in the Penguin *Sallust*. One volume in each of these series is devoted to Caesar's accounts of his campaigns in Gaul and in the Civil

War. The *Life* of Atticus by Cornelius Nepos can be found in the Loeb volume containing Florus. Plutarch's *Lives* of Sulla, Crassus, Pompey, Caesar, and Cicero feature in the Penguin *Plutarch: Fall of the Roman Republic*. They can also be found, with other relevant biographies, in the eleven Loeb volumes containing all of Plutarch's *Lives*. Suetonius' biography of Caesar is available in the Penguin volume *Suetonius: the Twelve Caesars* and in the first volume of the Loeb *Suetonius*.

MODERN WORKS

There are many modern accounts of this, the most richly documented period of the Roman Republic. They vary greatly in scope, emphasis, and level of detail.

Brief accounts in a long perspective can be found in the works of H. H. Scullard, P. A. Brunt, and M. H. Crawford, mentioned on p. 48.

For more detailed narrative, older works such as volume iv of the Everyman Edition of T. Mommsen's *History of Rome* (Engl. trans. 1880) and T. Rice Holmes, *The Roman Republic*, 3 vols. (Oxford, 1923), are still worth reading. The relevant chapters of the *Cambridge Ancient History*, vol. ix (1932), are still useful, though soon to be superseded by a new edition.

The great modern work on the fall of the Republic is Sir Ronald Syme's *The Roman Revolution* (Oxford, 1939), which concentrates especially on the later part of this period. A more recent analysis of political activity in the late Republic, combined with a penetrating, but controversial, diagnosis of the fall of the Republic, is contained in E. S. Gruen's *The Last Generation of the Roman Republic* (Berkeley, 1974). For a lively account of the working of Roman politics and of the mechanics and setting , see Lily Ross Taylor's *Party Politics in the Age of Caesar* (Berkeley, 1949) and *Roman Voting Assemblies* (Ann Arbor, 1966).

Much of the up-to-date and detailed analysis of the politics of the period is, however, contained in biographies of the leading figures. Most notable are those by M. Gelzer, of which only *Caesar, Politician and Statesman* (Oxford, 1968) is available in English. J. P. V. D. Balsdon's *Julius Caesar and Rome* (Harmondsworth, 1967) is brief and readable; Z. Yavetz, *Julius Caesar and his Public Image* (London, 1983), concentrates on his dictatorship. Several biographies of Pompey have appeared recently, by J. Leach (1978), R. Seager (1979), and P. Greenhalgh (1980–1), of which Seager's is the most detailed on politics at Rome. The unrewarding task of constructing a biography of Crassus has been attempted by B. Marshall (1976) and A. Ward (1977).

Cicero, the most feasible subject for a biography, has been well served in English. D. L. Stockton's *Cicero, a Political Biography* (Oxford, 1971) provides a useful account of his work as a statesman; D. R. Shackleton Bailey in *Cicero* (London, 1971) makes good use of his work on the letters in evoking Cicero the man; E. D. Rawson offers a sympathetic and well-rounded study in *Cicero, a Portrait* (London, 1975; repr. Bristol, 1983). Different aspects of

Cicero's life and work are illuminated in a collection of essays edited by T. A. Dorey (London, 1965).

Finally, it may be useful to list a few books that help to put the political life of the late Republic in a broader social and intellectual context: C. Nicolet, *The World of the Citizen in Republican Rome* (London, 1980); J. Crook, *Law and Life in Rome* (London, 1977); W. Liebeschuetz, *Continuity and Change in Roman Religion* (Oxford, 1979); K. Hopkins, *Conquerors and Slaves* (Cambridge, 1978); *Death and Renewal* (Cambridge, 1983); C. Wirszubski, *Libertas as a Political Idea at Rome* (Cambridge, 1960); E. D. Rawson, *Intellectual Life in the Late Roman Republic* (London, 1985).

5

The Poets of the Late Republic

ROBIN NISBET

Lucretius

EARLY in 54 BC Cicero ended a letter to his brother with a note
on his recent reading. 'Lucretius' poetry is just as you say; many
brilliances of natural genius, all the same much technique; but
more anon. If you read Sallustius' *Empedoclea* I'll think you
a man, but I'll not think you a human being' (*QF* 2. 10. 3). Here
we glimpse a society where some public men find time for new
literature, and comment on it without affectation. Both the
works mentioned are philosophical and scientific, reflecting the
intellectual curiosity of a small Hellenized élite, an enlightenment
that Cicero was to transmit but did not originate. The didactic
poem was a familiar form that continued the Alexandrian tradition of versified scholarship; Cicero himself in his youth had
produced a translation, innovating for its day, of the astronomical *Phaenomena* of Aratus. Such works were more noted
for technique than genius, but Lucretius in his six books *De
rerum natura* found a theme to engage both the reason and
the imagination, the now fashionable Epicurean explanation
of the universe. The poet himself is a shadowy figure, no doubt
comfortably born, certainly well educated, perhaps recently
dead; his poem will speak for him.

'Aeneadum genetrix, hominum diuumque uoluptas, /alma
Venus', 'Mother of Aeneas' race, pleasure of men and gods,

life-giving Venus' (1.1 f.): already in the resounding invocation we find the complexity of reference that was thereafter to characterize much of the greatest Roman poetry. Venus is the mythical and literary goddess of Love, the ancestress of the Roman People, the protecting deity of Memmius, the ambitious politician for whom the work is nominally written, but at a deeper level she personifies the creative forces in the world, and in particular *uoluptas* or pleasure, the prime impulse and supreme good of the Epicurean moral system. The poet tells how at the goddess's epiphany the inventive earth sends up fragrant flowers, and beasts bound through the lush pastures: the universality of the divine influence is described in conventional religious patterns, but the comprehensive sympathy suits a philosophy that sees man as part of nature. Then, as is appropriate in prayer, the suppliant relates Venus' powers to his own needs: 'forasmuch as without thee nothing rises to the radiant shores of light, nor does anything joyful or lovable begin ... grant, goddess, to my precepts a charm everlasting' (28 'aeternum da dictis, diua, leporem'); the archaic alliteration suits the solemnities of old Roman poetry, but 'charm' (here paradoxically combined with 'everlasting') suggests a more up-to-date awareness of beauty. Finally Lucretius prays that Venus may bring peace on earth by making love to the war-god Mars; once again he astonishes us by blending traditional religious diction with a sensuousness of description associated with the poetic movements of his own day (35 f. 'leaning back his shapely neck, and gasping at thee, goddess, he feeds his greedy gaze with love'). He conflates scandalous Homeric story-telling with a more sophisticated hint of Harmonia, the daughter of Mars and Venus; at the same time he includes a reference to the political anxieties of 60–55 BC, when Caesar was already subverting the Republic.

Lucretius next turns to a panegyric of Epicurus, who like Hercules ridding the world of monsters liberated oppressed mankind from the lowering menace of religion. In a typically Roman metaphor we are told how the philosopher's mind sallied forth through the walls of the world, and after scouring the universe like a reconnoitring raiding party, brought back 'a knowledge of what can be and what cannot': 'quare religio pedibus subiecta uicissim/obteritur, nos exaequat uictoria caelo' (78 f. 'and so religion in turn is crushed underfoot and victory raises *us* to heaven'). These fighting words are at odds with the mild piety of Epicurus, who recommended the observance of one's local form of worship, and Lucretius recognizes that his line of argument may be thought wicked; but he reflects that the true impiety is religion's. With suitably epic, or rather tragic, diction he pictures the fate of Iphigeneia, whose significance is of course symbolic rather than literally relevant to Roman cult: 95 ff. 'lifted by the hands of men she was escorted trembling to the altar, so that pure impurely, at the very time for her to marry, she might fall a sorrowing victim, slaughtered by her sire.' And so to the scathing summing up, not easily paralleled in antiquity, 'tantum religio potuit suadere malorum' (101 'so much evil could religion recommend').

The first two books are devoted to the atomic theory of Epicurus (Vol. 1, pp. 430 f.), which was itself derived from Leucippus and Democritus (Vol. 1, p. 138 f.). Lucretius copes skilfully with his technical problems, the poverty of his ancestral tongue ('patrii sermonis egestas') at least before Cicero standardized an abstract vocabulary, the clumsiness of Latin compared with Greek as a vehicle for subtle disputation, the constraints of the metre (for the hexameter was not indigenous in Rome and still could prove a recalcitrant medium). The theme required argumentation of a kind unusual in poetry, at least since the fifth-century Empedocles, and as suits a rationalist, there is an abundance of prosaic, logical words like 'for', 'whereas', 'nevertheless', 'moreover', 'finally', 'therefore'. Each book is ordered into self-contained sections, which ram home a point by repetition as well as deduction, often ending with a triumphant restatement of the propositions with which they began (for the procedures are more polemical than those of a technical philosopher); and as in the physical system that is being described, these sections interlock in larger structures. It would be quite wrong to suppose that the work consists of purple passages of eloquence stitched to a monotonous scientific fabric: when Lucretius talks of 'smearing honey on the medicine cup' (1.936 ff.), he is referring not to the set-pieces, but to the poetic form itself, which must have startled more professional Epicureans (their founder had rejected the arts as not conducive to happiness). But while some of the poet's qualities can be demonstrated, the grasp of reality, the passionate faith in reason, the actuality of the supporting illustration, no anthology can do justice to the interdependence and cumulative persuasiveness of the system as a whole.

The second book opens with an exposition of Epicurean ethics, for which the physical theory was simply the foundation. 'suaue, mari magno turbantibus aequora uentis, /e terra magnum alterius spectare laborem' (2.1 f. ' 'tis sweet, when the winds disturb the calm of the great sea, to look from land at the great tribulation of another'): here we have the Epicurean ideal of *ataraxia* (freedom from turmoil) expressed with the self-centredness of ancient moral philosophy. 'Sweet' is not just a conventional poeticism, but alludes to Epicurus' theory of pleasure, not the excited pleasure that he disapproved of, but the static sort which arises from the absence of pain and anxiety. To know the true pleasures of the body, men do not need a house shimmering with gold and silver, or panelled ceilings echoing to the lute, as they can enjoy themselves by lying on the soft grass, beside a stream of water, under the branches of a tall tree (29 f. 'prostrati in gramine molli/propter aquae riuum sub ramis arboris altae'); such passages show how far Epicurus was from the popular misconception of the epicure (Vol. 1, pp. 427 f.). Fame and riches do no more for the mind than for the body: you may see your legions swarming over the plain, and still be obsessed by religious scruples and the terror of death (40 ff.). Men are like children fearing phantoms in the dark: 'hunc igitur terrorem animi tenebrasque necessest/non radii solis neque lucida tela diei/discutiant, sed naturae species ratioque' (59 ff. 'this terror and darkness of the mind must be dispelled not by the rays of the sun or the shining shafts of day but by the outward appearance and inner rationale of nature').

Lucretius then reverts to his atoms, whose unseen collisions and reboundings he illustrates by characteristically memorable analogies: they manœuvre and fight like specks of dust seen in a sunbeam in a darkened room (114 ff.), but their motion is no more visible to the senses than that of sheep crawling on a far-off hill (317 ff.). They move in the first place because they have weight and fall; but if they fall in parallel lines, that does not explain the collisions that produce aggregations of matter (the poet is unaware of the possibilities of attraction). They cannot catch up with one another by falling at different speeds, for as they fall in a void they must all fall at the same speed (225 ff.). Lucretius is thus led to the theory of the *clinamen* or swerve which was Epicurus' most important contribution to atomic physics: 'at times quite undetermined and undetermined places they veer a little from their track, with the smallest possible change of course' (218 ff.). Cicero thought that nothing was as disgraceful for a scientist as to say that something happens without a cause, but modern physicists can understand an appeal to indeterminacy; they will be more shocked by Epicurus' ethical intention, a desire to exempt human volition from the shackles of determinism (Vol. 1, pp. 434 ff.).

The third book expounds the structure of the soul, and its mortality. Lucretius tells how Epicurus banished the fear of death: it is this that muddies the waters of life, clouding them with darkness, and leaving no pleasure clear and unpolluted. Men profess a disbelief in survival, but in adversity the mask is torn off, and they revert to their old superstitions (55 f.). Such remarks reflect a traditional preoccupation of the Epicureans, and Philodemus himself, the most distinguished contemporary member of the school, wrote a treatise *On Death*. Nor should one underestimate the credulity about an after-life in the poet's own society; it is true that Cicero mocks the Epicurean obsession ('what old woman is crazy enough to be afraid of such things?'), but he confines the issue to the fables of mythology, and his rational scepticism was untypical even of the governing class. Some have thought that Lucretius protests too much, but for a poet he seems remarkably clear-headed: St Jerome's story of his madness can be explained by the incomprehension of the Church.

Lucretius naturally rejects the mind—body dualism that has haunted the history of thought for so long; as Epicurus had uncompromisingly put it, 'soul is body'. He also opposes the more plausible view that the soul is simply a condition of the body, or *harmonia* as it was called ('attunement' gives the idea); he derisively comments that the *organici* or instrumentalists are welcome to keep the word (131 f.). Following the psychology of his master he distinguishes the *anima*, the vital principle that is common to all living creatures, from the governing *animus* or mind, that is found only in man; but as both are equally mortal, he does not always use his terms precisely. The soul can influence the body, and the body the soul; this can only be effected by physical contact, and touch is a property of body (161 ff.). The atoms of the mind are exceptionally small and smooth, as is shown by the speed with which volition can be translated into action; in the same way a puff of breath can scatter a heap of poppy seeds, while corn-ears are too big and spiky (196 ff.).

Lucretius now accumulates some thirty arguments to show that the soul cannot survive the body. As it consists of small atoms of exceptional mobility, when its vessel is shattered it must dissipate like smoke (425 ff.). The mind keeps in step with the body in its birth, development, and decay, as can be seen from children and old men; therefore it dies with the body (445 ff.). The body and mind are affected together by drunkenness (476 ff.) and epilepsy (487 ff.); the fact that the mind can be cured, i.e. changed, by medicine is itself an indication of its mortality (510 ff). Sufferers from creeping paralysis lose sensation first in the toes and the feet, 'and then through the other limbs go haltingly the steps of cold death' (529 f.); as the soul cannot be concentrated in the sound part of the body (which does not acquire extra sensation), it must be mortal. The mind cannot originate in the head or the feet (Lucretius put it in the breast), but has a fixed place appointed for it where alone it can exist (615 ff.). If the soul is to have sensation when separated from the body it must be endowed with five senses, as poets and painters have portrayed the dead in the Underworld; but in isolation from the body it cannot have eyes or nostrils or hand or tongue or ears (624 ff.). When you cut through a snake, the severed part twitches, and similar things can be seen in chariot battles (a very Roman illustration); but if the soul can be severed it cannot be immortal (634 ff.). Plato and others had argued that the soul had a previous existence, but if it has forgotten its past, that is virtually equivalent to death (670 ff.); for the ancients the notions of pre-existence and after-life were closely connected, as they reasonably thought it implausible that what is born should be eternal. The different species of animals inherit temperamental as well as physical characteristics (741 ff.); this shows that the soul and body grow up together. It is ridiculous to suppose that at the moment of conception immortal souls are queueing up for a body to occupy (776 ff.).

Lucretius sums up the conclusion of his argument with an aphorism of Epicurus, 'nil igitur mors est ad nos' (830, 'therefore death is nothing to us'). If anyone takes it amiss that his body will rot in the grave or be consumed in the pyre, he must have some lingering belief in survival after death. And so to the mourners' memorable lament, which is meant to sound over-emotional and cliché-ridden, even if humanity seems to break in:

> Iam iam non domus accipiet te laeta neque uxor
> optima, nec dulces occurrent oscula nati
> praeripere et tacita pectus dulcedine tangent . . .
>
> (894 ff.)

Now no more will your household greet you joyfully, nor your best of wives, nor will your dear children race to snatch first kiss and touch your heart with a silent sweetness . . .

Epicurus had urged a serious and rational enjoyment of the

present ('life is whittled away in thinking of the morrow, and each of us dies before he has time to relax'). His sentiments are here echoed in a remonstrance from a personified Nature, who speaks with the derisive vigour of popular philosophy (931 ff.):

Away with your tears, you rascal, and muzzle your moans ... Because you always long for what you don't have and disregard what you have, your life has slipped away from you unfulfilled and unenjoyed ... Now give up things unsuited to your years and make way for younger men; for there is no escape.

(Lucretius emphasizes, as elsewhere, the natural cycles of growth and decay.) Then with a characteristic rationalization of myth he explains that the fabled punishments of the underworld represent the self-inflicted torments of life (978 ff.): the overhanging rock of Tantalus stands for the oppressive terrors of religion, the vultures that tear at Tityos are the desires of the flesh, Sisyphus pushing the stone up hill is the ambitious politician (what did Memmius make of that?). The sermon then turns to the staple of consolation through the ages, 'You are not the first'. Good King Ancus died, and Scipio, the terror of Carthage, and Epicurus himself, who dimmed the light of all men as the sun blots out the stars (1042 ff.). We spend our lives running away from ourselves, without understanding the cause of our discontent; peace of mind can only be attained when we accept that death is eternal.

The fourth book first defends the Epicurean theory of perception, by which objects give off a thin film of atoms (Vol. 1, pp. 373 f.), like heat from the sun or exhalations from the sea. Lucretius is at his vivid best in describing distortions of perception, the motion of hills when seen from a passing ship (389 f.), the continued rotation of hall pillars when children have stopped spinning (400 ff.), the bending of oars as they pass beneath the surface of the sea (440 'refracta uidentur'). 'A gathering of water no deeper than a finger's breadth, standing between the stones on the paved street, provides a view beneath the earth with a reach as far as the chasm of the sky stretches on high above the earth' (414 ff.): the image shows the child-like clarity of the poet's vision, and his ability to use minute observation to achieve immense perspectives. Yet in spite of strange cases Lucretius insists that knowledge depends on the senses, which are irrefutable. In yet another section he denies that the eyes were created to give us sight, a teleological explanation that is literally preposterous, as it confuses cause and effect: 'nothing grew in the body in order that we could use it, but what has grown generates a use' (834 f.). Here he is reacting against Aristotle and the Stoics, with an approach that went back to Empedocles and Democritus: Bacon and Darwin understood.

The latter part of the book provides a mechanical explanation of sex that is extended to the emotional concomitants; here Epicurean non-involvement is expressed with a cynicism that counters the growing romanticism of the poets.

Fathers' hard-won earnings turn into ribbons and head-scarves, . . . yet from the very fountain of enchantment a bitterness wells up ('surgit amari aliquid'), to bring anguish amid the blossoms, when the lover's mind is gnawed by the awareness that he is passing his life in idleness and going to ruin in brothels, or because she has left unclarified a word she has let fly that sticks fast in his passionate heart and ignites like a flame, or because he thinks she flaunts her eyes too freely or gazes at another, and he sees in her face the traces of a smile. (1129 ff.)

This leads to a satirical account of lovers' euphemistic endearments, which are expressed in the affected Greek of the girls concerned: 'the black is "honey-gold", the filthy and smelly "unadorned"' (1160 'nigra melichrus est, immunda et fetida acosmos'). Yet the poet concedes that even an unattractive woman may persuade you to live with her by her trimness and obliging ways; even without divine assistance habit can make you love her, like water dripping on a stone (1278 ff.). This cool conclusion may have encouraged the story, familiar from Tennyson's poem, that Lucretius was driven mad by an aphrodisiac administered by his wife.

The fifth book turns to the cosmos, which originated from the concourse of atoms and will one day disintegrate. The gods had no part in creating it, and no reason to think of such a thing (165 ff.): serene and immortal beings could not be dissatisfied with their previous condition. (Epicureans were not atheists, but their gods were indifferent to the world of men.) The natural order was not made for us: there is too much wrong with it (199). Much of the earth has been denied to man by mountains, forests, and the sea, as well as the extremes of cold and heat; and hard-won cultivation may be blighted by sun, frost, or wind.

Furthermore a baby, like a seafarer cast up by the cruel waves, lies naked on the ground, speechless and lacking all vital support, when once nature has ejected him on the shores of light by travail from his mother's womb, and he fills the place with woeful wailing, as is right for one who is destined in life to pass through so many troubles. But the different flocks and herds and wild beasts thrive without need of rattles, and none has to be treated to soothing lisps by a cherishing foster-mother (222 ff.)

Though Lucretius is far from idealizing the animals, he sees like others before him the particular helplessness of the human child.

The latter part of the book gives a non-theological explanation of the origin of life and the development of civilization. Grass and shrubs came first (783 ff.), and then animals, which grew up in wombs rooted in the soil (a curiosity derived from Epicurus himself). The poet more plausibly emphasizes the warmth, moisture, and fertility of the primeval world, which nowadays is like a woman past the age of child-bearing. Many individual monstrosities were produced (837 ff.), but if they could not find food or reproduce, they died out; Lucretius is using an idea of Empedocles, but rejects his fantastic belief in hybrids of men and beasts. The species that have survived have been preserved by cunning, courage, or speed (857 ff.), or, like dogs and sheep, by the protection of man. But in spite of the notion of natural selection, Lucretius has no idea of evolution: though the species were originally produced by chance, they remain for him distinct and immutable.

Primitive men had no agriculture or navigation, but lived in woods and caves off acorns and berries. They must often have been mangled horribly by wild animals (a good instance of the poet's constructive imagination), but thousands were never slaughtered in a single day's battle (999 ff.): Lucretius has no illusions that our first ancestors can have been anything but brutish, but he is also aware that technical innovation need not be accompanied by moral development. In due course men acquired huts and skins and fire, which was produced in the forest by lightning or friction. They were softened by family life (in his grim chronicle Lucretius finds a place for the Epicurean virtues of friendship and affection), and formal compacts for mutual support; these must have been kept for the most part (1025 ff.), otherwise the human race would not have been preserved (a sometimes forgotten aspect of the 'survival of the fittest'). Language was not arbitrarily invented but grew out of natural cries, as can be seen from the variety of sounds made by dogs:

when they set about licking their puppies fondly with their tongues or throw them about with their paws and as they go for them with bites put on a show of soft gobbling without using their teeth, they nuzzle up to them with eager moans that are very different from their baying when left alone in the house or their whimpers when with cringing body they shrink from a beating. (1067 ff.)

Here we have a poet who loves words and dogs and ideas all at once.

Towns were built and lands distributed, and men competed for wealth in a self-defeating search for security (1120 ff.). Kings rose, and were toppled by envy, and violence gave way to law. Men saw gods in visions and dreams, and falsely assumed that natural phenomena were devised by them (1183 ff.); that is why they still spatter altars with blood, and shiver at thunder, and pray in storms at sea. Metals were discovered in forest fires (1241 ff.), and then mined in the earth (first bronze, then iron). Horses were tamed for war (1297 ff.), and less successfully bulls and lions. Plaiting came before weaving, as looms need metal parts (1350 ff.); men worked wool before women, as they are the more ingenious sex. Then as things became easier, music was made in imitation of birds and the wind (1379 ff.); by Epicurean doctrine the inventiveness that was first prompted by necessity was extended to add the graces of life. Lucretius has no nineteenth-century belief in ever-continuing improvement, but following ideas current in the Hellenistic world he recognizes that progress has historically occurred: 'usus et impigrae simul experientia mentis /paulatim docuit pedetemptim progredientis' (1452 f. 'practice and with it the experimentation of the active mind taught men gradually as they felt their way forward').

After a eulogy of Epicurus and Athenian civilization, which serves as a climax to what has preceded, the sixth book expounds irregular natural phenomena, thunder and lightning, waterspouts and rain, earthquakes and volcanoes. Lucretius wishes to show that his system can provide rational explanations for these traditional puzzles, some of which were responsible for the terror and superstition that the Epicureans were so concerned to avert; if some of his details were now out of date, that simply underlines that he was a moralist and a poet rather than a scientist. Finally he turns to epidemics with a description of the plague at Athens four centuries before (1138 ff.); his treatment is less objective than that of Thucydides, on whom he depends, but he is not so concerned with a clinical scrutiny of the physical symptoms as with a rhetorical presentation of human nature under stress. The end of the work is gruesome and abrupt, with mourners fighting to lay their dead on other people's pyres, and some have suspected that the poet was interrupted by terminal illness; yet the passage implies a plan, as it sets off not only the panegyric of Athens at the beginning of the book but the joyous hymn to Venus at the beginning of the poem. Familiar themes recur, the mechanical causation of the calamity, man's social and self-seeking propensities, the terror of death, the uselessness of religion. If we are not explicitly offered the consolations of philosophy, that is not just because the plague came before Epicurus. Better simply to describe things as they are, and the limits of human capacity.

Catullus

There is much about humanity in Lucretius, but no people. The balance is redressed by his young contemporary Catullus, the second-greatest poet of the Republic.

> Marrucine Asini, manu sinistra
> non belle uteris: in ioco atque uino
> tollis lintea neglegentiorum.
> hoc salsum esse putas? fugit te, inepte:
> quamuis sordida res et inuenusta est ...
>
> (12. 1 ff.)

Asinius from the Abruzzi, that's not a nice thing to do with your left hand: in the middle of fun and wine you nick the napkins of the inattentive. So you think it's smart? You're making a big mistake, you clown: it's as nasty and unattractive a thing as you can think of.

Asinius has gone off with a table-napkin belonging to Catullus, who pretends to believe that he has stolen it deliberately. Episodes as personal and particular are·uncharacteristic of Hellenistic epigram, but a new generation of Roman poets had the individuality to make everyday occurrences a subject for verse. Such poems were too slight·to be categorized as lyrics; for the graceful metre with its eleven syllables ('hendecasyllables') one may refer to Tennyson's imitation, 'Oh you chorus of indolent reviewers'. The sometimes mannered vogue-words commend an informal elegance and wit, both in life and in poetry, and show a corresponding distaste for rusticity and ineptitude. Friends are treated as unique and precious individuals: the shift from teasing mockery of Asinius to over-exquisite affection for others is typical of this self-regarding coterie. The poem catches a society in transition as well as a literature: we are meeting here for the most part not the old Roman aristocracy but rich young men from Italy who are very conscious of their newly acquired metropolitan sophistication. Catullus himself, like other poets of the 'Neoteric' movement, (below, pp. 217 f.) came from beyond the Po (Cisalpine Gaul, as it was then called); his father was a leading citizen of Verona, with an estate at Sirmione on the Lago di Garda. Asinius may be derided as a countrified boor (1, 'Marrucine'), but his grandfather had led Italy against Rome in the Social War; his smart young brother Pollio was to become a tragedian, patron of Virgil, consul, *triumphator*, and historian.

Catullus provides a sketch-book of incidents and people that can be paralleled in antiquity only in Cicero. Among many vivid characters we meet the polished Suffenus, who yet writes poetry like a *caprimulgus* or goat-milker (22), Egnatius with the silly grin, who cleans his teeth in the Spanish manner (39), Sestius whose frigid oratory gave the poet a bad cold (44), Arrius who has trouble with his aspirates, and says 'hinsidiae' or 'hambushes' (84). Catullus tells how he boasted to a girl that he had acquired eight litter-bearers in Bithynia, only to be found out when she asked for a lift (10.33 f. 'you're a tactless, tiresome creature, not to let a fellow be careless'). He recalls to his brother-poet Calvus a competition of the previous evening (50.4 ff. 'the two of us played at writing verselets, now in one metre, now in another, tit for tat amid laughing and drinking'); the very fact that he explains the details shows that he is building up the occasion for a wider public. With the verbal and political licence of his day he directs ribald fantasies at his enemies, even Julius Caesar and his chief-of-staff: 57.6 ff. 'morbosi pariter gemelli utrique, /uno in lecticulo erudituli ambo, /non hic quam ille magis uorax adulter, /riuales socii puellularum' ('a couple of queers, both identical, two *cognoscenti* in one snug sofa, each an equally avid adulterer, partners in competing with the girlies of the town'). Caesar was not amused but knew the rules of the genre, and on receiving an apology asked the poet to dinner.

Catullus did not address all his poems to men. Of the dozen pieces on the lady he called Lesbia we may begin with one that is written without disillusionment:

Quaeris, quot mihi basiationes
tuae, Lesbia, sint satis superque.
quam magnus numerus Libyssae harenae
lasarpiciferis iacet Cyrenis
oraclum Iouis inter aestuosi
et Batti ueteris sacrum sepulcrum;
aut quam sidera multa, cum tacet nox,
furtiuos hominùm uident amores:
tam te basia multa basiare
uesano satis et super Catullo est,
quae nec pernumerare curiosi
possint nec mala fascinare lingua. (7)

You ask, Lesbia, how many kissings of you are for me enough and to spare. As many as the grains of the Libyan sand that stretch in silphium-bearing Cyrenaica between the oracle of sweltering Jove and the hallowed tomb of old Battus, or as many as the stars that when night is hushed look on the stealthy loves of mortals: so many kisses are enough and to spare for crazed Catullus to kiss you with, so that busybodies cannot count them up or an evil tongue cast a spell on them.

At a formal level this belongs to the same category as the poem to Asinius: *basia* is a colloquial word for kisses, unsuited to serious literature; the repeated 'enough and to spare' keeps up the informal tone; the pedantic formation *basiationes* and the mock-conventional 'silphium-bearing' or 'asafoetidiferous' are humorously pretentious; though the poet claims to be crazed, he has not lost his sense of proportion. But there is also a more serious note that raises the poem far above the level it professes. Sand and stars are the tritest of models for the innumerable, but here they evoke an atmosphere that is more important than the literal comparison: the ancient shrine in the desert heat and the dispassionate witnesses in the silent night suggest the tranquillity that envelops the lover's passion. The last couplet adds a typically wry assertion of self-sufficiency: if the kisses are too many to count, the gossiping tongue, like the evil eye, will lose its power to blight. The poem has an emotional range that belies its informal manner, but unlike the critics who write about him Catullus is content with fifty-seven words.

Love poetry of this sort has no precedent in Greek literature, and was conditioned by a novel combination of social circumstances. The Lesbia of Catullus was really Clodia, one of the spectacular sisters of the aristocratic demagogue Clodius, and probably the wife of Metellus Celer, the consul of 60 BC. Upper-class women had achieved greater emancipation than at any time in the ancient world, and Clodia had not only the style to inspire sophisticated poetry but the education to understand it. If she showed a conspicuous disregard for the ancestral proprieties, her lover could woo her with a sense of adventure and write about her with a lack of reticence impossible within the context of marriage. It is true that some Greek courtesans had been cultured and intelligent, but new elements were the Roman interest in the individual (witness Lucilius and Cicero's letters) and the outspoken independence of a privileged class. When Meleager writes elegant epigrams to his Zenophila or Heliodora, nobody cares whether they ever existed, but Catullus can build up a convincing series of poems about a real relationship in all its vicissitudes. Nothing like that had ever been done before.

Most of the Lesbia cycle is in fact poetry of disillusionment. What gives it its characteristic tone is not just the piquant blend of apparently incompatible emotions but the persistence of the rational voice: here we find subsisting together rueful self-examination, resolute self-exhortation, reasoned reproaches, and virulent hate. Catullus may start at the traditional level of epigram, but he ends by adding a new element to literature.

What a woman says to her eager lover should be written in wind and in swirling water (70. 3 f.)

I hate and yet love. You may wonder how I manage it. I don't know, but feel it happen, and am in torment. (85)

I loved you then not just as the world loves its girl but as a father his sons and sons-in-law (72. 3 f.)

Poor Catullus, you must stop being silly and cut your losses (8. 1 f.)

It's hard suddenly to put aside a long love; it's hard, but somehow you must accomplish it. This is the only way out, this fight you've got to win, this you must do whether it's possible or impossible (76.13 ff.)

Let her go and get on with it with those lechers of hers whom she clasps in her embrace, three hundred at once, loving none really but repeatedly bursting the loins of all of them, and let her not this time count on my love which has collapsed through her fault like a flower on the field's edge when touched by a passing ploughshare (11.17 ff.)

The modern world tends to regard such personal pieces as the poet's most significant achievement, but ancient critics would have set a higher value on his more elaborate artefacts. Catullus was a member of the so-called 'Neoteric' movement, which with its precision and preciosity suddenly made traditional narrative poetry seem old-fashioned; though there was an overlap with the writers of occasional short poems, the two trends were distinct in origin. The new movement, which had its roots in Callimachus, was stimulated by the Greek poet and mythographer Parthenius, who was brought to Rome as a prize of war about 65 BC; his captor Cinna has been identified with the Cisalpine poet of that name, who will be familiar to readers of Shakespeare's *Julius Caesar* ('tear him for his bad verses'). The young officer found Parthenian poetics so seductive that he spent nine years composing a short and obscure mythological poem on Zmyrna's passion for her father, and an admiring epigram by Catullus brings to life what the Neoterics were about (95):

My Cinna's *Zmyrna* has been published at last nine summers and nine winters after it was begun, when meanwhile Hortensius(?) has written half a million lines in a single month. *Zmyrna* will be sent as far as her waters of Satrachus [a river of Cyprus which figured in the poem], *Zmyrna* will long be read through by the white-haired centuries. But the *Annals* of Volusius [a conventional narrative poet] will expire at the mouth of the Po [where their author belonged], and will provide lots of loose wrappers for mackerel [i.e. to fry them in]. Dear to me be the small-scale memorials of *my* favourite writer, but the vulgar can rejoice in their bloated Antimachus [a verbose poet derided by Callimachus].

The Neoteric influence on Catullus may be seen at its simplest in a harmonious wedding-poem whose symbolism goes back to Sappho: 'ut flos in saeptis secretus nascitur hortis /ignotus pecori, nullo conuolsus aratro, /quem mulcent aurae, firmat sol, educat imber' (62. 39 ff. 'as a bloom grows secluded in a walled garden, unfamiliar to the herd, plucked by no ploughshare, that the breezes fondle, the sunshine builds up, the shower brings on'). A more fantastic specimen of the movement's tastes is a bizarre *tour de force* on the self-castration of Attis, which with its syncopated rhythms and accumulation of short syllables evokes the orgiastic music of Cybele's eunuch-priests:

Where the cymbals' voice is sounding, and the tambourines re-echoing,
And the Phrygian piper blaring with a curved pipe's cacophony,
Where the ivy-wearing Maenads toss heads energetically
And with shrilling ululations celebrate rites inviolable,
Where is wont to come cavorting Cybele's vagrant retinue,
It befits us there to hasten with accelerated three-step.   (63. 21–6)

In a more profound poem that was to become the prototype of Roman elegy Catullus relates the sorrows of his life to the paradigms of myth. Just as Laodamia's passionate marriage was unhallowed from the beginning, so Lesbia came to him with an omen of doom: 'my radiant goddess entered with dainty steps, and planting her gleaming foot on the worn threshold, halted there with a click of her slipper' (68. 70 ff.). In the same way an anguished couplet on his brother's death near Troy recalls the sufferings of the *Iliad*: 'Troia—nefas—commune sepulcrum Asiae Europaeque /Troia uirum et uirtutum omnium acerba cinis' (68. 89 f. 'Troy, oh horror, the common burial-ground of Asia and Europe, Troy the untimely dust of all true men and manhood'). Greek elegiac poetry was never as personal or as deeply felt.

Catullus' most ambitious work is the 'Wedding of Peleus and Thetis' (64), a poem in the hexameters of epic, but in accordance with neoteric principles lasting only for 400 lines. He begins with the wondrous voyage of the first ship Argo 'Phasidos ad fluctus et fines Aeeteos' (2 'to the floods of Phasis and the realm of Aeetes'); the exotic proper names and the slow quadrisyllabic line-ending already suggest the poem's languorous beauty. 'As soon as the ship ploughed the windy plain with her beak and churned by the oars the wave whitened with spume, there emerged strange faces from the shining deep, the Nereids of Ocean marvelling at the apparition. In that and no other dawn mortals saw with their own eyes nymphs with bared bodies protruding to their breasts from the white deep' (64. 12 ff.). Such was the first encounter of the mortal Argonaut Peleus with the divine sea-nymph Thetis, and the rest of the poem depicts the celebration of their wedding. Pindar says that Peleus then achieved the highest happiness known to mortals, but even he was doomed to sorrow: the child of the marriage, Achilles, was to die young at Troy. Catullus' poem cannot be understood unless we remember both the supreme felicity of the occasion and the implicit undercurrent of sadness.

After recording the arrival of the guests, Catullus turns to the splendours of the scene, in particular a tapestry on the bed that depicted the story of Theseus and Ariadne (50 ff.). First we see a windswept heroine on the shore of Naxos as she gazes out to sea at her departing lover. Then a flashback describes how she had first met Theseus and how he had slain the Minotaur. Then we return to Naxos and hear an emotional soliloquy from Ariadne on her lover's forgetfulness. Next comes a projection of Theseus' return to Athens: he had forgotten to signal his victory by hoisting white sails, an arrangement expounded in another flashback, so his father Aegeus jumped over a cliff. Then back to Naxos again, where Bacchus approaches Ariadne with his outlandish revellers. The happy ending is hinted at rather than stated: every literate person knew that the god would marry the heroine and translate her to the sky.

The presentation of this digression illustrates important characteristics of the Neoteric poets and their Hellenistic predecessors. The dislocations of chronological order show a lack of interest in story-telling for its own sake: organic unity of action now matters less than the effects of diversity and surprise, and the aesthetic balance of the composition as a whole. The significant moments are caught in a series of colourful tableaux which suggest the influence of a pictorial art that was romantic in conception and ultra-realistic in execution. The love interest is neither Homeric nor traditionally Roman but derives from the psychologizing of some Hellenistic poets, especially Apollonius in his *Argonautica*: so too the attempt of a male-dominated world to enter into a rejected woman's feelings, an approach that went back to the *Medea* of Euripides and was to influence Virgil's portrayal of Dido. The sheer length of the episode may seem curious (it takes up more than half the piece), but such digressions were regular in poems of this type. Nor need we speak of irrelevance unless we apply inappropriate criteria: in ancient poetry descriptions of works of art often include elements that foreshadow something in the main action, and Ariadne's change from misery to happiness, while it reverses the movement of the poem as a whole, underlines the vicissitudes of human experience.

The action resumes with the departure of the wedding guests, which is described in a simile which no earlier Roman poet could have written:

> hic, qualis flatu placidum mare matutino
> horrificans Zephyrus procliuas incitat undas,
> Aurora exoriente, uagi sub limina Solis,
> quae tarde primum clementi flamine pulsae
> procedunt, leuiterque sonant plangore cachinni,
> post uento crescente magis magis increbescunt,
> purpureaque procul nantes ab luce refulgent.
>
> (269–75)

Then just as the West Wind ruffles the calm sea with morning breath, and sets the waves rolling, as dawn rises, towards the portals of the roving sun, and driven by the gentle breeze they proceed slowly at first, and their ripples sound with a soft plash; then, as the wind freshens, they crowd thicker and faster, and as they float along, shimmer afar with the purple light.

The comparison primarily illustrates how a trickle of departing guests develops into a flood, and nobody who has taken in the poet's words will forget them on such occasions. But there are other points of correspondence: 'cachinni' suggests the guests' merry babble, 'purpurea' their fine clothes, 'nantes' their undulating movement. The luminosity of the passage is typical of the poem as a whole: Catullus has imitated the more glittering aspect of Hellenistic poetry and given it a delightfully new colour and freshness.

As the poem draws towards its close it appropriately includes an epithalamium, which is sung not by a choir of young girls (the usual practice), or by the Muses (as in Pindar's account of this particular wedding), but by those grisly spinstresses, the Fates. Their chant begins normally enough with a mention of the Evening Star, a commendation of wedded bliss, and an annunciation of the child of the marriage. But the prophecy of Achilles gradually assumes a sinister note: 'his surpassing merits and glorious deeds mothers will often acknowledge at the funerals of their sons, when they let fall dishevelled hair from grey heads and bruise withered breasts with palsied palms. Run, drawing the threads, run, spindles' (348 ff.). And to remove all doubt about the poet's stance, they predict that Achilles' tomb will be honoured by the sacrifice of a girl. The poet's revulsion at these barbaric deeds is all the more effective for the matter-of-fact way in which they are presented. The poem's limpid beauty, which suited so well the lost age of innocence, now takes on a characteristically ironic note: just as in some of the love poems, the subject-matter and the style have begun to pull in opposite directions.

In spite of their very different subjects, Lucretius and Catullus have much in common. Both are recognizably poets of the Republic, and can describe intellectual or emotional adventures with a candour difficult in later periods. Both write Latin with an elegant propriety that is sometimes lost in the subtleties of the Augustans. Both observe the world with an uncluttered directness that had been unknown for centuries, and was never quite recovered in antiquity. Lucretius' awareness of beauty shows the influence of the new poetry, and some of Catullus' descriptions are modelled on Lucretius. But though the Neoteric movement refined techniques and enlarged sensibilities, its effect on literature was not all good. When art is pursued for art's sake, there is a danger of forgetting the nature of things.

Further Reading

LUCRETIUS

The best way of finding what Lucretius was like is to buy M. F. Smith's revision (Cambridge, Mass., 1975), including text and translation, of W. H. D. Rouse's Loeb edition. The standard commentary is by C. Bailey (3 vols., Oxford, 1947, including text and translation); this is particularly informative on the Epicurean background, but is long for non-specialists. There is a good short commentary on Book III by E. J. Kenney (Cambridge, 1971).

E. J. Kenney has summarized the issues in a very useful pamphlet (*Lucretius*. Greece & Rome New Surveys in the Classics, no. 11, Oxford, 1977). D. West, *The Imagery and Poetry of Lucretius* (Edinburgh, 1969) encourages the reader to look closely at the Latin, and should be compulsory reading for all who wish to understand any Roman poetry. D. R. Dudley, *Lucretius* (London, 1965), includes articles of varying interest by different hands. P. Boyancé, *Lucrèce et l'épicurisme* (Paris, 1963), is a specialized account of the philosophy of the poem.

CATULLUS

The best introduction is G. P. Goold, *Catullus* (London, 1983); this contains a text that is more radical than most, and a facing translation that is both literal and literary. The best English commentary is by C. J. Fordyce (Oxford, 1961, revised 1973); this includes Mynors's Oxford text except for a number of poems that have been expurgated. The commentary by K. Quinn (London, 1970), which contains all the poems, is better on bibliography but less good on Latin.

A. L. Wheeler, *Catullus and the Traditions of Ancient Poetry* (Berkeley and Los Angeles, 1934) is full and informative, but old-fashioned in manner and some of its matter. K. Quinn, *The Catullan Revolution* (Melbourne, 1959; Cambridge, 1969) covers less ground but will appeal more to the literary reader. Perceptive criticism may be found in the relevant chapters of R. O. A. M. Lyne, *The Latin Love Poets from Catullus to Horace* (Oxford, 1980) and R. Jenkyns, *Three Classical Poets/Sappho, Catullus and Juvenal* (London, 1983); the latter helps the reader to appreciate the beauty of the poet's words. T. P. Wiseman, *Catullus and his World* (Cambridge, 1985) gives an expert and very readable account of the social and political background.

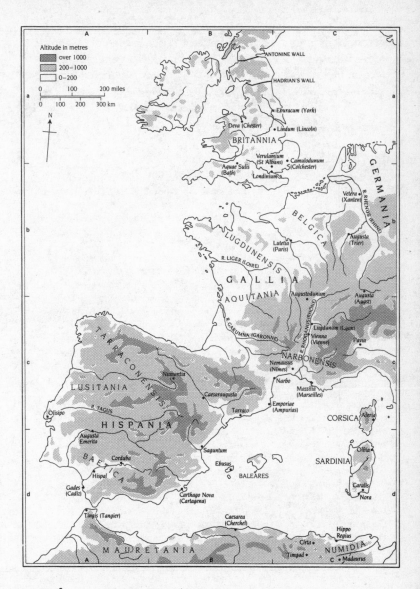

Altitude in metres
over 1000
200–1000
0–200

0   100   200 miles
0 100 200 300 km

N

A   B   C

ANTONINE WALL
HADRIAN'S WALL

Eburacum (York)
Deva (Chester) Lindum (Lincoln)
BRITANNIA
Verulamium Camulodunum
(St Albans) (Colchester)
Aquae Sulis
(Bath)
Londinium
GERMANIA

Vetera
(Xanten)
R. RHENUS (RHINE)
BELGICA
Lutetia Augusta
(Paris) (Trier)
LUGDUNENSIS
R. LIGER (LOIRE)
GALLIA
AQUITANIA Augustodunum Augusta
(Augst)
R. GARUMNA (GARONNE) Lugdunum (Lyon)
Vienna
(Vienne) Pavia
R. RHODANUS (RHONE)
NARBONENSIS
Nemausus
(Nîmes)
Narbo
Massilia ALeria
(Marseilles)
Emporiae CORSICA
(Ampurias)
TARRACONENSIS
Numantia
Caesaraugusta SARDINIA
LUSITANIA Tarraco Olbia
Olisipo
R. TAGUS
HISPANIA
Saguntum
Augusta
Emerita Corduba
Ebusus Caralis
BAETICA Hispal BALEARES Nora
Gades
(Cadiz) Carthago Nova
(Cartagena)
Tingis (Tangier)
Caesarea
(Cherchel)
Hippo
Regius
MAURETANIA Cirta NUMIDIA
Timgad Madaurus
A   B   C

MAP 3. THE ROMAN EMPIRE (WESTERN PROVINCES)

Altitude in metres
over 1000
200–1000
0–200

| 0 | 100 | 200 | 300 miles |

| 0 | 100 | 200 | 300 | 400 | 500 km |

Map labels:

RAETIA
NORICUM
PANNONIA
ILLYRICUM
DACIA
MOESIA
THRACIA
MACEDONIA
EPIRUS
ACHAEA
DALMATIA
ITALIA
BYZACENA
AFRICA
TRIPOLITANIA
CYRENAICA
LIBYA
SICILIA
CRETE
LESBOS
CHIOS
SAMOS

Augusta (Augsburg)
Carnuntum
Aquincum (Budapest)
Aquileia
Pavia
Arretium
Ancona
Salonae (Split)
Drobeta
R. DANUBE
Adamklissi
Perusia
Rome
Capua
Brundisium
Tarentum
Thessalonica
Doriscus
Pergamum
Thebes
Corinth
Athens
Sparta
Messana
Catana
Syracuse
Agrigentum
SICILIA
Carthage
Hadrumetum
Thapsus
MELITA (MALTA)
Sabratha
Oea
Leptis Magna
Ptolemais
Apollonia
Berenice (Benghazi)
Barca
Cyrene

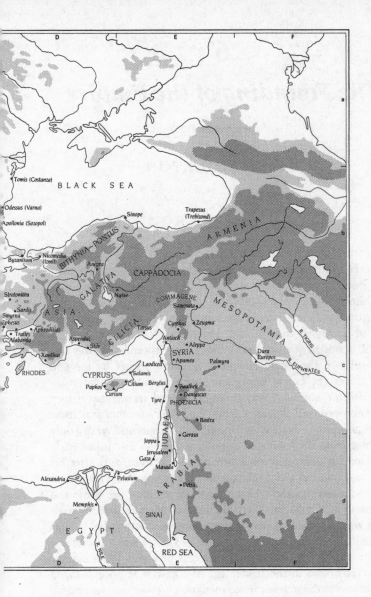

MAP 3. THE ROMAN EMPIRE (CENTRAL AND EASTERN PROVINCES)

6

The Founding of the Empire

DAVID STOCKTON

THE future Emperor Augustus was born at Rome in September 63 BC. His father, Gaius Octavius, held a praetorship two years later, but any hopes there may have been of a consulship died with him in 58 BC. The Octavii of Velitrae were well-to-do, but hitherto of only equestrian standing, and Octavius' wife Atia came of no higher than modest senatorial stock on her father's side; it is not surprising that a story later spread that the destined ruler of the world had been fathered on her by the god Apollo. Yet the boy's 'bourgeois' pedigree was singularly appropriate for one who was to engineer and secure the victory of the non-political classes of Italy. And Atia's mother was sister to Gaius Julius Caesar, who himself had no son and whose only daughter Julia died without surviving issue in 54. Julius early discerned his great-nephew's precocious promise, and after his death in 44 BC his will disclosed that the young Octavius was to be his adopted son and so keep alive the name of the noble and patrician Julii Caesares. Marcus Antonius sneered that his challenger was 'a mere boy, owing everything to a name', but he was only half right: the magic of the name of Caesar was a necessary, but not a sufficient, cause of the success of Gaius Julius Caesar Octavianus, who at the tender age of eighteen at once plunged head first into the maelstrom of intrigue and war that swirled all over the Mediterranean world.

By 30 BC, still little over thirty years old, Octavian had eliminated the last and most formidable of his rivals and, like his adoptive father before him, bestrode that world 'like a Colossus'. But this new Colossus did not have feet of clay. Julius had survived barely six months after his return to Rome from his final victory in Spain before he lay murdered beneath the statue of his great opponent Pompey. His assassins (they preferred the name of 'liberators') were an ill-assorted collection of ex-Pompeians, 'Republicans', and prominent adherents of the dictator himself, united by a shared fear or abhorrence of Julius' openly despotic authority. The new Caesar, in stark contrast, survived his own final victory at Actium by nearly half a century, and when he died in his bed in his seventy-sixth year he bequeathed to Rome and Italy and the Empire not civil war and insecurity, but that stable and durable system of government that we call the 'Principate'.

The Second Triumvirate

'If Caesar, for all his genius, could not find a way out, who is going to find one now?' The bleak pessimism of Julius Caesar's old friend Gaius Matius proved amply justified, for it was to be over thirteen years before the Roman world was delivered from disruption and uncertainty, pillage and slaughter, near-anarchy and the ever-present threat of disintegration, years in which the rule of law was set aside and justice was merely 'the interest of the stronger'.

Caesar's assassins, as Cicero saw at once, had been ingenuous in their hope that with his death 'normality' would return. Marcus Antonius soon gained control of the situation in Italy. Cicero's own cynically clever attempt to use Octavian against Antony and so divide the Caesarians against themselves backfired, and by the autumn of 43 Antony and Octavian and Marcus Aemilius Lepidus with his Gallic legions had reached the sensible conclusion that they must all hang together or all hang separately. The 'Second Triumvirate' which resulted was a three-

man legal dictatorship for five years; and Cicero's head was one
of the earliest to roll when the first proscription since Sulla's
day issued the death-warrants of some 300 senators and 2,000
knights, as the new masters of Rome sought security and a war-
chest. Leaving Lepidus to hold Italy, Antony and Octavian
moved to crush the only challenge to their dominance, and in
October 42 the last 'republican' leaders, Brutus and Cassius,
perished in defeat at Philippi in Macedonia.

While Antony left to set the East to rights, Octavian was
saddled with the unenviable task of finding land in Italy on
which to settle about 100,000 discharged triumviral soldiers.
Virgil's First *Eclogue* (below, pp. 246 f.) affords a glimpse of the
misery of the dispossessed, driven from their holdings to penury
and bitter exile. Antony's wife Fulvia and his brother Lucius
(consul 41 BC) tried to exploit Octavian's unpopularity, but were
briskly driven from Rome and starved into surrender at Perugia.
When Antony himself returned, a fresh civil war threatened, but
the legions had had enough of fighting each other, and the
diplomacy of Maecenas and Asinius Pollio patched together the
so-called 'Treaty of Brundisium' in October 40 BC. Lepidus was
fobbed off with Africa, and Antony, before returning to the East,
was married to Octavian's sister Octavia. The feeling of relief
produced by this reconciliation of the dynasts and the
widespread longing for a settled peace are perhaps mirrored in
Virgil's Fourth *Eclogue* (below, pp. 249 f.) with its vision of the
new Age of Gold that seemed about to dawn.

Such hopes quickly died. Pompey's son Sextus won naval
dominance in the western and central Mediterranean, and his
threat to the corn-routes compelled concessions—a five-year
proconsular command in Corsica, Sardinia, Sicily, and Greece.
But once Marcus Agrippa had secured Gaul for Octavian,
Sextus' days were numbered. After yet another open clash
between Antony and Octavian had been narrowly averted,
Octavian and Agrippa (who had built and trained a fleet out of
nothing) and Lepidus from Africa regained Sicily and destroyed
Sextus and his huge navy off Naulochus in north-west Sicily

(September 36 BC). A year earlier the tenure of the triumvirs had been retrospectively renewed for a further five years, but the three were now quickly reduced to two: Lepidus, with twenty-two legions at his back in Sicily, threw down the gauntlet in a bid for a larger share of the spoils, but his troops were not ready to shed more blood for him and preferred Octavian. Though his life was spared, Lepidus was stripped of his triumviral powers. The stage was now set for the final and decisive clash between the master of the West and the master of the East.

From 41 BC onwards Antony had had plenty of work to do. The northern marches of Macedonia had first to be secured against invaders; thereafter the Parthians never ceased to threaten Asia Minor and the Levant, where Rome's subjects were bled white by his heavy financial demands. He became increasingly dependent on the wealth of Egypt and on its Queen Cleopatra. In 37 he packed a pregnant Octavia off back to Italy, and shortly afterwards publicly acknowledged his twin children by Cleopatra, who was herself dreaming of recreating the great empire of her Ptolemaic ancestors. In the autumn of 34 he provocatively proclaimed Cleopatra's son Caesarion to be the legitimate issue of Julius Caesar, and much of the East was parcelled out to Caesarion and his mother, 'King of Kings' and 'Queen of Kings', and to his own two children by Cleopatra.

That gave Octavian a chance too good to miss: Antony could now be caricatured as a renegade apostate from the great traditions of Rome, the creature of an Egyptian she-devil. The Triumvirate was not renewed when it expired at the end of 33; Antony retained the title and claimed the powers, but Octavian eschewed both, posing as no more than the universally desiderated champion of the ordered West. Antony was enormously powerful in ships and men and money, for he 'held the East in fee': his splendid general Ventidius Bassus had driven the Parthians back over the Euphrates in 39, and in 34 Armenia briefly became a province of Rome. But he could not invade Italy as the consort and champion of the 'scarlet woman'. He planned to lure Octavian to defeat in north-west Greece, but, outguessed and outmanœuvred by Agrippa, he was beaten at sea off Actium in September 31, and escaped to Egypt with Cleopatra, leaving his massive, but leaderless, forces to surrender. By the summer of 30 Octavian was in Egypt, closing in for the kill. Antony took his own life, falsely believing Cleopatra to be dead, and died in her arms: she herself was taken prisoner, but preferred the deifying bite of an asp to the humiliation of being led in a Roman triumph. Two decades of civil war had at last come to an end. It remained to be seen if the new Caesar could find that way out which had eluded the old.

The Augustan Constitution

For three years or so after Actium Octavian's rule was essentially of a personal and irregular nature. He took care not to formalize his ascendancy and used this breathing space to tidy up loose ends in readiness for his first constitutional settlement in 28/7 BC, when he surrendered his supremacy and formally restored the government to Senate and People. As he himself expressed it later in his *Res Gestae* (34), the autobiographical inscription which he directed to be erected outside his mausoleum in the Campus Martius where the citizens could read and admire what their great leader had done for the Roman commons:

In my sixth and seventh consulships [28/7 BC], after I had stamped out the civil wars, and at a time when by universal consent I was in absolute control of everything, I transferred the *res publica* from my own charge ('ex mea potestate') to the discretion of the Senate and People of Rome. For this service I was given the name 'Augustus' by a decree of the Senate.

The Augustan Age had begun, and the quintessential character of the Augustan Principate was determined. The *princeps*, the 'first man' of the Roman Commonwealth, was to have no institutionalized authoritarian power, no perpetual dictatorship such as Julius Caesar had had himself voted early in 44, or anything like it. From Senate and People he accepted the charge of

Gaul, Spain, Syria, and Egypt, where the great bulk of the legions was stationed and which he could govern in absence through successive deputies chosen by, and immediately subordinate, to, himself. At Rome his overt authority rested on his repeated tenure of one of the two annual consulships, while his enormous personal wealth, patronage, influence, prestige, and diplomatic and political skills could be counted on to plug any gaps and to oil the wheels of government, and friends and confidants—most notably Agrippa and Maecenas—shared the burden of administration and policy-making.

Some four years later, in 23, after recovering from a near-fatal illness, Augustus resigned his consulship. (He was consul twice later, in 5 and in 2 BC, but on both occasions for only part of the year.) In its place he was voted tribunician power for life, and his command (*imperium*) as proconsul and governor of the 'imperial' provinces was specifically declared superior (*maius*) to that of any governor of a non-imperial or 'public' province. These changes and the reasons behind them have occasioned much argument: they were probably influenced both by the practical experience of the working of the earlier settlement and by certain dimly detectable, but elusive, stirrings in a section of the ruling aristocracy and even among his own leading supporters. Some have judged the revisions of 23 as constituting a tactical withdrawal by Augustus, to be balanced by a new advance in 19 with the grant to him in that year of the consular power for life. (His provinces were always voted him for set periods and renewed at ten- or five-year intervals.) Others see the grant in 19 as one merely of outward trappings and appearances rather than of any substance of power. In the long-term perspective it hardly matters which view one takes. Augustus had consular *imperium* from 28/7 BC until the day he died, either as consul or as proconsul. After 23 his *imperium* was not only explicitly superior to that of any other pro-magistrate, but also exercisable within Rome itself; and in that year he had received, not only a life tenure of the tribunician power with its wide discretion to veto the administrative and legislative acts of

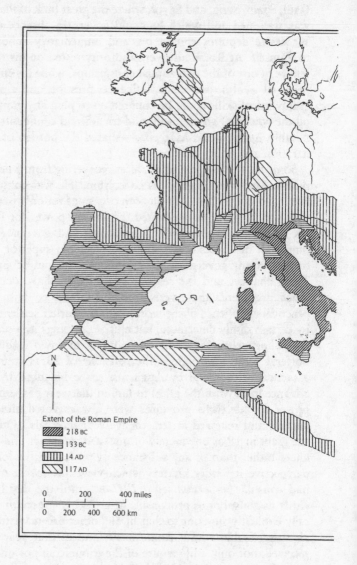

Extent of the Roman Empire

- 218 BC
- 133 BC
- 14 AD
- 117 AD

N

0   200   400 miles

0   200   400   600 km

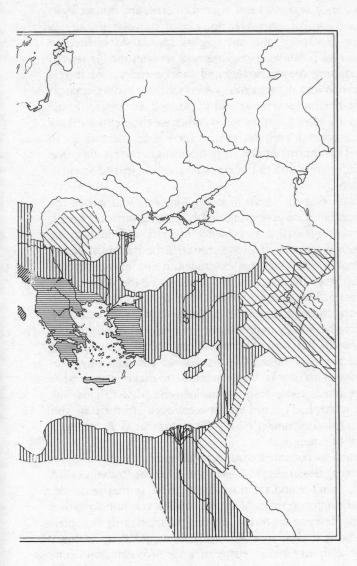

MAP 4. THE GROWTH OF ROMAN RULE

others, succour aggrieved and injured citizens, and initiate legislation in the tribal assembly, but also a consular priority in
convening the Senate and ordering its agenda. Moreover, we
later find him conducting censuses and revising the Senate-roll
and appointing commissioners and superintendents of several
new metropolitan departments. Given all that, his pre-eminent
and wide-ranging powers at and in, as well as outside, Rome
were and are plain for all to see, whether we choose to attribute
them to a general 'consular power' for life or alternatively to
piecemeal enactments empowering Augustus to use his *imperium*
in particular areas and to the gradual establishment of accepted
conventions.

It is plain that the *ciuilis princeps* Augustus understood the
great importance of preserving and respecting outward forms,
whether we regard this as evidence of craft and duplicity or
of tact and diplomacy. To have 'restored the Republic' in any
literal sense would have been misguided, if not impossible, and
as damaging to the loyalties and interests of the mass of the
inhabitants of Italy and the Empire as to any personal ambition
of Augustus himself. To have established an overt autocracy
would have been to fly in the face of five centuries of history and
discard much that was of immense psychological significance
and solid practical value. Augustus chose a middle way, preferring (one of his own favourite maxims) 'to make haste slowly'.
He appreciated, consciously or instinctively, that to close the
wide rift which had opened up between loyalty to the state and
loyalty to the government must call not just for skill, but for a
great deal of patience.

'Res publica' connoted constitutional government, the operation of recognized rules, as opposed to what the Romans called
'regnum', absolute and arbitrary domination. In that sense, the
claim that Augustus 'restored the *res publica*' was not altogether
hollow. By defining his formal powers, he necessarily delimited
them, making it clear in which areas he would exercise direct
and open authority and in virtue of what precedents and conventions; simultaneously, he advertised in which areas he did

not seek to exercise open authority. There were going to be rules, and the rules themselves were not new. Stable government and long-term policies demanded that he free himself effectively from those two fetters with which the Republican nobility had sought to restrain overgreat ambition: collegiality and limitation of tenure of powers. In practice, Augustus had no colleagues with equal power save for Agrippa and Tiberius, whom he himself chose to be his destined successors; and all his formal powers were his for life, although some—his provinces, for example—were renewed periodically, while others—like his influence over elections and his control of public finance—burgeoned gradually with the development of convention and interpretation. Augustus had come to power young, and time was on his side. Even in 23 BC, nobody much under sixty had been even a freshman member of the pre-Caesarian Senate; by AD 14 a man had to be over sixty even to have been born before Caesar crossed the Rubicon.

None of the foregoing is to be taken to imply that the sheer power of Augustus—his immense patronage, his 'party' following, his stupendous wealth, his control of the army—was not the ultimate guarantee of the stability of his new order. Had any rival been able to use the army against him, his formal prerogatives would have been of little or no avail. But in civilized societies rule is more than the possession of the biggest club to hit people on the head with. We do not take it amiss that modern governments can count on the loyalty and obedience of their military and police forces: it would be a sorry state of affairs if they could not. What worries us is the spectacle of a government which uses army and police to dominate a populace which otherwise would not tolerate it. There is no evidence at all that that was true of Augustus' government; quite the contrary, since we have good reason to believe that, apart from a very few ambitious men whose notions of what constituted 'liberty' were anything but egalitarian or democratic, the mass of the inhabitants of Italy and the Empire welcomed the peace and stability, material prosperity, and increased administrative efficiency which came with the Principate. Augustus took the army out of politics; but we may legitimately question whether his security and that of his regime would have been very long lived had he not also done much to remedy actual or potential social and economic distress and disaffection. For all its ambiguities, Augustus devised a system far more acceptable than the autocracies and anarchies which were the only practical alternatives. It was his achievement that what the Elder Pliny was to call 'the immense majesty of the Roman peace' gave to the Roman world a freedom from war and the fear of war unmatched in its duration, and that freedom under the law, one of the ideals of classical Greece and republican Rome, was still an ideal of the Principate; it grew gradually more remote, but survived to be transmitted to modern Europe. Thus, when the Emperor Claudius wanted to marry his own niece, he did not assume that he was above the law, but had the law changed so that any man could do the same: the distinction may appear slight, but on reflection can be seen to be of profound significance.

It was once accepted that one could talk of a 'dyarchy', a system in which power and executive responsibility were shared between two parties, *princeps* and Senate. That is now frowned upon, but it was certainly long accepted as the principle behind Augustus' new order. In his 'programme speech' to the Senate on his accession in AD 54, the young Nero declared his intention of abandoning the centralizing practices of his predecessor Claudius and returning to the true Augustan pattern:

he would not set himself up to be the judge in every case or issue, for a powerful few to grow fat behind the closed doors of one man's home at the expense of prosecutors and defendants alike; nothing in his household would be bought by money or open to intrigue; his private self and his public self would be kept quite separate from each other. The Senate would keep its traditional prerogatives, Italy and the public provinces should take their stand before the tribunals of the consuls, who would bring their business before the Senate for a hearing; he, the Emperor, would answer for the armies entrusted to his care. (Tacitus, *Annals* 13. 4)

And earlier Augustus' immediate successor, Tiberius, had been quite explicit about the Senate's role:

I say now what I have said often before on other occasions, conscript fathers: a good and healthful *princeps*, whom you have invested with such great discretionary power, ought to be the servant of the Senate, and often of the whole citizen body, sometimes even of individuals. Nor do I regret having said this; I have found you, and I still find you, good and fair and kind masters. (Suetonius, *Tiberius* 29)

It is indicative of a very important change in attitude that, while both Augustus and Tiberius are on record as having steadfastly refused to allow themselves to be addressed as 'dominus' ('master'), by Trajan's day at latest 'dominus' had become the customary form of addressing the *princeps*, as can be seen from Pliny's letters to that Emperor.

Between appearance and reality there was, however, a great gulf set. Although Augustus owed his formal powers to the granting of Senate and People, powers theoretically and constitutionally revocable by their grantors, Senate and People had in fact simply 'rubber-stamped' Augustus' own wishes, public opposition to which would have been, to say the least, ill-advised. It was only in the most trivial sense that Senate or People had invested Tiberius with 'such great discretionary power': his adoptive father had ensured that there could be no genuine alternative. Gaius (Caligula), Claudius, and Nero—all three total strangers to the long and distinguished record of public service and high responsibilities of which Tiberius could be proud on his accession—owed their elevation to factors over which the Senate had no control, and were duly voted *en bloc* the ever-growing powers and prerogatives which went with the office of *princeps*. Thus it is no surprise to find the Senate, during the confused power struggle that followed Nero's demise, tamely decreeing 'all the customary prerogatives of the *princeps*' to each usurper in turn, nor Vespasian preferring to date his reign from the day six months earlier when he had been saluted as 'imperator' by the legions at Alexandria.

The Emperor and the Senate

The organization of Rome's military forces under the Principate and their deployment, the growth and structure of an 'imperial secretariat' of equestrian officials and slave and freedman servants of the imperial household, the administration of the provinces and the consolidation and extension of Rome's imperial domains, and the spread of the rights and opportunities of Roman citizenship beyond the limits of Italy itself, all fall to be treated in Chapter 22. Here it must suffice to stress that in all these areas Augustus laid the solid foundations on which his successors were to build. But in the end all roads led to Rome, where by the time of Augustus' death new attitudes and expectations had become established. Ever since 5 BC, when Augustus was again consul after a gap of almost twenty years, with the names of a Caesar and a Sulla adding lustre to the date, there had been four consuls in nearly every year, holding office as successive pairs, a scheme regularly followed thereafter. This can be taken to mark the definitive 'arrival', a generation after Actium, of the 'new Italians' and the steepening decline of the old republican nobility. By now the overriding influence of the *princeps* on the choice of the highest magistrates was accepted, and in practice inevitable. It was from among ex-praetors and ex-consuls that he was constrained to select his provincial governors and legionary legates, senatorial curators and prefects, so that no *princeps* could fail to be vitally concerned about the stocking of the pool in which he must fish. Direct appointment to public magistracies was neither politic nor necessary: lip-service could be paid to constitutional forms while indirect methods and the *princeps*'s public and private support did their work—though in the less deftly sure hands of a Tiberius the legerdemain lacked conviction. Tiberius indeed effectively transferred elections to the Senate in AD 15, leaving to the popular assemblies a mere ceremonial role. But those assemblies had by then lost any effective role even in legislation, which became in practice the field of senatorial decrees and imperial edicts, rescripts, and constitutions. The free inhabitants of Rome and its immediate environs had long ceased to constitute a representative cross-section of Rome's widely scattered citizens; and among the consequences of this eclipse was a diminution of extravagant electoral expenditure and a decline in the influence of the political element among the *equites*. The latter also suffered from judicial changes, for before Augustus died cases of political importance had come regularly to be heard by the Senate sitting as a high court, instead of by the mixed courts of the late Republic and of the first part of his reign, while by Claudius' time the supreme and independent jurisdiction of the *princeps* had come to be exercised frequently.

The *de facto* subordination of the Senate itself was exposed in its helpless nakedness when an ageing Tiberius removed himself from Rome to Campania and then to Capri for the second half of his reign and ruled the world through his letters and the agents of his will. In the early books of his *Annals* Tacitus often underlines and castigates the servility, and even sycophancy, of the members of the Senate. Lacking as they did the hereditary self-contained power-bases of later European nobles or any formidable 'constituencies', hopelessly outgunned by the power and patronage of the Emperors themselves, and acutely aware that any 'dyarchy' was no more than a convenient fiction, they chose the line of least resistance. Yet what other possible counterweight could men see to the potential or actual misuse or abuse of the imperial prerogatives? The Senate enjoyed an important place in the constitution, and had gained a new role as a high court of justice; it handled much business of a routine nature from Italy and the public provinces; it numbered in its ranks nearly all the highest officers of state, as well as their recent predecessors and expected successors, not to speak of the great 'friends' (*amici principis*) who had the ear and the confidence of the Emperor; it had behind it half a millennium of independent history as Rome's great council of state and of imperial success. It is then not hard to appreciate that it remained a focus of opposition dreams, even when criticism of a *princeps* had to be whispered 'at private parties and in intimate gatherings' (Tacitus, *Annals* 3.54), or the repository of the hopes of independents like Thrasea Paetus in the early years of Nero, until men finally reconciled themselves to the 'futility of long speeches in the Senate, when the best men were quick to reach agreement elsewhere, and of endless haranguing of public meetings, when the final decisions were taken not by the ignorant multitude but by one man' (Tacitus, *Dialogus* 41). For all that, the Empire relied chiefly on senators to run it, and so no Emperor could be really secure unless his rule was founded on their consent or acquiescence. The Senate never lost its *esprit de corps*, and there was hostility to Emperors who were thought to abuse their great powers. As Tacitus expressed what was surely his own philosophy,

There can be great men even under bad emperors, and duty and discretion, if coupled with energy of character and a career of action, will bring a man to no less glorious summits than are attained by perilous paths and ostentatious deaths, with no advantage to the Commonwealth. (*Agricola* 42)

It may be that the weakness of the Senate went beyond what Augustus had desired. On more than one occasion, he tried to reduce its size to a really effective level, but in the end retired baffled from the task. He was probably well aware of the danger of distancing himself too far from average upper-class opinion. In the late Republic, the leading politicians had relied on informal 'cabinets' of friends and associates for discussion of policy and practicalities, and thus the constantly changing mosaic of politics had ensured a variety of experience and involvement not automatically guaranteed by the Augustan system. At some time before 4 BC Augustus had instituted a committee (*consilium semenstre*) made up of the consuls in office plus one each of the other magistrates and fifteen other senators selected by lot, serving for periods of six months, to help the *princeps* to prepare business for the Senate. Its random membership and relative informality should have made it a useful sounding-board; but its nature and composition changed significantly in the last year of his life, and it came to an end with Tiberius' withdrawal from Rome in AD 26. Of course, Augustus had always had an intimate circle of 'friends' and supporters (most of them senators, but including also *equites* such as Maecenas and Sallustius Crispus) whose advice and judgement and experience he valued—and needed, for 'no man is an island, entire of itself'—and with whom he could discuss in confidence the most sensitive and important issues and options; and this less institutionalized body continued under his successors. Outside Italy Tiberius was ready to devolve wide areas of delegated discretion and initiative for very long periods: the outstanding example was Poppaeus Sabinus who was left as virtual viceroy of the Balkans from AD 11 until his death in 35. But Tiberius was exceptional, and Poppaeus surely sometimes came back to Italy for leave and consultations.

The Emperor and the Gods

When M. Aemilius Lepidus, the erstwhile triumviral colleague of Octavian and Antony, long retired from public life, finally died in 12 BC, Augustus was elected to succeed him as Rome's Chief Pontiff (*pontifex maximus*), an office which now took its place among the imperial prerogatives. His election was the occasion for a massive demonstration of popular support, and this formal position as 'head of the national church' sat well with his programme of regeneration of traditional religion and morality. Already the very name 'Augustus' with its 'by the grace of God' overtones had marked him out as somewhat larger than life-size; and in 2 BC he was formally accorded the title of 'Father of the Fatherland' (*pater patriae*). Official deification had to await his death, but from very early days he had advertised that he was 'divi filius', the son of the deified Julius Caesar. For Virgil's Tityrus (*Eclogues* 1.7–8), 'He will always be a god, often will a tender lamb from my flock be sacrificed at his altar'; and for Horace (*Odes* 3.5.2–4), 'Augustus will be held to be a god here on earth with the addition to the empire of Britain and Persia.' The cult of his guardian spirit, his *genius* or *numen*, became established in many western municipalities, temples were set up in most provinces to 'Rome and Augustus', and oaths were regularly taken in his name. At Rome itself the splendid Altar of Augustan Peace (well worth seeing in its modern reconstructed form) portrayed the 'royal family' in simple and awesome majesty (below, pp. 422 f.). Nevertheless, there was a line which could not be overstepped, and the living Augustus was never formally and explicitly a god in Italy and the West. Things were different elsewhere: in Egypt he was as divine as the Pharaohs had been, and an inscription (*ILS* 8781) from Gangra in Paphlagonia preserves an oath of total and unreflecting devotion and loyalty to Augustus and his descendants which was taken in 3 BC 'at the altars of Augustus in the temples of Augustus' by all the inhabitants of the region (including resident Roman citizens), an oath in which Augustus is named along with 'all the gods and goddesses' as a guarantor of the oath and of the dreadful penalties for betraying it.

By and large, Augustus' policy was followed by his Julio-Claudian successors, although neither Tiberius nor Gaius nor Nero was posthumously deified. Tiberius indeed seems to have entertained a sceptic's distaste for such matters; but a temple to the living god Claudius was early established at Camulodunum in the new province of Britain (he had to wait for Vespasian's accession for a temple at Rome itself), and Gaius notoriously came to have exaggerated notions of personal divinity. Vespasian could take it all in his common-sense stride: as he lay dying, he blandly observed, 'My goodness, I think I am turning into a god!' He was right, as usual, and like subsequent Emperors whose memory was not officially damned he duly became 'divus'.

Augustus took pains to restore the gods, and especially the old deities of Rome and Italy, to their pre-eminent place in public life. Many decayed or dilapidated temples and shrines were rebuilt, many traditional rites and ceremonies renewed or reinvigorated. He aimed to restore public confidence in divine providence, duty to fatherland, and a secure sense of continuity and order and permanence. Yet here too the might and majesty of the *princeps* and his family were kept well in evidence. New temples of the Deified Julius, Mars the Avenger, Venus the Progenitress of the Julian line, and his own special patron Apollo enriched the capital; a temple and altar of Vesta, goddess of the sacred hearth of the commonwealth, actually formed part of his home on the Palatine; on his return to Rome from Greece and Asia in 19 BC an altar was dedicated to Fortune the Home-Bringer; vows were regularly offered to heaven for his safety, each new year and the various anniversaries of his birth and achievements were marked by solemn public prayers for his well-being and that of his family; throughout Rome his personal household tutelary spirit (*Lar*) was venerated in the various 'parish chapels' alongside the public *Lares Compitales*. The pomp and circumstance of the great priestly colleges (of all of which he was himself a member) were refurbished, and comparable institutions created and consolidated at lower levels of society. The glittering high-point was the magnificent celebration of the Secular Games in the summer of 17 BC, the tenth anniversary of the new order, a massive public thanksgiving for the past and present grandeur of Rome.

Domestic Policy

Hand in hand with this religious renaissance went a determination to restore that high moral seriousness and restraint which had, in pious memory or myth, assured the greatness of the old *res publica*. Sallust had not been the only man to incriminate and castigate, albeit over-ingenuously, the sad and steep decline from such sober standards as the root cause of the many and grave ills that had beset Rome in the febrile brilliance of the last generations of the Republic. However much we must allow for some measure of hypocrisy in this area, Augustus set a public example in the simplicity of his personal life-style, the modesty of his house on the Palatine and its furnishings (the austerity of

which later astonished Suetonius) in contrast with the splendour
of the public buildings with which he beautified Rome (below,
pp. 419 f.), and in his dress and table—a legacy, perhaps, of
his paternal ancestors and their solid municipal tradition at
Velitrae. Legislation was passed to visit severe penalties on
adultery, agents and accessories as well as the guilty parties
themselves. Marriage and the procreation of children to re-
stock the human wealth of Italy were encouraged by a blend
of 'stick and carrot', penalties for the celibate and rewards for
the philoprogenitive. Measures were taken to restrict ostentatious private extravagance and to check licence at public
shows. Historic noble names, some half-buried in the mists
of time, adorned the consulship (though the consulship was
not itself normally a preliminary to a great military command,
for Augustus prudently reserved such appointments in the provinces under his direct command to close relatives or 'new men'
in whose competence and loyalty he could trust). The public
dignity and display of the senatorial and equestrian orders were
actively promoted. The older and more respectable guilds were
encouraged, and Rome itself was organized in fourteen 'regions', subdivided in turn into 'districts' (*uici*) with their own
local officers (*uicomagistri*). The realization and exaltation of
a united Italy was nurtured with an ever-increasing number of
Italians entering the Senate and other levels of government service, civil and military, and a continuing move towards a greater
uniformity in municipal institutions. New building and traffic
regulations, a new Board of Public Works, the creation of a
Metropolitan Police Force and Fire Brigade, a Water Board to
ensure the needs of a city now approaching a million inhabitants, a Tiber Conservancy Board to dredge and embank the
river, and proper provision and supervision of the corn supply
are only the most noticeable of the benefits which could come
from a stable and effective government. Much of this spirit
and achievement of regeneration and progress is reflected in the
poetry of the period as well as in public architecture, statuary,
and inscriptions. Cicero had ruefully observed how most men at

all levels of society cared little about fighting despotism and valued above all else peace and stability in their lives; it is not surprising then to read in Tacitus (*Annals* 1.2) how Augustus contrived to seduce all and sundry with the sweet lure of tranquil security, and lead them to prefer the present and visible prosperity and security to the uncertain dangers of the old Republic, while the provinces too, where the power-struggle of the great at Rome and the greed of governors had destroyed any confidence in the institutions of the Republic, were no less ready to accept the tangible benefits of the new order.

The Problem of the Succession

A major question for Augustus to answer was how to provide for the continuity of his new order; for, as the event showed, he was concerned to do so, whether from altruistic motives or out of a sense of pride in his achievement or following the instinctive dynastic principles of a Roman noble. A formal hereditary succession was impossible, but it was not hard to associate a destined successor as a virtual vice-gerent and 'heir-presumptive' by having him voted the requisite offices and appointments, powers and dignities. His earliest choice seems to have lighted on M. Claudius Marcellus, only son of his sister Octavia, who was married in 25 BC to his only child, his daughter Julia, and in 24 marked out for more rapid acceleration up the ladder of office than Augustus' stepson Tiberius, who had been born in the same year (42 BC) as Marcellus. The obvious favour shown to his nephew/son-in-law may have occasioned some serious reactions, especially from his old and indispensable friend and general, M. Vipsanius Agrippa; but Marcellus' premature death in 23 removed that piece from the board. The immensely capable Agrippa now emerged as the obvious candidate; Augustus had handed him his personal signet-ring during his own grave illness in 23, and two years later he was married to the widowed Julia, who bore him three sons (Gaius and Lucius Caesar and Agrippa Postumus) and two daughters (Julia and Agrippina).

Entrusted in the same year with overall control of the eastern
half of the Empire, he moved subsequently to Gaul and then to
Spain, where he finally subdued the Cantabri. In 18 BC came the
grant of tribunician power for five years, followed by a renewal
for a further five years in 13, and his *imperium* was made either
superior (*maius*) like that of Augustus himself or at least equi-
potent (*aequum*) with that of all other provincial governors in
whichever part of the Empire his public duties might require
him to be.

Agrippa's death in 12 BC came as a surprise: he was only fifty,
and had been expected to outlive his exact coeval Augustus by
some years, for his robust health contrasted with Augustus'
somewhat delicate physique. His sons by Julia, Gaius and Lucius,
born in 20 and 17, had been adopted by their grandfather in the
latter year, but were still only children. So Augustus had to turn
to his thirty-year-old stepson Tiberius, requiring him to put
away his wife Vipsania (daughter of Agrippa by an earlier marriage) and marry the widowed Julia. In 6 BC Tiberius in turn was
granted tribunician power. But his marriage to the wayward and
imperious Julia was singularly loveless, and the one child of their
union, a boy, died in infancy; on top of that, it was clear that
Tiberius was cast as a stop-gap until Gaius and Lucius Caesar
should reach maturity. Whether through pride or apprehension
or calculation, Tiberius withdrew from public life to Rhodes—a
potentially risky move, but he probably counted on his formidable mother Livia, Augustus' wife, to keep him from serious
harm. Ill luck continued to dog Augustus: Lucius died at Marseilles in AD 2; and Gaius, consul for the whole year in AD 1 at
the age of nineteen and then sent on an important mission to the
East with experienced advisers to guide his early steps in high
responsibility, fell fatally ill in Lycia on his way home in February
AD 4. Two years before that, Tiberius had returned to Italy,
though not to public life. Now Augustus had to turn to him
again: there was no alternative, and he was himself already in
his middle sixties. Tiberius became Augustus' adopted son,
and received the tribunician power for ten years and an

imperium matching that of the *princeps* himself, both grants being subsequently renewed in AD 13.

Julia meanwhile had finally tried her father's patience too far and too often with her scandalous liaisons, and probably constituted a focus of attention for men with aspirations to become the ward and guardian of her young sons: expelled to the tiny island of Pandateria in 2 BC, she was allowed to return five years later only to the very tip of Italy at Rhegium, where she remained until her death in the early months of Tiberius' principate in an exile voluntarily shared by her mother, Augustus' first wife Scribonia. Still Augustus refused to relax his determination to secure the eventual succession of his own blood-line. Tiberius, who had a sixteen-year-old son, Drusus, by his first marriage, was required to adopt his eighteen-year-old nephew. Germanicus was the elder son of Tiberius' dead brother Drusus and Antonia Minor, younger daughter of Augustus' sister Octavia; and Germanicus' children by his wife Agrippina were Augustus' great-grandchildren, since Agrippina was the daughter of Julia.

Tiberius

Some ancient writers were apparently puzzled by a certain vagueness about the precise moment of Tiberius' assumption of the office of *princeps* in AD 14. In part that was due to the uniqueness of the occasion: no precedents existed, there was no time-honoured sequence of a 'The King is dead—long live the King' kind. Further, unlike his successors in the purple, Tiberius already shared the central powers of his adoptive father: ever since AD 4 he had been his 'partner in the *imperium* and the tribunician power'; these prerogatives were his by law and in his own right and not held by delegation, so that there could be no question of their lapsing with Augustus' death, though in theory they could have been revoked by Senate and People—but not in the teeth of a veto from Tiberius himself.

The next *princeps*, Gaius, came naked to empire, so that, as Dio (59. 3) observed, 'he had to be voted in a single day all the prerogatives which Augustus over so long a span of time had been voted gradually and piecemeal, some of which indeed Tiberius had declined to accept at all'; such too was the position of Claudius, Nero, and the four Emperors of 68/9. Hence later writers, puzzled by the absence of such an enabling grant for Tiberius, may have been left floundering or guessing, ascribing delay to a supposed concern about disaffection in the Rhine and Danube legions or wariness about what Germanicus might do— although such threats, had they been real, should have called for speed rather than indecision. Apart from that, the 'accession debate' (Tacitus, *Annals* 1. 11–13) was badly mismanaged, with Tiberius clumsily or deviously rehearsing or inviting other options (when in practice all that was needed was an expression of his readiness to take over the role of Augustus), and in the end not so much saying 'yes' as ceasing to say 'no'.

Tiberius had had an outstandingly successful military and administrative career from his early twenties, in the East, Germany, and the Balkans, interrupted only during the years of his retirement. He thus came to the task of government in his mid-fifties with excellent and unrivalled credentials. But his character was dour and introspective, poisoned by unhappy private experience, with more than a touch of melancholia and insecurity. Above all, he lacked the consummate political adroitness of Augustus, his self-confidence and prestige as the restorer of peace and security to a world shattered by civil war, his genial tact which had moved him to ask on his death-bed 'if everybody had enjoyed the play'. Men could never be quite sure what was going on in Tiberius' mind. This led to the view, particularly prevalent in Tacitus' *Annals* (below, pp. 282 f.), that he was a hypocrite, a master of dissimulation, a view sometimes ludicrous in its strained invention or innuendo. In fact, the true dissimulation stemmed not from the man, but from the system which he inherited, the product of the great illusionist Augustus; it was only underlined by his successor's maladroitness. Criticism, flinching from finding fatal flaws in the system itself, or seeing no practical alternative to it, turned instead on the failings of individual emperors once they were safely dead and adulation must be transferred to the new from the old master. Tacitus gave grudgingly good marks to the early years of Tiberius' rule; but the curse of premature mortality fell heavy on him as it had on Augustus, and by AD 23 first his adopted son Germanicus and then his true son Drusus were in their graves, leaving him with no younger shoulders to lean on as he approached old age. He came to rely heavily on his praetorian prefect L. Aelius Sejanus, especially after his withdrawal from Rome in 26. Sejanus used his chance and the vague, but deadly, charge of treason (*maiestas*) to pick off enemies and rivals, mostly adherents of Germanicus' strong-minded and ambitious widow Agrippina, sister of the dead Gaius and Lucius Caesar and grand-daughter of Augustus himself: she and the sons whom she fought to protect and advance were deported or imprisoned. Sejanus himself aspired to the hand of Claudia Livilla, Germanicus' sister and widow of Tiberius' son Drusus, in the hope no doubt of ruling as regent and guardian of Drusus' son Tiberius Gemellus (born AD 19) once the boy's grandfather was gone. Tiberius was too wary to allow that; but by AD 31 Sejanus had reached the consulship and had thoughts of the tribunician power, which Drusus had held for the year before his death. With the *princeps* now in his seventies and no 'heir apparent' in sight, more and more men must have looked to his great minister as the star to steer by. Then came swift and utter ruin: Antonia, the widow of Tiberius' brother Drusus, penetrated the fence which Sejanus had woven around the Emperor on his remote island retreat and alerted him to much of which he had been ignorant; Sejanus was out-guiled, arrested, and executed, and there followed a blood-bath of his supporters and associates, including his children.

The final years were years of gloom, intrigue, and uncertainty, over which loomed the cynical and suspicious shadow of a lonely old man encompassed by astrologers (and, so scabrous gossip would have it, the instruments of nameless sexual perversions) on the island of Capri. If we shift our sights from Rome, it is true, the Empire seems to have been well governed, prosperous, and (apart from a quickly suppressed revolt in Gaul occasioned by the greed of Roman financiers) secure; the Treasury was healthy, and Italy flourishing. But that something went wrong under Tiberius there is no doubt. The Augustan pattern was marred, above all, by Tiberius' neglect or refusal to imitate his predecessor in persisting in the search for a tried and trusted successor who could be trained for empire and give a secure sense of continuity and direction to men with longer horizons than the failing *princeps*. To have died leaving it virtually certain that Gaius must succeed is the blackest of all indictments, whether we seek an explanation in embittered cynicism, suspicious insecurity, or a lingering and misjudged 'constitutionalism' which saw it as the Senate's part to decide what must follow.

Gaius (Caligula)

Gaius was the son of Germanicus, and the great-grandson of both Augustus and Mark Antony: his nickname 'Caligula' he owed to the little soldiers' boots he wore as a child with his parents in the cantonments of the Rhine, 'Bootikins', an ironically innocent name. Just under twenty-five on his accession in AD 37, he lost little time in making away with the young Tiberius Gemellus, voiding the will in which Tiberius had named Gemellus as his coheir, and executing Macro, Sejanus' supplanter as praetorian prefect, who had been prompt in supporting Gaius' own accession. His brief reign has an air of melodramatic unreality: mental and emotional instability, vicious cruelty, incest, ridiculous indecision and waywardness as exemplified in the farce of his projected invasion of Britain, fantasies of divinity which *inter alia* bred unrest among the Jews. Within less than four years it was all over, and he and his fourth wife and his young daughter all lay dead in his palace. The murder was not part of a plan to seize power for a successor, and the Senate seemed to have a fleeting chance to reassert its authority. 'But while they deliberated, the praetorian guards had resolved.' In

January 41 Tiberius Claudius Nero Germanicus, Gaius' uncle and the brother of Germanicus, became the penultimate Julio-Claudian Emperor.

Claudius

Modern assessments of Claudius' principate vary widely. For some he was a strong ruler with a clear sense of direction, who had spent his long years of obscurity studying Roman history and reaching his own conclusions about the correct blending of tradition and innovation, concealing behind his unprepossessing physical exterior and manners an incisive and inventive intelligence; for them, his chief freedman secretaries, Pallas, Callistus, Narcissus, and the rest were the servants of the policies of a *princeps* who saw that the time was ripe for a forward development. But other scholars see him as a weak-willed, absent-minded, erratic, and malleable man, suddenly and quite unexpectedly bundled on to the throne at the age of fifty, totally devoid of any experience of the corridors of power and hence swiftly becoming the pliant tool of far more adroit and experienced manœuverers within the imperial household—in Dio's classic formulation, 'dominated by his slaves and his wives' (60–2); for them the increased centralization which marked his reign was the consequence not of his deliberate decision, but of his own ineffectual weakness and the ambitions of his ministers. It is impossible to be sure how much truth there is in these two contrasting pictures (and neither is likely to be completely false) since the overt facts can often be interpreted to suit either. But there is probably more truth in the less favourable portrait, which was certainly that recognized by many contemporaries, criticized in Nero's accession speech to the Senate, and caricatured by Seneca (below, pp. 300 f.) in his *Apocolocyntosis*. There can be no doubt that his freedmen achieved a far greater public prominence and influence than those of his predecessors and successors (there is, incidentally, no sound basis for the view that Claudius 'created' or even first organized an imperial bureaucracy), or that his wives exerted a potent influence; Messallina's public 'wedding' to the consul-designate Silius while her husband Claudius was out of Rome was so bizarre an affair that Tacitus felt compelled to reassure his readers twice in a single paragraph (*Annals* 11. 27) that his account was history and not a farcical fairy-tale; and Augustus' private correspondence shows that that shrewd and close observer, while recognizing some faint redeeming qualities in his young kinsman, had seen him as generally incoherent, absent-minded, easily influenced, and far from circumspect in his choice of models (Suetonius, *Claudius*, 4).

Not that Claudius' reign was a failure: whatever view we take, his chief advisers were clever and able men who had risen high in the imperial household by their own talents and energies. The invasion and conquest of southern Britain was a copy-book exercise, superbly well executed, commanded by generals of ability and dash; although the conquest made little economic or strategic sense, it was a resounding and valuable political success. Something was done to repair the damage Gaius had done to the susceptibilities of the Jews; the barbaric and potentially dangerous cult of Druidism was firmly repressed; citizenship was conceded widely, if not always wisely, with the Emperor's personal advocacy of the importance of this large-minded approach, though in a speech remarkable for its banality and irrelevance; public finances were buoyant; and Mauretania and Thrace were brought from indirect to direct rule. But the judicial carnage among senators and *equites* was heavy (quite a number of them had been implicated in Scribonianus' abortive revolt in Dalmatia a few months after Claudius' accession); and for all his good intentions, which need not be denied, it seems that only too often Claudius' left hand did not know what his right hand was doing. Thus it was all very well for him to adjure senators not to behave like 'yes-men'; but Tacitus (*Annals* 11. 23–5) makes it clear, for instance, that the possible admission of some leading men from Gaul to the senatorial order had been discussed and already decided on in the Palace before

Claudius brought it to the Senate, where the *princeps*'s somewhat incoherent speech was promptly followed by the automatic assent of his docile audience.

Nero

Claudius' death in October 54 was quite possibly due to poisoning by his second consort, his niece the younger Agrippina, whose son by her earlier marriage to Domitius Ahenobarbus (consul AD 32) now came to the Principate one month short of his seventeenth birthday. Like Gaius before him, Nero (or his mother—some of the imperial females were more ruthless than their kinsmen) lost no time in dispatching Britannicus (four years younger and Claudius' son by his earlier marriage to Messallina). For some time, however, all seemed fair. Nero's old tutor Seneca, and Agrippina's sometime favourite Burrus, sole praetorian prefect since 51, got the better of the Empress Dowager in the struggle to dominate the adolescent *princeps*, and presided over a period of stability and sound administration—although Thrasea Paetus, as already noted, stoutly deplored their neglect to exploit the chance to recruit the Senate's influence and authority. The first serious storm signal was hoisted when in 59 Nero grew impatient of his mother's insistent meddling and had her murdered. Three years later Burrus died, and was replaced by a pair of praetorian prefects, one of them the infamous Tigellinus, who secured a maleficent influence over the Emperor he was in the end to abandon. At this point Seneca retired, and soon Octavia, Claudius' daughter and Nero's wife, was ousted by the scheming Poppaea and later murdered. Nero was free to indulge his artistic and aesthetic pretensions, surrounded by a claque of corrupt and greedy advisers and toadies, some base-born, like the Sicilian Tigellinus, many others Greek or Levantine freedmen. His extravagance and their unscrupulous venality—not to mention the expense of warfare in Britain, where Boudicca's uprising was sparked off by Roman avarice and greed, and later in Asia Minor, where an ill-thought-out and mismanaged forward move in Armenia ended in a thinly disguised surrender of actual Roman sovereignty and the collapse of Augustus' 'diplomatic solution'—led to depreciation of the coinage and the quasi-judicial fleecing of rich victims. The Great Fire of AD 64 gave Nero the opportunity to start building his grotesquely expensive 'Golden House' (below, pp. 429 ff.) on the ruins of much of the capital: rumours that he had started the fire himself 'to clear the site' and had celebrated the occasion with poetry and song induced him to make the newly spreading Christian community of Rome, no longer seen as merely a dissident sect within Judaism, the innocent scapegoats.

Understandably, men steeled themselves to the perils of conspiring to remove a ruler who had strayed so far from the Augustan path. But in 65 a plot to replace him with the noble and popular Calpurnius Piso was uncovered, and Piso and the others involved or implicated (they included Seneca himself and his nephew, the poet Lucan) were executed. A legacy of suspicion and apprehension led to further deaths, most notably those of Gaius Petronius, 'the arbiter of elegance', and the prominent Stoics, Thrasea Paetus and Barea Soranus. When in the next year the great general Corbulo, mirror of Rome's ancient military virtues and victories, was ordered to take his own life, who could feel safe? An increasingly insecure Nero had committed the cardinal sin of unsettling his own ruling class and army commanders.

The Year of the Four Emperors

It was a descendant of an enfranchised princely house of Aquitania, Julius Vindex, the legate of Gallia Lugdunensis, whose inhabitants had, like those of Spain, suffered heavily from Nero's recent exactions, who raised the standard of rebellion in March 68 against an Emperor who had suddenly and sulkily to be summoned back to Rome from an 'artistic tour' of Greece. Vindex had appealed for support to other legates, without much response; but in Spain the seventy-one-year-old Servius Sulpicius

Galba, the sole direct descendant of a Republican noble house—apart from Nero himself—holding high office, agreed to accept the headship of the movement and styled himself 'Legate of the Senate and People'. In Africa Clodius Macer threw off his allegiance. Even so, had the legions and their commanders been firmly and competently handled, Vindex and Galba must have been overwhelmed. A mysterious collision, perhaps unintended by their commanders, at Besançon between Vindex's ill-trained Gallic levies and the crack legions from Upper Germany saw the insurgents scattered like chaff: Vindex took his own life, and Galba meditated imitating him when he heard the appalling news. But Nero's house of cards was tumbling down, and few retained any confidence in him. Verginius Rufus marched his legions back to Germany, waiting on events; Tigellinus turned his coat and suborned the praetorian guard. Before other help could arrive, Nero panicked and ran, and committed suicide. On 9 June 68 the Julio-Claudian line died with him.

Against all the odds, Galba had succeeded. But his power-base was perilously narrow: he had not won a war, he had marched through an open and undefended gate. His urgent need was to consolidate his position; but a combination of short-sighted ineptness and stiff-necked disciplinarianism and parsimony served him ill. His choice of a lightweight young noble, Piso, as his successor added nothing but the empty lustre of an historic name, and antagonized the energetic and ambitious Marcus Salvius Otho. The victorious German legions were neglected and unrewarded, the Gallic tribes opposed to Vindex alienated, the praetorians denied their expected donative. Throughout the Empire those who had remained loyal to Nero urgently needed a reassurance which they did not receive. Aulus Vitellius, sent by Galba to take command in Lower Germany, was saluted as Emperor by his troops on 2 January 69, and the legions of Upper Germany promptly followed suit. At Rome and on the Danube, Otho's intrigues bore fruit, and he was himself hailed as Emperor a fortnight later. Galba and Piso were murdered, and with them died the last pretensions of the old nobility. The advance elements of Vitellius' forces under Caecina and Valens won a bloody victory over Otho's army at Bedriacum near Cremona, and Otho took his own life on 16 April. But 'the long year' was far from over.

Over a century earlier, the refugees from Pompey's beaten army at Pharsalus had included a centurion or re-enlisted veteran called Titus Flavius Petro, who made his way back home to Sabine Reate where he spent the rest of his life in the humble calling of a collector of moneys due to bankers and auctioneers. His son spent most of his life as an agent of the customs-farmers of the province of Asia, and later became a money-lender in a small way in Switzerland. Of his two sons, the elder, Flavius Sabinus, reached the consulship and the command in Moesia before becoming Prefect of the City in the latter years of Nero; the younger, Flavius Vespasianus, after brilliantly commanding the left wing of the Claudian invasion of Britain, was also a consul and a governor of Africa before Nero appointed him in 67 to a special command to suppress the Jewish rebellion. Both brothers may stand as exceptional examples of the sort of opportunities which were opened to able, ambitious, but sensible 'new men' under the new system. Cut off by space and time from the rapidly changing pattern of events to their west, Vespasian and Gaius Licinius Mucianus, the legate of Syria, composed earlier disagreements and along with Tiberius Julius Alexander, an apostate Jew who was currently Prefect of Egypt, put together a powerful coalition of military, logistic, and financial strength and high experience, which also offered a second chance to all those who had 'backed a wrong horse' previously. Mucianus set off through Asia Minor and the Balkans, while Vespasian headed for Alexandria, where he was saluted as Emperor on 1 July.

Events now moved far more quickly than anyone could have expected. The southward march of the Vitellian army from Germany to north Italy had savagely scarred the regions which it traversed, and Vitellius himself behaved more like a conqueror than a saviour. He also made the mistake of humiliating Otho's troops, but not disbanding them. The bulk of the powerful Danubian armies had not arrived in time to make their weight felt decisively at Bedriacum. The meteoric Marcus Antonius Primus now took a hand, and what an Aquitanian Roman had begun a Roman from Toulouse finished. Something of a rapscallion, he had been exiled under Nero for his part in a scandalous testamentary fraud, but recalled by Galba and given the command of one of the Pannonian legions. War, confusion, and intrigue were his true *métier*; he had little difficulty in getting the disgruntled Danubian troops to declare for Vespasian, and he used them with a speed and *élan* worthy of Julius Caesar himself. Scorning caution and delay, which could also have strengthened the enemy, he declined to await the arrival of the eastern armies and drove at full speed into Italy, catching his opponents off guard and crushing Vitellius' army, itself demoralized by the recent dismissal of its general Caecina on suspicion of treachery, in a second battle at Bedriacum in October. Vitellius fell back on Rome, where Vespasian's brother Sabinus all but persuaded him to abdicate, but was himself killed when rampaging German auxiliaries overran the Capitol. After a furious resistance and some murderous street-fighting, Primus stormed to victory. Vitellius was hunted down and butchered, and a few days later Mucianus at last reached Rome, cut Primus down to size, and established a provisional government for the sixty-year-old Vespasian, whose two grown sons Titus and Domitian offered a prospect of continuity which the childless Mucianus could not match. 'The long year' ended at last in December 69. The task of rebuilding the shattered Empire was now in the hands of a hard-headed, down-to-earth, experienced, and immensely capable man who was to prove himself the first truly worthy successor to Augustus and who was, like Augustus, *princeps* by his own making and on his own merits.

Further Reading

I

Tacitus (*Annals* and *Histories*) and Suetonius (*Lives* of the individual Emperors) provide the most complete coverage. The standard edition and commentary on

Tacitus' *Annals* is that of H. Furneaux in two volumes (second editions respectively 1896 and 1907); *Histories* 1 and 2, and 4 and 5 are equipped with a *Historical Commentary* by G. E. F. Chilver (Oxford, 1979, 1985); book 3 with one by K. Wellesley (Sydney, 1973). Other important sources are Cassius Dio's *Roman History* and the works of Velleius Paterculus and Seneca, Strabo and Pliny the Elder. All of these are available in the Loeb Classical Library. Augustus' own *Res Gestae Divi Augusti* can be consulted in the excellent edition, with translation and commentary, by P. A. Brunt and J. M. Moore (1967). A selection of the most important epigraphical evidence is to be found (untranslated) in Ehrenberg and Jones, *Documents Illustrating the Reigns of Augustus and Tiberius* (2nd edn. repr. with addenda, Oxford, 1976) and E. M. Smallwood, *Documents Illustrating the Principates of Gaius, Claudius and Nero* (Cambridge, 1967).

II

Pre-eminent place must be given to the two great works of Sir Ronald Syme: *The Roman Revolution* (Oxford, 1939) and *Tacitus* (2 vols., Oxford 1958); and mention should also be made of his *History in Ovid* (Oxford, 1978). The *Cambridge Ancient History* devotes the whole of its tenth volume (1934) to this period (44 BC–AD 70). The later chapters of H. H. Scullard, *From the Gracchi to Nero* (5th edn., 1982) constitute the best and most reliable concise treatment of the years down to AD 68. On a slightly larger scale, A. Garzetti, *From Tiberius to the Antonines* trans. J. R. Foster (London, 1974), is to be commended. T. Rice Holmes, *The Architect of the Roman Empire* (vol. I, Oxford, 1928; vol. II, 1931) covers the reign of Augustus in detail and with full citation of evidence; more recent studies in *Caesar Augustus* (Oxford, 1984) ed. F. Millar and E. Segal. For Tiberius, see R. Seager, *Tiberius* (London, 1972) and B. M. Levick, *Tiberius the Politician* (London, 1976); for Gaius, J. P. V. D. Balsdon, *The Emperor Gaius (Caligula)* (Oxford, 1934); for Claudius, A. Momigliano, *Claudius, The Emperor and His Achievement*, tr. W. D. Hogarth (repr. Cambridge, 1961) and V. M. Scramuzza, *The Emperor Claudius* (Cambridge, Mass., 1940); for Nero, B. W. Henderson, *The Life and Principate of the Emperor Nero* (London, 1903), B. H. Warmington, *Nero, Reality and Legend* (London, 1969), and Miriam Griffin *Nero: the End of a Dynasty* (London, 1984). Finally, K. Wellesley, *The Long Year A. D. 69* (London, 1975) takes us through to the accession of Vespasian.

H. M. Pelham, *Essays on Roman History* (1911), remains excellent reading, especially his chapter on 'The Domestic Policy of Augustus'; so too do chapters x and xi by H. M. Last in vol. XI of *The Cambridge Ancient History*. On public and private law, see H. F. Jolowicz and B. Nicholas, *Historical Introduction to the Study of Roman Law* (3rd edn. Cambridge, 1972); on emperor-worship, L. R. Taylor, *The Divinity of the Roman Emperor* (Middletown, 1931); on the Greek cities, A. H. M. Jones, *The Cities of the Eastern Roman Provinces* (Oxford, 1937, revd. 1971) and *The Greek City* (Oxford, 1940); on the municipalization of Italy and the spread of citizenship outside Italy, A. N. Sherwin White, *The Roman Citizenship* (2nd edn., Oxford, 1973); on economic matters in general. vols. ii–v of Tenney Frank, *An Economic Survey of Ancient Rome* (Baltimore, 1933–40).

The modern scholarly literature is enormous in its extent, and archaeology keeps uncovering new material, including inscriptions. References to such specialized work can be found in most of the books that have been mentioned. In particular, the detailed bibliographies for each chapter in H. H. Scullard's latest (paperback) edition of *From the Gracchi to Nero* (London, 1982) are comprehensive.

7

The Arts of Government

NICHOLAS PURCELL

The Principate from Nero to Gallienus

IN AD 193 the military and political crisis of AD 69 was repeated;
the commanders of provincial armies contended for the position
of *princeps*. The balance of power of the armies had shifted east
from the Rhine, but in almost every respect the conflicts were
very similar. The crisis of 193 exchanged Commodus, the last
of the Antonines in a succession of adoption and blood which
had been continuous since the accession of Nerva in 96, for
Septimius Severus, nominal heir to that tradition and founder
of a similar sequence of succession which lasted until 235. Many
have seen this disturbance as the harbinger of the chaos of the
middle of the third century. Nothing could be further from the
truth. In its resemblance to the turmoil of 69 the war of 193 is
one of our most striking indications of the stability of the high
principate.

In this period, to a large extent an 'age without history' in the
normal sense, the narrative of events (accessions, usurpations,
battles, deaths) actually obscures the tendencies and evolutions
on which the historian, whose job it is to explain, must concentrate. And stability and peace challenge explanation much more
than destruction and disaster. This stability had been created
above all by the Flavian Emperors Vespasian and Domitian
(69–79 and 81–96). Three achievements in particular may

be emphasized, though we should be wary of asserting that they were brought about by design or policy rather than by accidental development. First, the revenues of Empire were organized to a high enough specification for expenditure over several years to be planned ahead; this had never before been the case. In the process some degree of administrative organization had to be fostered (but it is argued in this chapter that this should not be mistaken for a bureaucracy). Second, the last client kingdoms were subjected to the process of provincialization which had been emerging for sixty years, and at last the Empire became a tessellation of provincial units within clearly demarcated boundaries. The armies were now permanently fixed on similarly clear frontiers which divided an increasingly self-conscious empire from the non-provinces beyond. Third, the Flavian Emperors, largely disembarrassed of the remnants of the republican high aristocracy by the political chaos of Nero's reign, and of municipal Italian origins themselves, regularized the recruitment and replacement of the upper classes at Rome and advanced the process by which, through an ever more refined set of public positions in the gift of the Emperor, the élites of the cities of the Empire increasingly came to feel part of the establishment. This was the process, recognized by Tacitus in its early stages in one of the most perceptive and sophisticated historical discussions in Latin (*Annals* 3.55), that completed the transformation of the conqueror of the world into its captial. The Flavian Emperors came from the municipal élites of rural Italy. While they lacked the luxurious sophistication and amoral superiority of the ancient aristocracy which supplied and continued to flourish under the Julii and Claudii, they failed also to maintain the ceremonious constitutionalism which had characterized the wiser of their predecessors. Their impatience with the forms of Roman political life rapidly led them into autocratic manners which in the end brought down their dynasty with the assassination of Domitian.

But it was too late to return to before the Civil War. The safely respectable senator Nerva was replaced, perhaps not wholly voluntarily, by Trajan, a second-generation senator whose origin was from the Italian diaspora in the provinces. Recruitment to the Roman governing class was becoming wider all the time. Men like Trajan, native Latin speakers of Italian stock who spent all their formative years in Roman public life, were less surprising newcomers than the increasingly numerous magnates from the cities of the Hellenic East, often the descendants of the client kings through whom that area had been ruled a century before. Greek and Latin mixed on more equal terms than ever before; the new cosmopolitanism was expressed by Trajan's successor Hadrian in the style of his personal appearance and the assiduity with which he travelled in every part of the Empire. The new cultural homogeneity found one of its most splendid expressions in the lavish beautification, from Vespasian to Antoninus Pius, of the world's capital in a cosmopolitan architectural style, though the advancement of so many provincials gave a boost to competitive display in cities all over the Empire. The result—'the glitter of our age' (*nitor saeculi*), as Pliny calls it—was the imperial architecture which forms such an important part of our picture of the ancient world (below, pp. 433 ff.) The political life of the time involved the intrigues of the court and the struggle for personal advancement among the Emperor's entourage more than it had done before, for the Augustan ideal of the Principate had finally ended, and with it had come the age in which we may first legitimately call the *princeps* Emperor. Paradoxically it was now that relations between *princeps* and Senate became most amicable; even the fluctuation in popularity of Emperors, the variations in their adherence to the increasingly clear rules for respecting senatorial autonomy, became an endlessly repeated pattern. With the concerns of the Emperor increasingly related to the provinces, it mattered much less whether he was 'good' like Pius (138–61) or 'bad' like Commodus (180–93): except, perhaps, that Commodus' murder precipitated the crisis referred to at the beginning of this account.

The concern of the Emperors for the provinces is a reflection of the new homogeneity of the Empire, not a sign of crisis. Disorders there were, Jewish revolt under Hadrian, and plague under Marcus Aurelius, but these did not do serious damage to the inert and enormously stable fabric of Empire. The imperial élites had the prosperity which comes from peace and an ever more sophisticated economy, and opportunities of upward social mobility to invest their wealth in. In foreign affairs, too, despite the hardening of the frontiers with the great defence works of Domitian and Hadrian, the Empire was not really more defensive in the second century than in the first. The clashes were all in similar places, victories came no less easily, defeats were no more common. We see a repeating pattern of warfare, against Parthia under Trajan, Verus, and Severus; on the Danube under Nero, Domitian, Trajan, and Marcus; on the margin of the Sahara under Tiberius, Claudius, Domitian, and Pius. Of real extensions of Empire there was only the conquest of gold-rich and fertile Dacia beyond the Danube under Trajan. The conquest of Parthia directly afterwards proved unassimilable—a significant fact. The task which Severus won for himself in 193 was no harder than that of Vespasian. Severus died at York in 211. That his family was of African background only makes it typical of the homogeneous world of that age. His power passed to men of Syrian connections, no more exotic than he, despite the colourful anecdotes attached to the name of Heliogabalus. If the Emperor's power during the succession of these individuals seems less effective and his position less secure, that is not the decadence of personalities or the feebleness of characters. At last the Roman world was reaping the whirlwind which sprang from the never resolved impracticalities of the fortuitous system by which it held together.

The disasters of the third century were the product of a set of coincidences. The homogeneous Empire was an ephemeral creation. The provinces, having been raised to a similar high level of importance and prosperity, began to drift apart and to behave independently. Their armies, recruited locally to an ever greater extent, became loyal to the regions, not to Rome. The soldiers became distanced socially and culturally from the new élite of the Graeco-Roman Empire. Chronic political instability cut short the reign of Emperor after Emperor. And all this at a time when the pressures of available manpower beyond the Empire, prevented by hard frontiers from entering the Empire unobtrusively to fill the vacancies of its perpetually falling population, posed a military threat which had not been seen for generations, and when the weak Parthian state had evolved into the ferociously effective Sassanian power in the East. The cumbersome and inefficient system of the high Empire could not cope. In the crisis economic disaster overtook most of the Empire (though many areas, including most of Italy, escaped physical devastation). But it is essential to realize that this catastrophe was sudden. The first and second centuries with their many problems and lackadaisical amateur government had been no golden age; but it was not the troubles of that age which multiplied into the chaos of the third century. The disasters were new.

The Arts of Government

'And it came to pass in those days, that there went out a decree from Caesar Augustus, that all the world should be enrolled to be taxed' (Luke 2: 1). The evangelist wants to emphasize the centrality in world history of the coming of the Messiah, and accordingly links the birth of Christ to the moment when the power of Rome seemed at its most universal. For him, as often for us, the power of Rome is most potently expressed by reference to its administrative activity. St Luke, however, was wrong. We know now that no such decree commanded a universal registration of the Roman world, at this time or any other; he exaggerated Roman omnipotence on the basis of the experience of a single province. It remains extremely easy for us too to misunderstand the scope, practice, and effects of Rome's governmental procedures. We mistake patterns of decision-making for policies and take hierarchical sequences of posts for career-structures. When we find the taking of minutes or the accumulation of archives, we immediately see a bureaucracy. Virtuosity in the public service is confused with professionalism. Recent work has been able to show well how far Rome's administration failed, or could be corrupted or subverted, or simply had no effect but oppression on thousands of provincials. There have been fewer examinations of the way in which the arts of government at which the Romans thought themselves that they excelled actually worked—imposing civilization and peace, leniency to the defeated, and war to the last with the proud (Virgil, *Aeneid* 6. 852–3). The analogies which spring most readily to our minds often mislead. Either, beguiled by the delightful portrayal of Roman administration in Evelyn Waugh's *Helena*, we see Imperium as Raj, or we transpose to Rome with W. H. Auden the perpetual movement of memos in the offices of Whitehall:

> Caesar's double-bed is warm
> As an unimportant clerk
> Writes 'I do not like my work'
> On a pink official form.

These images of government will fit neither the headquarters of the governor nor the imperial Palatine. What follows is an outline alternative.

Roman theories of government were not elaborate; the practice too was simple. Two broad categories cover almost all the activities of Roman rule: settling disputes between communities or individuals, and assembling men, goods, or money— jurisdiction and exaction. Antiquity recognized three main types of authority: magistrate, soldier, and master of a household; and all governmental activity in the Roman Empire can be linked with one of these. The first, deriving from the Greek city, covers both the immemorial officers of the city-state which Rome had been and the magistrates of the hundreds of essentially self-governing cities which made up nearly all the Roman Empire. In a *polis* magistrates ran the military; at Rome the usual citizen militia became under the Empire a permanent, institutionally separate army, whose officers played an ever greater part in government culminating in the militarization of the third century. Finally, in a slave-owning society the type of authority exercised within the household was naturally recognizably different, and also came to be of considerable importance in government. These three administrative approaches will be examined individually. But it was always through activities which we would hesitate to call governmental that Roman rule was most effectively maintained: through the involvement of the upper classes in public religion, spectacles, impressive patronage of architecture, philosophy, literature, painting; and in civil benefactions all over the Empire. The civilizing and beneficial effects of this should be remembered as we move on to find the actual administrative and executive structure of the Empire erratic and illiberal.

The City Magistrate at Home and Abroad

Rome had from the earliest times enjoyed very close contacts with the Greek world, and had, like most ancient cities, a tripartite political structure of magistrates, council (the Senate), and popular assembly. The importance of the last for our purpose is that its early power produced the uniquely Roman and constitutionally vital concept of *imperium*. The Roman people conferred upon its chosen magistrates the right to command it and the sanctions against disobedience—ever more strictly circumscribed—of corporal and capital punishment of its members. On this depended the powers of the magistrates, and therefore of the Emperor and of provincial governors under the principate. *Provinciae*, which were at first simply the military spheres of command of consuls or praetors, changed greatly towards the late Republic. Not only had access to, and tenure of, the commands been progressively regularized, but proconsuls and propraetors, encouraged no doubt by the opportunities for reasonable or unreasonable profit, found themselves deeply involved in diplomacy, in the settling of disputes, the managing of their province's finances, and the giving of justice. They often spent more time on what came to be a regular assize-tour of their province than on military matters. When Augustus, needing to take over practically all the armies of the Empire, left the provinces of senatorial governors almost without legions, there was no governmental difficulty. Some provinces came to be governed not by men who might command Roman soldiers, but by freedmen and by equestrians whose title, _procurator_, was drawn not from public law, but from the language of the household. Finally, from the Flavian period, governors who found themselves overburdened by military duties began to be assisted by special deputies who would see to the jurisdiction of the governor and were called _iuridici_. The subordination of the governors of the provinces to the Emperor—although in the case of the proconsular provinces some still showed signs of their old independence in the Julio-Claudian period—eventually also brought about the establishment of a fixed hierarchy of provinces and exact definition of their boundaries, so that the Antonines ruled an Empire which was a tessellation of exactly fitting administrative units which, it is interesting to note, showed a tendency to divide and subdivide in the second and third centuries. This exactly bounded Empire was, however, a recent creation, and until the Flavian period much remained vague about the boundaries of Empire and provinces alike. But despite the changes of the early Empire, in the second century there was still much in the government of the provinces that would have been familiar in the age of Scipio Aemilianus: proconsuls and propraetors, assisted by quaestors and assistants such as scribes and messengers drawn from public panels, and delegating their _imperium_ to deputies called, if senators, _legati_, and if equestrians, _praefecti_, still ruled much of the Empire. And this includes the legates and prefects appointed by the Emperor as proconsul of his enormous province. To that extent the Roman Empire was run by the magistrates of a city-state.

This is why Rome long retained the habit of dealing with her subjects with the respect deserved by the free, and why Roman rule so long remained indirect. To the end of antiquity most of the cities of the Empire and their territories were ruled by local magistrates many of whose domestic executive actions were taken as if they were independent; indeed they often needed to be reminded that there were limits to the licence they were allowed. Similarly Rome also long tolerated local kings and dynasts, and the survival of these dependent kingdoms and free cities contributed much to the fuzzy informality of the power structure of the Empire before the age of the Antonines. Even in the third century, tens of thousands of Rome's subjects would have contact with superior executive authority only through whatever magistrates had authority in their own city. It was in Italy that the autonomy of the cities was first seriously weakened; there, already before the end of the Republic, regulations define the limits of city magistrates' competence. More significant is the interference in the financial affairs of cities which becomes widespread during the second century AD. Governors in the provinces or the Senate or the Emperor had always been able to intervene in some such matters, but their competence was of course severely restricted by their limited time and knowledge. In the appointment from Rome from the end of the first century AD of senatorial or equestrian state guardians (*curatores rei publicae*) or accountants (*logistai*) in the cities we find a momentous departure from the traditional *laissez-faire* attitude to government which had hitherto prevailed. In Italy the change can be linked with other administrative policies, such as the setting up of charitable foundations for poor children or the centralizing of many local administrative functions on regions based on the great Italian highways, developments which confirm that a new attitude to government was being born. Because of the crisis of the third century and the different direction taken by the administration of the late Empire as a result of the reforms of the age of Diocletian (284–305), this attitude never evolved fully; but combined with the final stage in the evolution of the provinces and the maturing of the office of provincial governor, it forms one of the hallmarks of the Antonine Empire.

Of this world of diminishing autonomy and growing governmental solicitude the experience of the Younger Pliny in Bithynia is not untypical. But a reading of his correspondence with Trajan, which forms our best evidence for this acme of Roman administrative excellence, leaves an abiding impression of how arbitrary, haphazard, and superficial Roman government was even then.

Without direct rule, how did Rome maintain order? The answers are social and cultural rather than administrative. It was, for example, by her open policies of corporate status and individual citizenship that she succeeded where imperial Athens had failed. The Romans remembered without shame how the nucleus of Romulus' city had been collected from nationless vagabonds and runaways who had seized their womenfolk by main force. Historically, the Romans' power in Italy had been consolidated through the slow evolution of a sophisticated hierarchy of partly citizen status which they had been prepared to extend to whole communities. From the last century of the Republic this policy was followed elsewhere too, and with the enfranchisement of non-Roman troops, the personal gift of Roman citizenship to Rome's supporters in foreign cities, the founding of Roman towns in the provinces, and the grant of privileges or citizenship to foreign communities, a highly successful means of incorporating the most influential members of the subject peoples in the Roman system was evolved. The citizenship carried various privileges, often, as St Paul found, of considerable personal use; but most importantly it gave provincials access to public appointments. The subject was involved in government, and stability resulted. The wooing of the provincial élites was one of Rome's most successful tools.

At Rome itself, the growth of the Empire had brought about indirectly an ever growing population of slaves, freedmen, foreigners, and Italians, the ambitious, the curious, the needy, and the desperate. Quite apart from the very serious problem of keeping the peace, the nourishment of scores of thousands of people and the keeping of the city wholesome and habitable posed very serious difficulties. Fortunately proceeds of empire could be devoted to the building projects, above all the aqueducts, which alone made it possible for so large a population to survive. But such projects needed organization as well as capital. In the (usual) absence of the consuls and often of the praetors, the management of Rome, the *cura Urbis*, devolved on other magistrates. Their principal resource for the job was a distinctive Roman procedure for the letting of contracts, *locatio*. This needs some stressing because it always remained one of the main governmental activities of Roman administrators, and because it was through this that so much of the civil engineering which is so eloquent a testimony of Roman rule was carried on. It was also for a very long period the principal mode, through tax-farming, of collecting public revenues, that basic activity of ancient governments. Moreover it was unique to Rome in its developed form, and appeared to Polybius (6. 117) one of the most striking and effective aspects of Roman state activity, embracing all activities from the contract for feeding the sacred geese of Juno (always let first) to the taxes of the provinces or the resurfacing of main roads. Polybius saw this practice as a democratic aspect of Roman public life, no doubt because it involved in state business some prominent plebeians. For our purposes it is doubly important. First it encouraged the formation of semi-public corporate organizations, *collegia* and *societates*, the spirit of which contributed to Roman notions of how to form administrative institutions—and indeed it is from this world that the important late-Roman official title *magister* derives. Second, and even more importantly, we see again here the unwillingness of Roman magistrates to undertake themselves the direct overseeing of the activities which they sponsored. The wish to limit the public sphere and privatize official actions is again apparent.

There were occasional administrative improvements at Rome during the Republic; but simple coercion by their attendants, and jurisdiction thus enforced, remained the magistrates' only executive agencies. By contrast, under Augustus and his immediate successors a still further worsening of the city's problems prompted a connected series of institutional innovations. Some of the new expedients were of the highest importance to the government of the Principate; moreover, the exercise of institutional change itself acted as a precedent for the later proliferation of new posts and offices. The Augustan administrative revolution consisted in the creation of boards of senior magistrates in departments (*curae*) responsible for the management of the aqueducts, the roads of the city, the banks of the Tiber, and so on; in the systematization of responsibility by means of artificial compartments, such as the fourteen regions of Rome or the eleven of Italy; and in the appointment of senior assistants responsible to the *princeps* who would control military or paramilitary bodies permanently stationed in Rome or very near by, for political and civil security. The creation of the *curae* did away with the ancient principle of annual tenure, and provided something of a permanent staff in place of sole reliance on contract labour. The formal systems of administrative units diminished competitiveness between patrons and helped ensure uniformity, stability, and comparison of results of administrative activity. And in the creation of the much more powerful posts of prefect of the praetorian guard, prefect of the city, and prefect of the fire-brigade, Augustus equipped future *principes* with three great ministers, as well as judges whose courts would acquire an importance which helped to centralize large areas of Italy on Rome and relieve other magistrates of much of their jurisdiction. We happen to know that already by the reign of Nero the prefect of the city had acquired jurisdiction comparable to that of the urban praetor. This centralization of Italian administration in turn provided an example for the management of the provinces; it is significant that the *curatores* of Rome lent their name to the functionaries described above whose financial supervision came to infringe the cities' autonomy.

This Augustan administrative revolution, for which Greek theoretical and practical precedents are perhaps to be sought, was, however, unique. Moreover, the senatorial *curae* were in part created not for administrative excellence but to subordinate these potentially prestigious activities of great senators to Augustus' regime, and they flourished as status symbols for the successful senator, to be held often by corrupt, lazy, or incompetent men. Above all, despite all the innovation, and all the extra posts and increase in personnel, the main activities remained the letting of contracts, the giving of permissions, and the business of arbitration—new posts, more subtle hierarchies, but the same old jobs.

The Army

The second general group of associations which political authority had for the governed is connected with war. Even when mercenary troops had been important, fighting had, in the classical *polis* and its heirs, remained to a large extent the preserve of a citizen militia. Until the second century BC this had been true of Rome too. It followed that a city's magistracies were often very closely associated with military command, from which derived the vital Roman concept of *imperium*, which underlay the whole governmental activity of the Empire and actually gave it its very name.

As the Hellenistic cities came increasingly to group themselves in leagues or to submit to the control of their foreign affairs by the kings and eventually by Rome, military titles such as *stratēgos*, 'army-leader', often lost their military connotations. So at Rome the praetors first, and with the Empire the consuls, came to acquire what we would call civilian functions. From the middle Republic the praetors were mainly concerned with jurisdiction, though it is interesting to observe that the regular Greek term for praetor (the Greek equivalents of Latin constitutional terms are often very revealing) is in fact *stratēgos*. Lower down the social scale the post of superintendent of engineers (*praefectus fabrum*) was practically non-military by the Julio-Claudian age, and even some types of military tribune were military only in name. It is only in the third century that the process is reversed, and military titles spread in areas of government with no necessary connection with war; the eventual militarization of the Empire brings to an end the processes described here (though, significantly, military titles such as *praepositus* and *optio* spread earlier among the servants of the Emperor). But throughout the Emperor was called by the honorific military title *imperator*, first as an informal description, then as a name, finally as a formal title, and took on himself many of the military functions once carried out by the republican magistrates. Although we usually refer to him by his senatorial style of *princeps*, it was as *imperator* (*autocrator*, 'the ruler answerable to none' in Greek) that he was perceived by the Empire. And the Emperor's military power pervaded the government of the Empire.

In the ancient world, to question the rightnees of a standing army was unthinkable; and peace was the product of victory won by the soldier. But there is no easy way to translate 'civilian' into Greek or Latin, and this is because the legacy of the citizen army ensured an intermingling of the apparatus of warfare with the activities of peace. The distinction between soldier and civilian, so clear to our minds, and in our times possessing a moral as well as a practical flavour, did not exist before the triumph of the military, which began in the Severan period.

Augustus established the military system which lasted until the third century. The army was composed of two parts (and there was also a considerable fleet). The senior part was a citizen army of some thirty legions (about 165,000 men), each commanded by a senator of middling status, and subject to the more senior senatorial governors of the imperial and senatorial provinces. Gradually these legions became a permanent feature of the frontier areas in which they were established. They recruited mostly from those areas. Although some legions changed their bases, such moves were not overall very frequent. Rather more numerous were the auxiliary troops who from the reign of Claudius regularly received the citizenship on discharge. Rome had always relied on the military help of non-Romans, and the employment and incorporation of the auxiliaries became one of the most important ways in which the Empire acquired a cultural homogeneity. The regiments of auxiliaries, much smaller than legions, were commanded by citizens of equestrian rank, usually from the élites of Italy or the provinces and using these jobs to win further status and opportunities for themselves. The whole system was financed from a military treasury established by Augustus, one of the first and most fundamental steps towards financial planning taken by the Romans.

It follows that before the third century the military commanders provided from the Empire's élites were not what we would call professionals. The effectiveness and expertise of the army rested with the senior and junior centurions who often rose from the ranks and would serve as long as any ordinary soldier. It was, as far as we know, very unusual for such an officer to receive equestrian rank, and still rarer to proceed to equestrian military office. And equestrian commands, although important in the promotion game of the upper classes, were usually short and variegated, including horse and foot and in a whole range of different places. So too even with senators, whose military service as junior officer, legionary legate, or governor of a garrisoned province would usually occupy only a short period of their whole career, take place in many different areas, and give them little opportunity to become professional. This is true of almost all the military commanders we know, and it is clear that it became standard practice for the Emperor to ensure that no senator acquired too much familiarity with armies and warfare. This practice of drawing the high military command from essentially unmilitary personnel helped integrate the army into the more peaceful activities of the Empire.

The legionary army always remained part of the citizen body of Rome. Its communities, especially in non-citizen areas, enjoyed privileges like other citizen settlements, and expected the facilities—aqueducts, amphitheatres, baths, and so on—of any classical city. The *castellum* (fort) was originally an ordinary member of the sequence of possible settlement-institutions which ranged from village to city. The *colonia*, originally in the late Republic a town of discharged citizen veterans which was autonomous but expected to defend itself and the interests of Rome in case of trouble, and which came to be the coveted highest status attainable by a provincial city, helped to blur the distinction between camp and town still further. Outside fortresses, moreover, people congregated to form whole settlements dependent on the presence of the army, which often became independent. When not on active duty—which was more often than not, as in all armies—soldiers cultivated the land, engaged in trade, and generally lived their lives like ordinary citizens. This close contact between soldiers and other citizens and noncitizens was still further fostered by the direct involvement of soldiers in the day-to-day administration of the Empire.

A study of a system of government must not only concern itself with top level decision-making and the bureaucracy which may give it stability and effectiveness; it must also give some account of the actual execution of the directives which emanate from these two sources. Who, we must ask, actually put into effect the decisions of the Roman government? The Roman magistrates had immediate agents in their staff of strong-arm men, errand-runners, and announcers. But these were few, and it is only in the command of real soldiers, given to him by his *imperium*, that the executive power of the Roman official eventually lay.

The army was not exclusively deployed in the remoter or more barbarous provinces. True, in the mid second century Britain had three, the Rhine four, and the Danube ten of Rome's twenty-eight legions; but most of these were placed, even in this period when the frontiers were hardening, so that they commanded large areas of province as well as foreign soil; and before the Flavian period even more legionary bases were within the Empire. Detachments from these legions or auxiliary troops were anyway widely dispersed through the provinces, especially in their capitals. In the East the nine legions (above all in Egypt) were positioned even more clearly with control of the local

populace in mind; and settled Africa and Spain both retained a
legion each. Besides these, in coastal or riverine cities there were
large naval bases. Rome had its own huge, complex garrison.
Wherever the Emperor was there was a large body of troops.
There were always soldiers moving from one detachment to
another, above all on the great roads connecting frontier areas—
living off the land by permission, by the generosity of local
magnates, or by extortion, with their privileges (only military
courts tried soldiers) and the needs of imperial security to justify
even their crimes. 'Your teeth are shattered?' asks Juvenal,
'Face hectically inflamed, with great black welts? You know
the doctor wasn't too optimistic about the eye that was left.
But it's not a bit of good your running to the courts about it. If
you've been beaten up by a soldier, better keep it to yourself'
(16. 10 ff.). The government of the Roman Empire was what
we would call military rule.

It would have been hard, indeed, for the Roman Empire to
be run on any other system. Even the civil services of modern
states, like the British, have often developed from military
models, retaining, for example, the concept of leave. There were
few possible structures of authority available that could cope
with the scale involved in Roman administration: the city-state
had already proved an inadequate institution for world government, and the authority of the patriarchal family was too limited.
Participatory institutions there were, like the cartels which undertook the public contracts described above or collegiate organizations of city populations, worshippers, artisans, and so
on; and all these bodies played a part in imperial rule, since
through representatives they could deal with the rulers of the
state, make petitions, and receive replies; through their privileges and corporate influence security might be maintained in
sensitive areas like the larger cities of the Empire. But none of
these offered the convenient, disciplined, extensive structure of
the army, and so the army came to have the public image we
have just seen in Juvenal. Using its own courts, answerable only
to itself, privileged and greedy, it became a tyrannical force
because it was omnipresent in government.

Soldiers were involved in public building; they surveyed land; they manned the customs posts at provincial boundaries; and their value to the collection of other taxes is sufficiently demonstrated by the fact that they were from time to time forbidden to take part in it. During the second century a secret service of government spies, the so-called 'grain militia' (*frumentarii*) came into being, the predecessors of the sinisterly bland *agentes in rebus* of the later Empire. Examples could easily be multiplied, but it is enough to end by referring to the vivid testimony of two papyrus lists of soldiers' duties, in one happy case referring not to atypical Egypt, but to the Danube. From Moesia we hear of soldiers with corn-shipments, on mine duty, requisitioning horses, running prisons; and from Egypt of harbour-dredging work, duty at the mint, at the paper factory (so essential to Egyptian administration), and on general river-guard duty, a police activity further illuminated by the countryside surveillance attested in a new document of this kind. Altogether there were few places in the Empire where it will have been odd to meet a soldier. 'To the soldier, at his demand—500 drachmae' is a typical note in the pathetic list of protection payments made by a wretched Egyptian subject of this government. In this at least the Egyptians were by no means unusual.

Administration Household-Style

Most governmental actions were undertaken by a very few people in every ancient state. Ancient government was top-heavy, in that a great deal of what seems to us mundane work was done by the men with most authority; there was relatively little delegation or selection of business. In the Roman Empire in the second century AD only some hundred or so men actually held *imperium* by direct grant or delegation at any one time: on them in theory fell the whole burden of government. Indeed some senators did feel that their dignity should be reflected in their agenda, and that they should not debate trivial or demeaning subjects, but others considered that an exhaustive concern for every corner of the *res publica* had been the great ideal of the

statesmen of old. 'How every single thing mattered to our ancestors!' exclaims the Elder Pliny admiringly of a censorial re-
gulation about laundrymen passed in 220 BC (*NH* 35. 197).
The evidence suggests that the opinion of Pliny prevailed: even
if an issue came to the attention of the authorities, it was only at
the top that any consideration of it could take place. Hence the
hours that the Emperors, their high officials, and the provincial
governors spent in routine jurisdiction; the inscriptions recording minor local administrative decisions often taken at a very
high, even at an imperial level; the small issues discussed in the
surviving letters between the relatively few executives of the
Roman Empire; hence too, no doubt, the hundreds, thousands
of matters as important as those that did receive attention, that
simply went by default. There was a great reluctance to multiply
positions of authority or to complicate the business of government. There was little forward planning; new administrative
measures (sometimes) followed only on acute crisis. So it was
naturally to dependents that over-pressed office-holders looked
for their assistants; some of these might be equestrians or free
plebeian clients, but the total obedience of the unfree offered
much more extensive possibilities in a slave-owning society. It is
with the role of authority conferred within the household, but
applied to public life, that we are here concerned.

The Emperor was the most hard-pressed administrator of all;
Fergus Millar has demonstrated conclusively how his detailed
concern for specific matters and his virtually undivided responsibility for all the business for which he could find time left no
time for the creation of what we would call policy. His it was to
begin to deal, rather, with all the appeals, petitions, embassies
which reached him from below. Because it was only as judge that
he was expected to act, whole areas of government—education,
the economy, welfare, administration—only impinged on him
accidentally, and were treated unsystematically. Nevertheless
the volume of material reaching him required some management, and so it was that in the imperial household we have
our clearest example of an administrator's personal dependants

gaining responsibility for public affairs and enormous political power.

So great were the fortunes of some late-republican senators that the slaves or freedmen on whom they relied might find themselves in control of sums of money or tracts of land comparable in size to objects of the state's administration. This was naturally most true of Augustus, whose personal property and wealth was truly imperial in scale. The private estate of the Julio-Claudians was settled by the falling in of the shares allotted by Augustus to his family, above all to Livia and Antonia the younger, and by the policy of accumulating goods by inheritance and confiscation. Thanks to the ravages in the Roman upper class of Caligula, Nero, Domitian, Commodus, and Septimius Severus, this imperial *patrimonium* gave the Emperor control over a substantial proportion of the real estate of the Empire by means of direct ownership, not simply constitutionally sanctioned political control. Ownership entailed a different style of administration, and one which evolved very fast.

There were other ingredients as well. In Egypt royal land was a phenomenon which survived from the time of the Pharaohs. As their successors, the Emperors enjoyed in this province at least the experience of the direct management of a large proportion of the soil. Although Egypt was a very special case in this, as in so many ways, it provided a precedent, if not a model, for the running on behalf of the Emperors of other formerly royal lands, especially in the eastern part of the Empire, where royal lands had previously become public land of the Roman People. It would be very interesting to know how such tracts had been administered in the last years of the Republic. A good example is Galatia, where the extensive estates of the last king, Amyntas, became under Augustus an imperial property of a sufficient scale to make an impact on the organization of the province. The potential power of the supervisors of these estates is clearest in the case of geographically circumscribed areas like the Gallipoli peninsula (the Thracian Chersonese) which formed a single imperial property. In places like this the agent of the Emperor had to exercise functions not unlike those of a provincial governor, and we hear of the punishment of one such in Judaea in the reign of Tiberius who took it on himself to give orders to Roman soldiers as if he held *imperium* (Tacitus, *Annals* 4. 15). As we shall see, such licence was soon to be regularized. It was in Africa that the imperial estates reached their greatest extent, and epigraphic evidence from the second century, especially the *Lex Manciana*, reveals a good deal about their scale and management. But every province had them; they included mines, quarries, forests, as well as agricultural land; and Emperors were not slow to add to them. Septimius Severus, in particular, vastly increased the imperial holdings in the provinces, and the substitution of imperial for private markings on oil-jars from southern Spain eloquently reveals how sudden, complete, and economically important such a step could be. The inhabitants of these estates, through the hierarchy of procurators and bailiffs which separated them from the Emperor, had very much the same opportunities—or lack of them—for appeal and petition as ordinary provincials did through the governor.

It was natural that the administrators of imperial property should derive their titles from republican practice. But *procurator* remained a term of private law, and it will have sounded very strange to Roman ears to call the governors of public provinces by it. This practice, introduced for small equestrian provinces by Claudius, is a striking departure from the scrupulously traditionalistic tact of the Augustan constitutional changes. These governors had previously quite correctly been called *praefecti*. At times, too, other officials with the innovative title appear in other departments of the government as assistants to senators in their public capacities—in the various concerns of the urban administration of Rome, for example, and as financial assistants of the legates of the provinces to which the *princeps* as proconsul had to delegate governors (the 'imperial' provinces).

The change is of great importance because it made it possible for there to grow up from these domestic origins over the following two centuries what we may call a procuratorial service, in which there was available to men of equestrian rank a series of important governmental posts in the provinces and in the city of Rome, in charge of a great variety of imperial concerns, from the control of whole provinces to the running of mines, and as the assistants of senatorial functionaries. In the end there were, at any one time, some 170 of these posts, and it is here that Rome's administrative excellence, that elusive beast, used to be located. It is clear, however, that these posts did not constitute a hierarchical sequence linked by a regular promotion pattern, and that the holders of them needed no more expertise, knowledge, devotion, professionalism, or talent than their senatorial colleagues. Jurisdiction and financial watchfulness was what was expected of them too, not a serious businesslike approach different in kind from what was expected of a noble magistrate. A procurator of an Alpine district describes his job as 'the supervision of the law and the carrying out of the interests of the emperors' (*CIL* XII. 103). These posts were much less important as means of increasing the efficiency of imperial rule than as a way of incorporating in the life of government the upper classes of the provinces. Through these posts social advancement was obtained, and this secured the loyalty of the powerful men of the Empire. This cannot be overstressed: it was the ability to incorporate, not administrative excellence, that was Rome's greatest Art of Government.

Who the equestrian procurators were, and where they came from, therefore mattered. What they did mattered less. Recognition of this has sent the hunt for the supposed Roman bureaucracy into other fields. 'The description "imperial civil service" better fits the freedmen and slaves of Caesar', says a recent scholar. Here again the republican senator's dependence on his slaves and freedmen sets the precedent. The *familia* of Augustus and his successors acquired enormous power. Under Claudius and Nero in particular their influence with the *princeps* became notorious. The principal freedmen used titles derived from their principal occupations—secretary for letters, or for accounts, and the like—which became so closely associated with the

Emperor that it was considered treasonable for others to use them in their households. In reaction to the hostility shown to these men, the posts they had held gradually became the preserve of men of equestrian status; but the household—the *familia Caesaris*—remained highly influential. Two flattering poems of Statius (*Silvae* 3.3 and 5.1) give us an idea of their possible concerns, and we get further information from some 4,000 inscriptions, mostly recording simply the title of the slave or freedmen. These titles, intricate, technical, and specific, seem to give support to the bureaucratic view. But the hostility to the freedmen raises a doubt; it seems that the Emperor was not free to delegate important matters to his freedmen without infringing public opinion. It therefore seems appropriate to look more critically at what the *familia Caesaris* actually did. It is clear that they acquired a mastery of technical information. Augustus left a list of 'names of freedmen and slaves from whom accounts could be obtained'. Some freedmen are praised by courtiers like Statius for this. Another is described on his epitaph as 'occupied throughout his life with the utmost attention to the interests of the imperial palace' (at Formiae: *ILS* 1583). But this devotion to duty does not entail administrative professionalism, and the importance and quantity and nature of business handled by a freedman administrator need have been no different from that dealt with by a senator or equestrian in public office. The administrative jobs which they did were, however mundane, like those of their superiors, generally to be described under the heading *litterae*. Their copying, writing, recording, and transmitting of information was important: as an expert on the subject says, 'the *tabellarii* (secretaries) were without doubt a necessary cog in the administrative machine, but most of the others in the jungle that was the Palace service seem to have been somewhat less than indispensable to the efficient running of the Roman Empire'. But in that case we are entitled to ask where the machine of which the *tabellarii* were a cog actually was. The freedmen did not constitute an administrative cadre; they were not dogsbodies doing the 'real' work of running the

Empire. The specific titles that they enjoyed, great and humble alike, mislead; they reflect only the aspect of household life which gave them status, proximity to the Emperor. Hence, for example, the moral indignation of Epictetus (1. 17. 18–19) at the high authority of the man who empties the Emperor's chamber-pot. Epictetus, freedman of a freedman of the Emperor and famous—if unconventional—philosopher (below, pp. 352 ff.), embodies an important truth about this milieu. The successful retinue of the Emperor were, or aspired to be, part of the ordinary upper-class world of Rome, taking part in its literary and intellectual culture. The inscriptions show us imperial freedmen in all sorts of activities quite unconnected with the Palace. Like any influential Roman, they devoted themselves to government only in an amateur and part-time way, and when they reached, like Pallas and Narcissus, the councils of state, it was as the friends, advisers, and confidants of the Emperor, not as expert bureaucrats. It is because of their *personal* power that by the late Empire the imperial domestics like the Grand Chamberlain have acquired the legitimate public functions which make the court of that period begin to seem medieval.

Government and Litterae

The search for bureaucracy in the Roman world is vain. We should now look a little more closely at the concern with jurisdiction and exaction which Roman administrators really did have. Then, in conclusion, we can consider in general terms the nature of the governmental process and attempt to discover what really held the empire together.

Because Roman officials spent so much time in jurisdiction it was natural that Roman law should become more complicated and more sophisticated. The natural rule that jurisdiction gravitates to the highest available authority operated to increase the workload of governors, the great prefects at Rome, and the Emperor himself, and to hasten the adoption of Roman law. Even in the reign of Augustus, Strabo can already write that

Crete, despite its own venerable legal tradition, had come, like all the provinces, to use the laws of Rome (10. 4. 22). And the bitterest realism about conditions in the Roman Empire cannot overlook the advantages of the existence of a legal framework to imperial rule, which the Hellenistic kingdoms had lacked, and which offered the Empire's subjects at least the theoretical possibility of redress and restrained the arbitrariness of Rome's rule. Law too grew at Rome with the problems first of city and then of Empire, and legal expertise came to provide an entry to the governing class. Professional legal practice was eventually one of the activities which gave many provincials a place in government, and Roman law was one of the most tenacious legacies of imperial rule—its greatest codification was the product of the eastern Empire under Justinian. There is not space here to recount the gradual evolution of Roman law, but the long accumulation of legal interpretations and precedents in the annual edicts of the praetors, which, when codified by Hadrian, formed the foundation of the legal system, and the role of the Emperor as a source of law and patron of the great jurists of the late second and early third centuries need stressing. For our purposes, however, two connected things are important. First, at Rome there was no question of the separation of judiciary and legislature which is so important a liberal principle to modern political thinkers. The law at Rome was on the whole the creation of judges, not lawgivers. The second point follows from this: legal measures show the same variety, casualness, and lack of generality which we find in Roman administrative decisions, and indeed it is difficult to separate the two. There is no proper ancient equivalent of statute law. The result was that the law was not always sufficiently universal, and the under-privileged might well not reap its benefits. Jewish nationalist writers, for example, compare the hypocrisy of Rome to the ambiguous associations of the unclean pig: 'Just as a pig lies down and sticks out its trotters as though to say "I am clean" [because they are cloven], so the evil empire robs and oppresses while pretending to execute justice.'

For the burdens of Roman rule on the Empire were heavy and hated, and much of Roman government was devoted to ensuring their efficacy. The collection of tribute, direct and indirect tax, rents, levies in kind, recruits, protection money, requisitioning, and so on in total amounted to a very heavy oppression, even if the amount of tax formally due was not by comparative standards very high. Roman officials from the highest to the most menial were involved with these matters, and finance was a serious administrative concern. Augustus' great catalogue of his achievements is called in full *Res Gestae et Impensae* ('His Deeds and Expenditure'). And this is undoubtedly the view that most provincials had of the way the Empire worked. A prophecy of Rome's fall concentrated on both the exactions of the ruling power and—less often discussed but equally odious—drain of manpower to Italy via the slave trade: 'the wealth that Rome has received from tributary Asia threefold shall Asia receive again from Rome, which will pay in full the price of its insolent pride. And for each of those who labour in the land of the Italians twenty Italians shall toil in Asia as needy slaves', (*Oracula Sibyllina* 3.350 f). Given this hostility to the harsh realities of the Empire, and given the amateur nature of Roman government, how was stability achieved?

Communications have been described as the nervous system of the body politic. Compared with what had gone before and what followed the rule of Rome, the frequency of movement and the security of roads and harbours was most impressive (though banditry never completely disappeared even from Italy). The imperial posting system, a creation of Augustus refined over the following centuries, became so huge, authoritative, and elaborate that it represented one of the heaviest burdens on the provincials whose food, animals, and dwellings were constantly being requisitioned for passing officials, as inscriptions from a wide range of places and times bear eloquent witness. But there can be no doubt that the roads and harbours of the Empire were one of the most necessary organs of Roman rule.

The transmission, retrieval, and storage of information is

a still more basic ingredient of the stability, durability, and effectiveness of government. Max Weber called documents the bureaucrat's tools of production. The Roman Empire has won a reputation for bureaucratic sophistication. So what of its documents? Before the nineteenth century, it is interesting to note, this aspect of Roman imperial rule did not strike students of the period. It was the discovery of the *papyri* of Egypt which contributed to the view that Rome too had been a bureaucracy like those burgeoning in the excavators' homelands. Since then the spectacular complexity of the administration of Egypt has been further revealed, and evidence from other dry regions— Dura Europus on the Euphrates is a notable example—has shown that the volume of administrative paperwork in other eastern provinces was likewise very great. The figures can be astonishing. A third-century regional administrator's office in Egypt consumed 434 rolls of papyrus in a particular period of about a month. The archives of the fortress at Dura Europus occupied more than ten rooms. It is easy incautiously to assert that this society can truly be called bureaucratic'. But two problems must be faced. First, is the practice of either Egypt or Mesopotamia, where the accumulation of documents was an extremely ancient aspect of government, typical of the eastern Empire in general, and is the East typical of the Empire as a whole? Papyrus archives naturally would not survive elsewhere, but the absence of the potsherds which were also extensively used at the lowest level of the Egyptian administration, is a better testimony to the singularity of the Egyptian system, since pottery is virtually indestructible. But the second question is more important: how far is this accumulation of mounds of paper by dozens of officials evidence for a bureaucratic administration of the kind found in modern states? To answer that question it will be necessary to discover why records were accumulated and how they were then deployed. Are our ancient administrative documents from working bureaux, lumber rooms, or something in between?

Even the ability to write documents such as the papyri which survive was not common in antiquity. We even hear in Egypt of illiterate scribes. Not so absurd: to be a scribe was a significant status, worth aspiring to through fraud. Of Pharaonic Egypt we know that scribes were men of very great importance in the state, and the pairing of Scribe with Pharisee is a still more familiar example of the way in which the skills conferred status. In China the skills of scholar and scribe, regulated by an amazing system of public examinations, defined the governmental class. In neither Greece nor Rome does the scribe have this status. At Rome the scribes played a role of their own in the political and social life of the city. The Emperor's service employed numerous clerks and secretaries. But it was not the handlers or documents, the men with the skills, who rose high. It was much more the *cubicularii*, the personal servants, the confidants of the Emperor or of poweful men. And they rose not through skill, dedication, or inside information, but through the patronage which came from social contacts. None of this speaks of a bureaucracy.

The scribe of ancient Egypt is portrayed cross-legged, his writing equipment on his lap, ready to move wherever he may be required. The classical scribe likewise was always mobile: there were clerks, but no offices. No ancient office building and no ancient desk will ever be discovered. Strikingly, when ancient administrative departments acquired a metaphorical name, it was not that of an unportable item of furniture, but the scribe's portable roll-satchel, the *scrinium*. Administration revolved around people, not around places or buildings, and not, despite those mountains of papyrus, around documents.

The documents were stored in archive rooms, some of which are known archaeologically. But although papers were kept, there were no filing cabinets, card indexes, reference numbers, registration forms. Collections of documents were made by pasting them together in chronological or—by no means as often as convenience would dictate—in alphabetical order. The codex, the presentation of documents as a book, was occasionally used, but the cartulary, a choice of really important documents for frequent reference, was unknown. Papers were preserved in archives, but it was well known that in most conditions papyrus did not keep well. Why did these things not matter? Because retrieval of documents from the archive was not a particularly urgent consideration in its formation. The tax assessment notice, the letter from the commanding officer, the tax receipt, the birth registration were used only once, in the process of checking a particular tax collection, or implementing a decision. Access to the document *might* be required a second time, but probably only a tiny fraction of all documents was ever looked at twice. The consultation of a document was a serious matter: 'for which reason, pious and benevolent Caesar, order that I be given a copy from your *commentarii* as your father intended', says a petitioner to Hadrian (*ILS* 338). Administrative processes were a favour, a privilege, a wonder, which is why on documents like this, where only what does credit to the purchaser of the inscription appears, what seem to us to be banal details of this kind are recorded in full. So this one actually preserves Hadrian's orders to his secretaries: 'Stasimus, Dapenis, publish the decision or opinion from the recorded version (*edite ex forma*)'. Authentication was a serious problem, never entirely solved, which helped prevent reliance on documentary authority. The *sardonychus* or imperial signet-ring gave its name to a Palatine department (see, e.g., *ILS* 1677), but there were often rumours that it had fallen into unauthorized hands. The Emperors used codes, but only rather simple ones. One of the principal reasons for the abuse of the public post system was that there was no reliable way of ensuring that only a limited number of people possessed authentic licences to demand hospitality and service. Distribution was another problem. It is very hard for us to imagine how difficult, despite the efficiency of communications, the systematic exchange of documentary information was. A letter of Trajan to Pliny making an important administrative point need never have been known in next door Asia, let alone Germania Inferior. This is perhaps one reason why Pliny's heirs actually published his correspondence. This difficulty no doubt helped to discourage the formation of any monolithic imperial administrative structure.

Documents, once stored, were of surprisingly little use. Governmental acts could not afford to depend on such an unreliable basis. The archives represented continuity and stability, and were not for regular use. The truth appears well from the story of the disastrous fire of AD 192 at Rome, when the central imperial archives of the Palatine were completely destroyed (Dio 73. 24). There is no hint that Roman government was disrupted; but the event was taken as a token that the authority of Rome, embodied in these documents, would weaken. The omen is not so far removed from the association of Rome's universal rule with a census registration at the beginning of the Gospel of St Luke.

Another famous fire, this time not accidental, destroyed 3,000 inscribed tablets on the Capitoline during the Civil War of AD 69. Vespasian, by contrast with the events just described, saw to it that new texts were inscribed whenever another version of one of the perished documents could be discovered. State documents, we must not forget, included texts on stone and bronze and wood, and in the arts of government these were perhaps more important than the ones which were stacked in dusty muniment rooms. The ancient world was a uniquely epigraphic culture—otherwise our view of it, and especially of its institutions, would be very different. In classical Greece Athens had been exceptional in the extent to which it encouraged the publication on stone of official texts. During the Hellenistic period this important governmental act became a universal practice which was naturally enough adopted by Rome. The inscribing of a decision made it seem more permanent; it gained from the association of other venerable and welcome enactments inscribed nearby, and from the religious, political, or sentimental tone of the place in which it was set up. To give only one example: the patents of citizenship of discharged auxiliary soldiers were at first tacked in hundreds to the Temple of the Good Faith of the Roman People to its Friends, high on the Capitol in the very heart of the Empire, powerfully expressing the relationship of Rome to its loyal subjects. A collection of privileges, honours, even historical or—in at least one case—philosophical texts could be a source of pride even to those who could not read them. For although there are pieces of evidence that the inscription was a source of information to the public—it was a tyrant's trick to hang savage edicts out of clear sight—it is revealing that published Roman laws sometimes contained the provision that the text was to be read aloud at regular intervals. Similarly we may assume that it was the moment when herald, ambassador, or magistrate first read the Emperor's letter to the city that it had its effect: the inscribing was a symbol of the city's gratitude and appreciation, and of the measure's permanence.

Depositing a document in an archive was not so different an act. The record depository might be in a significant temple (at Rome death registrations were kept in the grove of the goddess of funerals). The main Roman archive was part of a prestigious complex of buildings on the sacred Capitoline hill, high above the Forum. The close connection between the perishable documents and the public inscription, and the purpose of preserving the text, is excellently shown by an epigraphic version from an Italian town, page by page with chapter headings, of a section of the town-council minutes relevant to the honorific purpose at hand (*ILS* 5918[a]). It emerges that the minutes themselves were less practical in purpose than a part itself of civic ceremony; it seems that a new roll would be formally started each year on Augustus' official birthday. The keeping of such records had very little to do with future practical utility.

If record keeping in antiquity is understood in this way, it begins to become clear that we should not be surprised at finding no serious bureaucracy and no administrative art as such in the ancient world. Those involved in government needed no special training. It is true that, for example, shorthands were developed, but it is revealing that they are associated at Rome with the names of two men of high culture, Cicero's amanuensis Tiro and Horace's patron Maecenas. But importantly, although so many papyri concern counting and taxation, the ancient world had no systematic knowledge of accounting, and no concept of numeracy. Book-keeping, hindered by the number systems of Greek and Latin, always remained primitive. It is very strange, when the marginal subsistence of the ancient poor is considered, how low a standard of accuracy is found in papyrus and epigraphical calculations. What was required of an administrator was (after loyalty and probity) *litterae*, the whole world of ancient literary culture. The Younger Pliny (*EP.* 1. 10. 9) is most revealing on the subject. As prefect of the Roman treasury he has to spend his time at the most banal and routine administrative business; his work is 'extremely uncultured'—but the word he uses to describe it is *litterae*, none the less.

That administration was *litterae* is an observation which will enable us to end on a rather more positive note: up to now we have been necessarily preoccupied, sadly, with abandoning Auden's image of the bored clerk's 'pink official form'. It has been stressed that ancient government was concerned with warfare, jurisdiction, and the management of private property. What kept alive this ideology was the aristocratic literary culture for which ancient civilization has always been most famous. The leader of men, the just judge, and the fair master had been ideals since Homer. For Herodotus the origin of the power of the Median—and hence the Persian—kingship was simply the impartiality and importance to society of the judgements of Deioces. There was no distinction between the Arts of Government and the other *technai*, *artes*, with which ancient élites concerned themselves. The art of rhetoric above all united what we see as these two distinct worlds. Eloquence is one of the main requirements of the ancient administrator. The Roman Emperor himself always expressed himself in the literary forms of letters or speeches, and spent most of his day listening to similar products of ancient literary culture. The generalizations and principles expressed in Roman governmental pronouncements are not a coherent ideology, and still less an indication of imperial policies, but simply commonplaces of moral or political thought deployed appropriately in a literary composition. It was not easy to aspire to participation in this sort of exercise. In fact, in its formal intellectual demands, membership of the Roman administrative élite was not after all so very different from the system which evolved in China.

Vitruvius, the architect in the public service, expressly praises his parents for the general philological and technical/artistic education which has made him what he is (6, pr. 4). Philostratus sneers at the lack of success of an imperial freedman whose inadequate literary attainments let him down, 'Celer, a writer of technical works and a good enough secretary of the emperor, but lacking in polish' (*VS* 1.22). For slaves and freedmen, equestrians and senators alike, culture was the sign of and often the way to social success, and at no level of the Roman administration do we find functionaries who are carrying out some sort of 'serious' administrative activity while their seniors indulge in cultural pursuits.

I have also emphasized the importance of Rome's inclusion of the élites of the Empire, above all of Greece, in her government. This too would not have been possible had Greek and Latin speakers not already come to share a common cultural heritage. It is therefore no coincidence that the age of the greatest governmental complexity of the ancient world and that flowering of culture which we call the Second Sophistic came together. The aristocratic ideals which underlay ancient government also required conspicuous expenditure on the part of rulers. Much that is familiar about the Roman world from Gibbon's portrait of the Antonine golden age derives from this. The enormous tomb which Claudius' freedman Pallas built for himself, the vast scale of the military engineering of Hadrian's Wall, and the great building projects of the Emperor at Rome and the urban upper classes in the hundreds of cities of the Empire are all themselves part of the great Art by which the Empire was maintained. The reciprocal relations of benefaction, competiton, and prestige among those who controlled the resources of the ancient world are found throughout antiquity, from the aristocracies of the archaic Greek cities to the Roman Emperors. In these relations were included the whole rangs of ancient cultural activities, from architecture and utilitarian building to the patronage of literature, music, and painting—and also to the entertainments of the circus and the amphitheatre and the religious festivals which were the setting of almost all these forms of display. This characteristic aspect of ancient society produced a type of bond between the élite and the peoples of the cities which was unique—a major source of the stability and continuity which we associate with the Greek and Roman world.

Unfortunately ancient culture had never rid itself of its uneasy companion, warfare. In the end this aspect came to be dominant. There came a time when scribes were soldiers, bishops were soldiers, local governors were soldiers, the Emperor was a soldier. At that point the end of the ancient world was in sight. It is therefore again no coincidence that the first great crisis of Roman rule and the cultural desert of the third century came together, even if it would be too simple to say that either brought about the other.

Further Reading

Fundamental is F. Millar, *The Emperor in the Roman World* (London, 1977), not only for the role of the Emperor but for very many aspects of Roman government. For the city-state M. I. Finley, *Politics in the Ancient World* (Cambridge, 1983) is suggestive and interesting though unreliable on Rome itself; on citizenship A. N. Sherwin-White, *The Roman Citizenship*[2] (Oxford, 1973) remains basic. For the Greek world A. H. M. Jones, *The Greek City* (Oxford 1940), and for Italy W. Eck, *Die staatliche Organisation Italiens* (Munich, 1979). On town statuses F. Abbott and A. C. Johnson, *Municipal Administration in the Roman Empire* (Princeton, 1926) is still very useful. On the definition of provinces and *imperium*, A. Lintott, *Greece & Rome* 28 (1981), 53 f. For governors' assizes, G. Burton, JRS 65(1975), 926. An account of how the Empire worked which complements what is said here will be found in P. Garnsey and R. P. Saller, *The Roman Empire, Economy, Society, and Culture* (London, 1987), ch. 2, 'Government without bureaucracy'.

For the military angle R. MacMullen, *Soldier and Civilian in the later Roman Empire* (Harvard, 1963), is crucial; and see now L. Keppie, *The Making of the Roman Army* (London, 1984), and J. B. Campbell, *The Emperor and the Roman Army* (Oxford, 1984); on the Emperor's military planning F. Millar, *Britannia* 13 (1982), 1 f. For *praefecti fabrum* B. Dobson, *Britain and Rome* ed.

B. Dobson and M. G. Jarrett (Kendal, 1966), pp. 61 f. Amateur commanders: J. B. Campbell, *JRS* 65 (1975), 11 f.

For slaves in the public service L. Halkin, *Les ésclaves publics chez les romains* (Liége, 1897); for the *apparitores* N. Purcell, *PBSR* 51 (1983), 125 f. On the imperial household A. M. Duff, *Freedmen in the Early Roman Empire* (Oxford, 1926); P. R. C. Weaver, *Familia Caesaris* (Cambridge, 1972). The quotation about the imperial civil service is from P. A. Brunt, *JRS* 65 (1975), 124 f., which establishes that the administrators of Roman Egypt had no particular qualifications for the job. On equestrian procurators H. G. Pflaum, *Les procurateurs équestres* (Paris, 1972) presents the results of a monumental survey. For reasons for promotion see R. P. Saller, *Personal Patronage under the Early Empire* (Cambridge, 1982), chs. 2–3, making a very strong case against promotion for merit. For status, not administrative function, as the way to understand the *familia Caesaris* G. Burton, *JRS* 67 (1977), 162 f. The quotation about the *tabellarii* is from Weaver, cit.

On law, J. Crook, *Law and Life of Rome* (London, 1967); A. N. Sherwin-White, *Roman Society and Law in the New Testament* (Oxford, 1963). For a detailed survey of imperial finance, P. A. Brunt, *JRS* 71 (1981), 161 f. The remark about the pig is quoted from N. de Lange, 'Jewish Attitudes to the Roman Empire', in P. Garnsey and C. Whittaker, edd., *Imperialism in the Ancient World* (Cambridge, 1978), p. 255. For the miseries of ancient provincial subjects R. MacMullen, *Roman Social Relations* (Yale, 1974). On benefaction and dependence, P. Veyne, *Bread and Games* (English edn. of *Le Pain et le cirque* (Paris, 1976), in preparation).

Roman Egypt: a useful survey is A. K. Bowman, *Egypt after the Pharaohs* (London, 1986). On documents and records E. Posner, *Archives in the Ancient World* (Cambridge, Mass., 1972). For Rome's fostering of the élites of the empire G. E. M. de Ste. Croix, *The Class Struggle in the Ancient Greek World* (London, 1981), who (p. 503) likens the behaviour of the rulers of the Empire to that of vampire bats.

8

Augustan Poetry and Society

R. O. A. M. LYNE

THIS is perhaps the most eventful period of Roman history, witness to civil wars, revolution, and, eventually, an imposed peace: Republic becomes Empire. Meanwhile, Latin literature produces its greatest works; Italy produces poets destined to achieve immortality. The present chapter offers a sketch of this extraordinary time. First, three divisions within the period must be identified.

Dates and Divisions

The triumviral period begins in 43 BC, when the Roman world was put into the hands of Octavian, Antony, and Lepidus 'for the purposes of setting the state in order'. Antony was defeated at the battle of Actium in 31 BC, but the first Augustan period may be said to begin in the year 27 BC when Octavian's imperial role is effectively, but discreetly, defined and he himself assumes the name Augustus. Another change is then discernible about 20 BC: Augustus exercises his monarchical power more assertively, and this has a large effect upon literature.

The works that will be considered below may now be assigned to these three divisions, though some of the assignations are approximate and some insecure. Into the first, the triumviral period, fall the *Eclogues* and most of the *Georgics* of Virgil, the *Epodes* and *Satires* of Horace; Propertius' Book 1 is published at the beginning of the first Augustan period, but much of it may have been composed earlier. Propertius' Book 2, Tibullus' Books 1 and 2, Horace's *Odes* 1–3, and Virgil's *Aeneid* are all substantially works of this first Augustan period (though the *Aeneid* is unfinished at Virgil's death in 19 BC); at the end of it we can place Horace's *Epistles* 1 and 2.2, and Propertius 3, and we can detect signs of the atmosphere of the second Augustan period in those works. To this second Augustan period we may then assign Propertius 4, and Horace's *Odes* 4, *Epistle* 2.1 (the *Epistle to Augustus*), and *Ars Poetica*. Ovid's *Amores* straddle the two Augustan periods, while the remainder of his works all belong to the second.

The Role of Poets

Our period sees the culmination of a process of change in the status of poets and poetry, a change of fundamental importance. Traditionally—let us say in the second century BC—poets, unlike historians, had been of low social status (foreigners or freedmen for example) and their works and profession were positively revered only in one particular respect, their power to confer lasting fame. Drama was of course valued as entertainment, and dramatists unlike other poets were directly paid; but in general philistinism towards poetry was endemic. Aristocrats with aesthetic taste and education like Scipio Aemilianus were exceptions. Even by the time of Cicero things have not much changed: Cicero has to tread cautiously in his defence of the poet Archias, presupposing philistinism in his audience. Nor is Cicero himself boundlessly aesthetic. Given a second life, he said, he would still not bother to read the Greek lyric poets.

When upper-class Romans do start to turn their hands to poetry, one gets the impression of amateurs, more or less condescending. Q. Lutatius Catulus and others toss off epigrams at the end of the second century, showing an acquaintance with Greek precedents, probably from anthologies; but Catulus at least, consul in 102 BC with C. Marius, had better things to do with his serious time. The satirist Lucilius is a much more significant figure (his literary *floruit* can be put in the 130s BC). He is rich and of high rank, great enough to be friend and foe of the greatest men of his generation—great enough also to utter his sometimes scarifying opinions on these great men, as well as on more humble figures, in his able and fluent verse. His development of the genre of satire is important in the history of Latin literature; so is his assertively autobiographical standpoint; so in particular is the importance he accords to the business of writing. Nevertheless I do not think we have in Lucilius an instance of an aristocrat seriously adopting the profession of poet. It was what he said that mattered to him; and, clothing his thoughts in a racy patchwork of Greek tags and often colloquial Latin and disposing all that in a range of metres, he found an eye-catching and ear-catching way of saying what he wanted to say. It was the message that mattered for him; he was a commentator on the contemporary scene rather than an artist—although as an artist he was, incidentally, pretty good.

In the shift in attitude towards poets and poetry it is the so-called Neoteric movement in the late Republic that is crucial: the group of poets comprising Catullus, Calvus, Cinna, and others. These are men of the provincial or Roman upper classes who take the profession of poetry with utmost seriousness. They at least think that it well befits an upper-class Roman simply to be a poet. Catullus, of course, we know most about. After a brief brush with active life he devoted his whole energies to poetry—and love. Symptomatic of his poetical professionalism is his interest in and knowledge of the professional poet and scholar of Alexandria, Callimachus (Vol. 1, pp. 414 ff.). Catullus is probably best known for his love poetry and for his lampoons and invectives; but arguably most indicative of him as an artist and certainly as a Neoteric are his intricate and highly wrought longer poems, such as 64 (the *Peleus and Thetis*), 68, and his translation of Callimachus, 66. But these poems are also indicative of something which went hand in glove, perhaps inevitably, with this new interest in the business of poetry: aestheticism, an interest in technique for technique's sake. This tendency was probably more pronounced in Cinna. His 'miniature epic' *Zmyrna* took nine years to write and attracted a scholarly commentary in the next generation.

Our period sees the final shift in attitude towards poetry and poets. Not only can poetry now appear a reputable full-time occupation for Romans of good class. Poets relinquish aestheticism, engage themselves with society, discover or profess commitment—or have to defend non-commitment. In short, the classical Greek view of poetry is again in play: it is the work of important people and may serve the citizens of the state in a moral and educative fashion. Virgil and his poetry will be glanced at below and discussed in another chapter. Of the elegiac poets (the term refers to their metre, cf. Vol. 1, pp. 108 f., and does not have the mournful overtones of the English 'elegy'), Tibullus is a knight, well off in Horace's eyes, though less so in his own; Ovid and Propertius were knights (*equites*), and Propertius had relations of senatorial rank and friends of consular standing. The attitude of these poets towards society will be discussed below. Horace is less grand than Propertius or Tibullus: he is the son of a freedman, but a freedman with enough cash to put him through the equivalent of a university education at Athens. Eventually Horace gained the status of a kind of poet laureate. He not only performs, with some intermission, the function of moral and educative poet; he expresses it in theory.

Given that poets were traditionally of low social status, and given that no system of royalties or the like existed in the Roman world (except for dramatists), how did poets live? The answer basically is: patronage. Poets attached themselves to, or were collected by, wealthy Roman aristocrats. The great epic poet Ennius, for example (above, pp. 86 ff.), was patronized by, among others, M. Fulvius Nobilior, and a catalogue of other poets could be adduced who wrote epics celebrating aristocratic generals and thereby gained their sustenance. Poets fitted into the general Roman client—patron system whereby great men were attended, cultivated, and in humble matters assisted by the humble, and in return bestowed their bounty and their protection. But even in early days there was a difference between poet-clients and ordinary clients. For what the patron got from the poet was something that was rather more estimable than that which other clients could offer: the perpetuation of their fame and glory. More than that: *memoria sempiterna*, 'being remembered for ever', was the way in which many Romans, including Cicero, viewed how they might 'live' after death; so what a poet might offer was in effect a chance of immortality. This is the keynote of Cicero's defence of Archias, mentioned above: Archias had provided immortality for Marius and Lucullus and, through them, for the Roman People. This aspect of the poet's function in Rome is a vital one, continuing into our period.

As the status of poet changes, so does the nature of patronage. Catullus, whose family is friendly with Julius Caesar and soon to become senatorial, has no economic need of a patron and does not have one. His circle is a coterie, a grouping of equals, and his address to Cornelius Nepos in his first poem is to be construed as a friendly or polite gesture, no more. Similarly Propertius, in his first book. But patronage does persist, even among the socially enhanced poets of the Augustan period.

The circle of the great orator, soldier, and statesman, M. Valerius Messalla, consul with Octavian in 31 BC, is indicative, exhibiting both continuity and change. There are in fact points of resemblance between his circle and a coterie such as that of Catullus. Pliny tells us that Messalla interested himself in the writing of erotic versicles, and we can observe him surrounded by other love poets and poetasters (coterie fashion), who include his aristocratic niece Sulpicia. On the other hand, if the author of the *Panegyricus Messallae* in the Tibullan corpus belongs to the circle and is talking of our Messalla (as is likely), then here is continuity in the role of poet as client: the client-poet immortalizes the great man. But it is the relation of the elegist Tibullus to Messalla that is most interesting.

Although Tibullus is vastly the social inferior of the noble Messalla, he is a knight, he does reflect the change in status of poets—and yet his relationship to Messalla resembles the old one of client and patron. He writes poems that, while not being technically panegyrics, devote themselves to the celebration of Messalla and his family (1.7 and 2.5), and scatters his other poems with laudatory allusions. Patronage survives the changes in status of poets and poetry. The phenomenon is of course observable in the circle of Maecenas, and elsewhere. So we ask ourselves: To what extent is this literary patronage like the old kind? What are both parties now getting out of it?

Some basic points can be inferred—Ovid, who was patronized early in his career by Messalla, is informative. These upper-class poets were not dependent economically in the way that their predecessors had been (though more on this anon). What they obtained was the encouragement of a great man usually himself a littérateur, the cachet of being associated with a well-known group of poets, access to such like-minded people (they would meet and some would even live in the great man's house), and perhaps above all publicity. Although at this time literature is intensely literate, written ultimately to be read and propagated in texts, an initial and important mode of communication is oral: various kinds of readings—private readings among the poets, semi-public and public recitations (formal public *recitationes* were instituted in Rome by Asinius Pollio). This was the scene in which a poet might make his name, and the chance to recite to an audience organized by a great patron was crucially important to a rising poet. Horace deplored both the institution of recitation and the fact that fame accrued thereby; but deploring it did not remove it, and even Horace himself recited. As for the patron, he had the natural satisfactions that such patronage brings, and he had, too, his chance of a piece of immortality. And in the circle of Maecenas something else was happening.

In the first Augustan period, Maecenas is the Augustan patron, mediating between poets and *princeps*. We can identify very important points of difference between his circle and, say, Messalla's. First, Augustus naturally wanted his heroic deeds enshrined in an epic—his piece of immortality. The trouble was that Maecenas' poets—Virgil, Horace, and subsequently Propertius—had to a varying extent scruples, moral and literary. The accommodating Tibullus could include celebrations of Messalla and his military exploits amongst his elegies in praise of love and peace. Not so Propertius. And, emphatically, he was not an epic poet. Nor was Horace. Neither, to begin with, was Virgil. This presented a problem. These men were not old-style client-poets to be booted into an uncongenial genre. But Augustus was, to put it mildly, powerful. How does one deal with, on the one hand, upper-class poets with scruples and, on the other, an Emperor who wants an epic? The answer is that one is diplomatic, one mediates, one explains; and it is greatly to Maecenas' credit that his poets had the freedom, for a time, to decline impositions or fulfil them in their own individual way (as will be illustrated below).

Besides the moral and artistic sensitivity of his poets, Maecenas' circle was different from others in other and crucial respects. First and simply, the scale of what was on offer. These poets were not humble paupers, but Horace at least needed a living, and all had lost property in the land confiscations of the triumviral period. What Maecenas and Augustus bestowed on Horace and Virgil was vast (particularly, it seems, in Virgil's case), enabling them to live in very comfortable leisure in town or country. A certain moral pressure must therefore have been felt by these morally sensitive artists. Secondly, the task towards which they were being pressured was not just to immortalize the heroic deeds of the greatest general. It was something unique to the circle of Maecenas, reflecting the unique nature of his and later Augustus' patronage. Augustus and the state were effectively synonymous. To be in his patronage, directly or indirectly, was to be in the patronage of government, and there was a pressure to publicize the government's policies and to burnish its image. This task could be seen as invidious, but it could also be seen as a challenging responsibility; and with varying degrees of enthusiasm and directness, these scrupulous poets tackled it.

The nature of patronage in the imperial circle changes with

the second Augustan period. Indeed this change may be seen to
be part-cause of the second period arising. The sophisticated
Maecenas, for reasons that cannot be defined with certainty,
fades in importance, and the poets come under the direct patronage of the Emperor. His hand was heavier, and it was becoming increasingly so. Political life around 20 BC reveals a
more confidently autocratic ruler (witness, for instance, the
marriage laws of 18 BC), and poetry, lacking the mediation of
Maecenas, must also respond to his touch. A fourth book of
Odes is elicited from an unwilling Horace, for example, containing what he had largely avoided in recent years: panegyric.
The 'educator of citizens' becomes the court poet—but he has
ways of striking back.

Virgil

Against this background I shall now outline the careers of the
individual poets. Virgil's place in the picture must be adumbrated, but with all brevity since a separate chapter (Ch. 9) is
devoted to him. His *Eclogues*, written in the triumviral period,
show him ambivalent between the aestheticism of the Neoterics
and an emerging sense of commitment. Elegant imitations of
Theocritean pastoral glance at the miseries caused by land
confiscations. While writing the *Eclogues* Virgil is not in the
patronage of Maecenas. While writing the *Georgics* he is; and
the *Georgics*, instigated or at least encouraged by Maecenas,
show that Maecenas was not immediately concerned to elicit
material that directly or crudely served Octavian. But the poem
is to a great degree a moral didactic, hence of potential if rather
indefinite use to a ruler; and it shows Virgil's strengthening sense
of his committed poetic role.

It also demonstrates an attitude towards country life, an
attitude which can be paralleled. Unlike Catullus and, say,
Propertius, Virgil loves and esteems rustic life. But whereas the
dominating reality of contemporary agriculture was large slave-
run estates, Virgil esteems the small independent farmer—and

exploits his way of life as a metaphor for morality. The simple point I want to stress is that in spite of the prevalence of great ranches, such small farmers were still around. Evidence testifies to their minority existence; and the policy of settling soldiers on confiscated property might, if it was successful (as it probably was not), have increased their numbers. So Virgil's affectionate view of the country is we might say old-fashioned, blinkered, even slightly romantic; but it is not a mere fiction or poetic convention.

I said above that no immediate pressure was being exerted by Maecenas for a poem directly to serve Octavian. But both he and Virgil would know that the great man would want his exploits celebrated in epic, and that is what Virgil seems to promise at the beginning of *Georgics* III. In fact, in the sophisticated atmosphere of the first Augustan period, he developed an indirect, mythical mode whose fruit was the *Aeneid*—and the Emperor was, perhaps rather surprisingly, well pleased.

Horace

In the triumviral period Horace writes his *Epodes*, in Archilochian *iambi*, and his *Satires*, his development of Lucilius' genre. We can still discern vestiges of republican libertarianism and non-alignment in them. *Epodes* 7 and 16 consider with neutral despair the imminence of civil war. Other *Epodes* are vicious attacks, in Archilochian vein. Some *Satires* too attack personages, but in general Horace's *Satires* are more general and genial than those of Lucilius, and neither *Epodes* nor *Satires* assail men of eminence. Horace had not the protection of rank; and besides, the triumviral period was a despotic one, with the added complication that one could not be sure which despot would come out on top.

This is, however, also the period in which Maecenas gathers Horace into his circle, and Horace is induced to commit himself enthusiastically to Octavian. *Epode* 9 is a celebration of the victory of Actium, and *Epode* 1, addressed to Maecenas, is the effusive poem of a man who definitely sees himself in a patronized position; it reminds one of Tibullus talking to Messalla. *Satire* 2.6 records with gratitude the gift of the famous Sabine estate, and *Satire* 1.1 is also addressed to Maecenas.

On the other hand, Horace is careful about himself and his image in his patronized position. In *Satire* 1.9 and 1.6, the poem in which he describes his acceptance into Maecenas' circle, he is careful to define that acceptance as an honourable process, based on merit, and the circle as one of like-minded men free from the debasing procedures which characterized many client–patron groupings. Indeed he terms himself the 'friend' (*amicus*) of Maecenas. Although the language of *amicitia* was convention-ally used between clients and patrons, and it would be quite clear who was the grand *amicus* and who was not, there is much evidence that Horace genuinely was friendly in the full sense of the word with Maecenas and even with Augustus. Indeed, he was familiar enough with Maecenas to allude in *Epode* 14 to an erotic liaison on the great man's part with an actor, Bathyllus.

In *Odes* 1–3, belonging to the first Augustan period, Horace assumes the role of a Roman Alcaeus. It was the usefulness of the image rather than the material of Alcaeus' texts that suggested this choice. Horace presents the image of Alcaeus, with discreet distortion, as follows (*Odes* 1.32). Alcaeus was an intensely committed citizen-poet, *engagé*, patriotically writing about the burning issues of his time; he also knew, however, that there was a place on the margins of life for leisure, for love and wine, and for poetry of leisure, poetry of love and wine; and he wrote such leisure poetry, as well as *engagé* poetry, knowing it to be leisure poetry, marginal poetry. Thus the image, and it was indeed useful to Horace. Committed at this time to his belief in the social and educative role of the poet and yet at the same time a delighted and delightful poet of love and wine, he could thus, as a Roman Alcaeus, justify his production. Like Alcaeus, he was the committed public poet, but he knew nevertheless that it could be appropriate to relax and not unseemly to write poetry for such occasions. It was vital, simply, to keep a sense of proportion, and not to let the life and literature of leisure usurp the position of the serious business of life. That was the mistake of the Elegists. Tibullus is read a lesson in this connection in the *Ode* immediately following the presentation of the Alcaean image.

Horace makes a couple of false starts in his public poetry: *Odes* 1.2 and 12 border on unpalatable panegyric, and 1.2 imputes divinity to an Augustus anxious to avoid such adoration. But during this period he evolved a satisfying and sophisticated method of public poetry, an 'indirect' method which bears comparison with Virgil's procedure in the *Aeneid*. Horace's method is a process of *association* and *substitution*. A good example is *Odes* 3.5, in which the sequence of thought is this: Augustus will be considered analogous to a god (that sort of expression was seemly) when he has conquered Britain and Parthia; mention of Parthia brings to mind Crassus' defeat at the hands of the Parthians in 53 BC and the shocking fact that Roman prisoners were now living among the Parthians as Parthians; this disgrace is, Horace implies, what Augustus will avenge. Then Horace is prompted to recall an event, almost a myth, from Roman history, the story of Regulus, a story which also involved a hated enemy, Roman prisoners, and a great Roman general; and the telling of this story occupies the rest of the *Ode*.

Now in fact the parallels between the two episodes are slight, extending not much beyond the broad features just mentioned. But by means of a glossing formula of transition and by the mere fact of juxtaposition, Horace manages to associate the two generals (Augustus and Regulus), to assimilate Augustus' imminent honourable action in the matter of Parthians and prisoners to Regulus' action in the matter of prisoners and Carthaginians. Indirectly, therefore, he presents Augustus as a new Regulus: Stoic, honourable—and republican, a useful suggestion. By this process of association he avoids the invidiousness of direct and implausible praise. By the process of substitution—eleven of the fourteen stanzas of the *Ode* are devoted to the associated figure of Regulus, who is thus substituted for the contemporary figure Augustus—he gives himself artistic and indeed moral liberty. In both artistic and moral terms it is hard to sing stirringly about the impending expedition of a contemporary general; much easier to evoke the heroic action of a quasi-mythical figure. Similarly in 3.4 Horace discreetly associates Augustus' victory at Actium with Jupiter's victory over the Giants, a traditional paradigm of the victory of civilized force over barbarism; and he then devotes his lyrical attention to this, the substituted story. What poet could not write epically about such a story? What poet, on the other hand, would not find difficulties in lauding a contemporary battle like Actium? Horace himself had, back in *Odes* 1.37.

That is Horace in public vein. Here is a taste of Horace as poet of love. The first three stanzas of the famous Pyrrha *Ode* (1.5) run thus:

> quis multa gracilis te puer in rosa
> perfusus liquidis urget odoribus,
>   grato, Pyrrha, sub antro?
>   cui flauam religas comam,
>
> simplex munditiis? heu quotiens fidem
> mutatosque deos flebit et aspera
>   nigris aequora uentis
>   emirabitur insolens,
>
> qui nunc te fruitur credulus aurea,
> qui semper uacuam semper amabilem
>   sperat nescius aurae
>   fallacis. miseri, quibus
>
> intemptata nites! . . .

What slim boy, Pyrrha, drenched in liquid scents presses you in an abundance of roses under some pleasing grotto? For whom are you binding back your blonde hair in simple elegance? Alas, how often will he bewail fidelity and the gods changed, and wonder amazed at the sea made harsh by dark winds, he who now trustfully enjoys golden you, he who expects you always available, always lovable—ignorant of the deceiving breeze. Wretched are they for whom you shine untried . . . !

That carries a typical Horatian message which Horace, unlike the gullible youth in the poem, knows only too well. Love, the occupation of leisure, is a fleeting, evanescent, untrustworthy thing, though it can be none the less painful for that.

Odes 3.28 gives a taste of Horace as poet of wine as well as love. It too carries a typical Horatian message: Horace announces that it is a holiday, the *Neptunalia*, and therefore leisure time. What is he to do? Answer: drink good wine, make music—and love. So, in Horace's view, leisure pursuits, love and wine, should not usurp the position of serious business; but it is equally his view, embodied in this *Ode*, that leisure is not leisure without them.

It will be noted that the girls in Horace's poetry of love and wine have Greek names. If we investigate these names, if we investigate other details in the poems, we find that this leisure poetry reflects—with discretion, stylization, romance—a real society: the Roman *demi-monde*, the *symposion* scene, where girls of probably slave or freedwoman class entertained with music and sex. This fact is important in two respects. It shows that Horace's erotic and sympotic poetry is not mere fancy and convention. And it also shows that Horace as a rule enjoyed, or liked to be seen to be enjoying, his erotic pleasures with women, or boys, of the lower classes employed for that purpose. That was considered correct at Rome. To attempt an erotic liaison with an upper-class *uirgo* was or should be an impossibility, and to have affairs with married ladies was in the Augustan age to become literally criminal. That point was not always well taken.

Many of Horace's *Odes* in Books 1–3 are concerned neither with affairs of state nor merely with leisure and pleasure, but with ethics on a private scale: how a man in his private capacity should conduct his life. After the production of *Odes* 1–3 Horace returns to the hexameter metre of his *Satires* and, in the late twenties BC, writes *Epistles* (Book 1) which are devoted to such ethical exploration and instruction. In his introductory *Epistle* to Maecenas he explains that, for this new production, he is giving up verse 'and other such frivolities'. The statement lacks neither ambiguity nor disingenuousness: for a start, Horace is at that very moment technically writing verse. It is nevertheless true that he does temporarily relinquish his role as public poet and the more overtly poetical mode of lyric. Why? Some reasons are stated, some may be inferred. Horace's dislike of the business of being a professional poet (recitations and so on) is affirmed in *Epistle* 1.19 and reaffirmed in the *Epistle to Florus* (2.2) of 19 BC. He also attests lack of public acclaim for *Odes* 1–3, due to his unwillingness to participate in such business; that too may have been discouraging. Then again, the question of private ethics had always been a preoccupation of his, in *Satires* as well as in *Odes*. There is perhaps one more factor: something to do with the role of public poet, the poet as immortalizer, the poet as educator. Horace may have experienced lack of confidence in the role, or perhaps disenchantment with it, as the Maecenas era drew to its close; whatever it was, the cap was no longer fitting. In Book 3 Horace had been the 'priest of the Muses', addressing future generations in public and edifying tones. In the *Epistle to Florus*, this same man turns to discuss the various reasons for writing poetry—the reasons that might induce him to turn professional again—and does not mention poetry's grand functions, its functions to immortalize and in particular to edify. The silence seems to me significant: for some reason, Horace was unhappy about the poet in this sort of role.

Not for long, or he was not allowed to be for long. The second Augustan period is upon us. For the Secular Games of the year 17 BC, the games to mark the New Age, Horace writes the public hymn, the *Carmen saeculare*. Next he is induced under the direct patronage of Augustus to compose a fourth book of *Odes* containing, as I have said, courtly poems directly panegyrical of the Emperor and his family. On the other hand—a gesture of conscious or unconscious self-assertion—the book contains some of Horace's finest poetry of love and wine. The very first poem movingly evokes Horace in love, in love again at fifty, in love with a boy called Ligurinus. Note that name. For once the love-object in a Horatian homosexual love poem does not have a

Greek name; so he is neither cloaked in disguise nor assigned to an acceptably lowly class. Ligurinus is a real Roman *cognomen*. The poem is assertively personal—and very beautiful. Another beautiful poem of love and wine, also affectingly personal, is poem 11; and, satisfyingly, it is built round the birthday of the once great figure of Maecenas.

I do not think that Horace took up his public pen again totally willingly in this second Augustan period; but perhaps he was not totally unwilling. The reasons for his retirement are not, as I have said, perspicuous, and his description of poetry as frivolity was disingenuous. Certainly he came to be proud of the *Carmen saeculare*. And his *Epistle to Augustus* (2.1, of 12 BC) asserts once more the educative function of the poet and the power of poetry to immortalize. An interesting, incidental fact: in this epistle Horace implicitly argues for classic status to be accorded the Augustan poets: Virgil, the now lost Varius, and presumably himself. Over the love elegists a significant veil of silence is drawn: Ovid was, for example, by now the rage, but there is not a word on him. Finally, the *Ars Poetica* of the last years of his life shows him seriously occupied with poetry as a serious business, both entertaining and educative.

Propertius

Propertius is socially grander than Virgil and Horace and strikes a provocatively unconventional stance in life and literature (these two facts will not be unconnected). He seems never to have been so devoted or complete a member of Maecenas' circle as Virgil and Horace were.

Pragmatic Roman attitudes held that a man should do something serious with his life: conventionally, in the upper classes, he should advance it either in political or in economic terms. That was one position that Propertius confronted. But our period also sees, as I have said, poets regaining their classical status as civically committed, useful to the state, estimable creatures. Propertius confronts that idea too. He professes himself unemployed and unemployable in any conventional sense outside poetry, and 'useful' as a poet in ways which the conventional would regard as worse than useless. Whereas, therefore, Catullus the man had been prepared simply to *be* at leisure, Propertius declares it assertively, makes a manifesto of it; whereas Catullus the poet had occupied a position of unconcerned aestheticism, Propertius, in the new climate of artistic commitment, makes an aggressive statement of what in effect was non-commitment. I look at these points separately.

In a sequence of poems in Book 1 (1, 6, 14), Propertius declares his position on life and love. In contradistinction to Tullus, his addressee, Propertius cannot, he says, engage upon an active career. He must devote himself to love, and neither military/ political nor economic advancement can distract him. He represents his love as something without sense, mad even; a disease, degradation. He takes upon himself all the condemnatory terms that Roman society customarily assigned to a hopelessly lost romantic lover. He even accepts for himself a title that society was not accustomed to fling around; he is the slave of his mistress. And yet he insists: this is for me. His position remains much the same in Book 2, and in some poems of Book 3. The commitment to love may be taken seriously; the self-condemnation less so. Later Romantics were to find that a willing espousal of wrong could be satisfyingly provocative. Propertius presents a programme of life designed to provoke—and to provoke not only stern moralists, but discreet proponents of acceptable *amour* such as Horace. Here was exactly what Horace decried: love, which should be the occupation of leisure, usurping the serious business of life, indeed becoming coterminous with life.

Before we consider Propertius' views on poetry we must consider the woman of whom he writes. Who is Cynthia? She is quite fully sketched: among other things she is described as a woman of fine artistic accomplishments, but fond too of the lower sympotic pleasures. Her exact social status is hard to pin down: she sounds like a high-class courtesan, but she may have been perhaps a divorcée or a widow of dubious morals. The point to be stressed about her is that she is sexually independent, or relatively so. Unlike the bought objects of Horace's erotic world she can and does dominate; she can dominate the besotted Propertius simply by the power of being able to say 'No'. She is an important figure. Without such a figure, the Propertian type of 'life of love' could not exist.

How does Propertius view his role as poet? In Book 1 (poems 7–9) he phrases it with a provocativeness to match the provocativeness of his programme for life. He bases himself on his premiss that love equals life. That allows him to describe the traditionally grand genre of epic as useless. Meanwhile, he claims, his elegy can perform the vital task of winning round a recalcitrant or errant mistress; and, because of the knowledge and experience it contains, it can benefit others. In other words, within the 'life of love' (the only life for Propertius), elegy is useful and indeed educational, in contrast to epic's uselessness. We should mark what Propertius is doing here. He is managing to assign to his poetry the traditionally esteemed functions of usefulness and edification, while denying them to their traditional recipient, epic. It is a neat turnabout; non-commitment is nicely phrased as commitment. In Book 3 we find him similarly misassigning, misusing (some would say) a grand view of poetry's function, the grand idea that poetry can immortalize. Poem 2 boasts the power of Propertian elegy to immortalize a *girl*. Horace would certainly be among those who would call this a misuse; and, a nice touch, Horace's own language of immortality is imported to phrase that misuse.

Such statements as these are designed to provoke rather than to offer serious information on the nature of Propertius' poetry. His love poems tend, particularly in Book 1, to be either dramatic, a 'staged' interaction between himself and Cynthia or another character, or rhetorical, speeches of indignation, pain, joy, and so on, to various addressees. They all frequently exploit mythological comparisons, the resonance of the mythical world. And their achievement is to offer insight into the personalities

of Cynthia and Propertius, insight into their feelings and relationship, insight into love.

For example, poem 2 of book 1 is a speech to Cynthia dis-
suading her from meretricious behaviour, in particular the use
of cosmetics, and Propertius' mode of tackling the topic reveals
much about his own personality, about Cynthia's personality,
and about how the two interrelate. Poem 16 shrilly enquires
of Cynthia why she cannot display the devotion of Calypso,
Hypsipyle, and other romantic figures from myth—and exposes
thereby a tension that pervades Propertius' life and fuels much
of his love poetry. For Cynthia of course is not a romantic figure
from myth. But that is something that the romantic Propertius
finds so hard to accept. For a sample of a rhetorical poem the
reader is referred to 2.8. There Propertius justifies the grief he
is exhibiting at the loss of Cynthia by an appeal to the vast grief
displayed by Achilles on the loss of Briseis.

In Book 1, much of which may have been composed in the
triumviral period, Propertius is non-aligned and non-attached.
He includes a bitter poem (21) on the Perusine war of 41 BC,
bitter at the expense of the victor Octavian. This sort of independence of spirit is something he never loses.

Independence of spirit notwithstanding, the quality and
popularity of Book 1 attracted the attention of Maecenas; and
Maecenas suggested, inevitably, that Propertius might be well
employed in putting Augustus' deeds into epic. The opening
poem of Book 2 (first Augustan period) is a response to Maecenas' approach. It contains several interesting features. First,
to decline the proposition of epic, Propertius employs a device
which had been invented by Virgil and was used by other poets,
including Horace. It is basically to say 'I would if I could', and to
explain the inability by appeal to poetic powers or lack of them,
or to poetic alignment. Propertius, like Virgil, claims an alignment with Callimachus and, as everyone knew, Callimachean
aesthetics excluded epic. It is, however, clear that Propertius
neither phrases his Callimacheanism seriously nor indeed (unlike Virgil) was seriously Callimachean; nor did he intend to

1. INTERIOR OF THE PANTHEON (*c.* AD 118–28). The great Hadrianic rotunda dedicated to the planetary gods is a fine example of the new interest in interior space and surface ornament which developed in imperial architecture.

2. ROUND TEMPLE BY THE TIBER (*left*), probably the temple of Hercules Victor: one of the rare examples of a Greek-style marble building in Rome before Augustan times.

3. PONT DU GARD (*below*), near Nîmes (late first century BC). This gigantic bridge endows functional architecture with nobility of form.

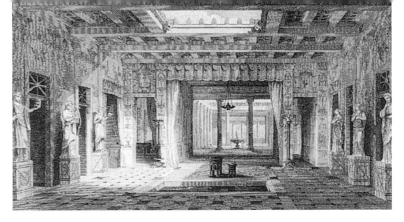

4. THE INTERIOR OF THE HOUSE OF PANSA AT POMPEII (*above*): looking through the atrium to the peristyle court beyond.

5. PAINTED WALL-DECORATION IN THE VILLA OF AGRIPPA POSTUMUS AT BOSCOTRECASE (*c.*10 BC) (*below*). A fine example of the early Third Style. The central panel contains a superb landscape painting of the sacro-idyllic type.

6. EMBOSSED SILVER WINE-CUP (*above*) from Hildesheim (first century AD). The finely worked Bacchic reliefs are wholly appropriate to the function of the vessel.

7. THE GEMMA AUGUSTEA (*below*), one of the finest examples of the large sardonyx cameos carved with propagandist reliefs by imperial court artists. The upper register shows Tiberius (stepping from his chariot) and the deified Augustus, while in the lower register Roman soldiers erect a trophy of victory.

8. STATUE OF A ROMAN WITH THE BUSTS OF HIS ANCESTORS (*left*), late first century BC.

9. POMPEY (CN. POMPEIUS MAGNUS) (*upper right*), the most powerful Roman general of the 70s and 60s BC and chief architect of the downfall of Sulla's political system.

10. C. JULIUS CAESAR (*lower right*), the conqueror of Gaul and dictator of 48–44 BC. He rose to power as a politician 'of the left', but achieved his ultimate triumph through brilliant generalship. He was assassinated in the famous Ides of March conspiracy.

11. THE ARA PACIS RELIEF: MOTHER EARTH (13–9 BC) (*above*). The fruitfulness of the earth is symbolic of the new Golden Age which Augustus sought to inaugurate and which recalls passages in the Augustan poets.

12. CAPTURED SPOILS FROM JERUSALEM (*below*), relief panel from the Arch of Titus (soon after AD 81). The two reliefs in the arch represent the Emperor Titus' triumphal procession after the defeat of the Jewish Revolt in AD 70.

13. BRIDGE ACROSS
THE DANUBE (*above*),
shown in a detail of the
reliefs from Trajan's
column (AD 113). The
bridge consisted of a
timber superstructure
carried on stone piers. In
the foreground the
emperor conducts a
sacrifice.

14. BRONZE STATUE
OF MARCUS AURELIUS
(*left*). The Roman
Emperor (AD 161–80)
was inspired by Stoic
philosophy and wrote
the *Meditations*.

15. DETAIL OF THE CANOPUS (*above*), Hadrian's Villa at Tivoli (between AD 124 and 133).

16. NILE BOAT-TRIP (*below*): mosaic panel from Tivoli (second century AD). General Nilotic subjects were popular in the Roman decorative arts.

be taken very seriously. He is simply declining a suggested imposition with grace and wit. And a bit of sting. When Propertius lists the heroic deeds of Augustus that he would have celebrated, had he been able, Maecenas must have felt relief that he did not. The list contains the ugliest episodes of the Civil War, including Perusia; and these, in the Augustan age, were best forgotten or reinterpreted.

Propertius declines the task of epic; but we must hereafter regard him as associated with the imperial circle—although this does not mean that his independence is snuffed. Poem 2.1 ends with the sort of praise for Maecenas that suggests the patronized: 'you whose favour all our young men covet and who are my true glory in life and will be when I die'; but the conclusion of the poem also insists on Propertius' role as a love poet—until he dies. Poem 2.7 rejoices in the abandonment of Augustus' first attempt at legislation to coerce Romans into marriage; and in 2.16, while making his characteristic noises about how shocking and degraded he is, Propertius associates himself with the shocking, degraded, romantic and magnetic figure of Mark Antony. Poem 2.34 celebrates the imminence of Virgil's *Aeneid* and, in the last couplet, celebrates Propertius himself as poet of Cynthia.

Book 3, written in the late twenties BC, opens with poems (1 and 3) that are a flamboyant assertion of Propertius' role as love poet and Callimachean. Not only flamboyant, pretentious: but one of the things Propertius is doing here is parodying Horace's just published and pretentious claims to be a Roman Alcaeus. Yet the book exhibits less interest in love poetry and, on the face of it, more concern with public issues. One scents the approach of the second Augustan period. But what Propertius gives with one hand, he takes with another—by irony and other methods. For example, poem 4 celebrates Augustus' expected Parthian victory. Propertius represents himself as the loyal observer of the triumph, reproducing an idea used by Horace and Cornelius Gallus. But he adds the slightly insolent touch that he will observe from the vantage point of his mistress's bosom; and he pairs the poem with one reminding us that Love is a god of peace.

In Book 4, which dates from the second Augustan period, we see the signs of Augustus' direct patronage. While Horace was induced to write a fourth book of *Odes*, the 'Callimachean' Propertius felt it prudent or compulsory to produce something rather more genuinely Callimachean—and patriotic. Poems on the causes or origins of institutions had absorbed Callimachus, and Propertius in his fourth book produces poems on the causes and origins of Roman institutions: he now styles himself the 'Roman Callimachus' explicitly, and with some justification. The time was of course no longer propitious for oppositional tactics of the type seen in Book 3; yet Propertius still preserves his integrity and sense of humour. For example, one 'origin' leads into a narrative of the battle of Actium, and it is told, not parodically (as some think), but exactly as a Roman Callimachus should tell it; the exotic, rococo result would have caused Propertius much pleasure and the Emperor no pain. It is perhaps one of his best compositions. In another fine poem the moral story of Tarpeia is given an erotic motive—again pleasure for Propertius and not much pain for the Emperor. In fact Book 4 contains much very good writing. Pressure, if it is not completely totalitarian, can inspire artists to creative ingenuity.

The final poem of the book is notable. It is a funeral elegy for a Roman lady, celebrating indirectly many of the moral virtues that Augustus was trying to inculcate. It should, we might think, bore, cloy, or irritate. It does not. In fact it is moving, and, for the reader of the entire Propertian collection, moving in a particular way. The dead lady speaks in the poem, and affirms how faithful, loving, and loyal she had been to her husband throughout her life—precisely the devotion that Propertius had sought and failed to find in Cynthia. Propertius' monument to an impeccable Roman lady is also therefore, by contrast, a monument to his own failure and sorrow: a pathetic irony. The poem provides a suggestive and moving end to the Propertian corpus.

Tibullus

I have touched upon Tibullus as the quasi-panegyrist of Messalla and his family. Beyond this, he hardly interests himself in national affairs, nor feels the need to explain his non-attention— a fact interesting in itself: imperial influence need not extend beyond the imperial circle. Nor is Tibullus interested in describing his role as poet, or his place in literary history. In discursive, associative elegies addressed mostly to the reader he writes of the country and his life of love.

Tibullus displays the same blinkered and slightly romantic love of the country as Virgil. But the feeling is none the less genuine, and a poem such as 2.1, a celebration of an annual rural festival, largely depends upon it. So indeed does much of Tibullus' poetry. Tibullus would in fact like to live in the country—so he says.

The first forty-four lines of the first poem of the first book are devoted to an expression of this wish. Exactly what the wish comprised should be identified. To begin with it sounds as if Tibullus actually wants to be a small-holding and labouring farmer ('Let me as a farmer set vines in the early season'). This is revealed to be a humorously intended feint. What he actually wants to do is to dabble with work, to be a dilettante, to live a life of, in fact, leisure in rural simplicity on his own estate. He sketches this estate for us in the first poem and subsequently. It has been reduced in size, perhaps in confiscations, but it is still sufficient, with slaves to run it. Tibullus therefore, like Propertius, wants—shocking fact—a life committed to leisure, a 'life of inaction', *uita iners*, as he actually terms it; and, like Propertius, he scorns military and mercantile activity. But unlike the urban and urbane Propertius he wants to spend his life of leisure in the country. This dissimilarity between them is one among many that Tibullus wishes us to discern.

Forty-four lines express this Tibullan wish. What, we might ask, of love? Where is its place? And why, we might also ask, does Tibullus not just up and go to his estate, instead of moaning elegiacally in Rome? The basic reason is—love.

Here is how the expression of Tibullus' rural dream continues:

> parua seges satis est, satis est requiescere lecto
> si licet et solito membra leuare toro.
> quam iuuat immites uentos audire cubantem
> *et dominam tenero continuisse sinu*
>
> (I. 1. 43–6)

A small crop is enough, it is enough if it is possible to rest in a bed and lighten the limbs on a familiar couch. How pleasant it is lying there to listen to wild winds, and *to hold my mistress in tender embrace.*

By 'mistress', *domina*, Tibullus means the woman to whom he as lover is slave (as Propertius was to Cynthia), and he has in mind the one he calls Delia. The exact social status of Delia can, like Cynthia's, be argued about. But she is not dissimilar to Cynthia, probably a freedwoman, and presented to us as highly materialistic and of course essentially urban. And yet we now learn that she is part of Tibullus' vision of rural life, indeed as poem 2 reveals to us, an essential part of his vision of rural life: he would wish to rough it in the country, he says, *provided* that Delia is there. Here is the reason why the rural wish cannot be realized: it proves to contain an incompatible element—Delia: 'But I am held a prisoner . . . and take my post as keeper at her door' (cf. 1. 55–6). In the first place this fact is offered as a reason why Tibullus cannot go on campaign with Messalla. But clearly a man bound to an urban mistress's door cannot simultaneously be a man of country pursuits on his rural estate.

Delia precludes Tibullus' wish being realized. So we have discovered. We have also discovered a source of tension that pervades Tibullus' life and fuels his poetry, and makes him a romantic visionary to be compared (and contrasted) with Propertius. Propertius tried to see in Cynthia a mythical figure, an attempt doomed to fail in the face of reality. Tibullus tried to see in Delia a figure compatible with his rural aspirations, an attempt also doomed to fail in the face of reality. And he, like

Propertius, had moments when he knew the truth only too well. Poem 5 provides the fullest description of Tibullus' rural and erotic vision: life in the country, with Delia taking a wifely part in the harvest, and so on. But the description concludes: 'haec mihi fingebam'—it was all a dream. Tibullus has been quoting his former vision with bitter irony, in a present mood of cruel self-knowledge.

Tibullus, we have sensed, is concerned to be different from Propertius in the way he provokes conventional sensibility. He is also concerned to be even more provoking. Take the question of 'servility': Propertius professes his slavery as an unwilling burden, and has in mind psychological bondage. Tibullus talks actually of the physical humiliations meted out to slaves, and seems masochistically willing to accept them at the hands of his mistress. Tibullus, too, moves on to a different and worse mistress: Nemesis, harder, more rapacious, and more mercenary than Delia.

We might have thought that esteem for the country and love of his own estate were constants in Tibullus' life. Not so. Through Nemesis Tibullus shows us that love can make the romantic abjure not only society's values but his own. In 2.3 a rival has taken Nemesis off to a country villa, at harvest time. Tibullus' response is to curse the country's fruitfulness, to curse what he has hitherto supremely valued. There are other instances like this—and Nemesis causes Tibullus to perform abrupt about-turns on other cherished points as well: for example, he will reverse his declared views on mercenariness in love, if that is what she wants. The most poignant reversal, however, comes in 2.4. Should Nemesis want it, he would even sell off the beloved family estate. Delia had rendered the rural aspiration unrealizable, by being part of it. Nemesis can make him simply and completely abandon it. Such can be the destructive power of romantic love. So Tibullus suggests.

Tibullus produces yet a third lover to whom he is exclusively devoted, a boy, Marathus; and for this boy he demonstrates as intense and abject a love as he and Propertius had for their mistresses. This is a remarkable fact. Of course, homosexual love is often enough professed, by Horace and Catullus among others. But among the love poets it is normally considered a slight business, a sideline, not a thing to engage emotions and passions. What we are observing is Tibullus once more upping the stakes in the game of provocation. Not only does he profess devoted love for three lovers. He exhibits himself as the abject romantic lover of a mere boy.

In fact the affair with Marathus presents Tibullus at perhaps his most abject—and amusing. The relationship is triangular: Tibullus loves Marathus, while Marathus loves a girl, Pholoe; and, to ingratiate himself, Tibullus gives the boy servile and humiliating assistance in his affair with the girl.

We need not doubt the real base of Tibullan poetry in Tibullan experience. But it is also clear that this experience is organized and orchestrated to interest and provoke, in particular in comparison with Propertius (Propertius, similarly, had presented his experience with an eye on Catullus): to interest and provoke—and, sometimes, to amuse. The word crept into the previous paragraph, and humour is perhaps quite pervasive in Tibullus. The kind and degree of Tibullus' humiliations, of his masochistic assertions, all neatly narrated, preclude total earnestness. There is hyperbole here, consideration for humorous effect. And it is all 'neatly narrated': Tibullus' grovelling words to his lovers, and indeed his prayers to be a rustic, are dressed in the urbanest of styles. That suggests a certain Tibullan distance from the Tibullan story, a wink in our direction.

Ovid

It has often been said that Ovid was anti-Augustan. The label is not exactly appropriate. Ovid was indeed irreverent towards Augustus' state, laws, image. But he was irreverent towards any solemn and sitting target.

Ovid came from an old equestrian family, and began a public career, but he soon abandoned it for poetry. He was assisted in his youth by Messalla, and his later books bow in the direction of Augustus and his house. But the evidence suggests that he never maintained a position with a literary circle, even to the extent that Propertius did. He had no need to: his work was instantly popular, and he had no economic problems. And his exuberant spirit was probably best served by such non-involvement.

His first poems, the elegiac *Amores*, were published in two editions: the first was begun about 25 BC and issued over the next ten years or so; the second and smaller edition (the one which we possess) was published about the turn of the millennium.

Ovid's irreverence is instantly visible in these poems, its potential catholicity already guessable. The most obvious targets here are, not conventional moralists, but the romantic elegists, the old protesters themselves. Ovid presents himself in the first book as a lover and poet in the tradition of Propertius and Tibullus, in devoted thraldom to one mistress, whom he calls Corinna. But what he actually gives us is parody. For example, Propertius and Tibullus had expressed their dissociation from public life, from war and the life of action ('soldiering'), by projecting themselves as 'soldiers' of love. Ovid gets hold of this expressive idea and probes it for ingenious and funny effects. How can a lover be represented as a soldier in detail? Poem 1.9, comparing lover and soldier, shows us. A sample:

> Tacticians recommend the night attack,
> use of the spearhead, catching the foe asleep . . .
> Lovers use them too—to exploit a sleeping husband,
> thrusting hard while the enemy snores.

This is a ludicrous, parodic exploitation of an elegiac motif. Other elegiac motifs (the slavery of the lover, the divinity of the beloved, and so on) are similarly treated. So is the Propertian use of myth: Propertius had evoked a romantic ideal of devotion by means of resonating myths; Ovid deploys resonating myths to depict beautiful legs.

In Books 2 and 3 of the *Amores* Ovid drops his mask and displays himself as a cheerfully promiscuous lover. Love is, or should be, simply fun—a game; and the books contain racy lectures and dramatic episodes illustrating it. In this we must observe, besides his dissimilarity to the romantic elegists, his similarity to Horace. Horace considered that love should be a game, even if it could turn out bitter-sweet. So Ovid is similar to Horace—but dissimilar too. Ovid took the game so to speak earnestly, committed time and trouble to it. He did not have things in perspective, Alcaeus-fashion. He even devoted a didactic treatise to the game of love, purporting to teach one how to play it—indulging an interest in the incongruous mixture of solemn didactic form and frivolous content that he displays in other works. This treatise was the 'Art of Love' (*Ars Amatoria*), first published about 9 BC and reissued about the time of the second edition of the *Amores*, not an auspicious time.

Such a didactic obviously affronts Horatian standards. And consistently and obviously, it affronts (once more) elegiac romanticism. And Ovid turns the knife. The cynical instructions of the *Ars* are repeatedly couched in terms that recall agonized elegiac devotion. For instance, the powerless elegist was forced to utter 'you are my only love'; Ovid instructs his pupils on how to *choose* someone to whom to say 'you are my only love'. But, in affronting the old protesters, the *Ars* also affronted Augustus, a very solemn target. So, probably, had the *Amores*.

The social status of Corinna and the other women in the *Amores* is as usual hard to pin down, but what seems clear is that she, and others, are described in a way that suggests they are legally married. The *Amores* therefore explicitly suggests adultery. Adultery, too, is obviously in mind in the *Ars*, despite an unconvincing statement to the contrary at the beginning of the poem and plangent protestations from exile. For exiled is what Ovid eventually was, and the *Ars* was adduced as part cause. His exile is hardly surprising. He writes in explicitly adulterous terms, in the second Augustan period, after Augustus' laws had made adultery criminal; he produces a second edition of *Ars*, and *Amores*, at about the time when Augustus' own daughter was banished for adultery (2 BC), and when the inefficacy of the laws was only too apparent. We can see that Ovid's adulterous line fits into a pattern of catholic and non-malicious irreverence—it is not 'anti-Augustan'. But to a gloomy and disappointed Augustus it might have appeared otherwise. It is perhaps a wonder that he took so long to react, but finally he did. In AD 8 Augustus' granddaughter was also banished for adultery, and Ovid, guilty of perpetrating some 'mistake' as well as his poem ('carmen et error'), was banished too, to Tomis, from whence he dispatched bookloads of not wholly laudable laments.

In between the *Amores* and the *Ars* come the *Heroides*, Ovid's first experiment with mythical narrative. This is safer fare, nevertheless congenial to read. Ovid's basic idea was to invent letters (in elegiacs) from mythical heroines to their lovers: Ariadne to Theseus, Phaedra to Hippolytus, Dido to Aeneas, Penelope to Odysseus, and so on. The examples cited show the wide range of situations that he dealt with, providing himself with wide scope for his rhetorical ingenuity and facile emotive ability. Nor is the irreverent spirit suppressed. Ovid takes pains to translate Virgil's Dido into a much more easily sympathetic figure, and one indeed who spots that Aeneas is vulnerable in the matter of his first wife's death.

At approximately this time Ovid composed his now lost tragedy *Medea*. His first extant attempt to compose on a larger and more ambitious scale is the *Fasti*. This work can reasonably be dated to the years AD 1–4; it is also reasonable to see in it an effort to balance the recently republished erotic works with something less *risqué*. The *Fasti*, also in elegiacs, aimed to go through the Roman calendar offering 'causes' for events and nomenclature in the Roman year. Thus Ovid, who had light-heartedly adopted a Callimachean stance in the *Amores*, felt as Propertius had done before him that it might be prudent to attempt something at once seriously Callimachean and patriotic: the calendar offered ample pegs on which to hang praise of

Rome and praise of Augustus. Irrepressible irreverence periodically mars or improves the poem, depending on one's point of
view. It was never finished. Disinclination seems to have moved
Ovid to abandon it, after six, instead of twelve, books. There
were external factors to support or cause disinclination. The
year AD 4 saw the adoption of Tiberius and therefore another
set of laudatory allusions to include; and, on the calendar, the
month of August loomed, a daunting prospect for a subject of
Augustus. Ovid gave up.

But he did not give up poetry, nor even Callimachean poetry.
Subsequent to the *Fasti* is the *Metamorphoses*, Ovid's great
hexameter poem in fifteen books. Here he assembles dozens of
attractive stories from myth, stories which end in the metamorphosis of characters into animals, plants, and other forms.
The stories are linked together with ingenious transitions, so
ingenious that progress can seem bewildering. The opening of
the poem seems sequential (from the creation of the world,
through Jupiter's punishment of sinful man, to Deucalion and
Pyrrha), but soon we find ourselves conducted through the
stories of Daphne, Io, Phaethon, and so on—all the way through
to the metamorphosis of Julius Caesar into a god in Book 15.

What is this poem? By a judicious choice of words at the
beginning Ovid surprisingly advertises it as something that Callimachus eschewed : a traditional epic. We expect, therefore, an
epic in which the plot is serious and a single, unified, action
unfolds objectively, an epic in which the consequences of actions
follow; hence, a moral poem. It very soon transpires that the
Metamorphoses is nothing of the sort. The advertisement was
a spoof. The action of the poem is neither single nor serious, but
a mass of disparate stories ingeniously, artificially linked and
subjectively told—told with Ovidian wit, humour, and gro-
tesqueness. And the consequences of actions do not follow. They
end in the fantasy of metamorphosis. The poem is a gloriously
amoral Callimachean collection got up in epic dress, an affront
to the traditional epic genre.

As always, Ovid affronts. Here, in particular, there is irrever-

ence towards Virgil's genre—and Virgil's material: in various
ways the material of the *Aeneid* gets mauled. Another sitting
and solemn target. There is, too, irreverence towards the house
of Augustus, despite overt but unconvincing flattery. Jupiter
compared to Augustus in one context is, within a few hundred
lines, chasing a girl in another. Nor does the company in which
Julius Caesar's 'metamorphosis' finds itself dignify it. And there
is irreverence, in a sense, towards life: it is simply the material
for amusing, amoral literature.

There is a great risk of assessing Ovid too negatively: he is, we
say, parodic, irreverent, unserious, unAugustan, amoral, even
immoral, merely rhetorical or ingenious. This can, and should
be, rephrased. Ovid is funny. His immorality serves humour,
and his parodies are the sort which direct laughter on to themselves, not the parodied original (see the example quoted above,
p. 239). Ovid is a poet of 'art for art's sake': Ovid reveres technique, reveres art; and amorality is indispensable to the construction of a self-contained artistic experience. UnAugustan? In
a sense Ovid is the Augustan poet *par excellence*, particularly of
the second period. Augustus' actions and legislations were designed to stem a tide, to combat a prevailing spirit. Ovid represents that spirit, pleasure-loving, sophisticated, and, it must
be admitted, cynical. Horace, twenty-two years older than Ovid
and belonging to a different generation, may draw a veil of
silence over him. But Ovid's contemporaries did not. They
praised him to the skies. For them he was the true Augustan
poet.

Further Reading

The Loeb Classical Library provides texts with facing translations of all the
poets discussed in this chapter. The following translations may also be recommended: Niall Rudd, *Horace, Satires and Epistles* (revd. edn. 1979); W. G.
Shepherd, *Horace's Odes and Epodes* (1983); Guy Lee, *Tibullus: Elegies* (2nd
edn. 1982), and *Ovid's Amores* (2nd edn. 1968); Rolfe Humphries, *Ovid, The
Art of Love* (1957), *The Metamorphoses* (1955).

Indispensable to a full understanding of Horace is E. Fraenkel's *Horace*

(Oxford, 1957), but David West's *Reading Horace* (Edinburgh, 1967) is perhaps the best introduction; comparably useful are Margaret Hubbard's *Propertius* (London, 1974) and L. P. Wilkinson's *Ovid Recalled* (Cambridge, 1955),
abridged as *Ovid Surveyed* (Cambridge, 1962). Tibullus lacks any balanced
introductory book; there is Francis Cairns's *Tibullus* (Cambridge, 1979) and
David F. Bright's *Haec Mihi Fingebam, Tibullus in his World* (Leiden, 1978),
but both these are idiosyncratic and the initiate is better served by the introduction to Guy Lee's translation.

The following books treat the period and its poetry (or aspects thereof) more
generally: R .O. A. M. Lyne, *The Latin Love Poets from Catullus to Horace*
(Oxford, 1980); K. Quinn, *Latin Explorations* (2nd edn. London, 1969); L. P.
Wilkinson, *Golden Latin Artistry* (Cambridge, 1963); G. Williams, *Tradition
and Originality in Roman Poetry*, (Oxford, 1968), abridged as *The Nature
of Roman Poetry* (Oxford, 1970). C. O. Brink, *Horace on Poetry*, vol. iii
(Cambridge, 1982), pp. 523 ff., offers a masterly overview of the period, and
vital illumination of the social background is provided by Jasper Griffin's *Latin
Poetry and Roman Life* (London, 1985)

9

Virgil

JASPER GRIFFIN

Preamble

PUBLIUS VERGILIUS MARO, in English normally called Virgil, was a celebrated figure in his own lifetime, and soon after his death a number of writers tried to satisfy the popular curiosity about the life of the greatest of Roman poets. We are consequently much better informed about him than about most poets in antiquity. Like most Roman writers, he was not born in Rome. He came into the world in 70 BC, near Mantua, in what was still called Cisalpine Gaul. Although thoroughly Romanized—we recall that Catullus came from Verona, and Livy from Padua (Patavium)—the area did not receive the Roman citizenship till 49, and it became officially part of Italy only in 42. Virgil's family seems to have been respectable though by no means prominent. The ultimate origin of the names 'Vergilius' and 'Maro' was probably Etruscan, but only the credulous will try to explain the poet's art or his character by invoking Etruscan ancestry.

It is worth looking at the period through which Virgil lived. Born in the year in which Pompey and Crassus forced their way into the consulship, he was seven when Catiline fell fighting at the head of a revolutionary army opposing the Roman legions. The gathering disorder of the 50s led to civil war; the assassination of Caesar to another, followed by proscriptions, by wars in Italy, and the eventual victory of Octavian, after a third civil war, in 31. As late as 19, the year of Virgil's death, there were serious riots in Rome. Of the fifty-one years of the poet's life, sixteen were years of civil war; the proscriptions which followed the battle of Philippi are said to have caused the deaths of at least 150 senators and 2,000 *equites*; considerable areas of Italy were devastated by fighting, by famine, and by the forcible expropriation of land. It was a terrible period, in which even the survival of Rome seemed to be in doubt, and that fact is of central importance for Virgil's poetry.

The Eclogues

His first published work was a collection of ten bucolic *Eclogues*, which proclaim themselves as in the tradition of Theocritus (Vol. 1, pp. 410 ff.), but which also echo and evoke many other poets, both Greek and Latin. The influence of Callimachus, for instance, is clear at the opening of the Sixth *Eclogue*, that of Lucretius in the middle of the same poem, that of Catullus in the Fourth. There were allusions to the work of other poets, contemporary or in the last generation, which we are not now in a position to recognize. Virgil is thus, at his first appearance, a learned poet. That was always to be his manner, and in antiquity some critics made names for themselves by sniping at the poet for his 'thefts', meaning plagiarism.

It is quite wrong to imagine that Virgil lacked originality, or that his poems are no more than imitations or distillations of the work of his predecessors. If we read the first five lines of the First *Eclogue* we find a good example of the creative reworking of a model. The countryman Meliboeus speaks to a friend who is singing of love, stretched out in the shade of a tree:

> Tityre, tu patulae recubans sub tegmine fagi
> siluestrem tenui Musam meditaris auena;
> nos patriae finis et dulcia linquimus arua:

nos patriam fugimus; tu, Tityre, lentus in umbra
formosam resonare doces Amaryllida siluas.

> Beneath a shady beech you may rehearse
> At ease, my Tityrus, your simple verse;
> I'm forced to leave my country and to roam,
> My Tityrus, from country and from home:
> You here can fill, at leisure in the shade,
> With Amaryllis' name the wooded glade.

At once we see that we both are, and are not, in the world of
Theocritus. The Greek poet is the source of the names, and of
the pastoral world of love and song; the languorously beautiful
hexameters, with their melodious vowels and artfully simple
repetitions, also owe a lot to Theocritus' inspiration. But the
world of reality, of politics and suffering, has invaded the
pastoral Arcadia in which nothing but love and song could
happen. Why is Meliboeus not able to stretch out and sing?
Because, it soon emerges, Rome has burst into his world. After
the defeat of Brutus and Cassius in 42, the Caesarian party had
to take care of the soldiers in the enormous armies which now
looked to them for their reward. What the soldiers wanted was
land, and that could only be found by ejecting its present owners.
A recent calculation estimates that a quarter of the land of Italy
changed hands in the proscriptions and evictions. Meliboeus,
despite his pretty Greek name, is sufficiently Italian and contemporary to be among the ejected victims:

> A godless soldier has my cherished fields,
> A savage has my land: such profit yields
> Our civil war. For them we worked our land!
> Ay, plant your pears—to fill another's hand.

Tityrus has miraculously escaped the general disaster, thanks to
a 'wonderful young man' in Rome, who secured him his land.
For that, Tityrus had to go to Rome:

> Urbem quam dicunt Romam, Meliboee, putaui
> stultus ego huic nostrae similem, quo saepe solemus
> pastores ouium teneros depellere fetus . . .

> I used to think the city men call Rome
> Was like our market-town, to which we come
> On market days, and drive our kids to sell.
> O foolishness . . .

The lines, standing on the very first page of Virgil's published work, have a prophetic ring. The poet, like his rustic speaker, will discover Rome; and will find that Rome is something very different from the innocent joys and sorrows of country life. The imperial city, with its fabulous wealth and power, can at will reward or destroy. That will be a central problem for the *Aeneid*.

The *Eclogues* form a unified work of art, with a structure of its own. The number of poems is itself not a random one: the first book of Tibullus contains ten poems, so does the first book of *Satires* of Horace. A poet was expected to organize his work into a pleasing shape. The First *Eclogue*, as we have seen, is in the form of a dialogue: so are all the odd-numbered *Eclogues*. The even-numbered ones, on the other hand, are monologues. The fifth poem ends with a little recapitulation, the speaker presenting his friend with the pipes on which, he says, he played the second and third poems. That marks the half-way point, and a little break, comparable to that after the third of Horace's six Roman odes (*Odes* 3. 1–6); as in that cycle of poems, the second half begins with a fresh scene of invocation, in this case not of the Muse but of Apollo. Another structure, also meant to be felt, centres on the Fifth *Eclogue* (allusion to the death and deification of Caesar), which is immediately framed by the two most ambitious and least simply pastoral poems (iv and vi), and at furthest remove framed by two poems on the evictions (i and ix). The last poem, in this structure, stands rather outside the rest; it is explicitly introduced as 'my last pastoral song'.

As we have seen, the Ninth *Eclogue* returns to the theme of the evictions. Menalcas, a singer and translator of Theocritus, has been turned out of his property near Mantua. So far from saving his land by means of his song, he was lucky to escape with his life. Ever since antiquity people have tried to make the two *Eclogues* on the evictions into an autobiographical account by the poet of his own ejection and restoration to his Mantuan property. But it is surely clear that Virgil did not mean to produce such an account. Tityrus, restored by a superhuman young man (who in real life could only be the nineteen- or twenty-year old Octavian) is elderly and a slave, in neither respect like Virgil; and he is balanced by Meliboeus, for whom no providential saviour averts disaster. And in the Ninth *Eclogue* Menalcas too, it seems, finds no remedy. The two poems would add up to a very odd way of saying 'Thank you' to Octavian. What Virgil has done, rather, is to show us scenes from the evictions, what is going on in the Italian countryside, filtered through the poetic medium provided by Theocritus. If we are to guess what happened to Virgil himself, it may seem likely that he lost his family land near Mantua, and was given by his patrons a property near Naples. That is where we find him living later on, one of a group of friends of the Epicurean philosopher Siro.

One point is a vital one for understanding Virgil. Already in the *Eclogues* he is working towards the special way of writing, which in the *Aeneid* he has perfected: a manner which allows the reader to see through the poetical surface to events and personalities of a different kind, which are never made fully explicit. So in the Fifth *Eclogue* two herdsmen sing of the death and deification of Daphnis, another name from Theocritus. Cruelly cut off and lamented by his mother, Daphnis becomes a god, a patron of peace, hailed as a divinity by all nature and by the country people. Daphnis was young, beautiful, a herdsman— a far cry from the middle-aged dictator Caesar. But so soon after the assassination and elevation to godhood of the most celebrated man in the world—descended from the goddess Venus—those spectacular events could not have been wholly out of the mind of Virgil's readers.

The Fourth *Eclogue* prophesies the return of the Golden Age. The poem is addressed to Asinius Pollio, an early patron of the poet, as a compliment to his entry on the consulship in 40 BC. Its exalted language draws on a wide variety of sources: oracles, Greek versions of Jewish prophecies, Etruscan techniques of divination, Platonic myths, Homer, Catullus. In Pollio's consulship the 'mighty months' will begin to roll: a child will be born, whose birth will be marked by miraculous signs, and whose growing up will be accompanied by the gradual blossoming of the age of Apollo. The earth shall produce all good things everywhere, without the need of agriculture; lions shall be harmless; venomous serpents shall cease to exist. War, too, shall cease, and the divine child shall rule the world. Many modern scholars think that this poem was written to celebrate the pact agreed at Brundisium in October 40 (above, p. 148), which included a marriage between Antony and Octavian's sister Octavia, and which averted the danger of war between the two men: the child of the poem will be the expected son of the new marriage. But a poem to honour a man's consulship should be ready for presentation on 1 January, not ten months later; and the striking parallels with Isaiah and other similar works show that this really is a Messianic poem. Such works are produced, not when successful political arrangements seem to have secured peace on earth, but when the earthly scene is so dark and hopeless that the mind turns away in despair to another order of thought. The Fourth *Eclogue* was for centuries believed to be a prophecy of the coming of Christ. The modern mind is unhappy with such notions; but perhaps that view comes closer to the real nature of the poem than it does to pin it to a specific political happening. Again Virgil is being deliberately evasive as to his exact meaning, and the suggestiveness of the poem is more effective than clarity would have been. And after all the treaty of Brundisium did not in the end mean lasting peace; while Octavia bore Antony two daughters, but no son. Virgil would have been surprisingly credulous if he had not thought of such possibilities.

The *Eclogues* can be ranged between two poles: some are fairly close to Theocritus (2, 3, and 7), others are further distanced but still Theocritean (8 and 9); at the other extreme some have very little contact with Theocritus at all (4 and 6). They all have in common a highly polished technique, in which Virgil shows that he has learnt everything that Theocritus, Callimachus, and Catullus had to teach him. The choice of words is punctilious, the sound of the verse is melodious, and there is a pervasive atmosphere of an exquisite and faintly melancholy beauty. The paintings of Claude Lorraine are perhaps the best analogy in another art; and he of course was much influenced by Virgil. It is a small but significant part of this that the first and last poems of the collection, and others in between, end with the coming of evening and the shadows lengthening from the hills.

Despite much scholarly endeavour, agreement is not possible on the order in which the *Eclogues* were composed. Their style does not enable us to extract many dates from the poems, which no doubt were polished to fit the positions they occupy in the final published collection. It is likely that the book of ten *Eclogues* was published about 38 BC; recent attempts to put the completion as late as 35 are not convincing. The poems seem to have been an immediate success. We are told that they were acted on the stage, and that the shy and evasive poet, on his rare appearances in Rome, was pointed at in the street. In the spring of 38, already an established writer, he introduced Horace to Maecenas, whose name does not appear in the *Eclogues*, but to whom Virgil was to dedicate his next work, the *Georgics*.

In the *Eclogues* Virgil addressed several great men: Asinius Pollio chiefly, but also Alfenus Varus. They both seem to be in the position of actual or potential patrons. In this respect Virgil resembles Horace rather than Catullus and (in his First Book) Propertius, who have no patrons but only friends. The poet Cornelius Gallus, who is praised in the Sixth *Eclogue*, also receives the supreme compliment of being the subject of the Tenth. In that poem Virgil presents the elegiac love poet as a pastoral lover in Arcadia, his amorous complaints transposed into Virgil's own metre, and the lover himself recalling Theocritus' Daphnis. The procedure seems strange to us in poetry, but it would surprise us less in music: Virgil has written a variation in his own style on a theme by Gallus.

The Georgics

All that is in the past, once we turn to the *Georgics*. Lesser patrons must give way to Maecenas, friends are no longer named, and Octavian—never named and barely hinted at in the *Eclogues*—is now in the centre of the poet's view. Ancient scholars claimed to know the contents of Virgil's will, and they report that he left the very large sum of 10,000,000 sesterces, with substantial legacies to Maecenas and Augustus. No doubt they were the source of the poet's wealth. But it would be wrong to think of the relationship as primarily a financial one. In the second half of the 30s the relative position of Octavian and Antony gradually changed. The ruthless young heir of Caesar, who 'kills and keeps his temper' (a phrase which Dryden put into the mouth of Antony in *All for Love*), was cleverly transforming himself into the defender of western values against an Antony dead to decent feeling and going native in the East. The war of propaganda was lost by Antony before the battle of Actium. Maecenas, personally a luxurious, even a decadent figure, wrote verse himself, as such men usually do, in the manner of the poets of his own youth; he was of great value as an intermediary between Octavian and the poets. An artist must be flattered when the holders of power express interest in his work, and much more when the master of the world (as Octavian was after 31) is anxious to recruit his support for a programme of reform and restoration, which is to replace civil wars and disasters with peace and the good life. In their different ways Virgil, Horace, and Propertius all responded, more or less, to that most seductive appeal.

Virgil refers to the *Georgics* as 'your exacting command, Maecenas' ('tua, Maecenas, haud mollia iussa', 3. 41). The phrase is hard to interpret. Obviously Maecenas did not 'command' the poet to write a poem in four books on agriculture, and Virgil also says of his writing:

Sed me Parnasi deserta per ardua dulcis
raptat amor; iuuat ire iugis, qua nulla priorum
Castaliam molli deuertitur orbita cliuo. (3. 291)

But over high Parnassus' lonely crest
Poetic rapture bears me: sweet to pass
Where never wheel has marked the tender grass.

He wanted to produce the poem, and he felt confident that
Maecenas would welcome it. For the poet it offered the challenge of a work on a large scale, some 2,000 lines in four roughly
equal books, far exceeding the length not only of the *Eclogues*
but also of anything ever attempted by Horace, Propertius, or
Tibullus. In a period deeply marked by the Callimachean rejection of the long poem (Vol. 1, p. 415), that was a striking
departure. The subject-matter was challenging, too. For Catullus and his friends, the word 'rustic' had stood for all that was
uncouth, ill-bred, boring—both in manners and in poetry.
Could the homespun rustic verse of Hesiod (Vol. 1, pp. 96 ff.)
be transformed into a Latin poem which would satisfy the
aesthetic demands of Virgil and his audience? He was not aiming to translate Hesiod, nor simply to paraphrase him and dress
him up in more elegant poetic form. Hesiod had made his practical instructions on sowing and reaping part of a moral picture
of life, with hard work and traditional piety. Virgil, too, will
produce a vision of a way of life, based on work, and embodying the old virtues which made Rome great: piety, tenacity,
patriotism, genuineness. It must combine exact vision and description of detail, without the golden haze of beautiful generality which so often marks the *Eclogues*, and also a grand
style, elevated but not hollow, for moral and poetical set-pieces.
As for Maecenas and Octavian, they would have preferred an
epic on Octavian's warlike feats: in the prologue to *Georgic* 3
Virgil promises that 'soon' he will write it. But the *Georgics* not
only praised Octavian in glittering eulogy, but also endorsed a
view of Italian and Roman life which was, in general terms,
highly acceptable to him. The age of civil war must be over, and
Octavian must heal a world turned upside down (1. 500). Then

the vices of ambition and greed must be rooted out in favour of modesty and hard work (2. 165 ff., 458 ff.). On all that, Virgil's poem and Octavian's policy were agreed. Of course, neither of them will have expected that educated readers of the *Georgics* would rush out to buy small farms and start ploughing with their own hands.

The *Georgics* were completed in 29 BC, and some passages were clearly written after the Battle of Actium. Virgil had been at work on the poem for seven years or so, a length of time which implies constant revision and slow progress. For facts he had prose works on agriculture at his disposal. Especially valuable was Varro's *De re rustica*, a systematic treatise packed with information, far more exhaustive and practically useful than the *Georgics*. Varro's work could also give the poet other hints, as the First Book opens with the characters looking at a map of Italy (cf. *Georg.* 2. 135 ff.), and ends with the random murder of one of them in the street, a vivid instance of the violence and lawlessness which Virgil laments in his poem.

The first book of the *Georgics* has some close echoes of Hesiod, to establish the colouring of the whole. 'Nudus ara, sere nudus' ('Strip to plough and strip to sow', 1. 299) which was found very comical in antiquity, is an exact translation of a quaint Hesiodic line. Hesiod told how Zeus made life hard for men as a piece of vengeance, and laughed aloud as he did so (Vol. 1, pp. 102 f.); Virgil prefers to tell how Jupiter made life hard for man's ultimate good, 'ut uarias usus meditando extunderet artes' ('that need and thought should useful arts devise', 1. 133). Virgil's Jupiter is more benevolent than Hesiod's Zeus. But even in this book there is far less of Hesiod than there is of Theocritus in the *Eclogues*. Lucretius, the great Latin poet of the last generation, is far more pervasive.

Virgil is careful to be selective. What appears to start out as a list of the necessary equipment (1. 160 ff.) actually includes only half a dozen tools, and those are mostly chosen for having a connection in Greek poetry which ennobles them: not 'a cart', but 'the slow rolling waggon of the Mother of Eleusis' (because in the great Eleusinian procession (Vol. 1, p. 322) waggons were used); not 'a winnowing fan', but 'the mystic fan of Iacchus' (a minor Eleusinian deity). Virgil is anxious to avoid being dragged down from the high style by his humble subject matter. He also embellishes his material by many stylistic devices. When, for example, he is explaining that it is important to rotate crops, as some plants exhaust the soil, he creates out of this unpromising idea an exquisitely shaped couplet:

> urit enim campum lini seges, urit auenae,
> urunt Lethaeo perfusa papauera somno.
>
> (1. 77–8)

Flax burns, and oats will burn, the fertile ground:
No less burn heavy poppies, slumber-drowned.

The repetition of the verb, the shaping of the sentence, the unusual rhythm of the last line which goes with the drowsy poppies, all work together to impose a formal unity and beauty.

He also varies the work with great skill. The passages on actual rustic work alternate with all kinds of more obviously 'poetical' passages—on the zones of the globe, on storms, on winter in the Scythian snows, on the glories of Italy. Some of them are both lengthy and highly ambitious in style, the poet trying his wings for his future epic. The most spectacular come at crucial points in the structure of the whole. Book 1 opens with an elaborate invocation of the gods, including a startlingly fulsome address to Octavian. Book 3 opens with a long passage on the epic which Virgil will write in the future. By designed contrast, the second and fourth books have very short introductions, and each has a long poetic excursus at the end. Book 2 closes with an emotional passage extolling the life of the farmer ('O all too happy, if they knew their luck!'), contrasting rustic innocence with the vicious luxury of the city, and extolling the lot of the poet who (like Virgil) knows the rustic gods. Book 4 ends with the epyllion of Aristaeus, to which we shall return. Other set pieces are darker in tone. At the end of Book 1, an account of the weather signs which the farmer needs to know runs into an emotional treatment of the fearsome portents which marked the divine anger at the assassination of Julius Caesar, the guilt of Rome which is punished by civil war, and a fervent prayer for the survival and success of Octavian, the only hope of the world. Book 3 closes with a grisly account of the ravages of plague among cattle, arising from some apparently simple instructions for preserving the health of one's animals. The four books thus end with alternating passages of gloom and hope, a structure which has often been compared to that of a great work of music.

It would be wrong, though, to think of the *Georgics* as consisting of unpoetical instruction, enlivened by purple patches of poetry. Virgil has shot through the instructions with all sorts of devices of variety. The tone is constantly changing, from mock-solemnity and humour to pathos and indignation. Vivid pictures—of clouds, snakes, birds, horses—are enlivened by echoes of military language, or Ennius, or Hellenistic verse. The poet constantly looks at events from the standpoint of the animals he describes. An example in Book 3: Virgil follows his sources in advising that bulls and stallions should be kept from dissipating their energies by sexual indulgence:

> The female saps their vigour as they gaze;
> The bulls look on her and forget to graze,
> So sweet are her enticements: in her sight
> The haughty rivals for her favour fight.
>
> (3. 215–18)

The passage goes on to develop the battle of the bulls, the chagrin of the loser 'in distant exile, groaning for the shame of defeat and the loss of his love', his practising, and his eventual thunderous return.

In the fourth book the bees are handled in much the same way. Varro's work shows that bee-keeping was only one branch of specialized farming, listing it along with the raising of chickens, pigeons, peacocks, dormice, hares, deer, edible snails, and fancy fish. Virgil ignores all but the bees: for they are an image of human life, orderly and public-spirited. They are treated with a mixture of sympathy, admiration, and irony. The book ends with a great surprise, the epyllion of Aristaeus. The poet tells that, if one's bees die, a new swarm will be forthcoming from the correct treatment of the corpse of an ox. This fantastic procedure was discovered by the legendary hero Aristaeus, whose bees all died to punish him (as he discovers) for causing the death of Orpheus' wife Eurydice. The story of Orpheus' descent to the Underworld to fetch her back, his fatal turning to look at her, his second and final loss, and his death, is told in Virgil's most magical verse. It seems to have been Virgil who first said that Orpheus failed to revive his wife. Why he ended the *Georgics* with this tale, narrated at a length of nearly 250 verses, is not easy to say. A possible reason is that he wanted to give another side of the vision of the virtuous, patriotic bees, 'little Romans' ('paruos Quirites') as he calls them: these impersonal creatures, sexless and free from passion, who kill themselves with work and gladly die for the community, can be brought back from death: 'the race is immortal', as the poet says. But something is irreparably lost: the beautiful Eurydice and her lover, the musician Orpheus. Irreplaceable individuals, passionate and creative, they are the prey of death. Such an interpretation would be in line with an important strand in the *Aeneid*, with its bitter awareness of the conflict between fate's impersonal purposes and the passions of the human heart.

The Aeneid

Virgil was still working on his epic when in 19 BC he died. We are credibly told that at the last he asked his friends to burn his unfinished poem. Antiquity did not share our romantic interest in fragmentary and suggestive works of art, and ancient writers, like ancient artists, aimed to offer the public works as perfect as they could make them. An obvious mark of its unfinished state is the presence, unevenly distributed through the poem, of metrically incomplete lines: lines, that is, to which the poet intended to return. Some of them are very effective, and romantic readers have been tempted to think that Virgil would have left them; but that is an idea which would not have occurred to him, any more than it occurred to any of his imitators in antiquity to include incomplete lines in their poems. He did not, however, intend to carry the story further forward than the point it reaches at the end of Book 12.

Maecenas tried to induce each of the poets to produce an epic on Augustus: none of them complied. That fact alone shows that the pressure was civilized. We are not in the world of Stalin and the Writers' Union. Virgil was unlike Horace and Propertius in that from the beginning he did talk in terms of writing a martial epic 'one day' (*Eclogues* 4. 54; 8. 6–10), whereas they always made it clear that they could not, or would not. In the introduction to the third book of the *Georgics* he seemed to undertake that he would write it 'soon'. But in the event he produced something quite different: a mythical epic on the ultimate origins of Rome. Augustus, we know, followed its progress with impatience, begging to be shown portions of it. He accepted, that is, that the *Aeneid* really was the fulfilment of his own wish; and he was right.

Virgil had come to see that it was not possible to write an epic of which Augustus should be the central figure, and which should satisfy the highest artistic demands. The framework of an epic must be the Homeric poems, and that entailed both the constant presence of the gods as characters, and also hand-to-hand fighting among heroic warriors. But to intrude divine councils and interventions into very recent history would be a jarring fault of taste, constantly risking bathos and absurdity; so, too, would the representation of Augustus mowing down thousands with his own strong right arm. Again, the plain fact was that the battle of Actium was unsatisfactory as a theme for verse. Not only did Augustan propaganda insist that it be represented not as a civil war but as a war with the Queen of Egypt, which was universally known to be untrue; there also apparently was hardly any fighting, some contingents changing sides at the last moment, and Cleopatra suddenly sailing away in flight. Nor, finally, could Virgil have found a central role for his great talent for pathos. If Augustus were the hero, there could be little sympathy for the defeated, and no ambiguity about his triumph. Cleopatra could not be treated as sympathetically as Dido. And Virgil was to succeed in making a natural flair for the pathos of loss and defeat into a central feature, not only of the decoration of the *Aeneid*, but also of its interpretation of imperialism and of history.

The chief difficulty about the creation of the *Aeneid* was that of writing a poem which at one level should be a mythical epic about the distant past, yet which should also be about the present and the future. The difficulty was so great that Virgil said in a letter that he must have been mad to attempt it. The poem was to be all-embracing, drawing upon both *Iliad* and *Odyssey*, Attic tragedy, Hellenistic poetry, and Latin predecessors, especially Naevius and Ennius; it was to be permeated by philosophical ideas from the Greek thinkers; it must be strongly marked by Roman history and characteristically Roman values; and Virgil was anxious also to include not only Rome but also Italy, with its geography, its peoples, and its virtues. Roman history must be presented as a crescendo leading up to Augustus, a thousand years in the future. Finally, the whole poem must be written in a style grand yet flexible, showing its author's familiarity with all preceding literature.

Romans believed that their city was founded in the eighth century BC, Romulus being the actual founder, but some places in Latium had for centuries believed that their origins went back to Troy: after the sack of the city, fleeing Trojans came to the West. Such beliefs were indeed widespread all over the Mediterranean, as non-Greek peoples became sophisticated enough to wish to attach themselves somehow to the great cycles of Greek legend. (In the Middle Ages this continued to be true: Britons descended from the Trojan Brut, for example.) Some aristocratic families at Rome claimed to have migrated there from other

Latin cities, and to trace their ancestry back to Troy, among them the Julii. Now, the story of Romulus was not very suitable for an epic, and it had no direct link with Augustus. Aeneas, who actually is a character in the *Iliad*, was a much better hero; and through the Julii he was Augustus' ancestor. A great drawback, however, was that Aeneas could not found Rome, as scholars put the fall of Troy 400 years earlier, in the twelfth century BC. Aeneas can only found Lavinium, from which in time Rome will derive. Virgil turns this difficulty to account brilliantly in Book 8, when Aeneas is entertained by an ally on the very site which will be that of Rome. The hero is shown the Capitol and all the places which will become opulent and celebrated, now green hills and trees. The touching scene is programmatic: Aeneas must live for a future he will not live to see.

The epic starts with Aeneas and his Trojans on their sea-journey to the West. The poet opens with a weighty introduction:

> Arms and the man I sing, who, forced by Fate
> And haughty Juno's unrelenting hate,
> Expelled and exiled, left the Trojan shore.
> Long labours, both on land and sea, he bore ...
>   (trans. Dryden)

A mighty warrior with a destined mission, the hero is persecuted by a hostile goddess: and more than that, he is 'famous for his *pietas*', and even that quality—in English 'sense of duty', 'devotion'—does not protect him. Virgil goes on to remonstrate, shocked by the theology of his own story:

> O Muse! tell why the queen of heaven began
> To persecute so brave, so just a man:
> What grievance must his suffering assuage?
> Can heavenly spirits feel such human rage?

The hostility of Juno arises, we learn, from personal pique: Ganymede, Jupiter's paramour, and Paris, who judged the beauty contest of the goddesses and gave the prize to Venus over Juno, were Trojans. But also she favours Carthage and hopes to frustrate the plan of Jupiter and Fate to confer dominion on Rome.

Aeneas had long been famous for his 'piety', and he was often depicted in the act of carrying his old father on his shoulders out of burning Troy. Virgil makes him also carry the Trojan *penates*, resident gods who are to take up their new home in Italy. *Pius* is his regular epithet in the poem (Virgil suggests but does not copy the Homeric use of 'formulaic' epithets: Vol. 1, pp. 66 ff.), meaning that he above all men identifies his will with the plans of Fate. His sufferings in the poem, in which he is shipwrecked, forced to fight a hateful war with the people of Italy, and to abandon the woman he loves, are thus clearly unjust. We hear him complain to his mother, the goddess Venus, when she has appeared to him in disguise: the episode will illustrate the way in which Virgil uses and transforms Homeric material. Asked who he is, Aeneas replies bitterly 'Sum pius Aeneas' ('I am the dutiful Aeneas') and goes on to complain that in obedient pursuit of his destiny he has seen his ships wrecked and himself cast up on an unknown African shore. His mother sharply rebukes him for his complaints. As she turns away and leaves him she allows him to recognize her, too late, and he pursues her with reproaches: why will she never stay with him? The scene, occurring in Book 1, is programmatic. It is based on several Homeric motifs: the scene in *Odyssey* 9 when Odysseus identifies himself to the listening Phaeacians ('I am Odysseus, famous everywhere for my clever tricks'); the relationship between Achilles and his goddess mother Thetis; and several scenes where gods allow their identity to be realized only as they turn away. But Odysseus' boast is a proud and justifiably confident one, and Thetis is a different sort of mother from Venus—she truly understands her son, comes when he calls, and never deceives him. Virgil has created from these Homeric hints a scene of great poignancy, which shows us the whole position of Aeneas. He is struggling to carry out the apparently arbitrary orders of heaven; and he is lonely. That combination is an explosive one, and we are meant to understand how it follows that the next thing that happens to Aeneas is that he falls in love.

He has been driven ashore at Carthage, where Dido, a glamorous and heroic widowed queen, is founding her new city. Aeneas' wife disappeared in the confusion at the fall of Troy. Humanly, the two seem made for each other, even without the interference of the meddling goddesses. Juno hopes that Aeneas will stay in Carthage and not found Rome; Venus, that Dido will be nice to her son. Together they push Dido to fall in love with Aeneas. Like Odysseus (*Odyssey* 9–12) he tells the story of his adventures, starting with Troy's fall (*Aen.* 2–3). Odysseus' audience listened with pleasure to the narration of exciting tales; Virgil adds the emotional point that, like Desdemona, Dido comes to love Aeneas as he tells her of the dangers he has passed. Juno is an unscrupulous enemy of the Trojans and anxious to frustrate the will of Jupiter and Fate, and we now see that Venus is essentially no different. She is on the right side because it happens that Aeneas is her son, but not for the right reason; and at Carthage she gets him into a terrible difficulty.

The fourth book of the *Aeneid* is the tragedy of Dido. Virgil is here strongly influenced by Euripides' Medea and by other unhappy heroines, including the Medea of Apollonius of Rhodes (Vol. 1, pp. 413 f.). Dido is overwhelmed by her love, and Aeneas (we infer) drifts into a passionate affair with her. He is seen by disapproving neighbours and gods dressed up in Carthaginian crimson and gold, Dido's gift, actually helping to found Carthage (4. 259). Dido, indeed, claims that they are married; though Aeneas is able to say, when the gods push him into leaving, that he never went through a regular marriage ceremony with her. Virgil was in a tight corner here. Aeneas cannot abandon a wife, but Dido cannot be allowed to carry on light-heartedly with a lover. The poet has dealt with the difficulty by constructing a situation which both is and is not a marriage. Out on a boarhunt, Dido and Aeneas are driven by a storm to take shelter together in a cave. Juno, goddess of marriage, is present as *pronuba* (matron of honour); the nymphs raise a cry; lightning flashes, and the sky was 'conscious witness to their union' ('conscius aether conubiis'). In a sense, that is a marriage; in another important sense it is not. But we are meant to think, when Aeneas advances that plea to her, that he has sailed very close to the wind. The book is dominated by a series of passionate speeches by Dido, of reproach, entreaty, bitterness, curses. The hero speaks only once, pleading the imperative instructions of Jupiter. There is nothing else he can say. He is right to go, but he does not cut a good figure. As he sails hastily away, Dido invokes eternal enmity between Carthage and Rome, and kills herself.

Aeneas finally lands in Italy in Book 6, and is immediately told to visit the Underworld. The sombre splendours of this book lead him through the stages of his past life, meeting his own dead, as well as the traditional inhabitants of the lower world. He is not spared a terrible encounter with Dido, who in death refuses to forgive him or to speak to him, and at last turns away to the company of her first husband, 'who answered her cares and matched her love'. A last bitter twist of the knife: even Dido is better off than the isolated Aeneas. This is the only happy marriage we ever see in the *Aeneid*; and it is among the dead. Aeneas is left in no doubt that he destroyed Dido, and he can only say that he did not intend it.

In the second half of the poem he will find himself destroying other things, too. Juno stirs up a fearful war with a coalition of Italian peoples, and Books 9 to 12 are full of epic fighting. Aeneas finds an unexpected ally, an aged Greek king named Euander, who entrusts his son Pallas to the hero, to learn from him to be a warrior. Pallas is killed, and Aeneas feels bitterly responsible. He himself is forced to kill the attractive young Etruscan prince Lausus, who persists in attacking him to rescue his own father: Aeneas weeps over Lausus' body. He tries repeatedly to make peace with King Latinus and his recalcitrant people, but they break the truce and force him into battle. His fighting rage is at last aroused, and he slaughters great numbers of the Italians; yet these are peoples who are to live together in

peace, and the war is horrible, a kind of civil war. The poem
ends with another masterly transformation of a Homeric scene.
The Italian champion Turnus finally comes face to face with
Aeneas, in a duel deliberately reminiscent of the duel between
Achilles and Hector. Turnus is wounded, he falls; he admits
defeat and begs for his life. Aeneas is about to spare him, his
fighting rage is subsiding—and then he sees round Turnus' waist
the belt which he stripped from the body of Pallas when he slew
him. Inflamed with anger, Aeneas avenges the death of his young
friend by killing Turnus, and the epic ends with the lines

> A deadly chill his loosening limbs invades:
> His soul lamenting passes to the shades.

Such an ending reminds us that in the *Iliad* Hector was killed in
Book 22, and that two books followed in which Achilles came
to terms, first with the other Achaeans, and then with his enemy
Priam. Here there is no such healing process of reconciliation,
and the work ends with the act of killing—an act which could
easily have been made less disturbing. Turnus is a killer, and his
death is just; but Aeneas would have liked to spare him, if he
could. That is Virgil's deepest reflection on the nature of imperialism: that it is a hard and lonely destiny, in which the conqueror repeatedly finds himself destroying what he would prefer
to spare. By his victory Aeneas wins the hand of the young
princess Lavinia, an *ingénue* who had been betrothed to Turnus,
and who never speaks in the poem. Unlike Odysseus' wife
Penelope, and unlike the Dido he has been forced to leave and
to destroy, this young girl will not be a wife to console the
loneliness of the battered hero—who in any case will live for
only three years.

It would be superficial to regard the *Aeneid* as anti-imperialist
or anti-Augustan. The message of the poem is that the domination of Rome over the world is willed by heaven, and that it
will impose peace and civilization (*mos, ius*). Virgil devises a
series of forward perspectives through history, to make this
vision real. In Book 1 Jupiter reveals to Venus the plans of Fate:

a Roman Empire without limits in time or space, and Augustus as its climax, a future god. In Book 6 Aeneas' dead father shows him the spirits of the unborn Romans of the future, who will conquer the world and, renouncing to the Greeks the fine arts, practise the arts of rule, putting down the proud and sparing the conquered. At the end of Book 8 Aeneas is brought a marvellous shield, the work of Vulcan, on which are depicted the wars of Rome, with the battle of Actium in the centre (brilliantly represented as a tableau, not a narrative). And in Book 12 Juno at last abandons her hostility to Rome, and she and Jupiter agree that the Italians, far from being simply defeated by the Trojans, shall contribute the native Italian toughness and valour to form the unique essence of Rome—'Italian hardihood shall make Rome great':

> Sit Romana potens Itala uirtute propago.

Other poets might have produced fine poetry on the greatness of conquest and dominion. The supremacy of the *Aeneid*, and its continuing importance when the Roman Empire has turned out after all to be less than eternal, depends on two things. One is the haunting beauty of Virgil's verse, never equalled in Latin literature; the other is his ability to present at the same time, with justice but also with passion, both the achievement of Empire and also its inevitable human cost. The exquisite balance comes out clearly when Aeneas is brought the shield, glittering with the representation of Rome's martial history, culminating in the figure of Augustus receiving tribute from a conquered world. Aeneas marvels at the wonderful work, but of course he cannot really understand it, as these events have not yet happened; but he must bear the weight of them:

> These figures, on the shield divinely wrought,
> By Vulcan laboured, and by Venus brought,
> With joy and wonder fill the hero's thought.
> Unknown the names, he yet admires the grace;
> His shoulder bears the fame and fortune of his race.
>
> (trans. Dryden, adapted)

Such was Virgil's fame that a number of spurious poems were ascribed to him. At least one, the *Culex*, was a deliberate fake, widely accepted as Virgilian within eighty years of the poet's death. Others make no pretence of Virgilian authorship, and it seems that the attribution was simply the result of an insatiable desire in the reading public for more poems by Rome's greatest writer. Several are quite interesting in their own right, notably the *Copa*, a short hedonistic piece about the charms of a dancer at a country inn, and the *Ciris*, a self-consciously decadent epyllion about a girl betraying her country for love. The only members of the collection with any chance of being by Virgil are one or two of the very short pieces collectively known as the *Catalepton* ('In the Slender Style'). Certainty about them will never be reached.

Further Reading

The standard text of Virgil is the Oxford Classical Text of R. A. B. Mynors. Dryden's translation is splendid in rhetoric and verse, though it is often rather far from the Latin, and his rhyming couplets inevitably impose a different movement on Virgil's hexameters. C. Day Lewis translated all of Virgil into readable modern verse: *Eclogues* and *Georgics*, with an Introduction by R. O. A. M. Lyne (Oxford, 1983); *Aeneid*, with an Introduction by J. Griffin (Oxford, 1986). There are good versions of the *Eclogues* by Guy Lee (Liverpool, 1980); of the *Georgics* by L. P. Wilkinson (Harmondsworth, 1982) and Robert Wells (Manchester, 1982); and of the *Aeneid* by Robert Fitzgerald (London, 1984).

Virgil is the subject of an immense modern literature, much of it speculative and idiosyncratic. J. Griffin's *Virgil* (Oxford 1986, in the Past Masters series) deals particularly with the poet's ideas. The *Cambridge History of Classical Literature* ii (1982), 297–369, gives a generally reliable account of the poet and his works (but it is not, as is there stated, certain that the *Eclogues* were published in 35 BC). The poet's early life is well treated in the second chapter of L. P. Wilkinson, *The Georgics of Virgil* (Cambridge, 1969: paperback); the historical and political background in R. Syme's classic, *The Roman Revolution* (Oxford, 1939: paperback).

The Introduction to Robert Coleman's edition of the *Eclogues* (Cambridge, 1977) is very helpful. L. P. Wilkinson's book on the *Georgics* is the best on that poem. A useful approach to the *Aeneid*: W. A. Camps, *An Introduction to Virgil's Aeneid* (Oxford, 1969: paperback). W. Y. Sellar, *Virgil* (Oxford, 1877) is a good example of solid Victorian criticism; Brooks Otis, *Virgil: A Study in Civilized Poetry* (Oxford, 1963) is more subjective. A good collection of papers: *Virgil, a Collection of Critical Essays*, edited by S. Commager (Eaglewood Cliffs, NJ, 1966; paperback). T. S. Eliot's essay 'What is a Classic?' appears in his book *On Poets and Poetry* (London, 1951). Gordon Williams, *Tradition and Originality in Roman Poetry* (Oxford, 1968) illuminates many passages in Virgil, and in other authors. See also R. O. A. M. Lyne, *Further Voices in Virgil's Aeneid* (Oxford, 1987).

Important commentaries have appeared recently: on *Aeneid* 1, 2, 4, and 6 by R. G. Austin; on 3 and 5 by R. D. Williams; on 7 and 8 by C. J. Fordyce (all Oxford University Press); also on 8 by K. W. Gransden (Cambridge, 1976). R. D. Williams has published a shorter commentary on the whole of the *Aeneid* (London, 2 vols., 1972).

Two classic works of German scholarship: R. Heinze, *Virgils epische Technik* (3rd edn., 1914), repr. 1957, and E. Norden's Commentary on *Aeneid* 6 (Stuttgart, 1927, repr. 1957).

10

Roman Historians

ANDREW LINTOTT

Origins

A small proportion of the works of the Roman historians has survived the hiatus in culture and learning that followed the decline of the western half of the Roman Empire. We have only about a half of Tacitus' major works, for example, thanks to precisely two manuscripts, and only thirty-five of the 142 books of Livy. Such is the fate of the acknowledged masters; our information about the pioneers and many other later historians is confined to brief comments and quotations. Greek historians by contrast fared much better as a result of Byzantine scholarship.

Generalization from this limited evidence is made easier by the homogeneity of what survives. A Roman historian was first and foremost a historian of Rome, 'rerum Romanarum auctor'. Like Thucydides or Xenophon, he dealt primarily with public affairs at home and abroad: 'vast wars, the sack of cities, the defeat and capture of kings, or in domestic history conflicts between consuls and tribunes, legislation about land and grain-distribution, the struggles of the aristocracy and plebs'—such in Tacitus' view was the subject-matter of the historians of the Republic. The basic aims of the historians were simple: to preserve the memory of Rome itself and to transmit to future generations the exploits and characters of her famous men. To quote Tacitus again, 'I think it a particular function of annals, that virtues should not be passed over in silence, while those responsible for wrong actions and words should be threatened with disgrace in the eyes of posterity.' This history was not purely secular, however; it also concerned Rome's relations with the gods who watched over her growth and prosperity, as revealed in the portents by which the gods communicated with mortals, and the cult practices which were the human response to them. Ideally the historian of public affairs was a man who had participated in them. With the occasional exception, notably Livy, Roman historians were senators or had held important positions in public life. Sallust claims that he was diverted from historiography by political ambitions but, when these failed and he was no longer committed to a particular faction, he readily devoted his retirement to history rather than to a life of leisure or the 'servile activities of agriculture and hunting'.

The most inspiring topic for a Roman historian was Rome's phenomenal rise to dominance over the Mediterranean during the Republican period. Yet it was only when they were approaching the zenith of this achievement that the Romans developed both the will and the ability to chronicle it properly. The first Roman historians, Q. Fabius Pictor and L. Cincius Alimentus, held public office during the second Punic War (Cincius was captured by Hannibal) and probably wrote their histories immediately afterwards, in the first decade of the second century BC. They wrote in Greek—Fabius has recently been discovered among a group of Greek historians commemorated by texts painted on wall-plaster at Taormina in Sicily. Fabius and Cincius did not merely write about their own lifetime, but tried to reconstruct Roman history from its origins. We must therefore briefly consider what sort of historical material survived from the past and how it affected the subsequent composition of histories.

The Romans maintained records of the consuls of every year (*fasti consulares*), which, as transmitted to us, stretched back to the founding of the Republic about 500 BC. These probably derive from the yearly registers said to have been kept by the chief priests, *pontifices maximi*, containing the magistrates and notable events of each year. Questions, which cannot be discussed here, inevitably arise about the genuineness of these early records and the extent to which, even if basically genuine, they were corrupted later; what is certain is that at best they were a bare factual account of wars, triumphs, portents (e.g. eclipses), and food-shortages. There was also a great stock of stories about Rome from its mythical origins onwards, some written down by Greeks like Timaeus (below, p. 271), others deriving from native traditions. By far the most significant of these were the family traditions preserved by the noble families. These had their particular origin in funerals, whose contribution to Roman self-consciousness of their military prowess was noted by the Greek historian Polybius. The dead noble was carried to the rostra in the forum amid mourners wearing the clothes and death-masks of his ancestors, and there his son or a close relative pronounced an encomium (*laudatio funebris*), which began with the dead man himself and then embraced the exploits of the other dead ancestors included in the gathering. These orations were preserved for future exploitation, but both Cicero and Livy complain of their corruption of history by the invention of achievements and improper genealogical claims.

As far as we can judge, the earliest histories were far from a mere chronicle. Their writers probably had two major purposes, corresponding to their two different readerships. Now that Rome had become the dominant power in the Mediterranean, the Roman version of recent conflicts was a useful adjunct to foreign policy. So was publicity about the nature and antiquity of the city. About this time a friend of Rome in Chios set up an inscription showing the genealogy of Romulus and Remus—interestingly, it was Fabius Pictor who first seems to have reconciled the Greek view that Aeneas had founded Rome with the Roman view that it was Romulus. At home the historians not only followed the poets in glorifying Roman virtues, but educated in another way by establishing the 'truth' about the Roman constitution and mores, so as to preserve these from erosion in a time of increasing foreign influence and one when many new families were reaching high office. Roman historiography was thus at the start essentially conservative in outlook.

Other senators followed Fabius and Cincius, the most noteworthy among them being the ex-consul and censor M. Porcius Cato from the town of Tusculum in Latium. Cato wrote his *Origines* in Latin. As the work's title suggests, he was concerned with the early history, not only of Rome, but of other Italian cities; but he then moved swiftly on to discuss the Punic Wars and his own lifetime (234–149 BC), enlivening the narrative with digressions on marvels, as Herodotus had done, and also versions of his own speeches. From Cato's time onwards Romans usually wrote their history in Latin, but they were still subject to Greek influences, of which three may be distinguished.

Polybius

The first of these, antiquarianism, was apparent in Roman historiography from the beginning. The obvious Greek example for the Romans was Timaeus of Tauromenium (Taormina), a Sicilian writer of the early third century BC, who in the course of his histories of Sicily and the western Mediterranean had become in effect the first historian of Rome. Secondly there was the 'tragic' approach associated with certain Hellenistic writers, whose chief features were pathos, sensationalism, and the cult of the bizarre. The third influence was Polybius of Megalopolis, a Greek taken to Italy as a political detainee in 168 BC, who became a close friend of Roman aristocrats there and set himself to describe how 'almost the whole inhabited world had come under the sole rule of the Romans within fifty-three years'. He aimed to write 'pragmatic' history, a political and military history, which would be of practical value for the serious reader, both because it explained the links of cause and motivation between events and because it judged critically the behaviour of men under stress as examples for future conduct. Because the whole history of the Mediterranean had become united through

Roman power, he believed it was possible to write a universal history which was at the same time coherent and had explanatory value. Polybius' work was thus the culmination of Hellenistic historiography, in that politico-military history, traditionally focused on the city-state, was given the breadth of a universal chronicle. His narrative, chronologically based on Olympiads and their constituent years, dealt successively with the different regions of the world known to the Greeks, cross-cutting in order to keep parallel stories in step with one another and stressing their interrelation and convergence. At the same time he transformed Greek historiography because his central theme was the rise of an alien empire.

Like Thucydides (Vol. 1, pp. 224 ff.), he is a historian's historian, self-conscious about the principles and methodology of his craft, but more ready to discuss openly problems such as the selection of material, composition of speeches, portrayal of character, and explanation of causes. His approach is in essence a reaffirmation of Thucydides' first priority, the search for the truth from the most authentic evidence possible—autopsy, the questioning of eyewitnesses, and the sifting of their accounts. However, he extended his researches to the past, especially the generation before his own, and he made critical use of other men's writings. Yet he also stresses the historian's personal contribution to history and, while in abhorring the fabulous and over-emotional he distances himself from both the antiquarians and the 'tragic' writers, he shares the latter's preoccupation with making an impression on his readers. He reconciles these beliefs by a theory centring on the Greek term *emphasis*, which covers the authoritative impression given by a writer, the vivid significance of the events he recounts, and the powerful impression left in the reader's mind. He believes that it is the truth of events which influences a reader more than rhetorical devices. Yet this requires the historian as a medium, selecting and presenting events with appropriate comment on motive, cause, and outcome. On the other hand, the historian's ability derives from his own political and military experience either in the events themselves or other events like them. So the good historian is writing out of his own experience, whatever he relates, and the resulting authenticity and explanatory power makes the impact on the reader, without which history is useless for the man seeking instruction.

The instruction Polybius gives is often explicit. He discusses technicalities such as the computation of the size of cities and the use of fire-signals; he moralizes on the fortitude of Regulus in disaster, the foolish presumption of the Aetolians, the arrogance of Philip V of Macedon; he illustrates the dangers of using mercenaries. One book is devoted to the relative merits of the Roman, Carthaginian, and Spartan constitutions. Individual political decisions are analysed directly: he claims to have avoided fiction in speeches, but to have selected from the available material the central arguments, on whose background and outcome he adds his own comments. His treatment of the causes of war is perhaps not quite sophisticated enough. Although he carefully distinguishes the preliminary acts of a war and the pretexts alleged by the combatants from the causes proper, he finds the latter only in the mental disposition of the aggressor and the circumstances which had so disposed him. No allowance is made for occasions when there is no long-term resolve to fight, but the diplomatic interaction of the two parties drives one or both of them over the brink, nor is enough weight given to complicity in the state attacked, for example Rome in the Second Punic War, when it acquiesces in, and plans for, the attack threatening it. Like Thucydides, Polybius refused to attribute to chance what can be rationally explained. However, he shared the fascination of his Hellenistic and classical predecessors with the paradoxes of fortune (*tychē*), that is, rapid changes in human circumstances, whose particular components can be rationally explained, but whose cumulative effect is unpredictable and awe-inspiring. Most strikingly, he states that the rise of Rome to world-domination was directed by *tychē*, though he argues elsewhere that chance played no part in Roman success, but it was to be expected in the light of their power, political stability, and enterprise. This apparent inconsistency can be explained. Polybius seems to have regarded Rome as the worthy victor in a contest which had, as it were, been promoted by *tyche* through the coincidence in time of several great and ambitious powers. But it was chance that the conflict in the West between Rome and Carthage, which had a causal nexus of its own, coincided in time with the expansion of Philip V and Antiochus III, and so political processes throughout the Mediterranean became enmeshed with each other.

The Late Republic

Roman historians did not share Polybius' interest in theory, nor did they match his universality in treating events. Nevertheless, he had put Rome firmly in the centre of world history, and the practical educational aim he ascribed to history would have ensured its respectability in Roman eyes. Furthermore, his desire that politicians and generals should write history, not men sitting in libraries, was in accordance with existing Roman tradition. How did Roman writing develop under these Hellenistic influences? In the late second century a distinction was drawn between *annales*, in the strict sense of a chronicle of events year by year, and *historiae*, which involved causal analysis. In due course the term 'historiae' was to be used by Sallust and Tacitus for works about their own lifetime, while 'annales' tended to mean ancient history. Cato had been the pioneer in turning history into a political weapon; by 100 BC politicians were writing memoirs to set the record right about themselves. This trend led in time to Caesar's commentaries and Augustus' autobiography and *Res Gestae*. Biography developed also: C. Gracchus wrote about his elder brother and in the late Republic great men—Caesar, Pompey, Cato, and Cicero, for example—were commemorated by their admirers. However, side by side with contemporary history antiquarian history flourished as never before. The material in the earlier annals was expanded by material culled from a variety of documents, whether genuine or forged, and supplemented by frequently stereotyped inventions, such as led Livy to wonder how the Volscians and Aequians had enough men to be slaughtered so often by the Romans.

No one could now complain of a shortage of Roman history, but in the view of Cicero's contemporaries what existed was not readable. Cicero's friends pestered him for a history—'a work in itself most suited to an orator'—and when he died, Cornelius Nepos (himself a writer of chronicles and short biographies) lamented that the chance of casting the rough and shapeless mass of material into a worthy literary form was lost. Cicero himself argued that Roman histories could not be compared with Greek because they lacked *ornatus*, attractive presentation. This comprised variations in colour and tone, good word-order, and an easy flowing style, in which ideally the rhythm of the sentences reproduced the rhythm of events. However, more than language was involved in Cicero's view: histories required proper chronological disposition and geographical descriptions, interpretations of policy and motive, and judgements on the execution of these policies. Although the fragments known to us of early annalists show spectacular language and a vigorous narrative skill, they lack the smoothness to beguile a reader over long periods. More important, they may not have given enough space to interpretation.

Julius Caesar

Caesar's commentaries on his Gallic and Civil Wars are the first good evidence we have of the progress of Roman historiography. Although they are memoirs with a political purpose, they share many of the characteristics of less committed histories: indeed tendentiousness and self-glorification are not vices unique to autobiography. Stylistically, Caesar seems to have improved on his predecessors. The narrative flows clearly and smoothly, but there is little variety of tone nor a great range of vocabulary, and the style generally resembles that of the official letters we find in Cicero's correspondence. Cicero praised their naked and austere beauty, precisely because they were stripped of verbal ornament. In organization and interpretation of his material Caesar meets Cicero's requirements more closely. Indeed the themes of Caesar's *Gallic War* are typical of mature Roman history. Caesar tells us of the expansion of Roman power in a successful war, enlivening the story with digressions on geography and the characteristics of foreign races, and explains its significance by comments in the first person and by speeches in which both he and his opponents justify their conduct. The whole work is a testimony to Roman virtue, not only that of Caesar himself, but of his troops, whose abilities are rarely portrayed so effectively elsewhere. There is a political message too. Although Caesar was radical and violent in his own political career, when discussing the Gallic communities he exalts established power and conservatism. Danger comes from ambitious men who solicit help from the plebs by largesse and aim at revolution. In spite of the irony which the reader can find in these remarks, Caesar would have written them quite sincerely: Rome had traditionally sought aid from the 'establishments' among her allies when securing her empire. The *Civil War* could not so easily be given a Roman interpretation. Yet once again Caesar's soldiers are heroes, and Caesar defends his own conduct according to traditional values: when his dignity was threatened and he was deserted by former friends, he took up arms in defence of the liberty of the Roman people against the machinations of a few powerful men.

Sallust

C. Sallustius Crispus (born 86 BC), a partisan of Caesar's who took to history about the time of the latter's murder, was more innovative stylistically and developed a terse epigrammatic style, which owed much to the short simple sentences and ponderous vocabulary of the early annalists, in particular Cato, but had greater variety of language and tone. Unfortunately his major work, the *Histories*, which dealt with late Republican history down to 67 BC, only survives in fragments, and we have to base our judgement of him mainly on the monographs *Catiline* and *Jugurtha*. In these Sallust makes plain his preoccupation with the portrayal of virtue; in fact he alludes to the importance of the death-masks of the nobility as inspiration for later generations, thus recalling the influence of Roman funerals on historical writing. However, to throw virtue into relief he gives as much emphasis to vice, and he does not limit himself to the character of individuals but portrays the mores of whole sections of society. Patriotically he gives Roman military glory its due, but contrasts this with the moral corruption which in his view attended the expansion of the Roman Empire. It was above all the aristocracy itself which through greed and ambition was not only self-destructive, but created injustice for the poor or encouraged corruption in them also. Rome was only saved by the outstanding virtue of a few of her leaders. Sallust also highlights conflicts between the nobility and the plebs, which had begun in the early Republic before corruption had set in, but returned in earnest in the late Republic after a brief period of harmony during Rome's most critical wars. He shows sympathy with plebeian sufferings (he had himself been tribune of the plebs and taken a popular stance at that time). Yet when writing of the late Republic, in a passage influenced by Thucydides, he denounces both those who claimed to defend the status quo of senatorial dominance and those who championed plebeian rights, for seeking in reality their own power. For Sallust vice and decadence were as important subjects as virtues and victories, and it was vice which gave him the greatest opportunities for extended portrayal of character, for example those of Catiline and Jugurtha themselves, and minor characters like Sempronia, the educated society woman in Sallust's *Catiline*. However, the analysis of the causes of decadence is comparatively superficial. Roman political organization and the Roman economy are but briefly mentioned. For Sallust the fundamental causes were prosperity and the lack of foreign enemies: these gave rein to a sort of original sin, which only the hardships of foreign wars could hold in check. This notion was not discovered by Sallust: it goes back to the politics and historiography of the second century BC. But Sallust transmitted it in a most memorable form.

Livy

T. Livius is the first annalistic writer whose work survives in any quantity, and it is through him and the elements of earlier writings discernible in his history that we are able to form judgements on the annals of the Republic. Moreover, his history was the last great annalistic history of the Republic written in Latin. Livy was born at Patavium (Padua) in 59 BC and wrote from about the age of thirty onwards after twenty years of civil war and the conversion of the Republic into a form of monarchy. A man of industry and learning rather than political or intellectual distinction, he came nearest to fulfilling the expectation which Cicero's friends had of Cicero—the production of a readable history of Rome. His resources in language and deployment of his material were everything that Cicero himself could have wished. Avoiding Sallustian abruptness, he yet contrived a swift and varied narrative built from a rich vocabulary and an immense flexibility of construction. His approach to his subject was conservative, as had probably been traditional among annalists: in wars he was patriotic, in politics he supported senatorial authority against the demagoguery of tribunes. Although he shows some sympathy with the *plebs* in his account of their struggle with the patricians, he shows an immense fascination with aristocratic hardliners who resisted inflexibly any concession to the *plebs* or deviation from tradition. It is likely that he retained this attitude in his lost books on the fall of the Republic and saw a reason for that fall in the failure of such men. One supreme example would have been Cato Uticensis, who opposed Caesar and had already been highlighted for selfless devotion to the Republic in Sallust's *Catiline*. Although Livy wrote in the aftermath of political failure and civil conflict, it was also a period when Roman imperial power was at its height. Faced by this discrepancy and by the coincidence of prosperity with the moral turpitude exemplified by the shedding of Roman blood, Livy, like Sallust, argued that Rome had succumbed to the weight of her own success.

As an interpreter of history in detail, Livy was unoriginal or simply defective in his treatment of causes. However, he substituted for explanation a vivid human sympathy shown in his portrayal of emotions both in the speeches he composed and in the narrative. This is essentially an imaginative skill. There was no evidence about the feelings of the people of Veii, when the Romans drove them from their city and razed it to the ground, or about what the Roman soldiers felt when sent under the yoke by the Samnites (both these episodes took place in the fourth century BC); there was probably little more about the Romans' reaction to their defeat by Hannibal at Trasimene in 217. Yet these are some of the most memorable passages in what survives of Livy. It was the 'tragic' approach to history that influenced him much more than the 'pragmatic' approach of Polybius. Livy carried his history down to 9 BC—a mammoth work never to be emulated, not least because in the meantime the Republic became a dead subject.

The Early Empire

The Principate of Augustus and his successors brought changes in political life and in literary style. Both the People and the Senate gradually lost the power to make effective political decisions on matters of importance: policies were formed by the Emperor and his intimates *in camera*; promotions ultimately depended on imperial favour. So secrecy led to ignorance of the *arcana* of the Empire among contemporaries and later historians and, to compensate, fed rumour and suspicion, while the court atmosphere encouraged intrigue and backbiting. Meanwhile the luxuriant oratory of men such as Cicero was abandoned in favour of a style pointed and abrupt, like Sallust's, but more striking in its phraseology, especially apt for lampoon and denunciation.

Some historians who chronicled the transition from republic

to monarchy maintained their independence from the new regime. One, Cremutius Cordus, had his books burnt under Tiberius and later reproduced under Gaius in a censored edition. In general, however, history, as Tacitus pointed out, was corrupted in two ways, by flattery of the present emperor and detraction of his predecessors. The former was stimulated by the requirement to deliver formal panegyrics of the Emperor in the consul's oration of thanks, instituted in Augustus' time (Pliny's *Panegyric* of AD 100 is the first surviving example). By contrast, Seneca's *Ludus* or *Apocolocyntosis* about the death and deification of the Emperor Claudius is a remarkable specimen of licensed defamation. Equally detrimental to the historian was the lack of traditional material. After Augustus' time most emperors did not seek major new conquests; at home there was no room for the great political conflicts of the Republic. The rivalries of the aristocracy centred on trials for treason, as they jockeyed for position in the Emperor's favour or the esteem of their equals. Important developments in the early Principate— changes in administration at home and abroad, the spread of citizenship and Graeco-Roman culture, the growth of cities— were not the stuff which had interested historians in the past and did not lend themselves to pathos or sensationalism. Yet Rome's greatest historian worked in what he himself believed was a narrow and inglorious field.

Tacitus

C. Cornelius Tacitus was born in the middle of the first century AD and reached senatorial rank and high office under the Flavian dynasty. He wrote mainly under the Emperor Trajan, in what was held to be an unexampled era of security and prosperity after the murder of the last Flavian Emperor, the 'tyrannical' Domitian. One early work was a written version of a funeral panegyric about his father-in-law Agricola. Both here and in his two major historical works—the *Historiae*, dealing with the Flavian period (AD 69–96), and the *Annales* on the Julio-

Claudian dynasty from AD 14 to AD 68—he proclaims his traditional concern with virtue and vice. 'The age was not so barren of virtues that it did not produce some fine examples of conduct.' These were not quite those of republican annals. 'Mothers accompanied their children into exile, wives followed their husbands . . . loyal slaves even gave insulting answers to their torturers.' Nevertheless, Tacitus' work is full of miniatures of the *Agricola* type—obituary notices of those who prospered under the regime or fell foul of it through treason trials. 'Let us make this concession to the reputation of famous men that, just as in their funeral rites they are kept apart from mass burials, so they may each have their own notice in the records of deaths.'

He aimed not only to give moral edification by parading virtue and vice, but to give practical instruction. This justified his attention to intrigue and treason trials. Under the Republic, he explains, when power was at one time with the *plebs*, at another with the Senate, one had to discover how to manage the masses and equally how to influence the nobles who dominated the Senate. By the same token under an autocracy it was helpful to understand how an Emperor's mind worked. It was for success in this respect that Tacitus was so admired by men like Machiavelli and Guicciardini in the Renaissance. Although he gave their due to those who were destroyed by Emperors, he reserved his greatest admiration for those like himself and his father-in-law Agricola, who survived. 'Let all those, whose habit is to admire acts of civil disobedience, realize that great men can exist under bad emperors, and that compliance and an unassuming demeanour, if backed by energy and hard work, can attain a pitch of glory, which the majority reach through an ostentatious and untimely death.' He had no illusions about the leading victims of the Julio-Claudians, pointing out how they tried to maintain status by self-display and extravagant spending, and contrasting them with the modest and parsimonious new men brought into the senate.

As a historian of the Empire he is most interesting for his ability to put the case for the opposition, not only denouncing the corruption of Roman rule (part of a Roman orator's stock-in-trade in so far as he had to appear for Rome's subjects in extortion cases), but also highlighting courageous independence and resistance to the blandishments of Roman civilization. 'If you wish to rule everyone, does it follow that everyone should accept slavery?' asks the captured British leader Caratacus. A feature of that slavery was 'the amenities that make vice agreeable—porticoes, baths, and sumptuous banquets'. On the other hand he could contrast the peace and justice that Roman rule brought with the insecurity of tribal rivalries. Most revealing, however, is the comment attributed to a Roman commander rejecting a plea from a German tribe to be allowed to settle in Roman territory. 'Men must obey their betters: the gods they invoked had empowered the Romans to decide what to give and what to take away, and to tolerate no judges but themselves.'

Tacitus lamented the lack of military material available to him. Yet, though he can give an exciting and not inaccurate account of a campaign (like Livy, he is especially effective in portraying the feelings of the men involved), his style leads to an irritating vagueness about detail. This style, however, was admirably suited to the portrayal of imperial politics. Two chief features were irony, used to contrast the appearances of public life with the underlying realities of power, and a deliberate cultivation of ambiguity. Tacitus delights in the deflating postscript. He also has an elaborate technique of providing alternative explanations—some his own, some ascribed to others—which do not clarify but increase the uncertainty over the motivation of those he describes. His classic achievement was his portrayal of Tiberius. His sources reported an Emperor who, in spite of great talents and a concern for the well-being of the Empire, ended his life with an intermittent grasp over his administration and abominated by his people. Tacitus seized on Tiberius' well-known hypocrisy as the answer to the enigma, and saw his life as the gradual peeling of skins of plausibility from a bitter and malevolent inner self. Tiberius was presented as a man of acute intelligence warped by his early life and love of domination. Guicciardini wrote, 'Cornelius Tacitus teaches very well every man who lives under a tyrant the way to live and manage his affairs prudently, just as he equally teaches tyrants the ways to found their tyranny.'

In spite of the supposedly happy era in which he wrote, Tacitus' attitude to history was pessimistic. The doom of the Republic was inevitable; the miseries under Tiberius were ascribed to divine wrath. Tacitus seems to have had genuine doubts about the free will of men, which should have subverted his endeavours to give them advice. Did the friendship or enmity of the Emperor depend on predestination and one's lot at birth or was policy of some avail? For Tacitus the world was either a realm of pure chance unmitigated by divine providence or else determined in its destiny, whether by rational chains of cause and effect, as the Stoics believed, or by the planets. Though not always complimentary to individual astrologers, Tacitus was respectful to the science itself, as were many of his contemporaries, including the Flavian Emperors. As for the old gods of Rome, Tacitus said little of religious ceremonies and his treatment of portents was equivocal. The disasters which befell the Roman people were proof that the gods had no care for their tranquillity, only for their punishment. In AD 69 there were 'monstrous animal births and numerous other signs and wonders of the kind that in primitive centuries were noted in peacetime, but now are only heard of when men are afraid.' It is hard to deduce a consistent religious or philosophical view from his work. However, this did not affect his moral purpose. Destiny might provide an explanation for human conduct, but not an excuse.

Suetonius

Tacitus' achievement was to adapt traditional principles to the history of the early principate and create a historical style which reflected the period. For over two centuries no one writing in Latin tried to match his achievement. Already in his lifetime literary fashion was turning from history to biography, where special attention could be given to psychology and personal relations, the subjects that had fascinated Tacitus himself. Moreover, from the point of view of the Roman upper class the lives of the Emperors were the main thread of history. Monographs might be written on their achievements, especially their campaigns. Fuller biographies would spice their official career with succulent details of their private life and judgements on their character. Tacitus' younger contemporary, C. Suetonius Tranquillus, is the most effective exponent of this literary genre known to us and he was followed by other writers, whose work was the basis for the creation in the late empire of the *Historia Augusta*, a collection of imperial biographies whose authorship and reliability are much disputed.

The core of Suetonius' work is the raw material of a Roman epitaph or funeral oration—the public record of an Emperor, his exploits at home and abroad, and the moral qualities revealed by these. Set against the official career is his private life. The domestic virtues of an Emperor had become a topic for panegyric by the time of the Younger Pliny. But there was much more scope there for detraction. Certainly, an Emperor was criticized for military failure, the waste of public money, and brutality towards the rest of the upper class (Suetonius did not on the whole judge the administrative reforms he recorded). Yet public faults could best be exploited as the result of the personal inadequacies of the Emperor, and his vices were revealed in his home, especially in his dining-room and bedroom. So we find in Suetonius catalogues of achievements placed side by side with scandalous descriptions of the Emperor's more intimate life, both copiously illustrated by anecdotes. In spite of the fact that these two elements are rarely well fused, an effective, though not necessarily accurate, character portrait often results.

Suetonius may be compared with a Greek contemporary of Tacitus, Plutarch of Chaeronea, the greatest biographer of antiquity (below, pp. 305 ff.) Most of Plutarch's biographies took the form of parallel lives, in which an eminent Greek was compared with an eminent Roman of the Republic. These were intended as character portraits (Plutarch specifically compares his work to both sculpture and painting), in which small faults were to be toned down without being completely omitted, in order that the requirements of truth should be fulfilled but the reader should not be distracted from the general outline of the man. To this end Plutarch did not simply recount the lives of his subjects from birth to death, but included general descriptions of their behaviour in certain contexts (it is here especially that, like Suetonius, he introduces anecdotes). The men are described and compared in terms of ethical concepts derived from Platonic and Aristotelian philosophy. Men should be brave, but not rash; modest, and not insolent in success; moderate and scrupulous in their use of wealth; and they should control the passions of their subordinates while not being themselves swept away by passion. The biographies seek to show the relative success or failure of great men in living up to such precepts. Compared with this, Roman biography is ethically crude. The values of the Roman historians had arisen not so much from a view of the good man, but from a view of the success of Rome, and utility to Rome was a narrow foundation on which to base judgements on personality.

Why did the flow of Roman history dry up after Tacitus? It is significant that the next great history of Rome was written in Greek by a Roman senator of Greek origins, Cassius Dio from Bithynia. This was a universal history of Rome up to the time of writing (the early third century AD), which was intended to emulate Thucydides' work in its explanations and political generalizations. By contrast, Roman explanations of their political history (in spite of Polybius' example) had rarely gone beyond the simplistic in political terms. Thus, once the history of a period had been eloquently written by a Livy or Tacitus there was little call to rewrite it. Since the Empire and the Principate were consolidated and apparently unlikely to change, the lives of the Emperors might be written as a series of appendices to a story already well told. Later, in the fourth century, a Syrian from Antioch, Ammianus Marcellinus, tried to make a new start by writing in Latin on the period from the end of Tacitus' work to his own day. The usual material is to be found there—wars, geographic and ethnographic descriptions, trials, seditions in Rome and other cities, and, not least, digressions on morals. Yet, in spite of the vivid and sensational presentation, little is said to explain the crises of the fourth century and the changes in society. This is perhaps one reason why the Roman upper class had abandoned writing history in the traditional fashion. They could find nothing new to say within the old framework.

Further Reading

English translations exist of most surviving historical works mentioned in this chapter; there is, however, no translation of the fragments of Roman historians. Apart from the translations facing texts in the Loeb Classical Library, the most complete range is now in the Penguin Classics. Especially good are those of Tacitus' *Annals* (M. Grant) and *Histories* (K. Wellesley), Sallust, Caesar (S. A. Handford), and Polybius (I. Scott-Kilvert), although this contains little of Polybius dealing with events after the Second Punic War. The best translation of Polybius is by E. S. Shuckburgh (2 vols., 1889/1962). Major translations of Tacitus include those of A. J. Church and J. Brodribb (London, 1882) and W. Fyfe (Oxford, 1912).

A *general survey* is provided by M. L. W. Laistner, *The Greater Roman Historians* (California, 1963). There are also useful collections of essays, *Latin Historians* and *Latin Biography* (ed. T. A. Dorey, London, 1966 and 1967), which contain chapters on Polybius and Plutarch respectively as well as on writers in Latin. A. Momigliano, *Essays in Ancient and Modern Historiography* (Oxford, 1977), especially chs. 4, 5, and 7, is important for both the historians themselves and their place in the development of historiography.

On *Early Historians* see E. Badian's chapter in *Latin Historians* (above) and Momigliano (above); for a more controversial study of early Roman records B. W. Frier, *Libri Annales Pontificum Maximorum. The Origins of the Annalistic Tradition* (Rome, 1979).

Polybius has been studied above all by F. W. Walbank. See his *Polybius* (California, 1972); also the introduction to *A Historical Commentary on Polybius*, vol. i. (Oxford, 1957). For Polybius' views of the historian's function see K. Sacks, *Polybius and the Writing of History* (California, 1981).

The best introduction to *Sallust* is D. C. Earl, *The Political Thought of Sallust* (Cambridge, 1961; Amsterdam, 1966). R. Syme, *Sallust* (Oxford, 1964), is a more detailed and wide-ranging investigation.

Caesar has been treated by F. E. Adcock, *Caesar as a Man of Letters* (Cambridge, 1956). P. G. Walsh, *Livy* (Cambridge, 1961), provides a concise and valuable general study of that author. Also useful is the introduction in R. M. Ogilvie, *A Commentary on Livy I–V* (Oxford, 1965).

R. Syme, *Tacitus* (2 vols., Oxford, 1958), is the major work in English on that historian. R. Martin, *Tacitus* (London, 1981), is a simpler work full of good sense. The introduction in H. Furneaux, *The Annals of Tacitus*, vol. i (Oxford, 1884), is also useful. B. Walker, *The Annals of Tacitus* (Cambridge, 1952, 1960), seeks to distinguish the factual and non-factual elements in the work. See also the collection of essays in *Tacitus*, ed. T. A. Dorey (London, 1969), and K. C. Schellhase, *Tacitus in Renaissance Political Thought* (Chicago, 1976).

On biography see A. Wallace-Hadrill, *Suetonius* (London, 1983); D. A. Russell, *Plutarch* (London, 1972); C. P. Jones, *Plutarch and Rome* (Oxford, 1971).

Other developments in imperial history and biography are most easily appreciated from reading *Latin Historians* and *Latin Biography* (above). On Ammanius see J. Matthews, *The Roman Empire of Ammanius* (London, 1989), especially ch. 18.

11

The Arts of Prose
The Early Empire

DONALD RUSSELL

Two Languages, One Literature

THE first two centuries of the Christian era produced an extensive and important prose literature, both in Greek and in Latin. Though the greatest genius, Tacitus, was a Roman whose ways of thinking seem peculiarly difficult to express in Greek, the two languages were in many respects vehicles of a single literature, and the Greek contribution is arguably the more significant of the two.

Not that Greek and Latin were at all on an equal footing. Native Greek speakers seldom troubled to learn Latin, except for the purposes of official life, and they seem to have found its nuances hard to grasp. 'Longinus' (*On Sublimity* 12. 4) wisely asks indulgence for trying to judge Cicero; Plutarch (*Demosthenes* 3) disclaims the ability to do so, and clearly had a struggle with his Latin. It was natural that there should be a steady demand for Greek books giving information on Roman subjects: Dionysius of Halicarnassus' *Roman Antiquities*, Plutarch's Roman *Lives*, Appian's *Wars of the Romans* catered for the need, which increased as the period advanced and more and more Greek speakers sought positions of influence in imperial administration and politics. Thus by the end of the second century Latin historiography has dried up, but Herodian and the much more competent Cassius Dio attest the vigour of Greek. Latin speakers, on the other hand, if they were destined for official position or literary education (and the two were always closely linked), learned Greek from childhood, and often preferred it, especially for philosophical or scientific purposes, to their native tongue. It is in no way surprising that the Emperor Marcus Aurelius wrote *To Himself* in Greek, nor that Pliny's friend Corellius Rufus announced his resolution to take his own life with the Greek word *Kekrika*, 'I have decided'. At the same time, there is an extensive literature conveying Greek learning and philosophy to a Latin public, pursuing the Ciceronian and Augustan ideal of making Latin literature a complete and self-contained expression of Graeco-Roman culture. Celsus' encyclopedia, Quintus Curtius' *Alexander*, Pliny's *Natural History* are examples of this.

But what was common to the two languages is more important than this difference. Both were self-consciously literary languages, diverging considerably from the spoken tongue. The difference was sharper in Greek. From the Augustan period onwards—indeed earlier—teachers of Greek grammar and rhetoric inculcated an ever closer approach to the precise linguistic and grammatical forms attested by the Attic classics of the fifth and fourth centuries BC, especially Thucydides, Xenophon, and the orators. This movement reached a high point in the middle of the second century, when the marvellous archaizing pastiches produced by great 'sophists' won the applause of packed theatres and the admiring patronage of Emperors. In Latin, the chronological perspectives were different. Latin literature had only recently reached what was quickly recognized as its classical maturity. Prose style had continued to develop naturally after Cicero, partly in reaction against the norms of sentence structure and decorum which he had tried to establish. This reaction lasted about a century, until Quintilian tried to reverse it. It was not till the Antonine period (AD 97–180) that the trickle of prose archaizers (*antiquarii*) became a flood, and something rather like Greek 'Atticism' developed. Before this happened, there had been much enrichment and experimentation; but the sources of this, it is important to notice, lay much more in poetry and in the devices of older Greek rhetoric than in the resources of everyday Latin speech. These remained largely untapped, though educated speech is clearly echoed in parts of Seneca, and Petronius (below, pp. 331 ff.) went so far as to make some of the characters in his comic novel speak the incorrect language of the uneducated: a unique experiment, so far as we know, whether in Latin or in Greek.

The salient point is that almost all the works of significance, in both languages, are written in what Eduard Norden, the scholar who has contributed most to our understanding of these matters, called *Kunstprosa*, 'prose of art' or 'formal prose', the product of assiduous teaching and imitation. The main mark of *Kunstprosa*, both in Greek and in Latin, is its dependence on deliberate choice made in advance by the writer for the particular task before him. He has to determine what is the appropriate stylistic level (*genus dicendi* or—in Greek—*charaktēr*) for the job; a common classification distinguished 'grand', 'middle', and 'delicate' styles, but this was by no means the only categorization that was possible. In any case, there was a choice to be made in vocabulary, and this was very much determined by literary precedent and association; there was also a choice of sentence-structure, between the long and elaborately organized 'periodic' sentence and a more simple pattern; and, most striking to the modern reader, there was the choice of rhythm. Some regularity in the quantitative pattern of sentence endings (*clausulae* in Latin) is to be seen in classical Greek prose; but it seems to have been the Hellenistic rhetors and their Roman pupils who systematized and enforced practices which had become second nature to writers of our period. Most Roman historians and some Greek sophists do, it is true, break all known rules; but this is itself an act of choice, dictated by the genre. Tacitus has regular Ciceronian 'clausulation' in his *Dialogue*, but not in his historical works. Quintilian (9. 15. 18) rationalizes this traditional preference—probably based on observation of Thucydides—by alleging that the speed of historical narrative makes the pauses marked by rhythmical *clausulae* inappropriate, because they slow the whole movement down.

Kunstprosa had already had a long history. Developed by the fifth- and fourth-century Greek sophists and orators, partly to give prose something of the dignity and affective power of poetry, but partly also to provide an unambiguous and elegant written language (*graphikē lexis*: Aristotle was the most important theorist who discussed this), it existed, in our period, in many different forms, and was a versatile and many-sided instrument. It was the vehicle, not only of the higher ranges of literature—history, oratory, *belles-lettres*—but of a great deal of technical and didactic writing. Dionysius' *The Arrangement of Words*, 'Longinus' *On Sublimity*, and Onasander's *The General* are good Greek examples, all of the first century; Celsus' encyclopedia (of which the medical books alone survive), Columella's treatise on farming, and Quintilian's manual of oratory are Latin ones of the same epoch. There are, however, works from which the signs of formality are absent, and which seem much less 'literary': Vitruvius' *Architecture* in Latin and Arrian's *Discourses of Epictetus* in Greek are notable instances. This lack of formality was itself often deliberate. Arrian wrote his *Expedition of Alexander* in Xenophon's Attic dialect, and his book on India in Herodotus' Ionic; so it was with the same deliberate selection of medium that he set down the discussions of the slave-philosopher Epictetus in the first-century technical language in which such things were actually expressed.

Critics and Rhetoric: The Sense of Decline

A literature with such exacting formal standards and so closely linked with education was bound to be self-conscious and self-critical. It is no wonder that this was the great age of literary criticism, though not, strictly speaking, of literary theory. In particular, the progress and decline of letters were anxiously monitored. Some saw improvement, more saw decline. This was a conventional pessimism, a literary application of the idea, which is as old as Homer and Hesiod, that men are 'not what they were'. Often a convenient mode of polemic, it is not therefore necessarily insincere.

Dionysius of Halicarnassus arrived in Rome very soon after Octavian's victory at Actium (31 BC). He settled there for a career which included rhetorical teaching, literary criticism, and the composition of an elaborate history of early Rome. In the preface to his series of studies on the Attic orators, he sets out the achievement of his age as he sees it. There have been great changes. The 'old philosophic rhetoric'—which embraces the Attic orators down to Demosthenes—was displaced 'after the death of Alexander the Macedonian' by an 'ill-bred' substitute, a new immigrant from some Asiatic hell-hole; but this vulgar and abandoned upstart has miraculously been put in her place by a revival of classical standards, the result of the good taste of the educated Roman governing class. This is a polemical picture, but it makes important points. The new mandarin prose is the expression of a rhetoric which is not just a bag of tricks, a technique of fallacious advocacy and intellectual blackmail, but 'philosophical rhetoric' (*philosophos rhētorikē*), a proper moral and social formation for an age of good government. Essentially, this was the ideal of Isocrates, 350 years earlier, restated for a larger world.

The three stages of development presupposed by Dionysius' account—acme of perfection, degeneration, and revival—are a familiar pattern in Greek theoretical accounts of literary and artistic history. It was at first not easy for the Romans to adapt this scheme to the circumstances of their own development. When Horace, Dionysius' contemporary, glories in the Augustan poetic achievement, his pride is in the techniques that have superseded the immaturity and imperfections of the past, not in the displacement of a corrupt or degenerate fashion. But it is not long before the pattern appears. In oratory, the Ciceronian age was seen to be the acme, corresponding to the period of Demosthenes. Everything that followed was a decline. The Elder

Seneca, writing under Tiberius or Caligula, is an early witness to the discussion of corruption and decline which is prominent in first-century speculation. He gave weight to three causes of deterioration: a political cause, the loss of republican liberty; a moral cause, the idleness and indiscipline of sensation-seeking youth; and finally the mere malevolence of the natural order which lets nothing stay at the peak of its development. His son, the philosopher Seneca, urged the moralists' view. Style, he thought, reflects a way of life, both in the individual and in the society: 'Where you see *oratio corrupta* give pleasure, you may be sure that morals also have strayed from the right path' (*Epistles* 114. 11). He wrote this in AD 62. A generation later, he himself is pilloried in the Roman replay of a sort of Dionysian classicism, initiated by the great teacher Quintilian (*c*.AD 35–100), in whose eyes the very charm of Seneca's faults makes him a particularly pernicious model. From Quintilian's point of view, this is not unjust. Seneca's short sentences, unselective vocabulary, and jaunty fluency make him the type of a Latinity radically opposed to Ciceronian dignity and decorum. But Seneca too, we must not forget, writes *Kunstprosa*; in no writer is the beat of the *clausulae* more insistent.

Quintilian's important *Institutio Oratoria*, in twelve books, describes the education and training of the orator in greater detail than any other ancient work. It insists on morality as the basis of oratory, and it is especially interesting on education. He also wrote a book, now lost, on the causes of 'corruption' in style, doubtless a statement of his programme. Tacitus' *Dialogue on Orators*, the dramatic date of which is AD 73 though it was probably written nearly thirty years later, is concerned to state both 'conservative' and 'modernist' points of view. Another statement of the problem is in Greek, in the last chapter of 'Longinus', *On Sublimity* (*Peri hypsous*). This little book is a detailed discussion of the means by which grand, solemn, and emotionally powerful effects may be obtained in literature. It is the most stimulating of ancient critical works, as well as one of the most influential. Some uncertainty about its date must be admitted. It is transmitted as the work of a famous third-century scholar and statesman; but this attribution is widely disbelieved, and with reason, for the links with first-century speculation and interests are unmistakable. 'Longinus' represents 'a philosopher' as advocating the view that the inferiority of contemporary oratory is due to loss of liberty and of 'democracy', but he himself, though rhetorician by trade and not philosopher, very pointedly takes the more moral line: it is the war of the passions and the corruption of the heart that inhibit the creation of great thoughts. It is difficult to cash these statements in terms of a specific historical situation. In a Greek context, *On Sublimity*, taken as a whole, makes sense as a reaction against Hellenistic extravagance and frivolity. Indeed, it seems a more sophisticated and profound reaction than Dionysius' frigid classical revival, because 'Longinus' puts the primary emphasis on the importance of emotional impact in oratory and in literature generally, and the thrust of his argument is to show how this is involved with high thinking and moral ideals. He thus makes a contrast between classical Greek literature, in which all the worthwhile models are to be found, and the rhetors and sophists of his own degenerate day, whose only chance of salvation lies in a supreme moral and imaginative effort.

In the closing chapter, however, the perspective seems rather to be Roman. The 'philosopher's' view that high oratory has been destroyed by loss of freedom seems to reflect the transition from Republic to Principate. The author's 'reply' to this then takes the debate away from political revolutions to personal ethics, but makes the point, clearly directed against his imagined opponent, that 'people like us' are perhaps better under control, lest our greed ruin the world. The combination of Greek and Roman perspectives is confusing, but typical of this bilingual culture.

The Uses of Formal Prose

The carefully fostered, and minutely monitored, arts of prose were used in this period for a wide range of purposes.

First, and most importantly, for history, as the preceding chapter has explained.

Secondly, for oratory. This was of course the original primary function; but critics such as 'Longinus' were clearly right in their perception that the age no longer offered political rewards for the orator. The great trials and debates in which Cicero's contemporaries had re-enacted the dramas of the Demosthenic age were in the past; imperial *causes célèbres* were less earth-shaking. First-century Roman oratory anyway is lost to us; we do not know how significant or innovative it was, and the classicizing revival at the end of the century caused a change of taste which consigned it to oblivion. We do, however, have two important dated works from the second century: Pliny's *Panegyricus* (102) and Apuleius' *Apologia* (157/8: below, pp. 334 ff.) The 'panegyric', spoken by Pliny as consul in the Senate before Trajan, shows what Quintilian's Ciceronianism, with a strong element of 'silver' ingenuity and point, could achieve in the 'epideictic' or ceremonial mode. The 'apology', in which Apuleius defends himself on a charge of using magic to secure the affections of a wealthy widow, shows forensic oratory turning into pure literature, a vehicle for verbal virtuosity, frivolous erudition, and emotive rhetoric. Pliny is of course inspired by the values of Roman public life, and Apuleius is steeped in old Latin learning; but they both exemplify here a Greek phenomenon, the use of rhetoric for entertainment, the typical activity of the 'sophists' of the age.

The history of oratory throughout this period is in fact much more a Greek than a Latin theme. Dio Chrysostom—that is, 'the golden-mouthed'—a leading citizen of Prusa in Bithynia, orator and moralist, harangued the citizens of Rhodes and Alexandria, calming passions and rebuking folly, around the end of the first century AD. Polemon of Laodicea, Favorinus of Arles, Herodes Atticus, and many others went on embassies, pleaded cases, taught pupils, and entertained multitudes with their ingenious historical or grimly comic fantasies, all in the Greek of Demosthenes or some other early classic. This period, with its celebrated travelling virtuoso orators, is often called the 'Second Sophistic': the great speakers were idolized like pop-stars. In the sight of posterity it has often seemed a vanity; in its time, it was a literary and social movement of great influence and significance.

A third use of *Kunstprosa* breaks new ground. This is the age in which what may be called the 'essay' flourished as a recognizable, though unnamed, literary form. Very many of the works of Seneca, Dio, Lucian, and Plutarch are best so described. They are short discourses, often dealing with ethical questions, but sometimes with literature or education or some antiquarian matter. They are, as a rule, very personal in tone, in the sense that the *persona* of the writer is prominent, though they admit also much allusive learning and literary elaboration. In style, they tend to the less periodic. Several traditions went to the making of this class of writing. One was that of the philosophical dialogue, not in the form Plato generally preferred, but in that used by Aristotle, with long speeches instead of sharp question and answer. The dialogue continued to be written throughout our period—Cicero, Tacitus, and Plutarch were notable practitioners—but its techniques and even its name (*dialogus*) were also applied to works in which the element of conversation was not present. Another ancestor was the less polished popular sermon or moral address—'diatribe' is the modern scholars' word—which seems to have flourished in Hellenistic times, and is especially associated with the Cynics. Bion of Borysthenes, acknowledged by Horace as an exemplar for his satire, certainly contributed to the technique of imagery and anecdote which Seneca and Plutarch deployed with such lavishness and enthusiasm. Though these urbane essays were, for the most part, philosophical in tone and content, this does not mean that they did not sometimes come within the province of the rhetorician. Philosophical *theses*—'on providence', 'on marriage', and the like—were an established part of the elementary rhetorical curriculum. Moreover, the popularity of the casual-sounding address led the teachers of rhetoric to lay down precepts for it much as they did for formal speeches; they called it *lalia*, 'chat', and prescribed simple style, an anecdote or simile to capture attention at the start, and studied concealment of rhetorical and logical structure.

Barely separable from the 'essay' is the letter (the fourth use), for the 'essay' is often cast in epistolary form. The letter was, however, a recognized genre, for which we have intelligent and careful instructions in the treatise of Demetrius *On Style*, probably to be dated around the beginning of our period. Artemon, who had published the letters of Aristotle, had said that the letter was 'one side of a dialogue'. Demetrius (223 ff.) disagrees: the dialogue-writer imitates an extempore speech, the letter is 'sent as a gift' and one must pay the recipient the compliment of care and art. The central consideration is that a letter is 'the image of one's mind'; more than any other kind of writing, it presents its author's personality. So it must not be too technical—'a treatise with an address at the top'—nor periodic in style like a forensic speech. In a word, it is 'a brief expression of affection, an exposition of a simple theme in simple words'.

The letter is a particularly important form in our period. Seneca used it for what is by common consent his best work, the *Epistulae morales*, written in retirement to his friend Lucilius. Epicurus' letters were an influence here; so were Cicero's letters to Atticus. Roman gentlemen recognized the letter as a form ideally suited to the amateur, an apt expression of the friendships and common interests of their class. Statius (*Silvae* 1. 3. 104) imagines his friend Vopiscus, in his country retreat at Tibur, writing epic or lyric or satire—or else a letter, as highly polished as any of these. He does not make it clear whether the letter is prose or verse; it may, we must remember, be the latter, in the model of Horace's or Ovid's 'epistles'. The Younger Pliny's stylish collection of letters is one of the most elegant and informative witnesses to the culture and education of the time. It is interesting, and perhaps surprising, that we have so little comparable Greek material. We have, it is true, a mass of Greek letters dating from this period; but these are fictions, purporting to be written by imaginary characters or historical figures. They are little more than rhetorical exercises, though occasionally (as in the *Letters of Crates* and *Chion of Heraclea*) we find sets of letters composed to form something like epistolary romance.

This may remind us that the last of the areas in which *Kunstprosa* was employed is pure fiction. This was a late development, despite the partial classical model of Xenophon's *Cyropaedia*. Origins and influences are hotly debated; whether the characteristic content is of 'oriental' origin and whether the stories were used as a vehicle for religious teaching, specifically that of the mystery religions, are questions which have been repeatedly raised and variously answered over the past century. What seems certain is that the novel, not being a part of the high classical tradition, originally had a different audience in view from history or philosophy. It gradually makes its way into more sophisticated circles, sometimes viewed patronizingly and parodied, sometimes taking its place as a serious successor to epic and drama. The surviving Greek novels are surprisingly similar in plot, and it is a plot which has the suggestiveness of myth. Two lovers undergo long travels, dangers, and separations, their chastity is sorely tried, but they are ultimately united and live happily ever after. Such is the framework of the novels of Chariton, Longus, Achilles Tatius, Xenophon of Ephesus, and Heliodorus. Their tones and settings of course differ: love, magic, violence, humour, the curiosities of distant countries and remote historical times, the rhetoric of trials and debates, are standard ingredients, present in varied degree. Most charming to modern readers is the pastoral romance of Longus, *Daphnis and Chloe*; most divergent from the common pattern are the two Latin examples, Petronius' *Satyrica* and Apuleius' *Metamorphoses*. The novel is, in many ways, the most intriguing literary achievement of the period; it looks forward to mediaeval romance, and it is one of the roots of modern prose fiction. But it is an escapist form; set in the past or at the ends of the earth, its fictions generally portray the human condition with the minimum of reference to the social and political structures within which its readers lived.

Seneca: Father and Son

The remains of this literature fill many volumes. Many of the Greek authors—Plutarch, Lucian, Aristides—were morally and stylistically ideal texts for Byzantine education, and their survival was assured. The Latins were less lucky. Though Pliny's *Natural History* and Seneca were much read in the medieval West, Tacitus survived by a singular accident, and much important historical writing has been lost. But, in both languages, there is a lot to read; and we must confine ourselves here to a brief indication of the qualities of some of the principal figures.

Given the association between education and power, literary success and political activity, it is no wonder that families figure largely in the story. A good example is the family of the Annaei, from Corduba in Spain, who held a high place in both literary and public life for three generations. L. Annaeus Seneca, 'the Elder', was born around the middle of the first century BC, studied at Rome in the triumviral and early Augustan period, and then divided his time between Rome and his native place. Like many writers of the time (Livy, Caecilius of Caleacte, Dionysius) he was both historian and rhetorician, though he was not a professional teacher of rhetoric. Late in life, he compiled for his three sons a collection of the brilliant rhetorical strokes he remembered from the 'declaimers' of his youth. His enthusiastic anthology has much charm. The prefaces and character sketches especially display an attractive shrewdness. I cite as a specimen a piece from the 'deliberative exercises' (*Suasoriae* 2. 17), in which he speaks of a connection of his own who made a fool of himself by his handling of the hackneyed theme of the Three Hundred Spartans at Thermopylae:

There was a person called Seneca—his name may have reached your ears—of a confused and disorderly cast of mind, who wanted to speak in the big style. In the end, this weakness obsessed him and made him ridiculous. He wouldn't have slaves unless they were big, or silver vessels unless they were big. Believe me, I'm not joking. His madness led him ultimately to wear shoes that were too big for him, to eat no figs except *mariscae* [these had a poor flavour, despite their size], and to have a mistress of vast proportions. He was nicknamed Seneca Grandio. Well, when I was a young man, he gave a version of this exercise. He posed the objection: 'All who had been sent from Greece ran away.' To answer it, he raised his hands, and stood on tip-toe (he used to do this, to seem bigger) and cried: 'I rejoice, I rejoice!' We wondered what piece of luck had come his way. 'Xerxes will be entirely mine', he cried.

That is to say, speaking in the role of a Spartan at Thermopylae, he welcomed the absence of reinforcements, on the ground that he would be able to fight Xerxes and his million men single-handed. Of the three sons to whom Seneca's anthology is addressed, one (Mela) was the father of the poet Lucan, one (Novatus) was adopted by Junius Gallio and appears in history as the proconsul of Achaea at the time of St Paul's stay in Corinth (Acts 18: 12), and the middle son, another L. Annaeus Seneca, became without question the leading literary figure of his generation, as well as a man of great wealth and influence, especially in the early years of Nero, whose tutor he was.

Growing up in the early years of Tiberius (*Epist.* 108. 22), the younger Seneca was much attracted by philosophy, especially the more ascetic kind. He became a vegetarian, influenced by Pythagorean ideas, and only desisted in deference to his father, who feared that such eccentricity would earn a black mark from people who mattered: it was one of the times when 'foreign superstitions' were under governmental attack. Seneca was in any case no rebel. His ambitions soared high. He was prominent enough to be. exiled for a court intrigue under Claudius, but was recalled, and was continuously in a position of influence from about AD 49 to AD 62. He then fell from grace, and spent the last three years of his life in study and writing: a retirement not unlike Cicero's, and perhaps modelled on it. His tragedies are discussed in Chapter 12. His surviving prose works (some interesting pieces are only known indirectly) include 'consolations'—notably that to his mother Helvia on his own exile—and a number of 'essays' on moral themes, some short, some (*On Anger, On Benefits, On Clemency*) elaborate treatises in several books. In his retirement he embarked on grander schemes: *Natural Questions*, a rhetorically elaborate account of current theories about winds, earthquakes, lightning, and similar phenomena; and a comprehensive study of ethics from the Stoic point of view, never executed, but reflected in many of the *Moral Letters*, which he addressed to his friend Lucilius and which are his most popular and readable work. When Macaulay said that reading Seneca was like dining on nothing but anchovy sauce, he expressed something of the pleasure in witty detail and the dissatisfaction with the whole that most readers experience; it is the smaller scale and more intimate tone of the *Letters* that saves them from the worst effects of Seneca's incontinent ingenuity. So repetitive a writer seems made for the anthologist; and I cite two passages from which his manner may perhaps be judged.

In the first (*Tranquillity of Mind* 12–13) he adapts a theme from the end of the third book of Lucretius, on restlessness of soul; Stoic though he is, he has no compunction about using the common stock of philosophic moralizing, even if it is of Epicurean origin. What he implies about taste in scenery in this passage is of interest; so is his incidental attack at the end on the cruel fashion for gladiatorial shows.

Some things give the body pleasure and pain at once, like turning over before one side is tired, or tossing in one position after another. Thus Achilles in Homer, now on his face, now on his back, makes himself comfortable in different ways. This is what sick people do, who cannot endure anything long and use change as medicine. Hence futile travels and coastal excursions. The inconsistency that hates whatever is at hand experiments with the sea one moment, with the country the next. 'Let's go to Campania.' Pretty scenery is a bore. 'Let's go to a wild place, let's head for the mountains of Bruttium (the Abruzzi) and Lucania.' But in the wilderness some softer charms are wanted, something to relieve an eye sated with the grimness of a savage land. 'Let's make for Tarentum, the harbour everyone admires, the mild winter resort, the countryside

that kept even its ancient population in affluence.' 'Now back to town!'
It is too long since he heard the applause and the uproar. Now he wants
the pleasure of human blood!

Secondly, one of the shorter *Letters* (60). The theme is the
vanity of human desire and the narrowness of our real needs.
The technique is very characteristic: exclamations, rhetorical
questions, allusion to a classic (here Sallust), examples from
the animal kingdom, personification of Nature, and a striking
epigram at the end.

I've a grievance, I'm taking you to court, I'm angry. Do you still wish
for what your nurse and your tutor and your mother wished for on
your behalf? Don't you understand how much harm they wished for?
How true it is that our friends' prayers are our enemies! All the more
so if they have been fulfilled. I no longer find it surprising if all our
troubles stay with us from childhood; we grew up amid our parents'
curses. Perhaps one day the gods may hear a disinterested prayer from
us! How long shall we go on asking them for something, as though
we could not yet feed ourselves? How long shall we go on filling the
territories of vast cities with our crops? How long shall a whole nation
harvest them for us? How long will all those ships from many a sea
supply the service of one man's table? The bull contents himself with
a few acres' pasture; a single forest feeds many elephants; does one
man need earth and sea to nourish him? Has Nature, having given us
so modest a physique, then endowed us with a belly so insatiable that
we surpass the greed of the hugest and hungriest of beasts? Indeed not.
How small a quantity it is that is given to Nature! She is cheaply dismissed; it is not our belly's hunger that costs dear, but our pride. So let
us count 'the belly's obedient servants', as Sallust calls them, as beasts,
not men— and some not even live beasts, but dead creatures! A man
who is of use to many is alive. A man who uses himself is alive. But for
those who hide away in torpor, home is no better than a tomb. You
might as well inscribe on marble at their door 'They predeceased their
death.'

Pliny: Uncle and Nephew

The Annaei suggest a comparison with a rather later literary
family, the Plinii. The earlier man of note is C. Plinius Secundus,

'the Elder Pliny', born about AD 23. He had a distinguished military and administrative career as an *eques*, serving in Germany under Claudius and Nero, but then retiring to a more private life until his friendship with Titus and Mucianus assured a succession of procuratorships under Vespasian. He died, as commander of the fleet at Misenum, in the eruption of Vesuvius in AD 79. He was curious to observe it, and went too far.

Pliny was not only an active official but a tireless student and writer. He wrote a history of the German wars in which he had served, a narrative history of Rome from AD 47 to AD 70, and a life of one of his commanding officers, the literary man Pomponius Secundus. All this is lost. What survives is a *Natural History*, in thirty-seven books, an encyclopedia of knowledge of the universe, the earth, man, animals, and plants, with large sections also on medicines and on the visual arts. It was a prime source of belief about the universe in the Latin Middle Ages and later, 'an immense register', as Edward Gibbon put it, of 'the discoveries, the arts, and the errors of mankind'.

Pliny's stylistic ambitions were not matched by competence or taste. He does not appear to have mastered either the periodic elegance in which, for example, Columella and Celsus wrote successfully on technical themes, or the staccato Senecan lucidity, which Seneca himself had used impressively for science. But he aims high; and, though a torment to translators, he has often tempted them, not only for his content but for a certain richness of language, especially in his many moralizing digressions and exclamations. His summary of Augustus' career (7. 147 ff.) reveals a talent for satire, and the syntax of Mr Jingle:

In Divine Augustus ... if all things were judged carefully many volumes of human destiny might be found; defeat in his uncle's time for the Mastership of the Horse; preference given to Lepidus over his candidature; unpopularity from the proscriptions; participation in the triumvirate with the most evil men—and in no equal share at that, but dominated by Antony; illness at Philippi, flight, three days' hiding in the marsh, ill and (according to Agrippa and Maecenas) swollen with

...eous water; Sicilian shipwreck; another concealment, this time
...ave; plea for death made to Proculeius in the rout at sea, with the
...emy fleet hard upon him; anxiety in the Perugian war; mutinies;
dangerous illnesses; suspicion of Marcellus' intentions; shocking exile
of Agrippa; all the plots against his life; accusations about his children's
deaths; mourning whose sadness was not due simply to bereavement;
daughter's adultery and the disclosure of her plans for parricide; his
stepson Nero's rude withdrawal from court; adultery again, in his
granddaughter; then a combination of evils—lack of revenue, rebellion
in Illyricum, call-up of slaves, shortage of recruits, plague in Rome,
famine in Italy, determination to die, four days without food, when
much of death entered his body; on top of this, disaster of Varus, foul
insults to dignity, Postumus Agrippa adopted, rejected, and then missed,
suspicion of Fabius and his betrayal of secrets, apprehensions concerning his wife and Tiberius. This was his last anxiety. In short, this god
who perhaps not only achieved heaven, but deserved it, died leaving his
enemy's son as his heir.

Pliny's nephew, 'the Younger Pliny', could never have written
this. A studious youth, who wrote a Greek tragedy at fourteen,
he describes himself, at the age of about eighteen, quietly reading Livy during the great eruption that killed his uncle. The boy
was a pupil of Quintilian and of a noted Greek rhetor Nicetes
Sacerdos. He went on to have a distinguished senatorial career,
culminating in a consulship under Trajan in AD 100, the honorific and important *cura* of the Tiber river-works and urban
drainage system, and finally the governorship of Bithynia. His
most famous work, his *Letters*, to some extent reflects his public life, especially his and others' advocacy in the courts. But it
is more a demonstration of what should be a cultured man's
interests and values than an image of an individual achievement
or personality. The letters have great elegance and finish. There
are certain links with Greek rhetoric. In the formal descriptions
(*ecphrases*), the reports of wonders of nature, and the technique
of anecdote, we recognize the skills of Greek sophists such as
Lucian. The general effect however is essentially Roman. Pliny
depicts, no doubt in an idealized form, the style of public duty
and literary taste that his generation felt to be its own. Literary

prestige is important to him. He writes to Tacitus (7.20) that he has read and commented on his book—it is probably a part of the *Histories*, just possibly the *Dialogue*—and hopes for the like service in return, such being the traditional function of Roman 'friendship' (*amicitia*) when the parties are men of letters. He is pleased with the thought:

How it delights me that, if posterity cares at all, it will always be told in what harmony, sincerity and loyalty you and I lived! It will be a rare and notable thing that two men, near equals in age and position, and of some repute in letters—for I must needs speak sparingly of you when I am also speaking of myself!—encouraged each other's studies.

Plutarch

Among Pliny's contemporaries, and sharing some of his acquaintance, was the most important Greek writer of the age. L. Mestrius Plutarchus—to give him his names as a Roman citizen (he was in fact of equestrian status)—was from mainland Greece. His was the leading family of the historic, but decayed, town of Chaeronea in Boeotia. The past of his native district was particularly real to him: he defends the ancient Thebans against Herodotus' innuendoes and accusations, and he sets up Epaminondas as an ideal of the philosopher statesman. But it was not enough to record the past, for there was a present revival to be fostered. Plutarch chose to teach his pupils philosophy at Chaeronea, he served the city whenever he could, and he worked hard for the restoration of the oracle and shrine at neighbouring Delphi, which enjoyed imperial patronage under Domitian and his successors. But for books and learned conversation—other than what he could gather around him at home—Plutarch had to visit Athens, where he learned his Platonist philosophy and enjoyed the company of the wise and the rich. Towards the end of his life, under Trajan and Hadrian, a happy age for many literary men, he received signal honours, notably the insignia of a consul (*ornamenta consularia*, a great distinction for an *eques*) and a post as procurator of Greece, nominally in charge of all imperial properties in the province. In later times it was well if a philosopher or scholar could claim descent from him; some did so even in the fourth century. This reputation was built on two foundations: personal charm and wisdom, and an immense activity of writing. Plutarch was not the man to command audiences like the great histrionic sophists of the age, nor did he wield any real political influence. His massive but superficial learning and his generous and unpedantic style served to project a conspicuously—some would say self-righteously—humane personality. We possess about half of what he wrote. He was popular in Byzantine times, but this was all that the thirteenth-century scholars managed to collect. All the same, it fills a dozen volumes. It falls into two parts: the great unified effort of the *Parallel Lives* and the seventy or so surviving miscellaneous works—mainly 'essays' and dialogues— which are usually called the *Moralia*.

The *Parallel Lives* were dedicated to Q. Sosius Senecio, an acquaintance of Pliny, and a great man—four times consul—of Trajan's reign. The plan was open-ended. Each book contained the lives of a Greek and a Roman whose careers had something in common: wisdom as lawgivers, courage, perseverance, eloquence, a period of exile, or a great fortune. Formal comparisons usually followed. The result was a presentation of classical history that, more than any other, created the Renaissance image of antiquity. Plutarch's purposes were confessedly moral. He sought to expound the virtues and vices of his great men and show how they responded to the challenges of fortune. He was not concerned with them as historical forces, only as men of certain qualities who were placed under the stress of great events and decisions. Whether it is Theseus or Pericles, Coriolanus or Caesar, the problem is seen in the same light, and (sources allowing) the biography follows more or less the same pattern: origin and childhood, introduction into public life, the career and its points of crisis, the death and posthumous reputation. It has often been pointed out that this partly echoes a well-attested rhetorical scheme for 'encomium'—origin, nature, character, actions and virtues, accomplishments, comparison with others—and this is of course true. But the distance between Plutarch's attitudes and that of rhetorical encomiast can hardly be exaggerated. 'Rhetors', said Cicero, 'are allowed to tell lies in history, so as to be in a position to say something clever.' This is what Plutarch never does. His respect for evidence should not be questioned, though his interpretation of it, and his view of what biographical evidence is, may excite surprise. We should not expect in him any recognition of the difference between a primary and a secondary source; and we must be willing to accept 'probability'—meaning accord with what one expects of a certain kind of person in certain kinds of circumstances—as a criterion for judging between alternative accounts of the facts. What makes the *Lives* live, however, is not their moral preoccupations, nor yet their evident concern to demonstrate the political as well as the intellectual greatness of classical Greece; it is above all Plutarch's narrative gift, his willingness to listen to his sources and his skill in choosing the telling detail. No one forgets the death of Cato at Utica, or the love of Antony and Cleopatra; and it is from Plutarch that these episodes came into the consciousness of the modern world.

Some of the *Moralia* provoke comparison with Seneca. Both men wrote on Tranquillity and on Anger, though with different philosophical outlooks and with different expectations of their readership: Plutarch is far richer in learned allusion and quotation, and is naturally critical of Stoic views. 'Essays' such as these, and the pieces on Curiosity, Talkativeness, and False Shame have been to many the most attractive of Plutarch's works. Through the translations of Amyot and Philemon Holland they have made a strong impact on the French and English essayists, from Montaigne to Emerson. But Plutarch himself would presumably have laid the weight elsewhere, on his more substantial philosophical exegesis (below, pp. 347 f.) and controversy, and especially on a group of dialogues which he wrote, it seems, towards the end of his life. Four of these have their setting in contemporary Delphi, and explore the antiquities of the oracle and the theory of prophecy. The most elaborate of them—'On those whom God is slow to punish'—rehearses views on the nature of evil, and concludes with a myth in the Platonic manner on the fate of the soul after death. Plutarch's revival of this theme—he used it twice besides in the works we have, and notably also in the lost *On the Soul*—is remarkable. His 'Underworld' has a stellar setting, and his descriptions are full of colour, light, and vividly imagined horror.

Philosophy and myth are not, however, the only elements in his dialogues: there is also a dramatic dimension. Thus he wrote *The Divine Sign of Socrates* with the liberation of Thebes from Spartan occupation in 379 BC as background (Vol. 1, p. 170). The adventure story, told again in the life of Pelopidas, is punctuated by discussions on prophecy and the most splendid of the myths. In the *Eroticus*, again, he weaves a contemporary intrigue—a widow has enticed a younger man to marry her—into a discourse on homosexual and heterosexual love, Platonic in detail but very un-Platonic in conclusions. For all their dependence on tradition—not only Plato's *Symposium, Critias*, and *Phaedrus*, but a Hellenistic inheritance, now only dimly discernible—Plutarch's dialogues are works of powerful originality. More than any of the other authors we have here selected for consideration, he is a witness to the deepening religious and theological consciousness of the age. In *The Decline of the Oracles*, he portrays a Spartan called Cleombrotus, freshly arrived in Delphi from the desert shores of the Red Sea. This personage advances views on 'demons' which there is good reason to think Plutarch does not take seriously; but the description of Cleombrotus' mission in life passes well for Plutarch's own:

Fond of seeing and learning, having adequate means and not thinking it worth while to acquire more, he employed his leisure for such travels, and assembled information (*historia*) to be the material of what he himself called 'philosophy with theology as its goal'.

Not that Plutarch would wish to seek out holy men in the desert. He stayed at home, and they came to him.

Lucian

The second great Greek writer of the period was born in Plutarch's latter years, around the beginning of the reign of Hadrian.

Lucian is in many ways Plutarch's antithesis. He came, not from the old heartland of Greece, but—much more typically of the period—from the more recently Hellenized East. His home was Samosata on the Euphrates, capital of the defunct kingdom of Commagene, one of whose princes—Philopappus—had been a friend of Plutarch's at Athens. His education would be quite different from Plutarch's, and this indeed is evident from their writing. Plutarch's Greek, allusive and classicizing as it is, is a link in a continuous tradition, passing through Hellenistic writing back to classical times. Lucian's—he claims it was his second language, Syriac being the first—is pure imitation (*mimēsis*) of the classical models, fascinatingly flexible, but clearly an artificial creation. There are other contrasts too. Plutarch takes religious belief, especially men's hopes and fears for what follows death, with great and humane seriousness. For Lucian all this is mockery. The judgement of the dead, the ferryman of the souls, 'and all the Vain, Infernal Trumpery', are for him simply the setting for a rather simple form of satire; visions, ghosts, magic are the contemptible inventions of charlatans whom it is the honest man's business to expose. Again: what Plutarch tells us of his life is evidently true. We believe in his regard for his father and his grandfather, his affectionate marriage, and his sorrow at his little daughter's death. Lucian, by contrast, gives us a stylized picture which it is foolish to treat as autobiography. We are not bound to believe in the family council that apprenticed him to his sculptor uncle, or his vision of Education (*Paideia*), or his abandonment of Rhetoric for Dialogue at the age of forty. We recall that Socrates too started as a sculptor, and Ovid's vision of Elegy and Tragedy (*Amores* 3. 1) is all too similar to Lucian's. A good deal of what Lucian says about himself is no more to be trusted than the voyage to the moon that he recounts so persuasively in the first person in *True Stories*.

Even his claim to have been the first to adapt the philosophical dialogue to comic purposes is hard to sustain. To go no further back, there is something of this in Plutarch—notably in *Gryllus*, where one of Circe's new pigs converses with Odysseus—and the evidence of Varro and Horace suggests the Hellenistic model of an earlier Syrian Greek, Menippus of Gadara, held by some to be a main source of Lucian's ideas. That Menippus' writings were a significant model is doubtful. More important than any such borrowing is Lucian's relentless exploitation of the limited range of classical texts that everybody knew, and his ingenuity in using the same motifs again and again. He does indeed have his originality, and it may well be that the 'miniature dialogue', in which he excelled, is one place where we should look for it. It was in this form that he composed his dialogues of the dead, of the gods, of the nymphs and deities of the sea, and of the educated prostitutes (*hetairai*) of comedy. Like the epigram, the letter, and the apophthegm—all of which flourished in this period—the miniature dialogue is directed at a readership which finds long texts trying. It has a clear connection with the elementary rhetorical exercises of narrative, anecdote, and description, and indeed with the even more elementary game of paraphrase. Yet in Lucian's hands it has real charm. We enjoy Doris' suggestion that Polyphemus really only likes Galatea because her complexion reminds him of the milk and cream cheese in which his riches lie. We admire the *ecphrasis* of Europa and the bull as seen with the eyes of Zephyrus, the West Wind, or Zeus' pleased revelation to Ganymede of who he really is. We relish the mild salaciousness of the conversations between the innocent young prostitute and her hopeful and ambitious mother—so long, that is, as we suspend any social feelings towards the widow whose only resource is to employ her daughter in this way. Lucian is sometimes regarded almost as a socialist before his time. This is to take him much too seriously. To see virtue in the poor and wickedness in the wealthy is a standard rhetorical pose of the age. And Lucian's consistent aim is to entertain.

Many of Lucian's dialogues are enlargements of the techniques of the 'miniatures'; but we also have—among nearly eighty books which seem to be genuine—not only purely rhetorical pieces ('talks', declamations, pastiches of Herodotus), but some works with a more serious link with the intellectual life of the time. These last include a 'life' of the Cynic Demonax, and devastating, though largely fictitious, accounts of two famous religious charlatans, Alexander of Abonuteichus, an inventor of Mystery Rites, and the cynic Peregrinus Proteus, who spectacularly burnt himself to death at Olympia in 167. But it is perhaps *True Stories*, an ancestor of science fiction, that best conveys the elegance of his imagination, the Lucianic blend of satire and fantasy that appeals to educated children of all ages. The following episode needs no explanation; its techniques of surprise are easily seen (1. 30—1).

Often, it seems, a change for the better heralds trouble. We had just two days' fair weather sailing. As the third day broke, we suddenly glimpsed against the sunrise a multitude of monsters and whales, the biggest of all being about 200 miles long. It was approaching with its mouth open, stirring up the sea, the foam breaking around it. It was displaying teeth taller than a human penis, sharp as rocks and white as ivory. We embraced one another and spoke our last farewells. Then we waited. It was upon us now, and it swallowed us up, ship and all. However, it failed to break the ship in pieces; she slid down through the gaps in the teeth into the interior. When we were inside, all was dark at first, and we could see nothing. After a while, however, the monster opened its mouth and we had sight of a high, broad area, large enough to accommodate a city of 10,000 people. In the middle, there were little fishes and many other animals, all chopped up, with ships' sails, anchors, human bones, cargoes, and, among all this, land and hills—formed, I imagine, out of the silt that had settled down. There was a wood and trees of all kinds, with vegetables growing, and they had the look of being cultivated. The circuit of the land area was 30 miles. Sea birds—gulls and halcyons—could be seen nesting in the trees.

Aelius Aristides

Neither Plutarch nor Lucian figures among the second-century 'sophists' whose lives Philostratus wrote, though both were on the fringe of the grand 'sophistic' world—Lucian indeed more closely involved. Aelius Aristides, Lucian's near contemporary, may stand as the typical Antonine sophist, wealthy, much travelled, flamboyant, egocentric. He has had little favour in modern times. Unravel his complexities—his style aimed especially at the density of thought of his models, Demosthenes and the speeches in Thucydides—and the labour seems wasted, so little is there left to grip the mind. We admire, but hardly wish to read twice, the subtle reconstructions of the political situations of 413 and 370 BC which underlie his 'Sicilian' and 'Leuctrian' declamations. It is no wonder that no complete translation of Aristides in any modern language has been attempted till recently; the magnificent scholarship of Willem Canter's Latin (1566) lay long unstudied and unappreciated. But it is all a little unjust. There are at least three claims that Aristides has on our attention. One—perhaps the best known—arises from his encomium of Rome, delivered in the summer of 144, a fine, flattering statement of the achievement of the Antonine Empire, from a grateful subject's point of view. A second rests on his achievement in extending the range of prose oratory to include the hymn, hitherto the prerogative of poets. He is proud of this, and not unjustly. His prose hymns to Sarapis, Athena, and Dionysus have many splendours; the hymn 'to the Aegean Sea', with its colourful vision of sea and islands, is perhaps the most attractive of all. Thirdly, Aristides is the author of a singular spiritual autobiography (*Hieroi Logoi*), the day-by-day record of the interventions of the god Asclepius in his life, as adviser and healer. Hypochondriacs are not attractive people; but the completeness of Aristides' record, his naïve vanity and credulity, and the vividness of his language (for once not elaborate, indeed hardly *Kunstprosa* at all) combine to produce a text which has claimed deserved attention from historians, psychologists, and students of the religious mind. Asclepius guided him in strange ways; here he is on a short, but stormy, voyage from Clazomenae to Phocaea, along the coast of Asia Minor (2. 12–14):

An easterly breeze got up, and, as we proceeded, a brisk east wind, which broke out in the end into a fearful gale. Up went the ship at the prow, and down at the stern. She nearly foundered. She was awash everywhere. Then she headed out to sea. Sweating and shouting from the sailors, screams from all on board—some of my friends were with me—but all I said was 'O Asclepius!' After many hazards, driven out to sea time and again when we were on the point of making port, and causing the people watching great anxiety, we finally reached land—safe and happy, but only just! When night came, the god commanded me to purge myself, and told me how. The purging was as complete as if I had taken hellebore, as those who had had experience of that drug told me. *Everything* was moved by the waves! The god now told me the whole truth, namely that I was destined to be shipwrecked and this was why these things had happened, and now, both for safety and to fulfil my destiny, I must get into a boat in the harbour and contrive that it should capsize and sink; someone would then rescue me and bring me ashore. I was of course happy to do this. Everyone was amazed at the ingenious fake shipwreck, coming on top of the real danger. We knew that it was Asclepius who had saved us from the sea. The purging was an additional blessing.

Conclusion

We began this survey by emphasizing that the prose literature of the period was one of highly professional art. Both in Latin and in Greek, the reading public expected accuracy, elegance, and virtuosity in a very elaborate verbal game. We conclude by making the complementary observation, to which the intimate detail of our last extract from Aristides particularly lends colour, that it was also a literature of personal statement. The letter, the essay, the speech that confesses a personality are, for the first time, leading literary forms. What unites these two features—which may at first sight seem ill matched—is the nature of the society on which the literature is based. This was a governing class of diverse origins but homogeneous education, for whom distinction in their studies both lent respectability to worldly success and often led to it. The members of this élite, whether in

Syria or in Spain, were of personal interest to themselves and to one another. Their feelings, their moral problems, even their illnesses were fit matter for writing. They shared a common range of cultural reference, and a common interest in the classical past.

It is hard to point to a prose genius, though common consent would except Tacitus. The Christian writers to come have a better claim. But the high level of skill, the charm and interest of the persons concerned, and the massive information they communicate about so many aspects of ancient life, in their own and earlier days, deserve appreciative readers and careful students. Seneca and Pliny, Plutarch and Lucian, and many others, are articulate witnesses to a state of civilization which has many affinities with our own. They look inwards upon themselves and backwards to the past, and in their two literary languages they have a superb instrument to express these two great concerns.

Further Reading

GENERAL

Besides the standard histories of literature etc. the following works are particularly useful for the whole period: E. Norden, *Die antike Kunstprosa* (3rd edn. Leipzig, 1915, repr. 1958); A. D. Leeman, *Orationis Ratio* (Amsterdam, 1963), on Latin prose; B. P. Reardon, *Courants Littéraires grecs des IIe et IIIe siècles* (Paris, 1971); G. Kennedy, *The Art of Rhetoric in the Roman World* (Princeton, 1972). Two older books may be added: J. P. Mahaffy, *The Silver Age of the Greek World* (Chicago–London, 1906); S. Dill, *Roman Society from Nero to M. Aurelius* (London, 1904). Both are still worth reading.

AUTHORS

Texts and translations of most of the works mentioned are available in the Loeb Classical Library (LCL). This, like the bilingual French Budé series, is of varying quality, but is particularly useful for late Greek authors, and contains some recent editions of great value, e.g. Seneca the Elder (M. Winterbottom), Pliny's Letters (B. Radice), Herodian (C. R. Whittaker). Authors *not* available in Loeb are asterisked in the following list. When an author is not mentioned, it may be assumed (i) that there is a Loeb; (ii) that there is no outstanding special study in English.

*Aristides: A. Boulanger, *Aelius Aristide* (Paris, 1923). Good discussions of the 'diary' of his illnesses in E. R. Dodds, *Pagan and Christian in an Age of Anxiety* (Cambridge, 1965); and in A. J. Festugière, *Personal Religion among the Greeks* (Berkeley and Los Angeles, 1954). LCL has a selection only; the most recent translation of the 'diary' is C. A. Behr, Aelius *Aristides and The Sacred Tales* (Amsterdam, 1968), which also contains a discussion of Aristides' career. A complete translation of Aristides by C. A. Behr is now available (Amsterdam, 1981).

Arrian: P A. Stadter, *Arrian of Nicomedeia* (Chapel Hill, 1980).

M. Aurelius: Good study by A. S. L. Farquharson, whose text, translation, and commentary are standard: *The Meditations of the Emperor Marcus Antoninus* (Oxford, 1944; reissued 1968).

Demetrius: Tr. G. M. A. Grube, *A Greek Critic* (Toronto, 1961). Also (part) by D. C. Innes in *Ancient Literary Criticism*, ed. D. A. Russell and M. Winterbottom (Oxford, 1972), where translations of other critical texts of the period (e.g. 'Longinus', Tacitus, extracts from Dionysius and Plutarch) may be found.

Dio Chrysostom: C. P. Jones, *The Roman World of Dio Chrysostom* (Cambridge, Mass., 1978).

Dio Cassius: F. Millar, *A Study of Cassius Dio* (Oxford, 1974).

Dionysius of Halicarnassus: S. F. Bonner, *The Literary Treatises of Dionysius of Halicarnassus* (Cambridge, 1939). LCL edn. of critical works not yet complete; Budé (G. Aujac) supplies the gap, also edns. of some treatises by W. Rhys Roberts (Cambridge, 1901; London–Edinburgh, 1910).

*Greek novelists: All important texts translated in B. P. Reardon, *Collected Ancient Greek Novels*, Berkeley and Los Angeles, 1989. General study: B. E Perry, *The Ancient Romances* (Berkeley, 1967); but E. Rohde, *Der griechische Roman* (Leipzig, 1876, 3rd. edn. 1914) remains a classic. See also G. Anderson, *Eros Sophistes* (*American Classical Studies* 9, 1982).

Greek letter-writing: Few of the 'epistolographi' are available in English: R. Hercher's edn. (Paris, 1873) remains standard. But note esp. I. Düring, *Chion of Heraclea* (Göteborg, 1951) which has a translation of this 'epistolary romance' and a useful introduction.

'Longinus': Ed. with commentary, D. A. Russell (Oxford, 1964; repr. 1982). For translation see under Demetrius.

Lucian: J. Bompaire, *Lucien écrivain* (Paris, 1958); G. Anderson, *Lucian: Theme and Variation*, and *Studies in Lucian's Comic Fiction*, *Mnemosyne*, suppls. 41 and 43 (1976); Penguin selection, tr. P. Turner. Complete Eng. tr. by H. W. and F. G. Fowler.

Philostratus: Abridged translation of *Life of Apollonius*—part novel, part pagan hagiography—by G. W. Bowersock (Penguin).

Pliny (the Younger): Comm. A. N. Sherwin White (2nd. edn. London, 1969).

Plutarch: C. P. Jones, *Plutarch and Rome* (Oxford, 1971); D. A. Russell, *Plutarch* (London, 1972); A. G. Wardman, *Plutarch's Lives* (London, 1974).

Penguin translation of many Lives. Elizabethan translation of Lives (Sir T. North) and 'Morals' (Philemon Holland), both important for English literature.
Quintilian: G. Kennedy, *Quintilian* (New York, 1969)
Seneca (the Elder): Recent studies by L. A. Sussman: *The Elder Seneca, Mnemosyne*, suppl. 51 (1978) and J. Fairweather (Cambridge, 1981).
Seneca (the Younger): M. T. Griffin, *Seneca: A Philosopher in Politics* (Oxford, 1976); A. L. Motto, *Seneca* (New York, 1973); also a collection of essays in *Seneca*, ed. C. D. N. Costa (London–Boston, 1974).

12

Silver Latin Poetry and the Latin Novel

RICHARD JENKYNS

The Silver Age: Problems and Solutions

THE word 'silver', applied to those Latin poets who wrote after the death of Augustus, is a modern label. Like all such labels, it can easily be misleading; time flows on continuously, and any attempt to divide the past into ages or periods is bound to be a more or less artificial attempt to impose simple patterns upon a complex and unceasing flux. None the less, the phrase 'silver age' has its uses. We customarily think of the Augustan age as a time of dazzling poetic achievement, but it is often forgotten that this achievement belongs largely to the first half of Augustus' long reign. During his last twenty-five years and more there was no major poet still active except Ovid; and there is evidence in his later work that Ovid saw himself as a lone survivor, the last of a line. The quarter century following Ovid's death is one of the most barren for poetry in Latin literary history; it is not unrealistic to think in terms of one chapter closing and another beginning.

The term 'silver age' is of course designed to contrast with the 'golden age' which preceded it. This implied contrast contains, once again, a truth and a danger. We should not let ourselves be trapped by a mechanical view of the rise and fall of cultures into supposing that the silver age was a second-rate period which necessarily produced second-rate literature; it includes, at the lowest estimate, at least one poet of genius and several distinctive talents of a lesser order, and it also gave birth to a great historian and by far the best prose fiction to come out of the ancient world. On the other hand, it is indeed true that the poets who came after the Augustans were faced with a peculiar difficulty and a peculiar challenge; and to understand what these were we must first recall the situation of their predecessors.

From the start the Latin poets wrote in the consciousness that the Greek achievement loomed large behind them; the shadow of a mighty past falls dark across their verses. The Greeks seemed to have mastered every field of literature; how could Latin poets hope to produce anything that would not seem a pale and lifeless imitation? That was their dilemma, and a number rose to the challenge by openly acknowledging their debt to Greece, sometimes boldly, sometimes with a studied modesty. The aim was to point the reader's attention to the Greek models, in order to draw out the no less significant divergences from those models; imitation could thus become a kind of originality. The supreme example of this technique is the *Aeneid*.

The silver poets inherited this situation, but with a new difficulty. There was now a mighty body of Latin classics as well. Virgil, Horace, and Ovid, in their different ways, had brought the various genres which they had attempted to such a pitch of perfection that it must have seemed impossible for their successors to develop them further. How could one now write an epic poem which would not read like a pastiche of Virgil, or lyric poetry which would not seem a mere shadow of Horace? It is interesting to find Velleius Paterculus, who wrote second-rate history during the reign of Augustus' successor Tiberius, observing that the highest achievements in any particular genre of literature all occur within a relatively brief period of time; he concludes that genius, despairing of surpassing what has already been perfected or seeking for new territory to conquer, passes on to new fields of endeavour. These remarks are significant precisely because Velleius was himself no genius: he reflects the attitudes of a more or less conventional literary gentleman. We find much talk of decline in the writers of the first century AD. Some of them assert that there has indeed been a decline, others indignantly deny it. Naturally there was no general agreement; what matters is that the state of contemporary literature was an issue that was in the air as never before.

It is intriguing, too, to find Statius, near the end of the century, concluding his epic *Thebaid* by insisting that his work is far inferior to the immortal *Aeneid*. What Statius is doing is dramatizing his dilemma and at the same time playing an elegant literary game by adapting a traditional motif to new circumstances. The theme of self-deprecating homage to a great predecessor had been heard often—Horace, for example, with nicely calculated humility contrasts himself with the torrential genius of Pindar—but never before in epic, where a pose of confidence was expected. Statius, however, who begins his poem by asking what story he shall take for his subject, concludes it on a note of self-doubt. More than ever, poetry has become reflective upon its own nature; the Augustan self-consciousness has been given a new twist.

Manilius' *Astronomica*, begun in the last years of Augustus and continued under Tiberius, illustrates the possibilities and the pitfalls. This is a didactic poem on the theory of astrology, conceived on a heroic scale. Lucretius' *De rerum natura* is the obvious exemplar, and its influence is patent throughout. Like Lucretius, Manilius speaks of struggling with the intractability of his subject-matter; the difficulty of putting arithmetic into verse is at once his problem and his delight. But whereas Lucretius' wrestle with the complexities of Epicurean physics is inspired by deep moral seriousnesss and driven forward by a formidable intellectual energy, the *Astronomica* seems to be at heart a literary exercise. The game of putting sums into polished hexameters is essentially pointless and quickly becomes tedious. In other parts of the work Manilius reveals himself as a poet of considerable talent, with a gift for the sonorous line and the piquant phrase; but his gifts have not found an adequate object.

The epic poet had two types of model before him, the mythological (such as the *Aeneid*) and the historical, such as Ennius' *Annales*. Silius Italicus (*c*.26–101) got the worst of both worlds by trying to combine the two: his *Punica*, which is (alas) the longest of classical Latin poems, relates Hannibal's invasion of Italy, but with the full mythological apparatus of divine interventions, a descent to the underworld, and so on. The result is painfully incongruous. The *Argonautica* of Valerius Flaccus (died *c*.92) and the *Thebaid* of Statius (*c*.45–96), both mythological epics, are better; but though both poets had talent, neither found a way of imparting genuine freshness and life to his subject. Few are those who have read to the end of either work for pleasure. Of Statius' other verse there survives the *Achilleid*, a fragment of an uncompleted epic, and the *Silvae*, a collection of mostly occasional poems, of which the shortest (5.4), nineteen lines addressed by the insomniac poet to the god of sleep, is deservedly well known.

But, as Martial unkindly observed (10.4), there was not much life left in the old mythology now: 'You who read of Oedipus and of Thyestes in the dark, of Colchian women and Scyllas, of what are you reading but monsters? . . . Why does the empty nonsense of a wretched sheet please you? Read this, of which life can say, "It is mine." You will not find Centaurs, Gorgons, or Harpies here; my page smells of man.' (Oedipus appears in Statius' *Thebaid*; Seneca had composed a *Thyestes*.) The one man who found a way to reinvigorate the epic genre was Lucan. He went to history for his theme, but to history told in a wholly new way.

Lucan

Lucan (39–65) is one of the most remarkable figures in Latin literature. He was compelled by Nero to take his own life at the age of twenty-six; by this time he had already composed numerous works, all of which have perished except for the ten books of his uncompleted epic on the civil war between Caesar and Pompey, known as the *Bellum civile* or *Pharsalia*.

Conventionally, the epic poet announces the heroic character of his theme in the first line, and even with the first word. Thus Virgil opens the *Aeneid* with the word 'arma' ('arms'), and Lucan, in apparently similar vein, begins 'bella' ('wars'). But then immediately he twists the theme in a new direction:

> Bella per Emathios plus quam ciuilia campos
> iusque datum sceleri canimus . . .

Of wars more than civil on the plains of Thessaly I sing, of legality granted to crime . . .

This will prove to be a heroic poem without a hero, for Caesar is portrayed as a villain, and though Pompey is more sympathetic, he is, as Cato is made to say, far inferior to earlier Romans in his respect for the bounds of law. (Cato himself, though the pattern of republican propriety, is of secondary importance only.) The staple of epic warfare had been the *aristeia*, in which an individual hero showed his prowess in a series of duels, each vividly described. Lucan allows none of his characters so much honour. There is not a single *aristeia* in his account of the battle of Pharsalus, and only one individual death is described; the rest is a senseless welter of mass slaughter. The gods, too, hitherto essential in epic, are given no place at all in the poem, but instead we see a world plunging to disaster, and at the climax of the action Lucan shouts out (7. 446 f.), 'The world is swept along by blind chance; we lie when we say that Jupiter reigns.'

In the same spirit, there is not the usual appeal to the Muse for aid and inspiration at the beginning of the work. After announcing his theme, Lucan turns instead to address the citizens of Rome with sorrow and indignation (1. 8): 'Quis furor, o ciues, quae tanta licentia ferri?' ('What was this madness, citizens, what was this great orgy of slaughter?') For this is to be not just a historical, but also a political, poem. Homer and Virgil had been remarkable for the breadth of their sympathies:

both Greeks and Trojans in the *Iliad*, both Trojans and Italians in the *Aeneid* excite our admiration and compassion. Lucan deliberately does away with this, admitting that his approach is partisan and his purpose to get his readers to favour one side against the other (7. 207–13).

In keeping with this outlook is the poet's declamatory method. The epic poet had traditionally kept his own personality out of his work, preserving an Olympian objectivity, but Lucan constantly involves himself with his characters, haranguing and mocking them. For example, Book 7 begins with one of Lucan's most moving passages: Pompey on the night before his defeat dreams of the triumphs of his earlier life. At first the scene is described without the author intruding his presence, but at line 24 he addresses the guards of the camp, urging them not to sound the reveille and disturb their general's slumbers. At line 29 he speaks to Pompey himself and continues addressing him until line 42. In line 43 he addresses the whole Roman nation; in line 44 he is back with Pompey again. He is like an advocate in court, turning to the gentlemen of the jury and then back to the witness in the box. Constantly we are aware of the poet's personal voice, harsh, passionate, and sarcastic.

On every page of the *Bellum civile* we find epigram, paradox, and bitter wit. Lucan carried to its extreme the fondness of the silver age for what Romans called the 'sententia', the pithy or pointed saying. The first line of the poem, besides asserting the work's epic character, announces this other element also, for it contains the poem's first epigram. The war is 'more than civil' because it is a conflict not just between fellow citizens but between members of the same family, Pompey having previously been Caesar's son-in-law. Lucan remodels epic to give it a sardonic and even a satiric tone.

The blend of political passion and rhetorical conceits is the essence of the *Pharsalia*. In the first book the character of Caesar is sketched in sharp terse phrases which recall Sallust. Cato's summing up of Pompey's career shows a historical sense, setting the great man in the context of his time and balancing virtues against faults with a dignified restraint:

> 'ciuis obit', inquit, 'multum maioribus impar
> nosse modum iuris, sed in hoc tamen utilis aeuo,
> cui non ulla fuit iusti reuerentia; salua
> libertate potens, et solus plebe parata
> priuatus seruire sibi, rectorque senatus,
> sed regnantis, erat.'

$$(9.\,190-5)$$

'A citizen has died', he said, 'far inferior to our ancestors in recognizing the limits of legality, but valuable in this present age, which has had no reverence for justice. He was powerful, and yet preserved liberty; he alone stayed a private citizen when the people were ready to be his slaves; he was ruler of the Senate, but of a Senate which kept the sovereignty.'

The last five words show how the *sententia* could be directed to the service of a political and historical theme: the difference between autocracy and dictatorship is put with admirable concision. Sometimes, too, the *sententia* displays a psychological acuity, as when the boy king of Egypt takes a child's delight at 'being grown up' and ordering the death of Pompey:

> adsensere omnes sceleri. laetatur honore
> rex puer insueto, quod iam sibi tanta iubere
> permittant famuli.

$$(8.\,536-8)$$

All voted for the crime. The boy king delights in the unaccustomed honour—that now his slaves should allow him to issue such important orders.

Unfortunately, though, an account of Lucan that dwelt only upon his virtues would be seriously misleading, for his faults are very gross. The promise of historical and political seriousness which the poem appears to make is for the most part unfulfilled; Caesar soon turns into a mere pantomime villain, a preposterous ranter hardly worth the compliment of our hatred. The rhetoric is often absurd, and the ceaseless search for paradox produces results that are often tedious and far-fetched; worst of all, the poem lacks variety of style and theme, and the unchanging note of sardonic bleakness becomes wearisome. The way in which Lucan allowed a taste for rhetorical smartness to run away with him can be seen (for example) in the speech of Pothinus at the court of Ptolemy (8. 484–535): for a line or two it looks as though this may be a powerful if cynical defence of expediency against absolute morality, but Pothinus quickly becomes a cardboard monster mouthing clever epigrams of the kind that would persuade nobody. Lucan is, apart from Ovid, the one major Latin poet surviving who composed with speed and fluency, and he has all the faults of the man who never blots a line. His early death leaves us with one of the most intriguing 'ifs' of Latin literary history: had he survived, would he have developed into a great master, or was he by nature one of those highly talented men who are for ever revealing unexpected shallows?

Tragedy

Quintilian (above, pp. 293 f.), while admiring Lucan's passion and epigrammatic brilliance, judged him more suitable for orators than poets to imitate. The influence of rhetoric has been commonly blamed for the vices of silver Latin poetry, and the charge has force; but it is wrong to regard rhetoric as the necessary enemy of poetry, and it should be clear that Lucan's virtues are as much the product of his rhetorical cast of thought as are his faults. In Juvenal rhetoric becomes an essential element of great poetry—as it does in the *Aeneid*, for that matter. If, on the other hand, we want to see what happens when the rhetorical manner is used in the absence of imagination, we may turn to the tragedies of Seneca. Ten plays have come down to us under his name, of which one is certainly and another probably spurious. The loss of all other Roman tragedies and the influence which Seneca's are supposed to have had on renaissance drama—an influence, however, which was probably much smaller than has usually been thought—have ensured for them a greater attention than their literary quality alone would deserve.

Like other Latin poets, Seneca develops a Greek genre in a

new direction: he turns Attic tragedy towards the gruesome, the sensational, and the extreme. The Hippolytus of Euripides is chaste, pure, puritan; Seneca's Hippolytus is a neurotic with an exaggerated aversion from city life. Euripides' *Medea* ends sensationally enough, but Seneca has a still more sensational, though much coarser, *coup de théâtre* in store for us: Medea, aloft, prepares to ascend into the skies in her chariot, and tosses down to Jason the bodies of their dead children; he closes the play by railing at her, 'Go through the lofty regions of high heaven, and bear witness where you ride that there are no gods' ('testare nullos esse, qua veheris, deos'—there is a savage punch in the very last word of all). Euripides' Theseus beholds the mangled body of his dying son Hippolytus; Seneca's Theseus tries to reassemble the corpse's scattered pieces, while the chorus add helpful advice, as though he were doing a jigsaw puzzle. In more talented hands such bizarreries might have a grotesque kind of power, and some critics have claimed to find unappreciated merits in these plays; but when we contemplate the amount of feeble rant that fills play after play, we may conclude that they have let faith triumph over plausibility.

Epigram and Satire

'I have not drenched my lips in the nag's spring,' declared Persius (34–62), in disrespectful allusion to the fountain Hippocrene, that classic symbol of poetic inspiration. Vitality came more easily to those poets who did not burden themselves with the pretensions of the more exalted genres. Persius himself, who wrote six satires before his early death, is a curious and intriguing figure. He describes himself as 'iunctura callidus acri' (5.14 'clever at the pungent combining of words'): his blend of a compressed, clotted style, thick with literary allusion, and a contorted moral seriousness makes difficult reading. He was much admired and imitated by the satirists of the English renaissance, and the reader of Donne's satires may catch something of his odd, pungent flavour.

Martial (*c.*40–101), as we have seen (above, p. 320), also took trouble to set himself at a distance from the grander poets; but he is, by contrast, easy and undemanding. Active mainly in the reign of Domitian, he is the father of the epigram in the modern sense of the term: the short poem, sometimes very short, with a witty point or a twist in the tail. For example:

> Hesterno fetere mero qui credit Acerram,
> fallitur: in lucem semper Acerra bibit.
>
> (1. 28)

He who thinks Acerra reeks of yesterday's wine is wrong: Acerra always drinks till dawn.

Sometimes the wit has a touch of Ovid's or (to look forward) of Herrick's charm:

> Intactas quare mittis mihi, Polla, coronas?
> a te uexatas malo tenere rosas.
>
> (11. 89)

Why, Polla, do you send me chaplets that you have not touched? I had rather hold roses that your hands had disturbed.

And sometimes he achieves pathos, still without losing his epigrammatic pointedness, as in his poem on the death of Erotion in childhood, which ends thus:

> mollia non rigidus caespes tegat ossa nec illi,
> terra, grauis fueris: non fuit illa tibi.
>
> (5. 34. 9 f.)

Let the turf be not hard that covers her soft bones; earth, be not heavy upon her; she was not heavy upon you.

On the other hand, a high proportion of his epigrams is obscene; and he cheerfully allows that his object is to titillate his readers.

We have seen that silver epic was most successful when, with Lucan, it shaded into satire; the finest fusion of rhetorical magnificence and epigrammatic harshness comes, however, in Juvenal, the greatest poet of the silver age. Little is known about his life: a fair hypothesis is that he was born around 65 or a little later and died around 130. His style is dense, muscular, declamatory. He seems to have composed slowly and laboriously, since he has left us just fifteen satires and a fragment of a sixteenth, probably unfinished.

Since Juvenal's is the Latin poetry most like satire in the modern sense, it should be stressed that he departed decisively from the traditions of Roman *satura*. Lucilius and Horace had adopted a rapid, discursive, informal manner; they offered, or purported to offer, a view of the poet off duty, with the quirks of his personality freely on display. Juvenal, by contrast, reveals very little of himself. His voice is exceedingly distinctive, but we learn next to nothing of the man behind it. The combination of impersonality and distinctive timbre recalls Lucretius; and it is again Lucretius whom of all Roman poets he most resembles in his blend of satiric sharpness with the grand manner. Many details of style and allusion show that the poet who most influenced him, surprising as it may at first seem, was Virgil, echoes of whom he sometimes uses to point an ironic contrast between the imaginary worlds of heroic or pastoral poetry and the ugly realities of the present time. Though he pays lip-service to the memories of Lucilius and Horace in his first satire, they seem to have made no substantial impression on his verse.

Much ink has been spilled on the question whether Juvenal was a genuine moralist or an opportunist who did not care what his target was, provided he could make a poem out of it; but the whole debate is to some extent misconceived. Though in a few of his later (and generally weaker) satires he assumes a high moral tone, he is for the most part concerned to excoriate human behaviour not for being wicked but for being sordid, vulgar, or disgusting. He is above all a social observer, who combines exactness of observation with imagination. We do not turn to him for wisdom, and he did not intend that we should.

In his first satire Juvenal presents himself as almost overwhelmed by the chaos of his own impression; and the sixth, a diatribe against the female sex almost 700 lines long, is (by design, we may suppose) a vast ramshackle edifice in which women are assailed for every vice from promiscuity to artiness, and even for being tediously virtuous. But he also liked to organize his satires along a particular line of argument illustrated by a mass of examples, a technique borrowed from the declaimers. Thus Satire 8 opens with the words 'What is the use of family trees?', and the entire poem argues the vanity of noble birth. Even the sixth satire is strung along a thread of this kind, however loosely: the poet purports to be giving an acquaintance the reasons for not marrying. This technique is seen at its most impressive in the tenth satire. 'What should a man pray for?' is the theme, and Juvenal passes one by one over the traditional objects of human aspiration—power, fame, conquest, long life, beauty—exposing the vanity of each by a succession of illustrations from history, mythology, and Roman life: Sejanus, Cicero, Hannibal, Alexander, Priam are all paraded before the reader's eyes.

Juvenal's favourite line of attack is to display things exactly as they are: to refuse to be deceived, as he sees it, by ideas and abstractions. What is military glory, with its processions of captured weaponry and triumphal arches, if you simply *look* at it? Juvenal gives us the answer (10. 133–6): 'The spoils of war, a corslet fastened to a stump as a trophy, a cheek-piece hanging from a broken helmet, a yoke shorn of its pole, the flagstaff of a captured trireme and a sad prisoner at the top of an arch . . .' Broken objects and wretched humanity—that is all there is to see, if one looks with Juvenal's dispassion.

In similar spirit, the first question that he asks about Hannibal is how much does his dust now weigh; the solid, physical world is what concerns him. And Hannibal's ambition—to ride in triumph through Rome—is viewed with the same harsh literalism: he wanted to plant his standard in the Subura, a shabby and crowded part of the city. The Carthaginian general had lost an eye, and he rode upon an elephant (a 'Gaetulian beast'). Juvenal puts these facts together, considers the picture that they make (notice the words 'facies' and 'tabella') and ends up with a vision both strange and ludicrous:

> o qualis facies et quali digna tabella
> cum Gaetula ducem portaret belua luscum.
>
> (157 f.)

What a sight it was, what a picture it would make, when the Gaetulian monster carried the one-eyed commander.

And the great man is finally dispatched in some famous lines:

> finem animae, quae res humanas miscuit olim,
> non gladii, non saxa dabunt nec tela, sed ille
> Cannarum uindex et tanti sanguinis ultor
> anulus. i, demens, et saeuas curre per Alpes
> ut pueris placeas et declamatio fias.
>
> (163–7)

Not swords, not stones or spears shall put an end to the life of this man who once threw human affairs into confusion, but that punisher for Cannae and avenger for so much blood, a little ring. Go, madman, run over the savage Alps, to become the schoolboys' favourite and become a subject for declamation.

This is magnificent rhetoric. The epigrammatic *sententia* which concludes the passage has an irony that embraces not just the boys in school but, more subtly, the poet as well: for what is he doing himself with Hannibal if not declaiming about him? The little word 'anulus', thin and scornful in its isolation at the beginning of a new line, contrasts admirably with the slow massive rhythm of the line before. But characteristically, the metrical technique serves a visual purpose as well: it is a *little* ring in which Hannibal kept poison ('anulus' is a diminutive, a fact which in the context is felt), and we are made to see how small an object has put an end to so great a life.

Juvenal is, indeed, a masterly observer, with a brilliant eye for the telling detail: a woman's ear-lobes pulled downwards by the weight of the pearls worn on them (6. 458 f.), the wife whose infidelity is betrayed to her husband by her glowing ears (11. 189), the soldiers' 'brawny calves drawn up to big benches' when their civilian victim appears before the military court

(16. 14). Often this vividness is enhanced by a touch of fantasy, and inanimate things are 'brought to life'. The windows seem to be watching the man rash enough to walk through Rome by night (3. 275); roast boar, piping hot, seems to be foaming like the living boar of Meleager (5. 115 f.); the figure on an equestrian statue seems to be in the act of aiming his lance (7. 128); a purse crammed with money 'swells with its mouth stuffed full' just like a greedy human being (14. 138). Some of his grimmest inventions are poetically suggestive, as in this picture of one of the Emperor Domitian's councillors (4. 109 f.): 'saevior illo/ Pompeius tenui iugulos aperire susurro' ('Pompeius, more savage than he [Crispinus] at slitting throats with his thin whisper'). The sinister sound of the verse matches the sinister compression of phrase which assimilates the thin sound of the informer's whisper to the thin edge of the razor cutting through flesh. Juvenal has often enough been praised as a satirist; he deserves to be more widely known for his powers of poetic imagination.

His contemporary Tacitus remarks (*Ann.* 4. 32), 'nobis in arto et inglorius labor' ('Mine is a narrow and inglorious task'). We catch a similarly self-contemptuous note in the poet; we are often reminded of Juvenal's claim that 'indignatio' inspired his verse, less often of the context in which that claim was made:

> si natura negat, facit indignatio uersum
> qualemcumque potest, quales ego uel Cluuienus.
>
> (1. 79 f.)

If nature denies, scorn makes such verses as it can—such as I write or Cluvienus.

In other words, the kind of verse that scorn produces is poor stuff. Yet both the poet and the historian, we may feel, protest too much. Tacitus would not really prefer, as he pretends, to be relating the glorious deeds of the Roman republic: the very bleakness and narrowness of his subject have a poetic grandeur of a novel kind. The same moral may be applied to Juvenal: his bitter, grating voice and narrowness of theme are not at odds with the splendour of his rhetoric but are the very essence of that splendour. The kind of sardonic grandeur that was achieved fitfully by Lucan was attained with full assurance by Juvenal. Political circumstances made men sour; literary circumstances demanded a new kind of poetry. Juvenal was the one poet, as Tacitus was the one historian, who found a theme and tone which answered to both the social and literary conditions of his age.

The Novel

Prose fiction was conventionally regarded as a very low form of art. Not one of the literary critics of antiquity thought it worth his consideration. Tacitus treated the life and death of Petronius in his *Annals* without deigning to mention that the man had written a novel; such things were below the dignity of history. We have seen that the poets who continued to work in the traditional or 'classic' genres were always liable to fall under the curse of academic art and become competent but lifeless. Perhaps we should not be surprised to find in the novel, the most despised of all genres, unfettered by literary convention, unencumbered by the legacy of great predecessors, a new sparkle and vitality. An ancestry can, it is true, be found for the Roman novel; in 'Milesian tales', stories of erotic or supernatural adventure; in Menippean satire, a genre which mixed prose and verse, as does Petronius; and, in the case of Apuleius at least, the Greek love romance. But all that we know about these often obscure ancestors suggests that our two surviving specimens of Roman novel-writing went far beyond them; they are gloriously original and uninhibited works, as unlike anything else in antiquity as they are unlike each other.

Petronius' date and identity have been disputed. Most scholars, though not all, believe him to be identical with Nero's 'arbiter elegantiae', compelled by the Emperor to take his own life in AD 66, and that is the assumption made here. Only one episode of the *Satyrica* (to give what is commonly called the *Satyricon* its correct title) has come down to us entire: this is what has become known as the *Cena Trimalchionis*, 'Trimalchio's dinner-party'. The rest of the *Satyrica* survives in very patchy fragments only. If it was written on the same scale as the *Cena*, it must have been an enormous work, far longer than any other novel of antiquity; but it is possible that the dinner party was a centre-piece, like the tale of Cupid and Psyche in Apuleius' *Golden Ass*, developed in far more detail than any other part of the story.

Since so much is lost, any account of the work as a whole has to be somewhat vague. The story is narrated by one Encolpius, thief, pervert, parasite, and man of the world. The novel charts his wanderings, along with his faithless catamite, the boy Giton, and his rival Ascyltus (all three names have sexual connotations): we find them by the Bay of Naples, on shipboard, and at Croton in the far south of Italy. A recurrent theme appears to be the hero's persecution at the hands of Priapus, the god of sexual potency. It has been suggested that the whole work is a kind of burlesque epic, with Encolpius as a disreputable Ulysses or Aeneas, and the ithyphallic Priapus taking the role of the more dignified gods Neptune or Juno.

Encolpius himself, cultivated and depraved, is scarcely a character in the modern sense but a pair of hard clever eyes through which we view an extraordinary comic world. Part of the *Satyrica's* fascination lies in its combination of low life with literary wit and social satire, all set out with a cold brilliant detachment. Some of the scenes are obscene, even monstrously obscene. There are grotesque inventions, as when Eumolpus, turning metaphor into actuality, decrees that his legatees must first eat the flesh of his corpse; but we also meet the rhetorician Agamemnon, who elicits from Encolpius a fruity declamation against declamation, while Eumolpus, for his part, is depicted as an obsessed versifier. Several times incidents are compared to scenes from mime, and there is something of the quality of pantomime, too, when members of the cast step out of character for the better entertainment of the audience. Encolpius, by turns rogue and literary gentleman, cynical and soft-hearted, is a protean figure who adapts to whatever role is suggested by the convenience of the moment; the blundering Eumolpus is allowed to tell the story of the widow of Ephesus in dashing style; Trimalchio's foolish astrology has a sharp edge to it (39): anyone born under the sign of the ram, he remarks, has 'a hard head, a brazen forehead, sharp horns. Many professors are born under this sign . . .'

In the conversation of the guests at Trimalchio's dinner, Petronius deploys a racy colloquial Latin to brilliant effect. The talk is fast and varied: dour, gossipy, and sentimental. We even catch a foretaste of Sam Weller. ' "Oro, te," inquit Echion centonarius, "melius loquere. 'Modo sic, modo sic' inquit rusticus; uarium porcum perdiderat" ' (45) (' "Please, please," said Echion the rag-merchant, "don't talk so gloomily. 'There's light patches and there's dark patches', as the yokel said when he'd lost his spotted pig" ').

Trimalchio himself is one of those characters, like Shylock, who ought to be a monster but turns out oddly endearing; whether Petronius designed this effect is perhaps an open question. His behaviour is self-contradictory, in this case not because the author has no consistent view of his character but because it is in the nature of that character to be a mass of inconsistencies. A former slave who has attained enormous, even preposterous riches (he contemplates buying property in Sicily so that he will be able to travel all the way to Africa on his own land (48)), he is anxious to play a part, but unable to decide what part to choose. At one moment he tyrannizes over his slaves, at another he apes the philosophers, declaring that slaves are human beings and have drunk the same milk as other men. He observes sagely that one should talk culture at dinner, and treats his guests to an outrageously confused account of the Trojan War; but he cannot forgo the rival pleasures of inverted snobbery: the epitaph he has composed for himself declares (71), 'Virtuous, brave and true, he began humbly, left 30,000,000 sesterces, and never listened to a philosopher.' He has skeleton brought in to remind him of his mortality (34)—a gesture which would be more impressive were the skeleton not made of silver. He is superstitious and sentimental, his puns are childishly awful, and his attempts to be stylish are disastrously vulgar (he uses a silver chamber-pot in public, and then wipes his hands on a slave's head). Some of his remarks are what Englishmen call Irish: he has cups depicting 'Cassandra's dead children' so skilfully engraved 'that you would think they were alive' (52); he has told his slaves that he means to free them in his will 'so that my household may love me now just as though I were dead' (71). Constantly he craves affection: 'No one in my house loves me more,' he says, as he feeds his dog (64). At the end of the feast, now thoroughly drunk, he decides to rehearse his funeral. Trumpeters are summoned, his shroud fetched, and lying on a heap of cushions he announces (78), 'Pretend I'm dead. Say something nice.' This is childish behaviour, certainly; perhaps childlike also. The scene seems an extravagant flourish on Petronius' part to mark the climax of Trimalchio's feast, so it is sobering to learn from Seneca's letters.of a certain Pacuvius who behaved in just such a fashion. It is Petronius' strength that he is a fantasist who does not lose touch with reality.

Apuleius was born at Madaurus in the province of Africa around 123 and was active in the second half of the century. Several works from his hand survive, including the *Apologia*, his self-defence on a charge of gaining his wife's love by the use of magic (below, p. 407); but his fame rests above all on his novel the *Metamorphoses*, also known as *The Golden Ass*. This is based on a Greek tale, *Lucius, or The Ass*, possibly written by Lucian, of which an abridged version is still extant. Comparison with the Greek story serves to demonstrate how brilliantly Apuleius enlarged and adapted his model. *The Golden Ass* is in eleven books and is told in the first person. After nearly three books of amorous and humorous incidents the narrator, as a consequence of an experiment with magic which goes wrong, finds himself transformed into a donkey; and the rest of the work consists of a series of picaresque adventures which befall the hero in his animal form, interrupted by a large number of other tales recounted by various of the characters who figure in the main narrative. The longest of these, the tale of Cupid and Psyche, occupies about a fifth of the entire work.

Finally, after a vision of the goddess Isis, the narrator Lucius is restored to his human shape. The last scenes of the novel provide one of the most remarkable accounts of religious experience to come down from classical paganism. It has often been thought that we see here the influence of Christian spirituality; on this supposition Apuleius was fighting Christianity but doing his best to steal the rival religion's clothes. The last book also presents the interpreter of Apuleius with his most teasing problem; no entirely satisfactory explanation has yet been given, and perhaps none is possible. How are we to reconcile the tone of the conclusion, with Lucius as an adept of the goddess, vowed to celibacy and simplicity of life, with the huge gusto with which the rest of the story is told? Lucius repeatedly tells us that he is 'curiosus' ('inquisitive'), or 'sititor . . . nouitatis' ('a thirster after novelty'); for this inquisitiveness he is punished and ultimately redeemed, but until the last book the whole atmosphere and style of the narrative encourages us to rejoice and share in this thirst for adventure and experience. The work begins, indeed, with an explosion of zest and hilarity: the narrator presents himself in ingratiating and persistent tones, almost as though he were a huckster pressing dirty postcards on a passer-by:

At ego tibi sermone isto Milesio uarias fabulas conseram auresque tuas beniuolas lepido susurro permulceam—modo si papyrum Aegyptiam argutia Nilotici calami inscriptam non spreueris inspicere—figuras fortunasque hominum in alias imagines conuersas in se rursum mutuo nexu refectas ut mireris.

Now then, I would like to stitch together a variety of stories in this Milesian tale and soothe your kindly ears with an elegant whisper—so long as you do not scorn to examine this Egyptian manuscript written with the neatness of a pen of the Nile—so that you may marvel at men's forms and fortunes changed into new shapes and then one with the other restored to themselves again.

Suddenly there is an interruption from the audience: 'exordior. "quis ille?" paucis accipe' ('I'll begin. "Who's this fellow?" I'll tell you briefly'). In elaborate and eccentric language the narrator explains that he is a Greek who learnt Latin at Rome in his adolescence. 'Lector intende; laetaberis', he concludes ('Reader, attend; you will be entertained'). All this passes in a very few sentences; everything speaks of briskness, energy, entertainment. And entertainment indeed is what we get, though often of a grotesque sort. Sex and magic, comedy and horror, elegant romance and coarse bawdy are blended into an intoxicating mixture: men are soused in urine or spattered with excrement; cuckoldry, castration, copulation are recurrent themes; the entire work is drenched in blood, torture, and hideous death.

The cement that holds this strange diversity together is provided by Apuleius' idiosyncratic style; it is his style, again, which prevents the work turning, as the Greek romances sometimes do, into mere vulgar titillation, by giving to the whole the gloss of an elaborate sophistication. The vocabulary is a weird blend of archaism, poeticisms, colloquialism, and neologism, elements which are curiously reminiscent of the babu English spoken in the last century by Indians who had educated themselves from a mixture of Shakespeare, newspapers, and modern slang imperfectly understood. That analogy is not as far-fetched as it may at first appear, for the narrator reveals that he is a Greek and apologizes for his imperfect command of the Latin language. 'Fabulam Graecanicam incipimus,' he explains ('I am beginning a Grecian tale'); characteristically he replaces the ordinary word for Greek, 'Graecus', with an uncommon form.

But of course the claim to imperfect Latin is all a feint; he is a stylistic virtuoso, a 'circus rider' by his own confession. With much adroitness he arranges his bizarre vocabulary into lilting mesmeric rhythms which sometimes have an almost incantatory effect. He loves assonances like 'sauia suauia' ('sweet kisses' 6.8) or, more elaborately, 'sordis infimae infamis homo' ('a notorious fellow of extreme squalor', 1.21). In place of the periodic structures and careful variations traditional in Latin art prose, he favours loose series of echoing phrases which on occasion even fall into the pattern of rhyming verse. Psyche's prayer to Ceres, for example, is a kind of coloratura aria (part of it is arranged here so as to bring out the rhyming effect);

Per ego te frugiferam tuam dexteram istam deprecor, per laetificas messium caeremonias, per tacita secreta cistarum et per famulorum tuorum draconum pinnata curricula et glebae Siculae sulcamina

et currum rapacem

et terram tenacem

et inluminarum Proserpinae nuptiarum demeacula

et luminosarum filiae inuentionum remeacula

et cetera quae silentio tegit Eleusinis Atticae sacrarium, miserandae Psyches animae supplicis tuae subsiste.

(6. 2)

I beseech you, by your right hand that bears the fruits of the earth, by your joyful ceremonies of harvest, by the unspoken secrets of your baskets, by the winged cars of the dragons your servants, by the furrows of the Sicilian soil, by the chariot that seized your daughter and the earth that held her, by the descent of Proserpine to a wedding unlighted by torches, by her ascent when she was found by the light of torches, by all else that the shrine of Eleusis in the land of Athens shrouds in silence, help the pitiable soul of Psyche, your suppliant.

Apuleius' rococo glitter is at its most dazzling in the story of Cupid and Psyche. On one level this is a fairy story, rich in folktale motifs, and opening with a disarming simplicity (4. 28): 'In a certain country there lived a king and queen' (it comes as small surprise that Psyche is the youngest and fairest of their three daughters, more lovely than Venus herself). On another level the tale hints at quasi-Platonic allegory: the marriage of Psyche, the soul, with Cupido, fleshly desire. On a third level the story is a comedy in the Ovidian manner, with Olympian goddesses constrained by the laws and etiquette of contemporary Rome; and on yet a fourth level it is the *ne plus ultra* of bejewelled preciosity. One of the virtues of Apuleius' high fantastical style is that it enables him to drift among these different levels of discourse.

Outside the story of Psyche, too, it enables him to create an atmosphere of his own, and to produce effects unlike anything else in Latin literature. His is a fantasy world, and yet it gives a curiously convincing picture of life under the Roman empire.

The scene in which Lucius falls for the slave-girl Fotis when he sees her stirring the porridge in a seductive manner is at once erotic and absurd (2.7). Lucius asks a cackling crone for directions to Milo's house; she answers with a terrible joke, but Lucius continues straight-faced with an elaborate gravity (1.21): ' "Remoto" inquam "ioco, parens optima, dic oro et cuiatis sit et quibus deuersetur aedibus" ' (' "Jesting aside, my good woman, " I answered, "tell me, pray, what manner of man he is and in what abode he lodges" '). Set against the comedy are glossy set-piece descriptions: the statues in Byrrhaena's house, so lifelike that they seem to be in motion (2.4); the beauty of a head of hair, glittering gold in the light, with shadows the colour of honey (2.9); the sheen of Cupid's dewy wings, with tender little downy feathers dancing tremulously at their edges as he sleeps (5.22). Many of Apuleius' stories are told with an outrageous insouciance, with loose ends left hanging all over the place. One might expect the result to be disordered ragbag, but the combination of mannerism and panache holds the work together. Apuleius is a curious figure with whom to end the account of a period; but it is stimulating to know that in the second half of the second century AD Latin literature could still throw up a writer so full of vitality and imagination.

Further Reading

Petronius has been translated by W. Arrowsmith (Ann Arbor, 1962); there are translations in the Penguin Classics series of Persius (together with Horace's *Satires* and *Epistles*) by N. Rudd; Petronius (together with Seneca's satire *Apocolocyntosis*) by J. P. Sullivan; selected epigrams of Martial by J. Michie; Juvenal by P. Green; and Apuleius, *The Golden Ass* by R. Graves. Marlowe translated Lucan's first book. Dryden's rendering of Persius and five satires of Juvenal (*The Poems of John Dryden*, ed. J. Kinsley (Oxford, 1958), vol. 2) are a part of English literature; his version of Juvenal gives a better idea of the grand declamatory manner than is possible in a modern idiom. Compare too Samuel Johnson's 'imitations' of *Satires* 3 and 10, 'London' and 'The Vanity of Human Wishes'. Walter Pater incorporated a translation of Apuleius' story of Cupid and Psyche into ch. 5 of his *Marius the Epicurean*; it conveys something of Apuleius' elegance, though not of his verve. The Loeb Classical Library contains none of Apuleius' works except *The Golden Ass*, but otherwise includes all the works discussed in this chapter.

G. Williams, *Change and decline: Roman literature in the early empire* (Berkeley, 1978) surveys the whole period. On individual poets see M. P. O. Morford, *The Poet Lucan: Studies in Rhetorical Epic* (Oxford, 1967); F. M. Ahl, *Lucan: An Introduction* (Ithaca, 1976); J. C. Bramble, *Persius and the Programmatic Satire: A study in Form and Imagery* (Cambridge, 1974); D. Vessey, *Statius and the Thebaid* (Cambridge, 1973); G. Highet, *Juvenal the Satirist* (Oxford, 1954); R. G. M. Nisbet, 'Persius' and H. A. Mason, 'Is Juvenal a classic?' in *Critical Essays on Roman Literature: Satire*, ed. J. P. Sullivan (London, 1963); R. Jenkyns, *Three Classical Poets: Sappho, Catullus and Juvenal* (London, 1982), part 3 'Juvenal the poet'; W. Anderson, *Essays on Roman Satire* (Princeton, 1982), which contains several pieces on Juvenal. On satire generally see M. Coffey, *Roman Satire* (London, 1976).

On the Latin novel: B. E. Perry, *The Ancient Romances: A Literary-Historical Account of their Origins* (Berkeley, 1967); P. G. Walsh, *The Roman Novel* (Cambridge, 1970); J. P. Sullivan, *The Satyricon of Petronius: A Literary Study* (London, 1968); J. Tatum, *Apuleius and The Golden Ass* (Ithaca, 1979); J. Winkler, *Auctor and Actor: a narratological reading of Apuleius's Golden Ass* (Berkeley, 1985).

13

Later Philosophy

=====

ANTHONY MEREDITH

General Tendencies

THE period with which this section is concerned is bracketed by
the lives of the two most interesting and important figures of
later philosophy, Posidonius of Apamea in Syria (d. 51 BC) and
Plotinus, an Egyptian by birth, who died in Rome in AD 270.
The former of these two was one of the most widely travelled
and deeply learned men of his age, who interested himself in a
whole range of subjects including rhetoric, geography, and recent history, taking over in the latter field where Polybius had
left off. He was also a philosopher and represents a tendency
present in a good deal of the philosophy of the period, to har-
monize the apparently conflicting views held by the main schools
of the age. So, though he was himself a Stoic, he seems to have
been willing to depart from the traditional views of his school in
two important matters, theology and anthropology. Unlike such
Stoics as Zeno and Chrysippus, he seems to have admitted the
existence of a god who was in some sense transcendent, and also
to have accepted the existence in man of the irrational appetites
as being truly human. In both of these areas he departs from the
monism and the intellectualism of the Stoic school as it is represented both in the founders of the fourth century and the
later Stoics, Epictetus and Marcus Aurelius, in the second
century AD. Plotinus, too, though an immeasurably greater

philosopher, indeed arguably the greatest since Aristotle and for a long time to come, was also prepared, as his biographer and pupil Porphyry tells us in his *Life*, to use the teachings of both Aristotle and the Stoics in addition to his master Plato.

In between these two towering figures crowd a host of lesser men whose main claim to fame is that they help to explain the genesis of Plotinus, but who also shed light both on the history of their respective schools and on the early growth of Christian reflection and doctrine. There are, however, certain overall features which can be found to a greater or lesser extent in all the writers of the period.

(a) The first two centuries after Christ were intensely conservative and traditional in their interests, and although it is doubtless true that under cover of a devotion to the past they intruded their own particular concerns, it cannot be denied that in all branches of their literary activity the writers of the age looked back to the great masterpieces of the golden age of Athens for their inspiration both in point of content and of style. It was their preoccupation with style that led many of the writers of the Second Sophistic to devote a good deal of attention to Plato, and it was perhaps for that reason that the philosophical renaissance of the age owes more to him than to Aristotle. As to content, most of the writers of the age can in general be classed as Platonists. The interest in the more dogmatic side of Plato can be dated to the earlier part of the first century BC and is connected with the figure of Antiochus of Ascalon, the first systematically to break away from the scepticism which had dominated the school since the days of Carneades (d. *c.*129/8 BC). The devotion to Plato shows itself in a number of ways, but above all in the constant use of quotation from him and in the general adherence to the main lines of his philosophy, the belief in the transcendence of God and in the immortality of the soul. So often were some of the commonplaces of Plato repeated by the writers of the period, above all by Plutarch, Maximus, and Albinus, that it has been thought by some scholars that they possessed a Platonic anthology, now lost, from which these excerpts were taken. It does not seem necessary to postulate such a book, but it still remains true that certain phrases, such as that from Plato's *Timaeus* 28 b 'To discover the maker and father of the universe is indeed a hard task, and having found him it would be impossible to tell everyone about him', recur with remarkable frequency in all the writers of the period, whether pagan or Christian.

(b) Alongside the intense traditionalism of the period may be found a strong tendency to amalgamate the central tenets of differing philosophical schemes, with the result of forming a united philosophical front. All the main schools must have had substantial followings over the period. Mention has already been made of Platonists and Stoics. But there was also a flowering of Pythagoreanism, again beginning at the opening of the first century BC with the figure of Nigidius Figulus (praetor in 58 BC). He was followed by men like the wandering preacher Apollonius of Tyana, whose biography, written by Philostratus for the Empress Julia Domna at the opening of the third century AD, came to be thought of as a rival to the Gospels. Another interesting Pythagorean of a slightly later date and more immediately philosophical interests was Numenius of Apamea, who made the interesting claim that Plato derived his doctrines from Pythagoras. He is therefore a witness to the belief that not only were Plato's doctrines derived, but also that underneath certain verbal differences all philosophers were saying the same thing. This mixture of appeal to antiquity, together with a desire to water down important divergences in favour of a common front, is characteristic of nearly all the writers of the age and is a mark of their learning, sterility, and general timidity.

(c) Most of the authors with whom we shall be concerned exemplify the revival in classical Greek style, known as the Second Sophistic Movement, of which Philostratus writes in his *Lives of the Sophists*. Marcus Aurelius wrote in Greek, and the 'cultured commonplaces' of Maximus were intended to help young men to develop the power of speaking elegantly in public on general themes. Again the interest of all the writers of the age, with the solitary exception of Plotinus, was practical. In Plutarch the moral and practical interest predominates, and in one of his *Discourses* Epictetus asks: 'But what is philosophy? Does it not mean making preparation to meet the things that come upon us?' It was for their lack of interest in giving practical help to the state that the Platonist philosopher Celsus was critical of Christians. Such a criticism would have sounded oddly from Plotinus, with his resolute and consistent exaltation of contemplation over action and his lack of interest in either the theory or the practice of politics. Finally, Plotinus differs from all his immediate predecessors in the systematic rigour that he brings to philosophy. Neither Plutarch nor Epictetus has any interest in speculation as such; for them philosophy subserves the life of action.

(d) The second-century sceptical writer Lucian (above, pp. 309 ff.), makes it clear that there was a good deal of religiosity in evidence in these years, and several of his essays are designed to poke fun at the various quacks and charlatans who thrived on some such atmosphere. *Essay* 42 deals with the false prophet Alexander of Abonuteichus who played grossly on the credulity of the period, and no. 55, 'On the death of Peregrinus', is an amusing account of a man who passed through Cynicism and Christianity to end up an Indian mystic. Lucian is hardly more merciful on grammatical pedants (*Essay* 41) or on philosophers (*Essay* 70, 'Hermotimus', a sustained attack on all philosophical schools). It was an era in which there appears to have been an abnormal flowering of many forms of occult piety, philosophical syncretism, and genuine religion. This sort of evidence has led E. R. Dodds to label it 'an age of anxiety', and to suggest that what led men and women to seek peace and revelation in all manner of mysteries was a sense of misery, a *fin de siècle* feeling, which encouraged such strange and unwonted outbursts. It is an attractive hypothesis, though it is hard to see why the age of the Antonines (AD 97–180) should be thought of as especially wretched. The historian Gibbon would hardly have subscribed to such a view. It is certainly true that many of the writers of the period seem to be very self-obsessed; some of them indeed like Herodes Atticus seem to have been pathological cases. It is also true that the age saw the rapid expansion of Christianity, but it would be hardly fair to label all Christians as either pathological introverts or seekers after secret and mystical revelation.

Platonism

It is possible to discern at least two widely different strands in the writings of Plato, the dogmatic and the critical: the Plato, in other words, who is responsible both for the theory of forms and the immortality of the soul on the one hand, and on the other the Plato who, in the tradition of his master Socrates, subjected all propositions to the sharpest criticism. Not long after his death in 347 the Academy which he had founded came under the influence of those who belonged for one reason or another to the second, sceptical stream. Partly in opposition to Stoic dogmatism, partly under the influence of Pyrrho, the leaders of the school, above all Arcesilaus (316/15–242/1) and Carneades, denied the possibility of any formal knowledge of anything. The last undisputed head of the Academy was Philo of Larissa (160/59–80), after whom, under the influence of his pupil Antiochus of Ascalon, the school lost its nerve and lapsed into dogmatism—a characteristic which it retained throughout the rest of its history right down to the closing of the Athenian Academy in AD 529 by order of the Emperor Justinian.

Of Antiochus we know very little, and that little is derived almost wholly from Cicero. He was born somewhere between 130 and 120 BC, and his death is put in 68. Our sources clearly regard him as a breakaway from the true Academy, largely if not entirely because he rejected the sceptical attitude to truth, which had been received 'doctrine' since the days of Arcesilaus, if not before. In another respect also he heralds a new age. He believed that there was fundamental agreement between the Old Academy of Plato and the Lyceum of Aristotle. Again this was a revolutionary step; and as we shall see, some Platonists, who might have been happy to admit the possibility of knowledge, regarded the proposed alliance between Plato and Aristotle with some distaste. The best known of the 'opposition' were Plutarch and Atticus. But beyond the fact that in these two respects Antiochus betrayed his immediate predecessors it is hard to be at all clear precisely what he taught.

Ironically enough, the clearest and most copious witness to the views of the Middle Platonists, as they are now called, is the Alexandrian Jewish writer Philo (*c*.25 BC–*c*.AD 45). From his lengthy allegorical commentary on the first five books of the Bible it is possible to extract a system which closely resembles the sort of picture which emerges from Plutarch and Albinus. It must, however, be remembered that, useful though he is for our purposes, Philo was a Jew and was thoroughly influenced by biblical ideas and images. Even so, in the first book of his commentary he provides us with a structured hierarchy of reality, beginning with the supreme God and ending with matter, like that which characterizes Middle Platonism. The question which the structure seeks to answer is 'How is it possible to derive the multiplicity which we see from the absolute unity which we believe to lie at the summit of the world?' The Bible, in common with all the great transcendental philosophers of classical antiquity, had assumed that above all there was a single indivisible self-sufficient principle; and although they might call it (him) sometimes God, sometimes Monad (Pythagorean), sometimes Absolute Beauty or the Idea of the Good (Plato's *Phaedrus* and *Republic*), sometimes the Unmoved Mover or Self-thinking Thought (Aristotle's *Metaphysics*), they were all agreed that it was single. The derivation of or relation to the One of the All was the problem. The theory of forms and the account of the making of the world in the *Timaeus* represent attempts at a solution. But Plato, Aristotle, and arguably the account of creation in the first chapter of Genesis, all tend to assume the eternity of matter as the condition of the possibility of the making of the world. Philo was perhaps the first to take the bold and interesting step of trying to present a picture of the making of the world which took into account all these insights. For him the maker of the world is the only one who is eternal in both senses of the word. That is, he held that God is both without beginning and without end (= durationally eternal) and also absolutely timeless. 'For God is the maker of time also, for he is the father of time's father. . . . Thus time stands to God in the relation of a grandson. . . . To the elder son, the intelligible universe, he assigned the place of the first-born.' This passage gives us in a nutshell the Philonic system. Beneath the first God and Father of all, who is incomprehensible and eternal, there comes a second God or Logos, who is described sometimes as the mind of God, sometimes as the place of the ideas or the intelligible world, sometimes as the first-born, sometimes as the agent in creation. Beneath him is the world of sense, created through the agency and on the model of the Logos. This last is less perfect and more multiple than is the world of forms.

It is clear what Philo is aiming at:

(a) He has replaced the confusing picture of three independent principles in the *Timaeus* with a neatly ordered pattern.
(b) He has achieved this by welding together rather disparate elements which he assumes enjoy a basic coherence.

Above all, the second principle draws together into one the creative word of Psalm 33:6, the Stoic Logos (though it is raised above and not identical with the material universe), the Platonic world of forms, and the Aristotelian self-thinking thought. On occasion he even calls the Logos 'God' and distinguishes him from the first God by the simple device of dropping the definite article. This distinction within the realms of the divine, which suggests the possibility of introducing degrees within the concept of God, was subsequently employed with considerable fruit and frequency by most of the later Middle Platonists and some of the Neoplatonist writers, notably by Albinus, Numenius, Plotinus, and the Christian Origen.

Plutarch was by birth a Greek and came from Chaeronea in

Boeotia. He studied philosophy in Athens and at a later date went to Rome, where he taught for a period, and then returned home. He spent the last thirty years of his life a priest at Delphi. He died *c*.AD 120 at about the age of seventy-five. Opinions about his philosophical seriousness vary from the declared and consistent, if not always orthodox Platonism attributed to him by Donald Russell, to the dismissive 'tea-table transcendentalist' of E. R. Dodds. A good example of this alleged incoherence is in his attitude to Stoicism. On the one hand he was sharply critical of much that the Stoics stood for. This is clear from two books of his *Moralia, Stoic Self-contradictions* and *On Common Conceptions*. So, for example, in the former book he argues that the Stoics believed that 'whatever is, is right', while believing at the same time that God chastises the wicked. On the other hand Plutarch owes a good deal of his belief in a benign providence to the Stoics, and to them also he, indirectly, owes his conviction that it is possible to know.

Plutarch's own attitude to the possibility of accounting for the existence of evil in a divinely ordered universe is not without its difficulties. His explanation of the origin of evil is not quite the same as Plato's, though he adduces passages in *The Laws* and *Timaeus* in defence of his own account. In his treatise *On Isis and Osiris*, an allegorical discussion of the Egyptian pantheon, he argues that there are two independent and eternal principles: Osiris, the principle of good, and Typhon, the principle of evil. This assertion of the existence of an eternal evil principle may be attributed to the influence of Xenocrates and could owe something to Iranian dualism, the eternal struggle between good (Ahura-Mazda), and evil (Ahriman); but it is at variance with the general tendency of Plato to deny to evil any place among the forms, and it is in clear conflict with the optimism of the Stoics and of Plotinus. In another treatise, *On the Obsolescence of Oracles*, Plutarch produces a slightly different explanation, attributing evil to the demons that exist between the divine world and that of the visible universe. Here we can see clear echoes of Plato's *Symposium*, with again the significant difference that Plato's demons are good or neutral, Plutarch's are evil.

In one final respect Plutarch's Platonism was modified by his Pythagorean teacher Ammonius, whose interpretation of the mysterious E at Delphi is related for us by Plutarch in his treatise of that name. According to Ammonius the purpose of the inscription is to identify the supreme principle of the universe with the utter simplicity of oneness that stands at the summit of the Pythagorean system. He concludes as follows: 'Under these conditions, therefore, we ought, as we pay Him reverence, to greet him and to address Him with the words, "Thou art"; or even . . . as did some of the men of old, "Thou art One".' This Pythagorean influence enables Plutarch to go beyond the other Middle Platonists; and in his insistence on the unity and simplicity of the supreme principle he closely approximates to the One of Plotinus.

Of all the Middle Platonist writers known to us the most characteristic and the most easily available is Albinus, sometimes called Alcinous. Of his life next to nothing is known, except that he lived in the middle of the second century AD and that he wrote two *Introductions* to the philosophy of Plato, both of which survive. His particular interest for us is that, unlike Philo and Plutarch, he seems to have been untouched by non-Hellenic influences. His work is decidedly eclectic in tone and marks a deliberate attempt to schematize his inherited Platonism on hierarchical principles. At the summit of the pyramid is the first God or Mind, ineffable, perfect, eternal, father of all. He fills the whole universe with himself because of his will. Beneath him comes second Mind: Mind, that is, in its active and passive side. After him comes the third principle, Soul. It should be noted that for Albinus the supreme God is both ineffable and personal and shares certain features in common with the first Mind of Aristotle, though differing from Aristotle in attributing to him both ineffability and personal involvement in the universe. Again, exalted though the God of Albinus is, he is not so utterly simple as the Pythagorean Monad of Philo and Plutarch, or the One of Plotinus. It is not surprising, therefore, to discover that he makes no use in his writings of the passage in *Republic* 509 b, on the source and nature of Being, of which later Platonists made so much.

From what has been said it is clear that Albinus, in common with Celsus and Maximus of Tyre, but unlike Plutarch and Atticus, believed in the fundamental harmony between Plato and Aristotle. This is clear not only from the willingness to treat the ideas of Plato as thoughts in the mind of Aristotle's god, but also from the extensive use made of Aristotle's logical works. On one further point of major importance the Aristotelianizing Platonists were at one. They all thought that the account of creation contained in Plato's *Timaeus* demanded an allegorical rather than a literal interpretation. The natural sense of Plato is that the making of the world took place in time. For Albinus such a suggestion implied some sort of change in God and must therefore be ruled out. It is of interest to note that on the three occasions when Plotinus discusses the problem of the making of the visible world he sides with Albinus. The same may also be said for the great Christian theologian Origen (185–254), who perhaps owed his views to Aristotelian influence.

The Middle Platonists hardly form a clear, organized body of thought. There is very little evidence that they exercised any influence on each other. It has indeed been suggested that Plotinus read Philo, but that is hardly likely. What unites them, rather, is the possession of certain common concerns and a general, if ill-defined, allegiance to Plato. The Bible, Pythagoras, and Aristotle were all thought of in their differing ways as being somehow in accord with Plato. The common concern that unites them is the desire on the part of all to interpret Plato in such a way as to overcome the crucial difficulty in his system; that of bridging the gulf created by the theory of forms between ultimate, static, reality and the changing unstable world of matter and sense. Connected with this is the effort towards transcendence manifested in differing ways by all the main authors: the incomprehensible God of Philo, the simple/complex Mind of Albinus, and the Monad of Plutarch.

Plotinus (204/5–270), the founder of Neoplatonism, is known to us both from the biography written by his devoted, but possibly not altogether comprehending pupil, Porphyry, and from the collections of his writings, organized topically into six volumes, *Enneads*, by the same pupil. He was by birth and early training an Egyptian and claimed to have learnt most of his philosophy from Ammonius Saccas. The content of this teaching is beyond recovery, since Ammonius left no writings behind him and speculation about him has yielded no certain results. In 244 Plotinus left Egypt for Rome, where he spent the rest of his life. His teaching was conducted by means of seminars, to which he attracted some of the influential men of his day. An index of the power of his views and personality is the fact that one of his auditors, a senator, Rogatianus, was persuaded to abandon his life of public service. This incident highlights the fact that politics was the only branch of ancient philosophy in which Plotinus showed no interest. Indeed at times he displays a positive antipathy towards it.

Plotinus thought of himself as a Platonist, and in much of his teaching Platonic influence is evident. Like Plato he believed in the superiority of intellect to sense and of the spiritual world to the material. In this area he consciously rejected precisely those philosophies which he thought undermined the basis of Platonic intellectualism, above all Scepticism, Stoicism, and Gnosticism (a body of esoteric doctrines which denied the reality of the flesh and the physical world). Against the first of these he insisted that we can know, and that our knowledge is neither derived from nor reducible to sense impressions, but comes on the contrary from a direct, ever present awareness of spiritual reality, which is always available to us if only we concentrate our minds upon it. Against the Stoics Plotinus argued that 'reality' is not primarily material but spiritual, and that the existence of matter results from the absence of form and spirit; in other words, that it is a negative rather than a positive thing. However, we are not to suppose that his critique of Stoicism made Plotinus into a despiser of the visible order. His third main opponents were the

Gnostics, whose devaluation of matter made it necessary for them to believe in the need to escape from this world. He also objected to their tendency to underrate the importance of choice and mind in their effort towards salvation. One of his grandest *Enneads*, 2.9, is directed against the Gnostics and has been described as a 'noble apology for Hellenism' in its insistence on the goodness and beauty of the visible order and its vindication of the centrality of freedom and reason in the good life. In his reactions to Stoicism and Gnosticism we can see Plotinus delicately or precariously balanced between two conflicting world views, tending respectively to the deification and vilification of the world we see.

Apart from the evident Platonism of the *Enneads* and the no less evident willingness to incorporate into this general system elements drawn from Aristotle and the Stoa, two other features need mention. The most widely known and distinctive of these is the One, the supreme principle which stands at the climax of the ladder of reality. The One is impersonal and beyond the reach of predication and of any direct knowledge, yet it is at the same time the source of all reality and all value. It combines the One of Plato's *Parmenides* and the Good of the *Republic*. It is from the One as the infinite and generous source of life and value that all else comes. In making this step Plotinus goes beyond both Plato and his own immediate predecessors. For them, absolute reality is both limited and static. For Plotinus, on the other hand, the One, and even more the second substance, the Mind, is boiling with life. On one occasion he writes that being is 'not a corpse, and not not-life and not not-thinking'.

The second feature of importance in Plotinus' system is that it is experienced rather than argued for. It was his own acute awareness of the One gained as the fruit of intense concentration that helped him to formulate the system above outlined. His biographer tells us two important things about him. He was strongly opposed to all forms of ritualistic religion and observed on one occasion that 'the gods must come to me, not I to the gods'. Towards the end of his biography Porphyry also says that during the time during which he knew him Plotinus experienced ecstasy. This state, which is described in great detail at the end of the last *Ennead*, entailed for him 'a simplification and sur- render of the self, an aspiration towards contact, which is at once a stillness and a mental effort of adaptation'. Union of this type is experienced only briefly and is the climax of a process of moral purification, introversion and contemplation of 'the vision that makes happy'. The culminating state of union, in which any awareness of distinction is for the time abolished, seems to have led Plotinus to postulate the One at the summit of the hierarchy of reality, as the only possible explanation for the variety we normally experience and for the state of exalted unification which he underwent on at least four occasions.

It is hard to exaggerate the importance of Plotinus. His system was the outcome both of the philosophical syncretism that pre- ceded him and of his own personal mystical experience. He is also significant because of his attempt to break down the layered vision of his immediate predecessors in favour of a dynamic, spiritual monism, in which as Dean Inge notes 'there are no straight lines drawn across the map of the universe'. The ten- sions in his own vision result almost entirely from his effort to break through the more static, dualistic presuppositions of his ancestors. Finally, it would be unfitting not to mention the extraordinary influence he exercised directly or indirectly on later Platonists, like Porphyry and Proclus, and on Christian writers of the stature of Denis the Areopagite and St Augustine.

Stoicism

Epictetus (*c*.AD 55–135) was a rough contemporary of Plutarch, but whereas Plutarch was a Boeotian aristocrat, Epictetus was by birth a slave. He belonged to Epaphroditus, the freedman and secretary of Nero, who later served Domitian until his murder in AD 95. Epictetus was allowed to attend the lectures of the celebrated Stoic Musonius Rufus, and in 89, together with all other philosophers, he was banished from Rome and took up residence at Nicopolis in Epirus. There he spent the rest of his life expounding the precepts of Chrysippus (Vol. 1, Ch. 15) and making his own comments on them. These comments were collected and organized by one of his hearers, Flavius Arrian, consul for 130, into eight books, four of which still survive. His work has a wider appeal than that of his predecessors; it was addressed to the humble and the poor rather than to the few and the self-reliant, and the main tenet of his teaching was the need to cultivate inner peace as the way to true freedom.

'With Posidonius the Stoa opened itself to Platonic influence.' The principal question to be asked about the philosophy of Epictetus is whether he continued in the direction mapped out by Posidonius, or whether he reverted to the pure doctrine of Zeno, Cleanthes, and Chrysippus, the founders of the school. On this central point opinions differ. Some scholars believe that in Seneca, Epictetus, and Marcus Aurelius, the Platonizing of the Stoa continues. Others, however, take the opposite line, at least for the central figure, and see in him a reversion to origins.

It cannot be doubted that a good deal of the language of Epictetus' *Discourses*, if taken literally, suggests a departure from the monistic position of Chrysippus. In some places, for example, God is described, not as a world process, as nature, but rather as the Other or Another. On the same point it is worth noting also that on many occasions reference is made to 'the God', 'the gods', and to 'Zeus'. It is not clear how far the use of such religious language implies belief in a god, or gods, existing separately from nature. Another arguably Platonizing element is the treatment of the soul. In *Discourse* 1.9.11 Epictetus speaks about our natural kinship to the gods, which we will be able to realize once we have dispensed with the fetters that bind us; that is, the body and its possessions. Such language is more akin to the 'body a prison' idea of Plato's *Phaedo* than to the doctrines of most of the Stoics, who denied such an opposition of soul and body. Again, therefore, the question must be asked: does such language express a profound metaphysical dualism, or has it some other function? In making a decision about the best method of understanding Epictetus' position three points should be noticed. First of all he was not primarily interested in the construction of an ontology but rather had an ethical concern, to which his metaphysical beliefs, if he had any, were not of the first importance. Then also, despite the appearance of transcendental, dualist language, such talk accounts for only a relatively small part of the actual usage of the *Discourses*. The old Stoic identification of 'God' and 'Nature' continues to be used (cf. fr. 1). Finally, it would be unfair to suggest that the existence of dualist language is restricted to Epictetus and the later Stoics. It also occurs in the *Hymn* to *Zeus* written by the unquestionably 'orthodox' Cleanthes somewhere towards the beginning of the third century BC. As Bonhoeffer notes, the Stoic school from its beginning had employed a dualist language alongside its basic monism. It seems therefore on the whole preferable to see in Epictetus, though arguably not in Seneca and Marcus Aurelius, a return to pure Stoicism, after the brief flirtation with Platonism evident in the Middle Stoicism of writers like Posidonius, Panaetius, the Pseudo-Aristotle, and the Book of Wisdom. If the above analysis is correct, it means that we see in Epictetus, and perhaps also in Cleanthes before him, a very interesting juxtaposition of two ways of talking, a metaphysical monism alongside a religious dualism.

The main concern of Epictetus is ethical. Like all the great moral philosophers of classical antiquity, he is concerned to ensure the happiness of those whom he addresses. But, unlike Aristotle, and to some extent unlike Plato, he subordinates philosophy to the cure of the soul. 'Men,' he writes, 'the lecture room of the philosopher is a hospital' (*Diss.* 3. 23. 30). Happiness is made to consist in peace of mind, a quality which is always within our power, and therefore must in no sense be made to depend upon things outside our control. Dependence upon external things, whether they be material possessions, the affection and esteem of others, even good health, necessarily impedes our own peace, because any of these things may be taken from us. Such a system, if it is to succeed, clearly relies on the power to make the fundamental distinction between what does and what does not lie within our power. In the first chapter of his *Encheiridion* or *Handbook* he writes as follows: 'Some things are under our control, while others are not under our control. Under our control are conception, choice, desire, aversion, and in a word, everything that is our doing; not under our control are our body, our property, reputation, office, and, in a word, everything that is not our doing.' This is all clear enough, though it might be objected that the clarity with which the distinction is made is a little deceptive. It is an often expressed corollary of this that the way to happiness is not straining after the impossible, but cutting down desires, not allowing yourself to be disturbed at all by the things that you cannot remedy, and even when you can remedy evil, not impairing your own peace of mind in the process. At *Diss.* 4.4.33 he writes:

And how shall I free myself?—Have you not heard many times that you ought to eradicate desire utterly; direct your aversion to things that lie within the sphere of the moral purpose, and these only; that you ought to give up everything, your body, your property, your reputation, your books, turmoil, office, freedom from office? For if once you swerve aside from your course, you are a slave, you are a subject.

It follows from all this that the root of our malaise is failure to make the correct judgements about what is and what is not in our power, and that the remedy for such errors is the formation of correct judgements and the control of the impressions that come into the mind. The aim of life and the way to happiness is for me to adapt myself to the particular expression of nature that is to be found in me. Once I have discovered that, I shall be in a position to live my life and adapt my moral purpose accordingly.

The system as outlined above clearly aims to offer the maximum of happiness, and at the same time it is highly intellectualist, in the best traditions of the primitive Stoa. Unlike Aristotle, and also unlike the Middle Stoics, Epictetus is not prepared to allow the emotions any part to play in the picture of man or in the end of the moral life. Again, an ethical system that consists largely in discovering where nature calls and following there, can hardly be prescriptive. In other words if 'whatever is, is right', there is little if any room left for any attempts to bring about the improvement of the world. By concentrating his efforts on the purification of the moral purpose—a central and new idea in him—Epictetus hardly preached a revolutionary system. Epictetus' ethics can be summed up not unfairly in the celebrated life formula 'Endure and Renounce'. Their restraint may echo his early life as a slave, where freedom of movement would have been greatly restricted; and it may be true that, as his translator observes, 'they hardly provide a sufficient programme for a highly organized society making towards a goal of general improvement'. Nevertheless there is something inexpressibly noble in the character they reveal and the programme they outline. In an age where the little man must have been made increasingly aware of his impotence in the face of a crushing imperial machine, Epictetus' invitation to win peace of soul, and with it happiness, by adapting oneself to one's circumstances and restricting one's desires within the bounds of the possible, must have sounded both wise and attractive. Conformity of such a sort reaches religious proportions when 'nature' becomes the same as 'God'.

Marcus Aurelius, born in AD 121, was adopted by the Emperor Antoninus Pius in 138 and himself became Emperor in 161. A good deal of his time in power was spent pacifying the northern and eastern frontiers of the Empire, and the twelve books of *Meditations* are almost certainly the result of his private self-communing during his campaigns. Book 2 was probably written 'among the Quadi on the Gran' and Book 3 at Carnuntum, now Haimburg, in Austria. This will give a date of somewhere between 171 and 173. Unlike the *Discourses* of Epictetus, they were not intended for an audience; but like them they are not composed in an orderly, schematic fashion. There seems to have been no idea in the mind of Marcus of future publication, and in that respect they differ from the *Letters* of Pliny or of Gregory of Nazianzus, which though perhaps initially meant for the immediate addressee, seem almost always, perhaps as a result of later revision, to have a wider audience in view. Marcus' *Meditations*, however, passed unnoticed until 350, and then they drop out of notice for 550 years. It was, in fact, only with their printing in 1558 that their popularity as a work of comfort and instruction began.

He presents the same sort of problems of classification as did his master Epictetus. He too uses from time to time dualistic language about the relation of body and soul, and personal transcendent language about the divine. *Meditation* 5.27 is a good example of this practice. 'Walk with the Gods. And he does walk with the Gods who lets them see his soul invariably satisfied with his lot and carrying out the will of that "genius", a particle of himself, which Zeus has given to every man as his captain and guide.' On the other hand *Med.* 4.23 seems to hold up as an ideal conformity with the Universe, which is taken as the equivalent of Nature and the city of Zeus. Such language is more monist in tone. In another traditionally Stoic passage Marcus writes 'For there is but one Universe, made up of all things and one God immanent in all things, and one substance and one law, one Reason common to all created intelligences, and one Truth.' There is also an unresolved ambiguity in his mind on the question of personal survival, an ambiguity which seems to distinguish him from Epictetus. Thus he can write 'What then remains [*sc.* of us] after death? To wait with a good grace for the end, whether it be extinction or translation.' One point, particularly connected with his moral advice, seems to distinguish him from his master, and to argue at the same time in favour of a slightly greater influence of Platonism. Marcus was a great advocate of introversion. 'Look within. Within is the fountain of Good, ready always to well forth if you are prepared to dig deep enough.' Introversion of this sort, and the reflexion it implies, would appear to rule out a purely material-istic concept of the soul, and this point, together with the distinct possibility of the existence of life after death, seems to tip the scales in favour of seeing in Marcus a Platonizing Stoic.

Despite the tendency to adopt certain Platonic ways of

thinking on occasion, it remains true that in the basic drive of his system Marcus keeps to the fundamental Stoic tenet that the way to well-being in this life is through obedience to nature and the suppression or mastery of passion. We ought to follow the god or the gods and live in agreement with nature. He uses the classic Stoic formula of 'life in accord with nature' only once; but the idea is always there in the background. On the whole Marcus prefers the more to the less personal expressions. He has less to say about curbing desire than does Epictetus, but being a person in supreme authority he had less obvious need to free himself from unsatisfiable wishes than his master. Among the precepts which he records there is one which expresses in a paradoxical way the ideal of the Stoic sage: 'At the same time to be utterly impervious to all passions and full of natural affection.' Noble though such an ideal undoubtedly is, it may be doubted whether it is at all attainable.

Stoicism, much more than Platonism, was devoted to helping men to live at peace with themselves and with the world, and was always in danger of toppling over into conformity, comfortable or otherwise. In accepting nature, or what happens, as the ultimate criterion of right and wrong, the Stoics were incapable on their own principles of criticizing society, and found some measure of peace in adapting themselves to its vagaries. This inevitably led them to pursue a sort of inner tranquillity through introversion, which represents at the same time a withdrawal from the external world and the assumption of an inner reality that lay beyond the reach of external tyranny. But in seeking such a peace it may be doubted if they remained true to the very principles of anti-dualism from which they began.

Scepticism

Despite Antiochus' abandonment of the sceptical position of the New Academy in favour of a Stoic belief in the possibility of certainty in perception and knowledge, it must not be supposed that the anti-dogmatic habit died at once to be resurrected only with the sixteenth century. Almost at the same time as the Academy abandoned the scepticism common to it since the days of Arcesilaus and Carneades, there arose at some time between 100 and 40 BC a champion of the ancient and true sceptic tradition—Aenesidemus of Alexandria. Little is known about his life except that he denounced, not surprisingly, Antiochus and, surprisingly, Arcesilaus and Carneades, because, he argued, they taught that scepticism was a dogma, whereas they should have said that it was a possibility, not a certainty.

The final flowering of Scepticism as a system took place in the second century and is available to us through the writings of Sextus Empiricus (d. *c.*AD 200). In the course of fourteen books he expounded the principles of Scepticism, and then took issue with all brands of dogmatists and instructors. His work and that of those he represents has been described somewhat eulogistically as the 'antecedent of freedom of conscience, rational criticism, and the absolute right of scientific thought'.

As in the other systems here described, the central aim was one of offering the maximum of happiness. It must be admitted at the outset that their conception of happiness is decidedly negative and owes a good deal to Epicureanism—a philosophy by no means dead, at least to judge from the massive inscription put up at the close of the second century AD by Diogenes of Oenoanda in his native city to instruct his fellow citizens in the Epicurean system. The aim of life is *ataraxia* or freedom from disturbance. The way to this state of mind is through suspension of judgement, which is arrived at by a realization that certainty is impossible and no argument incontrovertible. The main interest of the whole system is the way in which they thought this state of realization was to be achieved. It was supposed to happen through the ten celebrated 'tropes' of Aenesidemus. The aim of the tropes is to challenge the value, and even more the bare possibility, of going beyond the appearances and arriving at what Stoics and Platonists alike would have termed knowledge. Antisceptic though he was, Plotinus thought it necessary to refute their objections to the possibility of knowledge. In fact

Ennead 5.5.1 can be read as accepting their critique of Stoic sensualism, before he propounds his own theory. The principal type of argument proposed by Aenesidemus and Sextus is that, because the way in which objects appear to us differs from person to person, it is impossible to make absolute claims about the nature of the thing in itself. The first trope argues that, as the same object produces differing impressions on different living creatures, no valid inference about the actual object may be drawn from the report of our senses, and therefore that the only proper and possible attitude towards them is one of suspension of judgement, *epochē*. In his treatise *On the Drunkenness of Noah* Philo writes: 'These and similar phenomena are clear proofs of the impossibility of apprehension.' There is a certain rigour evident in the arguments of the Sceptics, which is in striking contrast to the somewhat incoherent dogmatism of the founders of Middle Platonism, notably Antiochus of Ascalon. As far as we know, no refutation was provided of the arguments of Sextus and Aenesidemus; nevertheless the school did not last. Perhaps it was thought of as too uncompromisingly destructive for an age which needed the support of a metaphysical or religious vision.

Further Reading

One of the best introductions to the thought and atmosphere of the whole period is *Conversion* by A. D. Nock (Oxford, 1933), a study in the Old and the New in Religion from Alexander the Great to Augustine of Hippo. To this should be added *Pagan and Christian in an Age of Anxiety* by E. R. Dodds (Cambridge, 1965), which offers an explanation of the success of Christianity in psychological categories. The chapters on philosophy by Nock and F. H. Sandbach in Vols. x and xi of the *Cambridge Ancient History* are also useful.

For more specifically philosophical treatment the last volume of Zeller's *History of Philosophy*, entitled *Stoics, Epicureans and Sceptics* (London, 1892), is still probably the most thorough and helpful treatment, though he does not deal with Plotinus. A good, though rather general, survey of the whole classical period of philosophy is also to be found in vol. i of *A History of Philosophy, Greece and Rome* (London, 1946) by F. C. Copleston. The most easily accessible account of Plotinus and of his immediate predecessors and followers, and also of Philo and of the main Christian philosophers of the first three centuries AD, is to be found in *The Cambridge History of Late Greek and Early Medieval Philosophy* (Cambridge, 1967) ed. A. H. Armstrong. More detailed accounts of imperial philosophy can be had in *Stoic Philosophy* by R. M. Rist (Cambridge, 1969) and in *The Middle Platonists, a Study in Platonism, 80 BC–AD 220* by J. Dillon (London, 1977), and *Neoplatonism* by R. T. Wallis (London, 1972).

Most of the authors of the period can be read in the Loeb Classical Library, which are often furnished with useful introductions and, in the case of Plutarch and Plotinus, with helpful analyses of the contents of the various treatises. The Stoics are represented by the *Discourses* of Epictetus (London, 1925) with an introduction and translation by W. A. Oldfather, and by the *Meditations* of Marcus Aurelius Antoninus (London, 1916), edited, translated, and introduced by C. R. Haines. The appendix contains the speeches and sayings of Marcus and a useful note on his attitude to Christians, in which Haines challenges the popular view that Marcus was hostile to them. Vol. i of Philo's works (London, 1929) edited by F. H. Colson and G. H. Whittaker has a particularly helpful introduction. Later Platonism is best illustrated by the *Moralia* of Plutarch, especially in vol. v (London, 1936), translated by F. C. Babbit, which contains *Isis and Osiris* and *The E at Delphi*. Neoplatonism is represented by the *Enneads* of Plotinus (1966), not yet all available, with translation and useful synopses of the complex argument by A. H. Armstrong. A good impression of the mind of Plotinus is available from *Ennead* 1.6 On Beauty and 2.9 Against the Gnostics.

14

The Arts of Living

ROGER LING

Introduction

THE object of the present chapter is to review those aspects of
Roman art and architecture which impinge upon life, and conversely those aspects of life which encroach upon the realms of
art. Thus, while Chapter 16 will deal with High Art and 'art for
art's sake', we shall here concentrate on topics such as houses
and gardens in so far as they affect and reflect life-style, on
fittings, furnishings, and interior decoration as documents of
contemporary taste and attitudes, on eating and drinking, on
personal effects and ornaments, and on household implements
and utensils. The field is vast and varied, and generalization is
inevitable. It is inevitable, above all, that much of the material
discussed will relate to Roman Italy and to the first and early
second centuries AD, for which we have an unparalleled abundance of evidence, both literary and archaeological. The literary
evidence is provided by social poets such as Persius, Statius,
Martial, and Juvenal, by novelists (Petronius), by encyclopedists
(the Elder Pliny), and by letter-writers (Pliny the Younger and,
for an earlier period, Cicero). The archaeological evidence comes
chiefly from the remarkable remains of two 'provincial' towns,
Pompeii and Herculaneum, buried by the eruption of Mount
Vesuvius in AD 79. There is, of course, much evidence from other
archaeological sites, for example second- and third-century

Ostia; but none of these supplies the same *embarras de richesse* as Pompeii, still less the same precision of dating.

Houses and Villas

The traditional middle- and upper-class town-house of republican and early-imperial Italy was the *domus*, a spreading

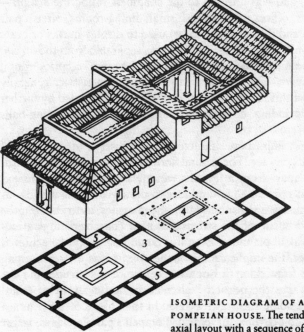

ISOMETRIC DIAGRAM OF A POMPEIAN HOUSE. The tendency to an axial layout with a sequence of roofed and unroofed elements is clearly emphasized: the entrance passage (1) leads to the front hall or *atrium* (2), behind which the reception room or *tablinum* (3) opens on to the colonnaded garden or peristyle (4). The recesses (*alae*) for the display of family portraits are at the back corners of the *atrium* (5).

mansion focused on two inner light-sources, the *atrium* at the front and a colonnaded garden or peristyle at the rear (see Plate 4). The *atrium*, the social and religious centre of the house, was the first open space to confront the visitor as he entered from the street, and it was fittingly endowed in most cases with majestic height, and sometimes with lofty columns framing the shallow rectangular catchwater basin (*impluuium*) in the centre of the floor. Light flooded through a central opening in the roof (*compluuium*) and was diffused to the chambers round the *atrium*— bedrooms, offices, store-rooms, small dining-rooms, often a pair of broad and deep recesses (*alae*) used to display masks or busts of the family's ancestors. At the back, separable from the *atrium* by a curtain or wooden partition, was the main reception room, the *tablinum*. The second light-source, the peristyle, generally lay behind this. Often of great size, it was surrounded by further rooms, including open-fronted *exedrae* and banqueting-halls (*oeci*).

The first important characteristic to observe in this kind of house is its privacy. The ground floor at least was entirely inward-looking; apart from a few slit windows at a high level, its exterior walls presented a blind face to the surrounding world—as much to insure against burglary, one imagines, as to shut out the noise and bustle of the streets. Another characteristic is a tendency to axial planning. Even if it could not always be achieved in practice, the implicit ideal of the *domus* was a vista running from the front door through the centre of the *atrium* and the *tablinum* into the peristyle, often focusing on an architectural feature of some form at the rear. In the House of the Faun, a grand double-*atrium* survivor of Pompeii's palmiest days, larger even than the royal palace at Pergamum, the main vista through the western *atrium* culminated in the columnar *exedra* paved with the Alexander mosaic. In other Pompeian houses a more ostentatious later generation installed a brightly coloured mosaic fountain-niche at the back of the garden, strategically placed to catch the eye of callers at the street-door. A further notable feature of the house was its strong contrasts of light and shade.

In the bright Mediterranean summer the aesthetic effect of the vista would have been conditioned by the alternation of deep shadow and dazzling sunlight, and even in the darker days of winter the rhythm of light and shade would have been a potent visual factor.

This last point leads naturally to the consideration of lighting, heating, and related amenities. In summer the cool, lofty rooms and the shady garden porticoes of the *domus* provided welcome relief from the heat and glare; but in winter the same rooms could be uncomfortably cold and dark. Although the chill of mosaic and mortar pavements could doubtless be alleviated with the aid of woven rugs, there was no entirely satisfactory way of heating living-rooms and bedrooms in early-imperial times. The underfloor heating systems which were employed in bath-suites were rarely introduced for other kinds of room, except (later) in the colder climes of the northern provinces. Generally householders had to rely on charcoal braziers, a source of heat which would have been unpleasantly smoky, especially in those chambers which were less well ventilated. At the same time the rarity of window glass, not widely available before the first century AD, created a lighting problem, since openings created to admit light would let out the heat. This is one reason why the older parts of houses had few and small windows. By the time of Seneca the darkness of old-style bathrooms was a matter for comment, but even now the problem of lighting must have remained in many rooms, whether in baths or elsewhere, if the owner could not afford the luxury of window glass and was obliged to employ shutters or hangings to retain the heat. The candelabra and oil lamps used in antiquity would have provided, at best, an inefficient light and would have contributed to the fumes emitted by braziers. Under the circumstances it was often felt appropriate to decorate the walls of badly illuminated rooms with light colour schemes; but there are just as many examples where the heavy polychromy of the murals increased the gloom.

Generally speaking, however, amenities improved as time

went on. The increasing use of window glass led to a better lit and more efficiently heated style of housing; the gradual introduction of more durable and fire-resistant building materials, notably (from Augustan times onwards) brick-faced concrete, brought new standards of stability and safety; and the steady expansion of aqueduct schemes provided running water to cities which had previously relied on wells and rainwater cisterns. Even now, however, running water reached very few private houses. In Pompeii, while well-to-do proprietors such as the Vettii and D. Octavius Quartio could service elaborate garden fountains and water-plays which looked forward across the centuries to the aquatic showpieces of Renaissance Italy, the vast majority of householders, including even the family which lived in the imposing House of the Menander, had to use rainwater or fill their pitchers at the streetside fountains.

The improvements in amenities were accompanied by general changes in the style of urban housing. The *domus*, laid out chiefly on one floor, was prodigal of space and belonged primarily to those periods and those cities in which there was plenty of room for expansion. But right from the first it was not the only, or even the predominant, mode of dwelling. In second-century BC Pompeii, a remarkably prosperous town, there were innumerable small 'lower-class' houses and shops, many of which consisted of only a couple of rooms or a single room containing a mezzanine storey; and in contemporary Rome population pressures were already promoting the development of 'high-rise' apartment blocks. We have a fascinating report in Livy of an ox which, as early as 218, climbed to the third storey of a house near the Roman cattle-market, whence it fell to its death; and in 191 two oxen in another quarter of Rome went up the stairs right to the roof (they survived the climb but were immolated for their efforts). By the late first century BC the architectural writer Vitruvius was able to refer to tower blocks with fine views, and Augustus was obliged, for safety reasons, to limit their height to 70 feet. An echo of this development is discernible at Pompeii, where upper storeys were added piecemeal to many of the older houses, and new blocks such as the Forum Baths, built soon after 80 BC, were provided from the start with upstairs flats accessible directly from the street. By AD 79 Herculaneum had at least two new-style shop-and-apartment blocks, one of which has survived to a height of three storeys. Pressure on space and the growth of the small commercial classes also led to the break-up of the old mansions, many of which, like the Victorian houses of modern Britain, came to be divided into independent rented units.

The housing of a major commercial city of the high imperial age is best studied at Ostia, largely rebuilt according to new building standards during the second and early third centuries AD. Here, although some single-storey *domus* still survived and new kinds of courtyard houses, complete with resplendent marble veneer, were added at a later date, the characteristic type of accommodation was the *insula*, or apartment block, three, four, or five storeys high. Unlike the *domus*, this faced outwards, with large windows often opening on to shallow balconies (not always accessible, however, and designed more to shelter the windows beneath than to provide extra space for the tenants). Its great virtue was its flexibility, both in plan and, as a consequence, in the life-style that it offered. It could take the form of a long narrow block, one living-unit in depth; of a rather deeper block, with two sets of living-units arranged back to back; or, where a building plot was particularly deep or neighbouring buildings obstructed the light, of a four-sided block round a central court. Within these basic formulae the variations were legion. A favourite treatment of the street front, foreshadowing the architecture of medieval and Renaissance Italy, was a succession of barrel-vaulted shops interspersed with stairways leading straight from the street to the upper storeys. The ground floor of the *insula* might, alternatively, be divided into two or four more or less identical self-contained flats, entered either directly from the exterior or from an internal dividing corridor. Sometimes, as in the House of the Muses and the House of the Painted Vaults, the whole, or a large part, of the ground floor constituted a single living-unit. In such cases the occupant was perhaps also the owner of the block, and the other occupants his tenants; at the very least he was himself a superior tenant, able to afford space and amenities denied to his upstairs neighbours, many of whom may have had very small apartments and even single rooms.

We know less about the quality of life in the Ostian *insulae* than we do for the houses of Pompeii, because so few of the furnishings and fittings survive. Doubtless standards of comfort were a great deal higher than in late-Republican Rome; and doubtless Juvenal's accounts of tumbling tenements and the constant danger of incineration in the Rome of his own day were somewhat exaggerated. But conditions in these multiple dwellings could not have been ideal. Even if water could be piped to the ground floor, upstairs tenants would still have been obliged to draw water from the public fountains or cisterns. Very few flats would have had private lavatories: the cry of 'gardyloo' was perhaps as familiar in the streets of Ostia as it was in eighteenth-century Edinburgh. Moreover there was enough timber in the upper floors and internal fittings to make the risk of fire a real one, especially since no truly safe means of heating and cooking were available. Lighting also remained a problem, as at Pompeii, for those tenants who could not afford window glass; many windows were filled with barely translucent panes of selenite or simply had wooden shutters.

Country residences, like town dwellings, ranged over the whole gamut of possibilities, from simple huts and cottages through small working farms to grand villas in which the management of an estate, though generally an important factor, was strictly segregated from a luxurious quarter in which the owner could maintain a life-style appropriate to his taste and station. This last type is well represented in the archaeological record, both in the countryside devastated by the eruption of Vesuvius, and in other parts of Italy and the Empire. We also see it portrayed in Pompeian paintings and read about it in the letters of Cicero and Pliny. Generalizations are difficult, but recurrent features included peristyle gardens, grand colonnaded façades, and (on sloping ground) a podium which Vitruvius calls the *basis uillae*, often containing an underground corridor (*cryptoporticus*). In the grandest examples, including the Villa of the Papyri at Herculaneum and the recently excavated villa at Oplontis, west of Pompeii, both of which have been attractively ascribed to leading families of the Roman nobility, no check was imposed upon the spatial extent of the buildings. At the same time such villas, unlike the aristocratic town-houses, were outward-looking; their colonnaded façades and terraces addressed themselves to a landscape or overlooked a garden. In the coolness and shelter of the portico the owner could stroll and philosophize, like the Younger Pliny, about the delights of nature, far from the toils of the city. A favourite form, especially renowned in the Bay of Naples and reflected in numerous murals, was the maritime villa, built along the sea-front or even terraced out into the sea; Pliny, for example, could dine in his Laurentine villa with 'a view from the front and sides, as it were, of three different seas'. In vain did Horace inveigh against the villa-builders of fashionable Baiae, whose concrete piers seemed almost to remodel the coast-line.

Interior Decoration

Interior decoration was an essential ingredient of the Roman life-style and can hardly be considered apart from domestic architecture. Its strictly art-historical aspects are dealt with elsewhere (Chapter 16); here we must examine its function and its meaning to the householder.

At the most mundane level a fine mosaic pavement or a set of painted murals were designed to beautify a room. The finest decorations were generally reserved for the main dining- and reception-rooms, but other areas of the house which were likely to be seen by visitors—the *atrium*, the peristyle, the baths, certain bedrooms—could also receive special treatment. Only in the more prosperous houses, however, was the majority of rooms elaborately decorated. Even in Pompeii the painted walls which conform to the four well-known styles were outnumbered by those with simple striped and panelled schemes and by walls with plain plaster, and the mosaic pavements were concentrated in a few particularly opulent dwellings, while the majority of floors were of mortar with perhaps at the most a sprinkling of inset tesserae or marble fragments. In less prosperous cities or societies, for instance in certain parts of Roman Britain, the house- or villa-owner concentrated most of his resources upon adorning one room: the central dining-room of the Lullingstone villa, with its Bellerophon and Europa mosaics, is a case in point.

At a more ambitious level the proprietor used decorations to transform and enhance his environment. This is particularly true of the Pompeian styles of wall-painting, in which the imitation veneering of the First Style echoed the real veneers of Hellenistic palaces. The porphyry columns and exotic architecture of the Second Style also evoked the grandeur of a court, though probably transmitted through the medium of stage-painting, and the baroque extravagances of the Fourth Style may have owed something to the theatre but were probably more a form of escapism into a world of pure imagination. The perspectival forms of both styles also, of course, seemed to enlarge the physical space within a room; and in some instances, by offering a glimpse of sky above the painted architecture, or by opening a window through it on to a mythical world, the decoration seemed to break right through the bounds of the wall. The ultimate expression of this is provided by those paintings, such as the garden murals from Primaporta, which turned the room into an open-sided pavilion set in a magic forest. The aesthetic value of such paintings in rooms which were often cramped and badly lit is easily appreciated.

Another role of interior decoration was to turn parts of the house into picture-galleries (*pinacothecae*). In Hellenistic times, copies of well-known paintings were carried out in mosaic to embellish the central fields of pavements, and the same tradition continued in certain cities of the east, such as Syrian Antioch, through the imperial age. But in the Roman west these copies were incorporated as painted panels within wall-decorations. Well-off Pompeians, such as the brothers Vettii and the owner of the House of the Tragic Poet, collected reproductions of Greek old masters in much the same way as more recent generations have collected copies of the Laughing Cavalier or the Mona Lisa. This was one means whereby the *nouveaux riches* could make a display of their culture. Truly cultured householders, like the owners of the villa at Boscotrecase just north of Pompeii, preferred original paintings in which the stories of Alexandrian and Ovidian elegy and the bucolic world of Theocritus' *Idylls* could be evoked in an altogether more subtle and mysterious manner.

Whether there are deeper meanings to be discerned in ancient wall-decorations is a question which has recently roused controversy. The Swiss scholar Karl Schefold argues from the Pompeian evidence, not only that painters or their patrons chose subjects which were relevant to the type of room being decorated, but also that the subjects within a decoration were normally linked in a consistent programme embodying deeply-felt moral or religious ideas. Thus one decoration will present a hymn to the great deities of love and fertility, Aphrodite and Dionysus; another will contrast the exploits of a divinely favoured hero with the sufferings of an offender against the gods. Landscape paintings are invariably sacred, still lifes are offerings to the gods, and so forth. The same idea is explored by Mary Lee Thompson, though with a more pragmatic approach: for her most of the programmes are on a relatively superficial plane, dealing with a particular hero such as Achilles, a particular locale such as Thebes, and particular conceptual combinations such as love and water. There is doubtless some truth in all this, for a strong religious element appears in many Roman murals (compare the cult-objects and sacrificants lurking in the painted architecture), and in some cases a thematic link between balancing paintings is unmistakable. The left *ala* of the House of the Menander at Pompeii contains a Trojan cycle in which paintings of the wooden horse and of the death of Laocoon, both allusions to warnings unheeded by the Trojans, are combined, as in a Greek tragedy, with the ruinous sequel: Priam watching griefstricken while Menelaus seizes Helen and Ajax assaults Cassandra. That the Romans often looked for thematic associations is illustrated by a picture gallery described by Petronius, fictional but perhaps based on fact, in which the story of Ganymede is grouped with those of Hylas and Hyacinthus, all three illustrating the love of immortals for beautiful youths and the resulting 'apotheosis' of the loved ones. But to try to apply such rules universally, and above all to look for recondite religious and ethical interpretations, is to expect too grave and profound an outlook in the ancient householder, whereas Pompeian painting contains much that is clearly humorous and much that appeals directly to the senses. It also leads very quickly to inconsistencies: to fit his theories Schefold has to argue that Medea is now contrasted with Penelope as a paradigm of false love, now compared with her as a beatified heroine.

The other main art form found in private houses is sculpture. Here we must distinguish between the religious statuettes of the household shrine (the *Lares*, the *genius* of the paterfamilias, and the protecting deities of the household) and works which were more purely decorative or ostentatious. The latter can again be divided. On the one hand there were small figurines designed to be kept on shelves or sideboards in private parts of the house, for example the terracottas including a gladiator, a porter, Venus arranging her hair, and two slaves carrying a litter, all less than 16 cm. high, found in the family quarters of the House of M. Lucretius at Pompeii, or the even smaller bronze figurines (a seated philosopher, an old man milking a goat, and an ape brandishing arms) from the ruins of the upper storey of the House of the Marbles, also at Pompeii. On the other hand there were the statues, statuettes, and reliefs which were displayed in gardens and other open parts of the house. These raise the same programmatic questions as wall-paintings and merit closer attention.

In most cases domestic sculptural displays were somewhat arbitrarily compiled and arranged. The need to 'shop around' for available pieces presented a totally different situation from that involved in commissioning a mural decoration and naturally led to heterogeneous collections. The great and wealthy imported works from Greece, but not always with great discrimination, as we can judge from Cicero's requests to Atticus to supply him with sculptures for his villa at Tusculum: 'anything you consider suitable for the palaestra and gymnasium . . . reliefs to be set in the plaster of the *atriolum* and a couple of figured well-heads'. Apparently almost any pieces would do so long as they were Greek. Even the sculptures of Hadrian's Villa at Tivoli seem to have been employed in a rather haphazard way. The statues round the Canopus ('Egyptian pool') included a splendid crocodile and much other appropriately Egyptian or egyptianizing material, but there were also very different items, for example copies of Classical Greek wounded Amazons, figures of Hermes and Ares, a statue group showing Scylla and her victims, and replicas of the Erechtheum caryatids. Since Hadrian and his successors were presumably better able than most patrons to get what they wanted, this heterogeneous assortment could hardly have been dictated solely by market forces.

The private collection about whose arrangement we know most is that of the Villa of the Papyri at Herculaneum, from which no fewer than eighty-seven sculptures were recovered and all their find-spots recorded. The late-Republican or early-Augustan aristocrat who formed the collection, perhaps L. Calpurnius Piso Pontifex, the consul of 15 BC, was clearly a man of culture rather than of great artistic sensibility: his penchant for busts of Attic orators, Stoic and Epicurean philosophers, and early-Hellenistic dynasts evinces an interest in humanistic studies, but the artistic quality of the collection was variable, ranging from excellent copies of Greek masterpieces to second-rate pastiches and decorative hackwork. Such programmatic arrangements as can be discerned were superficial and not consistently carried through (despite the efforts of modern commentators to argue otherwise). For example, in the large peristyle two figures of runners, a statuette of the seated Hermes, and busts of various philosophers evoked the idea of a gymnasium, but interspersed with them were Hellenistic *condottieri*, animal figures, and drunken satyrs—strange bedfellows indeed. Hermes actually sat back to back with one of the inebriates. Indeed this latter grouping illustrates the point that compositional balance, well exemplified by the favourite Roman device of pairing statues in mirror image, was more important to the householder than thematic correspondence.

The average Pompeian householder of the years before 79 did not lay claim to the literary culture of Piso: he preferred to concentrate on decorative subjects. Admittedly he might display a portrait herm of an ancestor in his *atrium* as a kind of guarantee of a respectable pedigree, but the bulk of his collection consisted of Bacchic figures, *putti*, herms, and animals, with perhaps the odd decorative statuette of a divinity such as Venus, Apollo, or Diana thrown in for good measure. Some of the items were inherited or bought from older collections, where no doubt they had been used in different roles; many, especially the marbles, were churned out by contemporary local workshops. A large number of them were designed or adapted to serve as fountain-pourers, in which capacity they could be set along the margins of the *impluuium* in the *atrium*, between the columns of the peristyle, or actually in the garden, where they discharged their water into ponds or marble basins. A good example is the satyr squeezing water from a wine-skin down the steps of a *nymphaeum* in the House of M. Lucretius. In addition to figures in the round, many collectors had reliefs, whether set in walls, displayed on top of pillars, or hanging in the form of shields between the columns of porticoes. Whatever the theme or function of the individual works, the householder's chief goals were to accumulate as many exhibits as possible and to place them so as to be visible from certain crucial vantage-points: thus the garden statuary of M. Lucretius is disposed for the benefit of visitors in the *tablinum* and the adjacent dining-room. Bronzes in particular, being more expensive and more highly prized, were flaunted in prominent positions.

If we combine the Pompeian material with evidence from elsewhere, we get a reasonable idea of decorative furnishings in use in imperial times. Tables in both bronze and marble, round or rectangular, were regularly supported by elaborate legs compounded of lions' paws, volutes, griffins' foreparts, and the like. Small bronze tripod stands, complete with raised rims to prevent things from rolling off, had deers' legs or (less tastefully) legs formed by ithyphallic satyrs. Couches were mainly of wood, which with one or two exceptions has perished, leaving only the bronze fittings: elegant lathe-turned legs, headboard ornaments with cast appliqués in the form of busts or horses' heads, and railings with silver inlay. Sometimes such fittings were in other materials, such as silver, tortoise-shell, or ivory, and a couch with reliefs of bone has recently been partially restored with the aid of remnants in the Fitzwilliam Museum, Cambridge. Bronze lamp-standards came in many more or less ornate types, among which the simplest consisted of a slender fluted column resting on three animal-paws and surmounted by some form of calyx, while more complicated versions had four or more arms, either in the form of volutes or shaped like tree branches, from which lamps were suspended. An especially ornate example from the Villa of Diomedes at Pompeii had a platform at the base, decorated with a figurine of a satyr on a prancing panther. Household chairs and stools, which were mainly of wood, have not survived, but interesting representations of armchairs in basketwork are known from later imperial times. Also of wood were cupboards and cabinets: examples from Pompeii and Herculaneum reveal that they were usually simple affairs divided by shelves into compartments and closed at the front by twin doors; but occasionally an architectural touch was bestowed by the addition of a gabled top or of flanking colonnettes. Even the family strongbox, a stout chest of wood or iron (or both) kept in the *atrium*, could be decorated with bronze plaques carrying figural and vegetal ornament.

Gardens

Ornamental gardening was not invented by the Romans: shrubs and trees had been used by the Greeks to beautify temple precincts and *gymnasia*, and a late-Hellenistic landscaped park has recently been identified outside Rhodes. But it was only in the Roman period that pleasure gardens became a major facet of the arts of living.

The term used by the Elder Pliny for ornamental gardening is *opus topiarium*, whose derivation from the Greek word *topia* (landscapes) reveals both the Greek origins of the art and one of its main themes. The original aim of the gardener was, in fact, to create attractive natural settings: in a famous passage Pliny seems to list varieties of landscape gardens as 'groves, woods, hills, fish-pools, canals, rivers, coasts'. But the artificial element soon came to play a predominant role, and we find increasing evidence for the use of statuary and garden furniture, the introduction of formal layouts and the shaping of trees, and the combination of plants with water displays.

The association of statuary and landscape began with works such as the Victory of Samothrace, set on a ship in a rock-filled pool, and continued with the sculpture-grottoes of the Rhodian park, a theme later carried to extremes of grandiloquence by Rhodian artists working in the service of the Emperor Tiberius at Sperlonga and on Capri. But the combination of statues with foliage soon became equally fashionable. When the word *topiaria* first appears in Latin literature, in a letter of Cicero dated to 54 BC, it is in connection with the growing of ornamental ivy as a backdrop to Greek statuary in one of his brother's villas at Arpinum. Such effects were doubtless employed by many of Cicero's illustrious contemporaries in the parks which they created in the area of Rome itself and round their luxury villas in the country; it was for Italian garden settings that the sculptured marble bowls and candelabra produced in Neo-Attic workshops were primarily designed.

Formal planning and topiary in the modern sense probably began in the time of Augustus. This is when, according to Pliny, one C. Matius invented *nemora tonsilia* ('barbered groves'). As the desire to impose formal shapes almost certainly went hand in hand with the desire to create formal plans, we can assume that the same period saw the first symmetrically planned gardens, especially as the improvements in the water-supply of Rome and other parts of Italy undertaken by Agrippa and his successors would have favoured the cultivation of low, ornamental plants. The first formal gardens in wall-painting belong to the first half of the first century AD, laid out in plots framed by hedges or trellis fences: an example in the *tablinum* of the House of M. Lucretius Fronto at Pompeii shows an enclosed flower-bed on either side of a focal tree, reflecting the symmetry of the villa-façade which overlooks it. Little archaeological evidence of formal gardens is known, though one fine specimen has been reconstructed in the villa at Fishbourne, with a central path bordered by hedges fashioned into a series of alternating rectangular and semicircular recesses. But that such gardens existed on a grander scale in Rome and its surroundings is demonstrated by examples represented on the Severan marble plan of the city (for example, in Vespasian's Temple of Peace) and by parts of a plaque now in Urbino preserving the plan of a funerary park. The further development of topiary, as distinct from formal plans, apparently knew no bounds. By the time that the *Natural History* was published Pliny could report not only that cypresses were clipped to form hedges but also that they were shaped into elaborate tableaux portraying 'hunt scenes, fleets of ships, and other images'; and in his nephew's villa at Tifernum in Tuscany there were box trees cut into the shapes of wild animals and into numerous other forms, including the letters of Pliny's and his gardeners' names. It was the description of the gardens at Tifernum that inspired the box parterres and labyrinths of the sixteenth and seventeenth centuries.

The same improvements in water-supply which favoured
diversification in types of planting also ushered in the age of the
garden fountain. Already in the wall-paintings from Boscoreale,
dated around 40–30 BC, we see a depiction of a piano-shaped

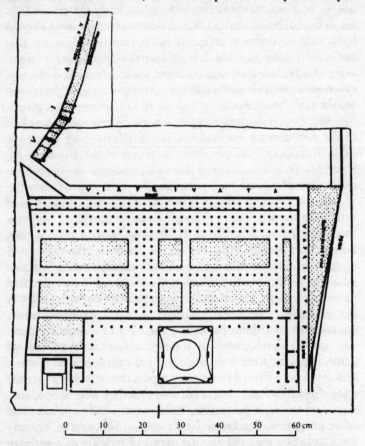

PLAN OF A FUNERARY GARDEN IN ROME: engraving on marble (third or
fourth century AD). The actual mausoleum, evidently a three-storeyed affair with
a square podium supporting a concave-sided structure crowned by a small rotunda, is shown at the bottom; behind it lies the garden, a formal arrangement
of lines of trees (indicated by small circles) and rectangular parterres.

marble fountain at the mouth of a vine-draped grotto; while Propertius, writing in the 20s, reveals that a fountain decorated with a sleeping Silenus played among the plane trees of Pompey's porticoes in Rome. The importance of water displays in Pompeian house-gardens has already been mentioned. In addition to statuettes pouring water into basins, many peristyles enclosed large ornamental pools fed by jets of water or fountain-niches at the rear, while other gardens, foreshadowing a vogue of the third and fourth centuries AD, had whole walls enlivened by a façade of niches and pavilions (*aediculae*) from which water flowed. Two large gardens in the east of the city, those of D. Octavius Quartio and Julia Felix, contained central canals with bridges at intervals, sculptures along the edges, and open pergolas bestriding them. On either side ran pathways overhung by climbing plants. A generation later the Younger Pliny took great pride in a fountain which played within a vine-arbour in his Tuscan villa and whose marble basin he and his guests used as a kind of supper table, resting larger dishes on the rim and allowing small dishes of hors d'oeuvres to float in the water.

The trees and plants cultivated in ornamental gardens put the accent on greenery rather than floral displays. Besides the box and cypress trees favoured by topiarists, the ancient sources mention plane trees, laurel, myrtle, hound's tongue, acanthus, maidenhair, butcher's broom (whose evergreen foliage, we are told, was sometimes used in wreaths to make up for a lack of flowers), and a shrub called 'Jupiter's beard' which had silvery leaves and could be trimmed into a round shape. Our picture is supplemented by the shrubberies represented in garden paintings; among the items identified by modern botanists are such flowering plants as poppies, oleanders, lilies, and viburnum. Roses, one of the few flowers attested in Pliny's garden at Tifernum, are shown next to fountain-basins in a mural in the House of the Floral Chambers at Pompeii.

An idea of the overall appearance of small private gardens in the early Imperial age is obtainable at Pompeii, where the recent work of Wilhelmina Jashemski, involving excavation, the study of carbonized plant-material, and pollen analysis, has opened a whole new perspective on the subject. A surprisingly large proportion of peristyle-gardens has turned out to contain fruit- and nut-trees, not to mention vines, all grown for food rather than for fancy; but purely ornamental gardens laid out to formal designs certainly existed in the better appointed houses. The more pretentious examples, combining shrubs, fountains, decorative statuettes, and often frescoes on the enclosing walls, reflect the aspiration of the wealthy middle class to import the villa life of Roman aristocrats into their urban homes. Thus the huge wall-paintings of wild animals which overlook many late-Pompeian gardens evoke the game- or safari-parks (*paradeisoi*) of the nobility, a theme which is also echoed by statuettes of dogs attacking wild boar amid the actual plants and fountains. Some details, such as marble ducks and ibises at the waterside, a bronze fisherman dangling his rod in a fountain, and a sleeping marble pixie amazingly akin to a modern garden gnome, are almost kitsch. The palm for vulgarity should perhaps be awarded to L. Ceius Secundus for commissioning a painting of a nymph who appears to empty her bowl of water into a real gutter in the pavement.

Eating and Drinking

Closely linked with the garden were the delights of dining. The U-shaped masonry dining areas (*triclinia*) found in Pompeian gardens, often accompanied by clam or snail shells and the bones of meat-animals, confirm that the modern Mediterranean practice of eating out of doors on hot summer evenings goes back to antiquity. Sheltered by an awning or by a vine-arbour and cushioned by mattresses and pillows, the diners would recline on their elbows in the Greek manner, picking titbits from a central table or, like Pliny's guests, from floating dishes in the form of little boats and water-birds; as night drew on, lamps would be lit in surrounding candelabra, some of them, as in the House of the Ephebe, suspended from the hands of bronze statues.

The banquets described by Martial, Pliny, Petronius, and others should not mislead us; the diet of the vast mass of the people was always frugal, and even the great men of affairs ate little before evening. But when occasion demanded meals could be splendid and cooking carried to the realms of fine art. A cookery book ascribed to the early-imperial gastronome M. Gavius Apicius gives some fascinating glimpses of Roman haute cuisine: for example, 'Sucking pig à la Frontinus: fillet, brown, and dress; put in a casserole of fish-sauce and wine, wrap in a bouquet of leeks and dill, pour off the juice when half-cooked. When cooked, remove and dry, sprinkle with pepper and serve.' Apicius was famous for his sauces and dressings, and gave his name to various cakes; he is also said by Pliny to have invented dishes of flamingos' tongues and mullets' livers, and to have pioneered a form of pâté de foie gras. It was one of the arts of the Roman chef to disguise dishes so that no one could divine their ingredients. This was taken to extremes at the feast described by Petronius, where a dish of pork was dressed up by Trimalchio's cook to look like a fattened goose garnished with fish and different kinds of birds ('If you want it, he'll make you a fish out of a sow's womb, a wood-pigeon out of bacon, and a turtle-dove out of a ham', brags the host), and the guests were treated to a whole sequence of unnerving surprises: peahens' eggs containing beccaficos rolled in spiced egg-yolk, a wild boar containing live thrushes, a pig full of sausages and black puddings, cakes and fruit filled with liquid saffron, thrushes made of pastry and stuffed with raisins and nuts, quinces decorated with thorns to look like sea-urchins. Each dish emerged in artistic form or with some histrionic display; the wild boar, for example, arrived with an escort of hunting dogs, and a boiled calf was sliced with a sword by a slave impersonating the frenzied Ajax. Such excesses, though inflated by the writer's fertile imagination, were certainly based upon the pageantry of real banquets. So too were some of the entertainments devised for Trimalchio's guests. The gold hoop laden with gifts which was let down from the ceiling recalls the revolving dome of Nero's Golden House which showered flowers on the diners below. The musicians, singers, acrobats, and dancing girls echo the performances provided at banquets such as the one that seduced a potential guest of Pliny: invited to a homely supper with a poetry recitation and a performance on the lyre, this philistine preferred the gourmet dishes and Spanish dancing-girls of another host.

The delights of more modest dinner-tables are celebrated by the succulent fruits, game-birds, and sea foods represented in Pompeian still-life paintings. These *xenia* ('guest-gifts'), named, according to Vitruvius, after the provisions Greek hosts supplied to visitors on self-catering holidays, call to mind menus described by Martial and Juvenal. Martial, for instance, offers a dinner in which the hors d'oeuvres are listed as mallows, lettuces, leeks, mint, rocket, sliced eggs and anchovies, and sows' udders in tunny sauce; the main course was a kid and cutlets with haricot beans and tender green-sprouts, with the addition of a chicken and the residue of a ham which had already served three suppers; and the dessert consisted of ripe fruit and a vintage Nomentan wine. Wine was, of course, the essential concomitant of good eating, and no meal was complete without a jar of a fine vintage—preferably the 'immortal Falernian', the Château Lafite of Roman Italy.

To serve a sumptuous repast the host needed the best silver and tableware (see Plate 6). Discoveries of silver hoards hidden by their owners in Pompeii and nearby Boscoreale at the time of the eruption of Vesuvius reveal both the quality of the plate in domestic use during the early imperial period and also the zeal with which it was prized and protected. The superb beakers, cups, bowls, and dishes decorated with repoussé reliefs of plant arabesques or mythological scenes, together with the simpler, but still elegant, spoons and ladles, lend significance to Petronius' gibes at the extravagance and tastelessness of his millionaire freedman Trimalchio, who used a chamber-pot of silver and gave orders for a silver dish which had been dropped during his banquet to be swept away like broken pottery. The quality of silverware was maintained during the later Empire. It is to this period that we must ascribe such masterpieces as the octagonal dish from Kaiseraugst in Switzerland, adorned with scenes from the life of Achilles.

If an owner could not afford silverware, the next-best thing was bronze or glass. Both these materials were in much wider use in the home than is generally realized, since the process of recycling has militated against the survival of specimens in domestic contexts. The excavations at Pompeii and Herculaneum have again done much to set the record straight; among the finds are numerous graceful bronze jugs and wine-jars with appliqué reliefs at the base of the handles, and a rich, but barely known, series of glass vessels of all types: bottles, phials, cups, beakers, plates, jugs, and the like, translucent or coloured, blown or cast, plain or decorated. Deluxe items of glassware are the so-called 'cameo-glass' vessels, of which the most famous are the Blue Vase from Pompeii and the mysterious Portland Vase, decorated with figures in white relief on a blue-black ground. During the second, third, and fourth centuries the use of glass became more widespread, largely replacing bronze-ware (the snobbish Trimalchio makes excuses for using glass-ware rather than antique Corinthian bronze), and the later imperial period saw the production of further expensive lines, such as various kinds of figured cut glass and the cage-cups with openwork decoration manufactured probably in Italy and the Rhineland.

Lack of space precludes a full examination of the domestic equipment of Roman times. Fine pottery, notably the red-gloss ware from Arretium (Arezzo) and (later) Gaul, imitated the embossed reliefs and even some of the subjects of figured metal-ware; but the careful moulded decoration of the first and second centuries tended to die away in many areas, to be replaced by simpler techniques including rouletting and relief motifs in applied clay. By the fourth century pottery was to a large extent overtaken by glass as the usual form of fine tableware. Other artistic products in domestic use included carved bone or ivory handles for knives and the ubiquitous bronze or terracotta lamps, with their simple figure-reliefs and distinctive wick-holding nozzles. Less artistic, but unambiguously geared to the pleasures of the table, was the extraordinary series of objects known as *gliraria*—large terracotta jars used to rear dormice, a delicacy which particularly appealed to the Roman palate. Surviving examples from Pompeii are provided with regular holes to admit air and with a spiral ramp round the interior wall to enable the animals to reach a pair of feeding trays near the rim.

Dress and Personal Effects

Dress is the aspect of the arts of living about which we are perhaps least well informed. We know from Roman writers that the ceremonial toga, a semicircular white woollen wrap between 5 and 6 m. in diameter, had to be donned with great art and no little difficulty, a circumstance which encouraged many men to view with relief those 'off-duty' occasions when they could wear the simple *tunica*. Portrait statues give us some idea of what the toga looked like, with its distinctive curving hem; and from the same source we get representations of the long dress, or *stola*, of the Roman matron. Other works of art illustrate further garments, such as the *pallium*, a version of the heavy Greek cloak; the *lacerna*, a short cape fastened at the neck with a brooch; and the *paenula*, a kind of hooded poncho. To the late-imperial period belong depictions of the long-sleeved tunic or dalmatic. But for all this comparative wealth of illustrative material there is little to convey the rich colours and embroideries, still less the fine fabrics (muslins and silks), worn especially by society ladies. The fragments of surviving textiles from Egypt, though instructive on the range of possible weaves, patterns, and colours, are mostly late in date (fourth or fifth centuries), while the pieces from other parts of the Roman world are rarely well preserved or of any artistic pretensions. Nor is there much information in the Latin authors beyond vague indications of cut or colour, for example the green tunic and red belt of Trimalchio's flunkey, the red tunic, yellow belt, and gilded slippers of his wife, and the close-fitting *lacerna* and well-tailored red, green, and purple cloaks given by Statius' friend Atedius Melior to his young favourite Glaucias.

We may know little of fine clothing, but fashionable hairstyles are well known from the sculptured portraits of Emperors and their womenfolk. These varied considerably over the years. In the first century the studied disorder of Augustus' hair gave way to the carefully styled waves and sideburns of Nero; and in the second century Trajan's 'Beatle' cut was replaced by the neat Hellenic beard and carefully cultivated coiffure of Hadrian, a fashion carried to extremes in the full beards and tightly crisped locks of his Antonine successors. The imperial ladies were not surprisingly even more fashion-conscious. Although Livia and the Julio-Claudian princesses favoured classicizing styles with gently waving hair running from a central parting to loose ringlets over the ears and a chignon at the nape of the neck, the *grandes dames* of Flavian and Trajanic times piled up elaborate edifices of spiral curls or interwoven plaits on wire frames. In the most extravagant examples these scaffoldings, like the *onkoi* of heroines in Greek tragedy, doubled the height of the head, and it must have been a great relief to all and sundry when the trend-setters of the second century reverted to simpler styles reminiscent of the Julio-Claudian period, albeit with a more deliberate crimping of the waves.

Beautification of the female did not, of course, stop with the hair. References in the Latin poets to tooth polish, painted cheeks, pencilled eyebrows, and eye-shadow have a familiar ring; and the wearing of excessive jewellery was a practice which legislators had long since given up trying to curb, though moralists still condemned it. Pliny rails against women who wore pearls on their fingers, on their ear-rings, and on their slippers, and reports with disapproval how Caligula's first Empress, Lollia Paulina, turned up to a feast wearing emeralds and pearls on her head, hair, ears, neck, and fingers. Similarly in Petronius' novel it is a mark of Trimalchio's lack of decorum that he flaunts his wife's gold jewellery—anklets, bracelets, and a gold hairnet. 'She must have six and a half pounds weight on her', he declares.

Numerous items of personal gold jewellery have survived. At Pompeii some of the objects, such as rings and bracelets in the form of snakes, continue the Hellenistic tradition, but new types also appear—ear-rings decorated with pendant clubs, hemispheres, or clusters of plasmas, and necklaces with crescent or wheel-shaped pendants. Generally speaking the use of inset stones remained popular in Roman times, but in place of a single species we find a profusion of colours and materials combined, for example sapphires, garnets, and crystals alternating in a single necklace. At the same time the fine techniques of filigree and granulation declined in favour, giving way to plain surfaces of gold or to a new openwork (*interrasile*) style of ornament. Finger rings were widely worn, both by women, as tokens of engagement, and by men, as signets. A popular device was an engraved portrait of the Emperor, and imperial gold coins or medallions were frequently set as bezels in rings; they also appeared as pendants on necklaces and as ornaments on brooches. Among the various types of brooches the most successful was the crossbow, widely worn in the fourth century. All this jewellery retains the technical quality of its Greek forerunners, but there is a certain reduction in artistic sensitivity in favour of bolder and showier effects.

This last comment, applicable also to other personal ornaments and effects, from combs and hairpins to toilet-boxes and mirrors, sums up what is a general characteristic of many of the arts of living discussed above. There is in them a certain lack of restraint, even a certain vulgarity—a love of immediate and over-elaborate effects which places imperial taste in the same bracket as that of the Victorian period. Like Victorian taste, it was the product of the fruits of world empire, for example of the free availabilty of exotic materials and commodities, from precious stones and metals to coloured marbles, tropical beasts, and (in the case of nineteenth-century England) American and oriental timbers. And, like Victorian taste, it was the prelude to an age of chaos and uncertainty, an age in which life and art suffered an almost total divorce.

Further Reading

For the ancient authors who give us information on this subject (Cicero in his letters, Petronius, Statius, Ovid, Martial, Juvenal, the Younger Pliny) see the translations etc. cited in the bibliographies of Chapters 4, 8, 11, and 12.

Pompeii and Herculaneum. The best book is T. Kraus and L. von Matt, *Pompeii and Herculaneum: the Living Cities of the Dead* (New York, 1975). Also valuable, though difficult to obtain, are the various editions of the exhibition catalogue *Pompeii 79* (London, 1976; Boston, 1978) edited by J. B. Ward-Perkins and A. Claridge. Brief popular surveys are M. Grant, *Cities of Vesuvius: Pompeii and Herculaneum* (London, 1971); A. De Franciscis, *The Buried Cities: Pompeii and Herculaneum* (London, 1978); R. Seaford, *Pompeii* (London, 1978); and J. J. Deiss, *Herculaneum: A City Returns to the Sun* (London, 1968). Still an important synopsis, though excluding the twentieth-century discoveries, is A. Mau, *Pompeii, its Life and Art* (transl. F. W. Kelsey, 2nd edn., New York, 1902).

Ostia. R. Meiggs, *Roman Ostia*, 2nd edn. (Oxford, 1973) includes much relevant material on housing. See further A. Boethius, *The Golden House of Nero* (Ann Arbor, 1955).

Many of the aspects covered in the present chapter are dealt with in the stimulating, but somewhat too gloomy, survey of J. Carcopino, *Daily Life in Ancient Rome* (New Haven, 1940). On domestic architecture the only general book is A. G. McKay, *Houses, Villas and Palaces in the Roman World* (London, 1975), which is confused and frequently at fault; much better are the relevant sections in J. B. Ward-Perkins, *Roman Imperial Architecture* (Harmondsworth, 1981). On gardens the fundamental work is now W. F. Jashemski, *The Gardens of Pompeii, Herculaneum and the Villas Destroyed by Vesuvius* (New York, 1979).

Decorative and luxury arts. See the general works cited in the bibliography of Chapter 16, especially M. Henig (ed.), *A Handbook of Roman Art* (Oxford, 1983). On specific themes the following are all useful studies: R. J. Charleston, *Roman Pottery* (London, 1955); R. A. Higgins, *Greek and Roman Jewellery* (London, 1966); G. M. A. Richter, *The Furniture of the Greeks, Etruscans and Romans* (London, 1966); D. E. Strong, *Greek and Roman Gold and Silver Plate* (London, 1966). The techniques of artists and craftsmen are examined in D. Strong and D. Brown (eds.), *Roman Crafts* (London, 1976).

15

Roman Life and Society

JOHN MATTHEWS

Distances and Diversity

In the year AD 333 a Christian pilgrim set out from his home city of Bordeaux for the Holy Land. Measuring the early stages of his journey by the 'leagues' still at this late date in use in south-western Gaul, he travelled by land across the Alps and north Italy, through the Balkans to Constantinople, and from there through Anatolia and Syria until, 170 days and 3,300 Roman miles (about 3,100 modern miles) after his departure, he came to Jerusalem. The pilgrim's journey is not merely testimony to the long-distance travel possible, and frequently undertaken, in all periods of the Roman Empire; it is also a challenge to the imagination. How did the pilgrim react to the different landscapes through which he travelled, the languages he heard spoken, the cities, towns, and way-stations in which he lodged as he passed from Bordeaux, penetrated by the Atlantic tides, to the edge of the Judaean wilderness? The modern historian, influenced perhaps by the Mediterranean perspective of his ancient informants and by his own knowledge of the future, tends to see the history of the Roman Empire in terms of the relationship between East and West, Greek and Latin; but a journey not much shorter than that of the Bordeaux pilgrim could be made from north to south, beginning at the militarized frontier region of Hadrian's Wall and passing through Celtic

Britain and Gaul through Romanized north Africa to the edge of the Sahara. Such a journey might take in the capital of the Empire and, in southern Italy and Sicily, enclaves of Greek speech in the west surviving from the colonial period. The traveller would find diversities of dress no less striking than those of climate and geography, from the wool-clad, hooded countrymen of the cool northern provinces, as we see them on grave reliefs and wall-paintings, to the bright oriental silks of a family from Edessa, shown with its Syriac names on a mosaic pavement from that city. The jurist Ulpian pronounced that it did not matter in what language certain legal documents were framed, citing Punic and Celtic as examples of languages that might be used, and in another he considered the legal status of statements made in Punic or Syriac 'or any other language' in reply to questions asked in Latin. If modern scholars are hesitant as to the actual extent of the franchise of Celtic and Punic by the time of these pronouncements in the early third century, no such uncertainty attends Syriac (better called Aramaic), a language spoken in its various dialects by Levantine easterners for centuries before its rise to become a great literary language. The same is true of Egyptian demotic, a spoken language for long before it acquired a script and, as Coptic, became a language of the written word. Celtic leaves no indigenous literature from ancient (as opposed to medieval) times, nor at any time does the language which modern scholars sometimes, though misleadingly, call 'Berber'—an indigenous African language commemorated on hundreds of inscriptions from one end of Roman north Africa to the other, and by a distinctive nomenclature attested as late as the fourth century.

A single city could present an extraordinary cultural diversity between the town and the surrounding country, and even within the town itself. Paul and Barnabas, performing a cure at Lystra in Lycaonia (Asia Minor), were hailed as Zeus and Hermes by the local people shouting 'in the Lycaonian language' (Acts 14:8 ff.). The priest of Zeus was all for making a sacrifice, as he brought oxen and garlands to the gates of the town from his temple outside the walls, but was dissuaded, and the evangelists' visit was terminated when hostile Jews from the cities of Pisidian Antioch and Iconium provoked the evidently volatile crowd into pelting them with stones. Despite this misadventure, the journeys of St Paul generally show him exploiting the modest social prestige of a man who had inherited the Roman citizenship from his father in the days when, as Tacitus remarked of a Gallic Roman citizen of the same period, that honour was given only rarely and in recognition of merit. A Jew from Tarsus, he nó doubt belonged at Jerusalem to that community of Jews from Greek cities who stirred up hostility to Stephen (Acts 6: 9 ff.). Then, after his conversion and decision to turn to the Gentiles— that is, to the non-Jewish Greek communities of the East—he travelled from city to city, attracted particularly to centres where Greek culture, philosophical learning, and Roman officials were to be found; finally using his status as a citizen to appeal to the Roman Emperor, he went to Rome and for a time lived there, among many thousands of Graeco-Orientals who had settled there before him. Jesus of Nazareth, in contrast with this picture of physical and cultural mobility, pursued his mission in the villages and townships of local communities, eventually meeting his death during his single known visit to Jerusalem as an adult, exchanged by an indifferent Pilate for a popular bandit chief and executed by a penalty reserved for slaves, brigands, and aliens of the lowest social status. The contrast between the social milieux of Acts and of the Gospels leaps to the eye at every turn.

It was precisely the achievement of the Roman Empire to have assimilated in one political and administrative system the immense diversities of the Mediterranean, and much of the northern European, worlds. The Bordeaux pilgrim undertook his journey to the Holy Land to see for himself the historical location of a religion that was within a few years of the conversion of Constantine (AD 312) to provide a coherent ideology for the entire Roman Empire. His near-contemporary, Eusebius of Caesarea, saw in the *pax Augusta* the providential dispensation of God to facilitate the expansion of Christianity through the Roman world.

For the power of the Romans [he wrote] came to its zenith at precisely the moment of Jesus' unexpected sojourn among men, at the time when Augustus first acquired power over all nations, defeating Cleopatra and putting an end to the succession of the Ptolemies. . . . From then also the Jewish nation has been subject to the Romans, that of the Syrians likewise, the Cappadocians and Macedonians, Bithynians and Greeks; to put it briefly, all the nations which now fall under the Roman Empire. (*Demonstratio Evangelica* 3. 7. 30 ff.)

With what difficulty, remarked Eusebius, would the disciples otherwise have travelled to foreign lands, 'the various nations being at war with one another, their diversities of government preventing relations between them'.

Eusebius' conception, for all its grandeur, fails even to mention the western and northern regions of the Roman Empire. It is not just that, by his time, the Empire was divided into largely self-contained administrative and political units. The reserved attitude of Greeks towards the West, the Latin language, and its literature, though modified when, in the fourth century, a Latin-speaking imperial court governed from Constantinople, is a fundamental aspect of ancient cultural history. Not that they otherwise allowed themselves to be inhibited, for in the republican and early-imperial age the intellectual and human current from east to west massively exceeded that in the reverse direction. In the three centuries before Eusebius' time, Greeks by the myriad had gone to the west to seek their fortune as artists, writers, teachers, and exponents of the other diverse skills mentioned by Juvenal: 'grammarian, orator, geometer, painter, wrestling-master, prophet, tightrope walker, medical man, wizard—he can do anything, your penniless Greek . . .' (*Satires* 3. 76–8). It was of course precisely his 'penniless' state that the humble Greek wished to remedy in going to Rome, and he had many examples, at the highest levels of distinction, to spur him on; Tiberius' astrologer, the famous mathematician Thrasyllus, Claudius' doctor Xenophon of Cos and his librarian Ti. Claudius Balbillus of Alexandria, not to mention the cohorts of literary men and scientists found at Rome under Augustus. In these professions, as Virgil had conceded in a famous passage (*Aeneid* 6.847 ff.), Greeks were allowed the supremacy.

Juvenal's attitude to Greeks is usually linked with his notorious allusion to the Orontes pouring into the Tiber, bringing its hordes of Greco-Syrian rhetoricians, musicians, religious fanatics, and prostitutes, but he goes on in later lines to mention also towns and islands of old Greece and Asia Minor, his examples (Sicyon, Amydon, Andros, Samos, Tralles, Alabanda) being chosen, no doubt, for their adaptability to hexameter verse and their ability to suggest the sound of Greek speech, but truly identifying the ancient homelands and colonial area as well as the Hellenized Orient as the origins of the Greeks who made their presence felt in imperial Rome. From the greater cities of Asia Minor, notably metropolitan centres such as Ephesus, Sardis, and Mytilene, had come ambitious dynasts (hardly 'penniless' Greeks) of the first and second centuries, to hold senatorial office, the consulship and provincial governorships (thereby refuting the second part of Virgil's prophecy, reserving for Romans the arts of government and administration). The historian Cassius Dio came from Nicaea in Bithynia. The son of a senator who had himself become consul and governed the province of Lycia-Pamphylia, Dio was twice consul and in the later 220s, as an old man, rather surprisingly made governor of Pannonia, a Danubian military province for whose inhabitants and culture he had little understanding or sympathy. A barbarous race, he thought them, their life enhanced by no liberal arts or any of the things that make an honourable life worth while. They produced only a little poor wine, drank beer, and lived in extreme cold. Dio wrote this (he claims) from personal observation of conditions among them, having been their governor, but his attitude is in reality as prejudiced as that of Juvenal towards Greeks, and with as little excuse. It betrays the depth of a Mediterranean man's, and a Greek civilian's, incomprehension of those non-Mediterranean military provinces of the Empire which, as events would quickly show, were crucial to its survival.

The limits to the cultural unity achieved, or attempted, by

the Roman government in its diverse regions and between its social classes, were then palpable—no less so, perhaps, than those between the Empire at its fringes and the barbarian world beyond; for the frontiers, generally based on rivers, which promote cultural exchange, rather than on mountain ranges, which prevent it, were far from impervious to the influence of foreign cultures. Yet the degree of uniformity of language and culture achieved within the empire, and the physical resources which made this uniformity possible, were extraordinarily impressive. Tacitus wrote of the Roman Empire as encircled by rivers and seas, every part—armies, provinces, navies—joined together as one system, and he was right. It was a rhetorical theme, sustained to the end of the Roman Empire, that Rome the city (*urbs*) had made the world (*orbis*) its own; conversely, that in Rome the city the entire world possessed a symbol of its identity. A commonplace sentiment perhaps, but a real one, and one with practical (if sometimes unexpected) consequences. It was not permissible, for example, for a man exiled from his own city to reside in Rome, for this was the 'common homeland' of all citizens. It is conventional to point to the sheer distances that were involved in travel between provinces, and between Rome and the frontiers, to the constant dangers of sea journeys and the inevitable slowness (given the nature of the available technology) of transport by land. But this is a relative matter; journeys like that of the Bordeaux pilgrim were undertaken, made possible by roads driven through provinces, over passes, across wide rivers. The bridge built by Trajan across the Danube at Drobeta (see Plate 13) was dismantled by Hadrian to prevent easy access to the Empire for hostile intruders; its piles were left in place and seemed to Dio, who had seen them, to show that there was nothing that could not be accomplished by human ingenuity. Its designer, Apollodorus of Damascus (below, pp. 436 f.) who was responsible also for the Forum of Trajan, with its column and library, was an architect of genius who would have been perfectly at ease in the company of Leonardo or Brunelleschi. He was certainly aware of his own abilities;

indeed. his contemptuous opinion of the architectural efforts of
Hadrian, a gifted amateur, was believed to have led to his
exile and execution by that jealous man when he became
Emperor.

The roads built by the Romans, originally for military purposes but in the nature of things quickly acquiring economic
uses, linked together distant regions by direct routes that were
not matched until modern times, for it is not every society that
has a frequent use for long-distance travel. Aerial views of the
Roman roads of Britain often show vividly the contrast between their direct, purposeful routes, professionally surveyed
for long-distance communications, and the local lanes and field-
boundaries of medieval and early modern England which adjoin
them, betraying the lines of an altogether more local economy.
The maintenance of the roads, once built, fell as a corvée on the
local communities through whose territories they passed, and
these communities naturally undertook the construction of sub-
sidiary roads, way-stations, and bridges. Of the latter, the most
'stupendous' (Gibbon's word), and certainly from a historical
point of view one of the most interesting, is the bridge over the
river Tagus at Alcantara in western Spain, standing high over
the river to accommodate winter spate and built, as an inscription shows, by the co-operative efforts of eleven Lusitanian
communities. The name of its builder, C. Julius Lacer, appears
in another inscription attached to the shrine of Trajan at the
bridge; his achievement, he there declared with a totally justified
pride, would 'last for ever through the ages'.

Along the roads of the Empire and across the pacified seas,
the Emperor sent his emissaries, confident that, whatever diversities of culture and language they traversed, they would
be understood by those to whom they were sent. In turn, and
perhaps still more to the point, provincial communities could
dispatch envoys to the Roman government with a similar confidence that, within the normal limits of human will and energy
and with only a small allowance for misadventure, they would
reach their destination; knowing too that within the mode of

communication established by Greco-Roman culture and maintained by the educated élite, their petitions would be understood. Such embassies, undertaken by leading citizens on behalf of their communities, are among the best-attested civic functions of Roman society. They reveal vividly the sheer physical movement required of subject as well as of Emperor in the administration of the Empire and show how this too was, from the point of view of the communities themselves, an expression of their social structure; for the ambassadors, filling their role as a social duty and deploying in its service the classical education which marked them out as members of the élite of their cities, returned (if successful) as the benefactors and patrons of their cities, leaving an enhanced prestige for their sons to inherit and, in their turn, surpass.

As all this implies, the comprehension of the Roman Empire as a rational social organization involves a marked simplification of its actual nature—a simplification in which the Emperors themselves and the leaders of local communities concurred, for it reinforced their power over outsiders and the less favoured classes. Celtic might still be spoken in Gaul and Britain, Aramaic in the Levant, demotic in Egypt, Libyan in large areas of north Africa, and who knows what in the remoter parts of Asia Minor; but all could be reached in one of two major languages. However diverse the physical nature of the communities of the Empire, they could be defined in terms of one civic status or another (*colonia, municipium, uicus, castellum*) and their inhabitants' status described in terms of Roman law, even if the actual law to which they were subject in minor matters was based on local practice and custom, administered by local magistrates. On major matters and before the Roman governor, no such concessions were envisaged. Pliny the Younger, encountering Christians in a town of Pontus, consulted Trajan on certain matters of legal procedure and social status, and on the question of anonymous denunciations posted in public places. In cases of admitted Christians of low social status, he had no hesitation in ordering immediate execution and was apparently prepared to treat 'pertinacious obstinacy' as a punishable offence. Pliny noted to Trajan that before his intervention the 'contagion' of Christianity had attacked not only the cities, but also the villages and the countryside of the province (it is the only reference to the countryside in his whole correspondence from Bithynia-Pontus); now, however, the temples were full of pious worshippers and sacrificial meat was again on sale in the markets. One wonders for how long *that* revival lasted, once Pliny had departed.

Town and Country

It is a natural instinct, encouraged somewhat by our sources, the products of city men, to see the Roman Empire as a vast confederation of city-states. If there is an over-simplification here it relates to the degree of uniformity to be found in the cities and in their economic functions, and in the different rates at which cities in fact developed. Tacitus in one passage shows himself aware of a process of urbanization which had in his own day become established in Numidia but had not yet begun in the time of Tiberius. The process is documented for just that region by the archaeology and epigraphy of cities such as Madaurus, Cuicul (Djemila), Milevis, and Sitifis, native settlements which progressed from municipal to colonial status at the turn of the first and second centuries. In Britain the governor Agricola encouraged the use of the toga, the building of houses and public amenities, and the use of the Latin language, and put his name to the forum building at Verulamium (St Albans) at a time when the settlement, though already a *municipium*, still consisted largely of wooden-framed structures and generally lacked properly made-up streets. Again according to Tacitus, the tribe of the Frisii in the Low Countries, having rebelled under Tiberius because of oppression in respect of their taxes, paid in elk-skins, were in the time of Claudius settled by the military governor and given 'senate, magistrates, and laws'. Presumably what is meant is some sort of civic foundation with a charter;

but we are left to imagine for ourselves what this new civic community actually looked like.

Everywhere in the West arose new cities. In central Gaul the Celtic *oppidum* of Bibracte (Mont Beuvray), inconveniently located in the hills of the Morvan, gave way to Augustodunum (Autun), a city of immense circuit built on an accessible site by the river Arroux. By the time of Tiberius the sons of the Gallic nobility were already receiving there an education in liberal studies—to pave their way (which, for reasons too complex to describe here, they never really took) into the high aristocracy of the Empire. Bibracte declined, not through coercion—for archaeology shows that the site was still inhabited after the foundation of Autun, and declined progressively—but through sheer inconvenience and the attractions of the new city. In similar fashion, the native settlement of the Magdalensberg in Noricum gave way to the new town and provincial capital of Virunum (just to the north of Klagenfurt). In the East little new city foundation was called for, nor did the activities of Hellenistic kings leave much room for it. With certain exceptions such as colonial foundations in areas of uncertain tranquillity like southern Asia Minor, the main influence in the East was the steadily increasing prosperity made possible by the *pax Augusta* rather than any particular intervention of the Roman power. The caravan cities of Palmyra, Gerasa, Bostra, and Damascus gained new prosperity as more settled Roman relations with the East encouraged economic activity and Roman control of the area became more definite. The spectacular urbanization of Palmyra, though its origins were in the Hellenistic period, was essentially a product of the Roman Empire, beginning in the time of Tiberius and ending only with the collapse of the Palmyrene Empire in the later third century.

It was above all in the West that living conditions were transformed, by the growth of cities and the development of those resources most conducive to public health, economic development, and organized leisure. Rome itself saw an immense change, achieved by huge capital outlay on the part of Augustus and his successors, which not only altered the appearance of the city, as Augustus rightly claimed for his own achievement, from one of brick to one of marble, but raised the quality and reliability of its food and water supplies to unheard-of levels. The gang of slave maintenance-workers assembled by Agrippa for the up-keep of the aqueducts was on his death inherited by Augustus and transferred by him to public ownership (that is, to the domain of the *curator aquarum*). We should not forget that in the cities of the Empire most men lived, not in palaces or the town houses of Pompeii and Herculaneum, with their gardens, fountains, statuary, and frescoed rooms, but in the plain tene-ment blocks best known to us from the remains of Ostia (above, pp. 367 f.). After the fire of Rome in 64, remedies were under-taken which have much to say about the general conditions of life in first-century Rome and, no doubt, in other large cities also. Limits were fixed to the permitted height of residential buildings, which must possess their own walls and not adjoin others directly; a proportion of the construction must be of fireproof stone, without timber frames; financial incentives were offered for early completion of building works; unauthorized tapping of the water system was prevented by government in-spectors, to ensure an adequate flow to the public supply, and householders were required to keep fire-fighting equipment in an easily accessible place. All agreed that the new city was more gracious than the old; some claimed (it being impossible to please everyone) that it was less healthy than the old city, whose narrow streets and high buildings had provided shade and cool-ness which the new open spaces did not allow. A more pertinent complaint might have concerned the area of the city taken up by Nero's dream, the 'Golden House' (below, pp. 429 ff.), with lawns, lakes, and rustic landscapes devised by its builders, as Tacitus said, to make good by art the deficiencies of nature.

Although the city was the fundamental unit of ancient social and administrative life, many were those who lived outside its range, in different ways; in tribal reservations which, at least in certain parts of north Africa, persisted to the late Empire and

beyond; in townships (*uici*) and the great villas which in the
northern provinces were quite as important a facet of the economic and social process of Romanization as were the cities. In
mountain areas, such as exist in north Africa (the Kabylie and
Aurès) and Isauria in southern Asia Minor, lived enclaves of
mountain folk hardly touched by Roman civilization but a threat
to it if economic conditions turned against them, for then they
would descend on the agricultural territories of Roman cities.
On the desert fringes to the south and to the east transhumant
peoples, and in the north barbarians, moved in and out of Roman territory in a way that paid little regard to the formal
barriers of the frontier systems.

In taking the cities and their articulate classes (and therefore
most of the surviving evidence) as the basis for the analysis of
Roman society, we risk ignoring the great majority of the population on whose labours the prosperity of the cities depended
but who do not make a proportionate impact on the surviving
source material: the rural peasantry. That the cities in fact depended on the economic exploitation of the peasantry is axio-
matic. But it would be a mistake to assume from this that the
cities and the countryside were in consequence divided by an
overt mutual enmity. The city, as a market, centre of distribution, source of occasional delights and pleasures, and, not
least, home of the major gods, was a real and active presence in
the life of the peasantry, even if a relatively small part of their
physical existence was spent there. In the fourth century John
Chrysostom remarked on the Syriac peasantry flooding into
Antioch on Christian feast days, 'divided from us in language
but at one in faith'; it is one of the few literary acknowledgments
we possess of the peasantry or, as in this case, of its non-classical
language, but the situation it evokes is evidently common and
immemorial. By the same token the local aristocracies, in whose
hands lay the conduct of civic politics and the provision of public services, were the owners of the land and spent much time
on their farms and country estates—a pattern of life illustrated
by Apuleius for second-century Oea (in Tripolitania) as much

as by the historian Ammianus Marcellinus for fourth-century Leptis Magna and Nisibis (in Mesopotamia). Among true 'city-dwellers' we should count professional men such as teachers and doctors, craftsmen, fortune-tellers and magicians, traders, merchants, and so on. For the activities of many of these professions, the value system of Greek and Roman society, rooted in the attitudes of landed amateurism, was reluctant to assign proper respect. At all levels of society, provincial and metropolitan, it was the landed interest that was most closely connected with the tenure of political office. The senatorial class of the early Empire was composed of landed magnates who came to politics with a census qualification that ensured they were men of substantial private means, and they embarked on careers that did not in general (though exceptions could always be made) require a specifically military, financial, or other expertise so much as all-round literary culture and general experience. In the domain of local politics trade secured no foothold even at Arles or Lyons, where it was a prominent and profitable activity; only at Ostia, an exceptional case because of its restricted territory and the overwhelming dominance of trade in the economy, did the trading interest make much impact on the conduct of its civic and political life.

A man who turned his back on politics to pursue commercial interests might be spoken of as following a life of *quies*, that is, the freedom to make money without the constraints and inhibitions imposed by the political life and its values. The two brothers Seneca and Mela, were prominent respectively in the senatorial and equestrian orders of later Julio-Claudian Rome, the latter expressing what Tacitus called a 'perverse ambition' in choosing to enrich himself by holding imperial procuratorships. Possibly the brothers were even cleverer than Tacitus acknowledged, in vesting their interests equally in the two great enterprises, politics and commerce. Cassius Dio alleged that among the causes of the revolt of Boudicca was Seneca's calling-in of loans of 40,000,000 sesterces he had made to the Britons, with an eye to the high interest rates he might extract. If true, or even plausible, it is an intriguing suggestion, not only of a senator indulging in speculative finance, but also, we may suspect, of the high costs to the leading men of the new province of their own Romanization. Buildings to construct and furnish, mosaicists to commission, statuary and luxury goods to import from all over (the early palace at Fishbourne gives an indication); there was a lot to pay for and not much money yet in the province.

The importance of trade, manufacture, and commerce in the actual conditions of life in the Roman provinces is as obvious as that of agriculture, which provided their economic base and of which they were very often the direct expression. So much is clear from many sources: from one of the most important inscriptions of any period of Roman history, the Edict of Maximum Prices by Diocletian in AD 301; from the patterns of ostentatious expenditure manifest in the great consuming cities of the Empire; from the incidence of discovered shipwrecks, rising to a peak in the late-republican and early-imperial periods; not least, from the illustration on large numbers of grave reliefs, especially from the western provinces, of a wide variety of trading, commercial, and generally professional enterprises, in which those commemorated evidently took pride and found respect (they would not otherwise have been shown on their tombstones). Viewed in another perspective, there are the various trades and occupations, more than a hundred of them, named on the inscriptions of a small town in south-east Asia Minor; and no less than 250 in the slice of life represented by a fourth-century manual of astrology. Why should we ever wish to apply to such modestly successful *petits bourgeois* a social attitude to trade, commerce, and manual labour formulated by the philosophers, and repeated by the rhetoricians, of a different social class—men freed by position, unearned income, and the labour of others from the need to contemplate the normal facts of economic life?

Yet it remains true that it was in the hands of the traditional aristocratic, rather than of the trading or commercial, interest that the physical maintenance and political conduct of the cities of the Roman Empire rested and also, therefore, much of what appears to us as its achievement. By generosity and munificence, these local aristocracies built their cities, sustained their physical amenities, patronized their literary culture by supporting municipal chairs of grammar and rhetoric, and provided their entertainments. They constructed aqueducts, porticoes, temples, theatres, built and provided the heating for public baths, kept the streets clean and lit at night. They maintained peace in the surrounding countryside, provided distributions of oil, grain, and cash and, at a personal expense recorded on many a commemorative inscription, employed professional gladiators and charioteers, acrobats and jugglers, singers and musicians, and imported exotic beasts to be hunted down in public shows for the general enjoyment. In return they were acclaimed by grateful multitudes as 'benefactors', 'providers', and 'patrons' of their cities in demonstrations of goodwill which ensured the continued influence of their families.

There was also the pressing need to channel into legitimate forms of expression the social tensions which, left unchannelled, could have destroyed civic life. Life in the ancient world did not possess the measured regularities of modern times—office hours and working weeks, factory shifts and teaching days, time-tabled transport, deep-frozen food stocks, and regulated prices; not to mention the instant communication of verbal and visual information (what did the Emperor even look like?), and a mode of political organization designed to promote class and economic interests by systematic process of election, discussion, and legislation. Ancient social life was more discontinuous, the role of government more passive and intermittent. Through provincial councils focused on the imperial cult, cities could periodically exchange views and explore their common interests, if necessary send an embassy to press their case before the Emperor; but for most of the time they lived separate lives, as often inclined to seize advantage over their neighbours as to co-operate with them. Disputes about provincial primacy, as between Ephesus and Smyrna, Nicaea and Nicomedia, or local economic rivalries, as between Lyons and Vienne, could impinge on the imperial administration because they led to disorder. They might occasionally affect the course of a civil war or campaign for the imperial throne by a pretender, a situation in which a mistaken judgement might lead a city into the need to make an expensive apology (or worse), but in which a correct one could enhance the status of a community and enrich those leading members who had guided its choice.

Even the financial situation of the landowning politicians contributed to the relative abruptness of civic life. It was in fact the fundamental cause of it, as the landowners drew incomes in cash rentals and the sale of market produce, in a society with few banking facilities, low liquidity ('I am totally involved in farming', said the Younger Pliny in explanation of his inability at short notice to raise 3,000,000 sesterces to purchase another estate), few possibilities for alternative investment, and a consequent need to dispose of their surpluses in whatever ways would give them satisfaction, add lustre to their material wealth, and increase their prestige.

The explosions of colour, pageantry, and popular demonstrations that mark ancient games and entertainments, not to mention their ritualized violence, reflect this discontinuous pattern of life, much as the disorder and rioting in the cities often reflect the abruptness of the economic conditions that framed it. It was not easy to be a recluse in an ancient town. Public life was conducted in specific locations, much of it out of doors in a particular area of the city (the *agora*, flanked by public buildings, temples, and the senate-house), and the leaders of the society would be known by personal appearance to the population; if things went wrong it would be known who was to blame. Famine, which could be sudden and extremely local in its incidence, could turn the affection of the people for its leaders into aggression, when mobs demonstrated in the streets and the landowning politicians fled for safety to their well-provided country estates. At such moments the upper classes show themselves in one of the more self-interested of their many roles, as they hoard grain supplies to secure high prices in times of shortage, by physical obstruction and specious argument resisting governors' attempts to bring down the price. For the historian of the city of Rome above all, social unrest and violence are to the end a central theme, their causes impressively consistent; partisanship over performers and factions in the public games and races provided by the Emperors and (in the late Empire) the resident aristocracy of Rome, and food shortages, especially of corn and wine. A new factor may be mentioned here, though it is beyond the scope of this survey; rioting and violence (on one notorious occasion resulting in 137 dead on the floor of a Christian basilica) over rival claims for the bishopric of the city. We might take these as the remote descendants of the late-republican battles between Clodius and Milo and the demonstrations in favour of rival triumvirs—just as the ritualized acclamations of the late Empire in circus and theatre descend from the political demonstrations so frequently mentioned in the *Lives* of Suetonius and described, with dubious political theory but fascinating examples, in the later chapters of the *Pro Sestio* of Cicero. At Alexandria, a city well known for its civic disturbances, riots in the fourth century between Christians and pagans, and between rivals for the bishopric, appear as the natural successors to the rioting of the early Empire between the Greek and Jewish communities.

Social Organization

The inequalities of wealth, social standing, and privilege between what a modern government might have called the 'socioeconomic categories' of the Roman world were immense. They embraced not only the physical conditions of life and the opportunities open to individuals for their self-betterment, but areas in which modern citizens, in theory at least, are equal: as in the differing legal penalties thought appropriate for different classes of men. Those described as 'more honourable' (*honestiores*) were in the course of the second century made exempt from such punishments as flogging, burning alive, exposure to wild beasts, and condemnation to the mines and quarries, penalties regularly imposed, by the most summary of legal procedures, on members of the lower classes. *Honestiores*, to be broadly identified with the order of local councillors of the cities of the Empire, might legally be executed only by the sword, and were able to claim rights of appeal to the jurisdiction of higher courts; in these respects they had inherited some of the privileges enjoyed by Roman citizens in the first century, before that class had become too extensive to make them worth while.

Had a programme of social reform ever been devised by the Roman government (which in fact never saw any need for such a thing), it would no doubt have identified a free urban citizenry consisting of the craftsmen, traders, and professional men whose activities were indicated earlier. Since it was usual for a craftsman to market his own products in a shop attached to the premises, there would be no need to separate sharply the means of production and of exchange, though it might be necessary to distinguish those people who, like porters, teachers, entertainers, and prostitutes, provided a service for a fee, and whose only asset might lie in physical strength or adroitness, intelligence, and the possession of an acquired skill. There were also the free labourers, whose numbers, for long underestimated, are in more recent study attaining their correct proportions; builders and manual workers, who ignored the contempt of Cicero for such occupations and worked for hire for any employer who would pay them. 'You must let me feed my people', said the Emperor Vespasian to an inventor who offered him a labour-saving device for the transport of building materials. We should no doubt consider separately the skilled workers, such as bakers, whose services to the community merited, and attracted, special attention. They and analogous workers, such as masons, silversmiths, wool-workers, undertakers (to select just four examples) belonged to trade associations, or *collegia*, which possessed social, religious, and sometimes quasi-political functions, as well as providing an organization for the businesses with which they were concerned. The city of Ephesus offers cases of silversmiths organizing demonstrations in the theatre against the preachings of St Paul in order not to lose their trade in the manufacture and sale of images of Ephesian Artemis and, in the second century, of the guild of bakers withholding their labour in pursuit of some aim of their own and being called to order by the proconsul. Considerations of public order prevented Trajan from agreeing to the formation of a fire brigade at Nicomedia, against the clearly implied advice of Pliny as governor of the province. Apart from the active political role implied by such episodes, the trade guilds were active in the ceremonial and pageantry of their cities. When Constantine entered Autun in 311, he was received by the usual crowds, and by the 'statues of the gods, music, and the emblems of the collegia'; the emblems were evidently not devised for this particular occasion, but indicate the regular part played by the trade guilds in their cities' public lives.

The countryside would be seen (from the socio-economic point of view here imagined) in far simpler terms, the more so because some of its most prominent figures, the local gentry, would already have been classified as urban dwellers, with the consequent over-simplification of their actual way of life mentioned earlier, and because the cities, the economic focus of the surrounding countryside, were also the centres for its administration. Yet here again we should not underestimate the diversity in the conditions of life found in the countryside. The peasants themselves might own their land or rent it from local or absentee landlords; in the fourth century Libanius (an influential professor of rhetoric at Antioch) draws the distinction for Syria between villages under 'one master' and those owned by 'many masters', that is by free peasant proprietors. Some were lessees of public land taken under long leases with preferential terms to encourage the planting of uncultivated or unsurveyed land, some were tenants of temple lands or of the Emperor. Such farmers, like the tenants of absentee landlords other than the Emperor, would normally be supervised (in some cases, which are documented for this reason, oppressed) by a land agent or bailiff or, in the case of imperial estates, the procurator of the province. As in the towns, so too in the country there would be a numerous free labour force, sometimes recruited as need arose from the surplus labour of nearby towns or from those local peasants who happened at a given time to be underemployed, sometimes migrant from region to region; and there were pastoralists following the seasons between upland and valley, desert and steppe. This is the context of a famous episode of republican history, the *calles siluaeque*, the 'tracks and forests' offered as a prospective command to the consuls of 59 in order to curb the ambitions of Julius Caesar. *Calles* are the droveways, in Italian *tratturi*, of transhumant shepherds, as described in an informative inscription of the time of Marcus Aurelius, from Saepinum in old Samnite country.

The women of the community would generally be seen in terms of the socio-economic categories assigned to the men. Their rights at law were however much more extensive than one might have expected, the institution of 'guardianship' of adult women, though it was not abolished, having by the late second century become a formality. It is already clear in the late Republic that women of senatorial status could in practice manage their own business and financial affairs, and with the early and almost universal acceptance of a form of marriage in which the woman retained her own legal identity rather than passing into the control of her husband, women had rights to own, inherit, and dispose of property which in modern Britain were not matched until the Married Women's Property Act of 1870. The marriage of Pudentilla of Tripolitanian Oea to the young philosopher Apuleius (above, pp. 334 ff.) in the mid second century was the occasion of a provincial *cause célèbre* from which Apuleius, accused before the proconsul by her first husband's relatives of having bewitched her by magic arts, was no doubt glad to escape. Pudentilla had for her part gone against their expressed wishes in choosing to marry Apuleius, which she was perfectly able to do. The real issue was that of the property, and Pudentilla's 'guardian' had to certify in court that a farm whose purchase he had formally authorized had been acquired not for Apuleius but for herself.

At less opulent social levels women are found frequently, in evidence that seriously under-represents their actual numbers, sharing in their husbands' work and its organization, particularly in the finer crafts and luxury trades such as silver-working and perfumery; and there were of course those service occupations in which opportunities to make a living, and even to achieve a certain scandalous distinction, conflicted with a social disapproval that was itself, as we should expect, shaped by that essential tool of a dominant class, moral hypocrisy. An early-fourth-century law on adultery took it for granted that the mistress of a tavern need not have sexual relations with the male clientele, while the serving-maids would normally be expected to, and so, unlike their mistress, were exempt from accusation as being 'unworthy of the cognizance of the laws'; and the same assumption was applied to women of the stage, whose immorality was held, again in Christian legislation of the fourth century, to preclude their returning to their profession after baptism. The social role of the woman was dominant, above all, in the home and in the day-to-day upbringing of children. The most intimate, if not the most endearing portrayal of this relationship, as of many other aspects of provincial family life, is Augustine's description of his mother Monica in the *Confessions*. It was not exclusively as an expression of personal affection, but of the normal patterns of family life in ancient cities, that Augustine's relations with his mother were so intense, and with his father so formal and distant by comparison.

A distinction in Roman society instantly recognizable through fundamental legal and social distinctions was that between slave and free. It is a truism hardly worth asserting, that Roman society was in some sense dependent on slave labour. But in what sense? One of the most important facets of the social and economic history of the Empire as opposed to the Republic is the declining rate of slave importation, the servile population being now to a far greater extent (one would not say entirely, in view of the evidence for the continuance of the slave trade under the Empire) maintained by reproduction among those who were already of this status, through what were in effect recognized as slave marriages. The effect of this is that the function of slavery in the Empire evolved within a wider social and economic pattern and was not imposed upon it. In whatever occupational milieu we find ourselves—among shopkeepers, building workers, members of *collegia*—we encounter a mixed population of slave, freedman, and free citizen. By a *senatusconsultum* of AD 52—introduced to the Senate by Claudius as the idea of his freedman Pallas—free women who entered into permanent relationships with slaves were themselves reduced to that status *if the master was unaware of the relationship*, or to that of freedwoman if he was aware and had given his consent. Though sometimes viewed as a socially oppressive measure, the *senatusconsultum* is more interesting to the historian for the situations it entitles him to visualize, of stable marital relationships freely undertaken between men and women of different legal status, but similar occupational groups, living (no doubt) in similar social conditions and in situations where the master might not know what was going on. The woman might find her legal status affected, but her marriage took her into the social network and protection afforded by the house to which her husband belonged; and in those frequent cases where the slave husband worked independently of his master, or under only indirect supervision, she might find her way of life little changed. Tacitus wrote of the disorder arising in Rome during the Civil War of AD 68 as affecting in opposite ways the stable part of the people connected with the great houses, and the spectacle-loving mob and the worst of the slave population. The first group, including by implication the 'better sort' of the slave population, welcomed the end of the reign of Nero and the prospect of better things to come; the second, used to Nero's extravagances, regretted his end, and, fearing the worst and fed on rumour, aggravated the general instability.

The social relations, expressed through various forms of

munificence, between the great houses of Rome (and so, on a lesser scale, in all cities of the Empire) and their dependants, and between the Emperor and his special clients, the people of Rome, provided a common interest for sectors of society that ought, on any rational calculation of economic advantage and disadvantage, to have been irrevocably opposed to each other. Yet this was only the tangible expression of the more extensive moral and legal relations between 'client' and 'patron' upon which ancient society was built. The failure of societies in which such inequalities are rampant, extreme, and blatant to the eye, to articulate their differences in terms of class conflict is a tribute (if that is the word) to the strength and flexibility of the relations between classes which can be summed up in the word 'paternalism': the art of extending social benefits and alleviating the effects of misfortune while enhancing the prestige and moral worth of the giver of the benefits, and thereby reinforcing rather than undermining the existing social structure. There were of course other means of 'alleviating the effects of misfortune', and it would be hard in conclusion to imagine a more vivid expression of the sheer variety of social relations and vicissitudes of human experience of which the historian must take account, than some questions envisaged on a late-third- or early-fourth-century papyrus as appropriate for putting to an oracle (the numbers are given on the papyrus):

72. Shall I get my pay? . . . 74. Shall I be sold up? . . . 78. Am I to get leave? 79. Shall I get the money? . . . 82. Is my property to be proscribed? . . . 85. Am I to be sold as a slave? 86. Shall I go into exile? 87. Shall I go on an embassy? 88. Am I to become a town councillor? 89. Is my escape cut off? 90. Shall I be separated from my wife? 91. Am I under a spell? . . . (*Oxyrhynchus Papyri*, No. 1477)

Further Reading

The literary sources mentioned are available in the Loeb Classical Library, and in most cases also in Penguin Classics, especially Tacitus, *Annals* (by Michael Grant, 1956) and *Histories* (by Kenneth Wellesley, 1964; all dates are those of first publication); Suetonius, *Lives of the Caesars* (by Robert Graves, 1957); Pliny the Younger, *Letters* (by Betty Radice, 1963). See also Lucian, *Satirical Sketches* (by Paul Turner, 1961) and Apuleius, *The Golden Ass* (by Robert Graves, 1950); the last two are extremely rewarding from a historical point of view, though their literary complexity makes them difficult to use. Particularly recommended is the splendid collection of source-materials, documentary and epigraphic as well as literary, by Naphtali Lewis and Meyer Reinhold, *Roman Civilization, Sourcebook II; the Empire* (paperback, New York, 1966). This collection contains hundreds of well-chosen passages, and responds equally well to browsing or to systematic reading; a real education in Roman history.

Fundamental both to the interpretation of Roman society and to the appreciation of the actual conditions of life in it is M. I. Rostovtzeff's *Social and Economic History of the Roman Empire* (2nd edn. by P. M. Fraser, Oxford, 1957); to be read (for it is a controversial work) with Arnaldo Momigliano's appreciation in his *Studies in Historiography* (London, 1966), pp. 91–104. Fergus Millar, *The Roman Empire and its Neighbours* (2nd edn., London, 1981) shares some of Rostovtzeff's emphasis on the provincial diversities of the Empire. G. E. M. de Ste. Croix's marvellously fertile *The Class Struggle in the Ancient Greek World* (London, 1981) in fact contains much directly on and relevant to the Roman imperial period. In Tim Cornell and John Matthews' *Atlas of the Roman World* (Oxford, 1982) are brief illustrated accounts of some of the issues mentioned above (for instance public shows, manufacture and trade, technology) and of the provinces of the Empire and the city of Rome. There is still much of interest in Ludwig Friedlander's old *Roman Life and Manners under the Early Empire*, especially in the Supplementary Volume with various excursuses (English tr. London, 1910).

On the conditions of travel in the Roman empire, see Lionel Casson's two books, *Ships and Seamanship in the Ancient World* (Princeton, 1971) and *Travel in the Ancient World* (London, 1974), with E. D. Hunt's fine *Holy Land Pilgrimage in the Later Roman Empire* (Oxford, 1982). On the role of Greeks in Roman Society, G. W. Bowersock, *Augustus and the Greek World* (Oxford, 1965) and *Greek Sophists in the Roman Empire* (Oxford, 1969) are both excellent books, concise, lively and well documented.

The economic functioning of the cities of the Empire is much discussed; see especially Chapters I and II of A. H. M. Jones, *The Roman Economy: Studies in Ancient Economic and Administrative History* (ed. P. A. Brunt, Oxford, 1974); R. Duncan-Jones, *The Economy of the Roman Empire: Quantitative Studies* (Cambridge, 1974) includes particularly full discussions of levels of civic munificence, and Philip Abrams and E. A. Wrigley (edd.), *Towns in Societies: Essays in Economic History and Historical Sociology* (Cambridge, 1978) contains a particularly good discussion by Keith Hopkins on the roles of trade and agriculture in the economic development of classical cities. The subject of Bruce W. Frier, *Landlords and Tenants in Imperial Rome* (Princeton, 1980) is urban leasehold law but he has much to say about the physical conditions of life, especially at Ostia; on which see Russell Meiggs, *Roman Ostia* (2nd edn., Oxford, 1973). Among the many interesting articles reprinted from the journal *Past and Present* in M. I. Finley (ed.) *Studies in Ancient Society* (London and Boston, 1974) is P. A. Brunt's splendid 'The Roman Mob' (pp. 74–102).

The debate about trade and labour and social attitudes towards them, reopened by Finley in *The Ancient Economy* (London, 1973), has been vigorously pursued; see, for instance, the collections of studies edited by Peter Garnsey, Keith Hopkins and C. R. Whittaker, *Trade in the Ancient Economy* (London, 1983), by Garnsey and Whittaker, *Trade and Famine in Classical Antiquity* (Cambridge, Philological Society, Suppl. Vol. 8, 1983), and by Garnsey, *Non-slave Labour in the Greco-Roman World* (ibid. 6, 1980); and John d'Arms, *Commerce and Social Standing in Ancient Rome* (Cambridge, Mass., and London, 1981). On the techniques of farming, K. D. White, *Roman Farming* (London, 1970).

On the role of law in social life, see J. A. Crook, *Law and Life of Rome* (London, 1967), and on the penal system of the Empire Peter Garnsey, *Social Status and Legal Privilege in the Roman Empire* (Oxford, 1970) and more generally A. N. Sherwin-White, *The Roman Citizenship* (2nd edn., Oxford, 1973). On slavery and social relations there are articles of interest in M. I. Finley (ed.) *Slavery in Classical Antiquity* (Cambridge, 1960); and see from a very different historical tradition Joseph Vogt, *Ancient Slavery and the Ideal of Man* (transl. Thomas Wiedemann, Oxford, 1974).

Social relations in general are discussed in two most illuminating books, written with characteristic zest and an eye for detail, by Ramsay MacMullen, *Enemies of the Roman Order; Treason, Unrest and Alienation in the Empire* (Cambridge, Mass., and London, 1967) and *Roman Social Relations, 56 B.C. to A.D. 284* (New Haven, Conn., and London 1974). Zvi Yavetz, *Plebs and Princeps* (Oxford, 1969) discusses the relations between the Emperor and People of Rome in the context of developments from the late Republic, and has most interesting material on modes of popular expression. Keith Hopkins, *Sociological Studies in Roman History*, I: *Conquerors and Slaves*, and II: *Death and Renewal* (Cambridge, 1978 and 1983) offers a radical approach to the evidential problems inherent in the writing of ancient social and economic history. Still more intractable are those relating to religious history, on which a stimulating introduction for the imperial age is E. R. Dodds, *Pagan and Christian in an Age of Anxiety* (Cambridge, 1965).

16
Roman Art and Architecture

R.J.A. WILSON

Republican Prolegomena

When the chaos and civil war which marked the collapse of the Roman Republic erupted in the third quarter of the first century BC, there had already been sown some of the seeds of architectural and artistic innovation which were to bear such remarkably productive fruit during the early years of Empire. Yet, architecture apart, the period of the Republic in central Italy down to the middle and later years of the second century BC was not marked by any brilliant outpouring of artistic creativity, or by many works which display striking originality: little that is genuinely and independently 'Roman' can be identified in the art of early- and middle-Republican Rome. Rather it was the twin cultural influences of Etruria and the Greek world that were dominant, the latter being by far the more significant. When, sometime around 300 BC, a Latin-speaking artist called Novios Plautios made in Rome a splendid bronze circular box (known as the 'Ficoroni cist'), his total dependence on the Greek artistic repertoire (the mythological scene on the body of the box, for example, or its fine lotus and palmette border), as well as his familiarity with the masterly Etruscan techniques of metal engraving, are abundantly clear. Etrusco-Hellenic influence was similarly at work in the Roman ('Italic') style temple as it emerged in the course of the third and second centuries BC after a long period of experimentation. The frontal emphasis and the lofty platform (*podium*), both features foreign to full-dress

Greek temples, are derived from Etruscan architecture, but the ornamental details, such as the use of engaged columns or pilasters to decorate the sides and back of the *cella*, as well as the architectural order itself, are almost invariably of Greek derivation and inspiration. A good surviving early example of the type is the second-century-BC 'temple of Fortuna' (probably dedicated to Portunus) near the Tiber in Rome.

By the time that this temple was built, Greek influence on the artistic life of the capital was all-pervasive. It had first made an impact in Italy in the sixth century BC, when it began to affect the development of Etruscan art, and some Greek artists are known from scattered literary references to have lived and worked in Rome from the fifth century BC onwards; but it was only in the third century BC, when Rome's political expansion brought her into direct contact with the Greek cities of southern Italy and Sicily (Tarentum's fall in 272 and Syracuse's in 212 being notable landmarks), that the steady trickle of Greek culture flowing into Rome became a constant stream; and that in turn reached flood proportions in the second century BC, when first Greece and then Asia Minor came within the orbit of Rome. Not only were Greek artists migrating westwards in increasing numbers in response to the demands of a new, large, and wealthy clientele; in addition, the craze for collecting Greek originals to adorn town and country houses grew to fever pitch, and led to the wholesale looting of masterpieces from their original settings. When originals were not to hand, copies could be manufactured, ever more faithful to their models thanks to continuing improvements in the pointing technique; and major workshops were already established in Athens, Rome, and elsewhere to meet this huge demand, which continued well on into the Empire. There were, of course, some commissions for new types, and the school of Pasiteles enjoyed modest success in producing pastiches of classical figures in novel arrangements, but free-standing sculpture in general at this period broke little fresh ground. Portraiture is quite another matter. Early in the first century BC there appear the first examples in a long and impressive series of marble portrait busts, in which the sitter is represented with striking fidelity, double chins, wrinkles, warts, and all (see Plates 9 and 10). This was a far cry from the bland, impersonal idealism of most (but not all) late classical and Hellenistic Greek portraits; the new type reflects, perhaps, a pragmatism, a rugged determination, and a certain ruthlessness in the Roman character, as well as a taste for unvarnished truth. The busts are generally of imported Greek marble, a material with which Italian sculptors were unfamiliar, and there can be little doubt that it was Greek sculptors working in Rome who were responsible for their execution; but although the strikingly uncompromising realism of this portrait-type has been seen as a reflection of the Greek artist's disgust for his sitter, the patron must have liked what he saw—otherwise the portrait sculptor would soon have been out of business, and the fashion would never have caught on.

One or two pieces of Roman relief sculpture in the last century of the Republic also show hints of a fresh approach, one that was to be fully developed only under the Principate. A pair of crisp but lifeless limestone reliefs depicting victory trophies, from the Capitoline hill in Rome, perhaps executed early in the first century BC in commemoration of African campaigns against Jugurtha, stand at the beginning of a long series of commemorative relief sculptures designed to leave a permanent, tangible record in stone of actual historical events. The approximately contemporary marble relief known misleadingly as the Altar of Domitius Ahenobarbus shows the hand of a Greek sculptor working none too confidently for a Roman patron. While three of the sides depict a playful marine scene wholly in the Hellenistic tradition, carved with confidence, even gusto, the fourth has the hitherto unfamiliar (and very Roman) scene of the sacrifice of pig, sheep, and bull (*suovetaurilia*), probably on the occasion of a military census-taking: the rather awkward arrangement of the figures and the disparity of scale between animals, humans, and 'props' such as the altar, betray the sculptor's unfamiliarity with his subject.

Wall painting, too, embarks on a dramatically different and more adventurous course from the beginning of the first century BC, again the fruit of successful co-operation between Roman patrons and (for the most part at least) Greek artists. Private houses up until *c*.100 had their walls rather monotonously decorated in imitation marbled blocks, sometimes simply painted, sometimes executed in moulded stucco as well (the so-called First Style of Roman painting). That gives way to an ambitious scheme of wall decoration which depends for its effect on a series of architectural frameworks and vistas in different planes, giving the illusion of space as the viewer looks out on a succession of often fantastic architectural creations receding into the distance. There can be little doubt that some of the features of this elaborate style came from the painted stage sets of the Hellenistic theatre, witnessed by such recurring features as the central door, the broken pediment, the circular pavilion, and above all the theatrical masks; indeed, a room in the villa at Boscoreale near Pompeii has paintings which correspond exactly with Vitruvius' description of the tragic, comic, and satyric sets of the Greek theatre. The originality of this style of painting (the so-called Second Style) lies not so much in its subject matter as such, as in the varying combinations of a stock repertoire of motifs to form new varieties of composition; and new, too, as far as we can tell, is the idea of placing these gaudy, overbearing architectural decorations within the intimacy of the private house. Some of the grand, large-scale, figured fresco cycles, such as the figures from another room at Boscoreale, or the frieze from which the Villa of the Mysteries at Pompeii takes its name, are also likely to owe much to lost Greek painting; but the adaptation of original models to suit both individual room sizes and the demands of the patron led in each case to a good deal of innovation and variation of the prototype or prototypes. Contemporary mosaic work tended to be somewhat sober, in order not to compete with the riot of colour and decorative detail on the walls, but the taste continued for set-piece, small-scale, figured panels of great intricacy (*emblemata*) in the centre of the floors of the more important rooms. This, however, was wholly a legacy of the Hellenistic tradition; Roman mosaic only begins to show major originality with the gradual development of a quite different black-and-white technique from Augustan times onward.

In the architecture of late Republican Italy, too, the impact of the Greek world was not inconsiderable. The regular town grid, with streets intersecting at right-angles, which first the Etruscans (from *c.*500) and then the Romans adopted for their new foundations, was with only minor adjustments the legacy of Greek orthogonal planning; and both the garden peristyle of the Roman house, introduced in the course of the second century BC, and many building-types in Roman public architecture, such as the stoa/portico, the theatre, and probably the basilica (its name means 'royal' in Greek), were more or less closely derived from Hellenistic Greek models. Much more significant, however, was the emergence in Italy of the new building technique of concrete, which (for once) owes nothing to the Greeks. In the second half of the third century BC, Italian architects discovered that when mortar was made with the volcanic brick-earth known as pozzolana, widely available in central and central-southern Italy, and added with lime and water to rubble aggregate, the result was an enormously strong (and waterproof) mass capable of bearing great stress. Expensive and cumbersome large-block ashlar construction could now be discarded in favour of concrete walling, the facing material of which was of no significant structural importance. At the same time the Romans first made use of another architectural feature they were to adopt very much as their own, the arch—an invention, in fact, of the Greeks, but never fully exploited by them. The more or less simultaneous discovery in central Italy of concrete and of the potential of the arch, prompted in turn the creation of the semicircular barrel vault in concrete, a revolutionary means of spanning a space which broke utterly free from the conventional timber beam-and-truss roof. An early maturity in the handling of serried ranks of barrel vaults with interconnecting arched openings is displayed in the gigantic warehouse in Rome of 193 BC, the Porticus Aemilia (some 487 m. long), and later in the second century it was concrete that made possible the creation of the finest surviving architectural complex of the Roman Republic, the great sanctuary of Fortuna at Palestrina. Here barrel vaulting was used to fashion a series of orderly terraces and retaining walls out of a rugged hillside, although, in contrast to the Porticus Aemilia, the concrete structures were for the most part concealed behind respectable colonnades in time-honoured Greek fashion. The traditional Greek orders were also used as a decorative frame for arched openings, an idea soon picked up and repeated in many other buildings (the Theatre of Marcellus, for example: p. 419). Concrete also played a vital role in the development of the Roman bath-house, in which concrete vaults were a more practical alternative to timber for roofing the heated rooms with their steamy atmosphere. The first surviving examples come from Campania, where the amphitheatre, another quintessentially Roman building, also made its earliest appearance, before the end of the second century BC (Pompeii's of c.80 BC being a well-preserved early example); but it was only after further advances in concrete architecture under the Empire that both building-types were to reach full maturity.

The Augustan Principate

When C. Octavianus (soon to take the title Augustus) emerged triumphant from the battle of Actium in 31 BC, he lost little time in embarking on a building programme the like of which Rome had never seen before. The reign of Augustus was an age of enormous architectural and artistic fervour, in which cautious conservatism was combined with revolutionary new ideas. The establishment of the Principate created for the first time a stability which enabled a long-term, coherent planning programme to be worked out for the monuments of the capital. The Emperor, with his family and associates, provided a motivated patronage which drew architects, sculptors, and painters to the capital, a patronage which was vital for creating the right conditions for works of art and buildings on the grand scale; and with that imperial patronage came the centralized control of state funds. Such conditions had of course existed before in the ancient world—in Periclean Athens, for example, and especially in the Hellenistic kingdoms such as Pergamum—but for Rome they were essentially new. Augustus was also not slow to realize the political overtones of a lavish architectural and sculptural programme: Caesar had already shown the way with his great vision of a monumental reorganization of the heart of Rome, and some of his projects were duly completed by Augustus. Caesar's adoptive son launched a building programme on an even more ambitious scale which, by his death in AD 14, had totally transformed the physical appearance of the capital. Mobilizing the building industry was one way of stimulating the economy; building theatres and amphitheatres, baths and basilicae, *fora* and temples, curried favour with a restless populace; and in the showpieces of the Augustan programme the potential for using monuments as vehicles of elaborate propaganda was exploited to the full.

Some idea of the scale of the new building programme can be judged from Augustus' astonishing claim that he built or restored no less than eighty-two temples in one year alone, quite apart from other types of building; add to that the projects sponsored by other energetic builders in his family, and one can gain some impression of the building fever that gripped Augustan Rome. Many of the new structures were essentially conservative, repeating the formulae already tried and tested in the late Republic. The Theatre of Marcellus, for example, begun by Caesar but not finished until *c*.13–11 BC, with its seats raised on concrete substructures and with an outer façade of superimposed arcades (each row framed by a continuous colonnade of engaged columns, a formula which much influenced architects from the sixteenth century onwards), was essentially the type of building already established at Rome by the earlier Theatre of Pompey (55 BC). Many of the temples, too, continued to use traditional materials, either travertine (a hard white limestone quarried near Tivoli) or one of the variety of local volcanic stones liberally covered with stucco. Such conservatism in the Augustan buildings programme would have delighted the contemporary architect, Vitruvius, whose ten books *On Architecture*, written between about 28 and 23 BC, enjoyed enormous fame from the Renaissance onwards, especially as a sourcebook for the Classical Greek orders. Conscious, but disapproving, of the radical changes going on around him, Vitruvius issued strictures against the haste and the boldness of the new generation of architects, while lavishing undiluted praise on the use of ashlar, on the materials of local quarries, even on the usefulness of mud-brick. Vitruvius was no progressive; his writings are more important for the light they shed on Greek and Roman Republican architectural practice than as a commentary on his own age.

For the materials on which Vitruvius pinned his faith were not to be those of the future. The Augustan age was an age of experiment, in using new materials and in exploring fresh uses for old. The quality of concrete, for example, was constantly being improved, and innovatory architects were trying out a new method of roofing, the hemispherical dome in concrete, which was to play such a vital part in the Roman architectural revolution of the next 150 years: the earliest surviving example, probably Augustan, is the so-called 'Temple of Mercury' at Baiae. Another arrival of lasting significance was kiln-fired brick, not a newly-invented material as such, but employed now for the first time as a continuous facing for concrete. In Rome it appears to have been used only modestly until after Augustus' death; real confidence in handling the new material was gained elsewhere, especially in Italian cities such as Turin. With brickwork, as with the dome, the significant developments were yet to come, but Augustan architects deserve credit for pointing the way forward.

A more immediate impact on the architectural scene was made by marble. Augustus boasted, according to Suetonius, 'that he found Rome a city of (mud-)brick and left it a city of marble';

and it is clear from the sheer number of marble-faced buildings which sprang up in the capital that this was no idle boast. Caesar had probably been the first to realize the potential of the rich Carrara marble quarries near Luna in north Italy, but their full-scale exploitation began only with Augustus' reign. Dead-white, crystalline, and clean-breaking (and therefore excellent for crisp carving and cutting), this handsome material won immediate and widespread popularity. Alongside Luna appeared an increasing range of polychrome marbles from abroad: yellow African marble, salmon-pink marble from Chios, and greeny-blue *cipollino* from Euboea, as well as Phrygian marble from Asia Minor. Marble had come to stay; and although the Augustan use of polychromatic effects, both for columns and in paving and wall veneers, remained restrained by comparison with later fashions, the new material gave a welcome touch of elegance and sophistication, as well as a splash of colour, which the architecture of the capital had hitherto lacked.

But the exploitation of marble brought with it a problem, lack of Roman expertise in handling it. That is why an army of Greek craftsmen were drafted into the capital: their role in shaping the distinctive creations of the Augustan programme is hard to overestimate. A new, precise language of architectural ornament, based on that of classical Greece, but with fresh variations and combinations, set the tone for the rest of the Empire and in turn was a source of inspiration for generations of Renaissance and Neo-classical architects. Even the one original Roman contribution to the classical orders, the Composite, with its blending of the volutes of Ionic with the acanthus leaves of Corinthian, makes its first known appearance in Augustan Rome and is hardly to be dissociated from the creative genius of Greek craftsmen in the capital.

The marriage of Greek skills and traditions with Roman taste and demands is nowhere more clearly documented than in the two monuments which mark the culmination of the Augustan programme, the Ara Pacis Augustae (dedicated in 9 BC), and the Forum of Augustus (2 BC). The forum in concept and planning is quintessentially Roman: the great Italic-style temple of Luna marble on a lofty podium dominates an open space flanked by porticoes, a formal, axial layout following the strict principles already established in Republican architecture. Roman too is the use of the forum as a portrait gallery of the great trail-blazers of Roman history, including Augustus himself, identified as just another hero in a long line of Republicans. As an ingenious and disingenuous piece of imperial propaganda and as a blueprint for architectural planning, the forum of Augustus was unmistakably Roman; yet its detail was no less unmistakably Greek: the textbook Corinthian capitals, the zoomorphic pilaster capitals with figures of Pegasus at the corners, most obviously of all the line of Caryatids above the colonnades, are closely matched in the Classical or late-Hellenistic architecture of Attica.

The Altar of Augustan Peace is an even more eloquent witness of the cultural interchange of Greece and Rome. The altar itself, set on a stepped platform, was surrounded on all sides by lofty screen walls broken by entrances on the west and east. Mythological panels flanked each entrance—Mother Earth (see Plate 11) with children on her lap and personifications of Ocean and Water at her side, a scene carved fully in the Hellenistic tradition and exuding the blessings of tranquillity and renewed fertility that accompanied the Augustan peace; Aeneas sacrificing at the spot where he first set foot on Italian soil. Just around the corner, near the head of the procession on the south side, is Augustus in the same act of solemn sacrifice: the propaganda message is being hammered home, that Augustus is the new Aeneas, the bringer of hope and the architect of a Rome reborn. The rest of the south side shows members of his family while magistrates and their families fill up the north side; it is a commemoration in marble of an actual procession and sacrifice that took place in 13 BC in thanksgiving for the Emperor's safe return after a provincial tour. The idea of historical relief sculpture to record a specific event had been tentatively explored during the late Republic, but it was to find full expression only during the Empire. As an exercise in political propaganda, the Ara Pacis succeeds brilliantly in presenting some of the essential values that Augustus stood for: *grauitas* witnessed by the solemnity of the occasion; *humanitas* witnessed by such touches as a tired child pulling at his father's toga and by the overall flavour of a 'family occasion'; above all *pax*, peace both in Italy and in the world at large. As a sculptural monument, too, the friezes of the Ara Pacis are superlative, a tribute to the skills of the Greek sculptors who worked on them. The influence, above all, of Athens is paramount: in the overall form of the altar, a copy on a more monumental scale of the Altar of Pity in the Athenian *agora* (*c*.420); in the processional friezes which inevitably recall those of the Parthenon; in the quiet solemnity reminiscent, perhaps, of Attic grave reliefs of the Classical age; and in the superbly disciplined yet exuberant floral scroll occupying the lower half of the screen wall, which, while at present most closely paralleled in Hellenistic Asia Minor, may well have been derived from now lost Attic models. The Ara Pacis epitomizes the Roman genius for borrowing freely from the Greek repertoire, but moulding it and adapting it into something new and distinctively Roman.

Another vital element of the new Roman propaganda machine was image-building; and Greek sculptors played a key role in fashioning a series of portrait-types of Augustus which were copied in vast numbers so that all corners of the Empire could be systematically bombarded with the image of the *princeps*. The types now created for Augustus and his family were not the ruthlessly realistic portraits of the late Republic, but a delicate blend of realism and statesmanly ideal. The mood might vary from the grim determination of the Capitoline Octavian, fashioned at a time before the total consolidation of his position, through the sober *auctoritas* of Augustus as *pontifex maximus*, carved some thirty years later yet with hardly a hint of ageing, to the supremely self-confident Primaporta Augustus, where the Emperor with expansive gesture harangues an unseen populace; but the overriding impression of a determined, efficient, authoritative leader is common to all.

In private life Augustus is reputed to have been a man of simple tastes who chose to dwell in a modest house unostentatiously adorned; certainly the property excavated on the Palatine and identified as his shows no greater luxury than comparable patrician residences of its day. In the fresco paintings of this and other properties of the imperial family, the overbearing architectural schemes which characterize the full-blown Second Style give way instead to decoration with a lighter touch, which favours architecture of less substantial form and an increasing emphasis on large central mythological 'panel' pictures as the focal point of each wall. The logical culmination of this trend was to deny altogether the illusion of depth and to emphasize instead the solidity of the wall. The new scheme of decor which thus emerged (the so-called Third Style) depended for its effect on intricate and often fanciful decorative detail, especially floral and abstract designs, usually interspersed with figured tableaux which varied a good deal in size and number, while architectural elements, if they survived at all, now became flimsy and unreal. The new decorative scheme can be seen fully developed at another imperial property, the country house at Boscotrecase near Pompeii (see Plate 5). The elegance and restraint of the frescoes here, in stark contrast to the excesses of the Second Style at its most extravagant, mark the culmination of a quiet but decisive revolution in artistic taste, achieved through the skill of court painters, but dictated, no doubt, by the personal preferences of the imperial family itself.

The individual ingredients of the new style of painting reflect the eclecticism of Augustan art as a whole. One ingredient was unashamedly classicizing: the wall schemes adopted by Augustan decorators, with their mythological panel pictures, large and small, were ideal vehicles for the widespread copying of Classical and Hellenistic Old Masters, and in this they set the tone for Roman wall painting for the next century. Another ingredient was the Egyptianizing element. This, like copying, was not entirely new, but it received an undoubted boost after the annexation of Egypt in 30 BC, when the curiosity value of things Egyptian ran high in Italy for a time. Some of the recurrent decorative features in Third Style compositions, such as sphinxes, ibises, cult objects, and figures of Isis, as well as vignettes of Nilotic scenes, were directly derived from the Egyptian repertoire. More controversial is the source of another popular ingredient in Augustan and later painting, the dreamy landscapes loosely referred to as 'sacro-idyllic' because they usually centre around a fanciful 'votive' column or flimsy shrine, with a variety of figures in attendance. Though they are often claimed as the products of Alexandrian mannerism, inspired by the bucolic poetry of Theocritus, no Hellenistic precedents in painting are so far known, and while some elements may well have had Hellenistic forerunners, the idea of peopling these artificial settings with shepherds, flocks, and dogs appears to begin only with the striking sacro-idyllic pictures from Boscotrecase; they may, therefore, be essentially an Augustan creation. Here the name of Studius is possibly relevant. He was the first, so Pliny tells us, who went in for the 'very charming paintings' of landscape gardens and the like filled with people engaged in the tasks of everyday life. This sounds like the sort of thing which crops up in several Augustan residences: tiny figures, depicted impressionistically in flat monochrome, walking and fishing and chatting and going about their daily business, in a setting of bridges, porticoes, and topsy-turvy pavilions. Certainly Studius did not invent landscape as such, nor can his name be associated with another masterpiece of Augustan painting, the 'garden of Livia' from her villa at Primaporta: here are no human figures, and so far from being impressionistic, the fruit and flowers of this wilderness of a paradise garden are executed with a loving care for naturalistic detail. Judgement must be suspended on this unique painting as to whether it, too, owes all or something to Hellenistic predecessors, or whether it is rather an exuberant product of the Augustan genius for originality.

The principal advances of Augustan art and architecture were worked out, of course, mainly in the capital; but the Augustan age saw in addition an enormous outpouring of building energy elsewhere in Italy and the Empire, especially in the western provinces. In many cases, indeed, we have to turn to these areas for preserved examples of buildings which are only fragmentary, or have vanished altogether, in Rome itself. One such is the triumphal arch, a characteristic monument of imperial propaganda of which several early examples still stand in north Italy and southern Gaul. Commemorative arches of a sort had been known in Republican Rome, but the developed form, articulated with columns, architrave, and attic bearing an inscription, is essentially an Augustan creation. Many of the buildings newly erected in the provinces at this time were based directly on metropolitan blueprints or from models elsewhere in Italy. Indeed in some instances (as at the famous Maison Carrée in Nîmes of AD 2–3) the presence of stonemasons and sculptors who had actually worked on the Augustan building programme in Rome can be argued. One of the most familiar of all Roman monuments, the stately Pont du Gard aqueduct near Nîmes (see Plate 3), a harmonious structure which vividly demonstrates that the aesthetics of appearance need not be divorced from practical function, is also an Augustan monument, erected in the last quarter of the first century BC. In the East, where urbanization was already deeprooted, the impact of Augustus was less dramatic; but in the West—above all in his creation of a road system and in his establishment or refounding of innumerable, carefully chosen towns in Yugoslavia, Gaul, the Iberian peninsula, and along the north-African littoral—Augustus left a decisive and enduring stamp on the map of western Europe.

The Julio-Claudians: Tiberius to Nero (AD 14–68)

Augustus died on 19 August AD 14, and within a month he had been deified. Among the trappings of the official state cult of *diuus Augustus* was a newly created iconographical language for depicting the deceased Emperor in the company of gods. An eloquent early expression can be seen in the cameo known as the Gemma Augustea (see Plate 7), a frank glorification of the dead Augustus, half draped, as befits his divine status, and surrounded by personifications of Rome, *Oikoumenē* (the inhabited world), Ocean, and Earth. Yet the new language rarely lost an opportunity to speak clearly also about the living, emphasizing the 'continuity factor' between the old regime and the new. On the Gemma Augustea, for example, Augustus looks across to his chosen successor Tiberius stepping from the chariot of victory, while the lower register alludes to Augustus' German wars, in which the prime architect of victory was none other than Tiberius. Some scholars claim that this and similar scenes were intended for private circulation during Augustus' lifetime; but that the man who himself shunned personal worship was instrumental in creating the new idiom seems unlikely. These scenes stand at the beginning of a long line of historical reliefs which use elaborate allegorical paraphrase to convey a political message.

Few monumental reliefs of Julio-Claudian date from Rome survive; those that do display a rather dry style entirely in the Augustan classicizing mould. The grand processional reliefs in the Villa Medici, for example, thought by some to be part of an Ara Pietatis ('Altar of Piety') of *c*.AD 22–45, are conceived and executed very much in the manner of the Ara Pacis; only in one major respect do they break fresh ground, in their detailed rendering of architectural setting, though the problem of providing this without sacrificing the prominence of the human figures has yet to be solved. A roughly contemporary relief showing a procession of city magistrates also marks an advance in its hesitant adoption of a slightly aerial perspective rather than a horizontal one: the heads of the second row are raised slightly above those in the foreground. Neither architectural setting nor vertical perspective was entirely new to the sculptural arts, but for the state reliefs of the capital they were a fresh departure, much exploited in the years to come.

Sculpture in the round was long to be dominated by the influence of Greek works and of the 'neo-Attic' school. Much of this was dreary and repetitive copying of the established

Classical and Hellenistic masterpieces, in constant demand for decorating the town and country houses of the rich, as well as public *fora*, gardens, and bath-buildings; what little originality existed was usually limited to feeble pastiches. Not all of this sculpture, however, lacked vitality: witness, for example, the outstanding work produced by the Rhodians Hagesander, Athanadorus, and Polydorus. One, the Laocoon, found in the Golden House of Nero, exerted a powerful influence on Michelangelo and his contemporaries; the other, a series of dramatic larger-than-life groups including the Blinding of Polyphemus and Odysseus' ship passing Scylla, adorned a grotto in Tiberius' villa at Sperlonga. None of this sculpture was probably wholly original, being best regarded as adaptations and reworkings from Hellenistic models; but nor is it derivative hack-work: it testifies to the continuing vibrancy, intensity, and superb technical quality of Hellenistic baroque at its best, well into the early years of Empire.

Magnificent sculpture of this sort was to play an increasingly important part in grandiose interior decoration; the more generous the setting, the more colossal the sculpture to suit it. Nor are other indications lacking of a growing luxury in Julio-Claudian interior decor: an expanding range of polychrome marbles for floor slabs and wall veneer, abandoning the comparative restraint of Augustan taste; wall mosaic using glass tesserae of dazzling colours, which was soon employed to good effect in sparkling fountains at Pompeii and elsewhere; mosaic work, too, to cover the soaring surfaces of concrete vaults, a medium with a long future down into Byzantine and early medieval times. Wall-painting, too, shared in the increasing desire for elaboration. One has only to compare some examples of the late Third Style, as in the House of Lucretius Fronto at Pompeii (*c*.34–45), with the early-Augustan versions of the same style (as at Boscotrecase) to appreciate just how significant a shift in taste had taken place: there is still the horizontal wall division into three, still the prominent mythological panel in the centre, but the restraint and elegant simplicity of an earlier generation has been replaced by a riot of contrasting sweeps of colour, and by a wide range of intricate, often fussy detail; while the virtuoso pavilions in the top register with their shifting planes look forward to the even more elaborate developments of the Fourth Style.

The transition to the fully developed Fourth Style seems to belong to the 50s; certainly its use on the grand scale is brilliantly seen a decade later in the frescoes of the Domus Aurea, the Golden House of Nero (AD 64–8), inspired creations of the court painter Fabullus. It is a style marked above all by the 'opening up' of the wall to provide once more an architectural vista, usually to each side of a central panel (more rarely in an 'all-over' composition). No longer, however, in the Fourth Style are the architectural forms grounded in reality. In the Golden House they form a scintillating essay in airy and insubstantial fantasy, creating a whimsical framework around full-length figures, mythological panels, landscapes, and patches of 'solid' wall in a dazzling *tour de force*. Enlivened too by dainty arabesques, the whole series of frescoes is executed with a light touch; while some of the vignettes, displaying deft and rapid brush-work, are masterpieces of the Roman impressionistic manner. Many of these features recur in varying degrees of elaboration in countless examples of Fourth Style paintings at Pompeii and Herculaneum; and another aspect of the frescoes of the Golden House, the use of white as the background colour, was also to be of lasting influence, for it gained increasingly in favour, espec-ially from the mid second century onwards. Even today, ravaged by the passage of time, the decoration of the Golden House makes a stunning impact on the visitor, just as it did nearly five centuries ago when Raphael and Giovanni di Udine, according to Vasari, 'were both seized with astonishment at the freshness, beauty, and excellent manner of these works'.

The Golden House of Nero was indeed no ordinary building. In the history of architecture, too, it represents a watershed, for the octagonal room in the east wing is roofed by the first surviving dome in the capital. This major achievement provided

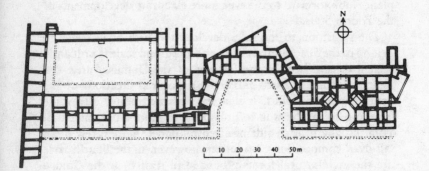

NERO'S GOLDEN HOUSE (AD 64–8): the Emperor's fabulous urban villa contained mechanical wonders and decorations 'all smeared with gold and picked out with jewels'; but more significant was its experimentation with new shapes and volumes within the basically rectangular plan. The novelty of the experiments is indicated by the presence of awkward, redundant triangular spaces between the main groups of rooms.

a novel flexibility in interior planning which at once opened up exciting possibilities for the future. The octagonal plan in itself (as also the five-sided court immediately to the west) is symptomatic of an impatience with the traditional rectangular room shapes which had long dictated architectural planning. Now, with concrete roofing a flexible tool in the hands of confident architects, the exploitation of circular, ovoid, and apsidal shapes in conjunction with stock rectangular ones created a variety in interior design that had not been possible before. In time, when the exterior shell was stripped away, the juxtaposition of widely differing room shapes with their medley of domes, semi-domes, barrel-vaults, and cross-vaults, often produced a positively ugly exterior. But the new Roman architecture is not an architecture of the exterior: rather it derives its dramatic impact from the interplay of light and space in the interior, so that the void becomes every bit as important as the solid envelope that encloses it. The dome of the Domus Aurea is but a small beginning, but it heralds the dawn of a new architectural approach which had a decisive influence on European architecture down to the present century.

The Golden House and its attendant pleasure park were created by an act of opportunism and imperial greed after the great fire of AD 64 had devastated the heart of Rome. That fire also presented Nero's city planners with a golden opportunity for revitalizing the domestic housing of the urban poor by replacing the sprawling tenement dwellings of the past with the tight, rational planning of the multi-storey rectangular apartment block (above, pp. 367 f.). It was a severely functional architecture, its sober façades rarely relieved by decorative detail; but it also has an uncompromisingly modern look, for the formula was repeated countless times in the urban housing of Renaissance and modern Rome. The material which made all this possible was brick-faced concrete, a winning combination which was strong, light and, as far as possible, fireproof. Having served its apprenticeship under the Julio-Claudians, brickwork was poised to sweep all before it and to take over as the principal facing material for major construction work in central Italy down to the very end of antiquity.

The Flavians, Nerva, and Trajan (AD 69–117)

In the autumn of 69 Vespasian established himself as sole master of the Roman world. A man of plebeian stock, he was a down-to-earth realist with the common touch, and it is probably not accidental that the best-known portrait of him, in Copenhagen, strips away the idealizing varnish and reveals a tough, experienced, ageing man, his leathery skin creased by long years of military campaigning. It is a frank portrayal in the Late Republican vein, shunning the blend of idealism and realism normally adopted in imperial portraits of the time.

Vespasian's name is indissolubly linked with the most celebrated of all Roman buildings, the Colosseum, the amphitheatre

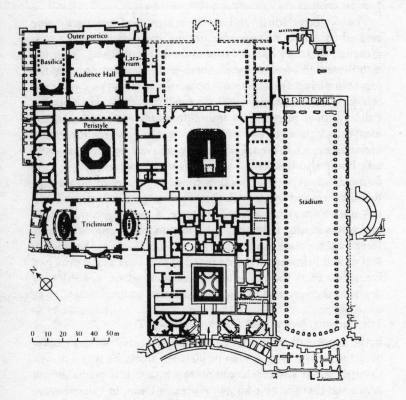

DOMITIAN'S PALACE (the Domus Augustana) in Rome (AD 81–92). The palace
consisted of three main blocks: at the left the official palace including the state
rooms; in the centre the Emperor's private residence; at the right the so-called
Stadium, a sunken garden in the form of a hippodrome. The detailed planning
shows a new facility in the integration of curvilinear and rectilinear shapes.

he provided for the entertainment and gratification of the Roman people. Only in its enormous size, however, which called for great architectural ingenuity to ensure efficient crowd control, does it break fresh ground; in other respects it is essentially conservative. Two other Flavian buildings are more important as trend-setters in the brick-faced concrete style. One is the public baths of Titus, which stands at or near the head of a distinguished line of imperial bath-buildings, each rationally and symmetrically arranged around its central short axis. The other is the imperial palace built by Domitian on the Palatine hill in the 80s and early 90s, a building which later spawned numerous provincial imitations. Within its tight rectilinear exterior, the Palatine palace enunciates many of the distinctive tenets of the new architectural thinking: confident handling of enormous masses of brick-faced concrete, grouped in split-level arrangement to take maximum advantage of a complex site; a continuing interest in the dome—three examples in all, each resting on walls which open out into alternating apses and rectangular recesses, now fully integrated with the maze of rooms beyond; and a delight in the curvilinear at the expense of the rectangular. All created novel visual and spatial effects, replacing the expected with the unexpected at every turn. But Domitian's palace was designed not just to surprise, but to impress. 'The edifice is august, immense, splendid,' wrote Statius, 'an edifice to stupefy the neighbouring abode of Jupiter the Thunderer'; and awe, even intimidation, was the keynote of such halls as the palace vestibule (down in the forum) with walls 98 feet high, the vast audience chamber, the dining-room only slightly smaller, and the 'basilica' in the north-west corner where the Emperor sat in judgement. This, with its apse and double row of columns, probably derives from the palaces of Hellenistic kings, but the distinctive plan was later to have a decisive influence on the layout of the early Christian church. Ablaze with brilliant polychrome marble, adorned, too, with enormous statues, these grandiose state apartments, among the largest interiors yet created by Roman architects, were designed to overwhelm, to make the visitor feel he was in the presence of a very god. Domitian paid the price of an assassin's dagger for such overt assumption of divine honours, and his immediate successors played down this inflated image of the imperial personage, even though they continued to live amid the splendour of his palace.

Domitian's conviction of his own divine status is further emphasized by one of the reliefs from the Papal Chancellery, where he sets out for war in the exclusive company of deities. There can be no doubt that this relief was carved in the Emperor's lifetime, as his head was later reshaped with the features of his successor Nerva. No earlier relief indisputably shows a living Emperor in such divine company; but the almost contemporary relief from the Arch of Titus, erected by Domitian in his brother's memory, is an equally frank glorification of the Emperor, showing him accompanied by Roma and other personifications rather than by ordinary mortals. From now on this elaborate allegorical shorthand became a fully fledged part of the grand tradition of historical relief sculpture, and by the time of Trajan a generation later the conventions are fully established, without hubristic overtones.

The Chancellery reliefs, competently carved but overall rather dull, are still firmly shaped by the mould of Augustan classicism. By contrast the lively reliefs on the Arch of Titus are brim-full of the excitement of a triumph in progress, especially in the procession of the spoils (see Plate 12), where the participants spring along past the spectator, placards waving, and wheel round through an archway into the distance. There is a new interest in the handling of depth here, with the figures carved in higher or lower relief according to their distance from the spectator; but the illusion of life and movement owes more, perhaps, to the Hellenistic tradition than to any immediately preceding Roman work, even though the subject matter is an entirely Roman one.

Nowhere, however, is a sense of life and movement more dramatically conveyed than on the stupendous 700-foot frieze of Trajan's Column in Rome. Dedicated in AD 113, and designed to commemorate the Dacian Wars of 101–2 and 105–6, it undoubtedly represents the very apogee of continuous narrative sculpture in the ancient world. The problem of receding space was not tackled in any consistent fashion; rather the designer's first priority was to present an almost uninterrupted flow of action-packed scenes. The constant switching between horizontal and bird's eye perspective, the frequent placing of figures 'above' and 'below' one another without perspective diminution, the incongruities of scale for some figures in relation to buildings, tend not to detract from the whole but to lend to it increased variety and vitality; the action relentlessly unfolds from bottom to top, never flagging despite its enormous length. Here, then, is a veritable textbook of the Roman army at work—gathering stores, preparing for the march, foraging for supplies, building camps, engaging the Dacian foe—delineated with supreme attention to detail (see Plate 13). When Trajan appears it is always as the calm, authoritative commander-in-chief addressing his troops, consulting his generals, performing sacrifices, receiving envoys: for on the column there is nothing of the majestic tone of the 'grand style' reliefs with their episodic treatment and full use of allegorical paraphrase; indeed personifications are entirely absent except when required for occasional scene-setting. The overall organization of the frieze called for imagination and dexterity of the highest order; and no less remarkable is the execution in very low relief of some 2,500 figures by a group of sculptors who (as on the Parthenon frieze) reached a uniformly high level of craftsmanship. The modelling of the figures is still firmly rooted in the Classical tradition, and some of the battle scenes can be traced back to late-Hellenistic groups, while other set-pieces are derived from the established repertoire of imperial iconography. But the overall effect is totally novel, a fully fledged product of pure Roman art, un-Greek in conception and execution. Most original of all is the use of a 100-foot column as a vehicle for propaganda sculpture, a bold stroke which marks the Column of Trajan with a touch of genius.

That touch of genius may well have been furnished by Apollodorus of Damascus, the architect of the forum in which the column stands. A man of forceful character, later to fall out with the Emperor Hadrian (who had strong, if idiosyncratic, architectural ideas of his own), Apollodorus was a first-rate structural engineer whose achievements included a half-mile-long bridge over the fast-flowing Danube, an amazing technical feat justly admired in antiquity. His forum too won high renown, not least for its impressive scale and the riot of gilded statues and polychrome marbles; but with the exception of the column and the integration of a basilica on the transverse axis (a novelty for the capital), the forum as a whole was closely linked with the past, consciously imitating the Forum of Augustus; and the relief sculpture, too, harks back to an Augustan dignity and simplicity of line. By contrast the friezes on a contemporary monument (the rebuilt temple in the Forum of Caesar) favour instead an ornate, highly decorative style with deep undercutting (intended to provide strong shadows and hence a powerful 'black and white' effect), a style with a longer future ahead of it in later Roman sculpture than restrained and sober classicism.

While Apollodorus' forum, however, looks decisively to the past, the accompanying market and shopping precinct terraced into the Quirinal hill looks no less emphatically to the future. Here is a complex where Apollodorus' mastery of the contemporary architectural idiom is displayed to the full: some 170 shops, offices, and storehouses, in brick-faced concrete up to four storeys high, brilliantly arranged on no less than six levels in an immensely complicated and irregular site. The jewel of the whole complex is a covered market-hall, roofed by one of the earliest large-scale examples of groined cross-vaulting to survive. This simple idea—a barrel-vault on the long axis intersected at right angles by a series of lesser barrel-vaults—marks an enormous architectural stride forward: for now the weight of the roof can be borne by great piers at intervals instead of by the entire length of the side walls, and windows can be opened up to the very crown of the vault, thus creating an imaginative, well-lit interior instead of the cavernous gloom of the usual barrel-vaulted hall. The first tentative steps in this direction were taken in the reign of Nero, but it needed the architectural ingenuity of a master-builder of Apollodorus' calibre to bring the idea to full fruition. Henceforth the cross-vault was to play a major role in Roman architecture, not least in the central halls of imperial bath-buildings with their impressive vistas opening off in all directions; and it is hardly surprising that the baths of Trajan, the first mature example of the axial type, three times the size of Titus' baths, were also the creation of Apollodorus himself.

Hadrian and the Antonines (AD 117–193)

It is tempting to link Apollodorus' name also with Hadrian's temple to all the gods, the Pantheon (see Plate 1), the construction of which was already in full swing within a year or so of Trajan's death; but no ancient authority does so, and the creator of what is unquestionably one of the great architectural masterpieces of all time remains anonymous. Characteristically it is not the exterior which wins admiration. The façade with its conventional portico and gable was very much run-of-the-mill for the temples of its time, and the radical conjunction of a rectangular porch with massive circular *cella* is positively disharmonious. Yet this incongruity is quite forgotten once one steps inside the enormous rotunda: for the impact of the interior, as any visitor to the Pantheon knows, is breathtaking. The eye is drawn up, immediately and irresistibly, to the superb lines of its coffered concrete dome, at 148 feet in diameter the largest man-made dome in the world until modern times. Sheer size is one element in the building's appeal: surprise is another. For the Pantheon is designed not along the lines of a coventional temple building dominated by a longitudinal, horizontal axis, but around a vertical axis, an invisible line joining the centre of the floor with the opening in the summit of the dome. Nothing is allowed to distract from this vertical aspect of the building, so that the articulation of niches and *aediculae* in the cylindrical drum wall is deliberately restless. Even the impact of the apse opposite the door is muted, no longer fulfilling its usual role as the focal point of a temple building. Yet despite this apparent complexity the essential geometry of the Pantheon is based on a simple, harmonious formula: the diameter of the whole building is identical to its height. Size, surprise, simplicity—these are three keynotes of this extraordinary temple. It is a building which embodies all the principal characteristics that define the specifically Roman contribution to architecture since Augustus: controlled use of polychrome marbles for columns, floor paving, and wall veneer, from Africa, Egypt, and Asia Minor; mastery of the properties of brick-faced concrete in its 20-foot-thick walls, constructed with numerous relieving arches and recesses to lessen the chances of settlement; mastery, too, in the pouring of some 5,000 tons of concrete for the soaring dome, with carefully graded ingredients ranging from strong basalt near its spring-line to light pumice at its summit. Above all the Pantheon is a supremely eloquent essay in the creation of interior space, and in the lighting of that space, through a single, bold opening at the very crown of the dome. More than any other Roman building it has inspired countless imitations and adaptations, starting in Hadrian's own reign with the Temple of Asclepius at Pergamum, and continuing on well into the present century.

The other architectural *tour de force* of Hadrian's reign is the sprawling stately home constructed by the Emperor near Tivoli over an enormous tract of rolling countryside. The whole bears the unmistakable stamp of the personality of its self-indulgent owner, who had at his disposal both the technical resources and the bottomless purse necessary to create the succession of luxurious living quarters, baths, pavilions, banquet halls, libraries, and grandiose ornamental pools (see Plate 15). Throughout the villa the variety of room shapes and the ingenuity shown in their interrelationship betoken a lively interest in the architecture of interiors; while in the central court of the pavilion in the Piazza d'Oro, or in the villa-in-miniature on its artificial island (where Hadrian could retreat when in reclusive mood), a delight in the curvilinear is carried to baroque extremes. Roofing, too, was the subject of fresh experiment: the dome in the vestibule of the Piazza d'Oro was no longer provided with an outer masonry skin to cloak its inner form (a frank admission that it was interior effect, not exterior appearance, which really mattered in Roman architecture); while the Serapeum has a spectacular example of the new 'pumpkin' dome, composed of distinct radiating segments alternately concave and flattened. Hadrian himself had a personal interest, possibly even a creative role, in this fresh variation of the dome, and an even more ambitious example occurs in another of his palaces, in the Gardens of Sallust at Rome.

While the architecture of Hadrian's villa was uncompromisingly Roman, the sculptural detail was no less uncompromisingly Greek. Hadrian was by far the most philhellenic of all Roman Emperors, and the enthusiasm which earned him the nickname of 'Greekling' carried him on occasion a little too far: his attempt to implant a temple of entirely Greek form, the Temple of Venus and Rome, in the very heart of the capital was widely regarded as an aesthetic failure. Sculpture, however, was a different matter; and such was the influence wielded by artistic patronage that the personal predilections of the Emperor could and did leave a decisive mark on the sculpture of the age. When Hadrian opted for a 'Classical revival' he stopped dead in its tracks for a generation the development of an authentically Roman sculptural style, such as was beginning to emerge on Trajan's Column. Instead he welcomed to Rome Greek sculptors and craftsmen on a scale not seen since Augustus' day, and evidence of their work can be detected in the embellishment of all the major projects associated with Hadrian. That evidence points to Asia Minor as the homeland of these gifted men, for the architectural ornament in Rome can sometimes be matched, detail for detail, with work at Pergamum, Ephesus, and elsewhere. Much of it was carved in the fine white marble (with a pronounced blue streak) from the quarries of Proconnesus near Istanbul, a material which arrived in Rome for the first time with these Asiatic craftsmen. Also carved by them on Italian soil was a wide range of sculpture both in relief and in the round, much of it with life and spontaneity suggestive of genuine creativity. Certainly it was to sculptors from the Greek world that Hadrian turned to perpetuate the melancholy beauty, diffident manner, and lithe and sensuous frame of his boyfriend Antinous, deified after drowning in the Nile in October 130. In original creations such as this Greek artists made a more important contribution to Hadrianic sculpture than did routine copies of Caryatids and other fifth-century Attic masterpieces which line the Canopus pool at the Tivoli villa, copies mechanically reproduced in Italian workshops long accustomed to demands of this kind.

The introduction of fresh currents from Greek lands into the mainstream of art and architecture was also symptomatic of an increasing cosmopolitanism in Rome and the Roman world under Hadrian and the Antonines. The second and third quarters of the second century were a particularly glorious age for the provincial cities of the Roman Empire, as self-confidence increased, living standards rose, and horizons widened. One graphic witness of the new outlook is provided by the rush to construct or refurbish in marble, which resulted in an astonishing boom in the export of coloured marbles. Its beginning can be dated to the early years of Hadrian's reign, and by the middle of the century nearly all new public buildings in major provincial cities were being constructed with marble columns and architraves and marble veneers. In some cases there is evidence that the imported materials were carved on arrival by craftsmen from the country of source, a process also documented later in the second century (as well as in the third) for the elaborate marble relief sarcophagi from Greece and Asia Minor, which were shipped in a roughed-out state and only worked in detail once they had reached their destination. This is no longer a Rome-centred world in which a metropolitan building type or decorative motif could be transmitted without substantial transmutation to a provincial centre: instead we are presented with an infinitely more complex and sophisticated organization which took architects, sculptors, and even jobbing masons far from their homes, with the resulting diffusion of fresh ideas and techniques into a common pool. Rome was no longer the only or even the dominant force in shaping provincial art and architecture: other vital creative centres had their part to play, leading to the emergence of an art which was no longer always

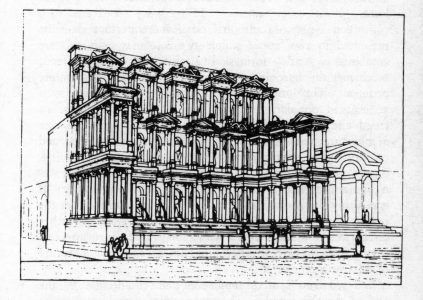

FOUNTAIN-BUILDING AT MILETUS (beginning of second century AD). The reconstruction reveals a number of features characteristic of Roman 'baroque' architecture: the elaborate play of advancing and receding entablatures, the sideways misplacement of pavilions so that those of the upper storeys straddle the spaces between those below, and the enlivenment of the whole façade with statue-niches. Such features were especially common in the eastern provinces.

individualistic along narrow provincial lines, but was common to widely separated parts of the entire Roman Empire.

That Asia Minor was among the most important of those creative centres has already been made clear. While art and architecture in the region generally retained its conservative, late-Hellenistic flavour during the first century, sparks of originality were also there: the recently discovered Sebasteion reliefs from Aphrodisias for example, dating to the fifties, glorify members of the imperial house in an individual style untramelled by the dictates of Italian state sculpture. But it was in architecture that the sparks of creativity really flew: and in such marble extravaganzas as the fountain building at Miletus (*c*.100) or the library of Celsus at Ephesus (*c*.117–20) we are treated to a controlled display of traditional, classical architectural elements presented in new guise: simple two-columnar *aediculae* are combined in straddle formation to achieve novel visual effects, heightened by baroque detail such as segmental and volute pediments. The notion of such elaborate columnar screens won widespread popularity, especially in theatre back-drops the length and breadth of the empire; while the language of baroque architecture finally became common currency during the second century in the architectural repertoire of the East, although it only occurred spasmodically in Italy or the West until Renaissance architects discovered it in the late fifteenth century. It is possibly also to the Hellenistic East that we must look for the origins of another highly influential idea, that of springing arches direct from columns, a device with a long and distinguished role to play from the early fourth century onwards in the architecture of the Christian church.

In fresco painting all the indications point to a decline after the end of the first century. There are some exceptions, but the monotonous frescoes from Ostia show that in general Hadrianic and Antonine interior decorators were content with repeating hackneyed decorative schemes which echo the Third and Fourth Styles of the previous century with increasing simplification and hardly a hint of originality—broad splashes of colour, especially red and yellow and white, but fewer and fewer mythological panels, which were gradually replaced completely by individual figures or motifs floating free in the centre of each zone. Ceiling decoration, by contrast, reached new heights of inspiration during the Antonine period: the strikingly detailed stuccoes from the Tombs of the 'Valerii', the Pancratii, and the Nasonii at Rome, all *c.*160, represent the very apogee of the Roman stucco-worker's craft. But it too seems to have declined thereafter, and by the early third century we have instances of walls and ceiling in the same room being painted with identical, humdrum, compartmentalized schemes, as in some of the early catacombs. Only in the occasional 'all-over' figured composition does second-century wall painting show signs of a different approach, as in a lively Hadrianic fishing scene from near the Porto Flumentano in Rome, but this appears to have become widespread only from early in the third century.

While painting was apparently in the doldrums, second-century mosaic work took on a new lease of life. The richly coloured, intricately figured panels of Hellenistic origin had continued to be made in Italy throughout the first century, and spasmodically even later, but they had been joined by modest black-and-white figural mosaics in a silhouette style from the Augustan period onwards. From about AD 110 fresh life was injected into this style, with ambitious and enormously success-ful wall-to-wall compositions, depending for their effect not on spatial depth or naturalistic detail but on superb draughtsman-ship. Outstanding Hadrianic examples include lively marine tableaux in the Baths of Neptune, and animal scenes in the Baths of the Seven Sages at Ostia; but the black-and-white style flourished throughout the Italian peninsula (and occasionally elsewhere) well into the third century. Purely ornamental mo-saics in black and white, also widespread in Italy, became increa-singly ornate, and both complicated curvilinear patterns and delicate floral arabesques enter the repertoire now. Ornamental designs were carried further in the experiments in polychromy that followed, both in Italy and the western provinces, from the mid second century; while the floral arabesque was adopted in polychromy by African workshops, which were already preparing the way for the enormous outburst of creativity that mosaicists there were to display during the third and fourth century. That story, however, lies outside our scope; but in the prelude to the full flowering of mosaic in late antiquity, the second-century mosaicists of Italy had a vital role to play.

In state sculpture too, the second century represents a crucial transition, heralding the emergence of a late antique style which breaks free from the shackles of the Classical heritage. We have seen how the personal tastes of Hadrian left a distinctive mark on the sculpture of a generation; and an entirely classicizing spirit, technically excellent but frigid and dull, can be seen on 'official' relief sculpture from his reign, such as two panels from a demolished triumphal arch (*c.*136–8). The subject of one depicting the apotheosis of his wife Sabina, borne to heaven by a winged female figure and watched by Campus Martius and an impassive Hadrian, is taken up again on the monumental base for Antoninus' Column, dedicated posthumously in 161. Here it is the deceased Emperor as well as his consort who are conveyed aloft on an even more preposterous winged figure, probably a personification of the Golden Age, with Campus Martius and Roma in attendance below. Again we are dealing with sculpture which shows consummate naturalistic handling of its material; yet the overall impression is static, pompous, even comic. The same serene and rather lifeless quality also pervades some of the reliefs dedicated by Marcus Aurelius, probably on an arch of 175–6; these display in addition an increasing simplification of composition and the beginning of a more frontal emphasis for the Emperor, a pose that was to become *de rigueur* by the fourth century. All these state reliefs, however, despite high technical skill, mark the very end of the road for the Classical tradition: sculptors now found themselves in a cul-de-sac, anxious for an avenue of escape from what was becoming routine and devoid of challenge. The earliest sign of the search for a new sculptural language comes on the Antonine Column base of 161, in two panels showing scenes of a funeral procession, each with ten footsoldiers of the Praetorian guard encircled by seventeen horsemen. The combination of horizontal and bird's eye perspective in a single scene is not in itself new, but on this scale it is novel, on a neutral background stripped of all setting; and the handling of the individual figures, with their large heads and dumpy bodies, also represents a new departure. The trend towards a fresh simplicity and abstraction of form is further developed on the Column of Aurelius, commemorating the Marcomannic Wars of 172–5 but not finished until 193. Inevitably compared unfavourably with the Column of Trajan, it lacks the involved action, the variety, the attention to detail of its forerunner. But its designer and sculptors were not seeking to make a duplicate of Trajan's Column. They intended to convey an impression of war rather than a detailed commentary on it, by presenting fewer episodes carved boldly and clearly, and instead of careful modelling we find rather flat surfaces, with grooved lines for drapery, and deep undercutting around the figures, designed to enhance the 'black-and-white' effect of the whole. A yet further stage in the development of what might be termed impressionistic sculpture can be seen on the Arch of Septimius Severus in the Roman Forum (AD 203). It is easy to dismiss the groups of ill-proportioned two-dimensional figures with their heavily drilled hair and clothing as native and degenerate products, representative of sculpture in decline; but as the figures of the Seasons or the Victory spandrels on the same Arch—or indeed the magnificent contemporary figured sarcophagi commissioned by private patrons—amply demonstrate, the sculptors of the period had not forgotten how to carve naturalistically; they were merely searching for a new and different means of expression. In this they paved the way for the transition to late antiquity, and ultimately, through Byzantium, to the cathedral sculpture of medieval Europe.

Further Reading

An excellent collection of source material in translation with brief linking commentary can be found in J. J. Pollitt, *Art of Rome* (Englewood Cliffs, NJ,

1966, reissued Cambridge, 1983). There is no up-to-date translation and commentary on Vitruvius, but M. H. Morgan's translation (1914; repr. New York, 1960) remains serviceable; for a brief discussion, A. McKay, *Vitruvius, Architect and Engineer* (London, 1978). For Rome there is a collection of ancient sources in translation in D. R. Dudley, *Urbs Roma* (London, 1967), and the reference work of S. B. Platner and T. Ashby, *Topographical Dictionary of Ancient Rome* (Oxford, 1929) and the photographic archive of E. Nash, *Pictorial Dictionary of Ancient Rome* (2 vols., 2nd. edn., London and New York, 1968) remain fundamental.

The best short introductions in English to Roman art are those of J. M. C. Toynbee, *Art of the Romans* (London and New York, 1965) and N. H. and A. Ramage, *Roman Art* (Cambridge, 1991); the most balanced longer account that of D. E. Strong, *Roman Art* (Harmondsworth, 1976, edited by R. Ling and reissued with full annotation 1988), but the latter was published posthumously and shows signs of being unfinished. Neither deals with architecture. M. Henig (ed.), *Handbook of Roman Art* (Oxford, 1983), is a well illustrated up-to-date account for the general reader with essays of uneven quality from several hands. The most lavishly illustrated single-volume treatment of Roman art, with copious colour and black-and-white photographs, is B. Andreae's *The Art of Rome* (New York, 1977; London, 1978), and there are also excellent illustrations in R. Bianchi Bandinelli's *Rome, The Centre of Power* and *Rome, The Late Empire* (London and New York, 1970 and 1971). Sir Mortimer Wheeler's *Roman Art and Architecture* (London and New York, 1964) has a lively if slightly idiosyncratic text and deals mainly with architecture, thematically by building type; the chapters on painting, sculpture, and the minor arts are very sketchy. Somewhat idiosyncratic, too, is the arrangement of material adopted by R. Brilliant, *Roman Art* (London, 1974). More balanced, well-illustrated accounts include G. M. A. Hanfmann, *Roman Art* (London and New York, 1964) and H. Kähler, *Rome and Her Empire* (London and New York, 1963), but both are now slightly out of date; so too is H. von Heintze, *Roman Art* (London, 1972, reissued 1990), also well illustrated but with a very brief text. A powerful and illuminating spotlight has recently been turned on Augustan art by German scholarship, with the publication of E. Simon, *Augustus: Kunst und Leben in Rom um die Zeitenende* (Munich, 1986), superbly illustrated with a lively if at times controversial text; and P. Zanker's *Kaiser Augustus und die Macht der Bilder* (Munich, 1987), a penetrating study of Augustan propaganda imagery, now translated as *The Power of Images in the Age of Augustus* (Ann Arbor 1988). O. Brendel, *Prolegomena to the Study of Roman Art* (New Haven and London, 1979), is especially useful on the different attitudes to Roman art from the eighteenth century onwards.

On the Republican background see the early chapters of the books quoted in the last paragraph. There are no full-length studies, except on the architecture, for which see A. Boethius, *Etruscan and Early Roman Architecture* (Harmondsworth, 1978); this is a revised version of the first part of A. Boethius and J. B. Ward-Perkins, *Etruscan and Roman Architecture* (Harmondsworth, 1970), now reissued as two separate books. The Etruscan background is best studied in O. J. Brendel, *Etruscan Art* (Harmondsworth, 1978), and G. M. A. Richter's *Ancient Italy* (Ann Arbor, 1955) studies inter alia the impact of Hellenistic art on the peninsula, a theme explored in depth in P. Zanker (ed.), *Hellenismus in Mittelitalien* (Gröningen, 1976), a conference proceedings with contributions in several languages.

On Roman imperial architecture, J. B. Ward-Perkins's *Roman Imperial Architecture* (Harmondsworth, 1981) is magisterial and will long remain the standard work; this is the revised version of the second part of the 1970 book mentioned above. J. B. Ward-Perkins's *Roman Architecture* (New York, 1977; reissued London, 1988) is a briefer. but no less lucid, account from the same hand. F. Sear, *Roman Architecture* (London, 1982, revised edition 1989), largely rehearses the same ground as Ward-Perkins with few fresh insights. Briefer essays include F. E. Brown, *Roman Architecture* (New York, 1961), and G. Picard, *Living Architecture: Roman* (London and New York, 1966); more specialized are W. L. MacDonald, *The Architecture of the Roman Empire* I (New Haven and London, 2nd edn., 1982), a detailed study of five buildings in Rome from Nero to Hadrian (especially good on vaulting), and the collection of essays on various topics by A. Boethius, *The Golden House of Nero* (Ann Arbor, 1960). MacDonald's essay on *The Pantheon* (Harmondsworth, 1976) provides not only a lucid analysis of that singular building but also an account of its many imitators down to the present century. There is also the same author's original and thought-provoking *The Architecture of the Roman Empire* II (New Haven and London, 1986), a study of urban public building and their visual interrelationship in town planning; it includes also an essay analysing the distinctive character of imperial architecture and its modes of expression. On baroque there is M. Lyttelton, *Baroque Architecture in Classical Antiquity* (London and Ithaca, NY, 1974), a theme also treated in W. L. MacDonald, *The Architecture of the Roman Empire* II (New Haven and London, 1986); the latter is a geographically wide-ranging work which primarily attempts to explore the function and interrelationship of public buildings in their urban setting.

On painting there is now the excellent monograph in English by R. Ling, *Roman Painting* (1991); G.-Charles Picard's *Roman Painting* (London and Greenwich, Conn., 1970) is superficial and, despite its title, does not deal exclusively with painting. Concise accouts of the Pompeian material can be found in the books cited in the Bibliography of Chapter 14. W. Dorigo's *Late Roman Painting* (London and New York 1971) deals with the post-Pompeian material and includes mosaic; although well illustrated, the discussion is verbose and, at times, wayward. On mosaics, K. M. D. Dunbabin's *Mosaics Of Roman North Africa* (Oxford, 1978) includes survey chapters on more general aspects of the medium and ranges outside Africa; while on the Italian black-and-white school, there is now J. R. Clarke, *Roman Black and White Figural Mosaics* (New York, 1978).

On sculpture, D. E. Strong, *Roman Imperial Sculpture* (London, 1961), remains the best introduction; A. W. Lawrence, *Greek and Roman Sculpture* (London and New York, 1972), is a fuller but more austere account. Notable essays on specific works include J. M. C. Toynbee's study of the Ara Pacis in *Proceedings of the British Academy* 39 (1953), 67–95, and her *The Flavian Reliefs from the Palazzo della Cancelleria in Rome* (Oxford, 1957). Trajan's Column has received monograph treatment in English from L. Rossi, *Trajan's Column and the Dacian Wars* (London and Ithaca, NY, 1971, with poor photographs), and from F. Lepper and S. Frere, *Trajan's Column* (Gloucester, 1988), while I. A. Richmond's classic 1935 treatment is now available in his *Trajan's Army on Trajan's Column* (London, 1982). The reliefs on the Antonine column base are fully discussed by L. Vogel, *The Column of Antoninus Pius* (Cambridge, Mass. 1973). The propaganda aspects in general of Roman sculpture are now exhaustively studied in N. Hannestad, *Roman Art and Imperial Policy* (Aarhus, 1986).

17

Envoi: On Taking Leave of Antiquity

HENRY CHADWICK

The ancient classical world is a large entity to take leave of. How did it all end? Or should one ask how it survived so long? What principally distinguishes 'ancient' history from that which we label medieval or modern? One obvious difference is that the available sources, though massive enough, are on a far smaller scale, so that the writing of ancient history is a distinct operation from writing modern history where the quantity of documents overwhelms the student. But that is of the accidents rather than the substance of what makes ancient classical studies a special and unique discipline. The rock whence western civilization is hewn is the old Mediterranean world, beginning with high achievements at the eastern end in the Nile valley, in the Assyrian and Persian worlds, in Judaea, but then seeing the centre of gravity move westwards: first to the Greeks, with a high peak of excellence in the fifth and fourth centuries BC, then to the Romans, whose power ultimately yields to the energy of the despised, crude, bibulous barbarians of the north and north-west.

Yet even the barbarian invasions of the fifth century AD fail to mark a decisive ending to the structures and values of classical Greece and Rome. If by 'the end of the ancient world' we mean the loss of a uniquely privileged position for Greek and Latin classics in western education and culture, then the shift cannot be described as decisive until the twentieth century, an age in which powerful forces are inimical to the very notion of a 'classic' of the past providing a model or criterion of judgement over the present. Even as the twentieth century draws to a close, the continued centrality of Rome and of the old Mediterranean world retains at least one living and undiminished symbol in the Papacy, presiding over a community of more than 700 million people, most of whom do not live in Europe. Until very recent times the renewal of high culture in the West has been linked with some direct contact with the prime sources of this culture in antiquity: in Greek philosophy, in Roman law and administration, in the universalism stremming from biblical monotheism.

That is not to say that these three main sources are, or were at the time felt to be, wholly harmonious and co-operative friends. The Romans, from Cicero to Pope Gregory the Great, regarded the Greeks as too clever to be honest. The Greeks, as is clear from Plutarch, admired the Romans, but did not greatly appreciate being conquered by them and would have preferred their own incompetent government to Roman efficiency and justice. Christian monotheism represented a disruptive challenge to immemorial local cults and social customs throughout the Empire, and was met by vigorous resistance in the form of philosophic criticism and state harassment.

It is astonishing that the Roman Empire survived the crisis of the third century AD. Already by 200 a serious trade recession had begun to hit the Mediterranean world, and people spoke anxiously of a falling birth-rate. In the middle years of the century the legions suffered fearful defeats from Persians, Goths, and other Germanic tribes; and the ferocity of internal civil wars brought the enterprise of imperial government to the verge of disintegration. This was averted by the new deal imposed first by Diocletian (Emperor 284–306, died 316 at Split), then by Constantine the Great (Emperor 306–37). From about 250 there was drastic inflation, which Diocletian vainly tried to check by fixing prices (which drove goods off the market altogether), and which Constantine fuelled when gold from pagan temple treasuries was allowed to flood the market. The repulse of the barbarians was achieved at the price of almost total concentration of power in the Emperor's hands and the decline in political significance of the old Senate, though senators remained in possession of their great estates and served in high offices of state. A rigid caste system enforced order. The graded rank of officials in the bureaucracy was marked by insignia in their clothing, particular shoes and girdles, and by special titles—in descending order *illustris, spectabilis, clarissimus, perfectissimus,* inferior officials in the secretariat being *deuotus* or *modestus,* and so on.

Diocletian divided the old provinces into two, thereby multiplying the costs of the civil service. Late Roman society felt the hand of bureaucracy heavy upon it, especially when even good bureaucrats, who felt themselves underpaid, took for granted a substantial tip from any whose interests they served. The worst officials expected 'protection money'. In the case of high officers of state whose support was indispensable in an important matter, a *douceur* would be substantial; we hear of petitioners landing themselves in huge debts at crushing interest rates, and perhaps even then not getting what they sought.

Usury was frowned on by Christian moralists. But the effect of making it difficult to obtain redress from a defaulter through the lawcourts must be to push interest rates higher, since the lender then spreads the risk over fewer customers. In practice loans continued with little restriction and became a target for sharp criticism when people of little means took out loans on the security of their houses or small holdings and ended by being evicted. Towards the end of the fourth century a series of infectious urban riots occurred which Jerome ascribed to the rage at wholesale evictions resulting from exorbitant interest rates. In the late Empire there was a constant tendency for land and property to be concentrated in fewer hands. Under pressure the weak sold to the strong, who competed with each other in the size of their estates.

There seems to have been no time in antiquity when corruption was excluded from the lawcourts and the tax system. Cyprian, bishop of Carthage (martyred 258), trenchantly described the system in which a man who had bought office felt justified in recouping his outlay and gathering more for the day when he fell from favour. The Emperors realized what inefficiency resulted from corruption and made intermittent attempts to stop it. One Christian preacher of about 370, probably at Edessa, illustrates the awesomeness of the last judgement by painting a word-picture of a provincial governor handing in his seals of office, standing trembling, white with fear, in the anteroom of the palace awaiting an interview with the Emperor. To check corruption Diocletian created an inspectorate, but they became merely a secret police, using power for their own advantage and at least as corrupt as anyone else.

The administration separated the Latin and Greek halves of the Empire, with two praetorian prefects in each half at the head of the civil services. They were responsible for justice and taxation, but not for the army. Under them were deputies (*uicarii*) administering groups of provinces called dioceses, and provincial governors. At court lay the central officers of State, the most influential being the Master of the Offices, responsible for intelligence services, the government postal service (not available to private individuals), arsenals, coastguards, keeping the Emperor informed, and seeing that his wishes were carried out. The civil service was organized in departments called 'cabinets' (*scrinia*). Other major officers were the Treasurer; the administrator of the Privy Purse; and, especially powerful, the Quaestor of the Palace, responsible for justice. Diocletian copied the Persian court, enhancing his authority by the mystery of elaborate ceremonial, with veils separating the anterooms from the audience chamber, and a series of silentiaries to guard the way. The number of veils to be passed was an index of the dignity of an official's place in the bureaucracy. Eunuchs became important as major-domos, not only in rich households, but also at court. In the office of High Chamberlain they would exercise an influence resented by high officers of state.

Diocletian's division of the Empire into two halves was reversed by Constantine, who by 324 had disposed of superfluous colleagues and made himself sole Emperor. But the division was later restored, and from 395 the western and eastern empires were in effect administered increasingly independently. People talked of 'both governments', recognizing the Empire to be a duality in more than language. In 476 the barbarian army commander Odovacer sent the Emperor Romulus Augustulus into pleasant retirement and assumed the insignia of regal office. The Ostrogothic king Theoderic, educated at Byzantium, was sent to remove Odovacer in 493, but he too found that his status in relation to the east-Roman Emperor Anastasius (491–518) was uneasy. There was regret at the ending of the line of Roman Emperors in the West, even though they had long been controlled by barbarian generals. Anastasius, Justin (518–27), and Justinian (527–65) aspired to restore Roman control. Two decades of desolating war were the price that Italy paid for having the Goths (whose administration under Theoderic (493–526) was pre-eminent) turned out by Justinian's armies under Belisarius and Narses. Soon the Goths were succeeded by the Lombards; and in the generations after Justinian's death Slavs and Avars poured into the Balkan peninsula (the Avars leaving a lasting mark in the name Navarino). The Emperor Heraclius exhausted the Empire's military strength in beating back the Persians and left the Jordan desert frontier defenceless against the Arabs. The Arabs had long been restless and marauding in Palestine and Egypt, but were now inspired by Islam and dreams of world conquest.

But until the Arab invasions of the seventh century the peoples of the Mediterranean world still felt themselves to be inhabiting a Roman world. The Vandals at Carthage were a nuisance for a hundred years of piracy, but Justinian's wars ended that. In the barbarian kingdoms of the West the Germanic tribes lived according to their own tribal law, while Romans continued under Roman law. The great aristocratic families served under the barbarian military authorities (the elevation of dukes above counts being one permanent consequence), and provided a civil service and lawcourts. Self-consciously they tried to educate their new masters, whom they found hard-drinking and mal-odorous. 'The Visigoths in southern Gaul and the Burgundians early in the sixth century produced legal codes, in the one case juxtaposing, in the other amalgamating, Germanic and Roman enactments. Thanks to the value placed on Roman imperial edicts in the Germanic kingdoms, there survives the law-code of the Emperor Theodosius II, published in the East on 15 February 438 and then also accepted in the West. The Theodosian Code was transmitted with a supplement of ad-ditional edicts or 'novels' for the years 438–58.

The 'end of the western Empire' in 476 was an event that no one at the time much noticed. There was no sudden collapse of Roman resistance against external barbarians. The barbarians had long been providing the army, and all that had happened was that the man with the real power assumed the ceremonial insignia as well. But the landed aristocrats of Italy and the Byzantine Emperors soon realized that the Gothic kingdom of Theoderic was much less Roman than they liked. We hear com-plaints of the appalling Gothic taste in music, of trousers and hair-grease. In the West the Church increasingly came to be the vehicle of Roman culture and civic values. It is characteristic, for example, that the clergy did not adopt barbarian dress at the time when their congregations were doing so, but continued to wear the 'Sunday best' of old Roman aristocrats—which we today think of as ecclesiastical vestments. It mattered little or nothing that Rome as a city had long given place to Milan and then Ravenna as the western Emperor's residence. Ravenna had the merit of being surrounded by marshes on the landward side, with a good port at Classis. Behind its walls Emperors felt safe. From there Theoderic administered Italy, and his palace chapel is now Sant' Apollinare Nuovo. There too in Justinian's time the exquisite church of San Vitale was erected and adorned with incomparable mosaic, including portraits of Justinian and Theodora.

The barbarian domination made people assertive about *Romanitas*. In Theoderic's Italy Boethius and Cassiodorus set about preserving ancient culture and philosophy. Boethius declared his 'fear that many things which are now known soon will not be'. At Constantinople Priscian wrote a Latin grammar which long educated the medieval West. Justinian's loudest assertion of Roman values was his code of laws superseding the Theodosian Code. All imperial edicts not included were declared invalid. In the Theodosian Code some edicts ('laws of citations') prescribed the legal authorities which could be cited as argument in court: Papinian, Paulus, Ulpian, Modestinus, Gaius, a majority among them being decisive. Under the great quaestor Tribonian, Justinian instructed his law commission of professional jurists to make a digest of the classical authorities, and this huge book remains the main source for our knowledge of classical Roman law. The way in which Tribonian's commissioners went about the task of compiling the *Digest* has given modern legal historians an unrivalled problem in detection and decoding, to which the utmost ingenuity has been applied. Justinian also put his name to a textbook of law, *Institutiones* or elementary instructions, designed to ensure that even students at law-school had a guidebook sealed with imperial authority. Both *Digest* and *Code* are Latin texts, though produced in the Greek East. The corpus of civil law had a third part, mainly in Greek, consisting of Justinian's further edicts or 'novels' promulgated subsequently to the *Code*, which appeared in 534 with a pompous fanfare of an introduction.

Historians of the law and of architecture cannot say an *envoi* to Justinian without a salute of deep admiration for his extraordinary achievements. The *Code* and *Digest*, Sancta Sophia at Istanbul, and San Vitale at Ravenna are enough to put the person responsible among the greater giants of western civilization. But one cannot help feeling about him as the Anglican

John Bramhall in 1658 felt about Henry VIII—that great good can come of the deeds of dreadful men. In the Church, especially in the West, many found the Emperor hard to bear. He loved to issue elaborate edicts on orthodox dogma, and then to summon large synods to ratify what he had prescribed. The horribly maltreated Pope Vigilius experienced Justinian as a disaster. Pagan intellectuals, not accustomed to agreeing with the Pope, found reason to dislike the Emperor very much. In 529 the Platonic Academy at Athens was led by the militantly anti-Christian Neoplatonist Damascius. Justinian closed the place down and confiscated the endowments, leaving Damascius, with Simplicius and other philosophers, to emigrate to the Persian Empire in a hope for liberty which was sadly unrealized. They all soon returned. At Alexandria the Neoplatonic school kept a much lower profile, writing commentaries on Aristotelian logic. Justinian did not interfere there at all. Moreover, among the Alexandrian exegetes of Aristotle was the Christian John Philoponus, with an intelligence that anticipated many of Galileo's discoveries. The most significant evidence of the way Justinian was regarded is the attitude of the principal chronicler of his military and architectural glories, Procopius of Palestinian Caesarea, an eloquent writer with a sardonic pen who served under Belisarius. How intense was his hatred of Justinian and Theodora stands out from every line of his *Anecdota* or 'Secret History', a portrait of a Stalin-like tyrant married to a grimly penitent harlot. Procopius thought the apotheosis of arbitrary autocracy unspeakable and appalling.

The imperial absolutism of Diocletian, Constantine, and their successors had long been presupposed by the Roman legal system. In the second century AD the jurist Gaius says explicitly that imperial decrees have the full force of law without needing further legitimation from the Senate. The supreme sovereignty of the Emperor was enhanced by the confusions and contradictions of edicts, of which the fourth-century historian Ammianus Marcellinus complains. Fourth-century Emperors were surrounded by lawyers, both civil and ecclesiastical, assuring them that their will was the sole source of valid law, and that they stood above it in the sense of not being bound by the enactments of their predecessors.

When those enactments were so full of contradictions, autocracy was no doubt a necessary doctrine. Naturally the Emperor was expected to preserve law and order and to defend the frontier. Tyrannical government made men remember old Stoic vindications of the right to tyrannicide. Christian writers like Ambrose of Milan, on the other hand, could appeal to the Emperor's status above the law to justify the Emperor Gratian (376–83) in suspending pagan cult at the Altar of Victory. If the Emperor Julian (355–63) chose to sit among the senators and spoke of himself as the enforcer of laws by which he felt himself bound, this was a criticism of his predecessor Constantius II, whose language and actions were at times absolutist, dangerously fortified by the belief that he was called to represent divine monarchy on earth, rather than a restatement of an older and more collegial political theory. In practice Julian's reversion to polytheism imposed on him a necessity to assert his unique position as the embodiment of public law and as principal exponent of a philosophical theology designed to vindicate pagan cults. Many students have been struck by the resemblance in political theory and practice between Julian and Justinian, both Emperors regarding religious dissent as a treason to society and the Empire. Paradoxical though it may seem, the 'democratic' ideal of populist participation came to our modern world more from Christian beliefs in the share of all the faithful in the society of the people of God than from Aristotle, the Stoics, or the Greek experience generally. Likewise surprising is the recognition that the Anglo-Saxon tradition of the common law owes more to the operations of ecclesiastical canon law than to classical Roman law.

The ancient political ideal was certainly very slow to die. When early in the fifth century Augustine of Hippo came to describe his ideal society, he did so in anachronistic terms of the classical city-state, with an autonomy that no city of the

Empire had enjoyed for some centuries past—an antiquarianism which emerges again in his description of Roman religion on the basis of Varro's work, in tactful silence about the contemporary scene. Augustine's attitude to imperial power was considerably indebted to the sombre pages of Sallust, and he writes with a hot and cold ambivalence about Rome's domination of the Mediterranean world: a manifestation of cupidity and lust to dominate on the one hand, yet, on the other, a beneficent force for centralized order and peace, without which human society would degenerate into jungle warfare. Augustine was well informed about Roman law, whose maxims and principles he cited with admiration. Friends to whom he turned for advice when questions of arbitration in civil cases were referred to him for judgement, included jurisconsults. He was aware that good Emperors can enact laws with unfortunate and unfair consequences, that bad Emperors may enact legislation that has a wholly beneficent effect, and that the problems of social justice are anything but simple.

Like his elder contemporary Jerome, Augustine was master of the classical literary tradition. Both men's writings abound in echoes and allusions to Cicero and Seneca, or the poets Virgil, Horace, Juvenal, and Tibullus. Terence was especially familiar. Though Augustine came from a small provincial town where a single schoolmaster taught all subjects to every child, the ancient educational system was not ineffective for him. He tells of one lifelong friend named Simplicius who 'knew Virgil backwards'; cite a line and he could tell you the preceding line, and he knew by heart several of Cicero's orations. A century later Boethius' prose and verse in the *Consolation of Philosophy*, written without access to a library in prison at Pavia, abounds in reminiscences of classical texts in which his mind was soaked. At one time in his youth Augustine taught grammar, and even wrote a textbook on the subject, together with other guides to the liberal arts of rhetoric, dialectic, geometry, and music (rhythm and metre, not pitch, on which he never wrote—Boethius was to take it up later). His writings show a sustained interest in grammar and diction. He could not but be acutely aware of the gulf between Ciceronian usage and the colloquial Latin of the Hippo waterfront.

Language

Before Diocletian introduced elaborate court ceremonial on the Persian model, Emperors were already being addressed as abstractions such as 'Your Majesty'. Powerful bureaucrats would be addressed as 'Your Excellency' or 'Your Eminence'. A tendency to verbal inflation went hand in hand with the debauch of the currency in the third century. Style became elaborate and formal. It was an indication of a person's importance if he was addressed in the third person rather than the second (a feature still apparent in Italian and German and in English etiquette for formal invitations). In the letters of Cyprian of Carthage, a man of upper-class origin, we see the use of similar courtesies entering ecclesiastical forms of address—'Your Holiness', or 'Your Beatitude'. By the fifth century the epithet 'venerabilis' is used for either Popes or Emperors. An Emperor is often 'serenissimus' or 'christianissimus', while a bishop is 'religiosissimus' and/or 'reverentissimus'. The plural form of self-designation and of address is adopted by Emperors and by Popes, who speak of themselves as 'we' and of their correspondent as 'you' (plural). Government chancellery formulas speak not of 'him', but of 'the aforesaid' or 'the above-mentioned', 'suprascriptus', 'memoratus', and so on. Instead of saying 'this', they write 'the present', 'praesens'. These and similar pedantries of formal style, familiar still in the formula books of European and American administrators, were established in this age.

The barbarian invasions of the fifth century had moments of tense military crisis, especially with the Vandals crossing the Rhine in 406, and later with the arrival of Attila, but for the most part the infiltration of the Germanic tribes was fairly gradual. Through service in the army a Vandal, Stilicho, could attain the summit of effective power. Such men learnt to speak and write fluent Latin; and in the West Latin remained a principal medium of communication among all well-educated men until the end of the medieval period, only gradually yielding to the vernacular. It required the zealous advocacy of Thomas More and William Tyndale (highly educated men who did not otherwise agree about much) to persuade English people that their language could be a proper medium for discussing serious subjects.

But at the everyday level Latin was by 700 in process of undergoing transformation into Romance. The travel diary of the pilgrim lady Egeria who in 384 journeyed from Spain to the Holy Land and ascended Sinai, or the sixth-century Rule of St Benedict, illustrates a colloquial idiom indifferent to the forms and syntax of Cicero. In the Carolingian renaissance after Alcuin had sent men back to school to learn formal Latin again, the rough colloquialisms of Benedict seemed vulgar and distressing to monks of high culture, so that a version of the Rule in correct Latinity had to be provided, saying, for instance, 'ausculta', not 'obsculta', for 'listen'. By Benedict's time plural nouns of the first declension use the accusative form for the subject of the sentence. Verbal forms have long become largely periphrastic; in fact, the auxiliary verb 'to be' mainly drops out of use, so that in some writers one meets long sentences with chains of participles and apparently no main verb. The spoken language in Italy was on the way to becoming Italian: one Roman inscription of the seventh century has 'essere abetis' for 'eritis'. The French definite article, in the forms *lo, la, lis*, is first attested in eighth-century Gaul. A council of bishops at Tours in 813 ruled that sermons be not in Latin but in 'rustica Romana lingua' so that everyone can understand. (The rest of the service evidently remained in Latin.) In sixth-century Merovingian Gaul the Latinity of Gregory of Tours, historian of the Franks, feels like a conscious act of resistance to demotic speech. Naturally, to admit the rustic Frankish form of pidgin Latin to the pulpit was to make possible a more rigorous purity of Latin for the educated élite in the government and the Church. From Alcuin on, a correct Latin was the preserve of this élite. To know it well, to be able to decorate a letter with a tag from Horace's *Ars Poetica* or the *Aeneid*, was to be elevated above the common herd and to have access to positions of considerable emolument.

Pronunciation of Latin varied regionally. When Augustine moved from Carthage to Milan, his African vowels brought comment from his Italian hearers. Africans made no distinction, as Italians still did, between long and short vowels. He astringently remarks that whether the third syllable of *ignoscere* is long or short is a matter of sublime indifference to a man crying to God for pardon. But only the educated in North Africa knew anyway, because the pronunciation would have been identical without regard to the quantity. In Gaul, on the other hand, there came to be a habit of marking *c* before *i* or *e* to sound *ts*. But among the northern barbarians in Britain the older hard *k* sound was kept for *c*. In the tenth century Abbo of Fleury (no mean logician) came to England to live for two years at Ramsey Abbey, and was pained by what seemed to him sad evidence of the uncivilized ways of the English who, though hospitable, were so uncultured as to pronounce *ce* and *ci* as *ke* and *ki*. It would have provoked incredulous astonishment to inform him that the crude barbarians of the north had preserved a more original usage than his own. It is likely that both Bede and Alcuin were accustomed to use the hard *k*, which was usual in the Irish schools, the isolation of which after the barbarian invasions produced deep conservatism.

In Augustine's mercantile congregation at Hippo (mainly sailors, dockers, and farm workers—very unlike Carthage, where he could address people who knew what a Stoic or Epicurean was), popular speech said 'dolus' for 'pain' when a grammarian would have prescribed 'dolor'. Having an identical pronunciation for both ōs, mouth and ŏs, bone, the people had replaced the latter by ossum. Although by training and every acquired reflex Augustine was acutely conscious of grammatical correctitude, he also knew, and liked to quote Horace to reinforce the point, that what is correct usage is determined by custom, the *consuetudo loquendi* which has a way of defying both logicians and grammarians with indifferent serenity. He reserved special scorn for people more offended by a linguistic vulgarism than by a fundamental breach of ethical principle. He admired the spontaneous vigour of popular Latin. While the Latinity of the *Confessions* is highly elaborate rhyming prose, never more sophisticated in rhetorical skill than when denouncing the meretricious arts of rhetoric, his sermons are in a direct style using short sentences and everyday idioms, usually with some apology and occasionally a swipe at scornful secular grammarians who did not know what was important in human life. In both Jerome and Augustine we find classical literature regarded as essentially secular. In Jerome's famous nightmare he dreamt of being arraigned before the Judgement Seat on a charge of being a Ciceronian, not a Christian. His promise of reform was ineffective. Augustine could also express reserve ('a certain Cicero', he wrote in the *Confessions*), but the Virgil who had first inflamed his heart as a schoolboy remained a lifelong love, together with Plotinus. He thought it very possible that the fourth *Eclogue* was a prophecy of Christ, the poet being inspired without being aware of the fact, and hoped the great sages and poets of the classical world had not only a providential role in the preparation for the gospel, but also a place in God's kingdom.

Augustine knew how to write moving Latin prose, whether simple or sophisticated. In the later Roman Empire there was a strong taste for a rococo style with out-of-the-way words and neologisms to challenge the reader's erudition and flatter his ingenuity in discovering the author's meaning. At its worst it became a tendency to say nothing as elaborately as possible. Literary allusions could provide a kind of esoteric code in letters between cultivated friends conscious of living in an increasingly unappreciative world. The Latinity of the pagan Martianus Capella, writing in Vandal Carthage about 470, or Ennodius, bishop of Pavia (*d*. 521), is not intended to communicate in the most direct terms with the ordinary reader. In Capella the technique is used as a mask for his essentially pagan sympathies. This mannerist style long continued. In the seventh century the

Italian Jonas, educated in the Irish monastery at Bobbio, composed a *Life* of his hero St Columban. His Latin style is full of poetic reminiscences and neologisms of the most *outré* kind, extravagant etymologies in which he takes special pleasure, and an impressive sprinkling of Greek words. All this is mingled with richly demotic usages—*pluriores* for *plures*, present participles used with passive force, confusions between similar-sounding words, and malapropisms such as *limes* for *limen*.

Nevertheless Jonas shows that classical literature was still being taught in schools. Augustine shows that the level of culture varied very much from place to place. At Carthage there were those who had read the *Aeneid* and could pick up an allusion. At Hippo no one except the bishop had read Virgil. His Hippo congregation knew the story of Dido, or ('a specially popular theme') the Judgement of Paris, from attending the local theatre, not from reading any books.

In the writing of Latin prose an awareness of the old rhythmic *cursus* was not lost. Schools continued to teach the rules. In Monte Cassino during the eleventh century proper prose rhythm even became something of an obsession. The replacement of quantity by accent, first seen coming in the third century, had decisive consequences for the writing of verse. Monastic and episcopal schools transmitted Latin through the most precarious age of the barbarian kingdoms, until they in turn gave ground to the newly founded universities. Medieval universities were directed towards vocational training in theology, law, medicine, and the *artes*. In them the study of classical Latin did not necessarily prosper better than it had done in the older episcopal schools. Until the twelfth century what was known in the Latin West about Plato came indirectly through Apuleius, Calcidius, Macrobius, Martianus Capella, and Boethius, who had also provided translations of Aristotle's *Organon* (only his versions of the *Categories* and *Interpretation*, and of Porphyry's *Isagoge* being generally known). The schoolmen's fascination with logic, stimulated further by contact with Muslim writers such as Avicenna and Averroes, also led them to coin neologisms of a repellent kind to meet their needs when negotiating a hesitant way over the *pons asinorum*.

The Renaissance reacted against the Schoolmen and their continual moulding of Latin to contemporary needs. Lorenzo Valla treats Boethius with a patronizing mixture of admiration and distaste—the last man to write decent Latin, but sadly tolerant of barbarisms. The Renaissance enthusiastically demanded classical Latin in its purity and beauty. Thereby, paradoxically, it reduced Latin to the status of a dead language. Once the churches of the Reformation required the vernacular, there was a further dethronement of the language from any ordinary employment. In the twentieth century even the Roman Catholic Church capitulated, and the Latin mass went the way of the steam engine.

The Greek language did not have so many problems to contend with, but underwent nevertheless a comparable development. The conquests of Alexander the Great might have made *koinē* Greek the normal means of communication in government administration and trade, but it was not used everywhere in the same way. The language of the Alexandrian waterfront or Syrian bazaars was very different from anything known to Aeschylus or Thucydides. One has only to pick up St Mark's Gospel to see that; he writes the demotic language of the streets. Pronunciation too varied in different regions. Lucian of Samosata was strongly conscious of his tell-tale accent; anyone could deduce he came from Syria. The educational system prescribed certain texts as pre-eminently suitable for educational purposes. The main corpus of classical Greek literature familiar to us today is the selection made by some anonymous schoolmasters, perhaps at Alexandria or Pergamum or Athens in the third century BC. The vast amount that is lost to us is what they omitted from their selection as unfitted for ordinary level work. The tension between poetry and philosophy, which surfaces in Plato's *Republic* and to which Plutarch devoted a tract, long continued into the Roman period.

The supreme model in poetry always remained Homer. Even

in eleventh-century Byzantium, according to the express testimony of Michael of Ephesus, schoolboys learnt each day between thirty and fifty lines of Homer by heart. An elementary school course normally included the first book of the *Iliad* and one play each of Sophocles, Euripides, and Aristophanes, with a few bits of Pindar and Theocritus thrown in. Byzantine schoolmasters of the twelfth century are found still debating the question keenly discussed a millennium earlier (for instance, by Dio Chrysostom) whether the superhuman elements in Homer's poetry required disbelief in the historicity of Odysseus and even of the Trojan War—a debate which Origen in 248 invokes as analogous to the debate about the miraculous element in the gospel narrative. A Homeric allusion always added a touch of class to the prose of any Byzantine author other than the most radically world-rejecting monk. In the fifth century Theodoret, bishop of Cyrrhus in Syria, who wrote a *Life* of the contemporary pillar saint Simeon Stylites, also composed urbane letters decorated with Homeric echoes to officers of the imperial consistory. Michael Psellos tells in his *Chronicle* how when the Emperor Constantine IX first introduced his mistress at court, one courtier quoted just two words from the Trojan elders' awe at the beauty of Helen. Everyone got the allusion except the lady, whose inferior education was revealed by the need to explain the highly sophisticated reference to her.

High style in the Byzantine world was necessarily marked by a self-conscious archaism. The demotic usages of the streets and farmyards were not appropriate for anyone with pretensions to be read in polite society. But the presence of the demotic element exerted a mounting pressure. Early in the seventh century a Cilician monk named John Moschos, intimate confidant of Sophronius the sophist, author of *Anacreontica*, and then first patriarch of Jerusalem under the Arab occupation, compiled an anthology of unusual, sometimes macabre stories about monastic heroes, entitled *Leimonarion*, the spiritual 'Meadow'. The work is fascinating not only for its folklore elements (one story reappears in the *Thousand and One Nights*), but also for the colloquial diction and syntax. Words and phrases characteristic of modern demotic Greek can go back a long way: *nero* for cold water appears in the apophthegms of the Desert Fathers of the fourth century. The eleventh-century epic *Digenes Akritas* ('the Borderer') used popular idioms, and regularly said *na* for *hina*. Beneath the surface veneer of high Byzantine style there was a popular speech uninfluenced by upper-class archaizing. Gradually poets and then prose writers came to have the confidence to use the demotic idiom. The twentieth-century tensions between demotic and *katharevousa* are in part a distant legacy of the divergence between the self-conscious correctness of the city of Constantinople with its literary élite and the everyday language of colloquial usage. Even in the seond century AD the grammarian Phrynichus was warning aspiring writers against admitting barbarous or uneducated words into their prose. A number of the usages which he specifically vetoes appear in the New Testament as ordinary unselfconscious speech. Throughout the history of the language, the conservative preservation of a pure and more archaizing or classical Greek is connected with the acknowledgement that in the classical age lie the supreme achievements of all Greek literature, history, and philosophy. To make the demotic language standard usage is obviously to weaken a link that gives wide access to that classical world, though at the same time it may prevent contemporary Greeks from thinking that they have inherited with their mother's milk a capacity to understand Aeschylus or Lycophron. In the continuous development of the Greek language since antiquity, an élite has always existed which wished to recite Homer and to write prose in the manner of Thucydides. Such a manner can be achieved only by some degree of affectation, and sophisticated Byzantine prose of the late-medieval period can be uncommonly difficult to interpret. It must have been found so at the time. Some neo-Latin writers of the Renaissance offer obvious parallels.

Philosophy and Religion

The Christian mission in the Graeco-Roman world, initially led by a Christian Jew from Tarsus whose followers were at times baffled by the profundity and dynamism of his understanding of Christ and the Church, met with a success sufficient to provoke government persecution and philosophical criticism. To their persecutors the Christians replied when in co-operative mood that an ethic which demanded stable family life and honesty in trade deserved encouragement, and that, provided one had no part in polytheistic cult which they thought honouring evil spirits, one could render to both God and Caesar whatever was their due. Indeed they recognized a religious obligation to pay taxes. They further claimed that the intellectual tradition of the classical past was not alien to them. They soon found ways to make it their own. Stoic ethics required attitudes to slavery or wealth that they found congenial. 'Seneca saepe noster' ('Seneca is often one of us'), said Tertullian. Platonic metaphysics affirmed divine transcendence, the freedom of the will, the immortality of the soul, and that virtue is necessary and sufficient for happiness. In Justin, Clement of Alexandria, and Origen, Platonism and Christian thought come to keep house together.

The marriage went with allegorical or symbolist exegesis of parts of the Pentateuch, already worked out in detail by the Jew Philo of Alexandria. This principle was soon extended to any part of the authoritative corpus of biblical writings accepted for reading in church lectionaries (this acceptance being a criterion of 'canonicity'). How deeply the first Christians pondered the complex relation between faith and history is apparent in St John's Gospel, where it is a general rule of interpretation that if anything can have two or more levels of meaning, it does: the history is a sacramental vehicle of spiritual truth. The Christians were not the first to discern a pattern in history that discloses the nature and meaning of human existence (Thucydides had already travelled that way); but symbolist writing in literature has its principal springs in the New Testament.

The dialogues of Plato that fascinated the Neoplatonists were *Timaeus*, *Parmenides*, and *Republic*. The *Timaeus* set out Plato's cosmogony and therefore a doctrine of the relation between the Creator and the cosmos. The *Parmenides* dealt with dialectical problems about being, identity, and difference. These two dialogues and the Neoplatonic commentaries on them were read by Christians with obvious sympathy.

The marriage of Platonism and Christianity, however, had its tiffs. The pagan Platonists were not in the least grateful for the hand of intellectual sympathy which the Christians stretched out towards them, and asked awkward questions about the compatibility of the notion of incarnation with divine immutability, which Plato had argued to be necessary to the concept of perfection. From the Christian side there was fierce criticism of the Platonic axiom of the eternity of the world, the belief that the soul possesses an eternity and immortality independent of the Creator, and, above all, the fatalism inherent in the notion of reincarnation.

Clement of Alexandria speaks of the Church as a river emerging from the confluence of Biblical faith with Greek philosophy. Apocalyptic hope, passing from late Judaism into early Christian preaching, is that element in Christianity which to a Platonist critic (Celsus) seemed most bizarre. Yet from apocalyptic the Christians brought to the western world the sense that the historical process is moving to a divine event—whether near or far off they disputed. In Romans 8 Paul sees the sufferings of this life as the birth-pangs preceding a new age.

Apocalyptic language implies a negative view of much of the world's way of going about its business. Neoplatonic ethics also encouraged world rejection and withdrawal. 'Plotinus always seemed ashamed of being in the body.' Before Plotinus' time Clement and Origen were articulating an ascetic ladder of the soul's ascent from passion and pleasure to a training and discipline of the character whose final goal is expressed in mystical terms of the vision of God granted to the pure in heart.

An accurate delineation of the distinctive features of early Christian ethics in comparison with the philosophical ethics of antiquity is intricate, certainly not susceptible of simplistic formulas. When the pagan Celsus dismisses Christian ethical teaching as having 'nothing new', Origen in reply is delighted to concede; for the gospel is a gift of the Creator for the realization of those duties or goods which the informed conscience recognizes, imprinted by the creative reason, the light that lightens every man coming into the world. The early Christians had not read Kant (though John Chrysostom anticipates verbatim Kant's dictum that God is discerned through the moral law within and the starry heavens above). They did not think moral reasoning a special way of exercising rational judgement separate from other deployments of the reason. They did not talk about the moral imperative as command coming from an alien force outside the soul and asking for blind obedience. The doctrine of man made in God's image, fused with Platonic language about the soul's 'affinity' with God, helped them to say that the soul naturally recognizes how right and rational it is to be good and just. The imperatives in the conscience are signposts to what the source of all goodness is like. But the Christians dissented deeply from the Socratic principle that none errs knowingly or deliberately, and saw human nature as a noble ruin whose self-inflicted misery called for a restoration transcending human powers. The stress on redemption and grace went with an insistence on obedience and humility of which Christ is model. But the main shift in ethical concern resulting from conversion to Christianity comes to lie in an intense interest in motive as the source of value. Augustine was especially fascinated by the fact that circumstances and motives are primary in evaluating the moral significance of an act.

The most striking manifestation of Christian detachment from the secular appears in the monastic movement of the fourth century. In a sermon of the mid third century Origen observed that renunciation of the world is not achieved by physically moving oneself out into the desert, a remark which suggests that already somebody thought otherwise. The complex motives that drove men and women to become hermits or, more commonly, to join communities of ascetics living under obedience are only partly visible to us. The fourth-century Church experienced the movement as a shock to its system. Many bishops opposed the weakening of urban or village congregations which resulted from the exodus of the most dedicated members into special separate communities owing an allegiance to their abbot and often showing a cool reserve to the ordinary life of the Church. The earliest document yet found to mention a monk is a papyrus from the Fayum of 6 June 324. Athanasius of Alexandria portrayed the hermit Antony in a *Life* which owed something to Pythagorean hagiography about their founder. In the Nile valley from about 320 the Copt Pachomius was establishing large communities of monks under virtually military discipline, some of which were embarrassingly successful in agriculture. In Asia Minor in the 360s and 370s Basil of Caesarea composed rules for communities under rule with a common habit and dedicated to the service of the outside community.

The monks enraged writers such as Libanius or the Alexandrian schoolmaster Palladas, whose embittered epigrams won a place in the *Palatine Anthology*, or in the West the poet Rutilius Namatianus. The Platonic Christian, Synesius of Cyrene, disliked their rejection of culture, and much misgiving was provoked by the readiness of some monks to form bands for the dismantling of pagan shrines. Augustine begs his people to win the minds and hearts of their pagan neighbours, not to infuriate them by insulting matters they held dear, even if obviously corrupt and superstitious.

The Church and the End of the Ancient World

The change of religion had some social consequences which affected the world from which the Church wished to be detached and independent. The capture of society, in principle largely achieved by 400 (though pockets of pagan resistance long continued), also affected the Church itself. Could the Church be respectable in class terms without losing its sense of obligation to and identification with the poor? The first charge on the local church chest was the maintenance of those whose names stood in the 'register of the poor' (the phrase is first attested in 422, but the thing is much earlier). Augustine knew that the alms of the faithful were inadequate to the problem of destitution, and longed for the imperial government to provide subsistence benefit, financed by redistributive taxation that, he felt sure, good men would be happy to pay. Rich benefactors usually preferred to see their money put into buildings or mosaic and marble decoration in basilicas. Then there were questions about compromise with the political and social system. Gregory of Nyssa boldly attacked the institution of slavery. Augustine thought the domination of man over his neighbour an inherent wrong, but saw no way of ending it and concluded that, since the ordering of society prevented the misery of anarchic disintegration, slavery was both a consequence of the fall of man and at the same time a wrong that providence prevented from being wholly harmful. Slaves were not a very large proportion of the ancient labour force, since the cost of a slave to his owner exceeded that of employing free wage-labourers. Slaves in a good household with a reasonable master enjoyed a security and standard of living that seldom came the way of free wage-labourers. But not all slaves had good masters, and in special cases bishops used the church chest to pay the costs of emancipation. Refusal on moral grounds to own slaves became a rule for monasteries.

The ancient Church deeply disapproved of capital punishment and judicial torture. A Roman church-order of about 200 forbids a Christian magistrate to order an execution on pain of excommunication. No Christian layman could tolerably bring a charge against anyone if the penalty might be execution or a beating with lead-weighted leather thongs. There was a tendency, first apparent in the fifth century, to modify rigorism against capital punishment in all circumstances; Pope Innocent I (405) ruled against excommunicating magistrates who imposed it, which was not to say that such penalties were welcome. Torture forced so many innocent people to confess to crimes they had not committed that the Christian hatred of it commanded wide assent. Nevertheless, by what were deemed necessities of state it continued. In the Merovingian period conciliar canons had to be content with forbidding clergy to be present in the torture chamber. The Bulgar king was probably little moved when in 866 Pope Nicolas I told him that torture is contrary to both divine and human law. The military impact of Islam first made some Christians argue the controversial thesis that one could resort to violence to withstand the infidel. Even after that had been admitted and implemented in the Crusades, in the West it was not effectively until the age of the papal monarchy that torture and execution began to be deployed against heretics, and there were those at the time who noted the break with immemorial tradition. Although Augustine justified coercion against the Donatist schismatics of north Africa, seeing how successful the policy was, nevertheless he laid down strict limits to the penalties that might be imposed, and refused all resort to force. The pain of his legacy arose from his need to reason out a theoretical justification of the coercion, and this survived the particular situation and his mitigating hand.

People bequeathed estates to churches and monasteries, and landownership brought responsibilities for the work-force and for correct financial trusteeship which were a source of anxiety to bishops and abbots, but nevertheless gave them powers of patronage. As the barbarian kingdoms took control in the West, aristocratic and cultured Romans, such as Sidonius Apollinaris in Gaul, found a bishopric a vantage-point for preserving independence and for protecting the secular interests of church members before an unsympathetic government. A bishop was not expected to confine himself to preaching good expository sermons. He had to be a community leader. In Syria Theodoret of Cyrrhus built porticoes, baths, two bridges, and an aqueduct for his little town. Christianity never shrugged off its origins as an urban religion moving from the town out into the surrounding countryside which was slow to be converted and tenacious of old peasant superstitions. The Church was joined by many women and manual workers, but never had a proletarian ethos. From the start (as I Corinthians shows) it contained a proportion of well educated people, capable of private Bible study at home. In a society where rhetoric was a part of the school curriculum eloquent sermons were appreciated, but it was often observed that sincerity and personal passion in the preacher mattered more than a fine turn of phrase. The bishops, based in the city, became identified with the city community in a way which, after the barbarian invasions, became socially important. Even by the third century bishops signed their names appending an adjectival form of the name of their town.

Among bishops the level of education varied by extremes. They were elected by their congregations subject to the veto of the consecrating bishops of the province under the metropolitan; they were local people, not brought in from outside or overseas, and closely reflected the style of their laity. Illiterate bishops—a favourite butt for the mockery of the half-educated, as Augustine once observed—were rare. By the mid fifth century a bishopric could be the destiny of a voluntarily retired praetorian prefect or a forcibly retired emperor. When Cyrus of Panopolis, a pagan poet who rose to be city prefect of Constantinople, fell foul of the chamberlain Chrysaphius, he saved himself by baptism and a Phrygian bishopric where the enraged population had lynched his four predecessors. Although individual bishops were occasionally unpopular, we hear more of the respect and affection in which their people held them. Like a rich patron, a bishop was expected to intercede with magistrates or tax authorities on behalf of his people and even to get employment for them. Augustine liked to quote a wise man's aphorism, that he had too much regard for his own reputation to vouch for other people's. He feared the dangers of his social role. When an acquaintance was elected to a bishopric, he wrote to warn him of the trappings of office, the raised throne with embroidered cloth, and the choir of nuns singing to welcome him; 'the honour of this world is passing away.'

The storms of the fifth-century invasions made all honour in this world seem infinitely precarious. The establishment of the barbarian kingdoms formalized a take-over which had long been reality. Even before Constantine's time Germanic tribes were providing some of the best soldiers for the legions. Julian's hymn of hate against Constantine includes the charge that he elevated barbarians to great offices of state. To the distress of the Roman aristocrats, Julian himself found it necessary to put a barbarian general into the prestigious post of consul. At the beginning of the fifth century the Vandal Stilicho held all real power in the West. Long before 476 collaboration had gone so far that resistance was no option. When the Goths poured into the Balkan peninsula to escape the Huns in 375, and shattered the imperial army of Valens at Adrianople (378), Ambrose of Milan saw the fulfilment of biblical prophecies of Gog and Magog coming from the north to ravage the city of God. Augustine would not accept this exegesis: 'the city of God had as much room for Goths as for Romans.'

The question has been repeatedly asked. Did Rome's conversion to Christianity directly cause or indirectly contribute to the end of the ancient world? Is there truth (even if now to be drastically reformulated in secular terms) in the contention of those whom Augustine sought to refute in the *City of God*, who thought Alaric's capture of Rome in 410 a consequence of Rome's abandonment of the old gods, the closing of the temples in 391, and the prohibition of pagan sacrifices?

In 412 the proconsul of Africa, Volusianus, later a Christian, but at that time still pagan, asked a friend of Augustine if the ethic of the Sermon on the Mount would bring the collapse of the Empire. Was war justifiable in self-defence or to recover stolen property? Augustine thought so, for it was in the cause of justice, and 'those who desire peace must first love justice'. Yet the wars of the Empire must be so conducted that afterwards the vanquished can enjoy justice and peace. Likewise mercy to prisoners of war is a fundamental principle. (The redemption of prisoners of war was a ground on which bishops thought it right to sell church plate given by wealthy benefactors.) There is no evidence that the Church denounced or discouraged the defence of the Empire against Attila. At this period we meet the first evidence for military chaplains attached to units of the Roman army. Augustine observed that Christ did not ask the centurion in the gospel to find a new career. But he might have felt strong misgivings had he seen the order of service prescribed for Toledo cathedral about 500 'when the Visigothic king goes forth to war'.

A more plausible answer than pacifism (or what Gibbon memorably called the Christian preaching of patience and pusillanimity) is that the Church provided an alternative society with a rival career structure and different loyalties. Warnings in ascetic texts betray awareness that bishoprics could be sought for reasons not exclusively religious. The Church competed for the available talent. It drew into its power structure men ambitious, not necessarily for themselves, but for the cause they served, who might well have been useful soldiers or administrators or traders or manufacturers increasing the material wealth of society instead of channelling it into poor relief or noble basilicas like the Ravenna churches. Even this answer to the question evidently rests on a concealed value judgement. In the second century Celsus thought the Church had too few educated people ready to accept public office. Was it that in the fourth and fifth century it employed too many?

The evidence of the time shows that the churches of late antiquity were desperately understaffed. Successive north-African councils deplored the shortage of clergy. Those whom they did have seem from Augustine's correspondence to be altogether unremarkable. There are obvious exceptions. Ambrose left a provincial governorship to become bishop at Milan, where his sermons instructed Valentinian II in his duties. He served as special envoy in matters of state. In that age bishops were often so used; there was an assumption that as negotiators they might be successful because they had divine aid. The millionaire Paulinus sold most of his estates to retire to Nola to write religious verse in honour of St Felix. His renunciation was not well regarded by all Christians; when he asked for a papal audience to tell the glad tidings, he was abruptly refused.

One could move from high positions in the world to become a

bishop, but it was not socially proper to move in the reverse direction. In later antiquity bishops did not, like their successors in the late Middle Ages or the Renaissance, combine spiritual office with major secular administration. It was thought highly unusual when Cyrus, the patriarch who surrendered Alexandria to the Arab invaders in 641, combined his patriarchate with the post of prefect of Egypt. He wore one shoe with the insignia of the patriarch, the other with those of the prefect—the ancient equivalent of wearing two hats.

There is one unquestionable respect in which conversion to Christianity brought to the administration of the Empire complexities it would prefer to have done without. The Christians tended to quarrel about ever more refined points of dogma and to take their disagreements to the crucial point of suspending eucharistic communion. That meant a denial that those with whom one refused to hold communion were part of the commonwealth of God; they were to be held as strangers and outsiders. From 311 until the coming of Islam at the end of the seventh century the great Church of north Africa was split between two rival groups, whose theological disagreement was enforced by rancour, by prohibitions on mixed marriages, and by one side wholly rejecting the validity of orders and sacraments on the other side. In the East also there were successive splinter groups, some only small but others very substantial. The followers of Nestorius flourished outside the Empire in Persia and across central Asia into China. At the opposite end of the theological spectrum the Monophysites, unable to accept the decisions of the fourth General Council at Chalcedon (451), set up a rival hierarchy against those in communion with the Orthodox patriarchates. The government harassed them in Egypt and Syria, and as a result, when these provinces first met the force of the Arab invaders from 634, the capacity of the Byzantine army and administration to resist was weakened by the deep alienation of many of its Monophysite citizens, who soon found their new rulers, though not always tolerant, at least much easier to live with than the Constantinople straitjacket. In Egypt the scale of apostasy to Islam so saddened one seventh-century monk on Sinai that in despair he took his life, and in the circumstances even suicide incurred no censure.

The Arab conquest of Syria, Egypt, north Africa, and then southern Spain and Sicily, ended the unity of the old Roman world as no other factor did. The Mediterranean was no longer a Roman lake.

Further Reading

The classic study of the 'end of the ancient world' remains Edward Gibbon's *Decline and Fall of the Roman Empire* (1776–88, best read in J. B. Bury's edn., London 1909–14); it is good until the sixth century, though Gibbon lacked a sense of history as process and had a complex personal attitude to sex and to Christianity. (Richard Porson's judgement stands: 'Mr Gibbon's humanity never slumbers unless when women are ravished or the Christians persecuted.') See also the early volumes of the *Cambridge Medieval History*. On the fourth century: N. H. Baynes, *Constantine the Great and the Christian Church* (2nd edn. London, 1973); D. Bowder, *The Age of Constantine and Julian* (London, 1978); T. D. Barnes, *Constantine and Eusebius* (Cambridge, Mass., 1981). On Julian: specialized studies by R. Browning: *The Emperor Julian* (London, 1975); G. W. Bowersock, *Julian the Apostate* (London, 1978); and P. Athanassiadi-Fowden, *Julian and Hellenism* (Oxford, 1981), which supplement the symposium edited by A. Momigliano, *The Conflict Between Paganism and Christianity in the Fourth Century* (Oxford, 1963). On social and economic history, especially the bureaucracy, see A. H. M. Jones, *The Later Roman Empire* (Oxford, 1964). On the barbarians, see J. B. Bury, *The Invasion of Europe by the Barbarians* (London, 1928); J. M. Wallace-Hadrill, *The Barbarian West* (3rd edn. London, 1967); *The Frankish Church* (Oxford, 1983); E. A. Thompson, *The Visigoths in the Time of Ulfila* (Oxford, 1966); *The Goths in Spain* (Oxford, 1969). C. E. Stevens, *Sidonius Apollinaris and his Age* (Oxford, 1933). On Spain, H. Chadwick, *Priscillian of Avila* (Oxford, 1976).

Of Augustine there is a striking portrait by Peter Brown: *Augustine of Hippo* (London, 1967). For his ideas see John Burnaby, *Amor Dei* (London, 1938 and repr.); É. Gilson, *The Christian Philosophy of St. Augustine* (ET London, 1961); H. A. Deane, *The Political and Social Ideas of St Augustine* (New York–London, 1963). On the sixth century: R. Browning, *Justinian and Theodora* (London, 1971); A. M. Honoré, *Tribonian* (paperback, London, 1981). Averil Cameron, *Agathias* (Oxford, 1970); H. Chadwick, *Boethius; The Consolations of Music,*

Logic, Theology, and Philosophy (Oxford, 1981); M. Gibson (ed.), *Boethius* (Oxford, 1981).

On the development of the languages: E. Löfstedt, *Late Latin* (ET Oslo, 1959); R. Browning, *Medieval and Modern Greek* (2nd edn. Cambridge, 1983).

Monks: Owen Chadwick, *John Cassian* (2nd edn. Cambridge, 1968); D. J. Chitty, *The Desert a City* (London, 1966); P. Rousseau, *Ascetics, Authority and the Church* (Oxford, 1978). On the Church in ancient society: H. Chadwick, *The Early Church* (Harmondsworth, 1967); *History and Thought of the Early Church* (London, Variorum, 1982).

TABLES OF EVENTS

TABLES OF EVENTS

GREECE

Only those events of importance to the Greeks in the West are mentioned here.

775–650 Greek colonization in the West
700–650 The diffusion of hoplite tactics
657–570 The age of tyrants
600   Foundation of Greek city of Massalia (Marseilles)

ROME

Early Rome

The dates and the reality of events in early Roman history are quite uncertain. Rome began as a community on the fringes of Etruscan culture; under the later kings she was in effect an Etruscan city dominating Latium. The establishment of the republic caused a decline in her power as she fought for survival against the Etruscans and sought to re-establish her dominance in Latium. The fifth century was a period of acute social tension. The destruction of Veii ended the Etruscan threat, and the sack of Rome by the Gauls proved only a temporary setback. By 338 Rome had incorporated Latium and moved into Campania.

753   Traditional date for
         foundation of Rome
753–509 Period of kings
616–579 Tarquinius Priscus
579–534 Servius Tullius; military

546–480	The flight of Ionian Greeks from Persia brings Greek philosophy and culture to the West: Xenophanes, Pythagoras, Parmenides active as philosophers, Alcmaeon of Croton as a doctor
540	Battle of Alalia; Carthaginians and Etruscans check Greek expansion in the western Mediterranean
524	Etruscans defeated at Cumae
508	Reforms of Cleisthenes at Athens
491–466	Tyrannies of Gelon and Hiero create a Greek power based on Syracuse
480	Great Persian Expedition by land to Greece; Carthaginians invade Sicily and are defeated at the battle of Himera
461	Radical reforms of the legal system at Athens by Ephialtes
431–404	Great Peloponnesian War between Athens and Sparta
415–413	Athenian expedition to Sicily is destroyed
405	Dionysius I becomes tyrant of Syracuse; peace between Syracuse and Carthage
367	Death of Dionysius I; Dionysius II becomes tyrant of Syracuse
359–336	Philip II of Macedon establishes Macedonian power over Greece
356–354	Dion, uncle of Dionysius and pupil of Plato, controls Syracuse
346–344	Second tyranny of Dionysius II
344–338	Timoleon arrives in Sicily, ends the tyrannies, and defeats the Carthaginians at Crimisus (341); revival of Greek Sicily
336–323	Alexander the Great overthrows the Persian Empire, and establishes Greek control as far as Russia, Afghanistan, the Punjab, and Egypt

	reforms and creation of Comitia Centuriata; treaty with the Latins and foundation of Temple of Diana on the Aventine
534–509	Tarquinius Superbus; draining of Roman forum suggests creation of an urban centre
509	Foundation of the Republic; first treaty with Carthage; foundation of Temple of Jupiter on the Capitoline
496	Latins defeated at battle of Lake Regillus; treaty with Latins
494–440	Struggle of the Orders
450	Publication of Laws of Twelve Tables
405–396	Siege and capture of Veii
390	Sack of Rome by the Gauls
366	First plebeian consuls
340	Latin War; Latin League dissolved
338	Campania incorporated into the Roman state

THE HELLENISTIC WORLD

ROME

POLITICAL EVENTS	CULTURAL DEVELOPMENTS	

Age of the Successors

The Colonization and Conquest of Italy

The struggles of the generals who divided Alexander's empire centred on the attempts of first Perdiccas and then Antigonus the One-Eyed to maintain the empire's unity. By 306 the family of Alexander had been eliminated, and the contenders felt sure enough to claim the title of king in their own areas; by 276 the three great powers of the Hellenistic world, Macedon, Egypt, and the Seleucid Empire were firmly established.

The period from 334 to 264 saw the gradual expansion of Rome to control by colonization, conquest, and alliance all of Italy south of the Po valley.

323–320	Perdiccas tries to maintain unity through his regency, but is killed in Egypt	325–300	Pytheas of Massilia circumnavigates Britain	
323–322	Athens and her allies attempt to free themselves from Macedon in the Lamian War	322	Deaths of Aristotle and Demosthenes Theophrastus becomes head of Lyceum	
		321–289	Career of Menander (poet of New Comedy)	
320–301	Antigonus the One-Eyed aims at universal empire	320–05	Hecataeus of Abdera writes first Hellenistic cultural history of Egypt	327–304 Second Samnite War against Samnites in the central Apennines
317–289	Agathocles tyrant of Syracuse	317–07	Demetrius of Phaleron (Peripatetic philosopher) is Macedonian governor of Athens	
317	Philip III half-wit half-brother of Alexander murdered	317	*Dyscolus* of Menander performed End of Attic gravestone series	
315	Olympias mother of Alexander murdered			

315–311	Coalition of satraps against Antigonus	314	Polemon becomes head of Academy on death of Xenocrates	310	Roman advance into Erruria
312	Seleucus captures Babylon; beginning of Seleucid era				
311	Peace between the successors recognizes in effect the division between Antigonus (Asia), Macedon/Greece (Cassander), Thrace (Lysimachus), Egypt (Ptolemy), and by omission the eastern satrapies (Seleucus)	310	Clearchus of Soli (Peripatetic philosopher) visits Aï Khanoum in Afghanistan(?)		
311–306	War between Agathocles and Carthage; invasion of Africa	310	Zeno of Citium establishes the Stoic school in Stoa *Poikilē* at Athens		
310	Murder of Alexander IV, son of Alexander the Great and last member of the dynasty	309	Philitas of Cos (scholar and founder of Alexandrian poetry) appointed tutor to future Ptolemy II		
307	Demetrius the Besieger, son of Antigonus, 'liberates' Athens	307–306	Exile and recall of Theophrastus from Athens		
306–304	Antigonus, Ptolemy, and Seleucus call themselves kings	307	Epicurus establishes his philosophical school at Athens		
305–304	Siege of Rhodes by Demetrius				

THE HELLENISTIC WORLD (cont.)

POLITICAL EVENTS		CULTURAL DEVELOPMENTS	
303	Seleucus cedes Indian territories to Chandragupta founder of Mauryan dynasty for 500 war elephants	302–290	Megasthenes (author on India) at court of Chandragupta
301	Destruction of power of Antigonus and Demetrius at battle of Ipsus; Antigonus killed	300	Ptolemy I founds Museum of Alexandria on advice of Demetrius of Phaleron Zenodotus royal tutor and first head of the Library Euhemerus writes his utopian romance Euclid (mathematician) active
297	Death of Cassander ruler of Macedon		
297–272	Career of Pyrrhus of Epirus	295	Tyche of Antioch; Colossus of Rhodes

ROME (cont.)

298–290 Third Samnite War

285	Demetrius the Besieger captured by Seleucus, dies of drink in 283	
283	Ptolemy I Soter dies; Ptolemy II Philadelphus succeeds	
281	Lysimachus killed	
	Seleucus assassinated; his son Antiochus I succeeds	
	Foundation of Achaean League	
279	Invasion of Macedon and Greece by Gauls	
276	Antigonus Gonatus, son of Demetrius, defeats the Gauls and becomes king of Macedon, founding the Macedonian dynasty	
290	Berossus (Babylonian priest) writes history of Babylonia	
287	Theophrastus dies; Strato head of Lyceum	
280	Duris of Samos (leading exponent of 'tragic history') active	
	Bion of Borysthenes (satirist) active	
276	Death of Polemon, head of the Academy	
280–275		Pyrrhus of Epirus crosses into south Italy to help the Greek cities against Rome, and is defeated by the Romans
		Earliest Roman coinage

THE HELLENISTIC WORLD (cont.)

POLITICAL EVENTS	CULTURAL DEVELOPMENTS

The Balance of Power

The third century saw the creation of an uneasy balance of power between the great kingdoms, with conflict confined to disputed areas: the Ptolemies and the Seleucids fought over Syria and Palestine, while the Greek cities of the Aegean area sought to manipulate the great powers in order to achieve independence. This was the great age of Hellenistic culture: philosophy was centred on Athens, while the patronage of Ptolemy II created Alexandrian literature and science. From the 230s there are signs of the re-emergence of non-Greek forces on the political scene.

274–271	First Syrian War between Ptolemy II and Antiochus I	271	Death of Epicurus
		270–242	Arcesilaus converts the Academy to scepticism
		270	Callimachus, Theocritus, Lycophron (or a century later), Aratus, and Posidippus active as poets
			Manetho (historian and Egyptian priest) lays foundations of Egyptian history
			Ctesibius of Alexandria (engineer) and Herophilus of Chalcedon (doctor) active
			Aristarchus of Samos proposes heliocentric theory of universe

ROME (cont.)

272	Surrender of Tarentum; alliance with Greek cities in south Italy
272–215	Hiero, lieutenant of Pyrrhus, elected general and then king (270) at Syracuse; Syracusan age of prosperity and building

267–262	Chremonidean War: Ptolemy unsuccessfully supports Greek independence from Macedon. Antigonus Gonatas enters Athens
269	Death of Strato, last head of Lyceum
265–235	Archive of Zeno illuminates economic life of Egypt

The First Punic War

	Rome begins to emerge on the western Mediterranean scene with her expansion into Sicily, Corsica, and Sardinia, and her response to the Carthaginian expansion in Spain
264	First gladiatorial show at Rome
	Roman army enters Sicily to help Mamertines against Carthage: First Punic War begins
263	Hiero of Syracuse becomes ally of Rome

263–241	Eumenes ruler of Pergamum founds independent power and begins building programme
262	Cleanthes succeeds Zeno as head of Stoics
261	Antiochus II succeeds to Seleucid kingdom
260–253	Second Syrian War between Ptolemy II and Antiochus II
260	Hieronymus of Cardia (historian of the Successors) dies aged 104; Timaeus of Tauromenium (historian of the west) dies aged ninety-six

THE HELLENISTIC WORLD (cont.)

POLITICAL EVENTS	CULTURAL DEVELOPMENTS	ROME (cont.)
	260 Apollonius of Rhodes writes *Argonautica* (epic) Herodas (author of mimes) active	
	Erasistratus of Ceos (doctor) understands action of heart and distinguishes motor and sensory nerves	
	260–212 Archimedes (mathematician and inventor) active	
		256–255 Expedition of M. Regulus to Africa ends in disaster
	256 Asoka, king of Mauryans (269–232), proclaims his Buddhist mission to the Greek world	255–249 Series of Roman naval disasters
	250 Ariston of Chios (Stoic philosopher) active at Athens	
251–213 Career of Aratus of Sicyon statesman and general of Achaean League		
246 Ptolemy III succeeds to kingdom of Egypt; Seleucus II succeeds to Seleucid kingdom	246 Eratosthenes becomes head of Library at Alexandria; literary scholar and pioneer of scientific geography, he calculates the circumference of the earth correctly	247 Hamilcar Barca begins Carthaginian offensive in Sicily
246–241 Third Syrian War between Ptolemy III and Seleucus II		241 Roman victory off Aegates Islands; end of First Punic War
244–241 Agis IV attempts to reform Sparta and is executed		

239 Demetrius II succeeds Antigonus Gonatas as king of Macedon War between Macedon and the Achaean and Aetolian Leagues		**240–207** Livius Andronicus (earliest Roman poet and playwright) active
239–130 Independent Greek kingdom established in Bactria		
238 Emergence of Parthia		
238–227 War of Attalus of Pergamum against Galatians; he becomes master of Asia Minor and takes royal title		
		237 Roman occupation of Corsica and Sardinia Hamilcar begins Carthaginian expansion in Spain, followed by Hasdrubal
	235 Apollonius of Perge (mathematician) active	**236** Naevius' first play produced
235–222 Cleomenes III king of Sparta; he reforms Spartan state in 227	**232** Chrysippus succeeds Cleanthes as head of Stoics	**228** Rome establishes protectorate over the Illyrian coast

THE HELLENISTIC WORLD (cont.)

POLITICAL EVENTS		CULTURAL DEVELOPMENTS	
223	Antiochus III succeeds to Seleucid kingdom	225	Eratosthenes of Cyrene (polymath) and Ariston of Ceos (Peripatetic philosopher) active
221	Philip V succeeds to kingdom of Macedon Ptolemy IV succeeds to kingdom of Egypt		
219–217	Fourth Syrian War between Ptolemy IV and Antiochus III Egypt is saved from conquest by Egyptian native troops at battle of Raphia		

ROME (cont.)

227	Sicily and Sardinia are made provinces
221	Hannibal, aged twenty-five, takes command of Carthaginian forces in Spain Rome allies with Saguntum in Spain
219	Siege and capture of Saguntum by Hannibal

ROME

THE EAST	THE WEST	CULTURAL DEVELOPMENTS

The Conquest of the Mediterranean

'There can surely be no-one so petty or so apathetic in his outlook that he has no desire to discover by what means and under what system of government the Romans succeeded in less than fifty-three years (220–167) in bringing under their rule almost the whole of the inhabited world, an achievement which is without parallel in human history' (Polybius). About 200 Rome began to develop a culture of its own, heavily dependent on Greek models.

THE EAST	THE WEST	CULTURAL DEVELOPMENTS
	218–201 Second Punic War / Hannibal invades Italy	
	217 Hannibal defeats Romans at Lake Trasimene	
	216 Hannibal defeats Romans at Cannae	
215 Philip V of Macedon allies with Carthage	215 Hannibal in south Italy / Roman victories in Spain / Carthage allies with Syracuse	
214–205 First Macedonian War between Rome and Philip	213 Romans besiege Syracuse	
212–205 Antiochus III campaigns in the east in an unsuccessful attempt to reconquer Parthia and Bactria	212 Romans besiege Capua	
211 Roman alliance with Aetolian League	211 Hannibal marches on Rome / Capua and Syracuse fall / Roman defeats in Spain	
209 Attalus I of Pergamum allies with Rome against Philip	211–206 Scipio Africanus defeats Hasdrubal in Spain / Spain divided into two provinces	
206–185 Revolt and independence of Upper Egypt		204–169 Ennius active at Rome as poet and teacher

ROME (*cont.*)

THE EAST		THE WEST		CULTURAL DEVELOPMENTS	
204	Ptolemy V succeeds in Egypt	204	Scipio invades Africa	204	Plautus' *Miles Gloriosus* performed
203–200	Philip and Antiochus make a secret alliance against Egypt; fifth Syrian War: Antiochus seizes Syria	203	Hannibal recalled from Italy		Career of Plautus 204–184
		202	Scipio defeats Hannibal at battle of Zama	202	Fabius Pictor writes first prose history of Rome in Greek
			Carthage becomes a dependent of Rome		
200–197	Second Macedonian War between Rome and Philip	202–191	Roman conquest of Cisalpine Gaul	200 onwards	Greek art begins to become known to the Romans
196	Rome declares the freedom of the Greeks at the Isthmus of Corinth	197–133	Wars in Spain	200	Aristophanes of Byzantium (scholar) becomes head of Library at Alexandria
196–179	Philip rebuilds the power of Macedon				
194	Romans evacuate Greece				
192–188	Syrian War between Rome and Antiochus				
187	Antiochus III dies			186	Senatorial edict against Bacchic rites
				184	Censorship of the Elder Cato
				179	Basilica Aemilia and Aemilian Bridge built at Rome
179	Philip V dies and is succeeded by his son Perseus				

175	Antiochus IV Epiphanes succeeds to Seleucid empire			
171–167	Third Macedonian War			
170–168	Sixth Syrian War			
167	Battle of Pydna ends kingdom of Macedon; Rome divides territory into four republics	167	Direct taxation of Roman citizens abolished	167	Polybius the historian arrives in Rome
	Rome orders Antiochus IV out of Egypt			
	Rome declares Delos a free port			
	Desecration of Temple at Jerusalem brings to a head Jewish resistance against Antiochus' policy of hellenizing the Jews			
	Maccabean Revolt		166–159	Plays of Terence produced Great Altar of Zeus and Athena built at Pergamum
164	Death of Antiochus IV; book of Daniel composed			

ROME (cont.)

THE EAST	THE WEST	CULTURAL DEVELOPMENTS
		155 Carneades (head of the Academy) comes to Rome on an embassy and introduces the Romans to philosophy
	149–146 Third Carthaginian War: Carthage destroyed by Romans; Africa becomes a province	150 Agatharchides of Cnidus (Ptolemaic geographer) flourished
148 Fourth Macedonian War and war against Achaean League; Corinth is sacked and Macedonia becomes a Roman province		149 Publication of Cato's *Origines* or history of Rome

AT HOME	ABROAD	CULTURAL DEVELOPMENTS

The Late Republic

The history of this period is the history of Rome *domi militiaeque*, at home and abroad. Rome exploited ruthlessly her control of the Mediterranean world; her generals led her citizens to ever richer conquests. But at home the strains of empire began to destroy republican government. Culturally Rome became the centre of patronage, and Latin literature flourished.

		CULTURAL DEVELOPMENTS
		145 Aristarchus (scholar and head of the Library) and other intellectuals flee from Alexandria on accession of Ptolemy VIII

Date	Events	Date	Events	Date	Events
136–132	First Sicilian Slave War	142	Independence of the Jews	144	Panaetius (Stoic philosopher c.185–109) arrives in Rome
133	Tribunate of Tiberius Gracchus	141	Parthians attack Babylon		
		137	Roman army defeated at Numantia in Spain	135	Nicander (medical poet) active
125	M. Fulvius Flaccus proposes enfranchising the Latins	133	Attalus III of Pergamum bequeaths his kingdom to Rome; it becomes the province of Asia (129)	133	Calpurnius Piso (Roman historian) consul; his work covered Roman history down to 146 / Lucilius (Roman satirist) active
123–122	Tribunates of C. Gracchus				
121	First use of *senatusconsultum ultimum* to authorize massacre of Gracchan supporters	130	Antiochus VII dies fighting the Parthians		
		121	Gallia Narbonensis becomes a Roman province	120–110	Temple of Fortuna at Praeneste built / Circular temple in Forum Boarium, Rome
		118–117	Roman campaigns in Dalmatia	118	Polybius dies soon after this
107–100	C. Marius consul six times; he reforms the army	114–110	Series of Roman defeats	106	Cicero born
104–102	Second Sicilian Slave War	112–106	War against Jugurtha of Mauretania ended by Marius		
100	Caesar born	102–101	Marius defeats the Teutones and Cimbri	100	Philo of Larissa becomes head of the Academy
				99	Lucretius born

ROME (cont.)

AT HOME		ABROAD		CULTURAL DEVELOPMENTS	
				95	Meleager of Gadara (poet and collector of earliest epigrams in the Greek Anthology) active
91–98	Attempted reforms of M. Livius Drusus lead to Social War between Rome and her Italian allies. Rome defeats the allies by force and offers of citizenship				
88	L. Sulla marches on Rome	88–85	Mithridates VI of Pontus massacres Roman citizens in Asia and seeks to free the Greeks from Rome	88–68	Antiochus of Ascalon becomes head of the Academy at Athens; Philo of Larissa leaves for Rome
87	Marius seizes Rome, but dies in 86	86	Sulla in the East captures Athens and Greece	87–51	Posidonius (philosopher, historian, and polymath) active in Rhodes and at Rome
				84	Catullus born
83–82	Sulla returns to Italy; civil war	83–82	Second Mithridatic War		
82–80	Sulla appointed dictator of Rome; Sullan reforms. He resigns in 80 and dies in 78	80–72	Sertorius, Marian supporter, controls Spain	81	Cicero's earliest extant speech
				78	Sisenna (Roman historian) praetor The Tabularium (record house) on the Capitoline built

73–71	Slave Revolt of Spartacus
70	Consulate of Crassus and Pompey; Trial of Verres
63	Consulate of Cicero; Catilinarian conspiracy; Caesar elected *pontifex maximus*
62	Pompey returns to Italy and disbands his army
61	Trial and acquittal of P. Clodius on religious charge
60	'First triumvirate' formed between Pompey, Crassus, and Caesar
59	Consulate of Caesar; legislation in favour of the triumvirs; Pompey marries Caesar's daughter, Julia

74–63	Third Mithridatic War
66–63	Pompey defeats Mithridates and reorganizes the East. End of Seleucid monarchy (64) and of independent kingdom of Judaea; provinces of Bithynia, Cilicia, Syria, Crete organized, and client kings established elsewhere

75–35	Philodemus (poet and Epicurean philosopher) active at Rome; Aenesidemus (Sceptic philosopher) active
70	Cicero's *Verrine Orations* delivered; Virgil born; Valerius Antias (Roman historian) active
68	Cicero's correspondence begins
65	Horace born
63	Cicero's *Catilinarian Orations* delivered; Augustus born
62	Cicero's *pro Archia* delivered
60–30	Diodorus of Sicily compiles his *Historical Library*
59–54	Catullus' poems to Lesbia

ROME (cont.)

	THE EAST		THE WEST		CULTURAL DEVELOPMENTS
58–57	Cicero's exile and return	58–49	Caesar campaigns in Gaul	58–52	Caesar writes his account of the *Gallic Wars*
56	Agreement between triumvirs renewed at Luca	55–54	Caesar's invasions of Britain	55	Death of Lucretius; his poem published posthumously; Theatre of Pompey completed
54	Julia dies; the link between Caesar and Pompey is severed	55–53	Crassus in the East, killed by Parthians at battle of Carrhae (53); his army destroyed	54	Cicero's *pro Caelio* delivered; Catullus dies
52	Clodius murdered by Milo in gang warfare	51	Parthian invasion of Syria	52	Cicero's *pro Milone* written
				51	Cicero writes his *de Republica*
				50	Andronicus of Rhodes discovers and begins editing the lost works of Aristotle; foundation of our modern knowledge of Aristotle
49	Civil War: Caesar crosses the Rubicon and Pompey leaves for East			49–27	M. Terentius Varro (antiquarian) active
48	Caesar defeats Pompey at battle of Pharsalus; Pompey murdered in Egypt				
47–44	Dictatorship of Caesar	47–45	Caesar campaigns against Republicans in the East, Africa, and Spain	46	Forum of Caesar begun in Rome; Cicero's *pro Marcello* delivered
45	Caesar returns from Spain			45–44	Cicero's main philosophical works published
44	(15 March) Caesar is murdered			44	Cicero's *de Officiis* written

THE ROMAN EMPIRE

POLITICAL EVENTS	CULTURAL DEVELOPMENTS

The Second Triumvirate and the Age of Augustus

Caesar's heirs struggled for control of the Roman world; the final victory of his nephew Octavian (later Augustus) saw the establishment of monarchy under the guise of a 'restored Republic'. His long reign was marked by consolidation and reform in every sphere of politics and culture. The great age of Latin poetry began with the Triumvirate and continued into the Augustan age.

POLITICAL EVENTS	CULTURAL DEVELOPMENTS
44 M. Antonius, surviving consul, controls Rome	44 Cicero attacks Antony in his *Philippics*
	44–AD 21 Strabo (geographer and historian) active

THE ROMAN EMPIRE (cont.)

POLITICAL EVENTS

43	Octavian seizes the consulate
	Second triumvirate of Antony, Lepidus, and Octavian formed; their opponents murdered in the proscriptions
42	Republicans defeated at battle of Philippi; Brutus and Cassius commit suicide
	Cisalpine Gaul incorporated into Italy
41–32	Antony in the East
40	Antony marries Octavia; pact of Brundisium
37	Renewal of Triumvirate
36–35	Campaigns against Sextus Pompeius, son of Pompey
32	Final breach between Antony and Octavian
31	Octavian defeats Antony at battle of Actium
30	Antony and Cleopatra commit suicide
	Annexation of Egypt by Rome
27	'The Republic restored': the first constitutional settlement. Octavian given the name *Augustus*
27–19	Agrippa completes conquest of north-west Spain
23	Conspiracy against Augustus and second constitutional settlement
20	Settlement with Parthia: Parthians return Roman standards
19	Constitutional readjustment of Augustus' powers
18	Augustan marriage and social reforms

CULTURAL DEVELOPMENTS

43	Murder of Cicero
	Birth of Ovid
40	Didymus (last great Alexandrian literary scholar) active
	Virgil's fourth *Eclogue*
38	*Eclogues* of Virgil published
37–30	Horace's *Satires* written
30	Horace's *Epodes* published
29	Virgil's *Georgics* and Propertius' *Elegies* 1 completed
28–23	Vitruvius *On Architecture* written
	Mausoleum of Augustus begun
26–16	Propertius' *Elegies* 2–4 written
25	Ovid begins writing *Amores*
24–23	Publication of Horace *Odes* 1–3
23	Effective end of Maecenas' patronage of poetry
20	Building of Temple of Mars the Avenger begun
	Horace's *Epistles* 1 published
19	Tibullus (elegiac poet) and Virgil die

17	Horace writes *carmen saeculare* for performance at Secular Games
13–11	Theatre of Marcellus
12	Horace *Epistles* 2.1 to Augustus published
9	First edition of Ovid's *Art of Love*
	End of Livy's history of Rome
	Dedication of Ara Pacis Augustae
8	Death of Maecenas and Horace
2	Second edition of Ovid's *Art of Love*
	Forum of Augustus dedicated
AD 1–4	Ovid's *Fasti* written
3	Maison Carrée at Nîmes built
8	Ovid banished to the Black Sea
	Manilius (astronomical poet) and Velleius Paterculus (historian) active
	Philo (Jewish writer) active
	Death of Elder Seneca (writer on oratory)

12	Death of M. Agrippa, heir apparent
	Augustus becomes *pontifex maximus* on death of Lepidus the triumvir
12–9	Tiberius campaigns in Pannonia
6–AD 2	Tiberius in retirement on Rhodes
2	Scandal of the elder Julia
AD 2–4	Lucius and Gaius Caesar die
	Final dynastic settlement: Tiberius is given tribunician power and adopts his nephew Germanicus
8	Scandal of the younger Julia
6–9	Pannonian Revolt
9	Disaster in Germany: Rhine becomes Roman frontier

The Julio-Claudian Dynasty

Despite the excesses of individual Emperors in Rome, the imperial governmental system was consolidated under a dynasty which claimed hereditary descent from Augustus.

TIBERIUS (14–37)

19	Death of Germanicus
23	Death of Drusus, Emperor's son
26	Tiberius retires to Capri
31	Sejanus, praetorian prefect and effective ruler of Rome, executed

GAIUS (CALIGULA) (37–41)

THE ROMAN EMPIRE (cont.)

POLITICAL EVENTS	CULTURAL DEVELOPMENTS
CLAUDIUS (41–54)	
43 Invasion of Britain under Aulus Plautius	49 Seneca (philosopher and tragedian) made tutor to future Emperor Nero
NERO (54–68)	
54–62 Burrus and Seneca control the young Emperor	54 Seneca's *Apocolocyntosis* published; Lucan (epic poet) and Persius (satirist) active
58–62 Conquest and loss of Armenia	
59 Murder of Agrippina on Nero's orders	
61 Revolt of Iceni in Britain under Boudicca	
62 Death of Burrus and end of Seneca's influence	
64 Fire in Rome for nine days; persecution of Christians	64–8 Building of Nero's Golden House
65 Pisonian Conspiracy against Nero	65 Suicides of Seneca and Lucan
66–73 Jewish Revolt	66 Suicide of Petronius (author of *Satyrica*)
	67 Josephus, rebel leader in Judaea and future author, deserts to the Romans

The Flavian Dynasty

With the Flavian dynasty power shifted to the bourgeoisie of Italy; luxury became unfashionable at Rome as the Emperor displayed 'old-fashioned standards'. Literature gives way to government as the art of Rome.

POLITICAL EVENTS	CULTURAL DEVELOPMENTS
69 The Year of the Four Emperors: Galba, Otho, Vitellius, and Vespasian struggle for power	
VESPASIAN (69–79)	
70 Destruction of Temple at Jerusalem	74 Frontinus (administrator and technical writer) consul
TITUS (79–81)	
79 Eruption of Vesuvius; destruction of Pompeii and Herculaneum	79 Death of Elder Pliny (administrator, naturalist, and encyclopedist) investigating eruption
80 Fire at Rome: destruction of Capitoline Temple	80 Inauguration of Colosseum

DOMITIAN (81-96)
78-85   Campaigns of Agricola in Britain
86-92   Domitian's wars against Dacians

Domitian's palace on Palatine hill built
Statius, Silius Italicus, Martial (poets), and Quintilian (writer on rhetoric) active

The Age of the Antonines

'If a man were called to fix the period in the history of the world, during which the human race was most happy and prosperous, he would, without hesitation, name that which elapsed from the death of Domitian to the accession of Commodus' (Edward Gibbon). Culturally the Greek world began to revive as city life prospered.

NERVA (96-8)

97   Tacitus consul

TRAJAN (98-117)
101-6   Trajan conquers Dacia (modern Romania)

Dio Chrysostom (Greek orator), Epictetus (moralist), and Plutarch (essayist and biographer) active in Greek literature
100-11 Pliny the Younger (orator and letter-writer) consul and governor of Bithynia
Tacitus writes *Histories* and *Annals*
112-13 Forum of Trajan and Trajan's Column dedicated

114-17 Trajan's Parthian War: Armenia and Mesopotamia annexed
115-17 Jewish Revolt
HADRIAN (117-38)
131   Hadrian establishes the Panhellenion, based on Athens, as a league of the Greek cities
132-5   Bar Kochba's revolt leads to final dispersal of Jews

Appian (historian), Lucian (satirist), and Ptolemy (astronomer) active in Greek literature; Suetonius (biographer) and Juvenal (poet) in Latin

The Pantheon (Rome), Hadrian's Villa (Tivoli), and Hadrian's Wall (Britain) built

ANTONINUS PIUS (138-61)

143   Pausanias writes his description of Greece
Herodes Atticus (Greek orator) and Fronto (Latin orator) consuls

THE ROMAN EMPIRE (*cont.*)

POLITICAL EVENTS

MARCUS AURELIUS (161–80)

162–6 Parthian Wars of L. Verus

165–7 Plague spreads through the Roman Empire

168–75 German Wars of Marcus

COMMODUS (180–92)

193 With the murder of Commodus four Emperors contend for power.

The Severan Dynasty

'Our history and the affairs of the Romans descend from an age of gold to one of iron and rust' (Cassius Dio, contemporary historian). The causes of the decline and subsequent transformation of the Roman world are complex. Militarization of the Empire and a shift of power from centre to outlying frontiers as barbarian pressure increased, brought strains which began to emerge under the Severans.

SEPTIMIUS SEVERUS (193–211)

208–11 Severus campaigns in Britain and dies at York

CULTURAL DEVELOPMENTS

144 Speech of Aelius Aristides (Greek orator) in praise of Rome

148 900th anniversary of founding of Rome

165 Apuleius (Latin writer) and Galen (doctor) active Justin (Christian apologist) martyred

174–80 *Meditations* of Marcus Aurelius

193 Column of Marcus Aurelius completed

Philostratus (literary biographer), Herodian (historian), Marius Maximus (biographer), Sextus Empiricus (Sceptic philosopher), Alexander of Aphrodisias (commentator on Aristotle), Tertullian and Clement of Alexandria (Christian writers) active Severus lavishly rebuilds his home town of Leptis Magna and builds the Arch of Septimius Severus in the Roman Forum

CARACALLA (212–17)

212	The *constitutio Antoniniana* grants citizenship to all inhabitants of the Empire

ELAGABALUS (218–22)

SEVERUS ALEXANDER (222–35)

226	Ardashir the Sassanian, crowned King of Kings in Iran, inaugurates 400 years of intermittent war with the Roman Empire

216	Baths of Caracalla completed
200–54	Origen (Christian philosopher) active
223	Murder of Ulpian, praetorian prefect and jurist, by his troops
229	Cassius Dio (historian) consul for the second time with the Emperor

The Late Empire

Fifty years of military anarchy (235–84, with nearly twenty Emperors) were ended by Diocletian's reforms and the establishment of the Tetrarchy. But intractable problems of frontier defence, heavy taxation, inflation, and excessive bureaucracy remained, and were not affected by Constantine's conversion to Christianity. The Late Empire was a new world in which from time to time Emperors such as Julian, or literary figures, sought to recapture the values of a lost society. Only a few leading events are mentioned in this brief list.

267	Heruli invade Greece
284–306	Diocletian re-establishes central power and founds the Tetrarchy
306–37	Career of Constantine the Great
312	Constantine wins battle of Milvian Bridge under the sign of the Cross: Christianity declared official state religion
324	Foundation of Constantinople
360–3	Julian the Apostate Emperor
378–95	Theodosius the Great Emperor
395	Division of the Empire between the sons of Theodosius

249–51	Decius' persecution of the Christians
258	Marryrdom of Cyprian
270	Death of Plotinus (Neoplatonist philosopher)
271	Aurelian Walls of Rome built
303–5	Great Persecution
307–12	Basilica of Maxentius in Rome, completed by Constantine
313–22	First Christian basilica built in Rome

THE ROMAN EMPIRE (*cont.*)

POLITICAL EVENTS		CULTURAL DEVELOPMENTS	
410	Sack of Rome by Alaric the Visigoth		
439	Rome formally renounces Britain Vandals conquer Carthage and Africa	430	Death of Saint Augustine
476	End of Roman Empire in the West		
527–65	Justinian, Eastern Emperor, seeks to reconquer Italy and Africa		The *Digest* of Roman Law is compiled
		529	Justinian orders the closure of the Academy at Athens
633–55	Arab conquest of Syria, Egypt, and the Sassanid Empire		
1453	Conquest of Constantinople by the Turks and end of the Eastern Roman Empire		

Index

References followed by grid letters (e.g. 10 Bd) are to maps. References in italics are to plans or figures.

Academy, Academicians, 344–5, 456, 485, 506
Achaean League, 485, 488
Achilles Tatius, 298
Acragas (Agrigentum), 12 Bd
Actium, battle of, 150, 215, 500; subject of Roman poetry, 223, 226, 234, 258, 265, 418
Adrianople, battle of, 474
Aenesidemus of Alexandria, 359–60, 497
Aesernia, 14 Bb; inscription, 31
Aetolia, Aetolians, 55, 491
Afghanistan, 481; *see also* Bactria, Aï Khanoum
Africa, Roman province of, 52, 61, 64, 144 Ad, 196, 492, 506
Agatharchides, 494
Agathocles, 482–3
agora, 403
Agricola, 280, 281, 396, 503
agriculture, 18, 20, 40–1
Agrippa, M. Vipsanius, 148–51, 155, 166, 398, 501
Agrippa Postumus, M. Vipsanius, 165
Agrippina, the elder, 165, 169
Agrippina, the younger, 173, 439, 502
Aï Khanoum, 483
Alalia, battle of, 481
Alaric, 474, 506
Albinus (or Alcinous), 348–9
Alcantara, bridge, 394
Alcmaeon of Croton, 481
Alcuin, 460–1
Alexander of Abonuteichus, 311, 343

Alexander of Aphrodisias, 504
Alexander of Macedon (the Great), 481; mosaic, 364
Alexandria, 71, 404, 456; as centre of literature, 484, 488, 492
Allegory, 467
Ambracia, 60
Ambrose of Milan, 457, 474, 475
Ammianus Marcellinus, 286, 400, 456
Ammonius, philosopher, 348, 350
amphitheatre, 433
Anastasius, 453
Andronicus of Rhodes, 498
Antigonids, 483
Antigonus Gonatas, 485–9
Antigonus the One-Eyed, 482–3
Antinous, 440
Antiochus I, 485; II, 487
Antiochus III, 51, 55, 61, 490–2
Antiochus IV, 51, 493
Antiochus of Ascalon, 341, 344–5, 496
Antonia, the younger, 169, 199
Antoninus Pius, 356, 503; column of, 444–5
Antonius, L., 148
Antonius, M. (Mark Antony), 68, 146–50, 499–500
Aphrodisias, 67, 145 Dc; Sebasteion reliefs, 442
Apicius, M. Gavius, 381
Apollodorus of Damascus, 393, 436–7
Apollonius of Perge, 489
Apollonius of Rhodes, 488
Apollonius of Tyana, 342
Appian, 54, 288, 503

Apuleius, 295, 298, 331, 334–8, 399, 407–8, 463, 504
Apulia, 14 Bd, 17–18
Arabs, 453, 476–7, 506
Aratus, Achaean statesman, 488
Aratus, poet, 486; translated by Cicero, 121
Arcesilaus of Pitane, 344, 486
archaism, 289–90
Archias, defended by Cicero, 216, 219
Archimedes of Syracuse, 488
architecture, 391–3, 417–18, 425–6, 430–4, 436–9, 442
Ariminum, 14 Ba, 31
Ariobarzanes, king of Cappadocia, 63
Aristarchus of Samos, 486
Aristarchus of Samothrace, 494
Aristides, Aelius, 299, 311–13, 504
Ariston of Ceos, 490
Ariston of Chios, 488
Aristophanes, librarian, 492
Aristotle, 16, 296, 345, 482, 498
Arles, 400
Armenia, 53, 145 Fb, 149, 174, 503
Arpinum, 15 Bb, 29
Arretium, 12 Ab, 99, 383
Arrian, 291, 353
Artemon, 297
Asia, Roman province of, 44, 52, 62, 143 Dc, 495
Asinius, 133
Asoka, 488
assemblies, 23
astronomy, 319–20
Athanasius of Alexandria, 470
Athanodorus of Rhodes, 428
Athens, 481, 482
Atia, 146
atomic theory, 125
Attalus I, 489
Atticus, 71, 93, 345
Attila, 459, 474
augures, 25
Augustine of Hippo, 94–5, 408, 457–9, 461–3, 470, 471, 473, 474–5, 506

Augustodunum, 143 Cc, 397, 406
Augustus, 13, 53, 72, 118, 146–67, 174, 184, 187, 190–1, 192, 193–4, 199, 215, 220–1, 224, 225–6, 228, 229, 240, 243, 252, 258, 366, 385, 398–9, 497, 501; art and architecture, 418–26; constitution, 150–7; Gemma Augustea, 427
Aurelius, Marcus, 183, 289, 342, 356–8, 504; column of, 445
Avars, 453
Averroes, 463
Avicenna, 463

Bactria, 491
Baiae, 360; 'Temple of Mercury', 420
Balbillus, Ti. Claudius, of Alexandria, 391
Balbus, L. Cornelius, 68
Balearic islands, 58, 143 Bd
Barea Soranus, 174
Barnabas, 389
Basil of Caesarea, 470
Bede, 461
Bedriacum, 7 Aa; battles of, 176, 177
Belisarius, 453, 456
Beneventum, battle of, 34
Berossus, 485
Bibracte (Mont Beuvray), 397
Bibulus, M. Calpurnius, 112–13
biography, 274, 284, 306–7
Bion of Borysthenes, 296, 485
Bithynia-Pontus, Roman province of, 52, 145 Db, 396, 497
Boethius, 455, 458, 464
Boii, 39
Boscoreale, 378–9, 382, 416
Boscotrecase, villa of Agrippa Postumus, 371, 424, 425, 428
Bostra, 145 Ec, 397
Boudicca (Boadicea), 173, 400, 502
Bovianum, 15 Bc, 44
Britain, 53, 143 Ba, 170, 172, 173, 195, 394, 395, 498, 503, 506
Britannicus, 173

Bruttians, 14 Be, 16, 38
Brutus, D., 58
Brutus, M., 63, 68, 500
bureaucracy, 184–92, 197–213, 505
Burgundians, 454
Burrus, 173, 502

Caecina, 176, 177
Caesar, Gaius, 166, 501
Caesar, Gaius Julius, 47, 53, 54, 57,
    58, 60, 64, 68, 91, 107–18, 134,
    146, 287, 419, 495–8
Caesar, Lucius, 166, 501
Caesarion, 149
Calcidius, 463
Cales, 14 Bc, 27
Caligula, *see* Gaius
Callimachus, 217, 232, 234, 486
Callistus, 171
Calpurnius Piso, 174, 495
Calvus, 134, 217
Campania, 12 Bc, 17, 27, 32, 58,
    418, 481; *ager Campanus*, 105–6,
    112
Camulodunum, 143 Ca, 162
Cannae, battle of, 14 Cb, 37, 491
Cantabri, 166
Capella, Martianus, 462, 463
Capri, 376
Capua, 14 Bd, 17, 18, 29, 32, 37, 491
Caracalla, 505
Caratacus, 282
Carneades of Cyrene, 62–3, 344, 494
Carnuntum, 144 Ba
Carrhae, battle of, 498
Carthage, 52, 62, 144 Ac, 481, 483,
    487, 489–92; Punic Wars, 34,
    37–8, 50, 487–91
Cassander, 483
Cassino, Monte, 463
Cassiodorus, 455
Cassius, 68, 500
castellum, 194–5
Catalepton, 266
Catalina, L. Sergius (Catiline), 98,
    107, 497
Cato, M. Porcius, elder, 22, 59, 60,
    64, 70, 71, 86, 271, 274, 433, 492

Cato, M. Porcius, younger, 94,
    105–6, 107, 108, 109, 274, 278
Catullus, 133–42, 217, 219, 230,
    245, 496–8
Catulus, Q. Lutatius, 216
Ceius Secundus, L., 380
Celsus, 289, 291, 343, 468, 475
Cenomani, 39
censors, 24, 102
centuriatio, 30
Centuripae, 12 Bd
Chandragupia, 484
Chariton, 298
Cherchel, 143 Bd
Chester, 15 Ba
China, 2–3, 207
Chion of Heraclea, 298
Christians, Christianity, 3, 7–8, 174,
    396, 450, 451, 454, 456, 466–76,
    502, 504, 505
chronicles, 270
Chrysaphius, 473
Chrysippus, 353, 489
Chrysostom, John, 399, 469
Cicero, 54, 57, 58, 60, 62, 67, 69, 71,
    72, 90–120 *passim*, 121, 125–6,
    147, 164–5, 216, 219, 270, 274,
    275–6, 289, 307, 368, 373, 376,
    404, 405, 495–500
Cilicia, 52, 145 Ec, 497
Cimbri, 44, 52
Cincius, Alimentus, L. 269
Cinna, poet, 137, 217
Cinna, L. Cornelius, 98
Ciris, 266
citizenship: in Italy, 20; Roman, 22,
    28–9, 43, 45, 71–2, 172
Claudia Livilla, 169
Claudii, 63, 181
Claudius, emperor, 156, 157, 162,
    168, 171–3, 183, 200, 409, 502
Claudius, Appius, 21
Claudius Caecus, Ap., 32
Cleanthes of Assus, 353, 354, 429
Clearchus, 483
Cleisthenes, 481
Clement of Alexandria, 467, 468,
    504

Cleomenes, 489
Cleopatra, 53, 149–50, 259, 500
clientela, 36
Cloatii, 67
Clodia, 136
Clodius, 112, 497, 498
Clodius Macer, 175
coinage, 32, 33, 42, 485
collegia, 190, 405–6
colonia, 195
colonization: Greek, 480; Roman,
    14 (map), 26–31 *passim*, 38–9, 41,
    194–5
Colosseum, 433, 503
Columella, 291
comedy, 74–86
Comitia Centuriata, 23, 481
Comitia Curiata, 23
Comitia Tributa, 23
Commodus, 182, 199, 504
Concilium Plebis, 23
concrete, 417–18
Constantine the Great, 390, 406,
    450, 453, 505
Constantine IX, 465
Constantinople, 455, 466, 506
Constantius II, 457
consuls, 22, 23, 192, 481
Copa, 266
Corbulo, 174
Corellius Rufus, 289
Corinth, 52
corn trade, 61
Cornelia, wife of Caesar, 108
Cornelius, C. 105
Corsica, 12 Ab, 50, 489
Cosa, 14 Ba, 28
Classus, L. Licinius, 93
Crassus, M., 53, 98, 101, 104,
    106–7, 498
Crates of Pergamum, 70
Cremona, 15 Aa, 39
Cremutius Cordus, 280
Crete, 204, 497
Crimisus, 481
Ctesibius of Alexandria, 487
cubicularii, 207
Culex, 266

Cumae, 14 Bd, 16, 33, 481
curae, 191–2
curatores rei publicae, 188, 191
Curtius, Quintus, 289
Cyprian, bishop of Carthage, 452,
    459, 505
Cyrene, Cyrenaica, 55
Cyrus of Alexandria, 476
Cyrus of Panopolis, 473

Dacia, 144 Ca, 183, 503
Dalmatia, 495
Damascius, 456
Damascus, 397
Daniel, Book of, 493
Decius, 505
Delos, 56, 59, 60, 493
Delphi, 34
Demetrius the Besieger, 483–5
Demetrius of Phalerum, 484
Demetrius, *On Style*, 297
dialogue, 94–5, 296, 307–8,
    309–11
Didymus, 500
Digenes Akritas, 466
Dio, Cassius, 167, 171, 209, 285,
    289, 392, 393, 400–1, 505
Dio Chrysostom, 295, 465, 503
Diocletian, 450–1, 459, 505; Edict
    of Maximum Prices, 401
Diodorus Siculus, 497
Diodotus, 93
Diogenes of Oenoanda, inscription,
    359
Dion of Syracuse, 481
Dionysius of Halicarnassus, 288,
    291, 292
Dionysius I of Syracuse, 481; II,
    481
Domitian, 177, 182, 183, 503;
    palace of, 432, 433–4
Domitii Ahenobarbi, 63
Donatus, 82
dress, 384–7
Drobeta, 144 Cb, 393
Druidism, 172
Drusus, Julius Caesar, 167, 169
Drusus, M. Livius, 45, 496

Dura Europus, 145 Fc, 206
Duris of Samos, 485

education, 70–1
Egeria, diary of, 460
Egypt, 51, 53, 55, 61, 195, 197, 206, 207, 481, 483, 490, 491, 492; *see also* Alexandria, Ptolemies
Elagabalus, 505
elegiacs, 218, 219, 229–41
Emerita, 143 Aa
Empiricus, Sextus, 359, 504
Ennius, 86–8, 218, 259, 491
Ennodius, bishop of Pavia, 462
Entella, inscriptions, 35
Epaphroditus, 352
Ephesus, 402, 442
Epictetus, 203, 291, 343, 352–6, 503
Epicurus, Epicureanism, 93, 483; in Lucretius, 122–33
epigrams, 133–7, 325–31, 470
Epirus, 59
Eratosthenes of Cyrene, 488–90
Eristratus of Ceos, 488
ethics, 354–8, 468–9
Etruria, Etruscans, 16–29 *passim*, 32, 33, 46–7, 99, 481, 483
Euclid, 484
Eumenes of Pergamum, 487
Eusebius of Caesarea, 390–1

Fabius Maximus Cunctator, Q., 87–8
Fabius Pictor, Q., 37, 269, 492
Fabullus, 429
familia Caesaris, 202
fashion, 384–6
fasti consulares, 269–70
Favorinus of Arles, 295
festivals, 403
Fishbourne, villa, 378, 401
Flamininus, T., 51, 62, 65, 66, 67
food, 380–4
freedmen, 171, 199, 201–3
Fregellae, 14 Bb, 31, 40
Frisii, 396
frumentarii, 197
Fulvia, 148

Fulvius Nobilior, M., 218
furniture, 374–6

Gabinius, 103
Gaius (Caligula), 157, 162, 167–8, 170–1, 501
Gaius, jurist, 456
Galatia, Galatians, 199
Galba, Servius Sulpicius, 174–5, 177, 502
Gallus, Cornelius, 251
Gangra, inscription, 162
gardens, 376–80, 431
Gaul: Cisalpine (Po Valley), 15 Aa, 31, 33, 36, 37, 39, 45, 50, 58, 107, 113, 492, 500; Roman province, 53, 62, 495; Transalpine, 53, 60, 498
Gauls, 13, 27, 34, 37, 485
Gela, 12 Bb
Gelon, 481
Genesis, Book of, 345
gentes, 36
geography, *see* Eratosthenes, Ptolemy, Strabo
Gerasa, 145 Ed, 397
Germanicus, 167, 169, 501
Germany, 501
glass, 366, 383
Goths, 453, 454, 474
Gracchus, C., 43, 52, 58, 61, 274, 495
Gracchus, Ti., 41–3, 52, 58, 103, 495
Gratian, 457
Gregory of Nyssa, 471
Gregory of Tours, 460
guilds, see *collegia*
Gytheum, 67

Hadrian, 182, 183, 204, 208, 212, 385, 393, 503; art and architecture, 373, 437–40
Hagesander of Rhodes, 428
Hamilcar Barca, 488–9
Hannibal, 37–8, 51, 490
Hasdrubal, 489
Hecataeus of Abdera, 482

Heliodorus, 298
Heliogabalus, 183
Hellenization, 68–72, 74–5,
   216–17
helots, 20
Heraclius, 453
Herculaneum, 362–83
   passim, 429, 502
Hernicans, 26
Herodas, 488
Herodes Atticus, 295, 344, 503
Herodian, 289, 504
Herodotus, 211
Herophilus of Chalcedon, 429
Hesiod, 254
Hiero, king of Syracuse, 34, 481,
   486–7
Hieronymus of Cardia, 487
Himera, 12 Bd; battle of, 481
historians, 268–86; see also
   individual historians
honestiores, 404–5
hoplites, *see* warfare, Greek
Horace, 161, 215, 216, 218, 220,
   221, 222, 223–9, 231, 243, 251,
   253, 292, 296, 318, 327, 369, 497,
   500–1
Hortensius Hortalus, 93, 98
houses, palaces, 362–9, 374–5,
   398–400, 429–34, 438–42
hunting, 402

Illyrians, 50, 489; First Illyrian
   War, 60
imperator, 193
imperialism, chs. 2, 4
imperium, 151–2, 166, 186–7, 197,
   200
Insubres, 39
Ionians, 481
Ipsus, battle of, 484
Italy, *vis-à-vis* Rome, 13–49
iuridici, 187

Jerome, St., 126, 451, 458, 462
Jesus of Nazareth, 390
jewellery, 385–6

Jews, Judaea, Judaism, 68, 145 Ed,
   170, 172, 183, 493, 495, 497,
   501–3; Jewish historical
   writing, 204
John, St., 467
Jonas, 463
Josephus, 502
Jugurtha, 45, 52, 63, 495
Julia, daughter of Agrippa, 165
Julia, daughter of Augustus, 165, 241
Julian, 457, 474, 505
Julius Lacer, C., 394
Justin, 453, 467, 504
Justinian, 453, 456, 457, 506
Juvenal, 196, 324, 326–31, 391, 503

king worship, 161–2
Kunstprosa, 290–1, 293, 296, 298,
   312

Labienus, 103
Lamian War, 482
language, 96–7, 459–64
Latins, Latium, 14 Ad, 16–17, 26–8,
   480, 481, 494; Latin status, 27
law: Greek, 481; Roman, 203–4,
   454–5, 506
Laws of Twelve Tables, 26, 481
legati, 187
Lepidus, M. Aemilius, consul
   78 BC, 99
Lepidus, M. Aemilius, triumvir, 104,
   147–8, 161, 500
letter writing, 90–1, 297–8, 301–2,
   304
Letters of Crates, 298
Lex de ambitu, 101
Lex Aurelia, 102
Lex Claudia, 56, 60
Lex Manciana, 200
Lex Tullia, 101
Lex Vatinia, 113
Libanius, 406, 470
libraries, 70
literary criticism, 291–4
Livia, 166, 199, 385; 'Livia's villa',
   see Primaporta
Livius Andronicus, 75, 87

Livy, 53, 54, 245, 269, 275, 278–9, 501
locatio, 190
logistai, 188
Lollia Paulina, 385
Lombards, 453
'Longinus', 288, 291, 293–4
Longus, 298
Lucan, 174, 320–4, 502
Lucania, Lucanians, 14 Bd, 16, 47
Luceria, 14 Cb, 31
Lucian of Samosata, 296, 299, 309–11, 343, 464, 503
Lucilius, 217, 327, 495
Lucretius, 95, 121–33, 495–7
Lucullus, L. Licinius, 104
Luke, St., 184, 209
Lullingstone villa, 370
Luna, marble quarries, 421
Lystra, 389

Maccabees, 493
Macedon, 38, 51, 55, 56, 61, 62, 64, 70, 148, 482, 485, 487; *see also* Alexander, Philip
Macro, 170
Macrobius, 463
Maecenas, 148, 151, 161, 220, 223, 229, 232, 233, 251, 252, 253, 258, 500
Magdalensberg, 397
magister, 190
magistrates, Roman, 186–92; *see also* consuls, quaestors, *etc.*
Manetho, 486
Manilius, *Astronomica*, 319–20, 501
Marcellus, M. Claudius (son of Octavia), 165; Theatre of Marcellus, 418, 419, 501
Marcellus, M. (consul 51 BC), 115
Marius, C., 43, 44, 52, 64, 98, 495
Mark, St., 464
Marsi, 16
Martial, 320, 326, 382, 503
Massilia, 52, 55, 68
Matius, C., 378
Matius, G., 118, 147
Mauretania, 143 Ad, 172, 495

Maximus of Tyre, 342
Megasthenes, 484
Mela, M. Annaeus, 300, 400
Meleager, 136, 496
Melinno, hymn to Rome, 67
Memmius, 122
Menander, 74, 76, 482
Menippus of Gadara, 310
Messalla, M. Valerius, 219, 239
Messallina, 172
Messana, 12 Cd, 34, 50
Metellus, L. Caecilius, *elogium* on, 35
Metellus, Pius, 104
metre, 133
Michael of Ephesus, 465
Miletus, 441, 442
Milvian Bridge, battle of, 505
Minturnae, 14 Bd, 28
misogyny, 327–8
Mithridates, 52, 98, 496–7; Mithridatic War, 67
Moesia, 144 Cb, 197
monks, 470
Monophysites, 476
mosaics, *see* painting
Moschos, John, 465–6
Mucianus, G. Licinius, 176, 177
Museum, *see* Alexandria, as centre of literature
Musonius Rufus, 352

Naevius, 87, 259, 489
Namatianus, Rutilius, 470
Narcissus, 171, 203
Narses, 453
Naulochus, battle of, 148
Neapolis, 14 Bd, 17
negotiatores, 56, 58, 60, 63–4, 67, 71
Neoplatonism, 350–2, 467–8
Nepos, Cornelius, 219, 275
Nero, 156, 162, 168, 171, 173–4, 183, 201, 385; *see also* Rome, places
Nerva, 181, 503
Nestorians, 476
Nicander, 495
Nicetes Sacerdos, 304

Nigidius Figulus, 342
Nîmes, 143 Cc, 426, 501
Nobilior, M. Fulvius, 218
Novatus, Annaeus, 300
novel, 298, 331-8
Numenius of Apamea, 342
Numidia, 143 Cd, 396

Octavia, sister of Augustus, 148, 149, 250, 500
Octavia, daughter of Claudius, 173
Octavianus, *see* Augustus
Octavius, G., 146
Octavius, M., 41
Odovacer, 453
Olympias, 482
Onasander, 291
Oplontis, villa, 369
Optimates, 102-3
Oracula Sibyllina, 205
oratory, rhetoric, 90-2
Origen, 349, 467, 468, 505
Ostia, 12 Bb, 28, 363, 367-8, 398, 400, 442, 443
Otho, M. Salvius, 175, 176, 502
Ovid, 216, 218, 220, 238-43, 309, 317, 318, 500-1

Pachomius, 470
painting and mosaics, 414, 416-17, 424-5, 429, 442-3; *see also* pottery and vase-painting
Palestrina, sanctuary of Fortuna, 418
Palladas, 470
Pallas, 171, 203, 212
Palmyra, 145 Ec, 397
Panaetius of Rhodes, 354, 495
Parmenides of Elea, 481
Parthenius, 137
Parthia, 53, 116, 149, 183, 225, 489, 491, 495, 498, 500, 503-4
Pasiteles, 414
pastoral, 245-52
patronage of literature, 218-20, 224
Paul, St., 189, 300, 389-90; *Corinthians*, 473
Paulinus, 475

Paullus, Aemilius, 51, 58, 70
Pausanius, traveller, 503
Peloponnesian Wars, 481
Perdiccas, 482
Peregrinus Proteus, 311
Pergamum, 41, 43, 51, 495; architecture, 438, 493
Perseus, king of Macedonia, 51, 55, 66, 433
Persia, 481, 503; and Greece, 481
Persius, 325, 502
Petro, T. Flavius, 176
Petronius, G. 174, 290, 298, 331-4, 372, 381-2, 386, 502
Pharsalus, 176, 498
Philip II of Macedon, 481; III, 482; V, 51, 55, 490-1
Philippi, battle of, 148, 500
Philo of Alexandria, 345-6, 360, 467, 501
Philo of Larissa, 344, 495
Philodemus of Gadara, 125
Philopappus, prince of Commagene, 309
Philoponus, John, 456
philosophy: Greek, 481; Roman, 93-7, 300-2; later, 340-60, 466-70
Philostratus, 212, 342, 442
Phrynichus, grammarian, 466
Picenum, 14 Bc, 103
pietas, 5, 260
Pietrabbondante, 18, *19*
Pilate, 390
pilgrimage, 460
Pindar, 139, 319
Piso Licinianus, L. Calpurnius, 175, 502
Piso Pontifex, L. Calpurnius, 373
Pius, Antoninus, 182, 183
Placentia, 15 Aa, 39
plague, 504
Plato, philosopher, 127, 341, 342, 463, 467-8
Platonism, 341-2, 344-52; and Christianity, 467-70
Plautios, Novios, 413
Plautus, 70-9, 85, 492

plebeian organization at Rome, 21–2

Pliny the Elder, 156, 198, 289, 302–4, 376, 378, 502

Pliny the Younger, 157, 189, 211, 280, 295, 297, 304–5, 368, 369, 378, 379, 385, 396, 403, 503

Plotinus, 340, 343, 350–2, 359, 468, 505

Plutarch, 54, 62, 67, 284–5, 288, 296, 299, 305–8, 311, 343, 345, 346–8, 450, 464, 503

Polemon of Athens, 483, 485

Polemon of Laodicea, 295

Pollio, G. Asinius, 134, 148, 220, 249–50, 251

Polybius, 34, 37, 50, 52, 53, 55, 56, 62, 66, 190, 270, 271–4, 493, 495

Polydorus of Rhodes, 428

Pompeii, 12 Bc, 58, 362–7 *passim*, 418, 428, 429, 502

Pompeius Magnus, Cn. (Pompey), 47, 52, 57, 63, 67, 68, 98–116 *passim*, 147, 497–8; Theatre of, 419–20, 498

Pompeius, Sextus, 148, 500

Pompeius Strabo, Cn., 45

pontifices, 24, 108, 270, 501

Pontus, 66, 496; *see also* Bithynia-Pontus

Poppaea, 173

Populares, 102–3

Porphyry, 340, 350, 352

Posidippus, 486

Posidonia (Paestum), 12 Bc, 33

Posidonius of Apamea, 340, 353, 435

Potentia, 15 Cc, 47

pottery and vase-painting, 32, 383–4

Po valley, *see* Gaul, Cisalpine

praefecti, 187, 200

praefectus fabrui, 192

Praeneste, 12 Bb, 18; sanctuary of Fortune, 495

praetors, 191

Primaporta, Livia's villa, 370, 425

Primus, M. Antonius, 177

princeps, 157–9, 182, 191

Priscian, 455

Proconnesus, marble, 440

proconsuls, 187

Procopius, 456

procuratores, 187, 200–1

Propertius, 215–16, 218, 221, 229–34, 252, 379, 500

propraetors, 187

prose rhythm, 290–1

Psellos, Michael, 465

Ptolemies, 483

Ptolemy I, 483–5

Ptolemy II, 483, 485–7

Ptolemy III, 488; IV, 490

Ptolemy, astronomer and geographer, 503

publicani, 56, 60, 67

Pudentilla of Oea, 407

Pulcher, Ap. 62

Punic Wars, *see* Carthage

Punjab, 481

Pydna, battle of, 51, 70, 493

Pyrrhus, 33, 34, 484–6

Pythagoras of Samos, 481; Pythagoreanism, 300, 342

Pytheas, 482

quaestors, 23, 187

Quintilian, 92, 289, 290–1, 295, 304, 324, 503

Rabirius, 108

Ravenna, 12 Ba, 455, 475; Sant'Apollinare Nuovo, 454; San Vitale, 454, 455

records, public, 268–70

religion, 24–5, 47, 161–3, 466–77

revolutions, 147–77, 180, 183

rhetoric, 246–9, 91, 291–4

Rhodes, 51, 60, 65, 71, 166, 376

roads, Roman, 42, 394–5

Rogatianus, 350

Romanitas, 455

Rome: 12 Bb, *passim*; early Rome, 13–49, 480–1; founding of republic, 481; expansion of, 50–72, 482, 491–2; 494–8; late republic, 90–118, 494–8; founding of empire 147–77;

Rome (*cont.*):
    arts of governments, 180–213
    places: Altar of Domitius
      Ahenobarbus, 415; Antoninus'
      column, 444, 445; Ara Pacis
      Augustae, 162, 422–3, 501;
      Ara Pietatis, 427; Aurelian
      Walls, 505; Aurelius' column,
      445; Colosseum, 433, 503;
      Domitian's Palace, 432, 433–4;
      forum, draining of, 481;
      forum of Augustus, 422, 501;
      forum Julium, 498; Golden
      House of Nero, 174, 382, 398,
      428, 429–31; Largo Argentina,
      40; Pantheon, 437–8, 503;
      Papal Chancellery reliefs, 434;
      Porticus Aemilia, 418,
      tabularium, 496; temple of
      Diana, 481; temple of Jupiter,
      481; temple of Mars Ultor, 500;
      theatre of Marcellus, 418, 419;
      Theatre and porticoes of Pompey,
      498; Titus' arch, 434; Titus'
      baths, 433, 437; Trajan's baths,
      437; Trajan's column, 435–6,
      439, 503; Trajan's forum,
      436–7, 503; Trajan's markets,
      436
Romulus Augustulus, 453
Roscius of Ameria, 98
Rubicon, 115, 155, 498
Rullus, 103
Russia, 481

Sabines, Sabinum, 14 Ac, 16–17
Sabinus, Flavius, 177
Sabinus, Poppaeus, 161
sacrifice, 415–16
Saepinum, 15 Bc, 44
Saguntum, 490
Sallust, 71, 97–8, 121, 155, 163,
    269, 274, 276–8
Sallustius Crispus, G. (adopted son of
    Sallust), 161
Samnites, Samnium, 14 Bd, 16, 17,
    18, 31, 33, 44, 47, 482–4
Samothrace, Nike, 376

Sardinia, 12 Ac, 34–5, 50, 489
Sassanians, 184
satire, 217, 223, 325–31
Saturninus, L. Apuleius, 43, 58
scepticism, 358–60
Scipio Aemilianus, P. Cornelius, 51,
    216
Scipio Africanus, P. Cornelius, 51,
    57, 491
scribes, 207
Scribonia, 167
Scribonianus, 172
sculpture, 414–16, 422–3, 426–8,
    434–6, 439–40, 441, 444–5
Sejanus, L. Aelius, 169, 170, 501
Seleucids, 488, 490
Seleucus I, 483–4
senate, senators, 46, 59–60, 61,
    156–61, 451, 495
Seneca, L. Annaeus, the elder, 292–3,
    299–300, 502
Seneca, L. Annaeus, the younger, 96,
    171, 173, 174, 280, 290, 293, 296,
    297, 299–302, 307, 320, 324–5,
    334, 353, 400, 502
Senecio, Q. Sosius, 306
Senones, 31, 39
Sentinum, battle of, 33
Septimius Severus, 504
Sertorius, 104, 496
Servius Tullius, 480–1
Severus Alexander, 505
Severus, Septimius, 180, 183,
    199; Arch of, 445
shops, 405
Sicily, 12 Bd, 34–5, 37–8, 50, 59,
    61–2, 481, 495–6
Sidonius Apollinaris, 472
Silius, G., 172
Silius Italicus, 320, 503
Simplicius, 458
slaves, slavery: in Roman world,
    58–9, 409, 497; Christian
    attitudes towards, 471; *see also*
    helots
Slavs, 453
Social War, 45, 496
societates, 190

Socrates, 111, 309
sophists, 290; Second Sophistic
  Movement, 342
Spain, 37, 38, 51, 58, 61, 64, 72, 143
  (map), 196, 490–2
Sparta, 18, 488
Spartacus, 104, 497
Sperlonga, statuary, 428
sport, 403
Statius, 202, 297, 319, 320, 385, 433,
  503
Stilicho, 459, 474
Stoicism, 352–8, 483, 487–9
Strabo, 59, 72, 203–4, 499
strategos, 192
Strato of Lampsacus, 485–7
Studius, 425
Suetonius, 157, 164, 172, 284, 285,
  404, 503
Sulla, L. Cornelius, 45, 47, 52, 61,
  64, 67, 98–100, 101, 102–3, 104,
  106, 107, 108, 496
Sulpicia, 219
Synesius of Cyrene, 470
Syracuse, 12 Bd, 37, 51, 414, 481,
  482, 486–7, 491
Syria, 51, 52, 145 Ec, 486–93, 497;
  see also Seleucids

tabellarii, 202
Tacitus, 159, 160, 165, 168, 169,
  172, 181, 200, 268–9, 274, 280–3,
  288, 290, 293, 296, 331, 390, 396,
  398, 400, 409, 503
Tarentum (Taranto), 12 Cc, 16, 18,
  33, 414, 486
Tarquinius Priscus, 20–1, 480
Tarquinius Superbus, 20–1, 481
Tauromenium (Taormina) 12 Bd
taxation 28, 61–2, 106, 205, 452,
  493, 505
Terence, 79–86, 493
terracottas, 372
Tertullian, 467, 504
Teutones, 43, 44, 52
Theocritus, 425, 486
Theoderic, 453, 454

Theodoret, bishop of Cyrrhus, 465,
  472
Theodosius the Great, 505
Theodosius II, law-code, 454
Thoephanes of Mytilene, 68
Theophrastus, 482–5
Thrace, 172, 483
Thrasyllus, 391
Thrasea Paetus, 173, 174
Thurii, 12 Cc
Tiberius, 155–70 *passim*, 183, 501
Tiberius Gemellus, 169
Tiberius Julius Alexander, 176
Tibullus, 216, 218, 219, 220, 235–8,
  500
Tigellinus, 173, 175
Timaeus of Tauromenium, 34, 270,
  271, 487
Timoleon, 481
Tiro, 210
Titus, 177, 502; *see also* Rome,
  places
Tivoli, Hadrian's villa, 373, 438–9,
  503
Tours, council of bishops, 460
town planning, 366–8, 417–18
trade, 54, 59–61; *see also* corn trade
tragedy, 324–5
Trajan, 182, 183, 385, 406, 503; *see
  also* Rome, places
Trasimene, battle of Lake, 491
Tribonian, 455
tribunes: military, 192; of the plebs,
  23
triumvirates, 109–14, 147–50, 497,
  499–501
Twelve Tables, 26, 481
tyranny, 480

Ulpian, 389, 505
Umbrians, 14 Ac, 17, 33
usury, 402

Valens, 176, 474
Valerius Flaccus, 320
Valla, Lorenzo, 464
Vandals, 453, 459
Varaino, Monte, 44

Varius, 229
Varro, 91, 254, 256, 310, 437, 498
Varus Alfenus, 251
vase-painting, *see* pottery and
  vase-painting
Vatinius, 113
vegetarianism, 300
Veii, 12 Bb, 18, 19, 26, 480, 481
Velleius Paterculus, 318–19, 501
Ventidius Bassus, 149
Verginius Rufus, 175
Verres, 63, 101; *Verrine Orations*,
  62, 497
Verulamium, 143 Bb, 396
Verus, 183, 504
Vespasian, 157, 162, 176, 177, 182,
  209, 405, 431, 433, 502
Vestal Virgins, 25
Vesuvius, 303, 368, 440
Via Appia, 32
villas and houses, 362–76; *see also*
  houses, palaces
Vindex, Julius, 174, 175
Vipsania, 166
Virgil, 86, 87, 221, 222–3, 229,
  245–66, 497, 500; *Aeneid*, 185,
  216, 223, 257–66, 318, 321, 392;

Eclogues, 148, 161, 215, 222,
  246–52, 258; *Georgics*, 215, 222,
  252–7, 258
Virunum, 397
Visigoths, 454
Vitellius, Aulus, 175–6, 177, 502
Vitruvius, 212, 291, 366, 369, 382,
  416, 420, 500
Volscians, 14 Bd, 26
Volusianus, 474

warfare: Greek, 481; Roman army,
  39–40, 192–7, 445; *see also*
  navies
women: in Roman empire, 407–8;
  beautification of, 384–6

Xenocrates, 483
Xenophanes, 481
Xenophon of Athens, 298
Xenophon of Cos, 391
Xenophon of Ephesus, 298

Zama, battle of, 38, 51, 492
Zeno of Citium, 483
Zeno, Ptolemaic agent, 487
Zenodotus, 484

Visit the
VERY SHORT
INTRODUCTIONS
Web site

www.oup.co.uk/vsi

➤ **Information** about all published titles

➤ News of **forthcoming books**

➤ **Extracts** from the books, including titles
not yet published

➤ **Reviews** and views

➤ **Links** to other **web sites** and main
OUP web page

➤ Information about **VSIs in translation**

➤ **Contact** the editors

➤ **Order** other **VSIs** on-line

ANCIENT PHILOSOPHY

A Very Short Introduction

Julia Annas

The tradition of ancient philosophy is a long, rich and varied one, in which a constant note is that of discussion and argument. This book aims to introduce readers to some ancient debates and to get them to engage with the ancient developments of philosophical themes. Getting away from the presentation of ancient philosophy as a succession of Great Thinkers, the book aims to give readers a sense of the freshness and liveliness of ancient philosophy, and of its wide variety of themes and styles.

> 'Incisive, elegant, and full of the excitement of doing philosophy, Julia Annas's Short Introduction boldly steps outside of conventional chronological ways of organizing material about the Greeks and Romans to get right to the heart of the human problems that exercised them, problems ranging from the relation between reason and emotion to the objectivity of truth. I can't think of a better way to begin.'
>
> **Martha Nussbaum, University of Chicago**

www.oup.co.uk/vsi/ancientphilosophy